FINANCIAL ACCOUNTING
In an Economic Context

JAMIE PRATT
Professor of Accounting
Chair, Department of Accounting and Information Systems
Kelley School of Business
Indiana University

John Wiley & Sons, Inc.

Acquisitions Editor: Jay O'Callaghan
Marketing Manager: Charity Robey
Senior Production Editor: Patricia McFadden
Design Director: Madelyn Lesure
Production Management Services: Lachina Publishing Services

This book was set in 10/12 Times by Lachina Publishing Services and printed and bound by Donnelley/Willard. The cover was printed by Von Hoffmann Press.

This book is printed on acid-free paper.

ISBN 0-470-00046-5

Printed in the United States of America

10 9 8 7 6 5 4 3 2

Brief Contents

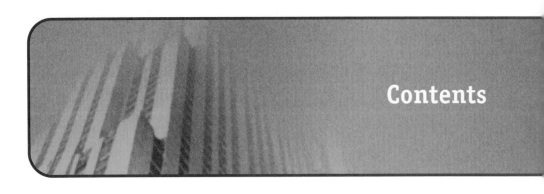

Contents

5 Using Financial Statement Information   179

PART 3: ASSETS: A CLOSER LOOK   235

8 Investments in Equity Securities 323

9 Long-Lived Assets 369

APPENDICES

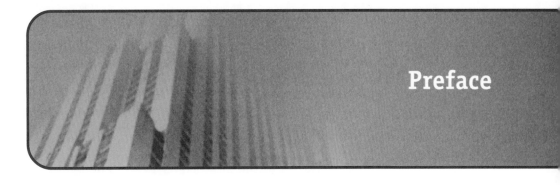

Preface

Financial Accounting in an Economic Context is a trendsetting textbook in the area of introductory financial reporting and analysis. Since the publication of the first edition in 1989, this text has become an important part of the curriculum at a large and impressive group of forward-thinking schools. The fifth edition continues to build upon the strengths of previous editions, while introducing several new ideas and refinements that better communicate the book's economic decision-making theme.

CONTINUING TO CHANGE THE WAY STUDENTS LEARN

The fifth edition contains several new elements designed to improve and sharpen the text's economic decision-making theme, and the real-world references have been updated to include substantial coverage of our Internet-based economy. For the most part, however, this fifth edition maintains the same style and content of the fourth edition, which was very well received by a wide variety of universities, colleges, and other institutions.

New to this Edition

In responding to our reviewers and adapting to the changing needs of students and faculty in their technological environment, the following changes have been made.

Updated Real-World References. The text contains hundreds of real-world references. Virtually every concept covered includes some reference to a real company, a real situation, or a real event. Current topics of concern to the SEC, the FASB, industry, the accounting profession, and various users of financial accounting information are woven throughout the discussion. A large percentage of these references has been updated to reflect the most current thinking in the area, including the dot-com boom and bust and the advent of the new Integrated Questions for Discussion and Review. Past editions have included a section at the end of each chapter containing Questions for Discussion and Review. This edition does not contain these sections but instead has integrated the questions into the chapter text itself, strategically placing them immediately after the coverage of the concepts to which they refer. The questions themselves are distinguished from the actual text by highlighted boxes, allowing the student to consider them without disrupting the flow of the text. Also, unlike in previous editions, these questions are no longer hypothetical; in every case they refer to some real-world company, event, or situation. This feature once again emphasizes and illustrates the timely and relevant nature of the text.

Real-World End-of-Chapter Exercises and Problems. Past editions have included sections at the end of each chapter containing Exercises, Problems, and Issues for Discussion. The Exercises and Problems asked students to perform computations and/or provide commentary on hypothetical situations; the Issues for Discussion asked students to perform computations and/or provide commentary on real-world situations. In this edition many additional Exercises and Problems have been added that ask students to respond to real-world information or situations. Thus the fifth edition's enhanced real-world emphasis is reflected not just in the Issues for Discussion; it is also reflected in the Exercises and Problems.

Minor Change in Chapter Sequencing. In the fourth edition Chapter 3 covered "Using Financial Statement Information," Chapter 4 covered "The Measurement Fundamentals of Financial Accounting," and Chapter 5 covered the "The Mechanics of Financial Accounting." Although *Financial Accounting in an Economic Context* continues to present these chapters in a manner that provides instructors with maximum flexibility, the sequencing of particular topics within chapters has been adjusted for additional ease of use. So although the independence of these three chapters has been maintained, measurement fundamentals are now covered in Chapter 3; mechanics is now covered in Chapter 4; and using financial statements is now covered in Chapter 5—a sequence believed by many users to be the best way to cover the material.

CONTINUING THE APPROACH

The fifth edition has retained and improved upon many of the popular features used in previous editions, such as ethics cases, Internet exercises, brief end-of-chapter real-world exercises and issues for discussion, and a set of interesting and challenging "quality of earnings" cases. This edition also includes a glossary considered by many to be the very best of its kind. But perhaps most importantly, this edition has maintained and improved upon its most distinctive feature—the economic decision-making approach and the balanced coverage of three important themes: economic factors, measurement issues, and mechanics.

Economic Factors

Financial accounting is meaningless without an understanding of the economic environment in which it exists. Each chapter in the fifth edition, therefore, includes frequent references to actual events and companies; quotes from well-known business publications and corporate annual reports; information about industry practices, debt covenants, compensation arrangements, and debt and equity markets; and in-depth discussions of legal liability, ethical issues, and management's incentives and influence on financial reports. The annual report of Wal-Mart, which is the subject of short case questions at the end of each chapter, is also provided at the end of the text. Further, ratio analysis and international issues are introduced early and integrated throughout the text, and the coverage still reflects a strong user orientation with a distinct "quality and persistence of earnings" flavor. The important role of the economic environment in this text makes it more than simply a study of financial accounting. It is a study of modern business management as seen through the financial accounting process.

Measurement Issues

As future managers and users, students must understand the measurement issues underlying the financial statements before they can interpret and meaningfully use them. The fifth edition devotes considerable attention to the conceptual and theoretical foundation of financial accounting measurement, with special emphasis on how the financial statements provide useful measures of solvency and earning power. Cash and accrual statements are treated as equally important, with the statement of cash flows being covered from the very beginning. Chapter 3 provides a framework for accounting measurement that is used throughout the remainder of the text.

Mechanics

Using financial statements without understanding the underlying mechanics is like trying to interpret a foreign language without knowing the vocabulary. Consequently, the fifth edition provides a strong mechanical foundation and stresses mechanics early and throughout the text. Journal entries and T-accounts play an important role, but they are never treated as a goal. Rather, they are characterized as an efficient way to communicate how economic events are reflected on the financial statements. A special coding is used throughout the text to link the form of each entry to the basic accounting equation and financial statements. Thorough mechanical coverage is especially important in a text that takes a user orientation, because effective users must be able to infer transactions from the financial statements. This mechanical skill, referred to as *reverse T-account analysis,* is covered several times in the text, and many exercises and problems are designed to test it.

Decision-Making Perspective

This text presents financial accounting in a way that helps managers make decisions—a decision-making perspective. At a fundamental level, managers make two kinds of decisions: attracting capital and investing capital. Simply put, managers must attract capital from debt and equity investors and then invest it in operations, producing assets, and investment securities. Successful management is defined by generating a return from these investments that exceeds the cost of capital. As depicted in Figure P–1, these two kinds of decisions can be matched with the three themes discussed above (mechanics, measurement issues, and economic factors) to produce six basic questions that must be answered by managers who use financial accounting information when making decisions.

In their effort to attract capital, managers must address three questions when considering whether to enter into certain transactions: How do the transactions affect the financial statements? (cell 1); How do these financial statement effects influence outside perceptions of the company's earning power and solvency? (cell 2); and How do these financial statement effects influence the decisions of outsiders as well as debt and compensation contracts? (cell 3). These questions must be answered if management is to understand the economic consequences of the transactions under consideration.

FIGURE P–1

	Management Decisions	
	Attract Capital	**Invest Capital**
Mechanics	1 How do the transactions affect the financial statements?	4 How are financial ratios computed and how can transactions be inferred from the financial statements?
Measurement Theory	2 How do these financial statement effects influence outside perceptions of the company's earning power and solvency?	5 How do the financial statements and ratios indicate a firm's solvency and earning power?
Economics	3 How do these financial statement effects influence decisions of outsiders as well as debt and compensation contracts?	6 What action should be taken (invest, extend credit, adjust loan terms)?

In their effort to invest capital, managers must address three different questions: How are financial ratios computed and how can transactions be inferred from the financial statements? (cell 4); How do the financial statements and ratios indicate a firm's solvency and earning power? (cell 5); and What action should be taken (e.g., invest, extend credit, adjust loan terms)? (cell 6). These questions must be answered if management is to understand how to use financial accounting information properly.

The decision-making perspective simply means that all six questions are addressed in this text. These are the areas where management decision making intersects with financial accounting information or, in other words, this is what managers need to know about financial reporting and analysis. It is this perspective that makes *Financial Accounting in an Economic Context* different from all other texts.

SUCCESSFUL FEATURES RETAINED FROM PREVIOUS EDITIONS

With few exceptions, the text retains the main features of previous editions. Below is a brief description of the most important ones.

Flexible Modules. Chapter 3 (The Measurement Fundamentals of Financial Accounting), Chapter 4 (The Mechanics of Financial Accounting), and Chapter 5 (Using Financial Statement Information) have been written so that they can be covered in any order. This modular structure adds an important dimension of flexibility to the text.

Reverse T-Account Analysis. An important user-oriented, analytical skill, called *reverse T-account analysis,* is covered in detail in Appendix 4B. This material shows students how to derive transactions from the financial statements, and many exercises and problems throughout the text require students to use it.

Ethics Vignettes. Each chapter closes with a short business scenario that introduces an ethical issue related to the material covered in the chapter. Several questions that follow each scenario are designed to encourage meaningful class discussion.

International Coverage. At the end of each chapter, we discuss timely, relevant, and important international issues. These sections encourage students to think more broadly about global business issues and how they relate to accounting.

Industry Data. Many of the chapters contain tables that compare accounting practices and show students the importance of accounting numbers and ratios across different industries and well-known companies. Updated in the fifth edition, these tables illustrate that the financial accounting issues faced by retailers, manufacturers, service enterprises, and financial institutions are quite different. A brief explanation of the operations of companies in different industries and how these operations give rise to different financial accounting concerns follows each table.

Excerpts from Business Publications and Professional Journals. Over 10,000 references from various business publications (*The Wall Street Journal, Forbes,* and other professional and academic journals) are integrated throughout the text. Updated to reflect the most recent developments, these references document and clarify important chapter concepts and introduce students to information sources that will be useful to them in their business careers.

Wal-Mart Annual Report. The 2001 annual report of Wal-Mart appears in Appendix A at the end of the text. In addition to being referenced periodically through out the text, each chapter contains an end-of-chapter case that requires students to relate the report to accounting issues covered in the chapter.

STUDENT LEARNING AIDS

Study Guide. Prepared by Joseph H. Anthony, Michigan State University, and Robin Clement, Louisiana State University. Designed to have a conceptual flavor that complements the text, this invaluable study aid includes for each chapter: (I) a review of key concepts and (2) a set of practice questions and exercises to enhance learning. This approach highlights important concepts and relations introduced in the text.

SUPPLEMENTS FOR THE INSTRUCTOR

Instructor's Manual. Prepared by Donald Loster, University of California–Santa Barbara. This instructor's resource includes a synopsis that highlights general chapter topics, a text/lecture outline that summarizes the chapter in detail, lecture tips for areas in which students commonly have difficulty, answers to chapter questions, and an assignment classification table. The manual also contains a checklist of key figures.

Test Bank. Prepared by Diane Tanner, University of North Florida. More than 1,700 questions are included in both the printed and microcomputer versions of the Test Bank. The questions are categorized by learning objectives and by question orientation (i.e., whether the questions test procedures, measurement concepts, or economic concepts).

Solutions Manual. Prepared by Terry Butler, Indiana University. This supplement provides complete solutions to all exercises and problems in the text.

Solutions Transparencies. This package includes 250 acetates that illustrate the solutions to all exercises and problems in the text.

Powerpoint Presentation Slides. Developed by Glenn Owen, University of California-Santa Barbara. Over 250 lecture slides highlight the major concepts of each chapter. The slides may be printed out for use on an overhead projector.

Financial Accounting Website at *http://www.wiley.com/college/pratt.* This password-protected instructor resource provides the Solutions Manual, Instructor's Manual, Test Bank, and PowerPoint Presentation Slides in an easily downloadable format.

For more information on these or other supplemental materials, please conact your local Wiley sales representative or visit us on the Web at www.wiley.com/college/pratt.

Acknowledgments

This text benefited significantly from the constructive and insightful comments provided by the individuals listed below.

Joe Anthony
Michigan State University

James Livingston
Southern Methodist University

Peter Bergevin
Valdosta State

David Malone
Texas Tech University

Joan Der
North Central College

Barbara Pierce
Florida Atlantic University

Gordon Duke
University of Minnesota

George Plesko
Massachusetts Institute of Technology

Elizabeth Eccher
Massachusetts Institute of Technology

Bal Radhakrishna
University of Minnesota

Paquita Friday
University of Notre Dame

Stephen Shanelin
Brigham Young University

Alan Glazer
Franklin & Marshall

Paul Simko
Emory University

William Heninger
Brigham Young University

Karen Smith
Arizona State University

Eric Hirst
University of Texas at Austin

Stuart Webster
University of Wyoming

Many other people deserve thanks and recognition for the contributions they have made to this text. I appreciate the efforts of all those who prepared ancillary material.

The editorial, design, and marketing staffs, including Rochelle Kronzek, Dan Silverburg, Ken Martin, Mark Sears, Malvine Litten, and Craig Ramsdell, represent a first-rate group of professionals. Their high-quality work helped to ensure that the manuscript was comprehensive, coherent, and completed in a timely and orderly fashion.

Special thanks go to my wife, Kathy, and children, Jason, Ryan, and Dylan. Their support and understanding were consistent throughout the seemingly endless development and production processes.

Jamie Pratt

Jamie Pratt is the KPMG Professor of Accounting at Indiana University in Bloomington, Indiana. He is also chair of the Department of Accounting and Information Systems. He received his undergraduate degree from Purdue University in 1973 and his doctoral degree from Indiana in 1977. Prior to joining the Indiana faculty in 1990, Jamie served on the faculties at the University of Washington in Seattle, Northwestern University, the University of Zurich (Switzerland), and INSEAD, an MBA program in Fontainebleau, France. Jamie teaches in executive programs throughout the world and has won numerous teaching awards and honors. He recently served as the Associate Editor of *The Accounting Review,* is very active in the American Accounting Association, and publishes frequently in the top academic journals in accounting. In addition to this text, Jamie has authored a variety of educational products, including a case book, a spreadsheet-based financial analysis simulation, and a state-of-the-art CD-ROM that contains a series of interactive financial reporting cases.

An Overview of Financial Accounting

In early 2000, Dell Computer, a high-performing computer manufacturer whose success has stemmed from its innovative cost-saving methods, warned in the *Wall Street Journal* that its days of sky-high revenue growth were at an end. The Texas PC maker expected to record net income well below the estimates of financial analysts who follow the company. Revenues were expected to increase by 30 percent but still fall $800 million below expectations, and sales were expected to slow for the entire year. In response to the announcement, Dell's stock fell 4.1 percent to $40.48 per share.

What are revenues and net income? What does it mean that net income was well below estimates of financial analysts? How can a company so successful at cost savings have its revenues increase by 30 percent and still experience a declining stock price? Answering such questions begins with an understanding of the business environment, investment decisions, and the financial statements—topics addressed in Part 1 of this textbook.

CHAPTER 1
Financial Accounting and Its Economic Context

CHAPTER 2
The Financial Statements

Financial Accounting and Its Economic Context

KEY POINTS

The following key points are emphasized in this chapter:

The economic role of financial accounting statements.

The standard audit report, management letter, and footnotes to the financial statements.

The four financial statements and the kind of financial information each provides.

The two forms of investment—debt and equity—and how the information on the financial statements relates to them.

Why ethics is important in the accounting process.

The Securities and Exchange Commission, the Financial Accounting Standards Board, and the development of generally accepted accounting principles.

The current status of international accounting practices and standards.

In March 2000, MicroStrategy, a prominent software company, announced that it was revising its financial results. Sales would be lowered by roughly 25 percent, from $205 million to about $150 million; and profits would be adjusted from a substantial gain to a substantial loss. The reaction was swift. MicroStrategy's stock plunged 62 percent, and many unwary investors lost huge sums of money. The company was bombarded by shareholder lawsuits. Some described this event as the endgame of the Internet investment boom.

The situation described above is all too common. Billions of dollars are lost each year by investors who base their investment decisions on misleading reported numbers. This text, beginning with this first chapter, explains how that could happen. It also describes how you can avoid the fate of those investors who, believing the profits reported by MicroStrategy, chose to invest their hard-earned money and lost much of it. The first step involves understanding the **financial accounting** process.

FINANCIAL REPORTING AND INVESTMENT DECISIONS

Financial reporting plays an important role in investment decisions.

1. *Profit-Seeking Companies*—Managers of profit-seeking companies prepare reports containing financial information for the owners of these companies. In addition to other information, these reports contain four financial statements: the balance sheet, the income statement, the statement of retained earnings, and the statement of cash flows.
2. *Owners and Other Interested Parties (Users)*—Although prepared primarily for the owners, these financial reports are available to the public and are read by other interested parties who use them to assess the financial condition and performance of the company as well as the performance of its managers. Such interested parties, called users in this text, include potential investors, bankers, government agencies, and the company's customers and suppliers.
3. *User Decisions*—Users obtain information from the financial reports that helps assess the company's past performance, predict its future performance, and control the activities of its managers. Financial reports, therefore, help users to make better decisions. Investors, for example, use financial reports to choose companies in which to invest their funds; bankers use them to decide where to loan their funds and what interest rates to charge.
4. *Effects of User Decisions*—User decisions affect the financial condition and performance of the company and the economic well-being of its managers. For example, a banker may use the information contained in a financial report to decide not to loan a certain company much-needed funds. Such a decision may cause the company to struggle and may cost managers their jobs and shareholders their investments.

Figure 1–1 illustrates how financial reporting relates to investment decisions. Note its dynamic nature: the financial information provided by managers of a profit-seeking company is used by interested parties to make decisions that, in turn, affect a company's financial condition and the economic well-being of its managers. Managers need to understand the process depicted in Figure 1–1 from two perspectives:

1. economic consequences
2. user orientation

FIGURE 1–1   Financial reporting and investment decisions

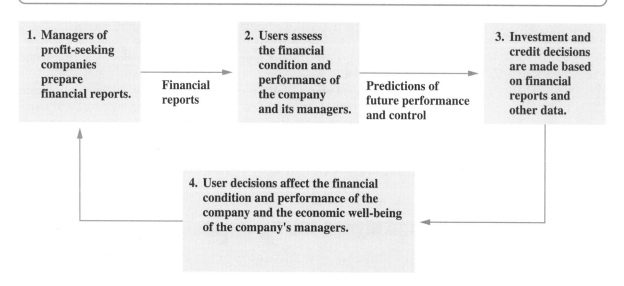

Economic Consequences

To run a company effectively, management must be able to attract capital from outsiders who use financial statements to evaluate the company's performance and financial health. Managers apply for loans from bankers, for example, who use the financial statements to determine whether to grant the loan and, if so, what interest rate to charge. Since using financial statements by outsiders leads to economic consequences for managers and the companies they operate (e.g., higher interest rates), it is important that they know how economic events (e.g., business decisions) affect the financial statements. Consider a case where management is deciding to either purchase or rent equipment. When making such a decision, an astute manager would consider how the choice affects the financial statements because it could influence the way in which the company is viewed by outsiders. Considering and understanding how such events affect the financial statements is referred to in this text as an **economic consequence perspective.**

User Orientation

Managers are also users of financial statements, such as when they are called upon to assess the performance and financial health of other companies. Questions such as the following are often answered by analyzing financial statements provided by those companies.

- Should we purchase a company?
- Should we use a company as a supplier?
- Should we extend credit or loan funds to a company?

Accordingly, managers also need to know how to read, evaluate, and analyze financial statements. We call this perspective a **user orientation.**

The next section develops a scenario designed to highlight issues that are particularly important to users of financial statements. That same scenario serves as the basis for further discussion of the environment of financial accounting, followed by a section focusing on management's point of view and the economic consequence perspective. The chapter concludes with a brief description of generally accepted accounting principles (GAAP), the standards that guide the preparation of financial accounting statements in the United States, and the general state of the financial accounting process in other countries. Appendix 1A introduces managerial, tax, and not-for-profit accounting.

Some claim that many Internet companies have chosen accounting methods that boost the profits they report to the public. Others have noted that it is difficult to place a value on Internet companies because financial statements do not do a good job of reflecting value for "new economy" firms. Which of the two statements takes an economic consequence perspective, and which takes a user orientation? Discuss.

THE DEMAND FOR FINANCIAL INFORMATION: A USER'S ORIENTATION

Suppose that you recently learned that a long-lost relative died and left you a large sum of money. You know little about financial matters, so you consult Mary Jordan, a financial advisor, to help you decide what to do with the funds. She tells you that you have two choices: you can consume it or you can invest it.

Consumption and Investment

In consuming your new fortune, you would spend the money on goods and services, such as a trip around the world, expensive meals, a lavish wardrobe, or any other expenditures that bring about immediate gratification. Consumption expenditures, by definition, are enjoyed immediately and have no future value.

In investing the fortune, you would spend the money on items that provide little in the way of immediate gratification. Rather, they generate returns of additional money at later dates. In essence, investments trade current consumption for more consumption at a later date. Examples include investing in stocks and bonds, real estate, rare art objects, or simply placing the money in the bank.

Where to Invest?

You decide to invest the money, and with a little direction from Mary, you begin to explore investment alternatives. You find that investments come in a number of different forms, however, and you quickly become overwhelmed, confused, and frustrated. Just as you are about to give up your search and put all your money in the bank, a man by the name of Martin Wagner knocks at your door. Through a mutual friend, Martin has heard of your recent windfall and states that he has an interesting offer for you.

Martin claims that he manages a very successful research company, called Microline, owned by a group of European investors. In its short, two-year history, the company has earned a reputation for innovation in software development. As Martin describes it, Microline's research staff is on the verge of designing a voice-activated word-processing system that will revolutionize word-processing in the future.

Martin has come to you for capital—$1 million, to be exact. The company's research and development efforts have run short of funds, and money is still needed to complete the design. With your money, Martin asserts that the software system can be completed and sold, producing millions of dollars of income, some of which will provide you with a handsome return on your investment. Without your capital, on the other hand, Martin believes that the project may have to be abandoned.

The Demand for Documentation

You have listened to Martin's story and now must decide what to do. Your first thought is that you simply cannot accept his word without some documented evidence. How do you really know that he has successfully managed this business for the past two years and that $1 million will enable the company to turn this design into a fortune in the future?

After careful consideration, you decide that you need to see some proof before making a final decision. You ask for specific documents to show that Microline has been run successfully for the past two years, is currently in reasonably good financial condition, and has the potential to generate income of the magnitude Martin suggests. He agrees to provide you with such documentation because he knows that if he does not, you will invest your money elsewhere, and both he and Microline will suffer.

Several days later, Martin returns with a set of financial statements prepared by Microline's accountants. He explains the meanings of the numbers on the statements and further claims that the records at his office can be used to verify them. Taken at face value, the figures look promising, but somehow Martin's explanation is not convincing. It occurs to you that Martin might fabricate or at least influence the figures. After all, Microline needs money, and who would blame Martin for showing you only the figures that make Microline's situation look attractive to a potential investor?

The Demand for an Independent Audit

You require that Martin go one step further. He must return again with financial statements that have been checked and verified by an independent outsider who is an expert in such matters. You insist that the person not be employed by Microline or have any interest whatsoever in the company and have the appropriate credentials to perform such a task. In essence, you demand that Martin hire a **certified public accountant (CPA)** to verify Microline's financial statements. You require, in other words, that Microline subject itself to an **independent audit.** Martin agrees because, once again, if he does not, you will take your money and invest it elsewhere. At the same time, however, Martin is somewhat troubled. He knows that hiring and working with a CPA can be very costly and time-consuming.

Martin and the CPA: Different Incentives

Time passes and you become concerned that Martin has taken too long to return with the financial statements. You have thought of several questions since Martin's last visit and decide to call on him in person. You arrive at Microline's office and are seated by Martin's secretary. While you are waiting, you hear Martin's voice through the partly open door to his office. He seems to be discussing Microline's financial statements with the CPA. While you cannot understand exactly what is being said, it is clear that they are not in complete agreement and that they are both strong in their convictions.

You wonder why Martin and the CPA might view the financial statements from different perspectives and speculate that perhaps the CPA recommended presenting Microline's financial condition in a way that was unsatisfactory to Martin. You reason that Martin should probably follow the CPA's recommendation because, after all, the CPA is the expert in financial reporting. You realize, however, that Martin wants the statements to be as attractive as possible and that he may have some influence over the CPA. Indeed, Martin did hire the CPA and does pay the CPA's fee.

Before long, the CPA leaves and Martin invites you into his office. During your short discussion, you mention nothing of what you think you have heard. Martin answers your questions confidently and assures you that the statements will be ready within the week. Satisfied, you return home.

The Auditor's Report, the Management Letter, and the Financial Statements

Martin arrives at your home with seven official-looking documents: (1) an **auditor's report,** a short letter written by the auditor that describes the activities of the audit and comments on the financial position and operations of Microline, (2) a **management letter,** signed by Martin, which accepts responsibility for the figures on the statements, (3) a balance sheet, (4) an income statement, (5) a statement of retained earnings, (6) a statement of cash flows, and (7) a comprehensive set of footnotes, which more fully explain certain items on the four statements listed above. You briefly review the documents and tell Martin that you will have a decision for him soon.

THE AUDITOR'S REPORT

You begin your examination by reviewing the auditor's report, from which you hope to learn how credible the financial statements actually are (see Figure 1–2).

Overall, you are reassured by the auditor's report. It indicates that the auditor reviewed Microline's records thoroughly and concluded that the statements (1) were prepared in conformity with generally accepted accounting principles and (2) present fairly Microline's financial condition and operations. You suspect that the auditor

FIGURE 1–2
The standard audit report

To the Board of Directors and Shareholders of Microline:

We have audited the accompanying balance sheet of Microline as of December 31, 2001 and 2000, and the related statements of income, retained earnings, and cash flows for the years then ended. These financial statements are the responsibility of the Company's management. Our responsibility is to express an opinion on these financial statements based on our audit.

We conducted our audit in accordance with generally accepted auditing standards. Those standards require that we plan and perform the audit to obtain reasonable assurance about whether the financial statements are free of material misstatement. An audit includes examining, on a test basis, evidence supporting the amounts and disclosures in the financial statements. An audit also includes assessing the accounting principles used and significant estimates made by management, as well as evaluating the overall financial statement presentation. We believe that our audit provides a reasonable basis for our opinion.

In our opinion, the financial statements referred to above present fairly, in all material respects, the financial position of Microline as of December 31, 2001 and 2000, and the results of its operations and its cash flows for the years then ended, in conformity with generally accepted accounting principles.

Arthur Price

Arthur Price, Certified Public Accountant
March 12, 2002

could have rendered a much less favorable report, such as that the statements were not prepared in conformance with generally accepted accounting principles, or that no opinion could be reached because Microline's accounting system was so poorly designed, or that Microline was in danger of failure. You also realize, however, that you know very little about either generally accepted auditing standards or generally accepted accounting principles and that Microline's management made a number of significant estimates when preparing the statements. This discovery is somewhat troubling because, even with the audit, it seems that Microline's management may have had some subjective influence on the financial statements.

THE MANAGEMENT LETTER

You next read the management letter, hoping to learn more about how the financial statements were prepared and audited (see Figure 1–3).

Once again, you are both reassured and troubled. It is comforting to know that Microline's management is accepting responsibility for the integrity of the statements, which have been prepared in conformance with generally accepted accounting principles, and that the company has an **internal control system** that safeguards the assets and reasonably ensures that transactions are properly recorded and reported. It is also nice to know that Microline's policies prescribe that its employees maintain high ethical standards. However, you still do not understand generally accepted accounting principles, are still concerned that the statements reflect management's estimates and

FIGURE 1–3
Management's letter

Management's Responsibilities:

Management is responsible for the preparation and integrity of the financial statements and the financial comments appearing in this financial report. The financial statements were prepared in accordance with generally accepted accounting principles and include certain amounts based on management's best estimates and judgments. Other financial information presented in this financial report is consistent with the financial statements.

The Company maintains a system of internal controls designed to provide reasonable assurance that the assets are safeguarded and that transactions are executed as authorized and are recorded and reported properly. The system of controls is based upon written policies and procedures, appropriate division of responsibility and authority, careful selection and training of personnel, and a comprehensive internal audit program. The Company's policies and procedures prescribe that the Company and all employees are to maintain the highest ethical standards and that its business practices are to be conducted in a manner which is above reproach.

Arthur Price, an independent certified public accountant, has examined the Company's financial statements, and the audit report is presented herein. The Board of Directors has an Audit Committee composed entirely of outside directors. Arthur Price has direct access to the Audit Committee and meets with the committee to discuss accounting, auditing, and financial reporting matters.

Martin Wagner

Martin Wagner, Chief Executive Officer
March 12, 2002

judgments, and have very little idea about the function of Microline's Board of Directors and Audit Committee.

THE FINANCIAL STATEMENTS

You briefly review the four financial statements (see Figure 1–4) and note first that dollar amounts are listed for both 2001 and 2000. This discovery is somewhat discouraging because only information about the past is included on the statements and is subject to the auditor's report and management letter. Nothing about Microline's future prospects is included in the financial statements—but the future is what inter-

FIGURE 1–4

Financial statements for Microline

Microline
Financial Statements
As of December 31, 2001 and 2000

	2001	2000
BALANCE SHEET		
ASSETS		
Cash	$ 100,000	$ 60,000
Accounts receivable	80,000	90,000
Equipment	330,000	300,000
Land	500,000	500,000
Total assets	$1,010,000	$ 950,000
LIABILITIES AND STOCKHOLDERS' EQUITY		
Short-term payables	$ 50,000	$ 30,000
Long-term payables	420,000	450,000
Common stock	400,000	400,000
Retained earnings	140,000	70,000
Total liabilities and stockholders' equity	$1,010,000	$ 950,000
INCOME STATEMENT		
Revenues	$1,650,000	$1,500,000
Expenses	1,450,000	1,350,000
Net income	$ 200,000	$ 150,000
STATEMENT OF RETAINED EARNINGS		
Beginning retained earnings balance	$ 70,000	$ 0
Plus: Net income	200,000	150,000
Less: Dividends	130,000	80,000
Ending retained earnings balance	$ 140,000	$ 70,000
STATEMENT OF CASH FLOWS		
Net cash flow from operating activities	$ 250,000	$ 120,000
Net cash flow from investing activities	(50,000)	(340,000)
Net cash flow from financing activities	(160,000)	280,000
Net increase (decrease) in cash	$ 40,000	$ 60,000
Beginning cash balance	60,000	0
Ending cash balance	$ 100,000	$ 60,000

ests you most. Whether Microline is able to provide an acceptable return on your $1 million investment depends primarily on what happens in the future. The past is often a poor indicator of the future.

You also observe that each statement emphasizes a different aspect of Microline's financial condition and performance. The balance sheet, for example, lists the company's assets, liabilities, and stockholders' equity. On the income statement, expenses are subtracted from revenues to produce a number called net income. The statement of retained earnings includes (1) the beginning and ending retained earnings balance, which can be found on the 2000 and 2001 balance sheets, (2) net income, which is the bottom line on the income statement, and (3) dividends. The statement of cash flows includes the beginning and ending balance of cash, which can be found on the 2000 and 2001 balance sheets, and net cash flows from operating, investing, and financing activities. It becomes clear quite quickly that you do not understand these terms and that you know very little about the information conveyed by these statements and, therefore, cannot begin to assess whether Microline would be a good company in which to invest.

THE FOOTNOTES

At this point you decide to examine the **footnotes,** hoping that they will clear up some of your uncertainty about the financial statements (Figure 1–5). They state that many of the numbers on the statements are the result of assumptions and estimates made by Microline's management, which does not surprise you because similar statements were made in both the audit report and the management letter. It is also clear from the footnotes that Microline was able to choose from a number of different acceptable accounting methods. While you know little about generally accepted accounting prin-

FIGURE 1–5 Notes to the financial statements	

Cash. **Cash consists of cash on hand and cash in a bank checking account.**

Accounts Receivable. **The balance in accounts receivable has been adjusted for an estimate of future uncollectibles.**

Equipment. **Equipment is carried at a cost and includes expenditures for new additions and those which substantially increase its useful life. The cost of the equipment is depreciated using the straight-line method over an estimated useful life of ten years.**

Land. **Land is carried at cost.**

Short-Term Payables. **Short-term payables consist of wages payable, short-term borrowings, interest payable, taxes payable, and an estimate of future warranty costs.**

Long-Term Payables. **Long-term payables consist primarily of notes that must be paid back after one year.**

Common Stock. **Common stock represents the contributions of the company's stockholders.**

Revenue Recognition. **Revenues from sales are reflected in the income statement when products are shipped. Revenues from services are estimated in proportion to the completion of the service.**

Expenses. **Expenses include selling and administrative expenses and estimates of uncollectible receivables and depreciation on the equipment.**

ciples, you confidently conclude that they do not ensure exact and unbiased statements. Alternative accounting methods as well as assumptions and estimates by Microline's management are very evident.

Descriptions of Financial Statements

After your initial examination, you decide that Microline may be a reasonable investment, but your lack of knowledge renders you incapable of making a confident choice. You decide to return to Mary Jordan, your financial advisor, for help. Perhaps she can explain the nature of the financial statements and improve your understanding of the decision that faces you. Mary begins by defining some of the fundamental terms used on the financial statements.[1]

The **balance sheet,** which lists Microline's assets, liabilities, and stockholders' equity, is a statement of the company's financial position as of a certain date. **Assets,** representing items that will bring future economic benefit to Microline, include the cash balance, the dollar amounts due from Microline's customers (accounts receivable), and the original cost of the equipment and land purchased by the company. **Liabilities,** which represent current obligations, consist of the amounts currently owed by Microline to its **creditors.** Satisfying these liabilities will generally require cash payments in the future. Common stock and retained earnings comprise the **stockholders' equity** section. **Common stock** represents the initial investments by Microline's owners, and **retained earnings** is a measure of Microline's past profits that have been retained in the business. Without the balance sheet, investors would have difficulty assessing the current financial condition of the company.

The **income statement** is divided into two components: **revenues,** a measure of the assets generated from the products and services sold, and **expenses,** a measure of the asset outflows (costs) associated with selling these products and services. The difference between these two amounts is a number called **net income (profit),** which measures the success of Microline's operations over a particular period of time. Without the income statement, investors would be unable to determine the company's performance during the period.

The **statement of retained earnings** describes the increases and decreases to retained earnings, which is a measure of Microline's past profits. The net income or profit amount from the income statement is first added to the beginning balance of retained earnings. **Dividends,** the assets paid to Microline's owners as a return for their initial investment, are then subtracted from this amount to compute ending retained earnings. The ending retained earnings amount appears on the balance sheet and becomes the beginning balance of the following period. The statement of retained earnings indicates in any given year how dividends compare to profit. Without the statement of retained earnings, investors may not clearly see the relationship between the company's net income and its dividends.

The **statement of cash flows** summarizes the increases and decreases in cash over a period of time. The beginning cash balance is adjusted for the *net cash flows* (cash inflows less cash outflows) associated with Microline's operating, investing, and financing activities. **Operating activities** are associated with the actual products and services provided by Microline for its customers. **Investing activities** include the purchase and sale of assets, such as equipment and land. **Financing activities** refers to the cash collections and payments related to Microline's *capital sources.* Examples

---

1. This section of the text provides basic definitions for important terms. These definitions are expanded upon in later chapters.

include cash borrowings and loan payments as well as collections from owners' contributions and the payment of dividends. Without the statement of cash flows, investors would have difficulty assessing the company's cash management strategies.

Analysis of Financial Statements

After defining the terms on the financial statements, Mary notes that Microline appears to be in reasonably strong financial shape. She focuses first on the statement of cash flows, pointing out that the company's cash position has been increasing and that operating activities have contributed $120,000 and $250,000 in cash in the last two years. She also notes that Microline has invested heavily in new assets since its inception and that $160,000 was paid during 2001 for dividends and to reduce outstanding debts. In short, Microline has demonstrated the ability to generate cash. Mary believes this is very important, because in order to remain solvent, the company must be able to generate enough cash to meet its debts as they come due. She comments that **solvency** is a requirement for financial health.

Mary then moves to the income statement and statement of retained earnings, noting that Microline has shown profits of $150,000 and $200,000 over the past two years and, at the same time, has paid significant dividends to its owners, specifically $80,000 in 2000 and $130,000 in 2001. These numbers show that Microline has demonstrated **earning power,** the ability to grow and provide a substantial return to its owners. Mary also notes that the balance sheets indicate Microline's assets have increased during the past year from $950,000 to $1,010,000, while its liabilities (payables) have decreased from $480,000 to $470,000. She indicates that such a trend is promising.

To further support Microline's financial strength, Mary computes a few ratios by using the dollar values on the income statement and balance sheet. She points out that net income as a percentage of revenues increased from 10 percent ($150,000/$1,500,000) in 2000 to over 12 percent ($200,000/$1,650,000) in 2001. Total payables as a percent of total assets decreased from over 50 percent ($480,000/$950,000) in 2000 to less than 47 percent ($470,000/$1,010,000) in 2001. Dividends as a percent of net income increased substantially over the two-year period—to 65 percent. After consulting some statistics covering the industry in which Microline is a member, Mary reports that Microline's financial ratios, in general, are stronger than those of many other similar firms.

In its 2000 annual report, Lands' End, a leading global clothing retailer that sells primarily through catalogs and its Website (landsend.com), reported sales of $1.3 billion; net income of $48 million; total assets and total liabilities of $456 million and $160 million, respectively; and net cash flows from operating activities of $123 million. On which of the financial statements were each of these values reported, and what values were reported for each of the following items: total expenses, stockholders' equity, and the net income to sales ratio?

What Form of Investment: Debt or Equity?

The definitions and analysis provided by Mary are encouraging, and you decide that Microline is a good investment. However, Mary states that now you must decide what form your investment should take. Should it be in the form of a loan, or should you purchase ownership (equity) in Microline? She explains that the risks you face and the potential returns associated with these two forms of investment are really quite different. Moreover, the relative importance to you of the different kinds of information disclosed on the financial statements depends on the kind of investment you make.

A DEBT INVESTMENT

You would make a **debt investment** if you loaned the $1 million to Microline. You would then become one of the company's creditors and would require that Microline's management sign a **loan contract,** specifying (1) the *maturity date,* the date when the loan is to be paid back; (2) the **annual interest** payment, the amount of interest to be paid each year; (3) *collateral,* assets to be passed to you in case the principal or the interest on the loan is in *default* (not paid back); and (4) any other **debt restrictions** you feel you should impose on Microline to protect your investment. The contract might specify, for example, that Microline maintain a certain cash balance throughout the period of the loan or that dividends during that period be limited.

As one of Microline's creditors, your first concern would be Microline's ability to meet the loan's interest and principal payments as they come due. Since such payments are made in cash, you would be especially interested in Microline's cash management record and its ability to generate cash over the period of the loan. Thus, the information in the statement of cash flows would be very relevant. You would also be interested in the selling prices of assets that could be used as collateral and in the amounts of the loans and other liabilities owed by Microline to other creditors. The balance sheet, therefore, which lists Microline's assets and liabilities, would also contain some useful information.

Mary reminds you, however, that many of Microline's assets are valued on the balance sheet at **historical cost,** the dollar amount paid when the assets were acquired, which, in many cases, was two years ago. This discovery is worrisome, because the historical cost of an asset is rarely the same as its current selling price, the relevant amount if an asset is to be considered as collateral for the loan.

AN EQUITY INVESTMENT

Rather than loaning Microline the $1 million, you may wish to purchase **equity** in the company. As an equity investor, you would become one of the owners, or **stockholders,** of Microline.

Equity investments give rise to considerations that are somewhat different from those of debt investments. As a stockholder, for example, your return would be primarily in the form of stock appreciation and dividends, which would tend to be large if Microline performed well and small, or nonexistent, if the company performed poorly. Unlike a loan investment, for which interest and principal payments are specified by contract, dividend payments are at the discretion of Microline's **board of directors,** which is elected annually by the stockholders to represent their interests. Such representation involves quarterly meetings where company policies are set, dividends are declared, and the performance and compensation of the company's upper management is reviewed. The board of directors has the power to hire and fire upper management as well as determine the form and amount of their compensation.

As a stockholder who could vote in the election of the board of directors, your primary concern would be the performance of Microline's management—specifically, its ability to generate and maintain earnings in the future. To achieve such an objective, management must both ensure that cash is available to meet debts as they come due and invest in assets that produce a satisfactory return in the long run. Consequently, stockholders are interested in the information contained in all four of the financial statements: the balance sheet because it indicates Microline's assets and liabilities, the income statement and statement of retained earnings because they indicate Microline's earning power and dividend payments, and the statement of cash flows because it provides a report of Microline's past cash management policies. As a stockholder, however, you would be especially interested in the income statement, since the board of directors often sets dividends as a percentage of income, which is generally considered to be the overall measure of management's performance and the company's earning power.

You would also be interested in the methods used to compensate Microline's upper management. You may wish, for example, to encourage the board of directors to institute a system of compensation that paid upper management on the basis of its performance. One way to implement such a system would be to set compensation levels at amounts expressed as percentages of net income. This would motivate Microline's management to increase net income and, accordingly, their compensation. Such a result should also mean increased earning power and greater dividend payments in the future. At the same time, however, you realize that management can influence the manner in which net income is measured.

A Decision Is Made, but Important Questions Still Remain

After a lengthy discussion with Mary, you decide to invest in the equity of Microline. From the information contained in the audit report, the management letter, the financial statements, and the footnotes, you have concluded that Microline is a legitimate operation that is solvent, has shown significant earning power, and has provided a reasonable return to its stockholders. You reason further that if Martin is correct in his prediction that their new voice-activated word-processing system will revolutionize the industry, there is a distinct possibility of large returns in the future. Stockholders would receive such returns in the form of larger dividends, while payments to creditors would be limited to the contractual interest and principal payments.

You thank Mary for her advice and feel satisfied with your decision. You realize, however, that the future is uncertain and that your investment involves risks.

The asset side of the balance sheet for the Bank of New York, as well as many other financial institutions, is comprised primarily of loans, while the Coca-Cola Company's assets include a large percentage of equity investments in other companies. What is the difference between these two kinds of assets and why would these two companies rely more heavily on one than the other?

THE ENVIRONMENT OF FINANCIAL ACCOUNTING

Figure 1–6 depicts the financial accounting environment. It illustrates the main points introduced in the previous scenario where you acted as the capital provider, Martin Wagner and Microline represented the company [manager], and Arthur Price was the auditor. The figure shows that providers of capital, in the form of debt and equity investors, invest in companies operated by managers and expect to receive interest, principal, and dividend payments. As a condition of these investments, the capital providers require that managers provide audited financial information and enter into debt and/or compensation contracts. Financial accounting information helps investors and creditors evaluate and predict the ability of managers to generate investment returns. It also provides numbers that are used in the debt and compensation contracts,

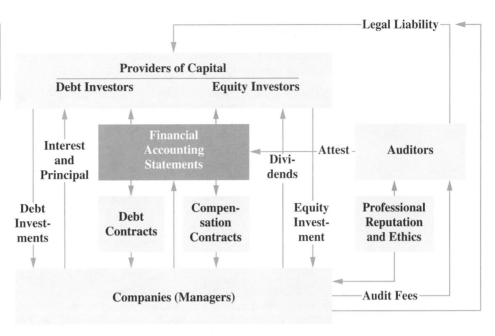

FIGURE 1–6

Basic relationships in the financial reporting process

which serve to protect the providers of capital by enabling them to exert control over the manager's activities. Note also that managers and auditors are guided by their professional reputations and ethics (the use of their specialized skill for the benefit of others) as well as the threat of legal liability. At the same time, auditors are in the ironic position of having a reporting responsibility to capital providers while their fees are paid by managers whose financial statements are being audited. Such conflicting goals create a tension that is part of everyday auditing. In the remainder of this section we provide more complete descriptions for each of the components in Figure 1–6.

Financial Accounting Information: More Than the Financial Statements

Financial accounting information extends beyond that which is contained in the four financial statements, the accompanying footnotes, the auditor's report, and the management letter. For example, **annual reports,** which are published each year by major U.S. companies, and the *Form 10-K,* which must be completed and filed annually with a government agency by companies whose securities are traded on the major U.S. stock exchanges, contain a wealth of information beyond what is contained in the financial statements alone.

ANNUAL REPORTS

Annual reports published by major U.S. companies include audited balance sheets for the two most recent years and audited statements of income, retained earnings, and cash flows for the three most recent years. They also include:

- Selected quarterly information.
- Summaries of selected financial information for the last five years.
- Descriptions of business activities.
- Separate information about each of a company's major segments.
- A listing of the members of the board of directors and the executive officers.

- Market prices of a company's stock for each quarterly period for the two most recent years.
- Management's discussion and analysis of the company's financial condition and results of operations.

The 2001 annual report of Wal-Mart is provided in Appendix A at the end of this text. Take a few minutes now to review it, especially the sections mentioned in the preceding paragraph, as we refer to this report frequently throughout the remainder of the text.

A VARIETY OF USERS

Annual reports are available not only to a company's stockholders but to the general public and can be obtained by virtually anyone interested in a company's financial condition and performance. Recall, for example, that management often uses the financial statements of other firms to assess whether to enter into business relationships with these firms. As you probably noticed when you reviewed the Wal-Mart annual report, however, financial accounting information can be complex and confusing. Consequently, many interested parties delegate the task of analyzing financial statement information to more knowledgeable representatives. _Financial and security analysts_ use financial information to evaluate equity and debt investments for individuals, companies, and other institutions. _Stockbrokers_ use it to buy and sell securities for their clients. _Bank loan officers_ and _credit analysts_ use it when deciding whether to loan money to individuals or businesses.

While investors, creditors, management, and their representatives are the largest group of financial information users, there are many others. Government bodies, like the Federal Trade Commission, often base regulatory decisions on information disclosed in annual reports, and public utilities normally base their rates (the prices they charge their customers) on financial accounting numbers such as net income. Labor unions often use accounting numbers to argue for more wages or other benefits, and companies often use their own financial statements to determine dividend payments, set company policies, and in general, to help guide operating business decisions. Indeed, financial accounting reports provide information to a variety of users, each with specific needs.

Providers of Capital: Investors and Creditors

Providers of capital represent people or organizations who have cash beyond what they need for current consumption. They seek ways to invest their extra funds so that they can increase their future levels of wealth and consumption. This group includes both current and potential equity and debt investors: individuals and entities who provide companies with the capital that they need to conduct operations. Equity investors (often referred to simply as investors) purchase shares of stock, which represent ownership interests in a corporation, with the expectation of receiving dividends and increases in the stock price in the future; debt investors (creditors) loan funds in exchange for interest and principal payments.

WHO HOLDS EQUITY AND DEBT INVESTMENTS?

Equity and debt investments are held by both individuals and entities. Millions of people in the United States, for example, hold shares of stock in large U.S. corporations which, in turn, hold shares of stock in each other. The equity securities of General Electric, for example, are held by over 500,000 individual stockholders, while General Electric as an entity holds 100 percent of the equity securities of the National

Broadcasting Company (NBC). Debt securities are held primarily by banks, who loan billions of dollars to individuals and corporations each year. For example, the balance sheet of Bank of America, a major U.S. bank, indicates that the company holds debt investments in the form of outstanding loans valued at over $364 billion. In addition, many debt securities in the form of bonds issued by large corporations are also held by individuals and institutions.

WHERE ARE EQUITY AND DEBT SECURITIES BOUGHT AND SOLD?

Stock markets, such as the New York Stock Exchange, NASDAQ, and the American Stock Exchange, provide forums for the buying and selling of equity and debt interests issued by major U.S. and foreign companies. Active markets also exist in virtually all major non–U.S. countries.

Companies (Managers)

Companies, operated by **managers,** provide goods and services that are consumed by individuals and other entities. They compete with each other for capital, attempting to convince investors and creditors that they offer the best potential return at the lowest level of risk. In 2000, for example, La-Z-Boy Incorporated collected over $175 million from creditors, much of which was used to finance expansion which, in turn, enabled the company to produce cash that was used to meet debt payments and pay dividends.

INDUSTRIES

Companies are often grouped into **industries** based on the nature of their operations. While there are many industry classifications, they can be summarized into three basic categories: manufacturing, retailing, and services (general and financial). Manufacturing firms such as General Motors, IBM, and PepsiCo acquire raw materials and convert them into goods that are sold either to consumers, usually through retailers, or to other manufacturers who use them as raw materials.[2] Retail firms like Wal-Mart, Kmart, Toys "R" Us, and J.C. Penney purchase goods from manufacturers and sell them to consumers. The service industry includes firms like Ameritech, MCI, Federal Express, and H&R Block, who provide general services, as well as firms like Citicorp, American Express, and Prudential Insurance, who provide financial services. Many of the "new economy" firms, such as America Online, Cisco Systems, and Amazon.com, are part of the service industry. We frequently refer to these firms and industry classifications throughout the remainder of the text.

What industry category would each of the following firms fall into? Boeing, Tommy Hilfiger, DuPont, American Express, General Electric, Microsoft, eBay, Delta Air Lines, and AT&T.

ECONOMIC ENTITIES: DIFFERENT KINDS

Financial accounting statements refer to a specific and definable *economic entity*. In this text we call this entity a *company* or *business* and limit our coverage to entities established primarily to generate profits. Such profit-seeking entities may be subdivided into segments and subsidiaries, each of which provides its own financial statements. For

2. Manufacturing also includes agriculture and mining.

example, in the annual report of The Limited, Inc., the financial statements are referred to as **consolidated financial statements,** which means that the total dollar amounts in the accounts on its financial statements include those of other companies, such as Victoria's Secret, Abercrombie & Fitch, and Mast Industries, which The Limited owns. These companies, called *subsidiaries,* prepare their own separate financial statements. Furthermore, The Limited is divided into twelve retail divisions, and financial reports on each of these can be compiled.

Accounting reports are also prepared for entities that are not established to make profits. Counties, cities, school districts, and other municipalities as well as charitable organizations and foundations are examples of **nonprofit entities.**

CONTRACTS

Capital providers require that managers, and the entities they manage, enter into contracts so that legal influence can be exerted over management's activities which, in turn, protects the interests of the capital providers. Debt (loan) and management **compensation contracts** are common examples. To illustrate, the annual reports of both Boeing and Owens Corning indicate that their long-term debt contracts require that both companies limit future dividends, capital expenditures, and borrowings. Violating these terms (i.e., defaulting on the contract) would give the debtholder the right to demand that the entire debt be paid immediately. DuPont's annual report discloses that the compensation of the company's executives is based, in part, on whether the company achieves certain net income goals. In both cases financial accounting numbers can be found in the contracts, thereby playing a critical role in shaping the behavior of corporate management.

Independent Auditors

Major U.S. companies incur considerable costs to have their financial statements audited by independent public accounting firms. Such audits lend credibility to the financial statements and are required by law for companies whose ownership shares are traded on the public stock exchanges. Five public accounting firms, known as the **"Big 5,"** audit most of the large companies. These firms and a selection of their major clients are listed in Figure 1–7. There are also many regional and local public accounting firms located throughout the United States. Their audit clients comprise the thousands of mid-sized and small companies who, for various reasons, wish to have their financial statements audited.

FIGURE 1–7 "Big 5" accounting firms and major clients	Accounting Firm	Major Clients
	Arthur Andersen & Co.	Oracle, Tristar Aerospace, Boise Cascade
	PricewaterhouseCoopers	eBay, Cisco Systems, DuPont
	Deloitte & Touche	Microsoft, Boeing, Merrill Lynch
	Ernst & Young	Wal-Mart, Intel, America Online
	KPMG Peat Marwick	US Airways, PepsiCo, Xerox

Relationships Among Capital Providers, Management and the Independent Auditor

Since investors and creditors demand the independent audit, it seems reasonable that they would choose the auditor and make sure that the audit was conducted in an independent manner. Such a solution is often impractical, however, because stockholders and creditors are often too widely separated and removed from the business to agree on an auditor and monitor the audit. As Figure 1–8 shows, in all major U.S. companies the stockholders elect a board of directors, which appoints a subcommittee of outside directors, called the **audit committee.** This committee, which is part of the board of directors and therefore represents the interests of the stockholders, works with management to choose an auditor. The committee monitors the audit to make sure that it is thorough, objective, and independent.

In spite of these controls, management still pays the audit fee and has considerable influence over whether the auditing firm is hired again. Such influence can threaten the auditor's independence. A recent issue of *Accountancy* reports that "auditors may be loath to report faults in their clients' operations for fear of losing their audit contract." Some managers have been known to "shop around" for favorable audit opinions. For example, when Broadview Financial Corporation, a large company in Ohio,

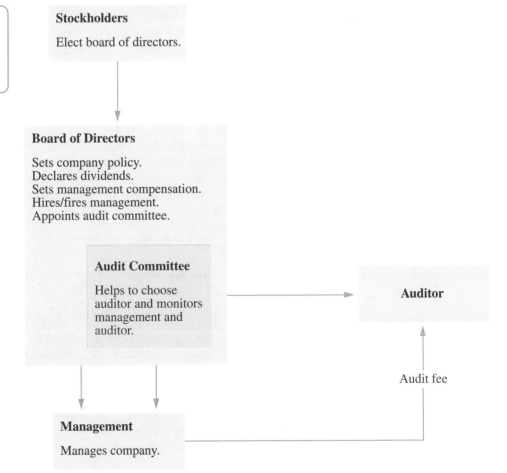

FIGURE 1–8

The role of the board of directors and the audit committee

Stockholders

Elect board of directors.

Board of Directors

Sets company policy.
Declares dividends.
Sets management compensation.
Hires/fires management.
Appoints audit committee.

Audit Committee

Helps to choose auditor and monitors management and auditor.

Auditor

Audit fee

Management

Manages company.

switched auditors, it was revealed later that the switch was due to disagreements about proper methods of accounting. Fortunately for investors, events like auditor changes must be disclosed in the SEC Form 8-K, which is available to the public.

Legal Liability

While pressure from management can threaten an auditor's independence, it is important to realize that there are federal regulations against "opinion shopping" and that auditors have a responsibility to the public to conduct a thorough and independent audit. Such responsibility gives rise to **legal liability,** which provides an economic incentive for auditors to conduct their work in a diligent and ethical manner.

Suppose in the Microline scenario that the company was not a legitimate operation and, for whatever reason, the auditor conducted an incomplete and careless audit and was influenced by Martin to write a favorable audit report. Trusting the report and the financial statements, you decide to invest your $1 million. In a short time the company fails and you lose your investment. It is revealed later that the statements were in error as of the time of the audit. In such a situation you would have a strong case for suits against both Martin and the auditor. Such suits can be very costly in the United States, and the auditor's legal liability seems to be increasing with each passing year. Several years ago, for example, the seventh largest accounting firm in the United States, Laventhol & Horwath, declared bankruptcy largely due to the costs of defending itself against lawsuits. Over several years prior to the failure, the firm paid approximately $50 million in claims to owners and creditors of clients who accused it of shoddy audit work. In addition, failures in the Savings & Loan industry, which cost taxpayers billions of dollars in the early 1990s, led S&L regulators to file suits against major accounting firms, seeking well over $1 billion in damages for fraud, negligence, and misconduct. *Business Week* reports that "In the wake of financial debacles, accountants are almost routinely sued, even though clients may have hidden relevant information from them." For example, Cendant, a New York–based marketing company, sued Ernst & Young for not discovering $500 million in fake revenues reported by the company. In 2000, Cendant faced liability suits from angry shareholders that totaled $2.5 billion to $3 billion.

Consequently, auditors have strong economic incentives to maintain their independence and not allow themselves to be influenced by pressures from managers. Similarly, the legal liability faced by managers encourages them to refrain from pressuring auditors too strongly.

Ethics and Professional Reputation

Financial accounting statements are one of several mechanisms designed to control management's business decisions and protect the interests of the shareholders. Others include the board of directors, the audit committee, regulations against "opinion shopping," and legal liability.

All these control devices suggest that a large amount of mistrust exists among shareholders, managers, and auditors. It is difficult to question such a conjecture when you realize that cases of management fraud and embezzlement have risen significantly in recent years and that audit firms have increasingly been found guilty of misconduct. Companies involved in recent well-known frauds include MicroStrategy, California Micro Devices Corp., Sunbeam, Waste Management, MiniScribe, Leslie Fay, and Crazy Eddie's. Some have even suggested that the United States is suffering from an ethics crisis. Indeed, businesspeople in general are often viewed as greedy, driven, and unscrupulous.

Notwithstanding these developments, there is little doubt that **ethics** is a major business asset and that ethical behavior is in the long-term best interest of managers, shareholders, and auditors. Indeed, Clifford Smith, a professor of finance at the University of Rochester, stated in the *Journal of Applied Corporate Finance* that "ethical behavior is profitable." In recognition of the value of ethics, major U.S. companies, such as Boeing, General Mills, and Johnson & Johnson, have instituted special programs designed specifically to instill ethical behavior in their employees. Harvard Business School and other well-known universities offer courses in ethics, commonly through their philosophy departments. The **American Institute of Certified Public Accountants** (**AICPA**), the professional organization of CPAs, has a strong professional code of ethics, designed to instill higher ethical standards in the members of the accounting profession.

Such efforts are not only moral, they are driven by sound economic logic. Companies like Merck, Wal-Mart, and Oracle with reputations for quality, service, and ethical business practices are valued highly by investors and creditors partially because their financial statements can be trusted. Such companies and their managers are sued less frequently. Indeed, the employee manual of Wetherill Associates states, "We do not try to make profits or avoid losses. Instead, we try to take the 'right action' in the best way we know; the profits are a natural by-product."

Auditors also benefit from ethical behavior and strong reputations. Independent and respectable auditors face fewer liability suits and can generally charge client companies higher fees, primarily because their audit reports are trusted by the public. Consequently, it is important to realize that while the financial accounting process is a system of control, and manager and auditor fraud will continue to occur, it is best to be ethical, from both a moral and an economic standpoint. Not surprisingly, the most successful companies and audit firms enjoy the best reputations for high ethical standards.

Recent federal rules require that public accounting firms stop cross-selling some big-ticket consulting services to audit clients. Discuss how this rule can improve the audit function.

ECONOMIC CONSEQUENCES: MANAGEMENT'S PERSPECTIVE

To run a company effectively, management must be able to attract capital from equity and debt holders at a reasonable cost. Since equity and debt holders use financial statements to evaluate and control management, which helps to determine this cost, the financial statements have direct economic consequences on management and the business. Real-world examples are provided below.

- Earnings reports have been coming up rosier than ever for the first quarter of 2000—up about 20 percent from the corresponding period last year. As a result, many market strategists believe that stocks will soon resume a steady upward climb (*New York Times,* April 14, 2000).
- Cisco Systems and Alcoa—whose real-time manufacturing saves them billions every year—also run their financial statements that way. Cisco tracks revenues and profits daily; it can close its books in a given day with hard numbers. Real-time accounting not only saves these companies bookkeeping costs, but more importantly it has changed the way they run their businesses (*Fortune,* June 26, 2000).

- The nation's main accounting rule-making body has decided to require companies to include shipping and handling costs in a category on the income statement that will reduce gross profit margins. "This is the last thing that e-retail companies need," said Tom Wyman of J.P. Morgan and Co. "It will cut Amazon.com's numbers by one-half and Etoys will likely see its margins for the year go from 21 percent to minus 3 percent" (*Dow Jones News Service,* June 2, 2000).
- The Boston law firm of Berman, DeValerio & Pease last week announced six separate class action lawsuits on behalf of investors against companies that have been accused of inflating their earnings with creative accounting (*Barron's,* June 26, 2000).
- Ever wonder why so many mergers make the CEO look superhuman? Odds are, it's not the strategic fit. It's the accounting (*Fortune,* April 26, 1999).

In each of these cases the reporting of financial statement numbers led to an economic consequence to the firm and its management. Astute managers should be aware of these consequences and attempt to anticipate them when making business decisions. Thus, managers should understand how their business decisions affect the financial statements and how the financial statements are used by capital providers and other outsiders.

These economic consequences can be far-reaching and in some cases create strong incentives for management to manage the perceptions of investors. The *Wall Street Journal* (May 23, 2000) reported: "Indeed, there is a growing trend by companies to emphasize whatever numbers make them look best—many unprofitable Internet companies, for example, focus on revenues or even the number of Web-site visitors, ignoring earnings."

It even happens that management sometimes goes beyond ethical boundaries in its attempt to make the financial statements appear as attractive as possible. In 1999, for example, Cendant, a well-known marketing company, disclosed that it falsified company books to inflate profits by $220 million. Unfortunately, such cases are not unusual, and financial statement users must be savvy to the possibility that management has influence over the reported statements. But rarely does falsifying the financial records lead to benefits for management in the long run. Indeed, recent academic research in accounting has shown that firms that use conservative accounting methods are valued more highly by the stock market, and as mentioned earlier, ethics is viewed by many as a prime business asset.

GENERALLY ACCEPTED ACCOUNTING PRINCIPLES

Generally accepted accounting principles (GAAP) play a critical role in the financial accounting process. They define the standards for external reporting, which produces greater uniformity in the accounting methods used by the variety of profit-seeking entities in the economy. Defining general reporting practices by a single set of standards facilitates meaningful comparisons of the financial performance of different companies. In addition, the level of credibility in the financial statements is largely determined by the extent to which their preparation follows GAAP. For example, if neither Coca-Cola nor PepsiCo followed GAAP in the preparation of their financial statements, not only would it be virtually impossible to compare their levels of performance because their measures of profit would be computed in different ways, but neither measure of profit would be very credible.

While the development of financial accounting and the need for reporting standards can be traced back to the beginning of record keeping, perhaps the most important single event occurred in 1929 when the U.S. capital markets collapsed, and the Great Depression followed. Many factors contributed to this dramatic economic downturn, and the lack of both credibility and uniformity in the financial accounting information available to investors and creditors did little to help the situation.

The Securities and Exchange Commission

In response to demands from the investing community for uniform and credible financial accounting information, in 1934 the U.S. Congress created the **Securities and Exchange Commission** (**SEC**). An agency of the federal government, the SEC was commissioned to implement and enforce the Securities Act of 1933 and the Securities Exchange Act of 1934. The Securities Act of 1933 requires that companies issuing securities on the public security markets file a registration statement (Form S-1) with the SEC prior to the issuance. The SEC Act of 1934 states that, among other requirements, companies with securities listed on the public security markets (*listed companies*) must (1) annually file audited financial reports with the SEC (Form 10-K), (2) file quarterly financial statements with the SEC (Form 10-Q), and (3) provide audited financial reports annually to the stockholders.

The Role of the Accounting Profession

The SEC was given broad powers by Congress to prescribe the accounting practices and standards to be used by companies within its jurisdiction. However, it has chosen not to assume this responsibility. Instead, it has allowed and encouraged the American Institute of Certified Public Accountants (AICPA), a nongovernment body, to take an active role. The AICPA has responded by establishing several standard-setting bodies since 1939: the Committee on Accounting Procedures (1939–59), the Accounting Principles Board (1959–71), and the Financial Accounting Standards Board (1973–present). Current GAAP contain standards established by all three of these boards. It is true, however, that the SEC still assumes an important oversight role and exerts a significant influence on the standard-setting process.

The Financial Accounting Standards Board

The **Financial Accounting Standards Board** (**FASB**) consists of seven well-compensated, full-time individuals who have severed all ties from previous employers and represent many business backgrounds. Since 1973 this private-sector body has issued well over 100 **statements of financial accounting standards** covering a wide variety of topics. In addition, the FASB has opened its deliberations to the public and initiated a number of procedural changes that specifically invite public participation. The process of establishing accounting standards now includes several points at which letters and personal presentations from the public are encouraged. Indeed, generally accepted accounting principles are the result of a joint effort among specialized experts, industry interests, government representatives, report users, auditors, academics, and the FASB.

Accounting Standard Setting: A Political Process

Even though the FASB is a private body, standard setting is very much a political process. Figure 1–9 illustrates its political nature. Policymakers, represented by the

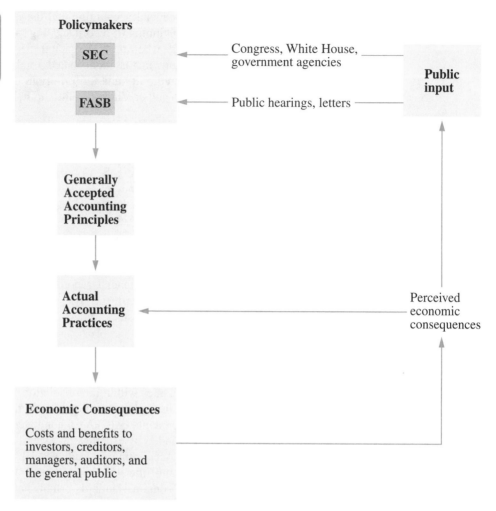

Source: Jamie Pratt, "The Economics of External Reporting: Three Frameworks for the Classroom," *Journal of Accounting Education* (1987), p. 182.

SEC and the FASB, are influenced in their deliberations by public input from Congress, the White House, government agencies, public hearings, and letters from interested parties. The result is generally accepted accounting principles, which, in turn, lead to actual accounting practices, the methods used by companies to account for their business activities. These methods, in turn, bring about **economic consequences,** the costs and benefits to investors, creditors, managers, auditors, and the general public associated with reported financial accounting information. Such costs and benefits play a special role in the political process because they create incentives for interested parties to provide public input to policymakers.

Reactions to Economic Consequences: Lobbying Accounting Numbers

Economic consequences, like the examples listed earlier, encourage interested parties, especially corporate management, to lobby the SEC and FASB in an attempt to influence generally accepted accounting principles. Corporations in the United States spend millions of dollars each year on such lobbying efforts by contacting Congressmen, appearing at public FASB hearings, and sending letters to the FASB and SEC. These efforts are often successful. Several years ago *The Wall Street Journal* reported: "When the FASB proposed that companies recognize the cost of executive options, corporate lobbyists steamrolled Congress and forced the FASB into a timid retreat."

The *Washington Post* (June 25, 2000) reported that a proposed FASB ruling would do away with a frequently used method of accounting for mergers. Affected companies say that the new rule would have "calamitous" results, reducing reported profits far into the future. Discuss some of the possible economic consequences of this ruling as well as industry's reaction.

INTERNATIONAL PERSPECTIVE: ACCOUNTING PRACTICES AND STANDARDS THROUGHOUT THE WORLD

The financial accounting process existing in the U.S. has evolved within a capitalistic system where markets are relatively free. Full disclosure is advocated and the decision needs of investors, creditors, and other outsiders are first priority. Financial accounting practices and standards used in other countries, however, are quite diverse.

Different Accounting Systems

Just as nations have different histories, economies, cultures, and political systems, they also have different systems of financial accounting. Indeed, accounting systems have evolved in response to the demands of the business environment, and the business environments faced by companies in different parts of the world are vastly dissimilar. For example, financial reporting in North America, the United Kingdom, and Australia tends to be oriented toward the decision needs of investors and designed to measure the effectiveness of management. The countries in this category tend to have large, well-developed securities markets, high levels of education, and a number of multinational corporations. A consumer orientation and a legal system that encourages litigation also tend to be more prevalent in these countries.

The accounting methods used in Japan and most of the countries in Western Europe are not oriented toward the needs of investors. Rather, they provide information that is used to satisfy government requirements, such as computing income taxes. Banks are very important providers of capital in these economies, and financial accounting practices tend to be largely at the discretion of management and tend to be highly conservative, sometimes withholding relevant information from the shareholders.

South American accounting methods are oriented toward the needs of government planners, and uniform rules are imposed on virtually all business entities. The most distinguishing feature about this system is that it includes periodic adjustments for inflation, a phenomenon that has plagued South America for many years.

For countries formerly in the communist bloc where there was limited private ownership, accounting rules were rigid and oriented to government planners. Financial statements were not prepared for outside investors and creditors. Instead, they were submitted to agency administrators who implemented the tight central economic controls of the communist system. The recent shift toward democracy and capitalism in these countries has encouraged greater economic exchange, less restricted markets, and more openness, resulting in greater levels of disclosure for investors and creditors.

International Accounting Standard Setting

The fact that so much diversity exists in worldwide accounting standards and practice makes it difficult for investors and creditors to compare the performances of companies operating in different countries. Comparing the performance of a South American textile mill to one from Australia, for example, is almost impossible because their financial reports are prepared using different accounting methods. Such differences can lead to a loss of credibility in the financial statements and investment decisions based on misunderstanding. It is also costly and time-consuming for financial statement users to educate themselves about the different accounting practices followed internationally.

Many efforts have been made to achieve greater international understanding and uniformity of accounting practices. The most active, and increasingly important, is the **International Accounting Standards Committee (IASC)**, formed in 1973 to develop worldwide accounting practices. This private-sector body, representing over ninety countries, can be viewed as the international counterpart of the FASB. It has issued a number of international accounting standards that are recognized as acceptable reporting by a large number of the major stock exchanges in the world. However, the SEC still does not recognize IASC standards as acceptable for the U.S. public exchanges.

The European Commission passed a rule in 2000 requiring that all companies in the European Union (EU), whose equity securities are traded on the public European markets, prepare their financial statements in conformity with International Accounting Standards (IAS) by the year 2005. At the time, only 275 companies in the EU used IAS; the commission hopes that the number will be 7000 by 2005. Discuss how this move could help investors, and how companies in the EU might be reacting to it.

APPENDIX 1A

THREE OTHER KINDS OF ACCOUNTING

This text is devoted almost exclusively to financial accounting. However, you should be aware of the three other kinds of accounting usually covered in other accounting courses: not-for-profit accounting, managerial accounting, and tax accounting.

Many economic entities do not have profit as an objective. Municipalities, such as cities, simply receive money from taxes, service fees, and debt investors and allocate it to address public needs. For example, a city allocates funds to a police department to ensure public safety. The process of recording these fund inflows and outflows and reporting them to the public is quite logically called **not-for-profit accounting.**

Managers need *internal information systems* to generate timely and accurate information that helps them plan and operate efficiently on a day-to-day basis. To guide their decisions, managers rely to some extent on the information produced by the financial accounting system. However, more important to such decisions is information that is not available to the public and is produced strictly for management's own use. Such information is referred to as **managerial accounting** information, and managerial accounting is usually covered in a separate course.

The area of accounting devoted to understanding and applying the tax law is known as **tax accounting.** Our complicated and constantly changing tax structure requires that thousands of accountants specialize in this area. Furthermore, tax law is extremely detailed and complicated;

even a moderate coverage of tax accounting requires a number of separate accounting or law courses.

An important distinction should be made between the income number resulting from applying income tax laws (called *taxable income*) and the income number that results from financial accounting (called *net income*). The *Internal Revenue Code* specifies the rules to be followed to calculate taxable income. An entity's tax obligation is then computed as a percentage of this taxable income. Financial accounting income, or net income, is determined by applying financial accounting principles and procedures, which differ in many ways from the tax laws stated in the Internal Revenue Code. As a result, net income is not necessarily equal to taxable income. Tax laws are enacted for purposes quite different from those that drive the development of financial accounting principles. Accounting students often confuse these two sets of rules.

Figure 1A–1 compares not-for-profit, managerial, and tax accounting to financial accounting. The top of the chart depicts a sequential process in which the managers of an economic entity follow certain accounting processes that convert financial facts about the entity into a set of financial statements. Interested parties then use this information for a variety of business decisions.

FIGURE 1A–1 Four kinds of accounting

Economic Entity →	Managers →	System →	Financial Information →	Recipients →	Decisions
FINANCIAL ACCOUNTING					
Profit-making companies	Finance or accounting department	Generally accepted accounting principles	Income statement Balance sheet Statement of retained earnings Statement of cash flows Other disclosures Auditor report	*External* Investors Creditors Suppliers Employees Managers Government General public	Equity and debt investments Contract negotiations Regulation Dividend payments
NOT-FOR-PROFIT ACCOUNTING					
Nonprofit entities	Finance or accounting department	Fund accounting principles	Balance sheet Funds flow statements	*External* Creditors Government General public	Debt investments Budget allocations
MANAGERIAL ACCOUNTING					
All entities	Internal accounting department	Company information system	Manager reports Production costs Performance evaluation, etc.	*Internal* Managers	Operating decisions
TAX ACCOUNTING					
All entities	Finance or accounting department	Internal Revenue Code	Official tax forms: 1040 for individuals 1120 for corporations	*External* Internal Revenue Service	Collection of government revenues

SUMMARY OF KEY POINTS

The key points of this chapter are summarized below.

○ *The economic role of financial accounting statements.*

Investors and creditors demand that management provide financial accounting information for two fundamental economic reasons. First, they need financial numbers to monitor and enforce the debt and compensation contracts written with management. Second, they need financial information to decide where to invest their funds. Companies incur the costs of providing the statements and having them audited because they need to attract capital from investors and creditors, and managers want to maintain their levels of compensation. Management hires auditors who must act independently because they face high levels of legal liability and must follow professional ethical standards.

○ *The standard audit report, management letter, and footnotes to the financial statements.*

The auditor's report is divided into three paragraphs. The first states that the financial statements are the responsibility of management, they have been audited, and the auditor's responsibility is to express an opinion on them. The second indicates that the examination of the company's records was made in accordance with generally accepted auditing standards and that the auditor has obtained reasonable assurance that the financial statements are free of material misstatement. The final paragraph states that the financial statements present fairly the financial position of the company, the results of operations, and its cash flows in conformity with generally accepted accounting principles.

The management letter normally states that the company's management is responsible for the preparation and integrity of the statements, that the statements were prepared in accordance with generally accepted accounting principles, and that certain amounts were based on management's best estimates and judgments. It further indicates that the company maintains a system of internal controls designed to safeguard its assets and ensure that all transactions are recorded and reported properly. The footnotes provide additional information about the dollar amounts on the financial statements. They indicate which accounting methods were used and where the numbers on the statements are the result of assumptions and estimates made by management.

○ *The four financial statements and the kind of financial information each provides.*

The four financial statements are (1) the balance sheet, (2) the income statement, (3) the statement of retained earnings, and (4) the statement of cash flows. The balance sheet lists the assets, liabilities, and stockholders' equity of a company at a given point in time. The income statement contains the revenues earned and expenses incurred by a company over a period of time. Revenues less expenses equal net income. The statement of retained earnings reconciles the retained earnings amount from one period to the next. Beginning retained earnings, plus net income, less dividends, equal ending retained earnings. The statement of cash flows reconciles the cash amount from one period to the next. It lists net cash flows from operating activities, investing activities, and financing activities.

○ *The two forms of investment—debt and equity—and how the information on the financial statements relates to them.*

There are two forms of investment: debt and equity. A debt investment is a loan, and debt investors are called *creditors*. When debt investments are made, management is normally required to sign a loan contract. Creditors are primarily concerned that the interest and principal payments are met on a timely basis. Since such payments are made in cash, creditors are interested in financial information that helps them to predict future cash flows over the period of the loan.

Equity investments involve purchasing ownership interests in a company. Equity owners of corporations are called stockholders. Their returns come in the form of dividends (or *stock price appreciation*), which tend to be large if the company performs well and small, or nonexistent, if it performs poorly. The primary concern of stockholders is the performance of the company's management—specifically, its ability to generate and maintain earning power in the future. To achieve this objective, management must ensure that cash is available to meet debts as they come due and also invest in assets that produce satisfactory returns in the long run. Consequently, stockholders are interested in the information contained in all four of the financial statements.

○ *Why ethics is important in the accounting process.*

The financial statements, debt and compensation contracts, the board of directors, auditors, and the audit committee all represent methods of controlling the business decisions of management in an effort to protect the investments of stockholders and creditors. While management and auditors have incentives to misrepresent the financial statements or exploit the system, there are compelling moral and economic reasons to act ethically. Ethical managers and auditors face less legal liability and are able to charge higher fees for their services than those whose behavior has been questioned. Accordingly, companies, universities, and the accounting profession have recently pursued efforts to enhance the ethical behavior of businesspeople.

○ *The Securities and Exchange Commission, the Financial Accounting Standards Board, and the development of generally accepted accounting principles.*

The SEC Act of 1934 established the Securities and Exchange Commission as the governmental body responsible for ensuring that listed companies prepare and file registration statements before they issue new securities, submit the annual Form 10-K, and prepare quarterly and annual reports for stockholders. The SEC also has broad powers to prescribe the accounting practices and standards to be employed by companies within its jurisdiction.

The SEC has allowed and encouraged the accounting profession to take an active role in setting standards. In 1973 the Financial Accounting Standards Board was established by a committee of the AICPA to assume responsibility for developing financial accounting standards. Since that time, the FASB, the third private body to develop standards of financial accounting, has issued over 100 standards and has received the full support of the SEC.

○ *The current status of international accounting practices and standards.*

Financial accounting practices and standards used in countries throughout the world are quite diverse due to different histories, cultures, economies, and political systems. There are four basic models: Anglo, Continental, South American, and Communist (which is disappearing). Each model represents a different orientation toward financial accounting measurement and disclosure, based primarily on the economic, political, and social characteristics of the constituent countries. Recent efforts by the International Accounting Standards Committee have attempted to bring greater uniformity to worldwide accounting practice, and many stock exchanges, except in the United States, have accepted these standards.

KEY TERMS

Note: Definitions for these terms are provided in the glossary at the end of the text.

American Institute of Certified Public
   Accountants (AICPA) (p. 21)
Annual interest (p. 13)
Annual reports (p. 13)
Assets (p. 11)
Audit committee (p. 19)
Auditor's report (p. 7)
Balance sheet (p. 11)
"Big 5" (p. 18)
Board of directors (p. 13)
Certified public accountant (CPA) (p. 6)
Common stock (p. 11)
Compensation contracts (p. 18)
Consolidated financial statements (p. 18)
Creditors (p. 11)
Debt investment (p. 13)
Debt restrictions (p. 13)
Dividends (p. 11)
Earning power (p. 12)
Economic consequence perspective (p. 4)
Economic consequences (p. 24)
Equity (p. 13)
Ethics (p. 21)
Expenses (p. 11)
Financial accounting (p. 3)
Financial Accounting Standards Board
   (FASB) (p. 23)
Financing activities (p. 11)
Footnotes (p. 10)
Generally accepted accounting
   principles (GAAP) (p. 22)
Historical cost (p. 13)

Income statement (p. 11)
Independent audit (p. 6)
Industries (p. 17)
Internal control system (p. 8)
International Accounting Standards
   Committee (IASC) (p. 26)
Investing activities (p. 11)
Legal liability (p. 20)
Liabilities (p. 11)
Loan contract (p. 13)
Management letter (p. 7)
Managerial accounting (p. 26)
Managers (p. 17)
Net income (profit) (p. 11)
Nonprofit entities (p. 18)
Not-for-profit accounting (p. 26)
Operating activities (p. 11)
Retained earnings (p. 11)
Revenues (p. 11)
Securities and Exchange Commission
   (SEC) (p. 23
Solvency (p. 12)
Statement of cash flows (p. 11)
Statement of retained earnings (p. 11)
Statements of financial accounting
   standards (p. 23)
Stock markets (p. 17)
Stockholders (p. 13)
Stockholders' equity (p. 11)
Tax accounting (p. 26)
User orientation (p. 4)

ETHICS IN THE REAL WORLD

While granting clean audit opinions on years of erroneous financial statements by Vienna software maker MicroStrategy, Inc., auditor PricewaterhouseCoopers was also serving as middleman in the sale of MicroStrategy products. Wearing those two hats can compromise the independence required of audit firms, which highlights a recent SEC concern that audit firms are increasingly putting themselves in positions of divided loyalty. In light of this finding, the SEC initiated a review of all the major accounting firms in 2000, finding that many accounting firm employees own stock in their client companies and perform for them a variety of non-audit services; both constitute direct violations of auditor independence rules. In settlement with the SEC, PricewaterhouseCoopers agreed to set up a $2.5 million education fund to be used to enhance awareness of the independence rules throughout the accounting profession.

ETHICAL ISSUE Is it ethical for the same firm to provide both an independent audit service for a client while providing business advisory services, and can an auditor maintain an independent perspective while owning equity securities in an audit client?

INTERNET RESEARCH EXERCISE

Recall the reference to MicroStrategy at the beginning of the chapter. Start with the MicroStrategy Website (www.microstrategy.com) and find out what revenues and profits MicroStrategy actually reported for 1999. How has the company done since that time?

ISSUES FOR DISCUSSION

ID1–1
Financial statement users

Financial accounting statements are used by many parties. Describe how each of the following parties might use them: security analysts and stockholders, bank loan officers, a company's customers and suppliers, public utilities, labor unions, and a company's managers.

ID1–2
Auditors and management fraud

The AICPA's list of red flags, alerting auditors to the possibility of management fraud, includes a "domineering management with a weak board of directors." Briefly explain the role of the board of directors and how such a situation could indicate management fraud. Why are auditors concerned with management fraud?

ID1–3
Audit committees

Explain the function of the audit committee and describe why it is important that it consist of outside (nonmanagement) directors.

REAL DATA
ID1–4
Financial statement relationships

In its 1999 annual report, PepsiCo reported that sales dropped from $22 billion to $20 billion while profits increased from $1.9 billion to $2 billion during the year. Total assets fell from $22.6 billion in 1998 to $17.5 billion in 1999, while stockholders' equity during the same time period increased from $6.4 billion to $6.8 billion. The company's cash balance increased $700 million with cash flows from operations (+$3 billion), investing activities (−$1 billion), and financing activities (−$1.3 billion). Discuss possible explanations for these developments.

REAL DATA
ID1–5
Debt covenants

As of December 31, 1999, Continental Airlines signed contracts with its major creditors (mostly banks) that require the company to maintain a minimum cash balance of $600 million, a minimum stockholders' equity balance of $972 million, and dividend payments restricted to no more than $576 million. Discuss why the creditors impose such restrictions on Continental.

REAL DATA
ID1–6
Managing reported profits

Fortune (March 20, 2000) ran an article titled "New Ethics or No Ethics? Questionable Behavior Is Silicon Valley's Next Big Thing," which recounts stories of Internet companies that aggressively inflate their revenues, delay the recognition of expenses, and report sales that are not exactly sales. In many cases the actions of these companies, while aggressive, are not in direct violation of generally accepted accounting principles. Discuss why companies might engage in such behavior, and comment on the ethical implications.

REAL DATA

ID1-7

Audit report

The following quote was taken from the audit report written by Ernst & Young on the financial statements of America Online:

In our opinion, the financial statements referred to above present fairly, in all material respects, the financial position of America Online at June 30, 2000 and 1999, and the results of its operations and its cash flows for each of the three years in the period ending June 30, 2000, in conformity with generally accepted accounting principles.

Explain the meaning of the quote and the terms used in it.

REAL DATA

ID1-8

Real-time financial information

An Associated Press report (March 22, 2000) notes that real-time data transmission and the information explosion has brought about a dramatic shift in the way financial information is disseminated. The audited financial statement and the independent audit, which evolved years ago to provide timely and relevant information about a company, now serve only to ratify financial information that has been in the public domain for some time. Meanwhile, the financial information disseminated through new channels is released without the benefit of an independent third party verifying the reliability and credibility of the information. Yet the investing public relies heavily on this information, and stock price movements are based on them. Discuss.

ID1-9

International accounting standards

Time International (February 14, 2000) reported that: "Most of the world has rallied around a set of 40 rules devised by the International Accounting Standards Committee. But the United States is reluctant to accept IASC standards, which it thinks pales in comparison to its own. It seems, however, that the rest of the world has little interest in adopting the U.S. model, which is viewed as outdated and over-laden with unnecessary prohibitions. Forces in the U.S. pushing for easier accounting standards include the New York Stock Exchange and the NASDAQ, who face growing competition from electronic markets and foreign exchanges, for companies to have their securities listed. Yet, the SEC has launched a recent attack on weak accounting rules and against firms that have been caught fiddling with their books. Discuss.

REAL DATA

ID1-10

Westernizing Japanese accounting

Japan's adoption of U.S.–style accounting methods is forcing many troubled companies to lift the veil from their balance sheets—and the results aren't pretty (Dow Jones & Co., February 29, 2000). How could the introduction of U.S.–style accounting methods give rise to such a situation in Japan?

ID1-11

Appendix 1A

Distinguish management accounting from financial accounting, and describe how the information provided by the two systems is used differently.

REAL DATA

ID1-12

The annual report of Wal-Mart

The Wal-Mart annual report is reproduced in Appendix A.

REQUIRED:

Review the 2001 Wal-Mart annual report, and answer the following questions.

a. Briefly describe the operations of Wal-Mart and indicate whether it is a manufacturing, retail, or service company.
b. Which accounting firm audits Wal-Mart? Briefly explain the contents of the audit report.
c. What dollar amounts for net income were reported in 2001, 2000, and 1999?
d. Compute Wal-Mart's liabilities as a percent of total assets in 2001 and 2000. Did the percentage increase or decrease.
e. How much cash was provided by operating activities during 2001, 2000, and 1999?
f. Comment on Wal-Mart's financial performance and condition.

The Financial Statements

CHAPTER 2

KEY POINTS

The following key points are emphasized in this chapter:

- *The three basic activities of a business and how they are reflected in the financial statements.*

- *The balance sheet, income statement, statement of retained earnings, and statement of cash flows and how these financial statements are used.*

In 1998, Air France announced profits of 1.87 billion francs ($315 million), attributed to stronger sales from a new Paris hub, increased domestic service, and tighter cost control. The French airline also cut its debt by more than half and dramatically increased its cash flow from several years earlier, when overstaffing and inefficiency made it Europe's least profitable major airline. The announcement was viewed as particularly good news by the French government, which was in the process of selling the company's shares to the public. These activities, so important to the success of Air France or any company, are reflected in different ways on the financial statements— the balance sheet, the income statement, the statement of cash flows, and the statement of retained earnings—that are the subject of this chapter.[1]

As you read this chapter, consider the following questions. How do operating, investing, and financing decisions affect the dollar amounts reported on the financial statements? What information on the financial statements can be used to assess solvency and earning power? How might investors and creditors use the dollar values shown on the financial statements to control and monitor the business decisions of managers? Is management able to influence the preparation of these statements so that solvency and earning power are depicted attractively? Such questions give economic meaning to financial statements and cannot be ignored by savvy managers.

BUSINESSES ARE LIKE FRUIT TREES

Note that a fruit tree is comprised of three parts: roots, trunk/branches, and fruit. The roots provide necessary nutrients to the trunk and branches which, in turn, bear fruit. A strong root system provides the required nourishment for a solid trunk and branching system, which can lead to plump, juicy, delicious fruit. The primary function of the root and trunk/branch systems is to produce and support the fruit, which can be consumed by the tree's owner or sold. Proceeds from fruit sales can be reinvested in the tree by hiring someone to prune and care for the trunk and branch system, and by purchasing and applying fertilizer to strengthen the roots.[2]

As depicted in Figure 2–1, businesses operate much like a fruit tree. To start a business, an **entrepreneur** must attract, or provide, capital in the form of equity or debt financing. Owners contribute cash and receive equity shares in return. Creditors loan cash in return for the promise of interest and principal payments. Note how equity and debt financing correspond to the root system of the fruit tree; they provide the nutrients necessary to support the entire process.

Once the capital (cash) is collected, it is then invested in producing assets, such as buildings, equipment, machinery, and vehicles, which produce and support the goods and services provided by the business. Note how the producing assets correspond to the trunk and branch system of the fruit tree in that they lead directly to the final product.

In a business the final product is a good or service, which is sold to customers. The net earnings from these sales can be used in three ways: (1) reinvested in the producing assets, (2) returned to the creditors in the form of debt payments, and (3) returned to the owners in the form of dividends. Note how the goods and services provided by a business are similar to the fruit, which can be sold and (1) reinvested in the trunk and branches, (2) used to strengthen the roots, or (3) consumed by the owners.

---

1. Major U.S. corporations are also required to prepare a statement of stockholders' equity. Due to its complexity, we do not cover this financial statement until Chapter 12. The earlier chapters refer to the statement of retained earnings, a part of the statement of stockholders' equity.

2. Interestingly, throughout its 1993 annual report PepsiCo, Inc., used a similar tree analogy to illustrate its variety of products.

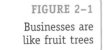

FIGURE 2–1

Businesses are like fruit trees

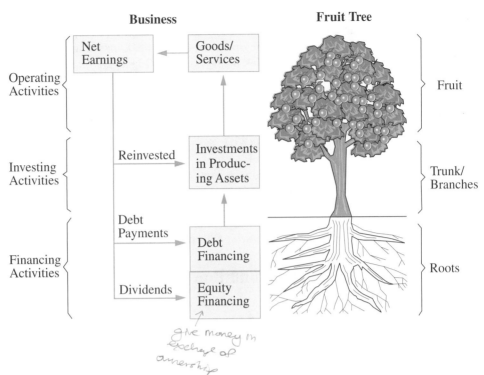

The comparison between businesses and fruit trees highlights three basic activities involved in conducting a business: (1) financing activities, (2) investing activities, and (3) operating activities. **Financing activities** involve the collection of capital through equity or debt issuances and any associated payments such as dividends and debt payments. These activities are the "roots" of the business. **Investing activities** involve the acquisition and sale of producing assets, the assets used to produce and support the goods and services provided. These activities are the "trunk and branches" of the business. **Operating activities** involve the sale of the goods and services and therefore are the "fruit" of the business. These activities produce additional capital that can be reinvested in the producing assets, used to service debt payments, and distributed to the owners in the form of dividends.

In its 2000 annual report, La-Z-Boy, a well-known furniture manufacturer, reported cash provided by operating activities of $58 million, cash used by investing activities of $104 million, and cash provided by financing activities of $27 million. Describe some of the transactions that led to each of these three cash flow numbers.

The remainder of the chapter is devoted to describing and interpreting the financial statements. As you study them, keep in mind that they are designed to measure different aspects of businesses and fruit trees, as depicted in Figure 2–1. The balance sheet includes assets (goods and producing assets) and financing sources (equity, debt, and reinvestments from net earnings) as of a point in time. It therefore represents a picture of the tree, including its trunk and root system. The income statement is a measure of operations, the activities involved in selling the goods and services, the "fruit" of the business. The statement of retained earnings measures the extent to which the business reinvests its net earnings and pays dividends (i.e., is the fruit reinvested in the tree or consumed?). The statement of cash flows reports the cash inflows and outflows associated with the operating (fruit sales), investing (trunk and branches), and financing (roots) activities of the business. Managers must understand the link between the financial statements and the company's financial condition and performance, as well as how their operating, investing, and financing decisions are reflected on the statements.

THE CLASSIFIED BALANCE SHEET

We now turn to more in-depth discussions of the four financial statements.[3] Figure 2–2 shows the balance sheet for Harbour Island Company as of December 31, 2002. It is entitled a **classified balance sheet** because the asset and liability accounts are grouped into classifications: current assets; long-term investments; property, plant, and equipment; intangible assets; current liabilities; and long-term liabilities.

A Photograph of Financial Condition

Think of the balance sheet as a photograph of the business at a specific point in time. The title includes a specific date (December 31, 2002). As of this date, the balance sheet measures the financial condition of Harbour Island Company. In fact, some companies refer to the balance sheet as the *statement of financial condition*. This "photograph" of financial condition shows that as of December 31, 2002, Harbour Island has $220 in cash, total assets of $18,615, contributed capital of $9,550, retained earnings of $1,385, and total liabilities plus stockholders' equity of $18,615.

The balance sheet lists Harbour Island's assets and their sources as of December 31, 2002. The company's total assets (valued at $18,615) came from three separate sources: (1) $7,680 (41 percent) came from various forms of borrowing (total liabilities) and must be repaid in the future, (2) $9,550 (51 percent) came from investments by stockholders (contributed capital), who expect some form of return in the future, and (3) $1,385 (8 percent), the dollar amount in the retained earnings account, was generated through the company's operating activities and not returned to the stockholders in the form of dividends.

Balance Sheet Classifications

Assets are divided into current assets ($1,415), long-term investments ($4,000), property, plant, and equipment ($11,500), and intangible assets ($1,700). These categories and the order of the accounts within them are listed in order of **liquidity.** The assets listed near the top of the balance sheet (e.g., current assets) are expected to be converted into cash within a shorter time period than those listed at or near the bottom. They are, therefore, considered to be more liquid. The assets in the current asset category are also listed in order of liquidity. Cash, the most liquid of all assets, is understandably listed at the top.

> Explain why total assets on the balance sheet of McDonald's Corporation consists of about 80 percent property, plant, and equipment.

---

3. The accounts that comprise the financial statements are discussed more thoroughly throughout the remainder of the text.

FIGURE 2–2

Classified balance sheet for Harbour Island Company

Liquidity
Highest at top

Harbour Island Company
Classified Balance Sheet
December 31, 2002

ASSETS

Current assets:			
Cash		$ 220	
Short-term investments		150	
Accounts receivable	$ 350		
Less: Uncollectibles	5	345	
Inventory		600	
Prepaid expenses		100	
Total current assets			$ 1,415
Long-term investments:			
Long-term notes receivable		$1,000	
Land		500	
Securities		2,500	
Total long-term investments			4,000
Property, plant, and equipment:			
Property		$6,000	
Plant	$ 4,000		
Less: Accumulated depreciation	1,100	2,900	
Equipment	$ 3,500		
Less: Accumulated depreciation	900	2,600	
Total property, plant, & equip.			11,500
Intangible assets:			
Goodwill		$ 800	
Patent		200	
Trademark		700	
Total intangible assets			1,700
Total assets			$18,615

LIABILITIES AND STOCKHOLDERS' EQUITY

Current liabilities:			
Accounts payable		$ 250	
Wages payable		25	
Interest payable		155	
Short-term notes payable		75	
Current maturities of long-term debts		60	
Deferred revenues		75	
Other payables		100	
Total current liabilities			$ 740
Long-term liabilities:			
Long-term notes payable		$1,500	
Bonds payable		3,500	
Mortgage payable		1,940	
Total long-term liabilities			6,940
Stockholders' equity:			
Contributed capital		$9,550	
Retained earnings		1,385	
Total stockholders' equity			10,935
Total liabilities and stockholders' equity			$18,615

Liabilities are divided into current liabilities ($740) and long-term liabilities ($6,940). These two categories, and the accounts within them, are also listed in order of liquidity. Those near the top (e.g., current liabilities) are expected to require the payment of cash within a shorter time period than those at or near the bottom. Study these categories and the order of the accounts contained within them. This is the general format required under generally accepted accounting principles, and it is important that you be familiar with it.

Assets

We now discuss the individual balance sheet accounts. This section reviews current assets; long-term investments; property, plant, and equipment; and intangible assets.

CURRENT ASSETS

Assets categorized as current are expected to be realized or, in most cases, converted into cash in the near future, usually within one year.[4] They are grouped into a separate category because they are considered to be highly liquid. The amount of highly liquid assets held by a company can be an indication of its ability to meet debt payments as they come due. Consequently, the current asset category is often reviewed by financial statement users who are interested in assessing a company's solvency position. **Current assets** include cash, short-term investments, accounts receivable, inventory, and prepaid expenses, and they often represent a significant portion of a company's total assets.

Explain why the current assets of Kmart, a major retailer, typically exceed 50 percent of total assets.   ↳ many pay on credit card

CASH. Cash represents the currency a company has access to as of the balance sheet date. It may be in a bank savings account, a checking account, or perhaps on the company premises in the form of petty cash. Cash amounts that a company can use immediately should be separated on the balance sheet from cash that is restricted. As a condition of granting a loan, for example, banks often require that the borrowing company maintain a certain cash balance with the bank while the loan is outstanding. Cash amounts of this nature, called *compensating balances*, are normally described in the footnotes to the financial statements so that readers can draw a distinction between available cash and restricted cash. Such a distinction can be useful when assessing how much cash is available to meet an outstanding debt. A recent financial report of Atlantic Richfield, for example, noted that "the company maintains compensating balances for some of its various banking services and products."

Compensating balances are required reserves to maintain for borrowing money — This is restricted cash

SHORT-TERM INVESTMENTS. **Short-term investments** include stocks (equity investments in other companies), bonds (debt investments in the government or other companies), and similar investments. These securities are both *readily marketable* (i.e., able to be sold immediately) and intended by management to be sold within a short period of time, usually less than one year. A company often purchases these kinds of securities to earn income with cash that would otherwise be idle for a short

liquid →

---

4. The actual definition of "current asset" is an asset expected to be converted into cash or used within one year or the operating cycle, whichever is longer. Operating cycles are discussed in Chapter 6.

time. The dollar value of this account is the total selling price (market value) of securities held by a company as of the balance sheet date. For purposes of solvency assessment, this dollar amount is normally viewed to be the same as available cash.

Why do you think that Aetna, an insurance company with assets of over $100 billion, carries short-term debt and equity investments of over $30 billion?

ACCOUNTS RECEIVABLE. The **accounts receivable** account represents the amount of money a company expects to collect from its customers. Such receivables arise from sales of products or services for which customers have not yet paid. These sales are often referred to as *credit sales* or *sales on account.* The dollar amount appearing on the balance sheet for this account is computed by taking the total dollar amount of the receivables owed and subtracting an estimate for *uncollectibles,* those accounts not expected to be received. The uncollectibles estimate is highly subjective, and users must be careful not to conclude that all reported receivables will necessarily lead to cash receipts.

they lend money as business

Briefly explain why Bank of America carries receivables in excess of $363 billion, which is well over 50 percent of the company's total assets.

INVENTORY. Inventory represents items or products on hand that a company intends to sell to its customers. It is often called merchandise inventory. The dollar value in this account is very important because a company's success often depends on its ability to sell these items. Users are very interested in the sales value of a company's inventory, but unfortunately, the balance sheet value of inventory is the cost of acquiring (purchasing or producing) it or the cost of replacing it as of the balance sheet date, whichever is lower.

Why do companies like Home Depot and Goodyear Tire & Rubber Company carry inventories that comprise most of their current assets and a large portion of total assets, while companies like Yahoo and Chase Manhattan Bank carry no inventories at all?

A second kind of inventory account is called *supplies inventory.* It represents items used to support a company's operations; office supplies and spare parts are two common examples. The dollar amount of this account on the balance sheet is usually the cost of acquiring the items. Major manufacturers often carry a substantial inventory of spare parts. Normally about 10 percent of The Boeing Company's total inventory is comprised of spare parts.

PREPAID EXPENSES. **Prepaid expenses** are exactly what the name suggests: expenses that have been paid by a company before the corresponding service or right is actually used. Insurance premiums, for example, are normally paid prior to the period of coverage. Similarly, rent is usually paid before the rental period. A prepaid expense, therefore, is considered an asset because it represents a benefit to be enjoyed by the company in the future; it is not considered an expense, appearing on the income statement, until it is used. Prepaid expenses are originally recorded on the balance sheet at the cost of acquiring them. For most companies, prepaid expenses are a very small, often insignificant, part of total assets. Also, prepaid expenses do not create future cash inflows, a fact that users must recognize when assessing a company's solvency position.

LONG-TERM INVESTMENTS

Long-term investments are acquired by companies to provide benefits for periods of time usually extending beyond one year. Examples include long-term notes receivable and investments in land and debt and equity securities.

The notes receivable account includes company receivables that are evidenced by promissory notes. *Promissory notes* are contracts (formal, legally enforceable documents) that state the face value of the receivable, the date when the face value is due, and the periodic interest payments to be made while the note is outstanding. The date when the receivable is due, called the *maturity date,* is often beyond one year, so this account is often listed in the long-term investment section of the balance sheet. However, if the maturity date of a note receivable is within one year, it should be disclosed as a current asset.

Notes receivable often arise because companies receive notes in exchange for the sale of expensive items. For example, The Boeing Company often receives notes in payment for sold aircraft and currently carries about $10 billion in long-term notes receivable. Alternatively, such notes can result from direct company loans to employees and others. It also happens that customers with large, overdue accounts are asked to sign promissory notes. Like accounts receivable, an estimate—often subjective—for uncollectibles must be provided for notes receivable.

The long-term investment section of the balance sheet can also include a number of other investments. Land, for example, may be purchased and held as a long-term investment. Investments in debt and equity securities that are not intended to be sold in the near future represent other common examples. Most major U.S. companies have made significant investments in the equity securities of other, usually smaller, companies, intending to exert long-term influence over their management. Owens Corning, for example, has major investments in the equity securities of over twenty different companies. Users should learn as much as possible about such investments, usually by reading the footnotes, because they signal areas where management has chosen to devote considerable attention.

PROPERTY, PLANT, AND EQUIPMENT

The property, plant, and equipment section of the balance sheet includes assets acquired for use in the day-to-day operations of the business. For many companies, especially manufacturers, this is the largest asset category on the balance sheet. For example, the property, plant, and equipment account for Exxon Mobil is valued at over $100 billion, which represents approximately 70 percent of its total assets. This account often contains the results of management's major investing activities, an important concern of financial statement users.

The **property** account represents the land on which the company conducts its operations. It is carried on the balance sheet at the original price for the land, which is not adjusted as the value of the property appreciates (i.e., increases). Be sure not to confuse this account with land in the long-term investment section. That land is held for investment purposes only and is not used in the operations of the business.

Plant and equipment represent the physical structures that a company owns and uses in its operations. The plant account, for example, includes the value of factory and office buildings and warehouses, while the equipment account includes machinery, vehicles, furniture, and similar items. The dollar amount in these accounts on the balance sheet is the original cost at the time the assets were purchased, reduced by an amount that loosely approximates the asset's lost usefulness or deterioration over time. This amount is called *accumulated depreciation.* Subtracting accumulated depreciation from the acquisition cost results in the *net value* or **net book value** of the assets. The excerpt below, which illustrates the methods used to disclose property, plant, and equipment, was taken from the 2000 annual report of Johnson & Johnson (dollars in millions).

IN MILLIONS	2000	1999
Land, Buildings, and Equipment:		
Land and improvements	$ 393	$ 375
Buildings	3,345	3,164
Machinery and equipment	6,065	6,070
Construction in progress	1,445	1,437
Total land, buildings, and equipment	$11,248	$11,046
Less accumulated depreciation	4,277	4,327
Net land, buildings, and equipment	$ 6,971	$ 6,719

INTANGIBLE ASSETS

Intangible assets are so named because they have no physical substance. In most cases they represent legal rights to the use or sale of valuable names, items, processes, or information. Many companies, such as Coca-Cola, have patents on certain formulas that grant them the sole legal right to produce and sell certain products. When NBC paid over $1 billion to acquire exclusive rights to broadcast the Olympics, it recognized an intangible asset on its balance sheet. In a similar way, a company's trademark (e.g., the golden arches of McDonald's) or its name (e.g., Goodyear Tire & Rubber) can also be valuable. Perhaps the most common intangible asset, called *goodwill,* represents the cost of purchasing another company over and above the total market price of that company's individual assets and liabilities. The goodwill account is prominent on the balance sheets of many major U.S. companies because they often purchase other companies, called *subsidiaries.* For example, when America Online purchased CompuServe, it recognized approximately $127 million in goodwill in the transaction. Similar to property, plant, and equipment, intangibles are of interest to users because they often represent the results of a company's major investing activities.

Intangible assets are carried on the balance sheet at net book value, which is equal to the cost of acquiring an intangible asset, reduced by a dollar amount, called *accumulated amortization,* which loosely approximates the asset's reduction in usefulness over time.[5] However, unlike accumulated depreciation on plant and equipment, accumulated amortization is usually not disclosed in a special account on the balance sheet; only the net book value of the intangible asset is disclosed. The excerpt below, which illustrates a method of disclosing intangible assets, was taken from the 2000 financial report of General Electric Company (dollars in millions).

	2000	1999
Goodwill	$11,962	$10,805
Other intangibles	462	457
Total	$12,424	$11,262

5. Certain intangible assets, including goodwill, are not subject to amortization.

A relatively large portion of the total assets of America Online is comprised of good-will. What does this fact tell you about the growth strategy used by AOL?

Liabilities

This section covers current and long-term liabilities. The dollar amounts disclosed in these sections of the balance sheet are very important to users who are interested in the timing of a company's future cash obligations, which is important when assessing whether a company can meet its debts when they come due. Total liabilities, as a percentage of total assets, varies significantly across companies in different industries. For example, Exxon Mobil carries liabilities of about 56 percent of total assets, while the liabilities of Bank of New York represent over 91 percent of total assets.

CURRENT LIABILITIES

Current liabilities are obligations expected to be paid (or services expected to be performed) with the use of assets listed in the current asset section of the balance sheet. Examples include Accounts Payable, Wages Payable, Interest Payable, Short-Term Notes Payable, Income Taxes Payable, Current Maturities on Long-Term Debts, and Deferred Revenues.

Accounts Payable are usually obligations to a company's suppliers for merchandise purchases made on account. Wages Payable are obligations to a company's employees for earned but unpaid wages as of the balance sheet date. Interest Payable and Short-Term Notes Payable are dollar amounts owed to creditors, often banks and other financial institutions. Income Taxes Payable are amounts owed to the government for taxes assessed on a company's income. **Current Maturities of Long-Term Debts** are portions of long-term liabilities that are due in the current period. They often arise when the principal amounts of long-term liabilities are due in installments over time. Deferred Revenues represent services yet to be performed by a company for which cash payments have already been collected.

Financial statement users often closely examine a company's current liabilities as they assess a company's solvency position because most current liabilities require cash payments in the short-term future. Retailers rely heavily on suppliers as a source of financing. For example, on the balance sheet of the GAP, Inc., the largest liability is accounts payable—over $1 billion and approximately 20 percent of total assets.

LONG-TERM LIABILITIES

Long-term liabilities are obligations expected to require payment over a period of time beyond the current year. These obligations are usually evidenced by formal contracts that state their principal amounts, the periodic interest payments, and maturity dates. The form of these debt contracts, however, can vary widely. Common examples include accounts like Long-Term Notes Payable, Bonds Payable, and Mortgage Payable.

Long-Term **Notes Payable** refer to obligations on loans that are normally due more than one year beyond the balance sheet date. They usually involve either direct borrowings from financial institutions or arrangements to finance the purchase of assets. **Bonds Payable** represent notes that have been issued for cash to a large number of debt investors (called *bondholders*). Issuing bonds is a common form of financing for many major U.S. companies, which often use the funds to expand operations.

During 1999, Federal Mogul, a manufacturer of automobile parts, issued $1 billion in bonds. The proceeds were used to finance capital expenditures and reduce other debt. **Mortgage Payables** are obligations that are secured by real estate and are usually owed to financial institutions. The contractual terms (e.g., interest notes and covenant restrictions) associated with long-term debts are particularly important to financial statement users because they identify short-term cash outflows and constraints that may inhibit management's future activities.

Provide a reasonable explanation for why the current liabilities of Bank of America are much larger than long-term liabilities and represent well over 50 percent of the total assets.

Stockholders' Equity

The **stockholders' equity** section of the balance sheet is basically divided into two parts: contributed capital and retained earnings. Note in Figure 2–2 that the total amount of stockholders' equity ($10,935) is equal to total assets ($18,615) less total liabilities ($7,680). This dollar amount is called the *net book value* of the company.

CONTRIBUTED CAPITAL

Contributed capital is a measure of the assets that have been contributed to a company by its owners.[6] Such contributions are made by purchasing the equity securities issued by the company, contributing cash or other noncash assets, or providing services. Whatever the form, the investor's contribution is exchanged for ownership interests (e.g., shares of stock) in the company. Such interests usually carry with them the right to have a voice in the management of the company (e.g., vote for the board of directors) as well as the right to receive assets (e.g., dividends), if they are distributed. In many cases, these ownership interests can be purchased and sold freely (e.g., through public stock markets), but such transactions have no effects on the company's balance sheet.

During the late 1990s, issuing stock was the principal form of financing used by Amazon.com. During 1997, 1998, and 1999, the company had three major common stock issuances, raising over $1 billion.

RETAINED EARNINGS

Retained earnings is a measure of the assets that have been generated through a company's operating activities but not paid out to stockholders in the form of dividends. This account is particularly troublesome to accounting students who tend to visualize it as a tangible pool of cash. Nothing could be further from the truth. The $1,385 in Harbour Island's retained earnings account in Figure 2–2 is not in the form of cash in the company treasurer's office or in the bank. In fact, it is not associated with any specific asset or group of assets. It is simply a measure of the amount of the assets appearing on the balance sheet that have been provided by profitable operations. All we know from the balance sheet in Figure 2–2 is that $1,385 of the $18,615 total in the asset account has been provided by the company's profitable operations.

The relative size of retained earnings on the balance sheets of major U.S. companies varies significantly across industries. Bank of America, for example, normally

6. Contributed capital is not used as a title of a balance sheet section. It encompasses a group of accounts that reflect owner contributions.

reports retained earnings of only 5 percent of total assets, while Microsoft is currently reporting retained earnings of about 50 percent of total assets. Users normally consider a large balance in retained earnings to be a positive sign because it indicates that the company has been profitable in the past and has chosen to reinvest those profits. However, young companies often report negative retained earnings because it takes several years to become profitable. Also, some very successful companies report relatively low levels of retained earnings because they pay large dividends.

As of the end of 1999, Amazon.com. reported a deficit in retained earnings of over $800 million. Explain how this could have occurred.

ORGANIZATIONAL FORM AND THE EQUITY SECTION

A business entity in the United States can be legally organized in either of two basic ways: as a corporation or as a partnership (called a *proprietorship* if there is only one owner).[7] A *corporation* is a legal entity that is separate and distinct from its owners. It can be taxed or sued, and the owners, called *stockholders* or *shareholders,* are legally liable only for the amount of their original contributions to the corporation. Stockholders acquire ownership interests by purchasing shares of stock in the corporation. Their interests give them the right to vote for its board of directors at annual stockholders' meetings as well as the right to receive dividends, which are distributed on a per-share basis, if declared by the board.

A *partnership,* or *proprietorship,* on the other hand, is not a legal entity. It can neither be taxed nor sued, and the legal liability of the owners, called *partners* or *proprietors,* is not limited to their original contributions. Asset distributions to partners are called *withdrawals.*

The differences between corporations and partnerships are reflected in differences in the equity sections of their balance sheets. The stockholders' equity section of a corporate balance sheet, as illustrated in Figure 2–2, draws a distinction between contributed capital, the measure of the assets contributed by the stockholders, and retained earnings, the assets generated through the company's operating activities and not returned to stockholders in the form of dividends.

On the other hand, the equity section on a partnership's balance sheet, called **owners' equity,** makes no distinction between contributed capital and retained earnings. Instead, it consists of separate accounts for each partner, which show the status of each partner's personal capital balance, reflecting all contributions and withdrawals. Figure 2–3 illustrates the differences between the stockholders' equity section of a corporation

FIGURE 2–3 Owners' equity: corporation vs. partnership	Corporation		Partnership	
	Stockholders' equity:		Owners' equity:	
	Contributed capital	$20,000	Capital account, Ms. A	$12,000
	Retained earnings	14,000	Capital account, Mr. B	15,000
	Total stockholders' equity	$34,000	Total owners' equity	$27,000

7. Other business forms exist that have characteristics of both partnerships and corporations. Examples include subchapter S corporations and limited liability corporations.

and the owners' equity section of a partnership with two partners. Throughout most of the text, the discussions and illustrations assume the corporate form of organization.

THE INCOME STATEMENT

The income statement measures operating performance over a particular period—the activities associated with the acquisition and sale of the company's inventories or services (i.e., "fruit"). An example, for the Harbour Island Company covering the year ended December 31, 2002, is illustrated in Figure 2–4. Note that it consists of three categories: operating revenues ($5,000), operating expenses ($3,895), and other revenues and expenses (−$20). The net amount of these three numbers yields a number called *net income* or *loss, net earnings,* or *profits* ($1,085). Net income is a very common and useful measure of operating performance. Indeed, most analysts, investors, creditors, and managers agree that net income is the most important number disclosed on the financial statements.

FIGURE 2–4
Income statement for Harbour Island Company

Harbour Island Company
Income Statement
For the Year Ended December 31, 2002

Operating revenues:		
Sales	$4,000	
Fees earned	1,000	
Total operating revenues		$5,000
Operating expenses:		
Cost of goods sold	$1,500	
Wage expense	1,000	
Rent expense	295	
Selling expense	300	
Depreciation expense	500	
Amortization expense	300	
Total operating expenses		3,895
Operating income		$1,105
Other revenues and expenses:		
Other revenues	$ 880	
Other expenses	900	
Net other revenues and expenses		(20)
Net income		$1,085

Operating Revenues

Operating revenues represent the inflow of assets (or decrease in liabilities) due to a company's operating activities over a period of time. Examples include sales and fees earned. The ability to generate operating revenues is often viewed as one of the important keys to success for a company. Indeed, in a recent annual report, John Chambers, CEO of Cisco Systems, noted that "Cisco's own ability to harness the power of the Internet . . . has resulted in exceptional value and returns for our shareholders . . . reported revenues exceeded last year by 43 percent!"

Sales is perhaps the most common revenue account. It represents a measure of asset increases (usually in the form of cash or accounts receivable) due to selling a company's products or inventories. If a company provides a service (e.g., a law firm or accounting firm) instead of selling a product, the revenue account reflecting such activity is called **Fees Earned** or **Service Revenue.** Walt Disney's income statement routinely includes both sales and service revenues. Sales are recognized when Disney products are sold, and service revenues come from its theme parks and films.

Operating Expenses

Operating expenses represent the periodic and usual outflow of assets (or creation of liabilities) required to generate operating revenues. Examples include cost of goods sold and expenses related to wages, rent, selling, depreciation, and amortization. As important as generating revenues, controlling expenses is also a barometer of a company's success. Dell is considered by many to be the number one computer-systems company in the world, largely because it does an excellent job of using the Internet to reduce operating costs.

The **cost of goods sold** account represents the original cost of the inventory items (purchase price or cost of manufacturing) that are sold to generate sales revenue. For retail and manufacturing companies, this *inventory expense* is normally separated from other operating expenses because it is comparatively large, and it is often compared to sales revenue to indicate the relationship between the selling price of the inventory and its cost. Users pay close attention to this percentage because it indicates by how much the sales price exceeds the cost of a good. Cost of goods sold as a percentage of sales for J.C. Penney, a large retailer, and Monsanto, a large manufacturer, is normally around 65 percent.

Why do you think that H&R Block, a firm that offers tax services, reports no cost of goods sold?

The remaining operating expenses differ based on the nature of a company's operations. For retailing companies, which simply purchase finished goods and then sell them (e.g., Wal-Mart), this expense category contains accounts reflecting the decrease in assets (or creation of liabilities) due to such items as commissions to salespersons, salaries, wages, insurance, advertising, rentals, utilities, property taxes, equipment maintenance, depreciation of plant and equipment, and amortization of intangible assets. Manufacturing companies, on the other hand (e.g., General Motors), typically include only selling and administrative expenses in this category. Note from the expenses listed on the income statement in Figure 2–4 that Harbour Island is a retailer.

Other Revenues and Expenses

The category *Other revenues and expenses* can include a number of items. It usually contains revenues and expenses from activities that are not central to a company's operations; therefore, the dollar amount of this category is also usually small. Other revenues include interest on bank accounts, rent collected on the rental of excess warehouse space, and book gains recognized when assets are sold for amounts that exceed those costs. Other expenses include interest on outstanding loans and book losses recognized when assets other than inventory are sold for amounts that are less than their original costs. It is very important that users appreciate the difference between revenues and expenses generated by core business activities and those generated by "one shot" transactions. Presumably, core activities can be expected to recur, while "one shot" transactions cannot.

In 1999, Honeywell International reported net income of $1.5 billion, but almost a third of that amount was due to items that would not be considered part of its core business. Explain how an analyst might react to that information.

THE STATEMENT OF RETAINED EARNINGS[8]

The statement of retained earnings, which is illustrated for Harbour Island in Figure 2–5, describes the activity in the retained earnings account over a period of time. Note that the beginning dollar balance in Retained Earnings, which comes from the December 31, 2001, balance sheet, is increased (decreased) by net income (loss), which comes from the 2002 income statement, and reduced by 2002 dividends, leading to the ending dollar balance, which can be found on the December 31, 2002, balance sheet. Thus, the balance in the retained earnings account at any point in time simply consists of past net income (earnings) amounts that have been retained in the business (i.e., not paid out in the form of dividends).

Companies retain profits to finance operations and capital expenditures and to pay off debts. The remaining profits are often returned to the shareholders in the form of dividends. Users are interested in the statement of retained earnings because it provides information about the company's dividend policy, specifically how dividends compare to reported profits.

It is important to realize that retained earnings is nothing in and of itself, but rather a measure of something else. It is not cash, nor is it an asset that can be touched or used. Instead, it is similar to an inch, a gallon, or a pound, all of which are measures of something tangible. An inch reflects a length of rope, the width of a table, or the height of a person, while retained earnings represents a measure of the assets, all of which are listed on the asset side of the balance sheet, that have been generated through profitable operations and retained in the business. Recall that assets can come

FIGURE 2–5	
Statement of retained earnings for Harbour Island Company	**Harbour Island Company** **Statement of Retained Earnings** **For the Year Ended December 31, 2002**

Beginning retained earnings balance (December 31, 2001)	**$ 500**
Plus: Net income	**1,085**
Less: Dividends	**(200)**
Ending retained earnings balance (December 31, 2002)	**$1,385**

8. The statement of retained earnings is actually a component of a larger statement—The Statement of Shareholders' Equity, which explains the changes in all shareholder equity accounts, including retained earnings, during a given period. This statement is discussed more completely in Chapter 12 of this text.

from three sources: borrowings, contributions from owners, and profitable operations. Retained earnings is a measure of the third source.

Johnson & Johnson consistently pays significant dividends to its shareholders—normally on the order of 30 to 40 percent of net income. How would this be reported on the financial statements, and what portion of earnings is normally reinvested in the business?

THE STATEMENT OF CASH FLOWS

The statement of cash flows is a summary of the activity in a company's cash account over a period of time. Understanding the statement of cash flows is simply a matter of recognizing that certain transactions entered into by a company during a given period increase the cash account, while others decrease it. The statement summarizes these transactions and, in the process, explains how the cash balance at the beginning of the period came to be the cash balance at the end of the period. The statement of cash flows for Harbour Island Company for the year ended December 31, 2002, appears in Figure 2–6.[9]

The statement of cash flows is divided into three basic categories: (1) operating activities, (2) investing activities, and (3) financing activities—the same categories of business activities introduced in the tree analogy earlier in the chapter. The transactions summarized within each of these three categories either increased or decreased cash during the period, and the net result of the three totals explains the change in a company's overall cash balance. For example, on Harbour Island's cash flow statement, operating activities increased cash by $1,470, investment activities decreased cash by $4,100, and financing activities increased cash by $2,750. The net result is $120 ($1,470 − $4,100 + $2,750), the increase in the cash balance during 2002.

The statement of cash flows provides important information to investors and creditors, especially those who are interested in assessing a company's solvency position. In a recent survey of over 60,000 companies that failed, over 60 percent blamed their failure on factors linked to cash flows.

Cash Flows from Operating Activities

Cash flows from operating activities include those cash inflows and outflows associated with the acquisition and sale of a company's products and services. The items found in this section are closely related to those found on the income statement because both measure operating inflows and outflows. However, the dollar amounts of these items on the statement of cash flows do not necessarily agree with the dollar amounts appearing for these items on the income statement. The statement of cash flows records only *cash* inflows and outflows; the income statement consists of revenues and expenses, which reflect more general *asset* and *liability* inflows and outflows. Cash is just one of a company's many assets.

9. The operating section of this statement of cash flows can be presented under either the direct or indirect method. The statement in Figure 2–6 uses the direct form of presentation. Most major U.S. companies use the indirect form of presentation, which is described in detail in Chapter 14.

FIGURE 2–6
Statement of cash
flows for Harbour
Island Company

Harbour Island Company
Statement of Cash Flows
For the Year Ended December 31, 2002

Operating activities:		
Cash collections from sales	$ 4,800	
Cash collections from rent	800	
Cash collections from interest	10	
Cash provided by operating activities		$5,610
Cash paid to suppliers	$(1,800)	
Cash paid to employees	(1,050)	
Cash paid for rent	(290)	
Cash paid for selling activities	(300)	
Cash paid for interest and taxes	(700)	
Cash disbursed for operating activities		(4,140)
Net cash increase (decrease) from		
operating activities		$1,470
Investing activities:		
Purchase of investment securities	$ (100)	
Purchase of property	(4,500)	
Proceeds from sale of investment securities	500	
Net cash increase (decrease) from		
investing activities		(4,100)
Financing activities:		
Proceeds from issuing equity	$ 3,100	
Principal payments on short-term notes	(100)	
Principal payments on long-term debt	(50)	
Cash dividends to stockholders	(200)	
Net cash increase (decrease) from		
financing activities		2,750
Increase (decrease) in cash balance		$ 120
Beginning cash balance (December 31, 2001)		100
Ending cash balance (December 31, 2002)		$ 220

Consider, for example, the sale of a service in exchange for a receivable. This transaction produces no cash; therefore, it has no effect on the statement of cash flows. It does, however, appear as a revenue on the income statement because an asset in the form of a receivable has been created. Consequently, net cash flow from operating activities on the statement of cash flows is rarely equal to net income on the income statement. In the case of Harbour Island, for example, net cash flow from operating activities in Figure 2–6 is equal to $1,470, while net income for the same period (see Figures 2–4 and 2–5) is equal to $1,085.

Two popular Web networks that emerged in the 1990s are Yahoo and Lycos. Yahoo showed negative cash flows from operations in its first few years, but began showing positive numbers in 1998. Lycos reported negative cash flows from operations throughout the 1990s. Where would these numbers be reported and how might an analyst react to them?

Cash Flows from Investing Activities

Cash flows from investing activities include the cash inflows and outflows associated with the purchase and sale of a company's investments. Cash effects from the purchase or sale of a company's marketable securities or property, plant, and equipment are common examples. Note in Figure 2–6 that Harbour Island used $100 and $4,500 to purchase long-term investment securities and property, respectively. It also generated $500 in cash by selling long-term investments. These transactions in total reduced Harbour Island's cash balance by $4,100.

In 1999, Yahoo reported net cash used by investing activities of $449 million, while Lycos reported cash inflows from investing activities of $27 million. What kind of transactions might have led to these two amounts?

Cash Flows from Financing Activities

Cash flows from financing activities include the cash inflows and outflows associated with a company's two sources of outside capital: liabilities and contributed capital. Cash proceeds from and cash principal payments on short- and long-term liabilities are reflected in this section of the statement of cash flows. As indicated in Figure 2–6, while Harbour Island borrowed no additional funds during 2002, it made cash principal payments on both short-term notes ($100) and long-term debt ($50). Cash proceeds from stockholder contributions, or equity issuances, and cash dividends to stockholders are also included in this section. Note that Harbour Island collected $3,100 in cash from issuing equity and paid cash dividends of $200.

In the 1990s, Yahoo and Lycos were both fast-growing companies that relied heavily on common stock issuances to raise capital. Do you expect that they showed positive or negative net cash flows from financing activities during this time period? Explain.

RELATIONSHIPS AMONG THE FINANCIAL STATEMENTS

Figure 2–7 presents a general overview of the four basic financial accounting statements and shows how they relate to each other. Take some time to study it.

Note the four statements indicated by the numbers: (1) balance sheet, (2) income statement, (3) statement of retained earnings, and (4) statement of cash flows. Note also that an additional balance sheet, prepared at the end of the period, is included on the right side of the figure. The account balances on this balance sheet are different from those on the balance sheet on the left. To explain how the balance sheet accounts changed during the year, examine the other three financial statements: the statement of cash flows, the statement of retained earnings, and the income statement.

The statement of cash flows explains the activity during the year in the company's cash account. At the beginning of 2002 the balance in the cash account was $100. During the year, operating, investing, and financing transactions affected the cash balance, and the end result was $220. The statement of cash flows ties into the cash accounts listed on the balance sheet at the beginning and end of 2002.

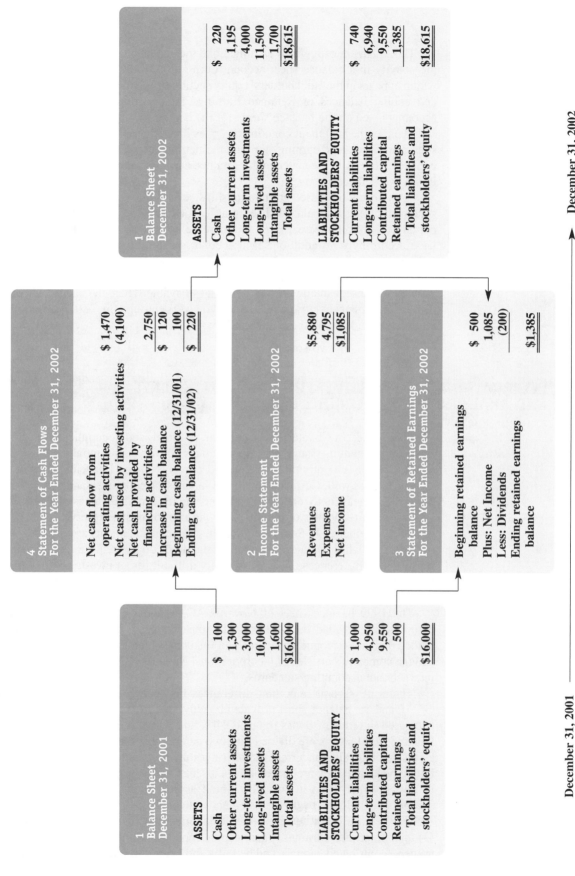

FIGURE 2–7 Relationships among the financial statements

1
Balance Sheet
December 31, 2002

ASSETS

Cash	$ 220
Other current assets	1,195
Long-term investments	4,000
Long-lived assets	11,500
Intangible assets	1,700
Total assets	$18,615

LIABILITIES AND STOCKHOLDERS' EQUITY

Current liabilities	$ 740
Long-term liabilities	6,940
Contributed capital	9,550
Retained earnings	1,385
Total liabilities and stockholders' equity	$18,615

4
Statement of Cash Flows
For the Year Ended December 31, 2002

Net cash flow from operating activities	$ 1,470
Net cash used by investing activities	(4,100)
Net cash provided by financing activities	2,750
Increase in cash balance	$ 120
Beginning cash balance (12/31/01)	100
Ending cash balance (12/31/02)	$ 220

2
Income Statement
For the Year Ended December 31, 2002

Revenues	$5,880
Expenses	4,795
Net income	$1,085

3
Statement of Retained Earnings
For the Year Ended December 31, 2002

Beginning retained earnings balance	$ 500
Plus: Net Income	1,085
Less: Dividends	(200)
Ending retained earnings balance	$1,385

1
Balance Sheet
December 31, 2001

ASSETS

Cash	$ 100
Other current assets	1,300
Long-term investments	3,000
Long-lived assets	10,000
Intangible assets	1,600
Total assets	$16,000

LIABILITIES AND STOCKHOLDERS' EQUITY

Current liabilities	$ 1,000
Long-term liabilities	4,950
Contributed capital	9,550
Retained earnings	500
Total liabilities and stockholders' equity	$16,000

December 31, 2001 ⟶ December 31, 2002

The statement of retained earnings, like the statement of cash flows, also explains the activity in a balance sheet account during 2002—the retained earnings account, which appears in the stockholders' equity section of each balance sheet. The beginning and ending balances of Retained Earnings tie directly into the retained earnings accounts listed on the balance sheets for the beginning and end of 2002.

The income statement contains revenues and expenses, which are reflected in the statement of retained earnings through the net income number. The income statement connects directly to the statement of retained earnings, which in turn connects directly to the two balance sheets.

As a result of these interrelationships, every transaction affecting the income statement affects the balance sheet in at least two places. Revenues and expenses are components of retained earnings and increase or decrease the Retained Earnings balance accordingly. In addition, each account on the income statement has a related account in either the asset or liability section of the balance sheet. Recognizing a sale, for example, can affect Cash and Accounts Receivable. Recognizing an expense, such as wage expense, can affect Cash and Wages Payable. Thus, the balance sheet and the income statement are closely related. As you work through this text, it is important that you clearly understand these relationships.

INTERNATIONAL PERSPECTIVE: FINANCIAL STATEMENTS AND ANALYSES IN OTHER COUNTRIES

We commented in Chapter 1 that cultural, political, and economic differences cause financial accounting standards and practices to vary substantially across different countries. Consequently, the formats and contents of the financial statements differ significantly as well. German, Swiss, and Japanese accounting standards, for example, encourage managers to intentionally understate the reported values of assets and overstate the reported values of liabilities, giving rise to special "reserve" accounts on the financial statements. In South America the financial statements are routinely adjusted for inflation, while Japanese accounting standards do not require a statement of cash flows. These differences make it extremely difficult for an investor or creditor who is unfamiliar with such practices to conduct meaningful evaluations of earning power and solvency.

The 1999 balance sheet of Novartis AG, a Swiss-based global pharmaceutical company, is provided below. PricewaterhouseCoopers conducted an audit and concluded that "the accounting records and financial statements . . . comply with the law and the company's articles of incorporation." Novartis follows neither U.S. GAAP nor international accounting standards.

There are several important differences between balance sheets based on U.S. GAAP and the balance sheet provided by Novartis. Note first that the balance sheet is expressed in terms of Swiss francs (CHF), and that U.S. dollar amounts are not provided. Second, assets are divided into two categories: financial and current. Financial assets refer to all noncurrent assets (investments; property, plant, and equipment; intangibles), and they are listed above current assets. Further, current assets are listed in reverse order—that is, the most liquid assets are at the bottom. Similarly, total equity (stockholders' equity) is listed above liabilities.

Total equity is divided into three categories: (1) share capital, (2) reserves, and (3) unappropriated earnings. Share capital represents funds contributed by the shareholders (contributed capital), and reserves and unappropriated earnings comprise what

Novartis AG
Balance Sheets (prior to profit appropriation)
(at December 31, 1999 and 1998)

	Notes	1999 CHF millions	1998 CHF millions
ASSETS			
Financial assets	4	$ 9,886	$ 9,829
Total long-term assets		9,886	9,829
Current assets			
Receivables from			
Subsidiaries		2,662	916
Others		1,525	207
Accrued income and other current assets		11	2
Marketable securities	5	1,688	1,016
Cash and short-term deposits		36	97
Total current assets		5,922	2,238
Total Assets		$15,808	$12,067
EQUITY AND LIABILITIES			
Equity			
Total share capital	6	$ 1,443	$ 1,443
Reserves			
Legal reserves	7		
General reserve		4,179	4,179
Reserve for treasury shares		2,800	608
Free reserves	8	—	905
Total reserves		6,979	5,692
Unappropriated earnings			
Net income of the year		5,650	2,491
Balance brought forward		935	1,726
Total unappropriated earnings		6,585	4,217
Total equity		15,007	11,352
Liabilities			
Provisions		532	532
Accounts payable and accrued liabilities			
Subsidiaries		61	52
Others		208	131
Total liabilities		801	715
Total Equity and Liabilities		$15,808	$12,067

The notes form an integral part of these unconsolidated financial statements.

we call retained earnings. Novartis breaks retained earnings down into various "reserve" accounts. The provisions account includes most of the company's liabilities.

The Novartis balance sheet departs from U.S. GAAP in two very important ways. First, the format is obviously different; and second, the provision and reserve accounts are used to record discretionary adjustments designed to "manage" the earnings number across time. Such adjustments are not allowed under U.S. GAAP. Many times later in the text, we return to how companies use discretion to manage earnings.

REVIEW PROBLEM

The following information was taken from the 2000 annual report of Lands' End. All dollar values are in millions.

Lands' End, Inc. & Subsidiaries
Consolidated Balance Sheet

(In thousands)	January 28, 2000	January 29,1999
ASSETS		
Current assets:		
Cash and cash equivalents	$ 76,413	$ 6,641
Receivables, net	17,753	21,083
Inventory	162,193	219,686
Prepaid advertising	16,572	21,357
Other current assets	16,477	25,536
Total current assets	$289,408	$294,303
Property, plant, and equipment, at cost:		
Land and buildings	102,776	102,018
Fixtures and equipment	175,910	154,663
Leasehold improvements	4,453	5,475
Total property, plant, and equipment	283,139	262,156
Less—accumulated depreciation and amortization	117,317	101,570
Property, plant, and equipment, net	165,822	160,586
Intangibles, net	966	1,030
Total assets	$456,196	$455,919
LIABILITIES AND SHAREHOLDERS' INVESTMENT		
Current liabilities:		
Lines of credit	$ 11,724	$ 38,942
Accounts payable	74,510	87,922
Reserve for returns	7,869	7,193
Accrued liabilities	43,754	54,392
Accrued profit sharing	2,760	2,256
Income taxes payable	10,255	14,578
Total current liabilities	$150,872	$205,283
Deferred income taxes	9,117	8,133
Shareholders' investment:		
Common stock, 40,221 shares issued	402	402
Other items	10,839	10,009
Additional paid-in capital	29,709	26,994
Retained earnings	454,430	406,396
Treasury stock, 10,071 and 10,317 shares at cost, respectively	(199,173)	(201,298)
Total shareholders' investment	296,207	242,503
Total liabilities and shareholders' investment	$456,196	$455,919

Lands' End, Inc. & Subsidiaries
Consolidated Statements of Operations

	For the period ended		
(In thousands, except per share data)	January 28, 2000	January 29, 1999	January 30, 1998
Net sales:	$1,319,823	$1,371,375	$1,263,629
Cost of sales	727,291	754,661	675,138
Gross profit	592,532	616,714	588,491
Selling, general and administrative expenses	515,375	544,446	489,923
Non-recurring charge (credit)	(1,774)	12,600	—
Income from operations	78,931	59,668	98,568
Other income (expense):			
Interest expense	(1,890)	(7,734)	(1,995)
Interest income	882	16	1,725
Gain on sale of subsidiary	—	—	7,805
Other	(1,679)	(2,450)	(4,278)
Total other income (expense), net	(2,687)	(10,168)	3,257
Income before income taxes	76,244	49,500	101,825
Income tax provision	28,210	18,315	37,675
Net income	$ 48,034	$ 31,185	$ 64,150

Lands' End, Inc. & Subsidiaries
Consolidated Statements of Cash Flows

	For the period ended		
(In thousands)	January 28, 2000	January 29, 1999	January 30, 1998
Cash flows from (used for) operating activities:			
Net cash flows from (used for) operating activities	$122,878	$ 74,260	$ (26,932)
Cash flows from (used for) investing activities:			
Cash paid for capital additions	(28,013)	(46,750)	(47,659)
Proceeds from sale of subsidiary	—	—	12,350
Net cash flows used for investing activities	$ (28,013)	$(46,750)	$ (35,309)
Cash flows from (used for) financing activities:			
Proceeds from (payment of) short-term debt	$ (27,218)	$ 6,505	$ 21,242
Purchases of treasury stock	(4,516)	(35,557)	(45,899)
Issuance of treasury stock	6,641	1,845	409
Net cash flows used for financing activities	$ (25,093)	$(27,207)	$ (24,248)
Net increase (decrease) in cash and cash equivalents	$ 69,772	$ 303	$ (86,489)
Beginning cash and cash equivalents	6,641	6,338	92,827
Ending cash and cash equivalents	$ 76,413	$ 6,641	$ 6,338

Comments on Lands' End earning power and solvency:

Net sales for Lands' End increased from 1998 to 1999, but dipped from 1999 to 2000. Gross profit also dropped off from 1999 levels. Income from operations, however, increased during 2000, primarily because selling, general, and administrative expenses declined and the nonrecurring charge recognized in 1999 was partially reversed. Interest expense was also much lower in 2000 than in 1999. The net effect of these differences is an overall profit increase, which might be encouraging, but 2000 profits are still much lower than 1998 profits, even though sales are higher. An analyst would be very interested in why expenses seem to be both rising and unstable.

The balance sheet shows virtually no growth in assets, but a relatively significant increase in cash. Other assets that are increasing include property, plant, and equipment. Decreases occurred in receivables and especially inventory. Current liabilities dropped off considerably as the company appeared to make payments on its lines of credit, providing an explanation for why interest expense on the income statement dropped off in 2000. The reduction in liabilities was offset by the increase in retained earnings. Overall, the company appears to be more liquid (have more cash available). Also, the inventory reduction, the lower reliance on lines of credit, and the increase in retained earnings could be signs of increased solvency and greater earning power.

The statement of cash flows shows a dramatic increase in the company's ability to generate cash from operations, which was used to purchase capital additions, reduce debt, and increase the cash balance. Lands' End does not appear to pay dividends to its shareholders.

SUMMARY OF KEY POINTS

The key points of this chapter are summarized below.

○ *The three basic activities of a business and how they are reflected in the financial statements.*

Businesses must first attract capital and then invest it in productive assets that can be used to produce saleable goods and/or services. The three basic activities involved in conducting a business are (1) financing activities, (2) investing activities, and (3) operating activities. Financing activities involve the collection of capital through equity or debt issuances and any associated payments, such as dividends and debt payments. Investing activities involve the acquisition and sale of producing assets, the assets used to produce and support the goods and services provided. Operating activities involve the sale of the goods and services. Operating activities produce additional capital that can be reinvested in the producing assets, used to service debt payments, and distributed to the owners in the form of dividends.

The balance sheet lists assets (goods and producing assets) and financing sources (equity, debt, and reinvestments from net earnings) at a particular point in time. The income statement is a measure of operations, the activities (revenues and expenses) involved in selling the goods and services. The statement of retained earnings measures the extent to which the business reinvests its net earnings and pays dividends. The statement of cash flows contains the cash inflows and outflows associated with the operating, investing, and financing activities of the business.

○ *The balance sheet, income statement, statement of retained earnings, and statement of cash flows and how these financial statements are used.*

The asset accounts reported on the balance sheet are listed in order of liquidity and are divided into four categories: (1) current assets, which include cash, short-term investments, accounts receivable, inventory, and prepaid expenses, (2) long-term investments, which include long-term notes receivable, land, securities, the cash value of life insurance, and special investment funds, (3) property, plant, and equipment, and (4) intangible assets, which include patents, trademarks, and other intangibles, such as goodwill.

Liabilities are divided into two categories: (1) current liabilities, which primarily include short-term payables, and (2) long-term liabilities, which include items such as long-term notes, bonds, and mortgages payable. The stockholders' equity section for a corporation contains contributed capital and retained earnings; the owners' equity section for a partnership contains an account for each partner that records the cumulative balance of the partner's contributions less withdrawals.

The income statement consists of two basic categories: revenues and expenses. Revenues, which represent asset inflows (or liability decreases) associated with operating transactions during a given period, include sales, fees earned, service revenues, and other revenues (e.g., interest, book gains). Expenses, which represent the asset outflows (or liability increases) required to generate the revenues, include cost of goods sold, operating expenses (e.g., wages, rent), and other expenses (e.g., interest, book losses). Revenues less expenses equal net income.

The statement of retained earnings has four components: (1) the balance in Retained Earnings at the beginning of the period, (2) net income (or loss), (3) distributions to stockholders, and (4) the balance in Retained Earnings at the end of the period. The statement of cash flows contains three categories: (1) cash flows from operating activities, (2) cash flows from investing activities, and (3) cash flows from financing activities.

This information enables external users to assess the earning power and solvency position of the company. Assets generate cash through their use and sale, and liabilities represent cash requirements. The income statement indicates how profitable the company's operations have been, and the statement of cash flows shows how the company's cash is managed. The statement of retained earnings provides information about individual payments relative to net income.

KEY TERMS

Note: Definitions for these terms are provided in the glossary at the end of the text.

Accounts payable (p. 42)	Entrepreneur (p. 34)
Accounts receivable (p. 39)	Fees earned (p. 46)
Bonds payable (p. 42)	Financing activities (p. 35)
Classified balance sheet (p. 36)	Intangible assets (p. 41)
Contributed capital (p. 43)	Investing activities (p. 35)
Cost of goods sold (p. 46)	Liquidity (p. 36)
Current assets (p. 38)	Long-term investments (p. 40)
Current liabilities (p. 42)	Merchandise inventory (p. 39)
Current maturities of long-term debts (p. 42)	Mortgage payables (p. 43)

Net book value (p. 41)	Property (p. 40)
Notes payable (p. 42)	Retained earnings (p. 43)
Operating activities (p. 35)	Sales (p. 46)
Owners' equity (p. 44)	Service revenue (p. 46)
Plant and equipment (p. 40)	Short-term investments (p. 38)
Prepaid expenses (p. 39)	Stockholders' equity (p. 43)

ETHICS IN THE REAL WORLD

German and Swiss companies (see the Novartis balance sheet at the end of the chapter) have long used accounting methods that allow them to "manage" earnings through discretionary adjustments. For the most part, the adjustments "smooth out" earnings variability across time, and most German and Swiss managers would argue that such adjustments are in the best interest of the firm, its stockholders, and the overall economy. Recently, these companies are coming under increasing pressure to adopt either U.S. GAAP or International Accounting Standards (IAS), neither of which allows these kinds of adjustments. Reuters English News Service (June 14, 2000), for example, recently reported that the "European Commission had chosen IAS rules as the way forward for Europe by the year 2005." Many believe that these reporting standards will encourage transparency between corporate management and the investing community. Nonetheless, many European companies will not be quick to adopt IAS rules, arguing that they will impose significant additional costs and simply make it more difficult for management to run their companies.

ETHICAL ISSUE Discuss the ethical issues facing a European manager who is trying to resist the pressure to adopt U.S. GAAP or IAS.

INTERNET RESEARCH EXERCISE

Provide a brief description and discussion of Air France's recent financial performance and core business. What world-famous airplane brand is owned and operated by Air France? Begin your search at www.Airfrance.com.

BRIEF EXERCISES

REAL DATA
BE2–1

Dividends as a percentage of net income

Revenues and expenses for PepsiCo during 2000 were $20.4 billion and $18.2 billion, respectively. The December 31, 1999 and 2000 balances in retained earnings were $14.1 billion and $15.5 billion, respectively. Compute dividends paid by PepsiCo during 2000. What percentage of net income did PepsiCo pay out in dividends during 2000?

REAL DATA
BE2–2

Financing assets

A summary of a recent balance sheet for Boeing Co. is provided below (dollars in billions):

Assets		Liabilities and Stockholders' Equity	
Current assets	$16	Liabilities	$23
Property, plant, and equipment	8	Contributed capital	3
Other assets	12	Retained earnings	10
Total	$36	Total	$36

What amount and what percentage of Boeing's assets were financed by (1) liabilities, (2) contributed capital, and (3) retained earnings?

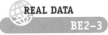

REAL DATA

BE2–3

Assessing solvency

In BE2–2, Boeing's current assets consisted primarily of cash and short-term investments of $3 billion, accounts receivable of $4 billion, inventory of $7 billion, and miscellaneous current assets of $2 billion; $14 billion of its liabilities are current. Does the company appear solvent? Why or why not? Can Boeing pay off its current liabilities with liquid assets? Would it be more or less solvent if the dollar amounts in accounts receivable and inventory were reversed?

REAL DATA

BE2–4

The statement of cash flows across time

Excerpts from the annual report of SBC Communications, Inc., parent of Ameritech, are provided below.

Statement of Cash Flows (Dollars in Millions)

	2000	1999	1998
Net cash from operating activities	$?	$16,578	$12,981)
Net cash from investing activities	(14,403)	?	(9,169)
Net cash from financing activities	252	(6,105)	(3,862)
Net change in cash	?	(104)	?
Cash balance at beginning of year	495	?	?
Cash balance at end of year	643	?	599

Compute the missing values and briefly discuss SBC Communications' sources and uses of cash during the three-year period.

EXERCISES

E2–1

Identifying financing, investing, and operating transactions

Listed below are eight transactions. In each case, identify whether the transaction is an example of financing, investing, or operating activities and which of the financial statements it would affect.

1. Common stock is issued for $500,000 in cash.
2. Twenty units of inventory are sold for $50 each.
3. Employee wages are paid.
4. A new warehouse facility is purchased.
5. Principal payments on outstanding debt are paid.
6. Dividends are paid to the shareholders.
7. A 4-year-old vehicle, used as a delivery truck, is sold for $9,000, its book value.
8. A utility bill for March is paid in April.

E2–2

Identifying financing, investing, and operating transactions

Listed below are eight transactions. In each case, identify whether the transaction is an example of financing, investing, or operating activities and which of the financial statements it would affect.

1. Company borrows $50,000 in cash, signing a 10-year note payable.
2. Twenty units of inventory are purchased from suppliers on account for $12,000.
3. The utility bill is paid at the end of the month, $5,200.
4. Services are performed and customers are billed for $13,000.
5. Five parcels of real estate are purchased for a total of $55,000 in cash.
6. A long-term investment in an equity security is sold for $4,500 cash.
7. Principal payments are made on outstanding debts.
8. Cash is received from customers for services completed in a previous period.

E2-3

Balance sheet or
income statement
account?

Listed below are accounts that may appear on either the balance sheet or the income statement.

a. Equipment
b. Fees Earned
c. Retained Earnings
d. Wage Expense
e. Patent
f. Cost of Goods Sold
g. Common Stock
h. Dividend Payable
i. Accumulated Depreciation

j. Prepaid Expense
k. Gain on Sale of Short-Term Investments
l. Rent Revenue
m. Supplies Inventory
n. Accounts Receivable
o. Land
p. Insurance Expense
q. Interest Payable
r. Deferred Revenue

For each account, indicate whether a company would ordinarily disclose the account on the balance sheet or the income statement.

REAL DATA

E2-4

Relationships
between retained
earnings and
revenues and
expenses across time

Cinergy is one of America's leading diversified energy companies. At the end of 1999 the company had a balance in its retained earnings account of $1.1 billion. Compute the missing amounts in the following table, and comment on the company's performance. Specifically, analyze the company's sales growth, profits, profits as a percentage of sales, and dividends declared as a percentage of net income (dollar amounts in billions).

	1999	1998	1997
Beginning retained earnings	$?	$1.0	$6
Revenues for the period	5.9	5.9	4.4
Expenses for the period	5.5	?	3.7
Dividends declared	.3	.3	?

REAL DATA

E2-5

Relationships
between retained
earnings and
revenues and
expenses across time

Young & Rubicam is a fast-growing advertising agency that recently sold its stock to the public. At the end of 1999 the company had a negative balance of $596 million in its retained earnings account. Compute the missing amounts in the following table, and comment on the company's performance. Specifically, analyze the company's sales growth, profits, profits as a percentage of sales, and dividends declared as a percentage of net income (dollars in millions).

	1999	1998	1997
Beginning retained earnings	$ (758)	$ (523)	$ (499)
Revenues for the period	?	1,522	1,383
Expenses for the period	1,550	1,608	?
Dividends declared	5	?	0

REAL DATA

E2-6

Using working
capital to assess
solvency

La-Z-Boy Incorporated included the following information in its 2000 annual report (dollars in millions).

	12/31/00	12/31/99
Cash	$ 14	$ 34
Accounts receivable	394	265
Inventory	246	97
Other current assets	37	30
Total current assets	$691	$426
Current liabilities	237	132
Current assets minus current liabilities	$454	$294

Define solvency and discuss how this information might be useful in assessing the company's solvency position. What drawbacks are associated with using this information in such a way?

REAL DATA

E2-7

The effects of
different forms of
financing on
financial statement
numbers and debt
covenants

Suppose that La-Z-Boy in E2–6 signed a debt covenant specifying that current assets must exceed current liabilities by $200 million. Assume further that in early January of 2000, the company planned to purchase a $300 million piece of machinery and had two possible methods of paying for it: (1) short-term note payable or (2) long-term note payable. Compute the effect of each of the alternatives on the difference between current assets and current liabilities, and discuss which method seems to be the most feasible.

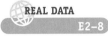

REAL DATA

E2-8

The statement of
cash flows across
time

The information below was taken from the 1999 annual report of Cisco Systems, a worldwide leader in networking for the Internet. As of the end of 1999, Cisco had a cash balance of $827 million. Compute the missing amounts in the following table. Describe and evaluate the company's cash management activities in each of the three years (dollars in millions).

	1999	1998	1997
Beginning cash balance	$ 580	$?	$ 0
Net cash flow from operating activities	4,438	?	1,448
Net cash flow from investing activities	4,937	(3,095)	?
Net cash flow from financing activities	?	497	(20)
Ending cash balance	$5,000	$ 580	$ 306

REAL DATA

E2-9

The statement of
cash flows across
time

US Airways is a major airline. The information below was taken from its 1999 annual report. As of the end of 1999, US Air had a cash balance of $246 million. Compute the missing amounts in the following table. Describe and evaluate the company's cash management activities in each of the three years (dollars in millions).

	1999	1998	1997
Beginning cash balance	$?	$1,094	$?
Net cash flow from operating activities	603	1,251	870
Net cash flow from investing activities	?	292	372
Net cash flow from financing activities	145	?	(355)
Ending cash balance	$246	$ 612	$?

E2-10

Preparing a
statement of
cash flows

From the following transactions, prepare a statement of cash flows for Lana and Sons in the proper form. The company began the year with a cash balance of $13,000. Describe and evaluate the company's cash management activities during the year.

1. The stockholders contributed $7,000 in cash.
2. Performed services for $5,000, receiving $4,000 in cash and a $1,000 receivable.
3. Incurred expenses of $4,000; paid $3,000 in cash and $1,000 is still payable.
4. Purchased machinery for $10,000; paid $3,000 in cash and signed a long-term note payable for the remainder.
5. Paid the stockholders a $1,500 dividend.

E2-11

Preparing a
statement of
cash flows

From the following transactions, prepare a statement of cash flows for Emory Inc. in the proper form. The company began the year with a cash balance of $25,000. Describe and evaluate the company's cash management activities during the year.

1. Borrowed $30,000 from a bank, signing a long-term note.
2. Performed services for $45,000, receiving $40,000 in cash and a $5,000 receivable.
3. Incurred expenses of $34,000; paid $23,000 in cash and $11,000 is still payable.
4. Purchased equipment for $28,000; paid $23,000 in cash and signed a long-term note payable for the remainder.
5. Paid the stockholders a dividend in an amount that ensured an ending cash balance of $25,000.

E2-12

Preparing financial statements from simple transactions

George began a business, and after collecting $6,000 from an equity investor and borrowing $5,000 from a bank, he purchased a piece of land for $8,000. During the year, he leased the land to Sheila and received $3,000 in cash. He paid $2,500 cash for expenses during the year and paid an $800 dividend to the equity investor.

Prepare an income statement, a statement of retained earnings, a balance sheet, and statement of cash flows for the period. What did George do that may have concerned the bank? Explain.

E2-13

Preparing financial statements from simple transactions

Mary began a business, and after collecting $30,000 from an equity investor and borrowing $15,000 from a bank, she purchased a piece of land for $40,000. During the year, she leased the land to Karl and received $12,000 in cash, paying $14,000 cash for expenses. She paid a $1,000 dividend to the equity investor at year-end.

Prepare an income statement, a statement of retained earnings, a balance sheet, and statement of cash flows for the period. Evaluate Mary's decision to pay the $1,000 dividend.

PROBLEMS

P2-1

Classifying balance sheet accounts

Presented below are the main section headings of the balance sheet:

a. Current assets
b. Long-term investments
c. Property, plant, and equipment
d. Intangible assets

e. Current liabilities
f. Long-term liabilities
g. Contributed capital
h. Retained earnings

REQUIRED:
Classify the following accounts under the appropriate headings, and prepare a balance sheet in proper form without account balances.

1. Dividend Payable
2. Payments Received in Advance
3. Allowance for Uncollectible Accounts

4. Inventories
5. Capital Stock
6. Accumulated Depreciation—Building
7. Bonds Payable
8. Machinery and Equipment
9. Accounts Receivable
10. Short-Term Investments
11. Buildings

12. Patents
13. Property
14. Investment Fund for Plant Expansion
15. Wages Payable
16. Cash
17. Accumulated Depreciation—Equipment
18. Prepaid Rent
19. Trademarks
20. Land Held for Investment
21. Current Portion Due of Long-Term Debt
22. Accounts Payable
23. Short-Term Notes Payable

P2-2

Classifying income statement accounts

Presented below are the main section headings of the income statement:

a. Sales
b. Fees earned
c. Other revenues

d. Cost of goods sold
e. Operating expenses
f. Other expenses

REQUIRED:
Classify the following descriptions under the appropriate headings and prepare an income statement in proper form without account balances.

1. Office salary expense
2. Sales of services provided

3. Insurance expense
4. Sales of inventories

(Continued)

5. Salespeople commission expense
6. Depreciation expense
7. Office supplies expense
8. Loss on sale of equipment
9. Income from interest on savings account
10. Income from dividends on investments

11. Advertising expense
12. Loss on sale of building
13. Interest expense on outstanding loans
14. Cost of sold inventories
15. Gain on sale of short-term investments

P2-3

Preparing a balance sheet in proper form

The following information is available relating to the activities of Johnson Co. as of December 31, 2002.

- Cash balance on 12/31/02 is $8,000.
- Short-term investments have a fair market value of $40,000 on 12/31/02.
- Accounts Receivable balance of $125,000 on 12/31/02 includes $2,400 that is not likely to be collected.
- Inventory costing $165,000 has a replacement cost (market value) of $161,000 on 12/31/02.
- Buildings having a fair market value of $68,500 were purchased for $35,000 and have accumulated depreciation of $8,000.
- Accounts Payable at year-end total $110,000.
- Taxes Payable at year-end total $29,400.
- Balance in the long-term notes payable account at the end of the period is $79,100.
- Fair market value of the Johnson Co. stock is $10 per share on 12/31/02. When originally issued, 12,500 shares were sold for $8 per share.
- The total amount of net income earned by Johnson Co. since its inception several years ago is $65,000. Over that same period, Johnson Co. has paid $24,900 in dividends.

REQUIRED:

Prepare a balance sheet as of 12/31/02 in proper form for Johnson Co. Would you invest in this company? Why or why not?

P2-4

Balance sheet and income statement relationships across five years

Compute the missing values for the following chart and analyze the financial performance and position of this company. The first year of operations is 1999.

	2002	2001	2000	1999
Assets:				
Cash	$500	$200	$ 300	$ 300
Accounts receivable	700	?	300	200
Inventory	400	400	?	500
Land	400	400	200	100
Property, plant, and equipment (net)	800	700	600	700
Liabilities and stockholders' equity:				
Accounts payable	?	500	300	200
Bonds payable	700	800	600	500
Contributed capital	600	600	400	?
Retained earnings	600	300	800	400
Sales	?	700	1,100	1,000
Expenses	(600)	?	?	(400)
Net income	?	(100)	400	?
Dividends	200	?	?	?

Using financial
statements to assess
solvency and
earning power

Excerpts from the financial statements for Supervalu, a major supermarket retailer, are provided below (dollars in millions).

	2000	1999
Cash	$ 11	$ 8
Accounts receivable	562	411
Inventory	1,490	1,068
Property, plant, and equipment	2,168	1,699
Other assets	2,049	1,080
Accounts payable	1,430	982
Other short-term debts	1,080	546
Long-term debt	2,164	1,438
Contributed capital	283	151
Retained earnings	1,323	1,149
Sales	20,339	17,420
Expenses	20,096	17,229
Dividends	69	64

REQUIRED:
Organize these numbers into financial statements (excluding the statement of cash flows), and comment on Supervalu's solvency and earning power positions.

Balance sheet value
and the fair market
values of the assets

Because of consistent losses in the past several years, Eat and Run, a fast-food franchise, is in danger of bankruptcy. Its most current balance sheet follows.

Assets		Liabilities and Stockholders' Equity	
Cash	$ 25,000	Accounts payable	$ 42,000
Short-term investments	15,000	Wages payable	20,000
Accounts receivable	35,000	Other short-term payables	34,000
Inventory	42,000	Long-term notes	75,000
Prepaid insurance	10,000	Mortgage payable	25,000
Property, plant, and equip.	82,000	Contributed capital	50,000
Other assets	50,000	Retained earnings	13,000
		Total liabilities and	
Total assets	$259,000	stockholders' equity	$259,000

Additional Information:
- The fair market value of the marketable securities is $19,000.
- The sale of the accounts receivable to a local bank would produce about $25,000 cash.
- A portion of the inventory originally costing $21,000 is now obsolete and can be sold for $3,000 scrap value. The remaining inventory is worth approximately $30,000.
- Prepaid insurance is nonrefundable.
- In the event of bankruptcy, the property, plant, and equipment owned by Eat and Run would be divided up and sold separately. It has been estimated that these sales would bring approximately $100,000 cash.
- Other assets (primarily organizational costs) cannot be recovered.

REQUIRED:
a. The book value (balance sheet assets less liabilities) of Eat and Run is $63,000. Comment on why this balance sheet value may not be a good indication of the value of the company in the case of bankruptcy.
b. If Eat and Run goes bankrupt, what would you consider the value of the company to be?
c. When a company goes bankrupt, the creditors are usually paid off first with the existing assets, and then, if assets remain, the stockholders are paid. If Eat and Run goes bankrupt, would the stockholders receive anything? If so, how much?

P2–7

Analyzing financial
statements

The chief executive officer of Romney Heights has included the following information from the financial statements in a loan application submitted to Acme Bank. The company intends to acquire additional equipment and wishes to finance the purchase with a long-term note.

	2003	2002
Balance Sheet		
Current assets	$ 14,000	$ 12,000
Long-term assets	50,000	43,000
Current liabilities	7,000	6,000
Long-term liabilities	26,000	21,000
Contributed capital	25,000	25,000
Retained earnings	6,000	3,000
Income Statement		
Revenues	$ 35,000	$ 32,000
Expenses	23,000	26,000
Statement of Cash Flows		
Net cash flow from operating activities	$ 15,000	$ 9,000
Net cash flow from investing activities	(14,000)	(12,000)
Net cash flow from financing activities	7,000	5,000
Change in cash balance	$ 8,000	$ 2,000
Beginning cash balance	3,000	1,000
Ending cash balance	$ 11,000	$ 3,000

REQUIRED:

Assume that you, a bank loan officer, review the financial statements and recommend whether Romney Heights should be considered for a loan. Support your recommendation with calculations.

P2–8

Analyzing financial
statements

Ted Tooney has operated a small service company for several years. The following information is from the financial statements prepared by Ted's accountant.

	2003	2002
Balance Sheet		
Current assets	$ 9,000	$ 8,000
Long-term assets	18,000	15,000
Current liabilities	7,000	4,000
Long-term liabilities	9,000	7,000
Contributed capital	9,000	9,000
Retained earnings	2,000	3,000
Income Statement		
Revenues	$92,000	$89,000
Expenses	78,000	72,000
Statement of Cash Flows		
Net cash flow from operating activities	$12,000	$15,000
Net cash flow from investing activities	(8,000)	(5,000)
Net cash flow from financing activities	(5,000)	(8,000)
Change in cash balance	$(1,000)	$ 2,000
Beginning cash balance	5,000	3,000
Ending cash balance	$ 4,000	$ 5,000

REQUIRED:

Assume that you have some capital to invest, and that Ted asked you to consider making an equity investment in his company. Review the financial statements and describe how you would respond to Ted's request. Support your recommendation with calculations.

P2–9

Debt covenants can limit investments and dividends

A summary of the December 31, 2002 balance sheet of Ellington Industries follows:

	2002
Assets	
Current assets	$12,000
Land investments	55,000
Total assets	$67,000
Liabilities and Stockholders' Equity	
Accounts payable	$ 9,000
Long-term liabilities	30,000
Stockholders' equity	28,000
Total liabilities and stockholders' equity	$67,000

On January 1, 2003, the company borrowed $40,000 (long-term debt) to purchase additional land. The debt covenant states that Ellington must maintain a current asset balance at least twice as large as its current liability balance over the period of the loan.

REQUIRED:

a. As of January 1, 2003, how much of the $40,000 can Ellington invest in land without violating the debt covenant?

b. Assume that Ellington invested the maximum allowable in land. Prepare Ellington's balance sheet as of January 1, 2003. Compute the following ratios—current assets/current liabilities and total liabilities/total assets.

c. Assume that Ellington invested the maximum allowable in land and that during 2003 it generated $150,000 in revenues (all cash), paid off the accounts payable outstanding as of December 31, 2002, and incurred $130,000 in expenses, of which $123,000 was paid in cash. The company neither purchased nor sold any of its long-term land investments, made no principal payments on the long-term debt, and issued no equity during 2003. Prepare a balance sheet as of the end of 2003, and compute how large a dividend the company can pay without violating the debt covenant. Compute total liabilities/total assets assuming the company declares the maximum allowable dividend.

ISSUES FOR DISCUSSION

REAL DATA

ID2–1

Relationships between cash flows, income, and dividends

For over a year, Center Energy Corporation, a utility company in Ohio, had negative cash flow from operating activities caused primarily by the escalating costs of one of its nuclear plants outside Cleveland. Yet, the company reported positive earnings and paid a dividend to its stockholders of $2.56 per share.

REQUIRED:

a. Briefly explain how a company could have negative cash flow from operating activities, have a positive net income, and still pay dividends.

b. Could a company continue such a strategy over an extended period? Why or why not?

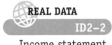

Income statement
classifications

The *Dow Jones News Service* (June 2, 2000) reported that the FASB has decided to require companies to include shipping and handling costs in the cost of goods sold category on the income statement, instead of in the section that includes selling and administrative expenses. Many e-retailers are objecting to this ruling. Tom Wyman, an analyst for J.P. Morgan & Co., notes: "Seattle online retailing heavyweight, Amazon.com, which drew cheers from analysts when it reported a first-quarter gross margin above 20 percent, will see that number cut in half. . . . Etoys, Inc. will likely see its margin for the year go from 21 percent to a negative 3 percent." Apparently, many e-companies are trying to discourage investors from focusing on the bottom line, since many of them are still unprofitable. Instead, they have been emphasizing gross margin as the most important indicator of their success.

REQUIRED:
Will this ruling affect the profit numbers reported by e-companies? Do shipping and handling costs tend to be more significant for e-retailers than traditional retailers? Why? Do you think that e-companies should object to this ruling?

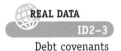

Debt covenants

The following excerpt was taken from a recent financial report of Cummins Engine Company, a manufacturer of heavy-duty truck engines.

Loan agreements contain covenants that impose restrictions on the payment of dividends and distributions of stock, require maintenance of a 1.25:1 current ratio, and limit the amount of future borrowings. Under the most restrictive covenants, retained earnings of approximately $351 million were available for payment of dividends.

REQUIRED:
a. Briefly explain the meaning of the above excerpt.
b. Why would a bank or other creditor impose such restrictions on a borrowing company?
c. Explain the role of financial accounting numbers in the restrictions described above.

Statement of cash
flow patterns across
companies

The following information was taken from the 1999 annual reports—statements of cash flows—of General Electric, Amazon.com, Lycos, Inc., and Coca-Cola (dollars in millions).

Company	Cash from Operations	Cash from Investing	Cash from Financing
General Electric	$24,593	$(42,179)	$21,823
Amazon.com	(91)	(922)	1,104
Lycos, Inc.	(38)	27	10
Coca-Cola	3,883	(3,421)	(471)

REQUIRED:
Each of these companies shows a different cash flow pattern for 1999. Explain what these patterns might indicate about each company.

Statement of cash
flow patterns
across time

The following information was taken from the 1999 annual report—statements of cash flows—of the Avis Group, a major company in the automobile rental and vehicle management industry (dollars in millions).

Year	Cash from Operations	Cash from Investing	Cash from Financing
1997	$ 416	$(1,079)	$ 679
1998	653	(967)	299
1999	1,098	(2,816)	1,852

REQUIRED:
What does this pattern of cash flows indicate about the business strategy followed by Avis from 1997 to 1999?

REAL DATA

ID2-6

Statement of
cash flows—
British format

The following balance sheet was taken from the 1999 annual report of GlaxoWellcome, a
British pharmaceutical company (British pounds in millions).

GlaxoWellcome Consolidated Balance Sheet			
	Notes	1999 £m	1998 £m
Goodwill	10	144	106
Tangible assets	11	3,720	3,633
Investments	12	483	98
Fixed assets		4,347	3,837
Equity investments	13	52	28
Stocks	14	1,537	1,154
Debtors	15	2,577	2,470
Liquid investments	16	1,697	1,617
Cash at bank	16	217	240
Current assets		6,080	5,509
Loans and overdrafts	16	2,250	1,317
Other creditors	18	3,013	2,828
Creditors: amounts due within one year		5,263	4,145
Net current assets		817	1,364
Total assets less current liabilities		5,164	5,201
Loans	16	1,260	1,804
Other creditors	18	116	161
Creditors: amounts due after one year		1,376	1,965
Provisions for liabilities and charges	19	595	468
Net assets	26	3,193	2,768
Called up share capital	22	910	906
Share premium account	22	1,249	1,149
Other reserves	23	983	647
Equity shareholders' funds		3,142	2,702
Equity minority interests		51	66
Capital employed		3,193	2,768

Approved by the Board
Sir Richard Sykes, Chairman
9th March 2000

REQUIRED:

Identify where the format of this balance sheet differs from that required under U.S. GAAP, and
prepare a balance sheet according to U.S. GAAP.

REAL DATA

ID2-7

The annual report
of Wal-Mart

The annual report of Wal-Mart is reproduced in Appendix A.

REQUIRED:

Review the 2001 Wal-Mart annual report, and answer the following questions.

a. Compute cost of sales, operating, selling and general and administrative expenses, interest
    costs, and taxes as a percent of revenues for 2001, 2000, and 1999, and explain why Wal-
    Mart's net income has increased over the three-year period.
b. Compute current and noncurrent assets as a percent of total assets, and explain how Wal-
    Mart's asset structure changed from 2000 to 2001.

c. Compute current and long-term liabilities as a percent of total assets, and explain how Wal-Mart's reliance on liabilities as a source of financing changed from 2000 to 2001.

d. Review the statement of cash flows, and comment on whether Wal-Mart is growing and which financing sources have financed this growth.

e. Approximately what portion of Wal-Mart's net income is paid to the shareholders in the form of dividends each year?

Measurement, Mechanics, and Use of Financial Statements

PART 2

Imation was formed in 1996, when 3M created a new company to house its information technology activities. In its 1997 annual report, Imation's chairman and chief executive officer, William Monihan, reported, "we are not pleased with the overall progress of the business [because] . . . we did not deliver the growth and financial performance that we expected to achieve in 1997." That same annual report disclosed a substantial stock price drop and deteriorating profits. He closed the letter to the shareholders by describing "the steps we are taking . . . to improve the execution of our business strategies." By the beginning of 2000, this dismal picture had reversed itself. Mr. Monihan was pleased to report that Imation's strategies—double-digit revenue growth, better control over expenses, and a host of new product introductions—had resulted in a dramatic 92 percent share price improvement. How do shareholders and potential investors assess such claims? Can analysts predict swings in performance like those experienced by Imation? How do the financial statements reflect the successes and failures of firm strategies? These kinds of questions are addressed in Part 2 of this textbook.

CHAPTER 3
The Measurement Fundamentals of Financial Accounting

CHAPTER 4
The Mechanics of Financial Accounting

CHAPTER 5
Using Financial Statement Information

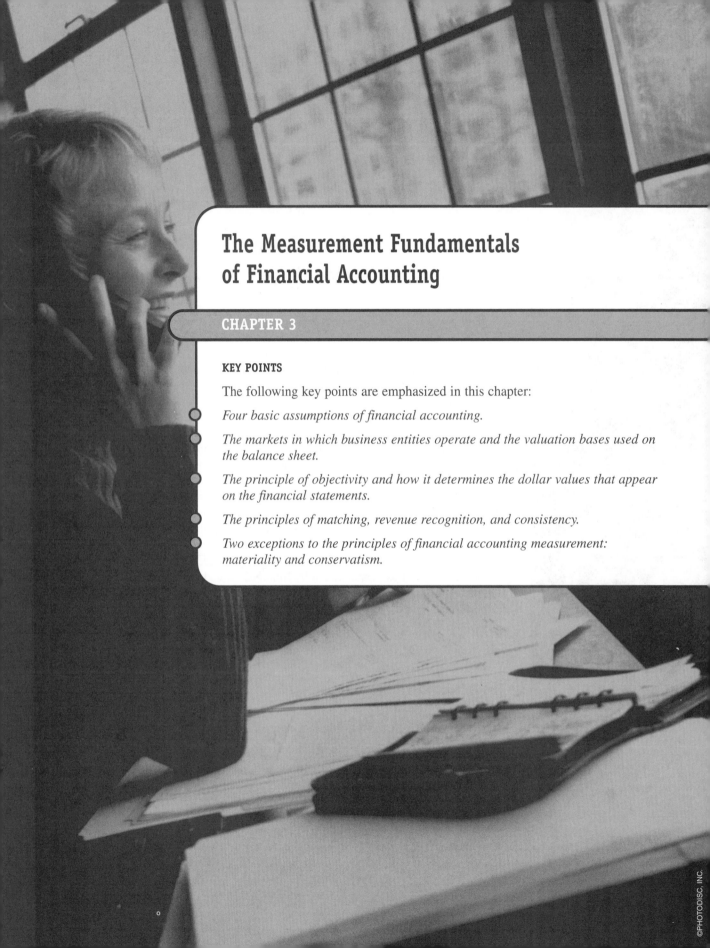

The Measurement Fundamentals of Financial Accounting

CHAPTER 3

KEY POINTS

The following key points are emphasized in this chapter:

Four basic assumptions of financial accounting.

The markets in which business entities operate and the valuation bases used on the balance sheet.

The principle of objectivity and how it determines the dollar values that appear on the financial statements.

The principles of matching, revenue recognition, and consistency.

Two exceptions to the principles of financial accounting measurement: materiality and conservatism.

Forbes (5/29/00) reported that ITT Educational Services, an Indianapolis company that runs sixty-eight technical institutes, was able to boost earnings and its stock price with aggressive revenue recognition practices. How can companies do this? This chapter answers that question and others like it by covering the measurement fundamentals of financial accounting, which consist of the basic assumptions, valuation issues, principles, and exceptions underlying the financial statements.

ASSUMPTIONS OF FINANCIAL ACCOUNTING

There are four basic assumptions of financial accounting: (1) economic entity, (2) fiscal period, (3) going concern, and (4) stable dollar. These assumptions are important because they form the building blocks upon which financial accounting measurement is based. Some are reasonable representations of the real world, and others are not. As each assumption is discussed, try to understand why it has evolved, and be especially aware of those that fail to capture the world as it really is.

Economic Entity Assumption

The most fundamental assumption of financial accounting involves the object of the performance measure. Should the accounting system provide performance information about countries, states, cities, industries, individual companies, or segments of individual companies? While it is important that each of these entities operate efficiently, financial accounting has evolved in response to a demand for company-specific measures of performance and financial position. Consequently, financial accounting reports provide information about individual, profit-seeking companies.

The process of providing information about profit-seeking entities implicitly assumes that they can be identified and measured. Individual companies must be entities in and of themselves, separate and distinct from both their owners and all other entities. This statement represents the **economic entity assumption,** the first basic assumption of financial accounting. This assumption provides an important foundation upon which the financial accounting system is built, and in certain situations, it plays a critical role in determining the scope of financial statements.

For example, after Walt Disney acquired the common stock of Capital Cities/ABC, Inc., a major broadcasting company, it included all of ABC's assets and liabilities on its consolidated balance sheet. For financial reporting purposes, therefore, ABC, which publishes its own separate financial statements, is included within the economic entity referred to as The Walt Disney Company. In fact, the consolidated balance sheet of Disney includes the assets and liabilities of many other companies, called *subsidiaries,* each of which prepares its own financial statements. NBC, another major broadcasting company, is a subsidiary of General Electric.

Nabisco is an entity called a holding company, consisting of three business segments: (1) biscuits, (2) the U.S. Food Group, and (3) the International Food Group. The company reports separate financial statements for each segment as well as a set of consolidated financial statements. Why might it be useful to maintain separate accounting records for each group? Might there be some difficulties maintaining separate records?

Fiscal Period Assumption

Once the object of measurement has been identified (i.e., the economic entity), we must recognize that to be useful, measures of performance and financial position must be available on a timely basis. Investors, creditors, and other users of financial information need periodic feedback if they are to monitor the performance of management as well as control and direct its decisions.

The need for timely performance measures underlies the **fiscal period assumption,** which states that the operating life of an economic entity can be divided into time periods over which such measures can be developed and applied. Most corporations, for example, prepare annual financial statements, providing yearly feedback and performance measures to their stockholders. The Securities and Exchange Commission requires that publicly traded companies provide financial statements (called *Form 10-Q*) to their stockholders on a quarterly basis.

TIMELY VS. OBJECTIVE FINANCIAL INFORMATION

The fiscal period assumption introduces a trade-off between the timeliness of accounting information and its objectivity. Users need timely information, and thus, they generally prefer fiscal periods that are relatively short. However, as the fiscal period becomes shorter, the applications of certain accounting methods become more arbitrary and subjective. The quarterly accounting reports published by major U.S. corporations, for example, are not audited and are generally more subjective than the audited annual reports. To illustrate, the Form 10-Q report published by Amazon.com, Inc., for the first quarter of 2000 contained the following statement:

The accompanying financial statements have been prepared by Amazon.com, pursuant to the rules and regulations of the Securities and Exchange Commission for interim financial reporting. The financial statements are unaudited. . . .

Cisco Systems and Alcoa have real-time financial information used exclusively for internal decision making. Cisco, for example, has hourly information on revenues, bookings, discounts, and product margins. While certainly there are advantages associated with real-time information systems, can you think of a possible disadvantage?

A CALENDAR YEAR OR FISCAL YEAR?

Another consequence of the fiscal period assumption is that companies must choose the dates of their reporting cycles. Most major U.S. corporations report on the calendar year. That is, they publish an annual report each year as of December 31, and their quarterly statements cover periods ending March 31, June 30, September 30, and December 31. However, a number of companies report on twelve-month periods, called **fiscal years,** that end on dates other than December 31.[1] In most cases a company chooses a fiscal reporting cycle because its operations are seasonal, and the financial statements are more meaningful if the reporting period includes the entire season.

---

1. According to a survey conducted by the American Institute of Certified Public Accountants, 37 percent of the merchandising and industrial companies in the United States close their books on dates other than December 31.

Large retailers, like Target, Kmart, and Toys "R" Us, for example, often end their fiscal years on January 31, after the completion of the Christmas season. Many companies in the food industry, such as Pillsbury, General Mills, and Quaker Oats, prepare annual financial statements in May or June, just after the winter grain crops are harvested. Companies in the automobile and farm machinery industries, such as Firestone and Deere & Co., close their books in September or October, following the summer season when sales are heaviest. Universal Leaf Tobacco, a major processor in the tobacco industry, ends its fiscal year on June 30, immediately after the previous year's tobacco crop has been cured.

Going Concern Assumption

The **going concern assumption** follows logically from the fiscal period assumption. If we assume that an entity's life can be divided into fiscal periods, we must further assume that its life extends beyond the current period. In other words, we assume that the entity will not discontinue operations at the end of the current period over which its performance is being measured. Taken to the extreme, this assumption states that the life of the entity will continue indefinitely.

The role of the going concern assumption in financial accounting is as fundamental as the definition of an asset. Recall that assets are defined to have *future* economic benefit; that is, benefits that extend beyond the current period. The cost of equipment, for example, is placed on the balance sheet because the equipment is expected to provide benefits in the future. The Financial Accounting Standards Board invoked the going concern assumption when, in Statement of Financial Concepts No. 3, it defined assets as "probable *future* economic benefits obtained or controlled by a particular entity as a result of past transactions or events."[2]

In the first quarter of 2000, Ernst & Young—a major professional service firm that performs audits on large companies—raised substantial doubt in its audit report about American Architectural Products' ability to continue as a going concern. What factors did Ernst & Young consider when reaching this conclusion, and why would they care about a client's ability to continue as a going concern?

Stable Dollar Assumption

To measure the dimensions, quantity, or capacity of anything requires a unit of measurement. Height and distance, for example, can be measured in terms of inches, feet, centimeters, or meters; volume can be measured in gallons or liters; and weight can be measured in pounds or kilograms. Mathematical operations, such as addition or subtraction, on any such measure require that the unit of measurement maintain a constant definition.

To illustrate, suppose that you weighed yourself at the beginning of the year and found that your weight was 120 pounds. At the end of the year, you weighed yourself again and noted that your weight was 128 pounds. You conclude that you gained 8 pounds during the year, but implicit in this conclusion is the assumption that the

---

2. Financial Accounting Standards Board, "Elements of Financial Statements of Business Enterprises," *Statement of Financial Concepts No. 3* (Stamford, Conn.: FASB, December 1980), xi and xii.

definition of a pound was the same at the beginning and the end of the year. Had a pound at the beginning of the year equaled 16 ounces, but 15 ounces at the end of the year, for example, you would actually have gained no weight at all. You would have weighed 1,920 ounces at both points in time.

The logical unit of measurement for the financial performance and condition of a company is the monetary unit used in the economic transactions entered into by that company. In the United States, for example, the monetary unit is the dollar. Consequently, the financial statements of U.S. companies are expressed in terms of dollars.

The measures of financial performance and position on the financial statements all involve the addition, subtraction, or division of dollar amounts. Total assets on the balance sheet, for example, represent the addition of the dollar values of all the individual assets held by a company at a particular point in time. The current ratio and the debt/equity ratio involve dividing certain balance sheet dollar amounts by other balance sheet dollar amounts. As with the measures discussed previously, valid use of these mathematical operations requires that the definition of the dollar be constant. Thus, a **stable dollar assumption** is implicit in the measures of performance and financial condition used to evaluate and control management's decisions.

INFLATION: THE DOLLAR'S CHANGING PURCHASING POWER

A dollar's value is defined in terms of its **purchasing power,** the amount of goods and services it can buy at a given point in time. During inflation, which has come to be a fact of life, the purchasing power of the dollar decreases steadily. Therefore, financial statements, which are based on the assumption that the purchasing power of the dollar is constant (i.e., no inflation), can be seriously misstated.

Suppose, for example, that on January 1 you have $1,000, and at that time the cost of rice is $1 per bag. You could purchase 1,000 bags of rice, but you decide instead to use the money to purchase (invest in) a small tract of land. During the year, the inflation rate is 10 percent. At year-end, the price of the rice is $1.10 per bag, and the value of the land is $1,100. You decide to sell the land, and on your income statement you recognize a gain on the sale of $100 ($1,100 − $1,000). You read your income statement and count the cash in your hand and conclude that your economic wealth has increased by $100. However, you use the $1,100 to buy rice and you are surprised to learn that it buys only 1,000 bags, the exact amount you could have purchased at the beginning of the year. Consequently, your wealth is not increased at all, even though your income statement indicates otherwise.

A LIMITATION IN THE FINANCIAL STATEMENTS

The stable dollar assumption is one instance in which the financial statements are based on an unrealistic assumption. Financial accounting standard–setting bodies have recognized this problem for many years and have attempted to solve it many times. The most recent effort occurred in 1979, when the FASB required certain large U.S. companies to provide information about the effects of inflation in their annual reports. However, this requirement was subsequently rescinded. Companies complained that the disclosures were costly, and financial statement users showed little interest in them, probably because they believed them to be unreliable. It is important that financial statement users at least recognize that this limitation exists and, in some cases, learn how to adjust financial statements for the effects of inflation. Indeed, in some countries inflation continues to be a problem, and financial statements need to be restated.

J.C. Penney's 1999 annual report indicates that "inflation and changing prices have not had a significant impact on the Company in recent years due to low levels of inflation." How could inflation, if significant, affect the way in which an investor might interpret J.C. Penney's financial statements?

Summary of Basic Assumptions

Our discussion of the basic assumptions of financial accounting is now complete. In summary, we have assumed the existence of a separate, measurable business entity (economic entity), whose infinite life (going concern) can be broken down into fiscal periods (fiscal period) and whose transactions can be measured in stable dollars (stable dollar). Each of these assumptions is briefly defined in Figure 3–1.

FIGURE 3–1
The basic assumptions of financial accounting

Assumption	Definition
Economic entity	**Profit-seeking entities, which are separate and distinct from their owners and other entities, can be identified and measured.**
Fiscal period	**The life of the economic entity can be divided into fiscal periods, and the performance and financial position of the entity can be measured during each of those periods.**
Going concern	**The life of the economic entity will extend beyond the current fiscal period.**
Stable dollar	**The performance and financial position of the entity can be measured in terms of a monetary unit that maintains constant purchasing power across fiscal periods.**

Now that the basic assumptions of financial accounting have been established, we can explain how dollar amounts are attached to the assets, liabilities, equities, revenues, expenses, and dividends of economic entities. In the course of this explanation we consider (1) valuations on the balance sheet and (2) the principles of financial accounting measurement.

VALUATIONS ON THE BALANCE SHEET

The dollar values attached to the accounts on a company's balance sheet are largely determined by the markets in which the company operates. To understand these markets, it is helpful to view a business entity in the following way.

Inputs ⟶ Entity Operations ⟶ Outputs
(purchase prices)   (sales prices)

A business entity operates in two general markets: an **input market,** where it purchases inputs (materials, labor, overhead) for its operations, and an **output market,** where it sells its outputs (services or inventories). Input market values (prices) are normally less than output market values (prices). For example, local automobile dealers purchase automobiles from manufacturers, such as General Motors, Daimler-Chrysler Corporation, and Ford Motor Company, and sell them to consumers. The prices paid for automobiles by dealers in their input market are generally less than the prices paid by consumers in the output market. A new Chevrolet, for example, may cost a dealer $15,000 in the input market and be sold to you, a customer, for $17,000 in the output market.

Moreover, input and output markets are defined in terms of specific entities: one entity's output market may be another entity's input market. DuPont, for example, supplies complete front and back assemblies for the General Motors cars produced at a GM plant near Kansas City, Missouri. When GM purchases these assemblies, the transaction takes place in the output market of DuPont and the input market of GM.

Viewing a business entity in terms of both its input and output markets introduces a number of different ways to value the accounts on the balance sheet. Should assets, for example, be valued in terms of prices from the input market or prices from the output market—or is there a way to reflect both input and output prices in their valuations? For example, should the value of the Chevrolet on the dealer's balance sheet be expressed in terms of the dealer's input cost ($15,000) or the selling price in the output market ($17,000)?

Four Valuation Bases

Four different **valuation bases** are used to determine the dollar amounts attached to the accounts on the balance sheet. They are (1) present value, (2) fair market value, (3) replacement cost, and (4) original cost. **Present value,** the computation of which is discussed and illustrated in Appendix B at the end of the text, represents the discounted future cash flows associated with a particular financial statement item. The present value of a note receivable, for example, is calculated by determining the amount and timing of its future cash inflows and then adjusting the dollar amounts for the time value of money. **Fair market value (FMV),** or sales price, represents the value of the item in the output market. **Replacement cost,** or current cost, is the current price paid for an item in the input market. **Original cost** represents the input price paid when the item was originally purchased. Figure 3–2 provides definitions of the four valuation bases in terms of an entity's input and output markets.

FIGURE 3–2 Markets and valuation bases	**Valuation Bases**
	1. **Present value—discounted future cash flows from input and output markets**
	2. **Fair market value—current sales price in output market.**
	3. **Replacement cost—current cost to replace in input market**
	4. **Original cost—historical cost in input market**

To illustrate, assume that on January 1, Watson Land Developers purchased an apartment building for $100,000, which an outsider recently offered to buy for $140,000. Watson estimates that if it continues to manage the apartment, it would produce net cash flows for the next ten years at a rate of $25,000 per year. The company also recently investigated replacing the apartment building with a comparable structure and learned that it would cost $175,000. The present value, fair market value, replacement cost, and original cost of the apartment building are provided below. In other words, Watson purchased an apartment building for $100,000 that could now be sold for $140,000 and/or replaced for $175,000. Continuing to manage the apartment would produce cash flows of $25,000 per year, which is equivalent to a present value of $153,614.

Present value   **= $153,614 ($25,000 × 6.14457*)**
Fair market value = $140,000
Replacement cost = $175,000
Original cost   = $100,000

*Present value factor (ten-year ordinary annuity, 10 percent discount rate)

> The Avis Group reports over $7 billion worth of vehicles on its balance sheet. Which of the four valuation bases does the $7 billion represent? Discuss how Avis could compute the present value, the fair market value, and the replacement cost of its fleet of vehicles, and describe how these different valuations might be considered useful information.

Valuation Bases Used on the Balance Sheet

All four of the valuation bases described in the previous section are contained in balance sheets prepared under generally accepted accounting principles. This point is illustrated in Figure 3–3, which provides a balance sheet with the valuation base for each account indicated in parentheses. The code for each valuation base is located below the balance sheet.

Cash and all current liabilities are valued using a specific form of fair market value called **face value.** This valuation reflects the cash expected to be received or paid in the near future. The statement of cash flows, which explains changes in the cash account, is completely expressed in terms of face value. Short-term investments are valued at fair market value. Accounts receivable are valued at **net realizable value,** another form of fair market value reflecting the amount of cash expected to be collected from the outstanding accounts. Inventories are valued at original cost or replacement cost, whichever is lower. This example of the conservative **lower-of-cost-or-market rule,** which ensures that the dollar value of this account is not overstated, illustrates that under certain circumstances replacement costs are found on the balance sheet.

Land, securities held as long-term investments,[3] and property used in a company's operations are all valued at original cost unadjusted for amortization or depreciation. Prepaid expenses, plant and equipment, and all intangible assets are carried on the balance sheet at their original costs (**historical costs**), reduced by accumulated amortization or depreciation. This adjusted cost dollar value is often referred to as *net book value.*

Long-term notes receivable and long-term liabilities are valued at present value. The dollar amount attached to each of these accounts is calculated by determining the amount and timing of the future cash flows associated with the account and adjusting the dollar amounts for the time value of money (see Appendix B).

Technically, the stockholders' equity section of the balance sheet is not valued in terms of any valuation base. It represents the residual interests of the stockholders or

---

3. A special method, called the equity method, is used to value certain long-term equity investments on the balance sheet. This method is based on the original cost of the investment, but certain additional adjustments to original cost are made periodically. This method is discussed and illustrated in Chapter 8, which covers long-term investments.

Harbour Island Company
Balance Sheet
December 31, 2002

ASSETS

Current assets:		
Cash	$ 220 (FMV)	
Short-term investments	150 (FMV)	
Accounts receivable	345 (FMV)	
Inventory	600 (LCM)	
Prepaid expenses	100 (OC)	
Total current assets		$ 1,415
Long-term investments:		
Long-term notes receivable	$1,000 (PV)	
Land	500 (OC)	
Securities	2,500 (OC)	
Total long-term investments		4,000
Property, plant, and equipment:		
Property	$6,000 (OC)	
Plant	2,900 (OC)	
Equipment	2,600 (OC)	
Total property, plant, and equipment		11,500
Intangible assets:		
Patent	$1,000 (OC)	
Trademark	700 (OC)	
Total intangible assets		1,700
Total assets		$18,615

LIABILITIES AND STOCKHOLDERS' EQUITY

Current liabilities:		
Accounts payable	$ 200 (FMV)	
Wages payable	150 (FMV)	
Interest payable	30 (FMV)	
Short-term notes payable	200 (FMV)	
Other payables	60 (FMV)	
Unearned revenues	30 (FMV)	
Dividends payable	70 (FMV)	
Total current liabilities		$ 740
Long-term liabilities:		
Long-term notes payable	$1,500 (PV)	
Bonds payable	3,500 (PV)	
Mortgage payable	1,940 (PV)	
Total long-term liabilities		6,940
Stockholders' equity		10,935
Total liabilities and stockholders' equity		$18,615

Valuation base code: FMV = fair market value; LCM = lower of cost or market; OC = original cost; PV = present value.

the book value of the company. In other words, the stockholders' equity section can be viewed simply as the difference between the total balance sheet value of the company's assets and the total balance sheet value of the company's liabilities.

So far we have assumed that economic entities can be identified and measured, their infinite lives can be divided into fiscal periods, and their performance and financial position can be measured in terms of stable dollars. We have also observed that a number of different valuation bases (face value, present value, fair market value, replacement cost, and original cost) are used to determine the dollar amounts of the accounts on the balance sheet. The next section presents the principles of financial accounting measurement, which explain why particular valuation bases are used for some accounts and not for others and how the valuation bases are used to measure net income.

Take a quick look at the 2001 balance sheet for Wal-Mart provided in Appendix A. Which of the four valuation bases accounts for the greatest dollar amount? Which accounts for the least?

THE PRINCIPLES OF FINANCIAL ACCOUNTING MEASUREMENT

There are four basic principles of financial accounting measurement: (1) objectivity, (2) matching, (3) revenue recognition, and (4) consistency.

The Principle of Objectivity

Financial accounting information provides useful measures of performance and financial position. In doing so, financial accounting statements must provide information about value: the value of entire companies, the value of company assets and liabilities, and the value of the specific transactions entered into by companies.

The economic value of an entity, an asset, or a liability is its present value, which reflects both the future cash flows associated with the entity, asset, or liability and the time value of money.[4] There is, however, one critical problem with the present value calculation: it assumes that future interest rates and future cash flows are perfectly predictable. This assumption presents no problems in theory, but users of accounting measures of performance and financial position need reliable measures that can be audited at reasonable costs.

For example, Union Carbide Corporation routinely invests over $700 million in plant assets. Reporting this investment on the company's balance sheet at present value would require an estimate of the net future cash flows generated by the new facilities, as well as an estimate of future interest rates. Such estimates, which would be the responsibility of the company's management, are simply too subjective for the financial statements. Auditors would be unwilling and unable to verify these subjective judgments, and the legal liability faced by both managers and auditors would make such verification potentially very costly.

The principle of **objectivity,** which is perhaps the most important and pervasive principle of accounting measurement, states that financial accounting information must be verifiable and reliable. It requires that the values of transactions and of the assets and liabilities created by them be objectively determined and backed by documented

---

4. The following discussion assumes that you understand the present value calculation. If not, refer to Appendix B.

evidence. Although it ensures that the dollar amounts disclosed on the financial statements are reasonably reliable, the principle of objectivity also precludes much relevant and useful information from ever appearing on the financial statements.

Many companies in the new Internet-driven economy are valuable because they have knowledge not possessed by other companies, often referred to as intellectual property rights. While most believe that these assets have value, they do not appear on the companies' balance sheets. Why not?

PRESENT VALUE AND THE FINANCIAL STATEMENTS

The principle of objectivity ensures that present value cannot be used as the valuation base for all assets and liabilities. In some cases, however, the future cash flows associated with certain assets and liabilities are predictable enough to allow for sufficiently objective present value calculations. Suppose, for example, that on December 31, The Boeing Company received payment from United Airlines for an order of jumbo jets in the form of a note receivable. The note states that United will pay Boeing $1 million at the end of each year for the next two years. Certainly, this note should appear as an asset (receivable) on Boeing's December 31 balance sheet and as a payable on the balance sheet of United, but at what dollar amount should it be reported?

If we assume a discount rate of 10 percent and realize that the note is actually a two-period $1 million cash flow, we can use the present value calculation to place a value on the note ($1.735 million = $1 million × 1.735 [Table 5: $n = 2$, $i = 10\%$]). Further, the auditors of Boeing and United would be willing to attest to this valuation because the future cash flows are objectively determined in a legal contract, entered into and signed by both Boeing and United in an *arm's-length transaction*. The auditors for the most part are protected from legal liability because the responsibility to provide the contractual payments rests with United. The result is that a $1.735 million note receivable would appear on Boeing's balance sheet and a $1.735 million note payable would appear on United's balance sheet. In this case, present value would be used to provide a balance sheet value for both an asset and a liability.

In general, present value is used on the financial statements only in those cases where future cash flows can be objectively determined. As illustrated, contractual agreements like notes receivable and payable represent cases that meet this criterion. Mortgages, bonds, leases, and pensions are other examples of contracts that underlie cash flows and remove much of the subjectivity associated with cash flow prediction.

Refer again to the balance sheet in Figure 3–3, and note that present value is used as the valuation base for long-term notes receivable, long-term notes payable, bonds payable, and mortgages payable.

The FASB has recently issued a standard that sets the parameters for deciding when and how to use present value to determine the fair market value of an asset or a liability when the amount or timing of future cash flows is uncertain. Comment on trade-offs that might be introduced by such a standard.

MARKET VALUE AND THE FINANCIAL STATEMENTS

Using market value (i.e., fair market value or replacement cost) as a valuation base for the accounts on the financial statements can be attractive because, in many cases, market value represents the best estimate of present value. If, for example, buyers and sellers in a given market use their individual estimates of present value when bidding on an asset, the resulting market price of the asset should approximate its actual present value. In addition, fair market value is often more objective than present value. Market prices for the equity securities of major U.S. companies, for example, are listed on public stock exchanges and can therefore be objectively verified. To illustrate, the market price of a share of DuPont common stock as of the end of trading on November 21, 2000, was $41.18.[5]

Unfortunately, while market values are sometimes objectively determinable, in most situations they are not objective enough for use in the financial statements. The market values of securities that are not traded on the major stock exchanges, most inventories, long-term investments, property, plant, and equipment, and intangible assets are not easily determined. The market values of such items may be very informative, but they fail to meet the principle of objectivity.

Refer again to the balance sheet in Figure 3–3, and note that market values are used in the valuation of relatively few accounts. Short-term investments are valued at fair market value, accounts receivable are valued at net realizable value, which approximates fair market value, and inventories are valued at original cost or market value, whichever is lower.

The Capital Markets Report (June 1, 2000) stated that a proposal requiring that financial instruments (e.g., securities) be reported at fair market value on the balance sheet drew a negative response from the financial services industry (e.g., banks, insurance companies, and savings and loans). Can you think of any reasons why?

ORIGINAL COST AND THE FINANCIAL STATEMENTS

Note also in Figure 3–3 that the remaining accounts on the balance sheet (Prepaid Expenses, Land, Securities, Property, Plant, and Equipment, and Intangible Assets) are valued at original cost, the price paid when the asset was originally acquired, or net book value, which is original cost adjusted for depreciation or amortization. Original costs can be objectively verified and supported by documented evidence. They are reliable, can be audited at reasonable cost, and do not violate the principle of objectivity.

The Principles of Matching and Revenue Recognition

Objectivity is the most pervasive principle of financial accounting. It affects all areas of measurement, including operating performance, which is the focus of the matching and revenue recognition principles.

The **matching** principle, which states that the efforts of a given period should be matched against the benefits that result from them, underlies the measures of operating performance. It is initiated when a company incurs a cost (e.g., pays wages, purchases equipment, invests in a security) to generate benefits, normally in the form of revenues.[6] If the revenues are generated immediately, the cost is treated as an expense, appearing on the income statement of the current period. If the revenues are expected to be realized in future periods, the cost is considered an asset, or capitalized, and

5. *The Wall Street Journal*, November 22, 2000.
6. Benefits can also be in the form of cost savings.

appears on the balance sheet. In future periods, as the revenues are realized, the assets are converted to expenses appearing on the income statements of the future periods. Thus, costs incurred to generate revenues are matched against those revenues in the time periods in which the revenues are realized. This process produces a periodic measure of net income, or company performance.

The most critical question in the matching process, as described in Figure 3–4, occurs at Step 2: In what time period will the revenue be realized? The cost incurred in Step 1 cannot be treated as an expense, and the matching principle cannot be applied until this question is answered. The answer, unfortunately, is not always obvious because there are many possibilities. The principle of **revenue recognition** provides the guidelines for answering this question.

FIGURE 3–4 Income measurement via revenue recognition and matching

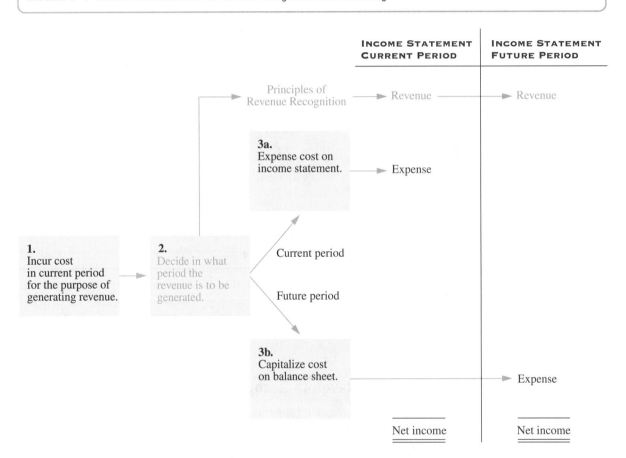

To understand the principle of revenue recognition, it is helpful to view the selling of a good or a service as involving the four steps illustrated in Figure 3–5. A good or service is (1) ordered, (2) produced, (3) transferred to the buyer, and then (4) paid for by the buyer. These four steps make a complete production/sales cycle.

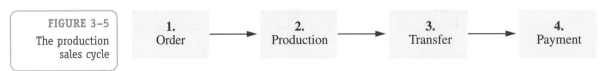

FIGURE 3–5
The production sales cycle

The principle of revenue recognition helps to determine at which of these four points the revenue from the sale of a good or service should be recognized on the income statement. The most common point of revenue recognition is Step 3, when the good or service is transferred to the buyer. At this point, a company has normally completed the earning process and is entitled to recognize the revenue. Yet, there are times when each of the other steps may be the point at which revenue should be recognized. The principle of revenue recognition states that four criteria must be met before revenue can be included in the income statement:

1. The company has completed a significant portion of the production and sales effort.
2. The amount of revenue can be objectively measured.
3. The major portion of the costs has been incurred, and the remaining costs can be reasonably estimated.
4. The eventual collection of the cash is reasonably assured.

While these guidelines are helpful, defining the point in time when all four criteria are met still requires much judgment and can be very important because it often dramatically affects the dollar amounts on the financial statements. In a story reported in *The Wall Street Journal,* for example, the SEC charged three former officers of Matrix Science Corporation with significantly inflating the company's earnings. The charges alleged that the officers were able to grossly overstate net income by recording revenues on products "that haven't been shipped, or in some cases, haven't even been assembled."

IBM, who has for years enjoyed a reputation as the epitome of financial conservatism, has been cited "for booking revenue when its products were shipped to dealers who could return them and sometimes even to its own warehouses." Many famous accounting frauds (e.g., Regina Vacuum Cleaners, Phar-Mor, MiniScribe, and Knowledge Ware) were based on exaggerating revenue and profit numbers by creating fictitious sales. Blockbuster Video has also been cited for aggressive revenue recognition practices, and the scenario described at the beginning of this chapter referred to the aggressive revenue recognition practices of ITT Education.

MicroStrategy, a prominent software company, provides software services for clients on contracts that extend over several years. At first, the company recorded the entire amount of revenue from these multiyear contracts in the first year. Later, its auditors forced the company to spread the recognition of the revenue over the lives of the contracts. How did the change affect MicroStrategy's reported income? Which of the two methods is a better example of the matching process?

The Principle of Consistency

Generally accepted accounting principles allow a number of different, acceptable methods to be used to account for the assets, liabilities, revenues, expenses, and dividends on the financial statements. For example, several acceptable methods may be used to account for each of the following assets: accounts receivable, inventories, long-term investments, and fixed assets. Such variety exists for two reasons: (1) no method is general enough to apply to all companies in all situations and (2) generally accepted accounting principles are the result of a political process in which interested parties who face widely different situations are allowed and encouraged to provide input.

The principle of **consistency** states that, although there is considerable choice among methods, companies should choose a set of methods and use them from one period to the next. Its primary economic rationale is that consistency helps investors, creditors, and other interested parties to compare measures of performance and financial position across time periods. Comparability is critical to effective financial analysis. Presumably, if a company does not change its accounting methods, outside parties can more easily identify trends across time. In addition, management rarely wishes to change accounting methods; it had reasons for choosing the existing methods in the first place, and changing from one method to another could be viewed by outsiders as an attempt to manipulate the financial statements, reducing credibility.

While consistency is important, it does not mean that companies never change accounting methods. If management can convince the independent auditor that the environment facing the company has changed to the point that an alternative accounting method is appropriate, the company is allowed to switch. However, such changes are not easily granted, and when approved, the effects of the change on the financial statements are clearly disclosed. The change is usually described in the footnotes and mentioned in the auditor's report, and its effect on income is disclosed in a separate category on the income statement.

In a recent annual report, for example, General Motors reported a change in its method of accounting for inventory. The change was mentioned in the audit report, and the increase in net income of $224 million was disclosed as a separate item on the income statement. The following excerpt describing the change was taken from the footnotes of General Motors' financial report:

. . . accounting procedures were changed to include in inventory certain manufacturing overhead costs previously charged directly to expense. The effect of this change on earnings was a favorable adjustment of $0.35 per share. . . .

Still, many of the recent accounting standards are designed to reduce the wide variety of methods used across companies. As reported in *The Wall Street Journal* (April 9, 1998), "the new standard for writing off start-up costs is aimed at ending the wide disparity in accounting for these expenses, which made it difficult for investors to properly compare financial results."

During America Online's period of tremendous growth, the company capitalized (treated as assets) all costs associated with acquiring new customers. In late 1999, the company chose to expense all such costs. This accounting change had a dramatic effect on the financial statements. Where in the annual report could an investor find information about this accounting change?

TWO EXCEPTIONS TO THE BASIC PRINCIPLES: MATERIALITY AND CONSERVATISM

Under certain circumstances, the costs of applying the principles of accounting exceed the benefits. In these situations, management is allowed (and, in some cases, required) to depart from the principles. All rules have exceptions, even the measurement principles of financial accounting. Two important exceptions are materiality and conservatism.

Materiality

Materiality states that only those transactions dealing with dollar amounts large enough to make a difference to financial statement users need be accounted for in a manner consistent with the principles of financial accounting. The dollar amounts of some transactions are so small that the method of accounting has virtually no impact on the financial statements and, thus, no effect on the related evaluations and control decisions. In such cases, the least costly method of reporting is chosen, regardless of the method suggested by the principles of accounting measurement. The dollar amounts of these transactions are referred to as immaterial, and management is allowed to account for them as expediently as possible.

For example, the matching principle indicates that the cost of a wastebasket should be included on the balance sheet and converted to expense over future periods because its usefulness is expected to extend beyond the current period. However, the cost of an individual wastebasket is probably immaterial, and it is costly in terms of management's time and effort to carry such items on the books. For practical reasons, therefore, the purchase price is immediately treated as an expense. Granted, such treatment misstates income for both the current period and the future periods of the wastebasket's useful life. This misstatement, however, is extremely small (i.e., immaterial) and would have no bearing on the decisions of those who use the financial statements. In this case, the costs of capitalizing and depreciating the purchase price of the wastebasket simply exceed the benefits it would provide.

While materiality is practical, it represents a major problem area in accounting because it requires judgments that can differ considerably among investors, creditors, managers, auditors, and others. The U.S. Supreme Court has provided one of the few guidelines, defining a material item as one to which "there is substantial likelihood that a reasonable investor would attach importance in determining whether to purchase a security."

In determining materiality, the size of an item is always considered, but whether it would affect the decisions of an investor or creditor is often unclear. A dollar amount that is too small to make a difference in a large company may be very significant in a small company, and not only must the size of an item be considered, but its nature can also be important. A small adjustment to the inventory account, for example, may be far more significant to financial statement users than a large adjustment to an account in the stockholders' equity section of the balance sheet. What about a very small accounting adjustment that allows a company to just achieve its earnings forecast? Would that be considered immaterial? Finally, the user must be considered. A creditor's definition of materiality, for example, may be very different from that of an investor.

In summary, materiality is an important and practical exception to the principles of financial accounting measurement. Indeed, the standard unqualified auditor's report states that "the financial statements are free of material misstatement." Materiality is, nonetheless, very ambiguous. As stated in *Forbes*, "Too often, investors miss important information because companies deem it 'immaterial.' What does this mean? Nobody knows—and that's a big problem." The article goes on to report that Rockwell International, a multibillion-dollar conglomerate, chose not to disclose a loss that could have been as large as $220 million because it was considered "immaterial."

For many years, companies used *quantitative* (object) methods to determine the materiality of a financial statement item (e.g., 5 percent of net income). In August 1999, the SEC issued a statement eliminating that practice, requiring instead the use of *qualitative* analysis when determining whether a reported item is material. In this context, what is the difference between quantitative and qualitative analysis?

Conservatism

Another important exception to the principles of financial accounting measurement is conservatism. Like materiality, conservatism is practical and has evolved over time in response to cost/benefit considerations. In its simplest form, **conservatism** states that, *when in doubt,* financial statements should understate assets, overstate liabilities, accelerate the recognition of losses, and delay the recognition of gains.

Conservatism does not suggest, however, that the financial statements should be intentionally understated. When given objective and verifiable evidence about a material transaction, the principles of accounting measurement should be followed, and no attempt should be made to intentionally understate assets or overstate liabilities. Only when there is significant uncertainty about the value of a transaction should the most conservative alternative be chosen.

The economic rationale for conservatism is partially driven by the liability associated with overstating incorrectly the financial condition and performance of a company. Jeffrey Block, a well-known attorney, has observed many lawsuits against firms that have overstated earnings, and he stated for the *Boston Globe* (April 12, 1998), "the lesson from all these cases is for executives to be more upfront and disclose negative news to shareholders a lot earlier."

There are many examples of conservatism in the financial statements. The lower-of-cost-or-market rule, which is used to value short-term investments and inventories, has already been mentioned in this chapter and is perhaps the most evident example. Others are discussed as they arise later in the text.

In 1999, Johnson & Johnson recognized an expense of $613 million in anticipation of costs expected to be incurred in the future. Would you consider this conservative reporting consistent with the conservatism exception? Why or why not?

INTERNATIONAL PERSPECTIVE: AN EXTREME FORM OF CONSERVATISM THAT ENCOURAGES INCOME MANIPULATION

In Japan and most of western Europe, most of the capital is provided by a few very large banks, who satisfy their needs for information in a direct way—through personal contacts and visits. National governments require some public disclosure, so companies prepare financial reports, but the required disclosures are limited and heavily oriented towards the needs of creditors. One relatively unique aspect of these reports is that they appear to be extremely conservative, containing intentional asset understatements and liability overstatements to reduce the chance that banks will grant loans that eventually are unpaid. By understating net income in certain years, this conservative reporting can also reduce the demand from shareholders for dividends.

In Switzerland, for example, federal law not only sets maximum limits for the values on the balance sheet at original cost, but expressly encourages management (1) to carry assets at less than original cost and (2) to set up "hidden reserves" through excessive depreciation or liability write-ups. Presumably, such discretion enables managers to ensure the continued prosperity of the enterprise through income smoothing—recording conservative adjustments in good years and ignoring them in poor years. Such conservatism can encourage income manipulation by allowing managers to create and use up their "hidden reserves" at will.

SUMMARY OF KEY POINTS

The key points of the chapter are summarized below.

○ *Four basic assumptions of financial accounting.*

The four basic assumptions of financial accounting are (1) the economic entity assumption, (2) the fiscal period assumption, (3) the going concern assumption, and (4) the stable dollar assumption. The economic entity assumption states that a company is a separate economic entity that can be identified and measured. The fiscal period assumption states that the life of an economic entity can be broken down into fiscal periods. The going concern assumption states that the life of an economic entity is indefinite. The stable dollar assumption states that the value of the monetary unit used to measure an economic entity's financial performance and position is stable across time.

○ *The markets in which business entities operate and the valuation bases used on the balance sheet.*

A business entity operates in two general markets: an input market, where it purchases inputs for its operations, and an output market, where it sells the outputs that result from its operations. The four valuation bases (present value, fair market value, replacement cost, and original cost) can be defined in terms of these two markets.

The present value of an asset or liability represents the discounted future cash flows associated with the asset or liability. Fair market value represents the sales price in the output market. Replacement costs (or current costs) are the current prices paid in the input market. Original costs are the input prices paid when the input was originally purchased.

The financial statements contain a wide variety of valuation bases. Face value is used to value cash and short-term liabilities. Short-term investments are carried at fair market value, and inventories are valued at the lower of cost or market. Accounts receivable are valued at net realizable value, a form of market value. Notes receivable, notes payable, and most long-term liabilities are valued at present value. Prepaid expenses, fixed assets, and intangible assets are valued at original cost less an adjustment for depreciation or amortization.

○ *The principle of objectivity and how it determines the dollar values that appear on the financial statements.*

The principle of objectivity requires that the values of transactions and the assets and liabilities created by them be verifiable and backed by documentation. It ensures that present value is reported on the financial statements only in cases, such as contracts, where future cash flows can be objectively determined. It also ensures that market values such as fair market value and replacement costs, which are often difficult to objectively determine, are rarely reported on the financial statements (e.g., the lower-of-cost-or-market rule applied to marketable securities and inventories). Objectivity also ensures that many accounts on the financial statements are valued at original costs.

○ *The principles of matching, revenue recognition, and consistency.*

The matching principle states that the efforts of a given period should be matched against the benefits they generate. In determining net income, benefits are usually represented as revenues, and efforts are represented by expenses, which cannot be matched against revenues until the revenues have been recognized. The principle of revenue recognition determines when revenues can be recognized. In short, the principle of revenue recognition triggers the matching principle, which in turn is necessary for determining the measure of performance. The principle of consistency states that accounting methods should be consistent across time.

○ *Two exceptions to the principles of financial accounting measurement: materiality and conservatism.*

Two important exceptions to the principles of financial accounting measurement are materiality and conservatism. Materiality suggests that the principles of financial accounting measurement can be violated if the dollar amount involved in a particular transaction is so small that it would not affect the decisions of financial statement users. Conservatism guides accountants, when in doubt, to understate assets, overstate liabilities, accelerate the recognition of losses, and delay the recognition of gains. These two exceptions guide departures from the principles of financial accounting measurement when the costs of following them exceed the benefits. Conservatism, in particular, makes economic sense because the legal liability facing auditors and managers imposes a high potential cost on errors due to overstating assets or understating liabilities. An extreme form of conservatism, which encourages the manipulation of income, is also practiced in Japan and many Western European countries.

KEY TERMS

Note: Definitions for these terms are provided in the glossary at the end of the text.

Conservatism (p. 88)
Consistency (p. 86)
Economic entity assumption (p. 73)
Face value (p. 79)
Fair market value (FMV) (p. 78)
Fiscal period assumption (p. 74)
Fiscal years (p. 74)
Going concern assumption (p. 75)
Historical costs (p. 79)
Input market (p. 77)
Lower-of-cost-or-market rule (p. 79)
Matching (p. 83)

Materiality (p. 87)
Net realizable value (p. 79)
Objectivity (p. 81)
Original cost (p. 78)
Output market (p. 77)
Present value (p. 78)
Purchasing power (p. 76)
Replacement cost (p. 78)
Revenue recognition (p. 84)
Stable dollar assumption (p. 76)
Valuation bases (p. 78)

ETHICS IN THE REAL WORLD

The American Institute of Certified Public Accountants (AICPA) recently passed a rule making it harder for software companies to recognize revenue immediately from contracts. Both the FASB and the SEC strongly supported the move, which forces companies to meet strict criteria before recognizing revenue and, in many cases, has put downward pressure on reported profits. Some have complained that the stricter rules are making it more difficult for small software makers to raise capital and thus compete with the industry leaders.

Others, like Microsoft, the largest software producer, have supported the rule. Due to its market strength, Microsoft has had no difficulty raising capital and has followed very conservative practices with respect to revenue recognition. Indeed, some have estimated that at any given point in time, Microsoft may have roughly a billion dollars in deferred revenue waiting to be recognized.

ETHICAL ISSUE Is Microsoft acting ethically when it supports rules, either through lobbying or financial support, that make it more difficult for small software manufacturers to compete in a market where Microsoft is an industry leader?

INTERNET RESEARCH EXERCISE

Find the most recent Form 10-K filed by ITT Educational Services with the Securities and Exchange Commission. Briefly describe the contents of the form, and identify the net income, total assets, and net cash from operations reported by the company. Begin your search at *www.sec.gov* and use the Edgar Database provided by the SEC. The database offers a complete listing of the filings required by the SEC for publicly traded companies.

BRIEF EXERCISES

REAL DATA

BE3-1

Accounting assumptions, principles, and exceptions

The following excerpts were taken from the annual reports of a variety of companies:

1. The company's reporting period ends on the Saturday closest to January 31 (The Limited).
2. The consolidated financial statements include the accounts of Federal Express and its wholly owned subsidiaries (Federal Express).
3. Substantially all merchandise inventory is valued at the lower of cost or market value (J.C. Penney).
4. Certain reclassifications have been made for prior years to conform with this year's presentation (Wendy's International).
5. Revenues from the distribution of motion pictures are recognized when motion pictures are exhibited (Walt Disney).
6. In an ongoing investigation, the Antitrust Division of the U.S. Department of Justice requested information from Microsoft concerning various issues. Management currently believes that resolving these matters will not have a material adverse impact on the Company's financial position or operations (Microsoft).
7. Flight equipment is depreciated on a straight-line basis over a 20-year useful life (Delta Air Lines).
8. Intangible assets are carried on the balance sheet at cost (Merck).

9. Property and equipment are recorded at cost (Lycos, Inc.).
10. Inflation rates, even though moderate in many parts of the world, continue to have an effect on worldwide economies but have had no effect on the Company's reported financial position and performance (Johnson & Johnson).

Match each of the ten assumptions, principles, and exceptions below with one of the ten excerpts.

Assumptions	Principles	Exceptions
Economic entity	Objectivity	Materiality
Stable dollar	Matching	Conservatism
Fiscal period	Revenue recognition	
Going concern	Consistency	

EXERCISES

E3-1

The effects of inflation on holding cash

In recent years, Boeing has maintained a cash balance of $3 billion to $4 billion. At an annual inflation rate of about 2 percent, does cash have more or less purchasing power at the end of a given year than at the beginning? By how much? Is such a gain or loss reflected on the company's financial statements? Why or why not? Why would Boeing want to keep its cash balance as low as possible? Why doesn't the company reduce its cash balance to zero?

E3-2

The effects of inflation on holding land

Palomar Paper Products purchased land in 1984 for $15,000 cash. The company has held the land since that time. In 2002 Palomar purchased another tract of land for $15,000 cash. Assume that prices in general increased by 60 percent from 1984 to 2002.

a. Assuming that Palomar made only these two land purchases, what dollar amount would appear in the land account on Palomar's balance sheet as of December 31, 2002?
b. Palomar used $15,000 cash to make each land purchase. Would $15,000 in 1984 buy the same amount of goods and services as $15,000 in 2002? If not, how much more or less, and why?
c. Explain how one could adjust the dollar amount reported in the land account as of December 31, 2002, if the stable dollar assumption were dropped.

E3-3

Valuation bases on the balance sheet

Name the valuation base(s) that are used for each of the asset and liability accounts shown here. Some assets and liabilities can use more than one valuation base.

	Original Cost	Fair Market Value (FMV)	Present Value	Replacement Cost
Cash				
Short-Term Investments				
Inventories				
Prepaid Expenses				
Long-Term Investments				
Notes Receivable				
Machinery				
Equipment				
Land				
Intangible Assets				
Short-Term Payables				
Long-Term Payables				

E3-4

Revenue recognition

Cascades Enterprises ordered 4,000 brackets from McKey and Company on December 1, 2002, for a contracted price of $40,000. McKey completed manufacturing the brackets on January 17 of the next year and delivered them to Cascades on February 9. McKey received a check for $40,000 from Cascades on March 14.

a. Assume that McKey and Company prepares monthly income statements. In which month should McKey recognize the $40,000 revenue from the sale?
b. Justify your answer in (a) in terms of the four criteria of revenue recognition.
c. Are there conditions under which the revenue could be recognized in a different month than the month you chose in (a)?
d. Provide several reasons why McKey's management might be interested in the timing of the recognition of revenue.

E3-5

The effects on income of different methods of revenue recognition

Lahmont Bridge Builders built a bridge for the state of Maryland over a two-year period. The contracted price for the bridge was $600,000. The costs incurred by Lahmont and the payments from the state of Maryland over the two-year period follow.

	Period 1	Period 2	Total
Costs incurred by Lahmont	$300,000	$100,000	$400,000
Payments from Maryland	400,000	200,000	600,000

a. Prepare income statements for Lahmont for the two periods under the following assumptions:
   (1) Revenue is recognized at the end of the project.
   (2) Revenue is recognized in proportion to the costs incurred by Lahmont.
   (3) Revenue is recognized when the payments are received.
b. Calculate the total net income over the two-year period under each assumption.

E3-6

Assets and depreciation—Which assumption and principle?

RDP and Brothers purchased a panel truck for $25,000 on January 1, 2002. It estimated the life of the truck to be five years, and it planned to depreciate an equal amount in each of the five years.

a. In line with generally accepted accounting principles, determine the amounts required here.

	2002	2003	2004	2005	2006
Original cost					
Depreciation expense					
Accumulated depreciation					
Net book value					

b. Why did you decide to initially recognize the cost as an asset rather than treat it as an expense? What basic assumption of financial accounting are you relying upon in this decision?
c. Why did you allocate a portion of the cost to each of the five years? What basic principle of financial accounting measurement are you relying upon in this decision?

E3-7

The concept of materiality

All large U.S. companies have policies in which all expenditures under a certain dollar amount are expensed. Many of these expenditures are for assets, items that are useful to the company beyond the period in which they were purchased.

a. Explain the proper accounting treatment for expenditures for items that are expected to generate benefits in the future.
b. Explain why it might make economic sense to expense some of these items. Upon what exception to the principles of financial accounting would such a decision be based?

E3–8

Changing
accounting methods
and net income

The net income amounts for Hauser and Bradley over the four-year period beginning in 2000 follow.

2000	2001	2002	2003
$21,000	$24,000	$23,000	$29,000

After further examination of the financial report, you note that Hauser and Bradley made accounting method changes in 2001 and 2003, which affected net income in those periods. In 2001, the company changed depreciation methods. This change increased the book value of its fixed assets in each subsequent year by $5,000. In 2003, the company adopted a new inventory method that increased the book value of the inventory by $9,000.

a. Calculate the effect of each of these changes on net income in the year of the change.
b. Prepare a chart that compares net income across the four-year period, assuming that no accounting changes were made by Hauser and Bradley. How would your assessment of the company's performance change after you learned of the accounting method changes?
c. What principle of financial accounting makes it difficult to make such changes? Describe the conditions under which Hauser and Bradley would be allowed to make changes in their accounting methods.

PROBLEMS

P3–1

The effects of
inflation on
reported profits

On January 1, 2002, you purchased a piece of property for $10,000. On December 31 of that year, you sold the property for $20,000. Assume that the general rate of inflation for 2002 was 10 percent.

REQUIRED:

a. According to generally accepted accounting principles, how much gain would be recorded in the income statement due to the sale of the property?
b. The $10,000 you used to purchase the property on January 1 could have been used to purchase any number of goods and services on January 1. Would the $20,000 you received at the end of the period enable you to purchase twice as many goods and services? Why or why not?
c. How much of the accounting gain computed in (a) could be attributed to inflation, and how much could be attributed to the fact that the property rose in value? Do generally accepted accounting principles make such a distinction? Why or why not?

P3–2

Inflation and
bank loans

Assume that on January 1, Bush Enterprises borrowed $4,760 from Banking Corporation, promising to pay $5,000 at the end of one year. The effective rate of interest on the loan is approximately 5 percent ([$5,000 − $4,760] / $4,760). Suppose that the general rate of inflation for that year was 10 percent.

REQUIRED:

a. How much interest revenue did Banking Corporation recognize for the year? (*Hint:* The difference between the cash payment and the face value of the note receivable is interest revenue that Banking Corporation will earn over the life of the note.)
b. Do you think that Banking Corporation is better off at the end of the year by the amount of the interest revenue? Did Banking Corporation have more or less purchasing power at the end of the year? How much?
c. Which of the two parties, Bush Enterprises or Banking Corporation, seems to have ended up with the better deal? Could one determine this from a careful examination of the financial statements prepared on the basis of GAAP? Why or why not?

P3-3

The irrelevance of original cost

Three years ago Yeagley and Sons purchased the three assets listed in the following table. The chief financial officer, Kathy Dillon, is presently trying to decide what to do with each asset. She has three choices for each asset: (1) sell it, (2) sell it and replace it with an equivalent asset, or (3) keep it. The following information is provided to aid her decision.

Asset	Original Cost	Replacement Cost	Fair Market Value	Present Value of Future Cash Flows Produced by Old Asset	Present Value of Future Cash Flows of Equivalent Asset
A	$4,000	$1,000	$1,500	$2,500	$5,000
B	1,500	2,000	500	2,500	3,500
C	2,000	3,500	3,000	2,500	5,000

REQUIRED:

a. Assuming that Kathy chooses to keep Asset A and Asset B and sell and replace Asset C, evaluate her decisions. What decisions should she have made? Support your choices.
b. How useful was the original cost of each asset in the evaluation of Kathy's decisions?
c. Assume that Kathy proceeds with her decisions. According to generally accepted accounting principles, at what dollar amount would each asset be carried on Yeagley's balance sheet? What principles of financial accounting would be involved?

REAL DATA

P3-4

The stable dollar assumption and sales growth

Sales data for 1997, 1998, and 1999 for Cisco Systems follows (dollars in billions).

	1997	1998	1999
Sales	$6.5	$8.5	$12.1

After reviewing the growth in sales, John Chambers, the company president, commented that according to the financial statements, sales almost doubled from 1997 to 1999. Assume that the general inflation rate as well as the price increase of Cisco's services for the period of 1997 to 1999 was 6 percent.

REQUIRED:

a. Considering price increases, did sales actually double from 1997 to 1999? By how much did the company's sales actually grow from 1997 to 1999? By what percentage did sales increase?
b. If prices had increased 10 percent from 1997 to 1999, by what percentage would sales have grown?
c. Describe how the stable dollar assumption could have misled the user's of Cisco's financial statements.

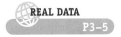

REAL DATA

P3-5

The economic value of a company vs. its book value

The December 31, 1999, balance sheet and the income statement for the period ending December 31 for Manpower, Inc., a world leader in staffing and workforce management solutions, follow (dollars in millions). (This problem requires knowledge of present value. Refer to Appendix B.)

Balance Sheet				Income Statement	
Current assets	$2,257	Liabilities	$2,068	Sales	$9,770
Long-lived assets	462	Common stock	1,304	Expenses	9,620
		Retained earnings	(653)	Net income	$ 150
		Total liabilities and			
Total assets	$2,719	stockholders' equity	$2,719		

You are interested in purchasing Manpower, and have analyzed the future prospects of the company, estimating that it should be able to maintain at least its current earnings amount for the next ten years, at which time the assets would be worthless. You also estimate that the discount rate over that time period will be 12 percent.

REQUIRED:

a.   Assuming that net income is equal to cash inflows, how much should you be willing to pay for Manpower?
b.   What is the book value of Manpower?
c.   Explain why there is a difference between the book value of Manpower and the amount you are willing to pay for it. What assumptions and/or principles of financial accounting are important here?

P3–6

Economic value and income vs. book value and income

On January 1, 2002, Barry Smith established a company by contributing $90,000 and using all of the cash to purchase an apartment house. At the time, he estimated that cash inflows due to rentals would be $65,000 per year, while annual cash outflows to manage and maintain it would be $45,000. He felt that the apartment house had a ten-year life and could be sold at the end of that time for $40,000. He also estimated that the effective interest rate during the ten-year period would be 10 percent. (This problem requires knowledge of present value. Refer to Appendix B.)

REQUIRED:

a.   What is the book value of the building as of January 1, 2002? Assuming that Barry's estimates are correct, what is the economic value of the building? In your opinion, did Barry make a wise investment?
b.   On December 31, 2002, Barry prepares financial statements and observes that his estimates were exactly correct. Assuming that cash inflows equal revenues, cash outflows equal expenses, and the net cost of the apartment, $50,000 ($90,000 − $40,000), is depreciated evenly over the ten-year period, prepare the income statement and balance sheet for Barry's apartment house.
c.   Calculate the economic income of the apartment building for 2002. Economic income equals the difference between the present value at the beginning of the year and the present value at the end of the year plus any cash received during the year. Why is there a difference between accounting income and economic income?
d.   What is the value on Barry's books of the apartment building at the end of 2002? What is the present value of the apartment building at that time?

P3–7

The differences between present value, book value, and liquidation value

The December 31, 2002, balance sheet of Myers and Myers, prepared under generally accepted accounting principles, follows. (This problem requires knowledge of present value calculations. Refer to Appendix B.)

Assets		Liabilities and Stockholders' Equity	
Cash	$ 10,000	Current liabilities	$ 8,000
Short-term investments	14,000	Long-term liabilities	20,000
Land	20,000	Common stock	80,000
Buildings and machinery	80,000	Retained earnings	16,000
		Total liabilities and	
Total assets	$124,000	stockholders' equity	$124,000

An investor believes that Myers and Myers can generate $20,000 cash per year for ten years, at which time it could be sold for $80,000. The FMVs of each asset as of December 31, 2002, follow:

Cash	$ 10,000
Short-term investments	14,000
Land	60,000
Buildings and machinery	40,000
Total FMV	$124,000

REQUIRED:

a. What is the book value of Myers and Myers as of December 31, 2002?
b. What is the value of Myers and Myers as a going concern (i.e., present value of the net future cash inflows) as of December 31, 2002? Assume a discount rate of 10 percent.
c. What is the liquidation value of Myers and Myers (i.e., how much cash would Myers and Myers be able to generate if each asset were sold separately and each liability were paid off on December 31, 2002)?
d. Discuss the differences among the book value of the company, the present value, and the liquidation value. Calculate goodwill, and explain it in terms of these three valuation bases.

P3–8

Three different measures of income

Suppose that Myers and Myers in P3–7 paid no dividends during 2003 and the December 31, 2003, balance sheet looks like the one below. (This problem requires knowledge of present value calculations. Refer to Appendix B.)

Assets		Liabilities and Stockholders' Equity	
Cash	$ 30,000	Current liabilities	$ 6,000
Short-term investments	20,000	Long-term liabilities	20,000
Land	20,000	Common stock	80,000
Buildings and machinery	76,000	Retained earnings	40,000
		Total liabilities and	
Total assets	$146,000	stockholders' equity	$146,000

Assume that the investor in P3–7 was correct (i.e., the company produced $20,000 cash during 2003) and that the investor's expectations at the end of 2003 are unchanged. Assume further that an objective appraisal of the company's assets revealed the following FMVs as of December 31, 2003:

Cash	$ 10,000
Short-term investments	20,000
Land	66,000
Buildings and machinery	32,000
Total FMVs	$148,000

REQUIRED:

a. What dollar amount did Myers and Myers report in 2003 for net income under generally accepted accounting principles?
b. Calculate net income during 2003, using fair market values as the asset and liability valuation bases (i.e., $FMV_{2003} - FMV_{2002}$).
c. Calculate economic income for 2003 (i.e., cash received during 2003 plus the change in present value). The discount rate is still 10 percent.
d. Discuss the differences among these three measures of income. Discuss some of the strengths and weaknesses of each measure.

P3–9

Comparing companies using different accounting methods

The net income and working capital accounts for two companies in the same industry, ABC Company and XYZ Company, follow:

	ABC	XYZ
1/1–12/31 Net income	$10,000	$24,000
12/31 Working capital	16,000	30,000

After reviewing the complete financial statements of the two companies, you note that ABC and XYZ use different inventory valuation and depreciation methods. ABC uses method A to value its inventory, while XYZ uses method B. Had ABC used B and XYZ used A, their inventory accounts would have been $10,000 greater and $10,000 smaller, respectively. Similarly, ABC uses method X depreciation, while XYZ uses method Y. Had XYZ used X and ABC used Y, their depreciation expenses for the year would have been $8,000 higher and $8,000 lower, respectively.

REQUIRED:

a.   Calculate net income and working capital for the two companies under the following assumptions.

Inventory Method	Depreciation Method	ABC Income/ Working Capital	XYZ Income/ Working Capital
B	Y		
B	X		
A	Y		
A	X		

b.   Given this information, which combination of inventory and depreciation methods gives rise to the highest income and working capital numbers? Can you think of reasons why a manager would choose one method over another? Would managers always choose the method that results in the highest income? Why or why not?

c.   If you were an investor attempting to decide in which company to invest, how would you treat the fact that the two companies used different methods to account for inventory and fixed assets? Is there a principle of accounting that covers this situation? Why or why not?

P3–10

Different methods of recognizing revenue

The Maple Construction Company agreed to construct twelve monuments for the city of Elderton. The total contract price was $2.4 million, and total estimated costs were $1,140,000. The construction took place over a four-year period, and the following schedule indicates the monuments completed, costs incurred, and cash collected for each period:

Year	1	2	3	4	Total
Monuments completed	2	6	3	1	12
Costs incurred	$380,000	$380,000	$285,000	$ 95,000	$1,140,000
Cash collected	$600,000	$900,000	$300,000	$600,000	$2,400,000

REQUIRED:

a.   How much revenue should Maple recognize in each of the four periods under the following three assumptions?
     (1) Revenues are recognized each year in proportion to the monuments completed.
     (2) Revenues are recognized each year in proportion to the percentage of costs incurred.
     (3) Revenues are recognized each year in proportion to the cash collected each year.

b.   For each of the three assumptions, match the appropriate amount of cost against the recognized revenue. Determine net income for each period under the three assumptions.

c.   Compare the total revenue, total cost, and total net income that result from each of the three assumptions. Note that although the timing of the recognition differs across the three assumptions, the total amount of income recognized is the same.

P3–11

Revenue recognition and net income

Hydra Aire, Inc., sells appliances to Seasons Department Store. A recent order requires Hydra Aire to manufacture and deliver 500 toasters at a price of $100 per unit. Hydra Aire's manufacturing costs are approximately $40 per unit. The following schedule summarizes the production and delivery record of Hydra:

Year	1	2	3	Total
Toasters produced	200	200	100	500
Costs incurred	$ 8,000	$ 8,000	$ 4,000	$20,000
Toasters delivered	150	200	150	500
Cash received	$10,000	$15,000	$20,000	$45,000

REQUIRED:
a. Assuming that Hydra Aire recognizes revenue when the toasters are produced, how much revenue should be recognized in each of the three years?
b. Assuming that Hydra Aire recognizes revenue at delivery, how much revenue should be recognized in each of the three years?
c. Calculate net income for the three periods under each of the two assumptions above.
d. If Hydra Aire's management is paid an income-based bonus, which of the two assumptions would be preferred?

P3-12

The economics of conservatism

Joe McGuire is a CPA who has recently completed the audit of Nelson Repairs, Inc. The audited balance sheet and income statement follow:

Balance Sheet

Current assets	$ 60,000	Liabilities	$ 80,000
Long-term assets	140,000	Stockholders' equity	120,000
		Total liabilities and	
Total assets	$200,000	stockholders' equity	$200,000

Income Statement

Sales	$160,000
Expenses	130,000
Net income	$ 30,000

During his examination, Joe learned that a lawsuit is soon to be filed against Nelson. The lawsuit accuses Nelson of negligence and asks for damages of $60,000 over and above the insurance. If Nelson were to lose the lawsuit, the future of the business would be in jeopardy. However, as the lawyers described it to Joe, the probability that Nelson will lose the lawsuit is very low, approximately 20 percent.

Joe is unsure about whether he should require Nelson to disclose the lawsuit on the financial statements. The president of Nelson does not want it disclosed because he believes that the disclosure would cause undue concern among the company's shareholders. Joe does not want to ignore the president's request because Nelson is his most important client. On the other hand, Joe knows that if he does not require disclosure, and Nelson loses the lawsuit, he may be legally liable for the losses of the stockholders. Joe constructed the following framework to help him make his decision.

	Lawsuit Outcome	
Decision	Win (80%)	Lose (20%)
Require disclosure	Error 1	Correct decision
Do not require disclosure	Correct decision	Error 2

REQUIRED:
a. Study Joe's framework, and note that he can choose to require or not to require disclosure. Requiring disclosure and winning the lawsuit gives rise to Error 1. Not requiring disclosure and losing the lawsuit gives rise to Error 2. Comment on the costs that Joe would incur from each of these two errors. Which of the two errors would be more costly? Which of the two outcomes (winning or losing the suit) is more likely to occur?
b. Suppose that Joe estimates that the cost of Error 1 is $10,000 and the cost of Error 2 is $50,000. Ignoring the costs and benefits of correct decisions, should Joe choose to require disclosure?
c. Explain the concept of conservatism in terms of Joe's framework.

ISSUES FOR DISCUSSION

REAL DATA

ID3-1

Revenue recognition
and matching

Most airlines offer promotional programs in which passengers accumulate miles over time; when they have earned enough miles, they receive free tickets. In the past, airlines did not make any accounting entries for these free tickets. The free rider merely uses available seats or, on occasion, displaces a ticketed passenger.

The FASB adopted a method of accounting for tickets issued under these programs. They require that a portion of the fare paid when a passenger in such a program pays for a ticket be deferred until the free ride is used. For example, if a passenger purchases a $200 ticket, a portion, say $20, would not appear as revenue to the airline until the free trip is taken. It would be considered unearned revenue until then.

REQUIRED:

a. Evaluate the accounting standard in terms of the principle of revenue recognition and matching. List the criteria of revenue recognition, and suggest when it would be appropriate to recognize the revenue from a ticket sale. Given your suggestion, how should the related costs be accounted for?

b. In 1999, Continental Airlines changed the way it accounts for "frequent flyer" credits, deferring more of the revenue it recognizes from this program until the service is actually provided. How would this change affect 1999 income, and does it appear to be a better application of matching? Why or why not?

REAL DATA

ID3-2

Aggressive revenue
recognition in the
Internet industry

Many Internet firms "gross up" their revenues by reporting the entire sales price a customer pays at their site, when in fact the company keeps only a small percentage of that amount. Take Priceline.com, for example, the company made famous by those William Shatner ads about "naming your own price" for airline tickets and hotel rooms. In its first quarter 2000 filings with the SEC, Priceline reported that it earned $152 million in revenues, but that included the full amount customers paid for tickets, hotel rooms, and rental cars. Traditional travel agencies call that amount "gross bookings," not revenues. And much like traditional travel agencies, Priceline keeps only a small portion of the "gross bookings," namely the difference between the customers' accepted bids and the price it pays for the merchandise or service. The rest, which Priceline calls "product costs," are paid to the airlines and hotels that supply the tickets and rooms. In the first quarter of 2000, those costs came to $134 million, leaving Priceline just $18 million. After subtracting other costs—like advertising and salaries—Priceline netted a loss of $102 million.

REQUIRED:

a. Comment on Priceline's method of booking "revenue."

b. Like Priceline, many Internet companies reported losses in the early years, forcing analysts to focus on other reported numbers. For example, at one time Priceline's stock price per share was 23 times its revenue per share, and 214 times its gross profit (revenue − product costs) per share. Can you think of a reason why Priceline might want to include "gross bookings" as revenue?

c. Why do you think that the SEC is clamping down on unethical accounting practices of Internet companies—most importantly, including as revenue "gross" versus "net" bookings?

REAL DATA

ID3-3

Revenue recognition

A report on Blockbuster Video commented that Blockbuster seems to have unusual success in opening new franchises during the Christmas season. It appears that during each of the past few years, product sales to new franchises have increased significantly in the fourth quarter. The report also noted, however, that Blockbuster recognizes revenue when products are shipped, and there is no indication that the new franchises receiving the merchandise were actually open for business.

The New York Times (Oct. 19, 1997) reported: "Like many other companies, U.S. Robotics reported revenue when it shipped items to dealers or wholesalers. The company's critics had suspected it was puffing up reported sales by stuffing inventory into dealers."

REQUIRED:

a. How could the policy of recognizing revenue when products are shipped enable a company like Blockbuster or U.S. Robotics to "manage" earnings?

b. Is recognizing revenue when products are shipped necessarily a violation of GAAP? Explain.

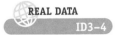

REAL DATA

ID3–4

Consistency and accounting changes

In 1998, Campbell Soup Company booked two special charges (reductions) to earnings totaling $29 million, one of which was a discretionary change in the way the company capitalized certain costs. The chart below shows the earnings numbers reported by the company for 1997, 1998, and 1999 (dollars in millions).

1997	$713
1998	660
1999	724

REQUIRED:

a. Recalculate net income for 1998, assuming that the accounting change had not been made. Which is the more appropriate comparison—the reported amounts or the recalculated amounts? Why?

b. In what three places in Campbell Soup's annual report would an investor be able to find a reference to this accounting change?

c. Does it appear that Campbell Soup is practicing any of the reporting strategies discussed earlier in the text? Which one and why?

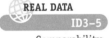

REAL DATA

ID3–5

Comparability

General Electric (GE) depreciates its fixed assets using a method that recognizes a relatively large portion of depreciation in the early years of an asset's useful life. IBM, on the other hand, uses the straight-line method.

REQUIRED:

Briefly describe the adjustments an investor would have to make when comparing GE's performance and financial position to that of IBM.

REAL DATA

ID3–6

Conservative reporting?

Forbes (June 20, 1994) reports: "Yes, there are hidden reserves in Switzerland, Germany, and Sweden. But that doesn't mean that there is more to these companies than meets the eye. Loosey-goosey reserves cut both ways. They could mean that a company's book value is understated. But they could also mean that the company's earnings are overstated. Reserves tucked away in earlier years could have been used to paper over last year's losses."

REQUIRED:

Explain the meaning of this quote, and provide several examples of how "conservative" reporting in a previous year may allow for "liberal" reporting in a future year. When viewed in this way, "conservative reporting" is actually part of a more general reporting strategy. Name that strategy.

REAL DATA

ID3–7

Matching in the Internet industry

Fast Company, a subsidiary of *U.S. News and World Report*, reported the following story (January 1, 2000): "In 1994 and 1995, America Online capitalized some of its customer acquisition costs—which means that it considered part of those costs assets. In other words, AOL was saying that, in acquiring new customers, it was creating a unique asset—one that would help the company become more profitable in the future. Financial analysts called that cheating! It was a new industry, competition was fierce, and analysts thought that AOL was trying to manipulate its earnings. Finally, in October 1996, AOL gave up and completely expensed its $385 million in customer-acquisition costs. As of January 1, 2000, AOL had a market value of $140 billion. Compare that with the $385 million that it tried to capitalize and it's almost humorous! And yet only five or six years previously, financial analysts were proclaiming that AOL was a cheat."

REQUIRED:
a.   Why did analysts believe that AOL was cheating?
b.   Do you agree? Express your response in terms of the matching principle.

REAL DATA

ID3–8

Fair value
accounting

In December 1999, the FASB unveiled a preliminary proposal calling for companies to report the fair value of their equity and debt securities on the balance sheets. The FASB described fair value as a market exit price—an estimate of the price an entity would have realized if it had sold the asset or paid if it had been relieved of the liability on the reporting data in an arm's-length exchange motivated by normal business conditions. The FASB acknowledged that such a change could result in changes in the income reported by companies.

REQUIRED:
a.   Which of the four valuation bases discussed in the chapter is the FASB suggesting that companies use for their equity and debt securities?
b.   Most of these securities are currently reported at cost. How would reporting them at fair value affect the income reported by companies?
c.   Do you agree with the FASB's proposal? Why or why not?

REAL DATA

ID3–9

The annual report
of Wal-Mart

The annual report of Wal-Mart is reproduced in Appendix A. This chapter listed and defined four basic assumptions, four principles of measurement, and two exceptions.

REQUIRED:
Review the 2001 Wal-Mart annual report, and find at least one example of each of the ten concepts. Also, indicate the accounts on Wal-Mart's balance sheet that use present value as a valuation base.

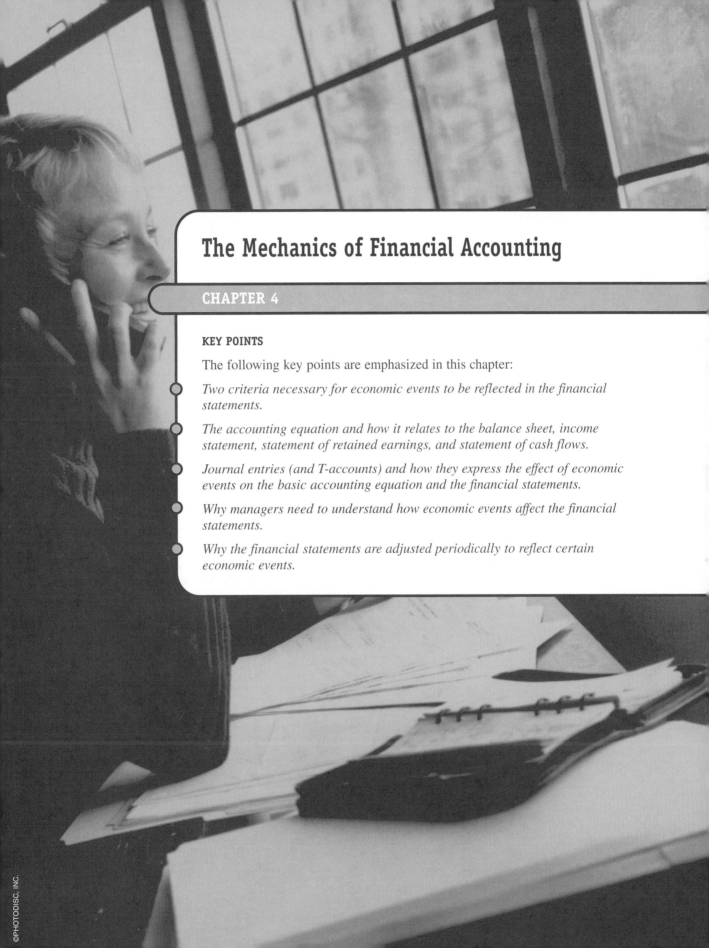

The Mechanics of Financial Accounting

CHAPTER 4

KEY POINTS

The following key points are emphasized in this chapter:

- *Two criteria necessary for economic events to be reflected in the financial statements.*

- *The accounting equation and how it relates to the balance sheet, income statement, statement of retained earnings, and statement of cash flows.*

- *Journal entries (and T-accounts) and how they express the effect of economic events on the basic accounting equation and the financial statements.*

- *Why managers need to understand how economic events affect the financial statements.*

- *Why the financial statements are adjusted periodically to reflect certain economic events.*

In early 2000, the Associated Press reported:

[T]he U.S. military says its owns $119.3 billion in ships, trucks, jet engines, and more. But its inspector general said he could not verify that because records lacked sufficient supporting documentation. The U.S. military's financial records are not in good enough shape to face an audit, let alone pass one, the inspector general said. As jumbled as its books are, the Pentagon is not alone: only 11 of 24 big federal agencies could produce reliable financial statements for the fiscal year that ended September 30, 1999.

This chapter covers the mechanics underlying the preparation of financial statements and how they help to ensure that a company's transactions are accurately and completely accounted for. After completing it, you should be able to construct financial statements from economic events. Those interested in additional coverage of accounting procedures should refer to Appendix 4A, which contains a complete description (and comprehensive example) of the accounting cycle and how it leads to the preparation of the financial statements.

Understanding the mechanics underlying the preparation of financial statements is crucial for effective management. Managers often choose among transactions, and such choices should not be made without considering the financial statement effects and the associated economic consequences. Consequently, managers must understand the mechanics that link transactions to the financial statements.

Managers must also understand how to read, interpret, and analyze financial statements. To do so effectively, it is useful to be able to infer from the financial statements events and transactions that occurred during the accounting period. A mechanical process, called T-account analysis, can enable users to make such inferences. This process is covered in Appendix 4B, titled "Mechanics: A User's Perspective."

ECONOMIC EVENTS

Economic events that are reflected in the financial statements must be both relevant to the financial condition of a company and objectively measurable in monetary terms.

Relevant Events

Relevant events have economic significance to a particular company and include any occurrence that affects its financial condition. Events of general economic significance, like the election of a new U.S. president, the passage of federal legislation, or the outbreak of war, could be considered relevant. Events that are more company-specific, like the signing of a new labor agreement, the hiring of a new chief executive officer, the sale of an item of inventory, or simply the payment of monthly wages, are also relevant. Each of these events could have a significant impact on the financial resources of a particular company. Anyone interested in the company's financial status (stockholders, investors, creditors, managers, auditors, and other interested parties) wants to be able to assess the financial impact of all such events.

Objectivity

Unfortunately, only a small percentage of all relevant events are reflected on the financial statements. The dollar values assigned to the accounts on the financial statements must be determined in an objective manner.

In general, a dollar value is considered objective if it results from an exchange in which two parties with differing incentives reach agreement. To illustrate, in 2000 The Boeing Company offered to purchase Hughes Space and Communications from Hughes's shareholders. Boeing and Hughes's shareholders had differing incentives because Boeing wanted to pay as little as possible, while the shareholders wanted to receive as much as possible. When they reached agreement on the value of Hughes, a transaction took place. Hughes passed to Boeing for a price of $3.75 billion. The price represented an objective valuation of Hughes because two parties with differing incentives reached agreement on it. The transaction was accompanied by documented evidence (e.g., receipts, canceled checks, vouchers, a bill of sale) that could be used to verify its entry into Boeing's financial records, and after the purchase, an investment of $3.75 billion was reflected on Boeing's balance sheet.

Unfortunately, the most relevant information is not always the most objective. King World Productions Inc., for example, is a television syndicator with the rights to *Jeopardy, Wheel of Fortune,* and *Oprah,* which generate millions of dollars in licensing fees. Yet, these rights are valued on the balance sheet at their purchase costs, less accumulated amortization, which are much less. Similarly, a partner at a major accounting firm recently noted: "Coca-Cola is one of the best-recognized trademarks in the world, but it is not on their books. It got that recognition through advertising, but you don't book advertising as an asset, because you don't know if it will have future value."

In the pharmaceutical industry, when a drug passes its clinical tests, huge value is created. In the software industry, when software passes a beta test, it suddenly becomes valuable. In these two examples, do the pharmaceuticals and the software companies become more valuable when these events occur? Are the events recorded in the financial statements? Explain.

THE FUNDAMENTAL ACCOUNTING EQUATION

The four financial statements are all based on a mathematical equation, which states that the dollar value of a company's assets equals the dollar value of its liabilities plus the dollar value of its stockholders' equity. In fact, the balance sheet is a statement of this equation.

Assets = Liabilities + Stockholders' Equity

The mechanics of accounting are structured so that this equality is always maintained. If the two sides of this equation are unequal, the books do not balance, and an error has been made. However, maintaining this equality does not ensure that the financial statements are correct; errors can exist even if the **accounting equation** balances.

Assets

Assets are items and rights that a company acquires through objectively measurable transactions that can be used in the future to generate economic benefits (i.e., more assets). Such acquisitions are usually made by purchase: an asset is received in exchange for another asset (often cash) or a payable. Assets include cash, securities, receivables from customers, land, buildings, machinery, equipment, and rights such as patents, copyrights, and trademarks. Simply, the left side of the accounting equation represents the dollar values of the items and rights that have been acquired by a company and are expected to benefit the company in the future.

Assets come from three sources: (1) they are borrowed, (2) they are contributed by stockholders (owners), and (3) they are generated by a company's operating activities. The right side of the equation, liabilities and stockholders' equity, represents the dollar values attached to these three sources. For each dollar amount on the asset side of the equation, a corresponding dollar amount is reflected on the liability and stockholders' equity side.

Liabilities

Liabilities consist primarily of a company's debts or payables. They are existing obligations for which assets must be used in the future. The dollar amount of the total liabilities on the balance sheet represents the portion of the assets that a company has borrowed and must repay.

Stockholders' Equity

Stockholders' equity consists of two components: (1) **contributed capital,** the dollar value of the assets contributed by stockholders, and (2) **retained earnings,** the dollar value of the assets generated by operating activities and retained in the business (i.e., not paid to the stockholders in the form of dividends). Operating activities are those transactions directly associated with the acquisition and sale of a company's products or services. Dividing stockholders' equity into its components, the fundamental accounting equation appears as follows:

Assets = Liabilities + Contributed Capital + Retained Earnings

That is, the dollar value of the assets is equal to the sum of the dollar amounts owed, the dollar amount of stockholders' contributions, and the dollar amount retained from profitable operations.

A summary of the 1999 balance sheet for Continental Airlines is provided below (dollars in millions). Describe it in terms of the basic accounting equation.

Current assets	$2,606	Liabilities	$6,630
Noncurrent assets	5,617	Contributed capital	479
		Retained earnings	1,114
Total	$8,223	Total	$8,223

BUSINESS TRANSACTIONS, THE ACCOUNTING EQUATION, AND THE FINANCIAL STATEMENTS

Companies conduct operations by exchanging assets and liabilities with other entities (e.g., individuals and businesses). These economic events are referred to as **business transactions.** Exchanging cash for a piece of equipment, for example, is a transaction that represents the purchase of equipment. Borrowing money is a transaction in which a promise to pay in the future (i.e., note payable) is exchanged for cash. The sale of a service on account is a transaction in which the service is exchanged for a receivable. In each of these exchanges, and in all business transactions, something is received and something is given up. *These receipts and disbursements affect the financial condition of a company in a way that always maintains the equality of the fundamental accounting equation. That is, each business transaction is recorded in the books so that the dollar values of a company's assets always equal the dollar values of its liabilities and stockholders' equity.*

Transactions and the Accounting Equation

The six transactions below were entered into by Joe's Landscaping Service during 2002, its first year of operations. Figure 4–1 shows how each transaction affects the accounting equation. Study it carefully and read the following discussion of each transaction.

FIGURE 4–1 Business transactions and the accounting equation

Transaction	Assets	=	Liabilities	+	Contributed Capital	+	Retained Earnings
(1)	$+10,000	=			$+10,000		
(2)	+ 3,000	=	$+3,000				
(3)	+ 5,000	=					
	− 5,000						
(4)	+ 8,000						
	+ 4,000	=					$+12,000
(5)	− 9,000	=					− 9,000
(6)	− 1,000	=					− 1,000
End-of-year balance	$ 15,000	=	$ 3,000	+	$ 10,000	+	$ 2,000

TRANSACTION (1). Joe, the owner of the company, contributes $10,000. This dollar amount increases the company's cash balance, an asset, by $10,000 and is also recorded on the right side of the accounting equation under contributed capital. Note that both sides of the accounting equation are increased by $10,000, so its equality is maintained.

TRANSACTION (2). $3,000 is borrowed from a bank. The dollar amount of this exchange also increases the company's cash balance, but in this case liabilities are also increased; the company now owes $3,000 to the bank.

TRANSACTION (3). The company purchases equipment for $5,000 cash. This exchange both increases and decreases the company's assets. It now has an asset called *equipment,* and its cash balance is reduced by $5,000. Still, the equality of the accounting equation is maintained because the asset side was both increased and decreased by $5,000.

TRANSACTION (4). The company performs a service for $12,000. This transaction increases the company's cash balance by $8,000 and creates a receivable of $4,000. Thus, total assets increase by $12,000. The corresponding $12,000 adjustment on the right side of the equation, which maintains its equality, is reflected in Retained Earnings because the company generated this $12,000 through its own operations.

TRANSACTION (5). The company pays $9,000 for expenses—wages, interest, and maintenance. This transaction decreases the company's cash balance by $9,000 and maintains the equality of the equation by decreasing Retained Earnings in the amount of $9,000. Retained Earnings is decreased because, as in Transaction 4, these expenses are associated with the company's operating activities.

TRANSACTION (6). Joe pays himself a $1,000 dividend as a return on his original investment. The dollar amount of the dividend reduces the company's cash balance by $1,000 and is also reflected on the right side of the equation by a $1,000 reduction in Retained Earnings. Retained Earnings is reduced because the fundamental objective of the company's operating activities is to provide a return for the owner, and Retained Earnings is the measure of the assets that have been accumulated through operations.

During 1999, the Coca-Cola Company purchased property, plant, and equipment in the amount of $1 billion. The company also borrowed $3.4 billion. How were these transactions reflected in the basic accounting equation?

The Accounting Equation and the Financial Statements

This section introduces and defines the concept of an account and describes the preparation of simplified versions of the balance sheet, statement of cash flows, income statement, and statement of retained earnings for Joe's Landscaping Service.

ACCOUNTS AND THE ACCOUNTING EQUATION

For purposes of recording transactions and preparing financial statements, the main components of the accounting equation (assets, liabilities, and stockholders' equity) can be further subdivided into separate categories called accounts. The general category of assets is normally divided into a number of accounts including, for example, a cash account, a receivables account, and an equipment account. Liabilities normally consist of various payable accounts, and as mentioned earlier, stockholders' equity can be divided into a contributed capital account and a retained earnings account.

Accounts serve as "storage units," where the dollar values of business transactions are initially recorded and later compiled into the financial statements. The accounts that appear on the financial statements represent a balance between enough detail to provide meaningful breakdowns of assets, liabilities, and stockholders' equity but not so much as to overwhelm the user.

In Figure 4–2, the main components of the accounting equation are divided into separate accounts for the purpose of recording the six transactions entered into by Joe's Landscaping Service. Note that Figure 4–2 is very similar to Figure 4–1. It differs only in that it records the transactions in more specific categories, which represent the accounts that eventually appear on the financial statements.

Note that total assets in Figure 4–2 ($15,000 = $6,000 + $4,000 + $5,000) equal total assets in Figure 4–1 as well as total liabilities plus stockholders' equity ($15,000 = $3,000 + $10,000 + $2,000). The components of the accounting equation have simply been divided into more specific "storage units." In the next sections, the information contained in Figure 4–2 is used to prepare the financial statements.

THE BALANCE SHEET

The balance sheet is the statement of the basic accounting equation as of a particular date: in this case, the end of 2002. It is called a balance sheet because assets are always

FIGURE 4-2 Accounts and the accounting equation

	Assets					=	Liabilities +		Stockholders' Equity		
Transaction	Cash	+	Receivables	+	Equipment	=	Loan Payable	+	Contributed Capital	+	Retained Earnings
(1)	$+10,000					=			$+10,000		
(2)	+ 3,000					=	$+3,000				
(3)	− 5,000				$+5,000	=					
(4)	+ 8,000		$+4,000			=					$+12,000
(5)	− 9,000					=					− 9,000
(6)	− 1,000					=					− 1,000
Total	$ 6,000	+	$ 4,000	+	$ 5,000	=	$ 3,000	+	$ 10,000	+	$ 2,000

in balance with liabilities plus stockholders' equity. That is, there is a source for each asset the company has acquired. Figure 4–3 shows the balance sheet for Joe's Landscaping Service at the end of its first year of operations. This balance sheet was prepared by simply listing and grouping the totals of the individual asset, liability, and stockholders' equity accounts, which appear at the bottom of Figure 4–2.

FIGURE 4–3

Balance sheet for Joe's Landscaping

Joe's Landscaping Service
Balance Sheet
December 31, 2002

ASSETS		LIABILITIES AND STOCKHOLDERS' EQUITY	
Cash	$ 6,000	Loan payable	$ 3,000
Receivables	4,000	Contributed capital	10,000
Equipment	5,000	Retained earnings	2,000
		Total liabilities and	
Total assets	$15,000	stockholders' equity	$15,000

STATEMENT OF CASH FLOWS

The statement of cash flows in Figure 4–4 was prepared directly from the activity recorded in the cash account in Figure 4–2. Each dollar value on the statement of cash flows corresponds to an increase or decrease in the cash account indicated in Figure 4–2. Note also that the ending cash balance of $6,000 on the statement of cash flows equals the balance in the cash account on the balance sheet. The statement of cash flows is nothing more than a summary of the activity in the company's cash account, divided into three sections—operating, investing, and financing activities.

INCOME STATEMENT

The income statement is a measure of the assets generated from the company's operating activities during a period of time. It compares *revenues* (the asset inflows due to operating activities) to *expenses* (the asset outflows required to generate the revenues).

FIGURE 4–4

Statement of
cash flows for
Joe's Landscaping

Joe's Landscaping Service
Statement of Cash Flows
For the Year Ended December 31, 2002

Operating activities:		
Sale of a service (4)	$ 8,000	
Payments for expenses (5)	(9,000)	
Net cash from operating activities		$ (1,000)
Investing activities:		
Purchase of equipment (3)	$ (5,000)	
Net cash from investing activities		(5,000)
Financing activities:		
Borrowings (2)	$ 3,000	
Owner contributions (1)	10,000	
Payment of dividends (6)	(1,000)	
Net cash from financing activities		12,000
Increase in cash balance		$ 6,000
Cash balance at beginning of year		0
Cash balance at end of year		$ 6,000

The difference between revenues and expenses is called *net income* or *net loss.* If revenues exceed expenses, there is net income or profit; if expenses exceed revenues, there is a net loss.

In terms of the accounting equation, revenues, expenses, and dividends are reflected in the retained earnings account. Like the general categories of assets, liabilities, and stockholders' equity, retained earnings can be further subdivided into revenue accounts, expense accounts, and dividend accounts. Recording a transaction in a revenue account increases retained earnings; recording a transaction in an expense or dividend account decreases retained earnings.

In the example of Joe's Landscaping Service, revenues in the form of cash and a receivable were generated in Transaction (4), the sale of landscaping services for $12,000. Expenses were recognized in Transaction (5), which reflects payments made for wages, interest, and equipment maintenance. The dollar amounts of these two transactions are recorded in the retained earnings account in Figure 4–2, but in practice they would be recorded in separate revenue and expense accounts, which are components of retained earnings. An income statement can be prepared by disclosing revenues and expenses in the manner shown in Figure 4–5.

FIGURE 4–5

Income statement
for Joe's
Landscaping

Joe's Landscaping Service
Income Statement
For the Year Ended December 31, 2002

Revenues: Fees earned for service	$12,000
Expenses: Wages, interest, maintenance	9,000
Net income	$ 3,000

STATEMENT OF RETAINED EARNINGS

The statement of retained earnings is similar to the statement of cash flows in that it is a record of the activity in a single balance sheet account over a period of time. Rather than explaining the activity in the cash account, however, it explains the activity in the retained earnings account. The statement of retained earnings in Figure 4–6 was prepared directly from the activity in the retained earnings account in Figure 4–2.

<table>
<tr><td>

FIGURE 4–6

Statement of
retained earnings

</td><td>

Joe's Landscaping Service
Statement of Retained Earnings
For the Year Ended December 31, 2002

Beginning retained earnings balance	$ 0
Plus: Net income	3,000
Less: Dividend to stockholder	1,000
Ending retained earnings balance	$2,000

</td></tr>
</table>

As indicated earlier, revenues, expenses, and dividends are reflected in the retained earnings account. On the statement of retained earnings, the dollar amount of revenues less expenses (i.e., net income) and the dollar amount of dividends are disclosed separately. Note that net income is also reported on the income statement and that the ending balance of retained earnings in Figure 4–6 is equal to the balance in the retained earnings account on the balance sheet in Figure 4–3.

A summary of the 2000 financial statements for Pier 1 Imports is provided below (dollars in millions). Discuss each statement in terms of the basic accounting equation.

Income statement:

Revenues	$1,231
Expenses	1,156
Net income	$ 75

Balance sheet:

Current assets	$ 415	Liabilities	$231
Noncurrent assets	256	Contributed capital	175
		Retained earnings	265
Total	$ 671	Total	$671

Statement of cash flows:

Cash from operations	$ 120
Cash from investing	(40)
Cash from financing	(71)
Increase in cash	9
Beginning cash	42
Ending cash	$ 51

Statement of retained earnings:

Beg. retained earnings	$ 201
Plus: Net income	75
Less: Dividends	(11)
End. retained earnings	$ 265

THE JOURNAL ENTRY

In the previous section, we demonstrated how economic events affect the accounting equation and, ultimately, the financial statements. **Journal entries** provide a more efficient way to represent such effects. They are used to represent relevant and measurable economic events, and their content and structure indicate how such events affect the accounting equation. The form of a typical journal entry follows:

	Debit	Credit
Equipment	5,000	
Cash		5,000

Purchased equipment for cash.

The affected accounts in this entry are Equipment and Cash, and the dollar amount of the transaction is $5,000. Placing the $5,000 assigned to Equipment on the left side of the entry indicates that the Equipment account has been increased by $5,000. That account is said to have been *debited*. In the terminology of financial accounting, to **debit** an account simply means to place the dollar amount assigned to it on the left side of the journal entry.

Placing the $5,000 assigned to the cash account on the right side of the entry, or crediting it, indicates that the cash account has been decreased by $5,000. To **credit** an account means to place it on the right side of the journal entry. The sample entry indicates that equipment was purchased for $5,000 cash.

Compound journal entries are treated in exactly the same way, but they involve more than two accounts. For example, if equipment is purchased for $5,000 cash and a $10,000 note payable, we would record the following compound journal entry:

	Debit	Credit
Equipment	15,000	
Cash		5,000
Notes Payable		10,000

Purchased equipment for cash and a note payable.

THE DOUBLE ENTRY SYSTEM

Note in the preceding journal entries that the total dollar value on the left side is always equal to the total dollar value on the right side and that at least two different accounts were affected. Both characteristics are true of all journal entries and illustrate the **double entry system,** which is the cornerstone of financial accounting. The equality of the debit and credit sides maintains the equality of the accounting equation, and the fact that at least two different accounts are affected indicates that in all exchange transactions, something is received and something is given up.

THE JOURNAL ENTRY BOX

A useful way to learn journal entries is to view them as shown in Figure 4–7, which provides a systematic way of converting exchange transactions to journal entries. The top of the box is an expression of the accounting equation. Answers to the three ques-

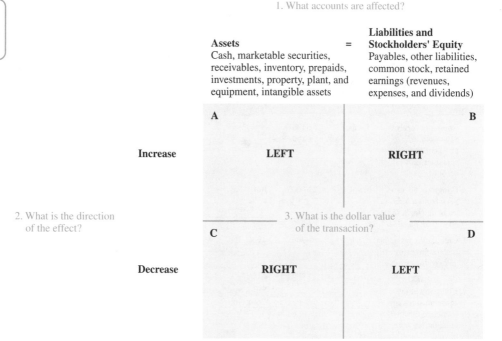

FIGURE 4–7

The journal
entry box

tions identify the three components of each transaction: (1) the accounts affected, (2) the direction of the effect, and (3) the dollar value of the transaction.

Increases in asset accounts (Cell A) and decreases in liability and stockholders' equity accounts (Cell D) are always represented on the debit (left) side of the journal entry. Decreases in asset accounts (Cell C) and increases in liability and stockholders' equity accounts (Cell B) are always recorded on the credit (right) side of the journal entry. It is important to recall that revenue, expense, and dividend accounts are all part of the stockholders' equity account Retained Earnings. Thus, revenues, which increase Retained Earnings, are recorded on the credit side of the journal entry. Expenses and dividends, which decrease Retained Earnings, are recorded on the debit side of the journal entry.

Figure 4–7 shows that journal entries have been devised so that transactions are recorded in a way that always maintains the equality of the accounting equation. Debits always equal credits, and accordingly, assets always equal liabilities plus stockholders' equity.

JOURNAL ENTRIES AND THE ACCOUNTING EQUATION: EXAMPLES

In Figure 4–8, seven different transactions give rise to seven different journal entries, affecting the accounting equation in seven different ways. The equality of the accounting equation is always maintained, and the debit side of each journal entry is exactly equal to the credit side. Note especially Transactions 5, 6, and 7, where the equality of the accounting equation is maintained through the effect of a revenue, an expense, and a dividend on retained earnings. The explanations on the right side of the chart indicate how the journal entry box was used to construct each journal entry.

FIGURE 4–8 Journal entries and the accounting equation

Transaction	Accounting Equation				Journal Entry	Debit	Credit	Explanation*
	Assets		=	Liabilities and Stockholders' Equity				
1. Company receives $100 cash in payment from a customer on account.	Cash Accts. Rec.	+100 −100 0	=	0	Cash (+A)** Accts. Rec. (−A)	100	100	Cash, an asset, is increased. Accts. Rec., an asset, is decreased.
2. Company borrows $500 from a bank in exchange for a short-term note payable.	Cash	+500 +500	=	Notes Pay.	+500 +500	Cash (+A) Notes. Pay. (+L)	500	500	Cash, an asset, is increased. Notes Pay., a liability, is increased.
3. Company pays $300 cash in payment of an account payable.	Cash	−300 −300	=	Accts. Pay.	−300 −300	Accts. Pay. (−L) Cash (−A)	300	300	Cash, an asset, is decreased. Accts. Pay., a liability, is decreased.
4. Company issues common stock in exchange for an outstanding note payable.		0	=	Notes Pay. Com. Stk.	−1,000 +1,000 0	Notes. Pay. (−L) Com. Stk. (+SE)	1,000	1,000	Notes Pay., a liability, is decreased. Com. Stk., an equity, is increased.
5. Company provides a service for which it bills its clients $2,000.	Accts. Rec.	+2,000 +2,000	=	Ret. Earn. via Fees Earned	+2,000 +2,000	Accts. Rec. (+A) Fees Earned (R, +SE)	2,000	2,000	Accts. Rec., an asset, is increased. Fees Earned, a revenue, increases Retained Earnings.
6. Company pays $500 in salaries to its employees.	Cash	−500 −500	=	Ret. Earn. via Salary Expense	−500 −500	Salary Exp. (E, −SE) Cash (−A)	500	500	Cash, an asset, is decreased. Salary Exp. decreases Retained Earnings.
7. Company declares an $800 dividend to be paid later to its owners.		0	=	Dividends Pay. Ret. Earn. via Dividends	+800 −800 0	Dividends (−SE) Dividends Pay. (+L)	800	800	Dividends Pay., a liability, is increased. Dividends decreases Retained Earnings.

Note: Accts. Rec. = Accounts Receivable; Accts. Pay. = Accounts Payable; Com. Stk. = Common Stock; Dividends Pay. = Dividends Payable; Notes Pay. = Notes Payable; Ret. Earn. = Retained Earnings; Salary Exp. = Salary Expense.
*See journal entry box in Figure 4–7.
**Typically, journal entries would not include the information in parentheses:
+ = increase and − = decrease; A = Asset; L = Liability; SE = Stockholders' Equity; R = Revenue; E = Expense; Ga = Gain; Lo = Loss;
Balance Sheet (A = L + SE)
Income Statement (R + Ga − E − Lo = NI)

The account names in each journal entry contained in Figure 4–8 are followed by parenthetical notations designed to indicate how the entry affects the fundamental accounting equation. We use this notation throughout the remainder of the text because it emphasizes the important relationship between the economic event represented by the journal entry and the accounting equation and, ultimately, the financial statements.

During 1999, Cisco Systems recorded revenues of $12.1 billion. Describe how these transactions would be represented in Figure 4-8.

T-ACCOUNTS

When analyzing the effects of many economic events on the financial statements, it is useful to keep running tallies of the balances for each asset, liability, stockholders' equity, revenue, expense, and dividend account. This can be achieved by creating a T-account for each of the financial statement accounts. **T-accounts** are so named because they are in the form of a T—the left side of the T represents the debit side of the entry, and the right side corresponds to the credit side. Since journal entries also have a debit and credit side, the debited and credited dollar amounts are easily transferred (posted) to their respective T-accounts. The following example demonstrates how financial statements can be prepared from a group of economic events (transactions), each of which is represented by a journal entry. The balances are maintained in T-accounts.

AN EXAMPLE. The December 31, 2002 balance sheet of Maple Services Company appears in Figure 4–9. The journal entries and associated T-accounts for ten transactions, entered into during 2003, are provided in Figure 4–10. Note first that the account balances from the balance sheet are the beginning balances in the T-accounts. Note also that the journal entries, numbered 1–10, are posted in the T-accounts. Review each journal entry and trace the dollar amounts of the debits and credits to the T-accounts. The financial statements, which appear in Figure 4–11, can be prepared directly from the T-accounts.

FIGURE 4–9
Maple Services balance sheet

Maple Services Company
Balance Sheet
December 31, 2002

ASSETS		LIABILITIES AND STOCKHOLDERS' EQUITY	
Cash	$12,000	Salaries payable	$ 4,000
Accounts receivable	9,000	Notes payable	6,000
Land	15,000	Common stock	21,000
		Retained earnings	5,000
		Total liabilities and	
Total assets	$36,000	stockholders' equity	$36,000

INCOME STATEMENT. The income statement for the period ending December 31, 2003 is prepared by subtracting the balances in the expense T-accounts (salary expense, rent expense, insurance expense, and interest expense) from the balances in the revenue T-accounts (service revenue), resulting in net income.

STATEMENT OF RETAINED EARNINGS. The statement of retained earnings for that same period consists of adding net income (or subtracting a net loss), which is taken from the income statement, to the beginning balance in the retained earnings T-account ($5,000), and then subtracting the balance in the dividends T-account ($1,000), which

FIGURE 4–10   Maple Services Company

JOURNAL ENTRIES

(1) Cash (+A)	5,000	(6) Rent Expense (E, −SE)	500
Common Stock (+SE)	5,000	Cash (− A)	500
Issued common stock.		*Paid rent.*	
(2) Land (+A)	7,000	(7) Insurance Expense (E, −SE)	100
Cash (−A)	7,000	Cash (−A)	100
Purchased land.		*Paid for insurance coverage.*	
(3) Salaries Payable (−L)	4,000	(8) Salary Expense (E, −SE)	3,000
Cash (−A)	4,000	Cash (−A)	3,000
Paid salaries owed at the end		*Paid salaries.*	
of 2003.		(9) Interest Expense (E, −SE)	500
(4) Cash (−A)	6,000	Notes Payable (−L)	2,000
Accounts Receivable (−A)	6,000	Cash (−A)	2,500
Received cash on outstanding		*Paid interest and principal on an*	
accounts receivable.		*outstanding loan.*	
(5) Cash (+A)	7,000	(10) Dividends (−SE)	1,000
Service Revenue (R, +SE)	7,000	Cash (−A)	1,000
Received cash for services provided.		*Paid cash dividend.*	

T-ACCOUNTS

Cash					Accounts Receivable			Land			Salaries Payable		
	12,000				9,000				15,000				4,000
(1)	5,000	(2)	7,000			(4)	6,000	(2)	7,000		(3)	4,000	
(4)	6,000	(3)	4,000		3,000				22,000				0
(5)	7,000	(6)	500										
		(7)	100										
		(8)	3,000										
		(9)	2,500										
		(10)	1,000										
	11,900												

Notes Payable			Common Stock			Retained Earnings		Service Revenue		
		6,000			21,000		5,000		(5)	7,000
(9)	2,000			(1)	5,000					
		4,000			26,000					

Salary Expense			Rent Expense			Insurance Expense			Interest Expense		
(8)	3,000		(6)	500		(7)	100		(9)	500	

Dividends		
(10)	1,000	

FIGURE 4–11

Financial statements for Maple Services Company

Income Statement
For the Year Ended December 31, 2003

Service revenue		$7,000
Expenses:		
Salaries	$3,000	
Rent	500	
Insurance	100	
Interest	500	
Total expenses		4,100
Net income		$2,900

Statement of Retained Earnings
For the Year Ended December 31, 2003

Beginning retained earnings balance	$5,000
Plus: Net income	2,900
Less: Dividends	(1,000)
Ending retained earnings balance	$6,900

Balance Sheet
December 31, 2003

ASSETS		LIABILITIES AND STOCKHOLDERS' EQUITY	
Cash	$11,900	Notes payable	$ 4,000
Accounts receivable	3,000	Common stock	26,000
Land	22,000	Retained earnings	6,900
		Total liabilities and	
Total assets	$36,900	stockholders' equity	$36,900

Statement of Cash Flows
December 31, 2003

Operating activities:		
Cash receipts for services	$ 7,000	
Cash receipts from accounts receivable	6,000	
Cash payments for salaries	(7,000)	
Cash payments for rent	(500)	
Cash payments for insurance	(100)	
Cash payments for interest	(500)	
Cash increase (decrease) due to operating activities		$ 4,900
Investing activities:		
Cash payment for purchase of land	$(7,000)	
Cash increase (decrease) due to investing activities		(7,000)
Financing activities:		
Cash receipt from issuing stock	$ 5,000	
Cash payment for loan principal	(2,000)	
Cash payment for dividends	(1,000)	
Cash increase (decrease) due to financing activities		2,000
Increase (decrease) in cash balance		$ (100)
Beginning cash balance		12,000
Ending cash balance		$11,900

represents the amount declared during the period. The result ($6,900) is the ending (December 31, 2003) balance in retained earnings.

BALANCE SHEET. The December 31, 2003 balance sheet consists of the balances in the asset (cash, accounts receivable, land), liability (notes payable), and stockholders' equity (common stock and retained earnings) T-accounts. Note that the ending balance in retained earnings ($6,900), which was computed on the statement of retained earnings, appears on the balance sheet.

The dollar amounts on the balance sheet represent the beginning balances for asset, liability, and stockholders' equity T-accounts for the next period (2004). Since the dollar amounts in the revenue, expense, and dividend accounts are reflected in the ending balance of retained earnings, the revenue, expense, and dividend T-accounts begin the next period (2004) with zero balances. The balance sheet accounts are described as *permanent* because their balances accumulate from one period to the next. The income statement and dividend accounts are described as *temporary* because their balances begin each new period at zero.[1]

STATEMENT OF CASH FLOWS. The statement of cash flows is prepared from the cash T-account. Each cash inflow and outflow is classified as operating, investing, or financing and then placed on the statement. This statement reconciles the change in the cash balance during the period, expressing it in terms of cash increases (decreases) due to operating, investing, and financing activities.

RECOGNIZING GAINS AND LOSSES

Companies often sell investments and noncurrent assets, receiving dollar amounts that do not match the amounts at which the investments are carried on the balance sheet. In such cases, a gain or loss must be recognized in the amount of the difference between the proceeds and the carrying amount. When McDonnell Douglas sold its North American Field Service business for $100 million, it recognized a $29 million gain because the investment was carried on the company's balance sheet at $71 million. Assuming that the business was acquired for $71 million, the following journal entries were used to record these events. (Dollar amounts are in millions.)

Investment (+A)	71	
Cash (−A)		71

Acquired North American Field Service for cash.

Cash (+A)	100	
Investment (−A)		71
Gain on Sale (Ga, +SE)		29

Sold North American Field Service for gain.

If McDonnell Douglas would have sold the business for an amount less than the $71 million carrying amount, $55 million for example, a loss would have been recognized in the following manner.

---

1. In actual accounting systems, the year-end balances in the revenue, expense, and dividend accounts are formally transferred to retained earnings through a series of journal entries. This closing process zeroes out the balances in the temporary accounts so that they begin at zero the next period. The closing process is part of the accounting cycle, which is covered in Appendix 4A.

Cash (+A)	55	
Loss on Sale (Lo, −SE)	16	
Investment (−A)		71

Sold North American Field Service for loss.

The gain or loss in the entry represents the profit or loss on the transaction in the amount of the difference between the proceeds and the balance sheet value of the investment. Note also that the gain or loss appears on the income statement, and the cash proceeds from the sale would appear on the statement of cash flows under cash flows from investing activities.

In 1998, the board of directors of PepsiCo approved a plan to sell off The Pepsi Bottling Group for $5.5 billion. The value of The Pepsi Bottling Group of PepsiCo's balance sheet prior to the sale was $4.5 billion. How did PepsiCo record this transaction?

PERIODIC ADJUSTMENTS

Up to now the discussion has focused on the financial statement effects of exchange transactions—transactions backed by documented evidence, in which assets and/or liabilities are transferred between parties. Assets and liabilities, however, are often created or discharged without the occurrence of a visible, documentable exchange transaction. They sometimes build up or expire as time passes. Interest, for example, is earned continually on bank savings accounts, and machinery depreciates as it is used in a company's operations. Such phenomena are not evidenced by exchange transactions, but they can be very important to a company's performance and financial condition.

Net income for a particular period is measured by (1) recognizing revenues when the earning process is complete and (2) matching against those revenues the expenses incurred to generate them. Under this view of performance, called the **accrual system of accounting,** revenues are booked when assets are created (or liabilities are discharged) and expenses are recorded when liabilities arise (or assets are reduced). In other words, revenues and expenses can be recognized either before or after the related cash is received or paid. The accrual system requires that periodic adjustments be made to the financial statements so that net income for a given period of time will be the result of a proper matching of the revenues and expenses within that period.

Periodic adjustments take one of three forms: (1) accruals, (2) deferrals, and (3) revaluations. The first two are covered in this chapter; revaluation adjustments are covered in subsequent chapters as they arise.

Accruals

Accruals refer to amounts in asset and liability accounts that build up over time. The term *accrue* simply means to build up gradually.[2] Two very common examples are accrued wages and accrued interest.

2. Note that the term accrual refers to a system of accounting that recognizes revenues and expenses as assets and liabilities are created or discharged, as well as one of two kinds of adjusting entries. The double meaning of this term can be a source of confusion, and it is important that you be aware of the context in which it is used.

ACCRUED WAGES

Suppose that employees of Taylor Motor are paid at the end of each week. The total weekly payroll is $10,000, which is earned at a rate of $2,000 per day for each of the five working days. Assume that December 31 falls on a Tuesday, and the financial statements are prepared as of that day. Figure 4–12 illustrates these facts and the journal entries that would be recorded under accrual accounting.

FIGURE 4–12 Accrued wages

	Period 1		Period 2		
	MONDAY (12/30)	**TUESDAY (12/31)**	**WED. (1/1)**	**THUR. (1/2)**	**FRIDAY (1/3)**
Wages Earned:	$2,000	$2,000	$2,000	$2,000	$2,000

Tuesday (12/31):
Adjustment
Wage Exp. (E, −SE) 4,000
   Wages Pay. (+L)   4,000
Recognized accrued wages.

Friday (1/3):
Wages Pay. (−L)   4,000
Wage Exp. (E, −SE) 6,000
   Cash (−A)   10,000
Paid accrued wages.

In applying the accrual system, it must be recognized that although no cash has been paid as of December 31, a liability has been created. The company owes its employees two days' worth of wages, or $4,000. This liability is recognized with an adjusting journal entry of the form indicated in Figure 4–12. Wage Expense of $4,000 is reflected on the income statement of the period ending on December 31 (Period 1). Wages Payable of $4,000 appears in the liability section of the December 31 balance sheet, and the amount is carried into Period 2. Note that on Friday, when the $10,000 cash payment for wages is made, $4,000 serves to remove the Wages Payable (the liability is discharged), and $6,000 is charged to Wage Expense of Period 2 and thus will appear on the income statement of Period 2.

The adjustment in this example achieves matching, in that it matches the cost of the effort expended by the employees in Period 1 with the revenues generated in Period 1. Wage expense of $4,000 is subtracted from Period 1 revenues in the computation of Period 1 net income. Similarly, the cost of the effort expended by the employees in Period 2 ($6,000) is matched against Period 2 revenues on the Period 2 income statement.

It is also important to realize that Taylor would prepare statements of cash flows for Periods 1 and 2 and the entire $10,000 cash payment would be reflected in the operating section of that statement in the second period only. None of it would appear on the statement of cash flows of Period 1. As Figure 4–13 indicates, the total resource

FIGURE 4–13
Expenditure recognition

Accounting System/Financial Statement	Period 1	Period 2	Period 3
Accrual/Income statement	$4,000	$ 6,000	$10,000
Cash/Statement of cash flows	0	10,000	10,000

expenditure recognized under the accrual system is the same as that recognized under the cash system. The difference lies in the timing of the recognition. Due to the adjustment, the accrual system recognizes $4,000 in Period 1 and $6,000 in Period 2.

ACCRUED INTEREST

Suppose that on December 1, Bank of America Corporation loans $12,000 to Exxon Mobil Oil Company at an annual interest rate of 10 percent. Assume that the accounting period ends on December 31 and that Exxon pays Bank of America in full (principal and interest) on January 31 of the next year. Figure 4–14 illustrates these facts and the journal entries that would be recorded under accrual accounting.

FIGURE 4–14   Accrued interest revenue

Period 1		Period 2
DECEMBER 1	**DECEMBER 31**	**JANUARY 31**
	Adjustment	Cash (+A) 12,200
Note Rec. (+A) 12,000	Interest Rec. (+A) 100	Interest Rec. (−A) 100
Cash (−A) 12,000	Interest Rev. (R, +SE) 100	Interest Rev. (R, +SE) 100
Received note for cash.	*Recognized accrued*	Note Rec. (−A) 12,000
	interest received.	*Received cash on*
		outstanding note.

Bank of America records an adjustment on December 31, to reflect the fact that an asset, Interest Receivable, has been created. The company has earned $100 ([$12,000 × 10%]/12 months) in interest during the month of December. Interest Receivable in that amount is recognized (debited), and Interest Revenue is credited. When the $12,200 cash payment is received on January 31, $12,000 serves to reduce the outstanding note receivable, $100 is charged against the Interest Receivable account, and the remaining $100 is recognized as Interest Revenue.

As in the example of accrued wages, the adjustment here helps to achieve a matching of revenues and expenses in the appropriate time period. It does so by dividing the total interest earned on the loan ($200) into two components, based on the periods in which it was earned and the time when the asset, Interest Receivable, was created. Half of the $200 interest payment was earned in Period 1 and therefore should appear as a revenue on the income statement of Period 1. The remaining $100 should appear as a revenue on the income statement of Period 2 because the loan was outstanding during one month of Period 2.

Consider again the effect of these transactions on the statements of cash flows for Periods 1 and 2. No cash inflow is recorded in Period 1, and therefore nothing would be reflected on the statement of cash flows for that period. Instead, all $200 would appear on the statement of cash flows in Period 2, when the cash is actually received. Once again, the total interest recognized across the two periods under the cash system ($200) is the same as that recognized under the accrual system, but the timing of the recognition is different. The adjusting journal entry prepared under the accrual system ensures that $100 is recognized on the income statement of Period 1, with the remaining $100 appearing on the income statement of Period 2.

Figure 4–15, using the same facts as Figure 4–14, considers the borrower's (Exxon Mobil's) point of view. Examine the journal entries, and note especially how the adjusting journal entry matches revenues and expenses in the appropriate time period and gives rise to expense recognition in a time period when no cash payment is made.

FIGURE 4–15 Accrued interest expense

| | **Period 1** | **Period 2** |

DECEMBER 1	**DECEMBER 31**	**JANUARY 31**

Cash (+A)   12,000
   Note Pay. (+L)   12,000
Borrowed cash and issued note payable.
	Adjustment
	Interest Exp. (E, −SE) 100
	   Interest Pay. (+L) 100
	Recognized accrued interest payable.
		Note Pay. (−L) 12,000
		Interest Pay. (−L) 100
		Interest Exp. (E, −SE) 100
		   Cash (−A) 12,200
		Paid interest and outstanding note.

Honeywell International, an advanced technology and manufacturing company, reported accrued liabilities of $3.5 billion on its 1999 balance sheet. Explain the meaning of that number.

Deferrals

The second type of adjustment is called a **deferral** (or **cost expiration**). Like accruals, these adjusting entries (1) are recorded in the books at the end of an accounting period to achieve an appropriate matching of revenues and expenses and (2) do not reflect cash exchanges. They are called deferrals because they are entries that serve to defer the recognition of an expense or revenue until the proper time.

ASSET CAPITALIZATION AND THE MATCHING PRINCIPLE

Before studying deferrals, you should understand one very important concept in financial accounting measurement—*asset capitalization* and how it relates to the matching principle. The **matching principle** involves a four-step process: (1) a cost is incurred in the current period for the purpose of generating revenue; (2) the revenue recognition principle determines the period in which the revenue is recognized; (3) if the revenue is recognized in the current period, the cost is **expensed** (appearing on the income statement as an expense); if the revenue is expected to be recognized in a future period, the cost is **capitalized** (appearing on the balance sheet as an asset); and (4) capitalized costs are converted to expenses (by recording cost expiration adjusting journal entries) in those future periods when revenue is recognized. Assets, by definition, are expected to generate economic benefits in the form of future revenues and, according to the matching principle, the costs of acquiring assets should be matched against those benefits when they are recognized. The accrual system of accounting accomplishes this matching by initially capitalizing the costs of assets and then converting them to expenses (through periodic adjustments) as their usefulness expires and their benefits are realized.

To illustrate the important difference between expensing and capitalizing a cost, consider a company with the following simplified balance sheet as of December 31, 2002:

Assets	$1,000	Liabilities	$ 600
		Stockholders' equity	400
Total	$1,000	Total	$1,000

During 2003, the company recognizes $2,500 in revenues and $1,500 in expenses. Near the end of the year, the company spends $500 on its facilities. Figure 4-16 provides the resulting financial statements if the company expenses or capitalizes the $500 expenditure, assuming that all transactions were in cash.

FIGURE 4–16
Expensing vs. capitalizing

	Expenses $500	Capitalizes $500
Balance sheet:		
Assets	$1,500	$2,000
Liabilities	600	600
Stockholders' equity	900	1,400
Income statement:		
Revenues	$2,500	$2,500
Expenses	2,000	1,500
Net income	$ 500	$1,000

Note the differences in total assets, stockholders' equity, expenses, and net income. Assets and net income are clearly much higher if the company chooses to capitalize the $500 cost. As illustrated in the next section, however, if the cost is capitalized it will have to be amortized against revenues in future periods, reducing reported net income in those periods.

EXPENSE OR CAPITALIZE EXAMPLES

Figure 4–17 illustrates the basic procedures used to account for expenses and capitalized costs. It is divided into two sections. The upper section depicts the matching process. The lower section consists of nine different transactions, each carried through the four steps involved in applying the matching principle.

CURRENT EXPENSES. The first three transactions (salaries, interest, and utilities) represent resource expenditures, either through the creation of a liability or the payment of cash, for which the benefit is assumed to be realized in the current period. Salaries and interest in this case are accrued at the end of the current period with an accrual adjusting journal entry, and the associated cash payments are expected to follow in a future period. The utility expense is both recognized and paid in the current period. Since the benefit from each of these three expenditures is assumed to be realized in the current period, all are expensed, regardless of the timing of the cash payment. These expenditures have not been capitalized and, therefore, Step 4 in the matching process, an adjusting journal entry, is not necessary.

SUPPLIES INVENTORY. The fourth transaction in Figure 4–17, the purchase of supplies, is capitalized because supplies are normally expected to be useful beyond the current period. Typically, at the end of each period, an inventory of the remaining supplies is taken, and a cost expiration adjusting journal entry is entered in the books to

---

FIGURE 4–17 Expense or capitalize?

1.
Incur cost in current period for the purpose of generating revenue.

2.
Decide in what period the revenue is to be generated.

3a.
Current: Expense on income statement.

3b.
Future: Capitalize on balance sheet. (Deferral)

4.
Cost Expiration: As revenue is generated, convert asset to expense via an adjusting journal entry.

Salaries	Current period (expense)	Salary Exp. (E, −SE) XX Salary Pay. (+L) XX	None required
Interest	Current period (expense)	Interest Exp. (E, −SE) XX Interest Pay. (+L) XX	None required
Utilities	Current period (expense)	Utility Exp. (E, −SE) XX Cash (−A) XX	None required

Purchase of supplies	Future period (asset)	Supplies Inv. (+A) XX
		    Cash (−A) XX
			Supplies Exp. (E, −SE) XX
			    Supplies Inv. (−A) XX
			Adjusted for supplies used.

Purchase of merchandise inventory	Future period (asset)	Merch. Inv. (+A) XX
		    Accounts Pay. (+L) XX
			Cost of Goods Sold (E, −SE) XX
			    Merchandise Inv. (−A) XX
			Adjusted for inventory sold.

Prepaid expenses (e.g., insurance, interest, rent)	Future period (asset)	Prepaid Rent (+A) XX
		    Cash (−A) XX
			Rent Expense (E, −SE) XX
			    Prepaid Rent (−A) XX
			Adjusted for rent period expired.

Payments received in advance	Future period (liability)	Cash (+A) XX
		    Unearned Rev. (+L) XX
			Unearned Revenue (−L) XX
			    Earned Revenue (R, +SE) XX
			Adjusted for service performed.

Purchase of property, plant, or equipment	Future period (asset)	Equipment (+A) XX
		    Cash (−A) XX
		    Note Payable (+L) XX
			Depreciation Exp. (E, −SE) XX
			    Accumulated Depr. (−A) XX
			Adjusted for useful life expired.

Purchase of intangible asset (e.g., patent, trademark)	Future period (asset)	Trademark (+A) XX
		    Cash (−A) XX
			Amortization Exp. (E, −SE) XX
			    Accumulated Amort. (−A) XX
			Adjusted for useful life expired.

reflect the cost of the supplies that were used (expired) during the period. This entry also restates the supplies inventory account on the balance sheet to reflect the supplies actually on hand at the end of the period.

To illustrate, assume that during 2002 Weyerhaeuser Company purchased materials and supplies to support the manufacture of forest products at a total cost of $700. On December 31, a count revealed that supplies in the amount of $300 remained on hand. If the company began the year with $500 in the supplies account, the cost of the supplies used during 2002 would be computed as shown below, and the following journal entries would have been recorded to reflect these facts.

Supplies Used	=	Beginning Inventory	+	Purchases	−	Ending Inventory
$900	=	$500	+	$700	−	$300

1997: Purchase of Supplies		Dec. 31: Cost Expiration Adjusting Entry	
Supplies Inventory (+A)	700	Supplies Expense (E, −SE)	900
Cash (−A)	700	Supplies Inventory (−A)	900
Purchased supplies.		*Recognized use of supplies.*	

In this situation, supplies in the amount of $300 would be reported on the company's December 31 balance sheet.

MERCHANDISE INVENTORY. The purchase of merchandise inventory is capitalized because inventories are expected to generate revenues in the future when they are sold. According to the matching principle, the cost of the merchandise should be converted to an expense, cost of goods sold, in the period when the inventories are sold. As with supplies, the end-of-period expiration adjusting journal entry reflects the cost of the inventories that were used (sold) during the period. It also serves to restate the inventory account on the balance sheet to reflect the merchandise that is actually on hand at the end of the period.[3]

To illustrate, assume that May Department Stores purchased $5,000 of merchandise inventory during 2002, and that a year-end inventory count revealed that inventories in the amount of $3,000 remained on hand. Assuming that the company began the year with inventories valued at $2,000, cost of goods sold would be computed as follows, and the following journal entries would be recorded to reflect these facts.

Cost of Goods Sold	=	Beginning Inventory	+	Purchases	−	Ending Inventory
$4,000	=	$2,000	+	$5,000	−	$3,000

2002: Purchase of Merchandise		Dec. 31: Cost Expiration Adjusting Entry	
Merchandise Inv. (+A)	5,000	Cost of Goods Sold (E, −SE)	4,000
Cash (−A)	5,000	Merchandise Inv. (−A)	4,000
Purchased merchandise.		*Adjusted for inventory sold.*	

In this example, May would report merchandise inventory of $3,000 on its 2002 balance sheet and cost of goods sold of $4,000 on its income statement.

PREPAID EXPENSES. Prepaid expenses represent costs such as insurance, interest, and rent that are paid in advance, before the associated benefit is realized. Insurance premiums, for example, are paid in advance and usually cover an entire year or more.

---

3. This chapter assumes that cost of goods sold is determined at the end of the year with a cost expiration adjusting journal entry. This procedure describes the periodic inventory method. The perpetual inventory method, which recognizes cost of goods sold each time inventory is sold, is discussed in Chapter 7, which covers inventories more completely.

Similarly, interest on loans is sometimes paid before the borrowed funds are used. In applying the matching principle, such prepayments are capitalized and then converted to expenses as the time period expires and benefits are realized. This periodic conversion is achieved through cost expiration adjusting journal entries.

To illustrate, assume that on January 1, 2002, Merck purchased a $1,000 insurance premium for a two-year period. The following journal entries would be made on the books of Merck over the life of the insurance coverage.

Jan. 1, 2002: Purchase of Insurance			Dec. 31, 2002 and 2003: Cost Expiration Adjusting Entry		
Prepaid Insurance (+A)	1,000		Insurance Expense (E, −SE)	500	
Cash (−A)		1,000	Prepaid Insurance (−A)		500
Paid insurance in advance.			*Adjusted for expiration of insurance.*		

In this example, Merck would report in the current asset section of its 2002 balance sheet $500 of prepaid (unexpired) insurance, which would be converted to an expense at the end of 2003.

UNEARNED (DEFERRED) REVENUES. Unearned revenues are the reverse of prepaid expenses. For every entity that prepays an expense before the associated benefit is realized, another entity receives a payment before it performs the required service. When applying the revenue recognition principle to the entity that receives payment and has yet to provide the service, a liability account, called **Unearned Revenues,** is credited when the cash is initially collected. This account is then converted to a revenue as the service is performed with an end-of-period adjusting journal entry.[4]

To illustrate, suppose that Delta Air Lines received $5,000 during 2002 for tickets not yet used. Delta's cash account would immediately increase by $5,000, but the company would not recognize revenue at that time because it had not yet performed the contracted service. Instead, Delta would recognize a $5,000 liability, indicating that it owed services in the form of airplane travel. Assume that as of the end of 2002, Delta had fulfilled 60 percent of the services. At that time, therefore, an adjusting journal entry would be recorded to remove 60 percent of the liability from the company's balance sheet and, at the same time, recognize 60 percent of the revenue. The following journal entries reflect these facts.

Receipt of Advance Payment			Cost Expiration Adjusting Entry		
Cash (+A)	5,000		Unearned Revenue (−L)	3,000	
Unearned Revenue (+L)		5,000	Fees Earned (R, +SE)		3,000
Received cash prior to providing *service.*			*Recognized revenue from providing* *service.*		

This sequence of journal entries would leave a liability for Unearned Revenues on Delta's 2002 balance sheet of $2,000, representing airline travel that Delta still had to fulfill.

PROPERTY, PLANT, AND EQUIPMENT. Transaction 8 in Figure 4–17 considers the costs of purchasing property, plant, and equipment. Since these assets are expected to

---

4. Technically, an unearned revenue does not represent a capitalized cost because it is not an asset, and therefore, the adjusting journal entry to convert it to a revenue is not a cost expiration adjusting journal entry. However, we have chosen to categorize it as such because the concept of deferring the recognition of a revenue until the service is performed is the same as deferring the recognition of an expense until the associated benefit is realized. Both are essential to implementing the matching principle.

help generate revenues beyond the current time period, the matching principle specifies that the acquisition costs be capitalized and systematically converted to an expense (**amortized**) over the estimated useful lives of the assets. At the end of each period of the estimated useful life, a cost expiration adjusting journal entry is recorded to amortize a portion of the capitalized cost. The process of amortizing the cost of property, plant, and equipment is called **depreciation.**

To illustrate, assume that Federal Express invested $10,000 in flight equipment on January 1, 2002. At the time of the purchase, FedEx management subjectively estimated that the equipment would have a useful life of ten years and chose to depreciate an equal amount of the capitalized cost ($1,000 = $10,000/10 years) at the end of each of the ten one-year periods. The following journal entries would have been recorded in FedEx's books.

Jan. 1, 2002: Purchase of Equipment			Dec. 31, 2002, 2003 . . . , 2011: Cost Expiration Adjusting Entry		
Equipment (+A)	10,000		Depr. Exp. (E, −SE)	1,000	
Cash (−A)		10,000	Accumulated Depr. (−A)		1,000
Purchased equipment.			*Adjusted for depreciation on equipment.*		

Note that the cost expiration adjusting journal entry involves a debit to Depreciation Expense that appears on the income statement for each of the ten years. It also involves a credit to an account called Accumulated Depreciation, instead of a credit to the equipment account itself. Accumulated Depreciation is a special account that appears on the asset side of the balance sheet. It offsets the asset account to which it applies (i.e., Equipment), maintaining an accumulated balance of the amount of depreciation taken on the asset up to the date of the balance sheet. Balance sheet accounts like Accumulated Depreciation, which are used to offset other balance sheet accounts, are called **contra accounts.** Subtracting the balance in the accumulated depreciation account from the original cost of the equipment on the balance sheet gives rise to a number referred to as **book value.**

Using the same information as in the preceding example, at the end of the second year (December 31, 2003) the equipment account would appear on FedEx's balance sheet as follows. The original cost of the equipment is $10,000, the accumulated depreciation is $2,000, and the net book value is $8,000.

Equipment	$10,000	
Less: Accumulated depreciation	2,000	$8,000

Estimating the useful life of property, plant, and equipment and choosing a method of allocating the capitalized cost to future periods is a subjective and difficult task for management. These choices can also have a significant effect on the amount of net income recognized each year because they have a direct bearing on the amount of depreciation expense that appears on the income statement. To illustrate the importance of such estimates, when Delta Air Lines decided to change the useful life estimate of its flight equipment from ten years to fifteen years, it disclosed in its financial report that the change decreased depreciation expense of that year by $130 million.

INTANGIBLE ASSETS. The final transaction in Figure 4–17 is the purchase of an intangible asset, such as a patent or trademark. The cost of this purchase is, once again, capitalized because the benefit of the purchase is expected to extend beyond the current period. Many intangibles have definable lives (often determined by law) over which the capitalized cost is typically amortized. The cost expiration adjusting journal entry consists of a debit to Amortization Expense and a credit to the contra account, Accumulated Amortization.

To illustrate, assume that Johnson & Johnson, a leading manufacturer of consumer health care products, purchased a patent for $20,000, which was determined by law to have a twenty-year life. The following journal entries would be recorded by Johnson & Johnson over the patent's legal life.

Purchase of Patent			End of Each of 20 Subsequent Years: Cost Expiration Adjusting Entry		
Patent (+A)	20,000		Amortization Exp. (E, −SE)	1,000	
Cash (−A)		20,000	Patent (−A)		1,000
Acquired patent.			*Adjusted for amortization*		
			of patent.		

Note that the Patent account is credited directly in the entry to amortize the cost of the patent. This practice is common, although GAAP recommends the use of a separate Accumulated Amortization account.

CAPITALIZING AND MATCHING: EXAMPLES

Figure 4–18 contains several examples in which cost expiration adjusting journal entries are used to apply the matching principle. Such entries are designed to convert capitalized costs to expenses in future time periods as the benefits (revenues) from the initial expenditures are recognized. The transactions illustrated in Figure 4–18 consider supplies, merchandise inventory, prepaid insurance, unearned revenue, equipment, and a patent.

Note in Figure 4–18 that equal amounts of the cost of the equipment and the patent are depreciated, or amortized, in each of the three time periods. For example, the $9,000 equipment cost is depreciated at a rate of $3,000 per period. This method is referred to as **straight-line depreciation.** It is almost always used to amortize intangible assets, but it is only one of several methods that can be used to depreciate the capitalized costs of property, plant, and equipment.

During 1999, Tommy Hilfiger Corporation booked revenues of $1.6 billion; paid interest costs on outstanding debt of $39 million; purchased inventory of $945 million; purchased property, plant, and equipment of $79 million; and recognized depreciation and amortization of $81 million. Explain each of these transactions in terms of Figure 4–17 and 4–18.

Revaluation Adjustments

At various points in the remainder of this text, we cover adjustments that do not fall into the categories of accruals or cost expirations. Such adjustments serve to restate certain accounts to keep their reported values in line with existing facts. For example, the balance sheet dollar amounts of short-term investments, accounts receivable, and inventories are sometimes adjusted when the market values of these assets change. The entries required in such situations are called **revaluation adjustments.**

FIGURE 4–18 Capitalize and match

| CAPITALIZE ➝ | ADJUSTING ENTRIES DURING COST EXPIRATION PERIOD ➝ | | | EXPLANATION |
	1	2	3	
Supplies (+A) 100 　Cash (−A) 100 *Purchased supplies.*	Sup. Exp. (E, −SE) 30 　Supplies (−A) 30 *Supplies costing $70 on hand.*	Sup. Exp. (E, −SE) 50 　Supplies (−A) 50 *Supplies costing $20 on hand.*	Sup. Exp. (E, −SE) 20 　Supplies (−A) 20 *No supplies on hand.*	The cost of supplies is converted to expense as the supplies are used up.
Inventory (+A) 600 　Accts. Pay. (−L) 600 *Purchased 6 items at $100 per item.*	COGS (E, −SE) 100 　Inventory (−A) 100 *One item sold.*	COGS (E, −SE) 200 　Inventory (−A) 200 *Two items sold.*	COGS (E, −SE) 300 　Inventory (−A) 300 *Three items sold.*	The cost of inventory is converted to expense (Cost of Goods Sold) as the inventory is sold.
Pre. Ins. (+A) 300 　Cash (−A) 300 *Paid 3 years of insurance coverage in advance.*	Ins. Exp. (E, −SE) 100 　Prepaid Ins. (−A) 100 *The first year of insurance coverage expires.*	Ins. Exp. (E, −SE) 100 　Prepaid ins. (−A) 100 *The second year of insurance coverage expires.*	Ins. Exp. (E, −SE) 100 　Prepaid Ins. (−A) 100 *The third year of insurance coverage expires.*	The cost of prepaid insurance is converted to expense as the insurance coverage expires.
Cash (+A) 240 　Un. Rev. (+L) 240 *Received $240 for services to be performed later.*	Un. Rev. (−L) 120 　Fees Earned (R, +SE) 120 *Half of the service is performed.*	Un. Rev. (−L) 60 　Fees Earned (R, +SE) 60 *One quarter of the service is performed.*	Un. Rev. (−L) 60 　Fees Earned (R, +SE) 60 *One quarter of the service is performed.*	Revenue is recognized as the service is completed.
Equip. (+A) 9,000 　Notes Pay. (+L) 9,000 *Purchased machinery with an estimated 3-year life and no salvage value.*	Depr. Exp. 　(E, −SE) 3,000 　Accum. Depr. 　(−A) 3,000 *First year passes, assuming straight-line depreciation rate.*	Depr. Exp. 　(E, −SE) 3,000 　Accum. Depr. 　(−A) 3,000 *Second year passes.*	Depr. Exp. 　(E, −SE) 3,000 　Accum. Depr. 　(−A) 3,000 *Third year passes.*	The cost of machinery is converted to expense (Depreciation Expense) as the estimated useful life passes.
Patent (+A) 900 　Cash (−A) 900 *Acquired patent with 3-year legal life.*	Amort. Exp. (E, −SE) 300 　Accum. Amort. (−A) 300 *First year passes, assuming straight-line amortization rate.*	Amort. Exp. (E, −SE) 300 　Accum. Amort. (−A) 300 *Second year passes.*	Amort. Exp. (E, −SE) 300 　Accum. Amort. (−A) 300 *Third year passes.*	The cost of obtaining the patent is converted to an expense (Amortization Expense) as the legal life passes.

FINANCIAL STATEMENT PRESENTATION IN A MULTINATIONAL ENVIRONMENT

In this chapter, we have covered the mechanics of preparing financial statements, measured in U.S. dollars, written in the English language, and using U.S. accounting principles. We now briefly discuss how **multinationals,** corporations that have their home in one country but operate and live under the laws of other countries as well, report to

stockholders, creditors, and other interested parties who transact in different currencies, speak different languages, and are familiar with different accounting principles.
There are five basic approaches:

1. do nothing,
2. translate the language only,
3. translate the language, and express monetary amounts in the foreign currency,
4. translate the language, express monetary amounts in the foreign currency, and
   restate accounting principles, and
5. prepare financial statements based on international accounting standards.

The first approach is followed by most of the multinational companies based in the
United States. These companies choose not to adjust their statements because they
raise most of their capital in the United States, and the English language, the dollar,
and U.S. accounting principles are well known throughout the world. The second and
third approaches are popular for multinationals based in Europe, whose capital
providers reside in any of a number of countries that use different languages and foreign currencies. These companies, such as the German-based Volkswagen Group, typically prepare English, French, German, and Spanish versions, expecting that any
reader will understand at least one.

Complete restatements, approach (4), are prepared by a number of Japanese multinationals, like Honda and Mitsubishi. Many of these companies list their common
stock shares on the New York and American stock exchanges, which require that all
registrants follow U.S. generally accepted accounting principles. A small number of
companies, like the oil giant Royal/Dutch Shell, prepare financial statements that
attempt to synthesize the "best" accounting practices of all countries. Such statements,
which are intended to satisfy all user needs on a global basis, are often based on the
accounting principles established by the International Accounting Standards
Committee (IASC).

There is controversy, however over whether these standards represent "best practices." *Time International* (February 14, 2000) reported:

*Most of the world has rallied around a set of 40 rules devised over the last 26 years
by the IASC, a London-based group of professional accountants representing 104
countries. But the United States is reluctant to accept the IASC standards, which it
thinks pale in comparison to its own. And that's the quandary. Global standards
snubbed by the U.S., with the world's largest, most vibrant equity markets, wouldn't
be truly global. But the rest of the world has little interest in adopting the U.S. model,
which is viewed as outdated and over-laden with unnecessary prohibitions.*

APPENDIX 4A

THE ACCOUNTING CYCLE—AN OVERVIEW

Figure 4A–1 illustrates the complete accounting cycle. It consists of sixteen steps that lead from
(1) the recognition of an economic event (i.e., a relevant and objectively measurable exchange
transaction) to the preparation of the (13) income statement, (14) statement of retained earnings,
(15) balance sheet, and (16) statement of cash flows.

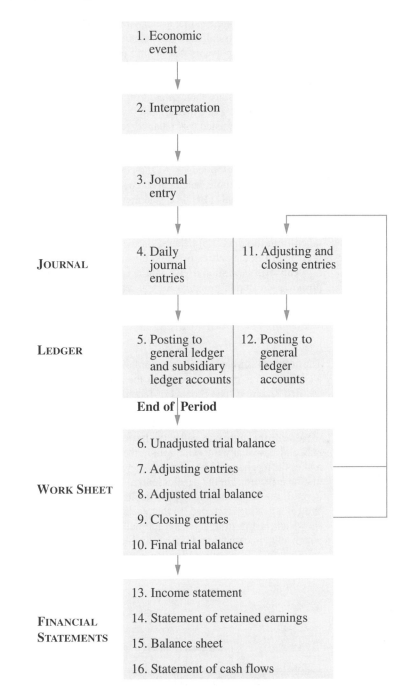

FIGURE 4A-1
The accounting cycle

1. Economic event

2. Interpretation

3. Journal entry

JOURNAL

4. Daily journal entries | 11. Adjusting and closing entries

LEDGER

5. Posting to general ledger and subsidiary ledger accounts | 12. Posting to general ledger accounts

End of Period

WORK SHEET

6. Unadjusted trial balance

7. Adjusting entries

8. Adjusted trial balance

9. Closing entries

10. Final trial balance

FINANCIAL STATEMENTS

13. Income statement

14. Statement of retained earnings

15. Balance sheet

16. Statement of cash flows

The accounting cycle begins when a relevant and measurable (1) economic event is (2) interpreted and (3) converted to a journal entry. Journal entries, the fundamental units of the accounting system, are recorded in the original book of record, (4) the journal, and are then posted in (5) the ledger. The process of recording journal entries and posting them to the ledger continues until it is time to prepare financial statements (monthly, quarterly, or annually).

At this time, denoted by *End of Period* in Figure 4A–1, a work sheet is prepared. Completing the work sheet encompasses Steps 6 through 10 in the accounting cycle. First, the account balances in the ledger are transferred to the work sheet. The list of the account balances on the work sheet is called (6) the unadjusted trial balance. The unadjusted trial balance is then adjusted for certain events that are not captured in the daily recording process (e.g., depreciation and earning interest). These (7) adjusting entries (or adjustments) are entered on the work sheet and added to the unadjusted trial balance, giving rise to (8) the adjusted trial balance. (9) Closing entries are then entered on the work sheet to transfer the balances in the income statement (revenue and expense) and dividend accounts to the retained earnings account. They are added to the adjusted trial balance, resulting in (10) the final trial balance, which completes the work sheet.

The adjusting and closing entries from the work sheet are now (11) recorded in the journal and (12) posted to the ledger. At the completion of Step 12, the financial statements are prepared. (13) The income statement can be prepared from the closing entries from either the work sheet or the journal. (14) The statement of retained earnings is prepared directly from the retained earnings account in the ledger. (15) The balance sheet is a collection of the final balances in the asset, liability, and stockholders' equity accounts in the ledger and can simply be taken from the final trial balance on the work sheet. (16) The statement of cash flows can be prepared from the entries listed on the cash account in the ledger.

This overview should give you a general feeling for the process. The following sections present each step thoroughly. As you read through the discussion, refer often to Figure 4A–1, so that you will know where each step fits into the process.

The Journal

The **journal** is a chronological record of the transactions, in journal entry form, entered into by a company. It is often referred to as the *book of original entry* because it is where transactions are first recorded. The process of recording transactions is called **journalizing.** As we mentioned earlier, journals can take many forms, depending upon a company's accounting system. While many companies use several different kinds of journals, for the purposes of this appendix we assume that only one, called the **general journal,** is maintained. We do so because all journals play essentially the same role in the accounting cycle, and the addition of special journals makes the mechanical procedures somewhat involved. For each transaction, the following information is recorded in the general journal: (1) the date, (2) the accounts that are debited and credited, (3) the dollar amounts of the debits and credits, (4) a brief explanation of the transaction, and (5) a posting reference, so that each journal entry can be traced to the ledger. Figure 4A–2 shows an excerpt from a general journal. The first entry describes the provision of a service for which $300 in cash and a $500 receivable were received. The second entry describes the buying on credit of $200 of office supplies.

FIGURE 4A–2
The general journal

GENERAL JOURNAL				PAGE 1
DATE	DESCRIPTION	POST. REF.	DEBIT	CREDIT
2003 Feb. 8	Cash (+A)		300	
	Accounts Receivable (+A)		500	
	Fees earned (R, +SE)			800
	Provided service for cash and on account.			
10	Supplies (+A)		200	
	Accounts Payable (+L)			200
	Bought supplies on account.			

The Ledgers

Immediately after the transactions are recorded in the journal, they are posted in the **ledger,** where a running balance for each asset, liability, stockholders' equity, revenue, expense, and dividend account is maintained. The ledger can be viewed, therefore, as a "scoreboard" that keeps track of the "score" in each account during the period.

It is useful to think of the ledger as containing a T-account for each account on the financial statements. T-accounts are so named because they are in the form of a T. The left side of the T represents the debit side of the entry, and the right side corresponds to the credit side. Since journal entries also have a debit and a credit side, the debited and credited dollar amounts are easily transferred (posted) to their respective T-accounts. Figure 4A–3 shows how the debits and credits in two journal entries are posted to their respective T-accounts.[1]

FIGURE 4A–3
Posting journal entries

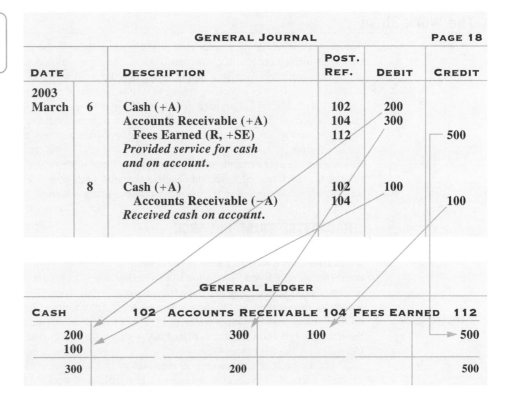

In the first entry, a service was exchanged for $200 cash and a $300 accounts receivable. Note that in the ledger the cash T-account is increased (debited) by $200, the accounts receivable T-account is increased (debited) by $300, and the Fees Earned T-account is increased (credited) by $500. In the second entry, $100 cash is received on an outstanding account receivable. Accordingly, the cash balance in the ledger is increased (debited) by $100, and the accounts receivable balance is decreased (credited) by that amount. Note how the final balances in each account in the ledger have been computed.

If every journal entry is immediately entered in the ledger, at any point in time the balance for a given account can be computed directly from its T-account. The balance is simply equal to the difference between the total dollar amount debited to the T-account and the total dollar amount credited. Having a convenient way to compute the account balances is particularly useful when it comes time to prepare the financial statements at the end of the accounting period.

---

1. For simplicity and to avoid getting into the specifics of bookkeeping, we have shown ledger accounts in the form of a T. While this is true in concept, manual bookkeeping systems in practice use ledgers that contain much greater detail.

Without an up-to-date ledger, computing the account balances and preparing the financial statements would involve tracing back through the journal to find each transaction that affected each account. For most companies, this would be time-consuming and tedious and could give rise to a number of recording errors.

We have described the ledger as containing one T-account for each account on the financial statements, which is actually a description of the **general ledger.** Companies also commonly use **subsidiary ledgers,** which contain T-accounts that relate to certain specific accounts in the general ledger. A $110 balance in an accounts receivable general ledger T-account, for example, may comprise a number of accounts associated with individual customers. Cindy Jones may owe $35 to the company, Jason Smith may owe $50, and Heather Johnson, $25. T-accounts for each individual would be kept in a subsidiary ledger, which is tied directly to the $110 (35 + 50 + 25) accounts receivable balance in the general ledger.

The Work Sheet

The process of recording journal entries and posting them to the appropriate ledger accounts continues throughout the **accounting period,** the time between the preparation of financial statements, which is usually a month, a quarter (three months), or a year. At the end of the accounting period, when the time comes to summarize the accounts and prepare financial statements, a work sheet is often prepared. A **work sheet** (see Figure 4A–4) is simply a piece of paper divided into a number of columns. It is used to transfer the account balances in the general ledger to the income statement, statement of retained earnings, and balance sheet in a systematic fashion.

A work sheet is certainly useful in preparing these three financial statements, but it is not necessary. The financial statements can be prepared without it. Nevertheless, work sheets of many kinds are important in the everyday practice of accounting.

UNADJUSTED TRIAL BALANCE

Transferring the ledger account balances to the financial statements begins by simply copying the general ledger account names in the column at the far left of the work sheet. Asset account names are usually listed first, followed by liability and stockholders' equity accounts, dividend accounts, revenue accounts, and expense accounts, in that order. The account balances from the ledger are then copied next to the account names in the adjoining two columns: debit balances on the left and credit balances on the right. The result (Step 6 in the accounting cycle) is called the **unadjusted trial balance.** Figure 4A–4 shows the unadjusted trial balance for Kimberly Company on an incomplete work sheet.

Note the order of the accounts in the unadjusted trial balance and that asset, dividend, and expense accounts have debit balances, while liability, stockholders' equity, and revenue accounts have credit balances. Keep in mind that these balances reflect the activities of Kimberly Company up to December 31, 2003, which have been journalized and posted in the ledger accounts. Note also that total debits ($42,000) on the unadjusted trial balance are equal to total credits ($42,000). If they are not equal, an error has occurred somewhere in the cycle.

ADJUSTING ENTRIES

In Step 7 of the accounting cycle, the unadjusted trial balance is adjusted to capture certain relevant economic events that are not normally recorded as they occur during the accounting period. Examples include year-end accruals and cost expirations. Assume that Kimberly Company recorded one of each on December 31, 2003—$400 of prepaid rent was expired during 2003, and $300 of salaries were payable as of December 31, 2003. The journal entries, which would be recorded in the journal and posted in the ledger, are provided and on the next page.

a. **Rent Expense (E, −SE)**   **400**
   Prepaid Rent (−A)   **400**
   Expired prepaid rent.

FIGURE 4A–4 Unadjusted trial balance for Kimberly Company (incomplete work sheet)

Kimberly Company
Work Sheet
For the Year Ended December 31, 2003

ACCOUNTS	UNADJUSTED TRIAL BALANCE DR.	CR.	ADJUSTING ENTRIES DR.	CR.	ADJUSTED TRIAL BALANCE DR.	CR.	CLOSING ENTRIES DR.	CR.	FINAL TRIAL BALANCE DR.	CR.
ASSETS										
Cash	11,900									
Accounts receivable	3,000									
Prepaid rent	500									
Land	22,300									
LIABILITIES										
Salaries payable										
Notes payable		4,000								
STOCKHOLDERS' EQUITY										
Common stock		26,000								
Retained earnings		5,000								
Dividends	1,000									
REVENUES										
Service revenue		7,000								
EXPENSES										
Salary expense	2,700									
Rent expense										
Insurance expense	100									
Interest expense	500									
Total	42,000	42,000								

b. **Salary Expense (E, −SE)**   300
    Salaries Payable (+L)   300
    Accrued salaries payable.

These entries would be recorded on the work sheet under "Adjusting Entries" in the manner illustrated in Figure 4A–5.

ADJUSTED TRIAL BALANCE

After entering the adjusting entries on the work sheet, the **adjusted trial balance** (Step 8) can be prepared. These columns simply result from adding the debits and credits from the adjusting entries to the debit and credit balances from the unadjusted trial balance. The resulting balance

FIGURE 4A–5 Adjusted trial balance for Kimberly Company (incomplete work sheet)

Kimberly Company
Work Sheet
For the Year Ended December 31, 2003

ACCOUNTS	UNADJUSTED TRIAL BALANCE DR.	CR.	ADJUSTING ENTRIES DR.	CR.	ADJUSTED TRIAL BALANCE DR.	CR.	CLOSING ENTRIES DR.	CR.	FINAL TRIAL BALANCE DR.	CR.
ASSETS										
Cash	11,900				11,900					
Accounts receivable	3,000				3,000					
Prepaid rent	500			(a) 400	100					
Land	22,300				22,300					
LIABILITIES										
Salaries payable				(b) 300		300				
Notes payable		4,000				4,000				
STOCKHOLDERS' EQUITY										
Common stock		26,000				26,000				
Retained earnings		5,000				5,000				
Dividends	1,000				1,000					
REVENUES										
Service revenue		7,000				7,000				
EXPENSES										
Salary expense	2,700		(b) 300		3,000					
Rent expense			(a) 400		400					
Insurance expense	100				100					
Interest expense	500				500					
Total	42,000	42,000	700	700	42,300	42,300				

for each account is carried over to the two columns to the right of the adjusting entries. Once again, the total dollar amount in the debit column equals the total dollar amount in the credit column. Figure 4A–5 shows the adjusted trial balance for Kimberly Company.

CLOSING ENTRIES AND THE CLOSING PROCESS

In the closing process (Step 9), the dollar balances in the revenue, expense, and dividend accounts are transferred, or *closed,* to the retained earnings account. Since this process is often difficult for students to understand, we first explain why closing is necessary, then distinguish permanent from temporary accounts, and finally describe and illustrate the actual procedures involved.

WHY IS CLOSING NECESSARY? Assume that Jenotech, Inc., (1) sold services for $500 cash, (2) paid $300 cash for miscellaneous expenses, and (3) paid a $100 cash dividend. These transactions would be recorded in the journal as follows.

1. **Cash (+A)**   500
       Fees Earned (R, +SE)   500
       Received cash for services provided.
2. **Miscellaneous Expenses (E, −SE)**   300
       Cash (−A)   300
       Paid cash for expenses.
3. **Dividend (−SE)**   100
       Cash (−A)   100
       Paid cash dividend.

Consider how these transactions affect the balance sheet and the accounting equation: assets = liabilities + stockholders' equity. Each involves cash and, accordingly, either increases or decreases assets. The accounts named *Fees Earned, Miscellaneous Expenses,* and *Dividends,* however, do not appear on the balance sheet. How are they handled so that the equality of the balance sheet and the accounting equation are maintained?

Until now we have answered this question by simply stating that retained earnings, which is part of stockholders' equity, is the net accumulation of past revenues, expenses, and dividends and is therefore adjusted when revenues, expenses, and dividends are recognized: revenues increase retained earnings, while expenses and dividends decrease retained earnings. These three transactions, therefore, would affect the accounting equation and the balance sheet as shown in Figure 4A–6.

FIGURE 4A–6 Revenues, expenses, dividends, and the accounting equation	Assets = Liabilities + Common Stock + Retained Earnings
	(1) +500 = +500
	(2) −300 = −300
	(3) −100 = −100

From a procedural standpoint, if revenues, expenses, and dividends are to be reflected on the balance sheet and, in the process, maintain the equality of the accounting equation, we need a method of transferring the end-of-period balances in the revenue, expense, and dividend accounts to the retained earnings account. This method is known as the *closing process.*

PERMANENT AND TEMPORARY ACCOUNTS. The need to transfer revenues, expenses, and dividends to retained earnings introduces an important distinction among the accounts on the financial statements. The balance sheet accounts (assets, liabilities, and stockholders' equities) are called *permanent accounts*; the income statement and dividend accounts (revenues, expenses, and dividends) are called *temporary accounts.* **Permanent accounts** have balances that accumulate from one accounting period to the next. The balance sheet, which consists of permanent accounts, reflects transactions that have occurred since a company's inception. It is a statement of a company's accumulated financial condition as of a particular point in time.

Temporary accounts accumulate only throughout a single period. At the end of that period their balances are reduced to zero, where they begin the next accounting period. For example, the income statement, which consists of temporary accounts, reflects transactions from only a single period.

The distinction between permanent and temporary accounts is at the heart of the closing process, in which a series of journal entries transfers the balances in the revenue, expense, and dividend accounts to the retained earnings account. The balances in the temporary accounts are zeroed out and transferred to a permanent balance sheet account, where they are accumulated.

THE PROCEDURES OF THE CLOSING PROCESS. The closing process consists of four basic steps:

1. *Create an income summary account.* A ledger T-account, called **Income Summary,** is created solely to execute the closing process.
2. *Close the revenue and expense accounts to Income Summary.* A series of **closing entries** transfers the balances in the revenue and expense accounts to the income summary account and sets the new balances in the revenue and expense accounts to zero.
3. *Close the income summary account to Retained Earnings.* A single journal entry closes the income summary account to Retained Earnings. As in the previous step, this entry simply transfers the balance in the income summary account to the retained earnings account and brings the income summary balance to zero.
4. *Close the dividends account to Retained Earnings.* A single entry closes the dividends account directly to Retained Earnings. Once again, the entry sets the dividends account to zero by transferring its balance to the retained earnings account.

Figure 4A–7 shows the procedures to close the revenue, expense, and dividend accounts for Kimberly Company at the end of 2003. The balances in the revenue, expense, dividend, and retained earnings accounts from the adjusted trial balance are indicated by *italics*. In Step 1, an income summary account is created. In Step 2, closing journal entry (1) debits Service Revenue for $7,000 and credits each expense account (Salary, Rent, Insurance, and Interest) for the amount of expense recognized during the year. When this entry is posted in the ledger, it brings the balances in the revenue and expense accounts to zero. In addition, this entry requires a credit of $3,000 to make the total credits equal the $7,000 debit. This amount is recorded in the income summary account and represents the dollar amount of the difference between the rev-

FIGURE 4A–7
 	
Kimberly
Company: The
closing process
	Step 1: Create income summary account.
	Step 2: Close revenue and expense accounts to income summary account.
	    Journal entry: (1) Service Revenue **7,000**
	                    Salary Expense **3,000**
	                    Rent Expense **400**
	                    Insurance Expense **100**
	                    Interest Expense **500**
	                    Income Summary (plug) **3,000**
	Step 3: Close income summary account to retained earnings account.
	    Journal entry: (2) Income Summary **3,000**
	                    Retained Earnings **3,000**
	Step 4: Close dividends account to retained earnings account.
	    Journal entry: (3) Retained Earnings **1,000**
	                    Dividends **1,000**

GENERAL LEDGER

Service Revenue		Salary Expense		Rent Expense		Insurance Expense	
(1) 7,000	*7,000*	*3,000*	(1) 3,000	*400*	(1) 400	*100*	(1) 100
	0	**0**		**0**		**0**	

Interest Expense		Income Summary		Dividends		Retained Earnings	
500	(1) 500	(2) 3,000	(1) 3,000	*1,000*	(3) 1,000		*5,000*
0			**0**	**0**		(3) 1,000	(2) 3,000
							7,000

enues and expenses recognized during the year, which incidentally is Kimberly's net income for 2003.

In Step 3, closing journal entry (2) is prepared, which, when posted to the ledger, brings the balance in the income summary account to zero and transfers $3,000 to Retained Earnings. Thus, it transfers the net amount of revenues and expenses (net income) to the retained earnings account. In Step 4, closing journal entry (3) is prepared, which, when posted, brings the balance in the dividend account to zero and reduces Retained Earnings by $1,000. Note that the ending balance in the Retained Earnings T-account ($7,000) is computed by adding net income ($3,000) to the beginning balance of retained earnings ($5,000) and subtracting the dividend ($1,000). This computation is exactly what appears on the statement of retained earnings.

Figure 4A–7 shows only the closing entries recorded in the journal and ledger. However, as the accounting cycle in Figure 4A–8 indicates, these entries are recorded first on the work

FIGURE 4A–8 Completed work sheet for Kimberly Company

Kimberly Company
Work Sheet
For the Year Ended December 31, 2003

ACCOUNT	UNADJUSTED TRIAL BALANCE DR.	CR.	ADJUSTING ENTRIES DR.	CR.	ADJUSTED TRIAL BALANCE DR.	CR.	CLOSING ENTRIES DR.	CR.	FINAL TRIAL BALANCE DR.	CR.
ASSETS										
Cash	11,900				11,900				11,900	
Accounts receivable	3,000				3,000				3,000	
Prepaid rent	500			(a) 400	100				100	
Land	22,300				22,300				22,300	
LIABILITIES										
Salaries payable				(b) 300		300				300
Notes payable		4,000				4,000				4,000
STOCKHOLDERS' EQUITY										
Common stock		26,000				26,000				26,000
Retained earnings		5,000				5,000	(3) 1,000	(2) 3,000		7,000
Dividends	1,000				1,000			(3) 1,000	0	
REVENUES										
Service revenue		7,000				7,000	(1) 7,000			0
EXPENSES										
Salary expense	2,700		(b) 300		3,000			(1) 3,000		0
Rent expense			(a) 400		400			(1) 400		0
Insurance expense	100				100			(1) 100	0	
Interest expense	500				500			(1) 500	0	
Income summary							(2) 3,000	(1) 3,000	0	
Total	42,000	42,000	700	700	42,300	42,300	11,000	11,000	37,300	37,300

sheet in the debit and credit columns to the right of the adjusted trial balance. When the work sheet is complete, these entries are recorded in the journal and posted to the ledger. The completed work sheet for Kimberly appears in Figure 4A–8.

THE FINAL TRIAL BALANCE

After the closing entries have been recorded on the work sheet and all the temporary accounts have zero balances, the only remaining balances are in the permanent asset, liability, and stockholders' equity accounts. In Figure 4A–8, these balances are carried to the **final trial balance** (Step 10). Asset accounts typically carry debit balances in the final trial balance, while liability and stockholders' equity accounts normally carry credit balances. Total debits ($37,300) will equal total credits ($37,300) if the entries have been recorded correctly.

Preparation of the Financial Statements

Preparing the income statement, statement of retained earnings, balance sheet, and statement of cash flows (Steps 13 to 16) at this point is a very straightforward procedure. Each statement comes directly from a segment of the accounting cycle.

THE INCOME STATEMENT

The income statement can be prepared directly from either the journal entry that closes the revenue and expense accounts (Figure 4A–7, journal entry [1]) or the closing entries on the completed work sheet (Figure 4A–8). These entries correspond to those on the income statement. The dollar amount initially recorded in the income summary account is equal to net income. Figure 4A–9 presents the income statement of Kimberly Company.

FIGURE 4A–9	Kimberly Company
Income statement for Kimberly Company	Income Statement
	For the Year Ended December 31, 2003

Service revenue		$7,000
Expenses:		
Salaries	$3,000	
Rent	400	
Insurance	100	
Interest	500	
Total expenses		4,000
Net income		$3,000

THE STATEMENT OF RETAINED EARNINGS

The statement of retained earnings can be prepared directly from the retained earnings T-account in the general ledger. Recall the reconciliation format of this statement: beginning balance, plus (minus) net income (net loss), less dividends, equals ending balance. The beginning balance of Retained Earnings for the current period is the dollar amount of retained earnings that appears on the previous balance sheet ($5,000). The entry to close the Income Summary to Retained Earnings represents the adjustment for net income ($3,000). The entry to close the dividends account to Retained Earnings reduces Retained Earnings in the amount of the dividend ($1,000). The ending balance in the retained earnings T-account, which also appears in the end-of-period balance sheet, is the net result of these adjustments. The statement of retained earnings for Kimberly Company appears in Figure 4A–10.

FIGURE 4A–10

Statement of
retained earnings
for Kimberly
Company

Kimberly Company
Statement of Retained Earnings
For the Year Ended December 31, 2003

Beginning retained earnings balance	$5,000
Plus: Net income	3,000
Less: Dividends	(1,000)
Ending retained earnings balance	$7,000

THE BALANCE SHEET

The balance sheet is prepared from the ending balances in the permanent asset, liability, and stockholders' equity accounts. These balances appear in the ledger and in the final trial balance on the work sheet. Figure 4A–11 shows the balance sheet of Kimberly Company.

FIGURE 4A–11

Kimberly Company
balance sheet

Kimberly Company
Balance Sheet
December 31, 2003

ASSETS		LIABILITIES AND STOCKHOLDERS' EQUITY	
Cash	$11,900	Salaries payable	$ 300
Accounts receivable	3,000	Notes payable	4,000
Prepaid rent	100	Common stock	26,000
Land	22,300	Retained earnings	7,000
		Total liabilities and	
Total assets	$37,300	stockholders' equity	$37,300

THE STATEMENT OF CASH FLOWS

The statement of cash flows can be prepared from the cash account in the ledger. Entries on the left of the cash T-account (debits) indicate cash inflows; entries on the right (credits) indicate cash outflows. Recall that the statement of cash flows is organized into three categories: cash flows from operating activities, from investing activities, and from financing activities. To prepare the statement, each of the cash inflows and outflows in the ledger must be placed in one of these three categories.

A statement of cash flows is not prepared for Kimberly Company because we do not provide the cash T-account. However, the next section provides a comprehensive example of the accounting cycle, including the preparation of the statement of cash flows.

A COMPREHENSIVE EXAMPLE OF THE ACCOUNTING CYCLE

In this comprehensive example of the entire accounting cycle, Figure 4A–12 represents the journal, containing eleven entries recorded during the accounting period (2003) and three closing entries recorded at the end of 2003. Figure 4A–13 represents the ledger, which contains a T-account for each financial statement account. Figure 4A–14 shows the work sheet, income statement, statement of retained earnings, balance sheet, and statement of cash flows.

The ledger indicates that ABC company began operations in 2003 with beginning balances in its asset, liability, and stockholders' equity accounts. For example, $600 was in the cash

FIGURE 4A-12 Comprehensive example: General journal entries

Entry	Date	Journal Entry			Description of Transaction
(1)	1/4/03	Accounts Receivable (+A)	300		*Provided services on account.*
		Service Revenue (R, +SE)		300	
(2)	1/7/03	Misc. Payable (−L)	50		*Paid misc. payable.*
		Cash (−A)		50	
(3)	1/8/03	Cash (+A)	500		*Provided service for cash.*
		Service Revenue (R, +SE)		500	
(4)	1/18/03	Cash (+A)	200		*Received payment on*
		Accounts Receivable (−A)		200	*outstanding receivable.*
(5)	1/20/03	Notes Payable (−L)	100		*Paid outstanding notes payable.*
		Cash (−A)		100	
(6)	1/22/03	Land (+A)	700		*Purchased two parcels of land*
		Cash (−A)		300	*for cash and signed a note*
		Notes Payable (+L)		400	*payable for balance.*
(7)	1/26/03	Interest Expense (E, −SE)	40		*Paid interest on notes payable.*
		Cash (−A)		40	
(8)	1/27/03	Cash (+A)	1,000		*Issued stock for cash.*
		Common Stock (+SE)		1,000	
(9)	1/29/03	Salary Expense (E, −SE)	350		*Paid salaries and other*
		Other Expenses (E, −SE)	200		*expenses.*
		Cash (−A)		550	
(10)	1/29/03	Cash (+A)	420		*Sold one parcel of land which*
		Land (−A)		350	*cost $350.*
		Gain on Sale (Ga, +SE)		70	
(11)	1/30/03	Dividends (−SE)	100		*Declared dividends to be paid*
		Dividends Payable (+L)		100	*in February.*
		Closing Entries			
(12)	1/31/03	Service Revenue	800		*Closed revenues and expenses to*
		Gain on Sale	70		*Income Summary.*
		Interest Expense		40	
		Salary Expense		350	
		Other Expenses		200	
		Income Summary		280	
(13)	1/31/03	Income Summary	280		*Closed Income Summary to*
		Retained Earnings		280	*Retained Earnings.*
(14)	1/31/03	Retained Earnings	100		*Closed Dividends to Retained*
		Dividends		100	*Earnings.*

account, $300 in Accounts Receivable, and a $400 (credit) balance in Retained Earnings. The beginning balances in the revenue, expense, and dividend accounts are zero because they were closed at the end of the previous accounting period (2002).

The journal entries numbered (1)–(11) represent the exchange transactions entered into by ABC during the month of January. Note that each entry has been posted in the ledger and is coded by an entry number. At the end of January, the ledger balances are totaled and transferred to the work sheet in the form of an unadjusted trial balance. We assume no adjustments, so the adjusted trial balance is the same as the unadjusted trial balance.

> FIGURE 4A–13 Comprehensive example: General ledger

ASSET ACCOUNTS

	Cash				Accounts Receivable				Land		
	600				300				1,500		
(3)	500	(2)	50	(1)	300	(4)	200	(6)	700	(10)	350
(4)	200	(5)	100		400				1,850		
		(6)	300								
		(7)	40								
(8)	1,000	(9)	550								
(10)	420										
	1,680										

LIABILITY AND STOCKHOLDERS' EQUITY ACCOUNTS

	Miscellaneous Payable				Dividends Payable				Notes Payable				Common Stock		
			100	(11)	100						400				1,500
(2)	50							(5)	100	(6)	400			(8)	1,000
			50				100				700				2,500

	Retained Earnings		
			400
		(13)	280
(14)	100		
			580

TEMPORARY ACCOUNTS

	Service Revenue				Interest Expense				Salary Expense		
		(1)	300	(7)	40			(9)	350		
		(3)	500			(12)	40			(12)	350
(12)	800										
			0		0				0		

	Other Expenses				Gain on Sale				Dividends				Income Summary		
(9)	200					(10)	70	(11)	100					(12)	280
		(12)	200	(12)	70					(14)	100	(13)	280		
	0						0		0				0		

The journal entries to close the temporary accounts (Revenues, Expenses, and Dividends) are numbered (12), (13), and (14) in the journal. These entries have been posted to the ledger and are also indicated on the work sheet. In entry (12) the revenue and expense accounts are closed to Income Summary. Entry (13) closes Income Summary to Retained Earnings, and entry (14) closes Dividends to Retained Earnings.

The income statement comes directly from journal entry (12), where the revenue and expense accounts are closed to Income Summary. The statement of retained earnings is simply a statement of the retained earnings T-account, and the final trial balance on the work sheet

FIGURE 4A–14 Comprehensive example: Work sheet and financial statements

ABC Company
Work Sheet
For the Year Ended January 31, 2003

ACCOUNT	UNADJUSTED TRIAL BALANCE DR.	UNADJUSTED TRIAL BALANCE CR.	ADJUSTING ENTRIES DR.	ADJUSTING ENTRIES CR.	ADJUSTED TRIAL BALANCE DR.	ADJUSTED TRIAL BALANCE CR.	CLOSING ENTRIES DR.	CLOSING ENTRIES CR.	FINAL TRIAL BALANCE DR.	FINAL TRIAL BALANCE CR.
ASSETS										
Cash	1,680				1,680				1,680	
Accounts receivable	400				400				400	
Land	1,850				1,850				1,850	
LIABILITIES										
Misc. payable		50				50				50
Dividends payable		100				100				100
Notes payable		700				700				700
STOCKHOLDERS' EQUITY										
Common stock		2,500				2,500				2,500
Retained earnings		400				400	(14) 100	(13) 280		580
Dividends	100				100			(14) 100		
REVENUES										
Service revenue		800				800	(12) 800			
Gain on sale		70				70	(12) 70			
EXPENSES										
Interest expense	40				40			(12) 40		
Salary expense	350				350			(12) 350		
Other expense	200				200			(12) 200		
Income summary							(13) 280	(12) 280		
Total	4,620	4,620	0	0	4,620	4,620	1,250	1,250	3,930	3,930

ABC Company
Income Statement
For the Period Ended January 31, 2003

Service revenue	$800
Gain on sale	70
Interest expense	(40)
Salary expense	(350)
Other expenses	(200)
Net income	$280

See closing entry (12).

ABC Company
Statement of Retained Earnings
For the Period Ended January 31, 2003

Beginning retained earnings balance	$400
Plus: Net income	280
Less: Dividends	(100)
Ending retained earnings balance	$580

See Retained Earnings T-account.

(continues next page)

> **FIGURE 4A-14** Comprehensive example: Work sheet and financial statements (*continued*)

ABC Company
Balance Sheet
January 31, 2003

ASSETS		LIABILITIES AND STOCKHOLDERS' EQUITY	
Cash	$1,680	Miscellaneous payable	$ 50
Accounts receivable	400	Dividends payable	100
Land	1,850	Notes payable	700
		Common stock	2,500
		Retained earnings	580
Total assets	$3,930	Total liabilities and stockholders' equity	$3,930

See final balances in asset, liability, and stockholders' equity accounts and final trial balance.

ABC Company
Statement of Cash Flows
For the Period Ended January 31, 2003

Operating activities:		
Cash collections from services	$ 500	
Cash from receivables	200	
Cash payments on misc. payables	(50)	
Cash payments for interest	(40)	
Cash payments for salaries	(350)	
Cash payments for other expenses	(200)	
Net cash increase (decrease) from operating activities		$ 60
Investing activities:		
Cash payments for land	$ (300)	
Cash proceeds from sale of land	420	
Net cash increase (decrease) from investing activities		120
Financing activities:		
Cash collections from issuing stock	$1,000	
Cash payments on notes payable	(100)	
Net cash increase (decrease) from financing activities		900
Net increase (decrease) in cash balance		$1,080
Beginning cash balance		600
Ending cash balance		$1,680

See cash T-account.

provides the data needed for the balance sheet. The statement of cash flows was prepared by categorizing the entries to the cash T-account as operating, investing, and financing. It may be helpful at this point to return to Figure 4A–1, the accounting cycle, and attempt to trace each of the sixteen steps in this comprehensive example. Also, make doubly sure that you are comfortable with the construction of journal entries. As this example illustrates, an error in a journal entry carries through the entire accounting cycle and is reflected in the financial statements.

APPENDIX 4B

MECHANICS—A USER'S PERSPECTIVE

Chapter 4 and Appendix 4A covered accounting mechanics from an economic consequence perspective. That is, we have discussed and illustrated how economic events affect the financial statements. Managers need such understanding to assess in advance the financial statement effects and associated economic consequences of transactions under their consideration. To be astute financial statement users, managers need an additional skill—one that involves working backward from the financial statements to identify underlying economic events. When evaluating solvency, earning power, and the quality of a company's management, it is often useful to be able to infer information that is not directly disclosed.

T-account analysis is employed by many financial statement users to infer economic events from the financial statements. It is a mechanical process that involves examining the activity in a given T-account to acquire information that is not directly disclosed on the financial statements or footnotes. Consider, for example, a situation where a financial statement user is analyzing the financial statements of Wildcat Industries, which are provided in Figure 4B–2.

Assume that the user is interested in the amount of cash paid during 2003 for salaries, information that is not disclosed anywhere on the financial statements. T-account analysis, as illustrated in Figure 4B–1, involves constructing a T-account for Salaries Payable and analyzing the activity in that account during 2003. Note first that the beginning and ending balances are $7,000 and $9,000, respectively, amounts that appear on the 2002 and 2003 balance sheets. Since salaries are accrued, the dollar amount for Salary Expense on the income statement indicates that during 2003 the salaries payable account must have been increased by $4,000. The entry to the left side of the T-account, therefore, must have been $2,000, the amount of cash paid for salaries during 2003. This $2,000 is disclosed nowhere on the financial statements (it is buried inside net cash provided by operating activities), yet it may be useful in assessing solvency and earning power.

In a second example, assume that the user is interested in the dollar amount of inventory purchased during 2003, additional information—not disclosed directly on the financial statements—that may be useful in assessing solvency and earning power. In this case, T-account analysis involves analyzing the activity in the inventory account, as shown in Figure 4B–3. Once again, the beginning and ending balances ($15,000 and $18,000, respectively) come

FIGURE 4B–1
T-account analysis of salaries payable account

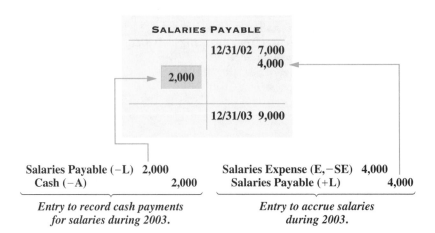

Entry to record cash payments for salaries during 2003.   *Entry to accrue salaries during 2003.*

FIGURE 4B–2

Financial
statements for
Wildcat Industries

Wildcat Industries
Abbreviated Financial Statements
For the Years Ended December 31, 2003 and 2002

	2003	2002
BALANCE SHEET		
ASSETS		
Cash	$ 4,000	$ 7,000
Accounts receivable	15,000	12,000
Inventory	18,000	15,000
Prepaid rent	5,000	3,000
Equipment	50,000	40,000
Less: Accumulated depreciation	(10,000)	(5,000)
Total assets	$82,000	$72,000
LIABILITIES AND STOCKHOLDERS' EQUITY		
Accounts payable	$ 8,000	$ 4,000
Salaries payable	9,000	7,000
Dividends payable	2,000	3,000
Unearned revenue	5,000	8,000
Long-term debt	35,000	30,000
Common stock	15,000	15,000
Retained earnings	8,000	5,000
Total liabilities and stockholders' equity	$82,000	$72,000

INCOME STATEMENT	
Revenues	$52,000
Less:	
Cost of goods sold	(30,000)
Salaries expense	(4,000)
Rent expense	(6,000)
Depreciation expense	(6,000)
Loss on sale of equipment	(1,000)
Net income	$ 5,000

STATEMENT OF RETAINED EARNINGS	
Beginning retained earnings balance (12/31/02)	$ 5,000
Plus: Net income	5,000
Less: Dividends	(2,000)
Ending retained earnings balance (12/31/03)	$ 8,000

STATEMENT OF CASH FLOWS	
Net cash provided by operating activities	$ 7,000
Net cash used by investing activities	(7,000)
Net cash used by financing activities	(3,000)
Change in cash balance	$ (3,000)
Beginning cash balance (12/31/02)	7,000
Ending cash balance (12/31/03)	$ 4,000

FIGURE 4B–3

T-account analysis
of inventory
account

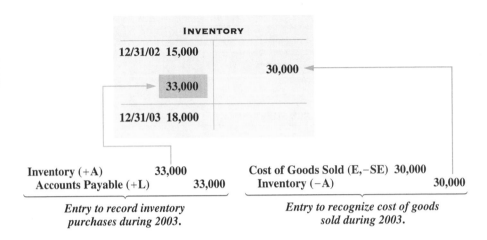

Inventory (+A)   33,000
    Accounts Payable (+L)   33,000

*Entry to record inventory
purchases during 2003.*

Cost of Goods Sold (E,–SE) 30,000
    Inventory (–A)   30,000

*Entry to recognize cost of goods
sold during 2003.*

directly from the 2002 and 2003 balance sheets. Since Cost of Goods Sold on the income statement represents the outflow of sold inventory, the inventory account must have been reduced
by $30,000 during 2003. Inventory purchases, therefore, must have been $33,000.

In the final example, assume that a user noticed on the income statement that Wildcat
incurred a $1,000 loss on the sale of equipment and was interested in reconstructing the trans-
action that produced that loss. Assume also that the footnotes indicate that Wildcat acquired
equipment at a cost of $15,000 during 2003. In this case, T-account analysis involves analyzing
both the Equipment and the Accumulated Depreciation accounts, as illustrated in Figure 4B–4.

As in the previous examples, the beginning and ending balances in the equipment and accumulated depreciation T-accounts come directly from the 2002 and 2003 balance sheets. The
footnotes indicate that Wildcat acquired equipment at a cost of $15,000, which explains the
$15,000 entry to the left (debit) side of the equipment account. Therefore, Wildcat must have
sold equipment with a cost of $5,000 during 2003. The income statement shows depreciation
expense of $6,000, which means that the accumulated depreciation T-account must have been
credited by $6,000 during 2003. To make this account balance, it must have been reduced by
$1,000, the amount of accumulated depreciation associated with the equipment that was sold
during 2003. Finally, the loss on the sale of equipment comes from the income statement, and
to make the journal entry balance, cash of $3,000 must have been received in the exchange.

In each of the three examples above, information not directly disclosed on the financial
statements was derived through a technique called T-account analysis, which normally includes
the following four steps.

1. One or more balance sheet accounts are identified for analysis depending on what the user
    wishes to learn.
2. T-accounts are created for each account, and the beginning and ending balances are taken
    directly from the balance sheets.
3. Additional information from various sources is used to recreate the activity (increases or
    decreases) that explains the change in the T-account balance. Sometimes the information
    can be found in the footnotes, and sometimes it is contained in the other financial state-
    ments. Often, the information is disclosed on the income statement, which includes certain
    accounts closely related to the T-accounts under analysis. For example, Salaries Expense is
    closely related to Salaries Payable; Cost of Goods Sold is closely related to Inventory; and
    Depreciation Expense is closely related to Accumulated Depreciation. These accounts are
    closely related because they often appear in the same journal entry. By recreating this jour-
    nal entry, the user can determine a portion of the activity in the T-account under analysis.
4. Given the information compiled in steps 1–3, the missing part of the activity in the T-
    account can be inferred because it represents the dollar amount needed to complete the
    explanation of the change in the T-account balance.

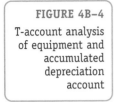

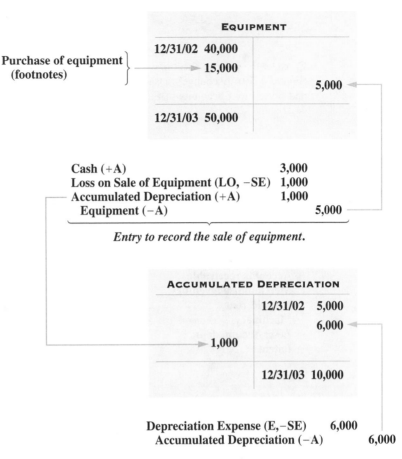

EQUIPMENT

12/31/02 40,000	
15,000	
	5,000
12/31/03 50,000	

Purchase of equipment (footnotes)

Cash (+A)   3,000
Loss on Sale of Equipment (LO, −SE)   1,000
Accumulated Depreciation (+A)   1,000
   Equipment (−A)   5,000

Entry to record the sale of equipment.

ACCUMULATED DEPRECIATION

	12/31/02 5,000
	6,000
1,000	
	12/31/03 10,000

Depreciation Expense (E,−SE)   6,000
   Accumulated Depreciation (−A)   6,000

Entry to depreciate equipment.

   In this section, we have only introduced T-account analysis and shown how it can be used to produce useful information in three relatively simple cases. It can involve highly sophisticated procedures, and for most accounting students it is a difficult concept that requires time, effort, practice, and experience before it can be mastered. The remainder of this textbook provides a number of opportunities to learn more about this technique and to practice it because it can significantly improve your ability to learn as much as possible from the financial statements.

Consider the balance sheet of a small retail company, Kelly Supply, as of December 31, 2002 (Figure 4–19). Exchange transactions that occurred during 2003 are recorded in Figure 4–20 and posted to T-accounts in Figure 4–21. The financial statements are contained in Figures 4–22 and 4–23.

FIGURE 4–19 Balance sheet for Kelly Supply	**Kelly Supply** **Balance Sheet** **December 31, 2002**

ASSETS			LIABILITIES AND STOCKHOLDERS' EQUITY	
Cash		$12,000	Accounts payable	$ 8,000
Accounts receivable		15,000	Wages payable	3,000
Merchandise inventory		12,000	Interest payable	1,000
Prepaid rent		3,000	Dividends payable	2,000
Machinery	$25,000		Unearned revenue	3,000
Less: Accum. depr.	5,000	20,000	Short-term notes pay.	5,000
Patent		5,000	Long-term notes pay.	10,000
			Common stock	30,000
			Retained earnings	5,000
			Total liabilities and	
Total assets		$67,000	stockholders' equity	$67,000

The December 31, 2002 balance sheet accounts are reflected in the T-accounts as beginning balances. The exchange transactions are numbered (1)–(11), and each is described and has been posted in the T-accounts.

At year-end, the adjusting journal entries are recorded and posted to the T-accounts. Adjusting entries are numbered (12)–(19). Entries (14), (17), and (18) are accruals, and entries (12), (13), (15), (16), and (19) are cost expirations.

The income statement contains revenues and expenses; the statement of retained earnings explains the change in the retained earnings balance; and the balance sheet consists of the ending balances in the asset, liability, and stockholders' equity accounts. The statement of cash flows was prepared directly from the entries in the cash T-account.

FIGURE 4-20 General journal for Kelly Supply

Daily Journal Entries			Adjusting Journal Entries		

Daily Journal Entries

(1) Cash (+A)   10,000
    Accounts Receivable (+A)   15,000
      Sales (R, +SE)   25,000
    Sold merchandise for cash and
    on account.

(2) Cash (+A)   8,000
      Accounts Receivable (−A)   8,000
    Received cash on account.

(3) Merchandise Inventory (+A)   10,000
      Cash (−A)   3,000
      Accounts Payable (+L)   7,000
    Purchased merchandise inventory
    for cash and on account.

(4) Accounts Payable (−L)   10,000
      Cash (−A)   10,000
    Paid cash on account.

(5) Wages Payable (−L)   3,000
    Wage Expense (E, −SE)   7,000
      Cash (−A)   10,000
    Paid accrued wages.

(6) Interest Payable (−L)   1,000
    Interest Expense (E, −SE)   1,000
      Cash (−A)   2,000
    Paid accrued interest.

(7) Short-Term Notes Pay. (−L)   2,500
      Cash (−A)   2,500
    Paid short-term note.

(8) Cash (+A)   10,000
      Long-Term Notes Pay. (+L)   10,000
    Issued long-term note for cash.

(9) Dividends Payable (−L)   2,000
      Cash (−A)   2,000
    Paid cash dividend.

(10) Machinery (+A)   1,000
      Cash (−A)   1,000
    Acquired machinery for cash.

(11) Dividends (−SE)   1,000
      Dividends Payable (+L)   1,000
    Declared dividends.

Adjusting Journal Entries

(12) Cost of Goods Sold (E, −SE)   9,000
      Merchandise Inventory (−A)   9,000
    Recognized $13,000 of inventory
    on hand.

(13) Unearned Revenue (−L)   2,000
      Sales (R, +SE)   2,000
    Recognized 2/3 of goods delivered.

(14) Interest Receivable (+A)   50
      Interest Revenue (R, +SE)   50
    Recognized accrued interest on
    savings account.

(15) Depreciation Expense (E, −SE) 3,000
      Accumulated Depr. (−A)   3,000
    Recognized depreciation on
    machinery.

(16) Amortization Expense (E, −SE)   500
      Patent (−A)   500
    Recognized amortization of patent.

(17) Wage Expense (E, −SE)   1,000
      Wages Payable (+L)   1,000
    Recognized accrued wages.

(18) Interest Expense (E, −SE)   2,000
      Interest Payable (+L)   2,000
    Recognized accrued interest on
    long-term note.

(19) Rent Expense (E, −SE)   1,000
      Prepaid Rent (−A)   1,000
    Recognized 1/3 of rent
    period expired.

FIGURE 4–21 T-accounts for Kelly Supply

Cash				Accounts Receivable				Interest Receivable				Merchandise Inventory	
	12,000				15,000			(14)	50				12,000
(1)	10,000			(1)	15,000							(3)	10,000
(2)	8,000												
		(3)	3,000			(2)	8,000						(12) 9,000
		(4)	10,000										
		(5)	10,000										
		(6)	2,000										
		(7)	2,500										
(8)	10,000	(9)	2,000										
		(10)	1,000										
	9,500				22,000				50				13,000

Prepaid Rent				Machinery				Accumulated Depreciation				Patent			
	3,000	(19)	1,000		25,000						5,000		5,000	(16)	500
				(10)	1,000					(15)	3,000				
	2,000				26,000						8,000		4,500		

Accounts Payable				Wages Payable				Interest Payable				Dividends Payable			
			8,000				3,000				1,000				2,000
		(3)	7,000	(5)	3,000	(17)	1,000	(6)	1,000	(18)	2,000	(9)	2,000	(11)	1,000
(4)	10,000														
			5,000				1,000				2,000				1,000

Unearned Revenue				Short-Term Notes Payable				Long-Term Notes Payable				Common Stock	
			3,000				5,000				10,000		30,000
(13)	2,000			(7)	2,500					(8)	10,000		
			1,000				2,500				20,000		30,000

Retained Earnings			Sales			Interest Revenue		
		5,000			(1) 25,000			(14) 50
					(13) 2,000			

Cost of Goods Sold		Wage Expense		Rent Expense		Interest Expense	
(12)	9,000	(5)	7,000	(19) 1,000		(6) 1,000	
		(17)	1,000			(18) 2,000	

Depreciation Expense		Amortization Expense		Dividends	
(15)	3,000	(16)	500	(11) 1,000	

FIGURE 4–22

Financial statements for Kelly Supply

Kelly Supply
Income Statement
For the Year Ended December 31, 2000

Revenues:		
Sales	$27,000	
Interest revenue	50	
Total revenues		$27,050
Expenses:		
Cost of goods sold	$ 9,000	
Wage expense	8,000	
Rent expense	1,000	
Interest expense	3,000	
Depreciation expense	3,000	
Amortization expense	500	
Total expenses		24,500
Net income		$ 2,550

Kelly Supply
Statement of Retained Earnings
For the Year Ended December 31, 2003

Beginning balance	$5,000
Plus: Net income	2,550
Less: Dividends	(1,000)
Ending balance	$6,550

Kelly Supply
Balance Sheet
December 31, 2003

ASSETS			LIABILITIES AND STOCKHOLDERS' EQUITY	
Cash		$ 9,500	Accounts payable	$ 5,000
Accounts receivable		22,000	Wages payable	1,000
Interest receivable		50	Interest payable	2,000
Merchandise inventory		13,000	Dividends payable	1,000
Prepaid rent		2,000	Unearned revenue	1,000
Machinery	$26,000		Short-term notes pay.	2,500
Less: Accumulated			Long-term notes pay.	20,000
depreciation	8,000	18,000	Common stock	30,000
Patent		4,500	Retained earnings	6,550
			Total liabilities and	
Total assets		$69,050	stockholders' equity	$69,050

FIGURE 4–23
Statement of
cash flows for
Kelly Supply

Kelly Supply
Statement of Cash Flows
For the Year Ended December 31, 2003

Operating activities:		
Collections from sales	$10,000	
Collections of accounts receivable	8,000	
Payments for inventory purchases	(3,000)	
Payments on accounts payable	(10,000)	
Payments for wages	(10,000)	
Payments for interest	(2,000)	
Net cash increase (decrease) from operating activities		$(7,000)
Investing activities:		
Purchase of machinery	$ (1,000)	
Net cash increase (decrease) from investing activities		(1,000)
Financing activities:		
Issuance of long-term notes payable	$10,000	
Payment of dividend	(2,000)	
Principal payments on short-term notes payable	(2,500)	
Net cash increase (decrease) from financing activities		5,500
Net cash increase (decrease) during 2003		$(2,500)
Beginning cash balance (December 31, 2002)		12,000
Ending cash balance (December 31, 2003)		$ 9,500

SUMMARY OF KEY POINTS

The key points of the chapter are summarized below.

○ *Two criteria necessary for economic events to be reflected in the financial statements.*

Economic events must be both relevant and objectively measurable in monetary terms if they are to be reflected on the financial statements. Relevant events have economic significance to the company. Objectively measurable events must be backed by documented evidence. Economic events must be relevant so that they can be used to evaluate the financial condition of the company; they must be objectively measurable so that they can be audited and viewed as credible by users.

○ *The accounting equation and how it relates to the balance sheet, income statement, statement of retained earnings, and statement of cash flows.*

The accounting equation states that assets equal liabilities plus stockholders' equity. The main components of the accounting equation (assets, liabilities, and stockholders' equity) are divided into subcategories, called *accounts,* in which transactions are recorded and from which the financial statements are compiled. When a business transaction occurs, two or more accounts are increased or decreased in such a way as to maintain the equality of the equation.

The balance sheet contains the balances as of a given point in time of all the asset, liability, and stockholders' equity accounts. It is a statement of the accounting equation.

The income statement contains a summary of the operating transactions, measured on an accrual basis, entered into by a company during a period of time. Operating transactions affect asset or liability accounts and always either increase or decrease retained earnings in the stockholders' equity section of the accounting equation.

The statement of retained earnings and the statement of cash flows summarize the transactions that affect the retained earnings and cash accounts, respectively. The statement of retained earnings includes the net effect of the operating transactions as well as asset distributions to stockholders (dividends). The statement of cash flows is composed of cash inflows and outflows and explains the change in the cash account during the period.

○ *Journal entries (and T-accounts) and how they express the effect of economic events on the basic accounting equation and the financial statements.*

Journal entries (and T-accounts) are structured to indicate three aspects about economic events: (1) the accounts affected, (2) the direction of the effect, and (3) the dollar amount of the effect. Increases (decreases) in asset accounts and decreases (increases) in liability and equity accounts are placed on the left (right) side of the entry. Recognized revenues (expenses) are always placed on the right (left) side of the entry because they are always accompanied by increases (decreases) in assets or decreases (increases) in equities, which are indicated on the left (right) side. Following these rules ensures that economic events will be recorded in a way that maintains the equality of the accounting equation, and understanding these rules enables one to efficiently communicate the effects of any economic event on the financial statements.

○ *Why managers need to understand how economic events affect the financial statements.*

Managers often face situations in which they must choose whether to enter into certain transactions or how to structure transactions. Such choices should not be made without considering their economic consequences. The financial statement effects of transactions can lead to important economic consequences because outsiders use financial statement numbers to control and evaluate the firm and its management. Therefore, astute managers must understand in advance how transactions and other economic events affect the financial statements.

○ *Why the financial statements are adjusted periodically to reflect certain economic events.*

A large number of economic events are not represented by exchange transactions (e.g., depreciation of productive assets, and accruals of salaries, interest, and rent), yet they meet the criteria (relevant and objective) for inclusion on the financial statements. These events require that adjustments be made to the financial statements periodically. Normally such adjustments are made to apply the principles of revenue recognition and matching. Revenue recognition states that revenues should be recognized when the earning process is substantially complete, not necessarily when cash is received. Matching states that expenses should be recognized in those periods when the associated benefit (revenue) is realized, not necessarily when cash is paid. These principles are fundamental to an accrual accounting system.

KEY TERMS

Note: Definitions for these terms are provided in the glossary at the end of the text.

Accounting equation (p. 105)
Accounting period (p. 134)
Accrual system of accounting (p. 119)
Accruals (p. 119)
Adjusted trial balance (p. 135)
Amortized (p. 127)
Assets (p. 105)
Book value (p. 127)
Business transactions (p. 106)
Capitalized (p. 122)
Closing entries (p. 138)
Compound journal entries (p. 112)
Contra accounts (p. 127)
Contributed capital (p. 106)
Credit (p. 112)
Debit (p. 112)
Deferral (cost expiration) (p. 122)
Depreciation (p. 127)
Double entry system (p. 112)
Economic events (p. 104)
Expensed (p. 122)
Final trial balance (p. 140)
General journal (p. 132)

General ledger (p. 134)
Income summary (p. 138)
Journal (p. 132)
Journal entries (p. 112)
Journalizing (p. 132)
Ledger (p. 133)
Liabilities (p. 106)
Matching principle (p. 122)
Multinationals (p. 129)
Permanent accounts (p. 137)
Relevant events (p. 104)
Retained earnings (p. 106)
Revaluation adjustments (p. 128)
Stockholders' equity (p. 106)
Straight-line depreciation (p. 128)
Subsidiary ledgers (p. 134)
T-accounts (p. 115)
T-account analysis (p. 146)
Temporary accounts (p. 137)
Unadjusted trial balance (p. 134)
Unearned revenues (p. 126)
Work sheet (p. 134)

ETHICS IN THE REAL WORLD

In an article about the subjectivity involved when deciding to capitalize or expense a cost, *Forbes* (February 24, 1997) reports:

A dollar spent on a toaster doesn't reduce wealth in the same way as one spent on a Twinkie. One lasts, the other doesn't. But where do toasters end and Twinkies begin in [today's] economy? . . . Accountants understand the general problem, but they do not know what to do about it. Capitalizing anything that you can't drop on your foot—software, worker training, America Online's marketing expense—can be hugely speculative. You never find out whether such things have real future value until the future arrives.

A case in point involves Fine Host Corp., who spent huge dollar amounts to obtain new food service contracts. The company listed these costs on the balance sheet and depreciated them over time. In late 1997, the company was accused of aggressive accounting, and the stock price dropped from $12 to $3 per share. *The Wall Street Journal* (February 9, 1998) reported that the food service contract costs should have been accounted for "as current expenses against revenue." Fine Host ended up restating its 1997 net income number, reducing it from $13 million to a loss of almost $18 million.

ETHICAL ISSUE Fine Host management was not convicted, nor even accused, of fraud. The company just subjectively called an asset what many in the financial community considered an expense. Was it ethical for Fine Host to do so? Was management acting in the interests of the stockholders?

INTERNET RESEARCH EXERCISE

The first paragraph of the chapter points out that there are some accounting problems in U.S. federal agencies. The government organization assigned to oversee budgeting and accounting for the federal government is the General Accounting Office (GAO). What is the GAO, what kind of reports does it provide, and how is it organized? Begin your search at **www.gao.gov.**

BRIEF EXERCISES

REAL DATA
BE4–1

Effects of transactions on the accounting equation

During 1999, Intel entered into the transactions listed below.

a.   On a separate sheet of paper, complete the following chart to show the effect of these transactions on the accounting equation and compute the net effect (dollars in millions).

Transaction	Assets = Liabilities + Stockholders' Equity
1. Paid $3,403 to purchase property, plant, and equipment.	
2. Issued common stock for $543.	
3. Recorded depreciation of $3,186.	
Net effect	

b.   Which one of the transactions did not appear to affect the accounting equation? Why didn't it?

REAL DATA
BE4–2

Effects of transactions on the accounting equation

During 1999, The Washington Post Company entered into the transactions listed below.

a.   On a separate sheet of paper, complete the following chart to show the effect of these transactions on the accounting equation and compute the net effect (dollars in millions).

Transaction	Assets = Liabilities + Stockholders' Equity
1. Borrowed $398 from banks, issuing long-term debt.	
2. Paid cash dividends of $53.	
3. Issued common stock for $25.	
4. Paid $425 to reduce long-term debt.	
Net effect	

b.   What was the net effect on the company's long-term debt balance? What two sources could have provided the cash to finance the net effect of these four transactions?

REAL DATA
BE4–3

Effects of transactions on the accounting equation

During 1999, Yahoo, Inc. entered into the transactions listed below.

a.   On a separate sheet of paper, complete the following chart to show the effect of these transactions on the accounting equation and compute the net effect (dollars in millions).

Transaction	Assets = Liabilities + Stockholders' Equity
1. Recognized service revenues of $588 in exchange for accounts receivable.	
2. Paid $214 for sales and marketing.	
3. Issued common stock for $238.	
4. Purchased marketable securities for $998.	
Net effect	

b.   Which of these transactions would be reflected on the income statement? Which of these transactions would be reflected on the statement of cash flows?

EXERCISES

E4–1

Effects of transactions on the accounting equation

On a separate piece of paper, complete the following chart to show the effect of each transaction on the accounting equation.

Transaction	Assets = Liabilities + Stockholders' Equity
1. Owners contributed $30,000 cash.	
2. Purchased land for $20,000 cash.	
3. Borrowed $9,000 cash from bank.	
4. Provided services for $8,000 on account.	
5. Paid $5,500 cash for expenses.	
6. Paid $500 cash dividend to owners.	

E4–2

Effects of transactions on accounts

Consider the same transactions as in E4–1, but this time complete the following chart, using a separate sheet of paper.

	Assets			=	Liabilities	+	Stockholders' Equity	
Trans.	Cash	Accounts Receivable	Land	=	Notes Payable	+	Contributed Capital	Retained Earnings
1.								
2.								
3.								
4.								
5.								
6.								

E4–3

Preparing the financial statements from the accounts

Total each asset, liability, and stockholders' equity account in E4–2, and prepare an income statement, a statement of retained earnings, a balance sheet, and a statement of cash flows. Assume that the current year is the company's first year of operations.

E4–4

Preparing the financial statements

Assume that Cathedral Enterprises, which is in its first year of operations, entered into the following transactions. Show how the five transactions affect the accounting equation, and prepare an income statement, statement of retained earnings, a balance sheet, and a statement of cash flows.

1.   Stockholders contributed $10,000 cash.
2.   Performed services for $8,000, receiving $6,000 in cash and a $2,000 receivable.
3.   Incurred expenses of $6,000. Paid $3,000 in cash, and $3,000 is still payable.
4.   Purchased land for $12,000. Paid $2,000 in cash and signed a long-term note for the remainder.

5.   Paid the stockholders $400 in the form of a dividend.
6.   Sold one-half of the land purchased in (4) for $7,000 cash.

E4–5

Which economic
events are relevant
and objectively
measurable?

The Brown Corporation experienced the following financial events on October 10, 2003:

1.   The company entered into a new contract with the employees' union that calls for a $2.00 per hour increase in wages, a longer lunch break, and cost-of-living adjustments, effective January 1, 2004.
2.   The company issued $200,000 in bonds that mature on October 10, 2013. The terms of the bond issuance stipulate that interest is to be paid semiannually at an annual rate of 10 percent.
3.   The company president retired and was replaced by the vice president of finance.
4.   The company received $10,000 from a customer in settlement of an open account receivable.
5.   The company paid $1,000 interest on an outstanding loan. The interest is applicable to September 2003 and is included on the books as a liability, "Accrued Interest Payable."
6.   The market value of all the company's long-lived assets is $275,000. They are currently reported on the balance sheet at $250,000.
7.   The company purchased a fire insurance policy for $1,500 that will pay the Brown Corporation $1 million if its primary production plant is destroyed. The policy insures the company from November 1, 2003, through October 31, 2004.
8.   The company placed an order to have $10,000 of inventory shipped on October 17, 2003.

Indicate whether each of these economic events has accounting significance (i.e., whether the company would prepare a journal entry for the event). In each case, explain why or why not.

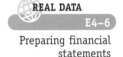
REAL DATA

E4–6

Preparing financial
statements

The following accounts and balances were taken from the records of US Airways (dollars in millions).

Flight equipment	$5,672	Accounts payable	$474
Passenger revenue	7,685	Common stock	101
Retained earnings	(551)	Fuel expense	727
Notes payable	2,113	Other revenues	761
Interest expense	193	Short-term investments	215
Accounts receivable	624	Depreciation expense	401
Dividends	0	Gain on sale of investment	274
Prepaid expenses	265		

Identify each account as an income statement or balance sheet account. Where is each account reflected in the basic accounting equation?

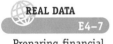
REAL DATA

E4–7

Preparing financial
statements

The following information was taken from the 2000 annual report of Bristol-Myers Squibb, a world-leading drug company (dollars in millions).

Cost of goods sold	$4,759	Cash and equivalents	$3,182
Net cash from operations	4,652	Short-term borrowings	162
Accounts receivable	3,662	Advertising and product expense	1,672
Gain on sale of business	160	Accounts payable	1,702
Net cash from financing	(4,157)	Long-term liabilities	2,766
Stockholders' equity	9,180	Net sales	18,216
Net cash from investing	16	Property, plant, and equipment	4,548
Research and dev. expense	1,939	Other current assets	2,777
Other noncurrent assets	3,206	Other current liabilities	887
Other expenses	1,435	Selling and adm. expenses	3,860
Marketable securities	203	Accrued payables	2,881

Prepare an income statement, balance sheet, and statement of cash flows, and comment on the financial performance and condition of the company.

E4–8

Preparing a statement of cash flows from the cash ledger

The following cash T-account for Miller Manufacturing summarizes all the transactions affecting cash during 2003.

Cash

Beginning balance	9,000	Equipment purchases	24,000
Sales of services	45,000	Rent payable payments	7,000
Receivables collections	50,000	Bank loan principal	12,000
Sale of land	7,500	Loan interest	3,000
Issuance of common stock	15,000	Salaries	26,500
Long-term borrowings	16,000	Dividend payments	4,000
		Miscellaneous expenses	13,000
		Long-term investment purchase	10,000

a. Compute the ending cash balance.
b. Prepare a statement of cash flows.

E4–9

Preparing a statement of cash flows from journal entries

Small and Associates, a small manufacturing firm, entered into the following cash transactions during January of 2003:

1. Issued 600 shares of stock for $25 each.
2. Sold services for $4,000.
3. Paid wages of $1,600.
4. Purchased land as a long-term investment for $9,000 cash.
5. Paid a $2,000 dividend.
6. Sold land with a book value of $3,000 for $3,500 cash.
7. Paid $1,500 to the bank: $900 to reduce the principal on an outstanding loan and $600 as an interest payment.
8. Paid miscellaneous expenses of $1,800.

a. Prepare journal entries for each transaction.
b. Prepare a cash T-account, and compute Small's cash balance as of the end of January. Assume a beginning balance of $5,000.
c. Prepare a statement of cash flows for the month of January.

E4–10

Preparing statements from transactions

The following transactions were entered into by Ed's Lawn Service during 2003, its first year of operations:

1. Collected $12,000 in cash from stockholders.
2. Borrowed $5,000 from a bank.
3. Purchased two parcels of land for a total of $10,000.
4. Paid $5,000 to rent lawn equipment for the remainder of the year.
5. Provided lawn services, receiving $10,000 in cash and $4,000 in receivables.
6. Paid miscellaneous expenses of $4,000.
7. Sold one parcel of land with a cost of $3,000 for $2,800.
8. Paid a $2,200 dividend to the stockholders.

a. In a manner similar to Figure 4–2, show how each transaction affected the fundamental accounting equation and prepare an income statement, a statement of retained earnings, a year-end balance sheet, and a statement of cash flows for 2003.
b. Journalize each transaction and post it in the appropriate T-accounts. From this information, prepare a year-end balance sheet, an income statement, a statement of retained earnings, and a statement of cash flows for 2003.

E4–11

Preparing the statement of cash flows from the cash T-account

The following cash T-account for Holcomb Manufacturing summarizes all the transactions affecting cash during 2003.

Cash

Beginning balance	8,000	Inventory purchases	27,000
Sales of inventories	34,000	Accounts payable payments	7,000
Receivable collections	40,000	Bank loan principal payments	10,000
Sales of long-term investments	12,500	Loan interest	3,000
Issuance of common stock	14,000	Wages	16,000
Long-term borrowings	9,000	Dividend payments	4,000
		Administrative expenses	12,000
		Equipment purchases	11,000

a. Compute the ending cash balance.
b. Prepare a statement of cash flows (direct method).

E4–12

Classifying adjusting
journal entries

Eaton Enterprises made the following adjusting journal entries on December 31, 2002:

1.	Rent Expense	1,200	
	Rent Payable		1,200
2.	Insurance Expense	5,000	
	Prepaid Insurance		5,000
3.	Depreciation Expense	20,000	
	Accumulated Depreciation		20,000
4.	Interest Receivable	1,500	
	Interest Revenue		1,500
5.	Unearned Revenue	200	
	Fees Earned		200

a. Give a brief explanation for each of the above entries.
b. Classify each of the above entries as either a cost expiration adjusting entry or an accrual adjusting entry.

E4–13

Classifying
transactions

Hog Heaven Rib Joint made the following journal entries on December 31, 2002:

1.	Wage Expense	6,000	
	Wages Payable		6,000
2.	Interest Expense	1,000	
	Cash		1,000
3.	Cash	10,500	
	Note Payable		10,500
4.	Rent Expense	1,500	
	Prepaid Rent		1,500
5.	Insurance Expense	2,800	
	Prepaid Insurance		2,800
6.	Cash	2,000	
	Unearned Revenues		2,000
7.	Equipment	9,000	
	Cash		9,000
8.	Supplies Expense	12,000	
	Supplies Inventory		12,000
9.	Accounts Payable	8,000	
	Cash		8,000
10.	Depreciation Expense	13,000	
	Accumulated Depreciation		13,000
11.	Advertising Expense	8,000	
	Cash		8,000
12.	Advertising Expense	3,000	
	Prepaid Advertising		3,000

Place each of the transactions above in one of the following five categories: (1) operating cash flow, (2) investing cash flow, (3) financing cash flow, (4) accrual adjusting journal entry, (5) cost expiration adjusting journal entry.

E4–14

Recognizing accrued wages

The Hurst Corporation pays its employees every Friday for the five-day week just ended. On January 2, 2004, the company paid its employees $70,000 for the week beginning Monday, December 29.

a. Assuming that the employees earned wages evenly throughout the week, prepare any adjusting journal entries that were necessary on December 31, 2003.
b. Prepare the journal entry that would be recorded on Friday, January 2, when the wages are paid.
c. Complete a chart like the following.

	2003	2004	Total
Wage expense			
Cash outflow associated with wages			

d. What is the purpose of the adjusting journal entry on December 31?

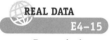

E4–15

Depreciating a fixed asset

At the beginning of 1999, Starbucks purchased equipment costing approximately $90 million. The company used straight-line depreciation and normally depreciates its equipment over three years.

a. Compute the book value of the equipment at the end of each of the three years.
b. Complete a chart like the following.

	1999	2000	2001	Total
Depreciation expense				
Cash outflow associated with the purchase of the equipment				

c. What is the purpose of the adjustments at the end of each period?

E4–16

The difference between accrual and cash accounting

Washington Forest Products began operations on January 1, 2002. On December 31, 2002, the company's accountant ascertains that the following amounts should be reported as expenses on the income statement:

Insurance expense	$20,000
Supplies expense	11,000
Rent expense	14,000

A review of the company's cash disbursements indicates that the company made related cash payments during 2002 as follows:

Insurance	$29,000
Supplies	27,000
Rent	8,000

a. Explain why the amounts shown as expenses do not equal the cash paid.
b. For each expense account, compute the amount that should be in the related balance sheet account as of December 31, 2002. *Hint*: Note that Forest Products began operations on January 1, 2002.

E4–17

The difference between net income and net cash flow from operations

The following journal entries were recorded by Lauren Retailing during the month of July:

1. Cash	**5,000**	
Accounts Receivable	**3,000**	
Sales		**8,000**
2. Cash	**2,000**	
Accounts Receivable		**2,000**
3. Inventory	**5,800**	
Accounts Payable		**5,800**
4. Accounts Payable	**2,800**	
Cash		**2,800**
5. Cost of Goods Sold	**3,700**	
Inventory		**3,700**
6. Accrued Expenses	**2,500**	
Accrued Payables		**2,500**

a. Prepare an income statement and the operating section of a statement of cash flows.
b. Explain why net income is not equal to net cash flow from operations, and reconcile the two numbers.

E4–18

Preparing a statement of cash flows from original transactions

Rahal and Watson, a small manufacturing company, entered into the following cash transactions during January of 2003:

1. Issued 800 shares of common stock for $30 each.
2. Collected $3,900 on outstanding accounts receivable.
3. Paid wages for the month of January of $1,530.
4. Purchased land as a long-term investment for $12,000 cash.
5. Paid a $6,000 dividend.
6. Sold a piece of equipment with a book value of $5,000 for $7,000 cash.
7. Paid $2,000 to the bank: $900 to reduce the principal on an outstanding loan and $1,100 as an interest payment.
8. Paid miscellaneous expenses of $5,000.

a. Prepare a journal entry for each transaction. Indicate the classification and the effect on the accounting equation.
b. Prepare a cash T-account, and compute the company's cash balance as of the end of January. Assume a beginning balance of $4,000.
c. Prepare a statement of cash flows (direct method) for the month of January.

E4–19

Cash and accrual accounting: comparison of performance measures

Peters Company was in business for two years, during which it entered into the following transactions:

Year 1:
1. The owners contributed $24,000 cash.
2. At the beginning of the year, rented a warehouse for two years with a prepaid rent payment of $12,000.
3. Purchased $10,000 of inventory on account.

4. Sold half the inventory for $24,000, receiving $20,000 in cash and an account receivable of $4,000.
5. Paid wages of $6,000 and also accrued wages payable of $4,000.

Year 2:
1. Paid the outstanding balance for the inventory purchased in Year 1.
2. Paid the outstanding wages payable balance.
3. Sold the remaining inventory for $30,000 cash.
4. Received full payment on the outstanding accounts receivable.
5. Incurred and paid wages of $12,000.
6. Returned the cash balance to the owners and shut down operations.

a. Prepare an income statement and a statement of cash flows for both Year 1 and Year 2.
b. Complete a chart like the following.

Performance Measure	Year 1	Year 2	Total
Net income			
Net cash flow from operating activities			

REAL DATA

E4–20

Assessing economic consequences

Condensed balance sheets for 1998 and 1999 and the 1999 income statement for Goodyear, the world's largest tire company, are provided below (dollars in millions).

	1999	1998
Current assets	$ 5,261	$ 4,529
Long-term assets	7,841	6,060
Total assets	$13,102	$10,589
Current liabilities	$3,960	$3,277
Long-term liabilities	5,525	3,568
Stockholders' equity	3,617	3,744
Total liabilities and stockholders' equity	$13,102	$10,589
Revenues	$12,881	
Expenses	12,640	
Net income	$241	

a. Early in 2000, assume that Goodyear is considering the following transactions. Treat each separately and compute how it would affect the company's current ratio and debt/equity ratio.
1. Purchase $1,000 in inventory on account.
2. Issue common stock for $2,000 cash.
3. Refinance a $500 short-term liability with a $500 long-term liability.
4. Purchase equipment in exchange for a $400 long-term note payable.
5. Pay a $1,000 short-term debt with cash.
b. Assume that the terms of Goodyear's long-term debt require the company to maintain a current ratio of 1.2. Is this covenant restriction relevant to whether the company should enter into any of the above transactions? Explain.
c. How much cash could Goodyear pay for a long-term investment and still be in compliance with the covenant?

E4–21

Appendix 4A:
Complete a
work sheet

Balmer and Associates has operated for one year. Its unadjusted trial balance follows.

Account	Unadjusted Trial Balance	
	Debit	**Credit**
Cash	4,200	
Accounts receivable	14,800	
Rent receivable	0	
Inventory	19,000	
Prepaid insurance	1,200	
Office equipment	42,500	
Accumulated depreciation		0
Accounts payable		8,500
Wages payable		0
Bonds payable		25,000
Common stock		35,000
Retained earnings		0
Sales		30,600
Rent revenue		1,100
Cost of goods sold	11,000	
Wage expense	7,500	
Depreciation expense	0	
Insurance expense	0	
Income summary		
	100,200	100,200

The following adjusting journal entries were recorded on December 31, 2003. Journal entry explanations have been omitted.

1.	Rent Receivable	600	
	Rent Revenue		600
2.	Insurance Expense	400	
	Prepaid Insurance		400
3.	Wage Expense	1,200	
	Wages Payable		1,200
4.	Depreciation Expense	2,000	
	Accum. Depr.		2,000

a. Create a work sheet, and transfer the adjusting journal entries to the work sheet.
b. Complete the work sheet and prepare the income statement, statement of retained earnings, balance sheet, and a statement of cash flows using the indirect approach.

E4–22

Appendix 4B:
T-account analysis

Excerpts from the financial statements of Dunbar Manufacturing are provided below.

Wages

Cash payments for wages during 2003	$35,000
Wages payable as of December 31, 2003	17,000
Wage expense on the 2003 income statement	39,000

Rent

Prepaid rent as of December 31, 2002	$12,000
Prepaid rent as of December 31, 2003	15,000
Rent expense on the 2003 income statement	21,000

Accounts Receivable

Cash collected from customers during 2003	$38,000
Accounts receivable as of December 31, 2002	14,000
Sales revenue on the 2003 income statement	45,000

a. Compute the wages payable as of December 31, 2002.
b. Compute the cash payments for rent during 2003.
c. Compute the accounts receivable as of December 31, 2003.

PROBLEMS

P4–1

Journal entries and
the accounting
equation

Below are several transactions entered into by Vulcan Metal Corporation during 2003. Unless otherwise noted, all transactions involve cash.

1. Purchased equipment for $150,000.
2. Paid employees $30,000 in wages.
3. Collected $15,000 from customers as payments on open accounts.
4. Provided services for $24,000: $16,000 received in cash and the remainder on open account.
5. Paid $50,000 on an outstanding note payable: $10,000 for interest and $40,000 to reduce the principal.
6. Purchased a one-month ad in the local newspaper for $5,000.
7. Purchased a building valued at $250,000 in exchange for $130,000 cash and a long-term note payable.
8. Sold investments with a cost of $20,000 for $35,000.

REQUIRED:

Prepare journal entries for each transaction and explain how each affects the accounting equation.

P4–2

T-accounts and the
accounting equation

The following T-accounts reflect seven different transactions that Rodman Container Company entered into during 2003:

Cash					Accounts Receivable					Equipment		
(a)	7,000	(c)	2,000		(a)	21,000	(f)	5,000		(d)	50,000	
(f)	5,000	(d)	20,000									
(g)	25,000	(e)	1,200									

Inventory			Accounts Payable					Notes Payable		
(b)	6,000		(c)	2,000	(b)	6,000			(d)	30,000

Common Stock			Sales Revenue				Rent Expense	
	(g)	25,000		(a)	28,000		(e)	1,200

REQUIRED:

For each transaction, describe what occurred and how it affected the accounting equation.

P4–3

Journal entries and
preparing the four
financial statements

Ryan Hope, controller of Hope, Inc., provides you with the following information concerning Hope during 2003. (Hope, Inc., began operations on January 1, 2003.)

1. Issued 1,000 shares of common stock at $95 per share.
2. Paid $2,600 per month to rent office and warehouse space. The rent was paid on the last day of each month.
3. Made total sales for services of $190,000: $65,000 for cash and $125,000 on account.
4. Purchased land for $32,000.

5. Borrowed $75,000 on December 31. The note payable matures in two years.
6. Salaries totaling $80,000 were paid during the year.
7. Other expenses totaling $40,000 were paid during the year.
8. $56,000 was received from customers as payment on account.
9. Declared and paid a dividend of $26,000.

REQUIRED:
a. Prepare journal entries for these transactions.
b. Establish T-accounts for each account, and post the journal entries to these T-accounts.
c. Prepare an income statement, statement of retained earnings, a December 31, 2003 balance sheet, and statement of cash flows for 2003.

P4–4

Preparing the four financial statements

The December 31, 2002 balance sheet for Morrison Home Services is summarized below.

Assets		Liabilities and Stockholders' Equity	
Cash	$10,000	Liabilities	$ 6,000
Receivables	4,000	Common stock	10,000
Long-term assets	10,000	Retained earnings	8,000
		Total liabilities and	
Total assets	$24,000	stockholders' equity	$24,000

During January of 2003, the following transactions were entered into:

1. Services were performed for $7,000 cash.
2. $3,000 cash was received from customers on outstanding accounts receivable.
3. $3,000 cash was paid for outstanding liabilities.
4. Long-term assets were purchased in exchange for a $6,000 note payable.
5. Expenses of $4,000 were paid in cash.
6. A dividend of $800 was issued to the owners.

REQUIRED:
a. Provide a journal entry for each transaction.
b. Treat each transaction independently and describe how each would affect Morrison's current ratio, return on equity, and debt/equity ratio.
c. Prepare the income statement, statement of retained earnings, the January 31 balance sheet, and the statement of cash flows for January.

P4–5

Effects of transactions on the income statement and statement of cash flows

Ten transactions are listed below.

Transaction	Accounts	Direction	Net Income	Net Operating Cash Flow
1. Issued ownership securities for cash.	Cash	+		
	Contributed			
	Capital	+	NE	NE
2. Purchased inventory on account.				
3. Sold a service on account.				
4. Received cash payments from customers on previously recorded sales.				
5. Purchased equipment for cash.				
6. Paid cash to reduce the wages payable account.				
7. Sold a service for cash.				
8. Paid off a long-term loan.				
9. Made a cash interest payment.				
10. Sold land for an amount greater than its cost.				

REQUIRED:

For each one, indicate what specific accounts are affected as well as the direction (increase or decrease) of the effect. Also indicate whether the transaction would increase or decrease both net income (revenues minus expenses) on the income statement and net cash flow from operations (operating cash inflows minus operating cash outflows) on the statement of cash flows. Use the following key: increase (+), decrease (−), and no effect (NE). The first one has been completed for you.

P4–6

The effects of adjusting journal entries on the accounting equation

Beta Alloys made the following adjusting journal entries on December 31, 2002.

1.	**Wage Expense**	**10,000**	
	Wages Payable		**10,000**
2.	**Insurance Expense**	**5,000**	
	Prepaid Insurance		**5,000**
3.	**Interest Receivable**	**1,000**	
	Interest Revenue		**1,000**
4.	**Unearned Rent Revenue**	**6,000**	
	Rent Revenue		**6,000**
5.	**Depreciation Expense**	**20,000**	
	Accumulated Depreciation		**20,000**
6.	**Supplies Expense**	**8,000**	
	Supplies Inventory		**8,000**
7.	**Unearned Subscription Revenue**	**2,000**	
	Subscription Revenue		**2,000**

REQUIRED:

Classify each adjusting entry as either an accrual adjustment (A) or a cost expiration adjustment (C), and indicate whether each entry increases (+), decreases (−), or has no effect (NE) on assets, liabilities, stockholders' equity, revenues, and expenses. Organize your answer in the following way. The first journal entry has been done for you.

Entry	Classification	Assets	Liabilities	Stockholders' Equity	Revenues	Expenses
(1)	A	NE	+	−	NE	+

P4–7

Preparing adjusting journal entries

The following information is available for M&M Johnson, Inc.:

a.   The December 31, 2002, supplies inventory balance is $85,000. A count of supplies reveals that the company actually has $30,000 of supplies on hand.

b.   As of December 31, 2002, Johnson, Inc., had not paid the rent for December. The monthly rent is $2,400.

c.   On December 20, 2002, Johnson collected $18,000 in customer advances for the subsequent performance of a service. Johnson recorded the $18,000 as unearned revenue, and as of December 31 two-thirds of the service had been performed.

d.   The total cost of Johnson's fixed assets is $500,000. Johnson estimates that the assets have a useful life of ten years and uses the straight-line method of depreciation.

e.   Johnson borrowed $10,000 at an annual rate of 12 percent on July 1, 2002. The first interest payment will be made on January 1, 2003.

f.   Johnson placed several ads in local newspapers during December. On December 31, the company received a $28,000 bill for the ads, which was not recorded at that time.

g.   On July 1, 2002, Johnson paid the premium for a one-year life insurance policy. The $350 cost of the premium was capitalized when paid.

REQUIRED:

Prepare the adjusting journal entries necessary on December 31, 2002.

P4-8

Inferring adjusting
journal entries
from changes in
T-account balances

The following information is available for Derrick Company:

Account	T-Account Balance Before Adjustments	T-Account Balance After Adjustments
Prepaid Rent	14,500	11,800
Prepaid Insurance	8,500	7,800
Accumulated Depreciation	36,000	38,400
Salaries Payable	1,300	2,500
Unearned Revenues	800	600
Fees Earned	87,600	87,800
Rent Expense	6,500	9,200
Insurance Expense	5,500	6,200
Depreciation Expense	0	2,400
Salary Expense	3,500	4,700

REQUIRED:

Prepare the adjusting journal entries that gave rise to the changes indicated.

P4-9

Reconciling accrual
and cash flow
dollar amounts

Burkholder Corporation borrowed $28,000 from its bank on January 1, 2002, at an annual interest rate of 10 percent. The $28,000 principal is to be paid as a lump sum at the end of the period of the loan, which is after December 31, 2003. This is the only interest-bearing debt held by Burkholder.

REQUIRED:

The chart below contains six independent cases, each related to the Burkholder Corporation. Compute the missing amount in each case, assuming that the loan described is Burkholder's only outstanding loan.

	Case 1	Case 2	Case 3	Case 4	Case 5	Case 6
12/31/02 interest payable balance	400	800	400	?	200	?
Cash interest payments—2003	3,000	?	2,300	2,600	?	2,500
12/31/03 interest payable balance	?	300	?	200	400	0

P4-10

Revenue
recognition, cost
expiration, and
cash flows

Prustate Insurance Company collected $240,000 from Jacobs Printing Corporation for a two-year fire insurance policy on May 31, 2002. The policy is in effect from June 1, 2002, to May 31, 2004.

REQUIRED:

a. Assume that Prustate Insurance Company recorded the $240,000 cash collection as a liability on May 31, 2002.
    1. Prepare the entry to record the cash collection.
    2. Prepare the adjusting entry necessary on December 31, 2002.
    3. What was the purpose of the adjusting journal entry on December 31, 2002?
    4. Complete a chart like the following:

	2002	2003	2004	Total

Insurance revenue
Cash receipts associated with insurance

b. Assume that Jacobs Printing Corporation recorded the $240,000 cash payment as an asset on May 31, 2002.
    1. Prepare the entry to record the cash payment.
    2. Prepare the adjusting entry necessary on December 31, 2002.
    3. What was the purpose of the adjusting journal entry on December 31, 2002?

(Continued)

4. Complete a chart like the following:

	2002	2003	2004	Total
Insurance expense				
Cash payments associated with insurance				

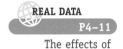

REAL DATA

P4–11

The effects of transactions on financial ratios

The balance sheet of Walgreens, a leading chain drugstore, as of August 31, 1999, appears as follows (dollars in millions):

Assets		Liabilities and Stockholders' Equity	
Cash	$ 142	Accounts payable	$1,130
Accounts receivable	487	Other short-term payables	794
Inventory	2,462	Long-term notes payable	499
Other noncurrent assets	2,816	Contributed capital	337
		Retained earnings	3,147
		Total liabilities and	
Total assets	$5,907	stockholders' equity	$5,907

REQUIRED:

Eight transactions that occurred the next year follow (dollars in millions). Indicate the effect of each transaction on net income (revenues minus expenses), the current ratio (current assets divided by current liabilities), working capital (current assets minus current liabilities), and the debt/equity ratio (total debt divided by total stockholders' equity) of Walgreens. Use the following key: increase (+), decrease (−), no effect (NE). Treat each transaction independently.

Transaction	Net Income	Current Ratio	Working Capital	Debt/Equity Ratio
1. Issued ownership shares for $132 cash.				
2. Purchased equipment costing $66 for cash.				
3. Paid off a $200 long-term note payable.				
4. Sold inventory costing $500 for $800 cash.				
5. Declared a $129 dividend but have not paid.				
6. Paid $200 in wages payable.				
7. Received $50 from customers on account.				
8. Incurred and paid $30 in interest on notes payable.				

P4–12

Effects of different forms of financing on financial ratios

The following condensed balance sheet for December 31, 2003, comes from the records of Buzz and Associates:

Assets		Liabilities and Stockholders' Equity	
Cash	$ 10,000	Current liabilities	$ 20,000
Other current assets	40,000	Long-term notes payable	20,000
Property, plant, and equipment	70,000	Contributed capital	30,000
		Retained earnings	50,000
		Total liabilities and	
Total assets	$120,000	stockholders' equity	$120,000

Buzz and Associates is considering the purchase of a new piece of equipment for $30,000. The company does not have enough cash to purchase it outright, so it is considering alternative ways of financing. As management sees it, it basically has three options: (1) issue 3,000 ownership shares for $10 per share, (2) take out a long-term loan (12 percent annual interest) for $30,000 from the bank, or (3) purchase the equipment on open account (must be paid in full in thirty days). Presently Buzz has 12,000 ownership shares outstanding.

REQUIRED:

a. Compute the present current ratio, the debt/equity ratio, and the book value of Buzz's out-standing ownership shares: (assets minus liabilities) divided by number of shares out-standing.

b. Compute the current ratio, debt/equity ratio, and book value per share under each of the three financing alternatives, and express your answers in the following format:

Financing Alternative	Current Ratio	Debt/Equity Ratio	Book Value per Share
1. Stock issuance			
2. Long-term note			
3. Open account			

c. Discuss some of the pros and cons associated with each of the three financing options.

d. The chairman of the board of directors stated at a recent board meeting that with $50,000 in Retained Earnings, the company should be able to purchase the $30,000 piece of equip-ment. Comment on the chairman's statement.

REAL DATA

P4–13

Effects of events on financial ratios

The following balances were taken from the December 31, 1999 balance sheet of Compaq, an Internet infrastructure company (dollars in millions).

Current assets	$13,849
Long-term assets	13,428
Current liabilities	11,838
Long-term liabilities	605
Stockholders' equity	14,834

Early in 2000, Compaq considered the financial effects of several events.

REQUIRED:

For each of the five events listed below, indicate how they would affect the financial ratios listed by completing the following chart. Assume that financial statements are prepared immediately after each event. Treat each event independently, and use the following key: Increase (+), Decrease (−), and No Effect (NE).

	Return on Equity	Current Ratio	Debt/ Equity
1. Purchase inventory on account.			
2. Sell assets for cash at a gain.			
3. Provide services to customers, receiving cash in return.			
4. Make a principal payment on an outstanding long-term liability.			
5. Issue common stock for cash.			

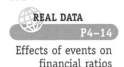

Effects of events on
financial ratios

The following balances were taken from the December 31, 1999 balance sheet of Manpower, Inc., a world-leading workforce provider (dollars in millions):

Current assets	$2,257
Long-term assets	462
Current liabilities	1,418
Long-term liabilities	650
Stockholders' equity	651

Early in 2000, Manpower considered the financial effects of several events.

REQUIRED:

For each of the five events listed below, indicate how each event would affect the financial ratios listed by completing the following chart. Assume that financial statements are prepared immediately after each event. Treat each event independently, and use the following key: Increase ($+$), Decrease ($-$), and No Effect (NE).

	Return on Sales	Quick Ratio	Debt/ Equity
1. Purchase equipment for cash.			
2. Purchase machinery in exchange for a long-term note payable.			
3. Pay salaries, which have not been accrued, to employees.			
4. Declare a dividend.			
5. Issue common stock to satisfy a current obligation.			

Effects of events on
financial ratios

The following balances were taken from the December 31, 1999 balance sheet of America Online (dollars in millions):

Current assets	$1,979
Long-term assets	3,369
Current liabilities	1,725
Long-term liabilities	590
Stockholders' equity	3,033

Early in 2000, America Online considered the financial effects of several events.

REQUIRED:

For each of the five events listed below, indicate how they would affect the financial ratios listed by completing the following chart. Assume that financial statements are prepared immediately after each event. Treat each event independently, and use the following key: Increase ($+$), Decrease ($-$), and No Effect (NE).

	Return on Assets	Current Ratio	Inventory Turnover (Times)
1. Purchase equipment in exchange for a note payable.			
2. Pay cash for marketing its services.			
3. Sell equipment for an amount less than its book value.			

	Return on Assets	Current Ratio	Inventory Turnover (Times)

4. **Pay wages that were accrued in a previous period.**
5. **Provide a service for which cash was collected in a previous period.**

P4–16

Appendix 4A: Completing the work sheet and preparing the financial statements

The following unadjusted trial balance is presented for J. Feeney, Inc., as of December 31, 2003.

	Unadjusted Trial Balance	
Account	**Debit**	**Credit**
Cash	88,000	
Accounts receivable	178,000	
Merchandise inventory	250,000	
Prepaid rent	18,000	
Supplies inventory	75,000	
Plant and equipment	500,000	
Accumulated depreciation		149,000
Accounts payable		104,000
Notes payable		50,000
Common stock		325,000
Retained earnings		501,000
Sales		875,000
Cost of goods sold	650,000	
Advertising expense	30,000	
Insurance expense	49,000	
Wage expense	146,000	
Dividends	20,000	
	2,004,000	2,004,000

J. Feeney used the following information to prepare adjusting journal entries on December 31, 2003.

1. Depreciation expense in the amount of $60,000 is recorded each year.
2. A physical count of the merchandise inventory indicates that $130,000 is on hand at the end of the year.
3. The company made an $18,000 rent payment on July 1, which covers the subsequent twelve-month period.
4. A physical count on December 31, 2003, indicates that $62,000 of supplies are on hand.
5. The company will pay employees $30,000 for wages earned for the thirty-day period ending January 15, 2004. Assume that the $30,000 is earned at a rate of $1,000 per day.
6. On November 1, 2003, the company began renting office space to a small insurance agency. The contract calls for rent receipts of $5,000 per month. No rent has been received as of the end of the year.
7. The $50,000 note payable was issued on August 1, 2003. It matures on January 1, 2004, and has a stated annual interest rate of 12 percent.

REQUIRED:
a. Prepare the adjusting journal entries necessary on December 31, 2003.
b. Prepare closing journal entries.
c. Prepare the 2003 income statement and the balance sheet as of December 31, 2003.

P4-17

Appendix 4A:
Comprehensive
problem

The following balance sheet is presented for J.D.F. Company as of December 31, 2002.

J.D.F. Company
Balance Sheet
December 31, 2002

ASSETS

Cash		$ 170,000
Accounts receivable		188,000
Merchandise inventory		200,000
Prepaid insurance		74,000
Supplies inventory		40,000
Long-term investments		160,000
Equipment	$480,000	
Less: Accumulated depreciation	98,000	382,000
Machinery	$950,000	
Less: Accumulated depreciation	230,000	720,000
Patent		75,000
Total assets		$2,009,000

LIABILITIES AND STOCKHOLDERS' EQUITY

Accounts payable	$220,000
Wages payable	73,000
Mortgage payable	300,000
Bonds payable	500,000
Common stock	500,000
Retained earnings	416,000
Total liabilities and stockholders' equity	$2,009,000

During 2003, J.D.F. entered into the following transactions.

1. Made credit sales of $1,350,000 and cash sales of $350,000. The cost of the inventory sold was $700,000.
2. Purchased $820,000 of merchandise inventory on account.
3. Made cash payments of $400,000 to employees for salaries. This amount includes the wages due employees as of December 31, 2002.
4. Purchased $110,000 of supplies inventory by issuing a six-month note that matures on March 12, 2004.
5. Collected $850,000 from customers in payment of open accounts receivable.
6. Paid suppliers $870,000 for payment of open accounts payable.
7. Sold a long-term investment for $37,000. The investment had been purchased for $30,000.
8. Paid $148,000 in cash for miscellaneous operating expenses.
9. Issued additional common stock for $120,000 cash.
10. On September 30, 2003, a customer gave the company a note due on May 1, 2004, in payment of a $72,000 account receivable.
11. The company declared and paid a cash dividend of $50,000.
12. The company purchased stock in Microsoft as a long-term investment for $50,000.

J.D.F. used the following information to prepare adjusting journal entries on December 31, 2003.

(a) Forty percent of the prepaid insurance on January 1 was still in effect as of December 31, 2003.
(b) A physical count of the supplies inventory indicated that the company had $40,000 on hand as of December 31, 2003.
(c) A review of the company's advertising campaign indicates that of the expenditures made during 2003 for miscellaneous operating expenses, $25,000 applies to promotions to be undertaken during 2004.
(d) The company is charged at a rate of $3,500 per month for certain operating expenses. It paid $36,000 for these expenses during the year.

(e) The company owes employees $43,000 for wages as of December 31, 2003.

(f) The $72,000 note receivable accepted in payment of an account receivable (see [10] above) specifies an annual interest rate of 9 percent.

(g) Equipment has an estimated useful life of ten years, and machinery has an estimated useful life of twenty years. The patent originally cost $125,000 and had an estimated useful life of ten years. The company uses the straight-line method to depreciate and amortize all property, plant, equipment, and intangibles.

(h) The note issued by the company (see [4] above) has a stated rate of 10 percent and was issued on September 12, 2003.

REQUIRED:

a. Open T-accounts for all balance sheet accounts as of January 1, 2003. Post beginning balances. Leave room for twenty-two additional T-accounts with nine lines per account.

b. Prepare journal entries for the activity during 2003. Post the entries to the ledger.

c. Prepare a work sheet and an unadjusted trial balance.

d. Prepare adjusting journal entries. Post these entries to the appropriate T-accounts and to the work sheet.

e. Prepare closing entries, and complete the work sheet. Post these entries to the appropriate T-accounts.

f. Prepare an income statement, a statement of retained earnings, a balance sheet, and a statement of cash flows using the direct and indirect methods.

P4–18

Appendix 4B:
T-account analysis

Excerpts from the financial statements of Tree Tops Services are provided below.

	2003	2002
Balance sheet:		
Accounts receivable	$ 2,500	$ 3,100
Unearned revenue	1,300	2,600
Income statement:		
Revenues from services	54,700	49,800
Statement of cash flows:		
Net cash from operations	62,400	58,700

Note: Net cash from operations consists of two components: (1) cash collections from services rendered and (2) cash payments due to operating activities.

REQUIRED:

For 2003, compute (1) cash collections from services rendered and (2) cash payments due to operating activities.

P4–19

Appendix 4B:
T-account analysis

Mayberry Enterprises has two sources of revenue. It sells advertising displays to retail firms and provides a consulting service on how to mount and use these displays. You represent a large manufacturing company that is considering purchasing Mayberry. You have reviewed Mayberry's most recent financial statements, excerpts of which are provided below, and are concerned about which of the two revenue sources is growing in importance for Mayberry. Mayberry's customers always pay for the consulting services in advance, indicating that the accounts receivable balance is associated only with sales of advertising displays.

	2003	2002	2001
Income statement:			
Revenues	$89,500	$76,000	$67,000
Balance sheet:			
Accounts receivable	29,500	32,200	35,000
Statement of cash flows:			
Collections from display sales	43,500	41,500	39,500

Which of the two revenue sources is growing in importance for Mayberry? Support your conclusion with calculations.

P4–20
Appendix 4B:
T-account analysis

You are a credit analyst for First American Bank, and Badger Business has applied for a loan. The company claims to have more than tripled profits from 2002 to 2003 and believes that it should be given prime credit terms. In addition, you note that Badger has expanded its operations, recently paying $37,000 for new equipment that replaced older equipment, which was sold that same year. No other transactions affected the company's equipment account. Excerpts from the company's 2003 financial statements are provided below.

	2003	2002
Balance sheet:		
Equipment	**$97,400**	**$84,800**
Accumulated depreciation	**(26,400)**	**(24,300)**
Income statement:		
Net income	**5,200**	**1,500**
Depreciation expense	**8,700**	**7,600**
Statement of cash flows:		
Proceeds from equipment sale	**23,400**	**0**

REQUIRED:
Reconstruct the journal entry to record the sale of equipment, and comment on Badger's claim that profits more than tripled in 2003.

ISSUES FOR DISCUSSION

REAL DATA
ID4–1

Journalizing a transaction and its effect on the accounting equation and balance sheet

When MCI Communications Corporation purchased Satellite Business Systems (SBS) from International Business Machines Corporation (IBM), it issued common stock to IBM, valued at $376 million, and signed a note payable for $104 million. MCI received miscellaneous assets valued at $52 million and the SBS system.

REQUIRED:
Respond to the following:

a. At what dollar amount was the SBS system recorded on MCI's balance sheet?
b. Describe how this transaction affected the accounting equation from MCI's point of view.
c. Describe how this transaction affected MCI's balance sheet.
d. Identify the financial statement accounts affected, the direction of the effect, and the dollar amount of the effect on each account.
e. Prepare the journal entry MCI recorded when the transaction took place.

REAL DATA
ID4–2

The effects of transactions on the accounting equation

In the late 1990s the Internet explosion sent the stock values of well-known Internet companies soaring. Many of these companies took advantage of the high prices by making major stock issuances and using the funds as their major source of financing. Lycos collected $111 million from a 1998 issuance; Yahoo collected over $800 million over a three-year period; and AOL topped them all, collecting over $1 billion. While each company used the proceeds a little differently, they all used some of it to reduce debt, update equipment, and increase current assets.

REQUIRED:
a. Describe how the issuance of stock to reduce debt, update equipment, and increase current assets affects the fundamental accounting equation.
b. Explain how the issuance of stock could increase a company's credit rating.

Cash flows and
business failures

The W.T. Grant Company was the nation's largest retailer until it filed for bankruptcy only one year after it had reported profits of over $20 million for more than ten consecutive years. Yet, cash flow provided by operations started dipping several years earlier and remained negative until the company's collapse.

REQUIRED:

a.   What kind of items might account for such a divergence between net income and cash flow provided by operations?

b.   What information on the financial statements could have provided some warning of the company's failure?

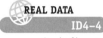

Capitalize or
expense?

An article published in *The Wall Street Journal* (October 21, 1992) titled "Polluted Numbers: Audit Report Shows How Far Chambers Would Go For Profits" describes how Chambers Development Co., a large waste-disposal firm, used inappropriate accounting methods to "report strong profits while actually losing money." From 1985 to 1992 the company overstated profits by a total of $362 million . . . "by grossly understating expenses [via capitalizing the costs of waste disposal improperly] and, in the process, violating generally accepted accounting principles. . . . The company also admitted capitalizing, as intangible assets, $43 million of internal costs relating to the acquisition of other companies, $65 million of interest cost that should have been expensed, and $27 million in start-up costs for new business and trash hauling routes. . . . Chambers put off recognizing $362 million in costs that other companies typically acknowledge as expenses."

REQUIRED:

a.   Explain how Chambers's accounting methods enabled it to grossly overstate its profits.

b.   The article further notes that in March of 1992 "the company disclosed it was abandoning its unorthodox accounting methods and taking a $27 million after-tax charge for 1991. Chambers's stock plummeted. In one day, the stockholdings of [the majority owners] lost $493 million in value." Explain how a $27 million charge could reduce the company's value by as much as $493 million.

c.   The accounting fraud at Chambers was not uncovered until 1991, when Grant Thornton, the company's external auditors, brought in a fresh team of auditors. The previous Grant Thornton auditors were recently hired by Chambers into top-level finance and accounting positions. An accounting professor at the University of Pittsburgh reacted to this situation by commenting: "If you're simultaneously auditing a company and looking for a job at that company, you may be less aggressive." Explain what the professor meant.

Watch cash flow

Herbert S. Bailey, Jr. published the following poem in *Publishers Weekly* (Jan. 13, 1975), which was written in the meter of Edgar Allen Poe's famous poem, *The Raven*.

Though my bottom line is black, I am flat upon my back.
My cash flows out and customers pay slow.
The growth of my receivables is almost unbelievable;
The result is certain—unremitting woe!
And I hear the banker utter an ominous low mutter,
"Watch cash flow."

REQUIRED:
Explain Mr. Bailey's message.

REAL DATA
ID4–6

International
accounting
standards

The chief accountant of the SEC, Lynn E. Turner, has commented that he supports the private standard-setting process and the FASB. He was also quoted in *The Wall Street Journal* (May 8, 1998) as intending to be. . . "fair, broad-minded and willing to listen to everyone." That same article noted that Mr. Turner "will negotiate with international rule-makers in London (IASC) who are trying to draft one set of accounting rules that companies anywhere in the world can use to list on any stock market around the globe."

REQUIRED:

a. What does it mean that Turner will negotiate with international rule-makers?

b. Imagine that you are the CFO for Bayer, a large German pharmaceutical, who would like to raise capital by issuing stock on U.S. security markets. You have recently shifted your financial reporting from German accounting standards to international standards, but you have been reluctant to adopt U.S. GAAP. Why do you think that Bayer is reluctant to shift to U.S. GAAP?

c. Why might the New York Stock Exchange want Bayer to be able to raise capital in the United States, while the SEC may resist it?

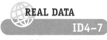

REAL DATA

ID4–7

Problems with the federal government's accounting systems

The *Associated Press* (March 4, 2000) reported:

The military's money managers last year made almost $7 trillion in adjustments to their financial ledgers in an attempt to make them add up, the Pentagon's inspector general said in a report released yesterday. The Pentagon could not show receipts of $2.3 trillion of those changes, and half a trillion dollars of it was just corrections of mistakes made in earlier adjustments. . . . The magnitude of accounting entries required to compile the financial statements highlights the significant problems [the Pentagon] has producing accurate and reliable financial statements with existing systems and processes . . . the military can't measure the results of closing a base; can't rationally decide whether to contract out a service or keep it in government hands; and may inaccurately peg the cost of programs under debate, from national missile defense to retirees' health care.

REQUIRED

Discuss problems that might arise due to the significant weaknesses of the Pentagon's accounting systems.

REAL DATA

ID4–8

Real-time accounting

According to *The Internal Auditor* (April 2000):

In the past, credible financial reports could be produced, audited, and published only on a periodic basis, because the information needed to generate such reports was either impossible or too costly to obtain on a real-time basis. However, a growing number of important items on financial statements have come under real-time management, as information technology has made such practices both economically feasible and competitively necessary for survival.

REQUIRED:

What does it mean that information can be obtained on a real-time basis? What items on the financial statements do you think have come under real-time management, and what advantages might real-time accounting create?

REAL DATA

ID4–9

The annual report of Wal-Mart

The annual report of Wal-Mart is reproduced in Appendix A.

REQUIRED:

Review the 2001 Wal-Mart annual report, and answer the following questions.

a. Estimate the cash received during 2001 from customers from the sale of goods (net sales).

b. Estimate the cash payments associated with inventory purchases during 2001. (Assume that accounts payable reflect accounts with inventory supplies only.)

c. Compute the cash outflow associated with operating, selling, and general and administrative expenses. (Assume that accrued liabilities and prepaid expenses are the balance sheet account related to operating, selling, and general and administrative expenses.)

Using Financial Statement Information

CHAPTER 5

KEY POINTS

The following key points are emphasized in this chapter:

Using financial accounting numbers to influence management decisions and predict future events.

Five steps of financial statement analysis.

Assessing the business environment.

Assessing earnings quality and persistence.

Analyzing financial statements.

Difficulties involved in using annual report information to identify mispriced securities.

Difficulties involved in using financial statements to compare the performance of companies operating in different countries.

When a company reports its earnings number, it had better beat the expectations of the analysts who follow that company. At least that's what Kenneth Heabner of CGM Capital Development Fund said in *The Wall Street Journal* (April 20, 2000). It seems that companies are getting better and better at reporting numbers that beat analysts' earnings predictions. In 1992, only 20 percent of all companies met or exceeded analysts' forecasts, and by 1999 that percentage had increased to 30. Why? It's simple. Companies that beat analysts' estimates see their stock rise, while those that miss "see the knees cut off their shares." To surpass analysts' expectations, companies either tell analysts that their earnings will be lower than they really believe, or they use accounting discretion to ensure that reported earnings meet or beat expectations. Earnings predictions are prepared regularly by analysts who closely follow companies, and they are compiled by groups like Thomson Financial Network and Nelsons. How do analysts make earnings predictions, and what role do financial statements play?

The information that appears in the financial statements is used in many ways by a variety of individuals and entities. Investors and creditors use it to evaluate company performance and to predict the amount and timing of earnings and the future cash flows (e.g., dividends and interest) associated with their investments. They also use financial information to influence and monitor the activities of management. As representatives of the stockholders, the boards of directors of many companies base executive compensation on various measures of income, while creditors protect their loan investments by writing debt covenants in terms of financial statement numbers. Public utilities use financial accounting numbers to set customer rates, and labor unions use such information to negotiate with management for higher wages and better working conditions. Credit-rating agencies, such as Standard & Poor's, Moody's, and Dun & Bradstreet, use financial statement information to determine credit ratings. Indeed, financial accounting information plays an important role in a number of different kinds of business decisions.

CONTROL AND PREDICTION

There are two fundamental ways in which financial accounting numbers are useful: (1) they help investors and creditors influence and monitor the business decisions of a company's managers, and (2) they help to predict a company's future earnings and cash flows.

Financial Accounting Numbers and Management Control

Investors and creditors, who provide a company with its capital, can direct and monitor the actions of its managers by requiring that their contracts be written in terms of financial accounting numbers. Stockholders have incentives to encourage management to act in ways that maximize future dividend payments and stock price appreciation. Since such returns depend on a company's earning power and long-term profitability, stockholders want management to make business decisions that maintain high levels of earning power. A common method used to attain such a goal is to base management's compensation on reported profits. Such compensation schemes, which are set by a company's board of directors, can lead to payments either in the form of cash or shares of stock. Exxon Mobil Corporation, for example, has implemented a management incentive program that pays eligible employees a percentage of the company's earnings if net income in a given year exceeds 6 percent of invested capital (as defined in the bonus plan). These bonuses have been paid in both cash and shares of Exxon Mobil common stock.[1]

Creditors are also interested in protecting their investments by influencing the business decisions of management. They are concerned that companies may not be able to meet their loan obligations because company assets may have been (1) paid to the shareholders in the form of dividends or purchases of outstanding stock, (2) pledged to other creditors, or (3) mismanaged. To reduce the probability of such events, a creditor may restrict certain business decisions of managers as a condition of the loan. Such restrictions are written into the loan contract and expressed in terms of financial accounting numbers.

For example, when Alcoa entered into an eight-year, $600 million revolving credit agreement with a group of banks, it required that during the period of the loan (1) the current ratio (current assets divided by current liabilities) not be less than 1:1 and (2) a minimum working capital (current assets − current liabilities) of $500 million be maintained. In other debt covenants, The Pillsbury Company is restricted with respect to paying dividends and purchasing its own common stock, and Delta Air Lines' covenants restrict its ability to grant liens, incur or guarantee debt, and enter into flight equipment leases.

Financial Accounting Numbers as Prediction Aids

Financial accounting numbers report on past events. In and of themselves, they are neither predictions nor forecasts. However, to the extent that past events are indicative of the future, financial accounting numbers can be used to make predictions about a company's future earnings and cash flows. Financial statement numbers, for example, have been used in statistical models to predict bankruptcy with reasonable accuracy, and such models are often used by auditors to predict whether potential clients will remain in business. Indeed, the main objective of financial reporting, as stated by the Financial Accounting Standards Board, is "to help present and potential investors and creditors and other users in assessing the amount, timing, and uncertainty of *future* cash flows."[2]

Business Times (June 9, 2000) reported that many dot-com companies fail to report profits in early years because they incur huge start-up costs, often related to advertising and marketing. Further, they are still young and "lack the sort of track record which would ordinarily be essential to inspire market confidence in their ability to create future value." Comment on the usefulness of financial accounting numbers for purposes of control and prediction in the dot-com industry. Do you think that dot-com managers are paid bonuses based on profits or any other financial statement numbers? Why or why not?

---

1. It is unclear whether basing management compensation on accounting measures of profit serves to maximize the long-term earning power of major companies in the United States. Some contend that such compensation schemes encourage management to manipulate reported profits and to make operating, investing, and financing decisions that increase profits in the short run, at the expense of long-term profitability.

2. Financial Accounting Standards Board, "Objectives of Financial Reporting by Business Enterprises," *Statement of Financial Accounting Concepts No. 1* (Stamford, Connecticut, 1979).

FRAMEWORK FOR USING FINANCIAL STATEMENTS TO PREDICT FUTURE EARNINGS AND CASH FLOWS

Equity investors use financial information to predict future earnings and cash flows in their efforts to identify securities that will provide high returns. Creditors use financial information to predict whether companies can generate enough cash in the future to cover debt payments. Future cash flows are at the heart of a company's true value, which is of interest to both investors and creditors. The balance sheet provides a measure of a company's value at a given point in time—its book value (assets – liabilities). Unfortunately, book value is a far cry from true value or even the stock market's estimate of true value. Recently, for example, the book value of Merck, a major pharmaceutical company, was $13 billion, while the total market price of its outstanding shares of stock was almost $200 billion!

As illustrated in Figure 5–1, there are three reasons why reported book value and true value differ: (1) the financial statements do not reflect the company's prospects within its business environment, (2) the financial statements do not reflect important unrecorded events, and (3) management prepares the reports in a biased manner.

FIGURE 5–1 Framework for financial statement analysis

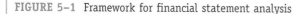

| Book value | + | **adjustments for:**
① Business environment
② Unrecorded events
③ Management bias | = | True value |

Business Environment

The major reason why book value fails to reflect "true value" is that the financial statements are backward looking, and what really matters in the valuation of a company is its future prospects. What is the prognosis for the economy—good or bad—and how closely are the company's fortunes tied to swings in the overall economy? What is the future for the industry in which the company operates: is it growing or dying? What is the company's strategy for generating profits within the industry? Does it compete by providing innovative products and/or services or by controlling its costs? The answers to these questions are critical in assessing a company's true value, and backward-looking financial statements are of limited use in answering them. It is often stated that trying to manage a company using the financial statements is like trying to drive a car by looking in the rear-view mirror. It works if the future is just like the past, but watch out if a big truck is stopped in front of you and there is no truck behind you!

Amazon.com posted losses in each of the four quarters in 1999. It also booked losses in 1998 and 1997. In fact, as of the end of 1999, the company was yet to book a profit. Interestingly, by the end of 1999 the company's stock price had grown to over $100 per share. While Amazon's stock price has since dropped considerably, briefly explain how a company with no profits could be valued highly by the stock market.

Unrecorded Events

The financial statements also leave out some current and historical information, which is relevant to assessing true value. For example, estimates of the value of a company's human resources are not included in the balance sheet. For many companies, especially those in the fast-growing service sector, human capital is the most important asset—yet, the balance sheet contains no asset called human capital. How can one assess the value of a basketball team without assessing the value of its players? How does one value a law firm or public accounting firm without considering the value of its professional staff?

Similarly, most of the assets on the balance sheet are carried at historical cost, not current market prices, and there is much doubt about the usefulness of historical costs for decision-making purposes. Consider, for example, land purchased ten years ago for $1,000 that now can be sold for $10,000. The land is carried on the balance sheet at $1,000, even though $10,000 is likely the more useful number.

It is also true that the financial statements ignore the effects of inflation and that they are not published in a timely manner. Normally, the annual reports of most U.S. companies are published several months after the balance sheet date, allowing many important—but unreported—transactions to occur in the meantime.

PR Newswire (June 16, 2000) reported: "Traditional standards of financial accounting—measuring a company's book value based solely on physical assets that appear on the balance sheet—is becoming obsolete. . . . Business commentator Thomas Stewart has written, 'Intellectual capital has become the one indispensable asset of corporations in this new knowledge-based economy.'" Explain.

Management Bias

Finally, the financial statements are limited by management's bias. Managers are not inherently unethical, and they do not attempt at every opportunity to exploit the investors and creditors who provide the company's capital. Indeed, it is in the manager's long-term best interest to report truthfully. However, it is well-known that managers choose accounting methods and estimates that report the results of operations in ways that protect and further their interests. They are fully aware that the financial statements are used by outsiders to evaluate and influence their actions and that their future levels of wealth are often directly tied to financial accounting numbers. Such influence may come in the form of choosing a particular accounting method or estimate and/or any number of other subjective operating, investing, financing, and reporting decisions.

The Wall Street Journal (May 23, 2000) reported: "Indeed, the dispute is a part of a growing trend of companies to emphasize whatever numbers make them look best—revenue or even the number of Web-site visitors, for example, in the case of unprofitable Internet start-ups. Established companies with Web businesses, critics say, are trying to have their cake and eat it, too—that is, gaining market recognition for having a sexy Internet site, while not being penalized by the losses." Why would companies engage in such practices, and how should astute analysts react to them?

ELEMENTS OF FINANCIAL STATEMENT ANALYSIS

Given that the use of financial statements for predicting future earnings and cash flows is limited due to the lack of forward-looking information, unrecorded events, and management bias, it is important that financial statement analysis address the following issues:

- Assessing the business environment.
- Reading and studying the financial statements and footnotes.
- Assessing earnings quality.
- Analyzing the financial statements.
- Predicting future earnings and/or cash flows.

In this chapter these issues are discussed in a given order, but keep in mind that different analysts use different methods. Indeed, financial statement analysis is an art, not a science, where judgment plays an extremely important role.

ASSESSING THE BUSINESS ENVIRONMENT

The analyst must first learn about the company, its industry, and how the company and industry relate to the overall economy. What is the nature of the company's operations, and what strategy is the company using to generate profits within its industry? What is the company's industry, who are the major players and the company's competitors, and is it easy or difficult for outside firms to enter the industry? What are the relationships between the company and its suppliers and customers, and who holds the bargaining power? Finally, when the overall economy booms or goes into recession, how are the company's sales and profits affected? How quickly do the company's sales and profits change when the indices of overall economic activity change? An astute analyst addresses these questions before reviewing the financial statements. The answers provide a forward-looking perspective on the company and create a useful context in which to interpret the financial statements. They also help the analyst to target key items in the financial statements for especially close examination.

One way to quickly gain a sense of a company's operations and how its future prospects are viewed by other experts is to access investment services, such as Moody's, Value Line, Dun & Bradstreet, and Standard & Poor's. These information sources provide extensive analyses of the operations and financial position of many companies, as well as ratings of the riskiness of their outstanding debts. These ratings reflect a company's future prospects within its business environment and have a direct bearing on its ability to issue debt with reasonable terms.

America Online made an important strategic move when it changed its customer pricing structure from fees assessed on a per-hour basis to a single price that allowed unlimited access to its online resources. This change drastically increased both the number of AOL customers and the average number of hours each customer used the system. AOL has two major revenue sources—monthly customer usage fees and receipts from companies that advertise on AOL sites. What do you think happened to the numbers on the company's financial statements after the pricing strategy was changed?

The Wall Street Journal reports almost daily that changes in a company's financial prospects influence its credit ratings, which in turn affects the prices of its outstanding stocks and bonds. DuPont stated in its 1999 annual report: "The company's strong financial position, as evidenced by its triple-A credit ratings from Moody's and Standard & Poor's . . . , provides a high degree of flexibility in obtaining funds at competitive terms."

READING AND STUDYING THE FINANCIAL STATEMENTS AND FOOTNOTES

After the analyst understands the company's business environment, financial statement information can be studied. This analysis consists of three steps: (1) read the audit report, (2) identify significant transactions, and (3) read the income statement, balance sheet, statement of cash flows, and footnotes.

The Audit Report

The audit report serves as the accounting profession's "seal of approval," stating whether, and to what extent, the information in the financial statements fairly reflects the financial position and operations of the company.

After reviewing the financial records of a company, the auditor usually renders a **standard audit report** stating that the financial statements fairly reflect the financial position and operations of the company. Such a report also states that all necessary tests were conducted in concluding that a company's financial statements conform to generally accepted accounting principles.[3] In such cases, the reader can be reasonably assured that the information in the statements is credible and that the company in question is in reasonable financial health.

Accounting Trends and Techniques (New York: AICPA, 2000) reported that, of the 600 major U.S. companies surveyed, over 90 percent received a standard report in 2000. The remainder of these companies received something other than a standard report. Auditors depart from the standard report for many different reasons, some of which can be quite serious. For example, in the United States, Andersen was the first major accounting firm to issue a qualified opinion on a dot-com company when it expressed "substantial doubt" about the ability of CDnow, a web-based music retailer, to continue as a going concern.

Not all companies are audited by certified public accountants. Only those companies whose equity securities are traded on public stock exchanges are legally required to do so. Such publicly traded companies tend to be the largest in the United States (in terms of annual sales or total assets), yet they represent only a small portion of the total number of U.S. companies. These other companies may or may not choose to have their statements audited. Many are required to do so as a condition for private equity issuances or bank loans, but most are not audited at all. A comprehensive audit by a public accounting firm can be very time-consuming and costly, and for many small companies, especially those that do not rely on outside sources of capital, the benefit from the audit simply does not justify the costs. In such cases, the financial statement user must proceed with extreme caution.

---

3. Examples of the standard audit report can be found in Chapter 1 of this text and in Appendix A, where Wal-Mart's annual report is located.

Significant Transactions

Predicting earnings and cash flows also involves reviewing significant transactions entered into by a company or significant recent events that might affect a company's performance. Such items can have an important effect on the future direction of a company and may distort the financial statements, making it more difficult to assess a company's financial position and operations. Examples include major acquisitions, the discontinuance or disposal of a business segment, unresolved litigation, major write-downs of receivables or inventories, offers to purchase outstanding shares (tender offers), extraordinary gains or losses, and changes of accounting methods. Usually, such transactions or events are discussed in the footnotes of the annual report and the financial effects are prominently disclosed on the income statement and/or statement of cash flows.

Analysts must pay careful attention to how these items affect the income statement. They can dramatically impact reported income yet reflect little about the company's future. An important concept in financial statement analysis is called **earnings persistence,** which refers to the extent to which an income statement item reported in the current period can be expected to reflect future income levels. An item with high persistence would be expected to relate closely to future income amounts and be useful in predicting them, while low persistence earnings are normally associated with "one-time," nonrecurring events.

The New York Times (May 14, 2000) reported that, in a recent quarter, Bank of America reported gains on equity investments as part of operating income. The article stated: "Although Bank of America can surely take pride in its investing prowess [which created those gains] such gains may not continue forever. So . . . investors should consider these types of gains as icing on the cake, rather than the cake itself." What does this quote mean?

Financial Statements and Footnotes

Financial statements were discussed in Chapter 2, and the information provided in the footnotes will be discussed and illustrated throughout the remainder of the text. There is, however, one important point worth mentioning here.

One of the goals of assessing a company's business environment is to identify key items on the financial statements. For example, success for companies in the retail industry, like Wal-Mart and Kmart, depends on the quality of inventory management. Consequently, inventory, accounts payable, and cost of goods sold—and the related footnotes—are particularly important financial statement accounts for these companies. In financial services, companies like Bank of America loan billions of dollars each year to customers, which makes the collectibility of receivables especially important. Software manufacturers, such as Microsoft, invest heavily in research and development, an income statement expense account that consistently generates considerable attention from analysts. Therefore, when reading the financial statements, it is important to recognize that the nature of the company's operations normally determines where the analysis should be focused. This is particularly true for Internet companies, like AOL, who invest heavily each year in the acquisition of new customers.

ASSESSING EARNINGS QUALITY

Earnings quality refers to the extent to which the reported financial statements deviate from the true financial condition and performance of the company. One aspect of assessing earnings quality involves determining the extent to which management's biases have influenced the financial statements. Four strategies used by managers to "manage" reported accounting numbers are well known. Each is discussed below.

Overstating Operating Performance

In certain situations, managers simply attempt to devise a more favorable picture by **overstating the performance** of the company. This is often achieved by accelerating the recognition of revenues or deferring the recognition of expenses. Young, fast-growing, aggressive companies sometimes use this reporting strategy to help them attract much-needed capital, and it is also common in situations where companies face financial difficulties. The quote below provides real-world evidence of this strategy.

Because Internet companies are judged on their revenue growth, that is where investors in such companies should go looking for aggressive accounting practices. (The New York Times, *May 14, 2000*)

Always keep in mind, though, that accelerating revenue in year 1 means that it will not be recognized in year 2.

Taking a Bath

When a company experiences an extremely poor year, it sometimes chooses very conservative accounting methods, estimates, or judgments (e.g., recognize an accounting loss) that, in turn, further reduce the company's reported financial condition and operating performance in that year. This strategy, called **taking a bath,** enables companies to recognize losses in years that are already very poor, in hopes that these losses may be less obvious. Furthermore, by recognizing losses in the current year, management will not have to recognize them in future years, which in turn may improve future financial statements. In the late 1990s, Compaq Computer Corporation faced significant business problems and profit deterioration. In 1998 and 1999, the company recognized over $4 billion in subjective charges to income that had minimal cash effects but reduced reported earnings dramatically.

Creating Hidden Reserves

Very conservative accounting methods, estimates, and judgments may also be used by management in years of extremely good performance. In such years, the recognition of accounting losses may help management to "smooth" reported earnings over time. Recognizing accounting losses in the current period ensures that reported earnings in that period are not too high and, in addition, guarantees that the loss will not have to be recognized in future periods when reported earnings may be less impressive. This strategy, called **creating hidden reserves,** is often practiced by companies who are doing well and fear possible political costs. *The Financial Post* (March 14, 2000) reported that General Electric has a history of "smoothing" earnings via "astute timing" of various charges. . . . "Such practices are often not legitimate," says the SEC.

Employing Off-Balance-Sheet Financing

Managers have been known to structure financing transactions and choose certain accounting methods so that debt need not be reported on the balance sheet. By avoiding the recognition of debt, such activities, called **off-balance-sheet financing,** may make the reporting company appear less risky. As noted in *Forbes,* "The basic drives of man are few: to get enough food, to find shelter, and to keep debt off the balance sheet."

RadioShack Corporation leases rather than owns most of its facilities. These leases involve insignificant contractual commitments to make payments far into the company's future—sometimes as long as ten or twenty years. Such commitments in the year 2000 totaled over $150 million. For the most part, these payments are accounted for on the income statement as rent expense as they are paid. Is there another way one might view these commitments, perhaps as a liability? Discuss.

Given such strategies, financial statement users must not only analyze the statements, but must also attempt to assess the extent to which management has had discretionary influence over the statements. To do so, users must examine the footnotes closely to identify the accounting methods that have been chosen, while being particularly aware of those areas in the statements that are most sensitive to the subjective estimates and judgmental reporting decisions of management. Users should also learn as much as possible about the situation faced by management or, in other words, put "themselves in management's shoes" by investigating incentive compensation contracts, debt covenants, and the general economic environment in which the company itself and its industry exist. With such information, users can better understand the economic incentives that may have determined the reporting strategies chosen by management.

Assessing the quality of a company's reported numbers is useful because it enables users to adjust the statements and thereby make more accurate assessments of a company's true value. Indeed, Baruch Lev, a prominent accounting professor from New York University, commented: "We have found that quality-adjusted earnings are much more closely related to the behavior of stock prices over time than are reported earnings. A deterioration in quality of earnings would suggest a deterioration in stock prices in the future."

Earnings Quality and Unrecorded Events

Assessing earnings quality also includes considering the unrecorded events not reflected on the financial statements. Once again, these limitations depend upon the nature of the company under analysis. The financial statements of professional service companies, where the value lies in the professional staff, may be quite limited because the balance sheet does not contain a value for human capital. In such cases, the analyst can improve the quality of the statements by estimating the value of human capital. Companies in the high-tech industry may have patents and formulas and other intangible assets that are not valued accurately on the balance sheet. Here again, analysts may wish to adjust the reported values of these assets. Such adjustments are highly subjective and often must be based on information available outside the financial statements (e.g., industry trade journals, asset appraisals). Nonetheless, the goal of earnings quality assessment is to improve the quality of the reported numbers, and the analyst should make some attempt to achieve it.

In today's economy, knowledge and intellectual capital are now the major sources of competitive advantage and the key to future profits. Yet, users must put a value on a company's intellectual resources without much help from the financial statements (*The Guardian*, March 25, 2000). Interpret this statement.

ANALYZING THE FINANCIAL STATEMENTS

Now that the analyst has assessed the business environment, read the financial statements, and assessed the quality of the reported numbers, the statements can be analyzed. Financial statement analysis is a broad and complex topic. In this chapter, we discuss comparison analysis, which includes common-size analysis and ratio analysis. Appendix 5A contains a framework designed to help in the analysis of ratios as a package (called the DuPont model). It also describes the basics of cash flow analysis.

Accounting numbers are not very meaningful in and of themselves. They become useful only when they are compared to other numbers. For example, suppose that you read in *The Wall Street Journal* that PepsiCo reported net income of $1 billion for 2001. Would you interpret that announcement as favorable or unfavorable news? This question is difficult to answer in the absence of a basis for comparison. Income of $1 billion is neither large nor small in an absolute sense. It depends on such factors as the amount of net income reported by PepsiCo in previous years, the amount of net income reported by other companies similar to PepsiCo, normally in the same industry, the size of PepsiCo's operations and capital base, or even the profit expected by analysts. Thus, financial accounting numbers are only meaningful when compared to other relevant numbers. Such comparisons can be made in three ways: (1) across time, (2) across different companies within the same industry, and (3) within the financial statements of the company at a given point in time against a benchmark or target.

Comparisons Across Time

Financial accounting numbers can be made more meaningful if they are compared across time. At a minimum, generally accepted accounting principles require that the financial statements of the current and the preceding years be disclosed side by side in published financial reports. Income statements, statements of cash flow, and statements of stockholders' equity are required for three years, while balance sheets are required for two. While this is helpful for identifying changes from one year to the next, many companies provide comparisons of selected items, accounting and nonaccounting, across five- or ten-year periods. Such disclosures can help a user to develop a "feel" for a company's activities and its general financial condition and, at the same time, can identify certain trends and turning points.

J.C. Penney Company, for example, provides a five-year comparison of most income statement items, selected per-share and balance sheet items, and the number of its employees. Delta Air Lines provides a ten-year comparison of most income statement items, selected per-share and balance sheet items, and such nonaccounting information as available seat miles, revenue passenger miles, and passenger load factor. Wendy's International provides a ten-year comparison of selected information about operations, financial position, per-share data, financial ratios (e.g., gross margin, current ratio, and debt/equity ratio), restaurant data (e.g., number of U.S. and international restaurants), and other data, including the numbers of shareholders and employees.

Comparison Within the Industry

A second type of comparison that can enhance the meaningfulness of financial accounting numbers is to compare them to those of similar companies. Similar companies are usually found in the same industry; thus, industry-wide statistics are often a useful basis for comparison. Information concerning industry averages is reported by such sources as (1) *Dun & Bradstreet's Key Business Ratios,* (2) *Robert Morris Associates' Annual Statement Studies,* (3) *Moody's Investors' Service,* and (4) *Standard & Poor's Industry Surveys.*

Differences in what are considered normal accounting numbers across industries can be very significant. For example, in the hobby, toy, and games industry, on average, current assets account for 80 percent of total assets, while in the telephone communications industry, the average percentage is only 31. Consequently, it is very important that the accounting numbers of a given company in a given industry be evaluated in terms of the norms established in that industry.

Comparisons Within the Financial Statements: Common-Size Statements and Ratio Analysis

A third way to analyze financial statement numbers is to compare them to other numbers on the financial statements of the company at a particular point in time. Such comparisons can take two forms: (1) common-size financial statements and (2) ratio analysis.

COMMON-SIZE FINANCIAL STATEMENTS

Financial statement numbers can be expressed as percentages of other numbers on the same statements. On the income statement, expense items and net income are often expressed as percentages of net sales. On the balance sheet, assets and liabilities can be expressed as percentages of total assets (or liabilities plus stockholders' equity). Presenting such information gives rise to **common-size financial statements.** Common-size income statements and balance sheets for La-Z-Boy Incorporated are contained in Figure 5–2.

Common-size financial statements can help to indicate why changes occur in a company's financial performance and financial condition. La-Z-Boy's sales and net income increased from 1999 to 2000. Expenses as a percent of sales shifted slightly—cost of sales increased by 1 percent, while expenses and charges decreased by 1 percent—leading to a constant profit as a percent of sales (5 percent). On the balance sheet, total assets grew significantly, and much of the growth was due to increased borrowings. Long-term liabilities almost quadrupled. Also, it appears that the mix of the company's assets shifted in favor of long-term assets.

FINANCIAL RATIOS

Preparing common-size financial statements is simply a matter of computing ratios in which income statement or balance sheet items act as numerators and sales or total assets serve as denominators. Computing additional ratios using two or more financial statement numbers is also a common and useful practice, generally known as **ratio analysis.**

FIGURE 5–2

Common-size financial statements— La-Z-Boy, Inc. (dollar amounts in millions)

	2000	%	1999	%
INCOME STATEMENT				
Net sales	$1,717	100	$1,288	100
Cost of sales	(1,284)	75	(947)	74
Expenses and charges	(345)	20	(275)	21
Net income	$ 88	5	$ 66	5
BALANCE SHEET				
Current assets	$ 692	57	$ 426	68
Long-term assets	526	43	202	32
Total	$1,218	100	$ 628	100
Current liabilities	$ 237	20	$ 132	21
Long-term liabilities	318	26	81	13
Stockholders' equity	663	54	415	66
Total	$1,218	100	$ 628	100

Two general points are particularly important when computing ratios. First, with only a few exceptions, there are no hard-and-fast rules for the computation of ratios. The ratios discussed here are merely representative of ratios that are widely used. Analysts can, and do, adjust them to fit different situations, and certainly other ratios might be equally or more relevant to a given decision.

Second, in the computation of many ratios, income statement numbers are compared to balance sheet numbers. Since the income statement refers to a period of time and the balance sheet refers to a specific point in time, in calculating these ratios it is usually best to compute an average for the balance sheet number. One way to compute such an average is to add the account balance at the beginning of the period to the account balance at the end of the period, and divide the result by 2. This method provides a simple average for the balance sheet dollar amount.[4] The following discussion divides the ratios into five categories: (1) profitability, (2) leverage, (3) solvency, (4) asset turnover, and (5) other ratios.

Profitability Ratios. Net income, or profit, is the primary measure of the overall success of a company. This number is often compared to other measures of financial activity or condition (e.g., sales, assets, stockholders' equity) to assess performance as a percent of some level of activity or investment. These comparisons are referred to as **profitability ratios** and are designed to measure earning power.

Return on Equity. Return on equity compares the profits generated by a company to the investment made by the company's stockholders.

Net Income[5] / Average Stockholders' Equity

Net income, which appears in the numerator, is viewed as the return to the company's owners, while the balance sheet value of stockholders' equity, which appears in the denominator, represents the amount of resources invested by the stockholders.

---

4. A weighted average, which is covered in advanced texts, may be more appropriate in certain cases.

5. Dividends paid on preferred stock are normally subtracted from net income in the numerator. However, because such dividends are normally small, we will assume that they are zero.

This ratio is considered a measure of the efficiency with which the stockholders' investment is being managed. As the ratio increases, management tends to be viewed as more efficient from the owner's perspective. Stockholders often compare this ratio against the returns of other potential investments available to them to determine whether their investment in a company is performing satisfactorily.

Return on Assets. Another measure of return on investment is return on assets. This measure is broader than return on equity because it compares the returns to both stockholders and creditors to total assets, the total resources provided by stockholders and creditors.

$$\{\text{Net Income} + [\text{Interest Expense } (1 - \text{Tax Rate})]^6\} / \text{Average Total Assets}$$

Accordingly, the numerator includes both the return to the stockholders (net income) and the return to the creditors (interest expense), while the denominator consists of the balance sheet value of total assets, which is equivalent to the investments of both the stockholders (stockholders' equity) and the creditors (total liabilities).

Return on Sales, or Profit Margin. Return on sales, or profit margin, is computed by dividing the return to the stockholders and creditors by net sales.

$$\{\text{Net Income} + [\text{Interest Expense } (1 - \text{Tax Rate})]\} / \text{Net Sales}$$

This ratio provides an indication of a company's ability to generate and market profitable products and control its costs. It reflects the number of cents in profit for every dollar of sales.

Leverage Ratios. **Leverage** refers to using borrowed funds to generate returns for the stockholders. A company that borrows $10,000 at an 8 percent interest rate and invests the funds to generate a 12 percent return is using leverage effectively. Leverage is desirable because it creates returns for the company's stockholders without using any of their money, but it increases risk by committing the company to future cash obligations. Three well-known leverage ratios are common equity leverage, capital structure leverage, and the long-term debt ratio.

Common Equity Leverage. Common equity leverage compares the return available to the stockholders to the returns available to all capital providers.

$$\text{Net Income}^7 / \{\text{Net Income} + [\text{Interest Expense } (1 - \text{Tax Rate})]\}$$

High levels of this ratio indicate that the shareholders are receiving a large portion of the total return generated by the company. These high levels are the result of the company either not using leverage (e.g., low levels of borrowing, and interest expense is very low) or using leverage very effectively (e.g., high levels of borrowing, but net income is still large relative to interest expense).

Capital Structure Leverage. Recall that a company can meet its financing needs in either of three ways: (1) borrowings, (2) stockholder contributions, or (3) undistributed profits. Capital structure leverage measures the extent to which a company relies on borrowings (liabilities).

$$\text{Average Total Assets} / \text{Average Stockholders' Equity}$$

---

6. Since interest is deductible for tax purposes, the actual cost of the interest is reduced by the tax savings.

7. Dividends on preferred stock are normally subtracted from net income in the numerator. In this chapter, however, we will assume that such dividends are zero.

This ratio increases above 1 as liabilities in the capital structure increase. It decreases toward 1 as liabilities decrease. High levels indicate that a company is using leverage—large potential earning power and high levels of risk.

Another equivalent and common way to measure capital structure leverage is called the **debt/equity ratio,** which compares liabilities to stockholders' equity, and is computed in the following way.

Average Total Liabilities / Average Stockholders' Equity

Long-Term Debt Ratio. The long-term debt ratio measures the importance of long-term liabilities as a source of asset financing.

Long-Term Liabilities / Total Assets

Companies that have large investments in long-term assets tend to finance those investments with long-term liabilities.

Solvency Ratios.
There is additional pressure on companies with high levels of leverage to manage their solvency, which refers to a company's ability to meet its debts as they come due. Four ratios are often used to measure this ability: (1) the current ratio, (2) the quick ratio, (3) interest coverage, and (4) accounts payable turnover.

Current Ratio. The current ratio compares current assets to current liabilities as of the balance sheet date.

Current Assets / Current Liabilities

It measures solvency in the sense that current assets, for the most part, can be used to meet current liabilities.

Quick Ratio. The quick ratio is similar to the current ratio, except that it provides a more stringent test of a company's solvency position. Current assets like inventories and prepaid expenses, which are not immediately convertible to cash, are excluded from the numerator.[8]

(Cash + Marketable Securities + Net Accounts Receivable) / Current Liabilities

Interest Coverage. The interest coverage ratio compares the annual funds available to meet interest to the annual interest expense.

(Net Income + Tax Expense + Interest Expense) / Interest Expense

Income before taxes and interest is used in the numerator because these funds can be used to pay interest. Increasing levels of this ratio signal that a company is becoming more solvent.

Accounts Payable Turnover. Many companies, especially in the retail industry, use their suppliers as an important source of financing. By delaying payments on inventory purchases to suppliers, companies can free up large amounts of cash. Accounts payable turnover measures how quickly, on average, suppliers are paid off or, in other words, the extent to which accounts payable is used as a form of financing.

Cost of Goods Sold / Average Accounts Payable

When computed in this way, the ratio indicates the number of times during the year that the accounts payable balance is paid off. Dividing this ratio into 365 days indicates the number of days, on average, that accounts payable balances remain outstanding.

---

8. The quick ratio is sometimes computed by excluding accounts receivable from the numerator.

Wal-Mart, for example, turns over its accounts payable approximately 29 times per year, or every 12.6 days (365 days/29).

Interpreting this ratio can be difficult. Slow turnover (i.e., few times per year or many days) can signify solvency problems in that the company may be having difficulty generating the cash to pay its suppliers. On the other hand, it may signify a financially strong company that has the negotiating power with its suppliers to use them as an inexpensive form of financing. Similarly, fast turnover can indicate financial strength or low negotiating power with suppliers. As is true for many ratios, the appropriate interpretation will depend upon an understanding of the company's business environment.

Asset Turnover Ratios. Asset turnover ratios—typically computed for total assets, accounts receivable, inventory, and fixed assets—measure the speed with which assets move through operations, or the number of times during a given period that assets are acquired, used, and replaced. As with accounts payable turnover, these ratios can be divided into 365 days to determine the number of days, on average, that it takes for given assets to be turned over. In general, high levels of asset turnover indicate efficient asset management—that is, a company is using a relatively low level of assets to generate returns for the shareholders. In some situations, however, low asset investments can constrain profitability.

Receivables Turnover. Receivables turnover reflects the number of times the trade receivables were recorded, collected, and recorded again during the period.

Net Credit Sales / Average Accounts Receivable[9]

It measures the effectiveness of the credit-granting and collection activities of a company. High receivables turnover often suggests effective credit-granting and collection activities, while low turnover can indicate late payments and bad debts, probably due to credit being granted to poor-risk customers and/or to ineffective collection efforts. A very high turnover, however, is not always desirable; it may indicate overly stringent credit terms, leading to missed sales and lost profits.

Inventory Turnover. Inventory turnover measures the speed with which inventories move through operations.

Cost of Goods Sold / Average Inventory

It compares the amount of inventory carried by a company to the volume of goods sold during the period, reflecting how quickly, in general, inventories are sold. Because profit (and often cash) is usually realized each time inventory is sold and substantial costs are often associated with carrying inventories, an increase in the inventory turnover is normally desirable. However, high inventory turnovers can indicate that inventory levels are too low, giving rise to lost sales and profits due to items being out of stock.

Fixed Assets Turnover. Fixed assets turnover measures the speed with which fixed assets are used up.

Sales / Average Fixed Assets

It compares the average level of fixed assets to the sales for the year, i.e., the level of fixed asset investment necessary to generate the annual sales volume.

---

9. Because credit sales are rarely disclosed by companies, analysts normally use total sales as a proxy for credit sales.

Total Asset Turnover. Total asset turnover measures the speed with which all assets are used up in operations, aggregating the turnover measures of the component assets (e.g., accounts receivable, inventory, and fixed assets).

Sales / Average Total Assets

It provides an overall measure of asset management efficiency.

Other Ratios. Several other ratios are used by the financial community to assess company performance: earnings per share, price/earnings ratio, dividend yield ratio, and stock price return.

Earnings per Share. Earnings per share is perhaps the best known of all the ratios, largely because it is often treated by the financial press as the primary measure of a company's performance. It measures profitability strictly from the standpoint of the common stockholders. Unlike return on equity or return on assets, which assess profitability relative to a measure of capital investment, this ratio assesses profitability relative to the number of common shares outstanding. According to generally accepted accounting principles, earnings per share must appear on the face of the income statement and be calculated in accordance with an elaborate set of complex rules that are beyond the scope of this book. The basic formula is provided below.

Net Income / Average Number of Common Shares Outstanding

Price/Earnings (P/E) Ratio. The price/earnings ratio is used by many financial statement analysts to assess the investment potential of common stocks.

Market Price per Share / Earnings per Share

Specifically, by relating the price of a company's common stock to its earnings, this ratio reflects the stock market's confidence that current earnings will lead to cash inflows in the future.

Dividend Yield Ratio. The dividend yield ratio relates the dividends paid on a share of common stock to its market price. It indicates the cash return on the stockholder's investment.

Dividends per Share / Market Price per Share

Stock Price Return. The annual return on investment provided by a share of common stock is computed by subtracting the market price at the beginning of the year (Market Price$_0$) from the market price at the end of the year (Market Price$_1$), adding the dividends per share paid during the year, and dividing the result by the market price at the beginning of the year:

(Market Price$_1$ − Market Price$_0$ + Dividends) / Market Price$_0$

This ratio provides a measure of the pretax performance of an investment in a share of common stock.

SUMMARY OF FINANCIAL RATIOS AND COMPANY RATIO PROFILES

Figure 5–3 contains a summary of the ratios discussed in this chapter, and Figure 5–4 contains selected ratios from seven well-known companies from various industries, computed from their 1999 financial statements. Consider the nature of each company's operations and think about why the ratio profiles differ across the companies.

Several concluding points about ratio analysis are important. First, ratios should never be interpreted in isolation; each ratio should be considered in the context of the

FIGURE 5–3 Summary of Important Financial Ratios

Ratio	Formula
PROFITABILITY RATIOS	
Return on equity	Net Income / Average Stockholders' Equity
Return on assets	{Net Income + [Interest Expense (1 − Tax Rate)]} / Average Total Assets
Return on sales (profit margin)	{Net Income + [Interest Expense (1 − Tax Rate)]}/Net Sales
LEVERAGE RATIOS	
Common equity leverage	Net Income / {Net Income + [Interest Expense (1 − Tax Rate)]}
Capital structure leverage	Average Total Assets / Average Stockholders' Equity
Debt/equity ratio	Average Total Liabilities / Average Stockholders' Equity
Long-term debt ratio	Long-Term Liabilities / Total Assets
SOLVENCY RATIOS	
Current ratio	Current Assets / Current Liabilities
Quick ratio	(Cash + Marketable Securities + Net Accounts Receivable) / Current Liabilities
Interest coverage	(Net Income + Tax Expense + Interest Expense) / Interest Expense
Accounts payable turnover	Cost of Goods Sold /Average Accounts Payable
ASSET TURNOVER RATIOS*	
Receivables turnover	Net Credit Sales / Average Accounts Receivable
Inventory turnover	Cost of Goods Sold / Average Inventory
Fixed assets turnover	Sales / Average Fixed Assets
Total asset turnover	Sales / Average Total Assets
OTHER RATIOS	
Earnings per share	Net Income / Average Number of Common Shares Outstanding
Price/earnings ratio	Market Price per Share / Earnings per Share
Dividend yield ratio	Dividends per Share / Market Price per Share
Stock price return	(Market Price$_1$ − Market Price$_0$ + Dividends) / Market Price$_0$

*Each turnover ratio can be converted to "days" by dividing by 365 days.

company's other ratios. Wendy's International, for example, maintains a current ratio well below 1.00, which if viewed by itself could signify a solvency problem. However, the company's strong earning power and cash flows provide adequate cash to meet the company's needs. Appendix 5A introduces a method for analyzing ratios as a package.

Ratio analysis is also limited in a number of significant ways. Financial ratios draw from financial statement information, which has important limitations. Limited inputs are rarely improved, and are sometimes made worse, when combined into ratios. Ratio comparisons within a firm across time, across firms at a given point in time, and across firms from different countries are fraught with difficulties and must be done with extreme caution. Thus, while ratio analysis is a valuable tool for the analyst, it must be conducted thoughtfully and carefully.

FIGURE 5-4   Selected Ratios for Well-Known Companies

	Colgate Palmolive	Microsoft	Dell	Home Depot	Amazon	Bank of America	AT&T
Return on equity	0.48	0.34	0.49	0.22	(3.56)	0.17	0.07
Return on assets	0.14	0.26	0.20	0.15	(0.41)	0.03	0.04
Profit margin	0.12	0.39	0.07	0.06	(0.39)	0.54	0.07
Common equity leverage	0.89	1.00	1.00	0.99	1.13	0.39	0.77
Capital structure leverage	3.85	1.32	2.41	1.45	7.70	13.83	2.19
Current ratio	1.04	2.32	1.48	1.75	1.37	0.24	0.49
Interest coverage	9.13	N/A	N/A	136.86	(7.51)	1.64	5.05
Receivables turnover	8.34	10.66	10.75	72.79	N/A	0.10	6.40
Inventory turnover	5.52	N/A	60.38	5.53	10.79	N/A	N/A
Asset turnover	1.21	0.66	2.75	2.52	1.05	0.06	0.54
Earnings per share	1.57	1.42	0.66	1.03	(2.20)	4.56	1.61
Price/earnings ratio	1.73	0.90	2.13	0.05	(0.01)	1.48	0.62

PREDICT FUTURE EARNINGS AND/OR CASH FLOW

After the analyst completes the first four steps (assessing business environment, reading and studying the financial statements, assessing earnings quality, and analyzing the financial statements), a prediction is normally prepared. Analysts who follow equity securities predict future earnings or cash flow, using these predictions in mathematical models that provide estimates of the value of a company's shares of stock. These estimates are compared to current market prices to determine whether a particular security is over- or underpriced. Credit analysts prepare cash flow predictions to see whether loan customers will be able to make their loan payments when they come due.

Predicting future levels of earnings or cash flow is a difficult and subjective process that is beyond the scope of this text. Nonetheless, it is very important for success, and astute financial statement analysis can improve these predictions significantly.

ANNUAL REPORT INFORMATION AND PREDICTING STOCK PRICES

It is well known that stock prices react to the disclosure of accounting information. Indeed, *USA Today* reported that "profits of public companies have the greatest and most immediate effect on the company's stock price," and in a number of accounting and finance research studies, stock prices of companies traded on the U.S. stock markets have been shown to react almost instantaneously to the disclosure of accounting information. It is important to understand, at the same time, that published annual reports are not available to the public until several months after the balance sheet date, and important numbers, such as net income, are announced quarterly and are available to the public almost as soon as they are determined. Thus, it is difficult, if not impossible, for investors to use the information contained in an annual report to identify undervalued stocks traded on the public securities markets. Such information is not timely enough because the market price has already reacted to important accounting numbers that were released at an earlier date.

While annual report information in and of itself may not be particularly helpful in identifying undervalued publicly traded securities, this certainly does not mean that it is useless. There is evidence, for example, that annual report information, if analyzed in a superior fashion, can lead to better-than-average returns in the stock market. Such analysis may also help an investor to better understand the expected risk and return levels associated with certain investments, to ascertain whether those levels are consistent with the investor's preferences. In addition, banks use financial statement analysis to guide loan decisions and to determine the terms of the loans they grant, and financial ratios have been used successfully by bankers and auditors to predict business failures. Financial statement analysis can also be useful when deciding whether to purchase equity or debt securities in companies that are not publicly traded. Finally, recall that financial statement numbers are used in contracts to influence the actions of managers.

INTERNATIONAL PERSPECTIVE: FINANCIAL STATEMENT ANALYSIS IN AN INTERNATIONAL SETTING

Recently, U.S. investors have shown increasing interest in foreign securities traded on foreign markets. Such securities often provide returns that exceed those available in U.S. markets, and holding foreign stocks can help reduce an investor's risk by diversifying the investment portfolio to include securities of companies from more than one country. In most cases, the choice to buy or sell a foreign security is based on financial information provided by the investee company which, in turn, presents the investor with the difficult challenge of analyzing and interpreting financial statements prepared according to foreign accounting and business norms.

In an earlier chapter we briefly discussed variations in the quality and extent of available accounting information across companies from different countries. We also mentioned and illustrated significant differences in the accounting practices of different countries. Clearly, an investor who uses accounting information to guide trading in foreign securities should attempt to reconcile these differences if meaningful comparisons are to be made among the almost limitless selection of foreign investments. One method of reconciliation would be to adjust the foreign statements to reflect U.S. accounting principles. Unfortunately, adjusting foreign financial statements to a common basis (e.g., U.S. GAAP) by itself may not be sufficient to achieve meaningful comparisons. Since the accounting system in a particular country is a product of the social, economic, legal, and cultural environment, it follows that differences across environments would further complicate the interpretation of the adjusted financial statements. In other words, not only must the financial statements of a foreign-based company be adjusted, but the resulting numbers can only be interpreted through an understanding of the foreign environment.

In an interesting study, Professor Frederick Choi and a number of colleagues from Japan, Korea, and the United States showed that understanding the institutional, legal, and cultural aspects of an environment is as important as adjusting the foreign financial statements for differences in accounting principles. The authors found that the Japanese and Korean firms, in general, were much more highly leveraged (higher debt/equity ratios) and less profitable (lower net income/sales) than their U.S. counterparts, but they noted further that important environmental and cultural characteristics explained these differences. For example, raising capital through equity issuances in Japan and Korea is relatively unusual for a number of reasons, one of which is that the local banks and government play a particularly important role in providing debt capital. The authors also reported that Japanese managers are much less concerned with short-term profits than U.S. managers, and are more likely to make investments that maximize long-term profitability, often at the expense of profits in the current period. As a result, Japanese and Korean firms may appear on the surface to be more highly leveraged and less profitable than U.S. firms, but in substance they may not be. They are simply products of a different business environment.

APPENDIX 5A

FINANCIAL RATIO (DUPONT) AND CASH FLOW ANALYSIS

This appendix provides a more complete description of financial ratio and cash flow analysis, two important tools for the analyst.

ANALYZING FINANCIAL RATIOS

We stated in the text that analyzing ratios involves comparisons—across time and across similar companies. In addition, it is difficult to reach meaningful conclusions by analyzing single ratios. When viewed as a package, however, ratios can provide a useful picture of the performance and financial condition of a company. A common method of analyzing ratios, used by many analysts, is called the DuPont model, which is illustrated in Figure 5A–1.

This method begins with return on equity (ROE), based on the premise that this ratio is an important indicator of whether management is increasing the wealth of the stockholders. When changes in ROE occur across time for a given company, or one company's ROE differs from another's, analysts are often interested in finding out why. The answer can be found by examining the changes in return on assets (ROA), common equity leverage (CEL), and capital structure leverage (CSL), because these three ratios, when multiplied together, equal ROE.

ROE	=	ROA	×	CEL	×	CSL
Net Income / Avg. Stock. Equity	=	Net Income + Interest / Avg. Assets	×	Net Income / Net Income + Interest	×	Avg. Assets / Avg. Stock. Equity

Note that when the expression ROA × CEL × CSL is computed, "Net Income + Interest" and "Average Assets" cancel out, leaving only ROE (Net Income / Average Stockholders' Equity). This equality means that changes in ROE can be explained by changes in one or more of its three components: ROA, CEL, and CSL.

Similarly, ROA can be broken down into its components: profit margin (PM) and asset turnover (AT). When PM is multiplied by AT, Sales cancels out and ROA (Net Income + Interest / Average Assets) is left. This equality means that changes in ROA can be explained by changes in PM and AT.

ROA	=	PM	×	AT
Net Income + Interest / Avg. Assets	=	Net Income + Interest / Sales	×	Sales / Avg. Assets

FIGURE 5A–1 Analyzing financial ratios

RETURN ON EQUITY	=	RETURN ON ASSETS	×	COMMON EQUITY LEVERAGE	×	CAPITAL STRUCTURE LEVERAGE
Net Income / Avg. Stockholders' Equity		*(Net Income + Interest) / Avg. Assets*		*Net Income / (Net Income + Interest)*		*Avg. Assets / Avg. Stock Equity*

PROFIT MARGIN
(Net Income + Interest) / Sales

ASSET TURNOVER
Sales / Avg. Assets

LONG-TERM DEBT /ASSETS

Cost of Goods Sold / Sales

Selling & Adm. Exp. / Sales

Interest Exp. / Sales

Taxes / Sales

Other Expenses / Sales

Receivables Turnover
Sales / Avg. Accounts Receivable

Inventory Turnover
Cost of Goods Sold / Avg. Inventory

Fixed Assets Turnover
Sales / Avg. Fixed Assets

Current Ratio
Current Assets / Current Liabilities

Quick Ratio
Quick Assets / Current Liabilities

Interest Coverage
Net Income + Interest + Taxes / Interest

Accounts Payable Turnover
Cost of Goods Sold / Avg. Accounts Payable

OPERATING PERFORMANCE

INVESTING PERFORMANCE

FINANCING PERFORMANCE

As illustrated in Figure 5A–1, these two expressions can be linked. That is, changes in PM and AT affect ROA, which in turn affects ROE.

We can take this idea even further by examining the components of PM, AT, and CSL. PM (Net Income + Interest / Sales) is closely linked to each income statement expense, expressed as a percentage of sales. A change in Cost of Goods Sold / Sales, for example, leads to a change in PM. Similarly, AT (Sales / Average Assets) is closely linked to the individual asset (receivables, inventory, and fixed assets) turnover ratios; CSL (Average Assets / Average Stockholders' Equity) is closely linked to the remaining leverage and solvency ratios.

When viewed as a whole, the entire framework shows how each ratio is linked to ROE. An analyst can see how changes in any one ratio affect the return to the company's stock-holders. A decrease in "Selling and administrative expenses" as a percentage of "Sales," for example, increases PM, which in turn increases ROA, which in turn increases ROE. Similarly, a reduction in inventory turnover will reduce AT, reducing both ROA and ROE.

Note also that the framework highlights ratios that measure operating, investing, and financing performance—the three key activities of the company. Companies that effectively and efficiently manage their operating, investing, and financing activities will create high levels of returns for their stockholders (ROE), and this framework shows how that process works.

EXAMPLE OF RATIO ANALYSIS: WAL-MART VS. KMART

Figure 5A–2 contains financial ratios taken from the 2000 financial statements of Wal-Mart and Kmart, organized in terms of Figure 5A–1. In the early 1990s Wal-Mart surpassed Kmart as the leading retailer of a variety of home products. Review the ratios and see if you can identify Wal-Mart's relative strengths.

Wal-Mart has a clear advantage in ROE. The reason appears to be its superior ROA as well as higher levels of CEL and CSL. Wal-Mart is much more profitable and a little more highly leveraged.

The advantage enjoyed by Wal-Mart in ROA is explained primarily by faster AT. Wal-Mart's PM is slightly higher than Kmart's, even though Kmart's "cost of goods sold / sales" is lower. Apparently, Kmart charges a higher markup on its goods, but Wal-Mart is more efficient in other areas—selling & administrative expenses as a percent of sales and lower interest charges. With respect to asset turnover, Wal-Mart turns over its inventories much faster than Kmart. Because these companies are in retailing, the inventory turnover difference is perhaps the most important and, to some extent, is driven by the fact that Wal-Mart charges a lower markup.

Wal-Mart's higher CSL appears to reflect higher long-term debt, but its interest costs seem to be less of a burden, suggesting superior lending terms. Interestingly, Kmart has a higher current ratio and faster accounts payable turnover. Unfortunately for Kmart, this is not particularly good news. The higher current ratio is due to more slow-moving inventory items, and the faster accounts payable turnover may be due to suppliers who insist on speedy payments.

Overall, the ratio analysis paints a relatively clear picture of why Wal-Mart is outperforming Kmart—faster inventory turnover, low levels of selling and administrative expenses, better lending terms, and stronger relationships with its suppliers.

CASH FLOW ANALYSIS

Analyzing ratios can indicate a great deal about a company's performance and financial position. However, it says little about the company's cash management performance. Companies, especially highly leveraged ones that rely heavily on debt financing, need to manage their cash flows prudently to ensure that cash is available when debt payments come due.

The investment community has become increasingly concerned with the assessment of solvency, concluding that it is not sufficient simply to analyze ratios. In large part this concern

FIGURE 5A–2 Wal-Mart vs. Kmart

(1) Wal-Mart
(2) Kmart

RETURN ON EQUITY

(1)	(2)
.245	.089

=

RETURN ON ASSETS

(1)	(2)
.106	.056

×

COMMON EQUITY LEVERAGE

(1)	(2)
.899	.771

×

CAPITAL STRUCTURE LEVERAGE

(1)	(2)
2.56	2.05

PROFIT MARGIN

(1)	(2)
.024	.023

×

ASSET TURNOVER*

(1)	(2)
2.74	2.45

LONG-TERM LIABILITY / ASSETS

(1)	(2)
.266	.247

Cost of Goods Sold / Sales

(1)	(2)
.786	.782

Selling & Adm. Exp. / Sales

(1)	(2)
.164	.182

Interest Exp. / Sales

(1)	(2)
.006	.008

Taxes / Sales

(1)	(2)
.020	.009

Receivables Turnover*

(1)	(2)
NR	NR

Inventory Turnover*

(1)	(2)
7.03	4.12

Fixed Assets Turnover*

(1)	(2)
5.33	5.83

Current Ratio

(1)	(2)
.944	2.00

Quick Ratio

(1)	(2)
1.24	.084

Interest Coverage

(1)	(2)
9.89	4.46

Accounts Payable Turnover*

(1)	(2)
11.1	13.2

OPERATING PERFORMANCE

INVESTING PERFORMANCE

FINANCING PERFORMANCE

* All turnover are times per year.

has stemmed from company failures, leading to huge investor, creditor, and auditor losses that may have been averted if better information about solvency had been available. For example, famous bankruptcies involving such companies as W.T. Grant, Sambo's Restaurants, Penn Central, AM International, and Wickes Lumber encouraged the FASB in 1981 to require the statement of changes in financial position, a predecessor to the statement of cash flows. Further, economic recession in the late 1980s brought down such corporate giants as Campeau Corporation (including Bloomingdales, Abraham & Straus, and Circle K convenience stores), R.H. Macy, and several major airlines.

Cash flow analysis, also called **solvency assessment,** involves estimating future cash flows and determining whether future inflows are timed so that adequate cash is available to cover future cash obligations. Three basic factors should be considered in this assessment: (1) operating performance, (2) financial flexibility, and (3) liquidity. Figure 5A–3 depicts how these factors relate to solvency.

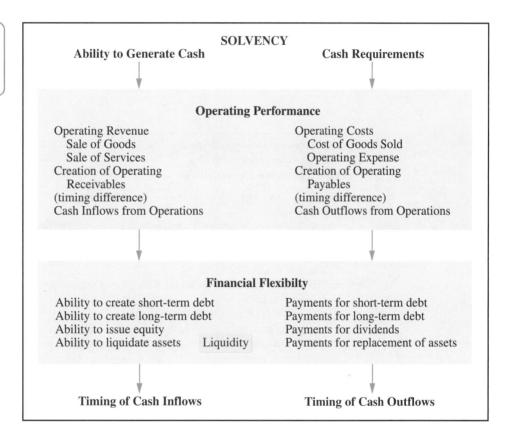

FIGURE 5A–3
Important factors in solvency assessment

Operating performance represents a company's ability to grow (increase its net assets) through operations. Since operations is perhaps the most important source of cash to a firm, this concept is very important for solvency assessment. The operating section of the statement of cash flows is especially useful here, as are the profitability and activity ratios discussed earlier.

Financial flexibility refers to a company's ability to produce cash through means other than operations: issuing debt, issuing equity, and selling assets. Companies capable of generating cash through a number of these options are considered financially flexible. Referring to the financial statement footnotes can be useful here because a company's ability to borrow and the condition of outstanding equity issuances are normally described in some detail. The balance sheet lists the assets of the company, but users must be cautious here because the assets are not carried at market value. The statement of cash flows may be helpful in assessing financial flexibility because it describes recent debt and equity issues and payments and recent asset acquisitions and sales.

Liquidity is part of financial flexibility. It represents the ability of a company to convert its existing assets to cash. Highly liquid assets increase a company's solvency position because they represent quick access to cash and can be used to secure outstanding loans. Liquidity can be assessed by reviewing the order of the assets listed on the balance sheet. A large percentage of current assets relative to total assets can indicate high liquidity. Also, the receivables and inventory turnover ratios reflect liquidity—high turnover normally indicates high liquidity.

CASH FLOW PROFILES

The statement of cash flows can also be used to identify the cash flow profile of a company. These profiles can indicate a company's strategy, position in its life cycle, or key characteristics of its current situation. Such profiles are defined simply by whether net cash from operating, investing, and financing activities are positive or negative. Note the eight combinations listed below. They are followed by a brief description of the company's activities, based on each profile.

	1	2	3	4	5	6	7	8
Net cash from operating activities	+	+	+	+	−	−	−	−
Net cash from investing activities	+	−	+	−	+	−	+	−
Net cash from financing activities	+	+	−	−	+	+	−	−

- *Profile 1.* This company is generating large amounts of cash, perhaps in anticipation of a large investment.
- *Profile 2.* This company is financing its growth through operations and by issuing debt and/or equity.
- *Profile 3.* This company is using operating cash and selling off long-term assets to reduce debt or pay stockholders.
- *Profile 4.* This company is financing both its growth and payments to capital providers with cash from operations.
- *Profile 5.* This company is selling off long-term assets and collecting cash from capital providers to finance operating cash flow losses.
- *Profile 6.* This company is collecting cash from capital providers to finance growth and operating cash flow losses.
- *Profile 7.* This company is selling off long-term assets to finance operating cash flow losses and payments to capital providers.
- *Profile 8.* This company is using its cash reserves to finance operating cash flow losses, payments to capital providers, and growth.

REVIEW PROBLEM

The information below was taken from the 2000 annual report of Pier 1 Imports, a leading retailer in home furnishings and gifts (dollars in millions). From the information, compute the ratios discussed in the chapter (excluding the market ratios) and comment on the change in Pier 1's earning power and solvency positions from 1999 to 2000. The company's tax rate during 2000 was approximately 35 percent.

	2000	1999	1998
Income Statement			
Net sales	$1,231	$1,139	$1,075
Cost of goods sold	(719)	(638)	(614)
Selling, general, and admin. expenses	(349)	(335)	(316)
Depreciation and amortization	(40)	(31)	(24)
Operating income	$ 123	$ 135	$ 121
Interest expense (net)	(5)	(5)	(7)
Other items			10
Income tax expense	(44)	(49)	(46)
Net income	$ 74	$ 81	$ 78
Balance Sheet			
Cash	$ 50	$ 42	$ 81
Accounts receivable	6	9	11
Inventories	269	259	225
Other current assets	90	72	66
Total current assets	$ 415	$ 382	$ 383
Noncurrent assets	256	272	270
Total	$ 671	$ 654	$653
Notes payable	39	0	0
Accounts payable	137	129	116
Total current liabilities	$ 176	$ 129	$ 116
Noncurrent liabilities	54	121	144
Stockholders' equity	441	404	393
Total	$ 671	$ 654	$ 653

SOLUTION A   Refer to the table below, which contains the 1999 and 2000 financial ratios for Pier 1 Imports. The definitions for these ratios can be found in Figure 5–3.

	2000	1999
Return on equity	.18	.20
Return on assets	.12	.13
Return on sales (profit margin)	.06	.07
Common equity leverage	.96	.96
Capital structure leverage	1.57	1.64
Long-term liabilities/assets	.08	.19
Current ratio	2.36	2.96
Quick ratio	.32	.40
Interest coverage	24.6	27
Accounts payable turnover	5.4	5.2
Receivables turnover	164	114
Inventory turnover	2.72	2.64
Fixed assets turnover	4.67	4.20
Asset turnover	1.86	1.74

The profitability ratios indicate that Pier 1 was a little less profitable in 2000. At the same time, the company reduced its leverage and, in particular, its reliance on long-term debt. Pier 1's solvency position fell off a bit during 2000, but the turnover ratios indicate faster turnover across the board. In sum, the company appears to be more efficiently using its assets, but unable to convert these efficiency gains into larger profits. Its leverage ratios also indicate relatively low levels of risk.

SOLUTION B

(To be reviewed in
conjunction with
Appendix 5A)

The ratios are displayed (using the format discussed in Appendix 5A) in Figure 5A–4. Note first that the drop in return on equity can be accounted for by decreases in both return on assets and capital structure leverage. Return on assets decreased because the proportional reduction in profit margin exceeded the proportional increase in asset turnover. The main problem appears to be the increase in cost of goods as a percent of sales. Partially offsetting this problem were improvements in selling and administrative expenses as a percent of sales and the asset turnover ratios, all of which increased. The leverage decrease was driven by a large decrease in long-term liabilities, while the company appears to be a bit less solvent. However, solvency levels seem adequate and Pier 1 is paying its suppliers back more quickly.

SUMMARY OF KEY POINTS

The key points of the chapter are summarized below.

○ *Using financial accounting numbers to influence management decisions and predict future events.*

Financial accounting numbers can be used in two fundamental ways: (1) they help investors, creditors, and other interested parties to influence the business decisions of a company's managers, and (2) they help to predict a company's future cash flows by providing an indication of earning power and solvency.

Investors and creditors use financial accounting numbers to influence managers by requiring that they enter contracts written in terms of financial accounting numbers. Stockholders encourage management to act in their interests by basing management's compensation on profits. Creditors constrain the actions of managers and protect their own interests by writing restrictions, expressed in terms of financial accounting numbers, into loan contracts.

Although financial accounting numbers report on past events, to the extent that past events are an indication of the future, financial accounting numbers can be used to predict a company's future cash flows. The income statement is designed to measure earning power, the balance sheet measures financial condition, and the statement of cash flows can be used to assess solvency—and all of these concepts relate to a company's ability to generate assets in the future.

○ *Five steps of financial statement analysis.*

The five steps of financial statement analysis are: (1) assessing business environment, (2) reading and studying the financial statements and footnotes, (3) assessing earnings quality, (4) analyzing the financial statements, and (5) predicting earnings and/or future cash flows.

○ *Assessing the business environment.*

The analyst must first learn about the company, its industry, and how the company and industry relate to the overall economy. Such analysis provides a forward-looking perspective on the company and creates a useful context in which to interpret the financial statements. It also helps the analyst to target the important parts of the financial statements for closer examination.

○ *Assessing earnings quality and persistence.*

Earnings quality refers to the extent to which the reported financial statements deviate from the true financial condition and performance of the company. For example, since

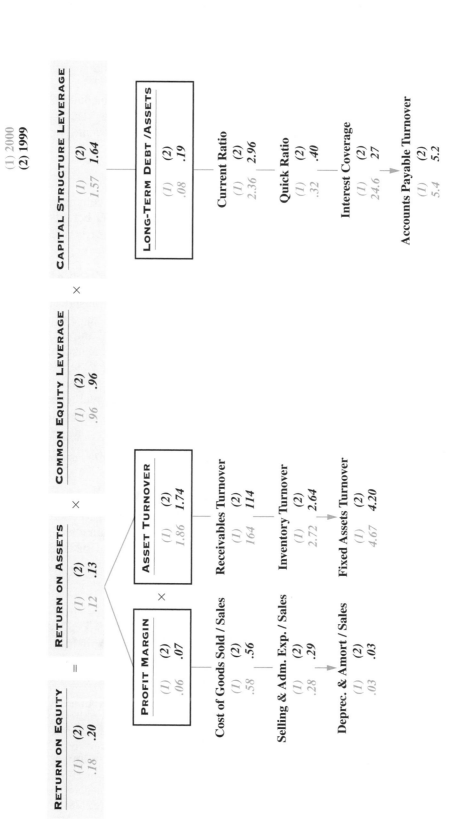

FIGURE 5A–4 Pier 1 Imports

(1) 2000
(2) 1999

RETURN ON EQUITY

(1)	(2)
.18	.20

=

RETURN ON ASSETS

(1)	(2)
.12	.13

×

COMMON EQUITY LEVERAGE

(1)	(2)
.96	.96

×

CAPITAL STRUCTURE LEVERAGE

(1)	(2)
1.57	1.64

PROFIT MARGIN

(1)	(2)
.06	.07

×

ASSET TURNOVER

(1)	(2)
1.86	1.74

LONG-TERM DEBT / ASSETS

(1)	(2)
.08	.19

Cost of Goods Sold / Sales

(1)	(2)
.58	.56

Selling & Adm. Exp. / Sales

(1)	(2)
.28	.29

Deprec. & Amort / Sales

(1)	(2)
.03	.03

Receivables Turnover

(1)	(2)
164	114

Inventory Turnover

(1)	(2)
2.72	2.64

Fixed Assets Turnover

(1)	(2)
4.67	4.20

Current Ratio

(1)	(2)
2.36	2.96

Quick Ratio

(1)	(2)
.32	.40

Interest Coverage

(1)	(2)
24.6	27

Accounts Payable Turnover

(1)	(2)
5.4	5.2

management prepares the reports, a certain bias may exist. There are other inherent limitations associated with the financial statements as well. Assessing earnings quality involves recognizing where these deviations occur and adjusting the statements accordingly.

Earnings persistence refers to the extent to which an income statement item (revenue or expense) is expected to persist in the future. Some items—low persistence—do not occur every year, and these items should be discounted when assessing the future prospects of the company.

○ *Analyzing financial statements.*

Comparison analysis consists of two components: (1) common-size analysis and (2) ratio analysis. Both involve comparisons across time, between companies, and within the financial statements. Ratio analysis consists of computing profitability, leverage, solvency, asset turnover, and market ratios.

○ *Difficulties involved in using annual report information to identify mispriced securities.*

It is difficult to use annual report information to identify mispriced (under- or over-valued) securities because annual reports are typically not available until several months after the balance sheet date. Important financial information, such as net income, is normally released to the public long before the annual report is published, and market prices react almost instantaneously to such news releases. Consequently, stock prices already reflect much of the annual report information by the time it is available. Notwithstanding the untimely release of the annual report, it is possible—with superior financial statement analysis—to improve a variety of equity and debt investment decisions.

○ *Difficulties involved in using financial statements to compare the performance of companies operating in different countries.*

It is difficult to make meaningful comparisons across companies operating in different countries because of the varying format of the financial accounting statements, the accounting methods, and the political, economic, and cultural environment. Analysts must understand these differences and restate the financial statements to comparable bases before analysis can be meaningfully conducted.

KEY TERMS

Note: Definitions for these terms are provided in the glossary at the end of the text.

Cash flow analysis (p. 204)	Off-balance-sheet financing (p. 189)
Common-size financial statements (p. 191)	Operating performance (p. 204)
Creating hidden reserves (p. 188)	Overstating the performance (p. 188)
Debt/equity ratio (p. 194)	Profitability ratios (p. 192)
Earnings persistence (p. 187)	Ratio analysis (p. 191)
Earnings quality (p. 188)	Solvency assessment (p. 204)
Financial flexibility (p. 204)	Standard audit report (p. 186)
Leverage (p. 193)	Taking a bath (p. 188)
Liquidity (p. 205)	

ETHICS IN THE REAL WORLD

Fortune(March 20, 2000) examined a series of recently published articles that explored increasingly common, and somewhat shady, business practices in the Internet world. These practices included: (1) how dot-coms intentionally inflate revenues, (2) how CEOs buy and sell large amounts of their own company's stock, (3) how boards of directors are often overly influenced by company management, and (4) how analysts who follow Internet companies are sometimes influenced by a company to make overly optimistic assessments of its future prospects.

ETHICAL ISSUE Why are these four business practices a possible violation of ethical business behavior?

INTERNET RESEARCH EXERCISE

Provide a brief description of Thomson Financial Network and explain what kind of information it provides for analysts. How might analysts use this information, and why are company managers interested in the information provided by Thomson about their companies? Begin your search at *www.thomson.com*.

BRIEF EXERCISES

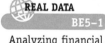
REAL DATA

BE5–1

Analyzing financial statements

The following information was taken from the financial statements of Coca-Cola and PepsiCo (dollar amounts in millions). Tax rates for Coca-Cola and Pepsi were 37 percent and 44 percent, respectively.

Coca-Cola	1999	1998
Income Statement		
Sales	$19,805	$18,813
Interest cost (net of tax)	337	277
Net income	2,431	3,533
Balance Sheet		
Assets	$21,623	$19,145
Stockholders' equity	9,513	8,403
PepsiCo	**1999**	**1998**
Income Statement		
Sales	$20,367	$22,348
Interest cost (net of tax)	363	395
Net income	2,050	1,993
Balance Sheet		
Assets	$17,551	$22,660
Stockholders' equity	6,881	6,401

a. Compute return on equity, return on assets, common equity leverage, capital structure leverage, profit margin, and asset turnover for each company for 1999. Discuss the comparison.

b. (Appendix 5A) For each company, what number results from the following: return on assets × common equity leverage × capital structure leverage?

c. (Appendix 5A) For each company, what number results from the following: profit margin × asset turnover?

d. (Appendix 5A) Compare Coca-Cola to PepsiCo. Which company has the higher return on equity and why? Which company has the higher return on assets and why?

EXERCISES

REAL DATA

E5–1

Analyzing financial statements

Excerpts from the 1999 financial report of Cisco Systems, a leading Internet networker, are provided below (dollars in millions).

Review the information, calculate relevant ratios from Figure 5–3, and explain why Cisco appears to be a good or poor investment. The tax rate was 37 percent.

	1999	1998	1997
Balance Sheet			
Current assets	$ 4,615	$ 3,814	$ 3,181
Long-term assets	10,110	5,158	2,312
Current liabilities	3,003	1,781	1,166
Long-term debt	44	43	2
Stockholders' equity	11,678	7,148	4,325
Income Statement			
Sales	12,154	8,448	6,452
Net income	2,096	1,355	1,051
Interest expense	0	0	0

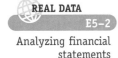

REAL DATA

E5–2

Analyzing financial statements

Excerpts from the 1999 financial report of Intel, a computer-processor manufacturer, are provided below (dollars in millions).

	1999	1998	1997
Balance Sheet			
Current assets	$17,819	$13,475	$11,782
Long-term assets	26,030	17,996	17,098
Current liabilities	7,099	5,804	7,096
Long-term debt	4,215	2,290	2,489
Stockholders' equity	32,535	23,377	19,295
Income Statement			
Sales	$29,389	$26,273	$25,070
Net income	7,314	6,068	6,945
Interest expense	36	34	27

Review this information, calculate relevant ratios from Figure 5–3, and explain why Intel appears to be a good or poor investment. The tax rate was 35 percent.

E5–3

Analyzing financial statements

The chief executive officer of Ginny's Fashions has included the following financial statements in a loan application submitted to Priority Bank. The company intends to acquire additional equipment and wishes to finance the purchase with a long-term note.

	2003	2002
Balance Sheet		
Current assets	$21,000	$14,000
Long-term assets	52,000	50,000
Current liabilities	9,000	7,000
Long-term liabilities	24,000	26,000
Contributed capital	25,000	25,000
Retained earnings	15,000	6,000
Income Statement		
Revenues	$74,000	$70,000
Expenses	56,000	53,000
Statement of Cash Flows		
Net cash from operating activities	$ 9,000	$15,000
Net cash from investing activities	(12,000)	(14,000)
Net cash from financing activities	5,000	7,000
Change in cash balance	$ 2,000	$ 8,000
Beginning cash balance	9,000	1,000
Ending cash balance	$11,000	$ 9,000

Assume that you, a bank loan officer, review the financial statements, and recommend whether Ginny's Fashions should be considered for a loan. Support your recommendation with financial ratios. Assume a tax rate of 30 percent. Interest expense is $2,000 in 2003 and $2,000 in 2002.

E5–4

Computing ratios and preparing common-size financial statements

The 2002 and 2003 financial statements of Ken's Sportswear follow:

Balance Sheet	2003	2002
Assets		
Cash	$ 9,000	$ 7,000
Accounts receivable	12,000	9,000
Inventory	18,000	15,000
Long-lived assets (net)	60,000	50,000
Total assets	$99,000	$81,000
Liabilities and Stockholders' Equity		
Accounts payable	$16,500	$12,000
Long-term liabilities	46,000	40,000
Common stock	20,000	20,000
Additional paid-in capital	5,000	5,000
Retained earnings	11,500	4,000
Total liabilities and equity	$99,000	$81,000

Income Statement	2003	2002
Sales (all on credit)	$72,000	
Less: Cost of goods sold	30,000	
Gross profit	$42,000	
Operating expenses	12,000	
Net income from operations	$30,000	
Interest expense	5,000	
Net income before taxes	$25,000	
Income taxes	8,500	
Net income	$16,500	
Dividends	$ 9,000	
Per-share market price	$ 36	$ 30
Outstanding common shares	2,000	2,000

a. Compute all relevant ratios for 2003.
b. Prepare common-size financial statements.
c. Evaluate the company's financial performance and condition.

REAL DATA

E5–5

Solvency and
the role of the
activity ratios

Financial information from the records of Gap Inc., a major clothing retailer, follows (dollars in millions).

	2000	1999	1998	1997
Cash	$ 450	$ 565	$ 913	$ 486
Inventory	1,462	1,056	733	579
Total current assets	$ 1,912	$1,621	$1,646	$1,065
Current liabilities	$ 1,753	$1,553	$ 992	$ 953
Sales (all on credit)	$11,635	$9,054	$6,508	$5,284
Less: Cost of goods sold	6,775	5,318	4,022	3,285
Gross profit	$ 4,860	$3,736	$2,486	$1,999

a. Compute the current ratio for each year.
b. Compute gross profit as a percent of sales for each year.
c. Compute inventory turnover and average days' supply of inventory.
d. Comment on the company's solvency position over the four-year period.

E5–6

Solvency and
the statement of
cash flows

Beecham Limited began operations in early 2001. Summaries of the statements of cash flows for 2003, 2002, and 2001 follow:

	2003	2002	2001
Net cash provided (used) by operating activities	$?	$(252)	$?
Net cash provided (used) by investing activities	150	?	$(400)
Net cash provided (used) by financing activities	(200)	400	800
Net increase (decrease) in cash balance	$?	$ (2)	$ 78
Beginning cash balance	76	?	0
Ending cash balance	$ 156	$ 76	$?

a. Compute the missing dollar amounts, and briefly comment on the company's cash management policies during the three-year period.
b. Does the company appear to have faced any solvency problems during the period? Explain your answer.

E5-7

Using solvency and activity ratios together

The following data are from the 2003 financial report of Generic Clothing Company:

	2003	2002
Current assets:		
Cash	$ 15,000	$ 30,000
Short-term marketable securities	225,000	10,000
Accounts receivable (net)	90,000	95,000
Inventory	50,000	225,000
Prepaid insurance	20,000	25,000
Total current assets	$400,000	$385,000
Current liabilities:		
Accounts payable	$ 75,000	$ 60,000
Wages payable	10,000	10,000
Current portion of long-term debt	375,000	100,000
Total current liabilities	$460,000	$170,000

a. Based upon the above data, compute the following for Generic Clothing Company for both 2002 and 2003:
    (1) The current ratio
    (2) The quick ratio
b. Assume that net credit sales for the years ended December 31, 2002 and 2003, were $780,000 and $800,000, respectively, and that the balance of Accounts Receivable as of January 1, 2002, was $100,000. Compute the receivables turnover for both years. Also compute the number of days outstanding.
c. Does it appear that the solvency position of the company improved or worsened from 2001 to 2003? Explain.

E5-8

Explaining return on equity with inventory turnover

PLP Corporation began operations on January 1, 2000. The initial investment by the owners was $100,000. The following information was extracted from the company's records.

	Net Income	December 31 Stockholders' Equity	December 31 Inventory	Cost of Goods Sold
2000	$510,000	$100,000	$200,000	$1,200,000
2001	490,000	290,000	255,000	1,350,000
2002	515,000	315,000	320,000	1,395,000
2003	505,000	510,000	365,000	1,400,000

a. Compute the return on equity for each year. Has the company been effective at managing the capital provided by the equity owners?
b. Does the information about inventory and the cost of goods sold indicate any reason for the trend in return on equity? Support your answer with any relevant ratios.

E5-9

Using ratios and the statement of cash flows to assess solvency and earning power

The financial information below was taken from the records of Lotechnic Enterprises. The company pays no dividends.

	2003	2002	2001	2000
Current assets	$ 35,000	$ 31,000	$24,000	$20,000
Noncurrent assets	93,000	86,000	64,000	33,000
Total assets	$128,000	$117,000	$88,000	$53,000

	2003	2002	2001	2000
Current liabilities	$ 30,000	$ 25,000	$13,000	$ 8,000
Long-term liabilities	40,000	40,000	35,000	15,000
Capital stock	20,000	20,000	20,000	20,000
Retained earnings	38,000	32,000	20,000	10,000
Total liabilities and stockholders' equity	$128,000	$117,000	$88,000	$53,000
Net cash provided (used) by operating activities	$ (2,000)	$ 3,000	$ 6,000	$ 7,000
Net cash provided (used) by investing activities	(10,000)	(20,000)	(31,000)	(12,000)
Net cash provided (used) by financing activities	15,000	15,000	25,000	8,000
Net increase (decrease) in cash	$ 3,000	$ (2,000)	$ 0	$ 3,000
Interest expense	$ 5,000	$ 5,000	$ 4,000	$ 2,000
Net income	24,000	21,000	14,000	13,000

a. Compute the current ratio, the debt/equity ratio, and return on assets for each of the four years. Assume that the year-end balances in 2000 reflect the average balances during the year. Assume a tax rate of 30 percent.
b. Prepare a common-size balance sheet for each of the four years.
c. Use the statement of cash flows, and analyze the earning power and solvency positions of Lotechnic.

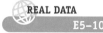

REAL DATA

E5–10

The effects of transactions on financial ratios

Lands' End, Inc., a leading global direct merchant, entered into the following transactions during 2001.

1. Purchased inventory on account.
2. Purchased plant machinery by issuing long-term debt.
3. Made a principal payment on long-term debt.
4. Paid wages.
5. Sold inventory on account for 20 percent over cost.
6. Issued stock for cash.

The 2000 balance sheet of Lands' End is provided below.

Assets		Liabilities and Stockholders' Equity	
Cash and marketable securities	$ 76,413	Current liabilities	$150,872
Other current assets	212,995	Long-term liabilities	9,117
Long-lived assets	166,788	Stockholders' equity	296,207
Total assets	$456,196	Total liabilities and stockholders' equity	$456,196

Fill in a chart like the one below by indicating whether each transaction would increase (+), decrease (−), or have no effect (NE) on the quick ratio, current ratio, and debt/equity ratio. Treat each transaction independently.

Transaction	Quick Ratio	Current Ratio	Debt/Equity Ratio
1.			

E5–11

Debt covenants limiting additional debt and dividend payments

At the end of 2002, Montvale Associates borrowed $120,000 from the Bayliner Bank. The debt covenant specified that Montvale's debt/equity ratio could not exceed 1.5:1 during the period of the loan. A summary of Montvale's balance sheet after the loan follows.

	2002
Assets	
Current assets	$130,000
Noncurrent assets	350,000
Total assets	$480,000
Liabilities and Stockholders' Equity	
Current liabilities	$130,000
Long-term liabilities	150,000
Stockholders' equity	200,000
Total liabilities and stockholders' equity	$480,000

a. Compute Montvale's debt/equity ratio immediately after the loan.
b. How much additional debt can the company incur without violating the debt covenant?
c. How large a dividend can the company declare and pay at the end of 2002 without violating the debt covenant?
d. If Montvale had declared, but not yet paid, a $20,000 dividend before it took out the loan, could the company pay the dividend afterwards without violating the debt covenant? Why or why not?

REAL DATA

E5–12

Examining market ratios over time

The information below refers to the financial records of McDonald's Corporation over a five-year period (dollar amounts in millions except share price).

	1999	1998	1997	1996	1995
Net income	$1,948	$1,550	$1,642	$1,573	$1,427
Dividends declared	$270	$245	$224	$213	$187
Closing per-share price	$40$5/16$	$38$7/16$	$23$7/8$	$22$11/16$	$22$9/16$
Number of shares outstanding	1,352	1,360	1,403[a]	1,417	1,441

a. Compute dividends declared as a percentage of net income during each of the five years.
b. Compute the price-earnings ratio, dividend yield, and stock price return for 1996, 1997, 1998, and 1999.
c. Comment on the performance of an investment in McDonald's stock from 1995 to 1999.

REAL DATA

E5–13

Computing ratios and the effect of transactions on return on equity

Merck, a major pharmaceutical, generated $5,890 million in net income for the year ended December 31, 1999.

1. The company declared and paid $2,629 million in dividends during 1999.
2. Merck stock was selling for $70 per share on January 1, 1999, and for $73 per share on December 31, 1999.
3. As of January 1, 1999, the company had 2,379 million shares of common stock outstanding. During 1999, the company repurchased 30 million shares. Assume that the purchases were made evenly throughout the year.

a. Compute the following ratios:
    (1) Earnings per share
    (2) Price/earnings
    (3) Dividend yield
    (4) Stock price return
b. What effect (increase, decrease, or no effect) did each of the three events above have on Merck's return on equity ratio?

E5–14

Appendix 5A:
Interpreting
financial ratios

The following ratios were computed from the financial statements of INSEAD Incorporated:

	2003	2002	2001
Return on equity	0.28	0.25	0.22
Return on assets	0.15	0.18	0.20
Common equity leverage	0.85	0.88	0.90
Capital structure leverage	2.20	1.58	1.22
Profit margin	0.09	0.08	0.07
Asset turnover	1.67	2.25	2.85

Use the DuPont model to analyze these ratios, and comment on the company's performance from 2001 to 2003 and why.

E5–15

Appendix 5A:
Interpreting
financial ratios

The following ratios were computed from the financial statements of LBS Products:

	2003	2002	2001
Return on equity	0.11	0.18	0.20
Return on assets	0.09	0.18	0.20
Common equity leverage	0.80	0.78	0.78
Capital structure leverage	1.50	1.30	1.30
Profit margin	0.06	0.13	0.13
Asset turnover	1.50	1.40	1.50

Use the DuPont model to analyze these ratios, and comment on the company's performance from 2001 to 2003 and why.

PROBLEMS

 REAL DATA

P5–1

Computing ratios
and the role of
market values

Imation, a global technology company, reported the following selected items as part of its 1999 financial report (dollar amounts in millions).

	1999	1998
Cash	$ 195	$ 64
Accounts receivable	252	326
Inventory	191	264
Total assets	1,128	1,313
Accounts payable	104	129
Accrued payroll	37	30
Other liabilities (long-term)	45	139
Contributed capital	809	830
Retained earnings (deficit)	(84)	(124)
Net sales	1,413	
Cost of goods sold	979	
Interest expense	2	
Net income before taxes	69	
Net income	44	

REQUIRED:

Compute the following ratios and briefly discuss.

1. Current ratio
2. Quick ratio
3. Receivables turnover
4. Interest coverage ratio
5. Return on assets
6. Inventory turnover
7. Return on equity

P5–2

Borrow or issue
equity: effects on
financial ratios

Edgemont Repairs began operations on January 1, 2001. The 2001, 2002, and 2003 financial statements follow:

	2003	2002	2001
Assets			
Current assets	$ 30,000	$10,000	$ 8,000
Noncurrent assets	83,000	45,000	41,000
Total assets	$113,000	$55,000	$49,000
Liabilities and Stockholders' Equity			
Current liabilities	$ 12,000	$ 7,000	$ 5,000
Long-term liabilities	50,000	10,000	10,000
Stockholders' equity	51,000	38,000	34,000
Total liabilities and stockholders' equity	$113,000	$55,000	$49,000
Revenues	$ 70,000	$45,000	$37,000
Operating expenses	27,000	24,000	24,000
Interest expense	5,000	1,000	1,000
Income taxes	13,000	6,000	6,000
Net income	$ 25,000	$14,000	$ 6,000
Dividends	$12,000	$10,000	$2,000
Number of shares outstanding	10,000	10,000	10,000

On January 1, 2003, the company expanded operations by taking out a $40,000 long-term loan at a 10 percent annual interest rate.

REQUIRED:

a. Compute return on equity, return on assets, common equity leverage, capital structure leverage, profit margin, and asset turnover.
b. On January 1, 2003, the company's common stock was selling for $20 per share. Assume that Edgemont issued 2,000 shares of stock, instead of borrowing the $40,000, to raise the cash needed to pay for the January 1 expansion. Recompute the ratios in (a) for 2003. Ignore any tax effects.
c. Should the company have issued the equity instead of borrowing the funds? Explain.

REAL DATA

P5–3

Percentage changes
and common-size
financial statements

You are considering investing in Eli Lilly, a major pharmaceutical. As part of your investigation of Lilly, you obtained the following balance sheets for the years ended December 31, 1998 and 1999 (dollars in millions):

	1999	1998
Assets		
Current assets:		
Cash	$ 3,700	$ 1,496
Short-term marketable securities	136	101
Accounts receivable	1,443	1,968
Inventory	900	1,000
Other current assets	876	842
Total current assets	$ 7,055	$ 5,407
Property, plant, and equipment	3,981	4,096
Other assets	1,789	3,093
Total assets	$12,825	$12,596
Liabilities and Stockholders' Equity		
Current liabilities:		
Accounts payable	$ 446	$ 1,186
Wages payable	489	704
Dividends payable	283	253
Income taxes payable	1,445	1,290
Other current liabilities	1,292	1,174
Total current liabilities	$ 3,955	$ 4,607
Long-term debt	3,877	3,559
Contributed capital*	(27)	(201)
Retained earnings	5,020	4,631
Total liabilities and stockholders' equity	$12,825	$12,596

*Net, including treasury stock and other adjustments.

REQUIRED:

a.   Compute the dollar change in each account from 1998 to 1999. Also compute the percentage change in each account from 1998 to 1999.
b.   Convert the balance sheets to common-size balance sheets. Also compute the percentage change in the common-size numbers of each account from 1998 to 1999.
c.   Does the information in (b) provide any additional data to that in (a)? Explain.

P5-4

**Comprehensive
ratio analysis**

You have just been hired as a stock analyst for a large stock brokerage company. Your first assignment is to analyze the performance of Gidley Electronics. The company's balance sheet for 2002 and 2003 is presented below and on page 219.

	2003	2002
Assets		
Current assets:		
Cash	$ 110,000	$ 115,000
Short-term marketable securities	175,000	220,000
Accounts receivable	350,000	400,000
Inventory	290,000	240,000
Prepaid expenses	55,000	35,000
Total current assets	$ 980,000	$1,010,000
Property, plant, and equipment	650,000	590,000
Less: Accumulated depreciation	(165,000)	(130,000)
Total assets	$1,465,000	$1,470,000

	2003	2002
Liabilities and Stockholders' Equity		
Current liabilities:		
Accounts payable	$ 60,000	$ 50,000
Wages payable	15,000	20,000
Unearned revenue	50,000	35,000
Income taxes payable	55,000	35,000
Current portion of long-term debt	110,000	135,000
Total current liabilities	$ 290,000	$ 275,000
Bonds payable	380,000	440,000
Common stock ($10 par value)	220,000	170,000
Additional paid-in capital	145,000	115,000
Retained earnings	430,000	470,000
Total liabilities and		
stockholders' equity	$1,465,000	$1,470,000

The company's income statement and statement of retained earnings for the years ended December 31, 2002 and 2003 are presented below.

	2003	2002
Income Statement		
Revenue:		
Net cash sales	$1,405,000	$1,255,000
Net credit sales	2,450,000	3,010,000
Total revenue	$3,855,000	$4,265,000
Cost of goods sold:		
Beginning inventory	$ 240,000	$ 300,000
Net purchases	1,755,000	2,005,000
Cost of goods available for sale	$1,995,000	$2,305,000
Less: Ending inventory	290,000	240,000
Cost of goods sold	$1,705,000	$2,065,000
Gross profit	$2,150,000	$2,200,000
Selling and administrative expenses:		
Depreciation expense	(95,000)	(100,000)
General selling expenses	(470,000)	(450,000)
General administrative expenses	(580,000)	(620,000)
Net operating income	$1,005,000	$1,030,000
Interest expense	150,000	165,000
Net income from continuing operations		
before taxes	$ 855,000	$ 865,000
Income taxes	345,000	350,000
Net income	$ 510,000	$ 515,000
Statement of Retained Earnings		
Beginning retained earnings balance	$ 470,000	$ 165,000
Plus: Net income	510,000	515,000
Less: Dividends	(550,000)	(210,000)
Ending retained earnings balance	$ 430,000	$ 470,000

The market prices of the company's stock as of January 1, 2002, December 31, 2002, and December 31, 2003, were $65, $69, and $54 per share, respectively. The January 1, 2002 balance in stockholders' equity was $450,000, there were no changes in the number of common shares outstanding or in accounts receivable during 2002, and the income tax rate was 40 percent for 2002 and 2003. Total assets as of January 1, 2002, were $1,450,000.

REQUIRED:
Answer the following questions (including any relevant ratios in your answers) for both 2002 and 2003. Unless the December 31, 2001 balance is provided, assume that the December 31, 2002 balance reflects the average balance during 2002.

1. How effective is the company at managing investments made by the equity owners?
2. Is the company using debt to the best interests of the equity owners?
3. Can the company meet its current obligations using current assets? using cash-like assets?
4. How sensitive are stock prices to changes in earnings?
5. How many days is the average account receivable outstanding? Are the days outstanding increasing or decreasing?

P5–5

Comparing companies on earning power

The following information was obtained from the 2003 financial reports of Hathaway Toy Company and Yakima Manufacturing:

	Hathaway Toy	Yakima Mfg.
Interest expense	—	$ 195,000
Net income	$ 875,000	755,000
Current liabilities	240,000	25,000
Mortgage payable	—	1,850,000
Common stock ($10 par value)	800,000	350,000
Additional paid-in capital	915,000	150,000
Retained earnings	745,000	325,000
Total liabilities and stockholders' equity	$2,700,000	$2,700,000

Assume that the only change to stockholders' equity during 2003 is due to net income earned in 2003.

REQUIRED:
a. Which company is more effective at managing the capital provided by the owners?
b. Which company is more effective at managing capital provided by all investors?
c. Compute the earnings per share for each company.
d. Is Yakima Manufacturing using its debt effectively for the equity owners?

REAL DATA

P5–6

Analyzing financial statements

Excerpts from the 1999 financial statements for Goodyear are provided below (dollars in millions):

	1999	1998	1997
Balance Sheet			
Current assets	$ 5,261	$ 4,529	$ 4,319
Long-term assets	7,842	6,060	5,451
Current liabilities	3,960	3,277	3,162
Long-term liabilities	5,526	3,567	3,212
Contributed capital	86	268	413
Retained earnings	3,531	3,478	2,983
Income Statement			
Revenues	$12,881	$12,626	$13,065
Expenses	12,640	11,944	12,506

	1999	1998	1997
Statement of Cash Flows			
Net cash from operating activities	$ 635	$ 439	$ 1,052
Net cash from investing activities	(1,802)	(702)	(789)
Net cash from financing activities	1,183	246	(206)
Change in cash balance	$ 16	$ (17)	$ 57
Beginning cash balance	279	296	239
Ending cash balance	$ 295	$ 279	$ 296

REQUIRED:

Assume that you have some capital to invest and that you are considering an equity investment in Goodyear. Review the financial statements and comment on Goodyear as an investment. Support your recommendation with financial ratios. Assume a tax rate of 30 percent. Interest expense is $179 in 1999, $148 in 1998, and $120 in 1997.

P5–7
Unusual items and financial ratios

The following selected financial information was obtained from the 2003 financial reports of Robotronics, Inc., and Technology, Limited:

	Robotronics, Inc.	Technology, Ltd.
Interest expense	$ 100,000	$ 175,000
Unusual gain (net of taxes of $320,000)	—	1,300,000
Net income (including unusual items)	610,000	1,675,000
Current liabilities	140,000	25,000
Bonds payable	725,000	0
Mortgage payable	1,490,000	405,000
Common stock	500,000	600,000
Additional paid-in capital	215,000	325,000
Retained earnings	290,000	515,000
Total liabilities and stockholders' equity	$3,360,000	$1,870,000

Assume that total assets, total liabilities, and total stockholders' equity were constant throughout 2003.

REQUIRED:
a. Assume that you are considering purchasing the common stock of one of these companies. Which company has a higher return on equity? Would your conclusion be different if the impact of the unusual item had not been included in net income? Should unusual items be considered? Why or why not?
b. Which company uses leverage more effectively? Does your answer change if you do not consider the impact of the unusual item on net income?

P5–8
Preparing the financial statements from financial ratios

Tumwater Canyon Campsites began operations on January 1, 2003. The following information is available at year-end. Assume that all sales were on credit.

Net income	$25,000	Return on sales	8%
Receivables turnover	8	Gross margin	40%
Inventory turnover	5	Quick ratio	50%
Accounts payable	$200,000		

REQUIRED:
Prepare an income statement and the current asset and current liability portions of the balance sheet for 2003. Current assets consist of cash, accounts receivable, and inventory. Accounts payable is Tumwater's only current liability. (*Hint:* Begin by using return on sales to compute net sales.)

P5–9

Common-size financial statements

Bob Cleary, the controller of Mountain-Pacific Railroad, has prepared the financial statements for 2002 and 2003, shown below and on the next page. The market prices of the company's stock as of January 1, 2002, December 31, 2002, and December 31, 2003, were $50, $45, and $70 per share, respectively. Assume an income tax rate of 34 percent and assume that interest expense was incurred only on long-term debt (including the current maturities of long-term debt).

REQUIRED:

a. Prepare common-size balance sheets and income statements for 2002 and 2003 and analyze the results.

b. Which income statement account experienced the largest shift from 2002 to 2003? Did this shift appear to have any impact on the balance sheet? Explain.

c. What benefits do common-size financial statements provide over standard financial statements?

Balance Sheet	2003	2002
Assets		
Current assets:		
Cash	$ 10,000	$ 312,000
Short-term marketable securities	125,000	120,000
Accounts receivable	500,000	150,000
Inventory	200,000	210,000
Prepaid expenses	50,000	75,000
Total current assets	$ 885,000	$ 867,000
Long-term investments	225,000	225,000
Property, plant, and equipment	430,000	540,000
Less: Accumulated depreciation	(65,000)	(100,000)
Total assets	$1,475,000	$1,532,000
Liabilities and Stockholders' Equity		
Current liabilities:		
Accounts payable	$ 10,000	$ 50,000
Wages payable	5,000	2,000
Dividends payable	125,000	5,000
Income taxes payable	50,000	35,000
Current portion of long-term debt	100,000	175,000
Total current liabilities	$ 290,000	$ 267,000
Mortgage payable	350,000	450,000
Common stock ($10 par value)	200,000	110,000
Additional paid-in capital	135,000	95,000
Retained earnings	500,000	610,000
Total liabilities and stockholders' equity	$1,475,000	$1,532,000

Income Statement	2003		2002	
Revenue:				
Net cash sales	$1,955,000		$2,775,000	
Net credit sales	4,150,000		1,410,000	
Total revenue		$6,105,000		$4,185,000
Cost of goods sold:				
Beginning inventory	$ 210,000		$ 300,000	
Net purchases	4,005,000		2,475,000	
Cost of goods available for sale	$4,215,000		$2,775,000	
Less: Ending inventory	200,000		210,000	
Cost of goods sold		4,015,000		2,565,000
Gross profit		$2,090,000		$1,620,000

Income Statement	2003		2002	
Selling and administrative expenses:				
Depreciation expense	$ 75,000		$ 90,000	
General selling expenses	575,000		600,000	
General administrative expenses	480,000	1,130,000	420,000	1,110,000
Net operating income		$ 960,000		$ 510,000
Interest expense		50,000		65,000
Net income from continuing operations before taxes		$ 910,000		$ 445,000
Income taxes		310,000		151,000
Net income before unusual items		$ 600,000		$ 294,000
Unusual loss—net of tax benefit of $60,000		115,000		—
Net income		$ 485,000		$ 294,000

Statement of Retained Earnings	2003	2002
Beginning retained earnings balance	$ 610,000	$ 326,000
Plus: Net income	485,000	294,000
Less: Dividends	(595,000)	(10,000)
Ending retained earnings balance	$ 500,000	$ 610,000

P5–10

Comparing ratios to industry averages

Mountain-Pacific Railroad, whose financial statements are presented in P5–9, is interested in comparing itself to the rest of the industry. Bob Cleary, the controller, has obtained the following industry averages from a trade journal. (The industry averages were the same for 2002 and 2003.)

Return on equity	0.500
Current ratio	3.100
Quick ratio	1.850
Return on assets	0.300
Receivables turnover	8.150
Earnings per share ($)	41.150
Price/earnings ratio	0.451
Capital structure leverage	1.770
Profit margin	0.072
Dividend yield	0.375
Return on investment	0.102
Interest coverage	9.890
Inventory turnover	21.700

REQUIRED:

a. Compute these ratios for Mountain-Pacific Railroad for both 2002 (using year-end balances) and 2003 (using average balances where appropriate). Identify significant trends. Could the company experience solvency problems? Explain.

b. Compare the ratios of Mountain-Pacific Railroad to the industry averages. Do you think that Mountain-Pacific Railroad is doing better, worse, or the same as the industry? Explain your answer, being as specific as possible.

P5–11

Assessing the loan risk of a potential bank customer

You have just been hired as a loan officer for Washington Mutual Savings. Selig Equipment and Mountain Bike, Inc., have both applied for $125,000 nine-month loans to acquire additional plant equipment. Neither company offered any security for the loans. It is the strict policy of the bank to have only $1,350,000 outstanding in unsecured loans at any point in time. Since the bank currently has $1,210,000 in unsecured loans outstanding, it will be unable to grant loans to both companies. The bank president has given you the following selected information from the companies' loan applications.

	Selig Equipment	Mountain Bike, Inc.
Cash	$ 15,000	$ 160,000
Accounts receivable	215,000	470,000
Inventory	305,000	195,000
Prepaid expenses	180,000	10,000
Total current assets	$ 715,000	$ 835,000
Noncurrent assets	1,455,000	1,875,000
Total assets	$2,170,000	$2,710,000
Current liabilities	$ 285,000	$ 325,000
Long-term liabilities	950,000	875,000
Contributed capital	790,000	910,000
Retained earnings	145,000	600,000
Total liabilities and stockholders' equity	$2,170,000	$2,710,000
Net credit sales	$1,005,000	$1,625,000
Cost of goods sold	755,000	960,000

REQUIRED:

Assume that all account balances on the balance sheet are representative of the entire year. Based upon this limited information, which company would you recommend to the bank president as the better risk for an unsecured loan? Support your answer with any relevant analysis.

P5–12

Issuing debt or equity: Effects on ratios and owners

Watson Metal Products is planning to expand its operations to France in response to increased demand from the French for quality metal products to use in production processes. Ben Watson, president of Watson Metal Products, and his consultants have estimated that the expansion will require an investment of $5 million. They have also estimated that this expansion will cause net income before interest expense to increase by $1,500,000. The company is considering financing the expansion through one of the following alternatives.

Alternative 1: Issue 200,000 shares of common stock for $25 per share.

Alternative 2: Issue long-term debt at an annual interest cost of 15 percent. The principal would be payable in ten years.

Alternative 3: Issue 100,000 shares of common stock for $25 per share and finance the remainder by issuing long-term debt at an annual interest rate of 15 percent. The principal would be payable in ten years.

The income statement for the year ended December 31, 2003, of Watson Metal Products was as follows:

Sales	$150,000,000
Cost of goods sold	(90,000,000)
Other expenses	(45,000,000)
Income from operations	$ 15,000,000
Interest expense	4,000,000
Net income before taxes	$ 11,000,000
Income taxes	4,400,000
Net income	$ 6,600,000
Earnings per share	$3.30

Prior to the expansion, the total debt of Watson Metal Products was $35 million, and total stockholders' equity was $45 million. There were no changes in total debt and total stockholders' equity other than those due to net income and the expansion project. Federal and state income tax rates total 40 percent.

REQUIRED:

a. Assume that the company's net income from non-French operations in 2004 equals the income earned in 2003 and that the estimated income from operations on the expansion is realized in 2004. Compute earnings per share, return on equity, return on assets, common equity leverage, and the capital structure leverage as of December 31, 2004, if the company finances the expansion through the following:

(1) Alternative 1
(2) Alternative 2
(3) Alternative 3

Assume that the December 31, 2004 balances equal average balances during 2004.

b. Assume that you are currently a stockholder in Watson Metal Products. Which expansion alternative would you prefer? Explain your answer.

c. What amount of net income would Watson Metal Products have to generate from the expansion project so that earnings per share would be the same before and after the expansion under each alternative?

P5–13

Preparing financial statement data from financial ratios

The following relationships were obtained for Boulder Mineral Company for 2003:

Current ratio	3:1
Inventory turnover (average days supply)	12.167
Quick ratio	2:1
Debt/equity	0.4:1
Return on equity	0.75:1
Return on assets	0.65:1
Return on sales (profit margin)	0.2:1
Receivables turnover	25
Earnings per share	$16.00

Additional Information:

1. Boulder Mineral Company generated $450,000 in net income during 2003.
2. Credit sales comprise 80 percent of net sales.
3. Cost of goods sold is 55 percent of net sales.
4. Current liabilities are 35 percent of total liabilities.
5. The balance in the cash account is $68,000.
6. The income tax rate was 34 percent.

REQUIRED:

Using the above information (and year-end balances), compute the following items.

a. Stockholders' equity
b. Total liabilities
c. Total assets
d. Interest expense
e. Net income before taxes
f. Net sales
g. Credit sales
h. Accounts receivable
i. Cost of goods sold
j. Inventory turnover
k. Inventory
l. Current liabilities
m. Current assets

(*Continued*)

n.   Marketable securities
o.   Noncurrent assets
p.   The number of shares of common stock outstanding

ISSUES FOR DISCUSSION

REAL DATA

ID5-1

Linking company
characteristics to
the financial
statements

Financial profiles, expressing the dollar values of financial statement accounts as a percentage of sales, are listed for four well-known companies:

1.   Toys "R" Us—retail toy store
2.   Kelly Services—provider of part-time employees
3.   J.P. Morgan—commercial bank
4.   Microsoft—software manufacturer

	1	2	3	4
Balance Sheet				
Cash	9%	61%	10%	529%
Accounts receivable	13	9	1	520
Inventory	—	3	22	—
Long-term assets	8	28	44	72
Current liabilities	9	15	25	984
Long-term liabilities	—	—	12	54
Stockholders' equity	21	86	40	83
Income Statement				
Sales of goods	—%	98%	100%	—%
Sales from services	100	2	—	100
Cost of goods sold	—	17	69	—
Operating expenses	97	33	20	30
Other expenses	1	25	43	56
Net income	2	25	6	14

REQUIRED:
Link each profile with a company, and explain your choices.

REAL DATA

ID5-2

Linking company
characteristics to
the financial
statements

Financial profiles, expressing the dollar values of financial statement accounts as a percentage of sales, are listed for four well-known companies:

1.   Lands' End—retail clothing store that sells through catalogs
2.   Walt Disney—amusement parks, films, and retailer of consumer products
3.   Ford Motor—manufactures and finances automobiles
4.   Hershey Foods—manufactures candy

	1	2	3	4
Balance Sheet				
Cash	1%	2%	26%	19%
Accounts receivable	8	1	16	112
Inventory	13	17	23	5
Long-term assets	59	11	70	47
Current liabilities	23	10	32	136
Long-term liabilities	5	1	44	31
Stockholders' equity	53	20	59	16

Income Statement

Sales of goods	100%	100%	16%	84%
Sales from services	—	—	84	16
Cost of goods sold	57	59	12	78
Operating expenses	30	33	68	11
Other expenses	6	3	9	8
Net income	7	5	11	3

REQUIRED:
Link each profile with a company, and explain your choices.

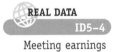

REAL DATA

ID5–3

Market and
book values

The following quote was taken from *Forbes* (April 21, 1997):

As stock values continue to diverge from book values, investors will be forced to realize . . . that stock prices have nothing to do with book values. The value of a company is determined by the present value of the cash that investors expect to get paid during the life of the firm. That value, less the company's debt, is what the company's equity is worth, regardless of the balance sheet. The key risk investors face is . . . buying an expected cash flow that fails to materialize because of competitive pressures or poor management. To properly evaluate those risks, investors will have to have a keen understanding of the companies they buy and the people who run them.

The market and book values—as of December 31, 1996—for three successful companies from three different countries are provided below. Monetary amounts are in billions.

	Market Value	Book Value	Market/ Book
AT&T—U.S. telecommunication services (U.S. dollars)	81	20	4.05
Carrefour—French retailer (French francs)	132	19	6.95
Bayer—German pharmaceutical manufacturer (Deutsch marks)	45	21	2.14

REQUIRED:
Use the quote to explain why the market and book values are not equal. Could the nature of the business or the home country of the company have anything to do with the difference?

REAL DATA

ID5–4

Meeting earnings
projections

Fortune (March 31, 1997) reported that seven of the eight companies in its 1997 Most Admired List—Coca-Cola, Merck, Microsoft, Johnson & Johnson, Intel, Pfizer, and Procter & Gamble—have missed making the analysts' consensus earnings forecast for their firm in only five quarters in the past five years. The same article noted that "for an unprecedented 16 consecutive quarters, more S&P (Standards & Poor's) companies have beat the consensus earnings estimates than missed them." And in most cases the companies seem to come in just above—not by too much—the consensus forecast.

REQUIRED:
a. What is a consensus earnings forecast, and why do companies wish to consistently beat it? What happens if they miss the forecast?
b. Why don't companies want to beat the forecast by too much?
c. Explain how management of a very successful company, like one of Fortune's Most Admired List, could help to ensure that the forecasts will be achieved year after year.

REAL DATA

ID5–5

The importance of
economic and
industry factors

On June 5, 1998, Motorola, the world's top cellular phone maker, announced that it would eliminate 15,000 jobs and issued a tough warning about hard times ahead in the semiconductor industry because of Asia's economic crisis. Also a leading chip maker, the company said it will fail to meet second-quarter earnings forecasts and reported its first loss since 1985, when the semiconductor industry slumped. As the company described it in the *International Herald*

Tribune, the loss is due primarily to a drop in semiconductor sales caused by the Asian down-turn and a special $1.95 billion charge.

REQUIRED:
a. Is it likely that this loss could have been anticipated by an analyst whose review of the company was limited to the 1997 financial statements, financial ratios, and footnotes? Discuss.
b. Why do you think that Motorola chose to book the $1.95 billion charge in a quarter that already was weak? Could the company be practicing any earnings management? If so, explain how it might work.
c. Name other U.S. companies whose financial successes and failures are linked to economies in other parts of the world.

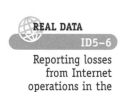

REAL DATA

ID5–6

Reporting losses from Internet operations in the retail industry

A retailer is posting strong earnings growth in its bricks-and-mortar business, but its fledgling Internet operation is posting losses. In making their earnings estimates, should Wall Street analysts ignore those losses and focus only on the profitable business or should they look at the company's retailing operations as a whole, which means lowering their profit forecasts to reflect the dot-com losses? That is the crux of the battle among a growing number of companies, and recently a behind-the-scenes conflict heated up because Staples, Inc., was able to persuade many analysts to submit estimates for the office supplier's first quarter of 2000, omitting losses from its Staples.com division. Most retailers, including Wal-Mart, lump their Internet results in with everything else. Staples's competitor, Office Depot, which is making money on its Internet business, rolls the Internet side into its overall results. Toys "R" Us and Blockbuster also include losses from their Internet operations in their overall results.

REQUIRED:
Explain why Staples might want to separate the losses from its new dot-com operation, and provide some reasons that company management may offer to justify the action. Do you think the losses should be reported, separated, included with the overall results, or ignored?

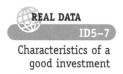

REAL DATA

ID5–7

Characteristics of a good investment

Fortune (June 26, 2000) ran an article on Bob Olstein, an investment analyst, who was particularly bullish at the time on several well-known stocks. He said the following indicators were the keys to his success: (1) a recent dramatic drop in the stock price, (2) company reports of positive free cash flow (net cash from operations minus capital expenditures), (3) conservative accounting methods, (4) a build-up in raw materials and partially completed inventory compared to finished inventory, (5) an increase in discretionary expenditures such as research and development, (6) undervalued assets on the balance sheet, (7) little or no debt combined with a high return on assets, and (8) consistency between what the president's letter said and what had actually happened over the past few years.

REQUIRED:
Explain how each of the eight items could provide a positive sign about a company.

REAL DATA

ID5–8

Financial accounting information in an efficient market

In an article published in the *Journal of Accountancy,* James Deitrick and Walter Harrison noted that the major markets for common stocks (e.g., the New York Stock Exchange, the American Stock Exchange) have been found to be efficient. That is, "common stock prices behave as if they fully incorporate all existing information quickly and without bias. This implies that information, old and new, has been impounded into security prices as a result of the analysis and collective wisdom of investors and their advisors." This finding has encouraged many accountants to contend that the information contained in financial reports cannot be used to identify undervalued common stocks in an efficient market.

REQUIRED:
a. Provide the rationale for why the information contained in financial reports cannot be used to identify undervalued securities.
b. Explain how financial accounting information can be useful even though it may not be helpful in identifying undervalued securities that are traded in efficient markets.

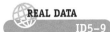

REAL DATA
ID5-9

Company value,
intangibles, and the
new economy

Baruch Lev, a well-respected accounting professor at New York University's Stern School of Business, has commented about the lack of relevance in today's financial statements. He notes that the 500 largest companies in the U.S. have market-to-book ratios (the ratio between the market value of the company and its balance sheet value [total assets − total liabilities]) that, on average, are greater than six. What this means is that the balance sheet reflects only 10 to 15 percent of the value of these companies. He claims that intangibles are fast becoming substitutes for physical assets. *PR Newswire* (June 16, 2000) reported: "The traditional standards of financial accounting—measuring a company's book value based solely on physical assets that appear on the balance sheet—is becoming obsolete."

REQUIRED:

What is Professor Lev referring to when he mentions intangibles, and explain the reasoning underlying his claim. Do you agree with him? Why or why not?

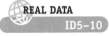

REAL DATA
ID5-10

Weak accounting

Billionaire investor Warren Buffet was quoted in the *Financial Post* (March 14, 2000) saying: "The reaction of weak management to weak operations is often weak accounting."

REQUIRED:

What does he mean? Provide some examples. What are the implications for financial statement users?

REAL DATA
ID5-11

Financial ratios,
earning power,
solvency, and
stock prices

An accounting professor at the University of California at Berkeley was quoted in *The Wall Street Journal* (December 17, 1990) as saying,

The most important items on the financial statements are trends in inventory, accounts receivable, and order backlogs. These are the strongest indicators and are more closely related to stock returns than reported earnings. In particular, investors should look at how companies' inventories of finished goods track their sales. If inventories are rising faster than sales, it's a bad signal. . . . For similar reasons, it pays to watch accounts receivable. . . . If these are rising faster than sales, not only can this signal trouble with sales but may show vulnerability to customer defaults.

REQUIRED:

a. Which of the financial ratios best captures the indicators suggested by the Berkeley professor?
b. Explain how these ratios provide information about solvency and earning power and why they might be more closely related to stock prices than earnings.

REAL DATA
ID5-12

Stock price
reactions to
earnings
announcements

Several years ago Compaq Computer reported a net profit of $971 million, a 24 percent increase above the previous year's first quarter. Unfortunately, the Company's stock price tumbled by over $9 when the news reached the market. In the third quarter of that same year, Chrysler reported an $82 million loss, yet on the day of the announcement, the Company's stock price jumped by 15 percent.

REQUIRED:

Explain why the stock market reacted negatively to Compaq's news and positively to Chrysler's news.

REAL DATA
ID5-13

Appendix 5A:
Analyzing the
financial statements
of Merck

On pages 230–232 are consolidated balance sheets and statements of income and cash flows taken from the 1999 annual report of Merck, a major pharmaceutical.

REQUIRED:

Analyze the statements by assessing the company's earning power and solvency position, and provide support for your assessment. In addition, list other kinds of information that would be useful for the analysis, and in each case, briefly explain why.

(Continued)

Merck & Co., Inc. and Subsidiaries
Consolidated Balance Sheet

December 31 ($ in millions) ASSETS	1999	1998
Current Assets		
Cash and cash equivalents	$2,021.9	$2,606.2
Short-term investments	1,180.5	749.5
Accounts receivable	4,089.0	3,374.1
Inventories	2,846.9	2,623.9
Prepaid expenses and taxes	1,120.9	874.8
Total current assets	11,259.2	10,228.5
Investments	4,761.5	3,607.7
Property, Plant and Equipment (at cost)		
Land	259.2	228.8
Buildings	4,465.8	3,664.0
Machinery, equipment, and office furnishings	7,385.7	6,211.7
Construction in progress	2,236.3	1,782.1
	14,347.0	11,886.6
Less allowance for depreciation	4,670.3	4,042.8
	9,676.7	7,843.8
Goodwill and Other Intangibles (net of accumulated amortization of $1,488.7 million in 1999 and $1,123.9 million in 1998)	7,584.2	8,287.2
Other Assets	2,353.3	1,886.2
	$35,634.9	$31,853.4

LIABILITIES AND STOCKHOLDERS' EQUITY		
Current Liabilities		
Accounts payable and accrued liabilities	$4,158.7	$3,682.1
Loans payable and current portion of long-term debt	2,859.0	624.2
Income taxes payable	1,064.1	1,125.1
Dividends payable	677.0	637.4
Total current liabilities	8,758.8	6,068.8
Long-Term Debt	3,143.9	3,220.8
Deferred Income Taxes and Noncurrent Liabilities	7,030.1	6,057.0
Minority Interests	3,460.5	3,705.0
Stockholders' Equity		
Common stock, one cent par value		
Authorized—5,400,000,000 shares		
Issued—2,968,030,509 shares	29.7	29.7
Other paid-in capital	5,920.5	5,614.5
Retained earnings	23,447.9	20,186.7
Accumulated other comprehensive income (loss)	8.1	(21.3)
	29,406.2	25,809.6
Less treasury stock, at cost		
638,953,059 shares—1999		
607,399,428 shares—1998	16,164.6	13,007.8
Total stockholders' equity	13,241.6	12,801.8
	$35,634.9	$31,853.4

Merck & Co., Inc. and Subsidiaries
Consolidated Statement of Cash Flows

Years Ended December 31 ($ in millions)	1999	1998	1997
Cash Flows from Operating Activities			
Income before taxes	$ 8,619.5	$ 8,133.1	$ 6,462.3
Adjustments to reconcile income before taxes to cash provided from operations before taxes:			
Acquired research	51.1	1,039.5	—
Gains on sales of businesses	—	(2,147.7)	(213.4)
Depreciation and amortization	1,144.8	1,015.1	837.1
Other	(547.7)	156.6	528.4
Net changes in assets and liabilities:			
Accounts receivable	(752.9)	(579.1)	(271.7)
Inventories	(223.0)	(409.5)	(53.5)
Accounts payable and accrued liabilities	404.5	250.1	321.8
Noncurrent liabilities	(150.9)	(13.0)	(29.4)
Other	69.9	9.8	29.9
Cash Provided by Operating Activities Before Taxes	8,615.3	7,454.9	7,611.5
Income Taxes Paid	(2,484.6)	(2,126.6)	(1,294.9)
Net Cash Provided by Operating Activities	6,130.7	5,328.3	6,316.6
Cash Flows from Investing Activities			
Capital expenditures	(2,560.5)	(1,973.4)	(1,448.8)
Purchase of securities, subsidiaries, and other investments	(42,211.2)	(29,675.4)	(22,986.7)
Proceeds from sale of securities, subsidiaries, and other investments	40,308.7	28,618.9	22,075.4
Proceeds from relinquishment of certain AstraZeneca product rights	1,679.9	—	—
Proceeds from sales of businesses	—	2,586.2	910.0
Other	(33.9)	432.3	(152.6)
Net Cash Used by Investing Activities	(2,817.0)	(11.4)	(1,602.7)
Cash Flows from Financing Activities			
Net change in short-term borrowings	2,137.9	(457.2)	431.3
Proceeds from issuance of debt	11.6	2,379.5	653.1
Payments on debt	(17.5)	(340.6)	(590.0)
Redemption of preferred stock of subsidiary	—	—	(1,000.0)
Purchase of treasury stock	(3,582.1)	(3,625.5)	(2,572.8)
Dividends paid to stockholders	(2,589.7)	(2,253.1)	(2,039.9)
Proceeds from exercise of stock options	322.9	490.1	413.3
Other	(152.5)	(114.1)	(153.9)
Net Cash Used by Financing Activities	(3,869.4)	(3,920.9)	(4,858.9)
Effect of Exchange Rate Changes on Cash and Cash Equivalents	(28.6)	85.1	(82.3)
Net (Decrease) Increase in Cash and Equivalents	(584.3)	1,481.1	(227.3)
Cash and Cash Equivalents at Beginning of Year	2,606.2	1,125.1	1,352.4
Cash and Cash Equivalents at End of Year	$2,021.9	$2,606.2	$1,125.1

Merck & Co., Inc. and Subsidiaries
Consolidated Statement of Income

Years Ended December 31 ($ in millions except per share amounts)	1999	1998	1997
Sales	$32,714.0	$26,898.2	$23,636.9
Costs, Expenses and Other			
Materials and production	17,534.2	13,925.4	11,790.3
Marketing and administrative	5,199.9	4,511.4	4,299.2
Research and development	2,068.3	1,821.1	1,683.7
Acquired research	51.1	1,039.5	—
Equity income from affiliates	(762.0)	(884.3)	(727.9)
Gains on sales of businesses	—	(2,147.7)	(213.4)
Other (income) expense, net	3.0	499.7	342.7
	24,094.5	18,765.1	17,174.6
Income Before Taxes	8,619.5	8,133.1	6,462.3
Taxes on Income	2,729.0	2,884.9	1,848.2
Net Income	$5,890.5	$5,248.2	$4,614.1
Basic Earnings per Common Share	$2.51	$2.21	$1.92
Earnings per Common Share Assuming Dilution	$2.45	$2.15	$1.87

Merck & Co., Inc. and Subsidiaries
Consolidated Statement of Retained Earnings

Years Ended December 31 ($ in millions)	1999	1998	1997
Balance, January 1	$20,186.7	$17,291.5	$14,772.2
Net Income	5,890.5	5,248.2	4,614.1
Common Stock Dividends Declared	(2,629.3)	(2,353.0)	(2,094.8)
Balance, December 31	$23,447.9	$20,186.7	$17,291.5

REAL DATA

ID5–14

Appendix 5A: Cash flow profiles and company life cycles

Cash flow profiles over a three-year year period are provided below for three well-known and very successful companies: Merck, Wal-Mart, and Sun Microsystems. Link each profile to one of the firms, explain what it means in terms of the company's cash management strategy, and describe how this analysis might reveal the company's age and maturity. Explain how three such different profiles can characterize three successful companies.

	1	2	3
PROFILE 1			
Net cash flow from operations	+	+	+
Net cash flow from investing activities	–	–	–
Net cash flow from financing activities	+	+	+
PROFILE 2			
Net cash flow from operations	–	–	–
Net cash flow from investing activities	–	–	–
Net cash flow from financing activities	+	+	+
PROFILE 3			
Net cash flow from operations	+	+	+
Net cash flow from investing activities	+	+	+
Net cash flow from financing activities	–	–	–

REAL DATA

ID5-15

The annual report
of Wal-Mart

The 2001 annual report of Wal-Mart is reproduced in Appendix A.

REQUIRED:

Review the 2001 Wal-Mart annual report, and analyze the financial statements by assessing Wal-Mart's earning power and solvency, and provide support for your assessments. Start by using the ratio framework illustrated in Figure 5–3.

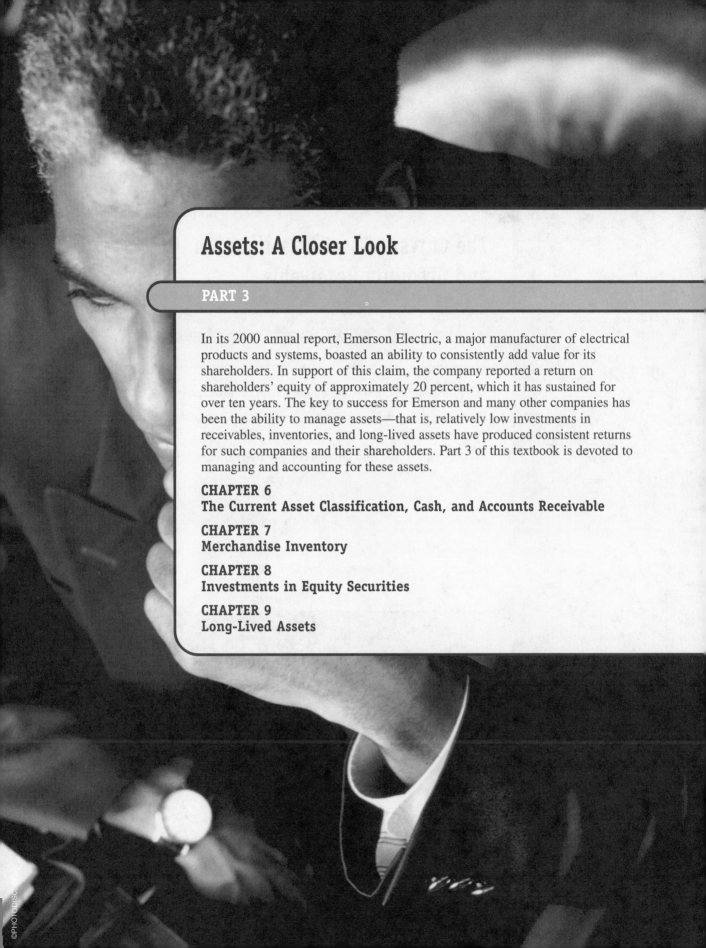

Assets: A Closer Look

PART 3

In its 2000 annual report, Emerson Electric, a major manufacturer of electrical products and systems, boasted an ability to consistently add value for its shareholders. In support of this claim, the company reported a return on shareholders' equity of approximately 20 percent, which it has sustained for over ten years. The key to success for Emerson and many other companies has been the ability to manage assets—that is, relatively low investments in receivables, inventories, and long-lived assets have produced consistent returns for such companies and their shareholders. Part 3 of this textbook is devoted to managing and accounting for these assets.

CHAPTER 6
The Current Asset Classification, Cash, and Accounts Receivable

CHAPTER 7
Merchandise Inventory

CHAPTER 8
Investments in Equity Securities

CHAPTER 9
Long-Lived Assets

The Current Asset Classification, Cash, and Accounts Receivable

CHAPTER 6

KEY POINTS

The following key points are emphasized in this chapter:

- *Current assets, working capital, current ratio, and quick ratio, and how these measures are used to assess the solvency position of a company.*

- *"Window dressing" and the reporting of current assets, working capital, and the current ratio.*

- *Techniques used to account for and control cash.*

- *Accounts receivable and how they are valued on the balance sheet.*

- *The allowance method for uncollectible receivables.*

- *Major concerns of financial statement users in the area of receivables reporting.*

The world economy revolves around credit; banks make loans and carry credit card debt, while large retailers, like Sears, grant lots of credit to their customers. These loans appear as receivables on retailers' balance sheets, but nobody really knows whether they will eventually produce cash. In three separate articles, *The Wall Street Journal* reported that banks wrote off almost 5 percent of their credit card loans, Swiss Bank Corporation—a major Swiss bank—wrote off almost $1.53 billion in bad loans, and Sears wrote off about $200 million in each quarter. More recently, Citicorp absorbed big credit card losses due to the financial crisis in Asia, where it maintains a large presence. Managing and accounting for outstanding receivables is an important and difficult problem that must be addressed by effective managers in today's business environment.

This chapter is divided into three sections. Section 1 covers the current asset classification and the measures of solvency and liquidity that use current assets. The dollar amounts in the cash and accounts receivable accounts make up an important part of current assets and are therefore important components of these measures. Sections 2 and 3 consider the definitions, disclosure rules, and methods of accounting for cash and accounts receivable. One appendix is included at the end of this chapter: Accounting for Receivables and Payables Expressed in Foreign Currencies.

THE CURRENT ASSET CLASSIFICATION

Current assets are so named because they are intended to be converted to cash (or consumed) in the near future. The exact definition of the near future is subjective, so the accounting profession has provided guidelines. According to professional standards, a **current asset** is defined as any asset that is intended to be converted into cash within one year or the company's **operating cycle,** whichever is longer.[1] As illustrated in Figure 6–1, a company's operating cycle is the time it takes the company to convert its cash to inventory (to purchase or manufacture inventory), sell the inventory, and collect cash from the sale. In other words, the operating cycle is the time required for a company to go through all the required phases of the production and sales process.

FIGURE 6–1
The operating cycle

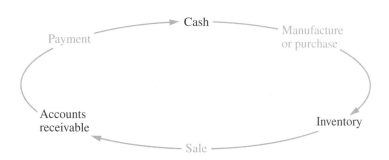

As the definition of current assets states, if the operating cycle is longer than one year, it serves as the time period for current assets. Companies with different operating cycles therefore use different time periods to define current assets. Compare, for example, the relatively short operating cycles of grocery chains like Safeway,

---

1. "Current Assets and Current Liabilities," *Accounting Research Bulletin No. 43, Restatement and Revision of Accounting Research Bulletin* (New York: American Institute of Accountants, 1953), Chapter 3A.

Albertson's, and Lucky Stores to the operating cycles of companies in the aerospace industry like The Boeing Company and Lockheed Martin, which require several years to manufacture aircraft. Indeed, the time periods for the current asset classification differ widely from company to company. However, the accounts included in the current asset section on the balance sheets of all companies are virtually the same. They are Cash, Short-Term Investments, Short-Term Accounts and Notes Receivable, Inventories, and Prepaid Expenses. The individual accounts that compose the current asset classification were briefly discussed and illustrated in Chapter 2.

Discuss the differences in the operations and the operating cycles of Tommy Hilfiger, a clothing manufacturer; Toyota, an automobile manufacturer; Young & Rubicam, an advertising agency; and Lycos, an Internet portal.

The Relative Size of Current Assets Across Industries

The relative size of current assets differs significantly across companies in different industries. Figure 6–2, which includes current assets as a percentage of total assets for selected well-known companies from various industries, shows that Merrill Lynch and Bank of America, financial institutions, have ratios of 70 to 90 percent. General services (SBC Communications and Wendy's) and manufacturing (GE and Chevron), on the other hand, are in the 15 to 30 percent range. The primary assets of financial services are short-term notes receivable and investments; the primary assets in the manufacturing and general services sectors tend to be property, plant, and equipment. Retailers, such as SUPERVALU and Tommy Hilfiger, carry relatively large amounts of inventory, and many of the Internet firms (Yahoo and Cisco) have large cash and short-term investment balances.

FIGURE 6–2
Current assets as a percentage of total assets

	Current Assets/Total Assets
MANUFACTURING:	
General Electric (Manufacturer)	.27
Chevron (Oil drilling and refining)	.20
RETAIL:	
SUPERVALU (Grocery retail)	.33
Tommy Hilfiger (Clothing retail)	.36
INTERNET:	
Yahoo (Internet search engine)	.57
Cisco (Internet systems)	.34
GENERAL SERVICES:	
SBC Communications (Telecommunications services)	.23
Wendy's (Restaurant services)	.16
FINANCIAL SERVICES:	
Bank of America (Banking services)	.70
Merrill Lynch (Investment services)	.91

Measures Using Current Assets: Working Capital, Current Ratio, and Quick Ratio

The distinction between current and noncurrent assets is useful because it provides an easy-to-determine, low-cost measure of a company's ability to produce cash in the short run. Current assets are often compared to current liabilities (the liabilities expected to require cash payments within the same time period as current assets) as an indicator of a company's solvency position.[2] Reasoning that current liabilities are a measure of short-run cash outflows, these comparisons appear to be logical. Three such comparisons, which were discussed in Chapter 5, are working capital and two solvency ratios, the current ratio and the quick ratio. **Working capital** is defined as current assets less current liabilities; the **current ratio** is equal to current assets divided by current liabilities; and the **quick ratio** divides the sum of cash plus short-term investments plus short-term receivables by current liabilities.

Selected current ratio balances are contained in Figure 6–3. The variances are quite large—some well above 1.0 and others below 1.0. Internet companies, like Yahoo and Cisco, tend to carry large amounts of cash and short-term investments and rely very little on short-term debt financing. Tommy Hilfiger's relatively large current ratio is driven by hefty cash and short-term investment balances, a large inventory of clothing goods, and a low level of accounts payable. Large companies in the high-tech telecommunications industry (SBC Communications) invest heavily in property, plant, and equipment, financing these investments with both short- and long-term debt. Such companies can afford to carry low current ratios because their operations can generate cash flows sufficient to meet their short-term debt payments. Also, they carry little in the way of inventories or receivables.

FIGURE 6–3

Current assets as a percentage of current liabilities

	Current Assets/Current Liabilities
MANUFACTURING:	
General Electric (Manufacturer)	.75
Chevron (Oil drilling and refining)	1.07
RETAIL:	
SUPERVALU (Grocery retail)	.87
Tommy Hilfiger (Clothing retail)	2.71
INTERNET:	
Yahoo (Internet search engine)	4.14
Cisco (Internet systems)	2.14
GENERAL SERVICES:	
SBC Communications (Telecommunications services)	.26
Wendy's (Restaurant services)	1.08
FINANCIAL SERVICES:	
Bank of America (Banking services)	.86
Merrill Lynch (Investment services)	1.17

2. Current liabilities were introduced and listed in Chapter 2 and are discussed extensively in Chapter 10.

Approximately two-thirds of RadioShack's total assets are considered current, while the same ratio for Hilton Hotels is only about 12 percent. Why?

The Economic Consequences of Working Capital, the Current Ratio, and the Quick Ratio

Managers must understand how transactions affect working capital, the current ratio, and the quick ratio because these measures are often used by investors, bankers, and other lenders (e.g., bondholders) to help assess a company's ability to meet current obligations as they come due. For example, Dun & Bradstreet, a widely used service that rates the creditworthiness of a large number of U.S. businesses, includes both the current ratio and the quick ratio as solvency measures in its list of fourteen key business ratios. Another of these key ratios, sales/working capital, is described as indicating whether a company has enough (or too many) current assets to support its sales volume. The formula used by Dun & Bradstreet to determine a company's credit rating, which in turn relates to the company's ability to borrow funds and the terms of its outstanding loans, includes these fourteen ratios.[3]

The measures of working capital and the current ratio also appear in loan contracts and debt covenants, where they specify certain minimum dollar amounts or ratios that a debtor company must maintain. For example, a recent financial report of Cummins Engine Company, a manufacturer of heavy-duty truck engines, indicated that loan agreements entered into by the company require maintenance of a 1.25 current ratio. This means that Cummins must maintain a current ratio of 1.25, or the creditor has the right to call for the immediate payment of the entire loan principal. Similarly, The Limited, which specializes in high-end clothing, has revolving credit agreements with a number of banks specifying that the company must maintain a certain level of working capital.

Working capital, the current ratio, and the quick ratio are also used by auditors. For example, an AICPA list of "red flags" alerting auditors to possible management fraud includes "inadequate working capital." The AICPA reasons that low amounts of working capital may put pressure on management to fraudulently manipulate the financial records in an effort to deceive stockholders, creditors, investors, and others. In addition, examining a company's working capital and current ratio can help an auditor assess whether there is substantial doubt about a company's ability to continue operations in the future. Information that helps to predict business failures is valuable to auditors because such failures lead to investor and creditor losses, which in turn can lead to costly lawsuits against auditors.

Limitations of the Current Asset Classification

While working capital, the current ratio, and the quick ratio are used extensively in business to assess solvency, they have a number of inherent and significant weaknesses. These limitations are related to the fundamental fact that current assets and

---

3. Many of the fourteen ratios were discussed in Chapter 5, but Dun & Bradstreet uses others as well.

current liabilities fail to accurately reflect future cash inflows and outflows, the essence of a company's ability to meet its debts as they come due. As noted by Leopold A. Bernstein,

The current ratio is not fully up to the task [of assessing short-term liquidity] because it is a static or "stock" concept of what resources are available at a given moment to meet the obligations at that moment. Moreover, working capital . . . does not have a logical or causative relationship to the future funds which flow through it. The future flows are, of course, the focus of our greatest interest in the assessment of short-term liquidity. And yet, these flows depend importantly on elements not included in the current ratio, such as sales, profits, and changes in business conditions.[4]

In addition, management has incentives to choose accounting methods and make operating decisions for no reason other than to "cosmetically" inflate the balances in the current asset accounts. For example, Datapoint, a computer manufacturer, once was charged by the SEC with materially overstating its receivables and revenues. The company was apparently shipping computers without customer authorization and thereby recording sales and receivables prematurely. Several years ago, General Motors changed its method of accounting for inventory and by doing so increased the dollar amount reported in its inventory account, and therefore its current assets, by $224 million. Such actions can have a significant impact on solvency ratios, which in turn may affect the company's credit rating as well as determine whether a company is in violation of a loan contract or debt covenant.

From these examples, it is clear that managers have discretion over the accounts in the current asset section of the balance sheet and thus have some control over measures like working capital, the current ratio, and the quick ratio. Exercising such discretion to inflate these measures is called **window dressing** and includes choosing accounting methods or making operating decisions that are designed solely to make the financial statements appear more attractive. Keep in mind, however, that while the practice of window dressing is widespread, it may not serve management's long-term interest. Managers who attempt to deceive by manipulating the dollar amounts on the financial statements risk reducing the credibility of the statements, which may actually hinder their abilities to raise debt and equity capital.

A MOVEMENT TOWARD CASH FLOW ACCOUNTING

In view of these limitations, measures like working capital, the current ratio, and the quick ratio are rarely viewed as the only ways to assess solvency. Cash flow numbers have gained popularity as indicators of a company's ability to meet its debts as they come due. The statement of cash flows, for example, which discloses the net cash flows from operating, investing, and financing activities, is also being used by investors and creditors to assess solvency. For example, Loyd C. Heath, an accounting professor at the University of Washington, states that "the emphasis in credit analysis has shifted from analysis of working capital position to dynamic analysis of future cash receipts and payments." A survey of investors published in *Management Accounting* notes that "investors use the statement of cash flows more, and the income statement less, than previously."

Nonetheless, solvency and liquidity measures based on the current asset classification are still important and widely used. Working capital, the current ratio, and the

---

4. Leopold A. Bernstein, "Working Capital as a Tool," *Journal of Accountancy* (December 1981), pp. 82, 84, 86.

quick ratio are low-cost surrogates for cash flow measures and are still used extensively by investors and creditors and in loan contracts and debt covenants. It is important, therefore, that you as a manager understand how transactions affect these measures and how these measures can be used to assess solvency and earning power. As we move now into discussions of each individual current asset, keep in mind that the accounting methods and operating decisions that affect these assets also affect working capital, the current ratio, and the quick ratio.

McDonald's carries a current ratio that is less than 50 percent, with relatively little investments in cash, receivables, inventories, and prepaid expenses. Explain why McDonald's is not in danger of going bankrupt even though its current liabilities far exceed its current assets.

CASH

The cash account is the first asset listed in the current asset section of the balance sheet. It consists of coin, currency, and checking accounts, as well as money orders, certified checks, cashier's checks, personal checks, and bank drafts received by a company. Remember also that cash is the standard medium of exchange and thus provides the basis for measuring all financial statement accounts.

Companies use a number of different titles to describe the cash account on their balance sheets. *Accounting Trends and Techniques* (2000) provided the summary contained in Figure 6–4 of the balance sheet captions of 600 of the largest companies in the United States. Note that the title *Cash* is decreasing in popularity, while *Cash and Equivalents* is becoming much more common.

FIGURE 6–4 Cash: Balance sheet captions		1999	1998	1997	1996
Cash		57	57	56	61
Cash and equivalents		504	502	501	488
Cash, including certificates of deposit or time deposits		8	5	5	9
Cash and marketable securities		29	31	32	35
No amount for cash		2	5	6	7
Total companies		600	600	600	600

Source: *Accounting Trends and Techniques* (2000).

The relative size of the cash account on the balance sheet varies across companies in different industries. Figure 6–5 reports that Yahoo, Cisco, Tommy Hilfiger, and Wendy's carry relatively large amounts of cash. Yahoo, Cisco, and Tommy Hilfiger, which have grown by purchasing other companies, may be holding cash intended for acquisitions, while Wendy's holds cash normally as part of its operations. Bank of America and Merrill Lynch are financial institutions that require cash balances to cover the cash needs of their depositors and clients.

Three issues concerning cash are particularly important to managers: (1) restrictions on the use of cash, (2) proper management of cash, and (3) control of cash.

	Cash/Total Assets	Cash/Current Assets
MANUFACTURING		
General Electric (Manufacturer)	.02	.07
Chevron (Oil drilling and refining)	.05	.23
RETAIL:		
SUPERVALU (Grocery retail)	.00	.01
Tommy Hilfiger (Clothing retail)	.13	.36
INTERNET:		
Yahoo (Internet search engine)	.20	.35
Cisco (Internet systems)	.13	.38
GENERAL SERVICES:		
SBC Communications (Telecommunications services)	.01	.03
Wendy's (Restaurant services)	.09	.53
FINANCIAL SERVICES:		
Bank of America (Banking services)	.04	.06
Merrill Lynch (Investment services)	.05	.06

FIGURE 6–5
Cash as a percentage of total assets and current assets

Restrictions on the Use of Cash

In general, cash presents few problems from a reporting standpoint. There are no valuation problems because cash always appears on the balance sheet at face value. The only reporting issue is whether there are restrictions on its use.

Restrictions placed on a company's access to its cash are typically imposed by creditors to help ensure future interest and principal payments. As part of a loan agreement, for example, a creditor may require that a certain amount of cash be held in **escrow;** that is, controlled by a trustee until the debtor's existing liability is discharged. In addition, banks sometimes require that minimum cash balances be maintained on deposit in the accounts of customers to whom they lend money or extend credit. These amounts are called **compensating balances.**

Cash held in escrow and compensating balances are examples of cash amounts that a company may own but cannot immediately use. Such restricted cash should be separated from the general cash account on the balance sheet, and the restrictions should be clearly described either on the balance sheet itself or in the footnotes to the financial statements. If the restricted cash is to be used for payment of obligations maturing within the time period of current assets, the separate "restricted cash" account is appropriately classified as a current asset. If it is to be held for a longer period of time, it should be classified as noncurrent.

Owens Corning, for example, once noted in its financial report that $85 million, almost 96 percent of its $89 million cash balance, was restricted. Approximately $70 million was held in escrow to be used in the following year for the payment of a long-term debt, and $15 million was temporarily "locked" in a Brazilian bank. That same year, Atlantic Richfield Company's financial report noted that "the company maintains compensating balances for some of its various banking services and products." Both Owens Corning and Atlantic Richfield included the restricted funds among their current assets. Manville Corporation, in its financial report, indicated that $278 million was placed in escrow in connection with bankruptcy proceedings. These funds were not included as current assets.

Proper Management of Cash

Proper cash management requires that enough cash be available to meet the needs of a company's operations, yet too much is undesirable because idle cash provides no return and loses purchasing power during periods of inflation. Maintaining a proper balance is one of management's greatest challenges. On one hand, enough cash must be available so that a company can meet its cash obligations as they come due. Purchases are often made in cash, and payments on accounts payable require cash. Wages, salaries, and currently maturing long-term debts must be honored in cash. Normally the cash needed for such operating activities is kept on the premises in the form of **petty cash** (small amounts of cash to cover day-to-day needs) or deposited in an interest-bearing checking account, where it earns a moderate rate of interest and can be withdrawn immediately as cash needs arise.

Cash in and of itself, however, is not a productive asset. Consider, for example, a popular TV game show that left $1 million under a plastic dome sitting out on the stage. The amount of annual interest income that was forgone by leaving that amount of cash idle, assuming a 10 percent interest rate, was $100,000 ($1,000,000 × 10%). Furthermore, during inflationary times, cash continually loses purchasing power. Assuming a 5 percent annual rate of inflation, it would require $1.05 million at the end of a year to buy the same goods and services that could have been purchased with $1 million at the beginning of the year. Consequently, cash over and above the amount needed for operations should be returned to shareholders as dividends or invested in income-producing assets such as short-term investments, inventories, long-term investments, property, plant, and equipment, and intangible assets.

A company that maintains a cash balance of more than is necessary for its day-to-day needs is not operating at its full potential. It is, of course, a desirable practice to keep a little extra in the checking account to meet unforeseen cash requirements, but in general, cash in excess of the amount necessary to cover day-to-day cash obligations should be invested in assets that produce a higher return. Determining this amount and where to invest the excess is a very important concern of a company's managers. Indeed, Andrew Long, head of global payments and cash management for Asia Pacific, notes, "If you are a treasurer of a company, one of the key concerns is managing cash . . ." (*Business Times,* March 15, 2000).

In the same article referred to above, Andrew Long notes that "cash management can cover a whole range of things." What does he mean?

Control of Cash

The control of cash is an important responsibility of a company's accounting system. It is a special concern for businesses such as grocery stores, movie theaters, restaurants, financial institutions, retail stores, department stores, and bars, which process frequent cash transactions. There are two aspects to the control of cash: record control and physical control.

RECORD CONTROL OF CASH

Record control refers to the procedures designed to ensure that the cash account on the balance sheet reflects the actual amount of cash in the company's possession. Problems of record control arise when many different kinds of transactions involve cash, and it is difficult to record them all accurately. Proper control of cash records requires that all cash receipts and disbursements be faithfully recorded and posted. Periodically, the dollar amount of cash indicated in the cash account in the ledger should be checked against and reconciled with the cash balance indicated on the statement provided by a company's bank.

PHYSICAL CONTROL OF CASH

Physical control of cash refers to the procedures designed to safeguard cash from loss or theft. Problems of physical control arise because cash is the standard medium of exchange; it is universally desired and easily concealed and transported. Cash embezzlement by a company's employees is always a threat. Separation of duties is an important part of a well-controlled system. It requires that employees responsible for recording cash transactions should not also be responsible for the physical control of the cash.

Proper physical control of cash may require that a minimum amount of cash be kept on a company's premises at any one time. Petty cash amounts used to cover day-to-day office expenses and cash receipts from sales or receivable payments should be handled by as few employees as possible and stored in a safe or locked cash drawer. Cash amounts in excess of petty cash requirements should be taken to the bank at frequent intervals.

Sarah Hogg, chairperson of Frontier Economics, commented that "ignoring cash control is accountants' Achilles' heel." Explain what she means.

ACCOUNTS RECEIVABLE

Accounts receivable arise from selling goods or services to customers who do not immediately pay cash. Often backed by oral rather than written commitments, accounts receivable represent short-term extensions of credit that are normally collectible within thirty to sixty days. These credit trade agreements are often referred to as **open accounts.** Often many such transactions are enacted between a company and its customers, and it is impractical to create a formal contract for each one. Open accounts typically reflect running balances, because at the same time customers are paying off previous purchases, new purchases are being made. If an account receivable is paid in full within the specified thirty- or sixty-day period, no interest is charged. Payment after this period, however, is usually subject to a significant financial charge. Credit card arrangements with department stores, like Sears and J.C. Penney, and oil companies, like Exxon Mobil and Chevron, are common examples of open accounts.

The following journal entries illustrate the recognition of accounts receivable from (1) the sale of merchandise[5] and (2) the sale of a service.

Accounts Receivable (+A)	500	
Sales (R, +SE)		500

Sold two items of inventory for $250 each on account.

Accounts Receivable (+A)	150	
Fees Earned (or Service Revenue) (R, +SE)		150

Provided consulting services for $150 on account.

Note that the recognition of the account receivable in each case is accompanied by the recognition of a revenue: sales or fees earned (service revenue). Both the balance sheet and the income statement are therefore affected when accounts receivable are established. Note also that the recognition of an account receivable is an application of the accrual system of accounting. Recall from Chapter 3 that revenues are recognized when the four criteria of revenue recognition are met.[6] Accounts receivable, therefore, are established in those cases where these four criteria are met prior to cash collection.

As the journal entry below illustrates, when cash is ultimately received, the accounts receivable balance is removed from the balance sheet and no revenue is recognized.

Cash (+A)	500	
Accounts Receivable (−A)		500

Collected cash on account.

The accounts receivable account therefore appears on the balance sheet during the time period between the recognition of a revenue and the receipt of the related cash payment.

Importance of Accounts Receivable

In our heavily credit-oriented economy, transactions that give rise to accounts receivable make up a significant portion of total business transactions. Figure 6–6 discloses the importance of accounts receivable to our selected group of well-known companies. Note first the sizable investment in receivables made by the financial institutions. Most of these are loans made to customers and clients. Similarly, General Electric owns a financial subsidiary that is used to provide financing to customers who purchase big-ticket items, such as home appliances. These receivables make up 35 percent of the company's total assets. The remaining companies included in Figure 6–6 do not tend to extend credit to their customers. Tommy Hilfiger and SUPERVALU, for example, do not issue their own credit cards, relying instead on cash sales, personal checks, and major credit cards such as VISA and Mastercard.[7] Some major retailers, like J.C. Penney, issue their own credit cards and consequently carry large balances of accounts receivable.

---

5. The sale of merchandise also involves the outflow of inventory, which must be recognized before financial statements are prepared.

6. The four criteria of revenue recognition are: (1) the earning process is substantially complete, (2) revenue is objectively measurable, (3) post-sale costs can be estimated, and (4) cash collection is reasonably assured.

7. When a customer uses a bank card to pay for an item or service (e.g., VISA or MasterCard), the selling company does not carry the receivable on its balance sheet. The receivable is "sold" to the finance company that issued the card. Such an arrangement is called *factoring*.

FIGURE 6-6		Receivables/ Total Assets	Receivables/ Current Assets
Receivables as a percentage of total assets and current assets	**MANUFACTURING**		
	General Electric (Manufacturer)	.35*	1.03*
	Chevron (Oil drilling and refining)	.09	.47
	RETAIL:		
	SUPERVALU (Grocery retail)	.09	.26
	Tommy Hilfiger (Clothing retail)	.09	.26
	INTERNET:		
	Yahoo (Internet search engine)	.04	.07
	Cisco (Internet systems)	.07	.21
	GENERAL SERVICES:		
	SBC Communications		
	(Telecommunications services)	.10	.03
	Wendy's (Restaurant services)	.04	.24
	FINANCIAL SERVICES:		
	Bank of America (Banking services)	.61	.87
	Merrill Lynch (Investment services)	.47	.52

Includes notes receivable.

In which of these three companies do you think accounts receivables management and control are most important and why—General Electric (major manufacturing), Kmart (discount retail), or Walgreens (pharmacies)?

Net Realizable Value: The Valuation Base for Accounts Receivable

The key factor in valuing accounts receivable on the financial statements is the amount of cash that the receivables are expected to generate. The cash is expected to be received in the future; in theory, therefore, present value should be used as the valuation base. The expected future cash receipt should theoretically be discounted. However, as indicated earlier, the period of time from the initial recognition of an account receivable to cash collection is normally quite short (thirty to sixty days). Consequently, the difference between the amount of cash to be received and the present value of the expected cash flows from the receivable is considered immaterial. For example, the difference between $100 and the present value of $100 to be received in one month, given a 10 percent annual interest rate, is approximately $0.76. Therefore, the face value of the receivable, the amount of cash to be collected, is judged to be a reasonable approximation of present value and, accordingly, provides the starting point for balance sheet valuation.

While the face value of the receivable represents a starting point, there are a number of reasons why it may not represent the actual amount of cash ultimately collected. Many companies, for example, offer cash discounts, allowing customers to pay lesser amounts if they pay within specified time periods. Other accounts receivable may produce no cash at all because customers simply refuse to pay (bad debts) or choose to return previously sold merchandise (sales returns). Each of these issues must be considered when placing a value on the accounts receivable account on the balance sheet.

Accordingly, the valuation base for the accounts receivable account is not the face amount of the receivables but rather the **net realizable value,** an estimate of the cash that is expected to be produced by the receivables.

Net Realizable Value of Accounts Receivable = Face Value − Adjustments for (1) Cash Discounts, (2) Bad Debts, and (3) Sales Returns

Cash Discounts

When a good or service is sold on credit, creating a receivable, the company making the sale naturally wants to collect the cash as soon as possible. To encourage prompt payment, many companies offer discounts (called **cash [sales] discounts**) on the gross sales price. There are benefits associated with offering these discounts because collected cash can be used to earn a return, and eliminating receivables quickly reduces the costs of maintaining records for and collecting outstanding receivables. Presumably, companies that offer cash discounts believe that these benefits exceed the reduction in future cash proceeds that results from the discount.

Cash discounts simply specify that an amount of cash less than the gross sales price is sufficient to satisfy an outstanding receivable if the cash is received within a certain time period. Certain sales on account, for example, may be subject to a 2 percent (of the gross sales price) cash discount if paid within ten days. Such terms are expressed in the following way: *2/10, n/30,* which reads "two-ten, net thirty." This expression means "a discount in the amount of 2 percent of the gross sales price is available if payment is received within ten days. To avoid finance charges over and above the gross price, payment must be received within thirty days." Other terms on cash discounts are also common: *3/20, n/30,* for example, means that a discount in the amount of 3 percent of the gross sales price is available if payment is received within twenty days, and finance charges over and above the gross price can be avoided if payment is received within thirty days; *n/10, EOM* means that the net amount of the sale (gross price less cash discount) is due no later than ten days after the end of the month.

CASH (SALES) DISCOUNTS VS. QUANTITY AND TRADE DISCOUNTS

Cash (sales) discounts, which can be viewed as incentives for prompt payment of open accounts, should be distinguished from quantity and trade discounts, which are simply reductions in sales prices. A **quantity discount** is a reduction in the per-unit price of an item if a certain quantity is purchased. "Cheaper by the dozen" is an example. Trade discounts are simply reductions in the sales price. A common form of trade discount, called a **markdown,** is quite common in retailing and normally is a sales price reduction due to decreased demand.

This distinction is important because cash (sales) discounts are reflected in the financial statements but quantity and trade discounts are not. To illustrate, in conjunction with an end-of-season sale, suppose that The Gap reduces the price of a certain line of shirts from $40 to $25. This $15 markdown is simply a reduction in the sales price of the shirts and would not be reflected in The Gap's books when the shirts are sold. The journal entry to record the sale would simply be:

Cash (or Accounts Receivable) (+A)   25
    Sales (R, +SE)   25
Sold merchandise for cash (or on account).

Note that the books give no recognition to the fact that the original sales price was $40. The asset (Cash or Accounts Receivable) and the revenue (Sales) are valued at the exchange price at the time of the transaction. The fact that the shirts were originally priced at $40 is ignored.

ACCOUNTING FOR CASH (SALES) DISCOUNTS

There are two ways to account for cash discounts: the **gross method** and the net method. Because the gross method is more straightforward and much more common in practice, we cover it only. Figure 6–7 illustrates the entries involved in the gross method.

FIGURE 6–7   Accounting for cash discounts

GIVEN INFORMATION:
Assume that Seller Company sells goods on account with a gross sales price of $1,000 to Buyer Company on December 15, 2002 (terms 2/10, n/30). The following journal entries would be recorded on the books of Seller Company using the gross method for two different cases.

Initial sale on December 15.

    Accounts Receivable (+A)   1,000
        Sales (R, +SE)   1,000
    Sold goods on account.

CASE 1:
Assume that Seller Company receives full payment on December 20 (within the ten-day discount period).

    Cash (+A)   980
    Cash Discount (−R, −SE)   20
        Accounts Receivable (−A)   1,000
    Paid on account.

CASE 2:
Assume full payment is received by Seller Company on January 3 (beyond the ten-day discount period).

    Cash (+A)   1,000
        Accounts Receivable (−A)   1,000
    Paid on account.

The gross method initially recognizes the transaction at $1,000, the gross sales price, and thereby is based on the assumption that Buyer Company, the customer, will not receive the cash discount. If Buyer Company pays within the ten-day discount period (Case 1), a cash discount account is used to balance the difference between the gross receivable ($1,000) and the cash proceeds ($980). Cash Discount is a temporary account that appears on the income statement of Seller Company. Its debit balance serves as a contra account to the credit balance in the sales account, giving rise to an income statement number called *net sales*. An example of the form of this disclosure follows.

Sales	$50,000
Less: Cash discounts	1,000
Net sales	$49,000

If Buyer Company misses the ten-day discount (Case 2), the $1,000 cash receipt after the expiration of the discount period exactly matches the gross amount in Seller Company's accounts receivable account.

An important caveat about cash discounts: In reality many companies pay little attention to their terms. Consider, for example, a major retailer like Wal-Mart who is an extremely important customer to a large number of its suppliers. While the suppliers may offer cash discounts, encouraging Wal-Mart to pay its bills quickly, there is little they can do if Wal-Mart chooses to pay the discounted amount after the expiration of the discount period. The suppliers are very dependent on Wal-Mart's business, and that dependence gives Wal-Mart an advantage that many businesses in similar situations tend to exploit.

The Allowance Method of Accounting for Bad Debts (Uncollectibles)

In an ideal world, all receivables would be satisfied, and there would be no need to consider bad debts. However, accounts that are ultimately uncollectible are an unfortunate fact of life, and companies must act both to control them and to estimate their effects on the financial statements. To give you some idea of the magnitude of bad debts, Figure 6–8 shows 2000 uncollectibles as a percentage of outstanding receivables for several major U.S. corporations.

<table>
<tr><td>

FIGURE 6–8

Bad debts as a percentage of outstanding receivables

</td><td>

Company	Bad Debts/ Outstanding Receivables
Bell Atlantic	9%
SUPERVALU	5%
General Electric	3%
Pier 1 Imports	1%

Source: 2000 annual reports.

</td></tr>
</table>

Controlling bad debts is a costly undertaking for many companies. The creditworthiness of potential customers can be checked by subscribing to credit-rating services such as Dun & Bradstreet, Moody's, or Standard & Poor's. Companies can create and maintain collection departments, hire collection agencies, and pursue legal proceedings. Certainly, each of these alternatives can improve cash collections, but each does so at a significant cost. In the extreme, management can institute a policy requiring that all sales be paid in cash. Such a policy would certainly eliminate collection costs and drive bad debts to zero, but it could also be extremely costly because it could dramatically reduce sales revenue. For most companies, then, bad debts are an inevitable cost of everyday operations that must be considered in the management of accounts receivable.

From an accounting standpoint, the inevitability of bad debts reduces the cash expected to be collected from accounts receivable. It thereby reduces the value of Accounts Receivable on the balance sheet. Bad debt losses also represent after-the-fact evidence that certain sales should not have been recorded, since the fourth criteria of revenue recognition (i.e., cash collection is assured) was not met for those sales. As a result, both Accounts Receivable and net income are overstated if bad debts are ignored. Proper accounting for bad debts, therefore, involves two basic adjustments: (1) an adjustment to reduce the value of Accounts Receivable on the balance sheet and (2) an adjustment to reduce net income.

"With China poised to enter the World Trade Organization, a fresh wave of foreign investors is preparing to take the plunge into its huge market. But as they do, these newcomers should learn a hard truth from their more seasoned, battle-worn predecessors: just because you make a sale doesn't mean you will get paid for it" (*Far East Economic Review*, 2000). Explain the meaning of this quote and how it might affect how U.S. companies do business in China.

The **allowance method** is used to account for bad debts. This method involves three basic steps: (1) the dollar amount of bad debts is estimated at the end of the accounting period, (2) an adjusting journal entry, which recognizes a bad debt expense on the income statement and reduces the net balance in Accounts Receivable, is recorded in the books, and (3) a write-off journal entry is recorded when a bad debt actually occurs. The following example illustrates the basic steps of the allowance method.

Suppose that during 2002, its first year of operations, Q-Mart had credit sales of $20,000 and a balance in Accounts Receivable of $6,000 as of December 31.

1. *Estimating bad debts.* After reviewing the relevant information, Q-Mart's accountants estimate that 2.5 percent ($500) of its credit sales will not be collected.
2. *Adjusting journal entry.* The following journal entry would be recorded on December 31.

   Bad Debt Expense (−R, −SE)   500
      Allowance for Doubtful Accounts (−A)   500
   Recognized provision for doubtful accounts.

3. **Write-off journal entry.** On January 18, 2003, Q-Mart is notified that ABM Enterprises has declared bankruptcy and will not be able to pay the $200 it owes to Q-Mart. The following journal entry would then be recorded in the books of Q-Mart.

   Allowance for Doubtful Accounts (+A)   200
      Accounts Receivable/ABM (−A)   200
   Wrote off uncollectible account/ABM.

STEP 1: ESTIMATING BAD DEBTS

The allowance method requires that the dollar value of bad debts be estimated at the end of each accounting period. The most common method of estimating bad debts for financial reporting purposes is the **percentage-of-credit-sales approach.**[8] This approach simply multiplies a percentage by the credit sales of the period. In the example given, $500 (2.5% × $20,000) of the credit sales during 2002 was estimated to be uncollectible.

8. Later in the chapter we discuss another method of estimating bad debts, called the *aging method.*

The percentage of credit sales used in the calculation of bad debt expense is based primarily on a company's past experience. For a company such as Q-Mart, which is in its first year of operations, the typical bad debt rate of the other companies in its industry may provide a useful benchmark. Nonetheless, the percentage is an estimate, which by definition is inexact and uncertain. These estimates represent an area of potential disagreement between managers, who often want the financial statements to be as attractive as possible, and auditors, whose professional ethics and exposure to legal liability encourage them to prefer conservative reporting.

The problem of estimating bad debts is significant for financial institutions, which have a large portion of their assets in outstanding loans. However, most service, retail, and manufacturing companies, especially those that have been in business for many years, can estimate bad debts with reasonable accuracy. The major retail companies, in particular, experience bad debts at a fairly constant percentage of credit sales across time. Bad debt expenses for J.C. Penney, for example, were less than 1 percent of sales in 1998, 1999, and 2000. Thus, while it may be difficult to predict whether an individual account will be uncollectible, many companies find it relatively easy to predict the percentage of bad debt losses from a large group of credit sales.

STEP 2: ADJUSTING JOURNAL ENTRY

The proper method of accounting for bad debts requires an end-of-period adjusting journal entry that reduces both net income and the balance sheet carrying value of Accounts Receivable.

The credit side of the adjusting journal entry recorded by Q-Mart in the previous example, Allowance for Doubtful Accounts, reduces the balance sheet value of Accounts Receivable by $500, the expected dollar amount of bad debts.[9] Allowance for Doubtful Accounts is a permanent contra asset account with a credit balance. It immediately follows and is subtracted from Accounts Receivable on the balance sheet. The form of this disclosure in the current asset section of the balance sheet follows.

Accounts receivable	**$6,000**
Less: Allowance for doubtful accounts	**500**
	$5,500

Disclosing the allowance for doubtful accounts account in this way reflects the fact that less cash than is indicated by the face value of the receivables is expected to be collected. In the case above, $5,500 of the outstanding receivables is expected to be received. Such disclosure helps to report Accounts Receivable at net realizable value.[10]

The debit side of the adjusting journal entry records a contra revenue on the income statement (Bad Debt Expense). Recognizing the $500 contra revenue in 2002 indicates that certain (unidentifiable as of December 31) credit sales should not have been recorded in 2002. It thereby serves to reduce revenues for sales that actually were never made.[11]

---

9. The account title "Allowance for Doubtful Accounts" is used in this text. However, in a survey of 600 major U.S. companies, *Accounting Trends and Techniques* (2000) reports that slightly less than half of these companies use this title. The remaining companies use any of eight different descriptions, including Allowance, Allowance for Losses, and Reserve for Doubtful Accounts.

10. Most major U.S. companies do not disclose the dollar amount in the allowance account explicitly on the balance sheet. Instead, they simply report the net amount of receivables, after the dollar amount in the allowance account has been subtracted.

11. The bad debt estimate represents revenues that should never have been recorded because the fourth criteria of revenue recognition (cash collection is reasonably assured) was not met—giving rise to a contra revenue account, which is subtracted from sales on the income statement. However, generally accepted accounting principles do not specifically address how this charge should be disclosed, and some companies record the adjustment as an expense.

STEP 3: THE WRITE-OFF JOURNAL ENTRY

The write-off journal entry recorded by Q-Mart reduces both the allowance account and the accounts receivable balance. It is particularly important to note that this entry has no effect on the income statement and only serves to remove from the books the specific account receivable of ABM.

The write-off entry has virtually no effect on the financial statements because it simply identifies a specific bad debt that (on average) was known to be uncollectible and was recognized as such at the end of the previous accounting period. Indeed, the entry does not affect the net accounts receivable balance, current assets, working capital, the current ratio, quick assets, or net income.

To illustrate, the February 26, 2000 net accounts receivable of SUPERVALU, the nation's tenth largest grocery retailer, appeared as follows (dollars in millions):

Accounts receivable	**$592**
Less: Allowance for doubtful accounts	**30**
	$562

The following year, assume that SUPERVALU receives notice that Catering Corporation will not be able to pay the $5 million it owes to SUPERVALU, and the following journal entry is recorded in SUPERVALU's books:

Allowance for Doubtful Accounts (+A)	**5**	
Accounts Receivable/Catering (−A)		**5**
Wrote off uncollectible account/catering.		

This write-off entry reduces the balance of both Accounts Receivable and Allowance for Doubtful Accounts by $5 million. Consequently, after the write-off entry, the net accounts receivable balance appears as follows:

Accounts receivable	**$587**
Less: Allowance for doubtful accounts	**25**
	$562

Note that the write-off entry had no effect on the net realizable value of Accounts Receivable. The net balance of $562 is unchanged because both Accounts Receivable and Allowance for Doubtful Accounts were reduced by the same dollar amount. As a result, current assets, the current ratio, working capital, the quick ratio, and net income are all unaffected. The financial statement effect occurred at the end of the previous period (Step 2) when the adjusting journal entry was recorded.

So far we have implied that bad debts are discovered when a specific event occurs. For example, in the preceding illustrations the bad debt write-offs were recorded when a company received notice that a given customer was bankrupt or could not pay for some other reason. While bad debt write-offs can be recorded in this manner, it is probably more common for companies to write off bad debts when they decide that given receivables have been outstanding too long and are too costly to pursue. The following excerpt, which summarizes a typical write-off policy, was taken from the 2000 financial report of J.C. Penney Company, Inc.:

The Company's policy is to write off accounts when the scheduled minimum payment has not been received for six consecutive months, or if any portion of the balance is more than twelve months past due, or if it is otherwise determined that the customer is unable to pay.

BAD DEBT RECOVERIES

Specific accounts that have been written off the books are occasionally recovered later. When such a receivable is reinstated, the write-off entry is simply reversed. This procedure corrects what was (in retrospect) recorded in error at a previous time. For example, the recovery of a previously written-off $5 million account receivable would be recorded as follows:

Accounts Receivable/Catering (+A)	5	
Allowance for Doubtful Accounts (−A)		5

Recovered $5 accounts receivable/catering.

Cash (+A)	5	
Accounts Receivable/Catering (−A)		5

Received $5 cash on account.

Inaccurate Bad Debt Estimates

Inaccurate bad debt estimates give rise to preadjustment balances in Allowance for Doubtful Accounts. For example, if a company estimates $4,000 of bad debts on December 31, 2002, and actually incurs only $3,400 during 2003, as shown in Figure 6–9, Allowance for Doubtful Accounts contains a $600 credit balance *before adjusting entries are recorded* at the end of 2003. If, instead of $3,400, bad debts of $4,400 actually occur during 2003, as shown in Figure 6–10, the *preadjustment December 31, 2003 balance* in Allowance for Doubtful Accounts is a $400 debit.

FIGURE 6–9 Overestimated bad debts

Allow. for Dbt. Accts. (+A) 3,400		Allowance for Doubtful Accounts		Bad Debt Exp. (−R, −SE) 4,000	
Accts. Rec. (−A)	3,400			Allow. for Dbt. Accts. (−A)	4,000
Wrote off accts. rec.—2003.			4,000	*2002 adjusting entry.*	
		3,400			
			Preadj.		
			bal. 600		

FIGURE 6–10 Underestimated bad debts

Allow. for Dbt. Accts. (+A) 4,400		Allowance for Doubtful Accounts		Bad Debt Exp. (−R, −SE) 4,000	
Accts. Rec. (−A)	4,400			Allow. for Dbt. Accts. (−A)	4,000
Wrote off accts. rec.—2003.			4,000	*2002 adjusting entry.*	
		4,400			
	Preadj.				
	bal. 400				

Because estimates are rarely correct, preadjustment balances in Allowance for Doubtful Accounts are common. But they are usually ignored because across time under- and overestimates in individual years tend to neutralize each other. However, a significant debit or credit accumulation in the preadjustment balance over several periods may indicate that the estimates are not only inaccurate but also biased. Consistent overestimates give rise to preadjustment credit accumulations (Figure 6–9), while consistent underestimates create preadjustment accumulations on the debit side of Allowance for Doubtful Accounts (Figure 6–10). Such accumulations, which often indicate that a company's estimating formula should be revised, can lead to balance sheet misstatements in the allowance account because they are reflected in the year-end, postadjustment balance. Users can detect these misstatements by comparing the amount in the allowance account to such numbers as sales and accounts receivable across time. Unusual deviations or well-defined trends may reveal a problem in estimating bad debts, which may raise questions about management's competence and/or incentives.

AN AGING SCHEDULE: ANOTHER METHOD OF ESTIMATING BAD DEBTS

Another common method of estimating bad debt losses is to establish an **aging schedule** of outstanding accounts receivable. This method categorizes individual accounts in terms of the length of time each has been outstanding and applies a different bad debt rate to each category. The bad debt rate applied to categories comprising older accounts is greater than that applied to categories comprising younger accounts, on the assumption that the longer an account has been outstanding, the more likely it is to be uncollectible.

To illustrate how an aging schedule can be used to estimate bad debts, assume that each of the accounts that make up a $4,000 end-of-year balance in Accounts Receivable is placed into one of three categories that represent the lengths of time the accounts have been outstanding: (1) six to twelve months, (2) three to six months, and (3) less than three months. It is the company's policy to write off accounts when they become one year old. Assume also that the percentage of uncollectibles expected for each of the three categories is 30 percent for Category 1, 10 percent for Category 2, and 2 percent for Category 3. The bad debt estimate for the entire accounts receivable balance is computed in Figure 6–11. The $324 estimate is computed by totaling the dollar amount of the bad debts expected from each of the three categories.

FIGURE 6–11
An aging schedule

Age of Accounts	Amount	Percent Uncollectible	Estimate	
6–12 months	$ 500	30%	$150	(500 × 30%)
3–6 months	1,300	10%	130	(1,300 × 10%)
Less than 3 months	2,200	2%	44	(2,200 × 2%)
Total	$4,000		$324	

AGING AS A MANAGEMENT TOOL

Maintaining control over outstanding accounts receivable is an important part of effective management for many companies. Because of the time value of money, receivables should be collected as quickly as possible. Bad debts should also be held to a minimum. Aging schedules help companies control bad debts in a number of significant ways.

An aging schedule, for example, can identify slow-moving accounts, thus direct-ing collection efforts and defining the maximum costs that should be incurred by those efforts. Collection efforts should be directed toward the accounts in the older cate-gories, but the costs associated with these efforts should not exceed the expected loss from the accounts. For example, a company may have $10,000 of accounts receivable that have been outstanding for over six months. Past experience indicates that 20 per-cent of such accounts are uncollectible. The $2,000 ($10,000 $\times$ 20%) expected loss from these accounts determines a maximum dollar amount for the costs incurred to collect them.

An aging schedule can also be helpful in estimating how much money a company is losing in potential interest charges. Such information can be useful in deciding whether to offer cash discounts and in determining the appropriate terms for such discounts.

Although aging schedules can provide useful information, keep in mind that they can be costly to establish and maintain. For companies that rely on credit sales to a wide variety of customers, maintaining the age and balance of each account can be quite time-consuming. Computerized accounting systems are almost a necessity for efficient aging analyses and receivables control. Most large companies, of course, have computerized their receivables accounting, and when small companies change from manual to computerized accounting systems, receivables applications are often used first to improve control over accounts receivable.

There is a growing trend among companies seeking greater efficiencies to sell their outstanding receivables to financial institutions, which are well equipped to deal with potential bad debts. As reported in *Crain's Chicago Business Journal* (June 2000), "The trend has been fueled by downsizing companies that no longer want to employ mid-level managers to oversee collection efforts, and the spread of sophisticated finan-cial management techniques is leading more firms to conclude that a smaller amount of money now is worth more than the possibility of a larger amount later." These developments underscore the significant costs associated with managing your own receivables.

As president and CEO of newly formed Hilco Receivables LLC, Bruce Passen plans to tap into a growing trend among businesses to sell delinquent accounts receivable rather than hire collection agencies to try to recover the money owed. Collection firms with a stomach for a little risk now have an opportunity for higher returns. What does Mr. Passen plan to do?

Accounting for Sales Returns

For many companies, it is common that merchandise sold on account is returned by customers at a later date. These returns are important in the retail industry, and text-book publishers are especially affected because customers can often return large amounts of product sixty days or more after the initial sale. When returned items were initially sold, the sale and the associated account receivable were recognized on the books. Because sales returns are usually accompanied by either the removal of the receivable or the granting of future credit, companies with significant returns must adjust both the income statement and Accounts Receivable on the balance sheet. The methods used to account for sales returns are similar to those used to account for bad debts; that is, at the end of each period an estimate of expected sales returns is made which, in turn, determines the dollar value of an adjusting journal entry that reduces income and establishes an allowance account. This account is disclosed on the balance sheet as a contra to Accounts Receivable. Actual returns are then debited against the allowance and credited against Accounts Receivable.

ACCOUNTS RECEIVABLE FROM A USER'S PERSPECTIVE

When accounting for short-term receivables, two general questions are of significant economic importance: (1) When should a receivable be recorded in the books? and (2) At what dollar amount should a receivable be valued on the balance sheet?

When Should a Receivable Be Recorded?

Revenues and related receivables are recognized when the four criteria of revenue recognition have been met. Establishing exactly when this occurs, however, is difficult and subjective, because managers have freedom to determine when and how a sale and the associated receivable are recorded. This freedom gives rise to widely different practices. For example, General Electric recognizes revenues when goods are shipped, while HarperCollins, a large book publisher, recognizes revenues when it invoices customers, sometimes a month before orders are shipped. Revenue recognition practices even differ among companies in the same industry. A survey of 200 software companies, for example, revealed that twenty-six (13 percent) companies waited until cash was received before recognizing a sale, while thirty (15 percent) companies recognized a sale as soon as an order was received.

Users of financial statements must realize that, even within the guidelines of generally accepted accounting principles, managers can use discretion to speed up or slow down the recognition of revenue. This concern is particularly important for transactions that occur near the end of an accounting period. Recognizing a receivable and a revenue on December 30 instead of January 2, for example, can significantly affect current assets, working capital, and net income on the December 31 financial statements.

To illustrate, suppose that current assets, current liabilities, and net income for Johnson and Sons as of December 29 are $45,000, $34,000, and $14,000, respectively. Johnson and Sons provides a service to Ace Manufacturing that is billed at $20,000. The service is ordered by Ace on December 30 and completed by Johnson and Sons on January 5. Payment is made by Ace after January 5. The current ratio, working capital position, and net income as of December 31 for Johnson and Sons are computed in Figure 6–12, assuming that (1) the revenue is recognized when the service is completed

FIGURE 6–12 The timing of revenue and receivable recognition		(1) Revenue Is Recognized on January 5.	(2) Revenue Is Recognized on December 30.
December 31 current ratio			
(current assets ÷ current liabilities)		1.32	1.91
December 31 working capital			
(current assets − current liabilities)		$11,000	$31,000
Net income, year ended December 31		$14,000	$34,000

on January 5 and (2) the revenue is recognized when the service is ordered on December 30.

Note that the timing of revenue recognition can have a significant effect on important financial statement numbers. Recognizing the sale in the earlier period increased the current ratio by 45 percent and working capital and net income each by $20,000. Such effects have economic significance because they may influence a company's credit rating or determine whether it violates the terms of debt agreements. Since the timing of revenue and receivable recognition has a direct effect on net income and current assets, financial statement users should pay special attention to it.

Extreme cases of premature revenue and receivable recognition, or the complete fabrication of sales, is often interpreted as management fraud. Bear and Stearns cited a 1999 study of over 200 corporate accounting fraud cases that occurred between 1987 and 1997, and concluded that the majority of these cases involved premature recognition of revenues (and receivables). In September of 2000 the SEC reported that it filed thirty enforcement actions for accounting abuses at a number of public companies, and many of these cases involved revenue recognition problems, such as booking revenue on shipments that never occurred. Two companies cited by the SEC were Raytheon, a defense contractor, and The Limited, a well-known clothing retailer, both of which have changed their revenue recognition practices. In each case the change led to the recognition of a major income write-down.

Other famous cases of inappropriate revenue recognition have involved such companies as MiniScribe, a software manufacturer, Regina Corporation, a well-known home appliance maker, and Orion Pictures, a motion picture studio that produced a number of box office hits. In all three cases, aggressive management, under intense pressure to perform, either fabricated sales or used questionable accounting practices to accelerate the recognition of revenues in an effort to increase reported profits and improve solvency measures. While these unethical behaviors may have delayed and obscured the companies' financial problems, they certainly did little to solve them and in most cases made matters much worse.

A special problem has arisen in the world of the Internet. Given that Internet startup companies are now routinely valued on their revenues—since most generate losses—the SEC has grown worried that some companies are overstating their revenues. When dot-com companies, for example, swap advertising with other Websites, the swapping companies often book offsetting revenue and expense amounts. While the practice does not affect earnings, it does tend to overstate revenues.

In 1994 California Micro Devices Corp. wrote off over half of its accounts receivable, causing a 40 percent drop in its stock price. A court hearing later revealed that in the face of aggressive revenue goals, the company booked revenues on products that had been sold but were not shipped until after the end of the year. In terms of the principles of revenue recognition, explain why this practice is inappropriate. How could it lead to a receivables write-off?

Balance Sheet Valuation of Receivables

The appropriate dollar amount at which to value receivables on the balance sheet is primarily a question of whether the outstanding receivables will, in fact, be paid. Companies like General Motors and General Electric have billions of dollars in outstanding receivables, many of which may never produce any cash. Estimating such uncollectibles, which can significantly affect both the income statement and the balance sheet, can be very subjective and can lead to substantial disagreements between management and its auditors. Several years ago, for example, a major auditing firm postponed rendering an opinion on Federal Home Loan Bank of Dallas because the bank carried $500 million of questionable receivables on its balance sheet. Bad debt write-offs can also be enormous. In the year 2000 alone, AOL wrote off over $50 million in bad debts. In addition, estimating bad debts involves judgment, and there is a real temptation for managers to use the estimate to report favorable earnings.

These examples suggest that (1) bad debts can be significant, (2) estimating bad debts is subjective, and (3) management is often unwilling to establish large bad debt provisions. Users must be aware of these concerns and pay close attention to the size and activity in the allowance account as well as the annual bad debt expense. For example, consider a case where the following information is taken from the financial statements of a company you are currently reviewing as a possible investment:

	2003	2002
Balance Sheet		
Accounts Receivable	$12,500	$13,200
Allowance for Doubtful Accounts	(1,300)	(1,500)
Income Statement		
Sales	$99,000	$82,500
Bad Debt Expense	(1,700)	(1,650)
Net Income	5,000	4,200

At first glance, the company's financial performance appears to be strong and improving. Both sales and net income increased by 20 percent during 2003, and accounts receivable decreased, which suggests that receivables collections may have improved. However, a closer look at the activity in the allowance account and bad debt expense raises a concern. Using T-account analysis, as illustrated in Figure 6–13, you can see that the bad debt expense was insufficient, $200 less than the write-offs during 2003. Further review shows that the expense, as a percent of sales, decreased from 2 percent in 2002 to 1.7 percent in 2003. Had 2 percent been used in 2003, the expense would have been $1,980, and net income would have been lower by $280. Also, the allowance amount, as a percent of accounts receivable, decreased from 11.4 to 10.4

FIGURE 6–13

Analyzing the allowance for doubtful accounts T-account

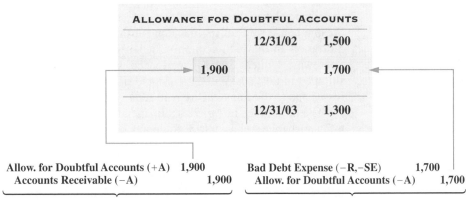

Write-off of Accounts Receivable.   Recognition of Bad Debt Expense.

percent. It seems that management reduced the bad debt expense, which increased reported net income, even though bad debt write-offs did not decrease during 2003. Users must be cautious in these situations because bad debt estimates are based on information about the creditworthiness of their customers, which is available only to management. It is virtually impossible for outsiders to assess these estimates.

The 2000 annual report of La-Z-Boy, a well-known furniture manufacturer, reports a profit of over $87 million, while reporting net cash from operations of only $8 million. One of the main reasons for the difference is a $49 million increase in accounts receivable during the year. What events may have accounted for the huge increase, and how might they influence an investor's interpretation of the company's current ratio and cash flow statement?

In summary, the methods used to account for accounts receivable can lead to significant economic consequences, affecting a company's credit rating, determining whether debt covenants are violated, accelerating bankruptcy proceedings, and introducing the potential for sizable lawsuits against managers and auditors. Recall from Chapter 5 that the combination of such economic effects and reporting subjectivity can encourage managers to use reporting strategies. Examples are overstating income and financial condition, "taking a bath," and building "hidden reserves," which can serve managers' interests at the expense of the stockholders. Recall also that practicing such strategies need not be fraudulent, because generally accepted accounting principles are sufficiently flexible to allow a large amount of management discretion.

FINANCIAL INSTITUTIONS AND UNCOLLECTIBLE LOANS

The collectibility of outstanding loans is a key concern for bank management and is at the heart of successful banking. In its 1999 financial statement, for example, Chase Manhattan reported approximately 172 billion in outstanding loans, which was about 43 percent of total assets. The company estimated that $3.5 billion of these loans would be written off, and in 1999 Chase recognized bad debt expense of $1.6 billion. Other financial institutions, such as savings and loans, insurance companies, and manufacturers that offer financing to their customers (Big 3 automakers, General Electric, Deere & Company), also carry significant receivables and face special collectibility problems. Such problems can involve much more than simply assessing the creditworthiness of customers. Major swings in the overall U.S. economy, certain sectors within the economy, or even entire countries and continents can have huge impacts on the financial health of these kinds of companies. Several years ago, for example, Westinghouse sold off its financial subsidiary due to nonperforming loans caused by a drop-off in the U.S. economy; banks with outstanding loans to companies in the Southwest United States experienced severe financial hardship when oil prices slumped in the '80s; and Citicorp and other major U.S. banks recently booked huge losses due to the financial crisis in Asia.

The difficulties in America's financial institutions have brought about several significant changes relevant to accountants. First, the FASB has ruled that banks both disclose the market values of their outstanding loans and create larger reserves for bad debts. This rule, which generated much opposition from the banking industry, has reduced the balance sheet value of most U.S. banks. Difficulties in the financial institutions have also imposed additional legal liability on the audit profession. Leading accounting firms have been sued for billions of dollars for their alleged roles in the failures of hundreds of savings and loan companies. Such suits were initiated by both savings and loan shareholders and government regulators. Indeed, the accounting issues surrounding receivables can lead to significant economic consequences.

APPENDIX 6A

ACCOUNTING FOR RECEIVABLES AND PAYABLES EXPRESSED IN FOREIGN CURRENCIES

As companies expand, they often search for new sources of supply and new markets in other countries. Most major U.S. companies operate in more than one country, and many have operations in countries throughout the world. IBM, for example, has operations in approximately eighty foreign countries. Such companies are called **multinational,** or **transnational, corporations.**

Consider, for example, Johnson & Johnson, which generated over $27 billion in worldwide revenues in 1999. Forty-four percent of the total was generated from operations in countries other than the United States. Figure 6A–1 compares the relative importance of foreign operations in the generation of sales, profits, and total assets for three well-known U.S. companies: McDonald's, General Electric, and Bristol-Myers Squibb.

FIGURE 6A–1		McDonald's	General Electric	Bristol-Myers Squibb
The importance of foreign operations in 1999 (dollars in millions)				
	Total sales	$13,259	$129,853	$18,216
	Foreign sales/total	62%	30%	33%
	Total operating income (before taxes)	$ 3,319	$ 20,686	$ 4,096
	Foreign operating income/total	56%	25%	28%
	Total assets	$20,983	$437,006	$17,578
	Foreign/total	54%	37%	40%

Source: 1999 financial reports.

The internationalization of business introduces an issue of major concern to accountants: that is, most transactions with foreign entities involve currencies other than the U.S. dollar. For example, when General Electric makes a sale to a Japanese customer, the receivable is often · expressed in Japanese yen. An accounting problem arises because the financial statements of General Electric, a U.S. company, must be expressed in terms of U.S. dollars, and the exchange rate between the U.S. dollar and the Japanese yen is constantly fluctuating. In this appendix, we explain exchange rates and describe how exchange rate changes affect receivables and payables held by U.S. companies that are expressed in foreign currencies.

Exchange Rates Among Currencies

An **exchange rate** is the value of one currency in terms of another currency. For example, as of May 23, 2001, $1.42 could be exchanged for one British pound, $0.56 could be exchanged for one Swiss franc, and $0.008 could be exchanged for one Japanese yen. Expressed in another way, as of that same date, $1 (U.S.) could have been exchanged for 0.70 (1/1.42) British pounds, 1.76 (1/0.56) Swiss francs, or 125 (1/0.008) Japanese yen. Like the prices of all goods and services, the exchange rates among currencies vary from one day to the next. Figure 6A–2 shows the rates at which selected foreign currencies could be exchanged for U.S. dollars on two different dates one year apart: Jan. 1, 2000, and Jan. 1, 2001.

FIGURE 6A–2
Foreign exchange rates (foreign currency per dollar)

	Jan. 1, 2000	Jan. 1, 2001	Percentage Change
Australia (dollar)	1.53	1.79	+.17
Britain (pound)	0.62	0.67	+.08
Canada (dollar)	1.44	1.50	+.04
Germany (mark)	1.94	2.08	+.07
Japan (yen)	102	114	+.12
Mexico (peso)	9.32	9.60	+.03
Switzerland (franc)	1.59	1.61	+.01

Observe the changes on the right side of the table and note that, in general, the value of the U.S. dollar rose over the time period. Fluctuations in exchange rates of this nature can give rise to economic gains and losses for individuals and entities that transact in these currencies.

To illustrate, suppose that you paid $1,613 to purchase 1,000 British pounds on Jan. 1, 2000, and on Jan. 1, 2001, you converted the pounds back into dollars. You would have received $1,493 in the exchange and therefore would have incurred an economic loss of $120 ($1,613 − $1,493) on the transactions. In essence, you held 1,000 British pounds during a period in which the value of the pound fell relative to the U.S. dollar. On the other hand, had you paid 1,000 British pounds to purchase $1,613 on Jan. 1, 2000, and on Jan. 1, 2001, exchanged the dollars back into pounds, you would have collected 1,081 pounds and enjoyed an economic gain of 81 (1,081 − 1,000) British pounds. In this case, the dollar strengthened compared to the pound, and it was beneficial to hold dollars, rather than pounds, during this time period.

Receivables and Payables Held in Other Currencies

Many U.S. companies engage in transactions with non-U.S. entities that give rise to receivables or payables denominated in foreign currencies. Since the exchange rate between the dollar and the foreign currency fluctuates, the values of the receivables or payables change, giving rise to gains or losses that must be recognized on the financial statements.

HOLDING RECEIVABLES EXPRESSED IN FOREIGN CURRENCIES[1]

Suppose that International Inc., a U.S. company that prepares financial statements expressed in U.S. dollars, sold inventories to Swiss Airlines and accepted a note receivable in return. The note states that Swiss Airlines is to pay International 5,000 Swiss francs. The note was signed on December 1, when one U.S. dollar was equivalent to two Swiss francs. The value of the transaction in terms of U.S. dollars as of December 1 was $2,500 (5,000/2); accordingly, International recorded a receivable at the time of the transaction in the amount of $2,500. The currency conversion calculation and the journal entry to record the sale are provided in Figure 6A–3.

FIGURE 6A–3
Recording a sale in a non-U.S. currency

Conversion of Swiss francs to U.S. dollars:
  $2,500 = 5,000 Swiss francs × (1 dollar ÷ 2 Swiss francs)

Dec. 1	Notes Receivable (+A)	2,500	
	Sales (R, +SE)		2,500
	Sold inventory for 5,000 Swiss francs.		

---

1. To make the computations easier, the exchange rates used in these examples are not realistic.

Assume further that on December 31, when International prepares financial statements, the rate of exchange between U.S. dollars and Swiss francs changed to one U.S. dollar per 1.8 Swiss francs. The note receivable that was recorded on the books at $2,500 on December 1 is now worth $2,778 (5,000/1.8, or $2,500 × 2.0/1.8). Therefore, International has enjoyed an economic gain of $278 ($2,778 − $2,500) because it held a right to 5,000 Swiss francs during a period of time in which Swiss francs increased in value relative to U.S. dollars. In simple terms, 5,000 Swiss francs can be exchanged for more U.S. dollars on December 31 than they could on December 1. The currency conversion calculation and the journal entry that would restate the note receivable and record the gain, an exchange gain, is provided in Figure 6A–4. The exchange gain would appear on International's income statement.

FIGURE 6A–4
 	
Recognizing an exchange gain on a receivable
	Conversion of Swiss francs to U.S. dollars:
	$2,778 = 5,000 Swiss francs × (1 U.S. dollar ÷ 1.8 Swiss francs)
	Adjustment: $2,778 − $2,500 = $278 (gain)
	
	Dec. 31 Notes Receivable (+A) 278
	          Exchange Gain (Ga, +SE) 278
	      Recognized exchange gain on a receivable
	      expressed in Swiss francs.

An exchange loss will be recognized on International's books if, at a later date, the value of the U.S. dollar rises relative to the Swiss franc. Assume that, as of January 31 of the following year, one U.S. dollar could be exchanged for 2.2 Swiss francs. In this case, the adjustment would be calculated and the adjusting journal entry recorded by International as in Figure 6A–5.

FIGURE 6A–5
 	
Recognizing an exchange loss on a receivable
	Conversion of Swiss francs to U.S. dollars:
	$2,273 = 5,000 Swiss francs × (1 U.S. dollar ÷ 2.2 Swiss francs)
	Adjustment: $2,273 − $2,778 = $505 (loss)
	
	Jan. 31 Exchange Loss (Lo, −SE) 505
	         Notes Receivable (−A) 505
	      Recognized exchange loss on a receivable
	      expressed in Swiss francs.

HOLDING PAYABLES EXPRESSED IN FOREIGN CURRENCIES

Exchange gains and losses can also occur from holding payables denominated in non–U.S. (foreign) currencies. Assume that on December 1, Cross Cultural, Inc., purchased inventory from a Japanese company, promising to pay 100,000 yen at a later date. At that time, 140 Japanese yen could be exchanged for one U.S. dollar. As of December 31 and the following January 31, there could be exchanged 125 and 160 yen, respectively, for one U.S. dollar. Assuming that Cross Cultural, Inc., held the payable throughout the two-month time period and prepared financial statements on December 31 and January 31, the journal entries and related calculations that are shown in Figure 6A–6 would have been recorded to reflect these changes in the exchange rates.

EXCHANGE GAINS AND LOSSES: FOUR POSSIBLE COMBINATIONS

To summarize, the recognition of an exchange gain or loss depends on the combination of two factors: (1) whether the U.S. company holds a receivable or payable that is denominated in a foreign currency, and (2) whether the foreign currency increases or decreases in value relative to the U.S. dollar. Figure 6A–7 illustrates the four possible combinations.

FIGURE 6A–6

Recognizing exchange losses and gains on payables

DECEMBER 1: PURCHASE OF INVENTORY

Conversion of Japanese yen to U.S. dollars:
  $714 = 100,000 yen × (1 U.S. dollar ÷ 140 yen)

| Dec. 1 | Inventory (+A) | 714 | |
| | Accounts Payable (+L) | | 714 |

Purchased inventory for 100,000 Japanese yen.

DECEMBER 31: COMPUTATION AND RECOGNITION OF EXCHANGE LOSS

Conversion of Japanese yen to U.S. dollars:
  $800 = 100,000 yen × (1 U.S. dollar ÷ 125 yen)
Adjustment: $714 − $800 = $86 (loss)

| Dec. 31 | Exchange Loss (Lo, −SE) | 86 | |
| | Accounts Payable (+L) | | 86 |

Recognized exchange loss on holding a payable expressed in Japanese yen.

JANUARY 31: COMPUTATION AND RECOGNITION OF EXCHANGE GAIN

Conversion of Japanese yen to U.S. dollars:
  $625 = 100,000 yen × (1 U.S. dollar ÷ 160 yen)
Adjustment: $800 − $625 = $175 (gain)

| Jan. 31 | Accounts Payable (−L) | 175 | |
| | Exchange Gain (Ga, +SE) | | 175 |

Recognized exchange gain on holding a payable expressed in Japanese yen.

FIGURE 6A–7

Exchange gains and losses

| | | Item held by U.S. Company | |
		Receivable	Payable
Change in the value of the foreign currency relative to the U.S. dollar	Increase	1.\ Exchange gain	2.\ Exchange loss
	Decrease	3.\ Exchange loss	4.\ Exchange gain

If a U.S. company holds a receivable denominated in a foreign currency, and the foreign currency rises in value relative to the U.S. dollar, the U.S. company recognizes an exchange gain on its income statement, as illustrated in Cell 1. Holding a receivable in a currency that decreases in value relative to the U.S. dollar, on the other hand, gives rise to an exchange loss, as illustrated in Cell 3. Holding a payable expressed in terms of a foreign currency produces exactly the opposite effect: that is, as the foreign currency rises in value, exchange losses are recognized, as illustrated in Cell 2. As the foreign currency drops in value, exchange gains accrue, as illustrated in Cell 4.

HEDGING AND THE ECONOMIC CONSEQUENCES OF FLUCTUATING EXCHANGE RATES

Exchange rate fluctuations are constant and often significant. As illustrated in the previous section, such erratic movement can give rise to exchange gains and losses that cause income and other reported values (e.g., receivables and payables) to vary substantially from one period to the next. Variations in exchange rates, as a result, can give rise to economic consequences through their effects on stock prices, credit ratings, management compensation, and debt covenants. Such consequences increase the economic risks associated with engaging in transactions that are denominated in foreign currencies.

While management has very little control over exchange rates, it can reduce some of the risks associated with holding receivables and payables denominated in foreign currencies. Multinational companies commonly use a strategy called hedging to reduce the variation in income due to fluctuating exchange rates. This strategy involves taking a position in a foreign currency in an amount that is equal and opposite to a particular receivable or payable expressed in that currency.

To illustrate, assume that on July 1, General Motors (GM) sells a group of automobiles to BPAmoco (BPA), receiving in exchange a note stating that BPA will pay GM 100,000 British pounds in one year. If the exchange rate as of July 1 is $1.70 per British pound, GM would record the following journal entry.

Conversion of British pounds to U.S. dollars:
  $170,000 = 100,000 British pounds × ($1.70 ÷ 1 pound)

July 1	**Notes Receivable (+A)**	170,000	
	Sales (R, +SE)		170,000
	Sold automobiles in exchange for a note		
	receivable expressed in British pounds.		

If GM chooses not to hedge this receivable, and the exchange rate changes to $1.50 per British pound as of December 31, GM will recognize a $20,000 exchange loss during the period when it records the following adjusting journal entry at the end of the year. This loss would appear on GM's income statement.

Conversion of British pounds to U.S. dollars:
  $150,000 = 100,000 British pounds × ($1.50 ÷ 1 pound)
  Adjustment: $170,000 − $150,000 = $20,000 (loss)

Dec. 31	**Exchange Loss (Lo, −SE)**	20,000	
	Notes Receivable (−A)		20,000
	Recognized exchange loss on a receivable		
	expressed in British pounds.		

GM could have negated the effect on income of this $20,000 loss if it had chosen to hedge the receivable. That is, GM could have borrowed 100,000 British pounds on July 1 and agreed to pay it back one year later. By doing so, GM would have taken a position in British pounds that was equal and opposite to the outstanding receivable. It would have entered into a payable (100,000 British pounds) that would have balanced the outstanding receivable (100,000 British pounds). Had GM adopted such a strategy, on December 31 it would have recognized a $20,000 exchange gain on the outstanding payable, which would have negated the effect on income of the $20,000 exchange loss recognized on the receivable. The journal entries to record the borrowing and the recognition of the exchange gain are provided in Figure 6A–8.

FIGURE 6A–8

Hedging an outstanding receivable

JULY 1:

Conversion of British pounds to U.S. dollars:
  $170,000 = 100,000 British pounds × ($1.70 ÷ 1 pound)

July 1	Cash (+A)	170,000	
	Notes Payable (+L)		170,000
	Borrowed 100,000 British pounds.		

DECEMBER 31:

Conversion of British pounds to U.S. dollars:
  $150,000 = 100,000 British pounds × ($1.50 ÷ 1 pound)
Adjustment: $170,000 − $150,000 = $20,000

Dec. 31	Notes Payable (−L)	20,000	
	Exchange Gain (Ga, +SE)		20,000
	Recognized exchange gain on a payable expressed in British pounds.		

Hedging is commonly practiced by U.S. multinationals to reduce the risks associated with holding receivables and payables in foreign currencies, where exchange rates are constantly fluctuating. General Motors, for example, holds long-term debt that is payable in Canadian dollars, Australian dollars, Swiss francs, Japanese yen, German marks, Spanish pesetas, Belgian francs, British pounds, and other currencies. Many of these payables were established by GM to hedge the effects on income and reduce the economic risks associated with holding outstanding receivables denominated in these currencies. The following excerpt from the 2000 financial report of 3M, a multinational manufacturer, describes how the company deals with fluctuating exchange rates:

The company engages in hedging activities to reduce exchange rate risks arising from crossborder cash flows denominated in foreign currencies.

REVIEW PROBLEM

This section provides a review problem that covers the methods used to account for bad debts. The facts given are accounted for using the allowance method with a percentage-of-credit-sales estimate.

Assume that Credit Inc. began operations on January 1, 2002. The relevant transactions for 2002 and 2003 are summarized in the accounts receivable T-account provided in Figure 6–14. Sales on account during 2002 totaled $10,000, and cash receipts for those sales equaled $6,000. The Accounts Receivable balance at the end of 2002 was $4,000 ($10,000 − $6,000). Sales on

FIGURE 6–14
Bad debt
review problem

General Ledger

Accounts Receivable

Beginning balance	0		
2002 credit sales	10,000		
		2002 cash receipts	6,000
12/31/02 balance	4,000		
2003 credit sales	12,000		
		2003 cash receipts	11,000
		2003 bad debt	500
12/31/03 balance	4,500		

Allowance Method
(percentage-of-credit-sales estimate)

December 31, 2002

$700 (7% × $10,000)

Estimate entry	Bad Debt Expense (−R, −SE)	700	
	Allow. for Doubt. Accts. (−A)		700

June 5, 2003

Write-off entry	Allow. for Doubt. Accts. (+A)	500	
	Accts. Rec. (−A)		500

December 31, 2003

$840 (7% × $12,000)

Estimate entry	Bad Debt Expense (−R, −SE)	840	
	Allow. for Doubt. Accts. (−A)		840

Allowance for Doubtful Accounts

		Beginning balance	0
		12/31/02	700
		12/31/02 balance	700
6/5/03	500		
		Preadj. balance	200
		12/31/03	840
		12/31/03 balance	1,040

account during 2003 totaled $12,000, and cash receipts during the same period, from sales made in both 2002 and 2003, were $11,000. On June 5, 2003, Credit Inc. received notice that a $500 account established in 2002 would not be collectible. This account was written off, and the December 31, 2003 balance in Accounts Receivable is $4,500 ($4,000 + $12,000 − $11,000 − $500). Assume that companies in Credit's industry typically experience bad debt losses of approximately 7 percent of credit sales.

The allowance method gives rise to end-of-period adjusting journal entries that decrease revenues in the appropriate period and reduce the value of Accounts Receivable on the balance sheet to net realizable value, the amount of cash expected to be collected from the receivables. The write-off entry on June 5, 2003, has virtually no effect on the financial statements of Credit Inc.

Note that the preadjustment balance in Allowance for Doubtful Accounts as of December 31, 2002, is a $200 credit ($700 estimate − $500 write-off). Either Credit overestimated its bad debt losses for 2002 or certain outstanding accounts created from 2002's credit sales may still be written off. If this preadjustment balance accumulates over a period of several years, Credit should review and possibly revise its estimating formula. Otherwise, it is ignored.

SUMMARY OF KEY POINTS

The key points in the chapter are summarized below.

○ *Current assets, working capital, current ratio, and quick ratio, and how these measures are used to assess the solvency position of a company.*

Current assets are assets that can be converted into cash within one year or the company's operating cycle, whichever is longer. Working capital is equal to current assets less current liabilities, which are the liabilities expected to be required for payment with the assets listed as current. The current ratio is equal to current assets divided by current liabilities. The quick ratio is equal to cash plus marketable securities plus accounts receivable, divided by current liabilities.

These low-cost measures are useful in assessing a company's solvency position because they compare a measure of short-term cash inflows to a measure of short-term cash outflows. They are often used by banks and other lenders, and they appear in many loan agreements and debt covenants, enabling lenders to protect their investments by requiring that management maintain certain levels of liquidity.

○ *"Window dressing" and the reporting of current assets, working capital, and the current ratio.*

Window dressing refers to management's use of discretion in reporting accounting numbers to make the financial statements appear more attractive. Such discretion is used, for example, to make it easier to attract capital, to increase bonus compensation, or to avoid violating the terms of debt contracts. There are three basic ways in which management can window dress: (1) management can choose to use accounting methods that improve the reported numbers, (2) it can bias the estimates required to apply a given accounting method, and (3) it can make operating, investing, and financing decisions that directly affect the reported numbers.

○ *Techniques used to account for and control cash.*

Cash held in escrow or compensating balances are examples of restrictions on a company's use of its cash. Such restrictions should be clearly disclosed on the balance sheet or in the footnotes, and restricted cash should be included in separate accounts.

There are two aspects to the control of cash that are largely the responsibility of the company's accountants: record control and physical control. Problems of record control arise because there are many transactions that involve the cash account, and it is often difficult to ensure that the cash account on the balance sheet reflects the actual amount of cash in a company's possession. Problems of physical control arise because cash is universally desired and easily concealed and transported.

○ *Accounts receivable and how they are valued on the balance sheet.*

Accounts receivable arise from transactions with customers who have purchased goods or services but have not yet paid for them. They are amounts owed by customers for goods and services sold as part of the normal operations of the business. Often backed up by oral rather than written commitments, accounts-receivable represent short-term extensions of credit that are normally collectible within 30 to 60 days. Accounts receivable are valued at net realizable value, the gross amount of the receivables less adjustments for cash discounts, uncollectibles, and sales returns.

○ *The allowance method for uncollectible receivables.*

Under the allowance method, the amount of uncollectibles is estimated at the end of each accounting period. Then an adjusting journal entry is made to reduce revenue via a contra revenue account, and a contra account to Accounts Receivable, Allowance for Doubtful Accounts, is credited. Later, when the uncollectible is actually realized, both the value of Accounts Receivable and the allowance account are reduced.

○ *Major concerns of financial statement users in the area of receivables reporting.*

For many companies, accounts receivable are a significant percentage of total and current assets. Accordingly, the methods used to account for them can have direct and often significant effects on such measures as current assets, working capital, the current ratio, the quick ratio, the collection period, and net income. Financial statement users must realize that managers can influence these measures by speeding up or slowing down the recognition of revenue and related receivables and that the estimate of uncollectibles is very subjective. Such practices can affect a company's credit rating, determine whether debt terms are violated, accelerate bankruptcy proceedings, and bring about sizable lawsuits against managers and auditors. In this area, users must pay close attention to the activity in Sales, Accounts Receivable, Bad Debt Expense, and Allowance for Doubtful Accounts.

KEY TERMS

Note: Definitions for these terms are provided in the glossary at the end of the text.

Accounts receivable (p. 243)
Aging schedule (p. 253)
Allowance method (p. 249)
Cash (sales) discounts (p. 246)
Compensating balances (p. 241)
Current asset (p. 235)
Current ratio (p. 237)
Escrow (p. 241)
Exchange rate (p. 259)
Gross method (p. 247)
Markdown (p. 246)
Multinational (transnational) corporations
   (p. 259)

Net realizable value (p. 246)
Open accounts (p. 243)
Operating cycle (p. 235)
Percentage-of-credit-sales approach (p.249)
Petty cash (p. 242)
Physical control (p. 243)
Quantity discount (p. 246)
Quick ratio (p. 237)
Record control (p. 243)
Window dressing (p. 239)
Working capital (p. 237)

ETHICS IN THE REAL WORLD

Allied Bancshares, a Houston-based group of banks, reported a string of 31 quarterly earnings increases. In an interview with three Goldman Sachs security analysts, one of the bank's senior officers explained that the bank intentionally overstates its bad debt expense in good quarters and understates it in poor quarters. In this manner, the fluctuations in earnings from one quarter to the next can be smoothed out. The bank's auditors have written clean opinions on the bank's financial statements over this time period, and this strategy maximizes the bonuses paid to the bank's executives. In addition, presumably it is in the best interest of the bank's shareholders, partly because it helps the bank maintain its legal reserve requirements.

ETHICAL ISSUE Is it ethical for companies like Allied Bancshares to intentionally overstate expenses in some periods and understate them in others to achieve consistent increases in reported net income across time?

INTERNET RESEARCH EXERCISE

For the most recent year, complete the chart below for Sears, Roebuck & Company. Begin your search at www.sears.com/

Activity in the *Allowance for Uncollectibles* account:

Beginning balance	_____?_____
Provision for uncollectible accounts	_____?_____
Write-offs (plug)	_____?_____
Ending balance	_____?_____

BRIEF EXERCISES

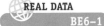

REAL DATA
BE6–1

Analysis of accounts receivable

The following information was taken from the 2000 annual report of Emerson Electric Co., a leader in the network power sector (dollars in millions):

	2000	1999
Balance Sheet:		
Receivables, less allowance for uncollectibles of $58 and $60, respectively	**$2,706**	**$2,516**

a. Compute total accounts receivable as of the end of 2000 and 1999, and compute the bad debt allowance as a percentage of total accounts receivable. Did the percentage increase or decrease?

b. The bad debt expense reported on Emerson's 2000 income statement did not equal $58. Explain why.

REAL DATA
BE6–2

Uncollectible accounts expense

The following information was taken from the publicly available records of General Electric concerning the allowance for uncollectible account (dollars in millions):

	2000	1999
Balance at Jan. 1	$ 3,708	$ 3,223
Increases	2,045	1,671
Decreases	(1,741)	(1,457)
Balance at Dec. 31	$ 4,012	$ 3,437

a. What dollar amounts of bad debt expense were recognized on the 2000 and 1999 income statements?

b. What dollar values of customer accounts were written off the books in 2000 and 1999?

c. By what percentage did the allowance account change from 1999 to 2000, and what are several reasons why this may have occurred?

REAL DATA

BE6–3

Uncollectible accounts expense

General Electric has its own financing subsidiary, called GECS (GE Capital Services). The purpose of GECS is to provide financing services for GE's customers. If you purchase a GE appliance, for example, you could finance it through GECS. In 2000, GECS generated over $66 billion in revenue and reported profits of over $5 billion. These numbers represented approximately 50 percent of the company's total revenues ($130 billion) and profits ($12 billion). In 1997, the bad debt provision reported on GE's income statement was $2 billion.

a. Compute bad debts as a percentage of revenues. Should you use GE overall revenues or revenues generated by GECS? Why?

b. If GECS prepared its own balance sheet, what would you expect to be the largest accounts?

c. Would you consider GE to be a manufacturing, retail, or service company? Discuss.

EXERCISES

E6–1

Classifying cash on the balance sheet

Boyer International is currently preparing its financial statements for 2002. The company has several different sources of cash and is trying to decide how to classify them. The sources of cash follow:

a. $30,000 in a checking account with The First National Bank.

b. $3,000 in checks dated December 4, 2002, received from customers.

c. $250,000 in certificates of deposit through The First National Bank, which are to mature on November 15, 2005.

d. $40,000 in a savings account with The First National Bank.

e. $1,000 in the petty cash fund. As of December 31, 2002, there are receipts totaling $600 in the petty cash drawer.

f. $50,000 held as a compensating balance for a loan with The First National Bank. The loan agreement requires Boyer International to maintain a compensating balance equal to 10 percent of the loan balance. During 2003, the outstanding principal balance will be reduced to $350,000.

g. $8,000 in a checking account with Interstate Federal Savings.

Indicate how each source listed should be classified on the December 31, 2002 balance sheet. Explain each answer.

E6–2

Classifying cash on the balance sheet

The following items were taken from the financial records of Melvin Construction Company.

a. $2,000 in a checking account.

b. $8,000 invested in a treasury note due to mature in 90 days.

c. $3,000 in a savings account that cannot be withdrawn until a $10,000 outstanding debt is paid off.

d. $18,000 invested in securities that will be sold in two years to finance an expansion of the plant.

e. $2,500 invested in IBM common shares. Management intends to liquidate this investment in less than six months.
f. $15,000 held in escrow by a bank, serving as earnest money that binds management to a real estate contract.
g. A $3,000 money order received in payment from a customer.

Classify each item as either (a) unrestricted cash, (b) restricted cash, or (c) investment.

E6–3

Accounting for
cash discounts

On December 12, Woodington sold goods on account for a gross price of $40,000. The terms of the sale were 2/10, n/30. As of December 31, when financial statements were prepared, no payment had been received by Woodington. Full payment was received on January 5 of the following year.

a. Prepare journal entries for these transactions.
b. Assume that full payment was received on December 20. Prepare journal entries and discuss how the timing of the cash receipt affected the income statement and statement of cash flows.

E6–4

Accounting for
cash discounts

On May 1, 2003, Crab Cove Fishing Company sold Maine lobster on account for a gross price of $30,000. On May 5, the company also sold cod on account for a gross price of $20,000. The terms of both sales were 3/10, n/30. Crab Cove received payment for the first sale on May 6, 2003, and payment for the second sale on May 31, 2003.

Provide all necessary journal entries.

E6–5

Bad debts under the
allowance method

Arlington Cycle Company began operations on January 1, 2002. The company reported the following selected items in its 2003 financial report:

	2003	2002
Gross sales	$1,400,000	$1,500,000
Accounts receivable	600,000	650,000
Actual bad debt write-offs	22,000	10,000

Arlington estimates bad debts at 2 percent of gross sales.

Analyze the activity in the allowance for doubtful accounts T-account, and comment on whether the bad debt estimate has been sufficient to cover the write-offs.

E6–6

Accounting for
uncollectibles

In its 2002 financial report, Sound Unlimited reported the following items:

1. A credit balance of $200,000 in Allowance for Doubtful Accounts.
2. A debit balance of $7,500,000 in Accounts Receivable.
3. Sales of $3,250,000.

During 2002, the company was involved in the following transactions that affected Allowance for Doubtful Accounts.

(1) Wrote off accounts considered uncollectible totaling $195,000.
(2) Recovered $45,000 that had previously been written off.

Assume that historically 5 percent of sales has proven to be uncollectible.

a. Compute the December 31, 2001 balance in Allowance for Doubtful Accounts.
b. Assume that all sales were on credit and cash collections from customers during 2002 totaled $4,200,000. Compute the 12/31/01 balance in Accounts Receivable.

REAL DATA

E6–7

Accounting for
doubtful accounts:
The allowance
method

The following items were extracted from the financial records of Bell Atlantic (dollars in millions):

Sales	$33,174
Accounts receivable	7,644
Allowance for doubtful accounts	619 (cr.)

During the following year, the company wrote off $580 of accounts receivable as uncollectible and then estimated, from historical data, that 2 percent of this year's sales will be uncollectible.

a.   Prepare the entry to record the bad debt expense.
b.   Compute the final balance in Allowance for Doubtful Accounts.

E6–8

Inferring bad debt write-offs and reconstructing related journal entries

The 2003 annual report of Johnson Services reveals the following information. The dollar amounts are end-of-year balances.

	2003	2002
Credit sales	$75,300	$61,500
Accounts receivable	9,400	9,200
Allowance for doubtful accounts	1,300	1,000
Bad debt recoveries	55	70

Johnson estimates bad debts each year at 2 percent of credit sales.

a.   Compute the actual amount of write-offs during 2003.
b.   Infer the journal entries that explain the activity in Accounts Receivable and the related allowance account during 2003.

E6–9

Preparing an aging schedule

Potter Stables uses the aging method to estimate its bad debts. Sherman Potter, the company president, has given you the following aging of accounts receivable as of December 31, 2003, along with the historical probabilities that the account balances will not be collected.

Account Age	Balance	Noncollection Probability
Current	$290,000	2%
1–45 days past due	110,000	5%
46–90 days past due	68,000	8%
Over 90 days past due	40,000	15%

Compute total receivables and expected bad debts as of December 31, 2003.

E6–10

Appendix 6A: Exchange gains/losses on outstanding receivables

On January 1, 2003, Outreach Incorporated sold services to a Canadian supply company and accepted a three-year note in the amount of 11,000 Canadian dollars. Exchange rates between the U.S. dollar and the Canadian dollar are provided below.

Date	U.S. Dollars Per Canadian Dollars
January 1, 2003	$.85
December 31, 2003	.90
December 31, 2004	.80

Provide the journal entries (in U.S. dollars) prepared by Outreach to record the receipt of the note and the exchange gains/losses recognized on December 31, 2003, and December 31, 2004. Ignore any interest on the note.

E6–11

Appendix 6A: Hedging to reduce the risk of currency fluctuations

Assume that Outreach (in E6–10) hedged the 11,000 (Canadian dollar) receivable by borrowing 11,000 Canadian dollars from a Canadian bank on January 1, 2003. Use journal entries to demonstrate how this transaction removes Outreach's exposure to the risk of fluctuating exchange rates. Explain.

PROBLEMS

P6–1

Classifying cash on the balance sheet

On September 30, 2002, Print-O-Matic Inc. entered into an arrangement with its bank to borrow $250,000. The principal is due on October 1, 2007, and the note has a stated annual interest rate of 10 percent. Under the borrowing agreement, Print-O-Matic agreed to maintain a compensating balance of $60,000 in a non-interest-bearing account. As of December 31, 2002, Print-O-Matic has an additional $225,000 in various savings and checking accounts that earn an annual rate of 6 percent. The controller intends to classify the entire $285,000 in cash as a current asset.

REQUIRED:

a. Do you agree with the classification of the $285,000 of cash as a current asset? Explain your answer.

b. Print-O-Matic reported interest expense associated with this note for the year ended December 31, 2002, in the amount of $6,250 [($250,000 × 10%) × 1/4]. Do you agree with this classification? Should any other factors be considered in the interest cost? Explain.

P6–2

Cash discounts

During the month of March, QNI Corporation made the following credit sales and had the following related collections. QNI prepares financial statements for the first quarter of operations at the end of March.

March	3	Sold goods to AAA company for a gross price of $1,400. The terms of the sale were 2/10, n/30.
March	8	Sold goods to BBB company for a gross price of $800. The terms of the sale were 2/10, n/30.
March	11	Received full payment from AAA.
March	28	Received full payment from BBB.
March	29	Sold goods to CCC Company for a gross price of $1,800. The terms of the sale were 2/10, n/30.

REQUIRED:

a. Prepare the journal entries to record these transactions.

b. Note that BBB missed the discount period by ten days. Compute the annual interest rate BBB paid for the use of the $800 for that ten-day period. Assuming that BBB can borrow money from the bank at 9 percent, what should BBB have done differently?

P6–3

Bad debts over time

Financial information for CNG Inc. follows:

	2003	2002	2001
Credit sales	$205,000	$200,000	$180,000
Actual bad debt write-offs	11,000	10,000	6,000

The company estimates bad debts for financial reporting purposes at 3 percent of credit sales. The balance in Allowance for Doubtful Accounts as of January 1, 2001, was $10,000.

REQUIRED:

a. Provide the journal entries related to Allowance for Doubtful Accounts for 2001, 2002, and 2003.

b. Compute the balance in Allowance for Doubtful Accounts as of December 31, 2003.

c. Comment on the sufficiency of the bad debt expense and allowance over the three-year period. How did you come to your conclusion?

P6-4

Accounting for
uncollectibles over
two periods

Glacier Ice Company uses a percentage-of-net-sales method to account for estimated bad debts. Historically, 3 percent of net sales have proven to be uncollectible. During 2002 and 2003, the company reported the following:

	2003	2002
Gross sales	$1,500,000	$1,800,000
Sales discounts	100,000	130,000
Sales returns	50,000	20,000

REQUIRED:

a. Prepare the necessary adjusting entry on December 31, 2002, to record the estimated bad debt expense for 2002.
b. Assume that the January 1, 2002 balance in Allowance for Doubtful Accounts was $65,000 (credit) and that $70,000 in bad debts were written off the books during 2002. What is the December 31, 2002 balance in this account *after adjustments?*
c. Prepare the necessary adjusting entry on December 31, 2003, to record the estimated bad debt expense for 2003.
d. What is the December 31, 2003 balance in Allowance for Doubtful Accounts? Assume that $85,000 in bad debts was written off the books during 2003.

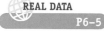
REAL DATA

P6-5

Analyzing the
activity in the
allowance account

The information below was taken from the footnotes of Chase Manhattan Corporation's 1999 annual report. The December 31, 1999 balance in the allowance account was $3,457 (dollars in millions).

	1999	1998	1997
Allowance at Jan. 1	$3,552	$3,624	$3,549
Provision for losses	1,621	1,343	804
Recoveries	254	373	292

REQUIRED:

Compute the actual write-offs recognized by Chase in 1998 and 1999.

P6-6

Ignoring potential
bad debts can lead
to serious
overstatements

The following financial information represents Hadley Company's first year of operations, 2002:

Income Statement		Balance Sheet	
Sales	$200,000	Cash	$ 5,000
Cost of goods sold	102,000	Accounts receivable	85,000
Gross profit	$ 98,000	Other assets	40,000
Expenses	65,000	Total assets	$130,000
Net income	$ 33,000	Current liabilities	$ 13,000
		Long-term notes payable	80,000
		Stockholders' equity	37,000
		Total liabilities and	
		stockholders' equity	$130,000

After reading Hadley's financial statements, you conclude that the company had a very successful first year of operations. However, after further examination, you note that the sales figure on the income statement was not adjusted for a bad debt expense. You also realize that a large percentage of Hadley's sales were to three customers, one of which, Litzenberger Supply, is in very questionable financial health, although still in business. Litzenberger owes Hadley $50,000 as of the end of 2002.

REQUIRED:

a. Adjust the financial statements of Hadley Company to reflect a more conservative reporting with respect to bad debts. That is, establish a provision for the uncollectibility of Litzenberger's account. Recompute net income. How does this adjustment affect your assessment of Hadley's first year of operations?

b. Why would auditors probably require that Hadley choose the more conservative reporting?

c. Hadley's chief financial officer claims that no bad debt expense should be recorded, because Litzenberger is still conducting operations as of the end of 2002. How would you respond to this claim?

P6–7

Estimating uncollectibles, financial ratios, and loan agreements

Excerpts from the 2002 financial statements of Finley, Ltd., a service company, follow:

Fees earned	**$240,000**
Accounts receivable	**68,000**
Allowance for doubtful accounts	**3,400**
Total current assets	**105,000**
Total current liabilities	**65,000**
Net income	**15,000**
Dividends declared	**5,000**
Bad debt expense	**3,400**

Auditors from Price and Company reviewed the financial records of Finley and found that a credit sale of $10,000 (for services rendered), which was included in the fees earned amount above, should not have been recognized until January 20, 2003. The auditors also noted that a more reasonable estimate of future bad debts would be 10 percent of the accounts receivable balance. The auditors have informed Finley's management that the audit opinion will be qualified if Finley does not adjust the financial statements accordingly.

REQUIRED:

a. Compute the effect of the auditors' recommended adjustment on the 2002 fees earned, accounts receivable, allowance for doubtful accounts, current ratio, working capital, and net income reported by Finley.

b. Assume that Finley has a loan agreement with a bank, requiring it to maintain a current ratio of 1.5 and limiting its annual dividend payment to 50 percent of net income. How might these restrictions have influenced the reporting decisions of Finley's managers?

P6–8

Uncollectibles: Ignoring an allowance

Fine Linen Service began operations on January 28, 1999. The company does not establish an allowance for doubtful accounts. It simply recognizes a bad debt expense when an account is deemed uncollectible. The company has written off the following items over the past five years:

July 6, 1999	**Wrote off $10,000 as uncollectible from a sale made on March 1, 1999.**
Feb. 3, 2000	**Wrote off $50,000 as uncollectible from a sale made on October 28, 1999.**
Mar. 11, 2001	**Wrote off $25,000 as uncollectible from a sale made on December 20, 1999 ($12,000) and a sale made on May 10, 2000 ($13,000).**
Mar. 24, 2001	**Recovered $5,000 that had been written off on February 3, 2000. It is company policy to credit Bad Debt Expense when an account is recovered.**
Aug. 8, 2002	**Wrote off $75,000 as uncollectible from sales made in 1999 ($20,000), in 2000 ($25,000), and in 2001 ($30,000).**
Dec. 2, 2002	**Wrote off $5,000 as uncollectible from a sale made on April 26, 2002.**
Sep. 19, 2003	**Wrote off $90,000 as uncollectible from sales in 1999 ($5,000), in 2000 ($30,000), in 2001 ($25,000), in 2002 ($20,000), and in 2003 ($10,000).**

Over the period 1999 to 2003, Fine Linen Service realized the following sales and reported the following ending balances in Accounts Receivable.

	Sales	Accounts Receivable
1999	$1,000,000	$ 950,000
2000	975,000	900,000
2001	1,025,000	1,200,000
2002	1,032,000	1,175,000
2003	990,000	1,095,000

At the beginning of operations, a consultant had informed Fine Linen Service that the company should expect not to collect 8 percent of total sales.

REQUIRED:

a. List the bad debt expense and the balance sheet value of Accounts Receivable for each year over the five-year period under both Fine Linen's current method and the allowance method. Use the following format:

	1999	2000	2001	2002	2003
Current method:					
Bad debt expense					
Accounts receivable value					
Allowance method:					
Bad debt expense					
Accounts receivable value					

b. Compute the total bad debt expense over the five-year period under the two methods. Why is the allowance method preferred to Fine Linen's current method?

P6–9

Accounting for uncollectibles and the aging estimate

In an attempt to include all relevant information for decision-making purposes, Merimore Company estimates bad debts using the aging method. However, for external reporting purposes, the company estimates bad debts as a percentage of credit sales. Merimore prepares monthly adjusting journal entries. From trends over the past five years, the company controller has estimated that 2 percent of monthly credit sales will prove to be uncollectible. Following are the monthly credit sales and bad debt write-offs for Merimore Company for 2002:

Month	Cash Collections	Credit Sales	Write-Offs
January	$ 1,200,000	$ 1,000,000	
February	1,050,000	925,000	
March	910,000	1,010,000	
April	1,000,000	975,000	$ 87,000
May	875,000	950,000	
June	1,080,000	1,200,000	
July	950,000	1,150,000	52,000
August	1,011,000	1,075,000	
September	1,105,000	1,025,000	
October	980,000	980,000	
November	1,100,000	900,000	
December	865,000	750,000	100,000
Total	$12,126,000	$11,940,000	$239,000

On December 31, 2002, the controller prepared the following aging of accounts receivable:

Account Classification	Balance	Percent Uncollectible
Current	$ 700,000	2.0%
1–30 days past due	1,200,000	5.5%
31–75 days past due	550,000	10.0%
Over 75 days past due	800,000	25.0%

The allowance for doubtful accounts balance on January 1, 2002, was a credit of $70,000.

REQUIRED:

a. Prepare the adjusting journal entry necessary on December 31, 2002, so that the statements will be in accordance with the company's external reporting policies. Remember that the company prepares monthly adjusting journal entries.

b. Compute the balance in Allowance for Doubtful Accounts after the entry in (a) has been recorded and posted.

c. Compute the balance in Accounts Receivable as of January 1, 2002.

d. Prepare the December 31 adjusting entry for bad debts, using the percentage-of-credit-sales method, and compute the estimated bad debts, using the aging method.

e. Why would a company want to estimate bad debts using two different methods? Which of the two methods is more costly and time-consuming to implement? Which provides more useful information?

P6–10

Inferring reporting strategies

Excerpts from the financial statements of Ticheley Enterprises are provided below.

	2003	2002	2001
Income Statement			
Bad debt expense	$ 1,700	$ 2,900	$ 2,100
Net income	15,800	15,300	14,400
Balance Sheet			
Accounts receivable	$27,400	$23,200	$23,100
Allowance for doubtful accounts (cr.)	2,100	3,000	2,300
Stockholders' equity	78,500	75,000	71,400

On December 27, 2002, Ticheley sent merchandise with a sales price of $8,500 to a major customer. The merchandise was in transit as of December 31. The cost of the inventory shipped was $2,900, and the company chose to record the sale and outflow of inventory on January 4, 2003, when the customer received the shipment. Ticheley's management is compensated partially on an annual bonus, where all managers share equally in a $10,000 bonus pool if reported net income exceeds 20 percent of shareholders' equity.

REQUIRED:

a. Ticheley's president recently stated in a letter to the shareholders that the company has reported profit increases consistently over the last three years. Comment on this statement.

b. Why would a company establish a management compensation system where a bonus is paid if reported income exceeds a certain percentage of stockholders' equity?

c. Identify any reporting strategy that Ticheley may be using, and support your position with calculations.

d. Explain why Ticheley may be using the strategy you mentioned above, and support your position with calculations.

P6–11

Appendix 6A: Exchange gains and losses

Hughes International is a U.S. company that conducts business throughout the world. Listed below are selected transactions entered into by the company during 2002.

1. Sold merchandise to Royal Equipment Company (a United Kingdom company) in exchange for an account receivable in the amount of 320,000 pounds. At the time, the exchange rate was 0.50 British pounds per U.S. dollar.

2. Sold merchandise to Honda Automobile Company (a Japanese company) in exchange for a note receivable that calls for a payment of 350,000 yen. The exchange rate was 150 yen to the U.S. dollar.

3. Purchased inventory from Venice Leathers (an Italian company) in exchange for a note payable that calls for a payment of 50 million lira. The exchange rate was 1,500 lira to the U.S. dollar.

4. Purchased inventory from B. C. Lumber (a Canadian company) in exchange for an account payable in the amount of 200,000 Canadian dollars. The exchange rate was 1.50 Canadian dollars per U.S. dollar.

On December 31, 2002, the exchange rates were as follows:

Foreign Currency	Currency Per U.S. Dollar
British pound	0.60
Japanese yen	140
Italian lira	1,600
Canadian dollar	1.20

REQUIRED:
a.   Convert each transaction above to the equivalent amount in U.S. dollars.
b.   Prepare journal entries to record each transaction.
c.   Assume that the receivables and payables are still outstanding as of December 31, 2002. Compute the amount of exchange gain or loss for each transaction.
d.   Why do fluctuating exchange rates give rise to exchange gains and losses?

P6–12
Appendix 6A: Fluctuating exchange rates, debt covenants, and hedging

International Services entered into a debt covenant requiring it to maintain a current ratio of at least 1.5:1. The company's condensed balance sheet as of December 31 follows:

Assets		Liabilities and Stockholders' Equity	
Current assets	$ 80,000	Current liabilities	$ 50,000
Noncurrent assets	200,000	Long-term liabilities	100,000
		Stockholders' equity	130,000
		Total liabilities and	
Total assets	$280,000	stockholders' equity	$280,000

International's primary customer is Buckingham, Ltd., a company located in Britain. As of December 31, Buckingham owed International 40,000 British pounds. The exchange rate as of December 31 between U.S. dollars and British pounds was $1.70 per pound.

REQUIRED:
a.   What dollar amount of International's current assets on the balance sheet is associated with the receivable owed by Buckingham?
b.   Assume that all account balances remain the same over the next year. Below what exchange rate (U.S. dollars per British pound) would International be in violation of the debt covenant?
c.   Assume that $1,600 of Accounts Payable on the balance sheet represents a debt of 1,000 British pounds to a British bank. Below what exchange rate would International be in violation of the debt covenant now? Consider both the receivable and the payable.
d.   Describe how International could hedge to reduce the risk of being in violation of the debt covenant.

ISSUES FOR DISCUSSION

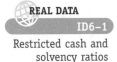
REAL DATA
ID6–1
Restricted cash and solvency ratios

In a recent financial statement, AMAX, Inc., a coal-mining company, reported the following:

Assets (in thousands)
   Cash and cash equivalents (Note 9) $46,700

Note 9:

AMAX had on deposit with commercial banks a total of $42 million of cash and equivalents that is restricted as to use. Of that amount, $15 million was held for the repurchase of common *shares from an affiliated company. The remainder represents a time deposit that is restricted to repayment of a short-term loan.*

REQUIRED:

a. Why would a potential investor or creditor reading AMAX's financial statements want to know about restrictions on cash?

b. Assume that the January 3 repurchase of common shares will result in a long-term investment. Should the restricted cash be disclosed as current or noncurrent? Why?

c. How might disclosure of such a restriction affect the calculation of working capital, the current ratio, and the quick ratio?

REAL DATA

ID6–2

Revenue recognition, ethics, and reputation

The Wall Street Journal (April 7, 1993) reported that "For more than ten years, IBM has quietly turned to Merrill Lynch & Co. and others to execute a rare financial maneuver that propped up the results of IBM's big leasing business. The maneuver allowed IBM to book immediately all the revenue from a long-term computer lease—even though the actual dollars would flow in over the life of the lease. That didn't break any rules, but some accountants term it an end-run that many blue-chip companies would avoid. [IBM's external auditors] called the revenue booster troubling . . . and urged IBM to take immediate action to use the maneuver less." Later, the article states, "Questions about IBM's accounting could be awkward for the wounded computer giant [because] IBM long enjoyed a reputation as the epitome of financial conservatism, with triple-A-rated debt and the bluest of blue-chip stocks."

REQUIRED:

a. Discuss how using an aggressive method to recognize revenue, like the one described above, might affect IBM's reputation as "the epitome of financial conservatism."

b. Discuss some of the economic consequences associated with the use of such a method, mentioning some of the benefits and costs affecting IBM and its management.

c. The article mentions later that IBM requires all employees to swear that they have read [the IBM] "Business Conduct Guidelines" manual that warns them against not only reporting information inaccurately but also organizing it in a way that is intended to mislead or misinform. Comment on whether this policy is consistent with the use of the aggressive revenue recognition method mentioned above.

REAL DATA

ID6–3

Working capital, debt covenants, and restrictions on management decisions

Excerpts from the June 30, 1994 balance sheet of The Quaker Oats Company are provided below (dollars in millions).

	1994	1993	1992
Current assets:			
Cash and short-term investments	$ 140.4	$ 61.0	$ 95.2
Receivables	509.4	478.9	575.3
Inventories	385.5	354.0	435.3
Other current assets	218.3	173.7	150.4
Current liabilities	1,259.1	1,105.1	1,087.5

REQUIRED:

a. The notes to the company's 1992 financial statements state that "under the most restrictive terms of the various loan agreements . . . minimum working capital of $150 million must be maintained." Compute how close The Quaker Oats Company came to this restriction at the end of 1992, and discuss what has happened since that time.

b. In Quaker Oats's 1994 annual report, it states "under the most restrictive terms of the Revolving Credit Agreements, the company must maintain total shareholders' equity greater than $300 million." Comment on possible explanations for the changing restrictions.

REAL DATA

ID6-4

Analyzing the allowance account

The footnotes to the 1997 financial statements of Bank of America contained the following table (dollars in millions):

| | **Allowance for Credit Losses** | | |
	1997	**1996**	**1995**
Beginning balance	$3,523	$3,554	$3,690
Credit losses (write-offs):			
Domestic consumer loans	$1,085	$1,023	$ 761
Domestic commercial loans	154	263	235
Foreign loans	66	39	15
Total	$1,305	$1,325	$1,011
Credit loss recoveries:			
Domestic consumer loans	$ 222	$ 231	$ 142
Domestic commercial loans	155	116	181
Foreign loans	27	60	99
Total	$ 404	$ 407	$ 422
Balance, end of year	$3,500	$3,523	$3,554

REQUIRED:

a. Compute the provision for credit losses (bad debt expense) recognized by Bank of America in 1997, 1996, and 1995, and comment on any trend across the three-year period.

b. As of the end of 1997, the company had outstanding loans (reported on the balance sheet) of $167,111—$74,109 in domestic consumer loans, $64,470 in domestic commercial loans, and $28,532 in foreign loans. Which of the three categories appears to be the riskiest?

c. Within the foreign loan category, 56 percent of the loans are in Asian countries, 3 percent are in Central and Eastern Europe, and the remainder are in Latin America. The greatest exposure is in Mexico, followed by Japan, Korea, and Brazil. Explain why this kind of information would be useful to an investor interested in Bank of America.

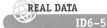

REAL DATA

ID6-5

Using the bad debt estimate to manage earnings

In November 1996, *The Wall Street Journal* stated that the success reported by Sears, the United States' second-largest retailer, over the past two years may not be as spectacular as it looks. The culprit is the $2 billion reserve for credit losses that Sears booked in 1993. As it turned out, the reserve was higher than it needed to be. In 1996, three years later, the company still had nearly twice the size of reserves (as a percentage of receivables) carried by most credit-granting retail companies.

REQUIRED:

a. Clearly explain how much of Sears's reported success in 1996 could be due to a $2 billion reserve booked in 1993. What reporting strategy does Sears seem to be practicing? Comment on the company's earnings quality.

b. Allen Lacey, Sears's chief financial officer, defended the company's actions by saying: "When you make estimates for something like credit-card debt, it can be higher or lower than what you actually experience . . . and Sears is operating well within the bounds of generally accepted accounting principles." Comment on Mr. Lacey's statement.

ID6-6

Auditors and receivable writeoffs

"For many auditors, the news would have set off alarm bells. California Micro Devices Corp., a highflying chip maker, disclosed that it was writing off half of its accounts receivable, mostly because of product returns. Its stock plunged 40 percent after the announcement, and shareholders filed suit alleging financial shenanigans. Nonetheless, the company's external auditors gave the chipmaker a clean bill of health. Within weeks it became clear that the auditors had missed an audacious accounting fraud, consisting of a dozen or more accounting tricks that various employees had deployed to keep the stock buoyant. They included one particularly bold one: booking bogus sales to fake companies for products that did not exist." (*Asian Wall Street Journal*, January 10, 2000)

REQUIRED

Explain the effect on the financial statements associated with "booking bogus sales to fake companies." After several years of booking such sales, what effect on the balance sheet might provide a clue that there may be a problem? Explain the effect on the financial statements of a receivables writeoff, and why might it be followed by a stock price decrease?

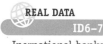

REAL DATA

ID6–7

Inernational banks
and bad
debt expense

The Wall Street Journal (September 1996) reported that Swiss Bank Corporation (SBC) unexpectedly said it will report a loss of about 1.9 billion Swiss francs ($1.53 billion) for 1996, after a radical change in its method of providing for bad debts. CEO Marcel Ospel said that the measure is being taken from a position of strength . . . and the company would have reported profit without the special one-time charge, which is being taken to cover the risks associated with repositioning its corporate business in Switzerland. The CEO noted further that the reforms should help produce net profit of about 1.7 billion francs in 1997 and that net profit should reach 2.5 billion by the year 2000.

REQUIRED:

Assume that you own stock in SBC. How would you interpret this announcement?

REAL DATA

ID6–8

Bad debt rates
over time

The following information was computed from the 1994 financial report of the merchandising division of Sears, Roebuck and Co. (dollars in millions):

	1994	1993	1992
Merchandise sales	$26,173	$23,811	$21,584
Credit sales as a percentage of total	59%	59%	57%
Bad debt expense	$ 650	$ 795	$ 872
Bad debt write-offs	$ 869	$ 821	$ 770

REQUIRED:

a. Assume that Sears uses a percentage-of-credit-sales method to estimate bad debts. Compute the percentages used by Sears in 1992, 1993, and 1994.

b. Assume that the merchandise division of Sears began 1992 with a $200 credit balance in Allowance for Doubtful Accounts. Prepare the journal entries that affected the allowance account for 1992, 1993, and 1994, and compute the balance as of December 31, 1994.

c. Have the rates used by Sears to estimate bad debts been consistently over or under its bad debt experience? How can you tell? Would you expect Sears's auditor to encourage the company to lower its bad debt estimate? Why or why not?

REAL DATA

ID6–9

Boosting earnings
with bad
debt estimates

Forbes (May 1997) notes that "Fairfield Company does set aside a reserve for bad debts, but last year it began tinkering with its provision for loan losses, reducing it from $6.5 million in 1995 to $5.39 million in 1996. It may not sound like much, but the reserve now covers only 4% of the company's time share sales, down from 6.5% in 1995—even though sales have increased by 30%. But, hey, that's tomorrow's problem. Today, Fairfield gets an extra $1 million in earnings."

REQUIRED:

a. Provide several reasons why a company may reduce its bad debt reserve from $6.5 to $5.39 million. Would these reasons seem to be as reasonable when sales have increased by 30 percent?

b. What does *Forbes* mean in the article by "that's tomorrow's problem"?

REAL DATA

ID6–10

Appendix 6A:
Accounting for
foreign currencies—
An economic
consequence

An article in *Forbes* noted that "accounting rules . . . can often change the way companies do business." Under the accounting rule covering receivables and payables denominated in foreign currencies, for example, "it is very important for companies to monitor their currency dealings." A case in point is R.J. Reynolds Industries, who "opened regional treasury offices in London and Hong Kong to keep tabs on worldwide cash flow and direct local borrowings." In that same article, a partner from a major accounting firm indicated that "more and more companies are centralizing their treasury-management function. Those that don't may be operating at a disadvantage."

REQUIRED:
a. Explain why the methods of accounting for foreign currencies might cause a company to centralize its treasury-management function and why those that don't may be operating at a disadvantage.
b. What is one of the main strategies used by U.S. companies to reduce the risks of holding receivables or payables denominated in non–U.S. currencies?
c. Explain how the strategy in (b) works. Specifically, how might it be used to reduce the possibility of violating a covenant on an outstanding debt?

ID6–11

The annual report of Wal-Mart

The 2001 annual report of Wal-Mart is reproduced in Appendix A.

REQUIRED:
Review the 2001 annual report, and answer the following questions.

a. Compute the change in Wal-Mart's current ratio and working capital from 2000 to 2001. Which accounts are the most important in explaining that change?
b. What is included in Wal-Mart's balance sheet cash account?
c. How large are Wal-Mart's receivables relative to current assets and total assets? How important is receivables management to Wal-Mart's operations? Explain.
d. Wal-Mart is moving aggressively into foreign markets. What currency risk does that move introduce and is there any evidence in the annual report that Wal-Mart is doing anything to control it?

Merchandise Inventory

CHAPTER 7

KEY POINTS

The following key points are emphasized in this chapter:

- *Inventory and how it affects the financial statements.*

- *Four issues that must be addressed when accounting for inventory.*

- *General rules for including items in inventory and attaching costs to these items.*

- *Differences between the perpetual and periodic methods and trade-offs involved in choosing between them.*

- *The three cost flow assumptions—average, FIFO, and LIFO.*

- *The lower-of-cost-or-market rule.*

Several years ago, the shareholders of Ann Taylor Stores, a national retailer of upscale women's clothing, brought suit against company management, accusing it of misleading investors by hiding the fact that it had accumulated huge amounts of excessive and overvalued inventory. Although the company reported disappointing results, surprising Wall Street, the company denied any wrongdoing. The financial press often reports incidents where management uses inventory accounting to manipulate earnings. This chapter covers inventory accounting, providing analysts the knowledge necessary to recognize when and how such manipulation influences the financial statements.

Inventory refers to items held for sale in the ordinary course of business. It is very important to retail and manufacturing enterprises, whose performance depends significantly on their sales. The demand for a company's products and the effectiveness of its inventory management are often the most important determinants of a company's success. Indeed, the 2000 annual report of Lands' End opened with the following comments from the company's chief executive. "The steps we took to put our company on the right track included reinvigorating our merchandise offerings and creative presentation, and a more disciplined approach to inventory management to improve gross profit margins.

Stockholders, creditors, managers, and auditors are all justifiably interested in the amount, condition, and marketability of a company's inventory. Stockholders are interested in future sales, profits, and dividends, all of which are related to the demand for inventory, and in the efficiency with which managers acquire, carry, and sell inventory. Creditors are interested in the ability of inventory sales to produce cash that can be used to meet interest and principal payments. Creditors may also view inventory as potential collateral or security for loans. Management must ensure that inventories are acquired (or manufactured) and carried at reasonable costs. Enough inventory must be carried and available to meet constantly changing consumer demands; yet carrying too much inventory can be very costly.[1] Auditors must ensure that the inventory dollar amount disclosed in the financial statements is determined using generally accepted accounting principles and reflects the value of the inventories actually owned. The value and marketability of a company's inventory can also provide an indication of its ability to continue as a going concern.

The Small Business Adviser in *Business Today* (Feb. 21, 2000) notes that "your inventory must be managed well to maximize profits. Uncontrolled inventories are inefficient and costly." What are "uncontrolled inventories" and how are they inefficient and costly?

THE RELATIVE SIZE OF INVENTORIES

Note in Figure 7–1 that financial institutions and Internet firms carry little or no inventories, while inventory is very important to retailers and to a lesser extent manufacturers. Inventory is by far the largest current asset for grocery store chains like SUPERVALU; and for retailers like Tommy Hilfiger, J.C. Penney, and Kmart, efficient and

---

1. In recent years U.S. manufacturers have become especially concerned with the levels of inventory they maintain. This concern is particularly important in the automobile industry, where U.S. automakers, like General Motors and Ford, compete with Japanese companies, like Honda, Toyota, and Mitsubishi, who are able to save substantial costs by carrying lower levels of inventory.

FIGURE 7–1

Inventory as a
percentage of
total assets and
current assets

	Inventory/ Total Assets	Inventory/ Current Assets
MANUFACTURING:		
General Electric (Manufacturer)	.02	.07
Chevron (Oil drilling and refining)	.03	.13
RETAIL:		
SUPERVALU (Grocery retail)	.23	.68
Tommy Hilfiger (Clothing retail)	.09	.26
INTERNET:		
Yahoo (Internet search engine)	.00	.00
Cisco (Internet systems)	.04	.11
GENERAL SERVICES:		
SBC Communications (Telecommunications services)	.00	.00
Wendy's (Restaurant services)	.02	.13
FINANCIAL SERVICES:		
Bank of America (Banking services)	.00	.00
Merrill Lynch (Investment services)	.00	.00

effective inventory management is the key barometer for their success. Manufacturers, like GE, invest in inventories because raw materials are necessary for the manufacturing process, but because carrying inventory is costly, they strive to minimize inventory levels, hoping to send their finished products to distributors and retailers as soon as possible. Similarly, companies that extract natural resources, like Chevron, attempt to ship their product to refineries and processing stations, and then to market, as soon as it is taken from the ground.

Both Hewlett-Packard, a world leader in technology development, and Yahoo, a well-known Internet portal and search engine, play important roles in today's high-tech business economy. One carries virtually no inventories while the other carries a substantial amount. Which is which? Explain.

ACCOUNTING FOR INVENTORY: FOUR IMPORTANT ISSUES

Figure 7–2 summarizes four important issues that must be addressed when accounting for inventory. At the top of the figure, the life cycle of inventory is divided into four segments. Inventory is (1) acquired, through purchase or manufacture, and then (2) carried on the company's balance sheet. It then either (3) is sold or (4) remains on the balance sheet as ending inventory. At each of these four points, an important issue in financial accounting must be addressed. The remainder of the chapter covers these four points in order.

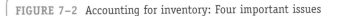

FIGURE 7-2 Accounting for inventory: Four important issues

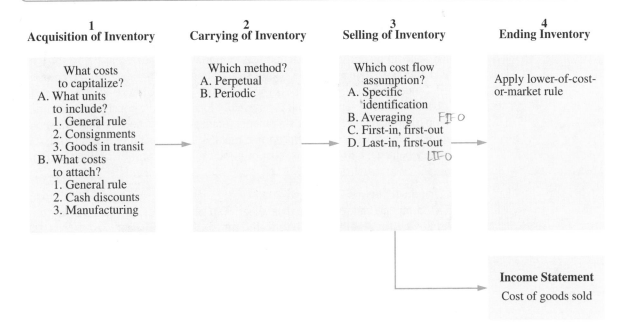

ACQUIRING INVENTORY: WHAT COSTS TO CAPITALIZE?

Inventory costs are capitalized because inventories are assets that provide future economic benefits. When inventories are sold, these benefits are realized. According to the matching principle, the capitalized cost should at this time be matched against the revenue recognized from the sale. Determining the amount of capitalized cost involves two steps: the number of items or units that belong in inventory must first be determined, and then costs must be attached to each item.

What Items or Units to Include?

Decisions as to what items or units to include in inventory are governed by a general rule. However, the general rule is not always simple to apply.

GENERAL RULE

Items should be included in a company's inventory if they are being held for sale and the company has complete and unrestricted ownership of them. Such ownership indicates that (1) the company bears the complete loss if the inventory is lost, stolen, or destroyed and (2) the company owns all rights to the benefits produced by the items.

In most cases, ownership is accompanied by possession: companies that own inventory are usually in possession of it. Under these circumstances, determining the number of units that belong in inventory is straightforward: the number of inventory units on the company's premises can simply be counted. In some cases, however, ownership is not accompanied by possession, and it becomes somewhat more difficult to find and determine the appropriate number of inventory units. Consignments and goods in transit are two common examples.

CONSIGNMENTS

In a **consignment,** a *consignor* (the owner) transfers inventory to a *consignee* (receiver), who takes physical possession and places the inventory up for sale. When it is sold, the consignee collects the sale proceeds, keeps a percentage of the proceeds for the service, and transfers the remainder to the consignor.

When accounting for consignments, it is important to realize that ownership, not physical possession, determines the balance sheet upon which consigned inventory is disclosed. Since consigned inventory is owned by the consignor, it belongs on the consignor's balance sheet, even though it is physically located on the consignee's premises. When preparing or using financial statements, managers must be sure that consigned inventory has been treated in the appropriate manner. Misclassifying it would misstate the inventory balance, current assets, cost of goods sold, gross profit, and net income.

Saks, a fashion retail store, reported 2000 consignment inventories of $87 million not reflected on the company's balance sheet. Explain what consignment inventories are and why they would not be reflected on Saks' balance sheet.

GOODS IN TRANSIT

When inventory is sold, the seller records a sale and the buyer records a purchase. Theoretically, both parties should record the transaction at exactly the same moment: the point in time when the ownership of the inventory transfers from the seller to the buyer. For practical purposes, however, most sales are recorded when goods are shipped, and most purchases are recorded when goods are received. Since goods are often in transit between the seller and the buyer for as long as several days, sellers and buyers often record the same transaction at two different points in time. This practice is acceptable except in cases where there are **goods in transit** at the end of an accounting period. For example, suppose that Buyer & Co. (located in Seattle, Washington) purchased goods on account from Seller Inc. (located in New York) on December 29, 2002. Seller delivered the goods immediately to XYZ Trucking Co., and the goods are in transit on December 31, the balance sheet date for both Buyer and Seller.

Accounting for this transaction in an appropriate manner involves determining who owns the goods while they are in transit. The most common way of determining ownership is to examine the freight terms associated with the shipment. These terms normally indicate which party bears the responsibility for shipping the goods and thereby owns them while they are in transit. The freight term of FOB shipping point (destination) indicates that the purchaser (seller) owns the inventory during transit.

FOB (free on board) shipping point indicates that the seller is responsible for the goods only to the point from which they are shipped. In the example, if the goods were shipped FOB shipping point, Seller Inc. would be responsible to deliver the goods to XYZ Trucking. From that point to Seattle, Buyer would be considered the owner of the goods, and their value would belong on Buyer's December 31 balance sheet. Both an inventory purchase on Buyer's books and a sale on Seller's books should be recorded.

FOB (free on board) destination indicates that the seller is responsible for the goods all the way to their destination. If the goods in the example were shipped FOB destination, Seller Inc. would be considered the owner of the goods until they reached Seattle. In this case, the goods would belong in Seller's inventory, and neither a purchase nor a sale would be recognized as of December 31.

Transactions near the end of an accounting period are often difficult to account for correctly. Managers must examine freight invoices and other related documents to ensure that sales and purchases are placed in the proper accounting periods and that, as of the balance sheet date, the number of inventory units on a company's balance sheet accurately reflects the inventory units actually owned. Similar to consignments, misclassifying goods in transit can misstate important financial statement numbers and ratios.

> The 2000 annual report of Kellogg Company states, "The company recognizes sales upon the shipment of its product to customers." What does this policy imply about goods in transit shipped by Kellogg? Explain how the revenue recognition policy influences the inventory amount carried on the balance sheet.

What Costs to Attach?

Once the number of items to be included in inventory has been determined, costs must be attached to these items to produce the total capitalized inventory cost. The general rule that guides this process and how it applies to inventory purchases and manufacturing operations is discussed in the following section.

GENERAL RULE

All costs associated with the manufacture, acquisition, storage, or preparation of inventory items should be capitalized and included in the inventory account. Included are the costs required to bring inventory items to saleable condition, such as the costs of purchasing, shipping in (called **freight-in** or **transportation-in**), manufacturing, and packaging. This rule is not difficult to apply in most cases, but two relatively common areas require further discussion. They are (1) accounting for cash (purchase) discounts on inventory purchases and (2) determining the costs of manufacturing inventories.

ACCOUNTING FOR CASH (PURCHASE) DISCOUNTS

Chapter 6 discusses accounting for cash (purchase) discounts from the seller's point of view. There we commented that the *gross method* establishes a credit sale and the corresponding account receivable at the gross price and recognizes a discount if payment is received within the discount period. Accounting for cash (purchase) discounts on inventory purchases is exactly the same, except now it is from the buyer's point of view. The inventory purchase is booked at the gross price, and if payment is made within the discount period, the carrying value of the inventory is reduced by the discount. If the discount is missed, the inventory is carried at the gross amount.

It is generally not advisable for companies to miss discounts. Under terms 2/10, n/30, for example, a purchasing company that makes a $1,000 payment 20 days after the expiration of the 10-day discount period would be paying a $20 financial charge. This situation is equivalent to borrowing cash at a 36.5 percent ([$20/$1,000] × [365 days/20 days]) annual rate of interest. Missing discounts, therefore, can be very expensive. Indeed, companies that miss discounts because they are short of cash would be better off to borrow from a bank at a rate much lower than 36.5 percent and use the proceeds to pay those suppliers offering cash (purchase) discounts. Consequently, most purchasing companies attempt to make payment within the discount period. Inability to do so can be a sign of mismanagement and/or serious financial problems.

An article published in the *Houston Chronicle* (June 2000) points out that inventory management and cash flow are closely related. Explain how good cash flow management can help to reduce the costs of inventory purchases.

DETERMINING THE COSTS OF MANUFACTURING INVENTORIES

Retail companies, like Sears, Wal-Mart, Kmart, May Department Stores, and J.C. Penney, simply purchase inventories (usually from manufacturers) and sell them for prices that exceed their costs. Retailers primarily provide a distribution service, rarely changing or improving the inventories they sell. As a result, the capitalized inventory cost for a retail operation consists primarily of only two components: (1) the purchase cost and (2) freight-in, the cost of shipping the goods to the retailer. If Kmart, for example, purchases merchandise for $5,000 cash and pays $500 to have the goods shipped to one of its stores, the following journal entry would be recorded:

Inventory (+A)	5,500	
Cash (−A)		5,500

Purchased inventory, including freight-in charges.

The operations of **manufacturing companies,** like IBM, General Electric, General Motors, Procter & Gamble, RJR Nabisco, and Johnson & Johnson, on the other hand, are much more complex. These companies purchase raw materials and use processes involving labor and other costs to manufacture their inventories. The capitalized inventory cost therefore includes the cost of acquiring the raw materials, the cost of the labor used to convert the raw materials to finished goods, and other costs that support the production process. These other costs, called **overhead,** include such items as indirect materials (e.g., cleaning supplies), indirect labor (e.g., salaries of line managers), depreciation of fixed assets, and utility and insurance costs.

The capitalized inventory costs of manufacturing operations include all costs required to bring the inventory to saleable condition. In this general respect, accounting for manufacturing operations is no different from accounting for retail operations. However, in manufacturing, virtually any cost that can be linked to the production process should be allocated to the inventory account. Therefore, costs like depreciation, wages and salaries, rent, and insurance are often capitalized as part of the inventory cost and, accordingly, are matched against revenues when the finished inventory is sold.

The 2000 annual report of 3D Systems Corporation provides the following information (dollars in thousands).

	2000	1999
Raw materials	$ 1,502	$1,633
Work in process	536	778
Finished goods	12,907	6,375
	$14,945	$8,786

Is 3D a retailer or manufacturer? What dollar amount appeared as inventory on the company's 2000 balance sheet? Briefly explain the differences across the three categories above.

Financial statement users should be aware that allocating overhead costs to inventory is a very subjective process, requiring expertise, that can have significant effects on important financial numbers and ratios. These allocations give management substantial influence over the financial statements. General Electric, for example, once reported in the footnotes of its annual report that it "changed its accounting procedures to include certain inventory costs [including depreciation and other product costs] previously charged directly to expense." The change increased reported net income by $281 million.

CARRYING INVENTORY: THE PERPETUAL OR PERIODIC METHOD?

Two methods are used to record and carry inventory on the books: perpetual and periodic. The **perpetual method** maintains a continuous record in the inventory account, recording inventory when it is purchased and allocating inventory costs to cost of goods sold when items are sold. Under the **periodic method,** inventory purchases are recorded as they occur, but the ending balance in the inventory account and cost of goods sold are not determined until the end of the period after an inventory count is taken. An example comparing the two methods appears in Figure 7–3, and the inventory T-account under the perpetual method is illustrated in Figure 7–4.

FIGURE 7–3   Perpetual and periodic methods

Given information:
Assume that inventory at the beginning of December is $2,500 (125 units at $20 per unit). The following transactions occurred during December.

	Perpetual Method		Periodic Method	
December 10: Purchased 100 units of inventory on account for $20 per unit.	Inventory (+A) Accts. Pay. (+L) *Purchased inventory on account.*	2,000[a] 2,000	Purchases (+A) Accts. Pay. (+L) *Purchased inventory on account.*	2,000[a] 2,000
December 20: Sold 50 units of inventory for cash at $30 per unit.	Cash (+A) Sales (R, +SE) *Sold inventory.*	1,500[b] 1,500	Cash (+A) Sales (R, +SE) *Sold inventory.*	1,500[b] 1,500
	COGS (E, −SE) Inventory (−A) *Recognized cost of goods sold and outflow of inventory.*	1,000[c] 1,000	(No entry recorded to reflect outflow of inventory.)	
December 31: Books are closed and financial statements are prepared.	(No journal entry required.)		COGS (E, −SE) Inventory (end.) (+A) Purchases (−A) Inventory(−A) *Recognized cost of goods sold and ending inventory.*	1,000[d] 3,500[e] 2,000 2,500

[a](100 units × $20)
[b](50 units × $30)
[c](50 units × $20)
[d]($2,500 + $2,000 − $3,500)
[e]An inventory count is required to determine the number of remaining units (175 units × $20).

FIGURE 7–4

Inventory
T-account: The
perpetual method

Inventory				
Beginning balance	2,500			
12/10 purchase	2,000			
		12/20 sale	1,000	
Ending balance	3,500			

As of December 31, the perpetual method provides an amount for cost of goods sold ($1,000) and an ending balance in the inventory account ($3,500). The periodic method, on the other hand, does not; it has to rely on an adjusting entry for these two amounts. In this example, the entry was recorded after an inventory count was taken, and it was determined that the ending balance in Inventory should be $3,500 (175 units × $20/unit). Cost of goods sold could then be determined by the following formula:

$$\text{Cost of Goods Sold} = \text{Beginning Inventory} + \text{Purchases} - \text{Ending Inventory}$$
$$\$1,000 \qquad\qquad \$2,500 \qquad\qquad \$2,000 \qquad\qquad \$3,500$$

In this example, the two methods come to the same dollar amounts for the ending balance in Inventory and Cost of Goods Sold. However, this occurred only because the inventory count (175 units × $20/unit) resulted in the same dollar amount as the ending inventory balance under the perpetual method ($3,500). More commonly, the inventory count does not match the ending inventory balance because items may have been lost, stolen, or damaged during the period. In such cases, the perpetual method is superior to the periodic method because it identifies these discrepancies, while the periodic method does not.

To illustrate, suppose that in the previous example the inventory count resulted in 150 units @ $20 per unit, or $3,000. Under the perpetual method, management would be able to see that the count resulted in an ending balance that was $500 less than the amount indicated in the inventory T-account ($3,500 − $3,000). This discrepancy would alert management to an inventory control problem that should be investigated. Under the periodic method, on the other hand, the discrepancy is not obvious, because there is no ending balance in the inventory T-account to compare to the results of the inventory count. In this case, cost of goods sold—as illustrated in the formula below—would simply be higher by $500 ($1,500 − $1,000), and management would not be made aware of the inventory control problem.

$$\text{Cost of Goods Sold} = \text{Beginning Inventory} + \text{Purchases} - \text{Ending Inventory}$$
$$\$1,500 \qquad\qquad \$2,500 \qquad\qquad \$2,000 \qquad\qquad \$3,000$$

This illustration represents just one of many ways in which the perpetual method provides more useful information than the periodic method. Although the perpetual method requires an additional bookkeeping procedure, computer systems have reduced the costs of such procedures significantly. As a result, more and more companies, even those that handle high volumes of widely diversified inventories, are moving toward the perpetual method for internal purposes. The major supermarket chains like Safeway, Giant Foods, and Lucky Stores, Inc., represent a case in point. Many have moved to automated bar code sensors, devices that reduce the cost of using the perpetual method for merchandisers who sell a wide variety of relatively low-cost items. Similarly, many of the major retailers like Kmart, Sears, and J.C. Penney have established perpetual systems. Interestingly, almost all of these companies still use the periodic method for financial reporting purposes.[2]

 Musicland Stores noted in its 1999 10K report that improved inventory management due to online tracking decreased inventory shrinkage and boosted gross margin. What kind of a system do you think Musicland is referring to, and how would a reduction in inventory shrinkage help to boost gross margin?

ERRORS IN THE INVENTORY COUNT

Under both the perpetual and periodic methods, inventory counts are made at the end of each period. But because many companies carry so many different kinds of inventory that each group of items cannot be counted at a reasonable cost, it is often difficult to ensure that such counts are accurate. In such cases, auditors and managers rely on estimates, and sometimes errors are committed.

An error in an inventory count will misstate both inventory on the balance sheet and net income on the income statement of that period. Such errors also misstate net income in the subsequent period by an equal dollar amount in the opposite direction. For example, an error in the inventory count taken at the end of 2002 that understates inventory by $2,000 will also understate 2002's net income by $2,000. In addition, this error if uncorrected will cause net income of 2003 to be overstated by $2,000. Such effects occur whether a company uses the perpetual method or the periodic method.

To illustrate using the periodic method, assume that Rainier Corporation began operations on January 1, 2002. Figure 7–5 summarizes the transactions entered into by the company during 2002 and 2003 and contains accurate inventory balances and income statements for the two years. Assume that the only expenses incurred by the company were the costs of sold inventories.

FIGURE 7–5
Rainier Corporation: Transactions for 2002–2003

	Inventory	Sales
2002		
(1) Purchased 500 units of inventory for $1 per unit	$500	
(2) Sold 200 units of inventory for $3 per unit	(200)	$ 600
Ending inventory	$300	
Sales ($600) − Cost of Goods Sold ($200) = Net Income ($400)		
2003		
Beginning inventory	$300	
(1) Purchased 600 units of inventory for $1 per unit	600	
(2) Sold 700 units of inventory for $3 per unit	(700)	$2,100
Ending inventory	$200	
Sales ($2,100) − Cost of Goods Sold ($700) = Net Income ($1,400)		

2. The reporting benefits firms obtain from using either LIFO or FIFO, discussed later, would be decreased if they used the perpetual method for reporting purposes.

Suppose that Rainier Corporation made no accounting errors during 2002 or 2003 except that it failed to include 20 items of inventory, each with a cost of $1, in its inventory count at the end of 2002. Inventory was thus determined incorrectly to be $280 instead of $300. Inventory was correctly counted at the end of 2003. The cost of goods sold and the inventory calculations for 2002 and 2003 appear in Figure 7–6. Income statements assuming accurate information and the miscounting error are shown in Figure 7–7.

FIGURE 7–6

Inventory errors: Periodic method

Cost of Goods Sold Calculation:

Cost of Goods Sold	=	Beginning Inventory	+Purchases	−	Ending Inventory
2002: $220	=	$0	+ $500	−	$280
2003: $680	=	$280	+ $600	−	$200

FIGURE 7–7

Comparative income statements: Rainier Corporation

	Accurate	Error
2002		
Sales	$ 600	$ 600
Cost of goods sold	200	220
Net income	$ 400	$ 380
2003		
Sales	$2,100	$2,100
Cost of goods sold	700	680
Net income	$1,400	$1,420

In summary, a single error in the counting of inventory caused net income of 2002 and net income of 2003 to be misstated by equal dollar amounts ($20) in opposite directions. Although both income statements are incorrect, the balance sheet as of the end of 2003 is properly stated. The accurate inventory count at year-end corrected the inventory balance, and the $20 understatement of retained earnings due to understated net income in 2002 was counterbalanced by a $20 overstatement to net income in 2003.

Inventory errors are not unusual and at times can be quite significant. For example, the auditor for Comnet Corp., a computer software and health-care products company, discovered that management had unintentionally overvalued inventories by $1.6 million on the company's financial statements. Consequently, Comnet's reported net income of $2.6 million was reduced to $1.0 million, and net income the following year was $1.6 million larger.

An article in *The Wall Street Journal* titled "Inventory Chicanery Tempts More Firms, Fools More Auditors" reported that "When companies are desperate to stay afloat, inventory fraud is the easiest way to produce instant profits and dress up the balance sheet . . . [and] the recent raise in inventory fraud is one of the biggest single reasons for the proliferation of accounting scandals." The article described how inventory frauds at Comptronix Corp., an Alabama electronics company, Laribee Wire Manufacturing, L.A. Gear, and the discount drugstore Phar-Mor were perpetrated simply by management creating fictitious inventories—undetected by the external auditor—that instantly increased profits. "Experts say that many companies overvalue obsolete goods and supplies. Others create phantom items in the warehouse to augment the assets needed for loan collateral. Still others count inventory that they pretend they have ordered but that will never arrive . . . [in these cases] the auditor was either taken or missed the obvious."

In its 2000 annual report, Pier 1 Imports reported ending inventory and net income of $269 million and $75 million, respectively. If Pier 1 had incorrectly counted its ending inventory at $300 million, what would have been its 2000 net income? (Do not account for income taxes.)

SELLING INVENTORY: WHICH COST FLOW ASSUMPTION?

Perhaps the most important and difficult question of inventory accounting involves how to allocate the capitalized inventory cost between the cost of goods sold and ending inventory. The examples so far have assumed that the cost of the sold inventory is known, but such situations are relatively unusual. In most cases, companies are unable to determine exactly which items are sold and which items remain in ending inventory. When this occurs, an assumption must be made about the cost flow of the inventory items. The assumption chosen can significantly affect net income, current assets, working capital, and the current ratio because it determines the relative costs allocated to the cost of goods sold and ending inventory.

This section first discusses the specific identification method, which is used when the cost of the sold inventory items can be determined. We then cover three cost flow assumptions that are used extensively in practice: averaging; first-in, first-out (FIFO); and last-in, first-out (LIFO).

Specific Identification

In some cases, especially with relatively infrequent sales of large-ticket items (e.g., jewelry, furniture, automobiles, land), it is possible to specifically identify which inventory items have been sold and which remain. In such situations, the allocation of inventory cost between the cost of goods sold and ending inventory is relatively straightforward. Suppose, for example, that on March 1, Used Cars & Co. had three 2002 Honda Accords for sale. Cars 1 and 2 were purchased from the same dealer at a cost of $10,000 each. Car 3 was purchased recently at an auction for $12,000. The three cars are in comparable condition, and the selling price for each is $18,000. The March 1 inventory for Used Cars & Co. follows.

Car	Cost
1	$10,000
2	10,000
3	12,000
Total	$32,000

Assume that on March 15, Sammy Sportsman agrees to purchase any one of the three cars for $18,000. Used Cars gives Sammy Car 3 (cost = $12,000), and the following journal entries (perpetual method) are recorded:

| Cash (+A) | 18,000 | |
| Sales (R, +SE) | | 18,000 |

Sold Honda.

| Cost of Goods Sold (E, −SE) | 12,000 | |
| Inventory (−A) | | 12,000 |

Recognized cost of goods sold for
Honda with cost of $12,000.

It is fairly clear in this situation that $12,000 should have been allocated to Cost of Goods Sold and $20,000 should remain in ending inventory. An inventory item (Car 3) with a cost of $12,000 was sold. Thus, the specific identification procedure is a relatively straightforward way to determine the cost of goods sold and ending inventory. Nonetheless, it does have limitations.

First, the **specific identification** procedure requires the tracking of specific inventory items, which can be difficult for some firms. A second limitation is that in many cases specific identification allows a manager to manipulate net income and the ending inventory value. Suppose in the example that the manager of Used Cars & Co. chose to give Sammy Sportsman either Car 1 or Car 2, instead of Car 3. Recall that Sammy was indifferent toward choosing among the three automobiles. In this situation, the following journal entries would have been recorded:

| Cash (+A) | 18,000 | |
| Sales (R, +SE) | | 18,000 |

Sold Honda.

| Cost of Goods Sold (E, −SE) | 10,000 | |
| Inventory (−A) | | 10,000 |

Recognized cost of goods sold for
Honda with cost of $10,000.

The decision to give Sammy Car 1 or Car 2 would have produced net income and ending inventory values that were $2,000 ($12,000 − $10,000) greater than the decision to give Sammy Car 3. The specific identification procedure allowed the manager to manipulate income and inventory by choosing which inventory item to deliver to the customer. While manipulating the financial statement in this way is not a misrepresentation, it does allow management to influence the timing of income recognition.

Three Inventory Cost Flow Assumptions: Averaging, FIFO, and LIFO

The inventories of many companies are acquired at so many different prices that it is often difficult to identify specifically the costs of the items sold and the costs of the items in ending inventory. In such cases, an assumption must be invoked. To illustrate and compare the three different cost flow assumptions, consider the following example. The chart in Figure 7–8 describes the inventory purchase and sales data for Discount Sales Company during its first year of operations.

Beginning inventory consisted of 20 units, a total of 60 units were purchased, and 35 units were sold during the year, producing an ending inventory of 45 units. Note that each unit of beginning inventory had a cost of $4, Purchase 1 was at a $5 unit cost, and Purchase 2 was at a $6 unit cost. Inventory costs increased during the period. Total capitalized inventory costs were $410, and $330 ($150 + $180) of those costs repre-

FIGURE 7–8 Inventory purchase and sales schedule: Discount Sales Company

Description	(1) No. Units	(2) Cost	(3) Sales Price	Total Costs (1) × (2)	Total Sales Proceeds (1) × (3)
Beginning inventory	20	$4		$ 80	
Purchase 1	30	5		150	
Sale 1	10		$15		$150
Purchase 2	30	6		180	
Sale 2	25		15	___	375
Ending inventory	45				
Capitalized inventory costs				$410	
Units sold	35				
Total sales proceeds					$525

sented new purchases. Sold units were priced at $15 each. The following assumptions each allocate the $410 of capitalized inventory cost to Cost of Goods Sold and Inventory in a different way.[3]

AVERAGING ASSUMPTION/PERIODIC METHOD: A WEIGHTED AVERAGE

The **averaging assumption** applied to the periodic method involves the calculation of the per-unit weighted average cost at the end of the period after the inventory count is taken. The total capitalized inventory cost ($410) is divided by the number of available units (80 = 20 + 30 + 30) to compute the per-unit average cost ($5.125 = $410/80 units). The weighted average ending inventory is calculated by multiplying the per-unit average cost by the number of units on hand ($231 = $5.125 × 45 units). Once the ending inventory is determined, the cost of goods sold can be calculated in the following manner. Note that the total capitalized inventory cost is allocated between cost of goods sold and the ending inventory.

Weighted average ending inventory = 45 units × $5.125/unit = $231

Cost of Goods Sold = Beginning Inventory + Purchases − Ending Inventory
$179   = $80   + $330   − $231

Cost of goods sold   = $179
Ending inventory   =   231
Total capitalized inventory cost   = $410

FIFO ASSUMPTION/PERIODIC METHOD

Under the **first-in, first-out (FIFO)** assumption, the costs of the units sold are assumed to be equal to the costs of the oldest available units in the financial records. The 45 units in ending inventory, therefore, are assumed to consist of those most

3. The calculations are based on the assumption that Discount Sales Company uses the periodic inventory method for reporting purposes. If the company used the perpetual inventory method, the dollar amounts of the differences across the three assumptions would be smaller but still in the same direction.

recently purchased: that is, the 30 units from Purchase 2 and the 15 units from Purchase 1. Ending inventory and cost of goods sold are computed as follows:

FIFO ending inventory = (30 units from Purchase 2 × $6/unit) $180
+ (15 units from Purchase 1 × $5/unit)   75
$255

Cost of Goods Sold = Beginning Inventory + Purchases − Ending Inventory
$155   = $80   + $330   − $255

Cost of goods sold	= $155
Ending inventory	= 255
Total capitalized inventory cost	= $410

LIFO ASSUMPTION/PERIODIC METHOD

Under the **last-in, first-out (LIFO)** assumption, the costs of the units sold are assumed to be equal to the costs of those most recently purchased. The 45 units in ending inventory, therefore, are assumed to consist of the oldest available in the financial records: that is, the 20 units from beginning inventory and 25 units from Purchase 1. Ending inventory and cost of goods sold are computed as below.

LIFO ending inventory = (25 units from Purchase 1 × $5/unit) $125
+ (20 units from beginning inventory × $4/unit)   80
$205

Cost of Goods Sold = Beginning Inventory + Purchases − Ending Inventory
$205   = $80   + $330   − $205

Cost of goods sold	= $205
Ending inventory	= 205
Total capitalized inventory cost	= $410

Inventory Cost Flow Assumptions: Effects on the Financial Statements

Figure 7–9 compares the averaging, FIFO, and LIFO cost flow assumptions with respect to the cost of goods sold, gross profit, net income, and ending inventory. Assume further that Discount Sales Company incurred $150 of expenses (excluding the cost of goods sold) during the period.

FIGURE 7–9

Financial statement effects of the three inventory cost flow assumptions

	FIFO	Averaging	LIFO
Sales (35 units × $15)	$525	$525	$525
Cost of goods sold	155	179	205
Gross profit	$370	$346	$320
Expenses	150	150	150
Net income before taxes	$220	$196	$170
Ending inventory	$255	$231	$205
Cost of goods sold	155	179	205
Total capitalized inventory cost	$410	$410	$410

Several features about the comparisons in Figure 7–9 are noteworthy. First, under all three cost flow assumptions, the entire $410 of capitalized inventory cost is allocated either to ending inventory or cost of goods sold. The three assumptions differ in that they give rise to different allocations.

Second, the relative dollar amounts on the financial statements produced by the three assumptions are driven by the changes in the inventory purchase costs that occurred during the period. In this illustration, for example, per-unit inventory purchase costs increased during the period from $4 for beginning inventory to $5 for Purchase 1 to $6 for Purchase 2. This cost increase caused ending inventory under FIFO ($255) to be greater than ending inventory under averaging ($231), which in turn was greater than ending inventory under LIFO ($205). Inventory cost increases also caused cost of goods sold under FIFO ($155) to be less than cost of goods sold under averaging ($179), which in turn was less than cost of goods sold under LIFO ($205). We chose to illustrate an inflationary trend because, in reality, prices tend to increase over time. However, it is important to realize that if inventory costs had decreased during the period, the orders shown above would have been reversed: the LIFO assumption would have resulted in the greatest ending inventory and the least cost of goods sold dollar amounts. In fact, had inventory costs remained stable throughout the period, no differences would have resulted: all three assumptions would have reported the same ending inventory and cost of goods sold amounts.

Finally, in the example, the FIFO assumption gave rise to the highest, and the LIFO assumption gave rise to the lowest, net income and ending inventory dollar amounts. In times of increasing inventory costs, therefore, using the FIFO assumption can boost important financial ratios, such as earnings per share, working capital, and the current ratio. Choosing LIFO, on the other hand, may value inventories at unrealistically low levels. Financial statement users should pay close attention to a company's inventory cost flow assumption because it can significantly distort important financial ratios.

Goodyear Tire & Rubber Company uses the LIFO cost flow assumption for most of its inventories. Inventory on the 1999 balance sheet was reported as $2.3 billion. Had the company used the FIFO assumption, ending inventory would have been $300 million higher. Explain why ending inventory can be so different under two acceptable assumptions.

Inventory Cost Flow Assumptions: Effects on Federal Income Taxes

As the previous example shows, if inventory costs are increasing, using the LIFO assumption gives rise to the lowest net income amount. During inflationary times, therefore, the LIFO assumption is an attractive alternative for determining a company's federal income tax liability, which is computed as a percentage of taxable income: less taxable income means less federal income tax liability.

Federal income tax law states that if a company uses the LIFO assumption for computing its tax liability, it must also use the LIFO assumption for preparing its financial statements. If a company uses a cost flow assumption other than LIFO for tax purposes, it can use the LIFO, averaging, or FIFO assumption for financial reporting. This regulation is called the **LIFO conformity rule,** and it causes most companies to use the same cost flow assumption for both income tax and financial reporting purposes. Companies that choose LIFO for tax purposes must use it for reporting purposes.

Companies that want to use FIFO for reporting purposes may not use LIFO for tax purposes.

Figure 7–10 shows the effects of the different cost flow assumptions on federal income taxes. The comparison uses the numbers from Figure 7–9, except that federal income taxes have been assessed as a percentage (34 percent) of net income before taxes and are listed as an expense on the income statement.

FIGURE 7–10

Income tax effects of the three inventory cost flow assumptions

	FIFO	Averaging	LIFO
Sales (35 units × $15)	$525	$525	$525
Cost of goods sold	155	179	205
Gross profit	$370	$346	$320
Expenses	150	150	150
Net income before taxes	$220	$196	$170
Federal income taxes (34%)	75	67	58
Net income after taxes	$145	$129	$112

Note in Figure 7–10 that, in times of rising inventory costs, if a company chooses to minimize its federal income taxes by using the LIFO assumption, it must report lower net income and inventory on its financial statements. The effects on the financial statements of using LIFO can be significant. For example, as of January 27, 2000, the inventories of Kmart, a LIFO user, were valued at about $360 million less than they would be under FIFO. In another example, DuPont reduced its current assets and reported net income by $612 million when it changed from FIFO to LIFO. On the other hand, companies using the FIFO assumption to boost reported net income and ending inventory must pay additional federal income taxes. These additional tax payments can be very significant.

Earlier we mentioned that Goodyear's 1999 inventory balance under LIFO was $300 million lower than it would have been under FIFO. Estimate how many dollars in taxes Goodyear has saved by using LIFO instead of FIFO. Assume a 30 percent income tax rate.

Choosing an Inventory Cost Flow Assumption: Trade-Offs

Most companies find it impractical to specifically identify the inventory items sold during a given period. Management must therefore choose from among the three assumptions discussed above. *Accounting Trends and Techniques* (2000) reports that of 600 major U.S. companies surveyed, 301 (50%) used LIFO, 404 (67%) used FIFO, and 176 (29%) used averaging for at least some of their inventories. Most of these companies used different methods for different kinds of inventory. Of those using LIFO, 183 (61%) used it for 50 percent or more of their inventories. The choice of a cost flow assumption is a difficult problem that depends on the situation faced by a given company.

Before considering the trade-offs involved in choosing an inventory cost flow assumption, remember that the assumption does not necessarily reflect the actual movement of the inventory. In fact, there is often no relationship between the assumption used to value the inventory for reporting purposes and the actual cost of the inventory on hand. Choosing a cost flow assumption is largely independent of the nature of the inventory itself.

It is also difficult to change a cost flow assumption once it has been chosen. As discussed in Chapter 3, the principle of consistency requires that accounting methods be consistent from year to year, and such changes, even when approved by an auditor, must be fully described in the footnotes, mentioned in the audit report, and their effect on income must be separately disclosed on the income statement. Recently, only a few major U.S. companies have changed their inventory cost flow assumptions. In 2000, for example, *Accounting Trends and Techniques* reports that only 2 of the 600 major U.S. companies surveyed chose to make such a change.

The trade-offs involved in choosing an inventory cost flow assumption are divided into two categories: (1) income and asset measurement and (2) economic consequences. *Income and asset measurement* refers to how well each assumption produces measures that reflect the actual performance and financial condition of a company. *Economic consequences* refer to the costs and benefits associated with using a particular assumption.

INCOME AND ASSET MEASUREMENT

In terms of income and asset measurement, neither LIFO nor FIFO is clearly preferred. The LIFO assumption is a better application of the matching principle than the FIFO assumption. LIFO allocates the most current purchase costs to cost of goods sold, where they are matched against current sales in the determination of net income. FIFO matches relatively old costs against current revenues.

FIFO, on the other hand, is generally viewed as producing a more current measure of inventory on the balance sheet. Ending inventory under FIFO reflects the costs of the most recent purchases; LIFO reports ending inventory in terms of older, less relevant costs. Using LIFO over a period of time, therefore, can give rise to ending inventory costs that are grossly outdated. Union Carbide's net worth (Assets − Liabilities), for example, was at one time understated by about 18 percent simply because it used LIFO, and the *inventory turnover* (Cost of Goods Sold ÷ Inventory) of Monsanto, another LIFO user, was overstated by approximately 50 percent.

ECONOMIC CONSEQUENCES

The economic consequences of choosing an inventory flow assumption relate to such factors as income taxes and liquidity problems, bookkeeping costs, LIFO liquidations and purchasing practices, debt and compensation contracts, and the capital market.

Income Taxes and Liquidity. Often the most important economic consideration when choosing an inventory cost flow assumption is the tax consequence. When inventory costs are rising, LIFO yields a lower net income number than FIFO, resulting in a lower tax liability. Consequently, choosing LIFO can improve a company's liquidity position by minimizing cash payments for income taxes. As mentioned earlier, the magnitude of such savings can be significant.

Using FIFO can create liquidity problems. In times of rising prices, FIFO produces higher income than LIFO because it matches relatively old costs against current revenues. Because old costs are lower than current costs, FIFO creates **paper profits**, profits that are due to rising inventory costs instead of efficient operations. Paper profits appear on the income statement, but they are not backed by cash inflows. Unfortunately, these inflated profits are also used to determine a company's tax liability, which must be paid in cash. As a result, operating cash inflows may not be sufficient to cover the required cash outflows, and the company's liquidity position suffers.

In the early 1970s, the United States experienced a dramatic economic downturn and double-digit inflation. That year over 400 companies, most with cash flow problems, switched from FIFO and LIFO. Explain why so many companies would make such a shift.

Bookkeeping Costs. While LIFO usually brings about a lower tax liability than FIFO, it requires more bookkeeping procedures and is generally more costly to implement. For example, one survey of FIFO users found that many companies did not adopt LIFO because the record-keeping requirements of LIFO were burdensome and costly. Indeed, short-cut methods for estimating LIFO have been devised to reduce the costs of maintaining LIFO records.

LIFO Liquidation and Inventory Purchasing Practices. The use of LIFO can give rise to grossly overstated net income amounts when inventory levels are cut back. Consider, for example, Atlantic Richfield, a giant in the oil industry and a long-time LIFO user. In the early 1980s, the dollar amount in the company's inventory balance consisted of costs that were very old, extremely low, and too outdated. Then an oil glut occurred, and the market price of oil decreased sharply. In response, Atlantic Richfield and a number of other oil companies cut inventory levels significantly. This action caused the low and outdated costs in inventory to be matched against Atlantic Richfield's current revenues. The result was a $105 million increase in the company's profits. That same year, the profits of Gulf Oil, Standard Oil of California, and Texaco, other LIFO users, were inflated for the same reasons, by $200 million, $165 million, and $315 million, respectively. Unfortunately, these high profits were due to the liquidation of LIFO inventories, not the effective and efficient operations of the oil companies or the condition of the oil industry, which at the time was suffering. Moreover, additional income taxes had to be paid on these profits.

Many LIFO users allow such inventory liquidations to occur, but other companies intentionally avoid them by maintaining their inventory purchases to prevent their inventory levels from diminishing. Such a practice avoids increased taxes, but at the same time, it can give rise to other problems. It may not be the appropriate time to purchase inventory. Inventory costs may be at a seasonal high, for example, or significant discounts may not be available. Further, such action does nothing to solve the problem associated with LIFO's understated inventory valuation; it merely postpones a problem that grows worse with each passing year.

Alcoa, a major steel manufacturer, recently reported that the reduction of its LIFO inventory quantities increased net income by $31 million, or eight cents per share. Explain how reducing inventory could increase income. As an analyst, why would you be interested in such a disclosure?

Debt and Compensation Contracts. FIFO may be attractive to management because, when inventory costs are rising, FIFO produces higher reported net income and higher inventory values than LIFO. Compensation paid to management expressed as a percentage of FIFO income tends to be higher than compensation based on LIFO income. In addition, debt covenants using ratios based on FIFO will impose less restrictive constraints on managers than those based on LIFO.

However, the relative effects of LIFO and FIFO on the financial statements are reversed when prices are decreasing. For example, the annual report of May Department Stores once noted: "We value our department store inventories using the LIFO (last-in, first-out) method. Usually, this decreases earnings . . . [however] in [the current year], we experienced deflation, which resulted in a pretax LIFO credit [earnings increase] of $46 million."

The Capital Market. Management may also choose FIFO over LIFO because it believes that FIFO's higher net income and inventory amounts are valued more highly by investors and creditors in the capital market. They reason that using FIFO could improve the company's credit rating, which may lead to better terms on its borrowings and higher prices for its outstanding debt securities. Some believe that FIFO may also bring about higher prices for the company's outstanding equity securities. For example, in the survey mentioned earlier when asked why [the company] did not use LIFO, one manager responded that using LIFO would depress the market price of its stock. If such assertions are correct, using FIFO would make it easier to raise capital as well as increase management's value in the managerial labor market.

The validity of this reasoning is still open to question. A number of research studies in accounting suggest that the stock market "looks through" a company's accounting methods and values the company on the basis of the underlying cash flows. Since using LIFO usually saves taxes, these studies suggest that companies using LIFO are more highly valued by the stock market than companies using FIFO. However, the evidence is mixed, and all such conclusions are still tentative.

Under generally accepted accounting principles, companies using LIFO are allowed to report in the footnotes to the financial statements what the value of their inventories would be if they used FIFO. Also, they are required to report the income effects of any LIFO liquidations during the year. The excerpt below was taken from the 1999 annual report of Solutia, a world-leading producer of plastics (dollars in millions).

	1999	1998
Finished goods	$260	$252
Goods in process	121	87
Raw materials	109	116
Inventories at FIFO	490	455
Excess of FIFO over LIFO	(119)	(124)
Inventories at LIFO	$371	$331

The cost of 67 percent of the inventories is determined by the last-in, first-out (LIFO) basis, which generally reflects the effects of inflation or deflation on cost of goods sold sooner than other inventory methods. The cost of the remaining inventories is generally determined by the first-in, first-out (FIFO) basis. Inventories at FIFO approximate current cost. The effects of LIFO inventory liquidations were not significant in 1999, 1998, and 1997.

The LIFO Reserve: A User Perspective. The Solutia footnote includes a line item called "Excess of FIFO over LIFO," which was $119 million in 1999 and $124 million in 1998. These dollar amounts are often referred to as **LIFO reserves,** and they provide useful information. For example, they enable users to compute the following for Solutia:

1. Inventory value if the company used FIFO in 1999. Adding the LIFO reserve to the LIFO inventory value produces the FIFO inventory value. Refer to the calculation

below to see Solutia's 1999 inventory value if it used FIFO (dollars in millions). This calculation can help users compare the financial performance and condition of Solutia to that of other FIFO users.

$$\begin{array}{ccc} \textbf{1999 Inventory (LIFO)} + \textbf{1999 LIFO Reserve} = \textbf{1999 Inventory (FIFO)} \\ \$371 \qquad + \qquad \$119 \qquad = \qquad \$490 \end{array}$$

2. Net income and the additional tax liability if the company switched from LIFO to FIFO in 1999. Multiplying the reserve by the company's effective tax rate (which can be found in the footnotes) provides an estimate of the additional tax liability associated with changing from LIFO to FIFO in 1999 (dollars in millions):

$$\begin{array}{ccc} \textbf{1999 LIFO Reserve} \times \textbf{Effective Tax Rate} = \textbf{Additional 1999 Tax} \\ \$119 \qquad \times \qquad 0.32 \qquad = \qquad \$38 \end{array}$$

Such a change would result in recognizing the firm's oldest (and lowest) inventory cost in the 1999 cost of goods sold, thereby increasing taxable income and the associated tax liability. This calculation shows that Solutia would have paid additional taxes of $38 million if it had chosen to switch to FIFO in 1999. Another way to interpret this calculation is that it represents an estimate of the taxes saved by Solutia from the time it adopted LIFO to the present, assuming constant tax rates.

3. FIFO net income in 1999 if the company had switched to FIFO in a prior year. An estimate of net income reported by Solutia if it had switched to FIFO in a prior year can be derived from multiplying the change in the LIFO reserve (from 1998 to 1999) by 1 minus the effective tax rate, and then adding that amount to net income reported under LIFO. Like the first calculation above, this calculation—provided below (dollars in millions)—can help users compare the financial performance and condition of Solutia to that of other FIFO users.

$$\begin{array}{ccc} \textbf{1999 Net Income (LIFO)} + \textbf{Increase in LIFO Reserve} &= \textbf{1999 Net Income (FIFO)} \\ & \times \textbf{Effective Tax Rate} & \\ \$206 \qquad + [(\$119 - \$124) \times (1 - 0.32)] = & \$203 \end{array}$$

ENDING INVENTORY: APPLYING THE LOWER-OF-COST-OR-MARKET RULE

The inventory cost flow assumption determines the capitalized cost allocated to ending inventory. However, inventories on the balance sheet are not necessarily carried at this dollar amount. Based on conservatism, ending inventory is valued at cost or market value, whichever is lower.

Applying the lower-of-cost-or-market rule to ending inventory is accomplished by comparing the cost allocated to ending inventory with the market value of the inventory. If the market value exceeds the cost, no adjustment is made and the inventory remains at cost. If the market value is less than the cost, the inventories are written down to market value with an adjusting journal entry.

Suppose, for example, that ABC Enterprises uses the FIFO assumption, which gives rise to an ending inventory of $100. If the market value of the inventory is $150, no adjusting journal entry need be recorded. The ending inventory remains at cost because cost ($100) is lower than market value ($150). If the market value of the inventories is $80, however, the inventory would have to be written down (reduced) from $100 to $80. The following journal entry represents one way of recording such a write-down:

Loss on Inventory Write-Down (Lo, −SE)   **20**
     Inventory (−A)   **20**
Wrote down inventory to market value ($100 − $80).

Inventory write-downs are fairly common and sometimes quite large. In a recent financial report, for example, Alcoa reported a write-down of approximately $213 million, while that same year Gerber Products Company recorded a $2.9 million charge to write down certain inventories to market value.

The 1998 annual report of Dayton Superior, the largest North American manufacturer and distributor, notes that the company provides reserves that reflect the company's best estimate of the excess of the cost over the market value of the inventory. The reserves were $1.6 million and $876 thousand for 1998 and 1997, respectively. Explain how the recognition of these reserves affected the company's reported net income in 1998 and 1997.

THE LOWER-OF-COST-OR-MARKET RULE AND HIDDEN RESERVES

The lower-of-cost-or-market rule is often criticized because it treats inventory price changes inconsistently. Price decreases, based on difficult-to-determine market values, are recognized immediately, while price increases are not recognized until the inventory is sold in an objective and verifiable transaction. This conservative, but inconsistent, treatment can create "hidden reserves" that managers can use to manipulate income.

Consider a company that is just about to complete a very good year. In fact, reported earnings are expected to be so high that management is seeking to reduce income and perhaps move some of the earnings to future periods that may be less successful. One way to execute this "income smoothing" strategy is to write down inventory in the current year and sell it in a future period. Suppose, for example, that management chooses to write down an inventory item with an original cost of $10 to its subjectively determined market value of $8. A $2 loss is immediately recognized, reducing the current year's net income. Assume further that during the following year, the inventory item is sold for $12, giving rise to a book gain that increases that year's net income by $4 ($12 − $8). Note that by writing down the inventory in the first year, management was able to transfer $2 of net income from the first to the second year. A "hidden reserve" was created by the write-down, which was realized in a subsequent period.

Certainly, the conservative and inconsistent nature of the lower-of-cost-or-market rule, combined with subjective inventory write-downs, can create "hidden reserves" that can be used to manage the reported values on the financial statements. However, it is important to keep in mind that conservative accounting is a response to the liability faced by those who must provide and audit financial statements. The potential costs to these parties associated with understating inventories and profits are typically less than those associated with overstating them. From an economic standpoint, therefore, the lower-of-cost-or-market rule may be justifiable, even though it produces questionable measures on the financial statements. In any event, investors, creditors, managers, auditors, and other interested parties must be aware of these weaknesses.

Earlier we noted that Dayton Superior recognized an inventory write-down (based on an estimate) of $1.6 million during 1998. If the company sold its inventory for full price during 1999, how would reported net income have been affected?

INTERNATIONAL PERSPECTIVE: JAPANESE BUSINESS AND INVENTORY ACCOUNTING

We have commented several times in this text that the business environment and practices in individual countries determine the accounting methods used in those countries. The situation in Japan with respect to inventories provides an interesting example. Japan has a long history of what might loosely be described in the United States as "corporate groups." Typically, such groups are made up of a number of different entities, many of which perform different functions and hold equity interest in the others. The board of directors of each company is normally comprised of representatives from each of the member entities. Mitsubishi, Sanwa, Nippon Steel, Hitachi, Nissan, and Toyota are all organized in such interlocking networks.

This group orientation, which is not evident in the United States, offers a number of significant advantages, most of which relate to planning and coordination among the group members. In most cases, for example, the presidents of the group companies hold meetings periodically to promote coordination and mutual understanding and to eliminate overlap in the activities conducted by the membership. These groups are then better able to share business risks, and when a company within a group faces difficulties, various means are pursued by other group members to assist it.

In many situations, such as in the Japanese auto and electronics industries, the group network contains both the manufacturer and its main suppliers. Proper coordination and planning among these parties can help to minimize material and product inventories as well as lead time and delivery items, giving rise to lower inventory carrying cost and better customer service. Just-in-time (JIT) inventory systems, which reduce the costs of carrying large amounts of inventory without jeopardizing customer service, have long been a characteristic of this Japanese system and have given the Japanese a definite advantage when competing against U.S. industry.

The implication for financial reporting is that Japanese manufacturers, in general, carry much lower levels of inventory that turn over at much higher rates than those in the United States. This difference decreases the importance of inventory accounting in Japan, making the effects on the financial statements of choosing among the various cost flow assumptions relatively insignificant. Consequently, unlike U.S. companies, who normally choose FIFO or LIFO for some significant economic reason, most companies in Japan use the averaging method.

REVIEW PROBLEM

On December 1, Jane Lee contributed $1,000 of her own funds to begin an Oriental grocery store that sells white rice. The rice is kept in a large bin, and customers help themselves by filling plastic bags with a large scoop. The transactions described in Figure 7–11 took place during December. Assume that Jane incurred cash expenses (excluding the cost of goods sold and inventory shortages) of $400 during December, and she pays income taxes at a rate of 30 percent of net income before taxes on December 31.

Jane purchased rice on two occasions at two different prices. By multiplying the number of pounds purchased by the cost per pound, the total capitalized inventory cost for January can be computed ($510). Three hundred pounds of rice were sold for a price of $5/lb., creating total sales of $1,500 (300 lb. × $5).

Date	Description	Total Inventory Cost
Dec. 1	**Jane Lee, owner, contributed $1,000.**	
7	**Purchased 300 pounds of rice for $1.00 per pound.**	**$300**
25	**Sold 250 pounds of rice for $5.00 per pound.**	
27	**Purchased 150 pounds of rice for $1.40 per pound.**	**210**
28	**Sold 50 pounds of rice for $5.00 per pound.**	
29	**Paid cash expenses of $400.**	
31	**Paid income tax liability.**	
Total capitalized inventory cost		**$510**

FIGURE 7–11

December transactions for JL Oriental Foods

On December 31, when financial statements are prepared, Jane is able to determine beginning inventory ($0) and total purchase costs ($510) because she recorded the purchases as they were made. Assume that Jane took an inventory at this time (i.e., weighed the rice) and noted that there were 150 pounds of rice on hand. The following figures (7–12 and 7–13) contain the income statements and balance sheets prepared by

FIGURE 7–12

Periodic method: FIFO assumption

JL Oriental Foods
Income Statement
For the Month Ended December 31, 2001

Sales (300 lb. × $5)	$1,500
Cost of goods sold	300[a]
Gross profit	$1,200
Expenses	400
Net income before taxes	$ 800
Income tax expense ($800 × 0.30)	240
Net income after taxes	$ 560

[a]Beginning inventory + Purchases   − Ending inventory
     $0   + ($300 + $210) − (150 lb. × $1.40)

JL Oriental Foods
Balance Sheet
December 31, 2001

Cash	$1,350[a]
Inventory	210[b]
Total assets	$1,560
Common stock	$1,000
Retained earnings	560
Total liabilities and stockholders' equity	$1,560

[a]Capital contribution − Purchases   + Sales   − Expenses − Taxes
     $1,000   − ($300 + $210) + $1,500 − $400   − $240
[b]150 lb. × $1.40

FIGURE 7–13
Periodic method:
LIFO assumption

JL Oriental Foods
Income Statement
For the Month Ended December 31, 2001

Sales (300 lb. × $5)	$1,500
Cost of goods sold	360[a]
Gross profit	$1,140
Expenses	400
Net income before taxes	$ 740
Income tax expense ($740 × 0.30)	222
Net income after taxes	$ 518

[a]Beginning inventory + Purchases   − Ending inventory
　　$0　　　　　 + ($300 + $210) − (150 lb. × $1.00)

JL Oriental Foods
Balance Sheet
December 31, 2001

Cash	$1,368[a]
Inventory (150 lb. × $1.00)	150
Total assets	$1,518
Common stock	$1,000
Retained earnings	518
Total liabilities and stockholders' equity	$1,518

[a]Capital contribution − Purchases   + Sales   − Expenses − Taxes
　　$1,000　　　　 − ($300 − $210) + $1,500 − $400　　 − $222

FIGURE 7–14
Comparison of
FIFO to LIFO

	FIFO/Periodic	LIFO/Periodic
Net income	$ 560	$ 518
Ending inventory	210	150
Cash balance	1,350	1,368

JL Oriental Foods under the periodic method with the FIFO and LIFO cost flow assumptions. In Figure 7–14, the net income, ending inventory, and cash balance produced under the two cost flow assumptions are compared.

Assume that on December 31 the market value of rice drops suddenly to $1.20 per pound. The total market value of Jane's 150 pounds of rice, therefore, is $180 (150 lb. × $1.20). If Jane used the FIFO assumption, she would record the following journal entry to apply the lower-of-cost-or-market rule:

Loss on Inventory Write-Down (Lo, −SE)　　30
**　Inventory (−A)　　　　　　　　　　　　　　　　　30**
Wrote down inventory to market value ($210 − $180).

If Jane used the LIFO assumption, she would record no journal entry, because the cost of the ending inventory ($150) is already below the market value ($180).

SUMMARY OF KEY POINTS

The key points of the chapter are summarized below.

○ *Inventory and how it affects the financial statements.*

Inventory includes asset items held for sale in the ordinary course of business. The ending inventory balance appears on the balance sheet and, for manufacturing and retail companies, is often the largest current asset. The methods used to account for inventory affect the allocation of the capitalized inventory cost between ending inventory and cost of goods sold. This allocation, in turn, affects net income and the ending inventory amount reported on the balance sheet. The effects of inventory accounting methods in the current and subsequent periods can be assessed by examining the following formula:

Cost of Goods Sold = Beginning Inventory + Purchases − Ending Inventory

The ending inventory valuation of the current period decreases cost of goods sold, and thereby increases gross profit and net income. Ending inventory of the current period becomes beginning inventory of the subsequent period. Beginning inventory increases cost of goods sold and decreases gross profit and net income.

○ *Four issues that must be addressed when accounting for inventory.*

Four issues that must be addressed when accounting for inventories are (1) what costs to include in the capitalized inventory cost (what items to include and what costs to attach to these items), (2) which method to use to carry the inventory (perpetual or periodic), (3) which cost flow assumption to use (specific identification, averaging, FIFO, or LIFO), and (4) how to apply the lower-of-cost-or-market rule.

○ *General rules for including items in inventory and attaching costs to these items.*

Items held for sale should be included in a company's inventory if the company has complete and unrestricted ownership of them. A consignment, though in the possession of the consignee, should be reported on the consignor's balance sheet. Shipping terms normally indicate how to account for goods in transit as of the balance sheet date.

Any cost required to bring an inventory item to saleable condition should be capitalized and treated as an inventory cost. This includes all costs that can reasonably be associated with the manufacture, acquisition, storage, or preparation of inventory items.

○ *Differences between the perpetual and periodic methods and trade-offs involved in choosing between them.*

The perpetual method keeps an up-to-date record of all inventory flows. Inventory purchases are recorded in the inventory account at cost, and Cost of Goods Sold is debited for the cost of items when they are sold.

The periodic method updates the inventory account at the end of each accounting period. Inventory purchases are recorded at cost, but the cost of goods sold is not recognized when the inventory is sold. Instead, at the end of each accounting period, an inventory count is taken and the inventory and cost of goods sold balances are updated.

The perpetual method requires more bookkeeping procedures than the periodic method and is therefore usually more costly to implement. Nevertheless, the perpetual method provides more up-to-date information. As computer systems have reduced the processing costs of maintaining inventory records, the perpetual method has become more popular.

○ *Three cost flow assumptions—average, FIFO, and LIFO.*

Under averaging, average costs are allocated to the goods sold and the goods that remain in ending inventory.

Under FIFO, the first items purchased are assumed to be the first items sold. This assumption matches old inventory costs with sales but places relatively up-to-date inventory costs on the balance sheet. In times of rising inventory costs, this assumption tends to inflate net income and increase a company's tax liability.

Under LIFO, the most recent items purchased are assumed to be the first items sold. This assumption matches current inventory costs with sales but tends to place old and outdated inventory costs on the balance sheet. LIFO can also be costly to implement and may encourage managers to purchase inventory items at inappropriate times. However, this assumption provides a reasonable measure of net income, and in times of rising inventory costs, it helps to minimize a company's tax liability. LIFO users also disclose the LIFO reserve, which allows the computation of FIFO inventory and net income as well as the accumulated tax savings associated with using LIFO.

○ *The lower-of-cost-or-market rule.*

Under the lower-of-cost-or-market rule, the cost of ending inventory is compared to its market value. If the cost is greater than the market value, the inventory is written down to market and a loss is recognized. If the cost is less than the market value, no write-down is necessary. The lower-of-cost-or-market rule is often criticized because it can be used to create hidden reserves, allowing managers to manipulate income, and it gives rise to reporting inconsistencies.

KEY TERMS

Note: Definitions for these terms are provided in the glossary at the end of the text.

Averaging assumption (p. 297)	LIFO reserves (p. 303)
Consignment (p. 288)	Manufacturing companies (p. 290)
First-in, first-out (FIFO) (p. 297)	Overhead (p. 290)
FOB (free on board) destination (p. 288)	Paper profits (p. 301)
FOB (free on board) shipping point (p. 288)	Periodic method (p. 291)
Freight-in (p. 289)	Perpetual method (p. 291)
Goods in transit (p. 288)	Retail companies (p. 290)
Last-in, first-out (LIFO) (p. 298)	Specific identification (p. 296)
LIFO conformity rule (p. 299)	Transportation-in (p. 289)

ETHICS IN THE REAL WORLD

It is well known that inventory fraud is an easy way for a company to produce instant profits and dress up the balance sheet. Indeed, many famous frauds have involved the creation of fictitious inventories.

An article in *The Wall Street Journal* reported that "auditors at even the top accounting firms are often fooled [by such shenanigans] . . . outside auditors can fail to catch inventory scams because they either trust management too much or fear they will lose clients by being tougher . . . spotting inventory fraud requires bigger staffs than some accounting firms . . . are willing to send out to do the inventory audits . . . If auditors were more skeptical of management claims, particularly in bad times, they would look at a far greater portion of the inventory in certain instances and do more surprise audits, which . . . nowadays are unusual."

On the other hand, auditors do face intense competition for clients, and audit fees have been reduced significantly in recent years. Accordingly, there is much pressure to control audit costs by reducing the number of audit hours in an effort to maintain profit levels, and inventory frauds are very difficult to uncover. Alan Winters, the AICPA's director of audit research, stated, "It is difficult if not impossible for the outside auditor to spot inventory fraud, [especially] if top management is directing it."

ETHICAL ISSUE Consider an auditor who has a large client in danger of being lost due to fee competition (i.e., a competitor has agreed to provide an audit for a lower fee). Is it ethical for this auditor to cut back on the number of hours devoted to auditing the inventory account so that the client can be charged a lower fee and a profit can still be made on this audit?

INTERNET RESEARCH EXERCISE

At the beginning of the chapter we noted that the management of Ann Taylor Stores had come under fire for intentionally inflating its inventory values. Briefly describe the operations of Ann Taylor Stores and comment on how the company has performed over the past several years. Begin your search with the Hoover's Company Finder, which can be found at *www.hoovers.com*.

BRIEF EXERCISES

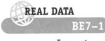

REAL DATA

BE7–1

Inventory

In its 2000 annual report, Hewlett-Packard reported beginning inventory of $4.9 billion, ending inventory of $5.7 billion on the balance sheet, and cost of goods sold of $29.7 billion on the income statement. Compute the inventory purchases made by Hewlett-Packard during 2000.

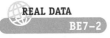

REAL DATA

BE7–2

Inventories

The information below was taken from the footnotes in the 1999 annual report of Johnson & Johnson.

	1999	1998
Raw materials and supplies	$ 663	$ 776
Goods in process	416	510
Finished goods	2,016	1,612
	$3,095	$2,898

a.   From information in the footnote alone, indicate whether Johnson & Johnson is a retailer, manufacture, or service firm. Explain.

b.   From information in the footnote alone, indicate whether Johnson & Johnson uses the LIFO or FIFO inventory cost flow assumption. Explain. (Hint: What disclosures are required under LIFO? under FIFO?)

REAL DATA

BE7–3

FIFO vs. LIFO

General Electric uses the LIFO inventory cost flow assumption, reporting inventories on its 2000 balance sheet of $7.8 billion and a LIFO reserve of approximately $.85 billion. What would GE's 2000 inventory balance be if it used the FIFO assumption instead? Why is the disclosure of the LIFO reserve useful to financial statement users?

EXERCISES

E7–1

Goods in transit as of the end of the accounting period

Dallas Manufacturing engaged in five transactions involving inventory at the end of 2002:

1. Ordered $50,000 of inventory on December 29, 2002. The goods were shipped on December 30, 2002, with the terms FOB shipping point. Dallas received the inventory on January 4, 2003.
2. Received an order to sell inventory with a cost of $40,000. The goods were shipped to the customer on December 31, 2002, and received on January 3, 2003. The terms of the sale were FOB shipping point.
3. Received an order to sell inventory with a cost of $15,000. The goods were shipped to the customer on December 29, 2002, and received on January 2, 2003. The terms of the sale were FOB destination.
4. Ordered $10,000 of inventory on December 27, 2002. The inventory was shipped on December 27, 2002, with the terms FOB destination. Dallas received the inventory on December 31, 2002.
5. Ordered $75,000 of inventory on December 30, 2002. The inventory was shipped on December 31, 2002, with the terms FOB destination. Dallas received the inventory on January 3, 2003.

Assume that Dallas included in inventory (12/31/02) all items from the five cases above. Explain how the resulting financial statements would be misstated.

E7–2

Accounting for inventory purchases

Nick's Fish Market purchased Maine lobster on account on October 10, 2002, for a gross price of $76,000. Nick also purchased Alaskan king crab on account on October 11, 2002, for a gross price of $36,000. The terms of both sales were 2/15, n/30. Nick paid for the first purchase on October 20, 2002, and for the second purchase on October 30, 2002. He uses the perpetual inventory method.
Prepare journal entries for each transaction.

E7–3

Accounting for inventory purchases

Baymont Corporation purchased inventory on account on March 3, 2002, for a gross price of $50,000. The company purchased additional inventory on account on March 10, 2002, for a gross price of $140,000. The terms of both sales were 3/12, n/30. Baymont Corporation paid for the first purchase on April 25, 2002, and for the second purchase on March 20, 2002. The company prepares monthly adjusting journal entries and uses the perpetual inventory method.
Prepare journal entries for each transaction.

REAL DATA

E7–4

Compute the missing values

The following information was extracted from the 2000 annual report of 3M.

	2000	1999	1998
Beginning inventory	?	?	2,327
Purchases	9,069	?	7,825
Goods available for sale	?	?	10,152
Ending inventory	?	2,030	?
Cost of goods sold	8,787	8,126	8,020

a. Compute the missing information.
b. Assuming that 3M uses the periodic inventory method to account for inventory, prepare the end-of-period adjusting entry to recognize the ending inventory and cost of goods sold for each year.

E7–5

Carrying
inventories:
Perpetual and
periodic methods

The following information comes from the records of Telly's Supply:

Beginning inventory	**$32,000**
Inventory purchases	**85,000**
Transportation-in	**4,300**

An inventory count taken at year-end indicates that inventory with a cost of $50,000 is on hand as of December 31, 2002.

a. Assume that Telly's uses the periodic inventory method. Compute cost of goods sold and prepare the year-end closing journal entry.

b. Assume that Telly's uses the perpetual method and that inventory purchases and transportation-in are both reflected in the inventory account, which shows an ending balance of $52,000. Compute cost of goods sold under the perpetual method along with any adjusting entries required at the end of the period.

c. Explain why the periodic method produces a value for cost of goods sold that is different from that produced by the perpetual method. What information does the perpetual method provide that is not provided by the periodic method?

REAL DATA

E7–6

The financial
statement effects of
inventory errors

Musicland Stores reported the following items in its 1999 financial report (dollars in millions).

	1999		1998	
Sales		**$1,891**		**$1,847**
Cost of goods sold:				
Beginning inventory	$ 447		$ 450	
Purchases	1,199		1,188	
Goods available for sale	$1,646		$1,638	
Less: Ending inventory	445		447	
Cost of goods sold		1,201		1,191
Gross profit		**$ 690**		**$ 656**

Assume that counting errors caused the ending inventory in 1998 to be understated by $50 and the ending inventory in 1999 to be overstated by $50.

a. Compute the impact of these errors on cost of goods sold for the year ended December 31, 1998, and on the inventory balance as of December 31, 1998.

b. Compute the impact of these errors on cost of goods sold for the year ended December 31, 1999, and on the inventory balance as of December 31, 1999.

c. What is the impact of these errors on cost of goods sold over the two-year period ended December 31, 1999?

E7–7

Income
manipulation under
specific
identification

Marian's Furs specializes in full-length mink coats. As of January 1, Marian had four top-of-the-line coats. Although the four coats are equivalent, they were purchased the previous year at different costs:

	Cost
Coat 1	**$8,400**
Coat 2	**7,100**
Coat 3	**7,600**
Coat 4	**6,800**

During January a customer decided to buy any one of the mink coats for $12,000. This was the only sale in January.

a. If Marian wished to maximize January's profits and ending inventory, which of the minks would she have sold to the customer? Compute the gross profit on the sale and January's ending inventory. Discuss why Marian might wish to maximize profits and ending inventory.

b. If Marian wished to minimize January's profits and ending inventory, which of the minks would she have sold to the customer? Compute the gross profit on the sale and January's ending inventory. Discuss why Marian might wish to minimize profits and ending inventory.

E7-8

Inventory assumptions and manipulating income under specific identification

Vinnie's House of Televisions has 75 identical 27-inch color monitors in stock on January 1, 2000. Vinnie maintains records of the serial number of each monitor to track its costs. Vinnie purchased the 75 monitors on December 5, 2002, for $450 each. He also purchased 50 on January 2, 2003, for $500 each and an additional 65 on January 15, 2003, for $600 each. Each monitor is priced to sell at $1,000. Vinnie sold 130 monitors during the month of January.

a. Compute gross profit and ending inventory for the month if the company uses the periodic method and adheres to each of the following:
   (1) FIFO cost flow assumption
   (2) Averaging cost flow assumption
   (3) LIFO cost flow assumption
b. Assume that Vinnie uses the specific identification method to compute the cost of goods sold. Explain how Vinnie could manipulate the gross profit number. What are the highest and the lowest gross profit amounts Vinnie could report? What are some possible factors that could motivate Vinnie to report either the highest or the lowest net income amount?

E7-9

Inventory cost flow assumptions

Watkins Corporation began operations on January 1, 2001. The 2001 and 2002 schedules of inventory purchases and sales are provided below.

2001:

Purchase 1	10 units @ $10 per unit	$100
Purchase 2	20 units @ $12 per unit	240
Total purchase costs		$340
Sales	15 units @ $30 per unit	$450

2002:

Purchase 1	10 units @ $13 per unit	$130
Purchase 2	15 units @ $15 per unit	225
Total purchase costs		$355
Sales	20 units @ $35 per unit	$700

Complete the following schedule, and briefly discuss the trade-offs associated with choosing an inventory cost flow assumption.

2001	FIFO	Weighted Average	LIFO
Cost of goods sold			
Gross profit (Sales − COGS)			
Ending inventory			

2002	FIFO	Weighted Average	LIFO
Cost of goods sold			
Gross profit (Sales − COGS)			
Ending inventory			

E7-10

Inventory flow assumptions over several periods and income taxes

Heller Bottling Company began business in 1999. Inventory units purchased and sold for the first year of operations and each of the following four years follow:

	Units Purchased	Cost per Unit	Units Sold
1999	10,000	$12	5,000
2000	12,000	16	16,000
2001	5,000	18	2,000
2002	10,000	21	10,000
2003	2,000	23	6,000

Inadequate cash flows forced Heller Bottling Company to cease operations at the end of 2003.

a.   Compute cost of goods sold for each of the five years if the company uses the following:
    (1) LIFO cost flow assumption
    (2) FIFO cost flow assumption
    (3) Averaging cost flow assumption
b.   Does the choice of a cost flow assumption affect total net income over the life of a business? Explain your answer.
c.   If the choice of a cost flow assumption does not affect net income over the life of a business, how does the choice of LIFO give rise to a tax benefit?

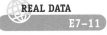
REAL DATA

E7–11

Using the LIFO
reserve

The following disclosure was included in the footnotes of Caterpillar's 1999 annual report. The company uses the LIFO cost flow assumption and reported net income of $966 for 1999. The company's effective tax rate is 35 percent (dollars in millions).

	1999	1998
Inventories at current cost	$4,594	$4,820
Less: Adjustment to LIFO basis	2,000	1,978
Inventories on LIFO basis	$2,594	$2,842

a.   Compute 1999 ending inventory for Caterpillar assuming it changed from LIFO to FIFO at the end of 1999.
b.   Compute the accumulated income tax savings enjoyed by Caterpillar due to the choice of LIFO as opposed to FIFO.
c.   Compute 1999 reported net income for Caterpillar assuming it changed from LIFO to FIFO in 1993.
d.   Explain how the information generated in (a), (b), and (c) could be useful.

E7–12

The lower-of-cost-
or-market rule and
hidden reserves

Central Incorporated has two items in inventory as of December 31, 2002. Each item was purchased for $40. Company management chose to write down Item #1 to $28, which at year-end was assessed to be its market value. Management did not write down Item #2 because its market value was estimated to be greater than $40. During 2003, each item was sold for $50 cash.

a.   Assume that the company uses the perpetual inventory method. Prepare journal entries for each activity (i.e., the write-down, the sale of Item #1, and the sale of Item #2).
b.   Compute the profit or loss associated with each item in 2002 and 2003.
c.   Explain how management could manipulate reported earnings when applying the lower-of-cost-or-market rule.

PROBLEMS

P7–1

Purchases and cash
discounts

On November 15 and 26, Brown and Swazey purchased merchandise on account for gross prices of $8,000 and $12,000, respectively. Terms of both purchases were 2/10, n/30. The company uses the perpetual inventory method, none of these items have been sold, and both accounts are paid in full on December 2.

REQUIRED:
Provide all the journal entries that would be recorded for these events.

P7–2

The gross method
and partial
payments

Stober Corporation made two purchases of inventory on account during the month of March. The first purchase was made on March 5 for $30,000, and the second purchase was made on March 10 for $60,000. The terms of each purchase were 2/10, n/30. The first purchase was settled on March 13, and the second was settled on July 18. The company uses the perpetual inventory method.

REQUIRED:

a. Prepare all the necessary journal entries associated with these transactions.

b. Assume that with respect to the second purchase, the company settled two-thirds of the accounts payable balance on March 19 and settled the remaining balance on August 7. The first purchase was settled on March 13. Prepare all the necessary journal entries associated with the second purchase.

REAL DATA

P7-3

The financial effects of inventory errors

The information below was taken from the records of Eli Lilly, a major pharmaceutical (dollars in millions).

	2000	1999	1998
Sales	$10,862	$10,003	$9,237
Cost of goods sold	2,056	2,098	2,015
Gross profit	$ 8,806	$ 7,905	$7,222
Expenses	5,748	5,184	5,124
Net income	$ 3,058	$ 2,721	$2,098

Assume that ending inventory was overstated by $500 in 1998, understated by $150 in 1999, and overstated by $320 in 2000. Assume that Lilly uses the periodic inventory method (1997 ending inventory was correctly stated).

REQUIRED:

Compute the corrected cost of goods sold and net income for 1998, 1999, and 2000.

P7-4

The financial statement and income tax effects of averaging, FIFO, and LIFO

The purchase schedule for Lumbermans and Associates is provided below.

Date	Items Purchased	Cost per Item
March 15	6,000	$1.30
July 30	9,000	1.50
December 17	7,000	1.60
Total	22,000	

The inventory balance as of the beginning of the year was $15,000 (15,000 units @ $1), and an inventory count at year-end indicated that 11,000 items were on hand. The company uses the periodic inventory method. Sales and expenses (excluding cost of goods sold) totaled $55,000 and $15,000, respectively. The federal income tax is 30 percent of taxable income.

REQUIRED:

a. Prepare three income statements, one under each of the assumptions: FIFO, averaging, and LIFO.

b. How many tax dollars would be saved by using LIFO instead of FIFO?

c. Assume that the market value of an inventory item dropped to $1.35 as of year-end. Apply the lower-of-cost-or-market rule, and provide the appropriate journal entry (if necessary) under the FIFO, averaging, and LIFO assumptions.

d. Repeat (a) above assuming that the costs per item were as follows:

Beginning inventory	$1.60
March 15	1.40
July 30	1.30
December 17	1.20

Which of the three assumptions gives rise to the highest net income and ending inventory amounts now? Why?

P7–5

The gross method,
the periodic
method, and the
LIFO and FIFO cost
flow assumptions

The Magic Teddy Bear Toy Company entered into the following transactions during January 2002:

January   3: Purchased 7,000 teddy bears at $20 each with the terms 2/10, n/30.
 3: Sold 2,000 teddy bears at $50 each for cash.
 9: Sold 4,000 teddy bears at $50 each on account.
 10: Settled the purchase made on January 3.
 15: Purchased 10,000 teddy bears. Three thousand of the bears were purchased for cash at $24.50 each, and the remaining bears were purchased on account for a gross price of $25.00 each (terms 2/10, n/30).
 19: Purchased 7,000 teddy bears at $26 each with the terms 2/10, n 30.
 23: Paid for one-half of the teddy bears purchased on account on January 15.
 27: Purchased 4,000 teddy bears at $28 each for cash.
 28: Settled the remaining open account from the purchase made on January 15.
 28: Settled the open account from the purchase made on January 19.
 29: Sold 6,000 teddy bears at $60 each for cash.
 30: Sold 5,000 teddy bears at $60 each on account.
 31: Purchased 2,000 teddy bears at $30 each for cash.
 31: Received a freight bill in the amount of $30,000, covering all purchases made during January 2002.

The Magic Teddy Bear Toy Company has 5,000 teddy bears on hand at $19 each as of January 1, 2002.

REQUIRED:

Assume that The Magic Teddy Bear Toy Company accounts for purchase cash discounts under the gross method and uses the periodic inventory method. Prepare all necessary entries, including adjusting journal entries, during January 2002, if the company uses the following:

a.   LIFO cost flow assumption
b.   FIFO cost flow assumption

(*Hint:* Compute the total cost per unit in order to calculate ending inventory and cost of goods sold.)

REAL DATA

P7–6

Using LIFO and
saving tax dollars

Financial statements as of January 2, 2000, for Johnson & Johnson are provided below. The company used the FIFO inventory cost flow assumption to prepare these statements (dollars in millions).

Income Statement

Sales		**$27,471**
Cost of goods sold:		
Beginning inventory	$ 2,898	
Purchases	8,639	
Goods available for sale	$11,537	
Less: Ending inventory	3,095	
Cost of goods sold		8,442
Gross profit		**$19,029**
Expenses		13,276
Net income before taxes		**$ 5,753**
Federal income tax (28%)		1,586
Net income		**$ 4,167**

Balance Sheet

Cash	$ 2,363	**Current liabilities**	$ 7,454
Inventory	3,095	**Long-term liabilities**	5,496
Other assets	23,705	**Stockholders' equity**	16,213
		Total liabilities and	
Total assets	$29,163	**stockholders' equity**	$29,163

Assume that on December 31, 1999, Johnson & Johnson decided to change from the FIFO to the LIFO inventory cost flow assumption. Assume that the ending inventory value under the LIFO assumption is $2,500.

REQUIRED:

a. Compute the change in Johnson & Johnson's current ratio associated with the change from FIFO to LIFO. Round to two decimal places.
b. Compute the change in Johnson & Johnson's gross profit and net income associated with the change from FIFO to LIFO. Assume that the dollar amount of the change is reflected in cost of goods sold.
c. How many tax dollars would be saved by the change from FIFO to LIFO?
d. Discuss some of the disadvantages associated with the change to LIFO.

P7–7

LIFO liquidations, income tax implications, and year-end purchases

Ruhe Auto Supplies began operations in 1989. The company's inventory purchases and sales in the first and subsequent years of operations are as follows:

Year	Units Purchased	Cost per Unit	Units Sold
1989	20,000	$ 5	4,000
1990	8,000	10	8,000
1991	7,000	15	9,000
1992	8,500	20	7,000
1993	6,000	25	7,500
1994	7,500	30	7,000
1995	9,000	50	8,000
1996	8,000	65	9,000
1997	9,500	70	9,000
1998	7,000	75	8,000
1999	8,500	80	8,500
2000	9,000	85	7,500
2001	8,500	90	9,500
2002	9,500	95	20,000

The company's federal income tax rate is 30 percent. For the year ended December 31, 2002, Ruhe Auto Supplies generated $3,000,000 in revenues and incurred $800,000 in expenses (exclusive of cost of goods sold). Ruhe Auto Supplies uses the periodic method and the LIFO cost flow assumption to account for inventory.

REQUIRED:

a. Compute ending inventory as of December 31, 2001. Identify the number of units in ending inventory and the costs attached to each unit.
b. Compute the company's 2002 income tax liability and net income after taxes for the year ended December 31, 2002.
c. Assume that Ruhe Auto Supplies was able to purchase an additional 10,500 units of inventory on December 31, 2002, for $95 per unit. Would you advise the company to purchase these additional units? Explain your answer.

P7–8

Using the LIFO
reserve

You are a financial analyst currently reviewing the financial statements of Danner International and Brady Enterprises, two companies of similar size within the same industry. Net incomes of $39,300 and $42,700 were reported for 2002 by Danner and Brady, respectively. After a thorough comparison of the accounting methods used by the two companies, you find that they are similar except for the inventory cost flow assumption—Danner uses FIFO and Brady uses LIFO. You conduct a further review of Brady's footnotes and discover the following. Inventories declined during 2001, causing a LIFO liquidation, which accounted for $8,000 of the before-tax net income reported in 2002.

	2002	2001
Inventories at current cost	$36,200	$42,400
Less: Adjustment to LIFO	3,500	4,800
Inventories at LIFO	$32,700	$37,600

Brady's effective tax rate is 35 percent.

REQUIRED:

a. Restate Brady's net income assuming there was no LIFO liquidation in 2002. How does the restated amount compare to Danner's net income?

b. Restate Brady's 2002 reported net income as if the company had always been a FIFO user. Is Brady's restated reported income higher or lower than Danner's reported net income? Explain.

c. As of the end of 2002, how much accumulated income tax had Brady saved due to its choice of LIFO instead of FIFO? How much as of the end of 2001? Does LIFO save taxes in every year? Explain.

d. Would it be advisable for Brady to change its cost flow assumption from LIFO to FIFO? Discuss.

P7–9

Avoiding LIFO
liquidations

IBT has used the LIFO inventory cost flow assumption for five years. As of December 31, 2001, IBT had 700 items in its inventory, and the $9,000 inventory dollar amount reported on the balance sheet consisted of the following costs:

When Purchased	Number of Items	Cost per Item	Total
1998	500	$12	$6,000
2000	200	15	3,000
Total	700		$9,000

During 2002, IBT sold 900 items for $75 each and purchased 350 items at $30 each. Expenses other than cost of goods sold totaled $20,000, and the federal income tax rate is 30 percent of taxable income.

REQUIRED:

a. Prepare IBT's income statement for the year ending December 31, 2002.

b. Assume that IBT purchased an additional 550 items on December 20, 2002, for $30 each. Prepare IBT's income statement for the year ending December 31, 2002.

c. Compare the two income statements, and discuss why it might have been wise for IBT to purchase the additional items on December 20. Discuss some of the disadvantages of such a strategy.

ISSUES FOR DISCUSSION

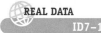

REAL DATA
ID7-1
Choosing FIFO
or LIFO

A partner from a major accounting firm made the following comment when asked about the accounting methods used by companies in the software industry: "Accounting policies that have adverse short-term effects on financial statements cannot help the industry raise capital."

After reading such a comment, one might conclude that managers who wish to raise capital by borrowing from banks or issuing equity or debt securities should choose the FIFO cost flow assumption instead of LIFO. Yet, others have written that they are "puzzled" about why thousands of U.S. companies use FIFO instead of LIFO.

REQUIRED:
Discuss the above comments.

REAL DATA
ID7-2
LIFO reporting

The information below was taken from the inventory footnote contained in the 1999 annual report of Solutia, a major plastics manufacturer.

	1999	1998
Finished goods	$ 260	$ 252
Goods in process	121	87
Raw materials	109	116
Inventories at FIFO	490	455
Excess of FIFO over LIFO	(119)	(124)
Inventories at LIFO	$ 371	$ 331

The cost of 67 percent of the inventories is determined by the last-in, first-out (LIFO) basis, which generally reflects the effects of inflation or deflation cost of goods sold sooner than other inventory methods. The cost of the remaining inventories is generally determined by the first-in, first-out (FIFO) basis. Inventories at FIFO approximate current cost. The effects of LIFO inventory liquidations were not significant in 1999, 1998, and 1997.

REQUIRED:
a. Why would a potential investor or creditor who is considering investing in Solutia be interested in the difference between LIFO and FIFO inventory values?
b. Explain why reducing certain inventory quantities, valued under LIFO, would increase net income and why an investor would be interested in such a disclosure.
c. Solutia's effective tax rate is 34 percent; approximately how much more income tax would Solutia have paid if at the end of 1999 it switched to FIFO for all of its inventory?

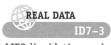

REAL DATA
ID7-3
LIFO liquidation and
hidden reserves

In the early 1980s, an oil glut caused Texaco, a LIFO user, to delay drilling, which cut its oil inventory levels by 16 percent. The LIFO cushion (i.e., the difference between LIFO and FIFO inventory values) that was built into those barrels over the year amounted to $454 million and transformed what would have been a drop in net income to a modest gain.

REQUIRED:
Explain how using LIFO could be interpreted as building "hidden reserves."

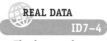

REAL DATA
ID7-4
The lower-of-cost-
or-market rule and
the recognition of
loss/income

TII Industries makes over-voltage protectors, power systems, and electronic products primarily for use in the communications industry. Several years ago, the company reported that it took "a substantial inventory write-down," resulting in a loss for its third quarter ending June 24. The write-down was estimated to be $12 million and stems from customers' changes in product specifications.

REQUIRED:

a. Provide the journal entry to record the write-down.
b. Assume that the original cost of the inventory was $52 million and that it was written down to its market value of $40 million. If TII Industries sells it for $48 million cash in the following period, what journal entries would be recorded? Assume that TII uses the perpetual inventory method.
c. Applying the lower-of-cost-or-market rule in this case would cause TII to recognize a loss in the period of the write-down and income in the subsequent period. Does such recognition seem appropriate? Why or why not?

Inventory write-down

The Wall Street Journal (April 17, 1998) reported that "Valero Energy Corp. said it will take a first-quarter charge of $37.7 million, or 43 cents per share, related to lower prices for crude oil and refined products. The energy-refining and marketing company characterized the write-down as an accounting 'to reduce the carrying value of our crude oil and refined products inventories to their market value.'"

REQUIRED:

a. What exception to the principles of financial accounting is being followed by Valero when it writes down its inventories?
b. How would the write-down affect the financial statements?
c. How would the write-down affect the company's current ratio and its inventory turnover ratio (increase, decrease, or no effect)?
d. Explain how such a write-down could be used to manipulate earnings and what two reporting strategies Valero could be following.

Interpreting the inventory footnote

The 1999 annual report of Sherwin Williams, a manufacturer of paint products, contained the following footnote.

Note 3-Inventories
Inventories are stated at the lower of cost or market. Cost is determined principally on the last-in, first-out (LIFO) method, which provides a better matching of current costs and revenues in periods of inflation. The following presents the effect on inventories and net income had the Corporation used the first-in, first-out (FIFO) cost method of inventory valuation adjusted for income taxes at the statuary rate. The information is presented to enable the reader to make comparisons with companies using the FIFO method of inventory valuation.

	1999	1998	1997
Percent of total inventory on LIFO	90%	91%	93%
Excess of FIFO over LIFO	$97,953	$96,235	$104,637
Increase (decrease) in net income due to LIFO	(894)	4,685	(3,604)

REQUIRED:

a. What does it mean that LIFO "provides a better matching of current costs and revenues in periods of inflation?"
b. Sherwin Williams reported inventories on the balance sheet at $703,388 (1999), $682,523 (1998), and $721,688 (1997). Compute the company's ending inventory had it shifted to FIFO at the end of 1999.
c. In 1998 the company's inventories decreased from $721,688 to $682,523. How did this liquidation affect reported net income?
d. Estimate the taxes saved by Sherwin Williams because it uses LIFO instead of FIFO. Assume a tax rate of 38 percent.

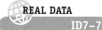

REAL DATA

ID7–7

Inventory
management

In an article devoted to small business management, the *Houston Chronicle* (June 6, 2000) noted: "To maximize profits, your inventory must be well managed. Uncontrolled inventories can become inefficient, ineffective, outdated, damaged, even stolen . . . in other words, costly. Old goods often have to be discarded and that translates into a drag on cash flow. A classic problem is unbalanced inventories—those with too many products in one category. To get rid of hard-to-sell items, you may have to resort to deep discounting, eliminating profit on those items. Your challenge is to maintain enough inventory to meet demand while preventing products from aging and moving too slowly."

REQUIRED:

a. What accounting entry would be required as old goods are discarded? How would you compute the dollar amount of this entry?

b. How could the perpetual inventory method be used to control some of the problems described above?

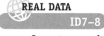

REAL DATA

ID7–8

Inventory and
the statement of
cash flows

The 1999 statement of cash flows for J.C. Penney reports net cash from operating activities of $1,258 (1999), $1,058 (1998), and $1,218 (1997). Included on the statement of cash flows (indirect method) in the computation of net cash from operating activities are adjustments for inventory of $169 (1999), $64 (1998), and −$395 (1997).

REQUIRED:

Explain the nature of these adjustments and what they tell us about J.C. Penney's inventory balances in 1999, 1998, and 1997. Discuss the cash flow implications of these inventory adjustments.

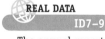

REAL DATA

ID7–9

The annual report
of Wal-Mart

The 2001 annual report of Wal-Mart is reproduced in Appendix A. Review the 2001 annual report, and answer the following questions.

REQUIRED:

a. How large is inventory compared to the other assets on Wal-Mart's balance sheet? Did inventory increase, decrease, or remain the same as a percent of total assets in 2001?

b. Did Wal-Mart appear to pay off its suppliers faster or slower during 2001 compared to 2000?

c. Does Wal-Mart use the LIFO or FIFO inventory cost flow assumption? Compute inventory values for both LIFO and FIFO as of the end of 2000 and 2001.

d. Compute 2001 net income, assuming that Wal-Mart changed its inventory cost flow assumption as of the end of 2001. Footnote 5 contains the company's effective tax rate.

e. Would you advise Wal-Mart to change its inventory cost flow assumption? Why or why not?

Investments in Equity Securities

CHAPTER 8

KEY POINTS

The following key points are emphasized in this chapter:

○ *Criteria that must be met before a security can be listed in the current assets section of the balance sheet.*

○ *Trading and available-for-sale securities and how the mark-to-market rule is used to account for them.*

○ *Why companies make long-term investments in equity securities.*

○ *The mark-to-market method, the cost method, and the equity method of accounting for long-term equity investments, and the conditions under which each method is used.*

○ *Consolidated financial statements, when they are prepared, and how they differ from financial statements that account for equity investments using the equity method.*

In early 2000, Cisco Systems boasted the greatest market value in the history of Wall Street—nearly half a trillion dollars, almost all of that wealth created since 1995. While Cisco is a great engineering company, well-managed and technically astute, almost all of its growth came from acquiring other companies. How it chose those companies has defined its corporate strategy; how it integrated them into its empire had defined its corporate politics; and how it retained the people acquired with the companies has defined its corporate culture. These acquisitions and others like it, where ownership is transferred, involve the purchase and sale of equity securities, the subject of this chapter.

An **equity investment** occurs when one company purchases another company's outstanding common stock. Recall from Chapter 1 that equity holders have the right to receive dividends, if declared, and to vote for the board of directors at the annual meeting of the stockholders. Companies make investments in equity securities for two basic reasons: (1) to earn investment income in the form of dividends and stock price appreciation and (2) to exert influence or control over the board of directors and management of the investee company. Relatively small equity investments are normally made to earn income over a short period of time, while larger, long-term equity investments often signal an attempt by the investing company to influence the operations of the target company.

To illustrate, as of December 31, 1999, Owens Corning, manufacturer of building materials and home care solutions, disclosed over $900 million in marketable securities from a wide variety of companies. At the same time, the company held investments in companies in which between 20 and 50 percent of the equity securities had been purchased. These holdings were carried on the balance sheet at about $65 million. During 1999 Owens Corning acquired other companies for a total price of $886 million, and sold a major interest in Alpha/Owens Company for $103 million.

The next section covers equity investments classified as current because they are readily marketable and intended to be sold within the time period of current assets. The chapter then discusses long-term equity investments and divides the coverage into three categories, based on the proportion of the common stock holdings: (1) equity holdings of less than 20 percent, (2) equity holdings from 20–50 percent, and (3) equity holdings of greater than 50 percent. As we note later, these three situations are accounted for differently. Appendix 8A is devoted to consolidated financial statements, which are prepared when a company holds more than 50 percent of the outstanding common stock in another company.

EQUITY SECURITIES CLASSIFIED AS CURRENT

Idle cash held by a company earns no return and during inflation actually declines in purchasing power. Nevertheless, proper cash management must ensure that enough cash is available to meet a company's day-to-day cash needs. Such cash needs tend to fluctuate, sometimes unexpectedly, making it difficult for management to consistently strike an appropriate balance between available cash and return-producing investments. In an effort to both earn a return and be able to produce cash on short notice, companies often purchase readily marketable securities. Companies also use these investments to offset the risks of changing interest rates associated with certain liabilities. The annual report of Intel, for example, notes, "The company maintains its short-term investment portfolio to offset change in certain liabilities." Such investments, which include stocks and bonds traded on public security exchanges, provide income through dividends, interest, or price appreciation and can be readily converted to cash when needed to meet current cash requirements.[1]

The relative size of short-term investments on the balance sheet varies significantly across companies in different industries. Retailers such as hardware, department, clothing, and sporting goods stores typically maintain dollar amounts of less than 3 percent of total assets. Financial institutions, insurance companies, and some services, on the other hand, which have greater needs for ready cash, often carry short-term investment portfolios that represent a larger percent of total assets. The 1999 annual reports of Gap, Inc. and Kmart show no holdings of short-term investments. Chase Manhattan carries short-term investments of about 30 percent of total assets. Biomet holds short-term equity investments of almost 6 percent of total assets.

Short-term investments are listed in the current assets section of the balance sheet. It is important to realize that they are distinct from long-term investments in equity and debt securities, which are included in the long-term investments section. Two criteria must be met for an investment in a security to be considered current and thus warrant inclusion as a current asset:

1. The investment must be *readily marketable.*
2. Management must *intend to convert* the investment into cash within the time period of current assets (one year or the operating cycle, whichever is longer).

If either criterion is not met, the investment must be included in the long-term investments section.

The 1999 annual report of Intel, a building block supplier to the world Internet economy, discloses short-term investments of $7.7 billion, representing about 18 percent of total assets. Describe the characteristics of these investments.

The Existence of a Ready Market

Readily marketable means that the security can be sold and converted into cash on demand. Stocks and bonds traded actively on the public stock exchanges (e.g., New York Stock Exchange, American Stock Exchange) usually meet this criterion. Objective market prices exist for such securities, which ensure that they can be sold on very short notice. In most cases, all a company must do is request that its stockbroker sell the security.

Some securities, on the other hand, are not publicly traded, often because there are restrictions on their sale. Common stocks of privately held corporations, for example, may have very limited markets because restrictions exist on who can own them (e.g., ownership is sometimes limited to family members). Objective market prices do not exist for such securities, and they cannot be readily converted into cash. Accordingly, they fail to meet the readily marketable criterion and should be listed in the long-term investments section of the balance sheet.

---

1. Short-term investments can also consist of certificates of deposit, money market accounts, and commercial paper. Certificates of deposit are usually purchased from banks in denominations of at least $5,000. They provide a fixed rate of return over a specified period of time. Money market accounts are similar to savings or checking accounts but provide a slightly higher rate of interest, and there are usually restrictions on the withdrawal of funds. Commercial paper is a short-term note issued by corporations with good credit ratings. They are usually issued in denominations of $5,000 and $10,000 and provide returns that exceed those of money market accounts.

The 1999 annual report of Intel discloses: "Non-marketable equity investments are included in other assets." Where do you think the other assets category is listed on Intel's balance sheet—current or noncurrent? Why would Intel list its nonmarketable investments in that section?

The Intention to Convert: Another Area of Subjectivity

The second criterion, **intention to convert** the investment to cash, is much more difficult to determine objectively. Consequently, it can be a very difficult area for the auditor, who must determine whether a company's financial statements conform with generally accepted accounting principles. Simply asking managers whether they intend to sell securities within the time period of current assets does not provide sufficiently objective evidence. Recall that managers have incentives to window dress, which in this case might consist of including what would appropriately be a long-term investment in the current assets section. Such a decision might be made to increase a company's quick ratio, current ratio, or working capital number—an issue that users should consider when they analyze financial statements.

Several years ago PepsiCo acquired two Canadian soft-drink bottling operations for $246 million. The company listed these investments as current assets on its balance sheet because "it was management's intention to resell these operations." The following year PepsiCo sold only one of the investments, and continued to include the remaining investment in the current assets section. In your opinion did PepsiCo violate an accounting standard? Discuss.

TRADING AND AVAILABLE-FOR-SALE SECURITIES

Investments in readily marketable equity securities are classified into one of two categories: (1) trading securities or (2) available-for-sale securities. **Trading securities** are bought and held principally for the purpose of selling them in the near future with the objective of generating profit on short-term price changes. Investments not classified as trading securities are considered **available-for-sale securities.** Trading securities are always listed in the current section of the balance sheet, while available-for-sale securities are listed as current or long-term, depending on management's intention.[2]

Both trading and available-for-sale securities are accounted for using the **mark-to-market rule,** which states that readily marketable securities be carried on the balance sheet at current market value.[3] The following example considers four separate events: (1) the purchase of the securities, (2) the declaration and receipt of related cash divi-

2. This chapter considers investments in equity securities, and this particular section is based on Statement of Financial Accounting Standards No. 115, "Accounting for Certain Investments in Debt and Equity Securities." Investments in debt securities are classified into one of three categories: (1) trading, (2) available-for-sale, or (3) held-to-maturity. The methods used to account for trading and available-for-sale debt securities are the same as those used for trading and available-for-sale equity securities, which are covered later in the chapter.

3. Until recently, the lower-of-cost or market rule was used in the United States to account for short-term investments, and it is still the predominant method used in other industrial countries.

dends, (3) the sale of the securities (at either a gain or a loss), and (4) changes in the prices of the securities on hand at the end of the accounting period. The first three events use the same methods to account for trading and available-for-sale securities. The fourth event, however, applies the mark-to-market rule differently.

Purchasing Trading and Available-for-Sale Securities

When trading and available-for-sale securities are purchased, they are capitalized and recorded on the balance sheet at cost. As with other capitalized assets (inventory, long-term investments, fixed assets, and intangible assets), cost includes the purchase price as well as any *incidental acquisition costs,* such as brokerage commissions and taxes.[4] For example, assume that Goodyear Tire & Rubber Company purchased three different kinds of securities (Dow Chemical, Abbott Laboratories, and Eli Lilly) on December 1, 2002. Each security is readily marketable, and the company intends to sell the Dow and Abbott investments in the near future. Thus, the investments in Dow and Abbott are classified as trading securities, and the investment in Lilly is classified as available-for-sale. The following prices were paid:[5]

10 shares of Dow Chemical at $10/share	**$100**
20 shares of Abbott Laboratories at $12/share	**240**
15 shares of Eli Lilly at $20/share	**300**
Total cost	**$640**

Assuming that all prices *include* brokerage commissions, the following journal entry reflects the purchase of the three sets of securities:

Trading Securities (+A)	**340***	
Available-for-Sale Securities (+A)	**300**	
Cash (−A)		**640**

Purchased trading and available-for-sale securities.

*$100 (Dow) + $240 (Abbott)

Declaration and Receipt of Cash Dividends

Cash dividends declared on trading and available-for-sale securities, to which Goodyear has a legal right, are initially recognized as a receivable and a revenue. When the cash dividend is received, the receivable is exchanged for cash. Continuing the example, suppose that on December 15, 2002, the board of directors of Abbott declared dividends of $1 per share, to be paid to the holders of its common stock on January 15, 2003. The following journal entries would be recorded in the books of Goodyear:

December 15—at declaration of dividend:

Dividend Receivable (+A)	**20***	
Dividend Income (R, +SE)		**20**

Recognized declaration of dividend.

*($1/share × 20 shares)

---

4. Actual brokerage commissions range from 1 to 5 percent.

5. For computational ease, the dollar amounts used in this example are unrealistically small. Multiplying the totals by 100 would produce numbers of a more realistic magnitude.

January 15—at receipt of dividend:

Cash (+A)	20	
Dividend Receivable (−A)		20

Received cash dividend.

Sale of Securities

When trading and available-for-sale securities are sold, the balance sheet value is removed from the books, and the difference between the balance sheet value and the proceeds from the sale is recognized as a realized gain or loss. If the proceeds exceed the balance sheet value, a **realized gain** is recognized; if they are less than the balance sheet value, a **realized loss** is recognized.

Continuing the example, assume that on December 4, Goodyear sold all ten shares of Dow Chemical stock for $13/share and ten of the fifteen shares of Eli Lilly stock for $10/share. Assuming that brokerage commissions have already been deducted from the sales price, these sales would give rise to the following journal entries:

Cash (+A)	130	
Trading Securities (Dow) (−A)		100*
Realized Gain on Sale of Trading Securities (Ga, +SE)		30

Sold Dow Chemical stock.
*($10/share × 10 shares)

Cash (+A)	100	
Realized Loss on Sale of Available-for-Sale Sec. (Lo, −SE)	100	
Available-for-Sale Securities (Lilly) (−A)		200*

Sold Lilly stock.
*($20/share × 10 shares)

The realized gain and loss accounts represent the difference between the sale proceeds and the balance sheet value of the sold securities and, therefore, provide a measure of management's performance with respect to the buying and selling of these securities. These accounts appear on the income statement and thus figure in the determination of net income. Chapter 13 points out that these book gains and losses, and others like them, appear in a special section of the income statement, titled "Other Revenues and Expenses."

Biomet, which designs, manufactures, and markets orthopedic products, reported dividend income and realized gains from short-term investments in the amounts of $4.3 million and $1.2 million, respectively, for 1999. Describe the transactions that gave rise to these two sources of income.

Price Changes of Securities on Hand at the End of the Accounting Period

At the end of each accounting period the current market values of all trading and available-for-sale securities held by the company are determined. Adjusting journal entries restate the balance sheet values of the securities to reflect their current market values. These adjustments give rise to **unrealized gains and losses,** often called **holding gains or losses.** In the case of trading securities, these gains or losses are considered temporary accounts, appear on the income statement, and are reflected in retained earnings. *In the case of available-for-sale securities, the **unrealized price changes** are considered permanent accounts and are carried in the stockholders' equity section of the balance sheet.*

END-OF-PERIOD ADJUSTMENTS: TRADING SECURITIES

Continuing the example, assume that Goodyear held all 20 shares of Abbott on December 31, 2002, the end of the accounting period. The shares were purchased for $12 each and are currently trading for $15 each. To mark the investment to market value, an adjusting journal entry of the following form would be recorded on December 31:

Trading Securities (Abbott) (+A)   **60***
   Unrealized Gain on Trading Securities (Ga, +SE)   **60**
Revalued Abbott securities to market.
*[($15 − $12) × 20 shares]

If instead of $15/share, the Abbott shares were trading for $10 each on December 31, the following adjusting journal entry would have been recorded:

Unrealized Loss on Trading Securities (Lo, −SE)   **40***
   Trading Securities (Abbott) (−A)   **40**
Revalued Abbott securities to market.
*[($12 − $10) × 20 shares]

The unrealized holding gain (loss) represents the extent to which Goodyear's wealth increased (decreased) due to holding Abbott securities from December 1 to December 31. Because the investment in these securities is classified as trading and therefore is expected to be sold in the near future, the unrealized holding gain (loss) is considered part of Goodyear's income for the accounting period. Note also that the balance sheet value of the investment in Abbott on December 31, 2002, reflects the current market price of the securities, which is carried into the next period and used in the determination of future realized and unrealized gains and losses.

END-OF-PERIOD ADJUSTMENTS: AVAILABLE-FOR-SALE SECURITIES

Assume that Goodyear held five shares of Eli Lilly stock on December 31, 2002, with a current market value of $22 each. (Recall that fifteen shares were originally purchased on December 1 at $20 each, and ten shares were sold on December 4 for $10 each.) To mark the investment to market value, the following adjusting journal entry would be recorded on December 31:

Available-for-Sale Securities (Lilly) (+A)   **10***
   Unrealized Price Increase on Available-for-Sale Sec. (+SE)   **10**
Revalued Lilly securities to market.
*[($22 − $20) × 5 shares]

If instead of $22/share, the Lilly shares were trading for $14 each on December 31, the following adjusting journal entry would have been recorded:

Unrealized Price Decrease on Available-for-Sale Sec. (−SE)   **30***
   Available-for-Sale Securities (Lilly) (−A)   **30**
Revalued Lilly securities to market.
*[($20 − $14) × 5 shares]

Again, the unrealized price increase (decrease) represents the extent to which Goodyear's wealth increased (decreased) due to holding Lilly securities from December 1 to December 31. However, because the investment in these securities is classified as available-for-sale and therefore is not expected to be sold in the near future, the unrealized price change is not considered part of Goodyear's income for the accounting period. Instead, it is *disclosed in the stockholders' equity section of the balance sheet.* Unrealized price increases (credits) increase stockholders' equity, while unrealized price decreases (debits) decrease stockholders' equity. Both the market value of the investment and the dollar amount of the unrealized price change in the stockholders' equity account are carried into the next accounting period and adjusted if the securities are sold or the market value of the securities changes. We illustrate below how the balance sheet values of the investment and unrealized price change accounts are adjusted under two separate conditions: (1) if the securities are sold in the next period and (2) if the market value of the securities changes in the next period.

(1) If the Available-for-Sale Securities Are Sold.
Assume as in the most recent example above that Eli Lilly shares were trading at $14 each as of December 31, 2002, and a $30 unrealized price decrease (debit) was disclosed in the stockholders' equity section of the December 31 balance sheet. If Goodyear sold all five Lilly shares for $16 each on April 5, 2003, the following journal entry would be recorded:

Cash (+A)	**80***	
Realized Loss on Available-for-Sale Sec. (Lo, −SE)	**20**	
Available-for-Sale Securities (Lilly) (−A)		**70****
Unrealized Price Decrease on Available-for-Sale Sec. (+SE)		**30**
Sold Lilly securities.		

*($16/share × 5 shares)
**($14/share × 5 shares)

Note first that Cash is debited for the proceeds of the sale ($16/share × 5 shares). The $30 unrealized price decrease and the balance sheet value of the available-for-sale securities account, which reflects the market value of the securities as of December 31 ($14/share × 5 shares), are both written off the books because Goodyear no longer holds the securities. The realized loss of $20 is the "plug" that brings the entry into balance, but more importantly, it represents the difference between the original cost ($100 = $20/share × 5 shares) of the securities and the proceeds from the sale ($80).

(2) If the Market Value of the Available-for-Sale Securities Changes.
Assume once again that Eli Lilly shares were trading at $14 each as of December 31, 2002, and a $30 unrealized price decrease was disclosed in the stockholders' equity section of the December 31 balance sheet. If on December 31, 2003, the securities are still held by Goodyear and the price has changed to $16, the following journal entry would be recorded:

Available-for-Sale Securities (Lilly) (+A)	**10***	
Unrealized Price Decrease on Available-for-Sale Sec. (+SE)		**10**
Revalued Lilly securities to market.		

*[($16 − $14) × 5 shares]

In this case, the available-for-sale account is adjusted to reflect its current market value and the unrealized price decrease account is reduced because the market price has increased since the previous balance sheet date. The December 31, 2003 balance in the unrealized price decrease account in the stockholders' equity section of Goodyear's balance sheet would be $20 ($30 − $10).

In its 1999 annual report, Biomet reported net unrealized gains on available-for-sale equity securities of $2.5 million. Where on the financial statements would this amount be reflected? Had the equity investments been considered trading securities, where on the financial statements would the amount be reflected?

Reclassifications and Permanent Market Value Declines

Companies sometimes choose to change the classifications of security investments from trading to available-for-sale, or vice versa. In such cases, unrealized holding gains or losses should be recognized immediately as income. When transferring securities from the trading to the available-for-sale classification, unrealized holding gains and losses that accrued since the most recent financial statement date should be recognized as income on the date of the transfer. When transferring securities from the available-for-sale to the trading classification, unrealized holding gains and losses from two sources should be recognized as income on the date of the transfer: (1) those that accrued since the most recent financial statement date and (2) the unrealized price change disclosed in the stockholders' equity section of the most recent balance sheet.

Investments sometimes suffer a permanent market value decline; the price declines and is not expected to recover. In such cases, the security should be written down to its market value and a *realized loss* that reduces net income should be recognized immediately whether the security is classified as trading or available-for-sale. Determining a permanent decline is very subjective, and GAAP provide very few guidelines. Perhaps the best way to assess such a decline is to consider the financial condition of the firm that issued the security. We return to this issue in Chapter 9, where we discuss permanent write-downs of fixed assets and how management can use its discretion in this area to manage reported financial numbers.

Mark-to-Market Accounting and Comprehensive Income

For years, accounting theorists have argued for a pure form of mark-to-market accounting, where assets are reported on the balance sheet at market value and changes in asset prices are included on the income statement. The methods used to account for trading securities are completely consistent with this approach, while the methods used to account for available-for-sale securities report market values on the balance sheet but do not reflect changes in market prices on the income statement.

In a move toward pure mark-to-market accounting, the FASB now requires companies to provide a statement of comprehensive income. No specific format is required for this statement, but it must be displayed with the same prominence as the other financial statements. Also, it must disclose total **comprehensive income,** which includes all nonowner related changes in stockholders' equity that do not appear on the income statement and are not reflected in the balance of retained earnings. Several items fall into this category, including adjustments to stockholders' equity for the holding gains and losses associated with available-for-sale securities. Thus, while unrealized price increases and decreases of available-for-sale securities are not reflected on the income statement, they are reported on the statement of comprehensive income. When combined with net income, which is reported on the income statement, comprehensive income provides investors, analysts, and others with an estimate of the overall change in a company's wealth during the period.

Major firms use a number of different methods to disclose comprehensive income on their annual reports. AT&T includes a statement of comprehensive income immediately after the statement of shareholders' equity; PepsiCo includes a line item called comprehensive income within the statement of shareholders' equity; Wendy's discloses a special financial statement devoted only to comprehensive income along with the other financial statements; and Johnson & Johnson includes a statement of comprehensive income in the footnotes to the financial statements. As an analyst, would you consider comprehensive income an important number, and how would you feel about the wide variety of disclosure options used by major companies?

LONG-TERM EQUITY INVESTMENTS

As indicated earlier in this chapter, companies make investments in the equity securities of other companies primarily for two reasons: (1) investment income in the form of dividends and stock price appreciation and (2) management influence, where the voting power of the purchased shares allows the investor company to exert some control over the board of directors and management of the investee company. The primary motivation behind the long-term equity investments for most major U.S. companies is reason (2), influence over the investee company's operations and management.

Most large, well-known U.S. companies are constantly involved in acquisitions, whereby they purchase all, or a majority of, the outstanding common stock of another company and then change the investee company's operations and/or management. Several years ago, for example, General Electric (GE) purchased for $6.4 billion all outstanding common stock of RCA Corporation, which at the time owned National Broadcasting Company (NBC). As reported in GE's financial report, "subsequent to the acquisition, GE sold . . . a number of RCA and NBC operations whose activities were not compatible with GE's long-range strategic plans."

In another example, Cisco Systems stated in its financial report that from 1997 to 2000 the company completed 16 major acquisitions for a total purchase price of $1.5 billion. These investments included majority interests of the outstanding common stock of American Internet Corporation and the Global Internet Software Group. In each case, Cisco made significant changes to either the operations or the management of the acquired companies.

It is also common to exert influence over the operations and management of a company by purchasing a significant portion, but less than a majority (51 percent), of the company's outstanding common stock. *Accounting Trends and Techniques* (New York: AICPA, 2000) reports that, of the 600 major U.S. companies surveyed, well over half reported such investments. For example, as of December 31, 2000, Walt Disney held a 39 percent ownership in Euro Disney, which operates the Disneyland Paris theme park and resort complex.

Accounting for Long-Term Equity Investments

Since long-term investments in equity securities are commonly made to exert influence over the operations and management of the investee company, financial accounting standards define the appropriate accounting method in terms of the potential for such influence—specifically, in terms of the percentage of outstanding voting stock owned by the investor company.

If the investor company owns less than 20 percent of the outstanding voting stock of the investee company, the potential for influence is relatively small, and the two entities can be viewed as independent. The equity investment, therefore, is accounted for using either the mark-to-market method or the cost method. When the percentage of ownership is between 20 and 50 percent, the investor company has the potential to exert "significant influence" over the investee company, and the two entities cannot be viewed as completely independent. The investor company uses the equity method to account for the equity investment. When the percentage of ownership is greater than 50 percent, the investor company has "control" over the investee company, and for accounting purposes, the two entities are viewed as one, and consolidated financial statements are prepared. Figure 8–1 summarizes the conditions that define the methods used to account for long-term equity investments.

The following discussion presents the mechanics involved in applying the cost and equity methods and the conditions under which each method is used.

<table>
<tr><td rowspan="6">**FIGURE 8–1**
Accounting for long-term investments in equity securities</td><td>**Percentage of Stock Ownership**</td><td>**Potential to Influence**</td><td>**Accounting Method**</td></tr>
<tr><td></td><td></td><td></td></tr>
<tr><td>**Less than 20%**</td><td>**Small**</td><td>**Mark-to-market or cost method**</td></tr>
<tr><td>**20%–50%**</td><td>**Significant**</td><td>**Equity method**</td></tr>
<tr><td>**Greater than 50%**</td><td>**Control**</td><td>**Consolidated financial statements**</td></tr>
</table>

The Cost Method

Some equity securities have no readily determinable market values. Equity securities in corporations whose securities are not publicly traded (i.e., closely held corporations or private companies), for example, may have restrictions on trading and therefore have no public market values. Relatively small investments (less than 20 percent of the outstanding voting stock) in such securities, which by definition cannot easily be liquidated, are accounted for using the **cost method.** It is impossible to apply the mark-to-market method to such securities because their market values cannot be determined.

Applying the cost method is very straightforward. Purchases of equity securities are recorded at cost, including incidental costs of acquisition; dividends are recorded as income when declared; and sales, when they eventually occur, give rise to realized gains or losses reflected on the income statement.

To illustrate, suppose that on January 15, 2002, Beldon Inc. purchased 100 equity securities in a closely held corporation for $10 per share. On December 15 Beldon received a $50 dividend that had been declared on November 29. No other activity occurred in the account until May 5, 2003, when Beldon sold the securities privately for $7 each. The journal entries contained in Figure 8–2 would reflect these transactions.

The Equity Method

Some companies have the ability to significantly influence the operating decisions and management policies of other companies. Such influence indicates a substantive economic relationship between the two companies and may be evidenced, for example, by representation on the board of directors, the interchange of management personnel between companies, frequent or significant transactions between companies, or the technical dependency of one company on the other. Significant investments in the

2002:			
Jan. 15	**Long-Term Investment in Equity Securities (+A)**	1,000	
	Cash (−A)		1,000
	Purchased 100 equity shares at $10 per share.		
Nov. 29	**Dividend Receivable (+A)**	50	
	Dividend Income (R, +SE)		50
	Recognized a declared dividend to be received.		
Dec. 15	**Cash (+A)**	50	
	Dividend Receivable (−A)		50
	Received previously declared $50 dividend.		
2003:			
May 5	**Cash (+A)**	700	
	Loss on Sale of Long-Term Equity Securities (Lo, −SE)	300	
	Long-Term Investment in Equity Securities (−A)		1,000
	Sold 100 equity shares, originally purchased at $10 each,		
	for $7 per share.		

equity securities (voting stock) of another company may also indicate significant influence and a substantive economic relationship. To achieve a reasonable degree of uniformity, the accounting profession concluded that an investment of 20 percent or more in the voting stock of another company represents a "significant influence" and that equity investments from 20 to 50 percent of the voting stock should be accounted for using the **equity method.**

The accounting procedures used to apply the equity method reflect a substantive economic relationship between the investor and the investee companies. The equity investment is originally recorded on the investor's books at cost but is adjusted each subsequent period for changes in the net assets of the investee. As the balance sheet value of the investee increases or decreases, so does the long-term equity investment account of the investor.

Specifically, the carrying value of the long-term investment on the investor's balance sheet is (1) periodically increased (decreased) by the investor's proportionate share of the net income (loss) of the investee and (2) decreased by all dividends transferred to the investor from the investee. In other words, the equity method of accounting acknowledges a close economic link between the two companies. Investee earnings, which indicate net asset growth, and investee dividends, which represent net asset reductions, are reflected proportionately on the balance sheet of the investor.

To illustrate, assume that on January 1, 2002, American Electric Company purchased 40 percent of the outstanding voting stock of Masley Corporation for $40,000. During 2002, Masley recognized net income of $10,000 and declared (Dec. 1) and paid (Dec. 20) dividends of $1,500 to American Electric. During 2003, Masley recognized a net loss of $5,000 and declared (Dec. 1) and paid (Dec. 20) only a $500 dividend to American Electric. Under the equity method, the journal entries contained in Figure 8–3 would be recorded on the books of American Electric.

It is important to understand how the equity method reflects a significant economic relationship between the investor and investee companies. The net income (loss) of the investee serves to proportionately increase (decrease) the investment account of the investor. Thus, the investee's net asset growth or decline is reflected on the investor's balance sheet and income statement. Note also that dividends transferred

FIGURE 8–3

The equity method of accounting for long-term equity investments

2002:

Jan. 1	Long-Term Investment in Equity Securities (+A)	40,000	
	Cash (−A)		40,000
	Purchased 40% of Masley's outstanding shares.		
Dec. 1	Dividend Receivable (+A)	1,500	
	Long-Term Investment in Equity Securities (−A)		1,500
	Recognized $1,500 dividend declared by Masley.		
Dec. 20	Cash (+A)	1,500	
	Dividend Receivable (−A)		1,500
	Received dividend declared on December 1.		
Dec. 31	Long-Term Investment in Equity Securities (+A)	4,000	
	Income from Long-Term Equity Investments (R, +SE)		4,000
	Recognized 40% of Masley's 1999 net income		
	($10,000 × 40%).		

2003:

Dec. 1	Dividend Receivable (+A)	500	
	Long-Term Investment in Equity Securities (−A)		500
	Recognized dividend declared by Masley.		
Dec. 20	Cash (+A)	500	
	Dividend Receivable (−A)		500
	Received dividend declared on December 1.		
Dec. 31	Loss on Long-Term Equity Investment (Lo, −SE)	2,000	
	Long-Term Investment in Equity Securities (−A)		2,000
	Recognized 40% of Masley's 2000 net loss		
	($5,000 × 40%).		

from the investee to the investor are not treated as revenue on the investor's books. Revenue is recognized when the investor's proportionate share of the investee's net income is recorded, not when the dividends are declared or transferred. Dividends are simply treated as an exchange of assets on the investor's books. The long-term investment account is decreased, Dividends Receivable is increased on the date of declaration, and the receivable is exchanged for cash on the date of payment.

Figure 8–4 indicates the importance of investments accounted for under the equity method, relative to total assets, to several major U.S. corporations as of December 31, 1999. Investee companies that are 20 to 50 percent owned by investor companies are often referred to as **affiliated** or **associated companies.**

FIGURE 8–4

The relative importance of investments in affiliate companies (selected U.S. companies)

Company	Amount of Investment (millions of dollars)	Percentage of Total Assets
Coca-Cola	$ 6,442	30%
AT&T	4,434	7
DuPont	1,459	4
General Electric	15,455	3
Goodyear Tire & Rubber Co.	115	1

Source: 1999 financial reports.

Income from equity investments can also represent a material percentage of net income. In recent annual reports, for example, Alcoa, J.C. Penney, and Dow Chemical reported income from affiliate companies (as a percentage of total net income) of 10 percent, 9 percent, and 3 percent, respectively. The following excerpt, taken from the 1999 financial report of Goodyear Tire & Rubber Co., describes how the company accounts for equity investments in affiliate companies:

The company's investments in 20% to 50% owned companies in which it has the ability to exercise significant influence over operating and financial policies are accounted for in the equity method. Accordingly, the company's share of the earnings of these companies is included in consolidated net income.

At the end of 1999, Coca-Cola reported investments under the equity method totaling over $6 billion (30 percent of total assets) primarily in bottling companies, the largest of which was a 40 percent investment in Coca-Cola Enterprises, the largest soft-drink bottler in the world. During 1999 Coca-Cola Enterprises reported net income of $56, while Coca-Cola reported an overall loss on its equity method investments of $184 million. How much profit did Coca-Cola report from its investment in Coca-Cola Enterprises? How well did the other bottling operations perform during 1999?

Some Cautions to Financial Statement Users About the Equity Method

Several features about the equity method should cause financial report users to view it carefully. First, the equity method provides another reason why a company's net income (loss) differs from its cash flow from operations. The income recognized from the investee company rarely equals the cash dividends received by the investor. *Forbes* magazine describes the equity method as "misleading" because "the investor company never really sees any nondividend cash from the investee company" on which it often recognizes substantial income.[6] For example, in 1999 Chevron recognized $526 million in income from affiliate companies, which represented 25 percent of its 1999 earnings. However, Chevron received only $268 million in cash dividends from the affiliates. An astute user can learn how much cash was received from affiliate investments by examining the operating section of the statement of cash flows. In Chevron's case, the $258 million difference between reported equity income ($526 million) and cash received ($268 million) was subtracted from net income in the calculation of net cash from operations and described as "distributions less than income from equity affiliates."

In addition, the equity method ignores price (market value) changes in the affiliate's equity securities. For example, price decreases, even if substantial, are not recognized on the investor's books and, in fact, may even be accompanied by the recognition of income and the receipt of dividends if the affiliate reports positive income and declares dividends during the period of the price decline. Informed users should keep track of the price changes of the affiliate's equity shares, if they are publicly available.

Third, the percent of ownership (20 to 50%) is not always a valid indication of "significant influence." Influence comes in many different forms. Time Warner, for

6. Aaron Bernstein, "Reading Between the Lines," *Forbes*, May 10, 1982, p. 78.

example, was able to block a bid by Turner Broadcasting Systems (TBS) to acquire CBS even though Time Warner owned less than 20 percent of TBS stock. Time Warner did, however, have two members on the TBS board of directors. Similarly, it is possible to exert a controlling influence with less than 51 percent of the stock, especially when the remaining stock is owned by stockholders who represent a wide variety of interests.

Finally, as we discuss later in this chapter, using the equity method can be considered a method of off-balance-sheet financing because it fails to reflect the liabilities of the affiliate on the balance sheet of the investor company. Financial accounting standards require that a summary of the financial statements of all affiliate companies be included in the footnotes of the investor's financial statements. Users should review these summaries to see if including the affiliate's assets and liabilities on the investor's balance sheet would affect solvency and liquidity ratios.

On its 1999 balance sheet, Exxon Mobil reported investments in affiliates of over $15 billion. The income statement reported equity income of $3 billion and the statement of cash flows (operating section) contained a line item "dividends received greater than equity in earnings of equity companies" of $146 million. How much cash in the form of dividends was received by Exxon Mobil from its affiliates during 1999?

Business Acquisitions, Mergers, and Consolidated Financial Statements

A **business acquisition** occurs when an investor company acquires a **controlling interest** (more than 50 percent of the voting stock) in another company. If the two companies continue as separate legal entities, the investor company is referred to as the **parent company,** and the investee company is called the **subsidiary.** Several years ago, for example, Benetton Group paid $330 million to acquire Benetton Sportsystem, which carries Rollerblade, Prince tennis racquets, and Nordica ski boots. Sportsystem now operates as a Benetton subsidiary. In such cases, the parent prepares **consolidated financial statements** (including the income statement, balance sheet, statement of retained earnings, statement of cash flows, and statement of stockholders' equity). Consolidated statements ignore the fact that the parent and the subsidiary are actually separate legal entities and, for reporting purposes, treat the two companies as a single operating unit.

Consolidated statements are prepared for financial accounting purposes only. The parent and the subsidiary maintain separate legal status. In many respects they may continue to operate as relatively independent entities, and the subsidiary maintains a separate set of financial statements. Only because the parent has a controlling interest over the subsidiary do professional accounting standards require that the financial condition of the two companies be represented to the public as one.

A **merger,** or **business combination,** occurs when two or more companies combine to form a single legal entity. In most cases, the assets and liabilities of the smaller company are merged into those of the larger, surviving company. The stock of at least one company, usually the smaller one, is often retired, and it ceases to exist as a separate entity. When Chemical Bank was merged into Chase Manhattan, for example, the surviving entity was named Chase Manhattan. Technically speaking, consolidated financial statements are not prepared after a merger because no parent/subsidiary relationship exists. At least one of the companies involved in the combination no longer exists. However, the financial statements of the surviving company do reflect the assets and liabilities of the merged entities.

Most business acquisitions and combinations consummate when cash and/or other assets (often stock) of the parent are paid to the stockholders of the subsidiary in exchange for the assets and liabilities of the subsidiary.[7] Such transactions are commonly accounted for under the purchase method, when the assets and liabilities of the subsidiary are recorded on the balance sheet of the parent at fair market value (FMV), and the difference between the purchase price and the net FMV of the subsidiary's assets and liabilities is recorded as goodwill.

For example, when Delta Air Lines, Inc., purchased all the outstanding shares of Western Air Lines, Inc., for $787 million, the purchase price consisted of $383 million in cash and Delta common stock valued at $404 million. Delta received the assets and liabilities of Western, which at the time of the transaction had fair market values as described in Figure 8–5.

FIGURE 8–5 Computation of goodwill		Fair Market Value (in Millions)
Current assets		$349
Property, plant, and equipment		748
Other assets		24
Less: Current liabilities	$310	
Long-term debt	431	(741)
Net FMV of Western's assets and liabilities		$380
Less: Purchase price		787
Goodwill (excess of purchase price over FMV of net assets)		$407

In the preparation of its consolidated statements, Delta recorded the purchase by making an adjustment similar to the following entry. The assets and liabilities of Western were then included on the consolidated balance sheet of Delta.

Current Assets (+A)	349	
Property, Plant, and Equipment (+A)	748	
Other Assets (+A)	24	
Goodwill (+A)	407	
Current Liabilities (+L)		310
Long-Term Liabilities (+L)		431
Cash (−A)		383
Common Stock (+SE)		404

Purchased Western Air Lines.

Accounting for business acquisitions and mergers and preparing consolidated financial statements are actually more complex than we have indicated here. Further discussion can be found in Appendix 8A and in intermediate and advanced financial accounting texts.

7. In the following discussion we use the terms *parent* and *subsidiary* to denote the investor and investee companies. In the case of business combinations, however, the term *parent* should be interpreted as the survivor company and the term *subsidiary* as the merged company.

The Equity Method or Consolidated Statements?

Accounting for an equity investment under the equity method can give rise to financial statements that are much different from those prepared as consolidated statements. The following example describes an equity investment, comparing the balance sheet produced under the equity method to a consolidated balance sheet.

Figure 8–6 shows the December 31, 2002 balance sheets of Megabucks, a large manufacturing company, and Tiny Inc., a smaller distribution outlet. Note initially that the debt/equity ratio of Megabucks is 67 percent ($20,000 ÷ $30,000). Assume that on December 31 Megabucks purchased the outstanding stock of Tiny Inc. for $10,000.

FIGURE 8–6

The balance sheets of Megabucks and Tiny Inc.

Megabucks
Balance Sheet
December 31, 2002

Assets	$50,000	Liabilities	$20,000
		Stockholders' equity	30,000
		Total liabilities and	
Total assets	$50,000	stockholders' equity	$50,000

Tiny Incorporated
Balance Sheet
December 31, 2002

Assets	$20,000	Liabilities	$15,000
		Stockholders' equity	5,000
		Total liabilities and	
Total assets	$20,000	stockholders' equity	$20,000

Under the equity method, Megabucks would record the following journal entry.

Long-Term Investment (+A)	10,000	
Cash (−A)		10,000

Purchased Tiny Inc. for $10,000.

Note that the journal entry to record the investment has no effect on the total assets, total liabilities, total stockholders' equity, or the debt/equity ratio of Megabucks. The transaction is simply recorded as an exchange of two assets, a long-term investment and cash. In future periods under the equity method, Megabucks' total assets will reflect the net incomes (losses) reported by Tiny Inc., less any dividends.

If Megabucks accounts for this acquisition as a purchase and prepares consolidated financial statements, it would record the transaction with the following journal entry. Assume that Tiny's assets and liabilities are reported on its balance sheet at FMV.

Assets (+A)	20,000	
Goodwill (+A)	5,000	
Liabilities (+L)		15,000
Cash (−A)		10,000

Acquired Tiny Inc. for $10,000.

In this case, both the assets and the liabilities of Megabucks would be increased by $15,000. The resulting consolidated balance sheet would appear as in Figure 8–7. Note that the debt/equity ratio is now 1.17 ($35,000 ÷ $30,000). Treating the transaction as a purchase and preparing a consolidated balance sheet, as opposed to using the equity method, increases the debt/equity ratio of Megabucks from 0.67 to 1.17.

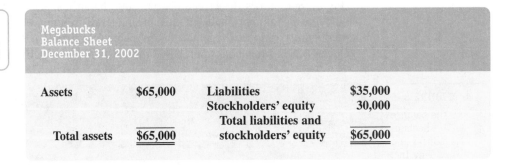

FIGURE 8–7
Consolidated balance sheet

Megabucks
Balance Sheet
December 31, 2002

Assets	$65,000	Liabilities	$35,000
		Stockholders' equity	30,000
		Total liabilities and	
Total assets	$65,000	stockholders' equity	$65,000

This difference between the equity method and preparing consolidated financial statements has encouraged many companies in the past to choose the equity method when possible, especially when the investee company carries considerable debt. Such a choice may come in the form of purchasing slightly less than 50 percent of the investee company's common stock, purchasing over 50 percent and claiming that "control is temporary or does not rest with the majority owner," or acquiring 100 percent and claiming that preparing consolidated statements would distort the financial statements because the subsidiary is so unlike the parent. The national director of accounting and auditing at Seidman & Seidman, a major accounting firm, once noted that the equity method can be viewed as a method of off-balance-sheet financing. He pointed out that using the equity method can "present a more favorable impression of debt/equity ratios, working capital ratios, and returns on assets invested in the business." Consequently, financial statement users and auditors should pay special attention to cases where some question arises about whether the equity method should be used or consolidated financial statements should be prepared.

As of the end of 1999, Coca-Cola owned approximately a 40 percent interest in bottling companies that reported accumulated assets of $50.6 billion and accumulated liabilities of $34.4 billion. The balance sheet of Coca-Cola listed assets of $21.6 billion and liabilities of $11.6 billion. If Coca-Cola increased its ownership interest in these bottling companies so that it was required to include their assets and liabilities in a set of consolidated financial statements, what do you think would happen to Coca-Cola's liability to total asset ratio?

Accounting for Equity Investments: A Summary

Figure 8–8 provides a framework that summarizes the methods used to account for investments in equity securities. It summarizes the appropriate accounting methods for all (short-term and long-term) investments in equity securities. In general, three questions must be answered before the appropriate accounting method and disclosure can be determined: (1) Is the security marketable? (2) Does management intend to liqui-

FIGURE 8–8 Accounting for equity securities

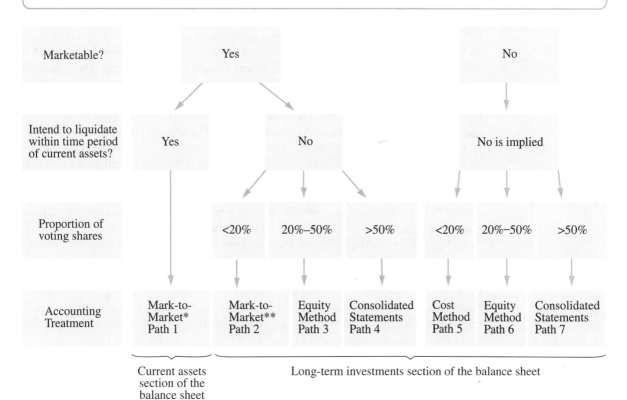

Marketable?
Yes   No

Intend to liquidate within time period of current assets?
Yes   No   No is implied

Proportion of voting shares
<20%   20%–50%   >50%   <20%   20%–50%   >50%

Accounting Treatment
Mark-to-Market* Path 1 | Mark-to-Market** Path 2 | Equity Method Path 3 | Consolidated Statements Path 4 | Cost Method Path 5 | Equity Method Path 6 | Consolidated Statements Path 7

Current assets section of the balance sheet   Long-term investments section of the balance sheet

*Trading or available-for-sale securities, depending on expected liquidations.

**Available-for-sale securities.

date the security within the time period of current assets? and (3) Is the proportion of ownership less than 20 percent, between 20 and 50 percent, or greater than 50 percent?

If the purchased equity securities are marketable, and management intends to liquidate them within the time period of current assets, the investment is considered short-term. This is regardless of the proportion of ownership and whether it is considered trading or available-for-sale, and it is carried on the balance sheet at market value (Path 1). If the purchased securities are marketable, but management does not intend to liquidate them within the time period of current assets, the investment is considered long-term. Such long-term investments, where less than 20 percent of the voting shares are held, are considered available-for-sale and are carried on the balance sheet at market value (Path 2). Long-term investments of between 20 and 50 percent of the voting shares are accounted for using the equity method (Path 3). Long-term investments of 50 percent or more of the voting shares give rise to consolidated statements (Path 4).

Equity investments that are not marketable are accounted for using the cost method if they represent less than 20 percent of the voting shares (Path 5), or the equity method if they represent an investment of between 20 and 50 percent (Path 6). Consolidated statements should be prepared if such investments represent 50 percent or more of the voting stock (Path 7).

GOODWILL ACCOUNTING: CONTROVERSY, CHANGE, AND INTERNATIONAL IMPLICATIONS

U.S. accounting rules require that when one company acquires another, goodwill must be recognized in the amount of the excess of the acquisition price over the fair market value of the acquired company's net assets (assets less liabilities). The goodwill account appears on the balance sheet of the acquiring company, and until quite recently U.S. GAAP required that goodwill be amortized to income over a period of time not to exceed forty years. The requirement to amortize goodwill generated much opposition in the United States. An article published in *Business Week* titled "Goodwill is making a lot of people angry," for example, reported that when Philip Morris acquired Kraft, Inc., it recognized over $11 billion of goodwill, virtually ensuring that Philip Morris would not report positive income for a number of years because the goodwill amortization expense would be at least $275 million per year. Similarly, AOL carried over $100 billion in goodwill, most of which related to the acquisition of Time Warner, which led to a whopping $7.5 billion amortization expense each year. U.S. firms like Philip Morris, AOL, and others claimed that goodwill amortization put U.S. companies at a disadvantage when competing for acquisitions against foreign companies whose goodwill accounting rules were much less damaging to earnings. For example, after several U.S. firms were outbid for Pillsbury by Grand Metropolitan, a large British firm, Peter Berger, a partner for Arthur Andersen, noted that U.S. executives were hesitant to get into bidding wars with their British counterparts because chief executive compensation is based on earnings, which makes them very wary about taking a big bite of goodwill.

In July 2001 the FASB passed an accounting standard that removes the requirement by U.S. firms to amortize goodwill and, as expected, U.S. industry reacted very positively to the change. No longer must U.S. executives worry about big charges to earnings related to goodwill recognized on major acquisitions. Some claim that it will make them more competitive in the international marketplace. Whether or not this is true, the accounting change passed by the FASB does provide an important example of a case where U.S. accounting standards appear to have moved closer to other accounting standards in place throughout the world.

APPENDIX 8A

CONSOLIDATED FINANCIAL STATEMENTS

Many companies expand by purchasing other companies and/or extending operations into other countries. For example, as of December 31, 1999, Johnson & Johnson, one of the world's largest consumer products companies, owned 37 different U.S. companies as well as more than 180 companies that operated in 60 different countries throughout the world. In a typical year, Johnson & Johnson spends $1 billion acquiring other domestic and foreign operations. Each of these acquisitions involved acquiring large amounts of the outstanding equity securities of the investee companies. This appendix covers the methods used to account for investments in excess of 50 percent of the investee company's outstanding voting stock.

Such transactions give rise to consolidated financial statements, which reflect the combined accounts of both the investor and the investee companies. Virtually all major U.S. corporations prepare financial statements on a consolidated basis. The following excerpt is from the 2000 financial report of IBM and is typical of the disclosures made by other major U.S. companies.

The consolidated financial statements include the accounts of International Business Machines Corporation and its U.S. and non-U.S. subsidiary companies. Investments in . . . other companies, in which IBM has a 20–50 percent ownership, are accounted for by the equity method. Investments of less than 20 percent are accounted for by the cost method.

Accounting for Business Acquisitions and Mergers: The Purchase Method

Equity shares in other companies can be acquired by paying cash or other assets, issuing stock, or issuing bonds to the acquired company's shareholders. Often some combination of these forms of payment is used. When Delta Air Lines acquired Western Air Lines, for example, the $787 million payment to Western's shareholders consisted of $383 million in cash and 8.3 million shares of Delta stock, each with a value of $48.75.

For simplicity, in the following examples we assume that cash is paid for the acquired stock. To illustrate how the purchase method is used to account for business acquisitions and mergers, assume that on December 31, 2002, Multi Corporation acquired a controlling interest in the equity shares of Littleton Company. The December 31 balance sheets for both companies and some additional information for Littleton Company appear in Figure 8A–1.

FIGURE 8A–1 Balance sheets for Multi Corporation and Littleton Company (before acquisition)

Multi Corporation
Balance Sheet
December 31, 2002

ASSETS

Cash	$ 65,000
Accounts receivable	70,000
Notes receivable	35,000
Inventory	120,000
Long-lived assets (net)	230,000
Total assets	$520,000

LIABILITIES AND STOCKHOLDERS' EQUITY

Accounts payable	$ 90,000
Long-term notes payable	130,000
Common stock	200,000
Retained earnings	100,000
Total liabilities and stockholders' equity	$520,000

Littleton Company
Balance Sheet
December 31, 2002

ASSETS

Cash	$ 6,000
Accounts receivable	9,000
Inventory	10,000
Long-lived assets (net)	35,000
Total assets	$60,000

LIABILITIES AND STOCKHOLDERS' EQUITY

Accounts payable	$14,000
Long-term notes payable	16,000
Common stock	22,000
Retained earnings	8,000
Total liabilities and stockholders' equity	$60,000

Additional information:
Common shares outstanding   8,000

When a parent company (Multi Corporation) purchases a controlling interest in a subsidiary (Littleton), the parent is essentially purchasing the assets and liabilities of the subsidiary. It is important to realize that the historical costs of the subsidiary's assets, which are included on Littleton's balance sheet in Figure 8A–1, are of little consequence to the purchase decision. The parent is actually purchasing the FMVs, not the historical costs, of the assets and liabilities of the subsidiary. An important rule, therefore, in understanding accounting for consolidated financial statements is the following: When a parent purchases a controlling interest in a subsidiary, the assets and liabilities of the subsidiary are recorded on the balance sheet of the parent at their FMVs.

Consequently, from Multi Corporation's standpoint, it is more appropriate to view the value of Littleton's net assets as shown in Figure 8A–2, where all assets and liabilities have been valued at their individual FMVs. As of December 31, 2002, there were 8,000 shares of Littleton common stock outstanding. The per-share market value of the net assets, therefore, is $5 ($40,000 ÷ 8,000 shares).

The following sections account for Multi Corporation's purchase of Littleton shares under the two most common scenarios: (1) purchase 100 percent of the common stock for a price greater than the per-share market value of the net assets, and (2) purchase between 50 and 100 percent of the common stock for a price greater than the per-share market value of the net assets.[8]

FIGURE 8A–2	
FMV of Littleton's net assets	**Littleton Company** **Schedule of Fair Market Values of Assets and Liabilities** **December 31, 2002**

Cash	**$ 6,000**
Accounts Receivable	**9,000**
Inventory	**15,000**
Long-Lived Assets	**40,000**
Accounts Payable	**(14,000)**
Long-Term Notes Payable	**(16,000)**
FMV of net assets	**$ 40,000**

CASE 1: PURCHASE 100 PERCENT OF STOCK AT A PRICE GREATER THAN THE PER-SHARE MARKET VALUE OF THE NET ASSETS

Assume that Multi Corporation purchased all 8,000 shares of the outstanding stock of Littleton for $8 per share, a total cost of $64,000. The purchase entry and illustrative adjusting entry appear in Figure 8A–3.[9]

FIGURE 8A–3			
Consolidated journal entries for Multi Corporation: Case 1	**Dec. 31 Investment in Subsidiary (+A)** Cash (−A) *Purchased 8,000 shares of Littleton common* *stock at $8.*	**64,000**	**64,000**

	Cash (+A)
	Accounts Receivable (+A)
	Inventory (+A)
	Long-Lived Assets (+A)
	Goodwill (+A)
	   Accounts Payable (+L)
	   Long-Term Notes Payable (+L)
	   Investment in Subsidiary (−A)
	Added assets and liabilities of Littleton at FMV and
	eliminated investment account.
		6,000
		9,000
		15,000
		40,000
		24,000*
			
			14,000
			16,000
			64,000

*$3 ($8 price per share − $5 per-share market value of net assets) × 8,000 sh.

---

8. It is unusual for a company to be purchased for less than the FMV of its net assets, and we do not cover such cases in this text. These situations are covered in advanced financial accounting texts.

9. The purchase entry would be recorded on Multi Corporation's books. The adjusting entry, however, is only for illustrative purposes. It is not actually on Multi Corporation's books. It is reflected only in the consolidation process, as illustrated in Figure 8A–4.

The purchase price in this case ($64,000) exceeds the FMV of Littleton's net assets ($40,000) by $24,000; therefore, goodwill of $24,000 is recognized on the acquisition. Multi Corporation apparently believes that Littleton is worth more than the FMV of its net assets. It paid $3 per share over and above the $5 ($40,000 ÷ 8,000 shares) per-share market value of the net assets, resulting in a total payment of $24,000 ($3/sh. × 8,000 shares) for goodwill, which Littleton had accumulated up to the date of the purchase. Goodwill, an intangible asset, appears on the asset side of the consolidated balance sheet, usually below fixed assets. The consolidated balance sheet would be prepared using a work sheet, as illustrated in Figure 8A–4.

FIGURE 8A–4 Work sheet for Multi Corporation: Case 1

Multi Corporation
Consolidated Work Sheet
December 31, 2002

ACCOUNTS	MULTI CORP.	LITTLETON CO.	ADJUSTMENTS AND ELIMINATIONS DR.	CR.	CONSOLIDATED BALANCE SHEET
Cash	1,000	6,000			7,000
Accounts Receivable	70,000	9,000			79,000
Notes Receivable	35,000	—			35,000
Inventory	120,000	10,000	5,000		135,000
Investment in Subsidiary	64,000	—		64,000	—
Long-Lived Assets	230,000	35,000	5,000		270,000
Goodwill	—	—	24,000		24,000
Total Assets	520,000	60,000	34,000	64,000	550,000
Accounts Payable	90,000	14,000			104,000
Long-Term Notes Payable	130,000	16,000			146,000
Common Stock	200,000	22,000	22,000		200,000
Retained Earnings	100,000	8,000	8,000		100,000
Total Liabilities and Stockholders' Equity	520,000	60,000	30,000		550,000

Transactions where 100 percent of a subsidiary's stock is purchased at a price that exceeds the per-share market value of the subsidiary's net assets are very common. In a recent year alone, Ralston Purina Company, for example, made four such acquisitions (Eveready Batteries, Drake Bakeries, Continental Baking Company, and Benco Pet Foods, Inc.).

CASE 2: PURCHASE BETWEEN 50 AND 100 PERCENT OF STOCK AT A PRICE GREATER THAN THE PER-SHARE MARKET VALUE OF THE NET ASSETS

Assume that Multi Corporation purchased 6,400 shares (80 percent) of Littleton's outstanding stock for $8 per share, a total cost of $51,200. The purchase entry and illustrative adjusting entry appear in Figure 8A–5.

In this case, both goodwill and minority interest are recognized. Goodwill is recognized because Multi Corporation paid $8 for each share, which is $3 more than the $5 per-share market value of the net assets. The total goodwill recognized by Multi Corporation on the transaction is $19,200 (6,400 shares × $3). Minority interest is recognized because Multi Corporation purchased only 80 percent of Littleton's stock. The amount of minority interest recognized on

Dec. 31	Investment in Subsidiary (+A)	51,200	
	Cash (−A)		51,200
	Purchased 6,400 shares (80%) of Littleton		
	common stock at $8.		
	Cash (+A)	6,000	
	Accounts Receivable (+A)	9,000	
	Inventory (+A)	15,000	
	Long-Lived Assets (+A)	40,000	
	Goodwill (+A)	19,200*	
	Accounts Payable (+L)		14,000
	Long-Term Note Payable (+L)		16,000
	Minority Interest (+L or +SE)		8,000**
	Investment in Subsidiary (−A)		51,200
	Added assets and liabilities of Littleton at FMV		
	and eliminated investment account.		

*$3 ($8 price per share − $5 per-share market value of net assets) × 6,400 sh.

**20% × $40,000

the transaction is computed by multiplying the FMV of Littleton's net assets ($40,000) times the percentage of Littleton's shares owned by the minority stockholders (20 percent).

The economic significance of minority interest is somewhat unclear. It can be interpreted as a liability in that it represents an interest held by outsiders in a portion of the net assets listed on the consolidated balance sheet. On the other hand, it resembles a stockholders' equity item because the interest held by outsiders is an equity interest held by outside stockholders. Consequently, minority interest is normally disclosed on the consolidated balance sheet between the long-term liability and the stockholders' equity sections.[10]

The consolidated balance sheet would be prepared using a work sheet, as illustrated in Figure 8A–6.

Acquisitions where both goodwill and minority interest are recognized occur periodically in the United States but are much less common than those where 100 percent of the subsidiary's stock is purchased. Often such transactions are followed quite closely by the acquisition of the outstanding minority stock. For example, when Alcoa acquired approximately 91 percent of the outstanding stock of TRE Corporation for $326 million, the transaction recognized both goodwill and minority interest, which were included in Alcoa's balance sheet. Shortly after the acquisition, Alcoa acquired the remaining outstanding stock, and TRE became a wholly owned subsidiary of Alcoa.

Other Issues Concerning Consolidated Financial Statements

Accounting for acquisitions and mergers is a very complex and detailed topic. In this appendix we have only scratched the surface. For example, transactions between a parent and subsidiary (intercompany transactions) must be eliminated when the financial statements of the two companies are consolidated. In the examples above, we focused only on consolidating balance sheets for transactions that occurred at year-end. Many acquisitions and mergers occur during the year, and of course, the income statement and statement of cash flows must also be consol-

10. There are several different views on how to account for purchases in which a parent acquires between 50 and 100 percent of the subsidiary's outstanding stock. As a result, the appropriate computation of minority interest and its classification as a liability or a stockholders' equity item on the consolidated balance sheet are also somewhat controversial. In this text, we have adopted primarily what is called an *entity view* because we believe it to be logical, consistent, and understandable. However, other views, which are discussed in advanced accounting texts, are followed by a significant number of U.S. companies.

FIGURE 8A-6 Work sheet for Multi Corporation: Case 2

Multi Corporation
Consolidated Work Sheet
December 31, 2002

ACCOUNTS	MULTI CORP.	LITTLETON CO.	ADJUSTMENTS AND ELIMINATIONS DR.	CR.	CONSOLIDATED BALANCE SHEET
Cash	13,800	6,000			19,800
Accounts Receivable	70,000	9,000			79,000
Notes Receivable	35,000	—			35,000
Inventory	120,000	10,000	5,000		135,000
Investment in Subsidiary	51,200	—		51,200	—
Long-Lived Assets	230,000	35,000	5,000		270,000
Goodwill	—	—	19,200		19,200
Total Assets	520,000	60,000	29,200	51,200	558,000
Accounts Payable	90,000	14,000			104,000
Long-Term Notes Payable	130,000	16,000			146,000
Minority Interest	—	—		8,000	8,000
Common Stock	200,000	22,000	22,000		200,000
Retained Earnings	100,000	8,000	8,000		100,000
Total Liabilities and Stockholders' Equity	520,000	60,000	30,000	8,000	558,000

idated. Finally, consolidations between parents and subsidiaries that operate in different countries can be complex because adjustments must be made for different currencies, and these adjustments sometimes are reflected on the income statement and sometimes only on the balance sheet. These topics are beyond the scope of this text and are normally covered in advanced accounting courses.

REVIEW PROBLEM I

The following information relates to the marketable security investments of Macon Construction. Securities held on December 31, 2002, are described in the table below. AAA and BBB are classified as trading securities, and CCC is classified as an available-for-sale security.

Securities	No. of Shares	Cost/Share	Total Cost	Value/Share	Total Market Value
AAA	10	$14	$140	$17	$170
BBB	25	15	375	14	350
CCC	15	8	120	10	150
			$635		$670

Early in 2003, Macon sold all of its investment in AAA securities for $18 per share. The company also sold five shares of BBB for $13 per share. During 2003, Macon received dividends of $3 per share on the remaining twenty shares of BBB, and dividends of $2 per share were declared, but not yet received, on the 15 shares of CCC stock. The per-share market values of BBB and CCC on December 31, 2003, were $12 and $9, respectively. During 2004, Macon sold the remaining 20 shares of BBB stock for $13 per share and the 15 shares of CCC for $11 per share.

The journal entries that would be required for 2002 under the mark-to-market rule follow.

1. **Trading Securities (AAA) (+A)**   30*
   Unrealized Gain on Trading Securities (R, +SE)   30
   Revalued AAA securities to market.
   *10 sh. × $3 per sh.

2. **Unrealized Loss on Trading Securities (Lo, −SE)**   25
   Trading Securities (BBB) (−A)   25*
   Revalued BBB securities to market.
   *25 sh. × $1 per sh.

3. **Available-for-Sale Securities (CCC) (+A)**   30*
   **Unrealized Price Increase on Available-for-Sale
   Securities (+SE)**   30
   Revalued CCC securities to market.
   *15 sh. × $2 per sh.

The journal entries that reflect 2003 activities involving short-term equity investments follow.

1. **Cash (+A)**   180*
   Trading Securities (−A)   170**
   Realized Gain on Sale of Trading Sec. (Ga, +SE)   10
   Sold ten shares of AAA stock at $18.
   *10 sh. × $18 per sh.
   **10 sh. × $17 per sh.

2. **Cash (+A)**   65*
   Realized Loss on Sale of Trading Sec. (Lo, −SE)   5
   Trading Securities (−A)   70**
   Sold five shares of BBB stock at $13 per share.
   *5 sh. × $13 per sh.
   **5 sh. × $14 per sh.

3. **Cash (+A)**   60*
   Dividend Receivable (+A)   30**
   Dividend Revenue (R, +SE)   90
   *Received BBB dividends and recognized
   dividends declared on CCC stock.*
   *20 sh. × $3 per sh.
   **15 sh. × $2 per sh.

4. **Unrealized Loss on Trading Securities (Lo, −SE)**   40
   Trading Securities (BBB) (−A)   40*
   Revalued BBB shares to market.
   *20 sh. × $2 per sh.

5. **Unrealized Price Increase on Available-for-Sale
   Securities (−SE)**   15
   Available-for-Sale Securities (CCC) (−A)   15*
   Revalued CCC shares to market.
   *15 sh. × $1 per sh.

The journal entries that reflect the sales of short-term equity investments follow.

1. **Cash (+A)**   260*
        Trading Securities (BBB) (−A)   240**
        Realized Gain on Trading Securities (R, +SE)   20
    Sold twenty shares of BBB stock at $13 per share.

    *20 sh. × $13 per sh.
    **20 sh. × $12 per sh.

2. **Cash (+A)**   165*
    Unrealized Price Increase on Available-for-Sale
    Securities (−SE)   15
        Available-for-Sale Securities (CCC) (−A)   135**
        Realized Gain on Available-for-Sale
        Securities (Ga, +SE)   45
    Sold fifteen shares of CCC stock at $11 per share.

    *15 sh. × $11 per sh.
    **15 sh. × $9 per sh.

REVIEW PROBLEM II

Trailor Corporation entered into the two transactions listed below on January 1, 2002.

a. On January 1, 2002, Trailor purchased 30 percent of the outstanding common stock of Rowers Company for $50,000. Income reported by Rowers during 2002 and 2003 was $15,000 and $8,000, respectively. Rowers declared and paid dividends to Trailor in the amount of $3,000 during each of the two years.

b. On January 1, 2002, Trailor purchased 100 percent of the outstanding common stock of Kleece Corporation for $20,000. The FMVs of the individual assets and liabilities of Kleece Corporation, as of the time of the acquisition, were $40,000 and $28,000, respectively.

The related journal entries that would be recorded for each transaction over the subsequent two-year period follow.

a. 2002:

Jan. 1   **Investment in Equity Securities (+A)**   50,000
                    Cash (−A)   50,000
        Purchased Rowers common stock.

Dec. 31   **Investment in Equity Securities (+A)**   4,500*
                    Income from Equity Investments (R, +SE)   4,500
        *$15,000 × 30%

                Cash (+A)   3,000
                    Investment in Equity Securities (−A)   3,000
        Recognized 30% of Rowers' income and
        *received dividends.**
        *Assume that dividends were declared and paid on the same day.

2003:

                Investment in Equity Securities (+A)   2,400*
                    Income from Equity Invest. (R, +SE)   2,400
        *$8,000 × 30%.

Cash (+A)	3,000	
Investment in Equity Securities (−A)		3,000

Recognized 30% of Rowers' income and
received dividends. *

*Assume that dividends were declared and paid on the same day.

b. 2002:

Jan. 1

Assets (+A)	40,000	
Goodwill (+A)	8,000	
Liabilities (+L)		28,000
Cash (−A)		20,000

Acquired Kleece Corporation.

SUMMARY OF KEY POINTS

The key points of the chapter are summarized below.

○ *Criteria that must be met before a security can be listed in the current assets section of the balance sheet.*

Two criteria must be met before an investment in a security can be listed in the current assets section of the balance sheet: (1) the security must be able to be converted into cash within the time period that defines current assets (i.e., the current operating cycle or one year, whichever is longer), and (2) management must intend to convert the security into cash within the time period that defines current assets.

○ *Trading and available-for-sale securities and how the mark-to-market rule is used to account for them.*

Trading securities are bought and held principally for the purpose of selling them in the near future with the objective of generating profit on short-term price changes. Investments not classified as trading securities are considered available-for-sale securities. Trading securities are always listed in the current assets section of the balance sheet, while available-for-sale securities are listed as current or long-term, depending on management's intention. In applying the mark-to-market rule to trading and available-for-sale securities, four separate events must be considered.

1. *Purchase of securities.* When the securities are purchased, they are capitalized and recorded on the balance sheet at cost. The cost includes the purchase price as well as any incidental acquisition costs, such as brokerage commissions and taxes.
2. *Declaration and payment of dividends.* Cash dividends declared on these securities are initially recognized as receivables and revenues. When a cash dividend is received, the receivable is exchanged for cash.
3. *Sale of securities.* When these securities are sold, their balance sheet value is removed from the books and the difference between this amount and the proceeds of the sale is recognized on the books as either a realizable gain or a realized loss.
4. *End-of-accounting period adjustment.* Both trading and available-for-sale securities are adjusted to current market value at the end of the accounting period. In the

case of trading securities, the related unrealized holding gain or loss is reflected directly in income; in the case of available-for-sale securities, the related unrealized price change is booked to stockholders' equity and included on the statement of comprehensive income.

○ *Why companies make long-term investments in equity securities.*

Companies make long-term investments in the equity securities of other companies for two primary reasons: (1) investment income in the form of dividends and/or stock price appreciation and (2) management influence, where the voting power of the purchased shares allows the investor company to exert influence or control over the board of directors and management of the investee company. The primary motivation behind the long-term equity investments for most major U.S. companies is reason (2), influence over the investee company's operations and management.

○ *The mark-to-market method, the cost method, and the equity method of accounting for long-term equity investments, and the conditions under which each method is used.*

The mark-to-market rule is used to account for trading securities, which are always considered current, and available-for-sale securities whether they are classified in the current or long-term assets section of the balance sheet.

Under the cost method, purchases of equity securities are recorded at cost, including incidental costs of acquisition, dividends are recorded as income when declared, and sales give rise to book gains or losses in the amount of the difference between the acquisition cost of the securities and the proceeds from the sale. The cost method is used for investments in nonmarketable securities that involve less than 20 percent of the investee company's voting stock.

Under the equity method, the purchase of equity securities is originally recorded at cost, and the carrying value of the long-term investment on the investor's balance sheet is (1) periodically increased (decreased) by the investor's proportionate share of the net income (loss) of the investee and (2) decreased by all dividends transferred to the investor from the investee. The equity method is used for investments in marketable or nonmarketable securities that involve from 20 to 50 percent of the investee company's voting stock.

○ *Consolidated financial statements, when they are prepared, and how they differ from financial statements that account for equity investments using the equity method.*

Consolidated financial statements represent the combined financial statements of a parent company and any companies acquired by the parent. Such acquisitions occur when the parent purchases a controlling interest (51 percent of the outstanding voting stock) in another company, or as the result of a merger, where the merged company ceases to exist. Consolidated statements should be prepared when a parent owns 51 percent or more of a subsidiary's outstanding common stock.

When the parent prepares consolidated financial statements, it includes the assets and liabilities of the subsidiary with its own. If the purchase price exceeds the FMV of the subsidiary's net assets, goodwill is also recognized on the balance sheet of the parent. Under the equity method, the assets and liabilities of the investee company are not included with those of the parent, and this, in turn, can represent a form of off-balance-sheet financing.

KEY TERMS

Note: Definitions for these terms are provided in the glossary at the end of the text.

Affiliated (associated) companies (p. 335)
Available-for-sale securities (p. 326)
Business acquisition (p. 337)
Business combination (p. 337)
Comprehensive income (p. 331)
Consolidated financial statements (p. 337)
Controlling interest (p. 337)
Cost method (p. 333)
Equity investment (p. 324)
Equity method (p. 334)
Holding gains or losses (p. 328)

Intention to convert (p. 326)
Mark-to-market rule (p. 326)
Merger (p. 337)
Parent company (p. 337)
Readily marketable (p. 325)
Realized gains/losses (p. 328)
Subsidiary (p. 337)
Trading securities (p. 326)
Unrealized gains/losses (p. 328)
Unrealized price changes (p. 329)

ETHICS IN THE REAL WORLD

Many countries, such as Switzerland, deduct goodwill directly from the stockholders' equity—avoiding the income statement altogether. Some claim that this treatment of goodwill gives Swiss companies advantages over U.S. firms when bidding to acquire other companies. The takeover battle for Gerber Products Co., for example, included bids by a number of U.S. companies, including Quaker Oats, which entered a bid of $35 per share. Swiss drug giant Sandoz Ltd. won the battle quickly, however, by raising the ante to $53 per share. Some investment bankers claimed that the favorable accounting treatment for goodwill practiced in Switzerland gave Sandoz the advantage it needed to outbid Quaker Oats.

These accounting differences also seem to have discouraged certain large foreign companies from raising capital on the U.S. stock exchanges. For example, Nestle, a Swiss food giant, says it is not willing to redo its financial statements to conform to U.S. GAAP (a requirement of the U.S. stock exchanges). The main reason is that its earnings would look about 10 percent lower.

These accounting differences have elicited complaints from U.S. businesses that certain foreign countries are allowing liberal accounting methods, which provide unfair trade advantages for their local companies and capital markets.

ETHICAL ISSUE Is it ethical for the government or standard-setting body in a particular country to set accounting standards that are designed to provide international economic advantages enjoyed solely by the companies and capital markets in that country?

INTERNET RESEARCH EXERCISE

The chapter began by noting that the extraordinary growth experienced by Cisco Systems in the late 1990s was fueled by acquisitions of other companies. How much has Cisco grown since 1999? Has Cisco maintained high levels of performance? Begin your search at *www.cisco.com*.

BRIEF EXERCISES

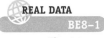

REAL DATA

BE8-1

Short-term investments

The table below was taken from the 1999 annual report of Merck & Company, a major U.S. pharmaceutical company (dollars in millions).

	1999	1998	1997
Net income	$5,891	$5,248	$4,614
Other comprehensive income (loss)			
Net unrealized (loss)	26	(6)	(18)
Other	4	(28)	(12)
Comprehensive income	$5,921	$5,214	$4,584

REQUIRED:

a. What is comprehensive income and how does it differ from net income?
b. This table indicates that Merck carries certain kinds of investments on its balance sheet. What are they, and what happened to the values of those investments in 1997, 1998, and 1999?

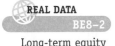

REAL DATA

BE8-2

Long-term equity investments

At the end of 1999, Merck & Company reported equity investments of $1.4 billion on the balance sheet and equity income from affiliates on the income statement of $762 million. The affiliates, in total, reported net income of $1.7 billion, and Merck received dividends of $412.

a. What percent of ownership interest, on average, does Merck hold in the affiliates?
b. Compute the total dividends declared by the affiliates. Comment on the relationship between affiliate income and dividends received by Merck.

REAL DATA

BE8-3

Goodwill

Procter & Gamble's 1997 balance sheet reported a goodwill balance of $3.9 billion. Describe what goodwill is, how it was originally recorded, and what it indicates about Procter & Gamble..

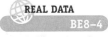

REAL DATA

BE8-4

Goodwill accounting

At the end of 1999, Kellogg purchased the outstanding common stock of Worthington Foods, a leading manufacturer of health foods, for $350 million. The $350 million purchase price was allocated in the following manner: current and noncurrent assets, $218 million; liabilities, $62 million; and the remainder to goodwill.

REQUIRED:

a. Compute the dollar amount allocated to goodwill.
b. Demonstrate how the transaction affected the basic accounting equation.

EXERCISES

E8-1

Accounting for short-term equity securities

Monroe Auto Supplies engaged in several transactions involving short-term equity securities during 2002, shown in the following list. The company had never invested in equity securities prior to 2002. All securities were classified as trading securities.

1. Purchased 1,000 shares of IBM for $50 per share.
2. Purchased 500 shares of General Motors for $80 per share.
3. Sold 750 shares of IBM for $60 per share.

4. Received a dividend of $1.50 per share from General Motors. Assume that the dividend was declared in a previous period.
5. Purchased 200 shares of Xerox for $40 per share.
6. Sold the remaining 250 shares of IBM for $30 per share.
7. Sold the 200 shares of Xerox for $58 per share.
8. Sold the 500 shares of General Motors for $60 per share.

a. Prepare journal entries for each transaction.
b. What effect did these transactions have on the company's 2002 net income?

E8–2

Mark-to-market accounting

The following information was extracted from the December 31, 2002 current asset section of the balance sheets of four different companies:

	Wearever Fabrics	Frames Corp.	Pacific Transport	Video Magic
Trading securities	$800,000	$490,000	$645,000	$210,000
Available-for-sale securities	130,000	40,000	250,000	85,000
Short-term equity invest.	$930,000	$530,000	$895,000	$295,000

There were no transactions in short-term equity securities during 2003, and as of December 31, 2003, the controllers of each company collected the following information:

	Wearever Fabrics	Frames Corp.	Pacific Transport	Video Magic
Trading securities	$820,000	$480,000	$625,000	$220,000
Available-for-sale securities	122,000	52,000	246,000	88,000
Short-term equity invest.	$942,000	$532,000	$871,000	$308,000

a. Compute the change in the wealth levels of each of the four companies due to the market value changes in their equity investments.
b. Compute the effect on 2003 reported income for each of the four companies due to the market value changes in their equity investments.
c. Explain why the answers to (a) and (b) are not the same.

E8–3

Mark-to-market accounting

The following information relates to the activity in the short-term investment account of Lido International, which held no short-term investments as of January 1.

1. **January 28**   Purchased ten shares of Able Co. stock at $14 per share.
2. **February 18** Purchased twenty shares of Baker Co. stock at $26 per share.
3. **March 15**   Received dividends from Able Co. of $1 per share.
4. **April 29**   Sold five shares of Able Co. for $15 per share.
5. **May 18**   Received dividends from Baker Co. of $2 per share.
6. **June 1**   Sold five shares of Baker Co. for $22 per share.
7. **June 30**   Market value of Able shares is $17 per share.
                    Market value of Baker shares is $20 per share.

a. Prepare journal entries for each transaction, excluding the June 30 adjusting entry. Use the asset account "Short-Term Investments," and assume that dividends were declared and paid on the same day.
b. Prepare the June 30 adjusting entry, and describe the effect on reported income, assuming that: (1) Able and Baker shares are both considered trading securities, (2) Able is considered a trading security, and Baker is considered an available-for-sale security, (3) Able is considered an available-for-sale security, and Baker is considered a trading security, and (4) both Able and Baker are considered available-for-sale securities.
c. Which combination in (b) depicts management as most successful in the current period? Explain.

E8–4

Activity in the
short-term
investment account
across time periods

On November 11, 2002, Wadsworth Company purchased 20 shares of ZZZ for $8 per share. Wadsworth held the investment for the remainder of 2002, and as of December 31, the per-share market value of ZZZ had risen to $10. During 2003, Wadsworth sold 10 shares of ZZZ for $9 each, and at the end of 2003, the per-share market price of the remaining 10 ten shares was $12. During 2004, the remaining shares of ZZZ were sold for $14 each. Assume that Wadsworth held no other equity investments during this time period.

a.   Complete the following chart. The first column assumes that the investment was classified as trading securities; the second column assumes that the investment was classified as available-for-sale securities.

	Trading	Available-for-Sale
2002 income		
12/31/02 balance sheet investment value		
2003 income		
12/31/03 balance sheet investment value		
2004 income		
Total income ('02 + '03 + '04)		

b.   Comment on the differences.

REAL DATA

E8–5

Available-for-sale
disclosures

Biomet, Inc., provided the following disclosures in Note D of its 1999 annual report. It describes the company's investments in available-for-sale equity securities (dollars in thousands).

		Unrealized	
	Cost	**Gains**	**Losses**
1999	$6,057	$2,998	$(544)
1998	5,101	2,982	(201)

a.   Compute the fair market value of Biomet's available-for-sale equity portfolio for both 1998 and 1999.
b.   What was the effect on the company's comprehensive income amount associated with its available-for-sale securities?
c.   Assume that Biomet sold its entire portfolio of available-for-sale securities at the end of 1999. How much income would be realized on the sale? Provide the journal entry.

E8–6

Reporting
problems with
mark-to-market
accounting
as applied to
available-for-sale
securities

Tom Miller and Larry Rogers each started separate businesses on December 1, 2002, by contributing $6,000 of their own funds. Early in December, both men purchased 120 shares of Diskette common stock, which was selling at the time for $26 per share, and classified the investment as available-for-sale securities. During December, they both also purchased $1,500 of inventory on account.

As of December 30, the market price of Diskette common stock had risen to $32 per share. Tom was delighted by the price increase but chose simply to hold the stock, expecting that the price would continue to appreciate for at least another month. Larry, on the other hand, sold his shares, but immediately repurchased them because he too believed that they would continue to appreciate.

a.   Prepare separate year-end balance sheets for both Tom and Larry.
b.   Compute net income, working capital, and the current ratio for both Tom and Larry.
c.   From the financial statements alone, which of the two appears to be in the better financial position? Why?
d.   Assume that there are brokerage commissions on all security purchases and sales. Which of the two is actually in the better financial position? Why?

E8–7

Classifying and accounting for equity investments

Hartney Consulting Services is involved in the following investments as of December 31, 2002:

1. Owns 40 percent of the common stock issued by Doyle Corporation. Doyle Corporation's stock is actively traded, and Hartney Consulting intends to hold this investment for at least five years.
2. Owns 55 percent of the common stock issued by Jacobs Automotive Parts Manufacturing. This stock is actively traded. Hartney Consulting intends to hold this investment indefinitely.
3. Owns 10 percent of the common stock issued by Markert Computers. Markert Computers is a closely held company with just two other stockholders.
4. Owns 45 percent of the common stock issued by Luther Brewery. Luther Brewery has just recently joined the New York Stock Exchange. Hartney intends to sell this investment to raise cash within the next five years.
5. Owns 15 percent of the common stock of Hartney Farms. The stock is publicly traded, but Hartney intends to hold the investment indefinitely.
6. On November 30, 2003, Hartney Consulting owned 18 percent of Whittenbach Industries. During December, Hartney Consulting purchased an additional 15 percent of the company. This company's stock is actively traded, and Hartney fully intends to hold this stock for four years.

a. Indicate whether each investment should be classified as short-term or long-term on the December 31, 2003 balance sheet. Also indicate the appropriate accounting treatment for each investment. Explain your answer.
b. Explain why the nonmarketable equity securities are disclosed in the long-term investment section of the balance sheet and are not carried at market value.

E8–8

The cost method

Mystic Lakes Food Company began investing in equity securities for the first time in 2002. During 2002, the company engaged in the following transactions involving equity securities. Assume that the stock of Thayers International and Bayhe Enterprises is not considered marketable and that ownership is less than 20 percent of the equity. Prepare journal entries to record these transactions.

1. Purchased 10,000 shares of Thayers International for $26 per share.
2. Purchased 25,000 shares of Bayhe Enterprises for $35 per share.
3. Thayers International declared a $2-per-share dividend to be paid at a later date.
4. Sold 4,500 shares of Bayhe Enterprises for $30 per share.
5. Sold 8,000 shares of Thayers International for $32 per share.

E8–9

Applying the mark-to-market rule

Refer to the data provided in E8–8.

a. Assume that the stock of Thayers International and Bayhe Enterprises is considered marketable, and Mystic Lakes Food Company wishes to hold all investments indefinitely. Prepare journal entries to record the transactions.
b. Assume that on December 31, 2002, the market values of Thayers International and Bayhe Enterprises are $25 and $32, respectively. Prepare the entry to adjust the company's long-term investments to market value.

E8–10

The equity method

On January 1, 2002, Nover Solar Systems purchased 10,000 shares of Reilly Manufacturing for $190,000. The investment represented 25 percent of Reilly's outstanding common stock. Nover intended to hold the investment indefinitely. During 2002, Reilly earned net income of $75,000, and during 2003, Reilly suffered a net loss of $6,000. Reilly paid dividends both years of $1.50 per share.

a. Prepare all relevant journal entries that would be recorded on Nover's books during 2002 and 2003.
b. Compute the book value of Nover's long-term equity investment account as of December 31, 2002, and December 31, 2003.

REAL DATA

E8-11

Inferring
information from
equity method
disclosures

PepsiCo accounts for its investments in bottling operations under the equity method, and as of December 31, 1999, PepsiCo reported equity method investments of $2.8 billion on its balance sheet. Equity income on the income statement totaled $83 million, and PepsiCo received no dividends from its bottling operations during the year.

a.   Assume that PepsiCo owns approximately 40 percent of the outstanding common stock of the affiliates. How much net income did the affiliates report for 1999?

b.   What disclosure would one find in the operating section (direct method) of PepsiCo's statement of cash flows?

E8-12

Inferring
information about
the equity method
from the financial
statements

Mainmont Industries uses the equity method to account for its long-term equity investments. The following information from the financial statements of Mainmont refers to an investment in the securities of Tumbleweed Construction, a company 30 percent owned by Mainmont:

	2002	2001
Long-term investment in equity securities	**$29,000**	**$25,000**
Income from equity securities	**12,000**	**7,000**

Mainmont neither purchased nor sold any equity securities during 2002.

a.   How much net income did Tumbleweed Construction earn during 2002?
b.   What was the dollar amount of the total dividend declared by Tumbleweed Construction during 2002?
c.   Provide the journal entries recorded by Mainmont during 2002 with respect to its investment in Tumbleweed Construction.

E8-13

Recording an
acquisition under
the purchase
method

Multiplex purchased 100 percent of the outstanding common stock of Lipley Company for $900,000. At the time of the acquisition, the fair market values of Lipley's individual assets and liabilities follow:

Cash	**$ 90,000**
Accounts receivable	**60,000**
Inventory	**160,000**
Plant and equipment	**560,000**
Payables	**300,000**

a.   Provide the journal entry recorded by Multiplex at the time of the acquisition.

b.   Assume that the book values of the assets and liabilities on Lipley's balance sheet as of the date of the acquisition were $550,000 and $300,000, respectively. Explain how the book value of Lipley could be less than the net FMV of Lipley's assets and liabilities, which in turn is less than the price Multiplex paid for Lipley's common stock.

E8-14

Appendix 8A: 100
percent purchases
in excess of the net
market value of the
assets and liabilities

The following chart describes six transactions where 100 percent of a subsidiary's voting stock was purchased for cash:

Purchase Price	Book Value	Net FMV in Excess of Book Value	Goodwill
1. ?	$ 7,000	$1,000	$1,000
2. $ 6,000	6,000	?	0
3. 12,000	?	4,000	3,000
4. 15,000	10,000	3,000	?
5. ?	2,000	1,000	3,000
6. 12,000	4,000	8,000	?

Provide the missing values.

E8-15

Appendix 8A:
Per-share book
and market value

The book value of a share of Camden common stock on December 31 is $12. The balance sheet value and the market value of the company's assets and liabilities as of that date follow:

	Balance Sheet Value	Market Value
Cash	$ 15,000	$ 15,000
Receivables	26,000	24,000
Inventories	15,000	25,000
Fixed assets	40,000	47,000
Liabilities	(60,000)	(60,000)
Net book value	$ 36,000	
Net market value		$ 51,000

On December 31, Conglomerate, Inc., purchased 100 percent of the outstanding stock of Camden for $22 per share.

a.   How many shares of common stock did Camden have outstanding as of December 31?
b.   Compute the per-share net market value of Camden's common stock.
c.   Why would Conglomerate pay more than the per-share market value for a share of Camden common stock?
d.   Prepare the entry that reflects the acquisition.

E8-16

Appendix 8A:
Computing goodwill
and minority
interest

Maxwell Industries paid $18 per share for 80 percent of the 10,000 outstanding shares of Kendall Hall. The balance sheet of Kendall Hall and additional market value information follow. Compute the amounts of goodwill and minority interest recognized by Maxwell.

	Historical Cost	FMV
Current assets	$125,000	$150,000
Noncurrent assets	65,000	80,000
Liabilities	70,000	70,000
Stockholders' equity	120,000	—

E8-17

Appendix 8A:
Completing
a consolidated
work sheet

Glover Chemical purchased 100 percent of the outstanding stock of Ward Supply on December 31 for $100,000 cash. As of that date, the FMVs of the inventory and fixed assets of Ward equaled $70,000 and $125,000, respectively. Assume that cash, accounts receivable, and the liabilities are on the books of Ward at FMV. Provide the information to complete the following consolidated work sheet, which already reflects the entry recorded at acquisition.

Accounts	Glover	Ward	Adjustments and Eliminations Dr.	Cr.	Consolidated Balance Sheet
Cash	73,000	10,000			
Accounts receivable	110,000	40,000			
Inventory	220,000	60,000			
Investment in subsidiary	100,000	—			
Fixed assets	615,000	120,000			
Goodwill	30,000	—			
Total assets	1,148,000	230,000			
Accounts payable	80,000	70,000			
Long-term notes	450,000	80,000			
Common stock	500,000	70,000			
Retained earnings	118,000	10,000			
Total liabilities and stockholders' equity	1,148,000	230,000			

PROBLEMS

P8-1

Applying the mark-to-market rule to investments in equity securities

O'Leary Enterprises began investing in short-term equity securities in 2002. The following information was extracted from its 2002 internal financial records. Houser and Miller were classified as trading securities, while Letter and Nordic were classified as available-for-sale securities.

Security	Purchases	Sales	Total Dividends Received	12/31/02 Market Value*
Houser Company	90 shares @ $22	60 shares @ $25	$40	$25
Miller, Inc.	180 shares @ $40	90 shares @ $30	85	35
Letter Books	75 shares @ $48	5 shares @ $55	30	46
Nordic Equipment	170 shares @ $70	145 shares @ $95	50	90

*Per share

REQUIRED:

Compute the effect on reported 2002 income from all investment transactions and price changes.

P8-2

Trading securities: purchases, sales, dividends, and end-of-period adjustments

Anderson Cabinets began operations during 1996. During the initial years of operations, the company invested primarily in fixed assets to promote growth. During 2002, H. Hurst, the company president, decided that the company was sufficiently stable that it could now invest in short-term marketable securities. During 2002, the company entered into the following transactions concerning marketable securities:

1. March 10   Purchased 1,000 shares of Arctic Oil & Gas for $28 per share.
2. March 31   Purchased 800 shares of Humphries Manufacturing for $10 per share.
3. May 26   Received a cash dividend of $1.25 per share from Arctic Oil & Gas.
4. July 10   Purchased 1,000 shares of Kingsman Game Co. for $18 per share.
5. September 11   Sold 800 shares of Arctic Oil & Gas for $35 per share.
6. September 27   Sold 500 shares of Humphries Manufacturing for $8 per share.
7. October 19   Purchased 1,000 shares of Quimby, Inc., for $25 per share.
8. November 6   Received a cash dividend of $1.25 per share from Arctic Oil & Gas.
9. December 8   Sold the remaining shares of Arctic Oil & Gas and Humphries Manufacturing for $30 and $15, respectively.
10. December 31   According to *The Wall Street Journal,* the market values of these securities at the close of business on December 31 follow:

Arctic Oil & Gas	$32
Humphries Manufacturing	14
Kingsman Game Company	15
Quimby, Inc.	26

REQUIRED:

a. Prepare the necessary journal entries for each of these transactions. Assume that any dividends were declared and paid on the same day.
b. Prepare the short-term equity securities section of the balance sheet as of December 31, 2002.
c. Compute the impact of these transactions on the income statement for the year ended December 31, 2002.

P8–3

Changing security
investment
classifications

On October 18, 2002, Daley Inc. purchased 100 shares of Orthon at $32 per share. The investment was classified as available-for-sale securities. The shares were held throughout the remainder of 2002 and 2003, and by December 31, 2002 and 2003, the per-share market price had risen to $40 and $50, respectively. On December 31, 2003, Daley decided to change the classification from available-for-sale to trading securities.

REQUIRED:

a. Provide the journal entries recorded at October 18, 2002; December 31, 2002; and December 31, 2003.
b. Assume that the investment was originally classified as trading securities and then changed to available-for-sale on December 31, 2003. Provide the journal entries recorded at October 18, 2002; December 31, 2002; and December 31, 2003.
c. Compute the 2002 and 2003 income effects under the two assumptions.

P8–4

Window dressing
and the mark-to-
market rule

Levy Company and Guyer Books made the same equity investment—200 shares of Watson Manufacturing at a cost of $12 per share—on November 18. On December 31, the market value of Watson had risen to $45 per share. Guyer Books held its investment in Watson, while Levy sold the shares and immediately repurchased them at the December 31 market value.

REQUIRED:

a. Compute the balance sheet value and income effect associated with these events recorded by the two companies, assuming that the investment was classified as trading and available-for-sale. That is, fill in the following chart with the appropriate dollar values.

	Guyer Books		Levy Co.	
	Balance Sheet Value	Income Effect	Balance Sheet Value	Income Effect
Investment classified as:				
Trading securities				
Available-for-sale				
securities				

b. Discuss the differences.

P8–5

Trading versus
available-for-sale
classifications

Rochester Enterprises purchased 500 shares of Newark Corporation for $15 per share on June 15, 2002, when Newark had approximately 10,000 equity shares outstanding. Rochester held the investment throughout 2002, and as of December 31, the per-share market price had risen to $18. On January 16, 2003, Rochester sold 300 shares for $19 per share, and on October 20 sold the remaining 200 shares for $13 each. The company held no other security investments during this time period.

REQUIRED:

a. Assume that Rochester classified the investment as trading securities, and provide the journal entries recorded on June 15, 2002; December 31, 2002; January 16, 2003; and October 20, 2003.
b. Assume that Rochester classified the investment as available-for-sale securities, and provide the journal entries recorded on June 15, 2002; December 31, 2002; January 16, 2003; and October 20, 2003.
c. Compute the net cash effect of these transactions across 2002 and 2003.
d. Compute the 2002, 2003, and total income effect, assuming that the investment was classified as trading securities.
e. Compute the 2002, 2003, and total income effect, assuming that the investment was classified as available-for-sale securities.
f. Comment on the difference between the two assumptions.

P8-6

Inferring from
balance sheet
disclosures

The following information was taken from the 1999 annual report of Orleans Enterprises:

	2002	2001
Trading securities	**$25,440**	**$27,000**

Related Footnote: The 2002 and 2001 balances in the trading securities account consist of 1,600 and 1,800 equity shares of Atwater Company, respectively. During 2002, in the only transaction related to these securities, 200 shares were sold for $15.50 each.

REQUIRED:

a. Compute the 2002 income effect related to the company's investment in Atwater. Divide the effect into its realized and unrealized components.
b. Repeat (a), assuming that the securities were classified as available-for-sale and that Orleans' first investment in these securities occurred on December 31, 2001.

REAL DATA

P8-7

Inferring
information about
trading and
available-for-sale
investments

Bank of New York carries portfolios of both trading securities and available-for-sale securities. At the end of 1999 and 1998, the trading securities were valued at $8.7 billion and $1.6 billion, respectively; and the available-for-sale securities were valued at $5.9 billion and $4.9 billion, respectively. Together, the investments comprise about 20 percent of the company' total assets as of December 31, 1999. Unrealized gains reported on the 1999 income statement totaled $199 million.

a. Trading securities are carried on the balance sheet at market value. Compute the net increase in the investment in trading securities during 1999.
b. The net increase in the investment in available-for-sale securities reported on the statement of cash flows during 1999 was approximately $800 million. Compute the unrealized net gains on the available-for-sale securities during 1999. On which financial statement would this dollar amount be found?

P8-8

Long-term equity
investments: The
mark-to-market
method versus the
equity method

A summary of the December 31, 2001 balance sheet of Masonite Tires follows:

Assets	$160,000	Liabilities	$ 70,000
		Stockholders' equity	90,000
Total	$160,000	Total	$160,000

On January 1, 2002, Masonite purchased 2,000 (20 percent of the outstanding common shares) shares of Bingo Boots for $40,000 and held the investment throughout 2002 and 2003. During 2002 and 2003, Bingo earned net income of $15,000 and $20,000, respectively. Bingo paid total dividends of $10,000 and $15,000 during 2002 and 2003. The per-share prices of Bingo common stock as of the end of 2002 and 2003 were $18 and $21, respectively. During 2002 and 2003, Masonite generated revenues (excluding revenues related to the investment in Bingo) of $85,000 and $75,000, respectively, and incurred expenses of $50,000 and $70,000, respectively. Assume that all these revenues and expenses involve cash. Masonite pays no dividends.

REQUIRED:

a. Assume that Masonite uses the mark-to-market method and the investment in Bingo was classified as available-for-sale.
    (1) Prepare a balance sheet as of January 1, 2002.
    (2) Prepare a balance sheet as of December 31, 2002, and an income statement for the year ended December 31, 2002.
    (3) Prepare a balance sheet as of December 31, 2003, and an income statement for the year ended December 31, 2003.
b. Assume that Masonite uses the equity method.
    (1) Prepare a balance sheet as of January 1, 2002.
    (2) Prepare a balance sheet as of December 31, 2002, and an income statement for the year ended December 31, 2002.

(Continued)

(3) Prepare a balance sheet as of December 31, 2003, and an income statement for the year ended December 31, 2003.

c. Identify some reasons why the management of Masonite may wish to use the mark-to-market method instead of the equity method. Describe why the equity method might be preferred. Does holding 20 percent of a company's outstanding common stock necessarily mean that the investor company can exert substantial influence over the investee?

P8–9

The equity method versus consolidated financial statements

A summary of the 2002 balance sheet of Alsop, Ltd., follows:

Assets	$180,000	Liabilities	$ 90,000
		Stockholders' equity	90,000
Total	$180,000	Total	$180,000

On January 1, 2002, Alsop acquired 100 percent of the outstanding common stock of Martin Monthly for $62,000 cash. At the time of the acquisition, the fair market values of the assets and liabilities of Martin were $86,000 and $64,000, respectively. During 2002, Martin operated as a subsidiary of Alsop; it recognized $15,000 of net income and paid a $10,000 dividend.

REQUIRED:

a. Account for the acquisition as a purchase. Provide the journal entry to record the acquisition, and prepare Alsop's consolidated balance sheet as of January 1, 2002.

b. Account for the acquisition using the equity method. Provide the journal entry to record the acquisition, and prepare Alsop's balance sheet as of January 1, 2002.

c. Compute the debt/equity ratios produced by the two methods of accounting for this investment. Explain why Alsop's management might wish to use the equity method instead of preparing consolidated financial statements.

P8–10

Inferring information from the financial statements

Excerpts from the financial statements of Macy Limited are provided below. (Numbers are in thousands.)

	2002	2001
BALANCE SHEET		
Assets:		
Short-term investments	$ 290	$160
Investment in affiliate	530	0
Stockholders' equity:		
Unrealized price decrease on short-term investments	(20)	0
INCOME STATEMENT		
Realized gain on short-term investments	$ 80	
Unrealized gain on short-term investments	30	
Income on equity investment	40	
STATEMENT OF CASH FLOWS		
Operating section (The following amounts were subtracted from net income in the calculation of net cash from operating activities.):		
Gains on short-term investments	$(110)	
Equity income in excess of cash received	(30)	
Investing section:		
Investment in affiliate	(500)	
Investment in short-term investments	(280)	
Sale of short-term investments	240	

Footnotes:

Short-term investments. As of December 31, 2001, trading securities were valued at $130, and during 2002, no available-for-sale securities were acquired or sold.

Investment in affiliate. On January 30, 2002, the company purchased 40 percent (50,000 shares) of the outstanding equity of Lehmon Financial Services at $10 per share.

REQUIRED:

Compute the following dollar amounts.

a. The 12/31/02 market value of the short-term equity investments classified as available-for-sale.
b. The balance sheet carrying value of the trading securities sold during 2002.
c. Compute the earnings-per-share dollar amount reported by the affiliate.
d. Compute the per-share dividend declared by the affiliate.

P8–11

Appendix 8A: 100 percent purchase and the recognition of goodwill

The condensed balance sheets as of December 31 for Rice and Associates and Rachel Excavation are provided below.

	RICE	RACHEL
ASSETS		
Cash	$ 196,000	$ 10,000
Accounts receivable	150,000	40,000
Inventory	300,000	40,000
Fixed assets	400,000	130,000
Total assets	$1,046,000	$220,000
LIABILITIES AND STOCKHOLDERS' EQUITY		
Accounts payable	$80,000	$ 20,000
Long-term liabilities	300,000	50,000
Common stock	400,000	90,000
Additional paid-in capital	140,000	10,000
Retained earnings	126,000	50,000
Total liabilities and stockholders' equity	$1,046,000	$220,000

As of December 31, the market values of Rachel's inventories and fixed assets were $70,000 and $120,000, respectively. Liabilities are at FMV on the balance sheet.

On December 31, Rice and Associates purchased Rachel Excavation for $180,000 cash. The preceding balance sheets were prepared immediately prior to the acquisition.

REQUIRED:

a. Prepare the journal entry recorded by Rice to recognize the acquisition.
b. Prepare a consolidated work sheet and a consolidated balance sheet.

P8–12

Appendix 8A: Minority interest and no goodwill

Assume that Rice and Associates in P8–11 purchased 80 percent of the outstanding stock of Rachel for $136,000 cash.

REQUIRED:

a. Prepare the journal entry recorded by Rice to recognize the acquisition.
b. Prepare a consolidated work sheet and a consolidated balance sheet.

P8–13

Appendix 8A: Minority interest and goodwill

Assume that Rice and Associates in P8–11 purchased 80 percent of the 10,000 shares of outstanding stock of Rachel for $140,000 cash.

REQUIRED:

a. Prepare the journal entries recorded by Rice to recognize the acquisition.
b. Prepare a consolidated work sheet and a consolidated balance sheet.

P8-14

Appendix 8A:
Allocating the
excess purchase
price among
tangible assets
and goodwill

Assume the same facts as in P8–11, except that the FMVs for the inventory and fixed assets of Rachel are not as precisely specified. That is, appraisers have indicated that the FMV of the inventory is between $65,000 and $75,000 and that the FMV of the fixed assets is between $115,000 and $125,000. You, as the accountant for Rice and Associates, can use any value within these ranges to record the acquisition.

REQUIRED:

a. Assume that you wish to maximize reported income in the next period. What dollar amounts would you allocate to Rachel's inventory, fixed assets, and goodwill when recording the acquisition? Explain.

b. Assume that you wish to minimize reported income in the next period (e.g., when preparing the transaction for tax purposes). What dollar amounts would you allocate to Rachel's inventory, fixed assets, and goodwill when recording the acquisition? Explain.

P8-15

Appendix 8A:
Minority interest
and goodwill

Groomer purchased a controlling interest in three companies during 2002. Financial information concerning the three companies follows:

	Company X	Company Y	Company Z
Cash	$ 6,000	$ 4,000	$ 2,000
Accounts receivable	12,000	9,000	7,000
Inventory	30,000	12,000	18,000
Fixed assets	70,000	30,000	15,000
Total assets	$118,000	$55,000	$42,000
Current liabilities	$ 7,000	$12,000	$ 5,000
Long-term liabilities	25,000	20,000	18,000
Common stock	50,000	10,000	15,000
Retained earnings	36,000	13,000	4,000
Total liabilities and stockholders' equity	$118,000	$55,000	$42,000
FMV:			
Inventory	$ 45,000	$18,000	$18,000
Fixed assets	75,000	35,000	15,000
Shares of stock outstanding before acquisition	10,000	1,000	2,000

All other assets and liabilities on the balance sheet are at FMV.

Groomer purchased 8,000, 600, and 1,500 shares of Company X, Company Y, and Company Z, respectively. The share prices and cash payments follow.

Company X   8,000 × $10.60 = $84,800
Company Y   600 ×   40.00 =   24,000
Company Z   1,500 ×   11.00 =   16,500

REQUIRED:

For each company, prepare the journal entry to record the acquisition by Groomer. Then, for each company, prepare a journal entry that could have been recorded to include the individual assets and liabilities on the books of Groomer.

P8-16

Appendix 8A:
Consolidated
statements, the
equity method, and
debt covenants

Mammoth Enterprises purchased 50 percent of the outstanding stock of Atom, Inc., on December 31 for $60,000 cash. On that date, the book value of Atom's net assets was $70,000. The market value of Atom's assets was $180,000, $20,000 above book value. Mammoth's condensed balance sheet, immediately before the acquisition, follows:

Assets		Liabilities and Stockholders' Equity	
Current assets	$150,000	Current liabilities	$ 30,000
Noncurrent assets	350,000	Long-term liabilities	200,000
		Common stock	100,000
		Retained earnings	170,000
		Total liabilities and	
Total assets	$500,000	stockholders' equity	$500,000

Mammoth entered into a debt covenant earlier in the year that requires the company to maintain a debt/equity ratio of less than 1:1.

REQUIRED:

a. Compute Mammoth's debt/equity ratio both before and after the acquisition. Consider minority interest a liability.

b. Explain why in this situation Mammoth would probably prefer the equity method instead of treating this transaction as a purchase and preparing consolidated financial statements.

ISSUES FOR DISCUSSION

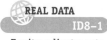

REAL DATA
ID8-1

Equity adjustments
for marketable
securities

H&R Block reported the following account on its statement of stockholders' equity (dollars in thousands):

	1997	1996	1995
Change in net unrealized gain on marketable securities	$157	$934	($5,291)

REQUIRED:

a. Did the market value of H&R Block's marketable securities increase or decrease in 1995, 1996, and 1997?

b. How could H&R Block manage its earnings by choosing when to sell certain of its marketable securities?

c. Explain how the FASB requirement on comprehensive income will influence the reporting practices of H&R Block.

REAL DATA
ID8-2

Available-for-sale
securities

The following footnote appeared in the 1997 annual report of H&R Block:

All marketable securities as of April 30, 1997, are classified as available-for-sale. Proceeds from the sales of available-for-sale securities were $23,852, $155,170, and $299,702 during 1997, 1996, and 1995, respectively. Gross realized gains on those sales during 1997, 1996, and 1995 were $600, $1,520, and $7,014, respectively. Gross realized losses were $146, $386, and $350, respectively. At April 30, 1997 and 1996, the net unrealized holding gain on available-for-sale securities included in stockholders' equity in the consolidated balance sheet was $1,326 and $1,169, respectively.

REQUIRED:

a. Describe the difference between trading securities and available-for-sale securities.

b. Compute the change in reported income assuming H&R Block accounted for the marketable securities as trading securities instead of available-for-sale securities.

c. How is the company's total comprehensive income affected by the dollar values reported in the footnote?

d. Compute the cost of the securities sold during 1995, 1996, and 1997.

REAL DATA
ID8-3
Equity method

The following excerpts were taken from the 2000 annual report of SBC Communications (dollars in millions):

	2000	1999
BALANCE SHEET		
Investment in affiliates	$12,378	$10,648
INCOME STATEMENT		
Equity in net income of affiliates	897	912
FOOTNOTES		
Dividends received from affiliates	5,193	
Total affiliate income	5,714	

REQUIRED:

a. What percentage ownership, on average, does SBC hold in its affiliates? Why might it be appropriate to use the equity method when the equity ownership percentage is less than 20 percent?
b. Explain why equity income is or is not a good measure of the cash SBC received from its equity investments.
c. Did SBC acquire any of its equity investments during 2000? How much?
d. The average liabilities/total asset ratio of SBC's affiliates is 76 percent. Provide one reason why Owens Corning may wish to hold less than 50 percent of the outstanding stock of its affiliates.

REAL DATA
ID8-4
Evaluating the equity method

In 1999, Chevron reported net income of $7.9 billion, $3 billion of which was income recognized on investments in affiliate companies accounted for under the equity method. In that same year, Chevron received much less than that amount in dividends from these affiliates. Some accountants have argued that the net income amount reported by Chevron from the equity method is distorted because the company received much less cash on its investment.

REQUIRED:

a. Comment on this criticism of the equity method. In your answer, explain the accounting procedures that characterize the equity method and why income is recognized that is not always backed up by cash receipts. Also explain why investors and creditors must be careful when analyzing financial statements that reflect the use of the equity method.
b. Chevron uses the indirect method of presenting the statement of cash flows. Indicate the direction of the adjustment to net income associated with earnings and dividends under the equity method that appears in the operating section of the statement.

REAL DATA
ID8-5
Consolidating a finance subsidiary's financial statement: Economic consequences

Prior to Financial Accounting Standard 94 in 1988, wholly owned finance subsidiaries of major U.S. companies were accounted for by the parent using the equity method. These companies justified the procedure by claiming that the operations of the subsidiaries were so unlike those of the parents that consolidating the subsidiaries' financial statements would distort those of the parents. At the same time, by using the equity method the parents were able to avoid including the subsidiaries' liabilities, which were often quite large, on their consolidated balance sheets. It was estimated, for example, that adding the liabilities of General Motors Acceptance Company, a finance subsidiary, to those of General Motors (GM), the parent, would have quadrupled GM's debt/equity ratio.

Forbes commented that if the FASB required such companies to consolidate their finance subsidiaries, it "could cause difficulties with bond indenture agreements and loan covenants requiring that certain ratios be maintained." Others have commented that such problems are of little concern because they can be avoided by writing debt covenants so that all financial ratios are defined in terms of generally accepted accounting principles. Moreover, most financial statement users are reasonably sophisticated and are already aware of the subsidiary's debt. Credit-rating agencies claim, for example, that as long as the debt of the subsidiary is disclosed, it matters little whether it is consolidated or not.

REQUIRED:

a. Briefly explain the difference between using the equity method and preparing consolidated financial statements, and describe how requiring the consolidation of subsidiary financial statements could "cause difficulties with bond indenture agreements."
b. How might the fact that most financial statement users are reasonably sophisticated affect the nature of the accounting standards developed by the FASB?

Mark-to-market accounting and hidden reserves

The *Capital Markets Report* (June 2000) suggests that Japanese banks, which carry large portfolios of short-term equity securities, are dreading the introduction of mark-to-market accounting. In the past, these investments have been carried on the balance sheet at cost or the lower of cost or market; thus, appreciated securities have not been written up to market value. The beauty of such a system, according to Japanese bank managers, is that it allows earnings to be managed by properly timing the sale of these securities because income is recognized only at the time of sale. Thus, a bank that had to absorb a particularly bad loan loss write-off could negate the income effects of that write-off by choosing to sell appreciated marketable securities. Immediately afterward, if the manager still wanted to hold the securities, they could be repurchased. This method of managing earnings disappears in a world of mark-to-market accounting because the income effects associated with appreciated securities is recognized when the price changes.

REQUIRED:

a. In your own words explain how the mark-to-market system of accounting reduces the ability of bank managers to manage earnings.
b. While it seems that bank managers may not favor mark-to-market accounting, do you think that analysts would feel the same way?
c. Consider the methods used to account for available-for-sale securities. Can you think of a way in which managers might be able to manage earnings by properly timing the sale of available-for-sale securities? Explain.

Marketable securities and stock market booms

The stock market boom in 1999 introduced an interesting phenomenon that appeared on corporate income statements. According to *The Wall Street Journal* (January 2000), U.S. mega companies like General Electric, General Motors, and Delta Air Lines, who carry large portfolios of marketable securities, reported huge unrealized gains on their 1999 income statements. Intel, for example, recently booked $327 million from sales of stocks it owns, and Microsoft had $773 million in profits from stock sales. Under mark-to-market accounting, the price appreciation brought on by the mammoth stock market rally went straight to the bottom line for trading securities and for available-for-sale securities, and profits are boosted as the securities are sold.

REQUIRED:

a. As an analyst, would you consider profits due to investment appreciation as significant as profits generated from a company's core operations? Why or why not?
b. The stock market took a major dive, especially in the high-tech sector, during 2000. How was this reflected on the financial statements of banks, who typically hold huge investments in trading securities, and on the financial statements of the nonfinancial companies that hold large portfolios of available-for-sale securities?

REAL DATA
ID8–8

2001 annual report
of Wal-Mart

The 2001 annual report of Wal-Mart is reproduced in Appendix A.

REQUIRED:

Review the 2001 annual report, and answer the following questions.

a. Does Wal-Mart carry investment portfolios in trading and available-for-sale securities?

b. How much goodwill did Wal-Mart report on its 2001 and 2000 balance sheets? From 1999 to 2000, Wal-Mart had a huge jump in goodwill. What does this indicate about Wal-Mart's growth strategy, and where on the statement of cash flow might you be able to find evidence of it?

c. How much did Wal-Mart invest in acquisitions during 2000, and how was this amount allocated?

Long-Lived Assets

KEY POINTS

The following key points are emphasized in this chapter:

○ *How the matching principle underlies the methods used to account for long-lived assets.*

○ *Major questions that are addressed when accounting for long-lived assets and how the financial statements are affected.*

○ *Major economic consequences associated with the methods used to account for long-lived assets.*

○ *Costs that should be included in the capitalized cost of a long-lived asset.*

○ *Accounting treatment of postacquisition expenditures.*

○ *How the cost of a long-lived asset is allocated over its useful life and the alternative allocation methods.*

○ *Disposition of long-lived assets.*

The Dow Jones Business News Service (March 6, 2000) reported that The Pepsi Bottling Group said its depreciation expense this year will be lower, boosting the bottom line, due to successful maintenance allowing changes in asset depreciation. Depreciation lives on manufacturing equipment, for example, are being changed to fifteen from ten years. The company said the change would reduce depreciation expense by about $58 million and increase earnings 22 cents a share in 2000. "The primary reason for this is that our extensive maintenance programs have enabled us to extend the operating lives of our assets well beyond their previous book lives," said company management.

The methods used to account for property, plant, and equipment vary greatly across companies and can have dramatic effects on reported income. These methods are covered in this chapter.

Long-lived assets are used in the operations of a business and provide benefits that extend beyond the current operating period. Included in this category of assets are land, buildings, machinery, equipment, natural resource costs, intangible assets, and deferred costs.

Land includes the cost of real estate used in the operations of the company. **Fixed assets,** such as buildings, machinery, and equipment, are often located on this real estate. **Natural resource costs** include the costs of acquiring the rights to extract natural resources. Such costs are very important in the operations of the extractive industries (e.g., mining, petroleum, and natural gas). **Intangible assets** are characterized by rights, privileges, and benefits of possession rather than physical existence. Examples include the costs of acquiring patents, copyrights, trademarks, and goodwill. **Deferred costs** represent a miscellaneous category of intangible assets, often including prepaid expenses that provide benefits for a length of time that extends beyond the current period, organization costs, and other startup costs associated with beginning operations (e.g., legal and licensing fees). These definitions are often firm specific. Land, for example, represents the inventory of a real estate firm, but it is a long-lived asset for a retailer. Similarly, Boeing carries aircraft in its inventory that when sold becomes a fixed asset on the balance sheet of United Airlines, the purchaser. The methods used to account for land, fixed assets, and natural resource costs (often using an account called Property, Plant, and Equipment) are covered in the main text of this chapter. Intangible assets and deferred costs are discussed in Appendix 9A.

Stockholders, investors, creditors, managers, and auditors are interested in the nature and condition of a company's long-lived assets because such assets represent the company's capacity to produce and sell goods and/or services in the future. Planning and executing major capital expenditures for such items as land, buildings, and machinery are some of management's most important concerns. Long-lived asset turnover (Sales/Average long-lived assets) is a financial ratio used to assess how efficiently a company uses its long-lived assets. In general, if the ratio is high, the company is generating large amounts of sales with a relatively small investment in long-lived assets. As discussed in the next section, this ratio may be particularly useful when comparing the relative performance of manufacturers and service enterprises.

THE RELATIVE SIZE OF LONG-LIVED ASSETS

As Figure 9–1 illustrates, investments in noncurrent assets tend to be large for services, manufacturers, and retailers, and relatively small for Internet firms and financial institutions. Services like SBC Communications must constantly invest in new technology, and restaurant services like Wendy's continually add and update facilities.

FIGURE 9–1		Property, Plant and Equipment + Intangibles/Total Assets
Property, plant, and equipment plus intangibles as a percentage of total assets	**Manufacturing:**	
	General Electric	.15
	Chevron (Oil drilling and refining)	.58
	Retail:	
	SUPERVALU (Grocery retail)	.57
	Tommy Hilfiger (Clothing retail)	.63
	Internet:	
	Yahoo (Internet search engine)	.16
	Cisco (Internet systems)	.16
	General Services:	
	SBC Communications (Telecommunications services)	.49
	Wendy's (Restaurant services)	.78
	Financial Services:	
	Bank of America (Banking services)	.03
	Merrill Lynch (Investment services)	.03

Retailers invest heavily in stores (SUPERVALU and Tommy Hilfiger); while natural resource production (Chevron) relies heavily on property, plant, and equipment. The relative size of the facilities for financial institutions is swamped by investments in securities and loans; the main infrastructure for Internet firms (Yahoo and Cisco) is largely electronic, not "bricks and mortar."

Chevron, Yahoo, and the Bank of New York are three well-known U.S. companies—one a major manufacturer, one an Internet company, and one a financial institution. Rank them in terms of how important fixed asset accounting is to their financial statements. Briefly explain.

LONG-LIVED ASSET ACCOUNTING: GENERAL ISSUES AND FINANCIAL STATEMENT EFFECTS

The matching principle states that efforts (expenses) should be matched against benefits (revenues) in the period when the benefits are recognized. The cost of acquiring a long-lived asset, which is expected to generate revenues in future periods, is, therefore, capitalized in the period of acquisition. As the revenues associated with the long-lived asset are recognized, these costs are **amortized** with a periodic adjusting journal entry. Stated another way, since expenses represent the costs of assets consumed in conducting business, at the end of each accounting period an entry is recorded to reflect the expense associated with the portion of the long-lived asset consumed during that period.

The form of journal entries to capitalize and amortize a piece of equipment follows. Assume that the equipment is purchased on January 1 for $10,000, and its cost is amortized evenly over its four-year useful life. Recall that amortization of a fixed asset is called **depreciation** and that the dollar amount of the Depreciation Expense recognized each year is accumulated in an Accumulated Depreciation account.

Jan. 1	**Equipment (+A)**	**10,000**	
	Cash (−A)		**10,000**
	Acquired equipment.		
Dec. 31	**Depreciation Expense (E, −SE)**	**2,500**	
	Accumulated Depreciation (−A)		**2,500**
	Recognized depreciation during first year.		

The preceding description and journal entries indicate implicitly that three basic questions must be answered when accounting for long-lived assets:

1. What dollar amount should be included in the capitalized cost of the long-lived asset?
2. Over what time period should this cost be amortized?
3. At what rate should this cost be amortized?

As the following illustration shows, the answers to these questions can have significant effects on the financial statements.

Assume that Rudman Manufacturing acquired equipment for a purchase price of $9,000 and paid an additional $3,000 to have it painted. Figure 9–2 compares the journal entries to record the acquisition and the depreciation charge and the resulting balance sheet value of the equipment in four different cases. In Case 1, Rudman capitalizes the entire $12,000 cost and depreciates it evenly ($4,000 per year) over a three-year period. In Case 2, Rudman capitalizes the $9,000 purchase cost, expenses the $3,000 painting charge, and depreciates the purchase cost evenly ($3,000 per year) over a three-year period. In Case 3, Rudman capitalizes the entire $12,000 cost and depreciates it evenly ($6,000 per year) over a two-year period. In Case 4, Rudman capitalizes the entire $12,000 cost and depreciates it over a three-year period using an accelerated rate, i.e., greater depreciation charges are recognized in the early years of the asset's life.

Comparing Case 1 to Case 2 illustrates the financial statement effects of varying the amount of capitalized cost. Note that increasing the amount of capitalized cost (Case 1) reduces the total expense recognized in Year 1, but this increases the depreciation expense recognized during each year of the asset's useful life.

Comparing Case 1 to Case 3 illustrates the financial statement effects of varying the estimated useful life. As the life estimate gets shorter (Case 3), the amount of depreciation expense recognized in each year increases. In the extreme case, estimating the useful life of an asset at one year is equivalent to expensing its cost.

Comparing Case 1 to Case 4 illustrates the financial statement effects of varying the depreciation rate. Using an accelerated rate (Case 4) increases the amount of depreciation expense recognized in the early years, but it gives rise to smaller amounts of depreciation expense in later years.

The differences among the four cases, with respect to the amount of expense recognized and the balance sheet value of the equipment, are summarized in Figure 9–3. Note that the total amount of expense recognized under the four cases is the same ($12,000). Varying the capitalized cost, estimated life, and depreciation rate affects only the timing of the expense recognition throughout the three-year period.

Choosing to capitalize and amortize or expense the costs associated with acquiring long-lived assets can have significant effects on the financial statements. When AOL chose to capitalize, instead of expense, its marketing cost, the company boosted earnings by $130 million. The major railroads, including Burlington Northern, CSX Santa

> FIGURE 9–2   The effects of depreciation period on the financial statements: Rudman Manufacturing

CASE 1: $12,000 cost is capitalized and depreciated evenly over a three-year period.

YEAR 1			YEAR 2			YEAR 3		
Equipment (+A)	12,000							
Cash (−A)		12,000						
Depr. Exp. (E, −SE)	4,000		Depr. Exp. (E, −SE)	4,000		Depr. Exp. (E, −SE)	4,000	
Accum. Depr. (−A)		4,000	Accum. Depr. (−A)		4,000	Accum. Depr. (−A)		4,000
Balance sheet value:*	$8,000		$4,000			$0		

CASE 2: $9,000 cost is capitalized and depreciated evenly over a three-year period.

YEAR 1			YEAR 2			YEAR 3		
Equipment (+A)	9,000							
Cash (−A)		9,000						
Maint. Exp. (E, −SE)	3,000							
Cash (−A)		3,000						
Depr. Exp. (E, −SE)	3,000		Depr. Exp. (E, −SE)	3,000		Depr. Exp. (E, −SE)	3,000	
Accum. Depr. (−A)		3,000	Accum. Depr. (−A)		3,000	Accum. Depr. (−A)		3,000
Balance sheet value:*	$6,000		$3,000			$0		

CASE 3: $12,000 cost is capitalized and depreciated evenly over a two-year period.

YEAR 1			YEAR 2			YEAR 3		
Equipment (+A)	12,000							
Cash (−A)		12,000						
Depr. Exp. (E, −SE)	6,000		Depr. Exp. (E, −SE)	6,000				
Accum. Depr. (−A)		6,000	Accum. Depr. (−A)		6,000			
Balance sheet value:*	$6,000		$0			$0		

CASE 4: $12,000 cost is capitalized and depreciated over a three-year period at an accelerated rate.

YEAR 1			YEAR 2			YEAR 3		
Equipment (+A)	12,000							
Cash (−A)		12,000						
Depr. Exp. (E, −SE)	6,000		Depr. Exp. (E, −SE)	4,000		Depr. Exp. (E, −SE)	2,000	
Accum. Depr. (−A)		6,000	Accum. Depr. (−A)		4,000	Accum. Depr. (−A)		2,000
Balance sheet value:*	$6,000		$2,000			$0		

*Balance sheet value, also known as book value, equals capitalized cost less accumulated depreciation.

Fe, Norfolk & Western, and Union Pacific, increased profits by an average of 25 percent when they chose to capitalize and amortize, instead of expense, the costs of laying track. The net income of Comserv, a Minneapolis-based maker of software systems, was boosted by $6.5 million because the company chose to capitalize and amortize, instead of expense, software development costs. Changing the useful-life estimate or adjusting the rate at which a long-lived asset is amortized can also significantly affect the financial statements and important financial ratios. The Pepsi Bottling Group

FIGURE 9–3

Comparative
expense amounts
and balance
sheet values

	Year 1	Year 2	Year 3	Total
CASE 1				
Expense	$4,000	$4,000	$4,000	$12,000
Balance sheet value	8,000	4,000	0	
CASE 2				
Expense	6,000	3,000	3,000	12,000
Balance sheet value	6,000	3,000	0	
CASE 3				
Expense	6,000	6,000	0	12,000
Balance sheet value	6,000	0	0	
CASE 4				
Expense	6,000	4,000	2,000	12,000
Balance sheet value	6,000	2,000	0	

decreased expenses by $58 million and increased earnings per share by 22 cents when it decided to depreciate the cost of its manufacturing equipment over a longer period of time. Blockbuster Video slowed the amortization period for its tapes from 9 to 36 months, a choice that added 20 percent to its reported income. Burlington Northern once disclosed that the company's net income was reduced by $336 million when it increased the rate at which it depreciated its railroad assets.

American Airlines once chose to extend the depreciation lives of its aircraft to conform more closely with practices in the airline industry. How did this choice affect American's reported income that year? Briefly explain.

AN OVERVIEW OF LONG-LIVED ASSET ACCOUNTING

Figure 9–4 summarizes and organizes the topics covered in the remainder of the chapter. As shown at the top of the figure, there are three points in time during the life of a long-lived asset when important accounting issues must be addressed: (1) when the long-lived asset is acquired (purchased or manufactured), (2) while the long-lived asset is in use, and (3) when the long-lived asset is disposed of.

ACQUISITION: WHAT COSTS TO CAPITALIZE?

The acquisition cost of a long-lived asset is determined by either (1) the fair market value (FMV) of the acquired asset or (2) the FMV of what was given up to acquire the asset, whichever is more readily determinable. In almost all cases, the FMV of what was given up is used because cash, which by definition is at FMV, is normally given up in such exchanges. Further, the capitalized cost (i.e., the FMV of what was given up) should include all costs required to bring the asset into serviceable or usable con-

FIGURE 9-4 Accounting for long-lived assets

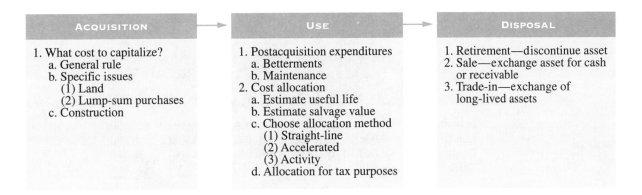

dition and location.[1] Such costs include not only the actual purchase cost of the asset but also costs like freight, installation, taxes, and title fees. For example, suppose that the purchase cost of a piece of equipment is $25,000, and it costs $2,000 to have it delivered, $1,500 to have it installed, and taxes and title fees total $500 and $300, respectively. The total capitalized cost of the equipment would then be $29,300 ($25,000 + $2,000 + $1,500 + $500 + $300), and the following journal entry would be entered to record the acquisition, assuming that cash is paid for the equipment.

Equipment (+A)	**29,300**	
Cash (−A)		**29,300**
Acquired equipment.		

The Acquisition of Land

All costs incurred to acquire land and make it ready for use should be included in the land account. They include (1) the purchase price of the land; (2) closing costs, such as title, legal, and recording fees; (3) costs incurred to get the land in condition for its intended use, such as razing old buildings, grading, filling, draining, and clearing (less any proceeds from the sale of salvaged materials); (4) assumptions of any back taxes, liens, or mortgages; and (5) additional land improvements assumed to be permanent, such as landscaping, street lights, sewers, and drainage systems. While the costs incurred to acquire land and prepare it for use are capitalized, *they are not amortized* over future periods. The process of amortization requires the estimate of a useful life. Because land is considered to have an indefinite life, its cost cannot be amortized.

Lump-Sum Purchases

A special problem arises when more than one asset is purchased at a single (lump-sum) price. In such situations, the total purchase cost must be allocated to the individual assets. If the FMVs of the purchased assets can be objectively determined, the total purchase cost can be allocated to each asset on the basis of its relative FMV. This cost allocation scheme is based on the assumption that costs vary in direct proportion to FMV.

---

1. Some costs (e.g., storage costs incurred waiting to put an asset into service) are not required to bring the asset into usable condition and therefore should be expensed.

To illustrate, assume that ABC Incorporated purchases three assets (inventory, land, and equipment) from Liquidated Limited, a company that is in the process of liquidation. The total price for the assets is $40,000. The individual FMVs of the three assets and the allocation of the $40,000 purchase cost to each asset appear in Figure 9–5.

FIGURE 9–5
Cost allocation on
the basis of
relative FMVs

	FMVs	Allocation Formula	Allocated Cost
Inventory	$20,000	[($20,000 ÷ $50,000) × $40,000]	$16,000
Land	10,000	[($10,000 ÷ $50,000) × $40,000]	8,000
Equipment	20,000	[($20,000 ÷ $50,000) × $40,000]	16,000
Total	$50,000		$40,000

Note that the cost allocated to each asset is in direct proportion to the asset's portion of the total FMV. The inventory, for example, accounts for 40 percent ($20,000/$50,000) of the total FMV and thereby receives 40 percent ($16,000/$40,000) of the total costs. The equipment is treated similarly. Land accounts for 20 percent ($10,000/$50,000) of the total FMV and receives 20 percent ($8,000/$40,000) of the total cost.

Two features about this cost allocation approach are very important. First, it is based on FMVs, which by nature are very subjective and therefore are often expressed in terms of ranges rather than precise estimates. Second, while all three costs in this example are capitalized, each is treated differently in the future. The $16,000 inventory cost will be converted to cost of goods sold when the inventory is sold, the $8,000 land cost is not subject to amortization, and the $16,000 equipment cost will be depreciated over the equipment's useful life. Taken together, these two features indicate that the subjective choice of FMVs can have significant effects on future net income amounts, a fact that management may be able to exploit. For example, if management wishes to maximize income, it can choose from within the FMV ranges values that allocate as much cost as possible to land, which will not be amortized, and as little as possible to inventory, which will be converted to cost of goods sold relatively soon. On the other hand, management can minimize income (e.g., income tax reporting, building hidden reserves, or taking a bath) by allocating as much cost as possible to inventory and as little as possible to land.

To illustrate, assume in the previous example that the FMV of equipment was assessed at $20,000, but the FMVs of inventory and land were expressed as being somewhere within the following ranges: inventory ($15,000–$25,000), land ($5,000–$15,000). Figure 9–6 compares the resulting costs under two allocation schemes: (1) "Maximize future income" where the lowest value for inventory ($15,000) and the highest value for land ($15,000) are used, and (2) "Minimize future income" where the highest value for inventory ($25,000) and the lowest value for land ($5,000) are used.

The procedure of allocating costs on the basis of FMVs is also used when a company acquires the assets and liabilities of another company (i.e., through the purchase of outstanding stock) and must allocate the purchase price to those assets and liabilities (see Chapter 8 and Appendix 8A). As illustrated in Figure 9–6, such allocations can be very subjective, giving management much reporting discretion in this area.

FIGURE 9-6
Comparing cost
allocation
methods

(1) Maximize Future Income:

	FMVs	Allocation Formula	Allocated Cost
Inventory	$15,000	[($15,000 ÷ $50,000) × $40,000]	$12,000
Land	15,000	[($15,000 ÷ $50,000) × $40,000]	12,000
Equipment	20,000	[($20,000 ÷ $50,000) × $40,000]	16,000
Total	$50,000		$40,000

(2) Minimize Future Income:

	FMVs	Allocation Formula	Allocated Cost
Inventory	$25,000	[($25,000 ÷ $50,000) × $40,000]	$20,000
Land	5,000	[($ 5,000 ÷ $50,000) × $40,000]	4,000
Equipment	20,000	[($20,000 ÷ $50,000) × $40,000]	16,000
Total	$50,000		$40,000

When Kellogg purchased the outstanding stock of Worthington Foods for $350 million, the purchase price was allocated to current and noncurrent assets ($218 million), liabilities ($62 million), and goodwill ($194 million). On what basis were these allocations made, and what kind of judgments were necessary to make them?

Construction of Long-Lived Assets

When companies construct their own long-lived assets, all costs required to get the assets into operating condition must be included in the long-lived asset account, including the costs of materials, labor, and overhead used in the construction process. The costs may also include interest on funds borrowed to finance the construction. Note the following excerpt from the 2000 annual report of Federal Express:

Interest on funds used to finance the acquisition and modification of aircraft and construction of certain facilities up to the date the asset is placed into service is capitalized and included in the cost of the asset.

Although determining the costs of materials and labor is relatively straightforward, allocating overhead and interest to the cost of long-lived assets can be difficult and is often arbitrary. Such issues are normally covered in management or intermediate financial accounting courses.

POSTACQUISITION EXPENDITURES: BETTERMENTS OR MAINTENANCE?

Costs are often incurred subsequent to the acquisition or manufacture of a long-lived asset. Such **postacquisition expenditures** serve either to improve the existing asset or merely to maintain it. Costs incurred to improve the asset are called **betterments,** and costs incurred merely to repair it or maintain its current level of productivity are classified as **maintenance.**

The following guidelines are used to distinguish betterments from maintenance expenditures. In order to be considered a betterment, a postacquisition expenditure must improve the long-lived asset in at least one of four ways:

1. Increase the asset's useful life over that which was originally estimated.
2. Improve the quality of the asset's output.
3. Increase the quantity of the asset's output.
4. Reduce the costs associated with operating the asset.

Betterments are usually infrequent and tend to involve large dollar amounts. Maintenance expenditures, on the other hand, fail to meet any of the criteria mentioned above and tend to be periodic. Also, maintenance items are normally small, but certain expenditures (e.g., replacing a building roof every ten years) can be significant.

Postacquisition expenditures classified as betterments should be capitalized, added to the cost of the long-lived asset, and then amortized over its remaining life. Expenditures classified as maintenance should be treated as current expenses. For example, note the following excerpt from the 2000 annual report of Adolph Coors Company:

Expenditures for new facilities and improvements that substantially extend the capacity or useful life of an asset are capitalized. . . . Ordinary repairs and maintenance are expensed as incurred.

Distinguishing between a betterment and a maintenance expenditure, even with the criteria mentioned above, is often difficult in practice, giving management reporting discretion in this area. In many cases, however, materiality plays an important role because postacquisition expenditures are frequently small, and in such situations they are expensed, regardless of their nature.

To illustrate the accounting treatment for betterments and maintenance expenditures, assume that Jerry's Delivery Service purchased an automobile on January 1, 2002, for $10,000. The purchase cost was capitalized, and the useful life of the automobile was estimated to be four years from the date of purchase. Each year, Jerry had the car tuned up and serviced at a cost of $300. During the second year, the muffler was replaced for $80, and during the third year, the car was painted at a cost of $450. At the beginning of the fourth year, Jerry paid $1,000 to have the engine completely overhauled. The overhaul increased the automobile's expected life beyond the original estimate by an additional year. Figure 9–7 traces the book value, depreciation, and maintenance expenses associated with the automobile over its five-year life.

Note that all postacquisition costs are treated as expenses except for the overhaul, which increased the automobile's life beyond the original four-year estimate. The $1,000 cost of the overhaul was capitalized at the beginning of the fourth year and, with the book value ($2,500) at that time, was depreciated evenly over the remaining two years of the car's useful life.

The 2000 annual report of Exxon Mobil states, "Repairs are expensed as incurred. Major renewals and improvements are capitalized." Which of these costs are considered betterments? Which are considered maintenance? Explain.

FIGURE 9–7

Betterments and
maintenance
expenditures:
Jerry's Delivery
Service

	2002	2003	2004	2005	2006
Book value (1/1)	$10,000	$7,500	$5,000	$2,500	$1,750
Overhaul				1,000	
Less: Depreciation	2,500[b]	2,500	2,500	1,750[c]	1,750
Book value[a] (12/31)	$ 7,500	$5,000	$2,500	$1,750	$ 0
Maintenance expenses:					
Tune-up	300	300	300	300	300
Muffler replacement		80			
Paint job			450		

[a]*Book value equals cost less accumulated depreciation.*
[b]2,500 = ($10,000 ÷ 4 years)
[c]1,750 = ($2,500 + $1,000) ÷ 2 years

COST ALLOCATION: AMORTIZING CAPITALIZED COSTS

Once the cost of a long-lived asset has been determined, it must be allocated over the asset's useful life. Such allocation is necessary if the costs are to be matched against the benefits produced by the asset. The allocation process requires three steps: (1) estimate a useful life, (2) estimate a salvage value, and (3) choose a cost allocation (depreciation) method.

Estimating the Useful Life and Salvage Value

Accurately estimating the useful life and salvage value of a long-lived asset is extremely difficult. An important consideration is the **physical obsolescence** of the asset. At what time in the future will the asset deteriorate to the point when repairs are not economically feasible, and what will be the asset's salvage value at that time? It is virtually impossible to predict accurately the condition of an asset very far into the future, let alone predict the **salvage value,** the dollar amount that can be recovered when the asset is sold, traded, or scrapped.

The problem of predicting useful lives and salvage values is complicated further by technological developments. The usefulness of a long-lived asset is largely determined by technological advancements, which could at any time render certain long-lived assets obsolete. **Technical obsolescence,** in turn, could force the early replacement of a long-lived asset that is still in reasonably good working order.

As a result, generally accepted accounting principles provide no clear guidelines for determining the useful lives and future salvage values of long-lived assets. In practice, many companies assume salvage value to be zero and estimate useful lives by referring to guidelines developed by the Internal Revenue Service. These guidelines, however, were established for use in determining taxable income and need not be followed in the preparation of the financial statements. Consequently, management can use its own discretion when estimating salvage values and useful lives. As long as the estimates seem reasonable and are applied in a systematic and consistent manner, auditors generally allow managers to do what they wish in this area. Sears, Roebuck

& Co., for example, depreciates its equipment generally over a five- to ten-year period and its real property over a forty- to fifty-year period. Figure 9–8 shows the range of estimated useful lives for different kinds of fixed assets reported by 600 major U.S. companies.

Buildings and improvements	10–50 years
Machinery and equipment	3–20 years
Furniture and fixtures	5–12 years
Automotive equipment	3–6 years

Source: Accounting Trends and Techniques (New York: American Institute of Certified Public Accountants, 1997).

These broad ranges can complicate the decisions of individuals who use financial statements to compare performance across companies. This problem is particularly evident in the airline industry, where the estimated lives used to depreciate aircraft often differ across companies. Delta Air Lines depreciates its planes over twenty years; other airlines, like Texas Air, estimate a life of twenty-five years for the same 727s that Delta writes off in twenty.

In *The New York Times* (May 14, 2000), Robert Olstein, a veteran accounting expert, noted, "Beware of companies that overestimate how much their fixed assets will be worth down the road. Optimistic assumptions allow a company to reduce the amount of depreciation it reports." Explain what he means. Who is he warning and why?

Revising the Useful-Life Estimate

Estimating the useful life of a long-lived asset when it is acquired is a very subjective process. After using such assets for several years, companies often find that their original estimates were inaccurate. For example, Delta Air Lines increased the estimated useful life of its aircraft. In these situations, the portion of the long-lived asset's depreciation base (cost − salvage value) that has not yet been depreciated is depreciated over the remainder of the revised useful life.

To illustrate, suppose that on January 1, 1997, ABC Airlines purchased aircraft for $110,000 and estimated the useful life of the aircraft and the salvage value to be ten years and $10,000, respectively. If the company depreciated equal portions ($10,000) of the amount subject to depreciation ($100,000) each year, it would have recognized $50,000 of accumulated depreciation by the end of 1998, and the aircraft would be reported on the 1998 balance sheet in the following manner:

| Aircraft | $110,000 | |
| Less: Accumulated depreciation | 50,000 | 60,000 |

Assume that as of January 1, 2002, the company believes that the aircraft will actually be in service through 2012, ten years beyond the present time, and fifteen years from the date of acquisition (1997). In other words, the company changed its original useful-life estimate from ten to fifteen years. At that point, ABC would not make a correcting journal entry to restate the financial statements of the previous periods. Instead, it would simply depreciate the remaining depreciation base ($60,000 [book value] − $10,000 [salvage value]) over the remaining life of the aircraft (ten years). The following journal entry would be recorded in the company's books at the end of 2002 and at the end of each year until and including December 31, 2011.

Dec. 31	Depreciation Expense (E, −SE)	5,000	
	Accumulated Depreciation (−A)		5,000
	Recognized depreciation on aircraft ($50,000/10 yr.).		

Depreciating the book value of the asset over the remaining useful life, as of the date of the estimate revision, is known as treating the revision *prospectively.* That is, no "catch-up" adjusting entry is recorded to restate the books. Estimate revisions are not considered errors, and therefore, the financial statements as of the time of the revision are not in need of correction. Instead, the new information that led to the revision affects only the manner in which the aircraft is accounted for in the future. However, if the revision gives rise to a reported net income amount that is materially different from what would have been reported without the revision, the company is required to describe the revision in the footnotes. The excerpt below was taken from the annual report of Delta Air Lines.

. . . the Company increased the estimated useful lives of substantially all of its flight equipment. . . . The effect of this change was a decrease of approximately $130 million in depreciation expense and a $69 million [after income taxes] increase in net income for the year ended. . . .

Cost Allocation (Depreciation) Methods

The useful-life estimate determines the period of time over which a long-lived asset is to be amortized. The salvage value estimate in conjunction with the capitalized cost determines the **depreciation base**[2] (capitalized cost − salvage value): the dollar amount of cost that is amortized over the asset's useful life. The cost allocation methods discussed in this section determine the rate of amortization or, in other words, the amount of cost that is to be converted to an expense during each period of a long-lived asset's useful life. Three basic allocation (depreciation) methods are allowed under generally accepted accounting principles: (1) straight-line, (2) accelerated, and (3) activity.

THE STRAIGHT-LINE METHOD OF AMORTIZATION (DEPRECIATION)

The discussion and most of the examples so far have assumed that equal dollar amounts of a long-lived asset's cost are amortized during each period of its useful life. This assumption, which is referred to as the **straight-line method,** is used by most companies to depreciate their fixed assets and by almost all companies to amortize their intangible assets.[3] The straight-line method can be chosen for several reasons: (1) management believes that the asset provides equal benefits across each year of its estimated useful life, (2) in comparison to the other methods, it is simple to apply, and (3) it tends to produce higher net income numbers and higher long-lived asset book values in the early years of a long-lived asset's life. The following example illustrates the straight-line method.[4]

---

2. *Depletion base* and *amortization base* are the terms used for natural resource costs and intangibles, respectively.

3. *Accounting Trends and Techniques* (New York: AICPA, 1997) reports that, of the 600 U.S. companies surveyed, 575 (96 percent) used the straight-line method to depreciate at least some of their fixed assets. The straight-line method is used predominantly to depreciate buildings.

4. The information from this example is also used in the illustrations of the accelerated methods that follow.

Assume that Midland Plastics purchased a van wagon for $15,000 on January 1, 1999. The life and salvage value of the wagon are estimated to be five years and $3,000, respectively. Under the straight-line method, the annual depreciation expense would be calculated as shown in Figure 9–9, which also includes the related adjusting journal entry.

FIGURE 9–9

The straight-line method: Midland Plastics

FORMULA

Straight-line depreciation = (Cost   − Salvage value)* ÷ Estimated life
$2,400 per year   = ($15,000 − $3,000)   ÷ 5 years

JOURNAL ENTRY

Depreciation Expense (E, −SE)   2,400
    Accumulated Depreciation (−A)   2,400
Recognized annual depreciation.

Depreciation base

Under the straight-line method, the same dollar amount of depreciation is recognized in each year of the asset's useful life. At $2,400 per year for five years, the total amount of depreciation taken would be $12,000, the depreciation base. At the end of the wagon's estimated life, its book value ($15,000 − $12,000) is equal to its estimated salvage value ($3,000).

DOUBLE-DECLINING-BALANCE METHOD

The next method discussed is the double-declining-balance method, an *accelerated method of amortization.* It is called an **accelerated method** because greater amounts of the capitalized cost are allocated to the earlier periods of the asset's life than to the later periods. Accelerated methods are used by some companies to depreciate fixed assets when preparing financial reports. Apple Computer, Inc., and Liz Claiborne, Inc., for example, use double-declining-balance as their primary depreciation method.[5]

To illustrate the **double-declining-balance method,** assume once again the facts of the preceding example. Figure 9–10 shows the general formula and calculations for each year.

Under the double-declining-balance method, each year's depreciation is computed by multiplying 2 by the book value of the asset (cost − accumulated depreciation) and dividing the result by N, the estimated useful life.[6] Note that salvage value is not part of the general formula. However, the book value of the asset cannot be reduced below the asset's estimated salvage value. In 2002, for example, only the amount of depreciation ($240) necessary to bring the asset's book value ($15,000 − $11,760) to its estimated salvage value ($3,000) was recognized. For this same reason, no depreciation expense was recognized in 2003.

5. Another accelerated method used by a few companies (e.g., General Electric) is called sum-of-the-years'-digits. Compared to double-declining-balance, it is a less extreme form of accelerated depreciation.
6. The formula for the double-declining-balance method can also be expressed as ([Cost − Accumulated depreciation] × [2 × the straight-line rate]). The straight-line rate is equal to the percentage of the depreciation base charged each year under the straight-line method (1/N). Using the numbers in the example above, this formula appears as follows: ($15,000 − Accumulated depreciation) × 40 percent.

FORMULA

Double-Declining-Balance Depreciation = (2 × Book Value) ÷ N
where   Book value = cost − accumulated depreciation
        N = the estimated useful life

CALCULATIONS

1999:	(2 × $15,000) ÷ 5 =	$ 6,000
	Accumulated depreciation = $6,000	
2000:	[2 × ($15,000 − $6,000)] ÷ 5 =	3,600
	Accumulated depreciation = $9,600 ($6,000 + $3,600)	
2001:	[2 × ($15,000 − $9,600)] ÷ 5 =	2,160
	Accumulated depreciation = $11,760 ($9,600 + $2,160)	
2002:	Reduce book value ($15,000 − $11,760) to salvage value ($3,000)	240
	Accumulated depreciation = $12,000 ($11,760 + $240)	
2003:	No depreciation recognized because book value cannot be	
	reduced below salvage value	0
	Total depreciation expense recognized	**$12,000**

STRAIGHT-LINE AND DOUBLE-DECLINING-BALANCE: A COMPARISON

This section compares the financial statement effects of the two cost-allocation methods discussed above. The general formulas, the depreciation expenses, and the related book values for each year of the estimated useful life under each of the two methods appear in Figure 9–11. This comparison uses the same information given in the previous examples.

The straight-line method results in the same amount of depreciation ($2,400) in each of the five years. The accelerated method shows greater amounts of depreciation in the early periods of the asset's life (1999 and 2000) and lesser amounts of depreciation in the later periods (2002 and 2003). Both methods recognize total depreciation

	Straight-Line			Double-Declining-Balance		
	SL = (C − SV) ÷ N			$\dfrac{2 \times BV}{N}$		
	EXPENSE	BOOK VALUE		EXPENSE	BOOK VALUE	
1999	2,400	15,000		6,000	15,000	
		− 2,400	12,600		− 6,000	9,000
2000	2,400	15,000		3,600	15,000	
		− 4,800	10,200		− 9,600	5,400
2001	2,400	15,000		2,160	15,000	
		− 7,200	7,800		−11,760	3,240
2002	2,400	15,000		240	15,000	
		− 9,600	5,400		−12,000	3,000
2003	2,400	15,000		0	15,000	
		−12,000	3,000		−12,000	3,000

of $12,000 over the five-year period and thus depreciate the long-lived asset only to its salvage value ($3,000).

Choosing between the two methods can have a significant effect on the timing of reported income. Assume that Midland Plastics, which purchased the wagon in the preceding examples, has revenues of $12,000 and expenses other than depreciation of $5,000 in each of the five years, 1999–2003. Figure 9–12 contains the income numbers for each of the two methods for each of the five years.

FIGURE 9–12

The comparative effects on net income of different depreciation methods

Methods	1999	2000	2001	2002	2003	Total
Straight-line	**$4,600**	**$4,600**	**$4,600**	**$4,600**	**$4,600**	**$23,000**
Double-declining-balance	**1,000**	**3,400**	**4,840**	**6,760**	**7,000**	**23,000**

Note: **The net income numbers were determined in the following manner:**

Net income = $12,000 (revenues) − $5,000 (other expenses) − depreciation expense
Straight-line method for all five years: $4,600 = $12,000 − $5,000 − $2,400

Note first that the total income recognized across the five-year periods is the same ($23,000) under each method because each method recognizes $12,000 ($15,000 − $3,000) of depreciation expense over the life of the asset. However, the amount of depreciation recognized in each period differs, giving rise to different income patterns over the life of the asset. The graph in Figure 9–13 compares these income patterns.

Note that compared to double-declining-balance, net income under the straight-line method is higher in the early periods and lower in the later periods of the asset's

FIGURE 9–13

Effects of depreciation methods on net income

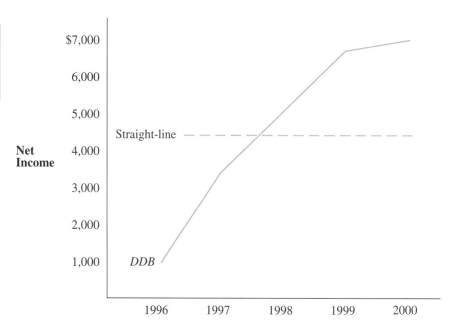

Note: DDB = Double-declining-balance.

estimated useful life. In the early periods, the double-declining-balance method produces low levels of net income that increase rapidly over the life of the asset.

Three major competitors in the aerospace industry include Boeing, Lockheed Martin, and Tristar. To depreciate its fixed assets Boeing uses primarily accelerated methods, Lockheed Martin uses accelerated for the first half of the assets' lives followed by straight-line, and Tristar uses straight-line. Discuss difficulties that are encountered by analysts who attempt to assess the relative performance of these three companies.

THE ACTIVITY (UNITS-OF-PRODUCTION) METHOD AND NATURAL RESOURCE DEPLETION

The **activity method**[7] allocates the cost of a long-lived asset to future periods on the basis of its activity. This method is used primarily in the mining, oil, and gas industries to **deplete** the costs associated with acquiring the rights to and extracting natural resources. The following excerpt, for example, was taken from the annual report of Pennzoil, a large oil and gas mining operation.

Provision for depreciation, depletion, and amortization is determined on a field-by-field basis using the units-of-production method.

The estimated life under the activity method is expressed in terms of units of activity (e.g., miles driven, units produced, barrels extracted) instead of years, as is done under the previous methods. In periods when an asset is very active (e.g., production is high), a relatively large amount of the cost is amortized. In periods when the asset is less active, relatively fewer costs are amortized.

To illustrate, assume that a company purchases mining properties for $1 million in cash. It estimates that the properties will yield 500,000 saleable tons of ore, and the company mines 10,000 tons during the first year of production. The computation of the depletion rate and the journal entries that would be made to record this series of events appear in Figure 9–14.

FIGURE 9–14 Depletion rate and related journal entries	

DEPLETION RATE

$1,000,000 ÷ 500,000 estimated tons = $2 per ton

JOURNAL ENTRIES

Mineral Deposits (+A)	1,000,000	
Cash (−A)		1,000,000
Acquired right to extract ore.		
Depletion Expense (E, −SE)	20,000	
Mineral Deposits (or Accumulated Depletion) (−A)		20,000
Recognized depletion for first year		
(10,000 tons × $2 per ton).		

---

7. Referred to as the *units-of-production method* in *Accounting Trends and Techniques* (New York: AICPA, 2000), p. 362.

Exxon Mobil is a multibillion-dollar U.S. oil company. It carries large investments in both oil reserves and property, plant, and equipment. In its annual report, the company reports that it uses both the activity method (units-of-production) and the straight-line method. Which method is used for which kind of asset, and why?

Cost Allocation Methods and the Matching Principle

Recall that the matching principle states that efforts (expenses) should be matched against the benefits (revenues) they produce. In terms of this principle, the straight-line method assumes that the revenues generated by the depreciated asset are constant across the asset's life; the accelerated method assumes that such revenues are high in early periods and low in later periods; and the activity method assumes that revenues are generated in proportion to the asset's activity. While each of these methods may represent the best application of the matching principle for certain assets, the activity method is probably the most consistent overall. Presumably, the more active an asset is, the more benefits it should produce. The extent to which a given amortization method is consistent with the matching principle is an important factor that should be considered by management when choosing an allocation method. Such consistency helps to improve the quality and usefulness of the reported financial numbers. However, other economic factors, discussed in the next section, are also considered when making such decisions.

AT&T uses accelerated methods to depreciate the digital equipment used in its telecommunications network, while it uses straight-line depreciation for all other plant and equipment. Why would AT&T use different depreciation methods for these two kinds of assets?

How Does Management Choose an Acceptable Cost Allocation Method?

Management may choose a given cost allocation method for a variety of economic reasons. Perhaps the most obvious is that the method has a significant and desired effect on important financial ratios, such as earnings per share, that are used by stockholders, investors, and creditors to evaluate management performance. When RTE Corporation, an electrical equipment manufacturer, more than doubled earnings per share by changing its depreciation method, its controller justified the action by stating: "We realize that compared to our competitors, our (past) conservative (accelerated) method of depreciation may have hurt us with investors because of its negative impact on net earnings." In a similar context, Inland Steel's controller commented, "Why should we put ourselves at a disadvantage by depreciating more conservatively (i.e., accelerated methods) than other steel companies do?"[8]

Note, however, that changing accounting methods, such as switching the depreciation method, to inflate net income in an effort to positively influence the assessments of investors and creditors may not be an effective strategy. When IBM shifted from the accelerated to the straight-line method, it increased reported earnings by $375 million. Did its share value increase? Some evidence suggests that stock market prices do not

8. Jill Andresky, "Double Standard," *Forbes*, November 22, 1982, p. 178.

react positively to such changes, and many accountants question whether credit-rating services, like Dun & Bradstreet, adjust their ratings. In fact, knowledgeable stockholders, investors, and creditors may interpret a change to a less conservative depreciation method (e.g., from accelerated to straight-line) as a negative signal, indicating that management may be attempting to hide poor performance that it anticipates in the future. It is also true that the use of accelerated methods can lead to the creation of "hidden reserves," giving management greater ability to manage reported financial numbers in the future.

Management may also consider compensation contracts based on net income and debt covenants when choosing a depreciation method. Compared to accelerated methods, straight-line, for example, would tend to produce greater amounts of net-income-based compensation in the early periods of an asset's useful life. Similarly, the depreciation method chosen may affect whether a company violates a debt covenant.

Delta Air Lines operates under a debt covenant where future borrowing may be restricted subject to the performance of the company. Explain how the choice of a depreciation method could determine whether this covenant is violated.

Depreciation Methods for Income Tax Purposes

Management is not required to choose the same depreciation method for income tax purposes that it uses for financial reporting. Indeed, many companies cannot use for financial reporting purposes the depreciation methods that they are allowed to use for tax purposes. Most companies, such as Sundstrand Corporation (aerospace) and Merck & Company, Inc. (pharmaceuticals), use the straight-line method for financial reporting and an accelerated method for tax purposes. *Forbes* reports:

Like most businesses, Anheuser-Busch keeps two sets of books, one for tax purposes and one for its owners. [The company] uses accelerated depreciation for taxes but straight-line for reporting to investors.

Using accelerated depreciation for tax purposes gives rise to significant tax savings for these companies. In a single year, for example, Anheuser-Busch normally saves millions of dollars in taxes by using accelerated depreciation instead of straight-line for tax purposes.

We have shown that estimating useful lives and salvage values in addition to choosing among alternative depreciation methods gives management considerable flexibility in reporting the amount of depreciation on the financial statements. However, the current rules specified in the **Internal Revenue Code,** which cover depreciation for tax purposes, are much less flexible.

According to tax law, a fixed asset is placed into one of eight categories, and each category is assigned a minimum allowable useful life and a depreciation method, as indicated in Figure 9–15.

Automobiles, for example, are placed in Category 2, which allows them to be depreciated over a five-year life, using the double-declining-balance method. Equipment and machinery are normally included in Categories 1, 2, 3, or 4 and therefore are depreciated over lives ranging from 3–10 years, using the double-declining-balance method. Apartments, buildings, and warehouses are generally classified in Categories 7 or 8, which are subject to the straight-line method over an estimated life of either 27.5 or 31.5 years.

FIGURE 9-15

Depreciation rules for income tax purposes

Category	Estimated Life	Allowable Depreciation Method
1	3 years	Double-declining-balance
2	5 years	Double-declining-balance
3	7 years	Double-declining-balance
4	10 years	Double-declining-balance
5	15 years	150% declining-balance*
6	20 years	150% declining-balance*
7	27.5 years	Straight-line
8	31.5 years	Straight-line

*Formula − [1.5 × (cost − accumulated depreciation)] ÷ life

For purposes of determining taxable income, management should use the depreciation strategy that provides the greatest economic benefit for the company, which normally means that management should choose the shortest allowable life and the most extreme form of accelerated depreciation. These choices are preferred for tax purposes because they save tax dollars in the early years of the asset's life and thereby minimize the present value of the stream of income tax payments.

To illustrate, refer back to Figure 9–12, which compares net income numbers produced by the straight-line and double-declining-balance methods of depreciation. Note that the total income recognized under the two methods is the same ($23,000). Now assume a corporate income tax rate of 30 percent. The income tax payments reported in Figure 9–16 would then be due under each of the methods for each of the five years. The table also provides the present value of each stream of tax payments, assuming a 10 percent discount rate.[9]

FIGURE 9–16 Income tax payments (Tax rate equals 30 percent of income)

Method	1999	2000	2001	2002	2003	Total	Present Value
Straight-line	$1,380	$1,380	$1,380	$1,380	$1,380	$6,900	$5,231
Double-declining-balance	300	1,020	1,452	2,028	2,100	6,900	4,896

The tax payments included in Figure 9–16 are simply the income numbers in Figure 9–12 multiplied by the 30 percent tax rate. The total tax payments are equal for each method ($6,900), but the present values of the tax payments are not. The double-declining-balance method has a lower present value ($4,896), which means that the present value of the tax cost is less under double-declining-balance. Thus, the depreciation method chosen for tax purposes should be the one that recognizes the greatest amount of depreciation in the early years of an asset's life.

9. Appendix B, at the end of the text, covers the time value of money and the concept of present value.

During 2000, PepsiCo, which uses accelerated depreciation for tax purposes, recognized $1.5 billion of tax-deductible depreciation expense. Had the company used straight-line depreciation, it would have recognized only about $1 billion of depreciation. For that year the company's effective income tax rate was 40 percent. How much money did the company save in taxes by using accelerated, instead of straight-line, depreciation?

DISPOSAL: RETIREMENTS, SALES, AND TRADE-INS

Long-lived assets are acquired at cost, amortized as they are used in the operation of a business, and eventually disposed of. The disposal can take one of three forms: retirement, sale, or trade-in. The accounting procedures followed in all three cases have much in common. The depreciation is recorded to the date of the disposal, the cost and accumulated depreciation (or *net cost,* as in the case of intangibles and natural resources) of the long-lived asset are removed from the books, and any receipt or payment of cash or other assets is recorded when the asset is disposed of.[10] A gain or loss on the exchange is recognized in the amount of the difference between the book value of the asset and the net value of the receipt. Such gains and losses are usually found in the "other revenues and expenses" section of the income statement. Consider, for example, the following excerpt from the 2000 annual report of Anheuser-Busch Co.:

When plant and equipment are retired or otherwise disposed, the related cost and accumulated depreciation are eliminated and any gain or loss on disposition is recognized in earnings.

Retirement of Long-Lived Assets

It is not unusual for companies to retire, close, or abandon their long-lived assets. **Retirement** of an asset can be due to obsolescence, the lack of a market for the asset in question, or closure by a regulatory body. In the early 1990s, for example, each of the "Big 3" automakers closed a number of plants in an effort to control costs. In such cases, the original cost and accumulated depreciation of the long-lived asset are simply written off the books. No gain or loss is recognized if the asset is fully depreciated at the time of the retirement. A loss is recognized if the asset is not yet fully depreciated.

Assume, for example, that Ajax and Brothers retired two pieces of equipment that were purchased ten years ago. Item 1 was purchased for $10,000 and was depreciated over eight years with no expected salvage value. At the time of its retirement, it was fully depreciated (i.e., accumulated depreciation was $10,000). Item 2 was purchased for $13,000 and was expected to have a $1,000 salvage value after its useful life of

---

10. Long-lived assets are rarely acquired or disposed of on the first or last day of the accounting period. In practice, therefore, companies must consider whether they wish to compute depreciation for partial periods. This text does not cover such computations for two reasons. First, many companies follow either of two policies: (1) recognize a full year of depreciation in the year of acquisition and zero depreciation in the year of disposition, or (2) recognize zero depreciation in the year of acquisition and a full year of depreciation in the year of disposition. Such policies eliminate the need to compute depreciation for partial periods. Second, computing depreciation for a partial period can get somewhat involved, especially under the accelerated methods, and we leave such discussion to intermediate accounting textbooks.

twelve years. At the time of its retirement, the accumulated depreciation account was equal to $10,000. The journal entries accompanying the retirement of the two pieces of equipment are provided below.

Accumulated Depreciation (+A)   **10,000**
     Equipment (−A)   **10,000**
Retired Item 1.

Loss on Retirement (Lo, −SE)   **3,000**
Accumulated Depreciation (+A)   **10,000**
     Equipment (−A)   **13,000**
Retired Item 2.

No gain or loss is recognized on the retirement of Item 1 because an asset with a book value of zero was simply abandoned. The $3,000 loss on the retirement of Item 2 is recognized because the disposal of an asset with a book value of $3,000 generated no benefit.

Accounting for asset retirements is highly subjective and controversial. Generally accepted accounting principles require that when the value of an asset is "permanently impaired," it should be written down, but recent guidelines are subject to judgment, leaving management much discretion over the amount and timing of such write-downs. Simply, it is very difficult to determine exactly when an asset has been permanently impaired and by how much. In addition, these write-downs can be huge. General Motors, Chrysler, Ford, Kmart, Westinghouse, and MCI have each recorded multibillion-dollar asset write-downs in recent years. Often part of an overall strategy to restructure company operations, management frequently chooses to record such write-downs in particularly poor years, enabling the company to "take the hit" when it does the least harm. This "taking a bath" strategy recognizes losses immediately that would normally be recorded as expenses (e.g., depreciation) in future years which, in turn, can improve future reported profits. *The Wall Street Journal* (November 2, 1994) reported that the FASB has "cracked down on corporate America's habit of seizing upon restructurings as an occasion to take a bushel of write-offs all at once, making an earnings turnaround look speedier and more significant when it happens."[11]

Management may also choose to record large "permanent impairment" write-downs in particularly good years. Polaroid, for example, recorded such a write-down in the same year it recognized a multibillion-dollar gain from a well-known legal settlement against Kodak for patent infringement. This reporting decision could be interpreted as "building a hidden reserve," which may enable Polaroid to "smooth" reported income over time. General Electric was cited in *The Wall Street Journal* (November 3, 1994) for using such write-offs frequently to "offset one-time gains."

During 2000, Bristol-Myers Squibb booked a $508 million restructuring charge against earnings—a $298 million accrual for employee termination benefits for approximately 5,200 laid-off workers, $136 million for write-downs of property, plant, and equipment, and $74 million for other accrued expenses. The charge involved no cash payment. Construct the entry recorded in the books of Bristol-Myers Squibb. Explain how the company could be practicing earnings management.

---

11. Recently, the FASB passed a financial reporting standard that set criteria for asset write-downs. While these criteria may have reduced abuses, they are still very subjective.

Sale of Long-Lived Assets

Accounting for the sale of a long-lived asset is essentially the same as accounting for its retirement, except that cash is received in the exchange. For example, Computer Services purchased office furniture on March 1, 1999, for $24,000. At the time of the purchase, the company estimated the useful life of the furniture to be ten years and the salvage value to be $4,000, and it used the straight-line method of depreciation. On July 1, 2002 (three years and four months later), Computer Services remodeled its office and sold all the original furniture for $13,000. The company policy on recognizing depreciation for partial periods is to recognize no depreciation in the year of acquisition and a full year's depreciation in the year of disposition. The relevant calculations and the related journal entries appear in Figure 9–17.

On the date of sale, the depreciation is updated and the sale recorded. The loss on the sale ($5,000) represents the difference between the updated book value ($24,000 − $6,000) and the cash proceeds ($13,000).

FIGURE 9–17

The sale of a long-lived asset: Computer Services

	Depreciation Computations	Depreciation Expense	Accumulated Depreciation
1999	(Year of acquisition)	$ 0	$ 0
2000	($24,000 − $4,000) ÷ 10 years	2,000	2,000
2001	($24,000 − $4,000) ÷ 10 years	2,000	4,000
2002	(Year of disposition)	2,000	6,000

JOURNAL ENTRIES

2002			
July 1	**Depreciation Expense (E, −SE)**	2,000	
	Accumulated Depreciation (−A)		2,000
	Recognized depreciation in year of disposition.		
1	**Cash (+A)**	13,000	
	Accumulated Depreciation (+A)	6,000	
	Loss on Sale (Lo, −SE)	5,000	
	Furniture (−A)		24,000
	Sold long-lived asset.		

Trade-Ins of Long-Lived Assets

With a **trade-in,** two or more long-lived assets are exchanged, and cash is often received or paid. The methods used to account for such transactions depend on whether the exchanged assets are similar or dissimilar. This text limits its coverage to exchanges of **dissimilar assets,** those that are of a different general type, perform different functions, and are employed in different lines of business. The methods used to account for exchanges of similar assets are normally covered in intermediate accounting textbooks.

In general, the accounting procedures described in the section on retirements and the section on sales of long-lived assets also apply when dissimilar assets are exchanged.[12] That is, the depreciation of the asset given up is updated, its capitalized

---

12. Keep in mind that a sale is simply the exchange of a long-lived asset for cash, a dissimilar asset.

cost and accumulated depreciation are written off the books, and the receipt or payment of cash is recorded. However, a problem arises when accounting for exchanges
because it is difficult to determine the dollar amount at which the asset received should
be valued on the balance sheet. This problem, in turn, makes it equally difficult to
measure the gain or loss that is recognized on the exchange.

The asset received in a trade-in should be valued on the balance sheet at either:
(1) the FMV of the assets given up or (2) the FMV of the assets received, whichever
is clearly more evident and objectively determinable. Applying this rule is often difficult because the list price of an asset does not necessarily reflect its FMV, and determining the FMV of the asset given up is normally very subjective. Often the accountant must consult industry publications or obtain data on recent transactions involving
similar assets to determine FMVs.

To illustrate, Mastoon Industries exchanged a delivery truck, which originally cost
$17,000 (accumulated depreciation = $9,000) for a new printing press. The dealer
agreed to accept the truck plus $12,000. Based on a list price of $18,000 for the printing press, the dealer claims to be granting a $6,000 ($18,000 − $12,000) trade-in
allowance on the truck. However, the accountant for Mastoon finds that recent sales of
comparable printing presses have realized, on average, $16,000, and a publication of
used truck prices indicates that the value of the truck is approximately $4,000.

Given these facts, there are two acceptable ways to value the printing press on the
balance sheet of Mastoon, each leading to the same result: (1) the FMV of the assets
given up ($16,000 = $12,000 cash + $4,000 value of truck) or (2) the FMV of the asset
received ($16,000, determined from recent sales). The resulting journal entry follows:

Printing Press (+A)	**16,000**	
Accumulated Depreciation (+A)	**9,000**	
Loss on Trade-In (Lo, −SE)	**4,000**	
Truck (−A)		**17,000**
Cash (−A)		**12,000**

Traded truck and cash for a press.

Note also that the list price ($18,000) was not used as the FMV of the printing
press. List prices are nothing more than invitations to negotiate, and astute buyers can
often bargain for lower prices. Is it normally economically prudent, for example, to
pay the list price for a new automobile? Moreover, since the actual FMV of the printing press seems to be $16,000 instead of $18,000, a better estimate of the trade-in
allowance on the truck is $4,000 ($16,000 − $12,000), rather than $6,000 ($18,000 −
$12,000). It is common for dealers, especially in the automobile industry, to lead cus-
tomers to believe that they are receiving more for their trade-ins than they actually are.

INTERNATIONAL PERSPECTIVE: LONG-LIVED ASSETS AND CURRENT VALUES

In the financial statements of U.S. companies, the property, plant, and equipment
account is carried at historical cost less accumulated depreciation. Several years ago,
a financial accounting standard was passed by the FASB that required certain large
companies to disclose in the footnotes the current values of their fixed assets and
inventories and to disclose with them depreciation and cost of goods sold amounts
based on those values. This standard was so controversial that after a few years it was
abandoned, and at present there appears to be no movement to reintroduce it.

In a number of foreign countries, however, fixed asset accounting is not based on historical cost. Instead, property, plant, and equipment revaluations based on current values are allowed and often practiced, and international accounting standards also allow such revaluations. In the Netherlands, the United Kingdom, France, and Australia, for example, depreciable fixed assets are often written up to their current values by recording an adjusting entry that debits the fixed asset account and credits stockholders' equity. Future depreciation charges are based on the revalued asset, which, in turn, can give rise to an accumulated depreciation balance that exceeds the asset's historical cost. The large and well-known Philips Company, which is based in the Netherlands, has practiced such accounting methods for over forty years.

Writing up fixed assets often requires considerable judgment that, in turn, can give foreign managers a certain amount of discretion over important financial numbers. To illustrate, *Forbes* reported that Australian-based News Corp., a global media company owned by the famous financial tycoon Rupert Murdoch, was able to reduce its debt/equity ratio from 3.4/1.0 to 0.8/1.0 by writing up certain fixed assets to reflect their market values and thereby increasing stockholders' equity. The article suggested that Murdoch may have chosen to record these revaluations to obscure the effect on News Corp.'s balance sheet of the excessive debt he incurred to finance a series of major acquisitions, including a number of magazines and publishing houses, Twentieth Century Fox, and Metromedia Broadcasting. It was further suggested that Murdoch's choice may have been motivated by the threat of violating debt covenants.

Such write-ups, however, make it difficult for foreign firms attempting to raise capital in the U.S. capital markets. When their financial statements are restated to U.S. GAAP, which is required by the major U.S. exchanges, their earnings numbers often fall. Several years ago, for example, *Forbes* reported that the restated earnings of Daimler-Benz, a large German company, was almost $1.5 billion less because it was required to value its fixed assets at historical cost. For a similar reason, Nestle, the Swiss chocolate giant, has decided not to list its shares on the New York Stock Exchange.

APPENDIX 9A

INTANGIBLE ASSETS AND DEFERRED COSTS

In Chapter 5 we noted that the value of a company as measured by the balance sheet (total assets − liabilities) rarely reflects its capitalization value (value of a company as measured by the stock market). As of December 31, 2000, for example, the balance sheet value of Emerson Electric was $6 billion, while the stock market valued the company at $28 billion. The difference, $22 billion in this example, is often referred to as "intangibles," referring to those features about the company that are valued by the market but ignored by the balance sheet. These intangibles include the quality of a company's management, the value of its brands, good relationships with its customers and suppliers, and other factors that are important to the company's future but very difficult to measure. Certainly, the absence of these kinds of "assets" is a balance sheet weakness, and many argue that for a variety of companies, especially those in the Internet sector where "knowledge" is a company's most important asset, that weakness is quite significant. Some countries allow companies to recognize certain of these kinds of assets. Britain allows companies to recognize the value of brands on the balance sheet and, as noted in the chapter, also allows fixed asset revaluations. For the time being, however, U.S. GAAP does not allow the recognition of these kinds of assets. The principle of objectivity in the United States is just too strict. Consequently, analysts reviewing companies traded on U.S. markets must be content to rely on financial statements that do not capture some very important information.

In this appendix we discuss intangible assets, but only those that can be measured objectively. They are characterized by the rights, privileges, and benefits of possession rather than by physical existence. Some accountants also suggest that intangible assets have a higher degree of uncertainty than tangible assets. Among other items, intangibles include the costs of acquiring copyrights, patents, trademarks, trade names, licenses, and goodwill. Deferred costs include prepaids, which extend beyond the current accounting period, and the costs incurred prior to the point when a company is fully operational (startup or organizational costs). Intangible assets and deferred costs are often reported on the balance sheet as "other assets." In general, the costs of acquiring such assets should be capitalized, and professional standards require that certain intangibles be amortized over their legal or useful lives, whichever is shorter. Most companies use the straight-line method to amortize intangibles for both reporting and tax purposes.

The useful life of an intangible asset is often difficult to estimate, and the decline in service potential is often almost impossible to measure. As a result, the allocation of the capitalized cost to future periods is very subjective, and different intangible assets are treated in different ways.

COPYRIGHTS, PATENTS, AND TRADEMARKS

Copyrights are exclusive rights granted by law to control literary, musical, or artistic works. They are granted for seventy years beyond the life of the creator. Patents are granted by the U.S. Patent Office, and they give the holders exclusive rights to use, manufacture, or sell a product or process for a period of twenty years. A trademark or trade name is a word, phrase, or symbol that distinguishes or identifies a particular enterprise or product. The right to use a trademark is also granted by the U.S. Patent Office exclusively to the holder. The trademark lasts for a period of ten years but can be renewed indefinitely. Kleenex, Pepsi-Cola, Excedrin, and Wheaties are just a few examples of trade names that are so familiar that they are now a part of our culture.

THE COSTS OF DEVELOPING COMPUTER SOFTWARE

Statement of Financial Accounting Standards No. 86 specifies that the costs of developing and producing computer software products that will be available for sale or lease should be capitalized and amortized over their economic lives. Prior to this standard, all such costs incurred prior to the development of a prototype were expensed, and many small software development companies claimed that this practice understated net income, making it very difficult to attract outside capital. This standard had a significant impact on the financial statements of many companies involved in the development of computer software. For example, consider the excerpt below from a financial report of Wang Laboratories, Inc. Note that the net effect of the change increased net income by $19.3 million.

The Company adopted a change of accounting for costs of computer software. The change was made in accordance with provisions of Statement of Financial Accounting Standards No. 86, which specifies that certain costs incurred in the development of computer software to be sold or leased to customers are to be capitalized and amortized over the economic life of the software product. Total costs capitalized during the year approximated $21.1 million, of which $1.8 million has been amortized and charged to expense.

GOODWILL

When one company purchases another for a dollar amount that is greater than the net FMV of the purchased company's assets and liabilities, goodwill is recognized on the purchasing company's balance sheet. Goodwill is a common asset on the balance sheets of major U.S. companies. *Accounting Trends and Techniques* reports that 515 of the 600 companies surveyed disclosed goodwill on their balance sheets. For many companies, such as Cisco Systems, Marriott Corporation, and General Electric, goodwill is quite significant. It can account for 10 percent or more of their total assets. As of December 31, 1999, goodwill represented over 11 percent of the total assets of Oracle.

To illustrate how goodwill is acquired, consider PepsiCo's acquisition of several major bottling operations from Philip Morris Companies and KFC from RJR Nabisco, Inc., for a total of $1,678.3 million. The FMVs of the physically identifiable assets and liabilities purchased by PepsiCo in these transactions were $1,191.4 million and $458.5 million, respectively. Accordingly, the transaction was accounted for as if the following journal entry (dollars in thousands) had been recorded on PepsiCo's books. Assets in the journal entry include cash, receivables, inventories, investments, and long-lived assets; liabilities include short-term payables and long-term debts.

Assets (+A)	1,191,400	
Goodwill (+A)	945,400	
Liabilities (+L)		458,500
Cash (−A)		1,678,300

Purchased bottling operations and
Kentucky Fried Chicken.

Note in the transaction that the amount of goodwill is simply the difference between the purchase price and the net value of the purchased companies' assets and liabilities. It represents PepsiCo's assessment that the purchased companies are worth more as working units than is indicated by the values of their individual assets and liabilities.

Until July 2001, goodwill was amortized over a period not to exceed forty years. As discussed at the end of Chapter 8, this rule was very controversial and led to huge charges against earnings for companies that made significant acquisitions. For example, AOL, after its acquisition of Time Warner, recorded goodwill amortization expense of over $7.5 billion annually. In *SFAS No. 142*, the FASB—in a very significant move—stated that goodwill results from the acquisition of an entity that becomes an integrated part of the parent, a going concern. Consequently, goodwill is not considered a "wasting asset," but rather has an indefinite useful life—similar to land. Accordingly, it should not be subject to amortization. However, if the market value of the acquired entity dips below the recorded amount, an asset impairment should be recognized; goodwill on the balance sheet should be written down, and a charge against earnings should be recorded.

ORGANIZATIONAL COSTS

Organizational costs represent another subjective area in accounting for intangible assets. These costs are incurred prior to the start of a company's operations, typically including fees for underwriting, legal and accounting services, licenses, titles, and promotional expenditures. It is relatively clear that such costs are incurred to generate future revenues, and therefore, it seems that organizational costs should be capitalized. However, the service potential of such an asset cannot be associated with any future revenue in particular, and thus, it is difficult to determine how it should be amortized. In a sense, organizational costs are of value to the company throughout its entire life. Does that mean that they should be left on the balance sheet indefinitely? Conceptually it may, but, similar to research and development costs discussed below, professional standards require that they be expensed.

RESEARCH AND DEVELOPMENT COSTS

Research and development (R&D) costs are incurred to generate revenue in future periods through the creation of new products or processes. Such costs are significant for many major U.S. manufacturers. In 2000, for example, Eli Lilly and Company invested $2 billion in research and development, which amounted to about 20 percent of sales.

The matching principle clearly suggests that R&D costs should be capitalized and amortized over future periods. However, it is difficult to match specific research and development expenditures with the creation of specific products or processes. Some R&D expenditures are for basic research, others lead to failures, and still others provide only indirect benefits, or benefits that could not have been foreseen when the expenditure was incurred.

Concerned with the wide variety of practices used by companies to capitalize and amortize R&D expenditures, the FASB published *SFAS No. 2* in 1974. This pronouncement required that expenditures for most types of R&D costs be expensed in the year incurred, rather than capitalized and amortized as intangible assets. While this pronouncement promoted uniformity of accounting practices in the area of R&D, relieved pressures on auditors and managers to subjectively determine which R&D costs should be capitalized, and reduced some of management's ability to manipulate the financial statements, it is definitely inconsistent with the matching principle. In line with this standard, many R&D costs that will clearly benefit future periods are being immediately expensed. As with organizational costs, accounting for R&D costs represents an example of theoretical measurement principles being compromised in the interest of practical considerations.

The requirement to expense all R&D costs can have significant effects on the financial statements. Had Boeing, for example, been allowed to capitalize half of its R&D expenditures in 1999, its net income would have increased by $700 million. There is also some evidence suggesting that the negative effects on net income and other important financial ratios of *SFAS No. 2* serve to discourage companies from making R&D expenditures. Boeing, for example, reduced its R&D expenditures by $500 million from 1998 to 1999. Some believe that the requirement to expense R&D may have been part of the cause.

REVIEW PROBLEM

Norby Enterprises purchased equipment on January 1, 2000, for $8,000. It cost $1,500 to have the equipment shipped to the plant and $500 to have it installed. The equipment was estimated to have a five-year useful life and a salvage value of $1,000. On January 1, 2003, the equipment was overhauled at a cost of $1,000, and the overhaul extended its estimated useful life by an additional year (from five to six years). On January 1, 2004, the equipment and $13,000 cash were traded for a dissimilar piece of equipment with a FMV of $15,000. Norby uses the straight-line method of depreciation. The computations and journal entries related to the acquisition, depreciation, overhaul, and disposal of the equipment appear in Figure 9–18.

> **FIGURE 9-18** Solution to review problem: Norby Enterprises

Description/Date	Journal Entry		Accumulated Depreciation	Book Value[a]
Acquisition of equipment (1/1/00)	Equipment (+A) Cash (−A)	10,000[b] 10,000	0	10,000
Depreciation[c] (12/31/00)	Depreciation Expense (E, −SE) Accumulated Depreciation (−A)	1,800 1,800	1,800	8,200
Depreciation[c] (12/31/01)	Depreciation Expense (E, −SE) Accumulated Depreciation (−A)	1,800 1,800	3,600	6,400
Depreciation[c] (12/31/02)	Depreciation Expense (E, −SE) Accumulated Depreciation (−A)	1,800 1,800	5,400	4,600
Overhaul (1/1/03)	Equipment (+A) Cash (−A)	1,000 1,000	5,400	5,600
Depreciation[d] (12/31/03)	Depreciation Expense (E, −SE) Accumulated Depreciation (−A)	1,533 1,533	6,933	4,067

Trade-in
(1/1/04)
	Equipment (new) (+A)
	Accumulated Depreciation (+A)
	Loss on Trade-In (Lo, −SE)
	    Equipment (old) (−A)
	    Cash (−A)
		15,000
		6,933
		2,067
		11,000
		13,000		

[a]Book value = Equipment cost − accumulated depreciation
[b]Equipment cost: $8,000 purchase + $1,500 shipping + $500 installation = $10,000
[c]Depreciation expense before overhaul: ($10,000 cost − $1,000 salvage) ÷ 5-year life = $1,800
[d]Depreciation expense after overhaul: ($4,600 book value + $1,000 overhaul − $1,000 salvage) ÷ 3-year remaining life = $1,533

SUMMARY OF KEY POINTS

The key points in the chapter are summarized below.

○ *How the matching principle underlies the methods used to account for long-lived assets.*

Long-lived assets are assets that are used in the operations of the business, providing benefits that extend beyond the current accounting period. Included are land (not held for resale), buildings, machinery, equipment, costs incurred to acquire the right to extract natural resources, intangible assets, and deferred costs.

According to the matching principle, efforts (expenses) should be matched against benefits (revenues) in the period when the benefits are recognized. Since the benefits provided by long-lived assets extend beyond the current period, the costs of acquiring long-lived assets are capitalized in the period of acquisition and then amortized as their useful lives expire.

○ *Major questions that are addressed when accounting for long-lived assets and how the financial statements are affected.*

Accounting for most long-lived assets consists primarily of answering three questions: (1) What dollar amount should be included in the capitalized cost of the long-lived asset? (2) Over what time period should this cost be amortized? (3) At what rate should this cost be amortized? These questions are addressed for all long-lived assets except land, which is not subject to amortization.

Answering these questions in various ways can have significant effects on the timing of asset and income recognition. Capitalizing instead of expensing a cost defers expense recognition, giving rise to higher asset values and net income in the period of acquisition. Similarly, allocating the cost of a long-lived asset over a long period of time defers expense recognition and creates higher asset and income values in the early years of the asset's life. However, these financial statement effects are a matter of timing, not magnitude. That is, a method giving rise to higher asset and income values in the early years of an asset's life will create lower asset and income values in the later years.

○ *Major economic consequences associated with the methods used to account for long-lived assets.*

The methods used to account for long-lived assets can have significant economic effects. The amount of cost to capitalize, the estimated useful life, the chosen amortization method, and the timing and amount of permanent write-downs can have significant effects on the timing of net income and important financial ratios. These numbers are used by interested parties to evaluate management and assess earning power, solvency, and determine credit ratings. They are also used in compensation contracts and debt covenants to control and direct management behavior.

○ *Costs that should be included in the capitalized cost of a long-lived asset.*

The acquisition cost of a long-lived asset is determined by either (1) the FMV of the acquired asset or (2) the FMV of what was given up to acquire the asset, whichever is more readily determinable. In almost all cases, the FMV of what was given up is used because cash, which by definition is at FMV, is normally given up in such exchanges. Further, the capitalized cost (i.e., the FMV of what was given up) should include all costs required to bring the asset into serviceable or usable condition and location. This includes not only the cost of purchasing a long-lived asset, but also costs such as freight, installation, taxes, title fees, idle time while the asset is being installed, the costs of preparing land for use in the business, indirect overhead costs incurred while manufacturing a long-lived asset, and interest costs on borrowed funds used to construct long-lived assets. When long-lived assets are purchased as part of a group of assets for a single, lump-sum price, the overall price is allocated to each asset on the basis of its relative FMV.

○ *Accounting treatment of postacquisition expenditures.*

Postacquisition expenditures are costs incurred subsequent to the acquisition or manufacture of a long-lived asset. Costs incurred to improve the asset (as defined by a set of criteria) are called *betterments* and should be capitalized as part of the cost of the asset and amortized over its remaining life. Betterments are usually infrequent and tend to involve relatively large dollar amounts. Costs incurred to repair an asset or maintain its current level of productivity are classified as maintenance and are immediately expensed. Maintenance expenditures tend to be periodic and relatively small. It is often difficult to distinguish between a betterment and a maintenance expenditure, so management has much reporting discretion in this area.

○ *How the cost of a long-lived asset is allocated over its useful life and the alternative allocation methods.*

To allocate the cost of a long-lived asset over its useful life, three issues must be addressed: (1) the useful life must be estimated, (2) the salvage value must be estimated, and (3) a cost-allocation method must be chosen. The useful-life estimate defines the period of time over which the asset's cost is to be amortized. The capitalized cost less the salvage value defines the amortization base, the total amount of cost to be amortized. The cost-allocation method determines the amount of cost to be amortized each period.

Three basic cost-allocation methods are considered systematic and reasonable: (1) straight-line, (2) accelerated, and (3) activity. The straight-line method recognizes equal amounts of depreciation each period throughout the life of the asset. Accelerated methods, including double-declining-balance, recognize larger amounts of depreciation in the early periods of an asset's life and smaller amounts in the later periods. The activity method bases the amount of amortization each period on the activity of the asset during that period. The life of the asset is expressed in terms of a unit of activity, and as each unit is produced, a portion of the asset's cost is amortized. This method is normally used to deplete the costs associated with mining natural resources.

○ *Disposition of long-lived assets.*

Long-lived assets are disposed of through retirement, sale, or trade-in. When a long-lived asset is retired, depreciation is updated, the original cost and accumulated depreciation of the asset are written off the books, and a loss is recognized if the asset is not fully depreciated as of the time of the retirement. Determining when and how to write down such assets is very subjective.

When long-lived assets are sold for cash, depreciation is updated, cash is debited, the original cost and accumulated depreciation are written off the books, and a gain or loss, which represents the difference between the book value of the asset and the proceeds, is recognized on the transaction.

When two dissimilar assets and cash are exchanged, depreciation is updated, the cash receipt or payment is recorded, the original cost and accumulated depreciation of the asset given up are written off the books, the asset received is given a dollar value, and a gain or loss is recognized on the transaction. The general rule for valuing the asset received is to use the FMV of the assets given up (cash and the asset given up) or the FMV of the asset received, whichever is more objectively determinable.

KEY TERMS

Note: Definitions for these terms are provided in the glossary at the end of this text.

Accelerated method (p. 382)
Activity method (p. 385)
Amortized (p. 371)
Betterments (p. 378)
Deferred costs (p. 370)
Deplete (p. 385)
Depreciation (p. 372)
Depreciation base (p. 381)
Dissimilar assets (p. 391)
Double-declining-balance method (p. 382)
Fixed assets (p. 370)
Intangible assets (p. 370)

Internal Revenue Code (p. 387)
Land (p. 370)
Maintenance (p. 378)
Natural resource costs (p. 370)
Physical obsolescence (p. 379)
Postacquisition expenditures (p. 377)
Retirement (p. 389)
Salvage value (p. 379)
Straight-line method (p. 381)
Technical obsolescence (p. 379)
Trade-in (p. 391)

ETHICS IN THE REAL WORLD

"With a simple bookkeeping change, companies can turn profits into losses—and vice versa. In many cases, the changes are perfectly justified, but the practice creates big opportunities for abuse."

So began a *Forbes* article that focused on the difficulty involved with determining the depreciation and/or amortization rates for long-lived assets and the level of discretionary judgment used by management in the area. Major U.S. companies, such as Cineplex Odeon, Blockbuster, General Motors, IBM, and Delta Air Lines, are cited in the article for the wide variety of methods they use. Blockbuster once changed the amortization period for its videotapes from nine to thirty-six months, adding nearly 20 percent to its reported income; GM added $2.55 to its earnings-per-share number by adjusting the way in which it amortizes its tools and

dies; IBM increased its "bottom line" by $375 million by changing from accelerated to straight-line; and Delta depreciates its planes over fifteen years, while most of the rest of the airline industry uses a twenty- to twenty-five-year useful life. In each case, the policies were disclosed and within the guidelines of GAAP, and the article notes further that "when it comes to amortization and depreciation, GAAP provides only the vaguest of guidelines."

However, the SEC chief accountant suggests that the disclosures are not adequate: "When a company says it's depreciating its plant over three to forty years, we don't know the intimate details and there is no practical way we could. I'd like accountants to take more responsibility for it."

ETHICAL ISSUE Is it ethical for management to use methods to account for long-lived assets that are within the guidelines of GAAP but fail to provide disclosure that is sufficient for stockholders to understand the financial condition and performance of the company?

INTERNET RESEARCH EXERCISE

The chapter makes the point that many companies are aggressively recognizing asset impairments, and some suspect that the companies are doing so as a way to manage earnings. The FASB recently established a standard to reduce these practices. Identify the number of this standard, when it was passed, and briefly describe its contents. Begin your search at www.rutgers.edu/accounting.

BRIEF EXERCISES

REAL DATA

BE9–1

Change in depreciation method

A footnote to the 1996 financial statements of Allegheny Teledyne Incorporated stated the following:

The straight-line method of depreciation was adopted for all property placed into service after July 1, 1996. Buildings and equipment acquired prior to that time are accounted for under accelerated methods. The company believes that the new method will more appropriately reflect its financial results by better allocating costs of new property over the useful lives of these assets. In addition, the new method conforms more closely to that prevalent in the industries in which Allegheny operates.

a.   What impact will the new method have on Allegheny's net income?

b.   Briefly discuss some of the reasons that may have caused Allegheny to change the method of depreciation.

c.   Where else in the annual report could one find evidence that Allegheny changed its method of depreciation?

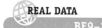

REAL DATA

BE9-2

Effect of
depreciation on
financial statements

Ford Motor Company recently reported $2.6 billion of depreciation and $3.3 billion of amortization for the year.

a.   Describe how the recognition of the amortization affects the basic accounting equation.

b.   As reported in the footnotes, Ford's accumulated depreciation balance grew during the year from $25.3 billion to $26.2 billion, and the company collected proceeds of $1 billion on sales of property, plant, and equipment with a cost of approximately $3 billion. Compute the gain or loss recognized by the company on these sales. On what financial statement would this appear, and how would these transactions affect the statement of cash flows?

REAL DATA

BE9-3

Acquisition of
fixed assets

The footnote below was taken from the 1999 annual report of Johnson & Johnson (dollars in millions).

	1999	1998
Land and land improvements	$ 586	$ 466
Buildings and building equipment	3,087	2,991
Machinery and equipment	5,936	5,686
Construction in progress	1,437	1,126
	$11,046	$10,269
Less accumulated depreciation	4,327	3,874
	$ 6,719	$ 6,395

a.   Approximately how much did Johnson & Johnson invest in land during 1999?

b.   Why did accumulated depreciation increase during 1999?

c.   The statement of cash flows indicates that Johnson & Johnson invested $1,728 in land, buildings, machinery and equipment, and construction during 1999. Estimate the cost of these kinds of assets sold during 1999.

d.   What dollar amount appeared on Johnson & Johnson's 1999 balance sheet for property, plant, and equipment?

EXERCISES

E9-1

Determining the
capitalized cost and
depreciation base

Lowery, Inc., purchased new plant equipment on January 1, 2002. The company paid $920,000 for the equipment, $62,000 for transportation of the equipment, and $10,000 for insurance on the equipment while it was being transported. The company also estimates that over the equipment's useful life it will require additional power, which will cause utility costs to increase $90,000. The equipment has an estimated salvage value of $50,000.

a.   What amount should the company capitalize for this equipment on January 1, 2002?

b.   What is the depreciation base of this equipment?

c.   What amount will be depreciated over the life of this equipment?

E9-2

Allocating cost on
the basis of relative
market value

AJB Real Estate purchased a ten-acre tract of land for $320,000. The company divided the land into four lots of two and one-half acres each. Lot 1 had a beautiful view of the mountains and was valued at $160,000. Lot 2 had a stream running through it and was valued at $120,000. Lots 3 and 4 were each valued at $60,000. Assume that each lot is sold for the values indicated. Compute the profit on each of the four sales.

E9-3

Which costs are
subject to
depreciation?

Firton Brothers purchased for $90,000 a tract of land that included an abandoned warehouse. The warehouse was razed, and the site was prepared for a new building at a cost of $10,000. Scrap materials from the warehouse were sold for $7,000. A building was then constructed for $140,000, a driveway and parking lot were laid for $32,000, and permanent landscaping was completed for $4,000. Firton Brothers depreciates fixed assets over a twenty-year period using the straight-line method.

a.   Compute the amount of cost to be placed in the land, land improvements, and building accounts.
b.   Assuming a salvage value of zero, compute the depreciation expense associated with the items above for the first year.

E9–4

Betterments or maintenance?

The following items represent common postacquisition expenditures incurred on machinery:

a.   Lubrication service
b.   Painting costs
c.   Cleaning expenditures
d.   Rewiring costs to increase operating speed
e.   Repairs
f.   Replacement of defective parts
g.   An overhaul to increase useful life
h.   Cost of a muffler to reduce machine noise
i.   Costs of redesign to increase output

Identify each item as a betterment or a maintenance item.

E9–5

How the matching principle affects the timing of income recognition

The condensed balance sheet as of December 31, 2002, for Van Den Boom Enterprises follows:

Assets		Liabilities and Stockholders' Equity	
Current assets	**$40,000**	**Liabilities**	**$35,000**
Land	**50,000**	**Stockholders' equity**	**55,000**
		Total liabilities and	
Total assets	**$90,000**	**stockholders' equity**	**$90,000**

Revenues and expenses (other than amortization) are predicted to be $65,000 and $20,000, respectively, for 2003, 2004, and 2005. All revenues and expenses are received or paid in cash. On January 1, 2003, Van Den Boom pays $40,000 cash for an item.

a.   Assume that Van Den Boom Enterprises engaged in operating activities only during 2003, 2004, and 2005. Prepare income statements for 2003, 2004, and 2005 and the balance sheet as of December 31 for 2003, 2004, and 2005, assuming the $40,000 cash payment is treated in each of the following ways:
(1) Immediately expensed.
(2) Capitalized and amortized evenly over two years.
(3) Capitalized and amortized evenly over three years.
b.   Compute the total income recognized over the three-year period under each assumption above.
c.   What is interesting about the 12/31/05 balance sheet prepared under all three assumptions?

E9–6

The effect of estimated useful life on income and dividends

Stork Freight Company owns and operates fifteen planes that deliver packages worldwide. The planes were purchased on January 1, 1999, for $1 million each. The company estimates that the planes will be scrapped after twelve years. Stork Freight uses straight-line depreciation.

a.   Assume that in a typical year the company generates revenues of $50 million and operating expenses (excluding depreciation expense) of $25 million. Prepare an income statement for a typical year.
b.   Assume that the company had originally estimated the useful life at six years instead of twelve. Prepare an income statement for a typical year. What is the percent change in net income?
c.   Assume that the company policy is to pay dividends in the amount of 30 percent of net income. Compute the difference in the dividend payment between the two cases above.

E9–7

Revising the estimated life

Portland Products purchased a machine on January 1, 1999, for $60,000 and estimated its useful life and salvage value at five years and $12,000, respectively. On January 1, 2002, the company added three years to the original useful-life estimate.

a. Compute the book value of the machine as of January 1, 2002, assuming that Portland uses the straight-line method of depreciation.
b. Prepare the journal entry entered by the company to record depreciation on December 31, 2002.

E9–8

Different amortization methods achieve different objectives

The controller of Elton Furniture Store is currently trying to decide what depreciation method to use for a particular fixed asset. The controller has prepared the following list of possible objectives that might be accomplished through a depreciation method. Which method(s):

a. most closely matches the asset's cost with the benefits resulting from the asset's use?
b. allocates the cost of the asset over the asset's useful life?
c. generates the largest net income in the last year of the asset's useful life?
d. does not directly use the asset's salvage value in computing the depreciation expense?
e. is best for tax purposes (i.e., minimizes the present value of future tax payments)?
f. recognizes an equal charge to expense every period?
g. generates the largest depreciation expense in the asset's last year?
h. does not allow the asset's book value to drop below the asset's salvage value?

Consider each objective independently, and indicate the depreciation method(s) that achieve each objective.

E9–9

Computing depreciation and choosing a depreciation method

Benick Industries purchased a new lathe on January 1, 2002, for $300,000. Benick estimates that the lathe will have a useful life of four years and that the company will be able to sell it at the end of the fourth year for $60,000.

a. Compute the depreciation expense that Benick Industries would record for 2002, 2003, 2004, and 2005 under each of the following methods:
(1) Straight-line depreciation
(2) Double-declining-balance depreciation
b. If you were the president of Benick Industries, what might you consider when choosing a depreciation method for financial reporting purposes? Why?

E9–10

Depreciation calculations and journal entries

Stockton Corporation purchased a new computer system on January 1, 2002, for $300,000 cash. The company also incurred $25,000 in installation costs and $10,000 to train its employees on the new system. The computer system has an estimated useful life of five years and an estimated salvage value of $70,000.

a. Prepare the entry to record the acquisition of the computer system.
b. Calculate the depreciation expense recognized each year over the life of the system for each of the following assumptions:
(1) Stockton uses straight-line depreciation.
(2) Stockton uses double-declining-balance depreciation.
c. Provide the journal entry recorded by Stockton at the end of 2002 under the double-declining-balance method.

E9–11

The activity method of depreciation

Apex Trucking purchased a truck for $100,000 on January 1, 2002. The useful life of the truck was estimated to be either five years or 200,000 miles. Salvage value was estimated at $20,000. Over the actual life of the truck, it logged the following miles:

Year 1   48,000 miles
Year 2   35,000 miles
Year 3   40,000 miles

Year 4   25,000 miles
Year 5   35,000 miles
Year 6   10,000 miles

At the end of the sixth year, the truck was sold for $12,000.

Prepare the journal entries to record depreciation over the life of the truck and its sale, assuming these methods:

1. Activity method
2. Straight-line method

E9–12

Depletion and matching

Natural Extraction Industries paid $4 million for the right to drill for oil on a tract of land in western Texas. Engineers estimated that this oil deposit would produce 100,000 barrels of crude oil.

a. During the first year of operations, Natural Extraction extracted 30,000 barrels of oil. Prepare the entry to record depletion for the first year.
b. During the second year, the company extracted 50,000 barrels. Prepare the entry to record depletion for the second year.
c. What dollar amount would Natural Extraction report on its balance sheet at the end of the second year for oil deposits?

E9–13

An error in recording the acquisition of a fixed asset

Lewis Real Estate purchased a new photocopy machine on January 1, 2002, for $120,000. The company's bookkeeper made the following entry to record the acquisition:

| Depreciation Expense (E, −SE) | 120,000 | |
| Cash (−A) | | 120,000 |

The photocopy machine has an estimated useful life of four years and an estimated salvage value of $20,000. Lewis Real Estate did not make any adjusting entry on December 31, 2002, or in any subsequent year associated with the photocopy machine. Furthermore, the company never discovered the error.

a. Assume that Lewis Real Estate uses the straight-line method to depreciate its fixed assets. Compute the values for the following chart:

Year	Depreciation Expense per Company's Books	Correct Depreciation Expense	Annual Difference	Cumulative Difference
2002				
2003				
2004				
2005				

b. In what direction and by how much will the account Accumulated Depreciation be misstated as of December 31, 2004?
c. In what direction and by how much will the account Retained Earnings be misstated *prior* to closing entries on December 31, 2004?
d. In what direction and by how much will the account Retained Earnings be misstated *after* closing entries on December 31, 2004?

E9–14

Fixed asset sales

Savory Enterprises reported the following information regarding the company's fixed assets in the footnotes to the company's 2002 financial statements:

| Office furniture | $500,000 | |
| Less: Accumulated depreciation | 300,000 | 200,000 |

a. Assume that Savory Enterprises sells all of its office furniture for $235,000 in cash on January 1, 2003. Prepare the entry to record the sale.
b. Assume that Savory Enterprises sells all of its office furniture for $185,000 in cash on January 1, 2003. Prepare the entry to record the sale.

E9-15

Retiring, selling, and trading in a fixed asset

Paris Company purchased equipment on January 1, 2000, for $25,000. The estimated useful life of the equipment is five years, the salvage value is $5,000, and the company uses the double-declining-balance method to depreciate fixed assets.

a. Provide the journal entry assuming the equipment is scrapped after three years.
b. Provide the journal entry assuming the equipment is scrapped after five years.
c. Provide the journal entry assuming the equipment is sold for $8,000 after three years.
d. Provide the journal entry assuming, at the end of the fifth year, the equipment and $28,000 cash are traded in for a dissimilar asset with an objectively determined FMV of $30,000.

E9-16

Reverse T-account analysis

The financial information below was taken from the records of White Bones, Inc.

	2002	2001
BALANCE SHEET		
Equipment	$37,500	$32,700
Less: Accumulated depreciation	17,600	14,300
Net book value	$19,900	$18,400

	2002	2001
INCOME STATEMENT		
Depreciation expense	$ 7,200	$ 6,800
Gain on sale of equipment	2,100	0

Note: The company purchased equipment for $12,000 during 2002.

a. How much cash was collected on the sale of equipment during 2002?
b. Reconstruct the entry that recorded the sale of equipment during 2002.

REAL DATA

E9-17

Inferring information from the financial statements

The information below was taken from the 1999 annual report of Intel, a world-leading supplier to the Internet economy.

	1999	1998
Property, plant, and equipment	$23,557	$21,068
Less: accumulated depreciation	11,842	9,459
Depreciation expense	3,186	2,807
Investments in property, plant, and equipment	3,403	3,557

a. From which of the financial statements was each figure taken?
b. Estimate the cost of property, plant, and equipment sold during 1999.
c. Estimate the accumulated depreciation associated with the property, plant, and equipment sold during 1999.
d. Assume the property, plant, and equipment was sold during 1999 for $100 million cash. Estimate the gain or loss recognized on the sale. On what financial statement(s) would this amount appear?

E9-18

Reverse T-account analysis

The financial information below was taken from the records of Frederickson and Peffer.

	2002	2001
BALANCE SHEET		
Equipment	$26,900	$23,400
Less: Accumulated depreciation	10,500	9,800
Net book value	$16,400	$13,600

INCOME STATEMENT

Depreciation expense	$ 3,800	$ 3,500
Loss on sale of equipment	900	0

STATEMENT OF CASH FLOWS

Cash received on sale of equipment	$ 4,300	$ 0

a. Reconstruct the entry that recorded the sale of equipment during 2002.
b. How much equipment was purchased during 2001?

E9-19

Appendix 9A:
Intangible assets:
Expense or
capitalize and
amortize?

Swift Corporation incorporated on January 1, 2002, and incurred $45,000 in organization costs.

a. Should Swift Corporation capitalize or expense these costs? Defend your answer.
b. If these costs are capitalized, over what period of time should they be amortized? Provide the amortization journal entry for a single year if the maximum period of time is chosen.
c. What arguments could be used to justify capitalizing organization costs but not allocating them to future periods?
d. Assume that during 2002, Swift acquired a patent for $65,000. Should this cost be expensed or capitalized? Why one and not the other?
e. Assume that during 2002, Swift invested $220,000 to research and develop new products. Should these costs be expensed or capitalized?
f. What arguments could be used to justify capitalizing research and development costs, and if capitalized, how should these costs be amortized to future periods?

E9-20

Appendix 9A:
The capitalized cost
of a patent

The following information was taken from the internal financial records of Southern Robotics regarding a patent filed in 2002 for a new robotics arm used for manufacturing:

1. Legal and filing fees of $50,000 were paid during 2002 for filing the patent.
2. Legal fees of $200,000 were incurred and paid during 2003 to defend the patent against infringement by another company.

The patent was granted on December 31, 2002. The company estimated that the patent would provide an economic benefit to the company for five years. It is company policy not to amortize intangible assets in the year of acquisition.

a. Assume that Southern Robotics successfully defended its patent against the infringement.
    (1) What amount should Southern Robotics report for this patent on the company's December 31, 2002 balance sheet?
    (2) What amount should Southern Robotics report for this patent on the company's December 31, 2003 balance sheet?
    (3) Prepare the entry to amortize the patent on December 31, 2003.
b. Assume that Southern Robotics was unsuccessful in defending its patent against the infringement.
    (1) What amount should Southern Robotics report for this patent on the company's December 31, 2002 balance sheet?
    (2) What amount should Southern Robotics report for this patent on the company's December 31, 2003 balance sheet?
    (3) Prepare the entry to write off the patent.

PROBLEMS

P9-1

Determining
capitalized cost
and the
depreciation base

Stonebrecker International recently purchased new manufacturing equipment. The equipment cost $1 million. The company also incurred additional costs related to the acquisition of the equipment. The total cost to transport the equipment to Stonebrecker's plant was $80,000, half of which was paid by Stonebrecker. The company also paid $8,000 to insure the equipment while it was being transported to its plant. The initial installation costs totaled $20,000. After installing the equipment, however, it was discovered that the floor under the equipment would have to be reinforced. Materials and direct labor to reinforce the floor totaled $15,000. While the equipment was being installed and the floor was being reinforced, the plant workers could not perform their normal functions. The cost to Stonebrecker of the employee downtime was $10,000. Stonebrecker estimates that the equipment will have a salvage value of $100,000 in ten years.

REQUIRED:

a. What dollar amount should Stonebrecker capitalize on its books for this equipment?
b. Prepare the journal entry to capitalize the equipment.
c. What is the depreciation base of this equipment?
d. Over the life of this equipment, what dollar amount will be depreciated under the straight-line method? under the double-declining-balance method?

P9–2

Lump-sum purchases and cost allocations

The JHP Company purchased a building, some office equipment, two cranes, and some land on January 1, 2002, for a total of $1 million cash. JHP has obtained the following appraisals of these assets:

Asset	FMV on 1/1/99	Estimated Life	Estimated Salvage Value
Building	$300,000	20 years	$75,000
Office equipment	150,000	3 years	35,000
Crane	75,000	5 years	15,000
Crane	75,000	5 years	15,000
Land	600,000	Indefinite	

JHP company uses the straight-line method to depreciate fixed assets.

REQUIRED:

a. Prepare the journal entry to record the purchase.
b. Prepare the journal entry to record depreciation expense for each type of asset for the year ended December 31, 2002.
c. Assuming that all of these assets are still held as of December 31, 2005, present these fixed assets as they would be shown on the December 31, 2005 balance sheet.

P9–3

Determining capitalized cost and depreciation

Gidley, Inc., purchased a piece of equipment on January 1, 2002. The following information is available for this purchase:

Purchase price	$950,000
Transportation	$100,000[a]
Installation	$130,000[b]
Salvage value	$50,000
Useful life	4 years

[a]**Included in the transportation cost is $1,000 for insurance covering the shipment of the equipment to Gidley.**
[b]**Included in the cost of installation is $80,000 in wages paid to employees who helped install the equipment.**

REQUIRED:

a. Compute the cost of the fixed asset that should be capitalized.
b. Prepare the entry to record depreciation expense for the year ended December 31, 2002, assuming the company uses each of the following:
   (1) Double-declining-balance depreciation method
   (2) Straight-line depreciation method

(Continued)

c. Assuming that the equipment was sold on January 1, 2003, for $250,000, prepare the entry to record the sale of the equipment using each of the following methods:
(1) Double-declining-balance depreciation method
(2) Straight-line depreciation method

P9-4

Expensing what should be capitalized can misstate net income

Westmiller Construction Company purchased a new truck on December 31, 2000, for $48,000. The truck has an estimated useful life of three years and an estimated salvage value of $12,000. When the truck was purchased, the company's accountant mistakenly made the following entry:

Depreciation Expense—Truck (E, −SE)   48,000
    Cash (−A)   48,000

Over the life of the truck, the company made no other entries associated with it.

REQUIRED:
a. What entry should Westmiller Construction Company have made on December 31, 2000?
b. Assuming that the straight-line method of depreciation should have been used and that the error was not discovered, in what direction and by how much was net income misstated in 2000 and 2001?
c. Assuming that the double-declining-balance method of depreciation should have been used and that the error was not discovered, in what direction and by how much was net income misstated in 2000 and 2001?

P9-5

Accounting for betterments and maintenance costs

McCartney Manufacturing purchased a dryer for $100,000 on January 1, 1999. The estimated life of the dryer is five years, and the salvage value is estimated to be $10,000. McCartney uses the straight-line method of depreciation.

On January 1, 2003, McCartney paid $160,000 to have the dryer overhauled, which increased the speed of the dryer and extended its estimated useful life to December 31, 2006. Each year, McCartney pays $1,000 to have the dryer serviced. On November 12, 2003, a major repair was required at a cost of $5,000. Salvage value is still estimated to be $10,000.

REQUIRED:
a. Provide the journal entry on January 1, 1999, to record the purchase of the dryer.
b. How should the service and repair costs be treated on the books of McCartney?
c. Compute the depreciation expense that would be recognized during each year of the dryer's eight years of useful life.

P9-6

Accounting for betterments

Hulteen Hardware purchased a new building on January 1, 1998, for $1.5 million. The company expects the building to last 25 years and expects to be able to sell it then for $150,000. During 2003, the building was painted at a cost of $5,000. Almost ten years after acquiring the building, the roof was destroyed by a storm. The company had a new roof constructed at a cost of $200,000. The new roof was completed on January 1, 2008, and it extended the estimated life of the building by five years, to a total of thirty years. All other estimates are still accurate. Hulteen Hardware uses the straight-line method to depreciate the cost of all fixed assets.

REQUIRED:
a. Prepare the entry to record the purchase of the building, assuming that the company paid cash.
b. Prepare the entry to record the purchase of the new roof on January 1, 2008.
c. Prepare the entry to record depreciation expense for the year ended December 31, 2008.
d. Prepare the journal entry that would be recorded if the building was sold for $1.2 million on December 31, 2013.

P9-7

Revising the estimated useful life

Burke Copy Center purchased a machine on January 1, 1997, for $180,000 and estimated its useful life and salvage value at ten years and $30,000, respectively. On January 1, 2002, the company added three years to the original useful-life estimate.

REQUIRED:

a. Compute the book value of the machine as of January 1, 2002, assuming that Burke recognizes the depreciation using straight-line.

b. Prepare the journal entry to record depreciation entered by the company on December 31, 2002, assuming that Burke uses straight-line.

REAL DATA

P9-8

Effects of an accounting change

Effective January 1, 1999, Guidant Corporation, a global leader in medical technology, adopted an accounting principle requiring that all startup costs be expensed as incurred. Prior to January 1, these costs were capitalized and depreciated over periods up to five years. This change in accounting principle resulted in a pretax cumulative adjustment of $5.3 million.

a. Provide the entry Guidant made to record this adjustment. Ignore taxes.

b. The after-tax adjustment was equal to $3.3 million. Compute Guidant's effective tax rate.

c. In what three sections in the 1999 annual report was this adjustment described?

P9-9

Why is double-declining-balance preferred for tax purposes?

Note: Knowledge of the time value of money is necessary for this problem (see Appendix B). Kimberly Sisters purchased equipment for $80,000 on January 1, 2002. Kimberly can use the double-declining-balance method for tax purposes but does not understand why it should be preferred over straight-line. The following information is available:

Estimated useful life	**4 years**
Estimated salvage value	**$20,000**
Expected revenues over each of the next four years	**$100,000**
Expected expenses (excluding depreciation) over each of the	
next four years	**$60,000**
Tax rate (percent of net income)	**35 percent**

REQUIRED:

a. Which of the two methods will give rise to the greater amount of depreciation over the life of the equipment? Support your answer with computations.

b. Which of the two methods will result in the payment of less taxes over the life of the equipment? Support your answer with computations.

c. Why is the double-declining-balance method preferred for tax purposes?

d. Assume a discount rate of 10 percent. How much money would be saved by using double-declining-balance instead of straight-line?

P9-10

The effect of depreciation on taxes, bonuses, and dividends

Bently Poster Company pays income taxes on net income at the rate of 32 percent. The company pays a bonus to its officers of 8 percent of net income after taxes and pays dividends to its stockholders in the amount of 75 percent of net income after taxes. On January 1, 2002, the company purchased a fixed asset for $400,000. Such assets are usually depreciated over a ten-year period. Salvage value is expected to be zero. Assume that the bonus payment is not included as an expense in the calculation of taxable income and reported income.

REQUIRED:

Assume that revenues and expenses (excluding depreciation) for 2002 are $250,000 and $140,000, respectively. Compute the tax, bonus, and dividend payment for 2002 if the company uses the following:

a. The straight-line method of depreciation

b. The double-declining-balance method of depreciation

c. The straight-line method of depreciation, assuming a five-year useful life

P9-11

Natural resources: Different methods of cost allocation depend on the nature of the asset

Garmen Oil Company recently discovered an oil field on one of its properties in Texas. In order to extract the oil, the company purchased drilling equipment on January 1, 2002, for $800,000 cash and also purchased a mobile home on the same date for $54,000 cash to serve as on-site headquarters. The drilling equipment has an estimated useful life of twelve years but will be abandoned when the company shuts down this well. The mobile home has an estimated useful life of seven years and an estimated salvage value of $5,000. The company expects to use the mobile home on other drilling sites after work on this site is completed.

Company geologists estimated correctly that the well would produce two million barrels of oil. Actual production from the well for 2002, 2003, and 2004 was 600,000 barrels, 750,000 barrels, and 650,000 barrels, respectively. All extracted barrels were immediately sold. This well is now dry, and Garmen Oil has shut it down.

REQUIRED:

a. Prepare the entry to record the purchase of the drilling equipment and the mobile home.
b. Prepare the entries to record depletion expense for the drilling equipment using the activity method for 2002, 2003, and 2004.
c. Prepare the entries to record depreciation expenses for 2002, 2003, and 2004 for the mobile home using the straight-line method. Why are different methods used to allocate the costs of the drilling equipment and the mobile home?
d. Assume that Garmen Oil discovered that the well was dry at the end of 2003 (i.e., the well produced only 1,350,000 barrels of oil). Repeat parts (b) and (c).

P9–12

Selling and trading in fixed assets

Webb Net Manufacturing purchased a new net weaving machine on January 1, 2000, for $500,000. The new machine has an estimated life of five years and an estimated salvage value of $100,000. It is company policy to use straight-line depreciation for all of its machines.

REQUIRED:

a. Assume that Webb Net Manufacturing sells this machine on January 1, 2003, for $325,000. Prepare the entry to record this transaction.
b. Assume that Webb Net Manufacturing sells this machine on June 30, 2003, for $320,000. Prepare the entry or entries to record this transaction.
c. Assume that Webb Net Manufacturing trades in this machine for a tract of land on January 1, 2003. The list price of the land is $250,000, and it has an appraised value of $210,000. The company is granted a trade-in allowance on the machine of $75,000 and pays an additional $175,000 in cash for the land. The net weaving machine is appraised at $75,000. Prepare the entry to record the trade-in, assuming that the land is valued as follows:
    (1) The FMV of the asset received.
    (2) The FMV of the assets given up.

P9–13

Appendix 9A: Recognizing goodwill

On January 1, 2002, Diversified Industries purchased Specialists, Inc., for $1.8 million. The balance sheet of Specialists, Inc., at the time of purchase follows:

Assets		Liabilities and Stockholders' Equity	
Current assets	$650,000	Liabilities	$250,000
Long-lived assets	330,000	Stockholders' equity	730,000
		Total liabilities and	
Total assets	$980,000	stockholders' equity	$980,000

The total FMV of the individual assets of Specialists is $1.35 million, and the liabilities are valued on the balance sheet at FMV.

REQUIRED:

a. How can the FMV of Specialists' assets exceed the value of the assets on the balance sheet?
b. Why would Diversified pay more for Specialists than the FMV of the assets less the liabilities?
c. Provide the journal entry to record the purchase.
d. In the recent past goodwill was amortized over a period of time not to exceed forty years. Provide an argument to challenge this position.

P9–14

Appendix 9A:
Goodwill accounting

On March 19, 1999, the Avis Group purchased the common stock of Rent-A-Car Incorporated for $1.918 billion. The fair market value of the assets acquired and liabilities assumed was estimated to be $4.810 billion and $4.272 billion, respectively.

a. Compute the goodwill acquired in the transaction.

b. Discuss why Avis paid significantly more for Rent-A-Car than was indicated by the fair market value of Rent-A-Car's net assets.

ISSUES FOR DISCUSSION

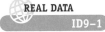

REAL DATA

ID9–1

Lump-sum sales and purchase

MGM Grand, Inc., purchased two Las Vegas casinos and the adjoining land for a total of $167 million. Soon afterwards, the company agreed to sell one of the casinos and 58.7 acres of adjacent land for $110 million.

REQUIRED:

a. What issues need to be addressed in order to determine the gain or loss resulting from the sale of one of the casinos? How should the cost of the sold casino be established?

b. Assume that each casino had a cost of $75 million and the adjacent land originally cost $17 million. Provide the journal entry prepared by MGM Grand to record the sale.

c. Explain how the casino and the land would each be valued on the balance sheet of the purchasing company.

d. Assume that an appraiser assesses the value of the land without the hotel to be $43 million. Compute the annual depreciation charge recognized by the purchasing company if it depreciates buildings using the straight-line rate over a period of twenty-five years. Assume no salvage value.

REAL DATA

ID9–2

Capitalizing marketing costs

Forbes (January 1997) reported that Seattle FilmWorks capitalizes the costs of its direct mailings to prospective customers, expensing them over three years rather than in the year they're incurred. There's nothing wrong with this practice per se. If the customers netted by mailing come back with repeat business year after year, you really have booked an asset. But there is no guarantee that the first-time customer will become a regular. Currently, $11 million worth of marketing costs sits on the company's balance sheet as an asset. If Seattle FilmWorks had deducted all fiscal 1996 marketing costs immediately, it would have netted less than $5.4 million, versus the $8 million it officially reported.

This situation is familiar to America Online shareholders. By spreading its marketing expenses over two years, AOL created artificially high earnings. In September the company finally changed its accounting policy. Result: A $385 million write-off and projected loss for fiscal 1997.

REQUIRED:

Discuss the trade-offs involved with capitalizing marketing costs from a matching standpoint and from the perspectives of management, the shareholders, and the auditors.

REAL DATA

ID9–3

Betterments or maintenance and subsequent depreciation

Ford Motor Company said it would spend $200 million to refurbish its Mustang assembly plant in Dearborn, Michigan. The aging factory had been discussed as a candidate for closing, but Ford's current capacity of Mustang production is barely able to keep pace with demand.

REQUIRED:

a. What issues must be considered when deciding whether to capitalize or expense the $200 million expenditures?

b. Under what conditions could the $200 million cost be expensed even if it improved instead of maintained the plant?

(Continued)

c. Assume that the $200 million cost is capitalized and that the refurbishment extends the useful life of the factory. Explain how Ford will compute depreciation on its factory over its remaining useful life.

REAL DATA

ID9–4

Expense vs.
capitalize

The 2000 annual report of Cisco Systems discloses that the company expenses all advertising and research and development costs, while capitalizing all software development costs.

REQUIRED:

Describe the effect of these two accounting treatments on the financial statements, discuss these treatments in terms of the nature of these particular costs and the matching principle, and comment on management incentives that might influence Cisco Systems to favor one or the other accounting treatment.

REAL DATA

ID9–5

Recognizing
depreciation and
economic
consequences

In the past, private colleges, which are subject to the accounting and reporting standards for not-for-profit entities, have not been required to recognize depreciation on their financial statements. However, *The Wall Street Journal* reported that "many of the nation's 1,500 private colleges are considering ignoring a new accounting rule that would require them to depreciate buildings and equipment.... Several colleges received assurances from Standard & Poor's Corp. and Moody's Investors Services, Inc., that the bond-rating agencies wouldn't lower the colleges' bond ratings based on noncompliance with the FASB Statement.... The FASB's rules have the informal blessing of the Securities and Exchange Commission and, if not followed, would result in a qualified (audit) opinion. Such qualifications could cloud the status of some college bonds by triggering spending limits in bond covenants."

REQUIRED:

a. Explain why colleges might not want to recognize depreciation on their financial statements.
b. Why would such institutions be interested in the assurances described above from companies such as Standard & Poor's and Moody's?
c. Why might an auditor qualify the audit opinion on a college that did not conform to this accounting rule?
d. Why would a spending limit be part of the bond covenant, and how could a qualified audit opinion trigger such a limit?

REAL DATA

ID9–6

Fair market value
accounting for
museums?

An article published in *The New York Times* several years ago, titled "Pricing the Priceless: Museums Resist, Accountants Insist," stated that "many museums' most valuable assets, from moon rocks to Michelangelos, are nowhere on their books." The FASB recently passed *SFAS Nos. 117* and *124*, both of which established reporting standards for not-for-profit entities. Now museums must follow these standards or risk qualified audit reports.

REQUIRED:

a. Do you believe that museums, not-for-profit institutions, should be required to have their art objects appraised and the values be placed on their balance sheets? Discuss.
b. Why would museums resist such a rule and be concerned about receiving unqualified opinions from their auditors?

REAL DATA

ID9–7

Corporate
restructuring

After being asked how General Electric has maintained such consistent earnings growth over the past decade, Dennis Dammerman, the company's chief financial officer, says, "We're the best company in the world." However, *The Wall Street Journal* (November 3, 1994) offered another explanation. It notes that from 1983 through 1993, General Electric recorded six discretionary restructuring charges, ranging in magnitude from $147 million to over $1 billion—totaling $3.95 billion. Coincidentally, in each of the years when a restructuring charge was recognized, GE booked a sizable one-time gain. In 1987, for example, the company recognized an $858 million one-time gain due to changes in accounting methods for taxes and inventory while taking a $1,027 million restructuring write-off. In 1993, GE matched a $1 billion restructuring charge against the $1.4 billion one-time gain it recognized on the sale of an aerospace unit to Martin Marietta. "To smooth out fluctuations, GE frequently offsets one-time gains from big asset sales with restructuring charges; that keeps earnings from rising so high that they can't be topped the following year. GE also times sales of some equity stakes and even acquisitions to produce profit gains when needed."

REQUIRED:

a. Determine what reporting strategy GE seems to be using, and explain how it works.
b. Explain how discretionary restructuring charges help GE to implement that reporting strategy and why the company would want to pursue it.
c. *The Wall Street Journal* (November 2, 1994) reported that "investors love restructurings" and that such charges seem to boost stock prices. Yet the FASB is seriously considering cracking down on this popular corporate practice. Explain why investors might love restructurings, why stock prices seem to rise when they are announced, and why the FASB is acting to limit such behavior.

REAL DATA
ID9–8
Current values?

As discussed in this chapter, U.S. accounting standards at one time contained a requirement that certain large companies disclose current values for inventories and fixed assets. Such disclosure included dollar amounts for cost of goods sold and depreciation that were based on current instead of historical cost. This requirement, however, was quickly abandoned in response to heated controversy.

REQUIRED:

a. Consider the case of News Corp. described in this chapter, and build an argument against requiring current values on the balance sheet.
b. Consider the usefulness of historical costs for decision-making purposes, and build a case for requiring current values on the balance sheet.
c. Which of the two arguments do you find most convincing?

REAL DATA
ID9–9
Subjective asset write-downs

In 1997, Kellogg, a maker of cereals and foods, hit its targeted earnings-per-share growth of 11 percent, and its stock price was up 25 percent over the year. In the fourth quarter of that year, the company took a significant "onetime" charge against earnings when it wrote down assets—mostly property, plant, and equipment—from its overseas operations. Interestingly, this write-down was the ninth such charge in the past eleven quarters. Some analysts believe that Kellogg was using these charges to manage earnings and estimated that the company's 1997 earnings should actually have been 24 percent below 1996 earnings.

REQUIRED:

a. Describe how Kellogg could use asset write-downs to manage earnings.
b. Explain why auditors may be less inclined to object to subjective asset write-downs compared to asset overstatements.
c. What is the FASB's position on asset impairments?

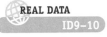

REAL DATA
ID9–10
The annual report of Wal-Mart

The 2001 annual report of Wal-Mart is reproduced in Appendix A.

REQUIRED:

Review the 2001 annual report, and answer the following questions.

a. What percentage of total assets do property, plant, and equipment make up?
b. What is the largest category of property, plant, and equipment?
c. How large is the depreciation expense relative to sales?
d. What estimated lives does Wal-Mart use for its buildings, fixtures, and transportation equipment?
e. Which method does Wal-Mart use to depreciate its property, plant, and equipment for financial reporting purposes? Which method for tax purposes?

f. How does Wal-Mart account for its software development costs? How does the company account for its advertising expenditures?

g. How much interest was capitalized during 2001, 2000, and 1999, and why would a company capitalize interest?

h. How much did Wal-Mart invest in property, plant, and equipment during 2001? How much was invested in international operations?

i. How much goodwill did Wal-Mart recognize in 2001?

Liabilities and Stockholders' Equity: A Closer Look

During 1998, Hewlett-Packard (HP) reported a drop in return on equity (ROE) from 21 to 17 percent. Return on assets (ROA) also decreased from 9.8 to 8.7 percent. While revenues increased by approximately $4 billion, profits fell from $4.3 billion to $3.8 billion. To some, HP suffered a pretty dismal year. Nonetheless, company management was upbeat in the 1998 annual report. Long-term debt was reduced in 1998 by almost 50 percent; over $2 billion was invested in the company's own common stock; and the shareholders received a hefty $625 million in dividends. It seems that management's optimistic outlook was based primarily on how HP's capital structure changed during 1998—less debt and lower levels of stockholders' equity. Do you think that management can justly claim success on the basis of capital structure changes in a year when ROE, ROA, and profits have fallen? The next three chapters—10, 11, and 12—describe the components of a company's capital structure, helping to explain the logic that may have underscored management's optimism.

CHAPTER 10
Introduction to Liabilities: Economic Consequences, Current Liabilities, and Contingencies

CHAPTER 11
Long-Term Liabilities: Notes, Bonds, and Leases

CHAPTER 12
Stockholders' Equity

Introduction to Liabilities: Economic Consequences, Current Liabilities, and Contingencies

CHAPTER 10

KEY POINTS

The following key points are emphasized in this chapter:

* *Definition of a liability.*

* *Economic consequences associated with reporting liabilities on the financial statements.*

* *Determinable and contingent liabilities.*

* *Current liabilities.*

* *Bonus systems and profit-sharing arrangements and the reporting incentives they create.*

* *Methods used to account for contingencies.*

Waste companies have great latitude in setting reserves (liabilities) for future environmental costs at their dumps. The process involves estimating how high the costs will be thirty years or more in the future and calculating how big a fund is needed in today's dollars to satisfy the future obligation. For example, Waste Management Inc., previously accused of using aggressive accounting methods, recently recorded a $173.3 million cost that lowered its third-quarter profit by 63 percent. The cost included $45 million to boost cleanup reserves for some dumps; $26 million to increase reserves for litigation; and $72.3 million to boost reserves for future claims. Does anybody really know how large the liability should be? This example illustrates the difficulties involved in measuring liabilities, the topic of Chapters 10 and 11.

Liabilities, defined as obligations of a company to disburse assets or provide services in the future, are divided on the balance sheet into two categories: current liabilities and long-term liabilities. Current liabilities primarily include short-term payables to suppliers, employees, banks, and others. Long-term liabilities relate to long-term notes, bonds, leases, retirement costs, and deferred income taxes. This chapter introduces liabilities in general and covers the methods used to account for current liabilities and contingent liabilities, which can be either current or long-term. Accounting for retirement costs and deferred income taxes is briefly reviewed in Appendices 10A and 10B, respectively. Chapter 11 is devoted to long-term notes, bonds, and leases. These three liabilities are covered in a single chapter because the same basic method, called the *effective interest method,* is used to account for them.

WHAT IS A LIABILITY?

The FASB has defined liabilities as "probable future sacrifices of economic benefits arising from present obligations of a particular entity to transfer assets or provide services to other entities in the future as a result of past transactions or events." The Board commented further that all liabilities appearing on the balance sheet should have three characteristics in common: (1) they should be present obligations that entail settlements by probable future transfers or uses of cash, goods, or services; (2) they should be unavoidable obligations; and (3) the transaction or event obligating the enterprise must have already happened.[1]

While the FASB's definition makes the measurement of most liabilities relatively straightforward, the liabilities listed on the balance sheet do encompass a wide variety of items, including credit balances with suppliers, debts from borrowings, services yet to be performed, withholdings from employees' wages and salaries, dividend declarations, product warranties, deferred income taxes, and a number of complex financing arrangements. As we will discuss later, there is some question whether all these items are liabilities in an economic sense as well as whether all the economic liabilities of a company are included on its balance sheet.

In its 2000 annual report, Emerson Electric reported that it leased certain of its fixed assets. The contracts associated with those leases specified that $99 million would have to be paid by the company in 2001. Yet this amount was not included in the liabilities listed on Emerson's balance sheet. Review the criteria for recognizing a liability and consider whether Emerson's accounting treatment was appropriate.

1. Financial Accounting Standards Board (FASB), "Elements of Financial Statements of Business Enterprises," *Statement of Financial Accounting Concepts No. 3* (Stamford, Conn.: FASB, 1980), pars. 28 and 29.

THE RELATIVE SIZE OF LIABILITIES ON THE BALANCE SHEET

Figure 10–1 contains liabilities as a percentage of total assets, often referred to as the **debt ratio,** for selected firms. The main financing source for financial institutions is clearly debt. Customer demand deposits and short-term debt are primarily responsible. General Electric's financial subsidiary, which is set up to provide financing to its customers on big-ticket sales, is basically a financial institution, accounting for GE's large debt ratio. Companies like SBC Communications and SUPERVALU invest heavily in property, plant, and equipment that is financed through debt, while Internet firms have generated most of their financing by issuing equity.

FIGURE 10–1 Liabilities as a percentage of total assets		Liabilities/ Total Assets
Manufacturing:		
General Electric (manufacturer)		.88
Chevron (oil drilling and refining)		.52
Retail:		
SUPERVALU (grocery retail)		.73
Tommy Hilfiger (clothing retail)		.46
Internet:		
Yahoo (Internet search engine)		.16
Cisco (Internet systems)		.19
General services:		
SBC Communications (telecommunications services)		.69
Wendy's (restaurant services)		.43
Financial services:		
Bank of America (banking services)		.93
Merrill Lynch (investment services)		.95

Internet companies like Yahoo and Lycos carry very little debt on their balance sheets, while large manufacturers like Exxon Mobil and General Electric have debt amounts that are well over 50 percent of total assets. Comment on why such differences might exist.

REPORTING LIABILITIES ON THE BALANCE SHEET: ECONOMIC CONSEQUENCES

The reported values of liabilities affect important financial ratios that stockholders, investors, creditors, and others use to assess management's performance and a company's financial condition. Seven of Dun & Bradstreet's fourteen key business ratios, for example, directly include a measure of liabilities: (1) quick ratio ([cash + marketable securities + receivables]/current liabilities), (2) current ratio (current assets/current liabilities), (3) current liabilities/net worth, (4) current liabilities/inventory, (5) total liabilities/net worth, (6) sales/net working capital, and (7) accounts payable/sales. These ratios and others that include liability measures are used by interested outside parties to determine credit ratings, assess solvency and future cash flows, predict bankruptcy and, in general, assess the financial health of an enterprise. In addition to using liability measures to evaluate the future prospects of a firm, stockholders, investors, creditors, and managers are interested in the reported values of liabilities for other important reasons, several of which are discussed in the following paragraphs.

Stockholders and Investors

Debt financing can be very valuable to shareholders because funds generated by borrowing can be used to generate returns that exceed the cost of the debt. Since interest is tax deductible (reducing the cost of debt), this strategy (called leverage) is very common. However, stockholders and investors must pay close attention to the amount of liabilities and the contracts that underlie them because debt increases the riskiness of the company. Interest payments must be met before dividends can be distributed, and, in the event of liquidation, outstanding payables must be satisfied before stockholders are paid. Many loan contracts restrict the amount of dividends that can be paid in any one year to the common stockholders. For example, The Boeing Company, an aircraft manufacturer, operates under debt covenants that restrict the payment of dividends and other distributions on the company's stock. As of December 31, 2000, these covenants limited Boeing's stockholder payments to less than 25 percent of retained earnings.

Creditors

The creditors of a company have a special interest in the liabilities held by others. These liabilities compete for the resources that must be used to satisfy the obligations owed to them. Creditors often protect their interests by writing terms in loan contracts that require collateral in the case of default or that restrict a company's future borrowings. A recent annual report of Owens Corning contained the following excerpt, which describes the debt covenants imposed by its bank lenders:

As is typical for bank credit, the agreements contain restrictive covenants, including requirements for the maintenance of working capital, interest coverage, and minimum coverage of fixed charges; and limitations on the early retirement of (certain) debt, additional borrowings, certain investments, payment of dividends, and purchase of Company stock. The agreements include a provision which would result in all of the unpaid principal and accrued interest of the facilities becoming due immediately upon a change of control in ownership of the Company. A material adverse change in the Company's business, assets, liabilities, financial condition, or results of operations constitutes a default under the agreements.

Management

Management views short- and long-term borrowings and the related liabilities as important sources of cash for operating, investing, and financing activities. An article in *Forbes* stated: *"Most companies spend lots of time figuring out when and how to borrow money. That makes sense. Proper timing of debt can save millions in interest payments."*

On its 2000 balance sheet, for example, General Electric disclosed about $381 billion of outstanding liabilities, representing almost 87 percent of its financing sources. That amount is certainly a significant sum that requires astute and careful management to ensure that sufficient cash is on hand to meet the required payments as they come due. In 2000 alone, General Electric paid approximately $12 billion in interest to service its outstanding debt. Effective management of such debt is critical to a company's success and can be used to great advantage. As noted earlier, practicing leverage is a very popular strategy.

While management often chooses to rely on borrowings for its financial needs, it has incentives to understate liabilities on the balance sheet. Indeed, a well-known article in *Forbes* began: *"The basic drives of man are few: to get enough food, to find shelter, and to keep debt off the balance sheet."*

Additional debt on the balance sheet, for example, can reduce a company's credit rating, making it increasingly difficult to attract capital in the future. Standard & Poor's Corp., an established credit-rating service, lowered the credit rating of Fleming Company because the company financed an acquisition with borrowings that increased its total debt by $375 million. In reaction to Standard & Poor's announcement, the market price of the company's outstanding stock immediately dropped.

Additional debt on the balance sheet can also decrease the current ratio, increase the debt/asset ratio, and increase the debt/equity ratio. Such changes could cause a company to violate its debt covenants and, in general, cause it to be viewed as more risky by outside investors and creditors. The national director of accounting and auditing at Seidman & Seidman, for example, points out: *"Removing large amounts of debt can present a more favorable impression of debt-to-equity ratios, working capital ratios, and the returns on assets invested in the business."*

There are also situations, however, when management may wish to accelerate the recognition of liabilities, booking them in a current instead of a future period. For example, by reporting additional liabilities in the current period, management may be able to report higher net income amounts in future periods. Such a reporting strategy is not unusual for companies that are experiencing exceptionally poor years as well as for those experiencing exceptionally good years.

While in the midst of bankruptcy proceedings, for example, LTV Corporation "took a bath" by accruing a number of significant liabilities, none of which were required at the time by generally accepted accounting principles. A spokesman for LTV was quoted in *The Wall Street Journal* as saying:

[The company] took the special charges because it believes it should record all its liabilities while in [bankruptcy] proceedings. It's a unique opportunity for us to take it at a time when it does the least harm. . . . LTV likely wants a fresh start when it emerges from bankruptcy-law proceedings.

Companies experiencing exceptionally good years may also choose to accrue additional liabilities. The article just cited also pointed out that a number of companies "with strong equity positions" may wish to take early recognition of certain liabilities and, in effect, "bite the bullet early." This reporting strategy, called "building hidden reserves," recognizes losses in a year when they will be overwhelmed by other items of income. It also avoids having to recognize the losses in later years that may not be so exceptional. Both General Electric and Microsoft have been cited for managing earnings through hidden reserves.

Auditors

Auditors must attest that all liabilities are identified and properly reported on the balance sheet. Auditors are particularly careful in this area because significant unreported liabilities may lead to future investor and creditor losses for which auditors may be held liable. For example, a major accounting firm withdrew its opinions on Bombay Palace Restaurants, Inc., accusing the company of supplying false information and invoice documents with respect to certain material liabilities. In a well-known case involving Phar-Mor drugstores, a major accounting firm was sued for millions of dollars for failing to uncover a fraud that grossly understated the company's liabilities.

In 1997, Whirlpool Corporation, maker of home appliances, accrued a $343 million liability and charge against income to "better align the company's cost structure with the global appliance market." That year Whirlpool reported a net loss of $15 million. In 1998 and 1999, the company's earnings rebounded, and Whirlpool reported over $300 million in profits in both years. In its 1999 annual report, it noted that a significant amount of the charge taken in 1997 still had not been realized (paid in cash). What earnings management strategy might Whirlpool be practicing and why should investors and the company's external auditors (Ernst & Young) be concerned?

CURRENT LIABILITIES

Current liabilities are obligations expected to require the use of current assets or the creation of other current liabilities. They normally include obligations to suppliers (accounts payable), short-term debts, current maturities on long-term debts, dividends payable to stockholders, deferred revenues (services or goods yet to be performed or delivered that are expected to require the use of current assets), third-party collections (e.g., sales tax and payroll deductions), periodic accruals (e.g., wages and interest), and potential obligations related to pending or threatened litigation, product warranties, and guarantees.

Note that current liabilities are defined in terms of obligations "expected to require the use of current assets." Thus, reported obligations that are not expected to require the use of current assets are not disclosed as current. For example, an obligation that is due within a year may not be disclosed in the current liabilities section if it is either (1) expected to be paid from assets that are presently listed as noncurrent or (2) expected to be replaced (refinanced) with a long-term liability or equity issuance. Such obligations would normally be disclosed as long-term.

The Relative Size of Current Liabilities on the Balance Sheet

Figure 10–2 shows that current liabilities are the main liabilities of financial institutions. As indicated earlier, customer demand deposits are the primary reason. Figure 10–1 indicated that Internet firms rely very little on debt, and in Figure 10–2 we see that almost all of that is current. In other words, Internet firms have almost no long-term debt. Tommy Hilfiger, Chevron, and GE carry relatively small amounts of current liabilities, choosing to create their leverage with long-term debt. Tommy Hilfiger and Chevron also carry relatively large investments in property, plant, and equipment.

Current liabilities as a percent of total liabilities for the Bank of New York and AT&T are approximately 80 percent and 40 percent, respectively. Explain why these two companies carry such different levels of current liabilities.

FIGURE 10-2
Current liabilities
as a percentage of
total liabilities

	Current Liabilities/ Total Liabilities
Manufacturing:	
General Electric (manufacturer)	.41
Chevron (oil drilling and refining)	.36
Retail:	
SUPERVALU (grocery retail)	.56
Tommy Hilfiger (clothing retail)	.29
Internet:	
Yahoo (Internet search engine)	.91
Cisco (Internet systems)	.82
General services:	
SBC Communications (telecommunications services)	.45
Wendy's (restaurant services)	.47
Financial services:	
Bank of America (banking services)	.88
Merrill Lynch (investment services)	.82

Valuing Current Liabilities on the Balance Sheet

Most liabilities involve future cash outflows that are specified by formal contract or informal agreement. They can therefore be predicted objectively, and present value methods can be used to value liabilities on the balance sheet. In the case of current liabilities, however, the time period until payment is relatively short and the difference between the **face value** (actual cash payment when the liability is due) of the liability and its present value (discounted future cash payment) is considered to be immaterial. Thus, in the interest of materiality, current liabilities are usually recorded on the balance sheet at face value.

Reporting Current Liabilities: An Economic Consequence

In most cases, the face value of a current liability is easy to determine and balance sheet valuation is straightforward. The primary problem is one of discovery, ensuring that all existing current liabilities are reported on the balance sheet. Failure to discover and report an existing current liability misstates the financial statements and any of the financial measures that include current liabilities. Two particularly important financial measures are the current ratio and working capital, which help investors and creditors to assess a company's solvency position because they match current obligations against the assets on hand to satisfy them. These ratios are frequently found in loan contracts, such as those disclosed in an annual report of Cummins Engine Co., a manufacturer of heavy-duty truck engines, requiring Cummins to maintain a current ratio of 1.25:1.

Such debt restrictions can discourage management from reporting current liabilities on the balance sheet. Consider, for example, JFP Company, which borrows $1 million from Thrift Bank. The loan contract states that the loan is in default if JFP's current ratio, as reported on the balance sheet, dips below 2:1. Defaulting on this loan could mean that JFP must immediately pay the outstanding balance; in most cases, however, the company would be forced to renegotiate the terms of the loan with Thrift Bank. Such renegotiations would probably require that JFP make costly concessions, normally in the form of less desirable loan terms (e.g., higher interest rates, additional collateral).

At year-end, JFP's accountants determine that current assets equal $100,000. If current liabilities are determined to be $50,000 or less, the current ratio will be at least 2:1, and the loan will not be in default. On the other hand, if current liabilities are determined to be greater than $50,000, the current ratio would dip below 2:1, and JFP would be in violation of the loan contract, which could lead to serious financial problems.

If JFP's management fails, either intentionally or unintentionally, to report a given current liability on the balance sheet, it can avoid violating the terms of the loan contract and the related consequences. Management, therefore, has an incentive either to ignore existing current liabilities, postpone them, or to structure transactions so that current liabilities do not have to be recorded. Auditors must make special efforts to ensure that all existing current liabilities are properly reported on the balance sheet, and financial statement users must be aware of these management incentives.

For many years the frequent-flyer programs offered by the major airlines have allowed customers to build up future flying credits—thus creating a liability for the airlines. That is, the airlines must provide free seats for its frequent flyers. Airlines now accrue current liabilities for these credits, but for many years they argued that it was unnecessary. Describe some of the economic consequences the airlines may have been trying to avoid by not accruing these liabilities.

DETERMINABLE CURRENT LIABILITIES

Determining the dollar amounts of all current liabilities, because they represent probable future outlays, involves an element of uncertainty. The relative degree of uncertainty gives rise to two current liability categories: (1) determinable and (2) contingent. Determining the dollar amount of a determinable current liability is relatively straightforward; determining the dollar amount of a contingent liability involves an estimate. Figure 10–3 provides an outline of the current liabilities covered in the next two sections.

FIGURE 10–3
Outline of
current liabilities

Determinable current liabilities
A. **Accounts payable**
B. **Short-term debts**
   1. **Short-term notes**
   2. **Current maturities of long-term debts**
C. **Dividends payable**
D. **Unearned revenues**
E. **Third-party collections**
F. **Income taxes**
G. **Incentive compensation**

Contingent liabilities
A. **Lawsuits**
B. **Warranties**

In general, **determinable current liabilities** can be precisely measured, and the amount of cash needed to satisfy the obligation and the date of payment are reasonably certain. Determinable current liabilities include accounts payable, short-term debts, dividends payable, unearned revenues, third-party collections, and accrued liabilities.

Accounts Payable

Accounts payable are dollar amounts owed to others for goods, supplies, and services purchased on **open account.**[2] They arise from frequent transactions that are normally not subject to specific, formal contracts between a company and its suppliers. These extensions of credit are the practical result of a time lag between the receipt of a good, supply, or service and the corresponding payment. The time period is usually short (e.g., thirty to sixty days) and is indicated by the terms of the exchange (e.g., 2/10, n/30).

Accounts payable are usually associated with inventory purchases, which were discussed in Chapter 7, and a recent Dun & Bradstreet survey found that accounts payable are the most popular source of financing for small business owners. The size of the balance in accounts payable can be an important indicator of a company's financial condition, especially in the retail industry where suppliers are heavily relied upon to provide merchandise. The 1990 Christmas season for R.H. Macy, for example, did not produce sufficient revenues to cover the outstanding accounts owed to Macy's suppliers, which, in turn, delayed payments and caused the company's accounts payable balance to increase. Many financial analysts used this information to accurately predict that the company would soon declare bankruptcy. Robert Campeau, who built a retail empire in the 1980s, experienced similar problems prior to the empire's collapse in 1990. His companies paid suppliers so slowly that they ceased sending shipments.

 J.C. Penney's accounts payable represent approximately 75 percent of its current liabilities while the percentage for Biomet, a manufacturer in the medical industry, is only 13. Explain why accounts payable are so much more important for J.C. Penney.

Short-Term Debts

Short-term debts (or short-term borrowings) typically include short-term bank loans, commercial paper, lines of credit, and current maturities of long-term debt. **Commercial paper,** a fast-growing means of providing short-term financing, represents short-term notes (30 to 270 days) issued for cash by companies with good credit ratings to other companies. A **line of credit** is usually granted to a company by a bank or group of banks, allowing it to borrow up to a certain maximum dollar amount, interest being charged only on the outstanding balance. Issued commercial paper and existing lines of credit are an indication of a company's ability to borrow funds on a short-term basis; thus, they are very important to investors and creditors who are interested in assessing solvency. Consequently, such financing arrangements are extensively described in the footnotes.

---

2. Accounts payable are often referred to as *trade accounts payable. Accounting Trends and Techniques* (New York: AICPA, 2000) reports that 112 of the 600 major U.S. companies surveyed used that phrase.

SHORT-TERM NOTES

Short-term notes usually arise from cash loans and are generally payable to banks or loan companies. In most cases, the life of a note is somewhere between thirty days and one year, and the bank or loan company lends the borrowing company less cash than is indicated on the face of the note. At the **maturity date** (when the loan is due), the borrowing company pays the lending institution the face amount of the note, and the difference between the face amount and the amount of the loan is treated as interest.

For example, suppose that on January 1, Freight Line Industries borrows $9,400 from Commercial Loan Company and signs a six-month note with a face amount of $10,000. The journal entry to record this transaction is provided below.

Cash (+A)	9,400	
Discount on Notes Payable (−L)	600	
Notes Payable (+L)		10,000

Issued short-term note payable.

The Discount on Notes Payable account serves as a contra account to Notes Payable on the balance sheet and represents interest that is not yet owed but will be recognized in the future. Assuming that financial statements are prepared monthly, one-sixth of the discount would be converted to Interest Expense each month by an adjusting entry of the following form:

Interest Expense (E, −SE)	100	
Discount on Notes Payable (+L)		100

Recognized accrual of interest on a short-term note ($600/6).

After this entry is recorded at the end of the first month, the balance of the discount would have been reduced to $500, and the balance sheet carrying amount of the note would be as follows:

Notes payable	$10,000	
Less: Discount on note payable	500	$9,500

CURRENT MATURITIES OF LONG-TERM DEBTS

Long-term debts are often retired through a series of periodic installments. The installments that are to be paid within the time period that defines current assets (one year or the current operating cycle, whichever is longer) should be included on the balance sheet as current liabilities. The remaining installments should be disclosed as long-term liabilities.

For example, assume that on December 31, 2002, Wright and Sons borrows $50,000, which is to be paid back in annual installments of $7,000 each. The first payment, which is due on December 31, 2003, will consist of $5,000 in interest and $2,000 in principal. On the December 31, 2002 balance sheet, the associated payable would be disclosed in the following way. Note that the $50,000 principal amount is divided up into $2,000, which is due in the current period, and $48,000, which is long-term. The $5,000 in interest will be accrued at the end of 2000 after the company has had use of the funds.

Current liabilities:	
Current maturity of long-term debt	2,000
Long-term liabilities:	
Long-term notes payable	48,000

Included as current liabilities in the 2000 annual report of Coca-Cola are accounts payable, accrued expenses, commercial paper, short-term notes payable, and current maturities of long-term debts. Define each of these items and explain why they are considered current liabilities.

Dividends Payable

A liability is created when the board of directors of a corporation declares a dividend to be paid to the stockholders. It is listed as current because dividends are usually paid within several weeks of declaration. The methods used to account for dividends are discussed in Chapter 12.

Unearned Revenues

Payments are often received before contracted services are performed. In such cases, an *unearned revenue, deferred revenue,* or *receipt in advance* liability is created because the companies receiving the payments are under obligations that must be fulfilled. This liability is then converted to revenue as the related services are performed or the relevant goods are delivered. Recall that one of the primary criteria of revenue recognition is that the earning process must be complete before a revenue can be recognized. If providing the related services or relevant goods is expected to require the use of current assets, the unearned revenue liability should be classified as current.

Unearned revenues arise from a number of different transactions: gift certificates sold by retail stores that are redeemable in merchandise, coupons sold by restaurants that can be exchanged for meals, tickets and tokens sold by transportation companies that are good for future fares, advance payments for magazine subscriptions, and returnable deposits. Two particularly interesting examples are common in the airline industry. Passenger tickets are frequently paid several months before they are used, often because special discount fares are available with prepayment. These receipts are not immediately treated as revenues by the airlines but are recorded as Air Traffic Liability and listed in the current liabilities section of the balance sheet. These liabilities are converted to revenue as the tickets are used. Similarly, the frequent-flyer programs offered by a number of the major airlines create obligations, as customers build up mileage credits that must be paid in the form of free airline tickets. While most airlines have neglected to do so, these liabilities should be recognized as the mileage credits are earned.

To illustrate the basic methods used to account for unearned revenues, assume that Seattle Metro Transit sells bus passes, good for one month, for $20 each. On December 15, the transit company sells 50 passes for a total of $1,000. The following journal entries would be recorded on December 15 and December 31, after one-half month had expired:

Dec. 15	Cash (+A)	1,000	
	Unearned Revenue (+L)		1,000
	Sold 50 bus passes for future service.		
Dec. 31	Unearned Revenue (−L)	500	
	Fees Earned (R, +SE)		500
	Recognized completion of one-half future service.		

On its 2000 balance sheet Continental Airlines reported a current liability titled "air traffic liability" that exceeded $1 billion. Explain the nature of this liability and distinguish it from accounts payable, another account that appears on the company's balance sheet.

Third-Party Collections

Companies often act as collecting agencies for government or other entities. The price paid for an item at Kmart, for example, includes sales tax, which Kmart must periodically remit to the proper government authority. Companies are also required by law to withhold from employee wages social security taxes as well as an amount approximating the employee's income tax.[3] These withholdings are periodically sent to the federal government. In addition to payroll tax deductions, companies often withhold insurance premiums or union dues, which in turn must be passed on to the appropriate third party. In each of these cases, a liability is created; the company receives or holds cash that legally must be paid to a third party. The liability is discharged when the cash payment is made. These liabilities are usually considered current because payment is expected within the time period of current assets.

To illustrate, assume that Sears, Roebuck sells a small tractor for $1,000, which includes $50 in sales tax. The proper journal entry to record the sale follows:

Cash (or Accounts Receivable) (+A)   **1,000**
      Sales Tax Payable (+L)   50
      Sales (R, +SE)   950
Sold merchandise and collected sales tax.

When Sears pays the sales tax to the proper government authority, the following entry is recorded:

Sales Tax Payable (−L)   50
      Cash (−A)   50
Paid sales tax.

Income Tax Liability

Income tax liability for a corporation is based on a percentage of taxable income in accordance with the rules stated in the Internal Revenue Code. The income tax rate currently paid by U.S. corporations is approximately 35 percent of taxable income. Most corporations are required by law at the beginning of each year to estimate their tax liabilities for the entire year and to make quarterly tax payments based on these estimates.

Incentive Compensation

Basing compensation on net income and/or stock prices is a very popular way to pay executives and managers. Such payments comprise a significant portion of the total

---

3. Companies must not only withhold employee social security taxes; they must also match them. That is, employers must pay to the government a dollar amount equal to that withheld from the employee's wages. Such payments can be quite large. General Motors, for example, pays well over $100 million each year in matched social security taxes.

compensation of virtually all upper-level executives in major U.S. corporations. Profit-sharing arrangements, which are also based on a measure of net income, are frequently used to compensate employees at lower levels of the corporate hierarchy. *Accounting Trends and Techniques* (AICPA, 2000) reported that virtually all major U.S. companies compensate their employees on some performance-based measure. "More and more, it's a system U.S. companies are using to recruit, keep, and motivate workers," says Whit Smith, owner of Whitney Smith Co. in Fort Worth (*Phoenix Newspapers*, 2000).

Incentive compensation plans can take a number of different forms. AMP Incorporated, for example, has two incentive bonus plans: (1) a stock plus cash plan and (2) a cash plan. Executive compensation under the first plan is related to the market value of the company's stock; compensation under the second is a percentage of the company's net income. The formula for Daimler-Chrysler's incentive compensation plan includes a provision of 8 percent of consolidated net income. Exxon's incentive program indicates that the total amount distributed cannot exceed 3 percent of net income or 6 percent of capital invested (as defined by the plan). Figure 10–4 describes the incentive compensation formulas for selected large U.S. corporations.

FIGURE 10–4 Bonus formulas of selected large corporations for executive compensation pools		
Aluminum Co. of America	15% of total cash dividends.
Ashland Oil	6% of after-tax net income.
The Boeing Co.	6% of before-tax net income.
Bristol-Myers Squibb	Lesser of 6% of before-tax net income or 8% of after-tax net income.
DuPont	20% of after-tax net income in excess of 6% of stockholders' equity.
Goodyear Tire & Rubber	10% of after-tax net income in excess of consolidated book value of outstanding capital stock.
ITT Corp.	12% of after-tax net income in excess of 6% of stockholders' equity.
International Paper	8% of after-tax net income in excess of 6% of stockholders' equity.
Rockwell International	2% of the first $100 million of before-tax net income plus 3% of the next $50 million of before-tax net income plus 4% of the next $25 million of before-tax net income plus 5% of the balance.
Unocal Corp.	3% of after-tax net income in excess of 6% of stockholders' equity.

From an accounting standpoint, liabilities associated with incentive compensation plans must be accrued at year-end because they are based on measures of performance (e.g., net income or stock prices) that cannot be determined until that time. They are listed as current on the balance sheet because they are typically distributed to employees early the following period, at which time the liability is discharged.

Suppose, for example, that Tom Turnstile, an executive for Maylein Stoneware, is paid a bonus each year in the amount of 3 percent of net income before income taxes. If net income before income taxes is determined at year-end to be $300,000, Turnstile's bonus is $9,000 ($300,000 × 0.03), and the following journal entry is recorded:

Bonus Expense (E, −SE)   **9,000**
    Bonus Liability (+L)   **9,000**
Accrued bonus liability.

When the bonus is paid the following year, the journal entry below is recorded.

Bonus Liability (−L)   **9,000**
    Cash (−A)   **9,000**
Paid bonus liability.

Incentive compensation plans are popular because they induce managers and employees to act in a manner consistent with the objectives of the stockholders. By basing compensation on net income or stock prices, such plans encourage management to maximize these measures of performance. Keep in mind, however, that managers have incentives to influence the measure of net income through operating decisions, the choice of accounting methods, estimates, assumptions, the timing of accruals, or even intentional misstatements.[4]

To illustrate, suppose in the previous example that Tom Turnstile, who receives a bonus equal to 3 percent of net income each year, is the chief financial officer for Maylein Stoneware. At year-end, rather than reporting net income at $300,000 as stated in the example, he overlooks a $20,000 accrued expense, chooses an accounting method that recognizes $20,000 less of expenses (e.g., FIFO), or postpones $20,000 in research and development expenditures. Any of these acts would cause expenses to be $20,000 less than otherwise and net income to be $320,000 instead of $300,000. Tom's bonus would then be $9,600 ($320,000 × 0.03) instead of $9,000 ($300,000 × 0.03), an increase of $600.

While executive compensation systems based on net income encourage management to act in the interests of the stockholders, they also encourage management to manipulate the measure of net income. In certain cases, such manipulations could be considered unethical, and furthermore, it may not even be in management's economic interest to do so. As illustrated throughout this text, accounting manipulations normally reverse themselves over time, and stockholders, investors, and creditors may discount the values of companies that provide financial statements of questionable credibility. Nonetheless, all interested parties should still be aware that management has incentives to manipulate income to increase compensation and often controls the mechanism to do so.

Incentive Compensation Using Stock Options

There is a growing trend to compensate executives in major U.S. corporations with **stock options.** These arrangements simply give executives an option to purchase company stock at a given price (say $10/share) for a given period of time (say ten years). If the price of the stock increases during that time period (say to $20/share), the executive benefits by purchasing the stock at $10/share and them immediately selling it at $20/share. If the stock price decreases, the executive loses nothing. Accounting standard setters have argued for years that options are costly to companies (and to shareholders) because they allow executives to buy stock at discounted values. Consequently, these costs should be accrued when the options are issued. While estimating these costs is quite subjective, Jack Ciesielki, an accounting expert, collected data

---

4. A number of research studies in accounting support the conclusion that management's choice of accounting methods (e.g., FIFO vs. LIFO; straight-line vs. accelerated depreciation) is influenced by the existence and nature of executive compensation plans.

showing what 1999 earnings for selected large U.S. companies would have been had the companies subtracted the cost of their options from reported earnings. Companies with sizable earnings overstatements included Lucent (20 percent), Kmart (13 percent), PepsiCo (12 percent), Morgan Stanley (12 percent), DuPont (9 percent), and Motorola (6 percent). While most believe that this problem is concentrated in the high-tech industry (e.g., Silicon Valley), where options have been a major form of executive compensation, these results show that many traditional U.S. companies suffer from earnings overstatements because they fail to recognize the cost of their executive stock options on the financial statements.

The San Diego Union-Tribune (June 17, 2000) reported that Graef Crystal, the nation's leading expert on executive compensation, remembers being booed and hissed by high-tech executives at a meeting in San Jose for wanting U.S. companies to accrue the cost of their stock options on their income statements and balance sheets. "The business community went ape," she recalled. They claimed that "our earnings will decline, and we will have to throw our little people out of the boat." Should the cost of stock options be included in the financial statements? Why would executives resist booking the cost of the stock options, and what do they mean by "throwing our little people out of the boat?"

CONTINGENCIES AND CONTINGENT LIABILITIES

As defined by the FASB, "a contingency is an existing condition, situation, or set of circumstances involving uncertainty as to possible gain or loss to an enterprise that will ultimately be resolved when one or more future events occurs or fails to occur."[5] A common example is an existing lawsuit that will be settled in the future by the decision of a court. If the possible future outcome represents an increase of assets or a decrease of liabilities, the existing condition is considered a **gain contingency.** If the possible outcome represents a decrease in assets or an increase in liabilities, the condition is considered a **loss contingency.**

Before discussing the methods used to account for contingencies, study the following scenario carefully. It is designed to illustrate some of the economic issues involved in reporting contingencies.

Contingent Liabilities: A Scenario

Suppose that Harry Jones, the accountant for Chemical Enterprises, is preparing the financial statements as of December 31, 2002. Chemical Enterprises is in need of cash and plans to submit the financial statements to First National Bank with an application for a sizable loan. First National has required that the statements Harry prepares be audited by an independent CPA. To conduct the audit, Chemical has hired the firm of Arthur Mitchell & Co.

The preparation of the statements has gone smoothly for Harry, except for one rather significant problem. Several months ago, evidence of a small amount of toxic liquid, allegedly from one of Chemical's plants, was found in the water supply of a small midwestern town. The extent of Chemical's responsibility and the nature and

5. Financial Accounting Standards Board (FASB), "Accounting for Contingencies," *Statement of Financial Accounting Standards No. 5* (Stamford, Conn.: FASB, 1987), par. 1.

extent of any physical harm to the town's residents are still uncertain, but the town has filed suit against Chemical for $1 million, a material amount, and a court case is currently in process. After reviewing the facts of the case, Chemical's lawyers estimate that there is a 70 percent chance that Chemical will successfully defend itself against the lawsuit.

Harry is uncertain how this lawsuit should affect the financial statements of Chemical as of December 31, 2002. As he sees it, the following alternatives represent the three possible ways to account for it.

1. Ignore the lawsuit on the financial statements.
2. Disclose and describe the lawsuit in the footnotes to the financial statements.
3. Recognize a loss on the income statement and a liability on the balance sheet in the amount of $1 million, and disclose and describe the lawsuit in the footnotes.

ALTERNATIVE 1: IGNORE

Under the first alternative, the lawsuit would not be mentioned anywhere in the financial statements. No loss has occurred as of December 31, 2002, and there is a 70 percent chance, according to the lawyers, that no loss will occur at all. Chemical's managers might be inclined to favor this alternative over the others because they suspect that disclosing the lawsuit (Alternative 2) or adjusting the financial statements to reflect it (Alternative 3) could endanger the bank loan or at least make the terms (e.g., interest rate) of the loan less favorable. Ignoring the lawsuit would avoid a negative effect on the financial ratios in general as well as on any contracts based on them.

However, the auditor, Arthur Mitchell & Co., is also aware of the lawsuit and is likely to render a qualified opinion on the financial statements unless some recognition is made of the potential loss. If it is not disclosed, and the auditor grants an *unqualified (clean) opinion* and the bank makes the loan, the auditor may be liable for any losses the bank incurs as a result of the litigation against Chemical. Ignoring the lawsuit would not be a conservative choice for either the auditor or management and may expose them both to significant legal liability.

ALTERNATIVE 2: DISCLOSE

The second alternative entails disclosing the nature and amount of the lawsuit as well as the opinions of Chemical's legal counsel. This alternative would describe the situation to the bank as well as other financial report users, but it would have no effect on the dollar amounts in the financial statements. Consequently, financial ratios and contracts written in terms of financial statement numbers would remain unaffected. However, the bank could make any adjustments it saw fit and thereby assess for itself the magnitude of the potential problem.

ALTERNATIVE 3: ACCRUE

The final alternative is to accrue the loss and the related liability on the financial statements. If Harry chooses this action, he would make the following adjusting entry on December 31, 2002:

Contingent Loss (Lo, −SE)   **1,000,000**
  Contingent Liability (+L)   **1,000,000**
Accrued contingent liability.

The contingent loss account is a temporary account that would appear on the income statement, reducing net income and, ultimately, stockholders' equity. The contingent liability account would appear on the liability side of the balance sheet and be classified as current if payment were expected to require the use of assets listed as current. If Chemical loses the suit and pays the residents of the town, the contingent liability would be written off in the following manner:

Contingent Liability (−L)	**1,000,000**	
Cash (−A)		**1,000,000**

Paid contingent liability.

Alternative 3 would probably be very unattractive to the management of Chemical. Having to recognize the contingent loss and the associated liability on the financial statements would not only endanger the bank loan but could make important financial ratios appear much less favorable. It could, therefore, put the company in technical default on existing debt covenants as well as reduce compensation from bonus and profit-sharing plans. Furthermore, the court might interpret accrual of the loss as Chemical's own admission that the suit is lost, reducing Chemical's chances of successful defense.

On the other hand, accruing the contingent loss is the most conservative choice. It would therefore substantially reduce the potential legal liability faced by both the auditor and Chemical's management and possibly increase the credibility of both parties in the view of financial statement users. Further, accruing the loss in this period would ensure that it would not have to be accrued in a future period.

Accounting for Contingencies

Choosing the appropriate accounting treatment for the situation depicted in the preceding scenario is not a simple matter. Each of the three alternatives is attractive in some respects and unattractive in others. The FASB addresses this problem in *Standard No. 5,* "Accounting for Contingencies," which provides guidelines that should be followed when accounting for contingencies. This standard first distinguishes between gain contingencies, which involve possible future gains, and loss contingencies, which involve possible future losses.

Figure 10–5 illustrates the methods used to account for both gain and loss contingencies. Note first that each is preceded by an initial event (e.g., the filing of a lawsuit). The probability of the related gain or loss is then assessed, usually by experts in the area, and classified as either "highly probable," "reasonably probable," or "remote." In all cases except highly probable contingent losses, this classification determines whether the gain or loss should be ignored or disclosed in the footnotes. In those cases

FIGURE 10–5 Accounting for contingencies

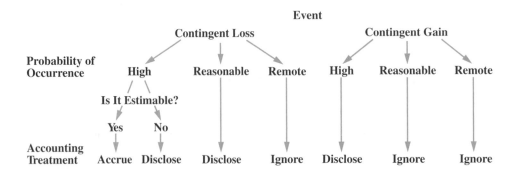

where a contingent loss is considered highly probable, the question of whether it can be estimated is also addressed. If the loss can be estimated, it is accrued and disclosed. If it cannot, information about the loss is simply disclosed.

GAIN CONTINGENCIES

Gain contingencies are almost never accrued on the financial statements and are rarely disclosed in the footnotes. They are not recognized until they are actually realized, which is consistent with both the principle of objectivity and the concept of conservatism. It avoids any subjective estimates involved in predicting the outcomes of contingent events and ensures that the financial statements do not reflect gains that may not actually occur.

LOSS CONTINGENCIES

Loss contingencies, on the other hand, are often disclosed, and when highly probable and estimable, they are accrued. The resulting liability is considered current if it is expected to require the use of assets that are listed on the balance sheet as current.

Classifying contingent losses as "remote," "reasonably probable," or "highly probable" and estimating the dollar amount of "highly probable" contingent losses is often quite subjective. Managers and auditors normally consult legal counsel or other experts, but in areas like lawsuits, it is difficult to predict outcomes accurately. Consequently, relatively few contingent losses stemming from lawsuits are actually accrued on the financial statements. The quote below, taken from an annual report of Johnson & Johnson, provides a typical example.

The Company is involved in numerous product liability cases in the U.S., many of which concern adverse reactions to drugs and medical devices. The damages are substantial [and] it is not feasible to predict the ultimate outcome of litigation. However, the Company believes that if any liability results from such cases, it will be substantially covered by the Company's reserves.

In those cases when losses are accrued, loss ranges are usually specified in the footnotes, and a "best estimate" within the range typically serves as the dollar amount for the accrual. Owens Corning, for example, accrued a huge liability for outstanding litigation related to asbestos claims dating as far back as 1960. The accompanying footnote described the range of possible settlements, and the amount of the accrual reflected "management's best estimate." If no "best estimate" can be agreed upon, the lowest amount in the range is normally used.

Some accrued losses can be very significant. For example, Paragon Trade Brands, a maker of generic diapers, booked a contingent loss related to a patent infringement case with Procter & Gamble that wiped out its entire stockholders' equity. In another example, Rockwood Holding Co. was issued a qualified opinion by its independent auditors "in connection with litigation related to credit insurance." As reported in *Forbes,* such qualifications are issued by auditors to "protect themselves from future litigation" by alerting investors and "bank credit officers to important footnotes" and material uncertainties about the future of the company.

A major current issue in contingency reporting involves environmental cleanup costs, which some have estimated to be as much as $800 billion. Through "superfund legislation," the U.S. government has established both a fund to clean up pollution and a mandate for companies to clean up existing waste sites. This legislation also empowers the Environmental Protection Agency (EPA) to clean up existing waste sites and then be reimbursed by any party deemed responsible for contaminating the site. Being designated a "potentially responsible party" by the EPA can result in the imposition of a huge liability. Some estimate that it will cost $65 billion to clean up existing waste sites, and each site is expected to cost an average of $25 million.

Environmental costs are a special concern for heavy manufacturing companies (e.g., petroleum products) and utilities (e.g., power plants) that have been in operation for many years. These companies are finding that they are increasingly being found responsible for environmental cleanup, often due to activities that occurred long before there was much public concern about the environment. While there is often great uncertainty about the actual dollar amount of these liabilities, more and more companies are incurring environmental cleanup costs and, at the same time, are disclosing and accruing contingent environmental liabilities in the annual report. The following excerpt was taken from the 1999 annual report of Goodyear Tire & Rubber Company.

The company expenses environmental expenditures related to existing conditions resulting from past or current operations and from which no current or future benefit is discernible. . . . The company determines its liability on a site by site basis and records a liability at a time when it is probable that it can be reasonably estimated. The company's estimated liability is reduced to reflect the anticipated participation of other potentially responsible parties in those instances where it is probable that such parties are legally responsible and financially capable of paying their respective shares of the relevant costs. . . . At December 31, 1999, the company had recorded contingent liabilities aggregating $72.6 million for anticipated costs, including legal and consulting fees, site studies, the design and implementation of remediation plans, postremediation monitoring and related activities. . . . At December 31, 1999, the Company had recorded liabilities aggregating $80.6 million for potential product liability and other tort claims.

In addition to litigation and environmental costs, the contingency framework applies to many other important areas of accounting. The allowance method used to account for uncollectibles, for example, treats bad debts as highly probable and therefore accrues estimable loss contingencies. In the next section, we consider warranties, another important area of accounting that relies upon the contingency framework.

The 2000 annual report of Bristol-Myers Squibb, a major pharmaceutical, reported that as of December 31, 2000, $186 million was included in current liabilities for breast implant product liability claims. What entry was made to record this liability, what conditions must have been met to justify this accrual, and what effect associated with this accrual would you expect to see on the statement of cash flows?

WARRANTIES: ACCRUED LOSS CONTINGENCIES

In a **warranty,** a seller promises to remove deficiencies in the quantity, quality, or performance of a product sold to a buyer. Warranties are usually granted for a specific period, during which time the seller promises to bear all or part of the costs of replacing defective parts, performing necessary repairs, or providing additional services. From the seller's standpoint, warranties entail uncertain future costs. It is unlikely that all buyers will take advantage of the warranties granted to them, but enough of them do so to consider the future costs probable and reasonably estimable. Thus, warranties are normally accounted for as accrued contingent losses.

For example, suppose that Hauser and Sons sold ten word processors on July 1 for $1,000 each. Each word processor is under warranty for parts and labor for one year, and based on past experience, the company estimates that, on average, warranty costs will be $100 per unit. During the remainder of the year, several machines require servicing, and as of December 31, $350 of warranty costs had been paid. The following entries would be recorded to reflect these events:

Cash or Accounts Receivable (+A)	**10,000**	
Sales (R, +SE)		**10,000**
Sold ten word processors (10 × $1,000).		
Warranty Expense (E, −SE)	**1,000**	
Contingent Warranty Liability (+L)		**1,000**
Recognized contingent liability (10 × $100).		
Contingent Warranty Liability (−L)	**350**	
Cash (−A)		**350**
Paid warranty liability.		

Several features about this accounting treatment are noteworthy. First, the contingent liability is created when the word processors are sold, because at that time Hauser and Sons are responsible for future services. Accordingly, the entire expected warranty expense related to the sale of the ten word processors is recognized in the period of sale, even though only a $350 cost is actually paid. The total warranty expense is thereby matched against sales revenue in the period of sale. Note also that the balance in the contingent warranty liability account at the end of the period is $650 ($1,000 − $350), indicating that costs of $650 are still expected during the following six-month period due to warranties. This amount would be listed as a current liability on the December 31 balance sheet. As the following entry illustrates, the $650 contingent liability is removed from the books when costs are incurred to service the warranties as they are exercised in the second period.

Contingent Warranty Liability (−L)	**650**	
Cash (−A)		**650**
Paid warranty liability.		

Fedders Corporation, a maker of air-conditioning systems, accrues the estimated costs of warranty coverage at the time sales are recorded. At the beginning of 1999, the company recorded a warranty liability of $2.5 million; at the end of the year, the amount was $4.8 million. Warranty expense during 1999 totaled $4.0 million. Justify Fedders's accounting treatment of warranties in terms of the matching principle. How much was paid during 1999 to meet the outstanding warranties?

INTERNATIONAL PERSPECTIVE: EXECUTIVE COMPENSATION AND U.S. BUSINESS IN THE GLOBAL MARKETPLACE

The Wall Street Journal Europe (June 6, 2000) noted: "Chief executive officers in Britain are falling further behind their U.S. counterparts in terms of total pay according to new data from Towers Perrin, an international human-resources consulting firm." It seems that a surge of long-term incentives, such as stock options, pushed the average pay raise for U.S. executives up by 21 percent, while a normal raise for British

CEOs was only 16 percent. The same appears to be true when U.S. pay is compared to CEOs on the Continent. "The U.S. currently places a greater emphasis on the role of the CEO in bringing about corporate success than Europe does," says Damian Carnell, head of Towers Perrin's European executive compensation practice. By far the greatest contributor to the pay gap between the U.S. and Europe is in the area of stock options—heavily relied upon in the U.S. and much less so in Europe.

Incentive compensation, excluding stock options (e.g., earnings-based bonuses), in Britain and Europe are rising faster than in the U.S., however, and base salaries rose by 11 percent in Britain and only 3 percent in the U.S. "As markets become truly global, you'll see the differences in compensation shrink," predicts Rae Sedel, a managing director of an executive search firm.

APPENDIX 10A

RETIREMENT COSTS: PENSIONS AND POSTRETIREMENT HEALTH CARE AND INSURANCE

This appendix briefly defines and describes how to account for pension and postretirement health care and insurance liabilities.

PENSIONS

A **pension** is a sum of money paid to a retired or disabled employee, the amount of which is usually determined by the employee's years of service. For most large companies, pension plans are an important part of the employees' compensation packages, and they are part of almost all negotiated wage settlements.[6] Pension plans are backed by contractual agreements with the employees and are subject to federal regulation.

Most pension plans are structured so that an employer periodically makes cash payments to a pension fund, which is a legal entity distinct from the sponsoring company. The cash, securities, and other income-earning investments that make up the fund are usually managed by someone outside the company, and the assets in the pension fund do not appear on the company's balance sheet. The employer's cash contributions plus the income generated through the fund's management (i.e., dividends, interest, capital appreciation) provide the cash that is distributed to employees upon retirement. The terms of the pension plan determine the amounts to which individual employees are entitled (benefits).

There are two primary types of pension plans: a defined contribution plan and a defined benefit plan. The definitions of these plans and the methods used to account for them are discussed below.

Defined Contribution Plan

Under a **defined contribution plan** an employer agrees only to make a series of contributions of a specified amount to the pension fund. These periodic cash payments are often based on employee wages or salaries, and each employee's percentage interest in the total fund is determined by the proportionate share contributed by the employer on the employee's behalf.

6. *Accounting Trends and Techniques* (New York: AICPA, 1997) reports that, of the 600 major U.S. companies surveyed, well over 80 percent disclosed the existence of a pension plan.

Under this type of plan, the employer makes no promises regarding how much the employees will receive upon retirement. The actual benefits depend upon the investment performance of the fund. The employer guarantees only the inputs (contributions), not the outputs (benefits). Most university business school professors are covered by such a plan.

Accounting for a defined contribution plan is relatively simple, because once the employer makes the contribution, the sponsoring company faces no further liability. The cash payment is simply expensed, as in the following journal entry:

Pension Expense (E, −SE)	**1,000**	
Cash (−A)		**1,000**
Paid to a defined contribution plan.		

Defined contribution plans have gained in popularity over the last several years. An Associated Press article (June 17, 1995) noted that in 1988, 36 percent of U.S. employees were covered by such plans, rising to 49 percent by 1993. Defined contribution plans, such as the very common 401(k)s, are considered much less expensive than defined benefit plans, which are covered in the next section. Wal-Mart, for example, contributed $429 million to its defined contribution pension plan during 2000.

Defined Benefit Plan

Under a **defined benefit plan** the employer promises to provide each employee with a specified amount of benefits upon retirement. Such a guarantee is somewhat more difficult than promising to make specified contributions because the benefits are received by the employees in the future and therefore are uncertain. The benefits must be predicted, and the employer must contribute enough cash so that the contributions plus the earnings on the assets in the fund will be sufficient to provide the promised benefits as they come due. The employees of most major U.S. companies are covered by defined benefit plans, but a survey conducted by the U.S. Labor Department indicates that the percent of U.S. employees covered by such plans . . . dropped from 63 percent in 1988 to 56 percent in 1995.[7]

In the past, many employers under defined benefit plans either set aside no funds or failed to set aside enough to cover their future pension obligations. They simply paid the obligations as they came due, often out of the company's current operating capital. This practice not only represented poor financial management but, on occasion, left retired employees short of their rightful pension benefits. To help assure that retired employees received what was promised them, Congress passed the **Employment Retirement Income Security Act (ERISA)** in 1974, which requires employers to fund their plans at specified minimum levels and provides other safeguards designed to protect employees.

The basic accounting procedures and the theories underlying accounting for defined benefit pension plans are really quite simple. In accordance with the matching principle, pension expense and the associated liability are accrued each period as employees earn their rights to future benefits (i.e., during the years when the employees provide services and help the company to generate revenues). The periodic adjusting entry to record this accrual takes the following form:

Pension Expense (E, −SE)	**800**	
Pension Liability (+L)		**800**
Recognized $800 pension liability.		

The periodic cash payments made by the employer to the pension fund simply reduce the pension liability as in the following journal entry, and the pension liability that appears on the balance sheet is simply the difference between the accrued liability and the cash payments. A

---

7. The social security system currently operating in the United States is a type of defined benefit pension plan; the federal government promises U.S. citizens a specified amount of benefits at age sixty-five. Presumably, these benefits are paid out of a fund that contains income-earning securities.

large pension liability indicates that a significant amount of the expected pension costs has yet to be funded.

Pension Liability (−L)   **500**
    Cash (−A)   **500**
Paid $500 to pension fund.

The primary difficulties in accounting for and managing a defined benefit plan are in (1) determining the appropriate dollar amount of the periodic accrual entry (i.e., Pension Expense debit and Pension Liability credit) and (2) deciding how much cash needs to be contributed to the pension fund to cover the eventual liability. The ultimate pension cost cannot be known for certain until the employees have received all the benefits to which they are entitled. This will not be known until the employees' deaths as well as the deaths of their survivors, who may also be entitled to certain benefits. Unpredictable factors such as employee life expectancies, employee turnover rates, future salary and wage rates, and pension fund growth rates all have a bearing on this determination.

Most companies hire actuaries (statisticians who specialize in such areas as assessing insurance risks and setting premiums) to establish estimates of the future pension costs and to provide methods for allocating those future costs to current periods (called *actuarial cost methods*). Generally accepted accounting principles require that an employer periodically recognize an expense and an associated liability in an amount that is established by one of many acceptable actuarial methods. The amount of this accrual is usually equal to an estimate of the present value of the pension benefits earned by employees during a given period. These amounts are very inexact, depending largely on subjective estimates and assumptions. As a matter of policy, contractual obligation, or law (ERISA), most companies make periodic cash payments to their pension plans in amounts that approximate the accruals they have chosen to record. Thus, the pension liability appearing on most balance sheets is either zero or relatively small.

In fact, recent gains in the stock market have boosted the fair market values of company pension plans, creating gains that are reflected in reported net income. As *Newsweek* (April 24, 2000) suggests, "these gains are expected to pad the profits of some big companies for years to come, . . ." including General Electric, SBC Communications, IBM, Lucent Technologies, and BellSouth. Analysts warn that income from appreciated pension assets is not part of the company's core activities. While the news is good for these companies, it is not quite the same as rising earnings due to success in a company's core business.

As specified in *Financial Accounting Standards Nos. 87* and *88*, the accounting methods and disclosure requirements for pension plans are more comprehensive and complex than indicated in this appendix. The following excerpt from the 1999 annual report of Delta Air Lines represents only a small portion of the required disclosures.

The retirement plans we sponsor include defined benefit pension plans. Selected disclosures are provided below (dollars in millions).

	1999	1998
Projected pension obligation	$8,872	$8,342
Fair value of plan assets	9,020	9,121
Amount of over funding	148	779
Pension expense	56	100

Accounting for pension plans is also quite subjective, relying heavily on estimates and assumptions. Further, a small change in an important estimate can have a significant effect on both the amount funded by the company and the pension expense and liability reported on its financial statements. For example, to determine what a company must contribute to the pension plan each year, company accountants must estimate the fund's future annual return. *The Wall Street Journal* reported that over a three-year period, GM predicted an annual return on its pension fund of 11 percent but realized only an 8.7 percent return. Missing that target understated the company's pension expense by "a couple hundred million" and led to a funding shortfall of similar size.

POSTRETIREMENT HEALTH CARE AND INSURANCE COSTS

Most large companies cover a portion of the health care and insurance costs incurred by employees after retirement. Similar to pensions, such coverage is part of employee compensation and is earned over an employee's years of service. According to the matching principle, therefore, such costs should be accrued over the employee's tenure with the company, and then the associated liability should be written off as the benefits are paid after the employee's retirement. The issues of estimating this liability, providing adequate funds to meet required future payments, and accounting for such transactions are actually very similar to those involved with pensions, and accordingly, the appropriate accounting methods are basically the same.

For many years most companies neither established funds to pay these future costs nor accrued the related liabilities as the employees earned the coverage. Unlike pensions, currently there is no federal law (like ERISA) requiring employers to establish funds for these liabilities. Standard practice in this area was to expense these costs simply as they were paid. Such a policy, which is contrary to the matching principle, is referred to as the pay-as-you-go approach.

The FASB, in a very controversial standard passed in 1990, required that companies accrue postretirement health care and insurance costs. Not only do the companies have to accrue a liability in the future as employees earn their benefits, but they are required to recognize existing liabilities that they had failed to accrue in the past. For certain companies, these unreported liabilities amounted to well over $1 billion. Indeed, *Barrons* (April 17, 1989) reported: "estimates of the size of this new liability [for the entire economy] range from $400 billion to $1 trillion, depending on whose . . . assumptions you accept."

The FASB, however, did grant the affected companies some latitude. The standard did not have to be implemented until 1993, and the "catch up" entry to recognize the liabilities that had not been accrued in the past could be booked over a period not to exceed twenty years.

Companies have implemented this standard in a number of different ways. While most chose to wait until 1993 and to record the "catch up" over several years, some companies actually adopted the standard early and recorded the entire "catch up" at once. Three notable examples include IBM, General Motors, and LTV, all of which experienced very poor years at the time they chose to book the liability, suggesting that in each case management may have been "taking a bath."

APPENDIX 10B

DEFERRED INCOME TAXES

We have noted that the rules for computing income and expenses for purposes of taxation, as specified by the Internal Revenue Service, are different from generally accepted accounting principles, which specify how financial accounting net income is to be measured. These differences can be divided into two categories: permanent and timing differences. Permanent differences never reverse themselves, while timing differences do. Premiums paid on life insurance policies covering key employees, for example, are not deductible for tax purposes, but they are charged against income for financial reporting purposes. Interest received on municipal bonds is not included in taxable income but is recognized as revenue on a company's income statement. The different treatments for tax and financial accounting purposes in these two examples are considered permanent, because in neither case will the effect on income of the different treatments reverse itself over the life of the asset.

One of many common temporary differences arises when a company depreciates its fixed assets using an accelerated method when computing taxable income and the straight-line method when preparing the financial statements. This strategy causes taxable income to be less than accounting income in the early periods of the asset's life, but as illustrated in Chapter 9, this difference reverses itself in the asset's later years. Many accountants believe that timing differences of this kind create a liability, called deferred income taxes, in the asset's early years, which is discharged in the later years.

THE CONCEPT OF DEFERRED INCOME TAXES

Suppose that Midland Plastics purchased a piece of equipment on January 1, 2000, for $9,000. The equipment is expected to have a three-year useful life and no salvage value. Midland computes depreciation using the double-declining-balance method for income tax purposes and straight-line for reporting purposes. In 2000, Midland's choice to use two different depreciation methods creates an income tax expense on the income statement, which is based on straight-line depreciation, that is greater than its income tax liability, which is based on double-declining-balance depreciation. In 2001 and 2002, the difference reverses itself, and the income tax expense is less than the income tax liability. Figure 10B–1 provides a schedule of these differences and, assuming an income tax rate of 30 percent, computes the tax effects associated with using double-declining-balance instead of straight-line for tax purposes.

	FIGURE 10B–1 Income tax effects due to DDB depreciation	Year	DDB Depr.[a]		SL Depr.[b]		Excess (Under) Depr.		Tax Rate		Tax Benefit (Disbenefit)
		2000	$6,000	–	$3,000	=	$3,000	×	30%	=	$ 900
		2001	2,000	–	3,000	=	(1,000)	×	30%	=	(300)
		2002	1,000	–	3,000	=	(2,000)	×	30%	=	(600)
		Total	$9,000		$9,000		$ 0				$ 0

[a][$9,000 – accumulated depreciation] × 2 [straight-line rate (33%)]
[b]$9,000/3 yr.

Note that the use of the double-declining-balance method, instead of straight-line, creates a tax savings of $900 in 2000, the first year of the equipment's useful life. In 2001 and 2002, however, this benefit reverses itself, giving rise to additional tax payments of $300 in 2001 and $600 in 2002. As of the end of 2000, Midland can view these additional tax payments as liabilities, because many consider them to be future obligations. Specifically, additional tax payments that total $900 ($300 + $600) are expected in 2001 and 2002. This liability is reported on the balance sheet and referred to as deferred income taxes. Midland Plastics, in other words, would report a deferred income tax liability of $900 in the liability section of its 2000 balance sheet.

During 2001 and 2002, as the tax benefit reverses itself and Midland pays the additional taxes, the deferred income tax liability is reduced by $300 in 2001 and by $600 in 2002. As of the end of 2002, therefore, after the useful life of the equipment has expired, the deferred income tax liability will have been reduced to zero.

ACCOUNTING ENTRIES FOR DEFERRED INCOME TAXES

Preparing the journal entry to record the recognition or discharge of deferred income taxes consists of three steps:

1.	Compute the future income tax disbenefit ($900 = $300 + $600) as illustrated in Figure 10B–1. This dollar amount is entered as a credit to the deferred income tax account. The dollar amounts of the reversals (2001: $300, 2002: $600) are entered as debits to the deferred income tax account in future periods.

2. Compute the company's income tax liability (taxable income × corporate income tax rate). This dollar amount is entered as a credit to the income tax payable account.

3. Enter a debit to the income tax expense account in an amount that brings the journal entry into balance.

To illustrate, assume in the preceding example that Midland Plastics recognized taxable income in the amount of $4,000, $8,000, and $9,000 in 2000, 2001, and 2002, respectively. At a 30 percent tax rate, the company's tax liability, therefore, is $1,200 (2000), $2,400 (2001), and $2,700 (2002). Given this information, Figure 10B–2 contains the journal entries and the balance sheet carrying values of the deferred income tax account for the three-year period.

FIGURE 10B–2 Deferred income taxes

2000		2001		2002	
Inc. Tax Exp. (E, −SE) 2,100*		Inc. Tax Exp. (E, −SE) 2,100*		Inc. Tax Exp. (E, −SE) 2,100*	
Deferred Inc. Tax (+L)	900	Deferred Inc. Tax (−L) 300		Deferred Inc. Tax (−L) 600	
Inc. Tax Pay. (+L)	1,200	Inc. Tax Pay. (+L)	2,400	Inc. Tax Pay. (+L)	2,700
Balance sheet excerpt:					
Deferred income tax	900	(900 − 300)	600	(600 − 600)	0

*plug

In 2000, a deferred tax liability of $900 is recognized because Midland, which uses the double-declining-balance method for tax purposes, expects to pay additional income taxes of $300 and $600 over the next two years. An income tax liability of $1,200 is also recognized, and Income Tax Expense is debited for an amount ($2,100) that brings the journal entry into balance. In 2001 and 2002, as Midland pays the additional taxes, the deferred income tax account is reduced.

DEFERRED INCOME TAXES: ADDITIONAL ISSUES

The size of the deferred income tax liability account is usually related to the size of a company's investment in fixed assets.[8] Note in Figure 10B–3 that large manufacturing companies, such as Exxon Mobil and Merck, often carry huge balances in their deferred income tax accounts. Such companies normally depreciate their fixed assets using accelerated methods for tax purposes and straight-line for financial reporting purposes, and the resulting differences between their tax liability and income tax expense can be quite large.[9] On the other hand, financial institutions, which carry limited investments in fixed assets, rarely show balances in the deferred income tax account. Indeed, Chase Manhattan Bank, the American Express Company, and Safeco Insurance report no deferred income taxes on their balance sheets.

8. The deferred income tax account can have a debit balance. When companies recognize expenses (revenues) for reporting purposes more quickly (slowly) than for tax purposes, a deferred tax asset is credited and disclosed on the balance sheet. Companies can carry deferred tax liabilities, deferred tax assets, or both on the balance sheet. Lands' End, for example, reported over $10 million in deferred tax assets on its 2000 balance sheet.

9. *Accounting Trends and Techniques* (New York: AICPA, 2000) reports that, of the 600 major U.S. companies surveyed, approximately 80 percent disclosed timing differences due to the use of a different depreciation method for reporting purposes than that used for tax purposes.

Company	Deferred Tax Liability (millions)	Percent of Total Assets
Exxon Mobil	$16,251	11%
Merck	7,030	20%
J.C. Penney	1,461	7%
Johnson & Johnson	287	1%

Source: 1999 annual reports.

As explained earlier, the deferred income tax account can be viewed as a liability, reflecting an obligation for additional income tax that must be paid in the future as certain tax benefits reverse. However, growing companies tend to purchase more fixed assets than they retire, which, in turn, causes fixed assets in the early (benefit) periods of their useful lives to exceed those in the later (disbenefit) periods. This phenomenon causes the credit balance in the deferred income tax account to accumulate, and many of the largest companies in the United States have amassed huge dollar amounts in deferred income taxes in this manner.

Another interesting aspect about deferred income taxes is that income statement gains and losses can be recognized when income tax rates change. Consider, for example, the General Electric (GE) Company, which at one time had accumulated excess depreciation (i.e., accelerated in excess of straight-line) of approximately $4 billion. At the then-current tax rate of 48 percent, these benefits translated to a deferred income tax liability of $1.92 billion ($4 billion × 48%), which GE reported on its balance sheet. However, when the corporate income tax rate was reduced to 34 percent, GE used the new tax rate and recalculated its deferred income tax liability to be $1.36 billion ($4 billion × 34%). Reducing the liability gave rise to an approximate gain of $560 million ($1.92 billion − $1.36 billion), which appeared on the income statement and was recorded with the following entry (dollars in millions):

Deferred Income Tax (−L)	560	
Gain on Change in Income Tax Rate (Ga, +SE)		560

Recognized gain due to reductions in future income tax rates.

Similarly, when corporate tax rates later went up from 34 percent to 35 percent, a number of companies were forced to recognize an additional liability and a charge to earnings. Coca-Cola Enterprises, for example, took a $40 million charge.

The methods used to account for deferred income taxes are controversial and actually much more complicated than indicated in this discussion. More in-depth coverage can be found in intermediate accounting texts. Nonetheless, this issue is important to all interested parties because calculating the amount of deferred income tax and reporting it as a liability or otherwise can have significant economic consequences. For example, should the computation of the debt/equity ratio include or exclude deferred income tax? Considering the size of the deferred income tax liability, how interested parties answer this question can certainly affect their solvency assessments of certain companies.

THE CONSERVATISM RATIO

An important theme in this text is that meaningful financial statement analysis cannot be conducted without assessing the extent to which management has used its discretion when preparing the financial statements. We have noted often that such discretion can be used to understate (report conservatively) or overstate the financial condition and performance of a company. A measure of the extent to which reported income is conservative, called the **conservatism ratio,** can be constructed from information disclosed in the annual report and is provided below.

Conservatism Ratio: Reported Income Before Taxes/Taxable Income

The intuition underlying this ratio is based on the premise that for tax purposes companies accelerate tax deductible expenses and defer taxable revenues as long as is allowable under income tax laws. Thus, taxable income (taxable revenues − tax deductible expenses), the denominator of the ratio, reflects a very conservative measure of a company's income in a particular year. The extent to which reported income before taxes, the numerator of the ratio, exceeds (or is less than) taxable income indicates how conservative reported income is. Ratio amounts around 1.0 or less indicate relatively conservative levels, while reported income becomes increasingly less conservative as the ratio grows larger than 1.0.

Figure 10B–4 provides 2000 conservatism ratios for three major U.S. companies. That year, income reported to the stockholders of all companies in the list was substantially higher than that reported to the IRS. Assuming that all three companies reported conservatively to the IRS, it appears that the financial reporting policies of SBC Communications were more conservative than those of General Electric, which were more conservative than those of Lands' End.

FIGURE 10B–4 Conservatism ratios		
MANUFACTURING		
General Electric	1.25	
SERVICE		
SBC Communications	1.18	
RETAILER		
Lands' End	1.41	
Source: 2000 annual reports.		

The conservatism ratio cannot be computed entirely from the dollar amounts on the financial statements; additional information contained in the footnotes is also required. Reported income before taxes, the numerator, can be taken directly from the income statement. Taxable income, the denominator, must be computed indirectly, as follows:

Taxable Income = Current Year's Tax Liability/The Effective Income Tax Rate

Both the current year's tax liability and the effective income tax rate are required disclosures under GAAP and can be found in the footnotes.[10] The excerpt below is selected information taken from the footnotes of General Electric's 2000 annual report, followed by the calculation of GE's conservatism ratio in Figure 10B–5 (dollars in millions).

Footnote 7. Provision for Income Taxes

	2000	1999	1998
Current tax expense	$4,560	$3,361	$3,042
Deferred tax expense	1,151	1,499	1,139
Tax expense	5,711	4,860	4,181
Actual income tax rate	31.0%	31.2%	31.0%

10. If the current year's tax liability is not immediately apparent in the footnotes, it can also be computed by subtracting the change in deferred income taxes on the balance sheet from the tax expense reported on the income statement. Increases (decreases) in net deferred income tax liabilities during the year should be subtracted from (added to) tax expense as reported on the income statement.

Conservative ratio computation (2000):

Taxable income   =   Current year's tax liability / Effective tax rate
$14,710   = $4,560   /   .31

Conservatism ratio = Reported income before taxes / Taxable income
     1.25   = $18,446*   / $14,710

*Reported on the 2000 income statement

The conservatism ratio provides a quick way to assess how conservative management's reporting choices have been in a particular year. Much more important, however, are the reasons and activities that explain the difference between reported income and taxable income, and these can be identified only through a close study of the footnotes.

REVIEW PROBLEM

Before adjustments and closing on December 31, 2002, the financial records of Martin Brothers indicated the following balances:

Cash	$23,000	Accounts payable		$13,000
Accounts receivable	14,000	Short-term notes	$10,000	
Inventory	32,000	Less: Discount on notes	1,000	9,000
		Unearned revenue		3,000
		Other current liabilities		13,000
Total current assets	$69,000	Total current liabilities		$38,000

The terms of an outstanding long-term note payable state that Martin must maintain a current ratio of 1.5, or the note will be in default. The current ratio computed from the information above is 1.82 ($69,000 ÷ $38,000). However, the following transactions are not reflected in the above balances:

1. Merchandise purchased on account for $5,000 was in transit as of December 31, 2002. The terms of the purchase were FOB shipping point.
2. One-half of the interest on the $10,000 short-term note payable should be accrued as of December 31.
3. A $4,000 installment on a long-term debt will be due on March 31, 2003. Martin Brothers intends to withdraw $4,000 from a fund, listed on the balance sheet as a long-term investment, to meet the payment.
4. One-third of the unearned revenue has been earned as of December 31.
5. Wages in the amount of $4,000 are owed as of December 31. Federal income and social security taxes withheld on these wages equal $800 and $400, respectively.
6. The total income tax liability for 2002 was estimated at year-end to be $34,000. Income tax payments during the year totaled $32,000.
7. Albinus, Inc., brought suit against Martin Brothers early in 2002. As of December 31, Martin's legal counsel estimates that there is a 50 percent probability that Martin will lose the suit in the amount of $8,000. If Martin loses the suit, payment will be due within the next year.

The journal entry, if necessary, for each additional transaction and the current ratio after all adjustments have been recorded are as follows:

Trans-action	Current Assets	Journal Entry			Current Liabilities
	$69,000				$38,000
1.	+5,000	Inventory (+A)	5,000		
		Accounts Payable (+L)		5,000	+5,000
2.		Interest Expense (E, −SE)	500		
		Discount on Note (+L)		500	+500
3.		No entry—not payable from current assets.			
4.		Unearned Revenue (−L)	1,000		
		Earned Revenue (R, +SE)		1,000	(1,000)
5.		Wage Expense (E, −SE)	4,000		
		Federal Income Tax Payable (+L)		800 ⎫	
		Social Security Tax Payable (+L)		400 ⎬	+4,000
		Wages Payable (+L)		2,800 ⎭	
		Tax Expense (E, −SE)	400		
		Social Security Tax Payable (+L)		400	+400
6.		Income Tax Expense (E, −SE)	2,000		
		Income Tax Payable (+L)		2,000	+2,000
		Recorded income tax liability.			
7.		Depends upon whether a 50 percent probability is considered "reasonably possible" or "probable."			
		If the loss is considered "reasonably possible," it is only disclosed and not included as a current liability.			
		If the loss is considered "probable," the contingent loss is accrued with the following journal entry:			
		Contingent Loss (E, −SE)	8,000		
		Contingent Liability (+L)		8,000	+8,000
	$74,000	Total current assets			
		Total current liabilities:			
		Not including contingent loss			$48,900
		Including contingent loss			$56,900

Current ratio not including contingent loss = 1.51 ($74,000/$48,900)
Current ratio including contingent loss = 1.30 ($74,000/$56,900)

Martin Brothers will be in default on the long-term liability if the contingent loss is accrued. The current ratio (1.30) will be below the ratio required in the debt covenant (1.5). If the contingent loss is only disclosed, the 1.51 current ratio will meet the requirements of the covenant.

SUMMARY OF KEY POINTS

The key points of the chapter are summarized below.

○ *Definition of a liability.*

The FASB has defined liabilities as "probable future sacrifices of economic benefits arising from present obligations of a particular entity to transfer assets or provide services to other entities in the future as a result of past transactions or events." All liabilities appearing on the balance sheet should have three characteristics in common: (1) they should be present obligations that entail settlements by probable future transfers or uses of cash, goods, or services; (2) they should be unavoidable obligations; and (3) the transaction or event obligating the enterprise must have already happened.

○ *Economic consequences associated with reporting liabilities on the financial statements.*

Disclosing a liability on the balance sheet affects important financial ratios (e.g., current ratio, debt/equity, debt/assets) that are used by stockholders, investors, creditors, and others (1) to assess the financial performance and condition of a company and (2) to direct and control the actions of managers through contracts. Each of these parties has an economic interest in the amount of debt that must be paid by a company. Financial ratios, which use balance sheet liabilities, are also found in debt contracts to protect creditors by limiting future borrowings, dividend payments, and other management actions. Such economic consequences create incentives that encourage managers in certain situations to either understate or overstate liabilities.

○ *Determinable and contingent liabilities.*

Determinable liabilities can be precisely measured, and the amounts of cash needed to satisfy the obligations and the dates of payment are reasonably certain. Examples include accounts and short-term notes payable, dividends payable, unearned revenues, third-party collections, and accrued liabilities. Determinable liabilities can also be conditional on certain events. Examples include liabilities associated with income tax and employee incentive compensation. Contingent liabilities result from existing conditions that can lead to negative outcomes in the future, depending on the occurrence of given events. Examples include lawsuits, uncollectibles, and warranties.

○ *Current liabilities.*

Current liabilities are obligations that are expected to require the use of current assets or the creation of other current liabilities. They include obligations to suppliers, short-term notes payable, current maturities of long-term debts, dividends payable to stockholders, unearned revenues, third-party collections, periodic accruals, certain conditional liabilities, and potential obligations related to pending or threatened litigation, and product warranties.

○ *Bonus systems and profit-sharing arrangements and the reporting incentives they create.*

Bonus systems are popular because they provide a means for stockholders to induce management and other employees to act in a manner consistent with the objectives of the stockholders. Such incentives are created by basing compensation on profits. Managers have some control, however, over the measure of profits through operating, investing, and financing decisions, the choice of accounting methods, estimates, assumptions, and the timing of accruals. They can use this control to increase their bonus compensation.

○ *Methods used to account for contingencies.*

Contingencies can be divided into two categories: gain contingencies and loss contingencies. Gain contingencies are rarely accrued and are only disclosed in the footnotes when they are highly probable. The probability of a loss contingency should be classified as either remote, reasonably possible, or highly probable. If the probability is remote, the loss need not be disclosed. If the event is reasonably possible, the potential loss and all relevant information about it should be disclosed in the footnotes. If the event is viewed as highly probable and the amount of the loss can be estimated, the potential loss and associated liabilities should be accrued on the financial statements and described in the footnotes. When a sale is made that includes a warranty, the sale is recorded. Because the warranty liability is highly probable and can be estimated with reasonable accuracy, warranty expense and the contingent warranty liability should be recognized in the amount of the estimated future warranty costs at the same time. As the warranty costs are paid, the contingent liability is reduced.

KEY TERMS

Note: Definitions for these terms are provided in the glossary at the end of this text.

Commercial paper (p. 424)
Conservatism ratio (p. 443)
Debt ratio (p. 418)
Defined benefit plan (p. 437)
Defined contribution plan (p. 436)
Determinable current liabilities (p. 424)
Employment Retirement Income Security
  Act (ERISA) (p. 437)
Face value (p. 422)

Gain contingency (p. 430)
Line of credit (p. 424)
Loss contingency (p. 430)
Maturity date (p. 425)
Open account (p. 424)
Pension (p. 436)
Stock options (p. 429)
Warranty (p. 434)

ETHICS IN THE REAL WORLD

Fortune (April 1999) reports that "because companies do not have to expense the cost of stock options, corporate directors are encouraged to overpay their CEOs and other corporate executives." Companies grant executives options on 300,000 or so shares every six months, for example, and then as the stock market rises, the value of the options also rises, and pretty soon the executives are wildly overpaid. If the stock price falls, the executive is no worse off, and options can then be reissued to the executive at the lower price—starting the process all over again. In essence, the executive has the chance to become very rich, there is no risk of loss, and under current accounting rules none of this has to show up on the financial statements.

ETHICAL ISSUE Is it ethical for a board of directors to compensate executives using stock options, and at the same time treat the options on the financial statements, which are provided to the public and the stockholders, as if they are costless? Discuss.

INTERNET RESEARCH EXERCISE

The costs associated with future environmental cleanup are significant, and companies like Waste Management, introduced at the beginning of the chapter, deal with estimating these costs continually. *SFAS No. 5* provides some guidance on accounting for these costs. When was the standard issued? Summarize its contents, and explain how it applies to the situation faced by Waste Management. You can begin your search at the FASB's home page (**www.FASB.org**).

BRIEF EXERCISES

BE10–1

Cash flow and accruals

3M reported interest expense of $111 million, $109 million, and $139 million for 2000, 1999, and 1998, respectively. Cash payments for interest were $104 million, $114 million, and $130 million for the same three years. Interest payable at the end of 1998 was $150 million.

a.   Briefly explain why the interest expense and cash payments for interest are not the same.
b.   What kind of liability is interest payable?
c.   Compute the interest payable balance for 1999 and 2000.

BE10–2

Inferring financial information

The following information was taken from the 1999 annual report of Kmart (dollars in millions):

	1999	1998
INCOME STATEMENT		
Cost of goods sold	$28,102	$26,319
BALANCE SHEET		
Inventory	7,101	6,536
Trade accounts payable	2,204	2,047

a.   Compute the inventory purchases made by Kmart during 1999. Record a single entry that reflects these purchases.
b.   How much cash did Kmart pay to its suppliers in 1999? Record a single entry that reflects these payments.

BE10–3

Cash payments for environmental cleanup

BF Goodrich's Footnote V in its 1999 annual report stated that the company accrued expenses for environmental cleanup of $125 million and $130 million for 1999 and 1998, respectively.

a.   Describe how the 1999 accrual affected the basic accounting equation.
b.   What accounting principle is being followed by BF Goodrich? Explain.

EXERCISES

E10–1

Why are current liabilities carried at face value instead of present value?

Winslow Enterprises reports $40,000 in Accounts Payable on the balance sheet as of December 31, 2002. These payables, on average, will be paid in ten days.

a.   Assuming a 12 percent annual discount rate, approximate the present value of the cash outflows associated with the accounts payable. (Note: Knowledge of present value [Appendix B] is required to do this exercise.)
b.   Why are accounts payable carried on the balance sheet at face value instead of present value?

E10–2

Financing with long-term debt, contract terms, and the current ratio

Darrington and Darling borrowed $100,000 from Commercial Financing to finance the purchase of fixed assets. The loan contract provides for a 12 percent annual interest rate and states that the principal must be paid in full in ten years. The contract also requires that Darrington and Darling maintain a current ratio of 1.5:1. Before Darrington and Darling borrowed the $100,000, the company's current assets and current liabilities were $130,000 and $80,000, respectively.

a. Compute the company's current ratio if it invests $50,000 of the borrowed funds in fixed assets and keeps the rest as cash or short-term investments. To what dollar amount can current liabilities grow before the company violates the debt contract?

b. Compute the company's current ratio if it invests $80,000 of the borrowed funds in fixed assets and keeps the rest as cash or short-term investments. To what dollar amount can current liabilities grow before the company violates the debt contract?

c. Compute the company's current ratio if it invests the entire $100,000 of the borrowed funds in fixed assets. To what dollar amount can current liabilities grow before the company violates the debt contract?

E10–3

Accruals, the current ratio, and net income

Lily May Electronics recognizes expenses for wages, interest, and rent when cash payments are made. The following related cash payments were made during December 2002.

1. December 1	Paid $1,100 for rent to cover the subsequent twelve months.
2. December 5 and 20	Paid wages in the amount of $7,500. Wages in the amount of $7,500 are paid on the fifth and the twentieth of each month for the fifteen days just ended. The next payment will be on January 5, 2000.
3. December 15	Paid $600 interest on an outstanding note payable. The note has face value of $10,000 and a twelve percent annual interest rate. Interest payments in the amount of $600 are made every six months.

As of December 31, the current assets and current liabilities reported on Lily May's balance sheet were $24,000 and $15,000, respectively. Lily May's income statement reported net income of $7,500.

Compute Lily May's current ratio and net income if the company were to account for wages, interest, and rent on an accrual basis.

E10–4

Short-term notes payable and the actual rate of interest

On December 1, Spencer Department Store borrowed $19,250 from First Bank and Trust. Spencer signed a ninety-day note with a face amount of $20,000. The interest rate stated on the face of the note is 15 percent per year.

a. Provide the journal entry recorded by Spencer on December 1.

b. Provide the adjusting entry recorded by Spencer on December 31 before financial statements are prepared. Show how the note payable would be disclosed on the December 31 balance sheet.

c. Compute the actual annual interest rate on the note. (*Hint:* Note that Spencer had the use of $19,250 only over the period of the loan.)

d. Why is the actual interest rate different from the rate stated on the face of the note?

E10–5

Current maturities and debt covenants

On January 1, 1998, Lacey Treetoppers borrowed $300,000, which is to be paid back in annual installments of $20,000 on December 30 of each year.

a. Assuming that Lacey has met all payments on a timely basis, how should this liability be reported on the December 31, 2002, balance sheet?

b. Assume that during December of 2002, the management of Lacey realizes that including the upcoming $20,000 installment as a current liability reduces the Company's current ratio below 2:1, the ratio required in a long-term note payable signed by the company. Discuss how management might be able to avoid classifying the current maturity as a current liability.

E10–6

Gift certificates and
unearned revenue

Norsums Department Store sells gift certificates that are redeemable in merchandise. During 2002, Norsums sold gift certificates for $88,000. Merchandise with the total price of $52,000 was redeemed during the year. The cost of the sold merchandise to Norsums was $32,000. Norsums sold gift certificates for the first time in 2002.

a.   Record the sale of the gift certificates.
b.   Record the redemption during 2002. Assume that Norsums uses the perpetual inventory method.
c.   Compute the balance in the unearned revenue account as of December 31, 2003, assuming that gift certificates were sold for $60,000 in 2003 and merchandise with a total price of $80,000 was redeemed.

REAL DATA

E10–7

Inferring a
cash payment

The information below was taken from the 2000 annual report of Lands' End, a leading global direct merchant that sells primarily through catalogs (dollars in thousands).

	2000	1999
Cost of goods sold	$727,291	$754,661
Inventory	162,193	219,686
Accounts payable	74,510	87,922

a.   Assume that accounts payable reflects only accounts with inventory suppliers, and compute the cash payments made to suppliers during 2000.
b.   Would this dollar amount be disclosed on the statement of cash flows? Explain.

E10–8

Gain and loss
contingencies

Zeus Power has brought suit against Regional Supply in the amount of $825,000 for patent infringement. As of December 31, the suit is in process, and the attorneys have determined that there is a greater than 50 percent chance that Zeus Power will win the entire $825,000.

a.   How should Zeus Power account for the situation described above?
b.   How should Regional Supply account for the situation described above? Briefly describe some of the factors that might affect how Regional Supply chooses to account for this situation.
c.   Why would the two companies account for the same facts in different ways?

E10–9

Bonus plans and
contingent losses

Jordan Brothers recently instituted a bonus plan to pay its executives. The plan specifies that net income must exceed $200,000 before any bonus payments are made. Cash in the amount of 10 percent of net income in excess of $200,000 is placed in a bonus pool, which is to be shared evenly by each of the executives. Ignore income taxes, and assume that the bonus payment is not included as an expense in the calculation of net income.

a.   Briefly describe why a company would institute a bonus plan, and compute the amount in the bonus pool if Jordan Brothers shows net income of $300,000. Prepare the journal entry that would be recorded to reflect the bonus liability at the end of the year.
b.   How much is in the bonus pool if Jordan Brothers shows net income of $180,000? Assume that Jordan Brothers is being sued for $60,000 as of the end of the year. The company's legal counsel believes that there is an 80 percent chance that Jordan will lose the suit and that the entire $60,000 will have to be paid. Assume also that the suit was ignored when the $180,000 net income was computed. Why might Jordan's management wish to accrue the loss from the suit in the current year instead of simply disclosing it?

E10–10

Warranty costs:
Contingent losses or
expense as
incurred?

During 2002, Seagul Outboards sold 200 outboard engines for $250 each. The engines are under a one-year warranty for parts and labor, and from past experience, the company estimates that, on average, warranty costs will equal $20 per engine. As of December 31, 2002, 50 engines had been serviced at a total cost of $1,400. During 2003, engines were serviced at a total cost of $2,600. Assume that all repairs used cash.

a.   Prepare the journal entries that would be recorded at the following times:
     (1) During 2002 to record the sale of the engines.

(2) During 2002 to accrue the contingent loss on warranties.

(3) During 2002 and 2003 to record the actual warranty cost incurred.

b. Assume that Seagul chose not to treat the warranty costs as contingent losses. Instead, it chose to expense warranty costs as they were paid. Compute the total net income for 2002 and 2003 for each of the two accounting treatments.

REAL DATA

E10–11

Deferred revenues and cash receipts

Delta Air Lines is paid in advance for its ticket sales, recognizing a deferred revenue, called air traffic liability, when it receives the cash. The liability is then converted to revenue when the passenger takes the flight. During 1999 Delta recognized passenger revenues in the amount of $13.4 billion. On the balance sheet Delta reported air traffic liabilities of $1.8 billion and $1.7 billion as of the end of 1999 and 1998, respectively.

a. Explain why Delta does not recognize revenue when it receives the payment from its customers.

b. What kind of a liability is air traffic liability? Discuss whether it should be considered current or long-term.

c. Compute the cash received by Delta from passengers during 1999.

E10–12

Appendix 10A:
Pension contributions and unfunded pension liability

Seasaw Seasons instituted a defined benefit pension plan for its employees three years ago. Each year since the adoption of the plan, Seasaw has contributed $16,000 to the pension fund, which is managed by Fiduciary Trust Associates. As of the end of the current year, it was estimated that contributions of $58,000 would have been necessary to maintain a fund large enough to provide the benefits promised to the employees when they retire.

a. Prepare the journal entries that were recorded by Seasaw as it contributed cash to the pension fund.

b. How much pension liability should be recorded on Seasaw's balance sheet as of the end of the current year?

E10–13

Appendix 10B:
Deferred taxes and the tax rate

Swingley Company uses an accelerated method to depreciate its fixed assets for tax purposes and the straight-line method for financial reporting purposes. In 2002, the accelerated method recognized depreciation of $35,000, while the straight-line method recognized depreciation of $20,000. Taxable income and net income before taxes for that year were $65,000 and $80,000, respectively.

a. If the federal income tax rate is 35 percent, prepare the journal entry recorded by Swingley to accrue its 2002 tax liability.

b. If the federal income tax rate is 30 percent, prepare the journal entry recorded by Swingley to accrue its 2002 tax liability.

c. Briefly explain why the deferred income tax account is considered a liability on the balance sheet and why it is less when the tax rate is 35 percent rather than 40 percent.

E10–14

Appendix 10B:
Conservatism ratio

The information below was taken from the annual report of Busytown Industries.

	2002	2001
BALANCE SHEET		
Deferred income tax liability	$ 9,700	$8,300
INCOME STATEMENT		
Income before taxes	$68,000	
Income tax expense	(20,400)	
Net income	$47,600	
Effective income tax rate: 38%		

a. Compute Busytown's conservatism ratio, and comment on how conservative the company's reporting methods are.

b. Explain why the conservatism ratio provides a measure of the extent to which a company's financial accounting methods are conservative, and provide examples of accounting treatments that may increase or decrease the ratio.

E10–15

Appendix 10B:
Conservatism ratio

The information below was taken from the annual report of Sega-Venus Enterprises.

	2002	2001
BALANCE SHEET		
Deferred income tax liability	$ 18,300	$19,400
INCOME STATEMENT		
Income before taxes	$145,500	
Income tax expense	(54,000)	
Net income	$ 91,500	
Effective income tax rate: 34%		

a. Compute Sega-Venus's conservatism ratio, and comment on how conservative the company's reporting methods are.
b. Explain why the conservatism ratio provides a measure of the extent to which a company's financial accounting methods are conservative, and provide examples of accounting treatments that may increase or decrease the ratio.

PROBLEMS

P10–1

Distinguishing
current liabilities
from long-term
liabilities

Beth Morgan, controller of Boulder Corporation, is currently preparing the 2002 financial report. She is trying to decide how to classify the following items.

1. Account payable of $170,000 owed to suppliers for inventory.
2. A $60,000 note payable that matures in three months. The company is planning to acquire a five-year loan from its bank to pay off the note. The bank has agreed to finance the note.
3. A $500,000 mortgage: $75,000 payable within twelve months, and the remaining $425,000 to be paid over the next six years.
4. The sum of $8,000 owed to the phone company for service during December.
5. Advances of $25,000 received from a customer. The contract between the customer and Boulder Corporation states that if the company does not deliver the goods within six months, the $25,000 is to be returned to the customer.
6. The sum of $15,000 due the federal government for income tax withheld from employees during the last quarter of 2002. The government requires that withholdings be submitted by the end of the next quarter to the Internal Revenue Service.
7. A $125,000 note payable: $30,000 is payable within twelve months, and the remaining $95,000 is to be paid over the next two years. Boulder Corporation plans to issue common stock to the creditor for the portion due during the next twelve months.
8. The company declared a cash dividend of $50,000 on December 29, 2002. The dividend is to be paid on January 21, 2003.

REQUIRED:

a. Classify each of the items as a current liability or as a long-term liability. (*Note:* Some items may be classified partially as current and partially as long-term.)
b. Compute the total amount that should be classified as current liabilities.
c. Compute the total amount that should be classified as long-term liabilities.

P10–2

Recognizing current liabilities can restrict dividend payments

Linton Industries borrowed $500,000 from Security Bankers to finance the purchase of equipment costing $360,000 and to provide $140,000 in cash. The note states that the loan matures in twenty years, and the principal is to be paid in annual installments of $25,000. The terms of the loan also indicate that Linton must maintain a current ratio of 2:1 and cannot pay dividends that will reduce retained earnings below $200,000. The balance sheet of Linton, immediately prior to the bank loan and the purchase of equipment, follows:

Current assets	$ 120,000	Current liabilities	$ 100,000
Noncurrent assets	1,500,000	Long-term liabilities	300,000
		Capital stock	1,000,000
		Retained earnings	220,000
		Total liabilities and	
Total assets	$1,620,000	stockholders' equity	$1,620,000

REQUIRED:

The board of directors of Linton is about to declare a dividend to be paid to the shareholders early next year. After accepting the loan and purchasing the equipment, how large a dividend can the board pay and not violate the terms of the debt covenant?

P10–3

Recognizing current liabilities and violating debt covenants

Before adjustments and closing on December 31, 2002, the current accounts of Seymour and Associates indicated the following balances:

	Debit	Credit
Cash	$40,000	
Accounts receivable	50,000	
Allowance for doubtful accounts		2,000
Inventory	52,000	
Accounts payable		30,000
Unearned revenues		25,000
Warranty liabilities		5,000
Other current liabilities		10,000

The terms of an outstanding long-term note payable state that Seymour must maintain a current ratio of 2:1 or the note will become due immediately. The following items are not reflected in the balances above:

1. Bad debt losses in the amount of 6 percent of the outstanding accounts receivable balance are expected.
2. The warranty liability on outstanding warranties is estimated to be $12,000.
3. Forty percent of the unearned revenue had been earned as of December 31.
4. Five thousand dollars, listed above under "Other current liabilities," is part of a line of credit and is expected to be immediately refinanced on a long-term basis when due.
5. The total income tax liability for 2002 was estimated at year-end to be $23,000. Estimated tax payments during the year totaled $20,000.
6. Trademans, Inc., brought suit against Seymour early in 2002. As of December 31, Seymour's legal counsel estimates that there is a 60 percent probability that the suit will be lost in the amount of $10,000. If the suit is lost, payment will most likely be due in the next year.

REQUIRED:

a. Prepare the journal entries that would be recorded (if necessary) for each of the six items listed.
b. After preparing the journal entries, compute the company's current ratio, assuming that the contingent liability described in (6) is not accrued.

(Continued)

c. After preparing the journal entries, compute the company's current ratio, assuming that the contingent liability described in (6) is accrued.

d. If you were Seymour's auditor, would you require that the contingent liability be accrued? Discuss.

P10–4

Issues surrounding the recognition of a contingent liability

While shopping on October 13, 2002, at the Floor Wax Shop, Tom Jacobs slipped and seriously injured his back. Mr. Jacobs believed that the Floor Wax Shop should have warned him that the floors were slick; hence, he sued the company for damages. As of December 31, 2002, the lawsuit was still in progress. According to the company's lawyers, it was probable that the company would lose the lawsuit. The lawyers also believed that the company could lose somewhere between $250,000 and $1.5 million, with a best guess of the loss at $742,000. The lawsuit was eventually settled in favor of Mr. Jacobs on August 12, 2003, for $690,000.

REQUIRED:

a. Discuss the issues that the Floor Wax Shop must address in deciding how to report this lawsuit in its 2002 financial report.

b. If you were auditing the Floor Wax Shop, how would you recommend that this lawsuit be reported in the 2002 financial report? Why?

c. Assume that a contingent liability of $742,000 is accrued on December 31, 2002. What journal entry would the company record on August 12, 2003, the date of the settlement?

P10–5

Accruing warranty costs before they are incurred

Arden's Used Cars offers a one-year warranty from the date of sale on all cars. From historical data, Mr. Arden estimates that, on average, each car will require the company to incur warranty costs of $760. The following activities occurred during 2002:

1. February 2   Sold five cars.
2. March 23   Sold ten cars.
3. May 30   Incurred warranty costs of $3,000 on four cars sold in 1998.
4. July 5   Sold eight cars.
5. September 2   Incurred warranty costs of $5,000 on five cars sold in 1999.
6. November 15   Incurred warranty costs of $6,000 on one car sold in 1999.
7. December 20   Sold twelve cars.

REQUIRED:

a. Assume that the cars were sold for cash for an average of $9,500. Prepare the entry to record the car sales during 2002 (combine all the sales and make one entry).

b. Prepare the individual entries to record the warranty costs incurred. Assume that the breakdown of warranty costs is 40 percent wages (paid in cash) and 60 percent parts.

c. Arden accrues its warranty liability with a single adjusting entry at year-end. Prepare that entry.

d. Compute the year-end warranty liability. The beginning balance in the warranty liability account was $3,500.

e. Explain why accountants estimate the warranty expense in the year of sale instead of recording the expenses as the costs are incurred.

P10–6

Advertising campaigns can give rise to contingent liabilities

To kick off its 2002 advertising campaign, Rachel's Breakfast Cereal is offering a $1 refund in exchange for five cereal box tops. The company estimates that the tops of 10 percent of the cereal boxes sold will be returned for the refund. The cereal boxes are sold for $2.00 each. During 2002 and 2003, 20,000 and 28,000 cereal boxes are sold, respectively, and 1,500 and 2,000 box tops are received for refunds during 2002 and 2003, respectively.

REQUIRED:

a. Prepare the journal entries to record the sale of the cereal boxes, the recognition of the contingent liability associated with the potential refunds, and the actual refund payments for 2002 and 2003.

b. Compute the liabilities associated with the potential refunds as of the end of 2002 and 2003.

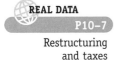

P10–7

Restructuring
and taxes

Bristol-Myers Squibb booked a $504 million restructuring charge during 2000. Approximately $372 million of the charge was an accrual for employee termination benefits to be paid in the future. The entire $504 million appeared on the company's statement of cash flows, in the operating section as an addition to net income in the computation of net cash from operations.

REQUIRED:

a. Provide the entry recorded by the company to recognize the future employee termination costs.
b. Explain why the entire restructuring charge appeared as an addition to net income in the operating section of the statement of cash flows.
c. Also in 2000, Bristol-Myers Squibb made income tax payments of $1.6 billion. The company's current tax expense was $1.3 billion, and income tax payable on the balance sheet was $794 million as of the end of 1999. Estimate the income tax liability as of December 31, 2000.

P10–8

Appendix 10A:
Accruing and
funding pension
liabilities

Shelby Company instituted a defined benefit pension plan for its employees at the beginning of 1998. An actuarial method that is acceptable under generally accepted accounting principles indicates that the company should contribute $40,000 each year to the pension fund to cover the benefits that will be paid to the employees. Shelby funded 80 percent of the liability in 1998 and 1999, 90 percent in 2000 and 2001, and 100 percent in 2002.

REQUIRED:

a. Prepare the journal entries to accrue the pension liability and fund it for 1998, 1999, 2000, 2001, and 2002.
b. Compute the balance in the pension liability account as of December 31, 2002.

P10–9

Appendix 10B:
Deferred income
taxes, changes in
tax rates, and
investment in
long-lived assets

Acme, Inc., purchased machinery at the beginning of 1998 for $50,000. Management used the straight-line method to depreciate the cost for financial reporting purposes and the double-declining-balance method to depreciate the cost for tax purposes. The life of the machinery was estimated to be four years, and the salvage value was estimated as zero. Revenue less expenses other than depreciation (for financial reporting and tax purposes) equaled $100,000 in 1998, 1999, 2000, and 2001. Acme pays income taxes at the rate of 35 percent of taxable income.

REQUIRED:

a. Prepare the journal entries to accrue income tax expense and income tax liability for 1998, 1999, 2000, and 2001. Indicate the balance in the deferred income tax account as of the end of each of the four years.
b. Assume that the tax rate was changed by the federal government to 20 percent at the beginning of 2000. Repeat the exercise in (a). Would it be appropriate to recognize a gain at the end of 2000 to reflect the tax rate decrease? Why or why not? If so, how much of a gain?
c. Assume that Acme purchased additional machinery at the beginning of 1999 and 2001. Each purchase was for $50,000, and each machine had a four-year estimated life and no salvage value. Once again, the straight-line depreciation method was used for reporting purposes and double-declining-balance for tax purposes. Repeat the exercise in (a) assuming a tax rate of 35 percent. Why is the deferred income tax account one of the largest liabilities on the balance sheets of many major U.S. companies?

P10–10

Appendix 10B:
Conservatism ratio

You are a security analyst for Magneto Investments and have chosen to invest in one firm from the semiconductor manufacturing industry. You have narrowed your choice to either Owen-Foley Company or Amerton Industries, firms of similar size and direct competitors in the industry. The information below was taken from their 2002 annual reports.

OWEN-FOLEY COMPANY	2002	2001
BALANCE SHEET		
Deferred income tax liability	$ 18,400	$16,600
INCOME STATEMENT		
Income before taxes	$163,000	
Income tax expense	(52,000)	
Net income	$111,000	
Effective income tax rate: 36%		

AMERTON INDUSTRIES	2002	2001
BALANCE SHEET		
Deferred income tax liability	$ 18,800	$19,800
INCOME STATEMENT		
Income before taxes	$158,500	
Income tax expense	(53,500)	
Net income	$105,000	
Effective income tax rate: 36%		

REQUIRED:

On the basis of this information, explain which of the two firms seems to have the stronger earning power.

REAL DATA

P10-11

Appendix 10B: Comparing conservatism ratios

The following information was taken from the 2000 annual reports of Lands' End and Pier 1 Imports (dollars in thousands).

	Lands' End	Pier 1 Imports
Net income before taxes	$76,244	$118,612
Income tax expense:		
Current	19,940	42,162
Deferred	8,270	1,725
Total	$28,210	$43,887
Effective tax rate	.37	.37

REQUIRED:

Compute the conservatism ratios for both companies and comment on the differences. Which company is more conservative, and why?

ISSUES FOR DISCUSSION

REAL DATA

ID10-1

Debt covenants and reporting current liabilities

Federal Express Corporation, a world leader in express mail services, reported the following in its 1997 financial statements (dollars in millions):

	1997
Current assets	$2,132
Current liabilities	1,962

The company's long-term debt contains restrictive covenants that require the maintenance of certain financial ratios. Assume that these covenants require that the company's current ratio be at least 1.0.

REQUIRED:

a. What additional dollar value of current liabilities could have been reported as of December 31, 1997, without violating the debt covenant?
b. List several current liabilities that management may have been able to control to ensure at year-end that the covenant was not violated, and explain how these liabilities could have been controlled.
c. Explain what could happen if the company violated the covenant.
d. Assume that at the end of 1997, Federal Express considered a $600 million inventory purchase. Assume also that the company has the necessary cash. Should the company pay cash or purchase the inventory on account, and why? Support your answer with calculations.

REAL DATA

ID10–2

Receipts in advance: Measurement theory and financial statement effects

Ingersoll-Rand manufactures specialized heavy-duty construction equipment. Included in a set of recent financial statements is the account "Customers' Advance Payments," with a balance of over $15 million. The notes to the financial statements indicate that, although payments are collected in advance from customers, revenues are recognized when products are shipped. Products are normally shipped within six months of the advance payments.

REQUIRED:

a. On what financial statement and in which section of that statement would the account "Customers' Advance Payments," be found?
b. Explain the accounting treatment associated with this account in terms of the principles of revenue recognition and matching.
c. Under this accounting treatment, how are important financial ratios, such as earnings per share, the current ratio, and the debt/equity ratio, affected (1) when the advance payments are received and (2) when the related goods are shipped?

REAL DATA

ID10–3

Contingency reporting in the tobacco industry

In a recent annual report, Philip Morris Companies, a major manufacturer of tobacco and food products, included footnote 16, which was almost five pages long. It consisted of a number of separate sections covering such topics as an overview of tobacco-related litigation, the type and number of cases, pending and upcoming trials, verdicts in individual cases, litigation settlements, smoking and health litigation, health care and cost-recovery litigation, and certain other tobacco-related litigation. During the year, over 500 smoking and health-related cases had been filed against the company, an increase of 30 percent over the previous year and 200 percent over the year before that. The company booked a pre-tax charge of over $3 billion, reducing reported net income to slightly over $5 billion.

REQUIRED:

Discuss Philip Morris's disclosure and accrual in terms of (1) the methods used to account for loss contingencies, and (2) the potential economic consequences associated with the disclosure and accounting treatment.

REAL DATA

ID10–4

Unreported assets

Several years ago, Lifschultz Industries, a small gas meter company, reported a book value of less than zero (i.e., reported liabilities exceeded reported assets). Yet, in late March, the company's stock price skyrocketed on news that it was pursuing a massive antitrust and racketeering lawsuit against three of the country's biggest trucking companies: Consolidated Freightways, Roadway Services, and Yellow Freight Systems. Lifschultz alleged that these trucking companies conspired to engage in anticompetitive activity, driving it out of the trucking business. The suit, filed in U.S. district court in South Carolina, sought $1.8 billion. The three trucking companies said nothing about the suit publicly other than to footnote it as a "contingency" in their annual reports.

REQUIRED:

a. Explain how Lifschultz can report negative book value and, at the same time, have its stock so highly valued in the stock market.

(Continued)

b. Explain the differences between how Lifschultz should account for the suit and how the three trucking companies should account for it.
c. Provide economic reasons why the plaintiff and defendants account for the same dispute differently.

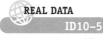

REAL DATA

ID10-5

The economic consequences of a technical default

The following quote refers to the problems of Campeau Corporation, a Canadian-based retail empire that later declared bankruptcy. At the time, Campeau's department store chains included Bloomingdale's, Rich's, Burdines, Abraham & Strauss, and Lazarus.

Campeau Corp.'s announcement Friday that its bankers believe it has technically defaulted on $2.34 billion in debt probably will freeze new spring shipments, apparel makers say. Citibank, leader of the bank syndicate providing much of Campeau's debt financing, informed Campeau by letter last week that Campeau had violated certain covenants on debt ... and unless Campeau can remedy the default by December 31, Citibank stated it may demand full repayment of the loans.

REQUIRED:

a. What is a "technical default," and how did Citibank react to it?
b. Explain why apparel makers might "freeze new shipments" and why this presented great problems for the Campeau organization.

REAL DATA

ID10-6

Reclassifying short-term notes as long-term debt

The 2000 annual report of General Mills reported the following (dollars in millions):

	2000	1999
Current assets	$1,190.3	$1,102.5
Current liabilities	2,529.1	1,200.3

Included in current liabilities are notes payable in the amount of $1,086 million and $524 million for 2000 and 1999, respectively. In the footnotes, the company discloses that the dollar amounts of short-term notes payable listed on the balance sheet are net of $480 million in 2000. Because the credit agreement covering these notes "provides us with the ability to refinance short-term borrowings on a long-term basis, we therefore have reclassified a portion of our notes payable to long-term debt."

REQUIRED:

a. Explain what is meant by the footnote disclosure.
b. What effect did the reclassification have on the company's 2000 current ratios?
c. Explain why one might claim that a short-term note may appropriately be classified in the long-term debt section of the balance sheet, and discuss how managers may use discretion in this area to serve their own interests. Note in particular the company's current ratio.

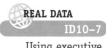

REAL DATA

ID10-7

Using executive compensation disclosures

The SEC requires additional information in the proxy statements that describe the compensation packages of a company's top executives. A *Wall Street Journal* article published soon after the requirement became effective offered a list of recommendations about how shareholders might use this additional information. Included in the list: compare executive pay with shareholder returns, check to see if executive compensation is linked to stock market performance, find out how much company stock is owned by the executives, and beware of changes in the auditor.

REQUIRED:

Explain what a proxy statement is, and discuss how each of the recommendations listed above may provide useful information to the shareholders.

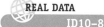

REAL DATA

ID10–8

"Taking a bath" during bankruptcy proceedings

A major defense contractor, LTV, faced with huge liabilities, once declared Chapter 11 bankruptcy protection. Under Chapter 11, a company continues to operate but is protected from creditors while it tries to work out a reorganization plan. At that time, the company's management chose to accrue a $2.26 billion liability to reflect the potential cost of medical and life insurance benefits for its 118,000 current and retired employees. At the time, this charge was not required by generally accepted accounting principles. *The Wall Street Journal* reported that the company chose to recognize the charge because "if the company waited until after it negotiated new credit agreements and emerged from bankruptcy law proceedings before taking the $2 billion charge, the additional liability could trigger violations of its debt covenants."

REQUIRED:

a. Provide the journal entry to record the $2.26 billion charge recognized by LTV.
b. Explain how taking the charge before negotiating new credit agreements could avoid violating debt covenants.
c. It was also reported that LTV took several other significant charges while it was under bankruptcy proceedings. In addition to its concern about debt covenants, in general, why might management have chosen to take these charges at this time?

REAL DATA

ID10–9

Replacing currently maturing debt with a long-term note

General Cinema Corporation operates the leading movie theater circuits in the United States, is an independent bottler of Pepsi Cola and related products, and also owns several "high-end" retail stores, including Neiman-Marcus. In its financial statements, the company reported the following in the current liabilities section:

Long-term liabilities—due within one year	**$ 7,014,000**
Total current liabilities	**339,304,000**

In the notes to the financial statements, the company profiled all the components of its long-term debt.

REQUIRED:

a. What kind of assets must General Cinema use to repay the long-term liabilities in order for the portion due within one year to be classified as a current liability?
b. If General Cinema plans in the foreseeable future to refinance the amount of currently maturing long-term debt by issuing long-term notes, should the debt be classified current or long-term? Why?
c. Why might management consider such a refinancing strategy? State your answer in terms of important financial ratios and debt covenants.

REAL DATA

ID10–10

Reversing contingent losses

The Wall Street Journal (April 23, 1998) reported: "Motive Power Industries Inc., maker of locomotives and other power-related components, posted net income of $6.6 million. . . . Results were helped by the addition of $1.2 million, or four cents per share, for a one-time item related to a 1994 contract liability that expired in the first quarter of 1998."

REQUIRED:

a. What is a contingency, and how did Motive Power account for this contingency in 1994—ignore, disclose, or accrue?
b. What entry did the company record in 1998?
c. As an analyst, how would you interpret the entry recorded by Motive Power in 1998?

REAL DATA

ID10–11

Performance-based compensation

Corporate America uses a wide variety of compensation plans to attract and motivate its executives. Most plans include a base salary, which is independent of the company's performance, as well as a performance-based component. Normally, the performance-based component is based on some measure of the company's success. Common examples include reported net income and the company's stock price. The *Wall Street Journal* (May 3, 2000) reports that "companies ranging from Coca-Cola to Toys "R" Us to Eli Lilly have linked their managers' compensation to economic value added," where the company's profit has to exceed the cost of its debt (interest) and equity capital before management bonuses are paid. Relatively recently, much of corporate America has moved to compensating executives with stock options, and one recent article in the *Arizona Republic* (March 27, 2000) notes that we are seeing an explosion in the growth of these kinds of plans, even for lower-level managers: "[M]ore and more, it's a system U.S. companies are using to recruit, keep, and motivate workers."

REQUIRED:

Discuss the various forms of performance-based compensation in terms of the risks and rewards available to managers, the management incentives they create, and how they are accounted for on the income statement and balance sheet.

REAL DATA

ID10–12

Appendix 10B: Changes in expected tax rates and net income

In the third quarter of 1994, General Motors posted net income of $552 million, compared with a loss of $112.9 million a year earlier. Over $200 million of the profit was due to an accounting adjustment in its North American operations because its expected taxes turned out to be lower than it had anticipated in earlier periods. David Healy, an analyst with S.G. Warburg & Co., was quoted in *The Wall Street Journal* (October 21, 1994) as saying, "Cynics would say that since they couldn't do it in the auto department, they did it in the accounting department."

REQUIRED:

a. Explain what Mr. Healy means.
b. Explain how a change in expected tax rates can lead to a positive effect on reported earnings.
c. Do you believe that the $200 million gain represents an increase in the overall wealth of GM?

REAL DATA

ID10–13

The annual report of Wal-Mart

The 2001 annual report of Wal-Mart is reproduced in Appendix A.

REQUIRED:

Review the 2001 annual report, and answer the following questions.

a. What is working capital and what is the trend in Wal-Mart's working capital position over the last ten years?
b. How much did working capital change as a percent of total assets over that time period?
c. What happened to Wal-Mart's current ratio between 2000 and 2001? What accounted for the change?
d. What are the most important current liabilities reported by Wal-Mart?
e. Compute Wal-Mart's accounts payable turnover (see Chapter 5) for the past two years. Comment on any change. (Note: The accounts payable at the end of 1999 totaled $11,997.)
f. What interest rate did Wal-Mart pay on its short-term borrowings? What is Wal-Mart's main type of short-term borrowing?
g. Is Wal-Mart concerned with any major contingencies?
h. (Appendix 10A). What kind of pension plan does Wal-Mart provide for its employees? How much did the company contribute to the plan in 1999, 2000, and 2001?
i. (Appendix 10B). Compute Wal-Mart's conservatism ratio for 1999, 2000, and 2001. What is interesting about the company's deferred taxes in 1999 and 2000? Does this indicate that the company was more or less conservative with its financial accounting choices?

Long-Term Liabilities:
Notes, Bonds, and Leases

CHAPTER 11

KEY POINTS

The following key points are emphasized in this chapter:

Long-term notes payable, bonds payable, and leasehold obligations, and how companies use these instruments as important sources of financing.

Economic consequences created by borrowing.

Different forms of contractual obligations.

The effective interest rate and how it is determined for contractual obligations.

The effective interest method.

How changes in market interest rates can lead to misstated balance sheet values for long-term liabilities.

Operating leases, capital leases, and off-balance-sheet financing.

Imation is a leader in developing, manufacturing, and marketing a wide variety of products in the information industry. When the company almost tripled its long-term debt to $320 million, it was in violation of certain restrictions in the credit agreement drawn up with its banks. After some negotiation, the company obtained a limited waiver from the lenders. They agreed that the debt need not be repaid immediately if the company put its assets up as collateral and paid additional fees.

Imation increased its debt position by increasing its reliance on notes payable, bonds payable, and leases—the topics covered in this chapter. **Notes payable** are obligations evidenced by formal notes that normally involve direct borrowings from financial institutions or arrangements to finance the purchase of assets. **Bonds payable** are obligations that arise from notes (bonds) that have been issued for cash to a large number of creditors, called *bondholders*. **Leasehold obligations** refer to future cash payments (e.g., rent) required for the use or occupation of property during a specified period of time. Each of these liabilities represents an obligation to disburse assets (usually cash) for a time that extends beyond the period that defines current assets. The formal contracts underlying such arrangements contain a number of terms including, for example, the principal amount of the debt, the periodic interest payments, the time period over which the interest and principal are to be paid, and security (e.g., collateral) and other provisions, many of which are designed to protect the interests of the lenders.

Long-term borrowing arrangements, such as notes, bonds, and leases, are a common and major source of capital and financing for companies throughout the world. Funds used to acquire other companies, purchase machinery and equipment, finance plant expansion, pay off debts, repurchase outstanding stock, and support operations are often generated by issuing long-term notes and bonds or entering into lease agreements. The Walt Disney Company, for example, recently increased long-term borrowing by over $500 million, primarily to finance theme parks, network television, and broadcast programming. In a typical year, U.S. companies will raise as much as $300 billion by issuing bonds.

Accounting Trends and Techniques (AICPA, 2000) reported that, of the 600 major U.S. companies surveyed, 450 (75 percent) disclosed long-term notes payable, 168 (28 percent) disclosed bonds payable, and 290 (48 percent) disclosed leasehold liabilities. In 1999, Kmart Corporation reported long-term liabilities of almost $4 billion, consisting primarily of notes, bonds, and leasehold obligations.

The 2000 statement of cash flows for Eli Lilly included the following disclosures (dollars in millions).

	2000	1999	1998
Proceeds from issuing long-term debt	$ 1.1	$843.5	$ 23.8
Repayments of long-term debt	(27.2)	(13.5)	(30.2)

Describe how this activity affected the company's 2000, 1999, and 1998 balance sheets.

THE RELATIVE SIZE OF LONG-TERM LIABILITIES

In Figure 11–1, we see again that Internet firms carry almost no long-term debt. It is also clear that while financial institutions rely very heavily on current liabilities (see

Figure 10–2), their long-term debt is still much greater than stockholders' equity. Recall from Figure 10–1 that the capital structure of financial institutions tend to be over 90 percent liabilities. GE has relied heavily on long-term debt primarily to finance its strategy to grow by acquiring other companies, and note that its long-term debt is more than four times stockholders' equity. Over the years GE has reduced the size of its stockholders' equity by repurchasing its outstanding stock, which we discuss in Chapter 12. As indicated earlier, Tommy Hilfiger and Chevron use long-term liabilities to finance large investments in property, plant, and equipment.

FIGURE 11–1

Long-term liabilities (LTL) as a percentage of total assets[1]

	LTL/ Total Assets	LTL/ Total Liabilities	LTL/ Stockholders' Equity
MANUFACTURING:			
General Electric (Manufacturer)	.52	.59	4.33
Chevron (Oil drilling and refining)	.33	.64	.69
RETAIL:			
SUPERVALU (Grocery retail)	.30	.44	1.11
Tommy Hilfiger (Clothing retail)	.33	.71	.61
INTERNET:			
Yahoo (Internet search engine)	.01	.10	.01
Cisco (Internet systems)	.03	.18	.04
GENERAL SERVICES:			
SBC Communications (Telecommunications services)	.37	.55	1.19
Wendy's (Restaurant services)	.17	.53	.30
FINANCIAL SERVICES:			
Bank of America (Banking services)	.11	.14	1.57
Merrill Lynch (Investment services)	.17	.18	3.4

Information from the 1999 balance sheets of the Bank of New York, Yahoo, and AT&T is provided below. Match each company with the proper profile and explain your reasoning.

	1	2	3
Fixed assets/total assets	1%	4%	46%
Current liabilities/total assets	76	13	25
Long-term liabilities/total assets	92	1	32

THE ECONOMIC CONSEQUENCES OF REPORTING LONG-TERM LIABILITIES

During the 1980s, the importance of long-term debt grew to unprecedented levels in the United States, brought on primarily by numerous takeovers, mergers, and acquisitions

1. Long-term liabilities on Figure 11–1 include deferred income taxes, but many accountants believe that deferred income taxes do not represent a liability in an economic sense. See Appendix 10B for further discussion on deferred income taxes.

that involved billions of dollars (referred to in the financial press as "merger mania"). Individuals like Henry Kravis, Robert Campeau, Michael Milken, Rupert Murdoch, Merv Griffin, and Donald Trump engineered mega-mergers that were financed by gigantic amounts of long-term debt. When the 1990s arrived, the surviving companies were left with the challenge of generating enough cash to meet the staggering debt payment schedules created by such borrowings.

In many cases, this situation has increased the pressure on companies to more carefully manage their debt payments and to pay special attention to how this debt is reported on the balance sheet. During the first quarter of 1991, for example, defaults on bond payments climbed to a record $8.2 billion, and corporate credit ratings, in general, sank to new lows. Many firms, including almost the entire auto and retail industries, experienced credit-rating downgrades, and well-known companies, such as R.H. Macy, Circle K, Pan Am Airlines, Eastern Airlines, and Campeau's retail empire (including Bloomingdale's, Abraham & Straus, and Lazarus), filed for bankruptcy protection.

Merger mania extended into the 1990s. *The Wall Street Journal* (August 1, 1995) reported: "Merger activity in the 1995 first half totaled $164.4 billion, the biggest first half on record." When Disney purchased Capital Cities/ABC in August 1995, for example, it added $10 billion to its balance sheet. More recently, WorldCom added over $6 billion in debt to its balance sheet when it acquired MCI in 1999.

In such a debt-laden environment, measures of solvency, like the debt/equity ratio, and debt covenant provisions take on a particularly important role. As such, management has strong incentives to manage financial statement numbers by employing reporting strategies like "off-balance-sheet financing."[2]

In response to this debt explosion and the threat of off-balance-sheet financing, the FASB passed a standard requiring companies to describe the risks associated with financing arrangements not disclosed on the balance sheet. While this standard falls far short of providing all the information necessary to assess this risk, users can now better assess a company's potential obligations, whether or not they appear on the balance sheet.

Honeywell, an advanced technology manufacturer, included in recent annual reports a section titled "Financial Instruments" in which the company described risks associated with fluctuating interest rates that could adversely affect the company, and how they are managed and controlled. Why is this disclosure necessary, and how is it useful to investors?

BASIC DEFINITIONS AND DIFFERENT CONTRACTUAL FORMS

Long-term obligations normally represent contractual agreements to make cash payments over a period of time. In addition to other terms, these contracts specify the period of time over which the payments are to be made as well as the dollar amount of each payment. Different contracts express these terms in different ways, giving rise to long-term obligations—and their associated cash flows—that take various forms.

---

2. Recall that "off-balance-sheet financing" involves the existence of debt obligations that are not listed in the liability section of the balance sheet.

Some contracts, called **interest-bearing obligations,** require periodic (annual or semiannual) cash payments (called **interest**) that are determined as a percentage of the **face, principal,** or **maturity value,** which must be paid at the end of the contract period. For example, a company may enter into an exchange in which it receives some benefit (e.g., cash, asset, or service) and, in return, promises to pay $1,000 per year for two years and $10,000 at the end of the second year. Such an obligation would have a life of two years, a **stated interest rate** of 10 percent ($1,000/$10,000), and a maturity, principal, or face value of $10,000. The cash flows associated with this contract are illustrated as follows.

Period:	0	──────────→	1	──────────→	2
Payment:	+Receipt		−$1,000		−$1,000
					−$10,000

Non-interest-bearing obligations, on the other hand, require no periodic payments, but only a single cash payment at the end of the contract period. For example, a company may enter into another exchange in which it receives a benefit and, in return, promises to pay $12,000 at the end of two years. This obligation, which is illustrated below, would have a life of two years, a stated interest rate of 0 percent, and a maturity, principal, or face value of $12,000. Although the stated rate is zero, we discuss later that these notes actually include an element of interest.

Period:	0	──────────→	1	──────────→	2
Payment:	+Receipt		−$0		−$0
					−$12,000

In an **installment obligation,** periodic payments covering both interest and principal are made throughout the life of the contract. For example, a company may enter into an exchange in which it receives a benefit and, in return, promises to pay $6,000 at the end of each of two years. The cash flows associated with this obligation are illustrated below.

| Period: | 0 | ──────────→ | 1 | ──────────→ | 2 |
| Payment: | +Receipt | | −$6,000 | | −$6,000 |

The contractual forms illustrated above represent three common ways to schedule the cash payments associated with long-term obligations. Further, each of these contractual forms may contain additional terms that specify assets pledged as security or **collateral** in case the required cash payments are not met (**default**), as well as additional provisions (**restrictive covenants**) designed to protect the interests of the lenders.

It is also useful to consider the nature of that which is received in exchange for the contractual obligation. In the examples above, we have simply referred to it as the "receipt." Often this "receipt" takes the form of cash, as in cases where companies borrow cash from financial institutions, promising to make payments in accordance with the terms of a loan contract. However, contractual obligations also can be exchanged for noncash items, such as long-lived assets, services, or other liabilities. Figure 11–2 illustrates the six possible kinds of notes that can be obtained by matching each of the three contractual forms with cash and noncash "receipts."

In the next section, we introduce the very important concept of the effective interest rate in the context of each of the six combinations illustrated in Figure 11–2. We then discuss notes payable, which can be related to all six combinations; bonds payable, which typically relate to 3A; and capital leases, which relate to 1B.

FIGURE 11-2

Six possible
kinds of notes

1. **Installment**
   A. Cash received (e.g., bank loan)
   B. Noncash received (e.g., lease or real estate purchase)
2. **Non-interest-bearing**
   A. Cash received (e.g., zero coupon bond)
   B. Noncash received (e.g., equipment purchase)
3. **Interest-bearing notes**
   A. Cash received (e.g., bond)
   B. Noncash received (e.g., equipment purchase)

EFFECTIVE INTEREST RATE

The **effective interest rate** is the actual interest rate paid by the issuer of the obligation. It may or may not equal the interest rate stated on the contract (for interest-bearing notes). It is determined by finding the discount rate that sets the present value of the obligation's cash outflows equal to the fair market value (FMV) of that which is received in the exchange.[3] When contractual obligations are exchanged for cash (1A, 2A, and 3A in Figure 11–2), the cash amount received represents the FMV of the receipt. When contractual obligations are exchanged for noncash items (1B, 2B, and 3B), the FMV of the noncash items must be determined through appraisals or some other means.[4] The following examples show how the effective interest rate is determined for the three notes illustrated earlier: installment, non-interest-bearing, and interest-bearing.

In its 2000 annual report, Lucent Technologies lists over $3 billion in long-term debt with annual interest rates ranging from 5.5 percent to 8 percent. The long-term debt include notes, bonds, and leases. Consider these three types of long-term debts and discuss whether you think that they are interest-bearing, non-interest-bearing, or installments. Are the interest rates indicated above stated rates or effective rates? Discuss.

Installment and Non-Interest-Bearing Obligations

Assume that Able Company entered into an installment obligation requiring the payment of $10,000 at the end of each of two years. In return, the company received a benefit (cash or noncash) with an FMV of $16,900. The cash flows associated with this exchange follow:

Period:	0	1	2
Payment:	+$16,900	−$10,000	−$10,000

In this case, the company has received a benefit of $16,900, promising to pay a $10,000, two-year, ordinary annuity. The effective (actual) interest rate on the obliga-

---

3. The material in this chapter requires an understanding of present value, which is covered in Appendix B.
4. If the FMV of the noncash item received in the exchange cannot be determined, the effective interest rate must be estimated by considering the effective interest rates of other similar contractual obligations.

tion is calculated by finding that interest rate which, when used to discount the two $10,000 payments, results in a present value (PV) of $16,900. The calculation can be set up in the following way:

PV   = Annuity Cash Payment × (PV Table Factor Ordinary Annuity: n = 2, i = ?)
$16,900 = $10,000   ×   ?

Rearranging,

PV table factor = $16,900 ÷ $10,000 = 1.69
Since n = 2, i = 12% (effective interest rate)

The effective interest rate is equal to 12 percent because a $10,000, two-year, ordinary annuity discounted at 12 percent is equal to $16,900, the FMV of the benefit received by Able in the exchange.

The method used to compute the effective interest rate for a non-interest-bearing obligation is the same as that used for an installment obligation, except that the table factor is taken from the Present Value of a Single Sum table instead of the Present Value of an Ordinary Annuity table. For example, if Baker Company entered into a non-interest-bearing obligation requiring a single $5,000 payment at the end of three years, receiving a benefit (cash or noncash) with an FMV of $3,969, the effective interest rate would be computed as follows:

PV   = Single Sum Cash Payment × (PV Table Factor Single Sum: n = 3, i = ?)
$3,969 = $5,000   ×   ?

Rearranging,

PV table factor = $3,969 ÷ $5,000 = 0.7938
Since n = 3, i = 8% (effective interest rate)

It is important to note in both cases that the effective interest rate of a given contractual obligation is determined by the FMV of the benefit received in the exchange. If, for example, the FMV of the benefit received in the non-interest-bearing case was $4,198 instead of $3,969, the effective rate would have been 6 percent instead of 8 percent. Similarly, in the installment case, if the FMV received was $17,355 instead of $16,900, the effective rate would have been 10 percent instead of 12 percent.

Interest-Bearing Obligations

Assume that Clyde Company entered into an interest-bearing obligation requiring interest payments of $1,000 at the end of each of two years and a principal payment of $10,000 at the end of the second year. In return, the company received a benefit (cash or noncash) with an FMV of $10,000. This obligation has a life of two years, a stated interest rate of 10 percent ($1,000/$10,000), and a maturity, face, or principal value of $10,000. The cash flows associated with this exchange follow:

Period: 0 ————————————→ 1 ————————————→   2
Payment: +$10,000   −$1,000   −$1,000
                                                         −$10,000

In this case, the company has received a benefit of $10,000, promising to pay a $1,000, two-year, ordinary annuity in addition to a $10,000 single sum payment at the end of two years. The effective (actual) interest rate on this obligation is calculated by finding that interest rate which, when used to discount all three payments, results in a present value of $10,000. The correct rate is 10 percent.[5]

Note in this case that the effective rate of interest (10 percent) equaled the interest rate stated on the obligation (10 percent). This equality occurred only because the FMV of the benefit received ($10,000) was equal to the maturity value of the obligation ($10,000). Had the FMV of the benefit received not equaled the maturity value, the effective rate of interest would not have equaled the stated rate. For example, had the FMV of the receipt equaled $9,662, the effective rate would have been 12 percent.

ACCOUNTING FOR LONG-TERM OBLIGATIONS: THE EFFECTIVE INTEREST METHOD

Understanding the effective rate of interest is important because it represents the actual rate of interest associated with an obligation. It is the foundation for the **effective interest method,** which is used to account for long-term contractual obligations—notes, bonds, and capital leases. This method consists of one basic rule:

The interest expense reported during each period of a long-term obligation's contractual life is computed by multiplying the effective interest rate by the balance sheet value of the obligation as of the beginning of the period.

The rationale underlying the effective interest method is that it leads to an interest expense amount each period that reflects the actual interest being paid on the obligation. In addition, it guarantees that the long-term liability on the balance sheet (note payable, bond payable, or lease liability) is reported throughout its life at the present value of its future cash flows, discounted at the effective interest rate. Recall from the discussion in Chapter 4 that present value is the theoretical goal of financial measurement.

At the end of 1999, Sherwin Williams reported long-term debt of $624 million on its balance sheet. At an average effective interest rate of 7 percent, estimate the interest expense associated with this debt reported by the company on its 2000 income statement.

ACCOUNTING FOR LONG-TERM NOTES PAYABLE

Issuing long-term notes is a popular way for major U.S. companies to raise cash. Both **secured** (backed by collateral) and **unsecured notes** are widely used. *Accounting Trends and Techniques* (AICPA, 2000) reported that, of the 600 major U.S. companies surveyed, 450 (75 percent) disclosed unsecured notes and 85 (14 percent) disclosed notes that were backed by collateral.

The issuance of notes normally involves only one or a small group of lenders (usually financial institutions) and can take a number of different contractual forms. Interest-bearing, non-interest-bearing, and installment notes are all quite common, and

5. The correct rate can be found using a trial-and-error approach—that is, trying different interest rates until the present value of the cash payments is equal to the fair market value of the benefit. Most of you, however, have calculators that can compute the answer directly.

they can be exchanged for cash and/or noncash items. A **mortgage,** for example, is a cash loan, exchanged for an installment note that is secured by real estate. Machinery and equipment purchases are often received in exchange for (financed with) installment notes. When a note payable is issued to satisfy another outstanding note payable, a **refinancing** has occurred.

The following example illustrates the methods used to account for a non-interest-bearing note exchanged for equipment (2B in Figure 11–2), which is almost identical to such a note being exchanged for cash (2A). Bonds are normally interest-bearing notes exchanged for cash, so the discussion of bonds later in the chapter will cover 3A in Figure 11–2. Capital leases are a form of financing the purchase of long-term assets with installment notes, so that discussion later in the chapter will cover 1B in Figure 11–2.

Assume that on January 1, 2002, Seabell Inc. acquired a piece of equipment with an FMV of $10,288 and, in return, signed a non-interest-bearing note payable with a maturity date of December 31, 2003, and a maturity value of $12,000. The transaction and the associated accounting entries are described in Figure 11–3.

FIGURE 11–3 Accounting for a non–interest-bearing note exchanged for equipment

---

Period: 1/1/02 ⟶ 12/31/02 ⟶ 12/31/03
Payment: +Equipment   −$0   −$0
                    (FMV = $10,288)   −$12,000

JOURNAL

Equipment (+A)	10,288	Interest Exp. (E, −SE)	823*	Interest Exp. (E, −SE)	889**
Disc. on Notes Pay. (−L)	1,712	Disc. on Notes Pay. (+L)	823	Disc. on Notes Pay. (+L)	889
Notes Pay. (+L)	12,000			Notes pay. (−L)	12,000
				Cash (−A)	12,000

BALANCE SHEET VALUE

Notes payable	$12,000		Notes payable	$12,000	
Less: Discount	1,712	$10,288	Less: Discount	889	$11,111

General Ledger   Discount on Notes Payable

(1/1/02)	1,712		
		(12/31/02 adj.)	823
(12/31/03)	889		
		(12/31/03 adj.)	889
	0		

*$10,288 × 8%
**$11,111 × 8%

When Seabell acquires the equipment and issues the note, the equipment is recorded at its FMV, the notes payable account is recorded at its maturity value, and a discount on notes payable account is debited for the difference. The discount is listed on the balance sheet directly under Notes Payable and subtracted from it in determining the balance sheet value of the note payable, as illustrated in Figure 11–3. The discount can be viewed as a form of "unaccrued interest" because Seabell agreed to pay $12,000 for a piece of equipment that at present is worth only $10,288. Accordingly, the discount is amortized into interest expense over the two-year life of the note.

The effective interest method is then used to account for the note over its two-year life. First, the effective interest rate must be determined, which is equal to 8 percent, the interest rate that equates the present value of the note's future cash flows with the FMV of the equipment ($10,288). Then, the effective interest rate (8 percent) is multiplied by the book value of the note at the beginning of 2002 ($10,288) to determine the interest expense for 2002 ($823). The adjusting entry at the end of 2002 serves to recognize interest expense and amortize a portion of the discount. The remaining amount of the discount ($889) is then subtracted from the notes payable account to determine the book value of the liability as of the end of 2002 ($11,111). The same procedure is then followed at the end of 2003 to recognize interest expense and amortize the remainder of the discount ($889), and the maturity value ($12,000) is paid off at the end of the second year.

Several features about this example are important. First, the accounting treatment would have been virtually the same had a cash amount of $10,288 been received instead of equipment with an FMV of $10,288. Only the initial entry would have differed, reflecting a cash receipt instead of equipment.

Second, even though the note payable has no stated interest rate, it has an effective (actual) interest rate of 8 percent, which must be recognized over the life of the note. In line with the effective interest method, the interest expense in each period is simply the effective rate multiplied by the balance sheet value of the note at the beginning of that period. The interest expense recognized in the second period ($889) is greater than that in the first ($823) because the balance sheet value of the note increased from $10,288 to $11,111. The company was one year closer to the ultimate $12,000 payment. Finally, the effective interest method ensured that the balance sheet value of the note throughout its life was equal to the present value of the note's future cash flows, discounted at the effective interest rate. For example, the present value of $12,000 discounted back one year at 8 percent is equal to $11,111 ($12,000 × .92593) and discounted back two years is equal to $10,288 ($12,000 × .85734).[6] These fundamental features are very important because they apply to other forms of notes as well as bonds and capital leases.

BONDS PAYABLE

Companies issue bonds to raise large amounts of capital, usually to finance expensive, long-term projects. For example, Lockheed Martin, an aircraft manufacturer, raised over $3 billion through bond issuances in 1999. Proceeds were used for working capital, capital expenditures, debt repayments, and acquisitions. Due to its first-rate AAA credit rating, the company was able to get excellent terms on the issuances.

6. Instead of the effective interest method, some companies amortize Discounts on Long-Term Obligations (e.g., notes and bonds) using the straight-line method. That is, they amortize equal amounts of the discount into interest expense during each period of the note's life. According to generally accepted accounting principles, the straight-line method is acceptable only if it results in numbers (i.e., interest expense and book value of the note payable) that are not materially different from those produced by the effective interest method. The straight-line method misstates periodic interest expense and the balance sheet value of the note because it fails to reflect the actual interest rate paid by the borrower.

Bonds are normally sold to the public through a third party (called an underwriter), such as an investment banker or a financial institution.[7] They are usually interest-bearing notes that involve formal commitments requiring the issuing company to make cash interest payments to the bondholder and a principal payment (usually in the amount of $1,000 per bond) when the bond matures. This is usually between five and thirty years from the date of issuance. After bonds are initially issued, they are generally freely negotiable; that is, they can be purchased and sold in the open market. Both the New York and the American Security Exchanges maintain active bond markets. Securities Data Co. calculates that the amount of new debt issued in 1996 set a new record of $300 billion.[8]

Bond Terminology

Figure 11–4 summarizes the important components of a bond. The **life** of the bond is the time period extending from the date of its issuance to its maturity date. At the **maturity date,** the end of the bond's life, an amount of cash equal to the face value (*principal, par value,* or *maturity value*) is paid to the bondholder. The *face value,* the amount written on the face of the bond, is usually $1,000. The **interest payment** (sometimes called coupon payment), which is paid to the bondholders on each semi-annual interest payment date, is computed by multiplying the annual interest rate stated on the bond (the stated or coupon rate) by the face value of the issuance. This amount is then divided by two because the stated rate is an annual rate, and the interest payments are made every six months. The **proceeds,** the amount collected by the issuing company when the bonds are issued, are equal to the price paid by the purchasers of the bonds multiplied by the number of bonds issued. This amount is usually net of the issuance costs incurred by the issuing company.[9]

To illustrate, assume that on January 1, 2000, Northern States Power Company issued 2,500 bonds, each with a face value of $1,000 and a stated interest rate of 5 percent, due to mature ten years later, on December 31, 2009. The company collected $990 on each bond, which totaled approximately $2.475 million for the entire bond issuance. In terms similar to those in Figure 11–4, the cash flows associated with this bond issuance and the calculations of the proceeds, the semiannual interest payment, and entire maturity value are shown in Figure 11–5.

In addition to the face value, maturity date, and stated interest rate, the bond contract may include a number of other important provisions. Three such provisions are described in Figure 11–4: restrictive covenants, security, and call provisions.

Restrictive **covenants** are imposed by bondholders to protect their interests and may restrict management in a number of significant ways. Nordstrom, a large specialty store operating throughout the United States, stated in its annual report that the company has entered into long-term debt agreements that (1) limit additional long-term debt and lease obligations, (2) require that working capital must be at least $50 million or 25 percent of current liabilities, whichever is greater, (3) limit short-term borrowings, and (4) restrict dividends to shareholders.

Security provisions also protect the interests of bondholders by ensuring that assets are pledged in case of default. As of December 31, 2000, for example, Lucent

---

7. Major underwriters include Merrill Lynch, Goldman Sachs, First Boston, Salomon Smith Barney, Shearson Lehman Hutton, Morgan Stanley, Prudential Bache, Kidder Peabody, Dean Witter, and Paine Webber.
8. *Business Week,* March 10, 1997.
9. To simplify the discussion, these issuance costs are assumed to be zero in the remainder of the chapter.

FIGURE 11-4 Bond terminology

Issuance Date	Time to Maturity					Maturity Date
0	6 months	1 year	6 months	2 years	(etc.) . . .	
Proceeds at Issuance	Interest Payment	Interest Payment	Interest Payment	Interest Payment	. . .	Interest Payment
						Face Value Payment

TERMS OF BOND CONTRACT

Life: Time period from date of issuance to the maturity date, usually from five to thirty years.

Maturity date: Date when the dollar amount written on the face of the bond (face value) and final interest payment are paid to the bondholder.

Face value: Dollar amount written on the bond certificate. Sometimes referred to as the *principal, par value,* or *maturity value,* the face value is usually $1,000.

Interest payment: The interest rate stated on the bond, multiplied by the face value. This rate is called the *stated rate,* or *coupon rate,* and it is usually fixed for the entire life of the bond.

Proceeds at issuance: Dollar amount collected when the bonds are issued, equal to the price the buyers paid for each bond multiplied by the number of bonds issued. This amount is usually net of issuance fees.

Effective interest rate: The actual interest rate paid on the bond. This rate, when used to discount the future interest and principal cash payments, results in a present value that is equal to the amount received by the issuer.

OTHER PROVISIONS OF THE BOND CONTRACT

Restrictions: The bond contract may restrict the issuing company in certain ways to ensure that the interest and principal payments will be made. For example, a certain current ratio or level of working capital may be required, dividends may be restricted, or additional debt may be limited.

Security: The bond contract may specify that collateral be paid in case of default (i.e., interest

or principal payments are not made). Unsecured bonds are called *debentures.*

Call provision: The bond contract may specify that the issuing company can buy back (retire) the bonds at a specified price after a certain date during the life of the bond. The specified price is usually greater than the face value.

Technologies had outstanding bonds with a balance sheet value of $116 million, which were secured by land, buildings, and equipment. Bonds with no assets backing them are called **unsecured bonds** or **debentures.** At December 31, 2000, Lucent had outstanding debentures valued on the balance sheet at $1.66 billion.[10]

10. Debentures with a very low priority for the issuing company's assets in case of liquidation are referred to as *junk bonds:* bonds rated by credit-rating agencies at lower than investment grade. Many of the mergers in the 1980s were financed with junk bonds. *The Wall Street Journal* (March 1991) reported that thirty-two U.S. companies defaulted on their junk bond payments in the first quarter of 1991. Such defaults had been rising due to the inability of debt-laden companies to repay, restructure, or refinance their debt.

FIGURE 11–5 Example of bond issuance: Northern States Power Company (dollars in thousands)

Issuance Date (1/1/00)		Time to Maturity: Thirty Years			Maturity Date (12/31/09)
0 —————→	6 months ——→	1 year ———→	6 months ——→	2 years . . . ——→	10 years
Proceeds	Interest	Interest	Interest	Interest . . .	Interest and face value
+$2,475,000ª	−$62,500ᵇ	−$62,500	−$62,500	−$62,500	−$62,500 −$2,500,000

ª2,500 bonds × $990 = $2,475,000
ᵇ(2,500 bonds × $1,000 × .05%) ÷ 2 = $62,500

A **call provision** grants to the issuing company the right to retire (repurchase) outstanding bonds after a designated date for a specified price. This provision serves to protect the interests of the issuing company, enabling it to remove the debt if economic conditions are appropriate. If interest rates and the economy fall, for example, a company may wish to repurchase outstanding bonds that require relatively high interest payments.

The following quote came from an annual report of CBS, a major television network:

The . . . debentures are due June 1, 2022 and may not be redeemed prior to June 1, 2002. On and after that date they may be redeemed, at the option of the company, as a whole at any time or in part from time to time, at specified redemption prices.

Interpret this quote and explain why CBS may want the option to redeem its outstanding long-term debt.

The Price of a Bond

Bond prices are basically determined by what potential bondholders are willing to pay for the right to receive the semiannual interest payments and cash in the amount of the face value at maturity.[11] The credit rating of the issuing company as well as the stated interest rate, covenants, security arrangements, call provisions, and many other terms of the bond contract directly influence the price at which bonds are issued. Bonds issued by companies with high credit ratings, offering high stated interest rates, and backed by collateral tend to sell for higher prices than unsecured bonds issued by companies with low credit ratings, offering low stated interest rates.

Bond prices are usually expressed as a percentage of the face value ($1,000) and may be less than, equal to, or greater than the face value. Bonds issued for less than $1,000 are issued at a *discount*. Bonds issued for $1,000 are issued at *face* (or *par*) *value*. Bonds issued for greater than $1,000 are issued at a *premium*.

---

11. A discussion of how bond prices are determined is contained in Appendix 11A.

As of the end of 1999, Exxon Mobil had long-term debt outstanding in the amount of $8.4 billion. Included in that amount were debentures due 2012 issued at a discount. What are debentures and under what circumstances would they be issued at a discount?

The Effective Rate and the Stated Rate

As with other interest-bearing obligations, the effective (actual) rate of interest paid on a bond is not necessarily equal to the stated rate. Recall that the effective rate is that rate which, when used to discount the future contractual cash payments, results in a present value that is equal to the FMV of the receipt (i.e., issuance price). Depending on the relationship between the issuance price and the face value, the effective rate of interest on a bond may be lower than, equal to, or higher than the stated interest rate. Figure 11–6 illustrates these three relationships.

FIGURE 11–6   Bond prices and the relationship between the effective rate and the stated rate (bond terms: $1,000 face value, a 6% stated rate, and a 5-year life)

Effective Rate		Stated Rate	Face Value	Price (Present Value)	Type of Issue
1. 8%	>	6%	$1,000	$ 919 = $30(8.1109) + $1,000(.6756)	Discount
2. 4%	<	6%	1,000	1,090 = $30(8.9826) + 1,000(.8203)	Premium
3. 6%	=	6%	1,000	1,000 = $30(8.5302) + 1,000(.7441)	Par

The effective interest rates of three different bonds are compared. Each bond has a $1,000 face value, a five-year life, and a 6 percent stated annual interest rate (paid semiannually). They differ in that #1 is issued at an $81 discount (91.9), #2 is issued at a $90 premium (109.0), and #3 is issued at par (100.0). In each case, the effective interest rate is determined by finding that rate which, when used to discount the interest and face value payments, results in a present value that equals the issue price.[12] The relationship among the price, the effective interest rate, and the stated interest rate is summarized below.

1. When the issuance price of a bond is greater that its face value (*premium*), the effective rate is less than the stated rate.

---

12. When using present value tables to infer an effective interest rate or to compute the price of a bond, keep in mind that interest payments are made on a semiannual basis. Accordingly, when finding the table factors for the interest payment annuity and the lump sum payment, the number of periods must be doubled and the discount rate must be halved. For example, the present value (PV) of a bond with a ten-year life, a $1,000 face value, and a 10 percent stated interest rate, discounted at 8 percent, would be computed as below. Note that the table factors are based on an *n* of 20 (10 × 2) and an *i* of 4 percent (8%/2).

PV = Semiannual interest (PV of annuity: n = 20, i = 4%) + Face value (PV lump sum: n = 20, i = 4%)
     = $50   (13.59)   + $1,000   (.456)
     = $679.50   + $456
     = $1,135.50

2. When the issuance price of a bond is less than its face value (*discount*), the effective rate is greater than the stated rate.
3. When the issuance price of a bond is equal to its face value (*par*), the effective rate is equal to the stated rate.

The effective interest rate on the debentures issued by Exxon Mobil, referred to earlier, was approximately 5 percent. Was the stated interest rate on the debentures above or below 5 percent? Explain.

Accounting for Bonds Payable

The effective interest method is used to account for bonds payable. The following examples use the effective interest method to account for three different bonds: one issued at face (par) value, one issued at a discount, and one issued at a premium. The following information is used in all three cases.

Assume that Webster International issues ten bonds, each with a face value of $1,000, a stated interest rate of 10 percent, and time to maturity of two years. Interest payments of $500 [($10,000 × 10 percent)/2] are to be made semiannually. In Case 1, the bonds are issued at face (par), so that the effective rate (10 percent) equals the stated rate (10 percent). In Case 2, the bonds are issued at a discount, so that the effective rate (12 percent) is greater than the stated rate (10 percent). In Case 3, the bonds are issued at a premium, so the effective rate (8 percent) is less than the stated rate (10 percent). Figure 11–7 shows the cash flows associated with the three bond issuances. Note that the cash flows are identical for all three bond issuances, except for the issuance price.

FIGURE 11–7 Cash flows for bonds payable: Three cases compared

Face value: 10 bonds × $1,000 per bond		= **$10,000**		
Semiannual interest payment: ($10,000 × 10%) ÷ 2 =		**500**		
Issuance Date	**6 months**	**1 year**	**6 months**	**Maturity Date**
Cash 1: Issued at $10,000 (face)				
+ 10,000	**−$500**	**−$500**	**−$500**	**−$ 500**
				− 10,000
Case 2: Issued at $9,654 (discount)				
+ 9,654	**− 500**	**− 500**	**− 500**	**− 500**
				− 10,000
Case 3: Issued at $10,363 (premium)				
+ 10,363	**− 500**	**− 500**	**− 500**	**− 500**
				− 10,000

CASE 1: BONDS ISSUED AT PAR

In Case 1, the bonds are issued at par ($10,000) and the effective rate (10 percent) is equal to the stated rate (10 percent). The journal entries, balance sheet values of bonds payable, and present value of the future cash flows discounted at the effective interest rate are shown in Figure 11–8.

FIGURE 11–8   Bonds issued at face value: Case 1

Date	Journal Entry			Balance Sheet Value	Present Value
Issue	Cash (+A)	10,000			
	Bonds Payable (+L)		10,000	$10,000	$10,000
	Issued bond.				
6 months	Interest Expense (E, −SE)	500			
	Cash (−A)		500	10,000	10,000
	Paid interest.				
1 year	Interest Expense (E, −SE)	500			
	Cash (−A)		500	10,000	10,000
	Paid interest.				
6 months	Interest Expense (E, −SE)	500			
	Cash (−A)		500	10,000	10,000
	Paid interest.				
Maturity	Interest Expense (E, −SE)	500			
	Cash (−A)		500	10,000	10,000
	Paid interest.				
	Bonds Payable (−L)	10,000			
	Cash (−A)		10,000	0	0
	Paid principal.				

Interest expense = Balance sheet value at beginning of period × [effective interest rate (10%) ÷ 2]
Cash interest payment = ($10,000 × 10%) ÷ 2
Balance sheet value = Face value ($10,000)
Present value = Remaining cash outflows discounted at effective interest rate (10%)

When bonds are issued at par, the journal entries are very straightforward because neither a discount nor a premium need be considered. The bonds payable account is simply carried on the balance sheet at $10,000 until maturity. Note that the present value of the remaining cash flows, discounted at 10 percent, is also equal to $10,000 throughout the life of the bond. The interest expense recognized in each six-month period ($500) appears on the income statement and is calculated by multiplying the effective interest rate (5 percent = 10 percent/2) by the balance sheet value of the bonds payable at the beginning of the period ($10,000). This calculation is the essence of the effective interest method and in this case gives rise to an amount equal to the $500 cash payment. These two dollar amounts are equal because the effective rate, which determines the interest expense, is equal to the stated rate, which determines the interest payment.

CASE 2: BONDS ISSUED AT A DISCOUNT

In Case 2, the bonds are issued at a $346 discount, and the effective rate of interest (12 percent) is greater than the stated rate (10 percent). Figure 11–9 shows the journal entries, balance sheet value of bonds payable, and present value of the future cash flows discounted at the effective interest rate.

FIGURE 11–9   Bonds issued at a discount: Case 2

Date	Journal Entry		Balance Sheet Value	Present Value
Issue	Cash (+A) Discount on Bonds Payable (−L) Bonds Payable (+L) *Issued bond.*	9,654 346 10,000	$ 9,654	$ 9,654
6 months	Interest Expense (E, −SE) Discount on Bonds Payable (+L) Cash (−A) *Paid interest and amortized discount.*	579 79 500	+ 79 9,733	9,733
1 Year	Interest Expense (E, −SE) Discount on Bonds Payable (+L) Cash (−A) *Paid interest and amortized discount.*	584 84 500	+ 84 9,817	9,817
6 months	Interest Expense (E, −SE) Discount on Bonds Payable (+L) Cash (−A) *Paid interest and amortized discount.*	589 89 500	+ 89 9,906	9,906
Maturity	Interest Expense (E, −SE) Discount on Bonds Payable (+L) Cash (−A) *Paid interest and amortized discount.*	594 94 500	+ 94 10,000	10,000
	Bonds Payable (−L) Cash (−A) *Paid principal.*	10,000 10,000	0	0

Interest expense = Balance sheet value at beginning of period × [effective interest rate (12%) ÷ 2]
Cash interest payment = ($10,000 × 10%) ÷ 2
Balance sheet value = Face value ($10,000) less unamortized discount
or
Balance sheet value at beginning of period + discount amortized during period
Present value = Remaining cash outflows discounted at effective interest rate (12%)

The Bond Payable is initially recorded at $10,000, which is greater than the $9,654 Cash Proceeds; consequently, a $346 **Discount on Bonds Payable** is recognized. This discount is disclosed on the balance sheet as a contra liability and is subtracted from the Bonds Payable account. It can be viewed as unaccrued interest waiting to be expensed over the life of the bond. The balance sheet disclosure of the Bonds Payable account and the discount at issuance appear as follows:

Bonds payable	**$10,000**	
Less: Discount on bonds payable	346	**$9,654**

In applying the effective interest method, interest expense is calculated each period by multiplying the effective interest rate (6 percent = 12 percent/2) by the balance sheet value of the bond liability at the beginning of the period. For example, at the end of the first six-month period, the $579 interest expense is computed thus: 6 percent × $9,654. The cash interest payment is only $500, so $79 is credited to the discount account. The $79 of amortized discount represents the interest cost, recognized in the first period, associated with receiving only $9,654 for a bond that requires a payment of $10,000 at maturity. The remaining (unamortized) portion of the discount ($267 = $346 − $79) is subtracted from Bonds Payable on the balance sheet to bring its balance sheet value to present value ($9,733).[13] This process is repeated every six months throughout the life of the bond, and eventually the entire discount is amortized into interest expense. Note also that the effective interest method ensures that the balance sheet value of the bond liability is equal to the present value of the remaining cash flows, discounted at 12 percent, throughout the life of the bond.

CASE 3: BONDS ISSUED AT A PREMIUM

In Case 3, the bonds are issued at a $363 premium, and the effective rate of interest (8 percent) is less than the stated rate (10 percent). The journal entries, balance sheet value of bonds payable, and present value of the future cash flows discounted at the effective interest rate appear in Figure 11–10.

The bond payable is initially recorded at $10,000, which is less than the $10,363 cash proceeds, so a $363 **Premium on Bonds Payable** is recognized. This premium is disclosed on the balance sheet as an addition to the bonds payable account. It can be viewed as a reduction in interest expense (or a deferred revenue) waiting to be recognized over the life of the bond. The balance sheet disclosure of the bonds payable account and the premium at issuance appear as follows:

Bonds payable	**$10,000**	
Plus: Premium on bonds payable	363	**$10,363**

In applying the effective interest method, interest expense is calculated each period by multiplying the effective interest rate (4 percent = 8 percent ÷ 2) by the balance sheet value of the bond liability at the beginning of the period. For example, at the end of the first six-month period, the $415 interest expense is equal to 4 percent × $10,363. The cash interest payment is $500, so $85 is debited to the premium on bonds payable account. The $85 of amortized premium represents reduced interest cost, recognized in the first period, associated with receiving $10,363 for a bond that requires a payment of only $10,000 at maturity. The remaining (unamortized) portion of the premium ($278 = $363 − $85) is added to Bonds Payable on the balance sheet to bring its balance sheet value to the present value ($10,278).[14] This process is repeated every six months throughout the life of the bond, and eventually the entire premium is amortized into interest expense. Note, once again, that the effective interest method keeps the bal-

13. Subtracting the unamortized portion of the discount from Bonds Payable is equivalent to adding the amortized amount of the discount to the balance sheet value, which is shown in Figure 11–9.

14. Adding the unamortized portion of the premium to Bonds Payable is equivalent to subtracting the amortized amount of the premium from the balance sheet value, which is shown in Figure 11–10.

FIGURE 11-10   Bonds issued at a premium: Case 3

Date	Journal Entry			Balance Sheet Value	Present Value
Issue	Cash (+A)	10,363			
	Premium on Bonds Payable (+L)		363		
	Bonds Payable (+L)		10,000	$10,363	$10,363
	Issued bond.				
6 months	Interest Expense (E, −SE)	415			
	Premium on Bonds Payable (−L)	85		− 85	
	Cash (−A)		500	10,278	10,278
	Paid interest and amortized premium.				
1 Year	Interest Expense (E, −SE)	411			
	Premium on Bonds Payable (−L)	89		− 89	
	Cash (−A)		500	10,189	10,189
	Paid interest and amortized premium.				
6 months	Interest Expense (E, −SE)	407			
	Premium on Bonds Payable (−L)	93		− 93	
	Cash (−A)		500	10,096	10,096
	Paid interest and amortized premium.				
Maturity	Interest Expense (E, −SE)	404			
	Premium on Bonds Payable (−L)	96		− 96	
	Cash (−A)		500	10,000	10,000
	Paid interest and amortized premium.				
	Bonds Payable (−L)	10,000			
	Cash (−A)		10,000	0	0
	Paid principal.				

Interest expense = Balance sheet value at beginning of period × [effective interest rate (8%) ÷ 2]
Cash interest payment = ($10,000 × 10%) ÷ 2
Balance sheet value = Face value ($10,000) plus unamortized premium
or
Balance sheet value at beginning of period − premium amortized during period
Present value = Remaining cash outflows discounted at effective interest rate (8%)

ance sheet value of the bond liability equal to the present value of the remaining cash flows, discounted at 8 percent, throughout the life of the bond.

ISSUING BONDS AT PAR, DISCOUNT, OR PREMIUM: A COMPARISON

Bond amortization tables for Case 1 (par), Case 2 (discount), and Case 3 (premium) are contained in Figure 11–11. Recall that the effective (semiannual) interest rates for Cases 1, 2, and 3 are 5 percent, 6 percent, and 4 percent.

The effective interest method ensures that the actual interest rate on a bond issuance is constant throughout its life. Note, however, that interest expense is constant when bonds are issued at par, increasing when bonds are issued at a discount, and decreasing when bonds are issued at a premium. This occurs because the effective rate is multiplied by the balance sheet value of the bonds payable, which is constant when

FIGURE 11–11 Bond amortization tables

Date	Interest Payment	Interest Expense	Amortization Discount/ Premium	Unamortized Discount/ Premium	Net Book Value
ISSUED AT PAR					
Issue					$10,000
6 months	$500	$500	0	0	10,000
1 year	500	500	0	0	10,000
6 months	500	500	0	0	10,000
Maturity	500	500	0	0	10,000
ISSUED AT DISCOUNT					
Issue				$346	$ 9,654
6 months	$500	$579	$79	267	9,733
1 year	500	584	84	183	9,817
6 months	500	589	89	94	9,906
Maturity	500	594	94	0	10,000
ISSUED AT PREMIUM					
Issue				$363	$10,363
6 months	$500	$415	$85	278	10,278
1 year	500	411	89	189	10,189
6 months	500	407	93	96	10,096
Maturity	500	404	96	0	10,000

KEY:

Interest payment = Stated (semiannual) interest rate (5%) × maturity value ($10,000)
Interest expense = Effective interest rate × net book value at beginning of period
Amortized discount/premium = Difference between interest payment and interest expense
**Unamortized discount/premium = Discount/premium of prior period minus amortized
  discount/premium**
Net book value = Maturity value ($10,000) minus unamortized discount or plus unamortized premium

bonds are issued at par, increasing when they are issued at a discount, and decreasing when they are issued at a premium. In all cases, the balance sheet value is equal to the face value ($10,000) when the bonds are paid off at maturity.

During 2000, La-Z-Boy issued $10 million in fifteen-year bonds to finance the construction of manufacturing facilities. The bonds had a stated rate of 5 percent and an effective rate of 6 percent. Assume that the bonds were issued on January 1 and compute the amount of interest expense recognized on the company's 2000 income statement.

The Effective Interest Method and Changing Interest Rates

We have stated on several occasions that the effective interest method ensures that long-term liabilities on the balance sheet are valued at the present value of the liability's future (remaining) cash flows, discounted at the effective interest rate *as of the date of issuance*. Under this method, the same effective interest rate is used throughout the life of the liability, even though interest rates in the financial markets may vary substantially. By ignoring changes in market interest rates, the effective interest method causes the balance sheet amount of the liability to equal something other than its actual present value. It fails to recognize economic gains and losses that affect the issuing company's financial condition.

To illustrate, assume that Olsen Foods issued ten bonds with a $1,000 face value for $1,000 each. The stated annual interest rate is 8 percent, and the bonds mature at the end of five years. Because the bonds were issued at face value, the effective interest rate is also 8 percent, and under the effective interest method, the following journal entry would be recorded at issuance:

Cash (+A)	**10,000**	
Bonds Payable (+L)		**10,000**
Issued bonds (10 × $1,000).		

Throughout their five-year life, the bonds payable would be carried on the balance sheet at $10,000, the present value (PV) of the remaining cash flows, discounted at 8 percent, the effective interest rate as of the issue date. If market interest rates fall by 2 percent during the first year of the bonds' life, however, the economic value of the bond liability becomes $10,702, the present value of the remaining cash flows discounted at 6 percent (8 percent − 2 percent).[15] As a result, Olsen would incur an economic loss of approximately $702 ($10,702 − $10,000). The intuition underlying such a loss is that Olsen is paying an effective rate of 8 percent on its outstanding bonds while market rates are somewhat lower. In addition, the liability on Olsen's balance sheet is understated by $702.

If market interest rates rise by 2 percent during the first year, the economic value of the bond liability becomes $9,354, the present value of the remaining cash flows discounted at 10 percent (8 percent + 2 percent).[16] Olsen, therefore, would enjoy an economic gain of approximately $646 ($10,000 − $9,354). In this case, Olsen is paying only 8 percent on its outstanding bonds while market interest rates are somewhat higher, and the liability on Olsen's balance sheet is overstated by $646.

The fact that fluctuating interest rates are not recognized is an important limitation of the effective interest method. Both net income and the balance sheet value of the outstanding liability are misstated. Financial statement users should be aware of this limitation and be able to improve the usefulness of the financial statements by adjusting reported income and liabilities to reflect such fluctuations. As discussed later, certain required disclosures may help users make such adjustments.

In its 2000 annual report, 3M discloses long-term debt with a balance sheet value $971 million and a fair market value of $950 million. Explain why the fair market value of the debt is less than its balance sheet value.

---

15. The economic value of the liability is equal to the liability's future cash flows discounted at the market rate.
$10,702 = $400 (PV annual: n = 8, i = 3%) + $10,000 (PV single sum: n = 8, i = 3%)
       = $400   (7.01969)   + $10,000   (.78941)
16. The economic value of the liability is equal to the liability's future cash flows discounted at the market rate.
$ 9,354 = $400 (PV annuity: n = 8, i = 5%) + $10,000 (PV single sum: n = 8, i = 5%)
       = $400   (6.46321)   + $10,000   (.67684)

Bond Redemptions

Bonds can be **redeemed** (repurchased or retired) on or before the maturity date. When this occurs, amortization of any discount or premium is updated, the dollar amount in the bonds payable account and any unamortized discount or premium are written off the books, a cash payment is recorded, and a gain or loss is recognized on the redemption if the cash payment differs from the net book value of the liability.

BOND REDEMPTIONS AT MATURITY

When bonds are redeemed at the maturity date, the issuing company simply pays cash to the bondholders in the amount of the face value and removes the bond payable from the balance sheet. At maturity, the bond payable is equal to the face value because, after the final entry to record interest expense, any discount or premium on the bonds will have been completely amortized. Journal entries to record bond redemptions at the maturity dates for bonds issued at face (Case 1), at a discount (Case 2), and at a premium (Case 3) appear in Figures 11–8, 11–9, and 11–10, respectively. Note that in all three cases, the journal entry to record the redemption takes the following form:

Bonds Payable (−L)	**10,000**	
Cash (−A)		**10,000**

Redeemed bonds with a $10,000 face value at maturity.

BOND REDEMPTIONS BEFORE MATURITY

Many companies exercise call provisions or purchase their outstanding bonds on the open market before the maturity date. As indicated earlier, as economic conditions (especially interest rates) change, companies may wish to retire long-term debts.

To illustrate, consider companies that issued bonds in the mid-1980s when interest rates, compared to recent rates, were relatively high. Many of these companies recently redeemed these bonds prior to maturity, recognizing losses because the market value of the debt exceeded its book value. Often new bonds were then issued at considerably lower rates. When Scott Paper Company, for example, retired $72.1 million of unsecured bonds (with an effective rate of 11.5 percent) prior to maturity, it recognized a $9.6 million loss on the transaction. That same year, Scott issued additional debt with effective rates that averaged 8 percent–9 percent.

To illustrate the redemption of a bond issuance prior to maturity at a loss, assume that bonds with a $100,000 face value and a $5,000 unamortized discount are redeemed for $102,000. The $7,000 loss on redemption would decrease net income and appear in a separate section of the income statement, referred to as *extraordinary items.*[17]

Bonds Payable (−L)	**100,000**	
Loss on Redemption (Lo, −SE)	**7,000**	
Discount on Bonds Payable (+L)		**5,000**
Cash (−A)		**102,000**

Redeemed bonds prior to maturity.

If bonds with a $100,000 face value and a $3,000 unamortized premium are redeemed for $102,000, the following journal entry is recorded, and a gain on the redemption is recognized on the income statement as an extraordinary item:

---

17. Extraordinary items are discussed in Chapter 13.

Bonds Payable (−L)	100,000	
Premium on Bonds Payable (−L)	3,000	
Cash (−A)		102,000
Gain on Redemption (Ga, +SE)		1,000

Redeemed bonds prior to maturity.

On its 1998 income statement, Georgia Pacific, a timber and building products man-ufacturer, reported an extraordinary loss from the early retirement of debt in the amount of $13 million. Explain what happened to result in the recognition of this loss.

FINANCIAL INSTRUMENTS AND OFF-BALANCE-SHEET RISKS

An FASB standard requires that companies disclose the market values of certain finan-cial instruments, whether or not they are recognized on the balance sheet. Financial instruments listed on the balance sheet include (1) short-term investments in equity securities, (2) notes receivable and investments in debt securities, and (3) long-term debts. Considering long-term debts, the market value is usually disclosed in a separate footnote and approximates the present value of the future cash outflows associated with the debt, discounted at the current market rate of interest for similar obligations. The excerpt below, which was taken from the 1997 annual report of Federal Express, illustrates this disclosure.

At May 31, 1997, the Company's long-term debt . . . had a carrying value of approx-imately $1,122,000,000 and fair value of approximately $1,223,000,000. The esti-mated fair value was determined based on quoted market prices or on the current rates offered for debt with similar terms and maturities.

In this case, the market (fair) value of the debt ($1.22 billion) exceeds its balance sheet value ($1.12 billion), suggesting that market interest rates have fallen since Federal Express issued the obligations. One could argue that Federal Express experi-enced a loss in the amount by which the market value exceeds the balance sheet value, even though no such loss appears on the income statement. Users may wish to reduce reported net income accordingly. Similarly, if the balance sheet value exceeded the market value, users may wish to increase the net income reported by Federal Express to reflect the gain.

The 2000 annual report of Johnson & Johnson contained the following: "The Com-pany uses financial instruments (called derivatives) to manage the impact of inter-est rate and foreign exchange rate changes on earnings and cash flows. The Com-pany does not enter into these financial instruments for trading or speculative purposes." Briefly explain what this quote means, and why the FASB wants compa-nies to provide such disclosures.

Many companies also carry financial instruments not listed on the balance sheet, many of which involve significant risks. Examples include commitments to guarantee the credit of third parties (e.g., subsidiaries) and commitments to provide financing to customers who purchase certain inventory items. Another example is financing arrangements often designed to reduce the risks associated with fluctuations in interest rates and the value of foreign currencies relative to the U.S. dollar. While these arrangements are normally covered in advanced texts, users should know that the public disclosures of most major U.S. companies contain extensive descriptions of these instruments and that such instruments often reflect risks borne by the company that are captured nowhere on the balance sheet.

LEASES

A **lease** is a contract granting use or occupation of property during a specified period of time in exchange for rent payments. Such contracts are a very popular way to finance business activities. Companies often lease rather than purchase land, buildings, machinery, equipment, and other holdings, primarily to avoid the risks and associated costs of ownership. *Accounting Trends and Techniques* (New York: AICPA, 2000) reports that, of the 600 major U.S. companies surveyed, 551 (2 percent) disclosed some form of material lease arrangement. Many of the major retailers, for example, lease most of the facilities in which they conduct operations. Kmart stores are almost always leased for terms of twenty years with multiple five-year renewal options. The company's annual lease payments approximate $1 billion. *Forbes* (September 8, 1997) notes:

Today, about a third of all capital spending is financial via leases rather than through direct ownership. A quarter of a trillion dollars worth of capital investment is owned by the 100 top leasing companies, a 17% increase over last year.

Operating Leases

In a pure leasing (or rental) arrangement, an individual or entity (*lessor*) who owns land, buildings, equipment, or other property transfers the right to use this property to another individual or entity (*lessee*) in exchange for periodic cash payments over a specified period of time. Normally, the terms of the lease are defined by contract, and over the period of the lease, the owner is responsible for the property's normal maintenance and upkeep. The lessee assumes none of the risks of ownership, and at the end of the lease, the right to use the property reverts to the owner.

These types of agreements are called **operating leases,** and accounting for them is straightforward. The property is reported as an asset on the owner's balance sheet, and the periodic rental payments are recorded as rent revenue on the owner's income statement. If applicable, as in the case of a fixed asset, the capitalized cost of the property is depreciated by the owner. The lessee, on the other hand, recognizes no asset or liability but simply reports rent expense on the income statement as the periodic rent payments are accrued.

During 2000, J.C. Penney paid $620 for its operating leases. How did the company account for these payments, and on which financial statements would activities associated with operating leases be reflected?

Capital Leases

Many contractual arrangements, which appear on the surface to be leases, are actually purchases financed with installment notes, where the risks and benefits of ownership have been transferred to the lessee. The present value of the periodic lease payments, for example, may approximate the FMV of the property. It is also possible that the property may revert, or be sold at a bargain price, to the lessee at the end of the lease period. Further, the period of the lease may be equivalent to the asset's useful life. In such situations, the lessee has actually purchased the property from the lessor and is financing it with an installment note, i.e., an asset has been received in exchange for an installment note payable. Such leases are referred to as **capital leases,** and they should be treated on the financial statements as purchases. That is, the leased property should be included as an asset on the balance sheet of the lessee, and the obligation associated with the future lease payments should be reported as a liability.

Suppose that on January 1, 2003, Hitzelberger Supply (lessee) signs an agreement to lease a bulldozer from Jones and Sons (lessor) for a period of two years. The contract specifies that Hitzelberger must pay $10,000 on December 31 of 2003 and 2004, and the bulldozer can be purchased by Hitzelberger at the end of the lease for a nominal sum. The market price of the bulldozer at the time of the agreement is $17,355, resulting in an effective interest rate of 10 percent, which is equivalent to the interest rate that would be charged if Hitzelberger borrowed funds to purchase the bulldozer.[18]

Hitzelberger should account for this arrangement as a capital lease because the present value of the lease payments discounted at the market rate of interest approximates the FMV of the bulldozer, and the company can purchase the bulldozer at the end of the lease period for a nominal sum. Although the transaction is described as a lease, in economic terms it is actually an installment purchase; stated another way, if Hitzelberger borrowed $17,355 from a bank to purchase the bulldozer and signed a two-year note with a 10 percent interest rate, the loan payment would be $10,000 per year for two years, the same payments required by the lease. Assuming that the bulldozer is depreciated on a straight-line basis over a five-year useful life, the entries shown in Figure 11–12 would be recorded by Hitzelberger over the life of the lease.

As with long-term notes payable and bonds payable, the effective interest method is used to compute the interest expense and amortize the lease liability. Specifically, the annual interest expense associated with the installment purchase is computed by multiplying the effective interest rate (10 percent) by the balance sheet value of the liability, and the dollar amount of the liability amortized each period is equal to the difference between the cash payment and the interest expense. This procedure ensures that the lease liability is carried on the balance sheet at present value throughout the life of the lease, assuming that market interest rates remain constant over that time period. Note also that Hitzelberger depreciates the cost of the machinery, reflecting that, for purposes of financial accounting, Hitzelberger is considered the owner of the bulldozer.

Kmart's 2000 balance sheet includes property under capital leases and capital lease obligations of $2,038 billion and $1.014 billion, respectively. Where on the financial statements would these numbers be found, and how did Kmart estimate them?

---

18. The effective rate of interest is determined by finding that rate which, when used to discount the future cash flows of the lease, results in a present value that is equal to the market price of the bulldozer. Refer to the discussion earlier in this chapter on the effective interest rate.

FIGURE 11–12

Accounting for a
capital lease:
Hitzelberger
Supply

GENERAL JOURNAL

2003	Jan. 1	Machinery (+A)	17,355	
		Lease Liability (+L)		17,355
		Recognized capital lease ($10,000 × 1.7355[a]).		
	Dec. 31	Depr. Expense (E, −SE)	3,471	
		Accumulated Depr. (−A)		3,471
		Recognized depreciation ($17,355 ÷ 5).		
		Interest Expense (E, −SE)	1,736[b]	
		Lease Liability (−L) (plug)	8,264	
		Cash (−A) (annual payment)		10,000
		Made first lease payment.		
2004	Dec. 31	Depr. Expense (E, −SE)	3,471	
		Accumulated Depr. (−A)		3,471
		Recognized depreciation ($17,355 ÷ 5).		
		Interest Expense (E, −SE)	909[c]	
		Lease Liability (−L) (plug)	9,091	
		Cash (−A) (annual payment)		10,000
		Made second lease payment.		

[a]Present value of annuity table: n = 2, i = 10%
[b]10% × $17,355
[c]10% × $9,091 [Unamortized lease liability ($17,355 − $8,264)]

Operating Leases, Capital Leases, and Off-Balance-Sheet Financing

Both operating leases and capital leases are commonly reported on the financial statements of U.S. companies. *Accounting Trends and Techniques* (New York: AICPA, 2000) reports that, of the 600 companies surveyed, 227 (38 percent) disclosed both operating and capital leases, 314 (52 percent) disclosed operating leases only, and 10 (2 percent) disclosed capital leases only.

Recall that from the lessee's standpoint, an operating lease simply gives rise to a periodic rent expense, while a capital lease involves the recognition of an asset, a leasehold liability, and an additional depreciation expense. Because accounting for capital leases increases liabilities and recognizes depreciation expense, which can negatively affect important financial ratios, companies have incentives to account for leases as operating. In 1977, the Financial Accounting Standards Board issued an accounting standard that identified a set of criteria for distinguishing capital from operating leases. In general, these criteria attempt to identify when a leasing arrangement actually represents an installment purchase and therefore should be treated as such (i.e., a capital lease) on the financial statements. Specifically, if any of the four criteria listed in Figure 11–13 are met, the lease should be treated as a capital lease.

FIGURE 11–13

Capital lease
criteria

1. **The lease transfers ownership of the property to the lessee.**
2. **The lease contains a bargain purchase option.**
3. **The lease term is 75 percent or more of the useful life of the property.**
4. **The present value of the lease payments equals or exceeds 90 percent of the FMV of the property.**

While these criteria are useful, they have not removed the effects of management's discretion on classifying leases. Indeed, a study sponsored by the Financial Accounting Standards Board, conducted four years after the FASB established the criteria, found that "a majority of the companies surveyed were structuring the terms of new lease contracts to avoid capitalization." Such attempts to finance asset acquisitions without having to report liabilities on the balance sheet may be economically sound in view of the importance of financial ratios in debt covenants and investor and creditor decisions. In one particular case, *Forbes* magazine reported that Dierckx Equipment Corporation, a small privately owned company, could "endanger its credit rating" by capitalizing its leases. Consequently, financial statement users should closely review the lease terms disclosed in the footnotes to financial statements and ascertain for themselves whether a leasing arrangement is in fact a rental agreement or an installment purchase. Furthermore, generally accepted accounting principles require that companies disclose in the footnotes the future cash payments associated with both their operating and their capital leases. Financial statement readers can use this information to ascertain the extent to which the financial statements are affected by the lease accounting method. For example, one could reconstruct the financial statements as if all leases had been accounted for as capital leases by computing the present value of the cash flow payments associated with the company's operating leases and including that dollar amount as both a liability and an asset on the balance sheet.

The disclosure below was taken from the 2000 annual report of May Department Stores, which includes a wide variety of well-known retailers, including Lord & Taylor and Payless ShoeSource. It describes the company's leasing activities.

Lease Obligations
The company leases approximately 27 percent of its gross rental footage. Rental expense for the company's operating leases consisted of:

(millions)	2000	1999	1998
Minimum rentals	$63	$48	$49
Contingent rentals based on sales	18	18	18
Real property rentals	81	66	67
Equipment rentals	4	3	3
Total	$85	$69	$70

Future minimum lease payments at February 1, 2001, were as follows:

(millions)	Capital Leases	Operating Leases	Total
2001	$ 7	$ 72	$ 79
2002	7	68	75
2003	7	65	72
2004	7	61	68
2005	7	55	62
After 2005	76	286	362
Minimum lease payments	111	$607	$718
Less imputed interest component	59		
Present value of net minimum lease payments, of which $2 million is included in current liabilities	$ 52		

The present value of operating leases was $414 million at February 1, 2001.

Property under capital leases is summarized as follows:

(millions)	February 1, 2001	February 3, 2000
Cost	$ 59	$ 65
Accumulated amortization	$(29)	$(32)
Total	$ 30	$ 33

This disclosure explains the rent expense recognized on May's operating leases ($85 million), the balance sheet liability recognized on its capital leases ($52 million), the present value of the future payments on operating leases ($414 million), and the net book value of the capital lease assets ($30 million). Approximately 87 percent of the lease payments are made on leases judged by May to be operating instead of capital. Had these leases been accounted for as capital leases, May would have recognized an additional $414 million in the long-term liability and asset sections of its balance sheet.

The information below was taken from the 1999 annual reports of Kmart and J.C. Penney (dollars in millions). Assume that the terms of each company's lease contracts are approximately equivalent, which company seems to be practicing off-balance-sheet financing more aggressively, and why?

	Minimum lease payments under:	
	Capital leases	Operating leases
Kmart	$2,790	$7,260
J.C. Penney	5,750	27

INTERNATIONAL PERSPECTIVE: THE IMPORTANCE OF DEBT FINANCING IN OTHER COUNTRIES

The nature of capital markets plays an important role in the determination of the accounting standards and practices in a given country. U.S. companies, for example, rely heavily on both debt and equity capital, which, in turn, influences the accounting systems to provide information for both equity and debt investors. Indeed, the importance of both earning power and solvency in the assessment of a company's financial health has been emphasized throughout the text.

In certain other countries, however, the sources of capital are not as balanced between equity and debt. In Japan, Germany, and Switzerland, for example, the environment is characterized by a few very large banks that satisfy the capital needs of most businesses. The local stock and bond markets, while increasingly becoming more active, are not as heavily relied upon as they are in the United States. The dependence on borrowing in Japan has caused the normal debt/equity ratio for a Japanese company to be well in excess of 75 percent, with most of the debt being in the form of long-term notes from one or more of the large banks.

This situation has had two significant effects on the accounting systems in such countries. First, the accounting disclosure requirements are not nearly as comprehensive as those in the United States, primarily because the information needs of the major capital providers (i.e., banks) are satisfied in a relatively straightforward way—

through personal contact and direct visits. In these countries, for example, it is not unusual for the banks to have members on the boards of directors of the companies for which they provide debt capital. Such direct access is an efficient and practical way to monitor a company's financial health, and it precludes the need for extensive accounting disclosures for external parties.

The second way in which the heavy reliance on debt affects the accounting system is that the disclosures and regulations that are required tend to be designed either to protect the creditor or to help in the assessment of solvency. For example, the Japanese Commercial Code, which determines the accounting rules, also sets a ceiling on the profits available for dividends to the stockholders. Such a regulation helps creditors by ensuring that there will be adequate cash available to meet debt payments on the company's outstanding loans.

APPENDIX 11A

THE DETERMINATION OF BOND PRICES

This chapter states that bond prices are determined by the dollar amount investors are willing to pay for them. That is, what will investors pay for the right to receive the semiannual interest payments and a cash payment in the amount of the face value at maturity? This appendix identifies and discusses factors considered by debt investors when deciding whether to purchase bonds. These factors have a direct bearing on bond prices.

Suppose, for example, that on June 9, 2003, you were reading *The Wall Street Journal,* looking to purchase a bond. You note that on that day Treetley Enterprises lists bonds with the following terms:

Face value	**$1,000**
Time to maturity	**18 years**
Stated annual interest rate (paid every 6 months)	**8%**
Current price	**$85\frac{1}{4}$, or $853**

The decision to buy the bond involves three steps: (1) determine the effective rate of return, (2) determine your required rate of return, and (3) compare the effective rate to the required rate.

Determine the Effective (Actual) Rate of Return

The procedure used to determine the effective rate of return is discussed in this chapter. Recall that the effective rate is that rate which, when used to discount the bond's future cash flows, results in a present value equal to the bond price. The effective rate of the Treetley bond is approximately 10 percent.

Determine the Required Rate of Return

Now that you have determined the effective rate, you must decide whether it is large enough to satisfy you. In other words, what rate of return do you require on a bond with these terms issued by Treetley Enterprises?

Your required rate of return is determined by adding the return you could receive from investing your money in a risk-free security (i.e., risk-free return) to the risk premium you would attach to the Treetley bonds:

Required Rate of Return = Risk-Free Return + Risk Premium

DETERMINE THE RISK-FREE RETURN

The **risk-free** (or **riskless**) **return** is the annual return you could receive by investing in a riskless security, a security where there is virtually no doubt that the interest and principal payments will be honored. Such securities are often backed by the federal government. The annual returns on **treasury notes,** which can be purchased from the federal government and mature up to six months from the date of issue, provide an approximation of the risk-free rate. The bank interest rate on savings accounts probably represents the lowest estimate of the risk-free return. The annual return on **certificates of deposit,** where a given amount of money is lent to a financial institution for a specified period of time, represents another, perhaps more relevant, example.

Keep in mind that the actual risk-free return can only be approximated and that it fluctuates from day to day, based on such factors as changes in the **prime interest rate** (the interest rate charged by banks to their best customers), changes in the **discount rate** (the lending rate charged to banks by the Federal Reserve Board), and the inflation rate expected in the future. Assume that on June 9, 2003, when you considered purchasing Treetley bonds, a reasonable approximation of the risk-free return was 7 percent.

DETERMINE THE RISK PREMIUM

The **risk premium** is expressed as a percentage and reflects the probability that Treetley will default on the periodic interest payments or face value payment at maturity. If this probability is high, these bonds would be considered "high risk" and the risk premium would be relatively large, say 5–10 percent. If the probability is low, the risk premium would be considerably less, say 1–3 percent.

The risk premium is associated specifically with the company issuing the bonds. It is determined by a number of factors, including the credit rating of the company and the bond issuance, the solvency and earning power of the company, future movements in the economy and how these movements may affect the operations of the company, and the terms of the bond issuance. For example, covenant restrictions on future debt and dividend payments as well as collateral and call provisions can affect the risk premium by changing the risk levels faced by the holder of the bonds. Analyzing financial statements is an important part of assessing the risk premium associated with investing in a particular company.

Assume that you have assessed the factors described above and have determined that the risk premium associated with the Treetley bonds is 2 percent.

Compare the Effective Rate to the Required Rate

The effective rate of return on the Treetley bond is 10 percent. You have determined that your required rate of return is 9 percent (7 percent risk-free rate + 2 percent risk premium). Since the effective rate exceeds the required rate, you will purchase the bond. The bond is selling for $853, and in fact, you would be willing to pay $920 for it, the present value of the bond's future cash flows discounted at 9 percent, your required rate of return. Had your required return been greater than 10 percent, either due to a higher risk-free rate or higher risk premium, you would not have purchased the bond and would not do so until the price decreased to the point where the effective rate exceeded your required rate.

Factors Determining Bond Prices

Bond prices, therefore, are determined by a market of investors, each assessing the economy-wide, risk-free rate as well as the risk premium associated specifically with the issuing company. Any factor affecting either of these two items affects bond prices. Factors that decrease either the risk-free rate or the risk premium tend to increase bond prices, while factors increasing either rate tend to decrease bond prices.

The Wall Street Journal often reports on how the actions of the Federal Reserve Board affect economy-wide interest rates. Almost without exception, when the Board acts to reduce interest rates, the bond market rallies, and when the Board acts to increase rates, bond prices fall. This relationship occurs because the Board's behavior has a direct effect on the risk-free rate of return. Indeed, the *New York Times* once reported that Merrill Lynch & Company, which holds a huge portfolio of bond investments, "lost $250 million in a given month because its bond investments plummeted in value when interest rates surged."

The close relationship between the risk premium and bond prices illustrates clearly why companies are so interested in their credit ratings. A decrease in a company's credit rating ordinarily leads to an increase in the market's assessment of the company's risk premium and, accordingly, a decrease in the value of the company's outstanding debt. For example, when Standard & Poor's downgraded $310 million of long-term debt issued by American Stores, the value of American's outstanding debt decreased substantially, making it more difficult for the company to raise debt capital in the future. Standard & Poor's justified the downgrade by claiming that American's "financial risk will increase sharply" as a result of its acquisition of Lucky Stores, Inc.

REVIEW PROBLEM

Assume that Southern Carbide issues 500 bonds, each with a $1,000 face value on January 1, 2003. The five-year bonds have an annual stated interest rate of 6 percent, to be paid semiannually on December 31 and June 30. The bonds are issued at 91.89, providing an effective annual interest rate of 8 percent. A call provision in the bond contract states that the bonds can be redeemed by Southern Carbide after December 31, 2003, for 96.0. Assume that Southern Carbide exercises this provision on July 1, 2004.

Figure 11–14 provides the cash flows, journal entries, discount balance, and net book value of the bonds from the time of the bond issuance to the redemption. An explanation of each calculation follows.

Cash Flow Calculations:

Proceeds. The proceeds of the bond issuance ($459,450) were calculated by multiplying the number of bonds issued (500) by the price per bond ($918.90).

Interest Payments. The semiannual interest payment ($15,000) was calculated by multiplying the number of bonds issued (500) by the face value of each bond ($1,000) by half the stated annual interest rate (3 percent).

Redemption Payment (7/1/04). The payment required to redeem the bonds on July 1, 2004 ($480,000) was calculated by multiplying the number of bonds issued (500) by the redemption price per bond ($960).

Journal Entry Calculations:

At Issuance. Cash ($459,450) was equal to the cash proceeds. Bonds Payable ($500,000) was calculated by multiplying the number of bonds issued (500) by the face value of each bond ($1,000). The discount ($40,550) represents an interest cost ("unaccrued interest") waiting to be recognized over the life of the bond. It arises because the bond issuance, which will require a $500,000 cash payment at maturity, generated only $459,450 at issuance.

Interest Payments and Discount Amortization. The calculation of the cash interest payments is described above. The effective interest rate (8 percent) was computed by finding the rate that produced a present value equal to the price ($459,450). The amount of interest expense recognized each period was calculated by multiplying half the effective interest rate (4 percent) by

FIGURE 11–14 Review problem

Terms: Number of bonds issued: 500
Face value: $1,000
Stated interest rate: 6%
Time to maturity: 5 years
Call Provision: Redeemable after 12/31/03 for .9600

Interest payment dates: Dec. 31, June 30
Issue date: January 1, 2003
Price: .9189 ($459,450)
Effective interest rate: 8%

CASH FLOWS

12/31/02 ———→ 1/1/03
+ $459,450
(proceeds)

———→ 6/30/03
−$15,000
(interest)

———→ 12/31/03
−$15,000
(interest)

6/30/04
−$15,000
(interest)

7/1/04
−$15,000
(interest)
−$480,000
(redemption)

GENERAL JOURNAL

Cash	459,450	
Discount	40,550	
Bonds Pay.		500,000
Issued bond.		

Int. Exp.	18,378	
Cash		15,000
Discount		3,378
Paid interest and amortized discount.		

Int. Exp.	18,513	
Cash		15,000
Discount		3,513
Paid interest and amortized discount.		

Int. Exp.	18,653	
Cash		15,000
Discount		3,653
Paid interest and amortized discount.		

Bonds Pay.	500,000	
Loss on R.	10,006	
Discount		30,006
Cash		480,000
Redeemed bond.		

DISCOUNT BALANCE

$40,550

$40,550 − $3,378
= $37,172

$37,172 − $3,513
= $33,659

$33,659 − $3,653
= $30,006 (before redemption)

NET BOOK VALUE

$500,000 − $40,550
= $459,450

$500,000 − $37,172
= $462,828

$500,000 − $33,659
= $466,341

$500,000 − $30,006
= $469,994 (before redemption)

Bonds Pay. = Bonds Payable
Int. Exp. = Interest Expense
Loss on R. = Loss on Redemption

the net book value of the bond payable ($500,000 − unamortized discount) at the beginning of the period. The credit to the discount represents the additional interest expense recognized each period because the bonds were issued at a discount.

Redemption (7/1/04). The calculation of the cash payment at redemption ($480,000) was described earlier. The balance sheet value of the bonds at the time of the redemption (Bonds Payable: $500,000, Discount: $30,006) is removed from the books. The loss on redemption ($10,006) represents the difference between the cash paid to redeem the bonds and the balance sheet value of the bonds as of July 1, 2004.

Discount Balance and Balance Sheet Value of Bonds Payable:

The ending discount balance each period was calculated by subtracting the amount of the discount amortized during the period from the balance at the beginning of the period. The balance sheet value of the bonds payable at the end of each period was calculated by subtracting the unamortized discount from the face value of the bond issuance ($500,000).

SUMMARY OF KEY POINTS

The key points of this chapter are summarized below.

○ *Long-term notes payable, bonds payable, and leasehold obligations, and how companies use these instruments as important sources of financing.*

Long-term liabilities include notes payable, bonds payable, and leasehold obligations. They represent obligations that require the disbursement of assets (usually cash) at a future time beyond the period that defines current assets. Notes payable refer to obligations evidenced by formal notes. They normally involve direct borrowings from financial institutions or an arrangement to finance the purchase of assets. Bonds payable are notes issued for cash to a large number of creditors called *bondholders.* Leasehold obligations refer to future cash payments (i.e., rent) that are required for the use or occupation of property during a specified period of time.

Long-term notes, bonds, and leases are common and major sources of capital for companies throughout the world. Funds used to acquire other companies, purchase machinery and equipment, finance plant expansion, pay off debts, repurchase outstanding stock, and support operations are often generated by issuing long-term notes, bonds, or entering into lease agreements.

○ *Economic consequences created by borrowing.*

The excessive borrowing in the United States during the 1980s forced managers to pay special attention to both their cash flow management policies and how the debt is reported in their financial statements. They entered into creative ways to generate sufficient cash to meet their debt obligations, and they managed the financial statement numbers by practicing strategies like "building hidden reserves," "taking a bath," and especially "off-balance-sheet financing."

○ *Different forms of contractual obligations.*

There are three basic forms of contractual obligations: interest-bearing, non-interest-bearing, and installment. Interest-bearing obligations require periodic (annual or semi-annual) cash payments (called interest) that are determined as a percentage of the face, principal, or maturity value, which must be paid at the end of the contract period. Non-interest-bearing obligations require no periodic payments but only a single cash payment at the end of the contract period. In an installment obligation, periodic payments covering both interest and principal are made throughout the life of the contract.

○ *The effective interest rate and how it is determined for contractual obligations.*

The effective interest rate is the actual interest rate paid by the issuer of the obligation. It is determined by finding the discount rate that sets the present value of the obligation's cash outflows equal to the fair market value (FMV) of that which is received in the exchange. When contractual obligations are exchanged for cash, the cash amount received represents the FMV of the receipt. When contractual obligations are exchanged for noncash items, the FMV of the noncash items must be determined through appraisals or some other means.

○ *The effective interest method.*

The effective interest method states that the interest expense reported during each period of a long-term obligation's contractual life is computed by multiplying the effective interest rate by the balance sheet value of the obligation as of the beginning of the period. It ensures that the long-term liability on the balance sheet is reported throughout its life at the present value of its future cash flows, discounted at the effective interest rate as of the issue date.

○ *How changes in market interest rates can lead to misstated balance sheet values for long-term liabilities.*

The effective interest method ensures that over the life of an obligation its balance sheet value is equal to the present value of the obligation's future cash flows, discounted at the effective interest rate as of the date the obligation was issued. If the market rate of interest remains constant over the life of the obligation, then the obligation's balance sheet value will equal its present value. When market interest rates fluctuate, however, the actual present value of the obligation, discounted at the market rate, differs from the balance sheet value of the obligation, which is discounted at the original effective interest rate. In such cases, the balance sheet value of the liability is no longer an accurate measure of its present value, and economic gains and losses are experienced by the issuing company but not recognized on the financial statements.

○ *Operating leases, capital leases, and off-balance-sheet financing.*

Operating and capital leases are categories created by generally accepted accounting principles that define the methods used to account for lease contracts. Four criteria that determine whether the lessor or lessee bears the risks and rewards of owning the leased asset are listed, and if any one of the criteria are met, the lease is considered a capital lease. Capital leases are treated as installment purchases for financial reporting purposes, requiring that the lessee record both an asset and a liability in the amount of the present value of the future lease payments, discounted at the effective interest rate. The asset is subject to depreciation, and the liability is amortized using the effective interest method. Operating lease payments are simply accounted for as rental expense by the lessee. Companies can practice off-balance-sheet financing by structuring lease contracts so that none of the four criteria are met, which, in turn, allows them to account for leases as operating that may in economic substance be capital. Such treatment keeps the liability associated with the lease off the balance sheet.

KEY TERMS

Note: Definitions for these terms are provided in the glossary at the end of the text.

Bonds payable (p. 462)
Call provision (p. 473)
Capital leases (p. 485)
Certificates of deposit (p. 490)
Collateral (p. 465)
Covenants (p. 471)
Debentures (p. 472)
Default (p. 465)
Discount on bonds payable (p. 477)
Discount rate (p. 490)
Effective interest method (p. 468)
Effective interest rate (p. 466)
Face, principal, or maturity value (p. 465)
Installment obligation (p. 465)
Interest (p. 465)
Interest-bearing obligations (p. 465)
Interest payment (p. 471)
Lease (p. 484)
Leasehold obligations (p. 462)

Life (p. 471)
Maturity date (p. 471)
Mortgage (p. 469)
Non-interest-bearing obligations (p. 465)
Notes payable (p. 462)
Operating leases (p. 484)
Premium on bonds payable (p. 478)
Prime interest rate (p. 490)
Proceeds (p. 471)
Redeemed (p. 482)
Refinancing (p. 469)
Restrictive covenants (p. 465)
Risk-free (or riskless) return (p. 490)
Risk premium (p. 490)
Secured notes (p. 468)
Stated interest rate (p. 465)
Treasury notes (p. 490)
Unsecured bonds (p. 472)
Unsecured notes (p. 468)

ETHICS IN THE REAL WORLD

A review of the financial statements of Kmart and Wal-Mart show that both companies lease a large portion of their facilities. A closer examination of the lease arrangements reveals that, while the contractual terms of the leases held by the two companies are quite similar, Kmart classifies a much larger percentage of its leases as "operating" leases, while Wal-Mart considers a larger percentage as "capital" leases.

According to GAAP, "capital" leases must be represented as balance sheet liabilities, while "operating" leases do not. While the FASB has provided criteria that should be followed when making such a classification, applying these criteria requires much judgment, and many companies structure their lease contracts in ways that give them the flexibility to classify them as "operating." Such a strategy can be construed as a form of "off-balance-sheet financing," enabling a company to raise debt capital without having to include it on the balance sheet as a liability. In this way, the company can avoid violating debt covenants, protect its credit ratings, and generally encourage stockholders and others to believe that the company is carrying less debt than it really is.

ETHICAL ISSUE Is it ethical for a company to structure its leasing contracts in a manner that allows it to avoid reporting debt?

INTERNET RESEARCH EXERCISE

Access Imation's current financial reports at www.imation.com. Briefly explain how the company has managed—since December 1997—the somewhat difficult situation introduced at the beginning of the chapter.

BRIEF EXERCISES

REAL DATA

BE11-1

Inferring debt
transactions

The following table was taken from the 1999 annual report of RadioShack.

Long-term debt (in millions)

	1999	1998
Notes payable (interest 5.8%)	$ 6.2	$ 9.1
Notes payable (interest 6.9%)	144.5	144.0
Medium-term notes payable	149.5	49.8
	$300.2	$202.9

a. Briefly explain the transactions entered into by RadioShack during 1999.
b. Approximately how much interest expense was recognized in 1999 on the 6.9 percent notes?
c. Assume that RadioShack paid $130 million to retire the medium-term notes in 1999. How much gain or loss would RadioShack have recognized on the transaction? Where in the financial statements would it be found?

REAL DATA

BE11-2

Bond issuance

In October 1997, Hewlett-Packard issued zero-coupon bonds with a face value of $1.8 billion, due in 2017, for proceeds of $968 million.

a. What is the life of these bonds?
b. What is the stated interest rate on these bonds?
c. Estimate the effective rate of interest on these bonds.
d. How many bonds did HP issue?

REAL DATA

BE11-3

Operating and
capital leases

During 2000, the SUPERVALU grocery chain paid approximately $172 million on its lease contracts—$60 million on capital leases and $112 million on operating leases.

a. How did the operating lease payments affect the income statement, balance sheet, and statement of cash flows?
b. How did the capital lease payments affect the income statement, balance sheet, and statement of cash flows?
c. Discuss whether SUPERVALU is practicing off-balance-sheet financing.

EXERCISES

E11-1

Disclosing debt and
debt covenants

The balance sheet as of December 31, 2002, for Melrose Enterprises follows:

Assets		Liabilities and Stockholders' Equity	
Current assets	$200,000	Current liabilities	$200,000
Noncurrent assets	700,000	Long-term liabilities	300,000
		Stockholders' equity	400,000
		Total liabilities and	
Total assets	$900,000	stockholders' equity	$900,000

During 2002, Melrose entered into a loan agreement that required the company to maintain a debt/equity ratio of less than 2:1.

a. How much additional debt can Melrose take on before it violates the terms of the loan agreement?

b. Assume that during 2003 Melrose had revenues of $950,000 and expenses of $800,000. Assume that all revenues and expenses were in cash. How much additional debt can Melrose take on before it violates the terms of the loan agreement?

c. Assume again that during 2003 Melrose has cash revenues of $950,000 and cash expenses of $800,000. If Melrose pays a cash dividend of $100,000, how much additional debt can it take on before violating the terms of the loan agreement? If Melrose declares, but does not pay, the dividend during 2003, does it make a difference in the amount of additional debt the company can take on?

E11–2

Annual or semiannual interest payments?

Hathaway Manufacturing issued long-term debt on January 1, 2002. The debt has a face value of $300,000 and an annual stated interest rate of 10 percent. The debt matures on January 1, 2007.

a. Assume that the debt agreement requires Hathaway Manufacturing to make annual interest payments every January 1. Set up a time line that indicates the timing and magnitude of the future cash outflows of this long-term debt.

b. Assume that the debt agreement requires Hathaway Manufacturing to make semiannual interest payments every July 1 and January 1. Set up a time line that indicates the timing and magnitude of the future cash outflows for this long-term debt.

c. Under the conditions of (a) and (b), compute the present value of these two debt agreements, assuming that the effective rate of interest is equal to the stated rate of interest.

E11–3

The relationship among the stated rate, effective rate, and issuance price of a liability

The stated and effective interest rates for several notes and bonds follow:

Note/Bond	Stated Interest Rate	Effective Interest Rate
1	10%	10%
2	7	8
3	9	8
4	11.5	9

Indicate whether each note/bond would be issued at a discount, par value, or a premium.

E11–4

Computing the proceeds from various notes

Compute the proceeds from the following notes payable. Interest payments are made annually.

Proceeds	Stated Interest Rate	Effective Interest Rate	Face Value	Life
?	0%	8%	$ 1,000	4 years
?	0	6	5,000	6 years
?	4	12	8,000	6 years
?	8	8	3,000	7 years
?	10	6	10,000	10 years

E11–5

Notes issued at a discount and the movement of interest expense

Tradewell Rentals purchased a piece of equipment with an FMV of $11,348 in exchange for a five-year, non-interest-bearing note with a face value of $20,000.

a. Compute the effective interest rate on the note payable.

b. Prepare the journal entry to record the purchase.

c. How much interest expense should Tradewell recognize on the note payable during the first year?

d. What is the balance sheet value of the note at the end of the first year?

e. Will the interest expense recognized by Tradewell in the second year be greater than, equal to, or less than the interest expense recognized in the first year? Why?

f. Will the interest expense recognized in the third year be greater than, equal to, or less than the interest expense recognized in the second year?

E11-6

Accounting for notes payable with various stated interest rates

Candleton signed a two-year, interest-bearing note payable with a face value of $8,000 and an effective interest rate of 8 percent. Interest payments on the note are made annually.

Provide the journal entries that would be recorded over the life of the note, assuming the following stated interest rates:

a. 8 percent
b. 0 percent
c. 6 percent

E11-7

Determining the effective interest rate

On January 1, 2003, Wilmes Floral Supplies borrowed $2,413 from Bower Financial Services. Wilmes Floral Supplies gave Bower a $2,500 note with a maturity date of December 31, 2004. The note specified an annual stated interest rate of 8 percent.

a. Compute the present value of the note's future cash flows at the following discount rates:
    (1) 8 percent
    (2) 10 percent
    (3) 12 percent
b. What is the effective interest rate of the note?
c. Determine the effective interest rate on the note if Wilmes Floral Supplies originally borrowed $2,500.

E11-8

Financing asset purchases with notes payable

Morrow Enterprises purchased a building on January 1, 2003, in exchange for a three-year, non-interest-bearing note with a face value of $693,000. Independent appraisers valued the building at $550,125.

a. At what amount should this building be capitalized?
b. Compute the present value of the note's future cash flows, using the following discount rates:
    (1) 6 percent
    (2) 8 percent
    (3) 10 percent
c. What is the effective interest rate of this note?
d. Explain how one could more quickly compute the effective interest rate on the note.

E11-9

Inferring an effective interest rate from the financial statements

The following information was extracted from the financial records of Leong Cosmetics:

	2004	2003
Balance Sheet		
Notes payable	$200,000	$200,000
Less: Discount on notes payable	12,000	14,400
Income Statement		
Interest expense	$ 16,400	$ 16,200

a. What is the effective interest rate on the notes payable?
b. Prepare the journal entry to record interest expense during 2004.

REAL DATA

E11-10

Bond discounts

During 1999, BF Goodrich issued ten-year notes with a face value of $200 million. The stated interest rate on the notes was 5 percent and they were issued at an effective rate of 7 percent.

a. Estimate the proceeds of the issuance.
b. Compute the interest expense associated with this note recorded in 1999.
c. Explain why the market paid less than $200 million for these bonds.

E11–11

Computing bond issuance proceeds and the movement of balance sheet value and interest expense over the bond's life

Three different bond issuances are listed here with interest payments made semiannually:

Bond Issuance	Face Value	Stated Interest Rate	Effective Interest Rate	Life
A	$100,000	6%	6%	10 years
B	$400,000	8	6	10 years
C	$600,000	6	8	5 years

a. Compute the proceeds of each bond issuance.
b. For each bond issuance, indicate whether the balance sheet value of the bond liability will increase, decrease, or remain constant over the life of the bond.
c. For each bond issuance, indicate whether the interest expense recognized each period will increase, decrease, or remain constant over the life of the bond.

E11–12

Accounting for bonds issued at face value

On January 1, 2002, Collins Copy Machine Company issued thirty $1,000 face-value bonds with a stated annual rate of 10 percent that mature in ten years. Interest is paid semiannually on June 30 and December 31. The bonds were issued at face value.

a. Prepare the entry to record the issuance of these bonds on January 1, 2002.
b. Prepare all the entries associated with these bonds during 2002 (excluding the entry to record the issuance).
c. Compute the balance sheet value of the bond liability as of December 31, 2002.
d. Compute the present value of the bond's remaining cash flows as of December 31, 2002, using the effective rate at issuance.
e. Repeat (c) and (d) as of December 31, 2003, and explain the relationship between the balance sheet value and the present value.

E11–13

Accounting for bonds issued at a discount

Tingham Village issued 500 five-year bonds on July 1, 2003. The interest payments are due semiannually (January 1 and July 1) at an annual rate of 6 percent. The effective interest rate on the bonds is 8 percent. The face value of each bond is $1,000.

a. Prepare the journal entry that would be recorded on July 1, 2003, when the bonds are issued.
b. Prepare the journal entry that would be recorded on December 31, 2003.
c. Compute the balance sheet value of the bond liability as of December 31, 2003.
d. Compute the present value of the bond's remaining cash flows as of December 31, 2003, using an effective interest rate of 8 percent. Explain the relationship between the balance sheet value and the present value. $(i = 4\%, n = 9)$

E11–14

Accounting for bonds issued at a premium

Coral Sands Marina issued 100 ten-year bonds on July 1, 2003. The interest payments are due semiannually (January 1 and July 1) at an annual rate of 8 percent. The effective rate on the bonds is 6 percent. The face value of each bond is $1,000.

a. Prepare the journal entry that would be recorded on July 1, 2003, when the bonds are issued.
b. Prepare the journal entries that would be recorded on December 31, 2003.
c. Compute the balance sheet value of the bond liability as of December 31, 2003.
d. Compute the present value of the bond's remaining cash flows as of December 31, 2003, using the effective rate at the time the bonds were issued. Explain the relationship between the balance sheet value of the liability and the present value of the future cash payments.

E11–15

Changing market interest rates and economic gains and losses

Treadway Company issued bonds with a face value of $20,000 on January 1, 2002. The bonds were due to mature in five years and had a stated annual interest rate of 8 percent. The bonds were issued at face value. Interest is paid semiannually.

a. As of December 31, 2002, market interest rates had decreased by 2 percent, and the market price of Treadway bonds reflected the entire change. Compute the present value of Treadway's bond liability as of that date, using the new effective interest rate (6 percent), and determine the economic gain or loss experienced by the company.

b. Assume instead that as of December 31, 2002, market interest rates had increased by 2 percent, and the market price of Treadway's bonds reflected the entire change. Compute the present value of Treadway's bond liability as of that date, using the new effective interest rate (10 percent), and determine the economic gain or loss experienced by the company.

c. What is the intuition underlying such gains and losses, and why are they not reflected on the financial statements? If you were analyzing the financial statements of Treadway, what could you do to improve the reported numbers?

E11–16

Redeeming bonds not originally issued at par

On September 10, 2000, Mooney Plastic Products issued bonds with a face value of $500,000 for a price of 96. During 2003, Mooney exercised a call provision and redeemed the bonds for 101. At the time of the redemption, the bonds had a balance sheet value of $490,000.

a. Prepare the journal entry to record the redemption.

b. Assume that the bonds were issued in 2000 for 102, and at the time of redemption they had a balance sheet value of $507,000. Prepare the journal entry to record the bond redemption.

REAL DATA

E11–17

Refinancing debt

In March 1998, Eli Lilly, a major pharmaceutical company, chose to refinance some of its outstanding bonds payable. In essence, the company paid off the outstanding debt and replaced it with a new bond issuance. At the time of the refinancing, the balance sheet value of the outstanding debt was approximately $35 million. On the company's 1998 income statement a loss of $7.2 million (net of $4.8 million in tax benefits) was reported.

a. Compute the payment made by Eli Lilly to retire the original debt.

b. How did the company benefit from the $4.8 million tax effect?

c. Lilly uses the indirect method of presentation for the statement of cash flows. How was the loss treated on that statement?

d. How was the loss disclosed on the income statement?

E11–18

Updating amortization and retiring a bond issuance

Marker Musical Products issued bonds with a face value of $100,000 and an annual stated interest rate of 8 percent on January 1, 2000. The effective interest rate on the bonds was 10 percent. Interest is paid semiannually on July 1 and January 1. As of December 31, 2002, the company reported the following dollar amounts for these bonds:

| Bonds payable | $100,000 | |
| Less: Discount on bonds payable | 3,546 | $96,454 |

Marker Musical Products retired the bonds on July 2, 2003, by repurchasing them for $91,700 in cash.

a. Provide the journal entry recorded on July 1, 2003, when the interest payment is made.

b. Prepare the journal entry to record the retirement of the bonds.

E11–19

Analyzing bond disclosures

The information below was taken from the balance sheet of Beasley Brothers as of December 31, 2002:

| Bond payable | $100,000 | |
| Less: Unamortized discount | 5,350 | $94,650 |

The bonds have a stated interest rate of 5 percent paid annually, and will mature on December 31, 2004. The market value of the bonds as of December 31, 2002, is $98,167.

a. Compute the effective interest rate when the bonds were issued.

b. What effective rate would an investor be earning by purchasing the bonds on December 31, 2002, at the market price and holding the bonds until maturity?

c. Assume that Beasley reported net income of $27,000 for the period ending December 31, 2002. Adjust net income for the gain or loss experienced by the company on these outstanding bonds due to the change in market interest rates. Ignore income taxes. Do you believe that the gain or loss represents an increase or decrease in the wealth of the company? Why?

d. Assume that Beasley retired the bonds by purchasing them on the open market. Record the journal entry, and compare the gain or loss recognized on the retirement with the gain or loss computed in (c) above. Discuss.

E11–20

Analyzing bond
disclosures

The information below was taken from the balance sheet of Cohort Enterprises as of December 31, 2003:

Bond payable   **$200,000**
Less: Unamortized discount   **6,941**   **$193,059**

The bonds have a stated interest rate of 5 percent and will mature on December 31, 2005. The market value of the bonds as of December 31, 2003, is $186,479.

a. Compute the effective interest rate when the bonds were issued.
b. What effective rate would an investor be earning by purchasing the bonds on December 31, 2003, at the market price and holding the bonds until maturity?
c. Assume that Cohort reported net income of $38,500 for the period ending December 31, 2003. Adjust net income for the gain or loss experienced by the company on these outstanding bonds due to the change in market interest rates. Ignore income taxes. Do you believe that the gain or loss represents an increase or decrease in the wealth of the company? Why?
d. Assume that Cohort retired the bonds by purchasing them on the open market. Record the journal entry, and compare the gain or loss recognized on the retirement with the gain or loss computed in (c) above. Discuss.

E11–21

Accounting
for leases

On January 1, 2002, Q-Mart entered into a five-year lease agreement requiring annual payments of $10,000 on December 31 of each year. The fair market value of the facility was estimated by appraisers to be $39,927.

a. Record the journal entries required over the five-year period, assuming that Q-Mart accounts for this arrangement as an operating lease.
b. Compute the effective interest rate on the lease, and record the journal entries required over the five-year period if Q-Mart accounts for this arrangement as a capital lease. Assume that the capitalized asset is depreciated over a five-year period, using the straight-line method with no salvage value.
c. Compare the effects of the two accounting methods on the financial statements. Discuss.

E11–22

Accounting for
leases and the
financial statements

Tradeall, Inc., leases automobiles for its salesforce. On January 1, 2002, the company leased 100 automobiles and agreed to make lease payments of $10,000 per automobile each year. The lease agreement expires on December 31, 2006, at which time the automobiles can be purchased by Tradeall for a nominal price. Assume an effective rate of 10 percent.

a. Compute the annual rental expense if the lease is treated as an operating lease.
b. Prepare the journal entry on January 1, 2002, if the lease is treated as a capital lease. What dollar amount represents an approximation of the fair market value of the automobiles?
c. Assume that the automobiles are depreciated over a five-year life, using the straight-line method with no salvage value. Compute the total rental expense (interest and depreciation) associated with the lease during the first year if the lease is treated as a capital lease.
d. Which of the two methods of treatment (operating or capital) would give rise to a higher net income in the first year? Which method would give rise to a lower debt/equity ratio?
e. Define off-balance-sheet financing, and explain how leases can be arranged to practice it.

E11–23

Financing asset
purchases

Watts Motors plans to acquire a building and can either borrow cash from a bank to finance the purchase or lease the building from the current owner. The sales price of the building is $149,388. If the company wishes to finance the purchase with a bank loan, it must sign a ten-year note with a face value of $149,388 and a stated interest rate of 12 percent. If the company leases the building, it must make an annual lease payment of a constant-dollar amount for ten years, at which time the building can be purchased for a nominal fee.

a. Compute the annual lease payment that would make the two alternatives equivalent. Ignore the nominal purchase fee at the end of Year 10.
b. Describe how the timing of the cash flows would differ between the two alternatives.
c. Provide the journal entries that would be recorded when the building is acquired if the company (1) finances the purchase with a bank loan, (2) leases the building and accounts for it as a capital lease, or (3) leases the building and accounts for it as an operating lease.
d. If the company leases the building and accounts for it as a capital lease, compute the balance sheet value of the lease liability after the second lease payment.
e. Compute the present value of the remaining lease payments as of the end of the second year.

E11–24

Inferring the effective rate of interest

Compute the effective rate of interest on the following long-term debts. Interest payments on the notes are made annually, and interest payments on the bonds are made semiannually.

Debt	Fair market value of receipt	Face value	Life	Stated interest rate
Note	$10,000	$ 10,000	6 years	8%
Note	35,056	100,000	8 years	0
Note	922	1,000	5 years	7
Bond	11,635	10,000	10 years	6
Bond	54,323	50,000	15 years	9

E11–25

Appendix 11A: The decision to purchase a bond

Dylander bonds are selling on the open market at 89.16. The bonds have a stated interest rate of 8 percent and mature in eight years. Interest payments are made semiannually.

a. Assume that your required rate of return is 12 percent. Would you buy the bonds? Why or why not?
b. At what required rate of return would you be indifferent to purchasing the bonds?

PROBLEMS

P11–1

Computing the face value of a note payable

On December 31, 2002, East Race Kayak Club decided to borrow $20,000 for two years. The Bend Bank currently is charging a 10 percent effective annual interest rate on similar loans.

REQUIRED:

a. Assume that the club borrows $20,000 and signs a two-year note with a 10 percent stated annual interest rate. What would be the face amount of the note payable?
b. Assume that the club borrows $20,000 and signs a two-year note with a stated annual interest rate of zero. What would be the face amount of the note payable?
c. Prepare the journal entry to record the note payable, assuming that the club signs
   (1) the note in (a).
   (2) the note in (b).
d. Prepare the entries necessary on December 31, 2004, assuming that the club signs
   (1) the note in (a) (interest payable on December 31).
   (2) the note in (b).

P11–2

Accounting for bonds with an effective rate greater than the stated rate

Hartl Enterprises issued ten $1,000 bonds on September 30, 2002, with a stated annual interest rate of 8 percent. These bonds will mature on October 1, 2012, and have an effective rate of 10 percent. Interest is paid semiannually on October 1 and April 1. The first interest payment will be made on April 1, 2003.

REQUIRED:

a. Without computing the present value of the bonds, will they be issued at par value, at a discount, or at a premium? Explain your answer.
b. Prepare the entry to record the issuance of the bonds on September 30, 2002.
c. Prepare any adjusting journal entries necessary on December 31, 2002.
d. Prepare the entry to record the interest payment on April 1, 2003.

P11–3

The balance sheet
value of debt and
the long-term
debt/equity ratio

The balance sheet as of December 31, 2002, for Manheim Corporation follows:

Assets		Liabilities and Stockholders' Equity	
Current assets	$ 85,000	Current liabilities	$ 70,000
Noncurrent assets	125,000	Long-term liabilities	40,000
		Stockholders' equity	100,000
		Total liabilities and	
Total assets	$210,000	stockholders' equity	$210,000

REQUIRED:

a. Compute Manheim Corporation's long-term debt/equity ratio.
b. Assume that Manheim Corporation is considering borrowing money and signing a five-year note with the following terms:

Face value	$40,000
Stated interest rate	0%
Effective interest rate	11%

   Compute the proceeds of the note, and compute the company's long-term debt/equity ratio if it decides to borrow the money.
c. Assume that Manheim Corporation is considering issuing bonds that mature on December 31, 2022. The bonds have a face value of $40,000, a stated interest rate of 10 percent, and an effective interest rate of 8 percent. Compute the proceeds from the bond issuance, and compute the company's long-term debt/equity ratio if it issues the bonds. The bonds pay interest semiannually.

P11–4

Accounting for
notes issued at a
discount and
at face value

Patnon Plastics needs some cash to finance expansion. Patnon issued the following debt to acquire the cash:

1. A five-year note with a stated interest rate of zero, a face value of $20,000, and an effective interest rate of 10 percent.
2. An eight-year note with an annual stated rate of 8 percent and a face value of $35,000. Interest is paid annually on December 31. The effective interest rate is 10 percent.
3. A ten-year note with an annual stated rate of 8 percent and a face value of $50,000. Interest is paid semiannually on June 30 and December 31. The effective interest rate is 8 percent.

All three notes were issued on January 1, 2003.

REQUIRED:

a. Compute the proceeds from each of the three notes.
b. Prepare the entries to record the issuance of each note.
c. Prepare the entry to record the interest paid on June 30, 2003, on the ten-year note.
d. Prepare the entries to record the interest paid on December 31, 2003, on the eight-year note and the ten-year note.
e. Prepare the adjusting entry required on December 31, 2003, to recognize accrued interest on the five-year note.

P11–5

The effects of
various notes
payable on the
financial statements

The balance sheet as of December 31, 2003, for Boyton Sons follows:

Assets		Liabilities and Stockholders' Equity	
Current assets	$ 40,000	Current liabilities	$ 30,000
Noncurrent assets	80,000	Long-term liabilities	60,000
		Stockholders' equity	30,000
		Total liabilities and	
Total assets	$120,000	stockholders' equity	$120,000

The company needs capital to finance operations and purchase new equipment. Boyton is not certain how much money it will need and is considering one of the following three-year notes payable. Each note would mature on January 1, 2007.

(A) Face value = $50,000   **Stated interest rate = 0%**   **Proceeds = $37,566**
(B) Face value = $50,000   **Stated interest rate = 10%***   **Proceeds = $50,000**
(C) Face value = $50,000   **Stated interest rate = 6%***   **Proceeds = $45,027**
*Interest paid annually.

REQUIRED:

a. Determine the effective interest rate of each note.
b. Compute the amounts that would complete the following table:

	Interest Expense (A)	Interest Expense (B)	Interest Expense (C)
Year 1			
Year 2			
Year 3			

c. Assume that Boyton can earn a 12 percent return on the borrowed money and that it reinvests all interest that it earns. Compute the annual income (return − interest expense) generated from each of the three notes.
d. Compute the amounts that would complete the following chart. (*Hint:* Consider the effect of annual income from (c) on stockholders' equity as well as the new debt.)

	Debt/Equity (A)	Debt/Equity (B)	Debt/Equity (C)
12/31/04			
12/31/05			
12/31/06			

e. Discuss some of the trade-offs involved in choosing among the three notes.

P11–6

The difference
between cash
interest payments
and interest
expense

Earl Rix, president of Rix Driving Range and Health Club, has provided you with the following information:

	2004	2003
Balance Sheet		
Notes payable	$800,000	$800,000
Less: Discount on notes payable	55,000	70,000
Income Statement		
Interest expense	$ 95,000	

The stated annual interest rate on the notes is 10 percent, and interest is paid annually on December 31. The $95,000 in interest expense is due solely on these notes. While reviewing the company's 2004 financial statements, Mr. Rix is having difficulty understanding why the amount charged to interest expense does not equal the amount of cash actually disbursed during 2004 in payment of the interest on these notes.

REQUIRED:

a. Assuming that Rix Driving Range and Health Club makes all of its interest payments on time, how much cash was actually disbursed during 2004 for interest payments on these notes?

b. Explain to Mr. Rix why interest expense does not equal the amount of cash disbursed for interest. What does the difference between the cash disbursed and the amount charged as interest expense represent?

c. What was the effective interest rate at the time the notes were issued?

d. Provide the journal entry to record the payment of interest on December 31, 2004.

P11–7

The effective interest method, interest expense, and present value

Hartney Enterprises issued twenty $1,000 bonds on June 30, 2003, with a stated annual interest rate of 6 percent. The bonds mature in six years. Interest is paid semiannually on December 31 and June 30. The effective interest rate as of June 30, 2003, the date of issuance, was 8 percent.

REQUIRED:

a. Compute the present value of the cash flows associated with these bonds on June 30, 2003, using the following format:

Face value	**XX**
Present value of cash payments at maturity	**XX**
Present value of cash interest payments	**+XX**
Less: Total present value	**XX**
Discount (premium) on bonds	**XX**

b. Compute the present value of the remaining cash flows associated with these bonds on December 31, 2003. What does the present value on December 31, 2003, represent?

c. What does the difference between the present value of the remaining cash flows associated with these bonds on June 30, 2003, and December 31, 2003, represent?

d. Prepare the entry to record the interest payment on December 31, 2003, using the effective interest method. Is the amount of Discount on Bonds Payable amortized in this entry the same as the amount found in (c)? Why or why not?

P11–8

The effective interest method and the straight-line method: Effects on the financial statements

Ross Running Shoes issued ten $1,000 bonds with a stated annual rate of 10 percent on June 30, 2003. These bonds mature on June 30, 2006. The bonds have an effective interest rate of 8 percent, and interest is paid semiannually on December 31 and June 30.

REQUIRED:

a. How much must Ross Running Shoes invest in a bank on June 30, 2003, at an annual rate of 8 percent, compounded semiannually, to meet all the future cash flow requirements of these bonds and have no money left after repaying the principal on June 30, 2006?

b. Prepare the entry to record the interest payment on December 31, 2003. Assume that the company uses the effective interest method.

c. Prepare the entry to record the interest payment on December 31, 2003. Assume that the company amortizes an equal amount of premium each year (i.e., straight-line method).

d. Which method (effective interest or straight-line) of amortizing the premium will allow Ross Running Shoes to recognize the higher amount of net income in 2003?

e. Which method (effective interest or straight-line) of amortizing the premium will allow Ross Running Shoes to recognize the higher amount of net income in 2006?

P11–9

Why the effective interest method is preferred to the straight-line method

Consider the three notes payable listed here. Each was issued on January 1, 2003, and matures on December 31, 2005. Interest payments are made annually on December 31.

Note	Face Value	Stated Interest Rate	Effective Interest Rate
A	$1,000	10%	6%
B	$1,000	10	10
C	$1,000	6	10

REQUIRED:

a. Compute the present value of the remaining cash outflows for each note at each date:

Note	1/1/03	12/31/03	12/31/04
A			
B			
C			

b. Compute the balance sheet values of each note payable at each of the above dates, using the effective interest method.
c. Compute the balance sheet values of each note payable at each of the above dates, using the straight-line method (i.e., amortize an equal amount of the discount or premium each year).
d. Why is the effective interest method preferred to the straight-line method for financial reporting purposes?

P11–10

Redemption and updating amortization

Ginny & Bill Eateries reported the following account balances in the December 31, 2002, financial report:

Bonds payable	$500,000
Premium on bonds payable	12,600

The bonds have a stated annual interest rate of 8 percent and an effective interest rate of 6 percent. Interest is paid on June 30 and December 31.

REQUIRED:

a. Compute the gain or loss recorded on January 1, 2003, if the bonds are called at 104.
b. Compute the gain or loss recorded on January 1, 2003, if the bonds are called at 108.
c. Compute the gain or loss recorded on July 1, 2003, if the bonds are called at 110.

P11–11

Call provisions and bond market prices

Ficus Tree Farm issued five $1,000 bonds with a stated annual interest rate of 12 percent on January 1, 2003. The bonds mature on January 1, 2008. Interest is paid semiannually on June 30 and December 31. The bonds were sold at a price that resulted in an effective interest rate of 14 percent. The bonds can be called for 103.5 beginning June 30, 2005.

REQUIRED:

a. Prepare the entry on January 1, 2003, to record the issuance of these bonds.
b. Prepare the entry on June 30, 2003, to record the interest payment.
c. Assume that Ficus wishes to retire the bonds on June 30, 2005. If the bonds are selling on the open market on that date at a price that would result in a return of 10 percent, should Ficus exercise the call provision or simply attempt to buy the bonds at the market price?
d. Is it likely that Ficus would be able to buy back all outstanding bonds on the bond market at market price?
e. Prepare the entries necessary on June 30, 2005, if Ficus chooses to exercise the call provision.

P11–12

Tax-deductible bond interest and the present value of cash outflows

Taylor Corporation is contemplating issuing bonds to raise cash to finance an expansion. Before issuing the debt, the controller of the company wants to prepare an analysis of the cash flows and the interest expense associated with the issuance. Taylor Corporation is considering issuing one hundred $1,000 bonds on June 30, 2003, that mature on June 30, 2007. The bonds will have a stated annual interest rate of 6 percent, and interest is to be paid semiannually on December 31 and June 30. The bonds will have an effective interest rate of 10 percent.

REQUIRED:

a. Compute the amounts that would complete the following table with respect to the bond issuance being considered by Taylor:

Date	Interest Expense	Cash Payment	Unamortized Discount	Balance Sheet Value
6/30/03				
12/31/03				
6/30/04				
12/31/04				
6/30/05				
12/31/05				
6/30/06				
12/31/06				
6/30/07				

b. Find the difference between the total cash inflow from issuing the bonds and the total cash outflows from interest and principal payments.

c. Recognizing that cash interest payments are tax deductible and assuming a tax rate of 34 percent, recompute the difference you found in (b).

d. Repeat (c), but now consider the time value of money by using the effective rate of these bonds to compute the present value of the net future cash outflows due to interest and principal payments.

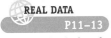

REAL DATA

P11-13

Capital and operating leases

As of January 31, 2000, Kmart reported balance sheet total liabilities and total assets of $12.9 billion and $15.1 billion, respectively. In the footnotes the company disclosed future operating lease payments of $7.2 billion. Future capital lease payments of $2.7 billion were discounted to $1.09 billion and disclosed at that amount on the balance sheet.

REQUIRED

a. Describe the difference between a capital lease and an operating lease.

b. Explain why a company might want to treat its leases as operating leases.

c. Compute the effect on Kmart's total liability/total assets ratio if the company treats all its leases as capital leases. Assume that future operating lease payments are discounted at the same rate as future capital lease payments.

d. Explain how this kind of analysis may be useful to an analyst trying to compare the financial position and performance of two companies that rely heavily on leasing.

P11-14

Accounting for a capital lease

Mackey Company acquired equipment on January 1, 2002, through a leasing agreement that required an annual payment of $30,000. Assume that the lease has a term of five years and that the life of the equipment is also five years. The lease is treated as a capital lease, and the FMV of the equipment is $119,781. Mackey uses the straight-line method to depreciate its fixed assets. The effective annual interest rate on the lease is 8 percent.

REQUIRED:

a. Compute the amounts that would complete the table:

Date	Balance Sheet Value of Equipment	Leasehold Obligation	Interest Expense	Depreciation Expense	Total Expense
1/1/02					
12/31/02					
12/31/03					
12/31/04					
12/31/05					
12/31/06					

b. Compute rent expense for 2002–2006 if the lease is treated as an operating lease.

c. Compute total expense over the five-year period under the two methods and comment.

P11–15

Some economic effects of lease accounting

The balance sheet as of December 31, 2002, for Thompkins Laundry follows:

Assets		Liabilities and Stockholders' Equity	
Current assets	$10,000	Current liabilities	$10,000
Noncurrent assets	60,000	Long-term liabilities	20,000
		Stockholders' equity	40,000
		Total liabilities and	
Total assets	$70,000	stockholders' equity	$70,000

The $20,000 of long-term debt on the balance sheet represents a long-term note that requires Thompkins to maintain a debt/equity ratio of less than 1:1. If the covenant is violated, the company will be required to pay the entire principal of the note immediately. On January 1, 2003, Thompkins entered into a lease agreement. The agreement provides the company with laundry equipment for five years for an annual rental fee of $5,000.

REQUIRED:

a. Compute Thompkins's debt/equity ratio as of January 1, 2003, if the company treats the lease as an operating lease.
b. Compute Thompkins's debt/equity ratio as of January 1, 2003, if the company treats the lease as a capital lease. Assume an effective interest rate of 12 percent.
c. Compare the expenses recognized during 2003 if the lease is treated as operating to the expenses recognized during 2003 if the lease is treated as capital. Assume that the leased equipment has a five-year useful life and is depreciated using the straight-line method.
d. Discuss some of the reasons why Thompkins would want to treat the lease as an operating lease. How might the company arrange the terms of the lease so that it will be considered an operating lease?

P11–16

Financing asset purchases with notes and inferring the effective rate of interest

Memminger Corporation purchased equipment on January 1, 2003. The terms of the purchase required that the company pay $1,000 in interest at the end of each year for five years and $20,000 at the end of the fifth year. The FMV of the equipment on January 1, 2003, was $17,604.

REQUIRED:

a. Prepare the journal entry that would be recorded on January 1, 2003.
b. Compute the effective interest rate on the note payable.
c. Prepare the journal entry that would be recorded when the first interest payment is made on December 31, 2003.
d. Compute the net book value of the note payable as of December 31, 2003.

P11–17

Appendix 11A: Determinants of bond market prices

Hodge Sports bonds are selling on the open market at par value. The bonds have a stated interest rate of 9 percent and mature in five years. You have determined that the risk-free rate is 7 percent.

REQUIRED:

a. What is the maximum risk premium you could attach to these bonds and still be willing to purchase them?
b. Assume that Standard & Poor's lowers the credit rating of Hodge Sports bonds, and this action causes you to increase your risk premium to 5 percent. The bonds have a face value of $1,000 and pay interest semiannually. What price would you be willing to pay for the bonds?
c. Independent of (b), assume that you read in *The Wall Street Journal* that the prime rate has been cut by 1 percent. All other factors being equal, would this news tend to increase or decrease the market price of Hodge Sports bonds? Why? Assume that reducing the prime rate by 1 percent reflects a reduction in the risk-free rate of 1 percent, and estimate the magnitude of this effect on the price of Hodge Sports bonds.

ISSUES FOR DISCUSSION

REAL DATA

ID11–1

Repurchasing
outstanding debt

Sun Company, an oil-refining concern, purchased all of its outstanding 8.5 percent (stated rate) debentures due November 15, 2000, as part of a restructuring plan. The balance sheet value of each outstanding debenture at the time of the repurchase was $875, and the company paid $957.50 for each $1,000 face value bond.

REQUIRED:

a. What is a debenture? Would such bonds tend to be issued at higher or lower prices than secured bonds? Why?
b. Briefly discuss why a company would repurchase its outstanding debt.
c. Explain how this repurchase would affect (increase, decrease, or no effect) the components of the accounting equation: assets, liabilities, stockholders' equity. Would a gain or loss be recognized on the transaction?
d. Would the gain or loss be recognized if Sun Company had not repurchased the bonds? Why or why not?

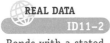

REAL DATA

ID11–2

Bonds with a stated
interest rate of zero

Several years ago, J.C. Penney Company issued bonds for 33.24, with a face value of $200 million and a stated interest rate of zero, which matured eight years later. That same year, Martin Marietta, Northwest Industries, and Alcoa also issued bonds with stated interest rates of zero.

REQUIRED:

a. Why would an investor purchase a bond with a stated interest rate of zero?
b. Compute the effective interest rate on the bond issuance.
c. In terms of its cash flows, explain why a company might wish to issue bonds with a stated interest rate of zero.
d. At what price would the bonds have been issued if the stated interest rate had been 5 percent? 18 percent? Assume that interest payments would be made annually.

REAL DATA

ID11–3

Buy or lease:
Financial
statement effects

Assume that United Airlines is planning to purchase a jet passenger plane with a price of $45,636,480 from The Boeing Company. United is considering structuring the transaction in one of two ways. In Alternative 1, United would borrow the necessary cash from Federal City Bank and sign a note requiring payments of $6 million at the end of each year for fifteen years. The proceeds from the loan would then be used to purchase the airplane. In Alternative 2, United would lease the airplane from Boeing and make annual lease payments of $6 million for fifteen years, at which time it could purchase the airplane from Boeing for a nominal sum. United depreciates its aircraft over a useful life of fifteen years, using the straight-line method.

REQUIRED:

a. Determine the effective interest rate on the note and the lease arrangement.
b. Provide the journal entries that would be recorded under Alternative 1 to reflect the borrowing and the purchase of the airplane.
c. Provide the journal entry that would be recorded under Alternative 2 when the lease agreement is signed if the lease is treated as a capital lease.
d. Compare the effects on the financial statements caused by (b) and (c).
e. Provide the journal entry that would be recorded under Alternative 2 when the lease agreement is signed if the lease is treated as an operating lease.
f. Which of the three alternative treatments (borrowing, capital lease, operating lease) could be considered off-balance-sheet financing? Explain why United might want to structure the transaction in this way.

REAL DATA

ID11–4

Financing
acquisition
with debt

"'Out on a limb, over his head'—that's the typical reaction every time Rupert Murdoch adds another debt-financed chunk to his global media colossus, News Corp. In the past five years, its reported assets have more than quadrupled, [but Murdoch is stepping] up to the plate again with a $1.4 billion offer for MGA/UA Communications Co. . . . Murdoch is rapidly approaching limits on his ability to borrow. News Corp.'s ratio of debt to equity [is] 0.98, up from 0.70, and not far below the 1.1 ceiling imposed by the large group of banks that make up News Corp.'s chief source of borrowing. A News Corp. insider estimates the company has only about $1 billion in additional borrowing power under the bank covenants." (*Business Week,* October 2, 1989)

REQUIRED:

a.   Explain why Murdoch's financing needs are handled by a large group of banks, rather than a single bank, and why these banks would impose a ceiling on News Corp.'s debt/equity ratio.

b.   The article states further that the company's "leverage may well be greater than [what is indicated by News Corp.'s debt/equity ratio]." Explain how this could be and how such a situation would affect the risk incurred by the banks who provide Murdoch's financing.

c.   The article also states that "in evaluating properties [to acquire], Murdoch considers their ability to generate cash . . . as a far more important variable than their asset value." Provide a plausible reason why Murdoch would consider the investment's ability to generate cash so important.

REAL DATA

ID11–5

Holding debt in
times of recession

As the United States slid deeper into a recession in the early 1990s, companies with high amounts of cash relative to their debt were coveted by the stock market, while companies with high levels of debt slashed dividends, payrolls, and capital expenditures to stay afloat. High debt, combined with slower sales and increasing energy and labor costs, proved to be a deadly combination for a number of companies. Standard & Poor's found that both dividend decreases and omissions were up. Defaults on corporate notes and bonds payable rose to a record level as companies missed debt payments. Moody's Investor Service noted that at the time an average of only 41 percent of the face value of defaulted debt was recovered by investors; secured bondholders recovered an average of 67 percent of the face value, while holders of debentures recovered an average of only 23 percent.

REQUIRED:

a.   U.S. corporations have dramatically increased their debt levels in recent years. Discuss how high levels of debt may influence the way in which a company is managed. That is, how might management concerns and decisions be different because a company is carrying a large amount of debt?

b.   Describe the financial statement effects of this borrowing activity, and explain how these effects could have helped investors and creditors to avoid the losses incurred during the recession in the early 1990s. How and why might the reported levels of debt on the balance sheet be less than the actual levels of debt carried by the company?

c.   Define a debenture and explain why defaults on debentures would lead to a lower recovery rate for investors than defaults on secured bonds.

REAL DATA

ID11–6

Adjusting ratios for
lease accounting

Albertson's and Safeway are leading retail food chains in the United States. Several years ago, Albertson's reported $3.6 billion in total assets and $1.9 billion in total liabilities, while Safeway reported $5 billion in total assets and $4.4 billion in total liabilities. Both companies, as is the case with most large retailers, lease most of their stores. At the time Albertson's incurred about $75 million per year in lease payments, treating about 70 percent of its leases as operating leases for financial reporting purposes. Safeway incurred about $170 million per year in lease payments and treated about 75 percent of its leases as operating leases. The approximate present value of the future cash flows associated with the operating leases of Albertson's and Safeway was $465 million and $820 million, respectively.

REQUIRED:

a. Compute the liabilities/total assets ratio for both companies.

b. Assume that both companies accounted for all their leases as capital leases, and recompute their liabilities/total assets ratios.

c. By how much did Safeway's adjusted ratio exceed that of Albertson's? Did the adjustment make much of a difference? Why or why not?

d. Explain why an analyst may wish to make the adjustments required above.

REAL DATA

ID11–7

Determinants of bond prices

Reuters English News Service (June 9, 2000) reported: "Paul DiNunzio, manager of North American and European funding at Ford Motor Credit Co., was surprised at how much investors wanted the $4 billion in bonds his company had planned to sell. So much so that DiNunzio sold them another $500 million, which investors gladly snapped up. After several reports suggested the U.S. economy is finally slowing down enough to mitigate the need for further interest rate hikes from the Federal Reserve, U.S. companies have flooded the market with $16 billion in bonds over the past three days. . . . Investors now believe they can worry less that rising yields may cause the value of bonds they buy to fall. For companies, which have regular financing needs, the shift is good because higher investor demand allows them to offer less yield to get investors to buy their bonds."

a. Why would an economic slowdown be good news for companies wishing to issue bonds?

b. How does higher investor demand allow companies to offer less yield to get investors to buy their bonds?

c. At about the same time, Western Resources chairman and CEO David Wittig said, "We believe that our outstanding debt is undervalued in the marketplace and this provides us an opportunity to purchase the debt at an attractive price." What factors would drive down the price of a company's outstanding debt, making it an attractive purchase opportunity?

REAL DATA

ID11–8

Market value of debt and managing risk

The passages below were taken from the footnotes of Alcoa's 1999 annual report (dollars in millions):

	1999	1998
Book value of long-term debt	**$2,657**	**$2,877**
Market value of long-term debt	2,526	2,902

Risk Management Activities. *The Company is exposed to market risk, including changes in interest rates, currency exchange rates, and certain commodity prices. To manage the volatility relating to these exposures, the Company enters into various derivative transactions pursuant to the company's policies in areas such as hedging.*

REQUIRED:

a. Why is there a difference between the book value and the market value of the company's long-term debt? What does this difference tell you about interest rates?

b. What transactions occurred during 1999 in the area of long-term debt, and on what financial statements would this activity be reflected?

c. What is meant by market risk due to interest rates and currency exchange rates?

d. Briefly describe the concept of hedging and how it can be used to reduce these risks.

REAL DATA

ID11–9

Lease accounting revolution

"It is time for a second overhaul of lease-accounting rules," says Peter Holgate (*Times of London*, June 22, 2000). In 1981, when the current lease rules were developed, there was a reasonably clear distinction between leases that were equivalent to purchasing an asset (capital leases) and others that were in the nature of short-term hire (operating leases). Though unpopular, the new rule was well accepted. Gradually, though, the leasing industry became more sophisticated: the capital/operating distinction became blurred through innovation as financial engineers sought to keep debt off the balance sheet. This was particularly prevalent in the

United States. A result of this innovation is that it is now time for another lease-accounting revolution. The basic idea is to abolish the distinction between capital leases and operating leases and require lessees to show all leases on the balance sheet as a liability and an asset.

REQUIRED:
a. What is the difference between a lease that is "equivalent to purchasing an asset and others that were in the nature of short-term hire?"
b. Why was the lease accounting rule that was passed in 1981 unpopular with industry?
c. How have financial engineers sought to keep debt off the balance sheet?
d. Do you agree with Mr. Holgate's proposal? Why or why not?

REAL DATA

ID11–10

The annual report
of Wal-Mart

The 2001 annual report of Wal-Mart is reproduced in Appendix A.

REQUIRED:
Review the 2001 annual report, and answer the questions below.

a. Compute Wal-Mart's long-term debt (include capital leases and deferred income taxes) to total asset ratio for 2000 and 2001. Discuss the change.
b. Compute the total interest costs (including capital leases) as a percent of revenues for 1999, 2000 and 2001. Discuss these changes.
c. What is the book value of the company's property under capital leases? What method is used to depreciate this amount?
d. Review the financing section of the statement of cash flows and comment on the change in the company's reliance on long-term debt.
e. Wal-Mart increased its reliance on long-term debt during 2001. Briefly describe the general terms of the additional debt incurred by the company.
f. Did Wal-Mart pay off any of its outstanding long-term debt during 2001? Discuss.
g. Describe any debt covenants referred to in the company's annual report.
h. How does Wal-Mart reduce the risk of interest rate fluctuations?

Stockholders' Equity

KEY POINTS

The following key points are emphasized in this chapter:

- *The three forms of financing and their relative importance to major U.S. corporations.*

- *Distinctions between debt and equity.*

- *Economic consequences associated with the methods used to account for stockholders' equity.*

- *Rights associated with preferred and common stock and the methods used to account for stock issuances.*

- *Distinctions among the market value, book value, and par (stated) value of a share of common stock.*

- *Treasury stock.*

- *Cash dividends and dividend strategies followed by corporations.*

- *Stock dividends and stock splits.*

After its market price dipped, Kellogg Company, the world's leading producer of cereal products, spent $1.8 billion to buy back its own shares. The main message in a *Wall Street Journal* article that covered the purchase was that analysts were somewhat cool to the move. It commented: "Nothing gets Wall Street's attention like a good share buyback, and nothing is applauded quite so indiscriminately. . . . Investors automatically cheer buybacks because of the mistaken premise that they necessarily contribute to a self-fulfilling circle of higher share prices. They would do better to think about who is paying for their so-called reward: namely, everyone who continues to own the stock."

This quote raises the issue about how shareholders respond when a company buys back its own shares. Such transactions are reflected in the stockholders' equity section of the balance sheet and, like many other transactions that affect stockholders' equity, provide useful signals about a company's financial performance and condition. This chapter covers these transactions.

Companies generate assets from three sources: (1) borrowings, (2) issuing equity securities, and (3) retaining funds generated through profitable operations. Each of these sources is represented on the right side of the basic accounting equation (balance sheet), which is depicted in Figure 12–1.

FIGURE 12–1
The basic
accounting
equation
	STOCKHOLDERS' EQUITY
	
	Assets = (1) Liabilities + (2) **Contributed Capital** + (3) **Earned Capital**
	                                         Preferred stock Retained earnings
	                                         Common stock
	                                         Additional paid-in

Chapters 10 and 11 were devoted to current and long-term liabilities, which represent the first of the three financing sources illustrated in Figure 12–1. This chapter is devoted to stockholders' equity, which comprises the other two financing sources: (2) contributed capital and (3) earned capital. **Contributed capital,** which reflects contributions from a company's owners, consists of three components: preferred stock, common stock, and additional paid-in capital. The major component of **earned capital** is retained earnings, a measure of the assets that have been generated through a company's profitable operations and not paid to the owners in the form of dividends. The total dollar amount of stockholders' equity is also referred to as a company's **net assets, book value,** or **net worth.**

Contributed and earned capital are important financing sources for many major U.S. companies. Funds used to acquire other companies, purchase machinery and equipment, finance plant expansion, pay off debts, and support operations are often generated by issuing preferred stock, issuing common stock, and retaining funds provided by profitable operations. *Forbes* reported that in the late 1990s corporate America issued new stock at the rate of $165 billion per year—2.37 percent of the gross domestic product, and close to an all-time high.

THE RELATIVE IMPORTANCE OF LIABILITIES, CONTRIBUTED CAPITAL, AND EARNED CAPITAL

Figure 12–2 illustrates the relative importance of the three forms of financing (liabilities, contributed capital, and retained earnings) for our selected firms. Overall, liabilities (with a few exceptions) are the primary financing source. Interest costs are tax deductible, reducing the cost of borrowing, and as discussed before, leverage is a popular way to provide returns to shareholders without using their capital. Internet firms, however, have not relied heavily on leverage for several reasons: (1) several years ago their stock prices were trading at huge premiums, which encouraged equity financing; (2) the speed of their growth created uncertainty associated with their future increased risks, discouraging debt capital providers; and (3) Internet firms had little collateral that could be used to secure loans.

FIGURE 12-2

The relative importance of liabilities, contributed capital, and retained earnings (percentage of total assets)

	Liabilities	Contributed capital	Retained earnings
Manufacturing:			
General Electric (Manufacturer)	.88	−.02	.14
Chevron (Oil drilling and refining)	.52	−.03	.51
Retail:			
SUPERVALU (Grocery retail)	.73	−.05	.28
Tommy Hilfiger (Clothing retail)	.46	.25	.29
Internet:			
Yahoo (Internet search engine)	.16	.82	.02
Cisco (Internet systems)	.19	.55	.25
General Services:			
SBC Communications (Telecommunications services)	.69	.12	.19
Wendy's (Restaurant services)	.43	.04	.62
Financial Services:			
Bank of America (Banking services)	.93	.01	.06
Merrill Lynch (Investment services)	.95	.01	.04

Note also that non-Internet firms rely very little on contributed capital; in fact, for GE, Chevron, and SUPERVALU, the percent under contributed capital is negative. These companies are well-established, successful firms that have repurchased large amounts of their outstanding shares over the years at prices far exceeding the price at which the shares were originally issued. As we discuss later in the chapter, these transactions reduce the value of contributed capital. Finally, the companies that rely heavily on retained earnings as a source of financing have had a history of high profitability and have chosen not to pay high levels of dividends.

The 1999 annual report for Lycos, Inc., an Internet search engine, shows total assets of $875 million and the following financing sources: current liabilities ($90 million), long-term liabilities ($58 million), contributed capital ($817 million), and negative retained earnings ($90 million). Explain what must have happened to create the company's capital structure since its inception in 1995.

DEBT AND EQUITY DISTINGUISHED

Chapters 10 and 11 presented the basic characteristics of the debt contracts between a company and its creditors. This section describes how the nature of this relationship differs from that between a company and its stockholders. As will be discussed later, such a distinction is important to investors, creditors, management, and auditors.

Characteristics of Debt

When a company borrows money, it establishes a relationship with an outside party, a *creditor* or *debtholder,* whose influence on the company's operations is defined by a formal legal contract containing a number of specific provisions. These provisions were discussed in Chapters 10 and 11, and they are summarized in Figure 12–3, along with characteristics of equity.

FIGURE 12–3
Characteristics of debt and equity

Debt	Equity
1. Formal legal contract	1. No legal contract
2. Fixed maturity date	2. No fixed maturity date
3. Fixed periodic interest payments	3. Discretionary dividend payments
4. Security in case of default	4. Residual asset interest
5. No direct voice in management; influence through debt covenants	5. Vote for board of directors
6. Interest is an expense.	6. Dividends are not an expense, but a distribution of retained earnings.

Characteristics of Equity

When a corporation raises capital by issuing stock, it establishes a relationship with an owner, often referred to as an *equityholder,* or *stockholder.* Unlike debt, an equity relationship is not evidenced by a precisely specified contract. There is no maturity date, because a stockholder is an owner of a company until it ceases operations or until the equity interest is transferred to another party. Dividend payments are at the discretion of the board of directors, and stockholders have no legal right to receive dividends until they are declared. In case of bankruptcy, the rights of the stockholders to the available assets are subordinate (secondary) to the rights of the creditors, who are paid in an order which can usually be determined by examining the terms in the debt contracts. The stockholders receive the assets that remain. That is, a corporation's owners have a **residual interest** in the corporation's assets in case of bankruptcy.

Stockholders, however, can exert significant influence over corporate management. Each ownership share carries a vote that is cast in the election of the board of directors at the annual stockholders' meeting. The board, whose function is to represent the interests of the stockholders, declares dividends, determines executive compensation, has the power to hire and fire management, and sets the general policies of the corporation. In addition, certain significant transactions, such as the issuance of additional stock, often must be approved by vote of the stockholders.

Finally, distributions by a corporation to the stockholders (dividends) are not considered operating expenses by either generally accepted accounting principles or the Internal Revenue Service. They are considered a return on the owners' original investments. Consequently, dividends are neither included as expenses on the income statement, nor are they considered deductible expenses in the computation of taxable income. On the financial statements, dividends serve to reduce retained earnings without passing through the income statement.

In its 2000 annual report KLM Royal Dutch Airlines reported interest expense of 381 million guilders (Dutch currency) and dividends of 45 million guilders. The interest expense appeared on the income statement, while the dividends appeared on the statement of stockholders' equity. Describe the difference between interest and dividends and explain why they are treated differently on the financial statements.

Why Is It Important to Distinguish Debt from Equity?

It is important to distinguish debt from equity for a number of different reasons, depending primarily on the perspective of the interested party: capital provider (investor or creditor), management, and accountant and external auditor.

DEBT VS. EQUITY: THE CAPITAL PROVIDER'S PERSPECTIVE

Capital providers include individuals and entities who hold debt and equity securities. Debt securities primarily include notes receivable and bonds, and equity securities include stocks. Active markets (e.g., the New York Stock Exchange) exist where such securities are purchased and sold.

Equity: Higher Risk. Owning an equity security is usually riskier than owning a debt security. The interest and principal payments associated with debt investments are backed by legal contracts and, in general, are more predictable and dependable than discretionary dividend payments. Debt contracts often include security provisions, and in case of bankruptcy, debtholders have higher priority claims to the existing assets than do equityholders, who are often left with nothing. As evidence of the riskier nature of equity securities, stock prices tend to be more volatile than bond prices on the major security exchanges.

Equity: Higher Returns. A characteristic of the additional risk associated with equity investments is that they can produce higher returns than debt investments. When companies perform exceptionally well, equity holders often receive exceedingly large returns, either in the form of dividends or price appreciation of their securities. Debtholders, on the other hand, are limited only to the interest and principal payments specified by the debt contract. Several years ago, for example, Microsoft had an exceptional year, during which the price of its common stock increased by over 312 percent. In contrast, during that same year the company paid less than a 9 percent return to its debtholders (i.e., interest rate on outstanding loans). Historically, annual equity returns have approximated 10–15 percent.

The Independent, a London newspaper, reported that "bonds have long been regarded as boring. Investors are only meant to buy them when they are too nervous of the excitement in the stock market." Explain the reasoning underlying this statement.

DEBT VS. EQUITY: MANAGEMENT'S PERSPECTIVE

The decision by management to raise capital by issuing debt or equity is complex. Factors such as present and future interest rates, the company's credit rating, the relative amount of debt and equity in the company's capital structure and balance sheet, the condition of the economy, and the nature of the company's operations are usually relevant.

Debt: Contractual Restrictions. Issuing debt limits a company in a number of important ways. Contractual interest and principal payments must be met in the future, and assets often must be pledged as security (collateral) during the period of the debt. At the end of 1999, for example, Kmart Corporation reported that capital lease obligations were expected to require future cash payments of approximately $2.8 billion. Additional debt may also lower a company's credit rating and reduce its ability to borrow in the future. Routinely, Standard & Poor's and Moody's Investor Service lower credit ratings of major U.S. companies when they incur large amounts of debt. Finally, the debt contract itself may restrict a company's future borrowing power, limit dividends, or require that certain accounting ratios be maintained at or above specified levels.

Debt: Less Expensive. On the other hand, raising capital by issuing debt is attractive because interest payments are *tax deductible*. General Electric, for example, saved over $3.6 billion in federal income taxes during 2000 because it was able to deduct for tax purposes the interest on its outstanding debts. Issuing debt, therefore, is generally considered less expensive than issuing equity, as dividend payments are not tax deductible. In general, if management can use debt capital to earn revenues that exceed the after-tax cost of the debt, it is using a concept called **leverage** to provide a return for the stockholders. As indicated in Figure 12–2, such a practice appears to be common in that many large U.S. corporations tend to rely more heavily on debt than on equity. The tax deductibility of interest, which significantly reduces the cost of issuing debt, is definitely one of the main reasons.

Equity: Dilution of Ownership. Another advantage of raising capital by issuing debt instead of equity is that issuing equity can dilute the ownership interests of the existing stockholders. Suppose, for example, that Mr. Jones owns 10 percent of XYZ Corporation, 1,000 of the 10,000 outstanding shares. If XYZ issues an additional 10,000 shares, and Mr. Jones purchases none, his ownership interest decreases from 10 percent to 5 percent (1,000/20,000).[1] Such **dilution,** if not accompanied by higher profits, can reduce both the future dividends paid to Mr. Jones and the market price of his shares. A few years ago, a 40-million-share stock issuance by Chrysler Corporation, for example, surprised some analysts because it did not depress the company's stock price. Others commented that the dilutive effect would be negated by increased auto sales.

Dilution also reduces the proportionate control of the existing shareholders and, accordingly, can increase the likelihood of a **takeover** by an outsider. In a takeover, another company, an investor, or group of investors (sometimes called a *raider*) purchases enough of the outstanding shares to gain a controlling interest in the purchased company. If the takeover is "hostile," the voting power attached to the acquired shares is often used by the "raider" to elect a new board of directors. Such action can be followed by the replacement of existing management and substantial changes in the nature of the purchased company.

Corporate managers whose jobs are threatened by takeovers are understandably concerned with the dilutive effects of equity issuances. In fact, many companies, like Kellogg Company, have entered into programs of buying back their own previously issued shares. Such transactions, called **treasury stock** purchases because the acquired

---

1. Some stock certificates carry with them a preemptive right, which allows existing shareholders to share proportionately in any new issue of stock. Also, additional stock issuances sometimes require the approval of the existing stockholders.

shares are often held in the corporation's treasury for reissuance at a later date, make a company less attractive as a takeover target by reducing its cash balance and increasing the proportionate control of the remaining stockholders. Several years ago, for example, the management of Safeway Stores, Inc., purchased all of its publicly traded outstanding stock to elude a takeover attempt by Dart Group Corporation. In other words, the company *went private*—the only shares left outstanding were those held by stockholder-managers who withdrew them from the public markets.

During 1998, 1999, and 2000, Verity, a relatively new provider of web-based portal solutions, made three equity issuances, raising over $115 million, while taking on no additional debt. As of the end of 2000, the company had contributed capital of $207 million and no long-term debt. Explain some of the reasons that may have encouraged Verity to rely on equity instead of debt financing.

DEBT VS. EQUITY: THE ACCOUNTANT'S AND AUDITOR'S PERSPECTIVE

The substantive differences between debt and equity give rise to different accounting treatments: (1) debt and equity issuances are disclosed in different sections of the balance sheet, and (2) debt transactions affect the income statement, while equity transactions do not.

Debt issuances are disclosed in the liabilities section of the balance sheet, while equity issuances are included in the stockholders' equity section. Proper classification is important because the debt/equity distinction affects a number of financial ratios, which are used by investors and creditors and in debt covenants and executive compensation agreements.

Interest payments on outstanding debts and book gains and losses, recognized when debt is redeemed, appear on the income statement and affect the computation of net income. In contrast, transactions involving equity securities, like dividends and the reissuance of treasury stock, do not enter into the computations of net income. Figure 12–4 summarizes why distinctions between debt and equity are important to investors and creditors, management, and accountants and auditors. These distinctions give rise to economic consequences that are discussed in the following section.

FIGURE 12–4

Distinctions between debt and equity from different perspectives

Interested Party	Debt	Equity

Investors and Creditors	Lower investment risk
	Fixed cash receipts
	    (contractual interest
	    and principal)
		Higher investment risk
		Variable cash receipts
		    (discretionary dividends
		    and stock appreciation)

Management	Contractual future cash
	    payments
	Effects on credit rating
	Interest is tax deductible
		Dividends are discretionary
		
		Effects of dilution/takeover
		Dividends are not tax
		    deductible

Accountants and Auditors	Liabilities section of
	    balance sheet
	Income statement effects
	    from debt transactions
		Stockholders' equity
		    section of balance sheet
		No income statement effects
		    from equity transactions

During 1999, Boeing paid $4.5 billion to capital providers—$400 million for interest, $700 million to reduce debt principal, $2.9 billion to repurchase outstanding common stock, and $500 million for dividends. Explain the effect of each payment on the basic accounting equation. Why are they accounted for differently?

THE ECONOMIC CONSEQUENCES ASSOCIATED WITH ACCOUNTING FOR STOCKHOLDERS' EQUITY

The economic consequences associated with accounting for stockholders' equity arise in part from the effects of financial ratios (e.g., debt/equity) that include the dollar amount of stockholders' equity or its components. Such ratios affect a company's stock prices, credit rating, and any debt covenants that restrict additional borrowings, the payment of dividends, or the repurchase of outstanding equity shares (i.e., treasury stock purchases). Some argue that return on equity (net income divided by stockholders' equity) is the most important indicator of whether management is creating value for the shareholders. Four of Dun & Bradstreet's fourteen key business ratios explicitly use the dollar value of stockholders' equity (net worth) in their calculations: (1) current liabilities/net worth, (2) total liabilities/net worth, (3) fixed assets/net worth, and (4) return on net worth. Dun & Bradstreet uses the values of these ratios to determine a company's credit rating, which in turn can affect the terms (e.g., market price, interest rate, security, restrictive covenants) of the company's debt issuances.

Many companies "manage" their debt/equity ratios to maintain or improve their credit ratings. In general, as a company's debt/equity ratio increases, its credit ratings fall. When American Stores, a supermarket and drugstore chain, acquired Lucky Stores, Inc., it raised additional capital, which it reported as debt on its balance sheet, increasing the company's debt/equity ratio. Moody's Investor Service responded by lowering the credit rating on American Stores' outstanding bonds, which was followed by a decrease in the market price of the company's stock.

On the other hand, as companies reduce their reliance on debt and increase their reliance on equity issuances and especially retained earnings as sources of financing, their credit ratings tend to rise. Indeed, General Motors claimed to "strengthen its balance sheet" when it announced plans to sell as much as $1 billion in stock. In its annual report, General Electric commented that during the year its debts were "substantially reduced," leading the major debt-rating agencies to evaluate the company's credit rating as being of the highest standing, *AAA*. Such a rating enabled General Electric to get the best possible terms on its debt issuances as well as maintain or increase the value of the company's outstanding debt securities. In one of its annual reports, May Department Stores commented: "Our strong capitalization ratios, primarily due to growth in retained earnings and the elimination of certain loans, are consistent with our capital structure objectives and provide us with substantial financial flexibility."

Another important economic consequence associated with the stockholder equity section of the balance sheet relates to restrictions on dividend payments and the repurchase of previously issued, outstanding stock imposed by certain debt covenants. Such restrictions can be very significant. Under the terms of covenants with its debtholders, Turner Broadcasting System, Inc., for example, has been prohibited from paying cash dividends altogether. Similar restrictions may be less binding. The 2000 annual report of Owens Corning states, "As is typical for bank credit facilities, the agreements . . .

contain restrictive covenants, including . . . limitations on . . . the payment of dividends and purchase of company stock."

Such restrictions protect the interest of creditors by keeping a company from paying all of its available cash to the shareholders through excessive dividends or stock repurchases. Note also that the methods used to account for stock issuances, dividends, treasury stock purchases, and retained earnings, which are covered later in the chapter, can determine whether such restrictions have been violated. Finally, recall that the methods used to account for assets and liabilities affect the recognition of expenses and revenues, which in turn affect retained earnings.

Some believe, as indicated above, that the most direct measure of value creation is return on stockholders' equity (net income/average stockholders' equity). During 2000, La-Z-Boy Incorporated, a furniture manufacturer, issued equity, bought back outstanding shares, and paid dividends. Assuming that these transactions all occurred at the end of the year, explain how each affected return on equity. How might these effects influence an analyst who considers return on equity an important metric of corporate performance?

ACCOUNTING FOR STOCKHOLDERS' EQUITY

The stockholders' equity section of a corporate balance sheet consists of two major components: (1) contributed capital, which primarily reflects contributions of capital from shareholders and includes the preferred stock, common stock, and additional paid-in capital[2] accounts, and (2) earned capital, which reflects the amount of assets earned and retained by the corporation and consists essentially of the retained earnings account. An example of the stockholders' equity section of a corporate balance sheet appears in Figure 12–5. Spend a moment to review it because it provides an outline of the remaining discussion in this chapter.

FIGURE 12–5 Stockholders' equity section of balance sheet			
Contributed capital:			
Preferred stock (authorized, issued, and outstanding shares, asset preference, dividend preference, par value, cumulative, nonparticipating)		$ 3,000	
Common stock (authorized, issued, and outstanding shares, par value/stated value/no par)		15,000	
Additional paid-in capital (preferred stock, common stock, treasury stock, stock dividends)		86,000	
Total contributed capital			$104,000
Earned capital:			
Retained earnings		$125,000	
Total earned capital			125,000
Less: Treasury stock (cost method)			(20,000)
Total stockholders' equity			$209,000

2. While the title *Additional Paid-In Capital* is the most common, there is some variation across companies. For example, The New York Times Company uses *Additional Capital*, Goodyear Tire & Rubber uses *Capital Surplus*, and Chevron Corporation uses *Capital in Excess of Par Value*.

Preferred Stock

Preferred stock is so called because preferred stockholders have certain rights that are not shared by common stockholders. These special rights relate to the receipt of dividends and/or to claims on assets in case of liquidation. **Preferred stock as to dividends** confers the right, if dividends are declared by the corporation's board of directors, to receive dividends. **Preferred stock as to assets** carries a claim to the corporation's assets, in case of liquidation, with a higher priority than the claim carried by common stock. The exact characteristics and terms of preferred stock vary from one issue to the next. The following sections describe some of the more important features of preferred stock.

AUTHORIZED, ISSUED, AND OUTSTANDING PREFERRED SHARES

Authorized preferred shares are the number of shares a corporation is entitled to issue by its corporate charter. Additional authorizations must be approved by the board of directors and are often subject to shareholder vote.

Issued preferred shares have been issued previously by a corporation and may or may not be currently outstanding. Some issued shares may have been repurchased by the corporation and held as treasury stock. **Outstanding** preferred shares are the shares presently held by the stockholders. Issued shares less repurchased shares equal outstanding shares. *Accounting Trends and Techniques* (AICPA, 2000) reports that, of the 600 major U.S. corporations surveyed, approximately 15 percent had outstanding preferred issuances.

The number of authorized, issued, and outstanding preferred shares should be disclosed in the annual report. Microsoft, for example, recently disclosed in its annual report that the shareholders had authorized 100 million shares of preferred stock, of which over 13 million had been issued and were presently outstanding.

Many major U.S. corporations have authorized preferred stock issuances but have chosen not to issue them. In such cases, the number of authorized shares should still be disclosed in the financial report. As of the end of 1999, for example, Goodyear Tire & Rubber Company (50 million shares), Hewlett-Packard (300 million shares), and Johnson & Johnson (2 million shares) disclosed authorized preferred shares, none of which had been issued.

PREFERRED DIVIDEND PAYMENTS

The terms of preferred stocks usually include a specific annual dividend that is paid to the preferred stockholders before any payments are made to the common stockholders, assuming that a dividend is declared by the board. The remaining amount of the dividend is then paid to the common stockholders. The amount of the preferred annual dividend payment is normally expressed as either an absolute dollar amount or as a percentage of a dollar amount referred to as the par value of the preferred stock.[3]

For example, if dividends are declared in a given year, the holder of one share of $5 preferred stock would receive a $5 dividend. The holder of one share of 4 percent preferred stock with a par value of $100 would receive a $4 (4% × $100) dividend. As of December 31, 1999, Sears had two kinds of preferred shares outstanding, differentiated by the per-share amount of the annual dividend payment: a $3.75 series and a series that paid an annual dividend of 8.88 percent of the $25 par value ($2.22).

---

3. The concept of par value is discussed more completely later in the chapter when we cover common stock. At that time, we point out that par value has little or no economic meaning. In the case of preferred stock, however, par value is meaningful in that it is sometimes used to determine the annual dividend payment to the preferred stockholders.

To illustrate the allocation of a dividend between preferred and common stock, several years ago the board of directors of DuPont declared and paid a total dividend of $802 million. During the year, approximately 1.68 million shares of $4.50 preferred stock, 0.7 million shares of $3.50 preferred stock, and 240 million shares of common stock were outstanding. The dividend allocation to the preferred and common stockholder is shown in Figure 12–6.

FIGURE 12–6

Allocation of a dividend between preferred and common stock

Preferred dividend:		
$4.50 preferred stock × 1.68 million shares	$7.55 million	
$3.50 preferred stock × 0.7 million shares	2.45 million	$ 10 million
Common dividend ($3.30 × 240 million shares)		792 million
Total dividend		**$802 million**

CUMULATIVE PREFERRED STOCK

With **cumulative preferred stock,** when a corporation misses a dividend, **dividends in arrears** are created in the amount of the missed preferred dividend. In future periods, as dividends are declared, dividends in arrears are first paid to the preferred stockholders, who then receive their normal, annual dividend. Finally, the common stockholders are paid from what remains. If the preferred stock is *noncumulative,* no dividends in arrears are created for missed dividends, and the preferred stockholders receive only their normal, annual dividend in future periods as dividends are declared.

It is important to realize that dividends in arrears are not liabilities to the corporation and therefore are not listed on the balance sheet. They do not represent legal obligations to the preferred stockholders, because dividends are at the discretion of the board of directors. The liability is created at the time the dividends are declared and only in the amount of the dividends. However, the corporation must keep track of dividends in arrears because they must be clearly disclosed in the financial report. Such information is particularly interesting to creditors as well as potential and existing stockholders because it may signal a shortage of cash in the corporation. The amount of dividends in arrears may also affect the dividends that common stockholders can expect to receive in the future.

The following excerpt was taken from a recent Sears annual report:

In the event that dividends payable on preferred stock are in arrears for six quarterly periods, holders of such stock shall have the right to elect two additional directors of the Company until all cumulative dividends have been paid or set apart for payment. Additionally, dividends cannot be paid on the Company's common shares if dividends on preferred shares are in arrears."

Who would insist on such a policy and why?

Almost all preferred stock issuances are cumulative, and among major U.S. companies, dividends in arrears are relatively rare. Several years ago, however, Stelco (Canada's second-largest steelmaker) omitted dividends on its cumulative preferred stocks as it attempted to turn around its money-losing operations. Accordingly, the company disclosed dividends in arrears in its financial report. The company had not missed a dividend payment in seventy-five years.

PARTICIPATING PREFERRED STOCK

If preferred stock carries a **participating** feature, the preferred stockholders not only have a right to the annual dividend payment, but they also share in the remaining amount of the dividend with the common stockholders. The extent to which the preferred stockholders participate in the remaining dividend is often expressed as a percentage of the par value of the preferred stock. Nonparticipating preferred stock, which is much more common, carries no rights to share in the remaining dividend.

PREFERRED STOCKS: DEBT OR EQUITY?

We have described how most preferred stocks (1) carry higher priority than common stocks in the event of liquidation, (2) specify annual dividend payments of a fixed amount, (3) are cumulative, and (4) do not contain a participation feature. In addition, preferred stocks normally do not carry a right to vote in the election of the board of directors, and many contain a call provision that allows the corporation to redeem the stock for a specified price after a specified date.

Recall the discussion earlier in the chapter on the characteristics of debt and equity (see Figure 12–3), and note how the features listed above closely resemble debt. In fact, in some cases the Internal Revenue Service has allowed corporations to deduct from taxable income the dividends paid on securities classified on the balance sheet as preferred stocks because such dividends were construed as interest. Preferred stocks are definitely hybrid securities, which have characteristics of both debt and equity. They are therefore difficult to classify on the balance sheet. In most cases, the preferred stock account is disclosed at the top of the stockholders' equity section, where it is located immediately below long-term liabilities. In some cases, however, preferred stocks are disclosed as debt. On its 1998 balance sheet, for example, NIKE, Inc., reported $300 million in preferred stock in the long-term liabilities section of the balance sheet. Financial statement users interested in computing ratios that involve distinctions between debt and equity (e.g., debt/equity) may find it more useful to treat the preferred stock account as a long-term liability.

Classifying hybrid securities, like preferred stocks, is indeed a difficult area for accountants and auditors, primarily because the distinction between debt and equity is not always clear-cut. Also, the guidelines specified by generally accepted accounting principles are not very specific. In an article in *Forbes*, the national director of accounting and auditing at a major accounting firm noted: "the distinction between debt and equity has become so muddied that the accounting rules seem more arbitrary than ever . . . preferred stocks are clever ways to raise cash . . . simply [a form of] off-balance-sheet financing masquerading as equity."

Consequently, by issuing certain kinds of preferred stock, management can raise what is essentially debt capital without increasing the liabilities reported on the balance sheet. Because preferred stock carries no voting power, such a strategy also avoids the problems of dilution and possible takeover associated with issuing common stock. As noted in *Forbes*:

Companies anxious to protect their credit ratings, and unwilling to issue more [common] stock for fear of diluting earnings per share or inviting takeover bids, have turned to these ingenious instruments [preferred stocks] to lower the cost of raising money. But pity the poor accountant who must categorize these hothouse hybrids.[4]

4. Jinny St. Goar, "Creative Paper," *Forbes*, June 3, 1985, pp. 178, 180.

In the liability section of its 1999 balance sheet, BF Goodrich, an automobile tire manufacturer, reported an account called "mandatorily redeemable preferred stock" in the amount of $271 million. Explain how something called stock could be reported in the liability section of the balance sheet. What does "mandatorily redeemable" mean, and how might that feature influence where it is reported on the balance sheet?

Common Stock

Unlike preferred stock, common stock is typically not characterized by a wide variety of features that differ from issuance to issuance. Moreover, common stock is not designed to provide a fixed return over a specified period of time. Rather, as a true equity security, common stock is characterized by three fundamental rights: (1) the right to receive dividends if they are declared by the board of directors, (2) a residual right to the corporation's assets in case of liquidation, and (3) the right to exert control over management, which includes the right to vote in the annual election of the board of directors and the right to vote on certain significant transactions proposed by management (e.g., the authorization of additional shares, large purchases of outstanding shares, major acquisitions).

The value of the common stock issued by a corporation can be described in a number of different and often confusing ways. This section clarifies some of this confusion by differentiating among the market value, book value, and par value of a share of common stock.

Market Value

The **market value** of a share of stock, common or preferred, at a particular point in time is the price at which the stock can be exchanged on the open market. This amount varies from day to day, based primarily on changes in investor expectations about the financial condition of the issuing company, interest rates, and other factors. The market prices of the common stocks of publicly traded companies must be disclosed in their financial reports. The 2000 annual report of Emerson Electric, for example, disclosed that the market price of the company's common stock fluctuated from a low of approximately $40 per share to a high of slightly over $70 during the year ending December 31, 2000.

Book Value

The **book value** of a share of common stock is determined by the following formula:

$$\text{Book Value of Common Stock} = \frac{\text{Stockholders' Equity} - \text{Preferred Capital}}{\text{Number of Common Shares Held by the Shareholders}}$$

It is simply the book value of the corporation (less preferred capital), as indicated on the balance sheet, divided by the number of common shares presently held by the shareholders. This value rarely approximates the market value of a common share, because the balance sheet, in general, does not represent an accurate measure of the market value of the company. As of December 31, 2000, the book value of Emerson common stock was $15 per share, considerably below the range of market value ($40–$70) indicated in the previous paragraph.

Market-to-Book Ratio

Dividing the market value of a company's common stock by its book value (**market-to-book ratio**) provides a ratio that indicates the extent to which the market believes that the balance sheet reflects the company's true value. Ratios equal to 1 indicate that a company's net book value (as measured by the balance sheet) is perceived by the market to be a fair reflection of the company's true value. More commonly, market-to-book ratios are somewhat larger than 1, indicating that the balance sheet is perceived to be a conservative measure of the company's true value. Large ratios can be attributed to a number of reasons: balance sheet assets are at cost, not fair market value; goodwill is ignored on the balance sheet; or accounting methods are conservative.

High market-to-book ratios also indicate that investors expect high growth relative to the invested capital indicated on the balance sheet. Market-to-book ratios vary substantially across and within companies. As of the end of 2000, for example, Emerson's market-to-book ratio was approximately 4:1, General Electric's was 10 to 1, and the ratio for 3M ranged from 4:1 to almost 7:1 during 2000.

Par Value

The **par value** (sometimes called stated value) of a share of common stock has no relationship to its market value or book value and, for the most part, has little economic significance. At one time it represented a legal concept, instituted by some states, that was intended to protect creditors, but over time the concept proved to be largely ineffective.[5] It is not uncommon for corporations to issue either no-par common stock or common stock with extremely low par values. For example, the par value of Emerson Electric's common stock is only $0.50 per share.

While the par (stated) value of a share of common stock has limited legal or economic significance, these values do have financial accounting significance. As the next section demonstrates, under generally accepted accounting principles, these values are used in the journal entries to record certain common stock transactions. Many believe that attributing any significance, accounting or otherwise, to the par or stated value of common stock is unwarranted.

As discussed above, as of the end of 2000, there were large differences among the market value, book value, and par value of a share of Emerson Electric common stock. What was each of the three values? Why are they so different?

ACCOUNTING FOR COMMON AND PREFERRED STOCK ISSUANCES

As with preferred stock, common stock issuances must be authorized in the corporate charter and approved by the board of directors and sometimes the stockholders. Similarly, the number of shares of common stock outstanding may differ from the number of common shares originally issued. As of December 31, 1999, for example, the corporate charter and stockholders of Johnson & Johnson had authorized over

---

5. In some states the concept of stated value was substituted for par value, but like par value, this concept has limited economic meaning. Note, however, that state laws differ in this area.

2 billion shares of common stock, 1.5 billion shares had been issued, and 1.4 billion shares were currently outstanding—approximately 140 million shares had been repurchased by the company and were held in the form of treasury stock.

The methods used to account for common stock issuances are essentially the same as those used for preferred stock. When no-par common or preferred stock is issued for cash, the cash account is debited for the proceeds and the common (or preferred) stock account is credited for the entire dollar amount. For example, when Apple Computer, Inc., issued 4.98 million shares of no-par common stock for an average price of $17.592 per share (total cash proceeds of $87.61 million), the company recorded the following journal entry (dollars in millions):

Cash (+A)	87.61	
Common Stock (+SE)		87.61
Issued no-par common stock.		

When common or preferred stock with a par value is issued for cash, the cash account is debited for the total proceeds, the common (or preferred) stock account is credited for the number of shares issued multiplied by the par value per share, and the additional paid-in capital (common or preferred stock) account is credited for the remainder. The dollar amount credited to the additional paid-in capital account represents the difference between the total issuance price of the stock and the par value of the issuance. For example, when Coca-Cola Enterprises issued 71.4 million shares of $1 par value common stock for $15.62 per share, the company recorded the following journal entry (dollars in millions):

Cash (+A)	1,115.27	
Common Stock (+SE)		71.40*
Additional Paid-In Capital, C/S (+SE)		1,043.87*
Issued $1 par value common stock.		

*71.4 million sh. × $1

When Weyerhaeuser Company issued 147,000 shares of $1.00 par value preferred stock for $11 per share, it recorded the following journal entry:

Cash (+A)	1,617,000*	
Preferred Stock (+SE)		147,000**
Additional Paid-In Capital, P/S (+SE)		1,470,000
Issued $1 par value preferred stock.		

*147,000 sh. × $11
**147,000 sh. × $1

In 1999, Cisco Systems issued 98 million shares of common stock. The stock was issued for $7.50 per share and had a par value of $0.001 per share. Explain how the issuance affected the basic accounting equation.

Treasury Stock

Outstanding common stock is often repurchased and either (1) held *in treasury,* awaiting reissuance at a later date, or (2) retired.[6] Repurchases of this nature normally must

---

6. Repurchased preferred shares are normally retired and are not held as treasury stock. Most repurchased common shares, on the other hand, are held in treasury. Treasury shares have the status of authorized and unissued shares.

be authorized and approved by a company's stockholders and board of directors. Treasury stock carries none of the usual rights of common stock ownership. That is, while common shares are held in treasury, they lose their voting power and their right to receive dividends.

WHY COMPANIES PURCHASE TREASURY STOCK

There are many reasons why corporations purchase outstanding common shares and hold them in treasury. Perhaps the most common is to support employee compensation plans. Johnson & Johnson, for example, purchased treasury stock in the amount of over $840 million in 1999. During that time period, treasury stock in the amount of $357 million was reissued as part of an employee compensation plan.

Other companies, such as Walt Disney, Avco, Gillette, and Safeway, have entered into common stock buy-back programs to fend off possible takeover attempts. We mentioned earlier that by purchasing its own outstanding common stock, a company can discourage takeovers by reducing its cash balance and increasing the proportionate control of the remaining shareholders. Gillette, for example, entered into a plan to purchase 11 million of its outstanding common shares. In doing so, the company blocked a takeover attempt by purchasing the 13.9 percent interest held at that time by the Revlon Group, Inc. Columbia Broadcasting System (CBS) blocked a takeover attempt by Ted Turner (Turner Broadcasting System, Inc.) by repurchasing a substantial portion of its outstanding common stock.

Purchasing treasury stock can also increase the market price of a company's outstanding stock. *Business Week* (May 12, 1997) reported:

It's a simple formula: announce plans for a $3.5 billion stock buyback . . . watch the stock soar. It worked for IBM.

Treasury stock purchases are often viewed as a sign of financial strength. In 1991, for example, when the economy took a downturn, companies with strong cash positions took advantage of the reduced prices on the stock market by purchasing large quantities of their own shares. Many of these shares were reissued later at much higher prices.

A treasury stock purchase can serve to increase a company's earnings per share (net income/outstanding common shares). *Business Week* (February 10, 1997) reported that "all told, IBM has spent some $10.7 billion on stock buybacks since 1995. . . . IBM's CFO claims that it has been an important contributor toward growing our earnings per share."

Finally, treasury stock purchases are often made to return cash to shareholders. In this sense, it is much like a dividend, especially if the treasury stock purchase is proportionate across the shareholders. Consider, for example, a company that has 6,000 common shares outstanding, held in equal amounts of 2,000 shares by three shareholders. Each shareholder owns one-third of the company. If 1,000 common shares are repurchased from each shareholder for $2 per share, each receives $2,000 and still maintains a one-third interest in the company—the exact result that would have occurred had the company paid a $1 per share dividend.

Between 1983 and 1997, aggregate repurchases of treasury shares represented 23 percent of corporate earnings, versus 3 percent in the 1973–1977 time period (*Barron's*, May 29, 2000). Explain why a company would buy back its own stock.

ACCOUNTING FOR TREASURY STOCK: THE COST METHOD

There are two methods of accounting for treasury stock: (1) the cost method and (2) the par value method. While either method is acceptable under GAAP, the cost method is covered below because it is simpler and more widely used.[7]

Purchasing Treasury Stock. Under the cost method, when a company purchases its own outstanding common stock and holds it in treasury, a permanent account, called Treasury Stock, is debited for the cost of the purchase.[8] This account is disclosed below retained earnings in the stockholders' equity section of the balance sheet (see Figure 12–5). For example, when Best Foods purchased treasury stock for a total cost of $265 million, it recorded the following journal entry (dollars in millions):

Treasury Stock (−SE)	265	
Cash (−A)		265

Purchased shares of treasury stock.

This transaction brought the total investment in treasury shares held by Best Foods to 2.1 billion, and the stockholders' equity section of Best Foods' 1999 balance sheet appeared as in Figure 12–7.

FIGURE 12–7
Disclosure of treasury stock

Best Foods
Balance Sheet
Stockholders' Equity Section
December 31, 1999
(in millions of dollars)

Preferred stock	$ 151
Common stock	98
Additional paid-in capital	109
Retained earnings	2,725
Less: Cost of common stock in treasury	$(2,145)
Total stockholders' equity	$ 938

The treasury stock account is disclosed immediately below retained earnings because in many states dividends cannot legally exceed retained earnings less the cost of all shares held in treasury. Such laws are designed to protect creditors by keeping a corporation from distributing all of its cash to the shareholders in the form of dividends or stock repurchases. By subtracting the dollar amount in the treasury stock account from retained earnings, financial statement readers can determine the maximum amount of cash that legally can be paid to the shareholders as of the balance sheet date.[9]

Reissuing Treasury Stock for More Than Acquisition Cost. Common stock held in treasury is often reissued at a later date. If it is reissued at a price greater than its acquisition cost, the cash account is debited for the proceeds, the treasury stock

---

7. *Accounting Trends and Techniques* (2000) indicated that almost 92 percent of the companies disclosing treasury stock use the cost method.

8. If outstanding stock, preferred or common, is repurchased and then retired, the stock account is debited and the cash payment is credited. If the payment exceeds the stock account, which is frequently the case, additional paid-in capital and/or retained earnings is debited to balance the entry.

9. Recall that debt covenants may further restrict the payment of dividends.

account is credited for the cost, and the difference is credited to the additional paid-in capital (Treasury Stock) account. For example, when PepsiCo, Inc., reissued 139,000 shares of treasury stock, which had an acquisition cost of $2.7 million, for a total of $5.3 million, the company recorded the following journal entry (dollars in millions):

Cash (+A)	5.3	
Treasury Stock (+SE)		2.7
Additional Paid-In Capital, T/S (+SE)		2.6

Reissued treasury stock.

Reissuing Treasury Stock for Less Than Acquisition Cost. If treasury stock is reissued for less than the acquisition cost, the cash account is debited for the proceeds, the treasury stock account is credited for the acquisition cost, and Additional Paid-In Capital (Treasury Stock) is debited for the difference, *if there is a sufficient balance in the account to cover this difference.* If the difference between the acquisition cost and the proceeds exceeds the balance in the additional paid-in capital (Treasury Stock) account, Retained Earnings is debited.

For example, several years ago Eli Lilly and Company reissued 1.2 million treasury shares, with an acquisition cost of $68.5 million, for $44.5 million. At the time of the transaction, the balance in the additional paid-in capital (Treasury Stock) account exceeded $24 million, the difference between the cost and the proceeds. The following journal entry, therefore, was recorded to reflect the transaction (dollars in millions):

Cash (+A)	44.5	
Additional Paid-In Capital, T/S (−SE)	24.0	
Treasury Stock (+SE)		68.5

Reissued treasury stock.

The Pillsbury Company reissued 300,000 shares of treasury stock, which had an acquisition cost of $12.9 million, for a total of $11.7 million. The balance in the additional paid-in capital (Treasury Stock) account at the time of the reissuance was zero. Accordingly, the following journal entry was recorded (dollars in millions).

Cash (+A)	11.7	
Retained Earnings (−SE)	1.2	
Treasury Stock (+SE)		12.9

Reissued treasury stock.

Note that in all three preceding examples, an income statement gain or loss is not recognized when treasury stock is reissued for an amount more than or less than the acquisition cost. Reissuing treasury stock is a capital transaction and as such should not affect the income statement.

The 1999 annual report of Guidant Corporation, a manufacturer of medical technology, reports a reissuance of treasury stock that decreased the treasury stock account by $147 million and decreased additional paid-in capital by $104 million. How much cash did Guidant receive from the stock issuance, and was the reissuance price above or below the original cost of the treasury stock?

THE MAGNITUDE OF THE TREASURY STOCK ACCOUNT

The dollar value of the treasury stock account on the balance sheets of major U.S. corporations is often quite significant. As indicated in Figure 12–8, it is not unusual for it to exceed the dollar value of the corporation's total contributed capital (preferred stock, common stock, and additional paid-in capital). This phenomenon can occur because treasury stock is often acquired at prices that are considerably higher than the original issuance prices of the shares.

FIGURE 12–8

The dollar value of treasury stock/total contributed capital (dollars in millions)

Company	Treasury Stock/ Contributed Capital
Eli Lilly	$\dfrac{109}{3,314} = .03$
SCB Communications	$\dfrac{2,071}{15,558} = .13$
3M	$\dfrac{4,065}{11,808} = .34$
Lands' End	$\dfrac{199}{38} = 5.24$
Emerson Electric	$\dfrac{1,923}{291} = 6.61$

Source: 2000 annual reports.

Stock Options

Recall from Chapter 10 that in the United States, **stock options** have become a very popular way to compensate corporate executives. This form of compensation is attractive to companies because it requires no cash payment and motivates executives to act in a manner that maximizes the company's share price—stock price increases create gains for the executive. Stock options are attractive to executives because, despite the great upside potential, there is no risk of loss. Recall also that current GAAP does not require the recognition of compensation expense at the issuance of most options even though most agree that something of value has passed from the company to the executives.

Most companies record no entry when stock options are initially issued. When executives exercise their options, they normally purchase stock from the company at prices below current market values. The proper method of accounting for these purchases depends upon whether the issued stock is classified by the company as "authorized but unissued," or treasury stock. If the stock is classified as "authorized but unissued," the transaction is treated simply as a stock issuance—cash is increased by the amount of issuance, and the common stock account is increased, as well as the additional paid-in capital account, if necessary. If the issued stock is classified as treasury stock, which is perhaps the most common situation, the transaction is treated as a reissuance of treasury stock.

As part of its employee incentive plan, Nabisco reissued 278,000 treasury shares with an original cost of $47 per share for $29 per share. During the period of the reissuance, the company had no additional paid-in capital. Provide the entry that Nabisco recorded, and explain why Nabisco might have reissued its shares at such a low price.

Retained Earnings

Retained earnings is a measure of previously recognized profits that have not been paid to the shareholders in the form of dividends. As indicated in Figure 12–2, major U.S. corporations rely heavily on internally generated funds as a source of capital. This section discusses two factors that affect the retained earnings balance: (1) dividends and (2) appropriations.

DIVIDENDS

Dividends are distributions of cash, property, or stock to the stockholders of a corporation. They are declared by a formal resolution of the corporation's board of directors (usually quarterly), and the amount is usually announced on a per-share basis. Cash dividends represent distributions of cash to the stockholders. Property dividends (dividends in kind) are distributions of property, usually debt or equity securities in other companies.[10] **Stock dividends** are distributions of a corporation's own shares. Cash dividends are by far the most common. *Accounting Trends and Techniques* (AICPA, 2000) reported that, of the 600 major U.S. companies surveyed, 497 (83 percent) paid cash dividends during 2000, 2 (.3 percent) paid property dividends, and 18 (3 percent) paid dividends in the form of stock.[11]

As Figure 12–9 shows, three dates are relevant when dividends are declared: (1) the **date of declaration,** when the dividends are declared by the board, (2) the **date of record,** which determines who is to receive the dividend, and (3) the **date of payment,** when the distribution is actually made.

FIGURE 12–9

Important dividend dates

Date of Declaration	Date of Record	Date of Payment
Board of directors declares dividend and liability is established.	Shareholders holding stock at this date receive the dividend when paid.	Dividend is paid to shareholders of record.

A typical dividend announcement reads as follows:

The Board of Directors of Bennet Corporation, at its regular meeting of March 10, 2000, declared a quarterly dividend of $5 per share, payable on April 20, 2000, to stockholders of record on April 2, 2000.

In this announcement, March 10 is the date of declaration, April 2, the date of record, and April 20, the date of payment.

Dividend Strategy. When and how much of a dividend to declare depends on a number of factors, such as the nature, financial condition, and desired image of the company, as well as legal constraints. If dividends are to be paid in cash, the board of directors must first be certain that the corporation has sufficient cash to meet the payment. Such a determination requires a projection of the operating cash flows of the company, including, for example, analyses of the company's current cash position, future sales, receivables, inventory purchases, and fixed-asset replacements. It is usu-

---

10. Accounting for property dividends is normally covered in intermediate financial accounting.
11. Some companies distributed more than one kind of dividend, and others distributed no dividends of any kind.

ally wise to make sure that the company's operating cash needs can be met before cash dividends are paid.

The goals of a corporation and the nature of its activities may also have a bearing on dividend policy. Some companies, like Toys "R" Us, Inc., Microsoft Corporation, and most of the Internet firms are relatively young, fast-growing companies that have adopted policies of paying no dividends. Such companies, often called growth companies, reinvest their earnings primarily to support growth without having to rely too heavily on debt and dilutive equity issuances. The shareholders receive their investment returns in the form of stock price appreciation. The following excerpt is from an annual report of Toys "R" Us, Inc.:

The Company has followed the policy of reinvesting earnings in the business and, consequently, has not paid any cash dividends. At the present time, no change in this policy is under consideration by the Board of Directors. The payment of cash dividends in the future will be determined by the Board of Directors in light of conditions then existing, including the Company's earnings, financial requirements and condition, opportunities for reinvesting earnings, business conditions, and other factors.

More established companies, such as General Electric and Johnson & Johnson, normally pay quarterly dividends in the amount of 30–40 percent of net income and also attempt to consistently increase their dividend payments from year to year. This policy, which provides a consistent dividend while retaining some funds to finance available growth opportunities, tends to reflect an image of stability, strength, and permanence. The following excerpt is from an annual report of General Electric:

Dividends paid totaled $1.777 billion [$1.29 per share]. At the same time, the Company retained sufficient earnings to support enhanced productive capability and to provide adequate financial resources for internal and external growth opportunities. [This increase] in dividends declared . . . marked the twelfth consecutive year of dividend growth.

Some companies consistently increase dividends from year to year, but the distributions do not represent a consistent percentage of net income. Eastman Kodak Company, for example, has increased its dividends each year since 1977. However, as a percentage of net income, dividend payments over that time period varied from around 40 percent to over 100 percent. Apparently, the boards of such companies believe that dividend payments should show consistent growth regardless of how well the company does from one year to the next.

State laws and debt covenants can also limit the payment of dividends. In most states, the dollar amount of retained earnings less the cost of treasury stock sets a limitation on the payment of dividends. In addition, the terms of debt contracts may further limit dividend payments to an even smaller portion of retained earnings. Several years ago, for example, Sears, Roebuck & Company had a balance of retained earnings of almost $9 billion. Yet, certain indenture agreements existing at the time limited dividend payments to a maximum amount of $8 billion.

AT&T consistently declares dividends of about 30–40 percent of net income. Delta Air Lines only pays dividends of about 2 percent of net income, and Cisco Systems has never issued a dividend. Does this mean that AT&T is a better investment than Delta and Cisco? Explain and briefly discuss dividend strategies.

Accounting for Cash Dividends. When the board of directors of a corporation declares a cash dividend, a liability in the amount of the fair market value of the dividend is created on the date of declaration. At this time, a cash dividend account is debited, and a current liability account, Dividends Payable, is credited for a dollar value equal to the per-share amount multiplied by the number of outstanding shares. Cash Dividend is a temporary account that is closed directly to Retained Earnings at the end of the accounting period. The dividends payable account is removed from the balance sheet when the dividend is paid on the date of payment. No entry is recorded on the date of record. The shareholders as of the date of record are simply the recipients of the dividend.

To illustrate, when the board of directors of Marriott Corporation declared a fourth-quarter cash dividend of $0.20 per share on 118.8 million common shares outstanding, the following journal entry was recorded (dollars in millions):

Cash Dividend (−SE)	23.76	
Dividends Payable (+L)		23.76

Declared a cash dividend (118.8 million sh. × $0.20/sh.).

Marriott recorded the following entry on the date of payment (dollars in millions):

Dividends Payable (−L)	23.76	
Cash (−A)		23.76

Paid a cash dividend.

Stock Splits and Stock Dividends. Corporations can distribute additional shares to existing stockholders by declaring either a stock split or a stock dividend. For practical purposes, there is very little difference between these two actions. In both cases, the existing shareholders receive additional shares, and in neither case are the assets or liabilities of the corporation increased or decreased.

In a **stock split,** the number of outstanding shares is simply "split" into smaller units, which requires the corporation to distribute additional shares. A 2:1 stock split, for example, serves to double the number of outstanding shares, which requires that the company distribute an additional share for each common share outstanding. A 3:1 stock split effectively triples the number of outstanding shares, which the company executes by distributing two additional shares for each one outstanding. In a 3:2 stock split, one additional share is issued for every two outstanding.

In a stock dividend, additional shares, usually expressed as a percentage of the outstanding shares, are issued to the stockholders. Large stock dividends have essentially the same effect as stock splits. Both a 100 percent stock dividend and a 2:1 stock split, for example, double the number of outstanding shares. Similarly, both a 50 percent stock dividend and a 3:2 stock split increase outstanding shares by 50 percent. Professional accounting standards recommend that relatively large stock dividends (over 25 percent) be referred to as **stock splits in the form of dividends.** Stock splits and stock splits in the form of dividends are relatively common. *Accounting Trends and Techniques* (AICPA, 2000) reports that, of the 600 major U.S. companies surveyed, 54 (9 percent) reported a stock split or a large stock dividend during 1999. Of those issuances, 5 were less than 3:2, 8 were 3:2, 36 were 2:1, and 5 were greater than 2:1. Relatively small stock dividends (less than 25 percent), which are somewhat less common than either stock splits or stock splits in the form of dividends, are referred to as **ordinary stock dividends.**

The Dow Jones News Service (March 28, 2000) reported: "With the long run bull run, many companies have stock prices well into triple digits that are daunting to investors, particularly retail customers and individuals. When stock prices are perceived as too high, companies may consider stock splits." How do stock splits work, and why might a company want to lower the average market price of its shares?

Accounting for Stock Dividends and Stock Splits. Stock dividends and splits can be divided into three categories: (1) stock dividends (<25 percent), (2) stock splits in the form of dividends (>25 percent), and (3) stock splits. While each category is accounted for in a slightly different manner, it is important to realize that such actions affect neither the corporation's assets nor its liabilities. Only the accounts within the stockholders' equity section (i.e., Common Stock, Additional Paid-In Capital, or Retained Earnings) are adjusted. Below, we cover ordinary stock dividends and stock splits.[12]

Ordinary Stock Dividends. When the board of directors of a corporation declares an ordinary stock dividend, a dividend account is debited for the number of shares to be issued multiplied by the fair market value of the shares, the common stock account is credited for the number of shares issued multiplied by the par value, and Additional Paid-In Capital is credited for the remainder.[13]

To illustrate, assume that ATP International has 100,000 shares of $1 par value common stock outstanding, each with a fair market value of $25. The company would record the following journal entry if the board of directors decided to distribute 5,000 additional shares by declaring a 5 percent stock dividend:

Stock Dividend (−SE)	125,000*	
Common Stock (+SE)		5,000**
Additional Paid-In Capital, Stock Dividend (+SE)		120,000
Declared five percent stock dividend.		

*(100,000 × .05) × $25/sh.
**5,000 sh. × $1/sh.

Note that no assets or liabilities are involved in the transaction; all of the activity takes place in the stockholders' equity section. Retained Earnings is reduced after the stock dividend account is closed at the end of the accounting period, and Common Stock and Additional Paid-In Capital (Stock Dividend) are both increased. In other words, Retained Earnings has been *capitalized.* Earned capital has been transferred to contributed capital. Note also that if the issued stock has a par value of zero, the entire amount of the stock dividend is credited to the additional paid-in capital account.

Stock Splits. Under generally accepted accounting principles, no entry is recorded in the books when stock splits are declared. The corporation should simply record the fact that the par value of the issued stock has been reduced in proportion to the size of the split. A 3:1 split, for example, triples the number of outstanding shares and reduces the par value of each share to one-third of its original value. If the stock has no par value, the par value need not be adjusted.

---

12. We do not cover stock splits in the form of dividends because we believe, as many others do, that they are effectively stock splits and should be accounted for as such.
13. We assume here that the stock dividend is declared and issued on the same day.

To illustrate, when the board of directors of Procter & Gamble approved a 2:1 stock split, the company recorded no journal entry to reflect the action. The 1.35 billion outstanding shares, each with a par value of $2.00, were simply replaced by 2.7 (1.35 × 2) billion outstanding shares, each with a par value of $1.00 ($2.00/2). In other words, one additional share with a par value of $1.00 was distributed for each share outstanding.

Why Do Companies Declare Stock Dividends and Stock Splits?
To understand the reasons behind stock dividends and stock splits, it is important to realize that (1) such actions do not distribute additional assets to the shareholders and (2) their proportionate ownership of the company after the dividend or split is the same as it was before the dividend or split. For example, a shareholder who owns 10 of a company's 100 outstanding shares, each with a market value of $6, owns 10 percent of the company that has a theoretical value of $600 (100 shares × $6). After a 2:1 stock split, the shareholder will own 20 shares of stock, but each share should drop in value to $3 and the 20 shares will still represent only 10 percent of the 200 outstanding shares. Consequently, unlike cash or property dividends, corporations do not declare stock dividends or stock splits to distribute assets to the shareholders.

Perhaps the most popular reason for declaring a stock split or a large stock dividend is to reduce the per-share price of the outstanding shares so that investors can more easily purchase them. When IBM, for example, declared a 4:1 stock split, which quadrupled the number of outstanding shares, the per-share price of IBM stock immediately decreased from $300 to $75 ($300/4). The managements of many corporations believe that such an action encourages better public relations and wider stock ownership. It is also true that a company's stock price often increases after a stock split is announced. *Business Week* (March 16, 1998) noted: "As the market booms, companies are increasingly splitting their stock to both make it more affordable and boost the price."

While it is unclear why stock prices jump when stock splits are announced, many believe that such announcements signal to investors that company management believes that it can maintain the value of the stock in the future. Perhaps this signal provides investors with positive information about the company's prospects that was unavailable prior to the announcement.

The reasons for stock dividends are even less clear. Such distributions have a relatively small effect on the number of outstanding shares and thus do little to reduce per-share prices and broaden stock ownership. They do not place assets in the hands of shareholders, which is supported by the IRS position of not considering stock dividends received as taxable income. It is possible that cash-poor corporations distribute stock dividends instead of cash dividends so that shareholders are at least receiving something, but this strategy could be interpreted simply as a publicity gesture. It may satisfy stockholders, especially if they believe that they have received additional assets, but more likely, it may signal financial problems. Finally, corporations may issue stock dividends to capitalize a portion of Retained Earnings. By reducing Retained Earnings, a stock dividend places a more restrictive limitation on future dividend payments.

During 1999, Hampton Industries declared a 10 percent stock dividend, while during that same year Tandy Corporation and Texas Instruments declared 2:1 stock splits. Briefly explain how each transaction affected the basic accounting equation, and discuss why a company might declare a stock dividend or a stock split.

APPROPRIATIONS OF RETAINED EARNINGS

An **appropriation of retained earnings** is a book entry that serves to restrict a portion of retained earnings from the payment of future dividends. It involves no asset or liability accounts and no stockholders' equity accounts other than Retained Earnings. Such entries are executed either at the discretion of the board of directors or in conformance with the terms of contracts (e.g., debt covenants).

Suppose, for example, that the board of directors of Rosebud Corporation plans to expand the company's main manufacturing plant. To save cash so that the expansion can be funded internally, the board has decided to place a restriction on the payment of future dividends. Accordingly, a resolution is passed stating that the company cannot pay dividends that reduce retained earnings below $300,000. Assuming that the balance in the company's retained earnings account before the appropriation was $500,000, the stockholders' equity section of Rosebud's balance sheet after the resolution would appear as in Figure 12–10.

FIGURE 12–10

Disclosing an appropriation of retained earnings

Rosebud Corporation Balance Sheet December 31, 1999		
STOCKHOLDERS' EQUITY		
Common stock		$1,200,000
Additional paid-in capital		2,500,000
Retained earnings:		
Restricted	$300,000	
Unrestricted	200,000	500,000
Total stockholders' equity		$4,200,000

Appropriations of retained earnings that result from contractual restrictions are disclosed in a similar manner. In practice, most companies simply disclose the existence, nature, and dollar amount of restricted retained earnings. Nordstrom, for example, disclosed the following information about restricted retained earnings in a recent annual report and chose not to adjust the balance of Retained Earnings:

Senior Note Agreements contain restrictive covenants which . . . restrict dividends to shareholders to a formula amount (under the most restrictive formula, approximately $247,342 of retained earnings was not restricted).

NEGATIVE RETAINED EARNINGS: A MIXED SIGNAL

The retained earnings account becomes negative if a company's accumulated net losses plus its dividends from previous years exceeds the accumulation of its past profits. Certainly, negative retained earnings can indicate serious company problems in that it reflects previous losses. However, young and ultimately very successful companies often experience losses in the early years as they start up their businesses, and these companies frequently show negative retained earnings on the balance sheet. At no time in recent history has this phenomenon been more common than in this era of high technology and the Internet. Well-known Internet providers like AOL,

Amazon.com, and others have consistently shown losses, yet their stock prices were extremely strong. Consider, for example, Verity, Inc.—recognized as a leading provider of corporate knowledge retrieval systems. As of the end of 1998, the company had not shown a profit during its relatively short history and had accumulated a deficit in retained earnings of over $51 million. Interestingly, the company's stock jumped from around $6 per share to over $40 in a matter of months during 1999, not because the company showed a profit and reduced its retained earnings deficit, but because the market seemed to sense something (e.g., a strong future) not captured on the financial statements.

The 1999 balance sheet of Yahoo, an Internet search engine, indicated an accumulated deficit in retained earnings of $11 million, down from $72 million the previous year. How could a well-known company like Yahoo accumulate a deficit in retained earnings, and what must have happened in 1999 to reduce the deficit?

RETAINED EARNINGS AND PRIOR PERIOD ADJUSTMENTS

All items on the income statement are eventually transferred (closed) to Retained Earnings, so net income (loss) appears as an adjustment to Retained Earnings on the statement of stockholders' equity. We have noted that the financial effects of other events, such as the declaration of dividends, the appropriation of retained earnings, and the sale of treasury stock for an amount less than its acquisition cost, are also booked directly to the Retained Earnings account.

In addition to these items, generally accepted accounting principles require that the financial effects of several rather unusual events be booked directly to Retained Earnings. The most common such event is the correction in the current period of an accounting error made in a previous period. When such a correction is made, a journal entry is recorded to correct the misstated asset or liability and the other half of the entry serves to increase or decrease Retained Earnings directly. The entry is called a **prior period adjustment.**

Cumulative Translation Adjustment

Multinational U.S. companies often own subsidiaries that operate in other countries and have financial statements that are expressed in foreign currencies. General Mills, for example, has major subsidiaries in France, Holland, Belgium, Spain, Canada, and Latin America, all of which publish their own financial statements denominated in their own local currencies. When General Mills prepares consolidated financial statements at year-end, the financial statements of these subsidiaries must be translated into U.S. dollars and then combined with the accounts of General Mills.

When the financial statements of a subsidiary that operates independently from the parent are translated into U.S. dollars, any gain or loss due to the translation is referred to as a **translation adjustment.** These adjustments are disclosed and accumulated in the stockholders' equity section of the balance sheet.

Translation adjustments can be quite large and either positive or negative. The excerpt below was taken from the 2000 annual report of Minnesota Mining and Manufacturing (dollars in millions):

	2000	1999
Cumulative translation—net		
Balance at beginning of year	*$(694)*	*$(518)*
Translation adjustment	*(220)*	*(176)*
Balance at end of year	*$(914)*	*$(694)*

During 1999 and 2000, the value of the foreign currencies, in general, declined against the U.S. dollar, giving rise to $176 million and $220 million decreases to stockholders' equity. It is important to note also that the translation adjustment each year, while not appearing on the income statement, is considered part of comprehensive income.

The 2000 annual report of Lands' End included the following information.

Accumulated comprehensive income

Beginning balance	$408,399
Net income	48,034
Foreign currency translation	92
Unrealized gains on securities	580
Ending balance	$457,105

What is comprehensive income, and how does it relate to retained earnings?

THE STATEMENT OF STOCKHOLDERS' EQUITY

Generally accepted accounting principles require that the changes during the period in the dollar balances of the separate accounts composing the stockholders' equity section be disclosed in the financial report. A company can either disclose such changes in the footnotes or in a separate financial statement called the **statement of stockholders' equity.** The consolidated statement of stockholders' equity for SUPERVALU stores appears in Figure 12–11.

INTERNATIONAL PERSPECTIVE: THE RISE OF INTERNATIONAL EQUITY MARKETS

We have referred many times in this text to the New York and American Stock Exchanges and the important roles they play in the buying and selling of equity securities in the United States. As the world of business has become internationalized, however, stock exchanges outside the United States have become increasingly important. The stock of J.C. Penney, for example, is traded not only on the New York Exchange, but also on exchanges in Antwerp and Brussels; General Electric is traded in New York, London, and Tokyo; Coca-Cola is traded in Frankfurt in addition to five different exchanges in Switzerland; and American Express stock is listed on no less than fifteen stock exchanges, eleven of which are outside the United States. It is also true that many companies outside the United States list their equity securities on U.S. exchanges. Approximately 50 percent of Sony's equity is held in New York, and each

FIGURE 12-11   Consolidated statement of stockholders' equity

SUPERVALU
Consolidated Statement of Stockholders' Equity
(In Thousands, Except Per Share Data)

	Preferred Stock	Common Stock	Capital in Excess of Par Value	Treasury Stock	Retained Earnings	Total
BALANCES AT FEBRUARY 22, 1997	$ 5,908	$150,670	$ 99	$(231,871)	$1,382,617	$1,307,423
Net earnings	—	—	—	—	230,757	230,757
Sales of common stock under option plans	—	—	(4,123)	51,623	—	47,500
Cash dividends declared on common stock—$.515 per share	—	—	—	—	(63,678)	(63,678)
Compensation under employee incentive plans	—	—	6,951	11,289	—	18,240
Purchase of shares for treasury	—	—	—	(338,337)	—	(338,337)
BALANCES AT FEBRUARY 28, 1998	5,908	150,670	2,927	(507,296)	1,549,696	1,201,905
Net earnings	—	—	—	—	191,338	191,338
Sales of common stock under option plans	—	—	(5,902)	35,497	(3,667)	25,928
Cash dividends declared on common stock—$.5275 per share	—	—	—	—	(63,985)	(63,985)
Compensation under employee incentive plans	—	—	1,057	10,914	—	11,971
Treasury shares exchanged for acquisition	—	—	1,918	2,167	—	4,085
Purchase of shares for treasury	—	—	—	(65,603)	—	(65,603)
BALANCES AT FEBRUARY 27, 1999	5,908	150,670	—	(524,321)	1,673,382	1,305,639
Net earnings	—	—	—	—	242,941	242,941
Sales of common stock under option plans	—	—	(5,181)	10,738	—	5,557
Cash dividends declared on common stock—$.5375 per share	—	—	—	—	(68,952)	(68,952)
Compensation under employee incentive plans	—	—	(1,802)	9,408	—	7,606
Treasury shares exchanged for acquisitions	—	—	139,209	318,293	—	457,502
Redemption of Preferred Stock	(5,908)					(5,908)
Purchase of shares for treasury	—	—	—	(122,906)	—	(122,906)
BALANCES AT FEBRUARY 26, 2000	$ —	$150,670	$132,226	$(308,788)	$1,847,371	$1,821,479

See notes to consolidated financial statements.

year billions of dollars are raised through equity issuances on U.S. stock exchanges by non–U.S. companies. Indeed, a "world stock exchange" seems to be emerging. In the words of Neil Osborn, author of *The Rise of the International Equity:* "It is quite possible to trade in a Japanese stock with a buyer in Saudi Arabia, a seller in London, and a U.S. broker without the transaction going near Tokyo."

The increasing level of international equity trading has important implications for accountants who must provide the financial reports necessary to support this investment activity. Each stock exchange, for example, has different reporting requirements, and issuing companies must prepare their financial statements and supporting disclosures in a manner that conforms to those requirements. To date, the requirements of the U.S. exchanges have been the most difficult to meet, which, in turn, has discouraged many companies from listing their securities on the U.S. exchanges. *The Wall Street Journal* (August 29, 1995) noted that "the major roadblock to foreign companies listing their overseas stock on U.S. exchanges has long been the big difference between accounting standards in the U.S. and abroad."

However, international accounting standards, as set by the International Accounting Standards Committee (IASC), are becoming increasingly important because more and more non–U.S. exchanges are accepting them. In addition, the S.E.C. is under increasing pressure from the New York Stock Exchange and large non–U.S. companies to list firms whose financial statements comply with IASC standards.

REVIEW PROBLEM

The following data pertain to the stockholders' equity transactions of Pike Place Corporation over its first three years of operations: 2001, 2002, and 2003. Transactions are described and followed by the appropriate journal entries. The stockholders' equity section of the balance sheet is shown for each of the three years.

2001

(1) The company issued 1,000 shares of $1 par value stock for $70 per share.

Cash (+A)	**70,000***	
Common Stock (+SE)		**1,000****
Additional Paid-In Capital, C/S (+SE)		**69,000**

Issued common stock.

*1,000 sh. × $70/sh.
**1,000 sh. × $1 par value/sh.

(2) The company issued 500 shares of no par value, $5, cumulative preferred stock for $50 per share.

Cash (+A)	**25,000**	
Preferred Stock (+SE)		**25,000**

Issued preferred stock (500 sh. × $50/sh.).

(3) Net income during the year = $2,000
Dividends = $0

Pike Place Corporation
Balance Sheet
December 31, 2001

STOCKHOLDERS' EQUITY

Preferred stock (500 sh., no par value)	$25,000
Common stock (1,000 sh. @ $1 par value)	1,000
Additional paid-in capital (C/S)	69,000
Retained earnings	2,000
Total stockholders' equity	$97,000

Note: Dividends in arrears on cumulative preferred stock = $2,500 (500 sh. × $5/sh.)

2002

(1) The company purchased 200 treasury (common) shares for $60 per share.

Treasury Stock (−SE)	12,000	
Cash (−A)		12,000

Acquired treasury stock (200 sh. × $60/sh.).

(2) Net income for the year = $20,000
Dividends = $6,600: $5,000 for preferred stockholders [$2,500 dividends in arrears and $2,500 (500 sh. × $5/sh.)] for 2002, and $1,600 for the common stockholders (800 outstanding sh. × $2/sh.). The dividends were declared and paid.

Preferred Dividends (−SE)	5,000	
Common Dividends (−SE)	1,600	
Dividends Payable (+L)		6,600

Declared dividends.

Dividends Payable (−L)	6,600	
Cash (−A)		6,600

Paid dividends.

Pike Place Corporation
Balance Sheet
December 31, 2002

STOCKHOLDERS' EQUITY

Preferred stock (500 sh., no par value)	$25,000
Common stock (1,000 sh. @ $1 par value)	1,000
Additional paid-in capital (C/S)	69,000
Retained earnings	15,400*
Less: Treasury stock (200 sh. × $60/sh.)	(12,000)
Total stockholders' equity	$98,400

$2,000 + $20,000 − $6,600

2003

(1) The company reissued 100 treasury shares for $65 each.

Cash (+A)	6,500*	
Treasury Stock (+SE)		6,000**
Additional Paid-In Capital, T/S (+SE)		500

Reissued treasury stock.

*100 sh. × $65/sh.
**100 sh. × $60/sh.

(2) The company reissued 50 treasury shares for $40 each.

Cash (+A)	2,000*	
Additional Paid-In Capital, T/S (−SE)	500	
Retained Earnings (−SE)	500	
Treasury Stock (+SE)		3,000**
Reissued treasury stock.		

*50 sh. × $40/sh.
**50 sh. × $60/sh.

(3) The company declared a 10 percent stock dividend. There were 950 common shares outstanding at the time of the split, each with a fair market value of $5.

Stock Dividend (−SE)	475*	
Common Stock (+SE)		95**
Additional Paid-In Capital (+SE)		380
Declared stock dividend.		

*Closed to Retained Earnings
**95 sh. × $1 par value/sh.

(4) The company entered into a debt covenant that required a minimum retained earnings balance of $30,000. The board of directors voted to restrict retained earnings of $30,000.

(5) Net income at the end of the year = $35,000
Dividends = $4,590: $2,500 to preferred stockholders and $2,090 to common stockholders (1,045 sh. outstanding × $2/sh.). The dividends were declared but unpaid at year-end.

Preferred Dividends (−SE)	2,500	
Common Dividends (−SE)	2,090	
Dividends Payable (+L)		4,590

Pike Place Corporation
Balance Sheet
December 31, 2003

STOCKHOLDERS' EQUITY

Preferred stock (500 sh., no par value)		$ 25,000
Common stock (1,045 sh. @ $1 par value)		1,045[a]
Additional paid-in capital		69,380[b]
Retained earnings:		
Restricted	$30,000	
Unrestricted	14,835	44,835[c]
Less: Treasury stock		(3,000)[d]
Total stockholders' equity		$137,260

[a]*$1,000 + $45*
[b]*$69,000 + $500 − $500 + $380*
[c]*$15,400 − $500 − $475 + $35,000 − $4,590*
[d]*50 sh. × $60/sh. or $12,000 − $6,000 − $3,000*

SUMMARY OF KEY POINTS

The key points of the chapter are summarized below.

○ *The three forms of financing and their relative importance to major U.S. corporations.*

Companies can generate assets from three sources: (1) borrowings, (2) issuing equity securities, and (3) retaining funds generated through profitable operations. Borrowings are represented by liabilities on the balance sheet, equity issuances are represented by contributed capital (preferred stock, common stock, and additional paid-in capital), and retaining funds is represented by earned capital (retained earnings). Major U.S. corporations generally rely more heavily on liabilities as a form of financing than on the combined total of contributed and earned capital. Earned capital is typically more important than contributed capital.

○ *Distinctions between debt and equity.*

Debt involves a contractual relationship with an outsider. The contract usually states a fixed maturity date, interest charges, security in case of default, and additional provisions designed to protect the interests of the debtholders. Interest is an expense on the income statement and is deductible for tax purposes. In case of liquidation, creditors have rights to the company's assets before owners. Creditors do not vote in the annual election of the board of directors.

Equity involves a relationship with an owner. There is no legal contract, no fixed maturity date, and no periodic interest payment. Dividends are at the discretion of the board of directors. They are not considered an expense on the income statement and are not tax deductible. Equity holders have lower asset priority than debtholders in case of liquidation, but they have a direct voice in the operation of the company, primarily through voting power over the board of directors.

Distinguishing debt from equity is important to investors and creditors because equity investments are generally riskier than debt investments but offer the potential for higher returns. From the company's perspective, issuing debt involves the commitment of future cash outflows, but interest is tax deductible. Issuing equity, while avoiding fixed contractual cash outflows, dilutes the ownership of the existing shareholders and makes it easier for outside investors to gain significant control. From the accountant's perspective, debt and equity are classified in different sections of the balance sheet, and unlike interest payments and debt redemptions, exchanges of equity are never reflected on the income statement.

○ *Economic consequences associated with the methods used to account for stockholders' equity.*

The economic consequences associated with accounting for stockholders' equity arise from the effects of financial ratios that include the dollar amount of stockholders' equity or its components on a company's stock prices, credit rating, or any debt covenants that restrict additional borrowings, the payment of dividends, or the repurchase of outstanding equity shares. Such ratios are also commonly used to define restrictions in debt covenants imposed on management. The use of financial ratios in these ways can encourage management, for example, to structure debt financing in a way that resembles equity so that additional debt need not be reported on the balance sheet. Issuing certain forms of preferred stock and other hybrid securities may represent such a strategy.

⊙ *Rights associated with preferred and common stock and the methods used to account for stock issuances.*

Stock that is preferred as to dividends carries the right, if dividends are declared by the board, to receive a certain specified dividend payment before the common stockholders receive a dividend. If the preferred stock is cumulative and the corporation misses a dividend, dividends in arrears are created in the amount of the missed preferred dividend. In future periods, as dividends are declared, dividends in arrears are paid first to the preferred stockholders, the preferred stockholders are then paid their normal, annual dividend, and finally, the common stockholders are paid from what remains. If the preferred stock carries a participating feature, the preferred stockholders not only receive their initial specified amount, but they also share in the remaining dividends with the common stockholders. Stock that is preferred as to assets carries a claim to the corporation's assets, in case of liquidation, that has higher priority than the claim carried by common stock. In many ways preferred stock resembles debt.

Common stock is characterized by three fundamental rights: (1) the right to receive dividends if they are declared by the board, (2) a residual right to the corporation's assets in case of liquidation, and (3) the right to exert control over corporate management, which is exercised primarily by voting in the election of the board at the annual stockholders' meeting.

When preferred or common stock with no par value is issued for cash, the cash account is debited for the proceeds, and the stock account is credited for the entire dollar amount. When stock with a par (or stated) value is issued for cash, the cash account is debited for the total proceeds, the stock account is credited for the number of shares issued multiplied by the par value per share, and the additional paid-in capital account is credited for the remainder.

⊙ *Distinctions among the market value, book value, and par (stated) value of a share of common stock.*

The market value of a share of stock is the price at which the stock can be purchased and sold on the open market. The book value of a share of stock is equal to the book value of the corporation, as indicated on the balance sheet (stockholders' equity or net assets), less preferred capital and divided by the number of common shares outstanding. The par (stated) value of a share of stock has no relationship to its market value or book value and, for the most part, has limited economic significance.

⊙ *Treasury stock.*

Outstanding common stock is often repurchased by companies. Such stocks are either (1) held in treasury, to be reissued at a later date, or (2) retired. Treasury stock purchases normally must be authorized and approved by the company's board of directors and stockholders. While held in treasury, stock shares carry none of the usual rights of ownership.

Companies purchase treasury stock to support employee compensation plans, to fend off possible takeover attempts, to prepare for merger activity, to increase the market price of the company's outstanding stock, to increase the company's earnings per share (net income/outstanding common shares), and to distribute cash to the shareholders. In general, treasury stock purchases reduce the scale of a company's operations.

When a company purchases its own outstanding common stock under the cost method, a permanent account, called Treasury Stock, is debited for the cost of the purchase. This account is disclosed below retained earnings in the stockholders' equity section of the balance sheet. If treasury stock is reissued at a price greater than its original cost, the cash account is debited for the proceeds, the treasury stock account is credited for the cost, and the difference is credited to the additional paid-in capital (Treasury Stock) account. If treasury stock is reissued at an amount less than the original cost, the cash account is debited for the proceeds, the treasury stock account is credited for the original cost, and Additional Paid-In Capital (Treasury Stock) is debited for the difference, if there is a sufficient balance in the account to cover the difference. If the difference between the cost and the proceeds exceeds the balance in the additional paid-in capital account, Retained Earnings is debited.

⬤   *Cash dividends and dividend strategies followed by corporations.*

Cash dividends represent distributions of cash to the stockholders. When a cash dividend is declared, a cash dividend account is debited and a current liability account, Dividends Payable, is credited on the date of declaration. The dollar amount is equal to the cash dividend per share multiplied by the number of outstanding shares. The dividend account is a temporary account that is closed directly to Retained Earnings at the end of the accounting period. On the date of record, no entry is made in the books of the corporation. The shareholders as of this date are the recipients of the dividends. On the date of payment, the cash dividend is paid, and the dividends payable liability is removed from the balance sheet.

When to declare a dividend and how much to declare depend on the nature, financial condition, and desired image of the company, as well as legal constraints. If dividends are to be paid in cash, the board of directors must first be certain that the corporation has sufficient cash to meet the payment. Some companies have adopted policies of paying no dividends. Such companies reinvest their earnings primarily to support growth without having to rely too heavily on debt and equity financing. Other companies pay quarterly dividends at the rate of a relatively fixed percentage of net income and also attempt to increase their dividend payments consistently from year to year. Some companies consistently increase dividends from year to year, but the distributions do not represent a consistent percentage of net income.

⬤   *Stock dividends and stock splits.*

In a stock split, the number of outstanding shares is simply split into smaller units, which requires the corporation to distribute additional shares. In a stock dividend, additional shares, usually expressed as a percentage of the outstanding shares, are issued to the stockholders. Professional accounting standards recommend that relatively large stock dividends (over 25 percent) be referred to as stock splits in the form of dividends and that relatively small stock dividends (less than 25 percent) be referred to as ordinary stock dividends.

Stock splits or stock dividends in the form of splits are often declared to reduce the per-share price of the outstanding shares so that investors can more easily purchase them. The reasons for small stock dividends are less clear. Such distributions have a relatively small effect on the number of outstanding shares and do little to reduce per-share prices and broaden stock ownership. Corporations that are short of cash may distribute stock dividends instead of cash dividends so that the shareholders are at least receiving something. Corporations may also issue stock dividends to capitalize a portion of retained earnings, rendering them unavailable for future dividends. In any case, the issuance of a stock split or stock dividend does not involve a distribution of assets to the shareholders.

KEY TERMS

Note: Definitions for these terms are provided in the glossary at the end of the text.

Appropriation of retained earnings (p. 537)
Authorized (shares) (p. 522)
Book value (of company/share) (p. 514)
Contributed capital (p. 514)
Cumulative preferred stock (p. 523)
Date of declaration (p. 532)
Date of payment (p. 532)
Date of record (p. 532)
Dilution (p. 518)
Dividends in arrears (p. 523)
Earned capital (p. 514)
Issued (shares) (p. 522)
Leverage (p. 518)
Market-to-book ratio (p. 526)
Market value (of stock) (p. 525)
Net assets (p. 514)
Net worth (p. 514)

Ordinary stock dividends (p. 534)
Outstanding (shares) (p. 522)
Par value (p. 526)
Participating (preferred stock) (p. 524)
Preferred stock as to assets (p. 522)
Preferred stock as to dividends (p. 522)
Prior period adjustment (p. 538)
Residual interest (p. 516)
Statement of stockholders' equity (p. 539)
Stock dividends (p. 532)
Stock options (p. 531)
Stock split (p. 534)
Stock splits in the form of dividends
  (p. 534)
Takeover (p. 518)
Translation adjustment (p. 538)
Treasury stock (p. 518)

ETHICS IN THE REAL WORLD

In both 1998 and 1999, Hampton Industries, a men's clothing manufacturer that relies heavily on low-cost labor in third-world countries, declared 10 percent stock dividends. Although no assets were transferred to shareholders, millions of dollars were transferred from retained earnings to the common stock and paid-in capital accounts. Recently, the company has faced some very difficult times, and in 2000 and 2001, it vio-lated debt covenants and entered into a plan to liqui-date assets. Some have speculated that the board of directors declared the stock dividends to mislead the stockholders into believing that the company was still able to distribute something of value even though prof-its were down and falling fast, perhaps in an attempt to delay an inevitable stock price collapse.

ETHICAL ISSUE Does a stock dividend represent some-thing of value? Was the board of directors acting ethi-cally if it attempted to delay an inevitable stock price collapse by issuing a stock dividend?

INTERNET RESEARCH EXERCISE

Kellogg Company manufactures products on six continents, and these products are sold in more than 160 countries. Review the company's most recent annual report, specifically the statement of stockholders' equity, which can be found at **www.kelloggs.com**. Briefly describe the main transactions between the company and its shareholders over the previous three-year period. Has the company issued stock, declared stock splits, purchased its own shares, or declared divi-dends, and have the company's executives exercised any stock options?

BRIEF EXERCISES

REAL DATA

BE12-1

Inferring stockholders' equity transactions

The information below was taken from the statement of stockholders' equity of May Department Stores (dollars in millions).

	Common Stock	Additional Paid-In Capital	Retained Earnings	Stockholders' Equity
Beginning balance	124		4,461	4,585
Net earnings			755	755
Dividends paid			(305)	(305)
Common stock issued	3	258		261
Purchase of treasury stock				(869)

a.   What portion of net income was paid out in dividends during the year?
b.   Explain how the issuance of common stock affected the basic accounting equation.
c.   Explain how the purchase of treasury stock affected the basic accounting equation.
d.   How much cash was distributed to the company's shareholders during the year?
e.   What was the dollar balance of the retained earnings account on the balance sheet?

REAL DATA

BE12-2

Stock splits and market values

In 1999, Tandy (RadioShack) Corporation announced a 2:1 stock split. Just prior to the split, the company had 97 million shares outstanding, trading at $100 per share.

a.   Estimate the number of shares outstanding and market price per share immediately after the split.
b.   Estimate the company's overall market value, and explain whether you expect that the company's overall market value will change due to the split.

REAL DATA

BE12-3

Treasury stock purchases

The information below was taken from the 1999 annual report of Office Max (dollar amounts in thousands).

	Treasury Shares	Dollar Amount
Balance 1/25/97	0	$0
1997 Share repurchases	100,000	1,279
1998 Share repurchases	8,135,000	77,499
1999 Share repurchases	4,467,100	34,841

a.   At what average price did the company repurchase its shares in 1997?
b.   At what average price did the company repurchase its shares in 1998?
c.   During 1999 the company reissued treasury shares to support employee compensation plans in the amount of $3,154. Compute the dollar amount in the treasury stock account as of the end of 1999.

EXERCISES

E12-1

The effects of transactions on stockholders' equity

The following are possible transactions that affect stockholders' equity:

1.   A company issues common stock above par value for cash.
2.   A company declares a 3-for-1 stock split.
3.   A company repurchases 10,000 shares of its own common stock in exchange for cash.
4.   A company declares and issues a stock dividend. Assume that the fair market value of the stock is greater than the par value.
5.   A company reissues 1,000 shares of treasury stock for $75 per share. The stock was acquired for $60 per share.

6. A company pays a cash dividend that had been declared fifteen days earlier.
7. A company generates net income of $250,000.

For each transaction above indicate the following:

a. The accounts within the stockholders' equity section that would be affected.
b. Whether these accounts would be increased or decreased.
c. The effect (increase, decrease, or no effect) of the transaction on total stockholders' equity.

E12-2

Debt, contributed and earned capital, and the classification of preferred stock

The balance sheet of Lamont Bros. follows:

ASSETS		LIABILITIES AND STOCKHOLDERS' EQUITY	
Current assets	**$ 85,000**	**Current liabilities**	**$ 52,000**
Noncurrent assets	**315,000**	**Long-term note payable**	**35,000**
		Preferred stock	**50,000**
		Common stock	**80,000**
		Additional paid-in capital:	
		Preferred stock	**50,000**
		Common stock	**100,000**
		Retained earnings	**113,000**
		Less: Treasury stock	**(80,000)**
		Total liabilities and	
Total assets	**$400,000**	**stockholders' equity**	**$400,000**

a. What portions of Lamont's assets were provided by debt, contributed capital, and earned capital? Reduce contributed capital by the cost of the treasury stock.
b. Compute the company's debt/equity ratio. Compute the debt/equity ratio if the preferred stock issuance was classified as a long-term debt.
c. In most states, to what dollar amount of dividends would the company be limited?

E12-3

Authorizing and issuing preferred and common stock

Deming Contractors was involved in the following events involving stock during 2003:

1. Authorized to issue: (a) 100,000 shares of $100 par value, 8 percent preferred stock; (b) 150,000 shares of no-par, $5 preferred stock; and (c) 250,000 shares of $5 par value, common stock.
2. Issued 10,000 shares of $5 par value common stock for $30 per share.
3. Issued 25,000 shares of the $100 par value preferred stock for $150 per share.
4. Issued 50,000 shares of no-par preferred stock for $50 each.

Prepare entries, if appropriate, for each event, describe how each event affects the basic accounting equation, and explain the economic significance of par value.

REAL DATA

E12-4

The effects of treasury stock purchases on important financial ratios

At the end of fiscal 2000, Wendy's purchased approximately 7 million shares of its outstanding stock for $187 million. Immediately before the purchase, 126 million shares were outstanding, and the financial statements appeared as below (dollars in billions).

INCOME STATEMENT:

Revenues	$2.072
Expenses	1.905
Net income	.167

BALANCE SHEET

Assets	$2.070
Liabilities	.818
Stockholders' equity	1.252

a. Provide the entry for the treasury stock purchase.
b. Compute the ratio of total liabilities to stockholders' equity before and after the purchase.

c. Compute earnings per share before and after the purchase.

d. Comment on why a company might choose to purchase treasury stock at year-end.

E12–5

Reissuing
treasury stock

Twin Lakes incorporated on April 1, 2003, and was authorized to issue 100,000 shares of $5 par value common stock and 10,000 shares of $8, no-par preferred stock. During the remainder of 2003, the company entered into the following transactions.

1. Issued 25,000 shares of common stock in exchange for $500,000 in cash.
2. Issued 5,000 shares of preferred stock in exchange for $60,000 in cash.
3. Purchased 3,000 common shares for $15 per share and held them in the form of treasury stock.
4. Sold 1,000 treasury shares for $18 per share on the open market.
5. Issued 1,000 treasury shares to executives who exercised stock options for a reduced price of $5 per share.

The company entered into no other transactions that affected stockholders' equity during 2003.

a. Prepare entries for each of the transactions.

b. Assume that Twin Lakes generated $500,000 in net income in 2003 and did not declare any dividends during 2003. Prepare the stockholders' equity section of the balance sheet as of December 31, 2003.

E12–6

Reissuing
treasury stock

The stockholders' equity section of Rodman Corporation as of December 31, 2002, follows:

Common stock	**$ 80,000**
Additional paid-in capital (C/S)	**10,000**
Retained earnings	**60,000**
Total stockholders' equity	**$150,000**

During 2003, the company entered into the following transactions:

1. Purchased 1,000 shares of treasury stock for $60 per share.
2. As part of a compensation package, reissued half of the treasury shares to executives who exercised stock options for $20 per share.
3. Reissued the remainder of the treasury stock on the open market for $66 per share.

a. Provide the journal entries for each transaction, and prepare the stockholders' equity section of the balance sheet as of December 31, 2003. Rodman Corporation generated $20,000 in net income during 2003 and did not declare any dividends.

b. What portion of the additional paid-in capital account is attributed to treasury stock transactions?

E12–7

Treasury stock
exceeds contributed
capital

In 1993, Stuart Corporation began operations, issuing 100,000 shares of $1 par value common stock for $25 per share. Since that time, the company has been very profitable. The stockholders' equity section as of December 31, 2002, follows:

Common stock	**$ 100,000**
Additional paid-in capital (C/S)	**2,400,000**
Retained earnings	**4,500,000**
Total stockholders' equity	**$7,000,000**

In 2003, the company entered into a program of buying back some of the outstanding shares. During the year, the company purchased 30,000 outstanding shares at a price of $95 per share.

a. Prepare the journal entry to record the purchase of the treasury shares.

b. Assuming that net income of $350,000 was earned and dividends of $50,000 were declared during the year, prepare the stockholders' equity section of the balance sheet as of the end of 2003.

c. Explain how the dollar value of the treasury stock account can be larger than the dollar amount of contributed capital.

E12–8

Book value per
share, stock
issuances, and
treasury stock
purchases

The condensed 1999 balance sheet of Honeywell International follows (dollars in millions):

Assets	$23,527	Liabilities	$14,928
		Stockholders' equity	8,599
		Total liabilities and	
Total assets	$23,527	stockholders' equity	$23,527

Seven hundred and fifty million shares of common stock and no preferred stock were outstanding. The following requirements are independent:

a. Compute the book value per common share.
b. Compute the book value per common share if the company issues 50 million shares of common stock at $32 per share.
c. Compute the book value per common share if the company issues 50 million shares of common stock at $20 per share.
d. Compute the book value per outstanding share of common stock if the company purchases 50 million shares of treasury stock at $32 per share.
e. Compute the book value per outstanding share of common stock if the company purchases 50 million shares of treasury stock at $20 per share.
f. What effect does issuing stock have on the book value of the outstanding shares? Upon what does this effect depend?
g. What effect does purchasing treasury stock have on the book value of the outstanding shares? Upon what does this effect depend?

E12–9

Inferring equity
transactions from
the statement of
stockholders' equity

The information below was taken from the statement of stockholders' equity of Chinook Furs:

	2003	2002
Preferred stock (no par)	$ 700	$400
Common stock ($1 par value)	1,000	900
Additional paid-in capital:		
Common stock	40	20
Treasury stock	10	—
Less: Treasury stock	130	150

Provide the journal entries for the following:

a. The issuance of preferred stock during 2003.
b. The issuance of common stock during 2003.
c. The sale of treasury stock during 2003.

E12–10

Inferring equity
transactions from
the statement of
stockholders' equity

The information below was taken from the statement of stockholders' equity of Zielow Siding as of December 31, 2003. The par value of the Zielow stock is $5, and as of the beginning of 2003, the company held 400 shares in treasury.

	Common Stock	Additional Paid-In Capital	Retained Earnings	Treasury Stock
Beginning balances	$10,000	$25,000	$34,000	$ 8,000
Acquisition of Timeco	5,000	23,000		
Treasury share purchases				4,000
Exercised stock options	1,000	800		
Net income			5,600	
Cash dividends			(3,520)	
Ending balances	$16,000	$48,800	$36,080	$12,000

a. Zielow issued common stock at one time prior to 2003. How many shares were issued and at what price per share?
b. Zielow purchased treasury stock at one time prior to 2003. How many shares were purchased and at what price?

c. During 2003, Zielow acquired Timeco and issued its own shares as payment in the transaction. How many shares were issued and what was the market value of Timeco at the time of the acquisition?

d. At what price were the stock options exercised, and how did that price compare to the market value of Zielow stock at the time?

e. Compute the per-share dividend rate paid by Zielow during 2003. Assume that treasury shares acquired in 2003 were purchased at the same price per share prior to 2003.

E12–11

Inferring equity transactions from the statement of stockholders' equity

The information below was taken from the statement of stockholders' equity of Kidd Sports as of December 31, 2003. The par value of Kidd stock is $1, and as of the beginning of 2003, the company held 1,500 shares in treasury.

	Common Stock	Additional Paid-In Capital	Retained Earnings	Treasury Stock
Beginning balances	$8,000	$32,000	$27,000	$18,000
Exercised stock options			(2,750)	(3,000)
Net income			5,600	
Cash dividends			(3,500)	
Stock dividend	700	9,800	(10,500)	
Ending balances	$8,700	$41,800	$15,850	$15,000

a. Kidd issued common stock at one time prior to 2003. How many shares were issued and at what price per share?

b. Kidd purchased treasury stock at one time prior to 2003. How many shares were purchased and at what price?

c. At what price were the stock options exercised, and how did that price compare to the market value of Kidd stock at the time? Assume that the stock options were exercised immediately prior to the issuance of the stock dividend, which was recorded at market value.

d. Compute the per-share dividend rate paid by Kidd during 2003, assuming that the cash dividends were declared prior to the stock dividend but after the stock options were exercised.

E12–12

Issuing cash dividends on outstanding common stock

The board of directors of Enerson Manufacturing is in the process of declaring a dividend. The company is considering paying a cash dividend of $12 per share. Enerson Manufacturing is authorized to issue 800,000 shares of common stock. The company has issued 375,000 shares to date and has reacquired 50,000 shares. These 50,000 shares are held in treasury.

a. How many shares of common stock are eligible to receive a dividend?

b. Assume that the board declares the dividend. Prepare the appropriate journal entries on the (1) date of declaration, (2) date of record, and (3) date of payment.

E12–13

Cumulative preferred stock and dividends in arrears

The stockholders' equity section of Mayberry Corporation, as of the end of 2003, follows. Mayberry began operations in 1999. The 5,000 shares of preferred stock have been outstanding since 1999.

Preferred stock (10,000 sh. authorized, 5,000 issued,	
** cumulative, nonparticipating, $5 dividends, $10 par value)**	$ 50,000
Common stock (500,000 sh. authorized, 200,000 sh. issued,	
** 50,000 held in treasury, no par value)**	1,600,000
Additional paid-in capital (P/S)	140,000
Retained earnings	110,000
Less: Treasury stock	(80,000)
** Total stockholders' equity**	$1,820,000

The company has paid the following total cash dividends since 1999:

1999	$ 0
2000	30,000
2001	80,000
2002	15,000
2003	40,000

a. Compute the dividends paid to the preferred and common stockholders for each of the years since 1999.
b. Compute the balance of dividends in arrears as of the end of each year.
c. Should dividends in arrears be considered a liability? Why or why not?

E12–14

Stock dividends and stock splits

The stockholders' equity section of Pioneer Enterprises as of December 31, 2003, follows:

Common stock (10,000 shares issued @ $6 par)	**$ 60,000**
Additional paid-in capital (C/S)	**100,000**
Retained earnings	**60,000**
Less: Treasury stock (2,000 shares @ $12)	**(24,000)**
Total stockholders' equity	**$196,000**

Prepare journal entries for the following *independent* transactions:

a. The company declares and distributes a 2 percent stock dividend on the outstanding shares. The market price of the stock is $70 per share.
b. The company declares a 3:2 stock split on the outstanding shares.
c. The company declares a 10 percent stock dividend on the outstanding shares. The market price of the stock is $80 per share.
d. The company declares a 2:1 stock split on the outstanding shares.
e. Compute the ratio of contributed capital to earned capital after independently considering each of the four actions listed above. Reduce contributed capital by the cost of the treasury stock. Comment on the difference between a stock dividend and a stock split.

E12–15

Why do companies declare stock dividends?

The December 31, 2000, balances in Retained Earnings and Additional Paid-In Capital for Railway Shippers Company are $135,000 and $50,000, respectively. Five thousand, $10 par value common shares are outstanding with a market value of $85 each. The company's cash position at year-end is lower than usual, so the board of directors is considering issuing a stock dividend instead of the normal cash dividend. They are considering the three options listed below.

Option 1: A 10 percent stock dividend: 500 new shares would be issued.
Option 2: A 20 percent stock dividend: 1,000 new shares would be issued.
Option 3: A 2:1 stock split: 5,000 new shares would be issued.

a. Prepare the journal entries for Options 1 and 2 above, and comment on why these alternatives may not be attractive. Why do companies issue stock dividends?
b. What effect would Option 3 have on the financial statements?
c. Why do companies split their stock?

E12–16

Appropriating retained earnings

Taylor Manufacturing entered into a borrowing arrangement that requires the company to maintain a retained earnings balance of $500,000. The company also wishes to finance internally a major plant addition in the not-too-distant future. Accordingly, the board of directors has decided to appropriate $350,000 of the retained earnings balance. Prior to the board's action, the balance in the retained earnings account was $800,000.

a. Why would the board of directors appropriate retained earnings in the situation described above, and why might an auditor insist that it be done?
b. Show how retained earnings would be disclosed on the balance sheet after the appropriation.
c. Discuss the constraints with respect to dividend payments that have been imposed on the board by the debt covenant and the appropriation.

PROBLEMS

P12–1

Hybrid securities and debt covenants

Lambert Corporation issued 1,000 shares of $100 par value, 8 percent, cumulative, nonparticipating preferred stock for $100 each. The stock is preferred to assets, redeemable after five years at a prespecified price, and the preferred stockholders do not vote at the annual stockholders' meeting. The condensed balance sheet of Lambert prior to the issuance follows:

Assets	$580,000	Liabilities	$250,000
		Stockholders' equity	330,000
		Total liabilities and	
Total assets	$580,000	stockholders' equity	$580,000

Lambert has entered into a debt agreement that requires the company to maintain a debt equity ratio of less than 1:1.

REQUIRED:

a. Provide the journal entry to record the preferred stock issuance, and compute the resulting debt/equity ratio, assuming that the preferred stock is considered an equity security.
b. Compute the debt/equity ratio, assuming that the preferred stock is considered a debt security.
c. What incentives might the management of Lambert have to classify the issuance as equity instead of debt? Do you think that the issuance should be classified as debt or equity? What might Lambert's external auditors think?

P12–2

The effects of treasury stock transactions on important financial ratios

The balance sheet of Alex Bros. follows:

Assets	$840,000	Liabilities	$300,000
		Preferred stock	50,000
		Common stock	300,000
		Additional paid-in capital (C/S)	100,000
		Retained earnings	130,000
		Less: Treasury stock	(40,000)
		Total liabilities and	
Total assets	$840,000	stockholders' equity	$840,000

Of the 200,000 common shares authorized, 50,000 shares were issued for $8 each when the company began operations. There have been no common stock issuances since; 45,000 shares are currently outstanding and 5,000 shares are held in treasury. Net income for the year just ended was $45,000.

REQUIRED:

a. Compute the par value of the issued common shares.
b. Compute the book value of each common share.
c. At what average price were the treasury shares purchased?
d. Alex is considering reissuing the 5,000 treasury shares at the present market price of $10 per share. What effect would this action have on the company's debt/equity ratio, book value per outstanding share, and earnings-per-share ratio?

P12–3

The significance of par value

Several independent transactions are listed below.

1. 10,000 shares of no-par common stock are issued for $50 per share.
2. 10,000 shares of $1 par value common stock are issued for $40 per share.

3. 10,000 shares of $10 par value common stock are issued for $30 per share.
4. 5,000 shares of no-par preferred stock are issued for $80 per share.

REQUIRED:
a. Prepare journal entries for each transaction.
b. What is the significance of par value from a financial accounting standpoint? Is par value significant in any economic sense?

P12–4

Cash and stock dividends

Royal Company is currently considering declaring a dividend to its common shareholders, according to one of the following plans:

1. Declare a cash dividend of $15 per share.
2. Declare a 10 percent stock dividend. Royal Company would distribute one share of common stock for every 10 shares of common stock currently held. The company's common stock is currently selling for $50 per share.

Royal Company is authorized to issue 100,000 shares of $10 par value common stock. To date, the company has issued 55,000 shares and is currently holding 8,000 shares in treasury stock.

REQUIRED:
a. How many shares of common stock are eligible to receive a dividend?
b. Prepare the entries necessary on the date of declaration, date of record, and the date of payment for the cash dividend.
c. Prepare the entry to record the stock dividend, assuming that the dividend is declared and issued on the same date.
d. Describe how each dividend would affect Royal's debt/equity ratio.
e. Which of the two dividends would you as a shareholder prefer to receive? Why?

P12–5

Dividend payments and preferred stock

The following information was extracted from the financial records of Maverick Corporation:

Preferred stock: 15,000 shares outstanding, 10 percent, $50 par value
Common stock: 50,000 shares outstanding, $15 par value

Maverick began operations on January 1, 1997. The company has paid the following amounts in cash dividends over the past seven years:

1997	$ 65,000
1998	100,000
1999	70,000
2000	50,000
2001	125,000
2002	110,000
2003	99,000

REQUIRED:
Prepare a sheet to contain the following schedule.

Year	Total Dividends Declared	Dividends to Preferred	Dividends to Common	Dividend per Share (Preferred)	Dividend per Share (Common)

a. Complete this schedule for each year from 1997 through 2003, assuming that the preferred stock is noncumulative and nonparticipating.
b. Complete this schedule for each year from 1997 through 2003, assuming that the preferred stock is cumulative and nonparticipating.

P12–6

The maximum dividend

The following selected financial information was extracted from the December 31, 2002 financial records of Cotter Company:

	Debit	Credit
Cash	25,000	
Short-term investments (2,500 shares of Oreton Corporation)	80,000	
Common stock ($10 par value, 100,000 shares authorized, 50,000 issued)		500,000
Additional paid-in capital (C/S)		100,000
Retained earnings (before closing)		245,000
Net income for 2002		43,000

The company's board of directors is currently contemplating declaring a dividend. The company's common stock is presently selling for $40 per share.

REQUIRED:

a. Given the present financial position of Cotter Company, how large a cash dividend can the board of directors declare?
b. How large a stock dividend can the board legally declare?
c. Assume that the dividends are declared and issued on the same day. Prepare the journal entry to record the maximum dividend in each case above.
d. If the company sold its short-term investments, how large a cash dividend could it declare and pay? The current selling price of Oreton Corp. is $50 per share.

P12–7

Stock splits and stock dividends

Stevenson Enterprises is considering the following items:

1. The company may declare a 10 percent stock dividend, issuing an additional share of common stock for every ten shares outstanding; the common stock is currently selling for $25 per share.
2. The company may issue a 2:1 stock split.

Prior to these events, Stevenson Enterprises reports the following:

Common stock ($6 par value, 650,000 shares authorized, 70,000 issued, 60,000 outstanding, and 10,000 held as treasury stock)	$ 420,000
Additional paid-in capital (C/S)	525,000
Retained earnings	695,000
Less: Treasury stock	(100,000)
Total stockholders' equity	$1,540,000

REQUIRED:

a. Assume that Stevenson Enterprises declares the stock dividend but not the stock split. Prepare the necessary journal entry. Prepare the stockholders' equity section of the balance sheet to reflect the stock dividend.
b. Assume that Stevenson Enterprises declares the stock split but not the stock dividend. Prepare the stockholders' equity section of the balance sheet to reflect the stock split.
c. Assume that Stevenson Enterprises declares the stock dividend and then the stock split. Prepare the necessary journal entries. Prepare the stockholders' equity section of the balance sheet to reflect both actions.
d. Assume that Stevenson Enterprises declares the stock split and then the stock dividend. Prepare the necessary journal entries. Prepare the stockholders' equity section of the balance sheet to reflect both actions. Assume that the market price of Stevenson's stock drops to $12.50 per share following the stock split.

P12-8

Stock issuances

The 1999 annual report (statement of stockholders' equity) of Starbucks, the coffee maker, included the following information concerning its common stock (amounts in thousands).

	Shares	Dollar amount
Beginning balance	**161,116**	**$391,284**
1998:		
Exercised stock options	**2,834**	**$31,245**
Sale of common stock	**272**	**4,649**
1999:		
Exercised stock options	**3,523**	**52,420**
Sale of common stock	**492**	**9,386**

REQUIRED:

a. Compute the average prices at which the shares in 1998 and 1999 were issued.
b. Were the shares to exercise stock options issued at a higher or lower price than the shares issued for the sale of common stock? Explain how the two sets of shares could be issued at different prices.

P12-9

Miscellaneous stockholders' equity transactions

The stockholders' equity section of Rudnicki Corp. contained the following balances as of December 31, 2002:

Preferred stock (10%, $10 par value, cumulative)	**$1,000**
Preferred stock (12%, $10 par value, noncumulative)	**1,500**
Common stock ($1 par value, 5,000 shares	
authorized, 3,500 issued and 400	
held in treasury)	**3,500**
Additional paid-in capital:	
Preferred stock (10%)	**1,050**
Preferred stock (12%)	**1,275**
Common stock	**2,345**
Retained earnings	**4,256**
Less: Treasury stock	**(5,750)**
Total stockholders' equity	**$9,176**

During 2003, Rudnicki Corp. entered into the following transactions affecting stockholders' equity:

1. On May 13, the company repurchased 50 shares of its common stock in the open market at $20 per share.
2. On September 26, the company issued 200 shares of its 10 percent preferred stock at $19 per share.
3. On October 19, the company reissued 30 shares of the stock held in treasury. They sold for $22 per share; all of the shares reissued were purchased prior to May 13 for $12 per share.
4. On December 2, the company declared a cash dividend of $750, which was paid on December 27. The company has not declared a dividend since 1998. (Rudnicki Corp. uses a separate dividend account for each type of stock.)
5. On December 27, the company pays the dividend declared on December 2.
6. On December 29, the company declares a 2:1 stock split on the company's common stock.

REQUIRED:

a. Prepare the necessary entries for each transaction.
b. Assume that Rudnicki Corp. earned net income of $899 during 2003. Prepare the stockholders' equity section as of December 31, 2003.

P12–10

Inferring transactions from the balance sheet

The stockholders' equity section of Buzytown Industries balance sheet reports the following:

	2003	2002
Preferred stock (9%, $100 par value)	$ 200,000	$ 110,000
Common stock ($10 par value, 750,000 shares authorized, 90,000 issued and 5,000 held in treasury)	900,000	750,000
Additional paid-in capital:		
Preferred stock	150,000	35,000
Common stock	465,000	298,000
Retained earnings	575,000	495,000
Less: Treasury stock	(110,000)	—
Total stockholders' equity	$2,180,000	$1,688,000

REQUIRED:

a. How many shares of preferred stock were issued during 2003? What was the average issue price?

b. How many shares of common stock were issued during 2003? What was the average issue price?

c. Prepare the entry to record the repurchase of the company's own stock during 2003. What was the average repurchase price?

d. Assume that the treasury shares were purchased on the last day of 2003. Did the purchase increase or decrease the book value of the outstanding shares? By how much?

P12–11

Inferring stockholders' equity transactions from information on the balance sheet

Tracey Corporation reports the following in its December 31, 2002, financial report:

	2002	2001
Cumulative preferred stock (10%, $100 par value)	$ 400,000	$ 400,000
Common stock ($10 par value, 11,000 shares authorized, issued, and outstanding)	110,000	70,000
Additional paid-in capital:		
Common stock	625,000	500,000
Treasury stock	124,000	55,000
Retained earnings	975,000	250,000
Less: Treasury stock	(84,000)	(105,000)
Total stockholders' equity	$2,150,000	$1,170,000

The total balance in Treasury Stock on December 31, 2001, represents the acquisition of 1,500 shares of common stock on March 3, 2000.

REQUIRED:

a. Compute the number of shares of common stock issued during 2002.

b. Compute the average market price of the common shares issued during 2002.

c. Assume that Tracey Corporation earned net income of $2 million during 2002. Compute the amount of dividends that were declared during 2002.

d. If Tracey Corporation did not declare or pay any dividends during 2001, and again assuming a net income during 2002 of $2 million, compute the amount declared as dividends to common stockholders during 2002.

e. Prepare the entry that would have been necessary on March 3, 2000, to record the purchase of the treasury stock.

f. Assume that all shares of treasury stock reissued during 2002 were reissued at the same time and at the same price. Prepare the entry to record the reissuance of the treasury stock.

g. At what per-share price was the treasury stock reissued?

P12–12

Stockholders'
equity over a
four-year period

Aspen Industries incorporated in the state of Colorado on March 23, 2000. The company was authorized to issue 1 million shares of $6 par value common stock. Since the date of incorporation, Aspen Industries has entered into the following transactions that affected contributed and earned capital:

1. On March 23, 2000, the company issued 50,000 shares of common stock in exchange for $15 per share.
2. On December 5, 2000, the company issued a 10 percent stock dividend. The market value of the stock is $18 per share.
3. On May 6, 2001, the company issued 60,000 shares of common stock in exchange for $22 per share.
4. On September 24, 2001, the company repurchased 15,000 shares of its own stock for $25 per share.
5. On December 1, 2001, the company reissued 5,000 shares held in treasury for $27 per share.
6. On February 14, 2002, the company declared a 3:1 stock split and adjusted the par value of the stock. (*Hint:* Consider the effect of the stock split on treasury stock.)
7. On August 19, 2002, the company reissued 8,000 shares held in treasury for $10 per share.
8. On December 27, 2002, the company declared a cash dividend of $50,000.
9. On January 3, 2003, the company paid the dividend declared on December 27, 2002.
10. On October 31, 2003, the company reissued 2,000 shares held in treasury for $15 per share.

REQUIRED:

a. Prepare the necessary journal entries to record these transactions.
b. Prepare the stockholders' equity section of Aspen's balance sheet as of December 31, 2003. Assume that net income for 2000, 2001, 2002, and 2003 was $400,000, $100,000, $100,000, and $20,000, respectively.

P12–13

Blocking takeovers
and treasury stock
purchases

Five shareholders together own 35 percent of the outstanding stock of Edmonds Industries. The remaining 65 percent is divided among several thousand stockholders. There are 400,000 shares of Edmonds stock currently outstanding. A condensed balance sheet follows:

ASSETS		LIABILITIES AND STOCKHOLDERS' EQUITY	
Cash	$ 3,150,000	Liabilities	$ 1,250,000
Other current assets	4,200,000	Common stock	8,000,000
Noncurrent assets	8,220,000	Retained earnings	6,320,000
		Total liabilities and	
Total assets	$15,570,000	stockholders' equity	$15,570,000

It has become known that Vadar, Inc., is planning to take over Edmonds by purchasing a controlling interest of the outstanding stock. Vadar hopes to gain enough control to elect a new board of directors and replace Edmonds' current management. The current board of directors, on which the five major stockholders serve, is considering how to block the apparent takeover attempt.

REQUIRED:

a. Describe how the company might be able to block the takeover attempt through a program of treasury stock purchases. How many shares would the company need to purchase to concentrate ownership enough to keep Vadar from acquiring a controlling interest? Assume that the other members of the board own no stock.
b. The current market price of the outstanding stock is $45, but the board feels that any major buyback would have to be at a premium—approximately $50 per share. How much cash would Edmonds need to purchase enough shares to block the takeover attempt?

(*Continued*)

c. Assume that Edmonds was able to borrow $4 million and used the cash to buy back the necessary number of shares. Prepare the balance sheet of Edmonds after stock had been purchased.

d. Compute the debt/equity ratio for Edmonds both before and after the treasury stock purchase. Comment on the effect of the purchase on the company's financial position.

P12–14

Bankruptcy and protecting the interests of the creditors

The balance sheet of Natathon International is provided below.

ASSETS		LIABILITIES AND STOCKHOLDERS' EQUITY	
Current assets	$200,000	Liabilities	$400,000
Fixed assets	500,000	Common stock	150,000
		Additional paid-in capital	50,000
		Retained earnings	100,000
		Total liabilities and	
Total assets	$700,000	stockholders' equity	$700,000

Although the balance sheet appears reasonably healthy, Natathon is on the verge of ceasing operations. Appraisers have estimated that, while current assets are worth $200,000, the fixed assets of the company can be sold for only $450,000. There are 1,000 outstanding shares of common stock owned by ten stockholders, each with a 10 percent interest (i.e., 100 shares). Before ceasing operations, the board of directors, which is comprised primarily of the major stockholders, is considering several alternative courses of action.

1. Liquidate the assets, declare a $250-per-share dividend, and distribute the remaining assets to the creditors.
2. Liquidate the assets, declare a $400-per-share dividend, and distribute the remaining assets to the creditors.
3. Liquidate the assets, purchase the outstanding shares for $250 each, and distribute the remaining assets to the creditors.
4. Liquidate the assets, and purchase the outstanding shares for $650 each.

REQUIRED:

a. Prepare the journal entry to reflect the write-down of the fixed assets.
b. Prepare the journal entry to accompany each of the alternative courses of action.
c. Comment on the legality of each of the board's proposals, and explain how the assets should be distributed after liquidation.

ISSUES FOR DISCUSSION

REAL DATA

ID12–1

Do stock dividends represent economic exchanges between a corporation and its shareholders?

In 1999, Hampton Industries declared a 10 percent stock dividend. After the stock dividend, the number of shares outstanding increased to approximately 6.2 million. Assume that the stock dividend was declared and paid on the same day.

REQUIRED:

a. How many shares of stock were outstanding prior to the dividend?
b. The market price of the stock was approximately $4 per share and the par value was $1.00 per share on the day the dividend was declared and paid. Provide the journal entry to record the distribution.
c. Compute the value of Hampton if all outstanding shares, prior to the stock dividend, could have been sold for $24 each. Using this value, compute the per-share value of the company's outstanding shares after the stock dividend.

(Continued)

d. Assume that Mr. Jones owned 1 million shares prior to the stock dividend. How many shares did Mr. Jones own after the stock dividend? What percent of the company did Mr. Jones own before and after the stock dividend? What was the value of Mr. Jones's total shareholdings before and after the stock dividend based on the amounts from part (c)?

e. Does a stock dividend actually represent an economic exchange between a corporation and its shareholders? Why or why not?

f. Provide several reasons why a company would issue a stock dividend.

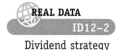

ID12–2

Dividend strategy

When companies cut dividends, it is usually a bad sign for the stock. But apparently not at Monsanto. Several years ago, the company cut its dividend and the stock price went up.

REQUIRED:

Explain how a dividend cut could lead to increasing stock prices.

ID12–3

Economic consequences of treasury stock purchases and cash dividends

The Wall Street Journal once reported, "Philip Morris Cos., in an aggressive move to boost its stock price, announced a $6 billion stock buyback plan and raised its quarterly dividend nearly 20%. . . . The announcement, which came after a regularly scheduled board meeting, raised the company's stock to a 52-week high. . . . Separately, rating agencies Standard & Poor's Rating Group and Moody's Investors Service Inc. confirmed their ratings on Philip Morris's debt. While both agencies said Philip Morris is continuing to generate strong cash flow, Moody's . . . placed Philip Morris at the low end of its current rating level."

REQUIRED:

Explain how this announcement can increase Philip Morris's stock price while at the same time reduce its credit rating.

ID12–4

Treasury stock purchases

Forbes (April 21, 1997) reported that, "U.S. corporations are announcing share buyback programs at a record pace. Last year, the total value of such announcements was $176 billion, up from $74 billion the year before—and up from just $20 billion as recently as 1991. . . . This means that almost the entire supply of stock from new stock offerings is being offset by corporate repurchase programs. . . . According to perhaps the best known study on the subject, the stock of the average corporation repurchasing its stock outperforms the rest of the market by 13 percent over the four years following the announcement of the repurchasing program. Even better, high book-to-price stocks that are being repurchased beat the market by 45 percent over the subsequent four years."

REQUIRED:

a. Explain why companies repurchase their own stock.

b. Provide some rationale for why the stock of companies that repurchase their own stock outperforms the rest of the market.

c. What is a high book-to-price stock, and why might such stocks perform even better?

ID12–5

Treasury stock

Business Week (April 13, 1998) noted that companies are saving their stockholders billions in taxes by buying back stock rather than paying dividends, and the article cites aggressive buyback programs by General Motors, Texaco, and Intel. The article closes with a CFO commenting that "stock buybacks should be a standard part of managing the balance sheet and the company."

REQUIRED:

a. Explain how a stock buyback affects the basic accounting equation and the balance sheet. Choose several key ratios (e.g., return on equity, return on assets, capital structure leverage) and explain how buybacks affect their values.

b. Stock buybacks and dividends both put cash in the hands of shareholders. How is it that stock buybacks save taxes for shareholders?

REAL DATA

ID12–6

Contracts based
on net worth

For twenty years, Westinghouse Electric Corp. used PCBs in the manufacture of electrical capacitors at its plant in Bloomington, Indiana. A federal consent decree has ordered the company to be prepared to build an incinerator in the future to destroy the PCB-contaminated materials. The decree, with which Westinghouse agrees, contains a clause stating that if Westinghouse's net worth (balance sheet assets less balance sheet liabilities) drops to $1.9 billion, the company is required to place in escrow (set aside) $325 million to ensure that funds will be available if and when the incinerator is built.

A pronouncement from the FASB required that Westinghouse as well as other companies change the way in which they account for certain employee retirement costs. After adopting this mandated change, Westinghouse's net worth plunged to $1.85 billion, which is below the dollar amount indicated in the consent decree. According to the agreement, therefore, Westinghouse should transfer $325 million to an escrow account. Westinghouse has refused to make the payment, however, claiming that the reduction in net worth was due to a new accounting standard not in effect at the time the agreement was signed.

REQUIRED:

Discuss this issue from the perspective of the following:

a. An executive of Westinghouse.
b. A representative of the federal government.
c. A resident of Bloomington, Indiana.

REAL DATA

ID12–7

Accounting for
stock options

In 1997, Microsoft presented to its shareholders an alternative income statement, both for the quarter ending in September and the most recent twelve months. For the quarter, the alternative income statement showed a loss of $60 million, while the main income statement showed a profit of $663 million. For the most recent twelve months, the alternative income statement showed a profit that was $0.60 per share lower than that shown by the main income statement. What accounts for the difference? Stock options. Microsoft was the first company to make a serious effort to estimate the real cost of the options that it hands out to nearly every employee. The company's chief financial officer noted in *The New York Times*: "We do recognize that options have a cost, and this is the company's best effort to help investors understand that cost. It is not perfect, but options are too uncertain to lend themselves to a perfect solution."

REQUIRED:

a. Summarize the controversy surrounding the methods used to account for stock options.
b. Explain why some believe that stock options have a cost.
c. Provide some rationale for why Microsoft, rather than other companies, is seriously attempting to communicate that cost to its shareholders.

REAL DATA

ID12–8

Boosting authorized
shares

"Citicorp wants to do it. So do Yahoo, Dow Chemical, Home Depot, Chevron, Motorola, and Amazon.com," reported the *Dow Jones News Service* in describing a major move in corporate America to increase the number of authorized shares. In April of 2000, no fewer than thirty-five companies got approval from their stockholders to increase the pool of authorized shares. Citicorp increased its shares from 6 to 10 billion; Home Depot doubled its shares from 5 to 10 billion; and Yahoo boosted authorized shares from 900 million to 5 billion.

REQUIRED:

a. What are authorized shares and how do they relate to issued and outstanding shares?
b. Why would a company have to seek shareholder approval to increase authorized shares?
c. List several reasons why a company might want to increase the amount of authorized shares.

REAL DATA

ID12-9

Off-balance-sheet
financing and
preferred stock

Business Week once noted that Rupert Murdoch's company, News Corp., was rapidly approaching limits on its ability to borrow, as indicated by covenants imposed by the large group of banks that provided most of the company's financing. An executive close to News Corp. commented that "Murdoch has several ways he can raise off-balance-sheet debt or reduce News Corp.'s debt. One favorite ploy: News Corp. has often raised cash by selling 'preference,' or preferred shares. Fully $1.4 billion worth of such shares were outstanding on June 30."

REQUIRED:

Describe the nature of preferred shares and explain how raising cash by selling them can be interpreted as off-balance-sheet financing. Why would Murdoch pursue such an activity, and how might a creditor adjust the reported financial statements to make them more representative of News Corp.'s financial position?

REAL DATA

ID12-10

Options, taxes, and
corporate earnings

The *National Post* (February 29, 2000) noted: "The earnings of many high-tech companies are expected to rise artificially in future years as a result of the way the federal government is changing the taxation of stock options given to executives as a form of compensation. This artificial growth in earnings will likely lead stock-market investors into believing that companies have made a real improvement in their performance, when it's only a tax effect, experts say."

Federal taxes paid by executives when they exercise options are being reduced. This reduction will increase the value of options, encouraging companies to issue more of them as compensation, instead of cash, to their executives. Since GAAP does not require that companies recognize an expense when the options are issued, compensating executives will become less costly—at least as indicated on the income statement. Net income, in turn, should increase.

REQUIRED:

a.   Why will executives be more inclined to accept stock options as payment instead of cash?
b.   Would you consider the boost in earnings described above as artificial? Discuss.
c.   Do you think that analysts should treat the boost in earnings associated with this change in tax law in the same way they treat other expense reductions?
d.   In what sense do stock options impose a cost on a company?

REAL DATA

ID12-11

Stock split and
stock prices

When Walt Disney Co. declared a 4:1 split of its common stock, the announcement boosted the entertainment company's shares up by $3.50 per share.

REQUIRED:

a.   What is a 4:1 stock split, and how did it affect the financial statements of Walt Disney Co.?
b.   Why should the market value of Disney's stock rise?
c.   *The Wall Street Journal* once reported that the stock split was "a psychological boost and an indication that management has confidence in their performance and that the stock price can be sustained." Explain how this explanation could account for the stock price increase.

REAL DATA

ID12-12

International
accounting
standards

The major roadblock to foreign companies listing their overseas stock on U.S. exchanges has long been the big difference between accounting standards in the United States and abroad. Several of the major accounting policymaking boards, including the FASB, have shown an interest in developing a separate set of accounting standards for companies that wish to raise equity capital outside of their home countries. The New York Stock Exchange (NYSE) appears to favor this proposal because it would encourage a number of foreign companies to have their securities listed in the United States. *The Wall Street Journal* (August 29, 1995) reported that this would "almost double" the NYSE's volume. However, some analysts fear that such a proposal would not be worth the price. That same article noted that "Pat McConnell, Bear, Sterns & Co.'s accounting guru, maintains that this gap would create the potential for big lies in financial statements of companies in foreign countries with weak accounting rules. Indeed, she frets that it would prevent U.S. investors from making meaningful comparisons of U.S. and foreign stocks."

Discuss this issue from the perspective of the following:

a. A foreign company wishing to raise capital in the United States.
b. A U.S. company that has equity securities already listed in the NYSE.
c. An executive of the NYSE.
d. An investment analyst who makes recommendations to buy and sell equity securities.

REAL DATA

ID12–13

The annual report
of Wal-Mart

The 2001 annual report of Wal-Mart is reproduced in Appendix A.

REQUIRED:

Review the 2001 annual report, and answer the following questions.

a. What percent of Wal-Mart's total assets were provided by liabilities, contributed capital, and retained earnings?
b. How many shares of preferred and common shares had been authorized, issued, and outstanding as of the end of 2001?
c. How much cash did the company use to purchase its outstanding stock and pay dividends during 1999, 2000, and 2001? Are those amounts growing or decreasing? Discuss.
d. Within what ranges did Wal-Mart's market price fall during 2000 and 2001, and what amount of dividends per share were paid during that period?
e. What happened in fiscal 1999 to dramatically increase the number of shares outstanding? How was that transaction accounted for?
f. At what average prices did the company issue stock in support of exercised stock options during 1999, 2000, and 2001?
g. What is Wal-Mart's accumulated balance of comprehensive income (other than retained earnings) as of January 31, 2001? What does the balance primarily consist of?

Income and Cash Flows

PART 5

Keebler Foods Company is the second-largest cookie and cracker manufacturer in the United States. From January 1, 1999, to January 1, 2000, company revenues rose from $2.2 billion to $2.6 billion—a nice 18-percent increase. Yet profits dropped by 7 percent, from $94.8 million to $88.2 million. During the same period, cash flows from operations increased from $145 million to $197 million. Three different measures of operating success seemed to be moving in vastly different directions. How can revenues shoot up, while profits lag and operating cash flows jump 36 percent? These kinds of questions are addressed in Chapters 13 and 14, which cover the income statement and statement of cash flows, respectively.

CHAPTER 13
The Complete Income Statement

CHAPTER 14
The Statement of Cash Flows

The Complete Income Statement

KEY POINTS

The following key points are emphasized in this chapter:

Economic consequences associated with reporting net income.

A framework for financing, investing, and operating transactions.

Categories that constitute a complete income statement and how they provide measures of income that address the objectives of financial reporting.

Intraperiod tax allocation.

Earnings per share disclosure on the income statement.

The 1999 annual report of Nabisco, currently a subsidiary of Kraft Foods, reported that net income increased from a $71 million loss in 1998 to a $357 million profit in 1999. Excerpts from the income statement are provided below (dollars in millions).

	1999	1998
Operating revenues	$8,268	$8,400
Operating expenses	(7,975)	(7,941)
Other expense items:		
Restructuring costs	67	(530)
Extraordinary item	(3)	—
Net income	$ 357	$ (71)

Did Nabisco really have such a substantial increase in profits during the year? Is it likely that such improved performance will continue in the future? The answer to this question requires one to analyze the items that comprise net income. Are they expected to occur again in the future, or are they one-time events? The rules governing income statement disclosure, which are covered in this chapter, are designed to help.

This chapter covers (1) the economic consequences associated with income measurement and disclosure, (2) conceptual issues of income measurement, and (3) the disclosure rules that must be followed when preparing an income statement.

THE ECONOMIC CONSEQUENCES ASSOCIATED WITH INCOME MEASUREMENT AND DISCLOSURE

Income is the most common measure of a company's performance. It has been related to stock prices, suggesting that equity investors use income in their decisions to buy and sell equity securities. An article in *The Journal of Accountancy* stated that "[accounting] research . . . has provided some well-established conclusions. Perhaps the most conclusive finding is the importance of accounting income to investors." Almost daily *The Wall Street Journal* reports how stock prices respond to corporate earnings reports.

Income has also been related to bond prices, which indicates that debt investors use income in their decisions to buy and sell corporate bonds. Credit-rating agencies, such as Standard & Poor's, Moody's, and Dun & Bradstreet, use income numbers to establish credit ratings. In response to "problematic profitability," for example, Standard & Poor's lowered the credit rating on McDonnell Douglas bonds from BBB+ to BBB which, in turn, lowered the market value of its outstanding debt. In addition, three of Dun & Bradstreet's fourteen key business ratios (return on sales, return on assets, and return on net worth) explicitly use a measure of income in the formula, and most of the numbers used in the remaining eleven ratios are indirectly affected by the dollar amount of reported income.

Due to the importance attached to income, periodic public earnings announcements, which appear in newspapers such as *The Wall Street Journal* and in corporate annual reports, are also considered important news items, having important effects on the economy. For example, an article in *USA Today* titled "Do Profits Matter?" noted:

Profit is the compass of the free enterprise system. When it dries up, the repercussions echo at every level of society. . . . Profits keep a free-market economy humming. They help pay for the development of new plants, products, and jobs. A sizable chunk of profits helps finance government in the form of taxes. Another chunk goes as dividends to shareholders—often the pension funds that pay for your retirement. Says an economist from the University of Chicago: "Economies . . . won't grow without corporate profit."

Various measures of income are also found in contracts written among stockholders, creditors, and managers. Such contracts are normally designed either to protect the interests of creditors or to control managers and encourage them to act in the interests of the stockholders. Loan agreements relating to the outstanding debts of Marriott Corporation, for example, limit the company's annual dividends to a portion of net income. Such covenants serve to protect the investments of corporate creditors by limiting the amount of cash that can be paid to stockholders in the form of dividends. The board of directors of May Department Stores encourages company employees to act in the stockholders' interests by providing incentive compensation in the form of a profit-sharing plan. As reported in the 2000 annual report, the payment of this compensation is based on changes in the company's annual earnings per share.

The measurement, definition, and disclosure of income is important to investors, creditors, managers, auditors, and the general public in a number of different ways. Students of accounting, therefore, must understand how it is measured and presented.

THE MEASUREMENT OF INCOME: DIFFERENT MEASURES FOR DIFFERENT OBJECTIVES

As stated in the *Statement of Financial Accounting Concepts No. 1,* the objectives of financial reporting are to provide information that is: (1) useful to those making investment and credit decisions who have a reasonable understanding of business and economic activities; (2) helpful to current and potential investors, creditors, and others in assessing the amounts, timing, and uncertainty of future cash flows; and (3) about economic resources, the claims to those resources, and changes in them.[1] There are three important features about this objective that are directly related to the income statement and the measure of income. It focuses on providing useful information to those who provide debt and equity capital to the firm; the information should help to predict future cash flows; and the information should reflect changes (increases or decreases) in the company's resources. No single measure of income can achieve this set of broad objectives, and income statements prepared under GAAP are designed to provide a variety of different measures of income. It is important that financial statement users understand how they differ and the situations under which each should be used.

To achieve this understanding, one must be familiar with several important definitions that appear in the *Statement of Financial Accounting Concepts No. 6.*[2] Figure 13–1 contains the definitions of ten key concepts, referred to as the elements of financial statements.

While you may be familiar with many of these definitions already, several points are noteworthy. Revenues and expenses, which are ongoing and central to the com-

---

1. "Objectives of Financial Reporting by Business Enterprises," *Statement of Financial Accounting Concepts No. 1* (Stamford, Conn.: FASB, November 1978), pars. 5–8.
2. "Elements of Financial Statements," *Statement of Financial Accounting Concepts No. 6* (Stamford, Conn.: FASB, December 1985), pp. ix and x.

FIGURE 13–1
Elements of the
financial
statements

Assets. **Probable future economic benefits obtained or controlled by a particular entity as a result of past transactions or events.**

Liabilities. **Probable future sacrifices of economic benefits arising from present obligations of a particular entity to transfer assets or provide services to other entities in the future as a result of past transactions or events.**

Equity. **Residual interest in the assets of an entity that remains after deducting its liabilities. In a business enterprise, the equity is the ownership interest.**

Investments by Owners. **Increases in net assets of a particular enterprise resulting from transfers to it from other entities of something of value to obtain or increase ownership interests (or equity) in it. Assets are most commonly received as investments by owners, but that which is received may also include services or satisfaction or conversion of liabilities of the enterprise.**

Distributions to Owners. **Decreases in net assets of a particular enterprise resulting from transferring assets, rendering services, or incurring liabilities by the enterprise to owners. Distributions to owners decrease ownership interests (or equity) in an enterprise.**

Comprehensive Income. **Change in equity (net assets) of an entity during a period from transactions and other events and circumstances from nonowner sources. It includes all changes in equity during a period except those resulting from investments by owners and distributions to owners.**

Revenues. **Inflows or other enhancements of assets of an entity or settlement of its liabilities (or a combination of both) during a period from delivering or producing goods, rendering services, or other activities that constitute the entity's ongoing major or central operations.**

Expenses. **Outflows or other using up of assets or incurrences of liabilities (or a combination of both) during a period from delivering or producing goods, rendering services, or carrying out other activities that constitute the entity's ongoing major or central operations.**

Gains. **Increases in equity (net assets) from peripheral or incidental transactions of an entity and from all other transactions and other events and circumstances affecting the entity during a period except those that result from revenues or investments by owners.**

Losses. **Decreases in equity (net assets) from peripheral or incidental transactions of an entity and from all other transactions and other events and circumstances affecting the entity during a period except those that result from expenses or distributions to owners.**

pany's operations, for example, are distinguished from gains and losses, which are peripheral or incidental to operations. Revenues and expenses occur frequently and are part of a company's core activities and, therefore, are related to the company's future cash flows. Gains and losses, on the other hand, tend to be infrequent and/or tangential to the company's core activities. Such items would not be expected to reflect future cash flows, yet they would be part of a company's comprehensive income and reflect changes in a company's resources.

To illustrate, consider two transactions entered into by a company: (1) sale of inventory with a cost of $50 million for $75 million, and (2) winning a settlement of $25 million in a one-time lawsuit. Both transactions increased the company's net assets by $25 million, making the company wealthier. Should they be included in income and reflected on the income statement? Transaction (1) involved the sale of inventory, a transaction that occurs frequently and is part of the company's core activities. It is likely to occur again, so it both reflects future cash flows and increases the company's resources. It seems that including this transaction on the income statement helps it to meet the objectives of financial reporting under almost any definition of income. Transaction (2) is a different story. The lawsuit was one-time, so it is not expected to occur again, and winning lawsuits is not part of the company's core activities. Consequently, this transaction would not be a good indicator of future cash flows, but it did increase the company's resources. It could be included, therefore, under a broad definition of income.

Refer to the Nabisco example introduced at the beginning of this chapter. What is a restructuring charge and should it be included on the income statement? How did including the restructuring charge in 1998 affect the apparent growth of Nabisco's earnings? As an analyst, would you consider the restructuring expense in the same way you consider operating expenses?

Comprehensive income represents a broad definition of income, including any change in the company's equity due to nonowner transactions. In June 1997, the FASB issued *SFAS No. 130,* "Reporting Comprehensive Income," which established standards for the reporting and display of comprehensive income and its components. This concept of income encompasses items not included in the computation of net income, such as foreign currency translation adjustments and unrealized gains and losses on available-for-sale securities (see Chapter 8). The standard does not change the display or components of net income, but it requires that the components of comprehensive income be displayed with the same prominence as the other financial statements. The disclosure below, which was taken from the 2000 annual report of Bristol-Myers Squibb, was placed immediately following the company's 2000 income statement. Many other firms have chosen to disclose it as a part of the statement of stockholders' equity (dollars in millions).

	2000	1999	1998
Comprehensive income:			
Net earnings from the income statement	$4,711	$4,167	$3,141
Other comprehensive income:			
Foreign currency translation	(282)	(212)	(86)
Tax effect	(5)	18	(3)
Comprehensive income	$4,424	$3,973	$3,052

This discussion demonstrates that there are different ways to measure income, and different measures of income address different objectives of financial reporting. It also shows that the nature of individual transaction must be considered to determine if and how they should be reflected in income. The following section develops a framework that describes different kinds of transactions and relates them to the different measures of income used in financial statements.

Financing, Investing, and Operating Transactions: A Framework

Financing and investing transactions basically involve setting up a company so that it can conduct operations, while **operating transactions** entail the actual conduction of the operations. In Chapter 2 of this text we referred to a company as a fruit tree: financing and investing transactions affect the size and structure of the tree (represented by the balance sheet), and operating transactions reflect the harvest and sale of the fruit (represented by the income statement). While these definitions are useful, some transactions are difficult to classify because they reflect some characteristics of each.

Figure 13–2 represents a continuum for classifying financing, investing, and operating transactions. Note that five categories of transactions are described, and each is placed at a point along the continuum. Category 1 at the extreme left contains purely financing transactions, and Category 5 contains operating transactions. Categories 2, 3, and 4 increasingly resemble operating activities. Later, we point out that operating transactions can also be subdivided into categories, based primarily on how germane they are to the normal, everyday operating activities of a company. Review the figure closely because we will be discussing it in detail in the following paragraphs.

FIGURE 13–2 Classifying financing, investing, and operating transactions

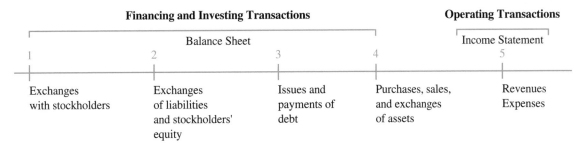

1. Exchanges with stockholders: stock issuances, stock redemptions, and dividend payments.
2. Exchanges of liabilities and stockholders' equity: debt refinancing and conversion of convertible bonds and stocks.
3. Issues and payments of debt: cash borrowings evidenced by notes payable, issuing bonds, and payments on debts, including the redemption of debt.
4. Purchases, sales, and exchanges of assets: purchases, sales, and exchanges of all assets.
5. Revenues: inflows of assets (or outflows of liabilities) due to operations.
   Expenses: outflows of assets (or inflows of liabilities) due to the generation of revenues.

(1) EXCHANGES WITH STOCKHOLDERS

Exchanges with owners include (1) issuances of preferred or common stock, (2) purchases, retirements, and reissuances of treasury stock, and (3) cash, property, and stock dividends. This group is located on the far left side of the continuum because these are purely financing transactions involved exclusively with the formation and dissolution of the company's equity capital and the returns (i.e., dividends) to the company's owners. The most distinctive and important feature about the transactions in this category is that they never affect the income statement. Even when treasury stock is reissued for an amount different from its cost, the dollar amount of the difference is not recognized as a gain or a loss on the income statement.

During 1999, Nabisco reissued treasury stock with a cost of $15 million, receiving $8 million. Did the company recognize a $7 million loss on the reissuance? Why or why not?

(2) EXCHANGES OF LIABILITIES AND STOCKHOLDERS' EQUITY

Exchanges of liabilities and stockholders' equity refer to transactions in which liabilities are exchanged for other liabilities (debt refinancing arrangements) or converted into stockholders' equity (conversion of convertible bonds or preferred stocks to common stock). Such exchanges are considered financing transactions because they deal only with a company's capital structure. Accordingly, they generally do not affect the income statement. However, these transactions are located to the right of exchanges with stockholders because in certain limited circumstances they can give rise to gains or losses that appear on the income statement.[3]

(3) ISSUES AND PAYMENTS OF DEBT

Issues and payments of debt include cash borrowings associated with the issuance of notes or bonds payable as well as the cash payments required to service or retire such liabilities. These transactions involve exchanges with a company's creditors and thus are reflected in the liabilities section of the balance sheet. They are considered financing transactions because they involve how a company pays for its operations through debt. However, these transactions are not completely separate from a company's operations. Interest payments on debt are directly reflected on the income statement through interest expense; book gains and losses are recognized when debt is retired; and premiums and discounts on notes and bonds are amortized to the income statement over the life of the debt. Consequently, this category of transactions is located to the right of exchanges of liabilities and stockholders' equity.

During 1999, Nabisco issued long-term debt in the amount of $777 million, and paid $203 million to redeem $200 million in debt. How did these two transactions influence the basic accounting equation, and how was the income statement affected?

(4) PURCHASES, SALES, AND EXCHANGES OF ASSETS

Category 4 includes the purchase, sale, or exchange of all assets. Such assets include marketable securities, inventories, prepaid expenses, long-term investments, and long-lived assets. These transactions, all of which are capitalized, represent both investing and operating activities. Activity involving long-term assets is considered investing, while activity involving short-term assets is considered operating. This category is located next to the operating section of the continuum because it is only a matter of time before these capitalized costs appear on the income statement. Prepaid expenses and long-lived assets, for example, are amortized, depleted, or depreciated on the income statement over their useful lives. Capitalized inventory costs, investments, and long-lived assets are matched against revenues when they are sold.[4]

---

3. The methods used to account for refinancing arrangements and the conversion of convertible bonds and stocks are complex and controversial, and we do not discuss them in this textbook. For our purposes, it is sufficient to note that, according to current generally accepted accounting principles, such transactions rarely give rise to income statement gains and losses.

4. Many companies also sell outstanding accounts receivable to financial institutions for immediate cash, and an income statement gain or loss is recognized in the amount of the difference between the book value of the receivable and the cash proceeds. These transfers accelerate cash collections from sales on account as well as pass on the risks and costs associated with uncollectible accounts to the financial institution. Such exchanges are called *factoring* arrangements. Sales made on credit using major credit cards, such as VISA, American Express, and MasterCard, represent factoring arrangements.

During 1999, Nabisco invested $241 million in property and equipment. How does this transaction affect the income statement in the current year and future years?

(5) REVENUES AND EXPENSES

The right side of the continuum includes exchanges that are considered operating transactions. Revenues represent inflows of assets (or outflows of liabilities) due to a company's operating activities, and in line with the matching principle, expenses represent outflows of assets (or inflows of liabilities) associated with the generation of the revenues.

Classifying Operating Transactions

Income statements include transactions ranging from those that are fundamental and necessary to a company's operations to those that are only marginally related to operations. Figure 13–3 shows three groups of operating transactions, based primarily on how germane the transactions are to the normal operations of a company and how frequently they occur.

FIGURE 13–3
Classifying operating transactions

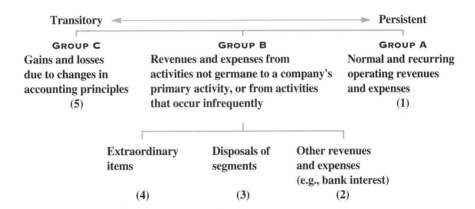

Group A contains revenues and expenses that result from transactions that are normal to company operations and occur frequently. Examples include the sale of the company's inventories or services and the payment and recognition of expenses due to such items as wages, utilities, rent, insurance, depreciation, and other administrative and selling activities.

Group B contains items that are much less germane to the normal activities of a company or that may occur infrequently. Examples include interest earned on bank savings accounts held by manufacturing, retail, and service companies; rent earned from temporarily leasing company property planned to be used later for other purposes; gains and losses recognized on sales of long-lived assets and debt retirements; and gains and losses related to such items as litigation, employee strikes, and infrequent natural disasters.

Group C contains gains and losses recognized from such activities as changes in accounting principles (e.g., from LIFO to FIFO, or from double-declining-balance to straight-line depreciation), which reflect very little about the operations occurring during the periods in which such changes were made. They are simply bookkeeping entries that do not reflect an economic event.

In the past, there was considerable controversy over the proper classification and disclosure of the transactions contained in Groups B and C. Some accountants argued that transactions from Group C should not enter into the computation of net income. Others took an even more extreme view and suggested that transactions in both Groups B and C were not germane to operations and, accordingly, should not appear on the income statement, which should be limited to operating revenues and expenses in the strictest sense.

In 1966, the accounting profession adopted the position that nonoperating items (Groups B and C) should be included on the income statement, but they must be separately and clearly disclosed in specific categories. Specifically, it was recommended that the income statement consist of five categories: (1) operating revenues and expenses, (2) other revenues and expenses, (3) disposals of business segments, (4) extraordinary items, and (5) changes in accounting principles. In terms of Figure 13–3, Category 1 corresponds to Group A, Categories 2, 3, and 4 come from Group B, and Category 5 corresponds to Group C.

The different categories on the income statement allow users to assess the significance of the items in each category and to choose to include or exclude them in the computation of net income as the situation dictates. The next section defines and illustrates the five categories of a complete income statement.

In recent years, AT&T has included the following items on its income statement—selling and administrative expenses, gain on sale of assets, restructuring charge, interest expense, and extraordinary loss. Classify each of these items in the groups illustrated in Figure 13–3.

A COMPLETE INCOME STATEMENT: DISCLOSURE AND PRESENTATION

Figure 13–4 provides an income statement that contains each of the five categories introduced in the previous section. Review the statement carefully. The following discussion considers first the income statement in general and then covers each category individually.

The computation of net income on the income statement involves five major components, each representing one of the five categories. In general, as one moves from the top to the bottom of the income statement, the events become increasingly less important to the operations of the business. Net operating income (operating revenues less operating expenses) reflects financial performance resulting from transactions that are both fundamental to a company's normal activities and occur frequently. Other revenues and expenses and disposals of business segments reflect the financial effects of events that are either not part of a company's normal operations or do not occur frequently. Extraordinary gains and losses result from events that are both highly unusual and infrequent, and gains and losses due to changes in accounting principles result simply from book entries.

The income statement is divided into these categories to enable users to distinguish transactions that are due to operations from those due to unusual, infrequent, and sometimes uncontrollable events (e.g., extraordinary items) or simply to changes in

FIGURE 13–4 A complete income statement[5]

XYZ Company
Income Statement
For the Period Ending December 31, 2003

Gross sales		$325	⎫
Less: Sales discounts and returns		25	⎬ 1. Operating revenues
Net sales		$300	⎭
Less: Cost of goods sold:			
Beginning inventory	$ 75		
+ Gross purchases	150		
− Purchase discounts and returns	(5)		
+ Freight-in	20		
− Ending inventory	(80)	160	
Gross profit		$140	
Operating expenses:			⎫
Wages and salaries	$ 30		
Advertising	10		
Insurance	8		⎬ 1. Operating expenses
State and local taxes	7		
Depreciation	25		
Utilities	20		
Miscellaneous	15	115	⎭
Net operating income		$ 25	
Other revenues		10	⎫
Less: Other expenses		(13)	⎬ 2. Other revenues and expenses
Net income from continuing operations before tax		$ 22	
Less: Federal income tax		7	
Net income from continuing operations		$ 15	
Income (loss) on segment up to disposal (net of tax)		(3)	⎫
Gain (loss) on disposal of segment (net of tax)		5	⎬ 3. Disposal of business segment
Net income before extraordinary items		$ 17	
Extraordinary gain (loss) (net of tax)		(5)	⎬ 4. Extraordinary item
Net income before change in accounting principle		$ 12	
Income effect due to change in accounting principle			
(net of tax)		7	⎬ 5. Changes in accounting principles
Net income		$ 19	
Earnings per share (100 shares outstanding):			
Net income from continuing operations			
(after tax)		$ .15	
Disposal of business segment		.02	
Extraordinary items		(.05)	
Change in accounting principle		.07	
Total earnings per share		$ .19	

5. Most real-world income statements are variations of two basic formats: (1) single-step or (2) multistep. This income statement uses the multistep format. Under the single-step format, all revenues and expenses above "net income from continuing operations" are grouped into two separate categories. Below "net income from continuing operations," the two formats are identical.

accounting principles (e.g., LIFO to FIFO). Presumably, measures of profit disclosed near the top of the income statement (e.g., net operating income) better reflect management's performance and are more indicative of the future than are those disclosed near the bottom of the statement (e.g., net income). The boards of directors of many companies, for example, express their management compensation agreements in terms of net operating income instead of net income. The boards apparently believe that if management acts to increase net operating income, it will increase the long-term earnings of the company and thus further the interests of the stockholders. Consider the following excerpt from the 2000 annual report of The Pillsbury Company:

Certain employees of the Company participate in compensation programs which include a base salary plus incentive payments based on the level of operating earnings.

(1) Operating Revenues and Expenses: Usual and Frequent

Operating revenues and expenses refer to asset and liability inflows and outflows related to the acquisition and delivery of the goods or services provided by a company. They are considered usual and frequent. The term **usual** refers to the normal operations of the business. If a company is in business to sell furniture, for example, *usual* revenues come from furniture sales. Automobile dealerships, on the other hand, are in business to sell and service automobiles; for them, revenues generated from selling office furniture would not be considered usual.

The term **frequent** refers to how often the revenue is generated or the expense incurred. Revenues and expenses are considered frequent if they are expected to recur in the foreseeable future. They are not "one-shot," unpredictable events. For many companies, the sale of a fixed asset or a long-term investment, for example, which can generate either a gain or a loss, is a transaction that tends to occur infrequently.

Which of the following two companies would likely consider a gain on the sale of investments a usual and frequent transaction—Bank of America or J.C. Penney? Why?

(2) Other Revenues and Expenses: Unusual or Infrequent

The section of the income statement headed "other revenues and expenses" contains revenues and expenses related to a company's secondary or auxiliary activities. The most common examples are interest income and interest expense, which relate to the company's investments and debt financing, respectively. While interest is certainly important and recurring, with the exception of financial institutions, it is not directly a part of the acquisition and selling of a company's goods and services. IBM Corporation and Coca-Cola Enterprises, like many other large U.S. companies, include both interest income and interest expense in this category. Another item commonly disclosed in this section is income (or loss) from long-term investments accounted for under the equity method. Both Scott Paper Company and Deere & Company, for example, disclosed equity earnings from associated companies in this manner on their 2000 income statements.

Other examples include dividend income from investments, gains and losses from sales of investments and long-lived assets, receivable and inventory write-downs, gains and losses on foreign currency transactions, losses due to employee strikes, income from the rental of excess warehouse space, and gains and losses due to litigation.[6] Many companies, like Kodak, Kmart, and American Brands, have restructured their operations and reported the associated costs in this section of the income statement. Several years ago, Exxon Mobil recorded a $2.5 billion charge for the Valdez incident in this way, and Johnson & Johnson reported a $140 million loss due to the write-down of inventory in the same manner. Over a recent three-year period, Goodyear Tire & Rubber Company recorded gains and losses from asset sales and write-downs, workforce reductions, and lawsuits in this section of the income statement.

The key feature about the items in this section of the income statement is that they are "unusual or infrequent, but not both." Interest and dividend income, for example, are considered unusual because they are not germane to the normal operations of the business. They are secondary to the major activities of most companies. At the same time, however, interest and dividend revenue may be recognized every year and are therefore considered to occur frequently. Receivables and inventory write-downs and losses from employee layoffs, on the other hand, while part of the normal business risks faced by virtually all companies, occur infrequently. They are, therefore, considered to be infrequent but not unusual.

The nature of a particular business and the environment in which it operates must be considered when deciding what is unusual and/or infrequent. Dividend and interest income, for example, are secondary to the operations of manufacturing, retailing, and service companies, yet they represent the primary revenues for financial institutions. Interest income for Bank of America Corporation, for example, normally represents 80–85 percent of total revenues generated by the company. Consequently, for Bank of America, interest income is an operating item, both usual and frequent.

In June 1999, United Airlines sold 17.5 million shares of Galileo International, resulting in a gain of $731 million. Total income for the company in 1999 was $1,235 million. In what section of the income statement did the gain appear, and why?

(3) Disposal of a Business Segment

A **business segment** is defined as a separate line of business, product line, or class of customer involving an operation that is independent from a company's other operations. Highly diversified companies consist of many independent segments. DuPont, for example, consists of nine different segments: agriculture, biomedical products, coal, fibers, industrial and consumer products, petroleum exploration, petroleum refining, marketing and transportation, and polymer products. Each of DuPont's segments generates well over $1 billion in revenue each year. The sale or discontinuance of any one of these segments would be referred to as a disposal of a business segment, and the related financial effects would be disclosed separately on the income statement. It is not uncommon for companies to sell major business segments. In recent years, for example, Whirlpool Corporation, Goodyear Tire & Rubber, and DuPont all disposed of major business segments. Indeed, in 1999, DuPont recognized a $7 billion gain on its sale of Conoco, a major petroleum business.

---

6. Book gains and losses due to foreign currency translations were discussed in Appendix 6A.

The disposal of a business segment is a significant and complex transaction that is subject to a number of detailed rules under generally accepted accounting principles. We do not cover these detailed rules here. For our purposes, it is sufficient to view the disposal of a segment as similar to the sale or retirement of a long-lived asset: more specifically, the sale or retirement of a large piece of equipment that generates revenues and incurs expenses that are independent of the company's other operations.

Note in the complete income statement in Figure 13–4 that two separate disclosures are associated with a disposed business segment. The first reflects the income or loss associated with the segment's operations for the time period extending from the previous balance sheet date to the point when the segment is actually disposed of. Since the segment is an independent entity, the expenses associated with it can be matched against its revenues to provide a net income or loss for that time period. The second disclosure reflects the gain or loss recognized when the segment is actually disposed of. At that time, the assets and liabilities of the segment are written off the books, the proceeds (if the segment is sold) are recorded, and a gain or loss on the disposal is recognized in the dollar amount of the difference between the book value of the segment and the proceeds. This dual disclosure allows users to separately ascertain both the profitability of the segment and the book gain or loss on the disposal.

To illustrate, on September 28, 2000, Bristol-Myers Squibb announced the sale of its Clairol and Zimmer businesses, which at the time were considered major business segments. Since the earnings reported by these segments will no longer be part of Bristol-Myers Squibb's normal and recurring operations, GAAP requires that these earnings be disclosed separately on the income statement along with the gain or loss on the actual sale. Consequently, the following disclosure appeared on the 2000 income statement of Bristol-Myers Squibb, immediately below "earnings from continuing operations (dollars in millions.)"

	2000
Net earnings on discontinued operations	$375
Net gain on disposal of segments	240
Earnings from discontinued operations	$615

(4) Extraordinary Items: Unusual and Infrequent

Extraordinary items are defined as material events of a character significantly different from the typical, customary business activities of an entity, which are not expected to recur frequently in the ordinary operating activities of a business. In other words, extraordinary items are both unusual and infrequent.

The most common extraordinary items reported by major U.S. companies are gains and losses resulting from early retirements of long-term debts.[7] *Accounting Trends and Techniques* (AICPA, 2000) reports that, of the 600 major U.S. companies surveyed, 62 (10 percent) disclosed at least one extraordinary item on the income statement, and 56 (90 percent) of these resulted from gains or losses recognized on early debt retirements. American Brands, for example, redeemed debt in both 1995 and 1996, reporting extraordinary losses in both cases.

---

7. The early retirement of long-term debt is a fairly common transaction for many major U.S. companies. Consequently, it does not always meet the infrequent criterion for an extraordinary item. A number of years ago, many corporations appeared to be manipulating income from continuing operations by timing their long-term debt retirements. Accounting policymakers combated this manipulation by requiring that the associated gains and losses be disclosed as extraordinary.

Other examples of extraordinary items include gains and losses from terminating pension plans; gains and losses from litigation settlements; losses resulting from casualties like floods, earthquakes, tornadoes, hurricanes, droughts, and volcanoes; and gains and losses resulting from expropriations (forced government takeovers or purchases of company property) and prohibitions under new law. Note, however, that losses due to employee layoffs, inventory write-downs due to obsolescence, receivables write-downs, and foreign currency translation gains and losses should never be classified as extraordinary according to generally accepted accounting principles. Such items are considered to arise from normal operating business risks.

As in the case of "other revenues and expenses," the nature of the company in question and the environment in which it operates are critical in determining what is, and is not, considered extraordinary. A company that operates in a low-land area where floods are common, for example, would not report a flood loss as extraordinary because it would not be infrequent. Similarly, gains and losses from lawsuits may or may not be considered extraordinary. Most large U.S. companies are constantly involved in various forms of litigation, so that gains and losses from lawsuits are considered unusual, but not infrequent. Many smaller companies, on the other hand, are infrequently involved in litigation, so resulting gains or losses would be considered extraordinary. However, the size of the settlement may also determine whether it is disclosed as extraordinary. Pennzoil, for example, reported as extraordinary a $1.66 billion gain which resulted from winning a legal claim against Texaco. As you can see, determining whether an item is extraordinary is often a judgment call, and management has much discretion in this area.

In 1998, Dole, a major food company with fruit groves in many warm-weather locations, reported two special charges—$100 million to reflect crop damage from Hurricane Mitch, and $20 million to reflect damage to citrus groves caused by freezing temperatures in California. In neither case did the company consider these charges extraordinary. Explain why.

(5) Changes in Accounting Principles

Chapter 4 defines the concept of consistency and mentions that once a company chooses an acceptable principle or method of accounting (e.g., straight-line depreciation, FIFO inventory valuation, etc.), it must continue to use that method consistently from one year to the next. Consistency helps to maintain the credibility of accounting reports, enabling investors, creditors, and other interested parties to make more meaningful comparisons and to identify more easily the trends in a company's performance across time.

If a company can convince its auditors, however, that the environment in which it operates has changed and another accounting method is now more appropriate than the one currently in place, it can change the accounting method and still be in conformance with generally accepted accounting principles.

The cumulative effects on net income due to changes in accounting methods can be very significant. For example, AT&T and Burlington Northern decreased net income by $175 million and $336 million (net of tax), respectively, when they changed to the units-of-production method of depreciation. General Electric increased net income by $858 million by changing its methods of accounting for deferred income taxes and inventories. In each case, the change was clearly described in the footnotes, the auditors concurred with and mentioned the change in the opinion letter, and the cumulative effect of the change on net income was separately disclosed on the income statement.

Nonetheless, financial statement users must still be careful not to overlook or be confused by such changes. As reported in *Forbes:* "When a company changes its accounting practices from one year to the next, all but the most diligent readers of annual reports can get lost." General Motors Corporation, for example, changed accounting methods five different times between 1986 and 1988. In each case, the changes served to increase net income. A GM spokesman commented: "Each change brings us more in line with the industry," [and that] "we're not trying to hide anything at all." An industry analyst, on the other hand, noted: "[GM's] management is under pressure to show a good financial performance, and these changes serve to make it harder to compare the company's financial results over time."

So far, this discussion has focused on discretionary accounting changes. That is, companies often voluntarily choose to change from one method to another. In 1999, Banta Corporation voluntarily changed from the LIFO to FIFO inventory assumption and Kmart changed its method of recognizing revenue on layaway sales. It happens frequently, however, that companies are forced by FASB mandate to change accounting methods. For example, in recent years the FASB issued new standards covering the methods of accounting for postretirement health care and insurance costs, income taxes, computer software, and pensions. In each case, a number of companies were required to change their accounting methods to conform with these new standards, and these changes were accompanied by prominent disclosure in the footnotes, on the income statement, and in the audit opinion. Sprint, for example, booked a $23 million gain due to adopting the new standard on income tax accounting, and it disclosed a $384 million loss due to adopting the FASB standard on postretirement health care costs.

Changes in accounting methods must be disclosed in three prominent places in the financial report: (1) the auditor's report to the shareholders must mention the change, (2) the footnotes to the financial statement must clearly describe the change, and (3) the cumulative effects of the change on net income must be disclosed (net of tax) separately on the income statement, immediately below extraordinary items. Figure 13–5 shows how 3M disclosed an accounting change in its 2000 annual report.

FIGURE 13–5	
3M excerpts from the annual report	**For the Year Ended December 31, 2000**

NOTES TO THE FINANCIAL STATEMENTS

During the fourth quarter of 2000, the company changed its revenue recognition policy. The effect of this change is reported as the cumulative effect of an accounting change in the fourth quarter of 2000.

AUDITOR'S REPORT TO THE SHAREHOLDERS

As discussed in Note 2 . . . the Company changed its method of revenue recognition.

2000 INCOME STATEMENT (MILLIONS OF DOLLARS)

Income before cumulative effect of accounting change	$1,857
Cumulative effect of accounting change	75
Net income	$1,782

Changes in accounting principles can make it more difficult to compare a company's financial performance across time because in the annual report the financial statements from periods prior to the change are prepared using the previous accounting methods. However, generally accepted accounting principles require that net income on a **pro forma (as if) basis** be disclosed on the face of the income statement for all periods presented, as if the newly adopted principle had been applied to those periods. This disclosure enables users to make more meaningful comparisons, at least across the periods presented on the face of the income statement.

One final point: it is important to realize that an accounting method differs from an accounting estimate, which is used to implement an accounting method. Straight-line depreciation, for example, is an accounting method, which is implemented by estimating the useful life and salvage value of a long-lived asset. The allowance method of accounting for bad debts is implemented by estimating the amount of bad debts at the end of each year. This section has discussed how to account for a change in an accounting method. How to account for revisions in accounting estimates was described in Chapter 9.

HON INDUSTRIES reported in its 1999 annual report that the company is now required under GAAP to capitalize certain software costs that were previously expensed. During the year, HON capitalized $3.5 million in software costs. Did this accounting change increase or decrease income, and where would information about it be disclosed in the company's 2000 annual report?

INTRAPERIOD TAX ALLOCATION

Federal income taxes, which do not include state and local taxes, are disclosed in two different ways on the income statement. The first income tax disclosure immediately follows net income from continuing operations (before tax). It represents the tax expense resulting from all taxable revenues and deductible expenses except for those listed below it on the income statement.[8]

The dollar amounts associated with the remaining items (disposal of business segments, extraordinary items, and changes in accounting principles) are all disclosed *net of tax.* Such presentation means that each of these revenue and expense items is disclosed on the income statement after the related income tax effect has been removed. The practice of including the income tax effect of a particular transaction with the transaction itself on the income statement is known as **intraperiod tax allocation.** It enables users to assess the total financial impact of these special transactions as well as the tax benefit or cost associated with them.

For example, when CBS Television Network retired long-term debt with a book value of $28.6 million for $29.1 million dollars, a loss of $0.5 million was recognized on the transaction with the following journal entry (dollars in millions):

Long-Term Debt (−L)	**28.6**	
Extraordinary Loss on Early Retirement of Debt (Lo, −SE)	**0.5**	
Cash (−A)		**29.1**
Retired long-term debt.		

---

8. Appendix 10B, which covers deferred income taxes, provides a more complete description of tax expense listed in the income statement.

The loss, however, was tax deductible and served to decrease CBS's tax liability by $0.2 million. This tax benefit was recorded in the books with the following journal entry, and a loss on early retirement (net of tax) of $0.3 million ($0.5 million − $0.2 million) was disclosed on CBS's income statement. This loss was disclosed on the income statement under extraordinary items.

Income Tax Liability (−L)[9]	**0.2**	
Extraordinary Loss on Early Retirement of Debt (−Lo, +SE)		**0.2**

Recognized tax benefit.

In another example, Ralston Purina Company sold its Van Camp Seafood division several years ago for $260 million. The book value of Van Camp was $147.3 million, and a gain of $112.7 million was recognized on the transaction with the following journal entry (dollars in millions):

Cash (+A)	**260**	
Net Assets of Van Camp Seafood (−A)		**147.3**
Gain on Disposal of Segment (Ga, +SE)		**112.7**

Sold business segment.

The gain, however, was included in Ralston Purina's taxable income and increased the company's tax liability by $42.5 million. The increase in tax liability was recorded with the following journal entry (dollars in millions), and Ralston Purina disclosed a $70.2 million ($112.7 − $42.5) gain on its income statement. The gain appeared under disposals of business segments.

Gain on Disposal of Segment (−Ga, −SE)	**42.5**	
Income Tax Liability (+L)		**42.5**

Recorded increase in tax liability.

The general formula for computing the net-of-tax dollar amount for a revenue or expense item is provided below.

Net-of-Tax Dollar Amount = (Gross Revenue or Expense) × (1 − Tax Rate)

If, for example, an accounting change leads to a book and tax gain or loss of $10,000, and the company's federal income tax rate is 35 percent, the net-of-tax dollar amount disclosed on the income statement would be calculated as follows:

$$\text{Net of Tax Dollar Amount} = \$10,000 \times (1 - 35\%)$$
$$= \$6,500$$

In 1999, SBC Communications changed its method of revenue recognition, creating a one-time pretax gain of $332 million. The company's effective tax rate at the time was 38 percent. What dollar amount was disclosed on the income statement, and where?

EARNINGS-PER-SHARE DISCLOSURE

Generally accepted accounting principles also require that earnings per share be disclosed on the face of the income statement and that the specific dollar amounts associated with (1) net income from continuing operations (after tax), (2) disposals of busi-

9. If the income tax effect of the transaction is not realized in the current year due to timing differences between tax rules and GAAP, the account "Deferred income taxes" is debited or credited.

ness segments, (3) extraordinary items, and (4) changes in accounting principles be disclosed separately. Note the form of this disclosure in Figure 13–4. The earnings-per-share amount for each category is calculated by dividing the dollar amount of the gain or loss associated with that category by the number of common shares outstanding. The income statement in Figure 13–6 was taken from the 2000 annual report of SBC

FIGURE 13–6 Illustrated income statement

Consolidated Statements of Income
SBC Communications
Dollars in millions except per share amounts

	2000	1999	1998
OPERATING REVENUES			
Landline local service	$22,099	$19,432	$17,506
Wireless subscriber	4,945	5,851	5,265
Network access	10,427	10,094	9,575
Long distance service	3,178	3,485	3,688
Directory advertising	4,439	4,266	3,929
Other	6,388	6,403	6,278
Total operating revenues	51,476	49,531	46,241
OPERATING EXPENSES			
Operations and support	30,985	29,380	27,177
Depreciation and amortization	9,748	8,553	7,841
Total operating expenses	40,733	37,933	35,018
Operating income	10,743	11,598	11,223
OTHER INCOME (EXPENSE)			
Interest expense	(1,592)	(1,430)	(1,605)
Interest income	279	127	182
Equity in net income of affiliates	897	912	613
Other income (expense)—net	2,561	(354)	1,702
Total other income (expense)	2,145	(745)	892
Income before income taxes	12,888	10,853	12,115
Income taxes	4,921	4,280	4,380
Income before extraordinary items and cumulative effect of accounting change	7,967	6,573	7,735
Extraordinary items, net of tax	—	1,379	(60)
Cumulative effect of accounting change, net of tax	—	207	15
Net income	$7,967	$8,159	$7,690
Earnings per common share:			
Income before extraordinary items and cumulative effect of accounting change	$2.35	$1.93	$2.27
Net income	$2.35	$2.39	$2.26
Earnings per common share – assuming dilution:			
Income before extraordinary items and cumulative effect of accounting change	$2.32	$1.90	$2.24
Net income	$2.32	$2.36	$2.23

The accompanying notes are an integral part of the consolidated financial statements.

Communications. Note, in particular, the earnings-per-share disclosure near the bottom. These breakdowns allow users to focus on the components of earnings-per-share.

Generally accepted accounting principles require an additional disclosure, called **diluted earnings per share,** for companies that have the potential for significant dilution. Many companies, for example, have issued and presently have outstanding options to purchase their common stocks or bonds that can be converted to common stocks in the future. If and when these options and conversion privileges are exercised, the number of outstanding common shares will increase, which, in turn, will dilute the ownership interests of the existing common stockholders. The calculation of diluted earnings per share, which is described in intermediate and advanced financial accounting textbooks, reflects these possibilities by essentially increasing the denominator of the earnings-per-share ratio and thereby reducing its dollar value. The extent of potential dilution, as measured by the difference between diluted and unadjusted (basic) earnings per share, can be useful information to existing or potential stockholders who are concerned with maintaining the value of their investments.

Review the income statement of SBC Communications in Figure 13–6 and estimate the number of common shares outstanding as of the end of 1998, 1999, and 2000. By how much would the number of shares increase if all potentially dilutive securities were converted to common shares?

INCOME STATEMENT CATEGORIES: USEFUL FOR DECISIONS BUT SUBJECTIVE

The income statement classifications discussed in this chapter introduce a very important concept to those who use financial accounting information to predict the future cash flows of an enterprise. The concept is called **earnings persistence,** and it reflects the extent to which a particular earnings dollar amount can be expected to continue in the future and, thus, generate future cash flows. Earnings amounts with high levels of persistence are expected to continue in the future, while those with low levels of persistence are not. The income statement classifications are useful because, for the most part, they are defined in terms of their persistence. Net operating income is the result of usual and frequent activities that can be expected to continue in the future; "other revenues and expenses" are considered to have somewhat less persistence; and disposals of segments, extraordinary items, and accounting changes are all considered to be "one-shot" events that should not be counted on in the future. Financial statement users cannot ignore these classifications since they contain valuable information about a company's future prospects.

In terms of the objectives of financial accounting, earnings numbers with high persistence are considered to reflect future cash flows, while low persistence earnings are not. Both kinds of earnings, however, reflect changes in the company's resources and in that respect are considered useful.

It is also important to realize, however, that income statement classifications can be quite subjective, and management has incentives to use its discretion to disclose the financial results of certain events in categories that serve its interests. For example, management may use its reporting discretion to include certain "gains" in the operating section and certain "losses" in the nonoperating sections of the income statement. By using such a strategy, management might influence users to believe that the "gains" are persistent while the "losses" are not. As noted in *Forbes* magazine: "clever accountants can find all sorts of different meanings in those simple sounding words [usual and frequent]. . . . It all comes down to a judgement."

Consider Western Savings of Phoenix, a savings and loan company that reported $49 million in *operating* income, almost half of which ($24 million) was due to the sale of one large investment. Many accountants agreed that this particular sale was nonrecurring and that similar gains could not be expected in the future. Consequently, the gain on this transaction should not have been included in the operating section of the income statement. *Forbes* pointed out that this and other accounting practices followed by the company suggested: "Western is a classic case of how reported profits can misrepresent economic reality."

The Wall Street Journal (January 30, 1996) noted that many companies use subjective restructuring charges to manage earnings. Often, they prematurely recognize expenses within a charge that is disclosed on the income statement outside of the operating section. This activity reduces future operating expenses and increases net income from operations. The article went on to say: "The most obvious way restructuring charges make companies' earnings look better is if the company can convince investors that operating earnings—before the charges—provide a more meaningful indication of trends."

The subjectivity associated with classifying gains and losses in different sections of the income statement can give rise to other significant economic consequences. We noted earlier in the chapter, for example, that The Pillsbury Company has instituted a compensation plan that rewards management on the basis of operating income. An important question is whether interest expense is considered to be an operating or a nonoperating expense in the measurement of operating income as defined by the plan. Including interest as an operating expense could discourage management from borrowing needed funds; including it as a nonoperating expense, on the other hand, could encourage managers to borrow too much. Classifying interest as operating or nonoperating is a subjective decision; yet it can influence the manner in which a company functions.

Robert A. Olstein, a veteran accounting expert and manager of the Olstein Financial Alert mutual fund, once noted in *The New York Times* (May 14, 2000): "We are always looking around and between the numbers to see what a company's real or repetitive earnings are." What does he mean, and how is the income statement designed to help him?

INTERNATIONAL PERSPECTIVE: INVESTMENTS AND INCOME STATEMENT DISCLOSURE

Many times in this textbook we have commented that U.S. businesses are increasingly investing in foreign markets and operations. Such investments introduce certain risks and opportunities that are different from those characterizing domestic business activities. The following quote from Coca-Cola's annual report provides an illustration:

The Company distributes its products in nearly 170 countries and [transacts in approximately 40 different currencies]. Approximately 80 percent of total operating income is generated outside the United States. International operations are subject to certain risks and opportunities, including currency fluctuation and government actions. The Company closely monitors its methods of operating in each country and adopts strategies responsive to changing economic and political environments.

Such a strong international presence increases the number of transactions that require special disclosure on the income statement. Owens Corning, for example, has significant investments in six different non–U.S. affiliated companies (two in Saudi Arabia, and one each in Canada, Japan, Brazil, and Mexico). A portion of the income reported by these affiliates is disclosed, under the equity method, as a special item on the company's income statement. Merck & Co., Inc., which has investments in foreign assets that total over $2.5 billion, has sold and restructured foreign subsidiaries frequently over the last several years. For example, the company sold subsidiaries in South Africa, Lebanon, and Nigeria and restructured operations in Argentina, Brazil, and Venezuela. These activities led to special disclosures in its income statement.

The unique risks associated with investments in countries with high inflation and volatile economies also often give rise to special income statement disclosures. Several years ago, Johnson & Johnson disclosed two special charges on the income statement: (1) a $104 million write-off for permanently impaired assets and operations in Latin America, which was disclosed in the operating section of the income statement, and (2) a $36 million loss from the liquidation of Argentine debt. The company's 2000 annual report also mentions the risks of foreign currency fluctuations and describes how the company hedges these risks.

In such an international investment environment, financial statement users must be particularly aware of, and carefully interpret, the special gains and losses that are reported on the income statement. They should attempt to completely understand the underlying transaction and appreciate the context in which it occurred. An article in *The Wall Street Journal* cautions investors about gains that arise from foreign currency translations in particular.[10]

Foreign exchange gains resulting from the dollar's [recent] tumble . . . raise questions about the quality of soon-to-be released earnings reports for those U.S. firms with big foreign operations. For example, American Family Corp., Gillette Co., American Brands Inc., and Colgate-Palmolive Co. all derive more than 60 percent of their sales from foreign operations. . . . Investors should [not overemphasize the importance of] currency-related earnings . . . because they're really a one-time gain that could easily reverse itself.

These issues underline the importance of carefully reading the footnotes in an annual report. Most of the information required to make the assessments discussed in this section is not disclosed on the face of the financial statements but is buried somewhere in the footnotes.

REVIEW PROBLEM

The operating revenues and expenses of Panawin Enterprises for 2003 follow, along with descriptions of and entries for several additional transactions. Assume that income taxes on income from continuing operations are $7,000, the effective income tax rate on other items is 34 percent, the balance in Retained Earnings as of December 31, 2002, is $106,000, and that dividends declared during 2003 total $16,000.

---

10. See Appendix 6A for a discussion of foreign currency gains and losses.

Operating revenues	**$85,000**
Operating expenses	**62,000**
Net operating income	**$23,000**

1. Machinery with an original cost of $14,000 and a book value of $11,000 was sold for $9,000. The transaction was considered unusual but not infrequent.

Cash (+A)	**9,000**	
Accumulated Depreciation (+A)	**3,000**	
Loss on Sale of Machinery (Lo, −SE)	**2,000**	
Machinery (−A)		**14,000**
Sold machinery.		

2. A separate line of business (segment) was sold on March 14, 2003, for $18,000 cash. The book values of the assets and liabilities of the segment as of the date of the sale were $10,000 and $4,000, respectively. The business segment recognized revenues of $18,500 and expenses of $14,000 from January 1, 2003, to March 14, 2003.

Revenues of the Segment	**18,500**	
Expenses of the Segment		**14,000**
Income Summary		**4,500**
Recognized business segment income		
(closing entry recorded at time of sale).		

Income Summary (E, −SE)	**1,530**	
Income Tax Liability (+L)		**1,530**
Recognized income tax liability related to		
1997 operations ($4,500 × 34%).		

Cash (+A)	**18,000**	
Liabilities (−L)	**4,000**	
Assets (−A)		**10,000**
Gain on Sale (Ga, +SE)		**12,000**
Sold business segment.		

Gain on Sale (−Ga, −SE)	**4,080**	
Income Tax Liability (+L)		**4,080**
Recognized additional tax liability ($12,000 × 34%).		

3. On September 12, 2003, Panawin retired, before maturity, outstanding bonds with a face value of $120,000, for a cash payment of $130,000. The bonds were originally issued at a premium, and the unamortized premium as of the date of retirement was $3,000. The loss on the retirement is considered extraordinary.

Bonds Payable (−L)	**120,000**	
Unamortized Premium (−L)	**3,000**	
Loss on Retirement (Lo, −SE)	**7,000**	
Cash (−A)		**130,000**
Retired outstanding bonds.		

Income Tax Liability (−L)	**2,380**	
Loss on Retirement (−Lo, +SE)		**2,380**
Recognized tax benefit ($7,000 × 34%).		

4. The company changed its inventory flow assumption from last-in, first-out (LIFO) to first-in, first-out (FIFO). This change increased the ending inventory balance for 2003 by $8,000.

| Inventory (+A) | 8,000 | |
| Income from Accounting Change (Ga, +SE) | | 8,000 |

Recognized change from LIFO to FIFO.

| Income from Accounting Change (−Ga, −SE) | 2,720 | |
| Income Tax Liability (+L) | | 2,720 |

Recognized additional tax liability ($8,000 × 34%).

The income statement is shown in Figure 13–7, and the reconciliation of retained earnings is shown in Figure 13–8.

FIGURE 13–7 Income statement for review problem

Panawin Enterprises
Income Statement
For the Year Ended December 31, 2003

Operating revenues	$85,000	(given)
Operating expenses	62,000	(given)
Net operating income	$23,000	
Loss on sale of machinery	(2,000)	
Net income from continuing operations before tax	$21,000	
Less: Federal income tax	7,000	(given)
Net income from continuing operations	$14,000	
Income from disposed segment (net of tax)	2,970	($4,500 − $1,530)
Gain on sale of segment (net of tax)	7,920	($12,000 − $4,080)
Net income before extraordinary items	$24,890	
Extraordinary loss on retirement of debt (net of tax)	(4,620)	(−$7,000 + $2,380)
Net income before change in accounting principle	$20,270	
Income effect from change from LIFO to FIFO (net of tax)	5,280	($8,000 − $2,720)
Net income	$25,550	
Earnings per share (10,000 shares outstanding):		
Net income from continuing operations	$ 1.40	($14,000 ÷ 10,000)
Disposal of business segment	1.09	[($2,970 + $7,920) ÷ 10,000]
Extraordinary item	(.46)	[$(4,620) ÷ 10,000]
Change in accounting principle	.53	($5,280 ÷ 10,000)
Total earnings per share	$ 2.56	($25,550 ÷ 10,000)

FIGURE 13–8

Reconciliation of retained earnings for Review Problem

Panawin Enterprises
Statement of Retained Earnings
For the Year Ended December 31, 2003

Beginning retained earnings balance	$106,000
Plus: Net income	25,550
Less: Dividends	(16,000)
Ending retained earnings balance	$115,550

SUMMARY OF KEY POINTS

The key points of the chapter are summarized below.

○ *Economic consequences associated with reporting net income.*

Income is the most common measure of a company's performance. It has been related to stock prices, suggesting that equity investors use income in their decisions to buy and sell equity securities. It has been related to bond prices, indicating that debt investors use income in their decisions to buy and sell corporate bonds. Income is also used by credit-rating agencies to establish credit ratings. Various income measures are also found in contracts written among stockholders, creditors, and managers. Such contracts are normally designed either to protect the interests of creditors or to encourage managers to act in the interests of the stockholders.

○ *A framework for financing, investing, and operating transactions.*

Financing and investing transactions involve setting up a company so that it can conduct operations. Operating transactions entail the actual conduct of the operations. The text identifies five categories of transactions: (1) exchanges with stockholders, (2) exchanges of liabilities and stockholders' equity, (3) issues and payments of debt, (4) purchases, sales, and exchanges of assets, and (5) operating transactions (revenues and expenses). Generally accepted accounting principles consider categories 1–3 as financing transactions, category 4 as investing transactions, and category 5 as operating transactions.

Exchanges with stockholders are involved exclusively with the formation and dissolution of the company's equity capital and the returns to the company's stockholders. Exchanges of liabilities and stockholders' equity deal only with a company's capital structure. Issues and payments of debt involve exchanges with a company's creditors and are reflected in the liabilities section of the balance sheet. Purchases, sales, or exchanges of assets are considered capital transactions because assets represent the capital base upon which operations are conducted.

○ *Categories that constitute a complete income statement and how they provide measures of income that address the objectives of financial reporting.*

The financial effects of five types of events warrant special disclosure and presentation on the income statement: (1) operating revenues and expenses, (2) other revenues and expenses, (3) disposals of business segments, (4) extraordinary items, and (5) changes in accounting principles.

These classifications highlight income numbers that vary in persistence. In terms of the objectives of financial accounting, earnings numbers with high persistence (e.g., operating earnings) are considered to reflect future cash flows, while low persistence earnings are not. Both kinds of earnings, however, reflect changes in a company's resources and, in that respect, are considered useful.

○ *Intraperiod tax allocation.*

Federal income taxes are disclosed in two different ways on the income statement. The first income tax disclosure immediately follows net income from continuing operations (before tax). It represents the tax expense recognized by the company due to taxable revenues and deductible expenses not related to the items listed below net income from continuing operations on the income statement.

The dollar amounts associated with the remaining items (disposal of business segments, extraordinary items, and changes in accounting principles) are all disclosed *net of tax*. Such presentation means that each of these revenue and expense items is disclosed on the income statement after the related income tax effect has been removed. The practice of including the income tax effect of a particular transaction with the transaction itself on the income statement is known as *intraperiod tax allocation*.

○ *Earnings per share disclosure on the income statement.*

Generally accepted accounting principles require that earnings per share be disclosed on the face of the income statement and that the specific amounts associated with (1) net income from continuing operations (after tax), (2) disposals of business segments, (3) extraordinary items, and (4) changes in accounting principles be disclosed separately. The calculation involves dividing the dollar amounts of each of the four items listed by the average number of shares outstanding during the accounting period.

KEY TERMS

Note: Definitions for these terms are provided in the glossary at the end of the text.

Business segment (p. 577)
Comprehensive income (p. 570)
Diluted earnings per share (p. 584)
Earnings persistence (p. 584)
Extraordinary items (p. 578)
Financing and investing transactions (p. 570)

Frequent (p. 576)
Intraperiod tax allocation (p. 581)
Operating transactions (p. 570)
Pro forma (as if) basis (p. 581)
Usual (p. 576)

ETHICS IN THE REAL WORLD

The boards of directors of most major U.S. companies have established executive compensation plans that base executive pay on some measure of company performance. While these plans differ widely across companies, a large percentage use some form of reported earnings as the measure of performance. Recognizing that there are many different ways to measure earnings, these compensation contracts must be very specific about which earnings measure is used. Pillsbury, for example, bases its formula on operating earnings, the result of subtracting operating expenses from operating revenues, excluding such items as interest expense, interest income, gains and losses on asset sales, extraordinary gains and losses, and the effects of accounting changes. Other companies, such as DuPont and Ashland Oil, base their formulas on net income after such items—the "bottom line."

Consider a company that has a compensation plan like that of DuPont, where compensation is a function of earnings after interest expense, and assume that management is analyzing how to finance a particular capital investment—that is, should it be financed with debt or equity? Management knows that if debt is chosen, net income and its compensation will be reduced by the interest expense recognized on the debt. On the other hand, if management chooses equity, there will be no interest expense to reduce its compensation amount.

ETHICAL ISSUE Is it ethical for management to consider the impact of the financing decision on its compensation amount, or should such impact be completely ignored when choosing between debt and equity?

INTERNET RESEARCH EXERCISE

In December 2000, Kraft Foods acquired all the common stock of Nabisco for $15 billion. Review the income statement of Kraft Foods for the previous three years and identify any non-operating items that should be carefully examined by an analyst. Begin your search at Kraft's home page (*www.kraft.com*).

BRIEF EXERCISES

REAL DATA

BE13–1

Nonrecurring items

In 1995, Sprint reported net income of $392.7 million, compared to $1.182 billion in 1996. The 1995 income statement contains an $87.6 million restructuring charge and a $565.3 million extraordinary loss, while the 1996 income statement contains no restructuring charge and an extraordinary loss of only $4.5 million.

a. Would you agree that Sprint performed almost three times better in 1996 than in 1995? Why or why not?
b. Briefly explain the nature of a restructuring charge and an extraordinary item.
c. How would you adjust the reported incomes in the two years to make them more comparable?

REAL DATA

BE13–2

Effects on the basic accounting equation

When Anheuser-Busch Company recognized a $160 million charge on its income statement for the closure of Tampa Breweries, it consisted of a write-down of plant assets of $113.7 million, employee severance costs of $19.4 million, and other disposal costs of $26.9 million. The following year the company disclosed a $54.7 million gain associated with the sale of the St. Louis Cardinals baseball team. The team was sold for $150 million.

For each of the elements of these disclosures, discuss how the basic accounting equation could have been affected.

REAL DATA

BE13–3

Following an FASB requirement

The FASB passed a requirement stating that costs of business process re-engineering be expensed. Up to that time, Owens Corning had capitalized these costs. The following year, Owens Corning was forced to recognize a $15 million charge (net of income taxes of $10 million) on its income statement.

a. What dollar amount was disclosed on the income statement, and where was it disclosed?
b. Describe how this event affected the basic accounting equation.
c. What was the gross amount of the write-off, and why is it reduced by the tax effect?

EXERCISES

E13–1

Which statement is affected?

Listed below are transactions or items that are frequently reported in financial statements.

1. Income effect due to changing from the double-declining-balance method to the straight-line method of depreciation.
2. Collection of accounts receivable.
3. Purchase of an insurance policy on December 31 that provides coverage for the following year.
4. Accrued wages earned by the employees.
5. Estimated uncollectible accounts receivable using the aging method.
6. Recognized a gain on the sale of plant equipment.
7. Recognized a loss when the government expropriated land for a highway.

8. Declared a dividend valued at $100,000.
9. Under the requirements of a debt covenant, appropriated a portion of retained earnings.
10. Received dividends on stocks held as a short-term investment. The dividends were declared and paid on the same day.
11. Recognized the cost of inventory sold during the year under the periodic method.
12. Paid rent for the current year.

a. Indicate whether each item would be included on the company's income statement, statement of stockholders' equity, or neither, using the following codes:
   IS   Income statement
   SE   Statement of stockholders' equity
   N   Neither
b. Indicate whether the items you coded IS would be considered (1) usual and frequent, (2) unusual or infrequent, (3) unusual and infrequent, or (4) other.
c. Provide a brief explanation of your choice in (b) of (1), (2), (3), or (4).

E13–2

Classifying
transactions

A number of transactions are described below.

1. Declaration of a stock dividend.
2. Purchase of 50 percent of the outstanding stock of another company.
3. Payment of previously accrued interest payable.
4. Accrual of interest expense.
5. Purchase of machinery.
6. Recognition of depreciation on machinery.
7. Purchase of treasury stock.
8. Sale of treasury stock at a price less than its original cost.
9. Conversion of debt to common stock.
10. Receipt of cash on an outstanding receivable.
11. Sale of inventory on account.
12. Purchase of inventory on account.
13. Declaration of dividends.
14. Receipt of dividends on short-term marketable securities.
15. Early retirement of outstanding long-term debt.

a. Refer to Figure 13–2 in the text, and classify each transaction in one of the following categories:
   (1) Exchanges with stockholders
   (2) Exchanges of liabilities and stockholders' equity
   (3) Issues and payments of debt
   (4) Purchases, sales, and exchanges of assets
   (5) Operating transactions
b. Briefly explain why the transactions are considered increasingly operating (or decreasingly financing) as the categories move from (1) to (5).

E13–3

Comprehensive
income

The December 31, 2003, balance sheet of Smedley Company is provided below.

Assets	$70,000	Liabilities	$15,000
		Stockholders' equity	55,000
		Total liabilities and	
Total assets	$70,000	stockholders' equity	$70,000

During 2004 the company entered into the following transactions:

1. Common stock was issued for $35,000 cash.
2. Services were performed for $50,000 cash.
3. Cash expenses of $24,000 were incurred.
4. Long-term liabilities of $15,000 were paid.
5. Dividends of $7,000 were declared and paid.

a. Classify each transaction as operating, investing, or financing and then prepare an income statement.
b. Compute comprehensive income, and compare it to the income amount calculated in (a).
c. Explain why the two dollar amounts are equal.

E13–4

Debt covenants expressed in terms of income

Morton Manufacturing maintains a credit line with First Bank that allows the company to borrow up to $1 million. A covenant associated with the loan contract limits the company's dividends in any one year to 20 percent of net income. The 2003 income statement data of Morton Manufacturing is provided below.

Net sales	**$840,000**
Less: Cost of goods sold	570,000
Gross profit	**$270,000**
Selling and administrative expenses	120,000
Net operating income	**$150,000**
Gain on sale of securities	14,000
Interest expense	(4,000)
Net income from continuing operations before tax	**$160,000**
Less: Income tax	51,200
Net income from continuing operations	**$108,800**
Extraordinary gain (net of tax)	22,000
Net income before change in accounting principle	**$130,800**
Income effect due to change in accounting principle	52,000
Net income	**$182,800**

a. Compute the maximum amount of dividends Morton can pay if the debt covenant is expressed as 20 percent of each of the following:
   (1) Net income
   (2) Income before change in accounting principle
   (3) Income before extraordinary items (from continuing operations)
   (4) Net operating income
b. Explain why the bank may wish to state the contractual limitation on dividends in terms of income from operations instead of net income.

REAL DATA

E13–5

Special items

In its 1999 annual report, Intuit, a world-leader in e-based financing solutions, reported net income of $68 million (1997), a net loss of $12 million (1998), and net income of $376 million (1999). In addition to the operating items listed on the income statement, the following special items also appeared: 1997—restructuring charge ($10 million), gain from sale of discounted operations ($71 million); 1998—gain on disposal of business ($4 million); and 1999—net gain on marketable securities ($579 million).

Describe each of the special items and comment on the trend of the company's operating income across the three-year period.

E13–6

Disposal of a business segment

LTB Enterprises consists of four separate divisions: building products, chemicals, mining, and plastics. On March 15, 2002, LTB sold the chemicals division for $625,000 cash. Financial information related to the chemicals division follows:

(1/1–3/15/02)		**(3/15/02)**	
Sales	$175,000	**Assets**	$1,850,000
Operating expenses	160,000	**Liabilities**	1,400,000
Net operating income (loss)	$ 15,000		

a. Provide the journal entry (or entries) to record the sale of the chemicals division. Assume an income tax rate of 35 percent.
b. Prepare the section of LTB's 2002 income statement that relates to the disposal of the business segment.

E13-7

Management choices and earnings persistence

It is December 2003, and Sharon Sowers, the CEO of Mallory Services, has decided to sell the clerical division. She has received an offer for $105,000 but is undecided about whether she wishes to complete the sale in 2003 or 2004. She is currently evaluating the effects of the sale on 2003 reported net income. Income from continuing operations for 2003 is estimated to be $950,000 (excluding the activities of the clerical division), and information about the clerical division is provided below. The company's tax rate is 35 percent.

Year Ended 2003		December 2003	
Revenues	$35,000	Assets	$93,000
Expenses	23,000	Liabilities	26,000

a. Prepare the 2003 income statement, beginning with net income from continuing operations, assuming that Sharon accepts the offer, and explain how a user might interpret the items on the income statement in terms of earnings persistence.
b. Prepare the 2003 income statement, beginning with net income from continuing operations, assuming that Sharon chooses not to sell the division in 2003, and explain how a user might interpret the items on the income statement in terms of earnings persistence.
c. Describe some of the important trade-offs faced by Sharon as she decides whether to complete the sale in 2003 or 2004.

E13-8

Management choices and earnings persistence

It is December 2003, and Rob Blandig, the CEO of Carmich Industries, has decided to sell the chemical division. He has received an offer for $350,000, but he is undecided about whether he wishes to complete the sale in 2003 or 2004. He is currently evaluating the effects of the sale on 2003 reported net income. Income from continuing operations for 2003 is estimated to be $1,930,000 (excluding the activities of the chemical division and management's bonus), and the company anticipates a weak year in 2004. Information about the division is provided below. The company's tax rate is 35 percent, and company management is paid a bonus each year in the amount of 20 percent $\times$ net income from continuing operations. For purposes of the bonus calculation, net income from continuing operations is not reduced by the bonus.

Year Ended 2003		December 2003	
Revenues	$145,000	Assets	$437,000
Expenses	120,000	Liabilities	218,000

a. Prepare the 2003 income statement, beginning with net income from continuing operations, assuming that Rob accepts the offer, and explain how a user might interpret the items on the income statement in terms of earnings persistence.
b. Prepare the 2003 income statement, beginning with net income from continuing operations, assuming that Rob chooses not to sell the division in 2003, and explain how a user might interpret the items on the income statement in terms of earnings persistence.
c. Describe some of the important trade-offs faced by Rob as he decides whether to complete the sale in 2003 or 2004.

REAL DATA

E13-9

Interpreting the income statement

The 1999 income statement for Honeywell International, an advanced technology manufacturing company, is provided below (dollars in millions).

Net sales	$23,735
Costs of goods sold	(18,495)
Selling and administrative expenses	(3,216)
Gain on sale of business	106
Equity income in affiliates	76
Gain on sale of investment	307
Interest charges	(265)
Income before taxes	2,248
Taxes on income	(707)
Net income	$ 1,541

a. Which of the items would you consider either unusual or infrequent or both, and why?
b. Estimate operating earnings for 1999.
c. Discuss why analysts might want to separate net income from operating earnings.

E13–10

Accounting for
unusual losses

You are currently auditing the financial records of Paxson Corporation, which is located in San Francisco, California. During the current year, inventories with an original cost of $2,325,000 were destroyed by an earthquake. The company was unsure how to record this loss and is seeking your advice. The loss is deductible for tax purposes, and the company's tax rate is 35 percent.

a. Prepare the journal entry (or entries) to record the loss of the inventory if the loss is not considered extraordinary.
b. Prepare the journal entry (or entries) to record the loss of the inventory if the loss is considered extraordinary.
c. Should the loss be classified as an extraordinary loss or as an ordinary loss? Explain.
d. Would your answer to (c) change if the plant had been located in Miami, Florida? Explain.

E13–11

Economic
consequences of an
extraordinary item

The management of Sting Enterprises shares in a bonus that is determined and paid at the end of each year. The amount of the bonus is defined by multiplying net income from continuing operations (after tax) by 12 percent. The bonus is not used in the calculation of income from continuing operations. During 2003, Sting was a defendant in a lawsuit and was required to pay $480,000 over and above the amount covered by insurance. The loss is tax deductible, and the company's tax rate is 35 percent. The company was last involved in a lawsuit five years ago. Net income from continuing operations (before tax) for 2003, excluding the loss from the lawsuit, was $800,000.

a. Compute management's 2003 bonus, assuming that the lawsuit is considered unusual but not infrequent.
b. Compute management's 2003 bonus, assuming that the lawsuit is considered extraordinary.
c. Repeat (a) and (b) above, assuming that Sting was awarded the $480,000 settlement instead of having to pay it.
d. Explain how the decision to include or not to include an item as extraordinary can have significant economic consequences.

E13–12

Earnings-per-share
disclosure

The following income statement was reported by Battery Builders for the year ending December 31, 2003:

Sales	**$85,000**	
Rent revenue	**23,000**	
Interest income	**7,000**	
Total revenues		**$115,000**
Cost of goods sold	**$52,000**	
Operating expenses	**24,000**	
Interest expense	**12,000**	
Loss on sale of fixed asset	**6,000**	
Total expenses		**94,000**
Income from continuing operations (before tax)		**$ 21,000**
Less: Income tax		**10,000**
Income from continuing operations		**$ 11,000**
Income from disposed segment (net of tax)		**3,000**
Gain on sale of disposed segment (net of tax)		**2,000**
Income before extraordinary items		**$ 16,000**
Extraordinary loss (net of tax)		**7,000**
Income before change in accounting principle		**$ 9,000**
Income due to change in accounting principle (net of tax)		**6,000**
Net income		**$ 15,000**

Show how Battery Builders would report earnings per share on the face of the income statement, assuming the following:

a. An average of 15,000 shares of common stock was outstanding during 2003.
b. An average of 25,000 shares of common stock was outstanding during 2003.
c. An average of 30,000 shares of common stock was outstanding during 2003.

E13–13

Intraperiod tax
allocation and the
financial statements

The following information was taken from the 2003 financial records of Rothrock Consolidated. All items are pretax.

	Debit	Credit
Operating Revenues		87,000
Operating Expenses	32,500	
Gain on Sale of Short-Term Investments		5,200
Loss on Sale of Business Segment	21,000	
Income Earned on Disposed Business Segment		3,000
Extraordinary Loss	5,000	
Income Due to Change in Accounting Principle		12,500
Retained Earnings (beginning balance)		72,000
Dividends Declared	18,000	

The company's income tax rate is 35 percent, and the items above are treated identically for
financial reporting and tax purposes.
Prepare the following:

a. A single-step income statement.
b. A reconciliation of retained earnings.

E13–14

Intraperiod tax
allocation

The following pretax amounts were obtained from the financial records of Watson Company
for 2003:

	Debit	Credit
Retained Earnings (1/1/00)		847,000
Sales Revenues		1,385,000
Rent Revenue		360,000
Cost of Goods Sold	475,000	
Administrative Expenses	100,000	
Depreciation Expense	250,000	
Selling Expenses	189,000	
Extraordinary Loss	202,000	
Loss on Sale of Fixed Assets	105,000	
Dividends Declared	460,000	

The company's tax rate is 35 percent.

a. Prepare an income statement for the year ended December 31, 2003, using the multistep
    format.
b. Prepare a statement of retained earnings for the year ended December 31, 2003.
c. What is the income tax effect associated with each item that is reported net of tax?
    Assuming that no taxes were owed at the beginning of 2003 and no tax payments were
    made during 2003, what is the total income tax liability at the end of 2003?

E13–15

Covenant
restrictions and
income reporting

Kennington Company has outstanding debt that contains restrictive covenants limiting dividends to 15 percent of net income from continuing operations. During 2003, the company
reported net income from operations of $235,000 after taxes, excluding the following items—
all of which ignore tax effects.

1. A $25,000 gain was recognized on the sale of an investment.
2. A $62,000 loss was recognized on a lawsuit.
3. A $38,000 loss was recognized on the early retirement of debt.

Assume that the gain in (1) is taxable, the losses in (2) and (3) are tax deductible, and the company's tax rate is 35 percent.

a. Provide the income statement, beginning at net income from operations, and compute the maximum amount of dividends that the company can declare, assuming that (1) the investment in (1) is a business segment that broke even during 2003, and (2) lawsuits are common for Kennington.
b. Provide the income statement, beginning at net income from operations, and compute the maximum amount of dividends that the company can declare, assuming that (1) the investment in (1) is a short-term equity security, and (2) lawsuits are very rare for Kennington.

E13–16

Stock market
reactions to
income reporting

Madigan International is planning a major stock issuance in early 2004. During 2003, the company reported net income from operations of $865,000 before taxes. The four items below describe major events that occurred during 2003. The company's accountants chose to include items (1) and (4) in the computation of net income from continuing operations and chose to disclose items (2) and (3) as extraordinary items.

1. A $42,000 gain was recognized on the sale of a subsidiary.
2. Inventory was written down by $53,000 due to earthquake damage.
3. An outstanding accounts receivable of $38,000 was written off when a major customer declared bankruptcy.
4. A $25,000 gain was recognized due to the change of an accounting principle.

Assume that items (1) and (4) are taxable, items (2) and (3) are tax deductible, and that the company's tax rate is 35 percent.

a. Present the income statement, beginning with net income from operations.
b. Critique the accounting treatment chosen by Madigan's accountants, and provide an income statement that is consistent with generally accepted accounting principles.
c. Discuss how Madigan's accounting treatment could influence the price at which the company's stock is sold in 2001, and provide a rationale for why Madigan may have made such choices.

PROBLEMS

P13–1

Classifying
transactions

Lundy Manufacturing produces and sells football equipment. The company was involved in the following transactions or events during 2003:

1. The company purchased $250,000 worth of materials to be used during 2004 to manufacture helmets and shoulder pads.
2. The company sold football equipment for a price of $500,000. The inventory associated with the sale cost the company $375,000.
3. One of the company's plants in San Francisco was damaged by a minor earthquake. The total amount of the damage was $100,000.
4. The company issued 10 ($1,000 face value) bonds at a discount (.98).
5. The company incurred $143,000 in wage expenses.
6. The company was sued by a high school football player who was injured while using some of the company's equipment. The football player will probably win the suit, and the amount of the settlement has been estimated at $10,000. This is the sixth lawsuit filed against the company in the past three years.

7. The company switched from the double-declining-balance depreciation method to the straight-line depreciation method.
8. The company declared and paid $50,000 in dividends.
9. The company incurred a loss when it sold some securities that it was holding as an investment.

REQUIRED:

a. Classify each of these transactions as financing, investing, or operating.
b. Refer to Figures 13–2 and 13–3 in the text, and identify the category in which each of the items listed should be placed.
c. Which of these items should be included on the company's income statement? Briefly describe how they should be disclosed.

P13–2

Bonus contracts based on income can affect management's business decisions

The managers of Martin House are paid a salary and share in a bonus that is determined at the end of each year. The total bonus is determined by multiplying the company's income from operations by 25 percent. The bonus is not considered an operating expense. Interest on borrowed funds is considered an operating expense when computing the bonus.

During 2003, the company decided to expand its plant facility. The estimated cost of the expansion was $1 million. To raise the necessary funds, the company could either borrow $1 million at an annual interest rate of 8 percent or issue 50,000 shares of common stock at $20 each. The company raised the funds using one of these two methods, and income from operations (excluding any interest charges) for 2000 was reported as follows:

Operating revenues	**$6,800,000**
Operating expenses (excluding interest)	**5,600,000**
Income from operations	**$1,200,000**

REQUIRED:

a. Assume that on January 1, 2003, Martin House borrowed the $1 million. Compute the total bonus shared by the company's managers.
b. Assume that on January 1, 2003, Martin House issued common stock to raise the $1 million. Compute the total bonus shared by the company's managers.
c. Why might management choose to issue equity instead of borrowing the $1 million? Is such a decision necessarily in the best interest of the company's stockholders?
d. Repeat (a) and (b) above, assuming that the interest expense is not considered an operating expense when computing the bonus.

P13–3

Financing, investing, and operating transactions

Raleigh Corporation began operations on February 10, 2003. During 2003, the company entered into the following transactions:

1. Issued $110,000 of common stock and $25,000 of preferred stock.
2. Performed services for $580,000.
3. Issued $475,000 in long-term debt for cash.
4. Incurred expenses: $125,000 for wages, $35,000 for supplies, $80,000 for depreciation, and $75,000 for miscellaneous expenses.
5. Purchased fixed assets for $250,000 cash.
6. Declared, but did not pay, cash dividends of $10,000.
7. Purchased fixed assets in exchange for a long-term note valued at $85,000.

REQUIRED:

a. Classify each transaction as either operating, investing, or financing.
b. Prepare an income statement.
c. Compute comprehensive income and compare it to the income reported on the income statement. Discuss.

Preparing an
income statement

Excerpts from Crozier Industries' financial records as of December 31, 2003, follow:

	Debit	Credit
Sales		977,000
Sales Returns	9,000	
Costs of Goods Sold	496,000	
Dividends	50,000	
Rent Expense	90,000	
Wages Payable		175,000
Loss on Sale of Food Services Division	2,000	
Loss Incurred by Food Services Division	10,000	
Depreciation Expense	100,000	
Cumulative Effect on Income of Change in Depreciation Methods	130,000	
Gain on Land Appropriated by the Government		92,000
Insurance Expense	12,000	
Inventory	576,000	
Administrative Expenses	109,000	
Prepaid Insurance	48,000	
Gain on Sale of Short-Term Investments		142,000

The amounts shown do not include any tax effects. Crozier's tax rate is 35 percent. Assume that all items are treated the same for accounting and income tax purposes.

REQUIRED:

a. Indicate which items should be included on the company's income statement. Classify each item to be included on the income statement as one of the following:
    (1) Usual and frequent
    (2) Unusual or infrequent
    (3) Disposal of business segment
    (4) Unusual and infrequent
    (5) Change in accounting method
b. Prepare an income statement using the single-step format, and assess the persistence of each item on the income statement.

Disclosing
extraordinary items

In its 2003 financial report, Meeks Company reported $850,000 under the line item "Extraordinary losses" on the income statement. The company's tax rate is 35 percent. The footnote pertaining to extraordinary losses indicates that the $850,000 loss, before tax, is comprised of the following items:

1. A loss of $260,000 incurred on a warehouse in Florida damaged in a hurricane.
2. A loss of $150,000 incurred when Meeks sold the assets of a business segment.
3. A loss of $225,000 incurred when a warehouse in Iowa was blown up by a disgruntled employee.
4. Accounts receivable written off in the amount of $125,000.
5. A loss of $90,000 incurred when one of the company's distribution centers in Arizona was damaged by a flood.

REQUIRED:

a. Discuss how each of these items should be disclosed in the financial statements, including whether or not they should be disclosed net of tax.
b. Show how the "extraordinary items" section of the income statement should have been reported.

P13-6
Intraperiod tax
allocation, income
tax expense, and
income tax liability

The following information has been obtained from the internal financial records of MTM Company:

Retained earnings, December 31, 2002	$1,259,000
Dividends declared and paid during 2003	100,000
Dividends declared during 2003 but not paid	75,000
Dividends declared during 2002 and paid in 2003	90,000
2003 income from continuing operations (before taxes)	850,000
Extraordinary losses in 2003 (before tax effect)	135,000

The company's tax rate is 35 percent. Assume that financial accounting income equals income for tax purposes.

REQUIRED:
a.   What is the company's net income for the year ended December 31, 2003?
b.   Compute income tax expense reported in MTM's 2003 income statement.
c.   Prepare a reconciliation of retained earnings for the year ended December 31, 2003.
d.   Assume that the income tax liability account had a balance of $70,000 on January 1, 2003, and that tax payments of $200,000 were made during 2003. What should be the balance in this account on December 31, 2003?

REAL DATA

P13-7
Earnings per share
and discontinued
operations

The lower portion of the 1999 income statement for Hewlett-Packard, a manufacturer of computer equipment, is provided below (dollars in millions).

Net earnings from continuing operations	$3,104
Net earnings from discontinued operations	387
Net earnings	$3,491
Basic net earnings per share:	
Continuing operations	$3.08
Discontinued operations	.38
	$3.46
Diluted net earnings per share:	
Continuing operations	$2.97
Discontinued operations	.37
	$3.34

REQUIRED:
a.   Why is there a distinction between net earnings from continuing operations and net earnings from discontinued operations?
b.   Estimate the number of common shares outstanding.
c.   Why is there a distinction between basic net earnings per share and diluted net earnings per share?
d.   Estimate the number of common shares that would be outstanding if all potentially dilutive securities were converted to common shares.

P13-8
Income effect due
to a change in
depreciation
methods

On January 1, 1998, Boxer Corporation purchased some manufacturing equipment for $3 million. The equipment was estimated to have a salvage value of $500,000 and a useful life of ten years. The company used the straight-line method of depreciation for both book and tax purposes. On December 31, 2002, Boxer Corporation decided that it should use the double-declining-balance method for both book and tax purposes. The company's tax rate is 35 percent.

REQUIRED:
a.   Compute depreciation expense and accumulated depreciation for 1998, 1999, 2000, and 2001, using both the straight-line method and the double-declining-balance method.
b.   Prepare the journal entry (or entries) that would be recorded on December 31, 2002, to record the change from the straight-line method to the double-declining-balance method for both book and tax purposes.
c.   How and where on the financial statements would the income effect of this change be disclosed?

P13-9

Disclosing net of tax, and the earnings-per-share calculation

Woodland Farm Corporation has the following items to include in its financial statements:

	Debit	Credit
Extraordinary Loss from a Flood	250,000	
Extraordinary Gain from Bond Retirement		55,000
Sale of Inventory		250,000
Loss on Disposal of Business Segment	100,000	
Income Effect Due to Change in Accounting Method		80,000
Advertising Expense	50,000	
Income Earned by Disposed Business Segment		150,000

None of the listed amounts include any income tax effects. The company's tax rate is 35 percent.

REQUIRED:

a. Describe how each item above would be disclosed on the income statement or statement of retained earnings.
b. Compute the tax effect of each of the items that should be disclosed net of tax. What dollar amount would be shown on the financial statements for each of these items?
c. Assume that income from continuing operations (after tax) was $600,000, and 200,000 shares of common stock were outstanding during the year. Provide the earnings-per-share calculation.

P13-10

Preparing an income statement

Tom Brown, controller of Microbiology Labs, informs you that the company has sold a segment of its business. Mr. Brown also provides you with the following information for 2003:

	Continuing Operations	Discontinued Segment
Sales	$10,000,000	$850,000
Cost of goods sold	2,500,000	600,000
Operating expenses	750,000	100,000
Loss on sale of office equipment	60,000	—
Gain on disposal of discontinued segment		250,000

The following information is not reflected in any of the above amounts:

1. Microbiology Labs is subject to a 35 percent tax rate.
2. Microbiology Labs switched from the straight-line to the double-declining-balance method of depreciation for financial reporting purposes. The company already uses double-declining-balance for tax purposes, and the cumulative effect of this change on income is a decrease of $230,000.
3. During 2003, Microbiology Labs retired outstanding bonds that were to mature in 2005. The company incurred a loss of $80,000, prior to taxes, on the retirement of the bonds.
4. Microbiology Labs owns several apple orchards as part of its operations. During 2003, the company's apple crop was destroyed by an infestation of a rare insect. This unusual and infrequent loss, prior to taxes, totaled $800,000.
5. Two million shares of common stock were outstanding throughout 2003.

REQUIRED:

Prepare an income statement for the year ended December 31, 2003, including the recommended earnings-per-share disclosures. In terms of the objectives of financial accounting, comment on the usefulness of each of the different measures of income.

REAL DATA

P13-11

Income management and special items

During 2000, Imation, a global technology company, booked a $22 million restructuring charge and changed the way it recognizes revenue to a more conservative method, creating a cumulative loss due to an accounting change of $3.4 million (net of a tax benefit of $1.7 million). Both charges were reported on the 2000 income statement. During that year the company recognized an overall net loss of $4.4 million.

REQUIRED:
a. Where on the income statement would one find the tax benefit associated with the restructuring charge?
b. Estimate the company's effective tax rate for 2000.
c. Imation booked large positive earnings in both 1998 and 1999. Is there an income management strategy that Imation may have used in 2000? If so, which one? Discuss.

P13–12

Comprehensive problem

Laidig Industries has prepared the following unadjusted trial balance as of December 31, 2003:

	Debit	Credit
Cash	$110,000	
Accounts Receivable	340,000	
Allowance for Doubtful Accounts		$ 50,000
Inventory (balance 1/1/03)	467,000	
Prepaid Insurance	60,000	
Fixed Assets	850,000	
Accumulated Depreciation		287,000
Accounts Payable		200,000
Dividends Payable		45,000
Bonds Payable		500,000
Common Stock		100,000
Retained Earnings		673,000
Sales		1,256,000
Gain on Sale of Land		76,000
Extraordinary Loss	35,000	
Income Effect Due to Change in Accounting Principle	60,000	
Purchases	750,000	
Administrative Expenses	100,000	
Selling Expenses	255,000	
Interest Expense	25,000	
Dividends	135,000	

ADDITIONAL INFORMATION:
1. A physical count of inventory on December 31, 2003, indicated that the company had $480,000 of inventory on hand.
2. An aging of accounts receivable indicates that $75,000 is uncollectible.
3. The company uses straight-line depreciation. The assets have a ten-year life and zero salvage value.
4. The company used a third of the remaining insurance policy during 2003.
5. The company pays interest for its bond payable on December 31 of every year. The coupon rate and the effective rate are both 10 percent per year.
6. The company's tax rate is 35 percent. All income tax charges are recorded at the end of the year.
7. 200,000 shares of common stock were outstanding during 2003.

REQUIRED:
Prepare the following:

a. The necessary adjusting and closing entries on December 31, 2003.
b. An income statement including recommended earnings-per-share disclosures.
c. A statement of retained earnings.
d. In terms of the objectives of financial accounting, discuss the usefulness of the various measures of income included on the statement.

ISSUES FOR DISCUSSION

ID13-1

Public earnings announcements

On November 17, 1995, *The Wall Street Journal* reported:

Kmart Corp., hurt by the cost of getting rid of discontinued merchandise and closing stores, posted a $69 million third quarter loss on a 2.5% sales increase. The discount retailer's loss would have been greater except for a $48 million gain from the sale of its equity interest in Sports Authority, Inc. . . . [However] . . . Wall Street did not punish Kmart's stock price.

REQUIRED:

a. Discuss the relevant issues involved in deciding where on the income statement to disclose the gain on the sale of the equity interest in Sports Authority, Inc.

b. The same week that Kmart announced its loss, DuPont posted a 19 percent increase in third quarter net income, which led to a 6 percent drop in its stock price. Explain how Wall Street could have viewed Kmart's announcement favorably and DuPont's unfavorably.

ID13-2

Accounting changes

The 1999 annual report of TJX Companies contained the following footnote:

Effective January 31, 1999 the Company changed its method of accounting for layaway sales in compliance with a Staff Accounting Bulletin issued by the Securities and Exchange Commission during the fourth quarter of 2000. Under the new accounting method, the Company will defer recognition of a layaway sale and its related profit to the accounting period when the customer picks up the merchandise. The cumulative effect of this change for periods prior to January 31, 1999 of $5.2 million (net of income taxes of $3.4 million), or $.02 per share, is shown as the cumulative effect of accounting change in the Consolidated Statements of Income.

REQUIRED:

a. Would you consider this accounting change discretionary or mandatory? Discuss how analysts might respond differently to discretionary and mandatory accounting changes.

b. Justify the accounting change in terms of the principles of revenue recognition.

c. Did the change increase or decrease reported income?

d. Estimate the company's effective income tax rate.

e. Where on the income statement would the cumulative effect of the change be reported?

REAL DATA

ID13-3

Extraordinary losses

Weyerhaeuser Company is principally engaged in the growing and harvesting of timber and the manufacture, distribution, and sale of forest products. When Mount St. Helens, a volcano located in Washington State, erupted, 68,000 acres of the company's standing timber, logs, buildings, and equipment were destroyed. As a result, the company recognized a $36 million (net of tax) extraordinary loss on its income statement.

REQUIRED:

a. What must have been true for Weyerhaeuser to classify this event as extraordinary?

b. If Mount St. Helens continues to erupt periodically, would future related losses necessarily be classified by Weyerhaeuser as extraordinary? Why or why not?

c. At the same time of the eruption, Weyerhaeuser's income tax rate was approximately 48 percent. Compute the entire loss (ignoring the tax effect) incurred by the company, and provide the journal entries prepared by the company's accountants to record the loss and the related income tax effect.

REAL DATA

ID13-4

Disclosing nonoperating items on the income statement

Several years ago, PepsiCo's earnings either rose or fell, depending upon the source of the information. Standard & Poor's reported that PepsiCo experienced a 25 percent earnings gain, while Value Line, another investor service, reported that PepsiCo experienced a 7 percent loss. The discrepancy involved a "normal but nonrecurring charge" taken by PepsiCo to write down foreign bottling assets. Standard & Poor's ignored the charge in its earnings calculation, while Value Line included the charge.

REQUIRED:

a. Provide reasonable arguments that could have been used by Standard & Poor's and Value Line to support the decision either to ignore or include the charge in the calculation of PepsiCo's income.

b. Briefly describe the categories comprising a complete income statement and explain how such categories are usually disclosed.

c. *Forbes* once reported that "most financial analysts [are not concerned about] the geographic location of such items on the income statement." It is only important that they be disclosed. Explain why financial analysts might take such a position; at the same time, however, provide an argument suggesting that the specific location of an item on the income statement is important in an economic sense. State your argument in terms of earnings persistence and how income numbers are used in contracts.

REAL DATA

ID13–5

Income statement classification

Many e-tailers (retailers via the Internet) were not profitable in their early years. Analysts who believed in the futures of these firms, therefore, were forced to focus on other positive metrics of performance, such as revenues and gross profit margins (sales less cost of goods sold). The *Dow Jones News Service* (June 2, 2000) reported that the FASB had recently come out with a new rule requiring companies to include shipping and handling costs, significant in the e-tailing industry, in the cost-of-goods-sold category instead of as part of selling and administrative expense. Even though this reporting requirement had no effect on the bottom line, e-tailers like Amazon.com lobbied aggressively against it.

REQUIRED:

a. Why might analysts be interested in companies that were not recording profits?

b. What specific effect did the new FASB rule have on the income statement of companies like Amazon.com, and why would these companies lobby aggressively against the rule?

c. What impact would this new rule have on the reported cash flows of the company?

d. Do you think that the stock market prices of e-tailers would decrease in response to this ruling by the FASB? Why?

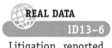

REAL DATA

ID13–6

Litigation, reported income, and stock prices

In 1990, Eastman Kodak recorded a third-quarter net loss of $206 million, but at the same time, it posted a 22 percent rise in operating earnings to $835 million. Much of the loss was due to a $909.5 million charge taken to cover the costs associated with a patent infringement ruling, at which time Kodak was ordered to pay almost $1 billion to Polaroid for infringing on Polaroid's instant photography patents. The dollar amount awarded Polaroid was far below the company's multibillion-dollar claim. Kodak's shares jumped $1.25 to $29.75 in response to the news.

REQUIRED:

a. Where on Kodak's income statement should the charge be disclosed, and should the amount be reported net of tax? If so, assume a 34 percent tax rate and compute the net amount.

b. The patent infringement case between Kodak and Polaroid was well publicized and extended over several years. How do you think this situation was reported in Kodak's 1989 annual report? In Polaroid's 1989 annual report?

c. Explain why Kodak's stock could have increased in value in response to news that the company reported a $206 million net loss for the quarter.

REAL DATA

ID13–7

Income statement categories

In its 2000 annual report, which included a statement of comprehensive income, Bristol-Myers Squibb reported the following items (dollars in millions):

Net earnings from discontinued operations	**$ 375**
Research and development	**(1,672)**
Foreign currency translation	**(282)**
Net gain on disposal of business	**240**

Provision for restructuring	**(508)**
Gain on sale of assets	**160**
Cost of products sold	**(4,759)**
Special charge to cover litigation claims	**(800)**

REQUIRED:

a. Explain the nature of each item, describe where they would be disclosed on the income statement (including comprehensive income), and state whether or not they would be reported net of taxes.

b. Discuss each item in terms of its persistence.

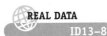

REAL DATA

ID13-8

Analyzing special income statement items

Indicate how the income effects of the following items would be disclosed on the income statement and whether they represent a wealth change and/or can be expected to persist in the future.

a. In 1997, Federal Express reported $17 million on operating gains from an insurance settlement for a DC-10 aircraft destroyed by fire.

b. From 1995 to 1997, Motorola reported net gains of $443 million on asset sales.

c. In 1997, Owens Corning reported a $68 million restructuring charge, equity in net income of affiliates of $11 million, and a $15 million cumulative effect of an accounting change.

d. In 1996, Owens Corning reported an $875 million charge related to expected litigation claims due to asbestos injuries.

REAL DATA

ID13-9

Writing off acquisition costs

The Wall Street Journal (September 1998) reported that the SEC is taking a tougher stance on companies that write off huge chunks of goodwill as purchased research and development. Apparently, when some companies acquire others, they write off the goodwill directly to the income statement rather than capitalizing it. They argue that they actually purchased research and development, which according to accounting principles must be expensed. A recent study from New York University shows that 389 companies, particularly high-technology and pharmaceutical concerns, wrote off part of their acquisition costs as R&D during the 1990s, compared to only three during the 1980s.

REQUIRED:

a. How should such write-offs be reported on the income statement?

b. Why would a company want to treat purchased goodwill as R&D, and why would the SEC want to take a stronger stand?

c. Do you think that purchased R&D should be written off immediately against income? Why or why not?

REAL DATA

ID13-10

The annual report of Wal-Mart

The 2001 annual report of Wal-Mart is reproduced in Appendix A.

REQUIRED:

Review the 2001 annual report, and answer the following questions.

a. Describe how nonoperating items affected Wal-Mart's reported net income in 1999, 2000, or 2001. Did they increase or decrease net income and by how much?

b. Describe the nonoperating items and classify them as "other" income items, extraordinary, discontinued operations, or changes in accounting methods.

c. What was the gross dollar amount of the cumulative accounting change? How much did Wal-Mart save in taxes by making this change?

d. How does Wal-Mart disclose other comprehensive income items? What are they?

e. How does Wal-Mart account for Sam's membership fee revenue? Discuss.

f. Briefly explain how Wal-Mart would disclose the sale if it chose to divest itself of Sam's Club.

The Statement of Cash Flows

KEY POINTS

The following key points are emphasized in this chapter:

The structure and format of the statement of cash flows.

Cash flows from operating, investing, and financing activities.

How the statement of cash flows complements the other financial statements and how it can be used by those interested in the financial condition of a company.

Important investing and financing transactions that do not appear on the statement of cash flows and how they are reported.

Economic consequences associated with the statement of cash flows.

Preparing a statement of cash flows from the information contained in two balance sheets, an income statement, and a statement of retained earnings.

MicroStrategy was a red-hot software company in the business-to-business Internet sector. Unlike many other Internet companies, MicroStrategy reported profits early and often. Then, the bottom fell out when news was released that MicroStrategy had been "cooking the books" by overstating revenues and profits. The stock price plunged and Zack's Research Report noted that, at the time, nine out of ten analysts had recently published "buy" or "strong buy" recommendations. Interestingly, well in advance of the stock price collapse, the company's cash flow from operations told a sobering story—negative $2.5 million instead of a profit of $9 million. Should the analysts have been looking at net cash from operations instead of net income? This chapter, which covers the statement of cash flows, answers that question, and discusses what cash flow is, how it should be used, and how earnings quality can be assessed by comparing net income to cash flow from operations.

The statement of cash flows contains a summary of a company's transactions that involve the cash account over a period of time. It is designed to highlight the cash flows associated with three aspects of the company's economic activities: (1) operations, (2) investments, and (3) financing. The basic structure of the statement of cash flows is provided in Figure 14–1. The reported numbers were taken from the 2000 annual report of Lucent Technologies Inc.

FIGURE 14–1 Sample statement of cash flows	**Lucent Technologies Inc.** **Statement of Cash Flows** **For the Year Ended December 31, 2000** **(in millions)**

Cash provided (used) by operating activities	$ 40
Cash provided (used) by investing activities	(2,480)
Cash provided (used) by financing activities	2,221
Increase (decrease) in cash	$ (219)
Cash—beginning of year	1,686
Cash—end of year	$1,467

Recall that the statement of cash flows has already been presented and briefly discussed. Chapter 1 introduced the statement and provided an example. Chapter 2 discussed the basic nature of the statement and related it to the income statement, balance sheet, and statement of retained earnings. Chapter 4 briefly explained how a statement of cash flows can be prepared from the cash T-account. Chapter 5 described how it can be interpreted to assess solvency. Thus, you have already been exposed to the fundamentals of the statement of cash flows. This chapter provides a more complete discussion of the nature of the statement, how it can be used, and how it is prepared.

The statement of cash flows is a relatively new addition to the set of financial accounting statements required under generally accepted accounting principles. It was established as a standard of financial reporting in 1987 when the Financial Accounting Standards Board decided (in FASB *Statement No. 95, Statement of Cash Flows*) to modify the statement of changes in financial position, which had been required since 1971.

On its 2000 statement of cash flows, Lands' End reported net cash flows from operating activities of $123 million. The same year, reported net income was only $48 million. Briefly explain how net cash flow from operating activities can be so much higher.

THE DEFINITION OF CASH

Chapter 6 of this text defines cash for purposes of balance sheet disclosure and points out that it consists of coin, currency, and available funds on deposit at the bank. Negotiable instruments such as money orders, certified checks, cashier's checks, personal checks, and bank drafts are also considered cash. The total of these items as of the balance sheet date is the cash amount that appears on the balance sheet.

When preparing the statement of cash flows, companies commonly consider as cash the items already mentioned as well as certain **cash equivalents,** which include commercial paper and other debt investments with maturities of less than three months.[1] They do so because these items can be converted to cash immediately; for all intents and purposes, therefore, they are virtually the same as cash. In the remainder of this chapter, where we illustrate the statement of cash flows, we will also treat cash equivalents as cash.

Bristol-Myers Squibb considers securities with maturities of less than three months to be cash equivalents. Would such securities be included in the cash account and reported on the statement of cash flows or in the marketable securities account on the balance sheet? Why?

A GENERAL DESCRIPTION OF THE STATEMENT OF CASH FLOWS

Take a moment now and refer back to Chapter 2. It describes the statement of cash flows in terms of the other financial statements, explaining the change in the cash balance from one balance sheet date to the next. Figure 14–2 illustrates the statement of cash flows more completely. This statement is divided into three sections (operating activities, investing activities, and financing activities) and shows the cash inflow and outflow categories that normally comprise each section.

Cash Provided (Used) by Operating Activities

Cash provided (used) by **operating activities** includes those cash inflows and outflows associated directly with the acquisition and sale of the company's inventories and services. This category includes the cash receipts from sales and accounts receivable as well as cash payments for the purchase of inventories, payments on accounts payable, selling and administrative activities, and interest and taxes. Under generally accepted accounting principles, there are two acceptable ways to present the operating section of the statement of cash flows: the direct method and the indirect method.

THE DIRECT METHOD

The statement of cash flows illustrated in Figure 14–2 was prepared using the **direct method.** It is so called because the computation of cash provided (used) by operating activities ($930) consists of cash inflows and outflows that can be traced *directly* to the cash T-account. For example, the $7,000 collected from customers, the $5,200 paid for

---

1. Commercial paper and short-term debt instruments were discussed in Chapter 10. Also, some corporations, like McDonnell Douglas, Eli Lilly, and Walt Disney, also include short-term investments, such as marketable securities, in the definition of cash for purposes of the statement of cash flows. Such a practice is acceptable under generally accepted accounting principles because marketable securities, by definition, are highly liquid.

FIGURE 14–2	**XYZ Corporation**
Standard statement of cash flows	**Statement of Cash Flows** **For the Year Ended December 31, 2002**

Operating activities:		
Cash received from customers	$ 7,000	
Cash paid for operations (to suppliers, employees, and others)	(5,200)	
Cash provided (used) by other operating items	(870)	
Net cash provided (used) by operating activities		$ 930
Investing activities:		
Cash outflows for the purchase of noncurrent assets	$(3,000)	
Cash inflows from sale of noncurrent assets	400	
Net cash provided (used) by investing activities		(2,600)
Financing activities:		
Cash inflows from borrowings	$ 3,000	
Cash inflows from stock issuances	2,000	
Cash outflows for debt retirements	(1,460)	
Cash outflows for treasury stock purchases	(1,550)	
Cash outflows for dividend payments	(200)	
Net cash provided (used) by financing activities		1,790
Net increase (decrease) in cash and cash equivalents		$ 120
Cash and cash equivalents at the beginning of the year		100
Cash and cash equivalents at the end of the year		$ 220

operations, and the $870 used for other operating items all represent aggregate totals of entries initially recorded in the journal and posted to the cash account in the ledger.

THE INDIRECT METHOD

Another method of computing and disclosing cash provided (used) by operating activities that is acceptable under GAAP is called the **indirect method.** Under this method, cash provided (used) by operating activities is computed *indirectly* by beginning with the net income figure, which appears on the income statement, and adjusting it for the differences between cash flows and accruals. The indirect method of computing cash from operating activities is illustrated in Figure 14–3.

FIGURE 14–3	
Cash from operating activities: Indirect method	

Operating activities:		
Net income		$1,085
Noncash charges to noncurrent accounts:		
Depreciation, amortization, and other noncash charges on noncurrent items	$ 400	
Book losses	50	
Book gains	(450)	0
Changes in current accounts other than cash:		
Net decreases (increases) in current assets	$ 105	
Net increases (decreases) in current liabilities	(260)	(155)
Net cash provided (used) by operating activities		$ 930

In general, items added back to net income in the computation of cash provided (used) by operating activities (e.g., depreciation, amortization, book losses, and decreases in current assets) decrease net income on the income statement but involve no cash outflows. Items subtracted from net income in this computation (e.g., book gains, decreases in current liabilities) increase net income on the income statement but involve no cash inflows. Note also that these adjustments are separated into two categories: (1) noncash charges to the noncurrent accounts and (2) changes in current accounts. The first category includes depreciation and amortization charges as well as book gains and losses recognized on the transfer of long-term assets and liabilities. The second category includes the changes during the period in the current asset and current liability accounts other than cash, marketable securities, and dividends payable.[2]

A depreciation charge of $53 million is included on the 2000 statement of cash flows for Imation, a global technology company. Does the company use the direct or indirect method of presenting the statement of cash flows? Why would an income statement expense like depreciation appear on the statement of cash flows?

THE FASB'S POSITION

Both the direct and the indirect methods result in the same dollar amount ($930) for cash provided (used) by operating activities; in that respect, they simply represent two different forms of presentation. In fact, when the FASB made the statement of cash flows a requirement, it allowed either the direct or the indirect method. If the direct method is chosen, however, the FASB requires that it be accompanied by a schedule of the adjustments that reconcile net income to cash provided (used) by operating activities. This schedule can appear either in the footnotes to the financial statements or on the face of the statement itself. Also, generally accepted accounting principles require that under either method cash amounts paid for taxes and interest must be separately disclosed.

Since the adjustments on this schedule are the same as those disclosed under the indirect method, the direct method (including the accompanying schedule) discloses more about the changes in the cash account than the indirect method. To encourage increased disclosure and what the FASB believes to be a more straightforward presentation, it has recommended that companies use the direct method. However, the vast majority of major U.S. companies choose not to follow this recommendation; they use the indirect method probably because it requires fewer disclosures.[3]

World Sources Online (2000) reported that the principal advantage of the direct method is that it shows operating cash receipts and payments, while the principal advantage of the indirect method is that it focuses on the differences between net income and net cash from operations. Explain how each advantage could be useful to an analyst.

---

2. Changes in marketable securities and dividends payable are reflected in the investing and financing sections, respectively.

3. *Accounting Trends and Techniques* (2000) reports that, of the 600 major U.S. companies surveyed, only seven used the direct form of presentation. The remaining 593 used the indirect form.

Cash Provided (Used) by Investing Activities

Cash provided (used) by **investing activities** includes the cash inflows and outflows associated with the purchase and sale of a company's noncurrent assets.[4] This section includes the cash effects from purchases and sales of long-term investments, long-lived assets, and intangible assets. The statement of cash flows in Figure 14–2, for example, shows that $3,000 was used to purchase such items, and $400 was collected from selling noncurrent assets. These cash inflows and outflows can all be traced to entries in the cash account in the company's ledger.

Cash Provided (Used) by Financing Activities

Cash provided (used) by **financing activities** includes cash inflows and outflows associated with a company's two sources of outside capital: liabilities and contributed capital. This category primarily includes the cash inflows associated with borrowings and equity issuances as well as the cash outflows related to debt repayments, treasury stock purchases, and dividend payments. The statement of cash flows in Figure 14–2 shows that the company borrowed $3,000, raised $2,000 by issuing stock, made principal payments on debt in the amount of $1,460, used $1,550 to purchase treasury stock, and paid cash dividends of $200. These cash flows can also be traced to the cash account in the company's ledger.

Note also that cash interest payments are not included in this section, even though they represent a cost of financing. Instead, such payments are included in the operating section of the statement of cash flows. This practice has been questioned because it confuses the distinction between financing and operating activities. Figure 14–4 provides an example of a recently published statement of cash flows prepared under the indirect form of presentation. It was taken from the April 29, 2000, annual report of La-Z-Boy, a well-known furniture manufacturer.

HOW THE STATEMENT OF CASH FLOWS CAN BE USED

The statement of cash flows is used primarily to assess performance in two basic areas: (1) a company's ability to generate cash and (2) the effectiveness of a company's cash management. The ability to generate cash is determined by the strength of the company's operating activities as well as its **financial flexibility,** which reflects the company's capacity to borrow, issue equity, and sell nonoperating assets (e.g., investments). During 2000, for example, 3M generated $2.3 billion through its operating activities, which was sufficient to finance $1.3 billion of additional investments, reduce $250 million of its outstanding debts, pay a $918 million dividend, and maintain its cash balance. On the other hand, Verity, a creator of web-based business portal solutions, needed to issue $107 million in common stock in 2000 to finance its investments of $116 million because cash from operations was only $8 million.

Effective cash management requires that two competing objectives be balanced. On one hand, cash must be available to meet debts as they come due. That is, **solvency** must be maintained. On the other hand, cash must be invested in productive assets that provide returns. Sources of cash include the sale of inventories and services, borrowings, equity issuances, and the selling of long-term assets. Uses of cash

---

4. Investing activities can include the purchase and/or sale of securities listed as short-term, but frequently these investments are included as cash equivalents, and in many cases they are not material.

FIGURE 14–4 La-Z-Boy Statement of Cash Flows

La-Z-Boy Incorporated
Consolidated Statement of Cash Flows

	Fiscal year ended		
	4/29/00	4/24/99	4/25/98
(Amounts in thousands)	(53 weeks)	(52 weeks)	(52 weeks)
Cash flows from operating activities			
Net income	$ 87,614	$66,142	$49,920
Adjustments to reconcile net income to			
net cash provided by operating activities			
Depreciation and amortization	30,342	22,081	21,021
Change in receivables	(42,595)	(26,875)	(14,090)
Change in inventories	(4,703)	(4,607)	(6,918)
Change in other assets and liabilities	(6,431)	28,287	2,374
Change in deferred taxes	(5,797)	(3,130)	3,177
Total adjustments	(29,184)	15,756	5,564
Cash provided by operating activities	58,430	81,898	55,484
Cash flows from investing activities			
Proceeds from disposals of assets	1,202	401	1,585
Capital expenditures	(37,968)	(25,316)	(22,016)
Acquisition of operating divisions, net of cash acquired	(57,952)	—	—
Change in other investments	(9,681)	(4,895)	(16,066)
Cash used for investing activities	(104,399)	(29,810)	(36,497)
Cash flows from financing activities			
Long-term debt	175,622	—	35,000
Retirements of debt	(110,319)	(6,786)	(24,653)
Capital leases	1,657	204	—
Capital lease principal payments	(856)	(1,403)	(2,017)
Stock for stock option plans	6,637	6,431	5,748
Stock for 401(k) employee plans	2,598	1,902	1,704
Purchases of La-Z-Boy stock	(31,046)	(30,460)	(16,391)
Payment of cash dividends	(17,447)	(16,417)	(15,029)
Cash provided by (used for) financing activities	26,846	(46,529)	(15,638)
Effect of exchange rate changes on cash	(74)	(709)	(31)
Net change in cash and equivalents	(19,197)	4,850	3,318
Cash and equivalents at beginning of the year	33,550	28,700	25,382
Cash and equivalents at end of the year	$ 14,353	$33,550	$28,700
Cash paid during the year			
—Income taxes	$ 52,210	$44,842	$29,025
—Interest	$7,128	$4,340	$4,235

The accompanying Notes to Consolidated Financial Statements are an integral part of these statements.

include purchasing and manufacturing inventories, covering selling and administrative costs, making debt interest and principal payments, purchasing long-term assets, purchasing treasury stock, and paying dividends. Effective cash management involves managing these cash sources and uses in a way that provides a high return without bearing too great a risk of insolvency.

Review Figure 14–4 and comment on La-Z-Boy's cash management over the three-year period covering 1998, 1999, and 2000.

Analyzing the Statement of Cash Flows

Questions like the following can be answered by referring to the statement of cash flows: Is the company's cash balance increasing or decreasing? What portion of the company's cash is generated through operations, the sale of investments, or the issuance of debt and equity securities? What portions of the company's cash payments go toward supporting operations, capital investments, repayments of debt, purchasing treasury stock, and dividends? In Chapter 5, we discussed cash flow analysis. There we distinguished between operating performance, financial flexibility, and liquidity, and illustrated how the statement of cash flows can be used to identify cash flow profiles of companies. You may wish to review this material now.

The Importance of Cash from Operating Activities

The amount of cash generated through operating activities is especially important to financial statement users because the successful sale of a company's services or inventories is a prerequisite for a successful business. Also, while cash flows from investing and financing activities tend to vary from one year to the next, operating activities, by definition, are normal and expected to recur. Consequently, positive net cash flows from operations, especially across several periods of time, can indicate financial strength.

It is generally desirable to finance asset purchases and debt payments with cash generated from operations. Companies able to follow such a strategy consistently tend to have higher credit ratings and are generally viewed as financially more stable than those unable to do so. DuPont, for example, one of the ten largest companies in the world with an AAA credit rating, commented in an annual report:

Cash provided by operations was sufficient to finance the company's capital expenditures, repurchase 1,968,000 shares of the company's common stock, reduce borrowings, and pay dividends.

The management of AT&T, the largest communications company in the world, stated:

Strong cash flow from operations permitted us to continue efforts toward increased financial flexibility. We redeemed $830 million of preferred stock and retired $147 million of long-term debt. Our external financing was limited to $343 million. Consequently, for the second consecutive year, we have reduced our utilization of external sources of financing.

The items that explain the difference between net income and net cash from operating activities can also be used to assess the quality of reported earnings in a given year. Review the operating section of La-Z-Boy's statement of cash flows, for example, and note that net income exceeds cash provided by operating activities by over $29 million. By far, the major reason for the difference is the significant growth in receivables during the year, a whopping increase of over $42.6 million. A review of the balance sheet and income statement shows that receivables grew by almost 50 percent while sales grew by only 33 percent. Normally, one would expect that receivables and sales would grow in roughly the same proportion, yet in this case receivables seems to be growing much faster. This development raises questions about the quality of both receivables and the company's reported net income. Do the excess receivables represent slow-paying customers, and should the bad debt expense be larger? Is La-Z-Boy aggressively recognizing revenue and the related receivables to inflate earnings? While we cannot provide definitive answers, items that create significant differences between earnings and operating cash flows can raise questions about the quality of La-Z-Boy's 2000 net income, and encourage analysts to investigate the situation more closely.

Business Credit (May 2000), a trade journal for analysts, states that financial analysis can be plagued by GAP ("games accountants play") in deriving the earnings number—the so-called "sins of accrual accounting." The effect of these actions is to either increase current profits or hide them for a later date. It is important for analysts to understand the effects of these games on cash flows. Explain how understanding these cash flows effects can be useful to analysts.

The Importance of Significant Noncash Transactions

The statement of cash flows includes only those transactions that directly affect cash or cash equivalents. Many important transactions, however, neither increase nor decrease cash and, as a result, are excluded from the face of the statement. For example, the purchase of a long-lived asset in exchange for a long-term note payable can be a significant capital transaction, yet as illustrated by the journal entry below, it has no effect on the cash account.

Equipment (+A)	20,000	
Notes Payable (+L)		20,000

Purchased equipment financed with a long-term note.

Similarly, the acquisition of land in exchange for a note payable, the acquisition of a subsidiary by issuing stock, the payment of a debt with common stock, and the declaration of a dividend are capital transactions that are not found on the statement of cash flows.

These kinds of capital transactions can be very important to a company's financial condition, and the FASB requires in its standard on cash flows that they be described clearly in the footnotes to the financial statements. It is important that such information be accessible to readers who are interested in examining the financing and investing activities of a company. For example, several years ago, MCI acquired Satellite Business Systems (SBS) and selected other assets from IBM. In exchange, MCI issued common stock and signed a note payable. No cash was exchanged in the transaction, and accordingly, neither the acquired assets nor the increases in the common stock and notes payable accounts appeared on MCI's statement of cash flows. However, the transaction was important enough to warrant disclosure, and MCI reported it directly below the statement of cash flows in the following manner:

Acquisition of SBS (in millions):

Common stock issued to acquire SBS	$ 376
Communications systems acquired	(428)
Other assets acquired	(52)
Current obligations assumed	104
Cash outflow to acquire SBS	$ 0

THE STATEMENT OF CASH FLOWS: ECONOMIC CONSEQUENCES

The economic consequences associated with the statement of cash flows result primarily from investors, creditors, and other interested parties using it to assess the investment potential and creditworthiness of companies and the equity and debt securities that they issue. *Forbes* magazine reported: "a number of stock advisers are basing their work in part on cash flow . . . an investor who ignores cash flow in picking stocks is being deprived of one of the most valuable tools in an arsenal." Further, many writers have claimed that had investors relied more heavily on cash flow numbers, instead of working capital and the current ratio, famous bankruptcies, like W. T. Grant, Penn Central, Sambo's Restaurants, AM International, and Wickes, might have been foreseen earlier. One survey found: "The evidence could not be clearer. Investors use the statement of cash flows more, and the income statements less, than previously."[5]

The increasing importance of cash flow information to investors and creditors creates incentives for management to **window dress** the statement of cash flows. Such incentives can be troublesome because in the short run it is relatively easy for management to present a favorable cash position. Delaying payments on short-term payables, for example, can significantly boost the amount of cash provided (used) by operating activities. Selling investments, even if it is not in the stockholders' long-term interests, can increase cash inflows from investing activities, while delaying debt payments and dividends can inflate cash from financing activities.

Those who use the statement of cash flows must be careful not to place too much importance on the cash flows of a particular period, which can be manipulated. However, such manipulation is much less effective when statements are viewed across several periods because payments that are delayed in one period must normally be paid in the next. For this reason, the FASB requires that cash flow statements from at least the previous three years be disclosed.

From management's standpoint, it is also important to realize that decisions designed to manipulate the disclosures on the statement of cash flows can be counterproductive. While such decisions may improve the appearance of a company's cash position in the current period, they can (1) represent poor business decisions, (2) make the cash position of the company look worse in the future, (3) reduce the credibility of the company and its financial reports in the eyes of investors, creditors, and other interested parties, and (4) if fraudulent, can expose management to future lawsuits. In addition, such manipulations may simply be unethical.

A *Wall Street Journal* (April 1, 1999) article titled "Analysts Increasingly Favor Using Cash Flow over Reported Earnings in Stock Valuations" describes how some analysts are losing faith in the earnings number, choosing instead to rely on various measures of cash flows in the assessments of a company's future performance. They claim that cash flow across time is less variable, less subject to manipulation, and easier to predict. Briefly discuss how cash flow from operations might be easier to predict than net income.

---

5. Marc J. Epstein and Moses L. Paun, "How Useful Is the Statement of Cash Flows?" *Management Accounting,* July 1992, p. 52.

DERIVING CASH FLOW FROM ACCRUAL FINANCIAL STATEMENTS

In Chapter 4 of this text, we prepared a simple statement of cash flows by focusing on the cash effects of the individual transactions of the period. That is, we prepared the statement from the entries to the cash T-account. This section demonstrates how the statement of cash flows can be prepared when the analysis of individual transactions is either impractical or, in some cases, impossible. We show that the statement can be prepared primarily from the information contained in two balance sheets, the intervening income statement, and the statement of retained earnings. This method is followed by most companies, and the resulting statement of cash flows is the same as that prepared from analyzing the entries to the cash T-account. In most cases, however, the method we illustrate here is far more practical. Figure 14–5 contains the December 31, 2002 and 2003 balance sheets of ABC Enterprises and the related income statement and statement of retained earnings. Additional information is disclosed in the section that appears below the statements.

FIGURE 14–5 The financial statements of ABC Enterprises	**ABC Enterprises, Inc.** **Balance Sheets** **For December 31, 2002 and 2003**	

	2003	2002
ASSETS		
Cash	$ 5,900	$ 8,000
Accounts receivable	23,200	12,000
Less: Allowance for doubtful accounts	(1,300)	(1,000)
Inventory	4,000	3,000
Prepaid insurance	1,000	2,000
Land	30,000	20,000
Machinery	6,000	8,000
Less: Accumulated depreciation	(2,500)	(2,000)
Building	30,000	—
Less: Accumulated depreciation	(1,500)	—
Patent	6,000	8,000
Total assets	$100,800	$58,000
LIABILITIES AND STOCKHOLDERS' EQUITY		
Accounts payable	$ 9,000	$12,000
Accrued payables	3,000	1,500
Income taxes payable	200	500
Payments in advance	—	3,000
Dividends payable	3,000	1,000
Notes payable	24,000	25,000
Less: Discount on notes payable	(1,800)	(2,000)
Common stock	42,000	10,000
Additional paid-in capital	19,300	2,000
Retained earnings	2,100	6,000
Less: Treasury stock	—	(1,000)
Total liabilities and stockholders' equity	$100,800	$58,000

FIGURE 14-5
(Concluded)

ABC Enterprises, Inc.
Income Statement
For the Year Ended December 31, 2003

Sales		$ 32,000
Fees earned		3,000
Cost of goods sold		(11,000)
Gross profit		$ 24,000
Operating expenses:		
Miscellaneous expenses	$11,000	
Insurance expense	1,000	
Bad debt expense	1,100	
Depreciation expense (machinery)	1,000	
Depreciation expense (building)	1,500	
Amortization of patent	2,000	17,600
Net operating income		$ 6,400
Nonoperating revenues and expenses:		
Loss on sale of machinery	$ 100	
Interest expense	2,000	2,100
Net income from continuing operations		
before taxes		$ 4,300
Less: Income tax expense		1,200
Net income		$ 3,100

ABC Enterprises, Inc.
Statement of Retained Earnings
For the Year Ended December 31, 2003

Beginning retained earnings balance		$ 6,000
Plus: Net income		3,100
Less: Cash dividends	$ 3,000	
Stock dividends	4,000	(7,000)
Ending retained earnings balance		$ 2,100

Additional information:
1. Two thousand shares of common stock ($10 par; $15 fair market value) were issued for a building early in 2003.
2. A 5 percent stock dividend on 4,000 outstanding shares was distributed late in 2003 when the fair market value of the $10 par value stock was $20 per share.
3. Treasury stock that was originally purchased for $1,000 was reissued for $1,300.

In the sections that follow, we prepare a statement of cash flows under both the direct and indirect methods from the information contained in Figure 14–5. Cash provided (used) by operating activities is derived first, followed by the cash provided (used) by investing activities, and cash provided (used) by financing activities. In the figures that appear throughout these sections, italics are used to indicate dollar amounts taken directly from the information in Figure 14–5.

Cash Provided (Used) by Operating Activities

This section analyzes the cash flows associated with each income statement account: Sales and Bad Debt Expense, Fees Earned, Cost of Goods Sold, Miscellaneous Expenses, Insurance Expense, Depreciation of Machinery and of Building, Amortization of Patent, Loss on Sale of Machinery, Interest Expense, and Income Tax Expense.

SALES AND BAD DEBT EXPENSE

The cash inflow from sales can be determined by analyzing the changes in Accounts Receivable and Allowance for Doubtful Accounts. Refer to the T-accounts and related journal entries in Figure 14–6.

FIGURE 14–6 Determining cash inflow from sales

Sales		Accounts Receivable			Allowance for Doubtful Accounts		Bad Debt Expense	
(1) 32,000		12,000				1,000	(2) 1,100	
		(1) 32,000				(2) 1,100		
			(3) 800	(3) 800				
			(4) 20,000					
		23,200				1,300		

Effect on Accounts:

Transactions	Accounts	Debit (Net)	Credit (Net)
(1)	Accounts Receivable	32,000	
	Sales		32,000
(2)	Bad Debt Expense	1,100	
	Allowance for Doubtful Accounts		1,100
(3)	Allowance for Doubtful Accounts	800	
	Accounts Receivable		800
(4)	Cash	20,000	
	Accounts Receivable		20,000

Cash collections from sales: $20,000

The beginning and ending balances in Accounts Receivable and the Allowance for Doubtful Accounts appear on the balance sheets in Figure 14–5. We assume that all sales were made on account, and therefore, $32,000 (see income statement) was debited to Accounts Receivable during the year. The $1,100 bad debt expense (see income statement) was credited to Allowance for Doubtful Accounts at year-end, which (when the beginning and ending balances in the allowance account are considered) implies that uncollectibles in the amount of $800 must have been written off and credited to Accounts Receivable. Therefore, an additional credit of $20,000 to accounts receivable must have been entered during the year. The corresponding debit represents cash receipts on outstanding accounts during the year.

FEES EARNED

The cash inflow related to Fees Earned can be determined by analyzing the change in the payments in advance account. Refer to Figure 14–7.

FIGURE 14–7
Determining cash inflow from fees earned

Fees Earned		Payments in Advance	
	(1) 3,000		3,000
		(1) 3,000	
			0

Effect on Accounts:

Transactions	Accounts	Debit (Net)	Credit (Net)
(1)	Payments in Advance	3,000	
	Fees Earned		3,000

Cash collections from fees earned: $0

The beginning ($3,000) and ending ($0) balances in the payments in advance account appear on the balance sheets in Figure 14–5. The recognition of $3,000 in Fees Earned (see income statement) involved a $3,000 debit to Payments in Advance. This entry accounts for the entire change in the payments in advance account, indicating that no cash inflow was associated with fees earned.

COST OF GOODS SOLD

The cash outflow associated with Cost of Goods Sold can be determined by analyzing the changes in the inventory and accounts payable accounts. Refer to Figure 14–8.

FIGURE 14–8
Determining cash outflow from inventory purchases

Cost of Goods Sold		Inventory		Accounts Payable	
(1) 11,000		3,000			12,000
			(1) 11,000		(2) 12,000
		(2) 12,000		(3) 15,000	
		4,000			9,000

Effect on Accounts:

Transactions	Accounts	Debit (Net)	Credit (Net)
(1)	Cost of Goods Sold	11,000	
	Inventory		11,000
(2)	Inventory	12,000	
	Accounts Payable		12,000
(3)	Accounts Payable	15,000	
	Cash		15,000

Cash paid to suppliers: $15,000

The beginning and ending balances in Inventory and Accounts Payable appear on the balance sheets in Figure 14–5. The $11,000 debit to Cost of Goods Sold (see income statement) was credited to Inventory, which (when the beginning and ending balances in the inventory account are considered) implies that inventory purchases of

$12,000 must have been made during the year. Assuming that all inventory purchases were made on account, $12,000 must have been credited to Accounts Payable. Considering the beginning and ending balances in Accounts Payable, an additional debit of $15,000 must have been recognized during the year. The corresponding credit represents cash payments of $15,000 on accounts payable during the year.

MISCELLANEOUS EXPENSES

The cash outflow related to Miscellaneous Expenses can be determined by analyzing the change in the accrued payables account. Refer to Figure 14–9.

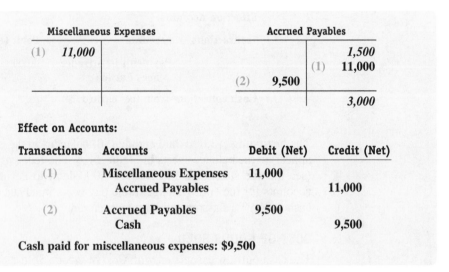

The beginning ($1,500) and ending ($3,000) balances in Accrued Payables appear on the balance sheets in Figure 14–5. Assuming that all miscellaneous expenses were accrued, the debit of $11,000 to Miscellaneous Expenses (see income statement) must have involved an $11,000 credit to Accrued Payables. Considering the beginning and ending balances in accrued payables, a $9,500 debit must have been entered in the account. The corresponding credit represents cash payments on accrued payables.

INSURANCE EXPENSE

The cash outflow related to Insurance Expense can be determined by analyzing the change in the prepaid insurance account. Refer to Figure 14–10.

FIGURE 14–10
Determining cash outflow related to insurance expense

Insurance Expense		Prepaid Insurance	
(1) 1,000		2,000	
			(1) 1,000
		1,000	

Effect on Accounts:

Transactions	Accounts	Debit (Net)	Credit (Net)
(1)	Insurance Expense	1,000	
	Prepaid Insurance		1,000

Cash paid for insurance: $0

The beginning ($2,000) and ending ($1,000) balances in Prepaid Insurance appear on the balance sheets in Figure 14–5. The debit of $1,000 to Insurance Expense (see income statement) involved a $1,000 credit to Prepaid Insurance. This entry accounts for the entire change in the prepaid insurance account, indicating that no cash was paid for insurance during the year.

DEPRECIATION OF MACHINERY, DEPRECIATION OF BUILDING, AMORTIZATION OF PATENT, AND LOSS ON SALE OF MACHINERY

There are no cash effects associated with depreciation, amortization, or book gains and losses.

INTEREST EXPENSE

The cash outflow related to Interest Expense can be determined by analyzing the change in the discount on notes payable account. Refer to Figure 14–11.

FIGURE 14–11
Determining cash outflow related to interest expense

Interest Expense		Discount on Notes Payable	
(1) **2,000**		**2,000**	
			(1) **200**
		1,800	

Effect on Accounts:

Transactions	Accounts	Debit (Net)	Credit (Net)
(1)	**Interest Expense**	**2,000**	
	Discount on Notes Payable		**200**
	Cash		1,800

Cash paid for interest: $1,800

The beginning ($2,000) and ending ($1,800) balances in the discount on notes payable account appear on the balance sheets in Figure 14–5. The $200 difference between the beginning and ending balances indicates that the discount was amortized in the amount of $200 during the year. Discounts are amortized into Interest Expense, as illustrated in Figure 14–11. Thus, $1,800 cash must have been paid for interest during the year.

INCOME TAX EXPENSE

The cash outflow related to Income Tax Expense can be determined by analyzing the changes in the income tax payable account. Refer to Figure 14–12.

The beginning ($500) and ending ($200) balances in the income tax payable account appear on the balance sheets in Figure 14–5. The debit of $1,200 to Income Tax Expense (see income statement), assuming that income taxes were accrued, involved a $1,200 credit to Income Tax Payable. Considering the beginning and ending balances in Income Tax Payable, $1,500 must have been debited to the account during the year. The corresponding credit represents cash payments for income taxes.

Cash Provided (Used) by Investing Activities

In this section, we determine the cash inflows and outflows associated with investing activities by analyzing changes in the long-lived asset accounts. Specifically, we analyze

FIGURE 14–12
Determining cash
outflow related to
income taxes

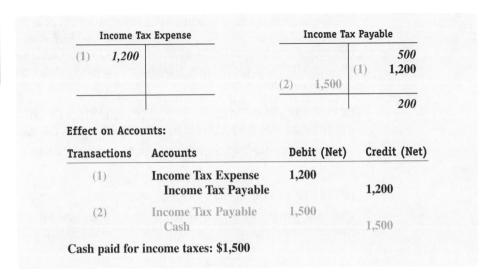

Income Tax Expense		Income Tax Payable	
(1) **1,200**			**500**
		(1) **1,200**
		(2) 1,500	
			200

Effect on Accounts:

Transactions	Accounts	Debit (Net)	Credit (Net)
(1)	Income Tax Expense	1,200	
	Income Tax Payable		1,200
(2)	Income Tax Payable	1,500	
	Cash		1,500

Cash paid for income taxes: $1,500

the $10,000 increase in the land account and the $2,000 decrease in the machinery account. The building was acquired in exchange for stock and involved no cash exchange, while the $2,000 decrease in the patent account reflects amortization, which also involved no cash receipt or payment.

PURCHASE OF LAND

The $10,000 increase in the land account (see Figure 14–5) indicates that land was acquired during the period. Since there is no indication that noncash assets were exchanged for the land or a liability was credited, we assume that the land was purchased for a $10,000 cash payment. Refer to Figure 14–13.

FIGURE 14–13
Determining cash
outflow for
land purchases

Land	
20,000	
(1) **10,000**	
30,000	

Effect on Accounts:

Transactions	Accounts	Debit (Net)	Credit (Net)
(1)	Land	10,000	
	Cash		10,000

Cash payment for land: $10,000

SALE OF MACHINERY

The cash inflow from the sale of machinery can be determined by using the available information to reconstruct the journal entry that recorded the transaction. Refer to Figure 14–14.

The beginning and ending balances in the machinery and accumulated depreciation accounts can be found on the balance sheets in Figure 14–5. Depreciation expense of $1,000 on the machinery (see income statement) was recognized during the period; accordingly, $1,000 must have been credited to Accumulated Depreciation. The accumulated depreciation account, therefore, must have been debited for $500 when the

FIGURE 14–14 Determining cash inflow from sale of machinery

Machinery	Accumulated Depreciation	Loss on Sale of Machinery	Depreciation Expense
8,000		2,000	(2) 100		(1) 1,000
(1) 2,000		(1) 1,000		
	(2) 500		
6,000		2,500		

Effect on Accounts:

Transactions	Accounts	Debit (Net)	Credit (Net)
(1)	Depreciation Expense	1,000	
	Accumulated Depreciation		1,000
(2)	Cash	1,400	
	Accumulated Depreciation	500	
	Loss on Sale of Machinery	100	
	Machinery		2,000

Cash receipt for sale of machinery: $1,400

machine was sold. Given the $100 loss on the sale (see income statement), the $2,000 reduction in the machinery account, and the $500 debit to Accumulated Depreciation, the journal entry to record the sale can be reconstructed and the amount of cash received ($1,400) can be determined.

Cash Provided (Used) by Financing Activities

In this section, we determine the cash inflows and outflows associated with financing activities by analyzing changes in the long-term liability and stockholders' equity accounts. Specifically, we analyze the $1,000 decrease in the notes payable account, the increase in the common stock and additional paid-in capital accounts, the issuance of treasury stock for $1,300, and the declaration of a $3,000 cash dividend.

PRINCIPAL PAYMENT ON NOTES PAYABLE

We have no indication that the $1,000 decrease in the notes payable account (see Figure 14–5) was due to anything other than the payment of cash. Refer to Figure 14–15.

ISSUANCE OF COMMON STOCK AND TREASURY STOCK

The cash inflows from the issuance of common stock and treasury stock can be determined by analyzing the changes in the common stock, additional paid-in capital, and treasury stock accounts. Note that the "additional information" section of Figure 14–5 indicates that a building was acquired for common stock, a stock dividend was distributed, and treasury stock was sold for $1,300. Refer to Figure 14–16.

The beginning and ending balances in Common Stock, Additional Paid-In Capital, and Treasury Stock appear on the balance sheets in Figure 14–5. The purchase of the

FIGURE 14–15

Determining cash
outflow from
payments
on notes

Notes Payable

		25,000
(1) 1,000		
		24,000

Effect on Accounts:

Transactions	Accounts	Debit (Net)	Credit (Net)
(1)	Notes Payable	1,000	
	Cash		1,000

Cash payment of notes payable: $1,000

FIGURE 14–16

Determining cash
inflow from
stock issuances

Building	Treasury Stock	Stock Dividend
0	1,000	(2) 4,000
(1) 30,000	(3) 1,000	
30,000	0	

Common Stock	Additional Paid-In Capital
10,000	2,000
(1) 20,000	(1) 10,000
(2) 2,000	(2) 2,000
	(3) 300
(4) 10,000	(4) 5,000
42,000	19,300

Effect on Accounts:

Transactions	Accounts	Debit (Net)	Credit (Net)
(1)	**Building**	**30,000**	
	Common Stock		**20,000**
	Additional Paid-In Capital		**10,000**
(2)	**Stock Dividend**	**4,000**	
	Common Stock		**2,000**
	Additional Paid-In Capital		**2,000**
(3)	Cash	1,300	
	Treasury Stock		1,000
	Additional Paid-In Capital		300
(4)	Cash	15,000	
	Common Stock		10,000
	Additional Paid-In Capital		5,000

Cash receipts from issuance of treasury stock: $1,300
Cash receipts from issuance of common stock: $15,000

$30,000 building increased Common Stock and Additional Paid-In Capital by $20,000
and $10,000, respectively. Common Stock and Additional Paid-In Capital each
increased by $2,000 when the $4,000 stock dividend was distributed. Additional Paid-
In Capital increased by $300 when the treasury stock was issued for $1,300 cash,
which was greater than its $1,000 cost. The additional information that follows the

financial statement in Figure 14–5 describes these three transactions. Given the ending balances in Common Stock and Additional Paid-In Capital, there must have been a stock issuance for cash in the amount of $15,000 during the year.

CASH DIVIDENDS

The cash dividend payment can be determined by analyzing the changes in the dividends payable account. Refer to Figure 14–17.

FIGURE 14–17
Determining cash outflow from dividend payments

Cash Dividends			Dividends Payable		
(1) **3,000**					**1,000**
		(2) 1,000	(1)		**3,000**
					3,000

Effect on Accounts:

Transactions	Accounts	Debit (Net)	Credit (Net)
(1)	**Cash Dividends**	**3,000**	
	Dividends Payable		**3,000**
(2)	Dividends Payable	1,000	
	Cash		1,000

Cash payment for dividends: $1,000

The beginning ($1,000) and ending ($3,000) balances in the dividends payable account appear on the balance sheets in Figure 14–5. The declaration of the $3,000 cash dividend (see statement of retained earnings) created a $3,000 dividend payable liability. Therefore, $1,000 must have been debited to Dividends Payable during the year, which represents cash payments to the stockholders.

THE COMPLETE STATEMENT OF CASH FLOWS

We have now derived the cash flows of the period and can prepare the statement of cash flows. The following sections cover the direct method and the indirect method.

The Direct Method

A statement of cash flows prepared under the direct method is provided in Figure 14–18. Note that the dollar amounts are identical to the cash flows derived in the previous section.

The Indirect Method

The statement of cash flows under the indirect method is exactly the same as the direct method, except for the presentation of the operating section and the derivation of net cash provided (used) by operating activities. The operating section presented under the indirect method for ABC Enterprises, Inc., is illustrated in Figure 14–19. Note first that the dollar amount of net cash provided (used) by operating activities is the same (−$7,800) whether the direct or the indirect method is used. The difference is in the way in which the amount is computed. Under the indirect method, net cash provided

FIGURE 14–18
Statement of cash flows for ABC Enterprises: Direct method

ABC Enterprises, Inc.
Statement of Cash Flows
For the Year Ended December 31, 2003

Operating activities:		
Cash collections from sales and accounts receivable	$ 20,000	
Cash paid to suppliers	(15,000)	
Cash paid on miscellaneous expenses	(9,500)	
Cash paid for interest	(1,800)	
Cash paid for income taxes	(1,500)	
Net cash provided (used) by operating activities		$(7,800)
Investing activities:		
Purchase of land	$(10,000)	
Sale of machinery	1,400	
Net cash provided (used) by investing activities		(8,600)
Financing activities:		
Proceeds from issuing common stock	$ 15,000	
Proceeds from sale of treasury stock	1,300	
Cash dividends	(1,000)	
Principal payment on outstanding note payable	(1,000)	
Net cash provided (used) by financing activities		14,300
Net increase (decrease) in cash balance		$(2,100)
Beginning cash balance		8,000
Ending cash balance		$ 5,900

FIGURE 14–19
Statement of cash flows: Indirect method

ABC Enterprises, Inc.
Statement of Cash Flows
For the Year Ended December 31, 2003

Operating activities:		
Net income	$ 3,100	
Noncash charges to noncurrent accounts:		
Depreciation of machinery	1,000	
Depreciation of building	1,500	
Amortization of patent	2,000	
Loss on sale of machinery	100	
Decrease in discount on notes payable	200	
Changes in current noncash accounts:		
Increase in net accounts receivable	(10,900)	
Increase in inventory	(1,000)	
Decrease in accounts payable	(3,000)	
Increase in miscellaneous expenses and taxes payable	1,200	
Decrease in payments in advance	(3,000)	
Decrease in prepaid insurance	1,000	
Net cash provided (used) by operating activities		$(7,800)

by operating activities (−$7,800) is computed by adjusting net income ($3,100), which appears on the income statement, for the timing difference between operating accruals and cash flows. As indicated earlier in this chapter, these adjustments are classified into two categories: (1) noncash charges to noncurrent accounts (e.g., depreciation, amortization, and book gains and losses) and (2) changes in the current noncash accounts (e.g., Accounts Receivable, Inventory, Accounts Payable, Income Tax and Miscellaneous Accruals, Payments in Advance, and Prepaid Insurance), except for short-term investments and dividend payable, which are reflected in the investing and financing sections, respectively.

The first category of adjustments, "noncash charges to noncurrent accounts," affected net income but did not affect cash flows. Depreciation and amortization charges, for example, simultaneously reduced the dollar amounts of long-lived assets and created expenses, which reduced net income. The entries to record depreciation and amortization, however, do not reduce cash. Consequently, when deriving cash flows from net income, as is done under the indirect method, depreciation and amortization charges are added back. Similarly, gains and losses on the disposal of long-lived assets do not affect operating cash flows. Note in Figure 14–19 that the loss on sale of machinery is added back in the computation of net cash provided (used) by operating activities. Such transactions often involve cash flows, but these cash flows are reflected in the investing—instead of the operating—section of the statement of cash flows. Other common examples, where changes in noncurrent assets affect net income—but not cash flow—include long-term investments accounted for under the equity method, deferred income taxes, and the amortization of discounts and premiums on long-term debt.

One way to better understand the adjustments included in the second category, "changes in current noncash accounts," is to refer to Figure 14–20. Here, four possible combinations are illustrated. Increases (decreases) in current assets and decreases (increases) in current liabilities are subtracted from (added to) net income in the computation of net cash provided (used) by operating activities. The logic is fairly straightforward. Increases in accounts receivable, for example, must mean that revenues are being recognized faster than cash is being collected from customers—that is, net income, not backed by cash receipts, is being recorded. Accordingly, an increase in accounts receivable is subtracted from net income in the calculation of net cash provided (used) by operating activities. Similarly, growing current payables must mean that expenses are being recognized faster than cash is being paid. Net income must be adjusted upward, therefore, in the computation of net cash provided (used) by operating activities. Note how Figure 14–20 explains each of the adjustments under the heading "Changes in current noncash accounts."

	Current Assets	**=**	**Current Liabilities**
Increase	**Subtract from** **Accrual Numbers**		**Add to** **Accrual Numbers**
Decrease	**Add to** **Accrual Numbers**		**Subtract from** **Accrual Numbers**

FIGURE 14–20

Explaining current adjustments to net income in the calculation of net cash provided (used) by operating activities

ANALYZING THE STATEMENT OF CASH FLOWS: AN APPLICATION

Now that the statement of cash flows has been prepared, we can use it to assess ABC Enterprises' cash management policies. ABC's cash position decreased (from $8,000 to $5,900) during 2003. For the most part, this decrease was caused by investing and operating activities, which required $8,600 and $7,800, respectively. Financing activities, which provided $14,300, almost made up for these cash deficits. While the exact sources and uses of cash in each of these three areas should be examined, the $7,800 cash deficit due to operating activities appears to be the most troublesome and definitely deserves special attention.

Summarizing the Cash Effects of Operating Transactions

ABC's income statement shows that net income for 2003 totaled $3,100. At the same time, the operations that produced net income reduced the cash balance by $7,800. Interestingly, these two measures produced significantly different numbers that are used to evaluate the same (operating) activities.

The statement of cash flows under the indirect method (Figure 14–19) explains the difference between net income and cash provided (used) by operations. Four items appear to be the most important: (1) the $10,900 buildup in net accounts receivable, (2) the $3,000 decrease in accounts payable, (3) the $3,000 decrease in payments in advance, and (4) the depreciation and amortization of the long-lived assets.

The net accounts receivable buildup increased net income but not cash. This could indicate aggressive revenue recognition policies. Coupled with the decrease in accounts payable, it indicates that ABC paid its suppliers more quickly than it received payments from its customers. Such a strategy can give rise to cash flow problems. The $3,000 decrease in payments in advance was reflected in revenues (and thus net income) but produced no cash. Presumably, the $3,000 was received some time before December 31, 2002. The depreciation and amortization of long-lived assets reduced net income by a total dollar amount of $4,500 ($1,000 + $1,500 + $2,000) but required no cash.

Keep in mind also that the management of ABC could have manipulated cash provided (used) by operating activities. For example, had management chosen to defer cash payment on accounts payable, cash provided (used) by operating activities would have been considerably higher. This particular decision would have had no effect on net income.

In the operating section of its 1999 statement of cash flows, Cisco Systems reported three items: depreciation and amortization ($+$486 million), provision for doubtful accounts ($+$19 million), and inventory write-downs ($+$151 million). Explain why each of these items is added back to net income in the computation of net cash provided by operations.

Summarizing the Cash Effect of Investing and Financing Transactions

ABC Enterprises relied heavily on stock issuances for its cash needs during 2003. The statement of cash flows shows that common stock was issued for cash in the amount of $15,000 and that the sale of treasury stock produced $1,300. Both issuances diluted ABC's outstanding stock. The sale of a piece of machinery produced $1,400.

The cash produced by the financing and investing sources was used primarily to cover the cash deficit from operating activities (−$7,800) and to purchase land ($10,000). Dividend and principal payments on outstanding loans amounted to $1,000 each.

Note that ABC Enterprises issued 2,000 shares of common stock, valued at $15 each, for a building (see Figure 14–5). While this transaction does not affect ABC's cash balance and does not appear on the statement of cash flows, it is nonetheless very important and should be reported in the footnotes to the financial statements. Apparently, ABC relied even more heavily on equity issuances and purchased more long-term assets than the statement of cash flows indicates.

During 1999, eBayInc. reported profits of only $10 million, yet boosted its investments by over $602 million. The company carries almost no long-term debt on its balance sheet. Explain how eBay must have financed these investments and indicate where one could find this information on the financial statements.

Two Additional Observations

Now that we have covered the nature, use, and preparation of the statement of cash flows, two additional observations might be helpful. First, the statement of cash flows provides very little new information over and above that provided by the balance sheet, income statement, and statement of stockholders' equity. After all, we just illustrated how the statement can be derived from two balance sheets and an income statement. Its significant value comes from the way in which it is organized and its focus on cash. It is the only statement that reports on the operating, investing, and financing activities of a business from a cash perspective, and many believe that cash management is a key to business success. Professor Loyd Heath, whose writings did much to motivate the development of the statement of cash flows, describes it as being "complementary to the income statement and balance sheet," and the project manager for the FASB once said that "cash flow is one of the best measures of corporate liquidity." A well-known article published in *The Wall Street Journal,* titled "Why Cash Is King in the Current Climate," noted that, during economic downturns, "companies with high amounts of cash relative to debt are likely to be coveted by investors as economic growth turns increasingly sluggish. Cash may be a new gauge of value in the stock market."

A second observation is that normally one cannot explain the adjustments in the operating section of the statement of cash flows (indirect method) of a major U.S. company by computing the changes in the current accounts on its balance sheet. For example, the 2000 statement of cash flows of SUPERVALU reported an accounts receivable increase of about $59 million. The change computed from the 1999 and 2000 balance sheets, however, indicated an increase of approximately $151 million. The difference can be explained by the consolidation process. When a company such as SUPERVALU acquires another company, the cash decrease is reflected in the investing section—not the operating section—of the statement of cash flows. When the accounts are consolidated at the end of the year, the current assets and liabilities of the acquired company are added to those of the parent. The result is an inconsistency. In the SUPERVALU case, the $151 million increase in accounts receivable indicated on the balance sheet reflects revenues that are being recognized faster than cash is being collected, but it also reflects receivables that have been purchased in other companies. The inconsistency arises because the cash outflows associated with these purchases are reflected in the investing section, rather than the operating section, of the statement of cash flows.

During 2000, Bristol-Myers Squibb sold off businesses for $848 million, and purchased businesses for only $196 million. Would you expect the change in receivables indicated on the statement of cash flows to be greater than or less than the change in receivables computed from the 1999 and 2000 balance sheets? Why?

INTERNATIONAL PERSPECTIVE: THE STATEMENT OF CASH FLOWS

The rise in international investing and other activities has introduced a number of important issues relevant to the statement of cash flows. In this section, we briefly discuss two such issues: (1) the disclosure requirements in other countries with respect to the statement of cash flows and (2) reporting foreign currency gains and losses on the statement of cash flows.

As mentioned earlier in the chapter, the statement of cash flows is a relatively recent addition to the required financial statements for U.S. corporations. It is not surprising, therefore, that the statement is not required in most other countries. Some countries, like Britain, require a "statement of sources and applications of funds." Other countries, like France, recommend a "sources and uses of funds statement," and still other countries, like Japan, are considering requiring a "statement of changes in financial position." While all of these statements resemble the statement of cash flows, they are different in many ways, and as you can see, they normally are not mandatory. In fact, in most countries no statement even resembling the statement of cash flows is required.

In the near future, however, it is likely that this situation will change. International accounting standards require a statement of cash flows, which will encourage companies in other countries to provide statements of cash flows. The importance of credit capital in many foreign countries also places a premium on cash flow information, which is important for credit analysis.

We have mentioned that U.S. corporations are increasingly conducting operations in foreign countries. These activities often involve transactions that are expressed in foreign currencies. A U.S. corporation, for example, may sell goods or services to a customer in a foreign country, giving rise to a receivable that is expressed in a foreign currency. When the value of the foreign currency changes relative to the U.S. dollar, the value of the receivable on the U.S. company's balance sheet must be restated, which, in turn, gives rise to a gain or loss that is reported on the income statement.[6]

Foreign currency exchange gains and losses, however, involve no cash flow. Consequently, when the statement of cash flows is prepared under the indirect method, an adjustment must be made to net income. Partly because these adjustments are becoming more and more significant, accounting pronouncements now require that they be disclosed separately at the bottom of the statement, immediately before "net increase (decrease) in cash and cash equivalents."

Refer to Figure 14–4, the statement of cash flows of La-Z-Boy, and find the adjustment for foreign currency exchange rate changes. What are the dollar amounts? Are they negative or positive, and what do they indicate?

6. The methods used to account for such transactions are covered in Appendix 6A.

REVIEW PROBLEM

Figure 14–21 contains balance sheets (December 31, 2002 and 2003) for XYZ Enterprises and the intervening income statement and statement of retained earnings. Following these statements are several selected pieces of information that more completely describe the activity of XYZ during 2003. The two forms of the statement of cash flows are contained in Figures 14–22

<table>
<tr><td rowspan="4" style="vertical-align:top">FIGURE 14–21
Financial statements for XYZ Enterprises</td><td colspan="3">XYZ Enterprises
Balance Sheets
For December 31, 2002 and 2003</td></tr>
</table>

XYZ Enterprises
Balance Sheets
For December 31, 2002 and 2003

	2003	2002
ASSETS		
Cash	$ 3,000	$ 2,500
Accounts receivable	4,500	4,000
Inventory	10,500	8,000
Prepaid rent	3,000	2,000
Fixed assets	40,000	35,000
Less: Accumulated depreciation	(12,000)	(10,000)
Patent	8,000	9,000
Total assets	$57,000	$50,500
LIABILITIES AND STOCKHOLDERS' EQUITY		
Accounts payable	$ 6,500	$ 3,000
Other current payables	7,000	10,000
Bonds payable	19,000	19,000
Plus: Premium on bonds payable	2,500	3,000
Common stock	15,000	10,000
Additional paid-in capital	4,000	3,000
Retained earnings	3,000	2,500
Total liabilities and stockholders' equity	$57,000	$50,500

XYZ Enterprises
Income Statement
For the Year Ended Dec. 31, 2003

Sales	$55,000
Less: Cost of goods sold	35,000
Gross profit	$20,000
Rent expense	(2,000)
Interest expense	(2,000)
Miscellaneous expense	(9,000)
Depreciation of fixed assets	(5,000)
Amortization of patent	(1,000)
Gain on sale of machinery	1,000
Net income	$ 2,000

XYZ Enterprises
Statement of Retained Earnings
For the Year Ended Dec. 31, 2003

Beginning balance	$2,500
Plus: Net income	2,000
Less: Cash dividends	(1,500)
Ending balance	$3,000

FIGURE 14–22 Statement of cash flows for XYZ Enterprises: Direct method

XYZ Enterprises
Statement of Cash Flows
For the Year Ended December 31, 2003

OPERATING ACTIVITIES:

INCOME STATEMENT		ADJUSTMENT/EXPLANATION	OPERATING CASH FLOWS	
Sales	$ 55,000	(500) [increase in accounts receivable]	$ 54,500	
COGS	(35,000)	(2,500) [increase in inventory]		
		+3,500 [increase in accounts payable]	(34,000)	
Rent	(2,000)	(1,000) [increase in prepaid rent]	(3,000)	
Interest	(2,000)	(500) [decrease in premium]	(2,500)	
Misc.	(9,000)	(3,000) [decrease in other current payables]	(12,000)	
Depreciation	(5,000)	[no cash effect]	0	
Amortization	(1,000)	[no cash effect]	0	
Gain	1,000	[no cash effect]	0	
Net income	$ 2,000	Net cash from operations		$ 3,000

INVESTING ACTIVITIES:

Sale of machinery		[see note below]	$ 3,000	
Purchase of machinery		[see note below]	(10,000)	
Net cash provided (used) by investing activities				(7,000)

FINANCING ACTIVITIES:

Issue of common stock		[increase in common stock and APIC]	$ 6,000	
Cash dividends		[see statement of retained earnings and no increase in dividend payable]	(1,500)	
Net cash provided (used) by financing activities				4,500
Increase (decrease) in cash balance				$ 500
Beginning cash balance				2,500
Ending cash balance				$ 3,000

NOTE:

		COST OF FIXED ASSETS	ACCUMULATED DEPRECIATION	
Beginning balance		$35,000		$10,000
Plus: Increases	(purchases)	10,000	(depreciation expense)	5,000
Less: Decreases	(sales)	(5,000)	(sold machinery)	(3,000)
Ending balance		$40,000		$12,000

Cash (+A)	3,000	
Accumulated Depreciation (+A)	3,000	
Machinery (−A)		5,000
Gain on Sale of Machinery (Ga, +SE)		1,000

(direct method) and 14–23 (indirect method). We have included relevant calculations on the statements to explain how the numbers were derived. Examine each cash flow statement closely, and trace the calculations back to the original financial statements and given information in Figure 14–21.

Additional information:
1. Purchased $3,000 of prepaid rent.
2. Sold a piece of machinery (cost: $5,000; accumulated depreciation: $3,000) for $3,000 cash. Purchased additional machinery for $10,000 cash.
3. Paid annual interest of $2,500 on note payable.
4. Issued 500 shares of $10 par value common stock for $12 per share.

FIGURE 14–23 Statement of cash flows for XYZ Enterprises: Indirect method	**XYZ Enterprises** **Statement of Cash Flows** **For the Year Ended December 31, 2003**

OPERATING ACTIVITIES:		
Net income	$ 2,000	
Noncash charges to noncurrent accounts:		
Depreciation of fixed assets	5,000	
Amortization of patent	1,000	
Gain on sale of machinery	(1,000)	
Decreases in premium	(500)	
Changes in current accounts other than cash:		
Increase in accounts receivable	(500)	
Increase in inventory	(2,500)	
Increase in prepaid rent	(1,000)	
Decrease in other payables	(3,000)	
Increase in accounts payable	3,500	
Cash provided (used) by operating activities		$ 3,000
INVESTING ACTIVITIES:		
Sale of machinery	$ 3,000	
Purchase of machinery	(10,000)	
Cash provided (used) by investing activities		(7,000)
FINANCING ACTIVITIES:		
Issue of common stock	$ 6,000	
Cash dividends	(1,500)	
Net cash provided (used) by financing activities		4,500
Net increase (decrease) in cash balance		$ 500
Beginning cash balance		2,500
Ending cash balance		$ 3,000

SUMMARY OF KEY POINTS

The key points of the chapter are summarized below.

○   *The structure and format of the statement of cash flows.*

The statement of cash flows explains the change in a company's cash account from one accounting period to the next. It is divided into three sections: (1) cash provided (used) by operating activities, (2) cash provided (used) by investing activities, and (3) cash provided (used) by financing activities. Each of these sections contains the cash inflows and outflows of the period that were associated with the indicated activity.

○   *Cash flows from operating, investing, and financing activities.*

Cash flows from operating activities include those cash inflows and outflows associated directly with the acquisition and sale of a company's inventories and services. Such activities include the cash receipts from sales and accounts receivable, as well as cash payments from the purchase of inventories, payments on accounts payable, selling and administrative expenses, and interest and taxes. The sale or purchase of inventory on account is an operating transaction that does not appear on the statement of cash flows.

Cash flows from investing activities include the cash inflows and outflows associated with the purchase and sale of a company's noncurrent assets. Cash activities include the cash effects from the purchase and sale of long-term investments, long-lived assets, and intangible assets.

Cash flows from financing activities include cash inflows and outflows associated with a company's two sources of outside capital: liabilities and contributed capital. Such activities include the cash inflows associated with borrowings and equity issuances as well as the cash outflows associated with debt repayment, treasury stock purchases, and dividends.

○   *How the statement of cash flows complements the other financial statements and how it can be used by those interested in the financial condition of a company.*

While the income statement provides a summary of a company's operating transactions on an accrual basis, and the balance sheet represents the accumulated accruals of the company's operating, investing, and financing transactions as of a particular point in time, neither statement indicates much about the cash effects of the company's operating, investing, and financing activities. The statement of cash flows is designed to fill this void by summarizing the cash effects of the company's operating, investing, and financing transactions.

The statement of cash flows is used primarily to evaluate a company's ability to generate cash (i.e., financial flexibility) as well as the effectiveness of its cash management policies. Financial flexibility reflects a company's ability to generate cash through operations, borrowings, issuing equity, or selling noncurrent assets. Effective cash management involves investing cash to provide a high rate of return while maintaining enough cash to meet debts as they come due (i.e., solvency). The statement of cash flows is helpful to this evaluation in three interrelated ways: (1) it explains the change in the cash balance, (2) it summarizes the cash effects of operating transactions, and (3) it summarizes the cash effects of capital (investing and financing) transactions.

○ *Important investing and financing transactions that do not appear on the statement of cash flows and how they are reported.*

The statement of cash flows includes only those transactions that either increase or decrease the cash account. Many important operating and capital transactions do not affect the cash account and are therefore excluded from the statement. For example, the purchase of machinery in exchange for a long-term note payable, the acquisition of land or the payment of a debt with capital stock, and the declaration of a dividend are all capital transactions that have no effect on the cash account and are therefore excluded from the statement.

The FASB requires that capital transactions that do not affect the cash account be described clearly in the footnotes to the financial statements. No special disclosures are required for operating transactions that do not affect the cash account, because the effects of such transactions can be inferred from the reconciliation of net income to net cash provided (used) by operating activities.

○ *Economic consequences associated with the statement of cash flows.*

The economic consequences associated with the statement of cash flows occur when investors, creditors, and other interested parties use it to assess the investment potential and creditworthiness of companies and the equity and debt securities they issue. The rising importance of cash flow information to report users creates incentives for managers to window dress the statement of cash flows. Such incentives can present problems, because in the short run, it is relatively easy for management to present a favorable cash position. Such manipulation is much less effective, however, when statements are viewed across several periods, because payments delayed in one period must normally be paid in the next. For this reason, the FASB requires that cash flow statements from at least the previous three years be disclosed in the financial report.

○ *Preparing a statement of cash flows from the information contained in two balance sheets, an income statement, and a statement of retained earnings.*

One can prepare the statement of cash flows, under either the direct or indirect method, by reconstructing the T-account for each balance sheet account, posting the transactions that are reflected on the income statement and statement of retained earnings, and deriving the related cash flows.

KEY TERMS

Note: Definitions for these terms are provided in the glossary at the end of this text.

Cash equivalents (p. 608)	Investing activities (p. 611)
Direct method (p. 608)	Operating activities (p. 608)
Financial flexibility (p. 611)	Solvency (p. 611)
Financing activities (p. 611)	Window dress (p. 615)
Indirect method (p. 609)	

ETHICS IN THE REAL WORLD

MicroStrategy, a software maker in the business-to-business Internet industry, was introduced at the beginning of the chapter. Since it revised its earnings numbers downward, the company has continued to report net losses. Its net loss in 2000, for example, was $261 million. Clearly, company management is under considerable pressure from stockholders, bankers, and the investment community to turn things around. The company's cash flow situation appeared somewhat more promising—a loss of only $33 million. However, a closer look at the numbers indicates that net cash from operations was buoyed by a huge increase in the company's accounts payable balance—that is, the accounts payable balance increased by 300 percent over the previous year while the accounts receivable balance increased by only 45 percent. It is possible that MicroStrategy intentionally delayed some payments to suppliers in an effort to put as positive a spin as possible on the company's cash flow position.

ETHICAL ISSUE Is it ethical for a company in weak financial condition to manage the timing of its cash receipts and payments to delay signaling that weakness to the public?

INTERNET RESEARCH EXERCISE

An article in *Forbes* (March 23, 1998) titled "Pick a Number, Any Number" indicated that the earnings quality of several well-known firms had fallen recently due to one-time charges, debatable methods of accounting for acquisitions, and aggressive revenue recognition practices. The companies cited were General Motors, Kellogg's, Boeing, Central Garden & Pet, FPA Medical, Signature Resorts, Ashworth, Penske, and Fine Host. Visit the Website for any two of these companies and find the most recent statements of cash flows. Trace the difference between reported net income and operating cash flow across the past three years. What are the reasons for the difference, and how could they reflect a "quality of earnings" problem?

BRIEF EXERCISES

REAL DATA
BE14–1

The indirect presentation

The 2000 statement of cash flows for Vectren, an energy company, reported net earnings of $72 million and net cash provided by operating activities of $40 million. Depreciation and amortization totaled $106 million. Vectren used the indirect form of presenting the statement of cash flows.

a.   How is depreciation disclosed on the statement of cash flows? Why?
b.   Why doesn't net earnings plus depreciation equal net cash provided by operating activities?
c.   Provide an estimate of the net change in current assets and current liabilities for Vectren during 2000.

REAL DATA
BE14–2

Cash vs. accruals

J.C. Penney reported retail sales for 1999 of $31 billion. During the year, accounts receivable decreased from $4.2 billion to $1.1 billion.
     Estimate the cash collected by J.C. Penney from its customers during 1999.

REAL DATA

BE14-3

Inferring inventory transactions

Pier 1 Imports reported cost of sales of $718 billion for 2000. Inventory increased during the year from $259 million to $269 million, and accounts payable (related to inventory purchases) increased from $129 million to $137 million.

a.   Estimate the cost of inventories purchased during 2000.
b.   Estimate the cash payments made to inventory suppliers during 2000.

REAL DATA

BE14-4

Interpreting the statement of cash flows

The information below was taken from the 2000 statements of cash flows for Agilent Technologies and Lucent Technologies (dollars in millions).

Company	Net Income	Cash from Operations	Cash from Investing	Cash from Financing
Agilent	$ 757	$838	$(1,117)	$1,275
Lucent	1,219	304	(2,480)	2,211

a.   Compute the change in the cash balance for both companies.
b.   Describe the cash management profile for each company; that is, what is the source of each company's cash, and how is each company using it?
c.   Discuss why cash from operating for Agilent exceeds net income and why cash from operating for Lucent is considerably less than net income.

EXERCISES

E14-1

Classifying transactions

Classify each of the following transactions as an operating, investing, or financing activity, even those that would not appear explicitly on the statement of cash flows. Some transactions may be classified in more than one category.

1. Purchase of machinery for cash
2. Issuance of common stock for cash
3. Sale of inventory on account
4. Purchase of outstanding stock (treasury stock) for cash
5. Sale of land held as a long-term investment
6. Purchase of a building for cash and a mortgage payable
7. Cash payment for principal and interest on an outstanding debt
8. Cash payment on accounts payable
9. Payment of a cash dividend
10. Payment of wages to employees

E14-2

Operating, investing, or financing activity?

The following are several activities that Wallingford, Inc., engaged in during 2003:

1. Wrote off an open receivable as uncollected.
2. Purchased a piece of plant equipment.
3. Reacquired 5,000 shares of its common stock.
4. Sold a building in exchange for a five-year note.
5. Declared, but did not pay, a cash dividend.
6. Retired bonds payable by issuing common stock.
7. Collected on a long-term note receivable.
8. Issued a stock dividend.
9. Recorded depreciation on fixed assets. (Assume that the direct method is used.)
10. Paid interest on long-term debt.
11. Purchased inventory on account.
12. Collected open accounts receivable.
13. Exchanged a building for land.
14. Issued 75,000 shares of preferred stock.
15. Purchased a two-year fire insurance policy.

Assume that each of these transactions involved cash unless otherwise indicated. Indicate in which section of the statement of cash flows each transaction would be classified. Classify each transaction as one of the following:

a.   An operating activity
b.   An investing activity
c.   A financing activity
d.   Not included on the statement of cash flows

E14–3

Cash management policies across companies

Summaries of the 2003 statements of cash flows for five different companies follow. For each company compute the missing dollar amount, and briefly describe the company's cash management policy for 2003.

| | Cash Provided (Used) by | | | Net Increase |
Company	Operations	Investments	Financing	(Decrease)
AAA	$320	?	$(180)	$ (38)
BBB	219	$(450)	190	?
CCC	?	(414)	80	$(137)
DDD	120	(130)	?	420
EEE	?	(120)	(100)	70

REAL DATA

E14–4

Cash management across companies

Excerpts from the 1999 statements of cash flows of Dole, Keebler, and Best Foods, three companies in the food industry, are provided below (dollars in millions).

Company	Cash from Operations	Cash from Investments	Cash from Financing	Net change in cash
Dole	$ 74	$?	$ 44	$ 7
Keebler	197	(97)	(103)	?
Best Foods	?	(477)	(697)	(74)

For each company compute the missing dollar amount, and briefly describe the company's cash management policy during 1999.

E14–5

Journalizing and classifying transactions

Presented below is a list of transactions entered into by Kaitland Manufacturing during 2003.

1.   Recorded depreciation expense of $170,000.
2.   Sold 10,000 shares of common stock ($10 par value) for $18 per share.
3.   Purchased 5,000 shares of IBM for $75 per share.
4.   Purchased a three-year insurance policy for $27,000.
5.   Purchased a building with a fair market value of $200,000 in exchange for a twenty-five-year mortgage. The agreement called for a down payment of $40,000.

Assume that each transaction is independent. Indicate how each transaction affects the accounting equation and how the cash effect, if any, would be disclosed on the company's statement of cash flows. That is, provide

a.   the dollar amount of the cash effect,
b.   whether it increases or decreases cash, and
c.   the section of the statement of cash flows in which it would appear.

E14–6

Converting accrual to cash numbers

The following are several account titles that could appear on an income statement:

1.   Cost of Goods Sold
2.   Insurance Expense
3.   Sales Revenue
4.   Rent Expense
5.   Dividend Revenue

6.   Wage Expense
7.   Supplies Expense
8.   Interest Expense
9.   Rent Revenue
10. Depreciation Expense

Several possible balance sheet accounts follow.

a.	Cash	m.	Deferred
√b.	Merchandise Inventory		Income Taxes
c.	Retained Earnings	√n.	Prepaid Rent
√d.	Unearned Sales Revenue	√o.	Wages Payable
√e.	Interest Payable	p.	Common Stock
√f.	Dividends Receivable	√q.	Supplies Inventory
g.	Fixed Assets	r.	Discount on Bonds Payable
√h.	Rent Payable	s.	Unearned Rent
√i.	Accounts Payable	t.	Marketable Securities
√j.	Accounts Receivable	√u.	Prepaid Interest
k.	Premium on Bonds Payable	v.	Bonds Payable
l.	Allowance for Doubtful	w.	Accumulated Depreciation
	Accounts	√x.	Prepaid Insurance

a. Assume that you wish to compute the cash inflow or outflow associated with each income statement account. Match each income statement account with the related balance sheet account (or accounts) that you would analyze in this computation.

b. For Sales Revenue, Cost of Goods Sold, and Interest Expense, indicate whether an increase in the related balance sheet accounts (identified in [a]) would be added to or deducted from the income statement item when computing the cash effect.

E14-7

Depreciation: A source of cash?

Your boss asks you to examine the following income statements of Hamilton Hardware and Watson Glass:

	Hamilton Hardware	Watson Glass
Sales	**$900,000**	**$900,000**
Cost of goods sold	**(400,000)**	**(400,000)**
Depreciation expense	**(50,000)**	**(100,000)**
Other expenses	**(200,000)**	**(200,000)**
Net income	**$250,000**	**$200,000**

In the notes to the financial statements, you notice that Hamilton Hardware uses the straight-line method of depreciation and that Watson Glass uses the double-declining-balance method.

a. Assume that the dollar amounts for sales, cost of goods sold, and other expenses reflect total cash collections from customers, total cash paid for inventory, and total cash paid for other expenses, respectively. Compute cash provided (used) by operating activities for each company, using each of the following:
    1. The direct method format
    2. The indirect method format

b. Why is the cash provided (used) by operations different from net income? Which of the two methods shows this more clearly?

c. Would you agree or disagree with the following statement? *"Depreciation is an important source of cash for most companies."* Explain your answer.

E14-8

Preparing a statement of cash flows from original transactions

Tony began a small retailing operation on January 1, 2003. During 2003, the following transactions occurred:

1. Tony contributed $20,000 of his own money to the business.
2. $60,000 was borrowed from the bank.
3. Long-lived assets were purchased for $25,000 cash.
4. Inventory was purchased: $25,000 cash and $15,000 on account.
5. Inventory with a cost of $25,000 was sold for $80,000: $20,000 cash and $60,000 on account.

6. Cash payments included $18,000 for operating expenses, $5,000 for loan principal, and a $2,000 dividend.
7. $15,000 in expenses were accrued at the end of the year.

a. Prepare journal entries for each economic event.
b. Prepare a balance sheet as of the end of 2003 and an income statement and statement of retained earnings for 2003 for Tony's business.
c. Prepare a cash T-account and a statement of cash flows using the direct method.
d. Prepare a statement of cash flows using the indirect method, but this time prepare it from the company's two balance sheets, the income statement, and the statement of retained earnings. Tony's first balance sheet contains all zero balances.

E14-9

Preparing a statement of cash flows from the cash account in the ledger

Driftwood Shipbuilders entered into the following transactions during 2003:

1. Sold $6,000 of no-par common stock.
2. Purchased $6,000 of inventory on account.
3. Purchased new equipment for $5,000 in cash.
4. Collections on accounts receivable totaled $10,000.
5. Made payments of $5,000 to suppliers.
6. Declared and paid dividends of $2,000.
7. Paid rent of $6,000 for the last six months of 2003 and $6,000 for the first six months of 2004.
8. Made sales totaling $100,000: $35,000 on account and the remainder for cash.
9. Paid $40,000 in cash for miscellaneous expenses.
10. Sold investments with a cost of $20,000 for $25,000.

a. Prepare journal entries for each transaction.
b. Prepare a cash T-account and post all transactions affecting cash to the account. Assume a beginning cash balance of $25,000.
c. Prepare a statement of cash flows (direct method) from the cash T-account.

E14-10

Computing cash outflows from accrual information

The following year-end totals were taken from the records of Landau's Supply House. Compute the cash outflows associated with insurance and wages during 2003.

	2003	2002
Prepaid insurance	$7,000	$4,200
Wages payable	6,000	0
Insurance expense	3,000	4,700
Wage expense	8,500	3,000

E14-11

Reconstructing a transaction and its cash effect

The following information was taken from the records of Dylan's Toys:

	2003	2002
Machinery	$ 45,000	$ 20,000
Accumulated depreciation	$(15,000)	$(10,000)
Depreciation expense	7,000	6,000
Gain on sale of machinery	2,000	500 ← *closed out*

Machinery with a cost of $8,000 was sold during 2003.

a. How much machinery was purchased during 2003?   *$33,000*
b. How much cash was collected on the sale of the machinery during 2003?   *$8000*
c. Provide the journal entry to record the sale of the machinery.

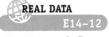

REAL DATA

E14-12

Compute cash flows
from accrual
numbers

Excerpts from the 2000 financial statements of SUPERVALU supermarkets is provided below (dollars in millions).

	2000	1999
Sales	$20,339	$17,420
Cost of sales	18,111	15,620
Accounts receivable	562	411
Inventory	1,490	1,067
Accounts payable	1,430	982

Compute estimates of cash receipts from customers, and cash payments to suppliers. Assume that all sales are on account and that accounts payable includes only accounts with suppliers.

E14-13

Computing cash
provided by
operations from
accrual information

Income statement and balance sheet excerpts of Shevlin and Liberty for the period ending December 31, 2003, follow. Compute cash provided (used) by operating activities for the period ending December 31, 2003. Use both the direct and indirect forms of presentation.

INCOME STATEMENT EXCERPTS

Sales		$48,000
Cost of goods sold		30,000
Gross profit		$18,000
Wage expense	$4,000	
Advertising expense	1,000	
Depreciation expense	2,000	7,000
Net income		$11,000

BALANCE SHEET EXCERPTS	2003	2002
Accounts receivable	$4,000	$ 5,000
Deferred revenues	0	3,000
Inventory	9,000	11,000
Accounts payable	3,000	4,000
Wages payable	1,800	900
Prepaid advertising	3,000	1,200
Accumulated depreciation	5,000	3,000

E14-14

Preparing a
statement of
cash flows from
information
contained in two
balance sheets, an
income statement,
and a statement of
retained earnings

The following information was taken from the records of Grimes Pools. Prepare a statement of cash flows (direct method) for the period ending December 31, 2003. Assume that all transactions involve cash.

	2003	2002
Cash	$ 4,000	$ 6,000
Noncash operating assets	15,000	15,000
Nonoperating assets	20,000	28,000
Operating liabilities	2,000	8,000
Nonoperating liabilities	6,000	4,000
Contributed capital	26,000	30,000
Retained earnings	5,000	7,000
Revenues	35,000	
Expenses	34,000	
Dividends	3,000	

E14–15

Preparing a
statement of cash
flows from
information
contained in two
balance sheets, an
income statement,
and a statement of
retained earnings

The following information was taken from the records of Romora Supply House. Prepare a statement of cash flows (direct method) for the period ending December 31, 2000. Assume that all transactions involve cash.

	2000	1999
Cash	$12,000	$ 5,000
Noncash operating assets	18,000	23,000
Nonoperating assets	27,000	23,000
Operating liabilities	7,000	2,000
Nonoperating liabilities	6,000	8,000
Contributed capital	35,000	32,000
Retained earnings	9,000	9,000
Revenues	64,000	
Expenses	61,000	
Dividends	3,000	

E14–16

Computing net
income from cash
provided by
operating activities

The operating cash flows and balance sheet excerpts of Schlee and Associates for the period ending December 31, 2000, follow. Compute net income for the period ending December 31, 2000.

OPERATING ACTIVITIES

Cash inflows from sales	$ 65,000
Cash payments for inventories	$(40,000)
Cash payments for wages	(6,000)
Cash payments for advertising	(1,000)
Cash provided (used) by operating activities	$ 18,000

BALANCE SHEET EXCERPTS	2000	1999
Accounts receivable	$ 3,000	$ 9,000
Deferred revenues	4,000	1,000
Inventory	18,000	10,000
Accounts payable	7,000	3,000
Salaries payable	2,100	1,300
Prepaid advertising	5,000	8,000
Accumulated depreciation	8,000	5,000

E14–17

Preparing the
operating section
of the statement
of cash flows:
direct and
indirect methods

The following balance sheet and income statement data were taken from the records of L. L. Beeno for the year ended December 31, 2000.

	2000	1999
BALANCE SHEET		
Cash	$ 3,000	$ 2,800
Accounts receivable	5,600	4,500
Inventory	7,500	7,800
Prepaid insurance	600	900
Total current assets	$16,700	$16,000
Machinery (net)	29,000	26,000
Total	$45,700	$42,000

	2000	1999
Accounts payable	$ 5,600	$ 7,300
Wages payable	4,500	3,400
Total current liabilities	$10,100	$10,700
Bonds payable (net)	14,000	14,800
Capital stock	5,000	5,000
Retained earnings	16,600	11,500
Total	$45,700	$42,000

INCOME STATEMENT

Revenues	$47,000
Cost of goods sold	25,000
Gross profit	$22,000
Wage expense	(6,200)
Insurance expense	(4,200)
Interest expense	(1,600)
Depreciation expense	(3,300)
Net income before taxes	$ 6,700
Tax expense	1,200
Net income	$ 5,500

Prepare the operating section of the statement of cash flows, and present it under both the direct and the indirect methods.

E14–18

Preparing the operating section of the statement of cash flows: direct and indirect methods

The following balance sheet and income statement data were taken from the records of Martland Stores for the year ended December 31, 2003.

	2003	2002
BALANCE SHEET		
Cash	$ 6,000	$ 1,400
Accounts receivable	12,000	13,500
Inventory	4,500	9,800
Prepaid insurance	900	1,200
Total current assets	$23,400	$25,900
Machinery (net)	38,000	37,500
Total	$61,400	$63,400
Accounts payable	$12,600	$13,100
Wages payable	9,500	7,400
Total current liabilities	$22,100	$20,500
Bonds payable (net)	17,000	17,000
Capital stock	15,000	15,000
Retained earnings	7,300	10,900
Total	$61,400	$63,400

INCOME STATEMENT

Revenues	$96,000
Cost of goods sold	64,000
Gross profit	$32,000
Wage expense	(18,600)
Insurance expense	(9,200)
Interest expense	(2,100)
Depreciation expense	(5,700)
Net loss	$ 3,600

Prepare the operating section of the statement of cash flows, and present it under both the direct and the indirect methods.

E14-19

Preparing the operating section of the statement of cash flows: direct and indirect methods

The following balance sheet and income statement data were taken from the records of Mako Retail Supply for the year ended December 31, 2003.

	2003	2002
BALANCE SHEET		
Cash	$ 6,000	$ 5,400
Accounts receivable	11,200	9,000
Inventory	15,000	15,600
Prepaid rent	1,200	1,800
Total current assets	$ 33,400	$31,800
Equipment (net)	58,000	52,000
Total	$ 91,400	$83,800
Accounts payable	$ 11,200	$14,600
Wages payable	9,000	6,800
Interest payable	1,500	2,200
Unearned revenue	6,500	4,700
Total current liabilities	$ 28,200	$28,300
Bonds payable (net)	28,000	28,400
Capital stock	10,000	10,000
Retained earnings	25,200	17,100
Total	$ 91,400	$83,800

INCOME STATEMENT	
Revenues	$109,100
Cost of goods sold	56,000
Gross profit	$ 53,100
Wage expense	(15,200)
Rent expense	(9,000)
Interest expense	(2,900)
Depreciation expense	(6,200)
Loss on sale of equipment	(4,200)
Net income before taxes	$ 15,600
Tax expense	4,400
Net income	$ 11,200

Prepare the operating section of the statement of cash flows, and present it under both the direct and the indirect methods.

E14-20

Preparing the operating section of the statement of cash flows: direct and indirect methods

The following balance sheet and income statement data were taken from the records of Steeler and Jones for the year ended December 31, 2003.

	2003	2002
BALANCE SHEET		
Cash	$ 6,400	$ 7,400
Accounts receivable	11,900	13,000
Inventory	14,100	15,600
Prepaid rent	1,300	900
Total current assets	$ 33,700	$ 36,900
Equipment (net)	52,000	66,000
Total	$ 85,700	$102,900

	2003	2002
Accounts payable	$ 9,200	$ 14,600
Wages payable	4,500	6,800
Interest payable	1,500	1,300
Unearned revenue	6,500	8,700
Total current liabilities	$ 21,700	$ 31,400
Bonds payable (net)	16,500	24,300
Capital stock	20,000	25,000
Retained earnings	27,500	22,200
Total	$ 85,700	$102,900

INCOME STATEMENT

Revenues	$ 87,400
Cost of goods sold	46,700
Gross profit	$ 40,700
Wage expense	$(13,200)
Rent expense	(11,000)
Interest expense	(1,900)
Depreciation expense	(5,700)
Plus: gain on sale of equipment	5,200
Net income before taxes	$ 14,100
Tax expense	4,800
Net income	$ 9,300

Prepare the operating section of the statement of cash flows, and present it under both the direct and the indirect methods.

E14–21

Preparing the operating section of the statement of cash flows: direct and indirect methods

The following balance sheet and income statement data were taken from the records of Harbaugh Auto Supply for the year ended December 31, 2003.

	2003	2002
BALANCE SHEET		
Cash	$ 10,100	$ 8,400
Accounts receivable	14,400	13,900
Inventory	21,600	18,700
Interest receivable	1,200	1,500
Prepaid rent	2,600	1,400
Total current assets	$ 49,900	$ 43,900
Investments	35,400	32,100
Equipment (net)	98,000	91,700
Total	$183,300	$167,700
Accounts payable	$ 18,700	$ 21,300
Wages payable	9,800	11,200
Interest payable	2,300	1,700
Dividend payable	1,700	1,200
Taxes payable	3,100	4,300
Unearned revenue	12,300	15,100
Total current liabilities	$ 47,900	$ 54,800
Long-term notes payable (net)	68,300	62,800
Capital stock	42,000	42,000
Retained earnings	25,100	8,100
Total	$183,300	$167,700

	2003	2002
INCOME STATEMENT		
Sales revenues	$ 47,500	
Service revenue	35,200	
Interest revenue	9,300	$ 92,000
Cost of goods sold		(21,200)
Wage expense		(17,600)
Rent expense		(15,300)
Interest expense		(6,200)
Depreciation expense		(11,500)
Add: Gain on sale of investments		13,200
Net income before taxes		$ 33,400
Tax expense		9,100
Net income		$ 24,300

The company sells goods and provides services. All sales are made on account, and cash is received in advance on services with service revenues being recognized after services are performed.

Prepare the operating section of the statement of cash flows, and present it under both the direct and the indirect methods.

E14–22

Preparing the operating section of the statement of cash flows: direct and indirect methods

The following balance sheet and income statement data were taken from the records of Standard Center Manufacturing for the year ended December 31, 2003.

The company sells goods and provides services. All sales are made on account, and cash is received in advance on services with service revenues being recognized after services are performed.

Prepare the operating section of the statement of cash flows, and present it under both the direct and the indirect methods.

	2003	2002
BALANCE SHEET		
Cash	$ 20,200	$ 22,800
Accounts receivable	28,800	34,800
Inventory	42,900	43,900
Interest receivable	4,100	6,300
Prepaid rent	3,900	1,200
Total current assets	$ 99,900	$109,000
Investments	18,200	23,500
Equipment (net)	43,900	62,500
Total	$162,000	$195,000
Accounts payable	$ 12,500	$ 8,600
Wages payable	11,100	11,500
Interest payable	1,800	2,100
Dividend payable	900	1,700
Taxes payable	1,200	3,200
Unearned revenue	7,200	9,600
Total current liabilities	$ 34,700	$ 36,700
Long-term notes payable (net)	75,400	97,300
Capital stock	25,000	25,000
Retained earnings	26,900	36,000
Total	$162,000	$195,000

	2003	2002
INCOME STATEMENT		
Sales revenues	$ 67,500	
Service revenue	28,200	
Interest revenue	7,300	$103,000
Cost of goods sold		(19,500)
Wage expense		(28,400)
Rent expense		(21,500)
Interest expense		(7,200)
Depreciation expense		(4,300)
Loss on sale of investments		(17,900)
Net income before taxes		$ 4,200
Tax expense		1,400
Net income		$ 2,800

PROBLEMS

P14–1

Placing transactions
on the statement
of cash flows

The following events occurred during 2003 for Frames Unlimited:

1. Purchased inventory for $60,000 in cash.
2. Recorded $40,000 in insurance expense for the portion of an insurance policy acquired in 1997 that expired during 2003.
3. Paid $40,000 for rental space that the company will not use until 2004.
4. Sold land with a cost of $80,000 for $94,000 cash.
5. Paid $90,000 on a long-term note. Included in the $90,000 is $15,000 in interest, $9,000 of which was accrued in 2002.
6. Recorded bad debt expense in the amount of $30,000 (allowance method).
7. Reissued 5,000 shares of treasury stock for $30 per share. The stock was acquired at $18 per share.
8. Declared and issued a stock dividend. 10,000 shares of common stock ($10 par value) were issued with a fair market value of $25 per share at the time.
9. Issued $500,000 face value bonds for cash at a total discount of $25,000.
10. Purchased a building for $100,000 in cash, $50,000 in common stock, and a note with a present value of $217,000.
11. Recorded $35,000 in sales to customers on account.

Frames Unlimited is in the process of preparing a statement of cash flows under the direct method.

REQUIRED:
Use a chart like the one at the top of the next page to indicate the following.

a. The section of the statement of cash flows in which each transaction should be listed. Use the following terms:
    (1) Operating—for operating activities
    (2) Investing—for investing activities
    (3) Financing—for financing activities
    (4) N/A—for items that would not be included on the statement of cash flows
b. Whether the transaction would involve an inflow or an outflow of cash.
c. The dollar amount, if appropriate, that the company would report on the statement of cash flows.

(Continued)

The first transaction is done for you as an example.

Transaction	Section	Inflow	Outflow	Amount
1.	Operating		X	$60,000

P14–2

Placing transactions on the statement of cash flows

Endnote Enterprises entered into the following transactions during 2003:

1. Sold merchandise for $52,000 in cash.
2. Purchased a parcel of land. The company paid $12,000 in cash and issued a $30,000 note payable for the remainder.
3. Purchased a three-year insurance policy for $30,000.
4. Purchased a building in exchange for a long-term note with a face value and present value of $115,000.
5. Collected $100,000 on a long-term note receivable. Included in the $100,000 is $6,000 in interest earned and accrued in the previous period and $4,000 in interest earned in the current period.
6. Collected from customers $45,000 that will not be earned until 2004.
7. Reacquired 5,000 shares of its common stock for $10 per share.
8. Declared and paid a cash dividend of $40,000.
9. Paid $25,000 for wages accrued in a prior year.
10. Retired $500,000 in bonds payable. The company gave the creditor $300,000 in cash and $200,000 in common stock.
11. Purchased $60,000 of inventory on account.
12. Wrote off an open account ($5,000) as uncollectible (allowance method).
13. Recorded $84,000 in depreciation expense for the year.

Endnote Enterprises is in the process of preparing its statement of cash flows under the direct method.

REQUIRED:

Use the chart format below to indicate the following.

a. The section of the statement of cash flows in which each transaction would be listed. Use the following terms:
   (1) Operating—for operating activities
   (2) Investing—for investing activities
   (3) Financing—for financing activities
   (4) N/A—for items that would not be included on the statement of cash flows.
b. Whether the transaction would involve an inflow or an outflow of cash.
c. The dollar amount, if appropriate, that the company would report on the statement of cash flows.

The first transaction is done for you as an example.

Transaction	Section	Inflow	Outflow	Amount
1.	Operating	X		$52,000

P14–3

Classifying transactions and their cash effects

MHT Enterprises entered into the following transactions during 2003.

1. Sold a piece of equipment with a book value of $8,000 for $1,200.
2. Purchased a parcel of land for $13,000.
3. Purchased a three-year insurance policy for $9,000.
4. Issued 1,000 shares of common stock at $7 per share.
5. Collected a short-term note, including interest, in the amount of $2,500.
6. Collected $3,000 from customers that will not be earned until 2004.
7. Purchased a building in exchange for a long-term note with a face value of $15,000 (the present value of the note is $12,000).

8. Declared and paid a cash dividend of $7,000.
9. Paid $5,000 in wages.
10. Converted an outstanding receivable into a short-term note receivable that matures in February 2004.
11. Purchased $4,500 of inventory on account.
12. Wrote off an account ($500) as uncollectible (allowance method).
13. Recorded $9,000 in depreciation expense for the year.

REQUIRED:

a. The controller of MHT Enterprises is trying to explain the change in the company's cash balance from January 1, 2003, to December 31, 2003. The controller has asked you to analyze each of the transactions. You are to indicate whether cash was provided, used, or not affected by each transaction. If the cash balance is affected by the transaction, indicate the dollar amount of the increase or decrease. Unless otherwise indicated, assume that all transactions involve cash.
b. Classify each transaction identified in (a) as affecting cash as one of the following:
   (1) An operating activity
   (2) An investing activity
   (3) A financing activity

REAL DATA

P14-4

Comparing cash flow policies across companies in the Internet industry

Cash flows from three well-known Internet companies are provided below (dollars in millions).

Yahoo:	1999	1998	1997
Operations	$ 216	$ 82	$(15)
Investing	(448)	(383)	15
Financing	236	440	54

Lycos:	1999	1998	1997
Operations	$ (38)	$ (3)	$ (2)
Investing	(27)	(1)	(2)
Financing	10	115	0

eBay:	1999	1998	1997
Operations	$ 67	$ 6	$12
Investing	(603)	(53)	(3)
Financing	718	72	0

REQUIRED:

a. Describe the similarities and differences of the cash flow policies across the three companies.
b. What appears to be distinctive about the cash flow policies of companies in this industry?

P14-5

Classifying transactions and their cash effects

Several transactions entered into by Travis Retail during 2003 follow.

1. Received $50,000 for wine previously sold on account.
2. Paid $55,000 in wages.
3. Sold a building for $100,000. The building had cost $170,000, and the related accumulated depreciation at the time of sale was $55,000.
4. Declared and paid a cash dividend of $70,000.
5. Repurchased 10,000 shares of outstanding common stock at $50 per share.
6. Purchased a two-year, $100,000 fire and storm insurance policy on June 30.
7. Purchased some equipment in exchange for 1,000 shares of common stock. The stock was currently selling for $75 per share.
8. Purchased $500,000 in equity securities considered to be long-term.
9. Issued $200,000 face value bonds. The bonds were sold at 101.
10. Owed $30,000 in rent as of December 31.

REQUIRED:

Record each transaction on a chart like the following. Classify the sections of the statement of cash flows as a cash flow from operating, investing, or financing activities. Transaction (1) is done as an example.

Transaction	Effect on Cash	Section of Statement	Explanation
1.	+50,000	Operating	Operations is defined in terms of inventory activity.

Ruttman Enterprises began operations in early 2001. Summaries of the statement of cash flows for the years 2001, 2002, and 2003 follow:

A company's cash management policy across time

	2003	2002	2001
Cash provided (used) by operating activities	$?	$(202)	$?
Cash provided (used) by investing activities	160	?	(500)
Cash provided (used) by financing activities	(150)	280	900
Increase (decrease) in cash	$?	$ (24)	$ 110
Cash balance at beginning of year	86	?	0
Cash balance at end of year	$ 176	$ 86	$?

REQUIRED:
a. Compute the missing dollar amounts.
b. Briefly comment on the company's cash management policy over the three-year period.

P14-7

Cash management across time

The information below was taken from the 2000 annual report of Imation, a global technology company (dollars in millions).

	2000	1999	1998
Cash provided (used) by operating activities	$192.0	$?	$ (6.4)
Cash provided (used) by investing activities	(58.3)	142.8	?
Cash provided (used) by financing activities	?	(97.1)	(280.5)
Increase (decrease) in cash	75.1	?	(39.3)
Cash balance at beginning of year	?	64.2	103.5
Cash balance at end of year	$269.7	$194.6	$?

REQUIRED
a. Compute the missing dollar amounts.
b. Comment on the company's cash management policies across the three-year period.

P14-8

Deriving the cash effects of investing transactions

Webb Industries reported the following information concerning the company's property, plant, and equipment in its 2003 financial report:

	2003	2002
Buildings	$ 750,000	$820,000
Accumulated depreciation	$(100,000)	(80,000)
Equipment	500,000	380,000
Accumulated depreciation	(75,000)	(85,000)
Land	250,000	250,000
Depreciation expense—buildings	40,000	25,000
Depreciation expense—equipment	15,000	12,000

Listed below are four independent cases involving buildings, equipment, and land during 2003.

1. The company purchased a building for $60,000.
2. The company sold equipment in December 2003 that was purchased for $50,000. It recorded a gain of $5,000 on the sale.
3. The company sold a piece of land for $300,000 at a gain of $75,000.
4. The company acquired a building in exchange for land. The land had a book value of $150,000 and a market value of $600,000.

REQUIRED:

a. For each case, explain the change from 2002 to 2003 in the affected buildings, equipment, and land accounts. (For example, in case [1] explain the change in the building account, the related accumulated depreciation account, and the balance in the related depreciation expense account.)
b. For each case, compute the effect on the cash balance, and indicate the appropriate disclosure on the statement of cash flows.

P14–9

Deriving the cash generated from a common stock issuance

The stockholders' equity section of Mountvale's Associates is provided below.

	2003	2002
Common stock ($1 par value)	$128,000	$100,000
Additional paid-in capital (C/S)	95,000	12,000
Retained earnings	41,000	35,000
Total stockholders' equity	$264,000	$147,000

The following selected transactions occurred during 2003:

1. 1/1/03: A 20 percent stock dividend was issued. The fair market value of the stock at the time was $3 per share.
2. 8/25/03: Land was purchased in exchange for 6,000 shares of common stock. The fair market value of the stock was $3 per share.
3. 12/31/03: Common stock was issued for cash.

REQUIRED:

How many shares of common stock did Mountvale issue on December 31, 2003, and how much cash did the issuance generate? Show all calculations clearly. (*Hint:* Calculate the number of shares of common stock issued for cash.)

P14–10

Converting cash flow numbers to accrual numbers and vice versa

Taylor Brothers began operations in 2002. The following selected information was extracted from its financial records:

	2003	2002
Sales returns	$ 25,000	$ 20,000
Cost of goods sold	375,000	250,000
Inventory	110,000	130,000
Accounts receivable	150,000	95,000
Insurance expense	50,000	35,000
Cash collected on sales	500,000	350,000
Accounts payable	115,000	105,000
Cash paid for insurance	90,000	65,000

REQUIRED:

a. Compute gross sales (accrual basis) for 2002 and 2003.
b. Calculate the amount of cash paid to suppliers during 2003 for inventory.
c. Compute the balance in the prepaid insurance account as of December 31, 2002, and December 31, 2003.

P14–11

Reconciling the income statement, the direct method, and the indirect method

Battery Builders, Inc., prepared statements of cash flows under both the direct and the indirect methods. The operating sections of each statement under the two methods follow:

DIRECT METHOD

Collections from customers	$ 26,000
Payments to suppliers	(13,000)
Payments for operating expenses	(10,000)
Cash provided (used) by operating activities	$ 3,000

INDIRECT METHOD

Net income	$ 9,000
Depreciation	3,000
Gain on sale of equipment	(2,000)
Increase in inventory	(3,000)
Increase in accounts receivable	(3,000)
Increase in accounts payable	1,000
Decrease in accrued payables	(2,000)
Cash provided (used) by operating activities	$ 3,000

REQUIRED:
Prepare an income statement from the information provided.

P14–12

Manipulating dollar amounts on the statement of cash flows

Pendleton Enterprises began operations on January 1, 2001. Balance sheet and income statement information for 2001, 2002, and 2003 follow:

	2003	2002	2001
Cash	$ 6,000	$ 9,000	$7,000
Accounts receivable	8,000	5,000	4,000
Accounts payable	5,000	3,000	2,000
Revenues	12,000	14,000	8,000
Expenses	14,000	9,000	6,000

REQUIRED:

a. Prepare the operating sections of the statement of cash flows for 2001, 2002, and 2003 under the direct method.
b. Assume that the $4,000 of outstanding accounts receivable on December 31, 2001, was actually collected before the end of 2001 but that the accounts receivable balances for 2002 and 2003 are unchanged. Prepare the statements of cash flows under the direct method for all three years.
c. Ignore the assumption in (b), and assume alternatively that the company deferred an additional $3,000 on the payment of accounts payable as of December 31, 2001 (i.e., accounts payable equal $5,000, and cash equals $10,000 on December 31, 2001). The accounts receivable balances for 2002 and 2003 are unchanged. Prepare the operating section of the statements of cash flows for all three periods.
d. How can managers manipulate cash provided (used) by operations, and what usually happens in the subsequent period?

P14–13

Preparing the statement of cash flows from two balance sheets and an income statement

The 2002 and 2003 balance sheets and related income statement of Watson and Holmes Detective Agency follow:

	2003	2002
BALANCE SHEET		
ASSETS		
Cash	$10,000	$ 6,000
Accounts receivable	7,000	2,000
Less: Allowance for doubtful accounts	(1,000)	(500)
Inventory	8,000	10,000
Long-lived assets	12,000	11,000
Less: Accumulated depreciation	(4,000)	(2,000)
Total assets	$32,000	$26,500
LIABILITIES AND STOCKHOLDERS' EQUITY		
Accounts payable	$ 5,000	$ 6,000
Deferred revenues	1,000	2,000
Long-term note payable	10,000	10,000
Less: Discount on note payable	(800)	(1,000)
Common stock	12,000	6,000
Retained earnings	4,800	3,500
Total liabilities and stockholders' equity	$32,000	$26,500
INCOME STATEMENT		
Revenues	$42,000	
Cost of goods sold	(24,000)	
Depreciation expense	(2,000)	
Interest expense	(3,000)	
Bad debt expense	(2,000)	
Other expense	(9,000)	
Net income	$ 2,000	

REQUIRED:

Prepare a statement of cash flows under both the direct and the indirect methods for 2003.

P14–14

Paying short-term debts: Effects on working capital, the current ratio, and the statement of cash flows

ISS Inc. began operations on January 1, 2003. It engaged in the following economic events during 2003:

1. Issued 6,000 shares of no-par common stock for $10 per share.
2. Purchased on account 20,000 units of inventory for $1 per unit.
3. Paid and capitalized $7,000 for rent covering 2003 and 2004.
4. Purchased furniture for $30,000, paying $20,000 in cash and signing a long-term note for the remaining balance.
5. Sold on account 8,800 units of inventory for $4 per unit.
6. Paid one-half of the outstanding accounts payable.
7. Received $12,000 from customers on open accounts.
8. Paid miscellaneous expenses of $10,000 for the year.
9. Depreciation recorded on the furniture totaled $5,000.
10. Accrued interest on the long-term note payable amounted to $1,000.
11. Declared dividends of $3,000 at year-end to be paid in January 2004.
12. Recorded entry for $3,000 of rent expired during 2003.

REQUIRED:

a. Prepare journal entries for these events.
b. Prepare an income statement, statement of retained earnings, balance sheet, and statement of cash flows (indirect method).

(Continued)

c. Compute working capital and the current ratio.
d. Assume that the company pays the outstanding accounts payable on the final day of
    2003. Recompute working capital, the current ratio, and cash provided (used) by operat-
    ing activities.

P14-15

Preparing the
statement of
cash flows and
reconciling the
operating section
with the income
statement

Sunshine Enterprises included the following statements in its 2003 financial report:

INCOME STATEMENT	2003	
Marketing revenue	$1,000,000	
Salary expense	(250,000)	
Office supplies expense	(175,000)	
Depreciation expense	(100,000)	
Insurance expense	(60,000)	
Rent expense	(120,000)	
Net income	$ 295,000	

BALANCE SHEET	2003	2002
Cash	$ 100,000	$ 120,000
Accounts receivable	150,000	105,000
Office supply inventory	75,000	85,000
Prepaid insurance	50,000	10,000
Office furniture	500,000	465,000
Less: Accumulated depreciation	(325,000)	$(225,000)
Total assets	$ 550,000	$ 560,000
Rent payable	$ 20,000	$ 8,000
Common stock ($10 par value)	100,000	100,000
Additional paid-in capital	125,000	125,000
Retained earnings	305,000	327,000
Total liabilities and stockholders' equity	$ 550,000	$ 560,000

REQUIRED:
a. Convert each of the accrual-basis income statement accounts to a cash basis. Would you
    classify this method as directly or indirectly computing cash provided (used) by operating
    activities?
b. Prepare a proof of results. That is, begin with net income and adjust net income to arrive at
    cash provided (used) by operating activities. Would you classify this method as directly or
    indirectly computing cash provided (used) by operating activities?
c. Refer to Figure 14–19 in the chapter, and use the same format to reconcile the income state-
    ment with operating cash flows.

P14-16

Preparing the
statement of cash
flows from two
balance sheets
and an income
statement: book
losses and
amortized discounts

The following information was extracted from the financial records of Bower Manufacturing
Industries:

INCOME STATEMENT	2003
Sales	$190,000
Cost of goods sold	(80,000)
Depreciation expense	(30,000)
Interest expense	(10,000)
Salary expense	(12,000)
Supplies expense	(7,000)
Loss on sale of marketable sec.	(4,000)
Loss on sale of fixed assets	(10,000)
Net income	$ 37,000

BALANCE SHEETS	2003	2002
Cash	$ 747,000	$ 593,000
Marketable securities	85,000	140,000
Accounts receivable	450,000	400,000
Supplies inventory	10,000	12,000
Inventory	150,000	175,000
Short-term notes receivable	100,000	50,000
Machinery and equipment	550,000	500,000
Less: Accumulated depreciation	(90,000)	(75,000)
Total assets	$2,002,000	$1,795,000
Accounts payable	$ 60,000	$ 95,000
Salaries payable	10,000	10,000
Bonds payable	500,000	500,000
Discount on bonds payable	(5,000)	(10,000)
Common stock ($10 par value)	200,000	100,000
Additional paid-in capital	900,000	800,000
Retained earnings	337,000	300,000
Total liabilities and stockholders' equity	$2,002,000	$1,795,000

The company purchased machinery in exchange for 10,000 shares of common stock. The stock was selling for $20 per share at that time. The short-term receivable was received from a customer in exchange for the sale of merchandise inventory.

REQUIRED:

Prepare a statement of cash flows for the year ended December 31, 2003, using both the direct and the indirect methods.

P14-17

Preparing the statement of cash flows from two balance sheets and an income statement: book gains and amortized premiums

The following information was extracted from the 2003 financial records of Price Restaurant Supply Company:

INCOME STATEMENT

Sales	$ 160,000
Cost of goods sold	(100,000)
Depreciation expense	(12,000)
Insurance expense	(10,000)
Interest expense	(11,000)
Gain on sale of plant equipment	10,000
Net income	$ 37,000

BALANCE SHEETS	2003	2002
Cash	$ 173,000	$120,000
Accounts receivable	60,000	65,000
Inventory	210,000	110,000
Prepaid insurance	14,000	24,000
Plant equipment	275,000	350,000
Less: Accumulated depreciation	(67,000)	(75,000)
Total assets	$ 665,000	$594,000

(Continued)

BALANCE SHEETS	2003	2002
Accounts payable	$ 51,000	$ 50,000
Bonds payable	200,000	200,000
Premium on bonds payable	3,000	5,000
Common stock ($10 par value)	75,000	40,000
Additional paid-in capital	125,000	95,000
Retained earnings	211,000	204,000
Total liabilities and		
stockholders' equity	$ 665,000	$594,000

The company sold a piece of plant equipment for cash that had originally cost $100,000. The accumulated depreciation associated with the equipment at the time of sale was $20,000.

REQUIRED:
Prepare a statement of cash flows for the year ended December 31, 2003, using both the direct and the indirect methods.

P14–18

Preparing the statement of cash flows and using it to set dividend policy

Lynch Engineering Firm provided the following income statement for 2003 in its annual financial report:

	2003		2002	
Sales		$5,967,000		$5,590,000
Salary expense	$2,025,000		$1,794,000	
Advertising expense	755,000		710,000	
Bad debt expense	275,000		260,000	
Administrative expenses	898,000		832,000	
Janitorial expense	132,000		120,000	
Supplies expense	281,000		299,000	
Depreciation expense	963,000	5,329,000	978,000	4,993,000
Net income		$ 638,000		$ 597,000

1. The company declared and paid a dividend of $550,000 in 2002 but did not declare any dividends in 2003.
2. 2002:
   (a) 35 percent of the sales were on account.
   (b) The accounts receivable balance decreased by $2,980,000 from January 1 to December 31.
   (c) As of December 31, the company still owed $145,000 in wages and $67,000 on the supplies used during the year.
3. 2003:
   (a) 75 percent of the sales were on account.
   (b) The accounts receivable balance increased by $1,671,750 from January 1 to December 31.
   (c) As of December 31, the company still owed $25,000 in wages and $50,000 in advertising.
   (d) On January 1, 2002, the company had a balance of $13,245 in cash.
4. The company had no write-offs on recoveries of accounts receivable during 2002 or 2003.

REQUIRED:
a. Prepare the operating section of the statement of cash flows for 2002 and 2003, using the direct method.
b. Assume that you are a member of the board of directors of the Lynch Engineering Firm. Several influential stockholders have called you and complained that the company generated more net income in 2003 than in 2002, yet chose not to declare a dividend in 2003. How would you explain the board's position on dividends in 2002 versus 2003?

P14-19

Preparing a
complete set of
financial statements
from a set of
original transactions

Mick's Photographic Equipment began operations on January 1, 2002. During 2002, the company entered into the following transactions:

1. Issued 50,000 shares of $15 par-value common stock for $30 per share in exchange for cash. Also issued, for cash, 1,000 shares of 10 percent, $100 par-value preferred stock for $102 per share.
2. Purchased $750,000 of fixed assets in exchange for cash.
3. Issued twenty bonds, each with a face value of $1,000, at 146 (annual coupon rate = 16 percent and annual yield rate = 10 percent). The bonds pay interest semiannually on December 31 and June 30.
4. Purchased land in exchange for 1,000 shares of $15 par-value common stock. The shares were selling for $40 per share at the time.
5. Purchased $2,000,000 of inventory on account. $1,075,000 was subsequently paid during 2002.
6. Sold $2,050,000 of merchandise in exchange for cash. The related inventory had cost $875,000.
7. Purchased a two-year insurance policy for $80,000.
8. Purchased short-term marketable securities for $250,000.
9. Sold $880,000 of merchandise on account. The related inventory had a cost of $490,000. $500,000 of the sales made on account were collected during the year.
10. Paid $500,000 in miscellaneous expenses (rent, utilities, and wages).
11. Declared, but did not pay, a $100,000 dividend.
12. Made the first interest payment on the bonds on December 31.

Adjusting entries include:

(a) The fixed assets were purchased on January 1 and had an estimated useful life and salvage value of five years and $50,000, respectively. The company uses the straight-line depreciation method.
(b) The company used one-fourth of the insurance policy during 2002.
(c) The market value of the marketable securities on December 31 was $225,000.
(d) As of December 31, the company had incurred, but had not yet paid, $75,000 in miscellaneous expenses.
(e) The company estimates that 8 percent of credit sales will prove uncollectible.
(f) The market value of the inventory was $5,000 less than the cost.

REQUIRED:

a. Prepare journal entries for each of the original and adjusting transactions. Establish T-accounts for each account. Post the entries to the T-accounts.
b. Prepare the necessary closing entries. Post these entries.
c. Prepare the income statement and balance sheet for Mick's Photographic Equipment for the year ended December 31, 2002.
d. Prepare the statement of cash flows for Mick's Photographic Equipment for the year ended December 31, 2002, using both the direct and the indirect methods.

ISSUES FOR DISCUSSION

REAL DATA

ID14-1

Using the cash flow
statement to spot
earnings quality
problems

An article in *Business Week* (October 30, 1995) described how Bob Olstein, a successful stock analyst, predicts that the prices of stocks issued by firms who "engage in aggressive accounting practices" will go down, stating that other "investors have unrealistic expectations of the earnings potential." He cites Mattel as an example by noting that big changes in net receivables, inventories, and deferred income taxes, as well as foreign currency translation gains that produced no cash, accounted for most of Mattel's earnings growth in the first half of 1995. The company's debt also jumped "from $440 million to $630 million in about two years."

REQUIRED:

a. Explain how the statement of cash flows, especially if prepared under the indirect format, can be used to identify "quality of earnings" and "earnings persistence" problems.
b. Specifically describe how the information mentioned above about Mattel was used to indicate these kinds of problems.
c. Do you think that it is possible to identify over- and undervalued stocks by identifying firms that use aggressive accounting practices?

REAL DATA
ID14-2

Equity in unconsolidated affiliates

As of December 31, 1999, The Washington Post Company held significant, but not controlling, interest in BrassRing, Inc., Bowater Mercy Paper Company, and the *International Herald Tribune.* These investments totaled $141 million on the company's 1999 balance sheet. In its 1999 annual report, The Washington Post Company included a statement of cash flows, presented in the indirect form, which covered the three-year period of 1999, 1998, and 1997. A line item was included in the operating section of that statement, titled "Equity in losses (earnings) of affiliates, net of distributions," and the dollar amounts for this item for 1999, 1998, and 1997 were $9,744, $9,145, and ($6,996), respectively.

REQUIRED:

a. Briefly describe the accounting methods used for unconsolidated affiliates, in which a company has a "significant influence." (For a review, see the equity method in Chapter 8.)
b. Explain why the 1999 and 1998 dollar amounts were added to net income on the statement of cash flows, while the 1997 dollar amount was subtracted.
c. What does the phrase "net of distributions" mean?
d. On the same statement of cash flows, The Washington Post Company reported another line item in the operating section, titled "Gain from disposition of business and marketable securities," which included dollar amounts for 1999, 1998, and 1997 of ($38,799), ($314,400), and ($44,560), respectively. Describe the transactions that led to these disclosures and explain why the three-dollar amounts are subtracted from net income in the calculation of net cash flow from operating activities. Would these amounts appear on any of the other financial statements, and if so, which one?

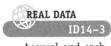

REAL DATA
ID14-3

Accrual and cash flow accounting

Loan Officer Han Blackford once commented that cash flow analysis has risen in importance due to a "trend over the past twenty years toward capitalizing and deferring more and more expenses. Although the practice may match revenues and expenses more closely, a laudable intent, it has also made it harder to find the available cash in a company—and easier for lenders to wind up with a loss." He further noted that recessions draw attention to the need for better warning signals of the sort cash flow analysis could provide.

REQUIRED:

a. Why would the process of capitalizing match revenues and expenses more closely, yet make it harder to find the cash available in a company?
b. Discuss the difference between earning power and solvency, why both are essential for a successful business, and how present-day financial accounting statements provide measures of each.
c. Explain why a wave of bankruptcies would draw attention to cash flow analysis.

REAL DATA
ID14-4

Analyzing the operating section of the statement of cash flows

SUPERVALU is the tenth-largest grocery chain in the United States. Its December 31, 2000, statement of cash flows included the following (dollars in thousands).

	Fiscal Year Ended		
	February 26, 2000 (52 weeks)	February 27, 1999 (52 weeks)	February 22, 1998 (53 weeks)
Cash flows from operating activities			
Net earnings	$ 242,941	$191,338	$230,757
Adjustments to reconcile net earnings to net cash provided by operating activities:			
Equity in earnings and gain on sale of ShopKo	—	—	(93,364)
Depreciation and amortization	277,062	233,523	230,082
LIFO (income) expense	8,253	(3,889)	2,403
Provision for losses on receivables	9,895	10,150	5,791
Gain on sale of assets	(163,662)	—	—
Restructuring and other charges	103,596	—	—
Deferred income taxes	(21,041)	16,520	22,680
Other adjustments, net	2,032	64	(3,476)
Changes in assets and liabilities, excluding effect from acquisitions:			
Receivables	(58,887)	(20,558)	(29,905)
Inventories	(195,192)	80,466	(25,700)
Accounts payable	61,997	14,623	38,453
Other assets and liabilities	74,178	37,703	15,214
Net cash provided by operating activities	341,172	559,940	392,935

REQUIRED:

a. Depreciation and amortization are added back to net earnings in the computation of net cash provided by operations. Does this mean that depreciation and amortization are sources of cash?

b. What method does SUPERVALU use to account for uncollectible accounts receivable? Explain why the provision is added back to net earnings.

c. Explain why the "gain on the sale of assets" is subtracted from net earnings, while "restructuring and other charges" are added. Describe the entries that led to these disclosures.

d. Comment on the trends across time of the company's current accounts, especially inventory.

e. Comment on the quality of the company's earnings over the three-year period.

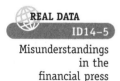

REAL DATA

ID14–5

Misunderstandings in the financial press

The financial press often uses the term cash flow to refer to a company's "net income + depreciation." In a well-known article in *Barron's* titled "No Substitutions, Please" (November 29, 1999), Intel was criticized for relying heavily on a number the company called "cash earnings," computed by adding amortization of goodwill and other intangible assets to net earnings.

REQUIRED:

Do you believe that using cash flow measures like the ones described above are superior to using net cash from operations as disclosed in the operating section of the statement of cash flows? Explain.

REAL DATA

ID14–6

Analyzing the statement of cash flows

Refer to the statements of cash flows for the years ending 1999, 1998, and 1997, taken from the 1999 annual report of Navistar International, a manufacturer of trucks and engines (dollars in millions).

Navistar International Corporation and Consolidated Subsidiaries
Statement of Cash Flow

FOR THE YEARS ENDED OCTOBER 31 MILLIONS OF DOLLARS	1999	1998	1997
CASH FLOW FROM OPERATIONS			
Net income	$ 544	$ 299	$ 150
Adjustments to reconcile net income to cash			
Provided by operations:			
Depreciation and amortization	174	159	120
Deferred income taxes	185	149	82
Deferred tax asset valuation allowance adjustment	(178)	(45)	—
Postretirement benefits funding less than (in excess of) expense	47	(373)	(128)
Other, net	(31)	(16)	(51)
Change in operating assets and liabilities:			
Receivable	(445)	(192)	(194)
Inventories	(129)	(13)	(25)
Prepaid and other current assets	(24)	(1)	4
Accounts payable	139	192	288
Other liabilities	20	202	137
Cash provided by operations	302	361	383
CASH FLOW FROM INVESTMENT PROGRAMS			
Purchases of retail notes and lease receivables	(1,442)	(1,263)	(970)
Collections/sales of retail notes and lease receivables	1,282	1,071	1,054
Purchases of marketable securities	(396)	(837)	(512)
Sales or maturities of marketable securities	726	521	557
Capital expenditures	(427)	(302)	(169)
Property and equipment leased to others	(108)	(125)	(42)
Investment in affiliates	(71)	(7)	8
Capitalized interest and other	(15)	(6)	(8)
Cash used in investment programs	(451)	(948)	(82)
CASH FLOW FROM FINANCING ACTIVITIES			
Issuance of debt	174	493	211
Principal payments on debt	(135)	(119)	(46)
Net increase (decrease) in notes and debt outstanding under bank revolving credit facility and commercial paper programs	88	348	(285)
Mexican credit facility	22	84	—
Debt and equity issuance costs	(3)	(26)	(7)
Purchases of common stock	(144)	(189)	(23)
Proceeds from reissuance of treasury shares	—	28	—
Redemption of series G preferred stock	—	(240)	—
Dividends paid	—	(11)	(29)
Cash provided by (used in) financing activities	2	368	(179)
CASH AND CASH EQUIVALENTS			
(Decrease) increase during the year	(147)	(219)	122
At beginning of the year	390	609	487
Cash and cash equivalents at end of the year	$ 243	$ 390	$ 609

See Notes to Financial Statements.

REQUIRED:
Analyze the company's cash management behavior and comment on the quality of the earnings
numbers across the three-year period.

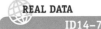

REAL DATA

ID14-7

Cash management
profiles
across time—
A mature firm

The following information was taken from the 2000 annual report and statement of cash flows of Eli Lilly, a major pharmaceutical (dollars in millions):*

	2000	1999	1998
Net income	$ 3,058	$ 2,721	$ 2,098
Net cash from operations	3,732	2,742	2,876
Net cash from investing activities	(1,057)	1,087	(369)
Net cash from financing activities	(2,229)	(1,575)	(2,984)
Change in cash	446	2,254	(477)

*Change in the cash balance does not always equal the sum of cash from operations, investing, and financing due to adjustments for exchange rate changes.

REQUIRED:

a. Discuss the cash management profile of Lilly across the three-year period. Where did the company get its cash, and what did it do with it?
b. Explain how the cash management profile relates to the company's financial condition and performance over this time period.

REAL DATA

ID14-8

Cash management
profile—
A young firm

Verity is a young, fast-growing company, recognized as a leading provider of corporate knowledge retrieval solutions. Excerpts from its 2000 statement of cash flows are provided below (dollars in thousands).*

	2000	1999	1998
Net income	$ 33,010	$ 12,130	$(16,510)
Net cash from operations	8,210	14,867	(9,044)
Net cash from investing activities	(116,448)	(19,614)	8,953
Net cash from financing activities	107,633	7,063	2,658
Change in cash	(724)	2,402	2,571

*Change in the cash balance does not always equal the sum of cash from operations, investing, and financing due to adjustments for exchange rate changes.

REQUIRED:

a. Discuss the cash management profile of Verity across the three-year period. Where did the company get its cash, and what did it do with it?
b. Explain how the cash management profile may be representative of a young, fast-growing company.
c. Comment on how this profile reflects the company's financial condition and performance.
d. Are there any possible quality-of-earnings issues? Explain.

REAL DATA

ID14-9

Reading the
operating section of
the statement of
cash flows

The operating section of the 2000 consolidated statement of cash flows for Imation Corp., a global technology company, is provided below (dollars in millions).

	2000	1999	1998
Net (loss) gain	$ (4.4)	$ 43.9	$ 57.1
Adjustments:			
Depreciation	53.5	72.4	110.5
Amortization	68.8	15.3	18.9
Restructuring charges	32.2		(16.8)
Gain on sale of image business			(65.0)
Accounts receivable	59.2	24.7	(57.6)
Inventories	46.6	10.2	46.3
Other current assets	16.0	(25.3)	(1.4)
Accounts payable	(19.7)	(6.8)	(29.6)
Accrued payroll	(48.3)	(25.3)	(89.7)
Other operating activities	(11.9)	(24.4)	20.9
Net cash provided (used in) operations	192.0	84.7	(6.4)

REQUIRED:

a. Review the trends across time of depreciation. Does the company's growth strategy seem to involve investing in property, plant, and equipment? Explain.
b. Why was the restructuring charge in 2000 added back to net income, while the gain on the sale of image business in 1998 was subtracted from net income?
c. Was the inventory balance growing or decreasing over the three-year period? Explain.
d. Comment on the financial performance of the company.

REAL DATA

ID14-10

The annual report
of Wal-Mart

The 2001 annual report of Wal-Mart is reproduced in Appendix A.

REQUIRED:

Review the 2001 annual report, and answer the following questions.

a. What are the major sources of cash for the company, and what is it doing with that cash?
b. Were there any significant transactions in 2000 that did not affect cash, but were reported on the statement of cash flows?
c. Analyze Wal-Mart's cash management policies across the three-year period (1999–2001).

A LOOK AT 2001 AND BEYOND

Dear Fellow Shareholder:

It is truly an honor to serve as President and CEO of Wal-Mart Stores, Inc., and I appreciate the opportunity to share with you some thoughts from fiscal 2001 and our outlook for the future. What a year of milestones it was! But before we get into the details, I'd like to touch on a few highlights from the year.

Net sales in fiscal 2001 increased almost 16 percent to more than $191 billion, representing a growth in revenue of more than $26 billion. In addition, net income reached $2 billion for the fourth quarter and almost $6.3 billion for the year, making it our first "two-billion-dollar-income quarter" and our first "six-billion-dollar-income year."

FORTUNE magazine named Wal-Mart the third "most admired" company in America and one of the 100 best companies to work for in America. Our Company also ranked fifth on *FORTUNE*'s Global Most Admired Companies list based on characteristics such as leadership, teamwork and the way we treat our people. In addition, Americans named Wal-Mart the company they think of first in supporting local causes and issues, according to Cone, Inc., a national research firm.

Whether it's our domestic or international Associates in the stores,

clubs and distribution centers, or those in the home office, our people truly deserve the credit for all these accomplishments. Let's look a little closer at what our Associates were able to achieve this year.

Fiscal 2001 was clearly one of the strongest years in recent memory for the SAM'S CLUB division. We saw growth in both sales and earnings. Moreover, earnings growth outpaced sales growth for the year. Membership renewals reached record levels, demonstrating strong loyalty and Member acceptance, and illustrating that a SAM'S membership is the best value in the warehouse club business. In fact, one in three households in America now has a SAM'S CLUB membership. SAM'S has made great progress over the past two years in upgrading our

facilities and adding services, including pharmacy, optical, 1-Hour Photo and fuel, to offer the highest quality shopping experience to our Members. In short, our Members continue to respond favorably to SAM'S unique, high-quality merchandise at exceptional values.

The International Division had an excellent year, growing sales by 41 percent and achieving more than $32 billion in revenues. As we travel internationally, it's exciting not only to see our stores and clubs operating at such high standards, but also to see the Wal-Mart culture being embraced throughout the world. This just shows that treating people with respect and raising their standard of living through Every Day Low Prices knows no boundaries.

I'll highlight the exceptional performances by our three largest international operations: Canada, Mexico and the United Kingdom.

Fiscal 2001 was a great year for our Canadian business. Sales and operating profit increased for the year by more than 14 percent, continuing the customer-focused retailing traditions established in the U.S. almost 40 years ago.

Mexico also had an outstanding year, exceeding both its sales and profit goals. Our Customers there have responded exceptionally well to the high level of customer service our Associates provide, and to the introduction of Every Day Low Prices in all our retail formats in Mexico.

In particular, I'd like to thank our ASDA Colleagues (Associates) in the United Kingdom for their exceptional performance over the last year. For the fourth straight year, ASDA was voted "Supermarket of the Year" by *Checkout* magazine. The division exceeded the objectives set at the time we acquired ASDA, and our Colleagues accomplished our ultimate goal – taking care of our Customers and providing them with an exceptional value in the marketplace.

The Wal-Mart Stores Division, by far our largest, features our Discount Store, Supercenter and Neighborhood Market formats. The year brought some truly bright spots for this division as well.

We've made exceptional strides in our food offerings through the Supercenters and Neighborhood Markets. This year, Wal-Mart became the largest retailer in the U.S. grocery industry, according to *Supermarket News*. That is truly a remarkable achievement, and I think Sam Walton would be proud. As always, we will continue to ensure that we are the *best* food retailer, not just the largest.

In July, we challenged our Associates to react to the slowing economy by reducing inventories by more than $1 billion, the majority of which would come from the Wal-Mart Division. Despite disappointing holiday sales, our Associates not only met this goal – they exceeded it.

The division had a strong first half of the year as our Associates built on last year's phenomenal growth. But as we moved through the second half of fiscal 2001, it became evident that consumer spending was slowing and would not recover in time for the crucial holiday shopping season. Our Associates reacted appropriately, however, by continuing our focus on customer satisfaction.

Although we did not end the year the way we would have liked, the keys to our ability to manage a slowdown in the economy remain simple and effective. They are what we have built our business on since the beginning.

First, we must maintain an in-stock level unequaled in the retail world. Our commitment is unchanged: provide the products our Customers want at the moment they want to make the purchase.

Second, we must provide the level of service our Customers expect and deserve. It's not enough to provide merchandise and a safe, comfortable environment in which to shop. We must generate the excitement and enthusiasm necessary to build a relationship with the Customer and make each shopping experience better than the one before. This includes simple things like saying thank you and greeting our Customers warmly as they enter the store. Sam Walton called it "aggressive hospitality," and it still works today.

Third, we must provide our Customers with top-quality merchandise and services at Every Day Low Prices. After all, that's what the sign says, and that's our commitment to our Customers.

Finally, it is a personal priority of mine to identify and develop the next generation of Wal-Mart leaders. For years, it was enough to just develop managers. But as the business environment becomes more challenging, it takes true leadership to guide a successful business. Sam Walton set the standard for our vision of leadership, and we are carrying it forward. We are committed to growing the leaders today who will propel this Company into tomorrow. It's the right thing to do for our Customers, our Associates and our Shareholders.

On a more personal note, I would like, on behalf of all Wal-Mart Associates, to thank David Glass for his leadership over the past 25 years. David served as Chief Executive Officer for 12 years and presided over more revenue and earnings growth than any other CEO in the history of retailing. We are fortunate that David has agreed to stay on in his present role, providing advice and counsel to me and the entire Wal-Mart team.

At Wal-Mart, we're passionate about delivering value to our Customers and Shareholders. As Shareholders, you play a vital role in our success as you invest in Wal-Mart stock and shop at our Wal-Mart stores and SAM'S CLUBS. While our history is rich with success, there's no question that our best years are yet to come, and this time next year I expect to report another record year for Wal-Mart. Thank you, and I look forward to visiting with you again next year.

Lee Scott

11-Year Financial Summary

(Dollar amounts in millions except per share data)	2001	2000	1999
Net sales	$ 191,329	$ 165,013	$ 137,634
Net sales increase	16%	20%	17%
Domestic comparative store sales increase	5%	8%	9%
Other income-net	1,966	1,796	1,574
Cost of sales	150,255	129,664	108,725
Operating, selling and general and administrative expenses	31,550	27,040	22,363
Interest costs:			
Debt	1,095	756	529
Capital leases	279	266	268
Provision for income taxes	3,692	3,338	2,740
Minority interest and equity in unconsolidated subsidiaries	(129)	(170)	(153)
Cumulative effect of accounting change, net of tax	–	(198)	–
Net income	6,295	5,377	4,430
Per share of common stock:			
Basic net income	1.41	1.21	0.99
Diluted net income	1.40	1.20	0.99
Dividends	0.24	0.20	0.16
Financial Position			
Current assets	$ 26,555	$ 24,356	$ 21,132
Inventories at replacement cost	21,644	20,171	17,549
Less LIFO reserve	202	378	473
Inventories at LIFO cost	21,442	19,793	17,076
Net property, plant and equipment and capital leases	40,934	35,969	25,973
Total assets	78,130	70,349	49,996
Current liabilities	28,949	25,803	16,762
Long-term debt	12,501	13,672	6,908
Long-term obligations under capital leases	3,154	3,002	2,699
Shareholders' equity	31,343	25,834	21,112
Financial Ratios			
Current ratio	0.9	0.9	1.3
Inventories/working capital	(9.0)	(13.7)	3.9
Return on assets*	8.7%	9.5%***	9.6%
Return on shareholders' equity**	22.0%	22.9%	22.4%
Other Year-End Data			
Number of domestic Wal-Mart stores	1,736	1,801	1,869
Number of domestic Supercenters	888	721	564
Number of domestic SAM'S CLUBS	475	463	451
Number of domestic Neighborhood Markets	19	7	4
International units	1,071	1,004	715
Number of Associates	1,244,000	1,140,000	910,000
Number of Shareholders of record	362,000	341,000	261,000

   * *Net income before minority interest, equity in unconsolidated subsidiaries and cumulative effect of accounting change/average assets*

  ** *Net income/average shareholders' equity*

*** *Calculated giving effect to the amount by which a lawsuit settlement exceeded established reserves. If this settlement was not considered, the return was 9.8%. See Management's Discussion and Analysis.*

1998	1997	1996	1995	1994	1993	1992	1991
$ 117,958	$ 104,859	$ 93,627	$ 82,494	$ 67,344	$ 55,484	$ 43,887	$ 32,602
12%	12%	13%	22%	21%	26%	35%	26%
6%	5%	4%	7%	6%	11%	10%	10%
1,341	1,319	1,146	914	645	497	404	262
93,438	83,510	74,505	65,586	53,444	44,175	34,786	25,500
19,358	16,946	15,021	12,858	10,333	8,321	6,684	5,152
555	629	692	520	331	143	113	43
229	216	196	186	186	180	153	126
2,115	1,794	1,606	1,581	1,358	1,171	945	752
(78)	(27)	(13)	4	(4)	4	(1)	–
–	–	–	–	–	–	–	–
3,526	3,056	2,740	2,681	2,333	1,995	1,609	1,291
0.78	0.67	0.60	0.59	0.51	0.44	0.35	0.28
0.78	0.67	0.60	0.59	0.51	0.44	0.35	0.28
0.14	0.11	0.10	0.09	0.07	0.05	0.04	0.04
$ 19,352	$ 17,993	$ 17,331	$ 15,338	$ 12,114	$ 10,198	$ 8,575	$ 6,415
16,845	16,193	16,300	14,415	11,483	9,780	7,857	6,207
348	296	311	351	469	512	473	399
16,497	15,897	15,989	14,064	11,014	9,268	7,384	5,808
23,606	20,324	18,894	15,874	13,176	9,793	6,434	4,712
45,384	39,604	37,541	32,819	26,441	20,565	15,443	11,389
14,460	10,957	11,454	9,973	7,406	6,754	5,004	3,990
7,191	7,709	8,508	7,871	6,156	3,073	1,722	740
2,483	2,307	2,092	1,838	1,804	1,772	1,556	1,159
18,503	17,143	14,756	12,726	10,753	8,759	6,990	5,366
1.3	1.6	1.5	1.5	1.6	1.5	1.7	1.6
3.4	2.3	2.7	2.6	2.3	2.7	2.1	2.4
8.5%	7.9%	7.8%	9.0%	9.9%	11.1%	12.0%	13.2%
19.8%	19.2%	19.9%	22.8%	23.9%	25.3%	26.0%	27.7%
1,921	1,960	1,995	1,985	1,950	1,848	1,714	1,568
441	344	239	147	72	34	10	9
443	436	433	426	417	256	208	148
–	–	–	–	–	–	–	–
601	314	276	226	24	10	–	–
825,000	728,000	675,000	622,000	528,000	434,000	371,000	328,000
246,000	257,000	244,000	259,000	258,000	181,000	150,000	122,000

The effects of the change in accounting method for SAM'S CLUB membership revenue recognition would not have a material impact on this summary prior to 1998. Therefore, pro forma information as if the accounting change had been in effect for all years presented has not been provided. See Management's Discussion and Analysis for discussion of the impact of the accounting change in fiscal 2000 and 1999.

The acquisition of the ASDA Group PLC and the Company's related debt issuance had a significant impact on the fiscal 2000 amounts in this summary. See Notes 3 and 6 to the Consolidated Financial Statements.

Management's Discussion and Analysis

Net Sales

Sales (in millions) by operating segment for the three fiscal years ended January 31, were as follows:

Fiscal Year	Wal-Mart Stores	SAM'S CLUB	International	Other	Total Company	Total Company Increase from Prior Fiscal Year
2001	**$121,889**	**$26,798**	**$32,100**	**$10,542**	**$191,329**	**16%**
2000	108,721	24,801	22,728	8,763	165,013	20%
1999	95,395	22,881	12,247	7,111	137,634	17%

The Company's sales growth of 16% in fiscal 2001, when compared to fiscal 2000, resulted from the Company's domestic and international expansion programs, and a domestic comparative store sales increase of 5%. The sales increase of 20% in fiscal 2000, when compared to fiscal 1999, resulted from the Company's expansion program, including a significant international acquisition, and a domestic comparative store sales increase of 8%. Wal-Mart Stores and SAM'S CLUB segments include domestic units only. Wal-Mart stores and SAM'S CLUBS located outside the United States are included in the International segment.

Costs and Expenses

For fiscal 2001, cost of sales as a percentage of sales decreased compared to fiscal 2000, resulting in increases in gross margin of 0.05% for fiscal 2001. This improvement in gross margin occurred primarily due to a $176 million LIFO inventory benefit. This was offset by continued price rollbacks and increased international and food sales which generally have lower gross margins than domestic general merchandise. Cost of sales, as a percentage of sales decreased for fiscal 2000 compared to fiscal 1999, resulting in increases in gross margin of 0.4% for fiscal 2000. The fiscal 2000 improvement in gross margin can be attributed to a favorable sales mix of higher margin categories, improvements in shrinkage and markdowns, a favorable LIFO inventory adjustment and the slower growth of SAM'S CLUB, which is our lowest gross margin retail operation. Management expects gross margins to narrow as food sales continue to increase as a percentage of sales both domestically and internationally.

Operating, selling, general and administrative expenses increased 0.1% as a percentage of sales in fiscal 2001 when compared with fiscal 2000. This increase was primarily due to increased maintenance and repair costs and depreciation charges incurred during the year. Operating, selling, general and administrative expenses increased 0.1% as a percentage of sales in fiscal 2000 when compared with fiscal 1999. This increase was primarily due to increased payroll cost incurred during the year. Additionally, in the second quarter of fiscal 2000, a $624 million jury verdict was rendered against the Company in a lawsuit. The Company settled the lawsuit for an amount less than the jury verdict. The Company had previously established reserves related to this lawsuit, which were not material to its results of operations or financial position. The settlement exceeded the Company's estimated reserves for this lawsuit and resulted in a charge in the second quarter of fiscal 2000 of $0.03 per share net of taxes.

Interest Costs

Debt interest costs increased .11% as a percentage of sales from .46% in fiscal 2000 to .57% in fiscal 2001. This increase is the result of increased fiscal 2000 borrowings incurred as the result of the ASDA acquisition and has been somewhat offset by reductions resulting from the Company's inventory control efforts. For fiscal 2000, debt interest costs increased .08% as a percentage of sales from .38% in fiscal 1999 to .46%. This increase resulted from increased fiscal 2000 borrowings as the result of the ASDA acquisition. See Note 3 of the Notes to Consolidated Financial Statements for additional information.

Wal-Mart Stores

Sales for the Company's Wal-Mart Stores segment increased by 12.1% in fiscal 2001 when compared to fiscal 2000 and 14.0% in fiscal 2000 when compared to fiscal 1999. The fiscal 2001 and fiscal 2000 growth are the result of comparative store sales increases and the Company's expansion program. Segment expansion during fiscal 2001 included the opening of 41 Wal-Mart stores, 12 Neighborhood Markets and 167 Supercenters (including the conversion of 104 existing Wal-Mart stores into Supercenters). Segment expansion during fiscal 2000 included the opening of 29 Wal-Mart stores, three Neighborhood Markets and 157 Supercenters (including the conversion of 96 existing Wal-Mart stores into Supercenters).

Fiscal 2001 operating income for the segment increased by 11.5%, from $8.7 billion in fiscal 2000 to $9.7 billion in fiscal 2001. Segment operating income as a percent of segment sales remained unchanged at 8.0% from fiscal 2000 to fiscal 2001. Operating income for fiscal 2001 was driven by margin improvements resulting from decreased markdowns and improved shrinkage. Offsetting these margin improvements were increased distribution costs, resulting from higher fuel, utility and payroll charges and higher overall payroll costs as a percentage of sales created by a holiday season with lower than anticipated sales. Operating income for the segment for fiscal 2000 increased by 20.2%, from $7.2 billion in fiscal 1999 to $8.7 billion in fiscal 2000. Fiscal 2000 operating income as a percentage of segment sales was 8.0%, up from 7.6% in fiscal 1999. The improvement in operating income in 2000 was driven by margin improvements resulting from improvements in markdowns and shrinkage. However, these margin improvements were somewhat offset by increased payroll costs in fiscal 2000. Operating income information for fiscal years 1999 and 2000 has been reclassified to conform to the current year presentation. For this reclassification, certain corporate expenses have been moved from the Other segment to the operating segments.

SAM'S CLUB

Sales for the Company's SAM'S CLUB segment increased by 8.1% in fiscal 2001 when compared to fiscal 2000, and by 8.4% in fiscal 2000 when compared to fiscal 1999. The fiscal 2001 and fiscal 2000 sales growth are the result of comparative club sales increases and the Company's expansion program. Due to rapid growth in the International segment, SAM'S CLUB sales continued to decrease as a percentage of total Company sales, decreasing from 15.0% in fiscal 2000 to 14.0% in fiscal 2001. Segment expansion during fiscal 2001 and 2000 consisted of the opening of 13 and 12 new clubs, respectively.

Operating income for the segment in fiscal 2001 increased by 10.8%, from $850 million in fiscal 2000 to $942 million in fiscal 2001. Due primarily to margin improvements, operating income as a percentage of segment sales increased from 3.4% in fiscal 2000 to 3.5% in fiscal 2001. In December 1999, the Securities and Exchange Commission issued Staff Accounting Bulletin No. 101 *"Revenue Recognition in Financial Statements"* (SAB 101). SAB 101 deals with various revenue recognition issues, several of which are common within the retail industry. As a result of the issuance of this SAB, the Company changed its method of recognizing revenues for SAM'S CLUB membership fees effective as of the beginning of fiscal 2000. Additionally, operating income information for fiscal years 1999 and 2000 has been reclassified to conform to the current year presentation. For this reclassification certain corporate expenses have been moved from the Other segment to the operating segments. After consideration of the reclassification and the effects of the change in accounting method for membership revenue recognition, operating income for the segment in fiscal 2000 increased by 22.7%, from $693 million in fiscal 1999 to $850 million in fiscal 2000. Operating income as a percentage of sales increased from 3.0% in fiscal 1999 to 3.4% in fiscal 2000. This improvement is primarily due to margin improvements. The pretax impact of the change in accounting method would have been $57 million in fiscal 1999 and was $16 million in fiscal 2000. The impact of the accounting method change is greater on fiscal 1999 due to an increase in the cost of SAM'S CLUB membership that occurred during that year. If the effect of this accounting change were not considered, operating income as a percent of segment sales would have increased by 22 basis points when comparing fiscal 1999 to fiscal 2000.

International
International sales accounted for approximately 17% of total Company sales in fiscal 2001 compared with 14% in fiscal 2000. The largest portion of the increase in international sales is the result of the acquisition of the ASDA Group PLC (ASDA), which consisted of 229 stores when its acquisition was completed during the third quarter of fiscal 2000. International sales accounted for approximately 14% of total Company sales in fiscal 2000 compared with 9% in fiscal 1999. The largest portion of this increase was also the result of the ASDA acquisition. Additionally, fiscal 2000 was the first full year containing the operating results of the 74 units of the German Interspar hypermarket chain, which were acquired in the fourth quarter of fiscal 1999.

For fiscal 2001 segment operating income increased by 36.1% from $817 million in fiscal 2000 to $1.1 billion in fiscal 2001. Segment operating income as a percent of segment sales decreased by .13% when comparing fiscal 2000 and fiscal 2001. This decrease was caused by the continued negative impact of store remodeling costs, costs related to the start-up of a new distribution system, excess inventory and transition related expenses in the Company's Germany units. Partially offsetting these negative impacts were operating profit increases in Mexico, Canada and the United Kingdom. After consideration of the effects of the change of accounting method for SAM'S CLUB membership revenues, the International segment's operating income increased from $549 million in fiscal 1999 to $817 million in fiscal 2000. The largest portion of the fiscal 2000 increase in international operating income is the result of the ASDA acquisition. As a percent of segment sales, segment operating income decreased by .89% when comparing fiscal 1999 to fiscal 2000. This decrease is the result of expense pressures coming from the Company's units in Germany. The Company's operations in Canada, Mexico and Puerto Rico had operating income increases in fiscal 2000.

The Company's foreign operations are comprised of wholly-owned operations in Argentina, Canada, Germany, Korea, Puerto Rico and the United Kingdom; joint ventures in China; and majority-owned subsidiaries in Brazil and Mexico. As a result, the Company's financial results could be affected by factors such as changes in foreign currency exchange rates or weak economic conditions in the foreign markets in which the Company does business. The Company minimizes exposure to the risk of devaluation of foreign currencies by operating in local currencies and through buying forward contracts, where feasible, for certain known transactions.

In fiscal 2001, the foreign currency translation adjustment increased from the fiscal 2000 level by $229 million to $684 million, primarily due to the dollar strengthening against the British pound and the German mark. In fiscal 2000, the foreign currency translation adjustment decreased from the fiscal 1999 level by $54 million to $455 million primarily due to the United States dollar weakening against the British pound and the Canadian dollar. This was partially offset by the United States dollar strengthening against the Brazilian real.

For 2001, expansion in the International segment consisted of the opening of 77 units. Expansion in the International segment in fiscal 2000 consisted of the opening or acquisition of 288 units. The Company also purchased an additional 6% ownership interest in its Mexican subsidiary, Wal-Mart de Mexico S.A. de C.V. (formerly Cifra S.A. de C.V.) in fiscal 2001.

See Note 6 of Notes to Consolidated Financial Statements for additional information on acquisitions.

Liquidity and Capital Resources Cash Flows Information
Cash flows from operating activities were $9,604 million in fiscal 2001, up from $8,194 million in fiscal 2000. In fiscal 2001, the Company invested $8,042 million in capital assets, paid dividends of $1,070 million, and had a cash outlay of $627 million primarily for the acquisition of an additional 6% ownership in Wal-Mart de Mexico S.A. de C.V. See Note 6 of Notes to Consolidated Financial Statements for additional information on acquisitions.

Market Risk
Market risks relating to the Company's operations include changes in interest rates and changes in foreign exchange rates. The Company enters into interest rate swaps to minimize the risk and costs associated with financing activities. The swap agreements are contracts to exchange fixed or variable rates for variable or fixed interest rate payments periodically over the life of the instruments. The following tables provide information about the Company's derivative financial instruments and other financial instruments that are sensitive to changes in interest rates. For debt obligations, the table presents principal cash flows and related weighted-average interest rates by expected maturity dates. For interest rate swaps, the table presents notional amounts and interest rates by contractual maturity dates. The applicable floating rate index is included for variable rate instruments. All amounts are stated in United States dollar equivalents.

Borrowing Information

At January 31, 2001, the Company had committed lines of credit with 78 firms and banks, aggregating $5,032 million, which were used to support commercial paper. These lines of credit and their anticipated cyclical increases combined with commercial paper borrowings should be sufficient to finance the seasonal buildups in merchandise inventories and other cash requirements. If the operating cash flow generated by the Company is not sufficient to pay the increased dividend and to fund all capital expenditures, the Company anticipates funding any shortfall in these expenditures with a combination of commercial paper and long-term debt. The Company plans to refinance existing long-term debt as it matures and may desire to obtain additional long-term financing for other uses of cash or for strategic reasons. The Company anticipates no difficulty in obtaining long-term financing in view of an excellent credit rating and favorable experiences in the debt market in the recent past. During fiscal 2001, the Company issued $3.7 billion of debt. The proceeds from the issuance of this debt were used to reduce short-term borrowings. After the $3.7 billion of debt issued in fiscal 2001, the Company is permitted to sell up to $1.4 billion of public debt under shelf registration statements previously filed with the United States Securities and Exchange Commission.

At January 31, 2001, the Company's ratio of debt to total capitalization, including commercial paper borrowings, was 41.6%. Management's objective is to maintain a debt to total capitalization ratio of approximately 40%.

Expansion

Domestically, the Company plans to open approximately 40 new Wal-Mart stores and approximately 170 to 180 new Supercenters in fiscal 2002. Relocations or expansions of existing discount stores will account for 100 to 110 of the new Supercenters, with the balance being new locations. The Company plans to further expand its Neighborhood Market concept by adding 15 to 20 units during fiscal 2002. The SAM'S CLUB segment plans to open 40 to 50 Clubs during fiscal 2002, approximately half of which will be relocations or expansions of existing clubs. The SAM'S segment will also continue its remodeling program, with approximately 80 projects expected during fiscal 2002. In order to serve these and future developments, the Company plans to construct seven new distribution centers in the next fiscal year. Internationally, the Company plans to open 100 to 110 units. Projects are scheduled to open in each of the existing countries, and will include new stores and clubs as well as relocations of a few existing units. The units also include several restaurants, department stores and supermarkets in Mexico. In addition, the Company's German operation will continue to remodel the acquired hypermarkets. Total Company planned growth represents approximately 40 million square feet of net additional retail space. Total planned capital expenditures for fiscal 2002 approximate $9 billion. The Company plans to finance our expansion primarily with operating cash flows and commercial paper borrowings.

Forward-Looking Statements

The Private Securities Litigation Reform Act of 1995 provides a safe harbor for forward-looking statements made by or on behalf of the Company. Certain statements contained in Management's Discussion and Analysis, in other parts of this report and in other Company filings are forward-looking statements. These statements discuss, among other things, expected growth, future revenues, future cash flows and future performance. The forward-looking statements are subject to risks and uncertainties including but not limited to the cost of goods, competitive pressures, inflation, consumer debt levels, currency exchange fluctuations, trade restrictions, changes in tariff and freight rates, interest rate fluctuations and other capital market conditions, and other risks indicated in the Company's filings with the United States Securities and Exchange Commission. Actual results may materially differ from anticipated results described in these statements.

Consolidated Statements of Income

(Amounts in millions except per share data)

Fiscal years ended January 31,	2001	2000	1999
Revenues:			
Net sales	$ **191,329**	$ 165,013	$ 137,634
Other income-net	**1,966**	1,796	1,574
	193,295	166,809	139,208
Costs and Expenses:			
Cost of sales	**150,255**	129,664	108,725
Operating, selling and general and administrative expenses	**31,550**	27,040	22,363
Interest Costs:			
Debt	**1,095**	756	529
Capital leases	**279**	266	268
	183,179	157,726	131,885
Income Before Income Taxes, Minority Interest and Cumulative Effect of Accounting Change	**10,116**	9,083	7,323
Provision for Income Taxes			
Current	**3,350**	3,476	3,380
Deferred	**342**	(138)	(640)
	3,692	3,338	2,740
Income Before Minority Interest and Cumulative Effect of Accounting Change	**6,424**	5,745	4,583
Minority Interest	**(129)**	(170)	(153)
Income Before Cumulative Effect of Accounting Change	**6,295**	5,575	4,430
Cumulative Effect of Accounting Change, net of tax benefit of $119	**–**	(198)	–
Net Income	$ **6,295**	$ 5,377	$ 4,430
Net Income Per Common Share:			
Basic Net Income Per Common Share:			
Income before cumulative effect of accounting change	$ **1.41**	$ 1.25	$ 0.99
Cumulative effect of accounting change, net of tax	**–**	(0.04)	–
Net Income Per Common Share	$ **1.41**	$ 1.21	$ 0.99
Average Number of Common Shares	**4,465**	4,451	4,464
Diluted Net Income Per Common Share:			
Income before cumulative effect of accounting change	$ **1.40**	$ 1.25	$ 0.99
Cumulative effect of accounting change, net of tax	**–**	(0.04)	–
Net Income Per Common Share	$ **1.40**	$ 1.20	$ 0.99
Average Number of Common Shares	**4,484**	4,474	4,485
Pro forma amounts assuming accounting change had been in effect in fiscal 2001, 2000 and 1999:			
Net Income	$ **6,295**	$ 5,575	$ 4,393
Net income per common share, basic	$ **1.41**	$ 1.25	$ 0.98
Net income per common share, diluted	$ **1.40**	$ 1.25	$ 0.98

See accompanying notes.

Consolidated Balance Sheets

(Amounts in millions)

January 31,	2001	2000
Assets		
Current Assets:		
Cash and cash equivalents	$ 2,054	$ 1,856
Receivables	1,768	1,341
Inventories		
At replacement cost	21,644	20,171
Less LIFO reserve	202	378
Inventories at LIFO cost	21,442	19,793
Prepaid expenses and other	1,291	1,366
Total Current Assets	26,555	24,356
Property, Plant and Equipment, at Cost:		
Land	9,433	8,785
Building and improvements	24,537	21,169
Fixtures and equipment	12,964	10,362
Transportation equipment	879	747
	47,813	41,063
Less accumulated depreciation	10,196	8,224
Net property, plant and equipment	37,617	32,839
Property Under Capital Lease:		
Property under capital lease	4,620	4,285
Less accumulated amortization	1,303	1,155
Net property under capital leases	3,317	3,130
Other Assets and Deferred Charges:		
Net goodwill and other acquired intangible assets	9,059	9,392
Other assets and deferred charges	1,582	632
Total Assets	$ 78,130	$ 70,349
Liabilities and Shareholders' Equity		
Current Liabilities:		
Commercial paper	$ 2,286	$ 3,323
Accounts payable	15,092	13,105
Accrued liabilities	6,355	6,161
Accrued income taxes	841	1,129
Long-term debt due within one year	4,234	1,964
Obligations under capital leases due within one year	141	121
Total Current Liabilities	28,949	25,803
Long-Term Debt	12,501	13,672
Long-Term Obligations Under Capital Leases	3,154	3,002
Deferred Income Taxes and Other	1,043	759
Minority Interest	1,140	1,279
Shareholders' Equity		
Preferred stock ($0.10 par value; 100 shares authorized, none issued)		
Common stock ($0.10 par value; 11,000 shares authorized, 4,470 and 4,457 issued and outstanding in 2001 and 2000, respectively)	447	446
Capital in excess of par value	1,411	714
Retained earnings	30,169	25,129
Other accumulated comprehensive income	(684)	(455)
Total Shareholders' Equity	31,343	25,834
Total Liabilities and Shareholders' Equity	$ 78,130	$ 70,349

See accompanying notes.

Consolidated Statements of Shareholders' Equity

(Amounts in millions except per share data)	Number of shares	Common stock	Capital in excess of par value	Retained earnings	Other accumulated comprehensive income	Total
Balance – January 31, 1998	2,241	$ 224	$ 585	$ 18,167	($ 473)	$ 18,503
Comprehensive Income						
Net income				4,430		4,430
Other accumulated comprehensive income						
Foreign currency translation adjustment					(36)	(36)
Total Comprehensive Income						$ 4,394
Cash dividends ($.16 per share)				(693)		(693)
Purchase of Company stock	(21)	(2)	(37)	(1,163)		(1,202)
Two-for-one stock split	2,224	223	(223)			–
Stock options exercised and other	4		110			110
Balance – January 31, 1999	4,448	445	435	20,741	(509)	21,112
Comprehensive Income						
Net income				5,377		5,377
Other accumulated comprehensive income						
Foreign currency translation adjustment					54	54
Total Comprehensive Income						$ 5,431
Cash dividends ($.20 per share)				(890)		(890)
Purchase of Company stock	(2)		(2)	(99)		(101)
Stock options exercised and other	11	1	281			282
Balance – January 31, 2000	4,457	446	714	25,129	(455)	25,834
Comprehensive Income						
Net income				6,295		6,295
Other accumulated comprehensive income						
Foreign currency translation adjustment					(229)	(229)
Total Comprehensive Income						$ 6,066
Cash dividends ($.24 per share)				(1,070)		(1,070)
Purchase of Company stock	(4)		(8)	(185)		(193)
Issuance of Company stock	11	1	580			581
Stock options exercised and other	6		125			125
Balance – January 31, 2001	4,470	$ 447	$ 1,411	$ 30,169	($ 684)	$ 31,343

See accompanying notes.

Consolidated Statements of Cash Flows

(Amounts in millions)

Fiscal years ended January 31,	2001	2000	1999
Cash flows from operating activities			
Net Income	$ 6,295	$ 5,377	$ 4,430
Adjustments to reconcile net income to net cash provided by operating activities:			
Depreciation and amortization	2,868	2,375	1,872
Cumulative effect of accounting change, net of tax	–	198	–
Increase in accounts receivable	(422)	(255)	(148)
Increase in inventories	(1,795)	(2,088)	(379)
Increase in accounts payable	2,061	1,849	1,108
Increase in accrued liabilities	11	1,015	1,259
Deferred income taxes	342	(138)	(640)
Other	244	(139)	78
Net cash provided by operating activities	9,604	8,194	7,580
Cash flows from investing activities			
Payments for property, plant and equipment	(8,042)	(6,183)	(3,734)
Investment in international operations (net of cash acquired, $195 million in Fiscal 2000)	(627)	(10,419)	(855)
Other investing activities	(45)	(244)	171
Net cash used in investing activities	(8,714)	(16,846)	(4,418)
Cash flows from financing activities			
Increase/(decrease) in commercial paper	(2,022)	4,316	–
Proceeds from issuance of long-term debt	3,778	6,000	536
Purchase of Company stock	(193)	(101)	(1,202)
Dividends paid	(1,070)	(890)	(693)
Payment of long-term debt	(1,519)	(863)	(1,075)
Payment of capital lease obligations	(173)	(133)	(101)
Proceeds from issuance of common stock	581	–	–
Other financing activities	176	224	(221)
Net cash provided by (used in) financing activities	(442)	8,553	(2,756)
Effect of exchange rate changes on cash	(250)	76	26
Net increase/(decrease) in cash and cash equivalents	198	(23)	432
Cash and cash equivalents at beginning of year	1,856	1,879	1,447
Cash and cash equivalents at end of year	$ 2,054	$ 1,856	$ 1,879
Supplemental disclosure of cash flow information			
Income tax paid	$ 3,509	$ 2,780	$ 3,458
Interest paid	1,319	849	805
Capital lease obligations incurred	576	378	347
Property, plant and equipment acquired with debt	–	65	–
ASDA acquisition cost satisfied with debt	–	264	–
ASDA acquisition cost satisfied with Company stock	–	175	–

See accompanying notes.

Notes to Consolidated Financial Statements

1 Summary of Significant Accounting Policies

Consolidation

The consolidated financial statements include the accounts of subsidiaries. Significant intercompany transactions have been eliminated in consolidation.

Cash and cash equivalents

The Company considers investments with a maturity of three months or less when purchased to be cash equivalents.

Inventories

The Company uses the retail last-in, first-out (LIFO) method for the Wal-Mart Stores segment, cost LIFO for the SAM'S CLUB segment, and other cost methods, including the retail first-in, first-out (FIFO) and average cost methods, for the International segment. Inventories are not recorded in excess of market value.

Pre-opening costs

The costs of start-up activities, including organization costs, are expensed as incurred.

Interest during construction

In order that interest costs properly reflect only that portion relating to current operations, interest on borrowed funds during the construction of property, plant and equipment is capitalized. Interest costs capitalized were $93 million, $57 million, and $41 million in 2001, 2000 and 1999, respectively.

Financial Instruments

The Company uses derivative financial instruments for purposes other than trading to reduce its exposure to fluctuations in foreign currencies and to minimize the risk and cost associated with financial and global operating activities. Contracts that effectively meet risk reduction and correlation criteria are recorded using hedge accounting. Unrealized gains and losses resulting from market movements are not recognized. Hedges of firm commitments are deferred and recognized when the hedged transaction occurs.

Advertising costs

Advertising costs are expensed as incurred and were $574 million, $523 million and $405 million in 2001, 2000 and 1999, respectively.

Operating, selling and general and administrative expenses

Buying, warehousing and occupancy costs are included in operating, selling and general and administrative expenses.

Depreciation and amortization

Depreciation and amortization for financial statement purposes are provided on the straight-line method over the estimated useful lives of the various assets. Depreciation expense, including amortization of property under capital lease, for the years 2001, 2000 and 1999 was $2,387 million, $1,998 million and $1,648 million, respectively. For income tax purposes, accelerated methods are used with recognition of deferred income taxes for the resulting temporary differences. Estimated useful lives for financial statements purposes are as follows:

Building and improvements	5 – 50 years
Fixtures and equipment	5 – 12 years
Transportation equipment	2 – 5 years
Internally developed software	3 years

Costs of computer software

During fiscal 2000, the Company adopted the Accounting Standards Executive Committee Statement of Position (SOP) 98-1, *"Accounting For the Costs of Computer Software Developed For or Obtained For Internal Use."* This SOP requires the capitalization of certain costs incurred in connection with developing or obtaining software for internal use. Previously, costs related to developing internal-use software were expensed as incurred. Under the new method these costs are capitalized and amortized over a three year life. The impact of the adoption of SOP 98-1 was to capitalize $27 million and $32 million of costs in fiscal 2001 and 2000, respectively, which would have previously been expensed. The impact of the change would not have a material effect on fiscal 1999.

Accounting for derivative instruments and hedging activities
On February 1, 2001, the Company adopted Financial Accounting Standards Board (FASB) Statements No. 133, 137 and 138 (collectively "SFAS 133") pertaining to the accounting for derivatives and hedging activities. SFAS 133 requires all derivatives to be recorded on the balance sheet at fair value and establishes accounting treatment for three types of hedges: hedges of changes in the fair value of assets, liabilities, or firm commitments; hedges of the variable cash flows of forecasted transactions; and hedges of foreign currency exposures of net investments in foreign operations. As of January 31, 2001, the majority of the Company's derivatives are hedges of net investments in foreign operations, and as such, the fair value of these derivatives has been recorded on the balance sheet as either assets or liabilities and in other comprehensive income under the current accounting guidance. As the majority of the Company's derivative portfolio is already recorded on the balance sheet, the adoption of SFAS 133 will not have a material impact on the Company's Consolidated Financial Statements taken as a whole.

Goodwill and other acquired intangible assets
Goodwill and other acquired intangible assets are amortized on a straight-line basis over the periods that expected economic benefits will be provided. This amortization period ranges from 20 to 40 years. Management estimates such periods of economic benefits using factors such as entry barriers in certain countries, operating rights and estimated lives of other operating assets acquired. The realizability of goodwill and other intangibles is evaluated periodically when events or circumstances indicate a possible inability to recover the carrying amount. Such evaluation is based on cash flow and profitability projections that incorporate the impact of existing Company businesses. The analyses necessarily involve significant management judgment to evaluate the capacity of an acquired business to perform within projections. Historically, the Company has generated sufficient returns from acquired businesses to recover the cost of the goodwill and other intangible assets.

Long-lived assets
The Company periodically reviews long-lived assets, if indicators of impairments exist and if the value of the assets is impaired, an impairment loss would be recognized.

Stock split
On March 4, 1999, the Company announced a two-for-one stock split in the form of a 100% stock dividend. The date of record was March 19, 1999, and it was distributed April 19, 1999. Consequently, the stock option data and per share data for fiscal 1999 and prior has been restated to reflect the stock split.

Net income per share
Basic net income per share is based on the weighted average outstanding common shares. Diluted net income per share is based on the weighted average outstanding shares adjusted for the dilutive effect of stock options (19 million, 23 million and 21 million shares in 2001, 2000 and 1999, respectively) (see note 7). The Company had approximately 2 million, .5 million and 6 million option shares outstanding at January 31, 2001, 2000 and 1999, respectively, that were not included in the dilutive earnings per share calculation because they would have been antidilutive.

Foreign currency translation
The assets and liabilities of all foreign subsidiaries are translated at current exchange rates and any related translation adjustments are recorded as a component of other accumulated comprehensive income.

Estimates and assumptions
The preparation of consolidated financial statements in conformity with generally accepted accounting principles requires management to make estimates and assumptions. These estimates and assumptions affect the reported amounts of assets and liabilities and disclosure of contingent assets and liabilities at the date of the consolidated financial statements and the reported amounts of revenues and expenses during the reporting period. Actual results could differ from those estimates.

New accounting pronouncement
In March 2000, the FASB issued Interpretation No. 44 ("FIN 44"), *"Accounting for Certain Transactions involving Stock Compensation - An Interpretation of APB Opinion No. 25."* FIN 44 clarifies the application of Opinion 25 for: (a) the definition of employee for purposes of applying Opinion 25, (b) the criteria for determining whether a plan qualifies as a noncompensatory plan, (c) the accounting consequence of various modifications to the terms of a previously fixed stock option or award, and (d) the accounting for an exchange of stock compensation awards in a business combination. FIN 44 became effective July 1, 2000, but certain conclusions cover specific events that occur after either December 15, 1998, or January 12, 2000. FIN 44 did not have a material effect on the financial position or results of operations of the Company.

Accounting principle change

In December 1999, the Securities and Exchange Commission issued Staff Accounting Bulletin No. 101, *"Revenue Recognition in Financial Statements"* (SAB 101). This SAB deals with various revenue recognition issues, several of which are common within the retail industry. As a result of the issuance of SAB 101, the Company changed its method of accounting for SAM'S CLUB membership fee revenue both domestically and internationally in fiscal 2000. Previously the Company had recognized membership fee revenues when received. Under the new accounting method the Company recognizes membership fee revenues over the term of the membership, which is 12 months. The Company recorded a non-cash charge of $198 million (after reduction for income taxes of $119 million), or $.04 per share, to reflect the cumulative effect of the accounting change as of the beginning of the fiscal year. The effect of this change on the year ended January 31, 2000, before the cumulative effect of the accounting change was to decrease net income $12 million, or almost $.01 per share. If the new accounting method had been in effect in fiscal 1999, net income would have been $4,393 million, or $.98 per basic or dilutive share.

The following table provides unearned revenues, membership fees received from members and the amount of revenues recognized in earnings for each of the fiscal years ended 1999, 2000 and 2001 as if the accounting change had been in effect for each of those years (in millions):

The Company's deferred revenue is included in accrued liabilities in the January 31, 2001 consolidated balance sheet. The Company's analysis of historical membership fee refunds indicates that such refunds have been de minimis. Accordingly, no reserve has been established for membership fee refunds at January 31, 2001.

Deferred revenue January 31, 1998	$ 258
Membership fees received	600
Membership revenue recognized	(541)
Deferred revenue January 31, 1999	317
Membership fees received	646
Membership revenue recognized	(626)
Deferred revenue January 31, 2000	337
Membership fees received	706
Membership revenue recognized	(674)
Deferred revenue January 31, 2001	$ 369

An additional requirement of SAB 101 is that layaway transactions be recognized upon delivery of the merchandise to the Customer rather than at the time that the merchandise is placed on layaway. The Company offers a layaway program that allows Customers to purchase certain items and make payments on these purchases over a specific period. Until the first quarter of fiscal 2001, the Company recognized revenues from these layaway transactions at the time that the merchandise was placed on layaway. During the first quarter of fiscal 2001, the Company changed its accounting method for layaway transactions so that the revenue from these transactions is not recognized until the Customer satisfies all payment obligations and takes possession of the merchandise. Layaway transactions are a small portion of the Company's revenue, therefore, due to the de minimis impact of this accounting change, prior fiscal year results have not been restated.

Revenue recognition

The Company recognizes sales revenue at the time the sale is made to the Customer, except for layaway transactions, which are recognized when the Customer satisfies all payment obligations and takes possession of the merchandise. Effective as of the first quarter of fiscal 2000, the Company began recognizing SAM'S CLUB membership fee revenue over the term of the membership, which is 12 months.

Reclassifications

Certain reclassifications have been made to prior periods to conform to current presentations.

2 Defined Contribution Plans

The Company maintains profit sharing plans under which most full-time and many part-time associates become participants following one year of employment and 401(k) plans to which associates may elect to contribute a percentage of their earnings. During fiscal 2001 participants could contribute up to 15% of their pretax earnings, but not more than statutory limits.

The Company made annual contributions to these plans on behalf of all eligible associates, including those who have not elected to contribute to the 401(k) plan.

Annual Company contributions are made at the sole discretion of the Company, and were $486 million, $429 million and $388 million in 2001, 2000 and 1999, respectively.

3 Commercial Paper and Long-term Debt

Information on short-term borrowings and interest rates is as follows (dollar amounts in millions):

Fiscal years ended January 31,	2001	2000	1999
Maximum amount outstanding at month-end	$ 6,732	$ 6,588	$ 1,976
Average daily short-term borrowings	4,528	2,233	256
Weighted average interest rate	6.4%	5.4%	5.1%

At January 31, 2001, short-term borrowings consisting of $2,286 million of commercial paper were outstanding. At January 31, 2000, short-term borrowings consisting of $3,323 million of commercial paper were outstanding. At January 31, 2001, the Company had committed lines of $5,032 million with 78 firms and banks, which were used to support commercial paper.

Long-term debt at January 31, consist of (amounts in millions):

		2001	2000
6.875%	Notes due August 2009	$ 3,500	$ 3,500
6.550%	Notes due August 2004	1,250	1,250
6.150%	Notes due August 2001	–	1,250
8.625%	Notes due April 2001	–	750
5.750%	Notes due December 2030	714	–
5.875%	Notes due October 2005	597	597
7.500%	Notes due May 2004	500	500
7.550%	Notes due February 2030	500	498
7.550%	Notes due February 2030	500	495
6.875%	Notes due August 2002	500	–
6.500%	Notes due June 2003	454	454
7.250%	Notes due June 2013	445	445
7.800% – 8.250%	Obligations from sale/leaseback transactions due 2014	373	398
6.750%	Notes due May 2002	300	300
7.000% – 8.000%	Obligations from sale/leaseback transactions due 2013	257	275
8.500%	Notes due September 2024	250	250
6.750%	Notes due October 2023	250	250
8.000%	Notes due September 2006	250	250
6.375%	Notes due March 2003	228	228
6.750%	Eurobond due May 2002	200	200
7.290%	Notes due July 2006	324	435
4.410% – 10.880%	Notes acquired in ASDA acquisition due 2002-2015	948	1,026
	Other	161	321
		$ 12,501	$ 13,672

The Company has two separate issuances of $500 million debt with imbedded put options. For the first issuance, beginning June 2001, and each year thereafter, the holders of $500 million of the debt may require the Company to repurchase the debt at face value, in addition to accrued and unpaid interest. The holders of the other $500 million issuance may put the debt back to the Company at any time. Both of these issuances have been classified as a current liability in the January 31, 2001 consolidated balance sheet.

Long-term debt is unsecured except for $155 million, which is collateralized by property with an aggregate carrying value of approximately $327 million. Annual maturities of long-term debt during the next five years are (in millions):

Fiscal year ended January 31,	Annual maturity
2002	$ 4,234
2003	1,362
2004	809
2005	1,926
2006	750
Thereafter	7,654

The Company has agreed to observe certain covenants under the terms of its note agreements, the most restrictive of which relates to amounts of additional secured debt and long-term leases.

The Company has entered into sale/leaseback transactions involving buildings while retaining title to the underlying land. These transactions were accounted for as financings and are included in long-term debt and the annual maturities schedules on the previous page. The resulting obligations are amortized over the lease terms.

Future minimum lease payments for each of the five succeeding years as of January 31, 2001, are (in millions):

Fiscal year ended January 31,	Minimum payments
2002	$ 94
2003	98
2004	93
2005	130
2006	94
Thereafter	499

At January 31, 2001 and 2000, the Company had letters of credit outstanding totaling $1,129 million and $902 million, respectively. These letters of credit were issued primarily for the purchase of inventory.

Under shelf registration statements previously filed with the Securities and Exchange Commission, the Company is permitted to issue debt securities aggregating $1.4 billion.

4 Financial Instruments
Interest rate instruments
The Company enters into interest rate swaps to minimize the risks and costs associated with its financial activities. The swap agreements are contracts to exchange fixed or variable rate interest for variable or fixed interest rate payments periodically over the life of the instruments. The notional amounts are used to measure interest to be paid or received and do not represent the exposure due to credit loss. Settlements of interest rate swaps are accounted for by recording the net interest received or paid as an adjustment to interest expense on a current basis.

USD notional (amounts in millions)	Fiscal maturity date	Rate received	Rate paid	Fair value 1/31/2001 (amounts in millions)	Fair value 1/31/2000 (amounts in millions)
Interest Rate Instruments					
$ 500	2001	5.9% (USD rate)	Rate A plus .245%	N/A	($1)
500	2001	5.7% (USD rate)	Rate A plus .134%	N/A	–
381 ($513 in FYE 2000)	2007	7.0% (USD rate)	Rate A	$ 17	(7)
250	2003	6.9% (USD rate)	Rate D minus .15%	14	N/A
250	2003	6.9% (USD rate)	Rate D minus .15%	14	N/A
230	2027	7.0% (USD rate)	Rate B	N/A	(14)
151	2027	Rate C	8.1% (USD rate)	N/A	(11)

Rate A – 30-day U.S. dollar commercial paper non-financial
Rate B – 6-month U.S. dollar LIBOR
Rate C – 3-month U.S. dollar LIBOR
Rate D – 1-month U.S. dollar LIBOR

Net Investment instruments

The Company has entered into cross currency interest rate swap agreements to hedge its net investments in Canada, Germany and the United Kingdom. The swap agreements are contracts to exchange fixed rate payments in United States dollars for fixed rate payments in foreign currencies. Settlements of currency swaps are accounted for by recording the net payments as an adjustment to currency translation adjustment. The fair value of these instruments are reflected on the balance sheet in other long-term assets, and as of January 31, 2001 and 2000, are as follows:

USD notional (amounts in millions)	FX notional (amounts in millions)	Fiscal maturity date	Rate received	Rate paid	Fair value 1/31/2001 (amounts in millions)	Fair value 1/31/2000 (amounts in millions)
Cross Currency Instruments						
$ 3,500	2,010 GBP	2010	6.9%	6.2%	$ 465	($17)
1,101	1,960 DEM	2003	5.8% (USD rate)	4.5% (DEM rate)	186	90
1,250	1,841 CAD	2005	6.6%	5.7%	57	N/A
1,000	630 GBP	2031	7.6%	5.9%	165	N/A
809	1,360 DEM	2004	5.2% (USD rate)	3.4% (DEM rate)	180	112
250	164 GBP	2024	6.8%	5.2%	29	N/A

The Company enters into forward currency exchange contracts in the regular course of business to manage its exposure against foreign currency fluctuations on cross-border purchases of inventory. These contracts are generally for short durations of six months or less and are insignificant to the Company's operations or financial position. There were contracts with notional amounts of approximately $292 million and $246 million outstanding at January 31, 2001 and 2000, respectively. These contracts had a fair value of approximately $6 million and ($1) million at January 31, 2001 and 2000, respectively.

The Company's risk management policy requires the Company to obtain collateral, generally cash deposits, from the counterparty when the fair value of the underlying swaps exceed certain limits.

In addition to the interest rate derivative financial instruments listed in the table on the previous page, the Company holds an interest rate swap with a notional amount of $500 million that is being marked to market through earnings. The fair value of this instrument was not significant at January 31, 2001.

Fair value of financial instruments

Cash and cash equivalents: The carrying amount approximates fair value due to the short maturity of these instruments.

Long-term debt: Fair value approximates $17.3 billion at January 31, 2001 and is based on the Company's current incremental borrowing rate for similar types of borrowing arrangements.

Interest rate instruments and net investment instruments: The fair values are estimated amounts the Company would receive or pay to terminate the agreements as of the reporting dates.

Foreign currency contracts: The fair value of foreign currency contracts are estimated by obtaining quotes from external sources.

5 Income Taxes

The income tax provision consists of the following (in millions):

Fiscal years ended January 31,	2001	2000	1999
Current			
Federal	$ 2,641	$ 2,920	$ 3,043
State and local	297	299	254
International	412	257	83
Total current tax provision	3,350	3,476	3,380
Deferred			
Federal	457	(71)	(655)
State and local	34	(3)	(28)
International	(149)	(183)	43
Total deferred tax provision (benefit)	342	(257)	(640)
Total provision for income taxes	$ 3,692	$ 3,219 (a)	$ 2,740

(a) Total provision for income tax includes a provision on income before the cumulative effect of accounting change of $3,338 and a tax benefit of $119 resulting from the cumulative effect of the accounting change.

Earnings before income taxes are as follows (in millions):

Fiscal years ended January 31,	2001	2000	1999
Domestic	$ 9,203	$ 8,414	$ 6,866
International	913	669	457
Total earnings before income taxes	$ 10,116	$ 9,083	$ 7,323

Items that give rise to significant portions of the deferred tax accounts at January 31, are as follows (in millions):

	2001	2000	1999
Deferred tax liabilities			
Property, plant, and equipment	$ 751	$ 748	$ 695
Inventory	407	393	286
International, principally asset basis difference	398	348	272
Acquired asset basis difference	65	314	–
Other	87	66	36
Total deferred tax liabilities	1,708	1,869	1,289
Deferred tax assets			
Amounts accrued for financial reporting purposes not yet deductible for tax purposes	865	1,098	985
Capital leases	74	193	188
International, asset basis and loss carryforwards	352	402	143
Deferred revenue	142	181	66
Other	153	215	184
Total deferred tax assets	1,586	2,089	1,566
Net deferred tax liabilities (assets)	$ 122	$ (220)	$ (277)

A reconciliation of the significant differences between the effective income tax rate and the federal statutory rate on pretax income follows:

Fiscal years ended January 31,	2001	2000	1999
Statutory tax rate	35.00%	35.00%	35.00%
State income taxes, net of federal income tax benefit	2.13%	2.18%	2.01%
International	-0.84%	-0.74%	-0.50%
Other	0.21%	0.31%	0.90%
	36.50%	36.75%	37.41%

Federal and State income taxes are not accrued on the cumulative undistributed earning of foreign subsidiaries because the earnings have been reinvested in the businesses of those companies. At January 31, 2001, undistributed earnings of the foreign subsidiaries totaled approximately $722 million. The determination of the amount of the unrecognized deferred tax liability related to the undistributed earnings is not practicable.

6 Acquisitions

On April 19, 2000, the Company purchased 271.3 million shares of stock in Wal-Mart de Mexico S.A. de C.V. (formerly Cifra S.A. de C.V.) at a total cash cost of $587 million. This transaction increased the Company's ownership percentage by approximately 6% and resulted in goodwill of $422 million, which is being amortized over a 40-year life.

During the third quarter of fiscal 2000, the Company completed it acquisition of the ASDA Group PLC (ASDA), the third largest retailer in the United Kingdom with 229 stores. The transaction has been accounted for as a purchase. The purchase price of approximately $11 billion has been allocated to the net assets acquired and liabilities assumed based on their estimated fair value. The resulting goodwill and other acquired intangible assets of approximately $7 billion are being amortized over 40 years. The results of operations are included in the consolidated Company results since the date of acquisition.

On January 1, 1999, the Company took possession of 74 units from the Interspar hypermarket chain in Germany. The units were acquired from Spar Handels AG, a German company that owns multiple retail formats and wholesale operations throughout Germany. The transaction has been recorded as a purchase and the results of operations are included beginning in fiscal 2000. The net assets and liabilities acquired are recorded at fair value. Resulting goodwill is being amortized over 40 years.

In July 1998, the Company extended its presence in Asia with an investment in Korea. The Company acquired a majority interest in four units previously operated by Korea Makro as well as six undeveloped sites. The transaction has been accounted for as a purchase. The net assets and liabilities acquired are recorded at fair value. The goodwill is being amortized over 40 years. The results of operations since the effective date of the acquisition have been included in the Company's results. In December 1999, the Company acquired most of the minority interest of its operation in Korea from its joint venture partner with the remaining minority interest being acquired during the first quarter of fiscal 2001.

The fair value of the assets and liabilities recorded as a result of these transactions is as follows (in millions):

	2001	2000	1999
Cash and cash equivalents	$ –	$ 195	$ 137
Receivables	–	16	–
Inventories	–	655	200
Prepaid expenses and other	–	403	–
Net property, plant and equipment	–	5,290	219
Net property under capital leases	–	612	–
Goodwill	452	7,020	576
Accounts payable	–	(1,159)	(112)
Accrued liabilities	–	(564)	(60)
Accrued income taxes	–	(283)	–
Long-term debt and obligations under capital leases	–	(1,272)	–
Deferred income taxes	–	(58)	32
Minority interest	165	–	(22)
Other	–	(7)	22
	$ 617	$ 10,848	$ 992

The following presents the unaudited pro forma results as if the ASDA acquisition had occurred at the beginning of the fiscal years ended January 31, 1999 and 2000. Adjustments to net income are primarily related to the amortization of goodwill and other acquired intangible assets and additional interest expense on the debt incurred to finance the acquisition. The ASDA results were converted from Great Britain pounds to United States dollars at the average exchange rate for the periods presented and range from 1.60 to 1.66.

The aggregate impact of other acquisitions in these periods are not presented due to the insignificant differences from historical results (amounts in millions except per share data):

Fiscal years ended January 31,	2000	1999
Sales	$ 172,295	$ 149,844
Net income	$ 5,551	$ 4,435
Net income per share – basic	$ 1.25	$ 0.99
Net income per share – diluted	$ 1.24	$ 0.99

7 Stock Option Plans

At January 31, 2001, 124 million shares of common stock were reserved for issuance under stock option plans. The options granted under the stock option plans generally expire ten years from the date of grant. Options granted prior to November 17, 1995, may be exercised in nine annual installments. Generally, options granted on or after November 17, 1995, may be exercised in seven annual installments. Options granted during fiscal 2001 may be exercised in five annual installments. The Company has elected to follow Accounting Principles Board Opinion No. 25, *"Accounting for Stock Issued to Employees"* (APB 25) and related interpretations in accounting for its employee stock options because the alternative fair value accounting provided under FASB Statement 123, *"Accounting for Stock-Based Compensation,"* (FAS No. 123) requires the use of option valuation models that were not developed for use in valuing employee stock options. Under APB 25, because the exercise price of the Company's employee stock options equals the market price of the underlying stock on the date of the grant, no compensation expense is recognized.

Pro forma information, regarding net income and income per share, is required by FAS No. 123 and has been determined as if the Company had accounted for its associate stock option plans under the fair value method of that statement. The fair value of these options was estimated at the date of the grant using the Black-Scholes option pricing model with the following assumption ranges: risk-free interest rates between 4.4% and 7.2%, dividend yields between 0.4% and 1.3%, volatility factors between .23 and .41, and an expected life of the option of 7.4 years for the options issued prior to November 17, 1995, 5.8 years for options issued thereafter and 2.0 to 4.0 years for options converted from ASDA stock options.

The Black-Scholes option valuation model was developed for use in estimating the fair value of traded options, which have no vesting restrictions and are fully transferable. In addition, option valuation methods require the input of highly subjective assumptions including the expected stock price volatility. Because the Company's associate stock options have characteristics significantly different from those of traded options, and because changes in the subjective input assumptions can materially affect the fair value estimates, in management's opinion, the existing models do not necessarily provide a reliable single measure of the fair value of its associate stock options. Using the Black-Scholes option evaluation model, the weighted average value of options granted during the years ending January 31, 2001, 2000, and 1999, were $22, $13, and $14, per option, respectively.

The effect of applying the fair value method of FAS No. 123 to the stock option grants subsequent to February 1, 1995, results in the following net income and net income per share (amounts in millions except per share data):

Fiscal years ended January 31,	2001	2000	1999
Pro forma net income	$ 6,235	$ 5,324	$ 4,397
Pro forma earnings per share – basic	$ 1.40	$ 1.20	$ 0.98
Pro forma earnings per share – dilutive	$ 1.39	$ 1.19	$ 0.98

Pro forma disclosures are not likely to be representative of the effects on reported net income for future years.

The following table summarizes information about stock options outstanding as of January 31, 2001:

Range of exercise prices	Number of outstanding options	Weighted average remaining life in years	Weighted average exercise price of outstanding options	Number of options exerciseable	Weighted average exercise price of exerciseable options
$ 5.33 to 8.84	50,000	<1.0	$ 6.45	50,000	$ 6.45
10.00 to 15.41	22,103,000	4.7	11.98	9,385,000	12.18
17.53 to 19.97	8,251,000	7.0	19.28	3,532,000	19.46
24.72 to 34.53	501,000	7.6	29.65	266,000	30.57
39.88 to 43.00	5,575,000	8.0	40.11	1,339,000	40.07
45.38 to 54.56	12,700,000	8.9	47.22	1,371,000	46.91
55.25 to 63.44	666,000	9.5	55.59	1,000	59.76
$ 5.33 to 63.44	49,846,000	6.6	$ 26.56	15,944,000	$ 19.42

Further information concerning the options is as follows:

	Shares	Option price per share	Weighted Average per share	Total
January 31, 1998	60,656,000	$ 3.59 – 19.97	$ 12.75	$ 773,213,000
(13,462,000 shares exerciseable)				
Options granted	9,256,000	12.63 – 43.00	33.02	305,646,000
Options canceled	(4,254,000)	4.39 – 39.88	13.74	(58,436,000)
Options exercised	(9,500,000)	3.59 – 19.09	10.92	(103,748,000)
January 31, 1999	56,158,000	$ 4.39 – 43.00	$ 16.32	$ 916,675,000
(12,357,000 shares exerciseable)				
Options granted	1,540,000	41.25 – 63.44	44.62	68,703,000
ASDA options converted to Wal-Mart options	4,250,000	46.17	46.17	196,244,000
Options canceled	(2,452,000)	5.33 – 43.00	17.27	(42,337,000)
Options exercised	(8,182,000)	4.39 – 39.88	11.44	(93,583,000)
January 31, 2000	51,314,000	$ 5.33 – 63.44	$ 20.39	$ 1,045,702,000
(12,967,000 shares exerciseable)				
Options granted	9,841,000	45.38 – 58.94	48.30	475,332,000
Options canceled	(3,444,000)	6.75 – 54.56	26.47	(92,274,000)
Options exercised	(7,865,000)	6.75 – 46.00	13.50	(106,145,000)
January 31, 2001	49,846,000	$ 5.33 – 63.44	$ 26.56	$ 1,322,615,000
(15,944,000 shares exerciseable)				
Shares available for option:				
January 31, 2000	71,918,000			
January 31, 2001	65,521,000			

Income tax benefit recorded as a result of the tax deductions triggered by employee exercise of stock options amounted to $118 million, $125 million and $49 million in fiscal 2001, 2000 and 1999, respectively.

8 Commitments and Contingencies

The Company and its subsidiaries are involved from time to time in claims, proceedings and litigation arising from the operation of its business. The Company does not believe that any such claim, proceeding or litigation, either alone or in the aggregate, will have a material adverse effect on the Company's financial position or results of its operations.

The Company and certain of its subsidiaries have long-term leases for stores and equipment. Rentals (including, for certain leases, amounts applicable to taxes, insurance, maintenance, other operating expenses and contingent rentals) under all operating leases were $893 million, $762 million, and $707 million in 2001, 2000, and 1999, respectively. Aggregate minimum annual rentals at January 31, 2001, under non-cancelable leases are as follows (in millions):

Fiscal year	Operating leases	Capital leases
2002	$ 564	$ 425
2003	540	421
2004	522	421
2005	514	419
2006	498	414
Thereafter	5,193	3,619
Total minimum rentals	$ 7,831	5,719
Less estimated executory costs		70
Net minimum lease payments		5,649
Less imputed interest at rates ranging from 6.1% to 14.0%		2,354
Present value of minimum lease payments		$ 3,295

Certain of the leases provide for contingent additional rentals based on percentage of sales. Such additional rentals amounted to $56 million, $51 million and $49 million in 2001, 2000 and 1999, respectively. Substantially all of the store leases have renewal options for additional terms from 5 to 30 years at comparable rentals.

The Company has entered into lease commitments for land and buildings for 17 future locations. These lease commitments with real estate developers provide for minimum rentals for 20 to 25 years, excluding renewal options, which if consummated based on current cost estimates, will approximate $22.3 million annually over the lease terms.

9 Segments

The Company and its subsidiaries are principally engaged in the operation of mass merchandising stores located in all 50 states, Argentina, Canada, Germany, Korea, Puerto Rico, and the United Kingdom, through joint ventures in China, and through majority-owned subsidiaries in Brazil and Mexico. The Company identifies segments based on management responsibility within the United States and geographically for all international units. The Wal-Mart Stores segment includes the Company's discount stores, Supercenters and Neighborhood Markets in the United States. The SAM'S CLUB segment includes the warehouse membership clubs in the United States. The Company's operations in Argentina, Brazil, China, Germany, Korea, Mexico and the United Kingdom are consolidated using a December 31 fiscal year end, generally due to statutory reporting requirements. There were no significant intervening events which materially affected the financial statements. The Company's operations in Canada and Puerto Rico are consolidated using a January 31 fiscal year end. The Company measures segment profit as operating profit, which is defined as income before interest expense, income taxes, minority interest and cumulative effect of accounting change. Information on segments and a reconciliation to income, before income taxes, minority interest and cumulative effect of accounting change, are as follows (in millions):

Fiscal year ended January 31, 2001	Wal-Mart Stores	SAM'S CLUB	International	Other	Consolidated
Revenues from external customers	$ 121,889	$ 26,798	$ 32,100	$ 10,542	$ 191,329
Intercompany real estate charge (income)	1,766	383	–	(2,149)	–
Depreciation and amortization	927	147	562	1,232	2,868
Operating income (loss)	9,734	942	1,112	(298)	11,490
Interest expense					(1,374)
Income before income taxes and minority interest					10,116
Total assets	$ 20,286	$ 3,843	$ 25,742	$ 28,259	$ 78,130

Fiscal year ended January 31, 2000	Wal-Mart Stores	SAM'S CLUB	International	Other	Consolidated
Revenues from external customers	$ 108,721	$ 24,801	$ 22,728	$ 8,763	$ 165,013
Intercompany real estate charge (income)	1,542	366	–	(1,908)	–
Depreciation and amortization	812	124	402	1,037	2,375
Operating income (loss)	8,701	850	817	(263)	10,105
Interest expense					(1,022)
Income before income taxes, minority interest and cumulative effect of accounting change					9,083
Total assets	$ 18,213	$ 3,586	$ 25,330	$ 23,220	$ 70,349

Fiscal year ended January 31, 1999	Wal-Mart Stores	SAM'S CLUB	International	Other	Consolidated
Revenues from external customers	$ 95,395	$ 22,881	$ 12,247	$ 7,111	$ 137,634
Intercompany real estate charge (income)	1,502	355	–	(1,857)	–
Depreciation and amortization	716	111	252	793	1,872
Operating income (loss)	7,238	693	549	(419)	8,061
Interest expense					(797)
Reverse adjustment for accounting change*	–	57	2	–	59
Income before income taxes and minority					7,323
Total assets	$ 16,950	$ 2,834	$ 9,537	$ 20,675	$ 49,996

For comparative purposes fiscal 1999 operating income has been adjusted to reflect the impact of the membership fee revenue accounting change described in Note 1. This is reversed for purposes of reconciling operating profit to income before taxes and minority interest.

Operating income information for fiscal years 1999 and 2000 has been reclassified to conform to current year presentation. For this reclassification, certain corporate expenses have been moved from the other category to the operating segments.

Domestic long-lived assets excluding goodwill were $29,741 million, $25,227 million and $21,929 million in 2001, 2000 and 1999, respectively. Additions to domestic long-lived assets were $6,374 million, $3,814 million and $3,317 million in 2001, 2000 and 1999, respectively. International long-lived assets excluding goodwill were $11,193 million, $10,742 million and $4,044 million in 2001, 2000 and 1999, respectively. Additions to international long-lived assets were $711 million, $7,070 million and $732 million in 2001, 2000 and 1999, respectively. The International segment includes all international real estate. All of the real estate in the United States is included in the "Other" category and is leased to Wal-Mart Stores and SAM'S CLUB. The revenues in the "Other" category result from sales to third parties by McLane Company, Inc., a wholesale distributor.

McLane offers a wide variety of grocery and non-grocery products, which it sells to a variety of retailers including the Company's Wal-Mart Stores and SAM'S CLUB segments. McLane is not a significant segment and therefore, results are not presented separately.

10 Quarterly Financial Data (Unaudited)

	Quarters ended			
Amounts in millions (except per share information)	April 30,	July 31,	October 31,	January 31,
2001				
Net sales	$ 42,985	$ 46,112	$ 45,676	$ 56,556
Cost of sales	33,665	36,044	35,694	44,852
Net income	1,326	1,596	1,369	2,004
Net income per common share, basic and diluted	$ 0.30	$ 0.36	$ 0.31	$ 0.45
2000				
Net sales	$ 34,717	$ 38,470	$ 40,432	$ 51,394
Cost of sales	27,241	30,123	31,606	40,694
Income before cumulative effect of accounting change	1,110	1,249	1,299	1,917
Cumulative effect of accounting change, net of tax	(198)	–	–	–
Net income	912	1,249	1,299	1,917
Net income per common share:				
Income before cumulative effect of accounting change	$ 0.25	$ 0.28	$ 0.29	$ 0.43
Cumulative effect of accounting change	(0.04)	–	–	–
Net income per common share, basic and diluted	$ 0.20	$ 0.28	$ 0.29	$ 0.43
Pro forma amounts assuming accounting change had been in effect for all of fiscal 2000:				
Net Income	$ 1,114	$ 1,251	$ 1,294	$ 1,916
Net income per common share, basic and diluted	$ 0.25	$ 0.28	$ 0.29	$ 0.43

Report of Independent Auditors

The Board of Directors and Shareholders,
Wal-Mart Stores, Inc.

We have audited the accompanying consolidated balance
sheets of Wal-Mart Stores, Inc. as of January 31, 2001
and 2000, and the related consolidated statements of
income, shareholders' equity and cash flows for each
of the three years in the period ended January 31, 2001.
These financial statements are the responsibility of the
Company's management. Our responsibility is to express
an opinion on these financial statements based on our
audits.

We conducted our audits in accordance with auditing
standards generally accepted in the United States. Those
standards require that we plan and perform the audit to
obtain reasonable assurance about whether the financial
statements are free of material misstatement. An audit
includes examining, on a test basis, evidence supporting
the amounts and disclosures in the financial statements.
An audit also includes assessing the accounting principles
used and significant estimates made by management, as
well as evaluating the overall financial statement
presentation. We believe that our audits provide a
reasonable basis for our opinion.

In our opinion, the financial statements referred to above
present fairly, in all material respects, the consolidated
financial position of Wal-Mart Stores, Inc. at January 31,
2001 and 2000, and the consolidated results of their
operations and their cash flows for each of the three
years in the period ended January 31, 2001, in conformity
with accounting principles generally accepted in the
United States.

Ernst & Young LLP

Tulsa, Oklahoma
March 26, 2001

Responsibility for Financial Statements

The financial statements and information of Wal-Mart
Stores, Inc. presented in this Report have been prepared by
management, which has responsibility for their integrity and
objectivity. These financial statements have been prepared in
conformity with accounting principles generally accepted in
the United States, applying certain estimates and judgments
based upon currently available information and management's
view of current conditions and circumstances.

Management has developed and maintains a system of
accounting and controls, including an extensive internal audit
program, designed to provide reasonable assurance that the
Company's assets are protected from improper use and that
accounting records provide a reliable basis for the preparation
of financial statements. This system is continually reviewed,
improved and modified in response to changing business
conditions and operations, and to recommendations made
by the independent auditors and the internal auditors.
Management believes that the accounting and control systems
provide reasonable assurance that assets are safeguarded and
financial information is reliable.

The Company has adopted a Statement of Ethics to guide
our management in the continued observance of high ethical
standards of honesty, integrity and fairness in the conduct of
the business and in accordance with the law. Compliance with
the guidelines and standards is periodically reviewed and is
acknowledged, in writing, by all management associates.

The Board of Directors, through the activities of its Audit
Committee consisting solely of outside Directors, participates
in the process of reporting financial information. The duties
of the Committee include keeping informed of the financial
condition of the Company and reviewing its financial policies
and procedures, the independence of the Company's
independent auditors, its internal accounting controls and
the objectivity of its financial reporting. Both the Company's
independent auditors and the internal auditors have free
access to the Audit Committee and meet with the Committee
periodically, with and without management present.

M Schoewe

Thomas M. Schoewe
Executive Vice President and Chief Financial Officer

Appendix B
The Time Value of Money

Financial accounting information is useful because it provides investors, creditors, and other interested parties with measures of solvency and earning power. In developing these measures, the valuation of the transactions in which the company participates and ultimately the valuation of a company's assets and liabilities as well as the company itself are very important. It is essential, therefore, that investors, creditors, managers, auditors, and others understand the concepts of valuation.

The economic value of an asset or liability is its present value. In computing present value, the future cash inflows and outflows associated with an asset or liability are predicted and then adjusted in a way that reflects the **time value of money** (i.e., a dollar in the future is worth less than a dollar at present). Financial accounting statements rely extensively on the concept of present value. In theory, providing measures of present value is the ultimate goal of financial accounting.

This appendix covers the time value of money and, specifically, the concept of present value. We first point out that money has a price (interest). The price of money gives it a time value; it ensures that money held today has a greater value than money received tomorrow. We then introduce the notion of compound interest and proceed to work a number of examples that equate future cash flows to present values. We conclude by discussing how present value fits into the financial accounting system.

INTEREST: THE PRICE OF MONEY

Money, like any other scarce resource, has a price. Individuals wishing to borrow money must pay this price, and those who lend it receive this price. The price of money is called *interest* and is usually expressed as a percentage rate over a certain time period (often per year but sometimes per month). The dollar amount of interest is the result of multiplying the percentage rate by the amount of money borrowed or lent (*principal*). For example, a 10 percent interest rate per year on a principal of $100 will produce $10 (10% × $100) of interest after one year.

TIME VALUE

In an environment that charges interest for the use of money, would you rather have one dollar now or receive one dollar one year from now? If you choose to receive the dollar immediately, you could lend it, and it would grow to some amount greater than one dollar after a year has passed. Someone, perhaps a bank, would be willing to pay you interest for the use of that dollar. Therefore, in a world where money has a price, a dollar today is worth more than a dollar at some time in the future. The difference between the value of a dollar today and the value of a dollar in the future is called the time value of money. For example, if the interest rate is 10 percent, $1 placed in a bank today will grow to $1.10 ($1 × 1.10) in one year. In this example, the time value of a dollar is $0.10.

Size of Time Value

Let's go one step further and explore the factors that determine the size of the time value of money. That is, what factors determine whether the time value of money is large or small? The first factor is obviously the price of money, or the interest rate. If there were no interest rate, the time value of money would be zero. Accordingly, as the interest rate gets larger, so does the difference between the value of a dollar today and the value of a dollar in the future. The higher the interest rate, the greater the time value of money. In the example above, a 20 percent interest rate would give rise to a time value of money equal to $0.20.

The second factor determining the magnitude of the time value of money is the length of the time period. Which do you think is larger: the difference in value between a dollar today and a dollar tomorrow or the difference in value between a dollar today and a dollar one year from now? Clearly, a dollar will grow much more in one year than it will in one day. Thus, the longer the time period, the greater the time value of money.

Inflation

One additional important point should also be noted. We have assumed in the discussion so far that interest is simply the price of money. You might view this price as a rental fee for the use of money. Just as you pay rent for the use of someone else's apartment, you must also pay rent for the use of someone else's money.

However, in addition to the rental price of money, there is another reason why someone would prefer a dollar today to a dollar in the future. In times of rising prices (inflation), for example, one would definitely prefer a dollar today to a dollar in the future because today's dollar will buy more goods than the future dollar. In inflation, the prices of today's goods are less than the prices for the same goods in the future. Thus, in an inflationary environment, there are actually two reasons why one would prefer a dollar today to a dollar in the future: (1) the rental price charged for using the dollar (time value) and (2) the erosion of the purchasing power of the dollar in the future (inflation).

In the real world, interest rates are set so that they reflect both factors. A 10 percent interest rate, for example, might be viewed as a 6 percent rental fee and a 4 percent inflation factor. Unfortunately, when using an interest rate to compute the time value of money, it is quite difficult to clearly separate the rental factor from the inflation factor. As a practical matter, there is little one can do other than to realize that both factors exist and that they are nearly impossible to separate accurately. As indicated previously in Chapter 3, financial accounting ignores this problem by assuming that inflation does not exist.

TIME VALUE COMPUTATIONS

Computations involving the time value of money can be viewed from either of two perspectives: (1) the future value of a sum of money received today or (2) the present value of a sum of money received in the future. The following sections discuss these two perspectives.

Future Value

In our discussion of the time value of money, we stated that $1 invested at a given interest rate for a period of time will grow to an amount greater than $1. This dollar amount is called the **future value.**

SIMPLE INTEREST

As in the example above, $1 invested at a 10 percent per year interest rate will grow to $1.10 ($1 × 1.10) at the end of one year. This $1.10 is referred to as the future value in one year of $1, given a 10 percent interest rate. In such a situation, an individual would be indifferent as to receiving $1 now or $1.10 in one year. A simple interest calculation for one year is illustrated below.

Now ────────▶ 1 year
$1 ────────▶ $1.10

COMPOUND INTEREST

If we wish to compute the future value of $1 at the end of more than one period (say, two years), given a 10 percent interest rate, we use the notion of **compound interest.** That is, in the second year, the 10 percent interest rate is applied to both the original $1 principal and the $0.10 interest earned in the first year. Here, the future value of $1 at the end of two years, given a 10 percent interest rate compounded annually, is equal to $1.21. An individual would be indifferent as to whether to receive $1 now, $1.10 in one year, or $1.21 in two years, given a 10 percent interest rate compounded annually. The computation is depicted below.

Now ────────▶ 1 year ────────▶ 2 years
$1 ────────▶ $1.10 ────────▶ $1.21

TABLE FACTORS

This same basic procedure could be used to calculate the future value of $1 for any number of periods in the future. After very many periods, though, this computation becomes quite time-consuming. Try, for example, to compute the future value of $1 in 40 years, given an 8 percent interest rate compounded annually. Fortunately, tables have been developed that expedite these calculations considerably. Turn now to the time value of money tables—specifically Table 1, located at the end of this appendix. (The factors in this table and in Tables 2, 3, 4, 5, and 6 are carried out to five digits beyond the decimal point. In our discussions, however, we round the factors to two or three digits beyond the decimal point to simplify calculations.) This is a future value table. It enables you to quickly compute the future value of any amount for any number of periods in the future. To compute a future value, first find the intersection of the interest rate and the number of periods. This amount is called the **table factor.** Then, simply multiply this table factor by the dollar amount. For example, find the table factor for a 10 percent interest rate and two periods. It equals 1.21. Multiplying this factor by $1 gives you the future value in two years of $1 invested at a 10 percent annual interest rate. Multiplying this factor by $20 gives you the future value in two years of $20 invested at a 10 percent annual interest rate.

Note that the table factor in this example (1.21) is equal to 1.10×1.10, or $(1.10)^2$. In general, the formula for the future value calculation is as follows:

Future Value = A $(1 + i)^n$
where   **A = money amount**
            i **= annual interest rate**
            n **= number of periods**

Figure B–1 illustrates the future value calculation of $100 invested at 8 percent, 10 percent, and 12 percent for one, two, and three periods.

| FIGURE B-1 |
| Future value |

The chart demonstrates three important points. First, it shows that the factors found on the future value table are nothing more than an individual interest factor $(1 + i)$ multiplied by itself for the number of periods $(1 + i)^n$. For example, the table factor for $n = 3$, $i = 12$ percent is 1.40 ($1.12 \times 1.12 \times 1.12$). Can you find the table factor for three periods and an 8 percent interest rate on the future value table? Can you derive it?

Note also in Figure B–1 that in each of the three time periods, as the interest rate gets higher, the time value of money is larger. In Period 3, for example, the time value of money at an 8 percent interest rate is $26 ($126 − $100). At 10 percent, it is $33 ($133 − $100), and at 12 percent, it is $40 ($140 − $100). And finally, as the time period becomes longer, the time value of money becomes greater. These last two points illustrate the idea mentioned earlier that the magnitude of the time value of money is determined by two factors: (1) the size of the interest rate and (2) the length of the time period.

FUTURE VALUE OF ORDINARY ANNUITIES

It often happens in business transactions that cash payments of equal amounts are made periodically throughout a period of time. Installment payments on loans, for example, are typically set up in this manner. A flow of cash payments of equal amounts paid at periodic intervals is called an **annuity.** If these payments are made at the end of each period, the flow of payments is called an **ordinary annuity,** or an *annuity in arrears.* An ordinary annuity is illustrated below. This five-year ordinary annuity shows $100 payments made at the end of each year for five years.

Now $\longrightarrow$ 1 $\longrightarrow$ 2 $\longrightarrow$ 3 $\longrightarrow$ 4 $\longrightarrow$ 5
            $100 $100 $100 $100 $100

How would one go about computing the future value of this entire ordinary annuity? What would an ordinary five-year annuity of $100 grow to at the end of five years, given a 10 percent interest rate compounded annually? There are basically three ways to approach this problem, and they are illustrated in Figure B–2: (1) you can view each payment separately and compute its growth over each individual time period, (2) you can view each payment separately and use the table for future value (Table 1), or (3) you can use the table for future value of an ordinary annuity (Table 2). Both tables appear at the end of this appendix.

As is evident from the illustration, all three methods bring you to the correct solution ($610). However, the use of Table 2 requires the fewest computations by far. The table factor for five periods and a 10 percent interest rate (6.10) is simply multiplied by the amount of the periodic annuity payment ($100). Note that this table factor is simply the addition of all the individual table factors used in Method 2 (6.10 = 1.46 + 1.33 + 1.21 + 1.10 + 1.00). Thus, the factor in Table 2 for a given time period is simply the summation of the individual time period factors in Table 1. Table 2 is merely a shortcut that makes it easier to compute the future values for ordinary annuities.

Think for a moment about the simple interest factor $(1 + i)$. As we have discussed, the factors in Table 1 are the simple interest factors compounded, or $(1 + i)^n$. A given factor in Table 2 for a specified length of time is the result of adding together the compound factors for each component time period. Thus, the simple interest calculation underlies the factors in both Table 1 and Table 2. In each, we have built upon the very fundamental notion of simple interest.

FUTURE VALUE OF AN ANNUITY DUE

Annuities are often paid at the beginning of each period rather than at the end. Such a series of equal cash payments is referred to as an **annuity due** and is frequently observed when, for example, lease agreements require payments in advance. Calculating the future value of an annuity due follows the same concepts as those for an ordinary annuity. The only difference comes from the obvious fact that annuity due payments come one period earlier and thus earn one period more of interest than ordinary annuities. Table 3 provides table factors for future value of an annuity due calculations.

In the same manner that Figure B–2 illustrated the future value of an ordinary annuity calculation, Figure B–3 illustrates three approaches to computing the future value of a five-year annuity due, given a 10 percent interest rate compounded annu-

> **FIGURE B-2** Future value of ordinary annuities

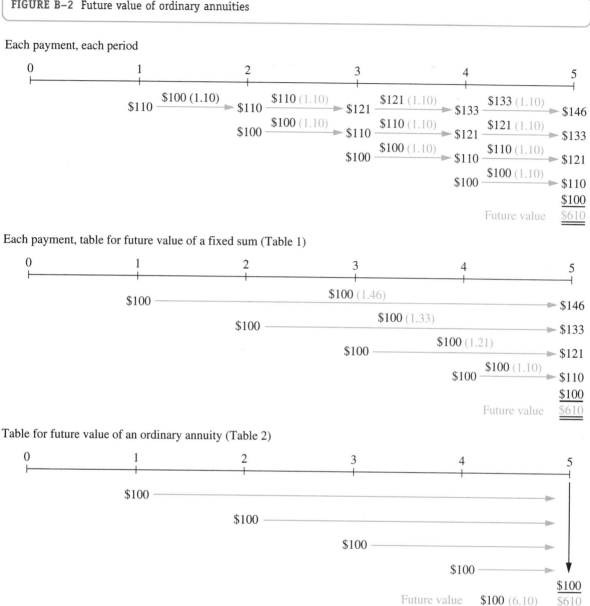

Each payment, each period

Each payment, table for future value of a fixed sum (Table 1)

Table for future value of an ordinary annuity (Table 2)

ally. Again, while all three methods come to the correct solution, Method 3, which uses the factor found on Table 3 (6.71), is by far the easiest.

Compare the computations on this chart to those illustrating the future value of an ordinary annuity on Figure B–2. The future value here is $61 ($671 − $610) greater than the ordinary annuity future value. Why? This difference occurs because each annuity due payment comes one period earlier than each ordinary annuity payment and thus earns more interest over the annuity's life. The fifth $100 payment earns an extra $10 over one period, the fourth payment an extra $11 over two periods, the third an extra $12 over three periods, the second an extra $13 over four periods, and the first an extra $15 over five periods (61 = 10 + 11 + 12 + 13 + 15).

FIGURE B-3 Future value of an annuity due

Each payment, each period

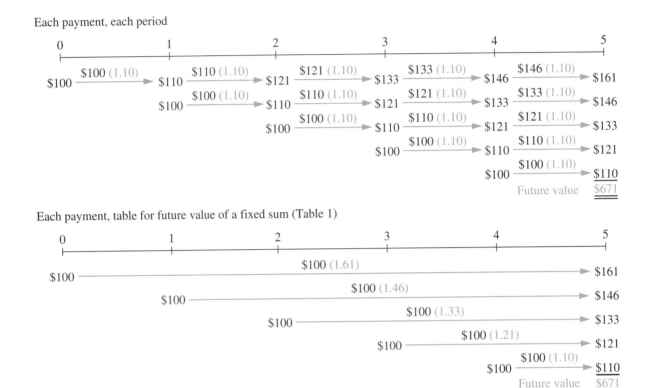

Each payment, table for future value of a fixed sum (Table 1)

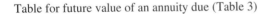

Table for future value of an annuity due (Table 3)

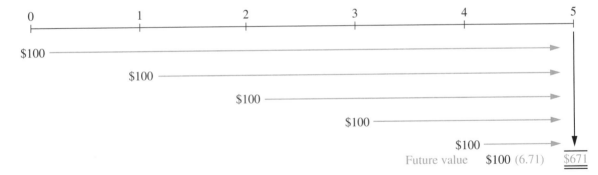

Present Value

Now that we have covered the concept of future value, it should be relatively easy to look at the "other side of the coin." Rather than asking about the future value of a current payment, we now focus on the question, "What is the present value of a future payment?"

In the original example, we stated that $1 would grow to $1.10 after one year, given a 10 percent interest rate. This relationship can just as easily be stated in the opposite way. That is, $1 is the present value of $1.10 received one year in the future, given a 10 percent interest rate. As investors, we would be indifferent between $1 now (the present value) or $1.10 (future value) one year in the future.

The computation of present value is exactly the reciprocal of the future value computation. Recall that the simple interest factor for the future value in one period at 10 percent interest is $(1 + i)$. The simple interest factor for present value is the reciprocal, $1 \div (1 + i)$. In the future value example presented earlier, $1 \times (1 + 0.10)$ equaled $1.10, the future value. To compute the present value, we simply multiply $1.10 by $1 \div (1 + 0.10)$ to arrive at $1. The present value computation is illustrated as follows.

Now ◄——————— 1 year
$1 ◄——————— $1.10

If the present value computation involves more than one period, just as in the future value case, the notion of compounding must be considered. The present value factor, once again, is simply the reciprocal of the future value factor, $1 \div (1 + i)^n$. A two-period, 10 percent interest rate example follows.

Now ◄——————— 1 ◄——————— 2
$1 ◄——————— $1.10 ◄——————— $1.21
$1 ◄—————————————————— $1.21

This example demonstrates that the present values of both $1.21 in two years and $1.10 in one year are equal to $1, given a 10 percent interest rate compounded annually. In such a case, an investor would be indifferent among having $1 now, receiving $1.10 in one year, or receiving $1.21 in two years. The example also shows that the present value of a future payment can be calculated in several different ways.

As for future values, there are tables (Tables 4, 5, and 6) designed to expedite the computations required to calculate present values. The factors contained in these tables are the reciprocals of the corresponding factors in the future value tables. Table 4 contains the table factors for the present values of single payments in the future. In the illustration above, one could use the table by multiplying $1.21 by 0.826 (Table 4, $n = 2$, $i = 10\%$) to arrive at the $1 present value. Obviously, as the number of time periods increases, the time savings from using the tables also increases.

Present values for ordinary annuities and annuities due must also be computed from time to time, and Table 5 (ordinary annuity) and Table 6 (annuity due) are designed for that purpose. As with future values, there are basically three ways to compute the present value of ordinary annuity and annuity due payment streams; they are depicted in Figures B–4 (ordinary annuity) and B–5 (annuity due). In both cases, a $100, five-year annuity at a 10 percent interest rate is illustrated.

Again compare the two charts and note that the present value of an annuity due is $38 ($417 − $379) greater than the present value of the ordinary annuity. The fact that each of the five payments in the annuity due is one period earlier than the corresponding ordinary annuity payment accounts for this difference.

An Illustration

You may quickly grasp the general concepts of future and present value, yet still have difficulty making the appropriate computations for a specific problem. We have designed the following example to demonstrate how straightforward future and present value computations can be and also how many different ways one can approach the same problem. We also introduce a concept we call **equivalent value.** It can be useful in understanding the notion of time value.

FIGURE B–4 Present value of an ordinary annuity

Each payment, each period

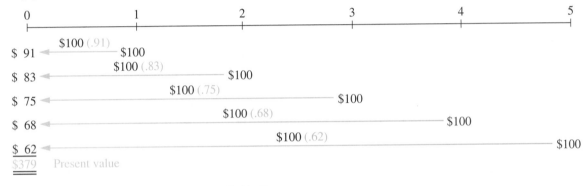

Each payment, table for present value of a fixed sum (Table 4)

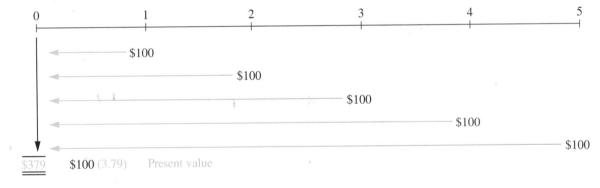

Table for present value of an ordinary annuity (Table 5)

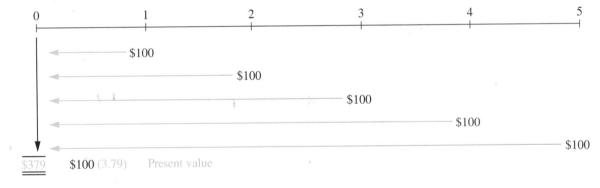

Assume a $500, five-year, ordinary annuity at a 12 percent interest rate compounded annually. The cash flows are illustrated below. Let's see how many different ways we can compute the future and present value of this payment stream. Five such examples are shown in Figure B–6.

0 ——— 1 ——— 2 ——— 3 ——— 4 ——— 5
         $500 $500 $500 $500 $500

FIGURE B–5 Present value of an annuity due

Each payment, each period

Each payment, table for present value of a fixed sum (Table 4)

Table for present value of an annuity due (Table 6)

Can you follow each of the five methods shown? Note that each method brings you to a future value of $3,176 and a present value of $1,804. No matter how many different ways one tackles this problem, the same future and present values emerge.

EQUIVALENT VALUE

To understand the concept of equivalent value, view the $500 annuity payments, the present value, and the future value as being indifference amounts. That is, in this example, an investor would be indifferent as to a five-year, $500 ordinary annuity, or

FIGURE B–6   Example calculations

FUTURE VALUE

1. Each payment, each period

$500 (1.12) (1.12) (1.12) (1.12) = $ 787
$500 (1.12) (1.12) (1.12) =   702
$500 (1.12) (1.12) =   627
$500 (1.12) =   560
$500 =   500
Future value $3,176

2. Each payment individually

$500 (1.574) = $ 787
500 (1.405) =   702
500 (1.254) =   627
500 (1.120) =   560
500 (1.000) =   500
Future value $3,176

3. Ordinary annuity table
Future value $500 (6.353) = $3,176

4. Compute present value, and then compute future value of present value

A. Present value
$500 (3.604) = $1,802

B. Future value
$1,802 (1.7623)   = $3,176

5. Compute equivalent value at Period 3, and then compute future value of that number

A. Value at Period 3
$500 (1.254) = $ 627
500 (1.120) =   560
500 (1.000) =   500
500 (.893) =   447
500 (.797) =   399
$2,533

B. Future value
$2,533 (1.254) = $3,176

PRESENT VALUE

Each payment, each period

$500 (.893) (.893) (.893) (.893) (.893) = $ 284
$500 (.893) (.893) (.893) (.893) =   318
$500 (.893) (.893) (.893) =   356
$500 (.893) (.893) =   399
$500 (.893) =   447
Present value $1,804

Each payment individually

$500 (.567) = $ 284
500 (.636) =   318
500 (.712) =   356
500 (.797) =   399
500 (.893) =   447
Present value $1,804

Ordinary annuity table
Present value $500 (3.604) = $1,802*

Compute future value, and then compute present value of future value

A. Future value
$500 (6.353) = $3,176

B. Present value
$3,176 (.5674)   = $1,802*

Compute equivalent value at Period 3, and then compute present value of that number

Value at Period 3
$500 (1.12) (1.12) = $ 627
$500 (1.12) =   560
500 (1.00) =   500
500 (.893) =   447
500 (.893) (.893) =   399
$2,533

B. Present value
$2,533 (.712) = $1,804

*Rounding difference

$1,804 now, or $3,176 five years from now. These three payments are, in other words, equivalent in value.

The idea of equivalent value is further illustrated in the fifth computation in Figure B–6. It involves two steps. We first compute the amount that would be equivalent to the five-year ordinary annuity if one lump sum were received at the end of Period 3 ($2,533). This amount is the equivalent value of this particular annuity at the end of Period 3. We then adjust this amount to present or future value by multiplying it by the appropriate table factor. Figure B–7 illustrates the equivalent values of the five-year ordinary annuity if lump-sum payments were made at the end of each of the five periods.

Figure B–7 demonstrates that given a 12 percent interest rate compounded annually, an investor would be indifferent among the following seven payments. Can you derive these amounts?

1. a five-year, $500 ordinary annuity
2. $1,804 now (present value)
3. $2,021 at the end of one year
4. $2,262 at the end of two years
5. $2,533 at the end of three years
6. $2,839 at the end of four years
7. $3,176 at the end of five years (future value)

FIGURE B–7 Equivalent values

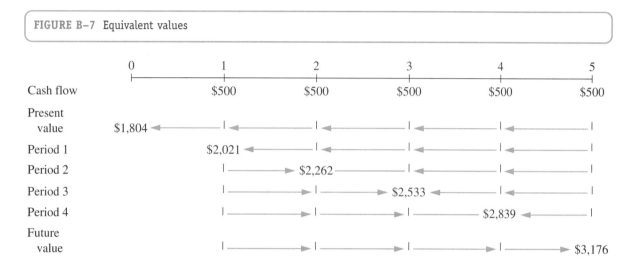

PRESENT VALUE AND FINANCIAL ACCOUNTING

We stated earlier that present value is the economic form of valuation. Investors, creditors, and managers use it to compare the values of alternative investments. Bankers, lawyers, and other business decision makers use it to derive the terms of contracts like mortgages, leases, pensions, and life insurance. Virtually any transaction that can be broken down into periodic cash flows utilizes the time value of money concept and can be reduced to present value, future value, and other equivalent values. The time value of money is covered in finance, economics, accounting, and other business courses. You may have already studied present value in previous courses, and you will probably see it again in the future. The uses of present value in business decision making are almost limitless.

The study of financial accounting and its reliance on the time value of money concept is no exception. As you already know, financial accounting information is useful because it helps investors, creditors, and other interested parties evaluate and control the business decisions of management. Such evaluation and control requires that financial accounting information be used to assess value: the value of entire companies, the value of individual assets and liabilities, and the value of specific transactions. Since present value is the economic form of valuation, financial accounting information must reflect present value if it is to be useful.

However, a critical problem is associated with using present value on the financial statements. The present value calculation requires that both future cash flows and future interest rates be predicted. In the vast majority of cases, predicting the future cash flows associated with a particular asset or liability with a reasonable degree of confidence is almost impossible. For example, how would one go about predicting the future cash inflows and outflows associated with the purchase of a specific piece of equipment like an automobile? Moreover, accurately predicting interest rates has for years eluded even the best economists. The predictions that management must make to apply present value are simply too subjective for financial statements that are to be used by those outside the company. Auditors are unwilling and unable to verify such subjective judgments. The legal liability faced by both managers and auditors makes such verification potentially very costly.

For these reasons, although present value remains the goal of financial measurement, most of the valuation bases on the financial statements represent surrogate (substitute) measures of present value. Historical cost, fair market value, replacement cost, and net realizable value can all be viewed as surrogate measures of present value. These valuation bases are used primarily because present value is simply too subjective and unreliable for a system that requires auditors to verify financial statements prepared by management for stockholders and other outside interested parties. Present value calculations, in general, violate the principle of objectivity.

In some cases, however, the future cash flows associated with an asset or a liability are predictable enough to allow for sufficiently objective present value calculations. As discussed in Chapter 3, contractual agreements like notes receivable and payable meet the criterion of objectivity. Mortgages, bonds, leases, and pensions are other examples of contracts that underlie cash flows and thus remove much of the subjectivity associated with cash flow prediction. In these cases, the present value calculation is used in the preparation of the financial statements.

In summary, there are two reasons why accounting students must understand present value. First, present value is the economic form of valuation and is therefore the ultimate goal of accounting measurement. It is the standard against which all financial accounting measurements must be compared and evaluated. Second, in those cases where cash flow prediction is sufficiently objective (e.g., contracts), present value methods are used, and present values are actually incorporated into the financial statements. The balance sheet valuation of the assets and liabilities arising from such contracts results from the present value calculation.

EXERCISES

EB-1

(Future value/ single sum)

If $150 were invested today, how large a sum could be withdrawn at the end of the following time periods at the following compound interest rates? Complete the following table.

	Time Periods (Years)		
Compound Interest Rates	5	10	15
5%			
10%			
15%			

EB–2
(Present value/ single sum)

Compute the present value of $10,000 received at the end of the following time periods at the following discount rates. Complete the following table.

	Time Periods (Years)		
Compound Interest Rates	5	10	15
5%			
10%			
15%			

EB–3
(Future value/ ordinary annuity)

If $150 were invested at the end of each year over the following time periods at the following interest rates, how large a sum could be withdrawn at the end of the final time period? Complete the following table.

	Time Periods (Years)		
Compound Interest Rates	5	10	15
5%			
10%			
15%			

EB–4
(Future value/ annuity due)

If $150 were invested at the beginning of each year over the following time periods at the following interest rates, how large a sum could be withdrawn at the end of the final time period? Complete the following table.

	Time Periods (Years)		
Compound Interest Rates	5	10	15
5%			
10%			
15%			

EB–5
(Present value/ ordinary annuity)

Compute the present value of $10,000 received at the end of each year over the following time periods at the following discount rates. Complete the following table.

	Time Periods (Years)		
Compound Interest Rates	5	10	15
5%			
10%			
15%			

EB–6
(Present value/ annuity due)

Compute the present value of $10,000 received at the beginning of each year over the following time periods at the following discount rates. Complete the following table.

	Time Periods (Years)		
Compound Interest Rates	5	10	15
5%			
10%			
15%			

EB–7
(Present value of different payment patterns)

Compute the present value of the payment patterns provided below, given an 8 percent discount rate.

a. $50 at the end of Year 2; $100 at the end of Year 5; $80 at the end of Year 8.
b. $100 at the end of Years 1, 2, 3, 4; $100 at the end of Year 8.
c. $60 at the end of Years 5, 6, 7, 8; $100 at the end of Year 10.
d. $90 at the end of Years 7, 8, 9.

EB-8

(Present value of
different payment
patterns)

Compute the present value of the payment patterns provided below, given an 8 percent discount rate.

a. $50 at the end of Year 2; $100 at the end of Year 5; $80 at the beginning of Year 8.
b. $100 at the beginning of Years 1, 2, 3, 4; $100 at the beginning of Year 8.
c. $60 at the beginning of Years 5, 6, 7, 8; $100 at the beginning of Year 10.
d. $90 at the beginning of Years 7, 8, 9.

EB-9

(Future and
present values)

Ben Watson found $25,000 lying on the sidewalk and decided to invest the money. He believes that he can earn a 10 percent rate (compounded annually) on his investment for the first four years, 12 percent for the following three years, and 15 percent for the following five years.

a. How much money will Ben have at the end of four years, seven years, and twelve years?
b. If someone offered to pay him $36,000 at the end of four years for the $25,000, should he accept? Why or why not?

EB-10

(Present value of
future bond
payments—
ordinary annuity
and annuity due)

Rudnicki Corporation raises money by issuing bonds. The bond agreement states that Rudnicki must make interest payments in the amount of $40,000 at the end of each year for ten years and make a $500,000 payment at the end of the tenth year. Assume that the discount rate is 10 percent.

a. What amount, as a lump sum, would the company have to invest today to meet the $40,000 annual interest payments and the $500,000 principal payment at the end of the tenth year?
b. What amount would have to be invested if the bond agreement stated that the interest payments were to be made at the beginning of each of the ten years and the $500,000 payment was still at the end of the tenth year?

EB-11

(The highest
present value)

Congratulations! You have just won the lottery. The lottery board offers you three different options for collecting your winnings:

1. You will receive payments of $500,000 at the end of each year for twenty years.
2. You will receive a lump-sum payment of $4,500,000 today.
3. You will receive a lump-sum payment of $1 million today and payments of $2,100,000 at the end of Years 5, 6, and 7.

Assume that all earnings can be invested at a 10 percent annual rate. Which option should you choose and why?

EB-12

(Comparing ordinary
annuities and
annuities due)

Consider a three-year, $700 ordinary annuity (the first payment is due one year from now) and a three-year, $700 annuity due (the first payment is due now). Assume a discount rate of 10 percent. For each of the two annuities, compute the equivalent value as of the following points in time.

a. Now
b. The end of Period 1
c. The end of Period 2
d. The end of Period 3
e. Which of the above is referred to as the present value?
f. Which of the above is referred to as the future value?
g. Which of the two annuities is most valuable and by how much?

EB-13

(Different terms
of financing)

Dunn Drafting Company is considering expanding its business by purchasing new equipment. Because of constraints on how much the company can spend for new equipment, the president wants to make sure that the company enters into the best possible deal. Dunn Drafting has four options for paying for the new equipment.

1. Make a lump sum payment of $240,000 today.
2. Make a lump sum payment of $500,000 eight years from now.
3. Make a lump sum payment of $600,000 ten years from now.

4. Make payments of $50,000 at the beginning of each year for six years. The first payment is due now.

a. Compute the present value of each option. Assume that the relevant interest rate is 12 percent.
b. If you were the president of Dunn Drafting Company, which option would you select?
c. Would your answer to (b) change if the annual interest rate was 8 percent? If so, which option would you now prefer?

EB–14

(Saving for a college education—future value)

The Croziers have a three-year-old son named Ryan, and they want to provide for Ryan's college education. They estimate that it will cost $40,000 per year for four years when Ryan enters college fifteen years from now. Assume that all investments can earn a 10 percent annual interest rate and that the four annual payments will be made at the beginning of each year.

a. How much would the Croziers have to invest today to meet Ryan's college expenses?
b. How much would the Croziers have to invest at the end of each year for fourteen years to meet Ryan's college expenses?
c. Answer questions (a) and (b) above, assuming an 8 percent annual interest rate.

EB–15

(Saving for a college education—future value)

The Smithsons have a nine-year-old daughter named Emily, and they wish to provide for her college education. They estimate that it will cost $30,000 per year for four years when Emily enters college ten years from now. Assume that all investments can earn an 8 percent annual interest rate and that the four annual payments will be made at the beginning of each year.

a. How much would the Smithsons have to invest today to meet Emily's college expenses?
b. How much would the Smithsons have to invest at the end of each year for nine years to meet Emily's college expenses?
c. Answer questions (a) and (b) above, assuming a 6 percent annual interest rate.

PROBLEMS

PB–1

(The value of common stock)

Christie Bauer is contemplating investing in South Bend Ironworks. She estimates that the company will pay the following dividends per share at the end of the next four years and that the current price of the company's common stock ($100) will remain unchanged.

Year 1	Year 2	Year 3	Year 4
$5	$6	$7	$8

Christie wants to earn 12 percent on her investment.

REQUIRED:
Assume that Christie plans to sell the investment at the end of the fourth year. How much would she be willing to pay for one share of common stock in South Bend Ironworks?

PB–2

(Computing future value, present value, and equivalent value)

Wharton Company is planning to make the following investments.

1. $1,000 at the end of each year for five years at a 10 percent annual rate. Wharton Company will leave the accumulated principal and earnings in the bank for another five years at a 12 percent annual rate.
2. $3,000 at the end of each year for seven years at a 15 percent annual rate. Wharton will not make the first $3,000 payment until four years from now.

REQUIRED:
a. How much money will Wharton have at the end of ten years?
b. How much would Wharton have to invest in a lump sum today to have an equivalent amount at the end of ten years, given a 12 percent annual rate of return?

PB-3

(Computing present value and equivalent value of contract cash flows)

The terms of three different contracts follow.

1. $8,000 received at the beginning of each year for ten years, compounded at a 6 percent annual rate.
2. $8,000 received today and $20,000 received ten years from today. The relevant interest rate is 12 percent.
3. $8,000 received at the end of Years 4, 5, and 6. The relevant annual interest rate is 10 percent.

REQUIRED:

a. Compute the present value of each contract.
b. Compute the equivalent value of each contract at the end of Years 5 and 10.

PB-4

(The highest present value?)

J. Hartney, president of Doyle Industries, has a choice of three bonus contracts. The first option is to receive an immediate cash payment of $25,000. The second option is a deferred payment of $60,000, to be received in eight years. The final option is to receive an immediate cash payment of $5,000, a deferred payment of $27,000 to be received in three years, and a deferred payment of $20,000 to be received in twenty years. Assume that the relevant interest rate is 9 percent. Which bonus option should Hartney accept and why?

PB-5

(Computing equivalent values)

Boulder Wilderness Adventures purchased rafting and kayaking equipment by issuing a note to Recreational Co-op, the seller of the equipment. The note required a down payment of $5,000, annual payments of $10,000 at the end of each year for five years (the first payment to be one year from now), and a final payment of $15,000 at the end of the fifth year (this payment is in addition to the $10,000 annual payments). Assume that 10 percent is the relevant annual interest rate.

REQUIRED:

Recreational Co-op is indifferent between receiving the cash flows described above or any other cash flow that represents an equivalent value. Compute equivalent values as of the following points in time:

a. Today
b. At the end of two years
c. At the end of four years
d. At the end of five years

PB-6

(Present and future values)

Assume an annual interest rate of 8 percent for each of the following independent cases. Compute the value at time 0 and the value at the end of the investment period for all the cash flows described.

a. $10,000 is invested and held for four years.
b. $2,000 is invested at the end of each year for eight years.
c. $5,000 is invested at the beginning of each year for three years.
d. $3,000 is invested at the end of each year for five years. The balance is left to accumulate interest for an additional five years.
e. A company will receive $25,000 at the end of seven years.
f. A company will receive $3,000 at the end of each year for two years.
g. A company will receive $4,000 at the beginning of each year for three years.

PB-7

(Present value of a note receivable and inferring the effective interest rate)

Joy Don Corp. sells a building to Trifle and Life in exchange for a note. The note specifies a lump sum payment of $300,000 ten years in the future and annual payments (beginning today) of $2,000 at the beginning of each year for ten years. Assume an annual interest rate of 10 percent.

REQUIRED:

a. Would Joy Don be wise to accept $110,000 now instead of the note? Why or why not?
b. At what interest rate would Joy Don be wise to accept the $110,000 instead of the note? (*Hint:* Use a trial-and-error approach. The answer is an integer.)

TABLE 1   Future value of $1 (future amount of a single sum)

Periods (n)	2%	3%	4%	5%	6%	7%	8%
1	1.02000	1.03000	1.04000	1.05000	1.06000	1.07000	1.08000
2	1.04040	1.06090	1.08160	1.10250	1.12360	1.14490	1.16640
3	1.06121	1.09273	1.12486	1.15763	1.19102	1.22504	1.25971
4	1.08243	1.12551	1.16986	1.21551	1.26248	1.31080	1.36049
5	1.10408	1.15927	1.21665	1.27628	1.33823	1.40255	1.46933
6	1.12616	1.19405	1.26532	1.34010	1.41852	1.50073	1.58687
7	1.14869	1.22987	1.31593	1.40710	1.50363	1.60578	1.71382
8	1.17166	1.26677	1.36857	1.47746	1.59385	1.71819	1.85093
9	1.19509	1.30477	1.42331	1.55133	1.68948	1.83846	1.99900
10	1.21899	1.34392	1.48024	1.62889	1.79085	1.96715	2.15892
11	1.24337	1.38423	1.53945	1.71034	1.89830	2.10485	2.33164
12	1.26824	1.42576	1.60103	1.79586	2.01220	2.25219	2.51817
15	1.34587	1.55797	1.80094	2.07893	2.39656	2.75903	3.17217
20	1.48595	1.80611	2.19112	2.65330	3.20714	3.86968	4.66096
30	1.81136	2.42726	3.24340	4.32194	5.74349	7.61226	10.06266
40	2.20804	3.26204	4.80102	7.03999	10.28572	14.97446	21.72452

Periods (n)	9%	10%	11%	12%	14%	15%
1	1.09000	1.10000	1.11000	1.12000	1.14000	1.15000
2	1.18810	1.21000	1.23210	1.25440	1.29960	1.32250
3	1.29503	1.33100	1.36763	1.40493	1.48154	1.52088
4	1.41158	1.46410	1.51807	1.57352	1.68896	1.74901
5	1.53862	1.61051	1.68506	1.76234	1.92541	2.01136
6	1.67710	1.77156	1.87041	1.97382	2.19497	2.31306
7	1.82804	1.94872	2.07616	2.21068	2.50227	2.66002
8	1.99256	2.14359	2.30454	2.47596	2.85259	3.05902
9	2.17189	2.35795	2.55804	2.77308	3.25195	3.51788
10	2.36736	2.59374	2.83942	3.10585	3.70722	4.04556
11	2.58043	2.85312	3.15176	3.47855	4.22623	4.65239
12	2.81266	3.13843	3.49845	3.89598	4.81790	5.35025
15	3.64248	4.17725	4.78459	5.47357	7.13794	8.13706
20	5.60441	6.72750	8.06231	9.64629	13.74349	16.36654
30	13.26768	17.44940	22.89230	29.95992	50.95016	66.21177
40	31.40942	45.25926	65.00087	93.05097	188.88351	267.86355

TABLE 2 Future value of an ordinary annuity of $1

Periods (n)	2%	3%	4%	5%	6%	7%	8%
1	1.00000	1.00000	1.00000	1.00000	1.00000	1.00000	1.00000
2	2.02000	2.03000	2.04000	2.05000	2.06000	2.07000	2.08000
3	3.06040	3.09090	3.12160	3.15250	3.18360	3.21490	3.24640
4	4.12161	4.18363	4.24646	4.31013	4.37462	4.43994	4.50611
5	5.20404	5.30914	5.41632	5.52563	5.63709	5.75074	5.86660
6	6.30812	6.46841	6.63298	6.80191	6.97532	7.15329	7.33593
7	7.43428	7.66246	7.89829	8.14201	8.39384	8.65402	8.92280
8	8.58297	8.89234	9.21423	9.54911	9.89747	10.25980	10.63663
9	9.75463	10.15911	10.58280	11.02656	11.49132	11.97799	12.48756
10	10.94972	11.46388	12.00611	12.57789	13.18079	13.81645	14.48656
11	12.16872	12.80780	13.48635	14.20679	14.97164	15.78360	16.64549
12	13.41209	14.19203	15.02581	15.91713	16.86994	17.88845	18.97713
15	17.29342	18.59891	20.02359	21.57856	23.27597	25.12902	27.15211
20	24.29737	26.87037	29.77808	33.06595	36.78559	40.99549	45.76196
30	40.56808	47.57542	56.08494	66.43885	79.05819	94.46079	113.28321
40	60.40198	75.40126	95.02552	120.79977	154.76197	199.63511	259.05652

Periods (n)	9%	10%	11%	12%	14%	15%
1	1.00000	1.00000	1.00000	1.00000	1.00000	1.00000
2	2.09000	2.10000	2.11000	2.12000	2.14000	2.15000
3	3.27810	3.31000	3.34210	3.37440	3.43960	3.47250
4	4.57313	4.64100	4.70973	4.77933	4.92114	4.99338
5	5.98471	6.10510	6.22780	6.35285	6.61010	6.74238
6	7.52333	7.71561	7.91286	8.11519	8.53552	8.75374
7	9.20043	9.48717	9.78327	10.08901	10.73049	11.06680
8	11.02847	11.43589	11.85943	12.29969	13.23276	13.72682
9	13.02104	13.57948	14.16397	14.77566	16.08535	16.78584
10	15.19293	15.93742	16.72201	17.54874	19.33730	20.30372
11	17.56029	18.53117	19.56143	20.65458	23.04452	24.34928
12	20.14072	21.38428	22.71319	24.13313	27.27075	29.00167
15	29.36092	31.77248	34.40536	37.27971	43.84241	47.58041
20	51.16012	57.27500	64.20283	72.05244	91.02493	102.44358
30	136.30754	164.49402	199.02088	241.33268	356.78685	434.74515
40	337.88245	442.59256	581.82607	767.09142	1342.02510	1779.09031

TABLE 3   Future value of an annuity due of $1

Periods (n)	2%	3%	4%	5%	6%	7%	8%
1	1.02000	1.03000	1.04000	1.05000	1.06000	1.07000	1.08000
2	2.06040	2.09090	2.12160	2.15250	2.18360	2.21490	2.24640
3	3.12161	3.18363	3.24646	3.31013	3.37462	3.43994	3.50611
4	4.20404	4.30914	4.41632	4.52563	4.63709	4.75074	4.86660
5	5.30812	5.46841	5.63298	5.80191	5.97532	6.15329	6.33593
6	6.43428	6.66246	6.89829	7.14201	7.39384	7.65402	7.92280
7	7.58297	7.89234	8.21423	8.54911	8.89747	9.25980	9.63663
8	8.75463	9.15911	9.58280	10.02656	10.49132	10.97799	11.48756
9	9.94972	10.46388	11.00611	11.57789	12.18079	12.81645	13.48656
10	11.16872	11.80780	12.48635	13.20679	13.97164	14.78360	15.64549
11	12.41209	13.19203	14.02581	14.91713	15.86994	16.88845	17.97713
12	13.68033	14.61779	15.62684	16.71298	17.88214	19.14064	20.49530
15	17.63929	19.15688	20.82453	22.65749	24.67253	26.88805	29.32428
20	24.78332	27.67649	30.96920	34.71925	38.99273	43.86518	49.42292
30	41.37944	49.00268	58.32834	69.76079	83.80168	101.07304	122.34587
40	61.61002	77.66330	98.82654	126.83976	164.04768	213.60957	279.78104

Periods (n)	9%	10%	11%	12%	14%	15%
1	1.09000	1.10000	1.11000	1.12000	1.14000	1.15000
2	2.27810	2.31000	2.34210	2.37440	2.43960	2.47250
3	3.57313	3.64100	3.70973	3.77933	3.92114	3.99338
4	4.98471	5.10510	5.22780	5.35285	5.61010	5.74238
5	6.52333	6.71561	6.91286	7.11519	7.53552	7.75374
6	8.20043	8.48717	8.78327	9.08901	9.73049	10.06680
7	10.02847	10.43589	10.85943	11.29969	12.23276	12.72682
8	12.02104	12.57948	13.16397	13.77566	15.08535	15.78584
9	14.19293	14.93742	15.72201	16.54874	18.33730	19.30372
10	16.56029	17.53117	18.56143	19.65458	22.04452	23.34928
11	19.14072	20.38428	21.71319	23.13313	26.27075	28.00167
12	21.95338	23.52271	25.21164	27.02911	31.08865	33.35192
15	32.00340	34.94973	38.18995	41.75328	49.98035	54.71747
20	55.76453	63.00250	71.26514	80.69874	103.76842	117.81012
30	148.57522	180.94342	220.91317	270.29261	406.73701	499.95692
40	368.29187	486.85181	645.82693	859.14239	1529.90861	2045.95385

TABLE 4   Present value of $1 (present value of a single sum)

Periods (n)	2%	3%	4%	5%	6%	7%	8%
1	0.98039	0.97087	0.96154	0.95238	0.94340	0.93458	0.92593
2	0.96177	0.94260	0.92456	0.90703	0.89000	0.87344	0.85734
3	0.94232	0.91514	0.88900	0.86384	0.83962	0.81630	0.79383
4	0.92385	0.88849	0.85480	0.82270	0.79209	0.76290	0.73503
5	0.90573	0.86261	0.82193	0.78353	0.74726	0.71299	0.68058
6	0.88797	0.83748	0.79031	0.74622	0.70496	0.66634	0.63017
7	0.87056	0.81309	0.75992	0.71068	0.66506	0.62275	0.58349
8	0.85349	0.78941	0.73069	0.67684	0.62741	0.58201	0.54027
9	0.83676	0.76642	0.70259	0.64461	0.59190	0.54393	0.50025
10	0.82035	0.74409	0.67556	0.61391	0.55839	0.50835	0.46319
11	0.80426	0.72242	0.64958	0.58468	0.52679	0.47509	0.42888
12	0.78849	0.70138	0.62460	0.55684	0.49697	0.44401	0.39711
15	0.74301	0.64186	0.55526	0.48102	0.41727	0.36245	0.31524
20	0.67297	0.55368	0.45639	0.37689	0.31180	0.25842	0.21455
30	0.55207	0.41199	0.30832	0.23138	0.17411	0.13137	0.09938
40	0.45289	0.30656	0.20829	0.14205	0.09722	0.06678	0.04603
50	0.37153	0.22811	0.14071	0.08720	0.05429	0.03395	0.02132
60	0.30478	0.16973	0.09506	0.05354	0.03031	0.01726	0.00988

Periods (n)	9%	10%	11%	12%	14%	15%
1	0.91743	0.90909	0.90090	0.89286	0.87719	0.86957
2	0.84168	0.82645	0.81162	0.79719	0.76947	0.75614
3	0.77218	0.75131	0.73119	0.71178	0.67497	0.65752
4	0.70843	0.68301	0.65873	0.63552	0.59208	0.57175
5	0.64993	0.62092	0.59345	0.56743	0.51937	0.49718
6	0.59627	0.56447	0.53464	0.50663	0.45559	0.43233
7	0.54703	0.51316	0.48166	0.45235	0.39964	0.37594
8	0.50187	0.46651	0.43393	0.40388	0.35056	0.32690
9	0.46043	0.42410	0.39092	0.36061	0.30751	0.28426
10	0.42241	0.38554	0.35218	0.32197	0.26974	0.24718
11	0.38753	0.35049	0.31728	0.28748	0.23662	0.21494
12	0.35553	0.31863	0.28584	0.25668	0.20756	0.18691
15	0.27454	0.23939	0.20900	0.18270	0.14010	0.12289
20	0.17843	0.14864	0.12403	0.10367	0.07276	0.06110
30	0.07537	0.05731	0.04368	0.03338	0.01963	0.01510
40	0.03184	0.02209	0.01538	0.01075	0.00529	0.00373
50	0.01345	0.00852	0.00542	0.00346	0.00143	0.00092
60	0.00568	0.00328	0.00191	0.00111	0.00039	0.00023

TABLE 5 Present value of an ordinary annuity of $1

Periods (n)	2%	3%	4%	5%	6%	7%	8%
1	0.98039	0.97087	0.96154	0.95238	0.94340	0.93458	0.92593
2	1.94156	1.91347	1.88609	1.85941	1.83339	1.80802	1.78326
3	2.88388	2.82861	2.77509	2.72325	2.67301	2.62432	2.57710
4	3.80773	3.71710	3.62990	3.54595	3.46511	3.38721	3.31213
5	4.71346	4.57971	4.45182	4.32948	4.21236	4.10020	3.99271
6	5.60143	5.41719	5.24214	5.07569	4.91732	4.76654	4.62288
7	6.47199	6.23028	6.00205	5.78637	5.58238	5.38929	5.20637
8	7.32548	7.01969	6.73274	6.46321	6.20979	5.97130	5.74664
9	8.16224	7.78611	7.43533	7.10782	6.80169	6.51523	6.24689
10	8.98259	8.53020	8.11090	7.72173	7.36009	7.02358	6.71008
11	9.78685	9.25262	8.76048	8.30641	7.88687	7.49867	7.13896
12	10.57534	9.95400	9.38507	8.86325	8.38384	7.94269	7.53608
15	12.84926	11.93794	11.11839	10.37966	9.71225	9.10791	8.55948
20	16.35143	14.87747	13.59033	12.46221	11.46992	10.59401	9.81815
30	22.39646	19.60044	17.29203	15.37245	13.76483	12.40904	11.25778
40	27.35548	23.11477	19.79277	17.15909	15.04630	13.33171	11.92461
50	31.42361	25.72976	21.48218	18.25593	15.76186	13.80075	12.23348
60	34.76089	27.67556	22.62349	18.92929	16.16143	14.03918	12.37655

Periods (n)	9%	10%	11%	12%	14%	15%
1	0.91743	0.90909	0.90090	0.89286	0.87719	0.86957
2	1.75911	1.73554	1.71252	1.69005	1.64666	1.62571
3	2.53129	2.48685	2.44371	2.40183	2.32163	2.28323
4	3.23972	3.16987	3.10245	3.03735	2.91371	2.85498
5	3.88965	3.79079	3.69590	3.60478	3.43308	3.35216
6	4.48592	4.35526	4.23054	4.11141	3.88867	3.78448
7	5.03295	4.86842	4.71220	4.56376	4.28830	4.16042
8	5.53482	5.33493	5.14612	4.96764	4.63886	4.48732
9	5.99525	5.75902	5.53705	5.32825	4.94637	4.77158
10	6.41766	6.14457	5.88923	5.65022	5.21612	5.01877
11	6.80519	6.49506	6.20652	5.93770	5.45273	5.23371
12	7.16073	6.81369	6.49236	6.19437	5.66029	5.42062
15	8.06069	7.60608	7.19087	6.81086	6.14217	5.84737
20	9.12855	8.51356	7.96333	7.46944	6.62313	6.25933
30	10.27365	9.42691	8.69379	8.05518	7.00266	6.56598
40	10.75736	9.77905	8.95105	8.24378	7.10504	6.64178
50	10.96168	9.91481	9.04165	8.30450	7.13266	6.66051
60	11.04799	9.96716	9.07356	8.32405	7.14011	6.66515

TABLE 6 Present value of an annuity due of $1

Periods (n)	2%	3%	4%	5%	6%	7%	8%
1	1.00000	1.00000	1.00000	1.00000	1.00000	1.00000	1.00000
2	1.98039	1.97087	1.96154	1.95238	1.94340	1.93458	1.92593
3	2.94156	2.91347	2.88609	2.85941	2.83339	2.80802	2.78326
4	3.88388	3.82861	3.77509	3.72325	3.67301	3.62432	3.57710
5	4.80773	4.71710	4.62990	4.54595	4.46511	4.38721	4.31213
6	5.71346	5.57971	5.45182	5.32948	5.21236	5.10020	4.99271
7	6.60143	6.41719	6.24214	6.07569	5.91732	5.76654	5.62288
8	7.47199	7.23028	7.00205	6.78637	6.58238	6.38929	6.20637
9	8.32548	8.01969	7.73274	7.46321	7.20979	6.97130	6.74664
10	9.16224	8.78611	8.43533	8.10782	7.80169	7.51523	7.24689
11	9.98259	9.53020	9.11090	8.72173	8.36009	8.02358	7.71008
12	10.78685	10.25262	9.76048	9.30641	8.88687	8.49867	8.13896
15	13.10625	12.29607	11.56312	10.89864	10.29498	9.74547	9.24424
20	16.67846	15.32380	14.13394	13.08532	12.15812	11.33560	10.60360
30	22.84438	20.18845	17.98371	16.14107	14.59072	13.27767	12.15841
40	27.90259	23.80822	20.58448	18.01704	19.94907	14.26493	12.87858
50	32.05208	26.50166	22.34147	19.16872	16.70757	14.76680	13.21216
60	35.45610	28.50583	23.52843	19.87575	17.13111	15.02192	13.36668

Periods (n)	9%	10%	11%	12%	14%	15%
1	1.00000	1.00000	1.00000	1.00000	1.00000	1.00000
2	1.91743	1.90909	1.90090	1.89286	1.87719	1.86957
3	2.75911	2.73554	2.71252	2.69005	2.64666	2.62571
4	3.53129	3.48685	3.44371	3.40183	3.32163	3.28323
5	4.23972	4.16987	4.10245	4.03735	3.91371	3.85498
6	4.88965	4.79079	4.69590	4.60478	4.43308	4.35216
7	5.48592	5.35526	5.23054	5.11141	4.88867	4.78448
8	6.03295	5.86842	5.71220	5.56376	5.28830	5.16042
9	6.53482	6.33493	6.14612	5.96764	5.63886	5.48732
10	6.99525	6.75902	6.53705	6.32825	5.94637	5.77158
11	7.41766	7.14457	6.88923	6.65022	6.21612	6.01877
12	7.80519	7.49506	7.20652	6.93770	6.45273	6.23371
15	8.78615	8.36669	7.98187	7.62817	7.00207	6.72448
20	9.95011	9.36492	8.83929	8.36578	7.55037	7.19823
30	11.19828	10.36961	9.65011	9.02181	7.98304	7.55088
40	11.72552	10.75696	9.93567	9.23303	8.09975	7.63805
50	11.94823	10.90630	10.03624	0.30104	8.13123	7.65959
60	12.04231	10.96387	10.07165	9.32294	8.13972	7.66492

Appendix C
Quality of Earnings Cases: A Comprehensive Review

CASE 1: LIBERTY MANUFACTURING

You have recently been hired by Capital City Bank as a credit analyst. One of the tasks of your new position is to review the financial statements submitted by loan applicants. You have been instructed to assess the solvency and earning power of the applicants as well as the quality and persistence of the reported earnings number. After completing your analysis, you should report your conclusions to your supervisor, recommending whether the applicant should be further considered for the loan and why.

Company Description

You are now asked to review the file of a loan applicant, Liberty Manufacturing, which has applied for a long-term $500,000 loan. This company is a medium-sized, family-run operation that manufactures a component used in a wide variety of engines. Liberty has been in existence for approximately twenty years and has grown consistently during that time, reporting profits in each of the last ten years. The company has recently begun to move into foreign markets and is seeking the loan to finance investments in property, plant, and equipment and to complete the acquisition of a small foreign supplier, Packer Technical.

The demand for Liberty's product seems stable, and the company has made recent technical advancements in product design that may lead to increased sales in the future. At present, the company appears to hold a solid position in its industry. Prices in the industry, both input and output, have been rising at an above-average rate, and the industrywide inflation rate in 2002 was approximately 5 percent.

Note from Your Supervisor

Contained in the file is a note from your supervisor, Anne Mayor, who has made a cursory review of the financial statements. In addition to your task of assessing Liberty's solvency, earning power, and quality and persistence of the reported earnings number, she raises several other points that you should address in your report.

First, Anne would like you to closely examine the investing activities entered into by Liberty in late 2001 and during 2002. It seems that the company both acquired and sold property, plant, and equipment, land, and short-term investments. It also made a large investment in an affiliate company, Packer, which it intends to increase with the proceeds from the loan under consideration. Is Packer a profitable company, and will this be a prudent investment? Perhaps your analysis can shed some light on why the company entered into these transactions and how they affect the financial statements.

Anne also notes that there were large changes in the accounts receivable, inventory, and accounts payable balances, and suggests that you should pay particular attention to these developments. With respect to receivables, for example, she wonders just how much cash was generated from customers and what was the dollar value of the actual bad debt write-offs during the year. Is the allowance for uncollectibles sufficient?

Finally, Anne is curious about the foreign currency translation gain reported by Liberty. Specifically, she wonders whether it can be considered persistent and what exchange rate between German deutsche marks and U.S. dollars as of the balance sheet date gave rise to the $12,500 gain.

Financial Statements

The financial statements and selected additional information are provided below and on the following pages. Based upon this information only, prepare a report for your supervisor. The following financial statements have been audited by a major public accounting firm and have received an unqualified opinion. Dollar amounts on the statements are in thousands.

ADDITIONAL INFORMATION

Short-Term Investments. Short-term investments are carried at market value and consist solely of an investment in a single firm, Fredericks Ltd., which has 500,000 shares outstanding. As of December 31, 2001, Liberty held 40,000 shares, which cost $2 per share when they were acquired in 2001, and all shares are accounted for as available-for-sale securities. On December 16, 2002, Liberty sold all 40,000 shares for $3 per share. The price remained constant for the next few days, and on December 20, Liberty purchased 46,667 Fredericks shares.

Receivables. Uncollectibles on accounts receivable are accounted for under the allowance method. On December 1, 2002, Liberty completed a service for Bundes A.G., a manufacturer located in Germany. Liberty received a note from Bundes promising a payment of 100,000 German deutsche marks within thirty days. On December 1, 2001, two deutsche marks exchanged for one U.S. dollar.

Inventories. The last-in, first-out (LIFO) method is used, and inventories are carried at the lower-of-cost-or-market value. Inventories at December 31, 2001, consisted of 10,000 units @ $6 each, 10,000 units @ $3 each, and 30,000 units @ $1 each. Inventory costs have risen consistently in recent years. During 2002, 50,000 units were sold @ $10 each, and 25,000 units were purchased @ $8 each. For reporting purposes Liberty uses the periodic inventory method.

Investments. On December 20, 2001, Liberty purchased a tract of land for $40,000; it sold the land on December 18, 2002. On January 2, 2002, Liberty purchased 100,000 shares of Packer Technical @ $2.50 per share. Packer has 250,000 shares outstanding (including those held by Liberty). As of December 31, 2002, the share price of Packer shares had fallen to $2 per share.

Property, Plant, and Equipment. Property, plant, and equipment is depreciated using the straight-line method.

Outstanding Debts. Interest rates on outstanding loans range from 9 percent to 12 percent.

Liberty Manufacturing
Statement of Cash Flows
For the Period Ended December 31, 2002

Operating activities:		
Net income	$ 79.5	
Depreciation	50.0	
Realized gain on short-term investments	(40.0)	
Gain on sale of plant	(5.0)	
Gain on sale of land	(2.0)	
Income not received in cash on equity investment	(15.0)	
Increase in net accounts receivable	(130.0)	
Decrease in inventory	95.0	
Increase in notes receivable	(62.5)	
Increase in accounts payable	60.0	
Net cash from operating activities		$ 30.0
Investing activities:		
Investment in property, plant, and equipment	$ (60.0)	
Sale of plant	7.0	
Investment in affiliate	(250.0)	
Sale of land	42.0	
Investment in short-term securities	(140.0)	
Sale of short-term securities	120.0	
Net cash used by investing activities		(281.0)
Financing activities:		
Issuance of long-term note	$ 300.0	
Payment of dividend	(30.0)	
Net cash from financing activities		270.0
Increase in cash		$ 19.0
Beginning cash balance		10.0
Ending cash balance		$ 29.0

Liberty Manufacturing
Statement of Retained Earnings
For the Period Ended December 31, 2002

Beginning balance in retained earnings	$150.0
Plus: Net income	79.5
Less: Dividends	(30.0)
Ending balance in retained earnings	$199.5

Liberty Manufacturing
Balance Sheet
December 31, 2002

	2002	2001
ASSETS		
Cash	$ 29.0	$ 10.0
Short-term investments	140.0	84.0
Accounts receivable	275.0	150.0
Less: Allowance for uncollectibles	(5.0)	(10.0)
Notes receivable	62.5	0
Inventory	25.0	120.0
Investment in affiliate	265.0	0
Investment in land	0	40.0
Property, plant, and equipment	550.0	500.0
Less: Accumulated depreciation	(142.0)	(100.0)
Total assets	$1,199.5	$794.0
LIABILITIES AND STOCKHOLDERS' EQUITY		
Accounts payable	$ 110.0	$ 50.0
Other short-term payables	90.0	90.0
Long-term liabilities	600.0	300.0
Common stock	200.0	200.0
Unrealized price increase on available-for-sale investments	0	4.0
Retained earnings	199.5	150.0
Total liabilities and stockholders' equity	$1,199.5	$794.0

Liberty Manufacturing
Income Statement
For the Period Ended December 31, 2002

Revenues:		
Sales	$500.0	
Fees earned	50.0	$550.0
Cost of goods sold		295.0
Gross profit		$255.0
Miscellaneous operating expenses		(120.0)
Interest expense		(45.0)
Depreciation expense		(50.0)
Bad debt expense		(20.0)
Gain on sale of plant		5.0
Realized gain on short-term investments		40.0
Gain on sale of land		2.0
Income on equity investment		20.0
Foreign currency translation gain		12.5
Net income before taxes		$ 99.5
Income taxes		20.0
Net income		$ 79.5

CASE 2: MICROLINE CORPORATION

You work in the finance and investment department of Mega Industries, which recently purchased several small high-tech companies. An additional company, Microline Corporation, is presently under consideration. You have been asked to serve on a project team that is preparing a recommendation to the chief financial officer about whether Mega should attempt to acquire Microline. Your duty on this team is to review the company's financial statements and write a memo to the team leader, Sharon Sonneborn. The memo should analyze Microline's solvency position, earning power potential, and the extent to which the reported financial statements reflect the company's "true" financial position and performance. After a brief review of Microline, Sharon believes that you should also address in your report the following important questions:

1. Is there any evidence that management's bonus caused it to enter into any transactions, especially at year-end, that may not have been in the shareholders' interest?
2. Has the debt covenant imposed any restrictions that may have influenced any of management's reporting choices?
3. What was the acquisition price of Littleton when it was purchased by Microline?
4. Is Microline's bad debt allowance sufficient?
5. How much cash was received by Ellery Inc. during 2002, and what percentage of Ellery's total income was paid out in the form of dividends?
6. How much cash was collected from customers during 2002?

Microline's most recent financial statements are as follows (dollars in thousands).

Microline Corporation
Income Statements
For the Periods Ending December 31, 2002 and 2001

	2002	2001
Sales	$120,000	$105,000
Cost of goods sold	68,000	63,000
Gross profit	$ 52,000	$ 42,000
Selling and administrative expenses	(45,500)	(35,000)
Bad debt expense	(500)	(700)
Depreciation expense	(5,000)	(4,200)
Interest expense	(2,000)	(1,200)
Other gains (losses)	10,500	2,500
Net income before taxes	$ 9,500	$ 3,400
Income tax expense	3,000	1,600
Net income	$ 6,500	$ 1,800
Earnings per share	$ 0.26	$ 0.072

FOOTNOTES (DOLLARS IN THOUSANDS)

Short-Term Equity Investments. Short-term equity investments consist of trading securities and available-for-sale securities. The trading securities were valued at

Microline Corporation
Balance Sheets
December 31, 2002 and 2001

	2002	2001
ASSETS		
Cash	$ 2,400	$ 2,200
Short-term investments in equity securities	5,000	2,000
Accounts receivable (net)	11,400	7,300
Inventory	13,500	10,500
Prepaid interest expense	700	1,500
Total current assets	$ 33,000	$23,500
Investment in affiliate	12,000	10,000
Land	15,000	12,000
Property, plant, and equipment	40,000	35,000
Less: Accumulated depreciation	(8,000)	(6,000)
Goodwill	10,500	10,500
Total assets	$102,500	$85,000
LIABILITIES AND STOCKHOLDERS' EQUITY		
Accounts payable	$ 8,000	$ 6,000
Dividends payable	3,000	2,000
Miscellaneous payables	3,000	3,000
Unearned rent revenue	12,000	14,000
Total current liabilities	$ 26,000	$25,000
Long-term notes payable	29,000	15,000
Common stock	25,000	25,000
Accumulated unrealized revaluations on equity inv.	500	0
Retained earnings	22,000	20,000
Total liabilities & stockholders' equity	$102,500	$85,000

$4,000 and $1,500 as of December 31, 2002 and 2001, respectively. The available-for-sale securities consists of 50,000 common shares of Acme Inc. that were held throughout 2002. During 2002, equity investments classified as trading securities were actively traded, and related sales generated $2,000 in cash.

Accounts Receivable. The allowance for bad debts was $800 and $700 as of December 31, 2002 and 2001, respectively. Microline estimates bad debts as a percentage of credit sales.

Inventory. Microline carries inventories using the LIFO cost flow assumption and the lower-of-cost-or-market method. The LIFO reserve was $2,800 and $2,500 as of December 31, 2002 and 2001, respectively.

Equity Investments. Microline acquired 40 percent of the outstanding voting stock of Ellery Incorporated, a highly leveraged financial institution, at the beginning of 2001. The corporation paid an amount equal to 40 percent of Ellery's book value at the time of the acquisition and uses the equity method to account for this investment. During 2001, Ellery reported income of $2,000 and declared and paid dividends of $800.

**Microline Corporation
Statement of Cash Flows
For the Period Ending December 31, 2002**

Cash flows from operating activities:		
Net income	$ 6,500	
Depreciation	5,000	
Loss on sale of machinery	1,800	
Unrealized revaluation of equity investments	500	
Gain on sale of land	(3,000)	
Undistributed affiliate income	(2,000)	
Increase in accounts receivable (net)	(4,100)	
Increase in inventory	(3,000)	
Decrease in prepaid interest expense	800	
Increase in accounts payable	2,000	
Decrease in unearned rent revenue	(2,000)	
Net cash from operating activities		$ 2,500
Cash flows from investing activities:		
Purchases of plant and equipment	$(20,000)	
Purchases of land	(8,000)	
Proceeds from sale of machinery	10,200	
Proceeds from sale of land	8,000	
Net cash used by investing activities		(9,800)
Cash flows from financing activities:		
Increases in long-term notes (net)	$14,000	
Dividend payments	(3,500)	
Net cash from financing activities		10,500
Increase in cash and short-term equity investments		$ 3,200
Beginning balance in cash and short-term equity investments		4,200
Ending balance in cash and short-term equity investments		$ 7,400

Land. Microline deals in land as an investment. The land is carried on the balance sheet at cost. As of December 31, 2002, the market value of the land was approximately equal to its cost. As of December 31, 2001, the market value of the land was approximately $3,000 in excess of its cost. Land values remained constant throughout 2002. Near the end of the year, Microline sold one parcel of land and immediately purchased another similar parcel.

Property, Plant, and Equipment. Microline depreciates its plant and equipment using accelerated rates for both financial reporting and income tax purposes.

Goodwill. Microline has acquired only one company, Littleton Enterprises, since its inception. Goodwill was recognized on the acquisition in the amount by which the purchase price exceeded the fair market value of assets and liabilities of Littleton. At the time of the acquisition, the net fair market value of the assets and liabilities of Littleton was $15,000.

Other Gains (Losses). The following chart provides further details about the other gains (losses) that Microline recognized during 2002 and 2001.

	2002	2001
Rent revenue	$ 4,800	$3,200
Inventory write-down		(1,500)
Realized gains on short-term equity securities	800	
Unrealized gains on short-term equity securities	200	
Gain on sale of land	3,000	
Foreign exchange gain	1,000	
Income from affiliate	2,500	800
Loss on sale of machinery	(1,800)	
Total	$10,500	$2,500

Exchange Gain. On December 3, 2002, Microline sold goods to a customer in Germany and agreed to accept 8,000 deutsche marks in payment. The receivable was still outstanding as of December 31, 2002, at which time the exchange rate of deutsche marks to dollars was 1.6dm/$1. No other transactions were conducted outside U.S. borders during 2001 or 2002.

Short- and Long-Term Debt. On November 15, 2002, Microline signed a 90-day note payable in the amount of $8,000. As of December 31, 2002, this note was classified as long term because Microline intends to refinance it indefinitely. Microline also signed a long-term note in the amount of $6,000. This ten-year note includes an interest rate of 8 percent and requires that Microline maintain a current ratio of greater than 1.0 over the ten-year life.

Income Taxes. Microline's effective income tax rate is 34 percent.

Executive Compensation. At the end of each year, Microline's executives share equally in a bonus, which is equal to 25 percent of the dollar amount by which the corporation's net income exceeds 10 percent of the stockholders' equity dollar amount at the beginning of the year.

Revenue Recognition. All sales made by Microline are on credit, and Microline recognizes revenue when goods are shipped.

CASE 3: TECHNIC ENTERPRISES AND SONAR-SUN INC.

You are an investment analyst for Timken Brothers, a small brokerage firm. Recent developments in the medical equipment industry have caused a number of Timken's customers to inquire about two particular companies, Technic Enterprises and Sonar-Sun Incorporated. You have been asked to analyze the financial statements of these two companies and—on that basis only—rate them on a scale from 1 (very weak) to 10 (very strong) with respect to (1) solvency position, (2) earning power and persistence, and (3) earnings quality. In addition to the ratings, you have been asked to provide a memo stating why the ratings on these three dimensions do (or do not) differ between the two companies. The ratings and the memo will comprise part of a report that will be used by Timken's brokers to guide their buy/sell recommendations. The financial statements of Technic Enterprises and Sonar-Sun Inc. follow.

Technic Enterprises

The financial statements of Technic Enterprises and selected additional information are provided on the following pages. Dollar amounts are in thousands.

Technic Enterprises
Statement of Retained Earnings
For the Period Ended December 31, 2002

Beginning balance in retained earnings	$3,000
Plus: Net income	1,830
Less: Dividends	(830)
Ending balance in retained earnings	$4,000

Technic Enterprises
Statement of Cash Flows
For the Period Ended December 31, 2002

Operating activities:		
Net income	$ 1,830	
Depreciation	1,000	
Gains on short-term investments	(1,100)	
Gain on sale of building	(80)	
Gain on sale of land	(200)	
Equity income in excess of cash received	(300)	
Increase in net accounts receivable	(2,600)	
Decrease in inventory	1,300	
Increase in notes receivable	(1,250)	
Increase in accounts payable	1,700	
Increase in other short-term payables	600	
Net cash from operating activities		$ 900
Investing activities:		
Investment in property, plant, and equipment	$(1,040)	
Sale of building	120	
Investment in affiliate	(5,000)	
Investment in land	(700)	
Sale of land	1,000	
Investment in short-term investments	(2,800)	
Sale of short-term investments	2,400	
Net cash used by investing activities		(6,020)
Financing activities:		
Issuance of long-term note	$ 6,000	
Payment of dividend	(830)	
Net cash from financing activities		5,170
Increase in cash		$ 50
Beginning cash balance		200
Ending cash balance		$ 250

Technic Enterprises
Balance Sheets
December 31, 2002 and 2001

ASSETS	2002	2001
Cash	$ 250	$ 200
Short-term investments	2,900	1,600
Accounts receivable	5,500	3,000
Less: Allowance for uncollectibles	(100)	(200)
Notes receivable	1,250	0
Inventory	1,100	2,400
Total current assets	$10,900	$ 7,000
Investment in affiliate	5,300	0
Investment in land	700	800
Property, plant, and equipment	10,900	10,000
Less: Accumulated depreciation	(2,900)	(2,000)
Total assets	$24,900	$15,800

LIABILITIES AND STOCKHOLDERS' EQUITY	2002	2001
Accounts payable	$ 2,700	$ 1,000
Other short-term payables	2,400	1,800
Total current liabilities	$ 5,100	$ 2,800
Long-term liabilities	12,000	6,000
Common stock	4,000	4,000
Unrealized price decrease on short-term investments	(200)	0
Retained earnings	4,000	3,000
Total liabilities and stockholders' equity	$24,900	$15,800

Technic Enterprises
Income Statement
For the Period Ended December 31, 2002

Revenues:		
Sales	$10,000	
Fees earned	1,000	
Less: Bad debt charge	(400)	$10,600
Cost of goods sold		(5,900)
Gross profit		$ 4,700
Miscellaneous operating expenses		(2,400)
Interest expense		(900)
Depreciation expense		(1,000)
Income on equity investment		400
Miscellaneous gains and losses (net)		1,480
Net income before taxes and accounting change		$ 2,280
Income tax expense		700
Net income before accounting change		$ 1,580
Income effect of change in inventory costing method		250
Net income		$ 1,830

FOOTNOTES (DOLLARS IN THOUSANDS, EXCEPT PER SHARE AMOUNTS)

Revenue Recognition. All sales of inventory are on credit and are recorded in the sales account when goods are shipped. Services are exchanged for short-term notes and recorded in the fees earned account when the service is substantially complete.

Uncollectibles. The allowance method is used to account for bad debts, and accounts are written off when payment is not made within one year.

Notes Receivable. On November 15, 2002, Technic completed a service for Belton A.G., a manufacturer located in Germany. Technic received a note from Belton promising payment of 2,000 German deutsche marks within 30 days, and on that date two deutsche marks exchanged for one U.S. dollar. Technic has no other exposure to foreign currency exchange risk.

Short-Term Investments. Short-term investments are carried on the balance sheet at market value and consist of equity securities classified as either trading or available-for-sale. As of December 31, 2001, trading securities were valued at $1,300. During 2002, no available-for-sale securities were acquired or sold.

Inventory. Technic uses the first-in, first-out (FIFO) cost flow assumption and carries inventories at the lower-of-cost-or-market value. All inventory purchases are made on account and recorded as accounts payable.

In addition, during 2002, Technic changed the method used to allocate labor costs to cost of goods manufactured. To achieve a better matching of revenues and expenses, the company now allocates certain of these costs to inventory that previously were charged directly to operating expenses. The change increased 2002 net income by $250, net of applicable income taxes.

Investment in Affiliate. On January 30, 2001, Technic purchased 40 percent (50,000 shares) of the outstanding equity of Lehmon Financial Services @ $100.00 per share. No goodwill was recognized on the purchase. The information below refers to Lehmon Financial Services.

	2002	2001
Assets	$9,900.00	$8,300.00
Liabilities	8,300.00	7,500.00
Stockholders' equity	1,600.00	800.00
Stock price per share (Dec. 31)	8.50	10.35

Land Investments. During 2001, Technic invested in ten equivalent parcels of land, paying approximately $80 for each parcel. In November of 2002, the company sold these parcels, but chose to repurchase seven of them in December, when it revised its estimate of future real estate appraisal rates.

Property, Plant, and Equipment. Technic uses the straight-line method of depreciation and depreciates property, plant, and equipment over time periods ranging from five to forty years.

Miscellaneous Gains and Losses. Miscellaneous gains and losses consist of the following items:

Write-down of inventory to market value	$ (150)
Gain on sale of building	80
Realized gain on short-term investments	800
Unrealized gain on short-term investments	300
Gain on sale of land	200
Foreign currency translation gain	250
Total	$1,480

Additional Information. Interest rates on outstanding loans range from 6 percent to 10 percent, and general inflation during 2002 was approximately 5 percent. The company's effective income tax rate is 34 percent.

Sonar-Sun Inc.

The financial statements of Sonar-Sun Inc. and selected additional information are provided on the following pages. Dollar amounts are in thousands.

Sonar-Sun Inc.
Statement of Cash Flows
For the Period Ended December 31, 2002

Operating activities:		
Net income	$20,700	
Depreciation	10,000	
Write-down of equipment	2,000	
Dividends received over income from affiliates	700	
Increase in accounts receivable	(3,500)	
Increase in prepaid insurance	(1,000)	
Increase in inventory	(6,000)	
Increase in accounts payable	11,000	
Increase in unearned revenues	10,000	
Increase in other short-term payables	1,000	
Net cash from operating activities		$44,900
Investing activities:		
Investments in equity securities	$(2,000)	
Acquisition of Wallingford Atlantic	(24,000)	
Sale of real estate	2,000	
Net cash used by investing activities		(24,000)
Financing activities:		
Issuance of common stock	$ 5,000	
Dividends paid	(20,000)	
Net cash used by financing activities		(15,000)
Increase in cash balance		$ 5,900
Beginning cash balance		2,600
Ending cash balance		$ 8,500

Sonar-Sun Inc.
Income Statement
For the Period Ended December 31, 2002

Sales	$145,000
Revenues from services	35,000
Income from affiliate	4,000
Cost of goods sold	(63,000)
Operating expenses	(65,000)
Depreciation expense	(10,000)
Bad debt expense	(1,000)
Write-downs	(5,000)
Loss on translation of foreign currencies	(1,500)
Interest expense	(5,800)
Net income before taxes	$ 32,700
Income tax expense	(12,000)
Net income	$ 20,700

Sonar-Sun Inc.
Balance Sheet
December 31, 2002 and 2001

	2002	2001
ASSETS		
Cash	$ 8,500	$ 2,600
Accounts receivable (net)	17,200	13,700
Inventory	39,000	33,000
Prepaid insurance	4,000	3,000
Total current assets	$ 68,700	$ 52,300
Equity investments	7,000	4,000
Investments in affiliate	11,300	12,000
Real estate	28,000	25,000
Property, plant, and equipment (net)	44,000	37,000
Goodwill	13,000	8,000
Total assets	$172,000	$138,300
LIABILITIES AND STOCKHOLDERS' EQUITY		
Accounts payable	$ 24,000	$ 13,000
Dividends payable	12,000	13,000
Unearned revenues	15,000	5,000
Other payables	15,000	14,000
Total current liabilities	$ 66,000	$ 45,000
Long-term bank notes	45,000	40,000
Common stock	20,000	15,000
Unrealized price increase on equity investments	1,000	0
Retained earnings	40,000	38,300
Total liabilities and stockholders' equity	$172,000	$138,300

FOOTNOTES (DOLLARS IN THOUSANDS)

Revenue Recognition. All sales of inventory are made on account. Sonar-Sun recognizes revenue on such sales when goods are shipped. Revenues on services, where cash is received in advance, are estimated at year-end, based on the extent to which the service is completed.

Accounts Receivable. Sonar-Sun uses the allowance method to account for uncollectible accounts. The dollar value in the allowance account as of the end of 2002 was $800. Outstanding receivables are written off when they are deemed uncollectible, and during 2002, $500 of such accounts were removed from the books.

Inventory. Inventory is carried at the lower-of-cost-or-market rule using the last-in, first-out (LIFO) inventory cost flow assumption. Current costs of the inventory as of the end of 2002 and 2001 were $45,000 and $37,000, respectively.

Equity Investments. Equity investments listed as noncurrent are considered available-for-sale securities. No sales of such securities were made during 2002.

Investment in Affiliate. Sonar-Sun owns 25 percent of the outstanding voting stock of EDM Suppliers, and this investment is carried on the financial statements under the equity method.

Property, Plant, and Equipment. Sonar-Sun uses accelerated methods to depreciate its plant and equipment for both reporting and tax purposes. At the end of 2002 and 2001, accumulated depreciation totaled $12,000 and $8,000, respectively.

Wholly Owned Subsidiaries. Sonar-Sun owns 100 percent of the outstanding voting stock of two companies: Kenworth South and Wallingford Atlantic. The stock of Kenworth South was purchased for cash on January 1, 1999. The stock of Wallingford Atlantic was purchased near the end of 2002. The purchase price consisted of $24,000 in cash and a $5,000 long-term note. Wallingford was comprised of machinery and real estate only.

Write-Downs. Sonar-Sun reduced the book value of its inventory by $3,000 to replacement cost in accordance with the lower-of-cost-or-market rule. It also wrote off certain equipment at a book loss of $2,000.

Foreign Currency. Sonar-Sun purchases a considerable portion of its inventory from a French supplier, paying its accounts in French francs. Certain accounts payable owed to this supplier were revalued as of year-end to reflect the advance of the French franc against the dollar from 6 francs per dollar to 5 francs per dollar.

Income Taxes. Sonar-Sun's effective tax rate is 34 percent.

CASE 4: AVERY CORPORATION

Tracy Sellers, a retired musical artist, and his two brothers own a substantial amount of the outstanding common stock of Avery Corporation, a young and fast-growing manufacturer of cartons, containers, and a wide variety of packaging materials. The company's home office is in Cleveland, Ohio, and regional sales offices are operating at several locations across the United States.

   Tracy and his brothers, who recently inherited the stock from their aunt, know very little about the business. Just a few days ago, each received the company's 2002 annual report, and Tracy plans to attend the annual stockholders' meeting in

Cleveland, scheduled next month. He would also like to take an active part at the meeting—representing both his own and his brothers' interests—especially because doubts about the quality of the company's board of directors and management have recently been raised. However, he knows very little about analyzing annual report information and has hired you to help him prepare for the meeting.

Tracy begins by showing you Avery's 2002 annual report, which includes a letter from Avery's chief executive officer, Arnold Tennenden, a set of consolidated financial statements, and the related footnotes. He cautions you that he wonders whether the CEO's letter accurately characterizes the company's performance and financial position, and he is asking you to ascertain whether this letter reasonably represents Avery's financial situation. Tracy suspects that many of the comments made by Arnold at the upcoming stockholders' meeting will be similar to those contained in the annual report letter, and he hopes to be able to accurately evaluate and respond to them. The CEO's letter is provided below.

Letter from the Chief Executive Officer

To the Shareholders:

Avery has just completed another successful year, demonstrating strong earning power. Total revenues increased by almost 8 percent, and profits increased by a whopping 30 percent. The profit rise would have been even greater had management chosen not to record a highly unusual $5 million write-off due to the obsolescence of certain inventory items.

The company used the cash generated from these earnings to make an important acquisition, to increase its investment in property, plant, and equipment, and to increase common shareholder dividends. Indeed, Avery has grown substantially in this recent year and the shareholders have prospered. It is particularly impressive that Avery has been able to maintain its rate of growth without relying heavily on debt financing. The company's debt/equity ratio as of the end of 2002 is only 0.65, and profits are more than adequate to cover debt interest payments.

In sum, I am proud to report to you that Avery is an extremely solvent company with great earning power potential. Management plans to keep it that way far into the future.

Arnold Tennenden
Chief Executive Officer

Tracy has also attempted to review the statements himself, and in addition to evaluating the CEO's letter, he would like you to answer the questions listed below.

1. Why did the company's 2002 earnings-per-share number decrease even though net income seems to have increased?
2. How many shares of stock were issued in the 2002 stock dividend, and how did this issuance affect the assets and liabilities of the company?
3. Is it likely that the company will exercise its option to call its outstanding bonds in the near future? Why?
4. The company's debt/equity ratio as of December 31, 2002, is only 0.65. Is that ratio an accurate measure of the company's actual debt position?
5. Is the 2002 sales number disclosed in the footnotes a measure of the cash collected from customers during 2002? If not, how much cash was actually collected from customers in that year? How much cash was paid in 2002 to Avery's suppliers for inventory purchases?

6. Inventory and accounts receivable levels have increased dramatically over the past two years. Is that a positive sign?
7. Are the elements that make up the increase in profits from 2001 to 2002 likely to persist in future years?
8. What was the value of Buckeye's property, plant, and equipment when Buckeye was acquired by Avery in 2002?
9. What was the book value of the equipment that was sold by Avery in December of 2002?
10. How much cash did Avery contribute to its pension fund during 2001?

Avery Corporation
Consolidated Statement of Cash Flows
(in thousands of dollars)
For the Years Ended December 31, 2002 and 2001

	2002	2001
Operating activities:		
Net income	$ 7,333	$ 5,626
Depreciation	5,000	5,000
Inventory write-down	5,000	—
Income in excess of cash from affiliate	(1,050)	(900)
Amortization of bond discount	467	424
Gain from sale of property, plant, and equipment	(6,000)	—
Deferred income taxes	(41)	476
Increase (decrease) in unfunded pension liability	2,000	3,000
(Increase) decrease in net accounts receivable	(9,950)	(9,950)
(Increase) decrease in inventory	(15,000)	(15,000)
Increase (decrease) in accounts payable	7,800	2,200
Increase (decrease) in accrued payables	8,000	(1,700)
Increase (decrease) in unearned revenues	(8,000)	8,000
Net cash used by operating activities	$ (4,441)	$ (2,824)
Investing activities:		
Cash payments for acquisitions	$(50,000)	$ —
Cash payments for equipment purchases	(14,000)	—
Cash from equipment sales	20,000	—
Net cash used by investing activities	$(44,000)	$ 0
Financing activities:		
Cash from preferred stock issuance	$ —	$80,000
Cash from exercise of executive stock options	10,000	—
Cash payments for treasury stock purchases	—	(18,000)
Cash payments for dividends	(6,000)	(4,000)
Net cash from financing activities	$ 4,000	$58,000
Increase (decrease) in cash balance	$(44,441)	$55,176
Beginning cash balance	58,676	3,500
Ending cash balance	$ 14,235	$58,676

Footnotes to the Financial Statements

1. Revenue Recognition. The company recognizes revenue when goods are shipped, and all sales are made on credit. The dollar amounts for operating revenues

Avery Corporation
Consolidated Balance Sheet
(in thousands of dollars)
December 31, 2002, 2001, and 2000

	2002	2001	2000
ASSETS			
Cash plus marketable securities	$ 14,235	$ 58,676	$ 3,500
Accounts receivable	45,000	35,000	25,000
Less: Allowance for uncollectibles	(600)	(550)	(500)
Inventory	55,000	45,000	30,000
Investment in affiliate	11,950	10,900	10,000
Property, plant, and equipment	94,000	50,000	50,000
Less: Accumulated depreciation	(19,000)	(20,000)	(15,000)
Goodwill	15,000	—	—
Total assets	$215,585	$179,026	$103,000
LIABILITIES AND STOCKHOLDERS' EQUITY			
Accounts payable	$ 16,000	$ 8,200	$ 6,000
Accrued payables	14,000	6,000	7,700
Unearned revenues	—	8,000	—
Unfunded pension liability	7,339	5,339	2,339
Bonds payable	50,000	50,000	50,000
Less: Unamortized discount	(4,868)	(5,335)	(5,759)
Deferred income taxes	3,155	3,196	2,720
Preferred stock	50,000	50,000	—
Common stock	5,350	5,000	5,000
Additional paid-in capital	64,900	55,000	25,000
Retained earnings	27,709	31,626	30,000
Less: Treasury stock	(18,000)	(38,000)	(20,000)
Total liabilities and stockholders' equity	$215,585	$179,026	$103,000

Avery Corporation
Consolidated Statement of Stockholders' Equity
(in thousands of dollars)
For the Years Ended December 31, 2002 and 2001

TRANSACTION	PREFERRED STOCK	COMMON STOCK	ADDITIONAL PAID-IN CAPITAL	RETAINED EARNINGS	TREASURY STOCK
Beginning balance (12/31/00)	$ 0	$5,000	$25,000	$30,000	$(20,000)
Net income				5,626	
Cash dividends				(4,000)	
Issue of preferred stock	50,000		30,000		
Purchase of treasury stock					(18,000)
Ending balance (12/31/01)	$50,000	$5,000	$55,000	$31,626	$(38,000)
Net income				7,333	
Preferred stock dividend				(6,000)	
Exercise of stock options					10,000
Issue for acquisition			5,000		10,000
Stock dividend		350	4,900	(5,250)	
Ending balance (12/31/02)	$50,000	$5,350	$64,900	$27,709	$(18,000)

Avery Corporation
Consolidated Income Statement
(in thousands of dollars, except per-share numbers)
For the Years Ended December 31, 2002 and 2001

	2002	2001
Operating revenues	$130,800	$121,500
Less: Cost of goods sold	(60,500)	(60,000)
Selling and administrative expenses	(23,000)	(25,000)
Depreciation expense	(5,000)	(5,000)
Accrued pension expense	(10,000)	(8,000)
Bad debt expense	(500)	(450)
Operating lease expense	(10,000)	(10,000)
Net income from operations	$ 21,800	$ 13,050
Loss due to inventory write-down	(5,000)	—
Interest expense	(4,467)	(4,424)
Pretax income from continuing operations	$ 12,333	$ 8,626
Income tax expense	5,000	3,000
Net income	$ 7,333	$ 5,626
Earnings per share:		
From continuing operations	$ 3.20	$ 3.75
Due to extraordinary loss	(1.30)	—
Total	$ 1.90	$ 3.75

reported on the consolidated statement of income include the following items (dollars are in thousands):

Item	2002	2001
Sales	$115,000	$120,000
Income from affiliate	1,800	1,500
Gain on sale of equipment	6,000	—
Special services	8,000	—
Total	$130,800	$121,500

2. Inventory. Inventory is carried at lower of cost or market under the first-in, first-out cost flow assumption. Inventory purchase costs have risen consistently over the past several years. The company wrote off certain inventories during 2002 due to obsolescence.

3. Property, Plant, and Equipment. Property, plant, and equipment are carried at cost less accumulated depreciation. Depreciation is calculated on a straight-line basis, assuming no salvage value and a ten-year useful life. In December of 2002, the company sold equipment with a cost of $20 million and soon thereafter purchased additional equipment for $14 million.

4. Acquisitions. In December of 2000, the company acquired 30 percent of the outstanding common stock of Spartan Savings, a highly leveraged financial institution, for $10 million. The company has held this interest through December of 2002.

In early December of 2002, the company acquired 100 percent of the outstanding common stock of Buckeye Corporation, which consisted primarily of property, plant, and equipment and goodwill. The purchase price included $50 million cash and 1,000,000 shares of the company's common stock, which had been held in treasury. The stock had a market value at the time of the acquisition of $15 per share.

5. Employee Pension. The amount of pension expense accrued each year is based on a number of actuarial assumptions regarding the life expectancy of the current workforce and other factors. Payments to the pension fund have met all regulatory requirements.

6. Bond Issuance. In January of 2000, the company issued 5,000 bonds, each with a face value of $1,000, a stated interest rate of 8 percent, and a maturity date of January 2003. The bonds sold for $877.10 each, producing an effective interest rate of 10 percent. The terms of the issuance state that beginning in 2003, and thereafter, the company can call the bonds for 2 percent above the face value. Current market interest rates are 8 percent.

7. Deferred Income Taxes. The deferred income tax account arises solely from the company's choice to use straight-line depreciation for financial reporting purposes and double-declining-balance for income tax reporting purposes. For both purposes property, plant, and equipment are assumed to have a ten-year life and no salvage value. The company's effective tax rate is 0.38.

8. Leases. The company leases certain facilities in which operations are conducted. Under the lease contract, the company is responsible for maintenance and can acquire the leased properties at the end of the lease term for an amount that is equal to 50 percent of the market value at that time. The current lease was entered into in January of 1999 and will expire in January of 2009. Lease payments are set at $10 million per year over the period of the lease.

9. Stock Transactions. In 2000, the company was authorized to issue 10,000,000 shares of $1 par-value common stock, and it chose to issue 5,000,000 shares for a price of $6 per share. Later that year, the company repurchased 2,000,000 of these shares for $10 per share and held them in treasury. Additional treasury shares were purchased in 2001 for $12 per share.

In December of 2001, the company issued 1,000,000 shares of $50 par-value preferred stock for $80 per share. Annual dividend payments are set at 12 percent of par value, and the shares are callable at par value by the company in 2006. There are 1,000,000 authorized but unissued shares of preferred stock.

Company executives are paid bonuses in the form of options to purchase common stock. In 2002, 1,000,000 options were exercised. Five million options are outstanding as of December 31, 2002.

10. Stock Dividend. At the end of 2002, the company declared and issued a 10 percent stock dividend on all outstanding common shares. At the time of the issuance, the common stock had a market value of $15 per share.

CASE 5: ZENITH CREATIONS

It is early in January 2003. You have just been hired by Zenith Creations and assigned to the accounting department. The company specializes in creative sales displays used to market point-of-purchase goods, and it has several large customers that annually hire Zenith to design and manufacture displays for retail outlets. The company has grown quickly and recently has moved from a pure manufacturing firm to one that provides both manufacturing and creative services. In fact, the company's name was just changed from Zenith Manufacturing.

Recently, two giant companies in the industry have shown a serious interest in acquiring Zenith, which has caused Zenith's management to be particularly concerned with how the financial statements are interpreted by outside parties—especially the potential buyers, who will likely base their offers on assessments of Zenith's financial condition and performance. At the same time, management is considering several actions and wants to know in advance how these actions will affect the financial statements, financial ratios, and outsider evaluations of Zenith's financial condition and performance. The actions are listed below.

*   Purchase treasury stock at the current market price.
*   Write off a relatively large uncollectible accounts receivable.
*   Issue a 20 percent stock dividend.
*   Redeem the remaining notes payable for $23,200,000.
*   Sell the real estate received in the acquisition of Lyon Real Estate for $12,000,000.
*   Change the inventory cost flow assumption from LIFO to FIFO.

Your supervisor has asked you to prepare a memo that will be part of a report presented to Zenith's board of directors concerning the possible acquisition. Your memo should consist of two parts: (1) an objective evaluation of Zenith's financial condition and performance, and (2) an assessment of how each of the actions listed above will affect that evaluation. Zenith's financial statements and related footnotes are contained on the following pages.

Zenith Creations
Consolidated Income Statement
(in thousands of dollars, except per-share numbers)
For the Years Ended December 31, 2002 and 2001

	2002	2001
Operating revenues	$109,800	$125,800
Less: Cost of goods sold	(47,000)	(52,000)
Selling and administrative expenses	(27,000)	(23,000)
Depreciation expense	(6,000)	(5,000)
Accrued pension expense	(8,000)	(7,500)
Bad debt expense	(1,500)	(1,000)
Operating lease expense	(8,000)	(8,000)
Net income from operations	$ 12,300	$ 29,300
Interest expense	(3,848)	(3,771)
Loss on inventory write-down	(2,000)	—
Restructuring charge	(15,000)	—
Pretax income (loss) from continuing operations	$ (8,548)	$ 25,529
Income tax expense	500	6,000
Net income (loss) from continuing operations	$ (9,048)	$ 19,529
Extraordinary loss due to debt retirement	2,462	—
Net income (loss)	$(11,510)	$ 19,529
Earnings (loss) per share:		
From continuing operations	$ (1.24)	$ 1.86
Due to extraordinary loss	(.23)	—
Total (excludes stock dividend)	$ (1.47)	$ 1.86

Zenith Creations
Consolidated Balance Sheet
(in thousands of dollars)
December 31, 2002, 2001, and 2000

	2002	2001	2000
ASSETS			
Cash plus marketable securities	$ 43,933	$ 30,260	$ 3,500
Accounts receivable	15,900	16,800	28,000
Less: Allowance for uncollectibles	(1,400)	(800)	(1,000)
Inventory	22,500	23,500	30,500
Investment in affiliate	4,900	5,600	6,000
Property, plant, and equipment	82,000	85,000	60,000
Less: Accumulated depreciation	(14,000)	(20,000)	(15,000)
Goodwill	20,000	20,000	—
Total assets	$173,833	$160,360	$112,000
LIABILITIES AND STOCKHOLDERS' EQUITY			
Accounts payable	$ 19,000	$ 6,000	$ 3,000
Accrued payables	14,700	9,700	7,700
Unearned revenues	4,000	8,000	5,000
Restructuring reserve	14,000	—	—
Unfunded pension liability	5,900	3,900	2,400
Notes payable	25,000	50,000	50,000
Less: Unamortized discount	(5,335)	(11,518)	(12,289)
Deferred income taxes	4,920	6,420	5,220
Preferred stock	12,500	—	—
Common stock ($1 par value)	13,555	12,500	10,000
Additional paid-in capital	61,605	47,500	25,000
Retained earnings	23,488	47,658	35,969
Less: Treasury stock	(19,500)	(19,800)	(20,000)
Total liabilities and stockholders' equity	$173,833	$160,360	$112,000

Footnotes to the Financial Statements (Dollar Amounts, Except per Share, in Thousands):

1. Revenue Recognition. The company recognizes revenue when goods are shipped or services are provided, and all sales are made on credit. The dollar amounts for operating revenues reported on the consolidated statement of income include the following items:

Item	2002	2001
Sales	$110,000	$120,000
Income (loss) from affiliate	(200)	800
Loss on sale of equipment	(4,000)	—
Special services	4,000	5,000
Total	$109,800	$125,800

2. Inventory. Inventory is carried at lower of cost or market under the LIFO cost flow assumption. LIFO reserves for 2000, 2001, and 2002 are $1,400, $1,250, and

Zenith Creations
Consolidated Statement of Cash Flows
(in thousands of dollars)
For the Years Ended December 31, 2002 and 2001

	2002	2001
Operating activities:		
Net income (loss)	$(11,510)	$ 19,529
Depreciation	6,000	5,000
Affiliate distributions over earnings	700	400
Amortization of bond discount	848	771
Loss from sale of property, plant, and equipment	4,000	—
Loss on debt retirement	2,462	
Noncash restructuring charge	14,000	
Deferred income taxes	(1,500)	1,200
Increase (decrease) in unfunded pension liability	2,000	1,500
(Increase) decrease in net accounts receivable	1,500	11,000
(Increase) decrease in inventory	1,000	7,000
Increase (decrease) in accounts payable	13,000	3,000
Increase (decrease) in accrued payables	5,000	2,000
Increase (decrease) in unearned revenues	(4,000)	3,000
Net cash from operating activities	$ 33,500	$ 54,400
Investing activities:		
Cash payments for acquisitions	$ —	$(10,000)
Cash payments for equipment purchases	(15,000)	(10,000)
Cash from equipment sales	2,000	—
Net cash used by investing activities	$(13,000)	$(20,000)
Financing activities:		
Cash from preferred stock issuance	$ 15,000	$ —
Cash from exercise of executive stock options	300	160
Cash payment to retire debt	(22,127)	—
Cash payments for dividends	—	(7,800)
Net cash used by financing activities	$ (6,827)	$ (7,640)
Increase (decrease) in cash balance	$ 13,673	$ 26,760
Beginning cash balance	30,260	3,500
Ending cash balance	$ 43,933	$ 30,260

$1,100, respectively. The company has experienced LIFO liquidations in each of the three years, but the effects on income due to the liquidations have been immaterial. The company wrote off certain inventories at the end of 2002 due to obsolescence.

3. Property, Plant, and Equipment. Property, plant, and equipment are carried at cost less accumulated depreciation. Depreciation is calculated on a straight-line basis, assuming no salvage value and a ten-year useful life. During 2002, the company sold equipment with an original cost of $18,000.

4. Acquisitions. In January of 2000, the company acquired 40 percent of the outstanding common stock of University Services for $5,000. The company has held this equity interest through December of 2002.

In December of 2001, the company acquired 100 percent of the outstanding common stock of Lyon Real Estate, which consisted of land and goodwill. The purchase

Zenith Creations
Consolidated Statement of Stockholders' Equity
(in thousands of dollars)
For the Years Ended December 31, 2002 and 2001

TRANSACTION	PREFERRED STOCK	COMMON STOCK	ADDITIONAL PAID-IN CAPITAL	RETAINED EARNINGS	TREASURY STOCK
Beginning balance (12/31/00)	$ 0	$10,000	$25,000	$35,969	$(20,000)
Net income				19,529	
Cash dividends				(7,800)	
Issue for acquistition		2,500	22,500		
Exercise of stock options				(40)	200
Ending balance (12/31/01)	$ 0	$12,500	$47,500	$47,658	$(19,800)
Net loss				(15,510)	
Exercise of stock options					300
Issue of preferred stock	12,500		2,500		
Stock dividend		1,055	11,605	(12,660)	
Ending balance (12/31/02)	$12,500	$13,555	$61,605	$19,488	$(19,500)

price included $10,000 cash, and the company issued 2,500,000 shares of common stock. The stock had a market value at the time of the acquisition of $10 per share.

5. Employee Pension. The amount of pension expense accrued each year is based on a number of actuarial assumptions regarding the life expectancy of the current workforce and other factors. Payments to the pension fund have met all regulatory requirements.

6. Note Payable. In December of 2000, the company signed a note with a face value of $50,000, a stated interest rate of 6 percent, and a maturity date of December 2010. The annual effective interest rate is 10 percent, and the proceeds at issuance were $37,711. Half of the notes were redeemed in December 2002, and a loss of $2,462 was recognized on the redemption.

7. Deferred Income Taxes. The deferred income taxes are recognized on timing differences between taxable income and reported net income. The company's effective income tax rate is 35 percent.

8. Leases. The company leases certain facilities in which operations are conducted. Under the lease contract, the company is responsible for maintenance and can acquire the leased properties at the end of the lease term for an amount equal to 90 percent of the market value at that time. The current lease was entered into in January of 1996 and will expire in January of 2016. Lease payments are set at $8 million per year over the period of the lease.

9. Stock Transactions. The company is authorized to issue 25 million, $1 par value, common shares. During 2000, in its only treasury stock purchase, the company acquired 2 million shares at $10 each.

In December of 2001, the company issued 500,000 shares of $25 par value preferred stock for $30 per share. Annual dividend payments are set at 10 percent of par value, and the shares are callable at par value by the company after 2006. There are 500,000 authorized but unissued shares of preferred stock.

10. Executive Compensation. Company executives are paid bonuses in the form of options to purchase common stock. The option price is equal to the per share market price at the time options are issued to the executives. Certain of these options were exercised in 2002 and 2001.

11. Stock Dividend. At the end of 2002, the company declared and issued a 10 percent stock dividend on all outstanding common shares.

12. Restructuring. During 2002, the company began a major restructuring and chose to accrue certain future costs associated with employee layoffs, plant closings, and equipment replacement. A $15,000 charge was taken against 2002 income, and a restructuring reserve was established for the future costs. The portion of the reserve due to expected layoffs is considered a current liability.

CASE 6: PIERCE AND SNOWDEN

Pierce and Snowden is an established manufacturer of a wide variety of household items that are sold through retailers all over the United States. Wellington Mart and Wagner Stores, two retailers, have recently expressed an interest in carrying a number of Pierce and Snowden products. While these two potential customers could generate considerable volume for the company, both retailers would require the extension of a significant amount of credit, and in general, retail sales throughout the United States have been somewhat slow for several years.

You work in the finance department of Pierce and Snowden and have been asked to serve on a team whose task is to make a recommendation to management about whether, or how much, credit should be extended to Wellington Mart and Wagner Stores. The recommendation in part will be based on the solvency position and earning power of these two companies.

Your assignment is to analyze the financial statements of these two companies and—on that basis only—rate them on a scale from 1–10 (weak to strong) with respect to solvency position, earning power and persistence, and earnings quality. In addition to the ratings, provide a memo to the team captain stating why the ratings on these three dimensions do (or do not) differ between the two companies. The financial statements of Wellington Mart and Wagner Stores follow.

Wellington Mart
Consolidated Statement of Stockholders' Equity
(in thousands of dollars)
For the Year Ended December 31, 2001

TRANSACTION	PREFERRED STOCK	COMMON STOCK	ADDITIONAL PAID-IN CAPITAL	RETAINED EARNINGS	TREASURY STOCK
Beginning balance (12/31/00)	$50,000	$20,000	$35,860	$44,680	$(36,080)
Net loss				(19,878)	
Stock dividend		2,100	8,400	(10,500)	
Stock issue for options			3,900		7,500
Stock issue for acquisition		6,000	24,000		
Ending balance (12/31/01)	$50,000	$28,100	$72,160	$14,302	$(28,580)

> **Wellington Mart**
> **Consolidated Balance Sheet**
> **(in thousands of dollars)**
> **December 31, 2001 and 2000**

	2001	2000
ASSETS		
Cash	$ 1,870	$ 2,650
Trading securities	2,000	3,500
Net accounts receivable	18,450	12,000
Inventory	4,200	15,800
Investment in affiliate	28,700	34,200
Investment in real estate	45,500	10,500
Buildings, machinery, and equipment	122,500	119,500
Less: Accumulated depreciation	(7,900)	(12,400)
Goodwill	45,000	—
Total assets	$260,320	$185,750
LIABILITIES AND STOCKHOLDERS' EQUITY		
Accounts payable	$ 22,400	$ 8,900
Accrued payables	25,200	11,200
Current maturities of long-term debts	6,100	6,100
Income tax liability	3,050	5,050
Long-term notes payable	26,100	12,200
Bonds payable	16,788	16,540
Retirement liability	6,200	—
Deferred income tax	9,500	11,300
Preferred stock	50,000	50,000
Common stock	28,100	20,000
Additional paid-in capital	72,160	35,860
Retained earnings	23,302	44,680
Less: Treasury stock	(28,580)	(36,080)
Total liabilities and stockholders' equity	$260,320	$185,750

Footnotes to the Financial Statements of Wellington Mart (Dollar Values, Except Per-Share Amounts, Are in Thousands)

1. Revenue Recognition. The company recognizes revenue when goods are shipped, and all sales are made on credit.

2. Other Revenues and Expenses. Other revenues and expenses consist of the following items (dollars in thousands):

Gain on sale of trading securities	$ 2,000
Unrealized gain on trading securities	500
Translation gain on outstanding accounts payable	1,500
Income from affiliate	2,500
Inventory write-down to market	(1,600)
Restructuring charge	(9,000)
Total	$(4,100)

Wellington Mart
Income Statement
(in thousands of dollars, except per-share numbers)
For the Year Ended December 31, 2001

	2001
Sales	$150,000
Cost of goods sold	(90,000)
Gross profit	$ 60,000
Selling and administrative expenses	(45,000)
Depreciation	(7,500)
Bad debt expense	(1,550)
Interest expense	(2,328)
Net loss from operations	$ (3,622)
Other revenues and expenses	(4,100)
Net loss before taxes	$ (478)
Income tax expense	(4,200)
Net loss before change in accounting method	$ (4,678)
Write-off due to change in accounting method	
(net of tax)	(6,200)
Net loss	$ (10,878)
Loss per outstanding common share:	
Before write-off due to change in accounting method	$ (5.49)
Write-off due to change in accounting method	(2.68)
Total	$ (8.17)

3. Trading Securities. In the only transaction involving trading securities during 2001, 50 common stock shares of Mammoth Corporation were sold in April.

4. Accounts Receivable. A further breakdown of the net accounts receivable balances is provided below.

	Gross Accounts Receivable	Allowance	Net
12/31/00	$12,300	$300	$12,000
12/31/01	19,400	950	18,450

5. Inventory. Inventory is carried at lower of cost or market under the LIFO cost flow assumption. Inventory purchase costs have remained relatively constant over the past several years. The LIFO reserve was $730 and $750 as of December 31, 2001 and 2000, respectively. The company wrote off certain inventories during 2001 due to obsolescence.

6. Affiliate. The company owns 49 percent of the outstanding voting stock of Ellery, Inc. A condensed balance sheet for Ellery as of December 31, 2001, is provided below (dollar amounts are in thousands).

Current assets	$24,000	Current liabilities		$21,000
Noncurrent assets	46,000	Long-term liabilities		35,000
		Stockholders' equity		14,000
Total assets	$70,000	Total liabilities and stockholders' equity		$70,000

Wellington Mart
Consolidated Statement of Cash Flows
For the Year Ended December 31, 2001

	2001	
Operating activities:		
Net loss	$(10,878)	
Depreciation	7,500	
Noncash restructuring charge	8,000	
Write-off due to change in accounting method	6,200	
Amortization of discount on bonds payable	248	
Dividends from affiliate (net of income recognized)	5,500	
Decrease in deferred income taxes	(1,800)	
Increase in net accounts receivable	(6,450)	
Decrease in inventory	11,600	
Increase in accounts payable	13,500	
Increase in accrued payables	14,000	
Decrease in income tax liability	(2,000)	
Net cash flow from operating activities		$45,420
Investing activities:		
Investment in buildings	$ (8,000)	
Investment in machinery and equipment	(15,000)	
Acquisition of Marilyn Real Estate	(50,000)	
Net cash flow used by investing activities		(73,000)
Financing activities:		
Increase in long-term notes payable	$13,900	
Stock issuances for exercised options	11,400	
Net cash flow from financing activities		25,300
Decrease in cash and trading securities		$ (2,280)
Beginning balance in cash and trading securities		6,150
Ending balance in cash and trading securities		$ 3,870

7. Buildings, Machinery, and Equipment.

Buildings, machinery, and equipment are carried at cost less accumulated depreciation. Depreciation is calculated on a straight-line basis over estimated useful lives ranging from five years for machinery and equipment to twenty years for buildings. The cost and related accumulated depreciation for buildings and for machinery and equipment are provided below.

	12/31/00	Increases	Decreases	12/31/01
Buildings:				
Cost	$65,000	$ 8,000	$20,000	$53,000
Accumulated depreciation	10,400	3,000	12,000	1,400
Machinery and equipment:				
Cost	54,500	15,000	—	69,500
Accumulated depreciation	2,000	4,500	—	6,500

In December of 2001, the company closed a plant with an original cost of $20,000. A loss, which included cash payments required to complete the closure, was recognized in 2001 as a restructuring charge.

8. Acquisitions. In January of 2001, the company acquired 100 percent of the outstanding common stock of Marilyn Real Estate. The company paid cash and issued 600,000 common shares to the shareholders of Marilyn in the acquisition, and the $80 million purchase price was allocated between real estate and goodwill.

9. Long-Term Debt. Long-term notes outstanding as of December 31, 2000, are being paid off in equal installments of $6,100, of which the current portion is listed as a current liability. The interest rate on these notes is approximately 5.5 percent, and the book value of the notes is approximately equal to the market value. An additional note payable was issued during 2001.

The outstanding bond liabilities listed on the balance sheet were issued on January 1, 1996. The bond issuance has a face value of $18,000, an annual stated interest rate (payable semiannually) of six percent, and a maturity date of December 31, 2005. The bonds were issued to yield an annual effective rate of return of eight percent. As of December 31, 2000, the annual market rate of interest on similar bond issuances was ten percent, and the company has the right to call the bonds any time after December 31, 2000, at face value. A covenant in the bond indenture requires that the company's ratio of total liabilities to total assets cannot exceed 0.60 during the term of the bonds.

10. Accounting Changes. The company recognized a large accrual for retirement costs at the end of 2001. The present value of the future liability associated with these costs was estimated, and the entire dollar amount of the liability was charged against income. Previously, the company accounted for these costs on the cash basis.

11. Deferred Income Taxes. Deferred income taxes are recognized on timing differences between income recognized for tax purposes and income for financial reporting purposes. Increases to the deferred tax liability arise primarily because the company uses straight-line depreciation for financial reporting purposes and accelerated depreciation for income tax reporting purposes. Decreases to the deferred income tax liability arose from charges to reported income for restructuring, retirement costs, inventory write-downs, and certain bad debt expenses. The company's effective tax rate for 2001 was 34 percent.

12. Stockholders' Equity Transactions. In December of 1999, the company issued 500,000 shares of eight percent preferred stock, each with a par value of $100. The shares are callable, cumulative, and nonparticipating. As of December 31, 2001, dividends in arrears on these shares totaled $4,000.

As of December 31, 2001, the company was authorized to issue 3,000,000 shares of $10 par value common stock; 2,810,000 have been issued; 2,310,000 were outstanding; and 500,000 were held in treasury. During 2001, the company issued 600,000 common shares in the acquisition of Marilyn Real Estate, issued 300,000 treasury shares to executives who exercised stock options, and on December 20, 2001, declared a ten percent common stock dividend.

13. Employee Pension. The company has a defined contribution pension plan that covers all employees, and the payments associated with this plan are expensed as incurred.

14. Leases. The company leases certain facilities in which operations are conducted. Under the lease contract, the company is responsible for maintenance, and at the end of the lease term, it can either acquire the leased properties for an amount equal to 25 percent of the market value or renew the contract. The current lease was entered into in January of 1998 and will expire in January of 2008. Required lease payments, included in selling and administrative expenses, are equal to $12 million per year over the period of the lease and are paid at the beginning of each period.

15. Contingencies. The company is currently under investigation by the Environmental Protection Agency for toxic waste management violations. In several cases, the company has been identified by the agency as a "potentially responsible party," and it is likely that the company will be required to clean up certain waste sites in the future. It is also possible that the company will be subject to certain fines and punitive damages. At this time, there is no way to reliably estimate these possible costs, which management believes to be somewhere between $1 million and $25 million.

Wagner Stores
Income Statement
(in thousands of dollars, except per-share numbers)
For the Year Ended December 31, 2001

	2001
Sales	$72,000
Cost of goods sold	(28,000)
General operating expenses	(14,000)
Operating leases	(6,200)
Insurance expense	(2,800)
Depreciation	(1,200)
Bad debt expense	(150)
Income tax expense	(6,300)
Operating income	$13,350
Other income (losses)	(5,267)
Net income	$ 8,083
Earnings per share*	$16

Net income divided by the weighted average of the common shares outstanding during 2001.

Wagner Stores
Statement of Stockholders' Equity
(in thousands of dollars)
For the Year Ended December 31, 2001

TRANSACTION	PREFERRED STOCK	COMMON STOCK	ADDITIONAL PAID-IN CAPITAL	RETAINED EARNINGS	TREASURY STOCK
Beginning balance (12/31/00)	$5,000	$ 6,400	$4,200	$ 9,850	$(3,200)
Net income				7,983	
Cash dividends				(3,000)	
Stock dividend issued		500	100	(600)	
Common stock issuance		5,000	800		
Exercise of stock options			(1,000)		1,800
Treasury stock purchases					(2,500)
Ending balance (12/31/01)	$5,000	$11,900	$4,100	$14,233	$(3,900)

Wagner Stores
Consolidated Balance Sheet
(in thousands of dollars)
December 31, 2001 and 2000

	2001	2000
ASSETS		
Cash	$ 4,920	$ 6,200
Trading securities	1,050	800
Accounts receivable (net)	7,250	9,400
Inventory	16,700	12,300
Prepaid insurance	1,800	2,500
Notes receivable	2,586	3,320
Investment in affiliate	10,600	8,000
Property, plant, and equipment (net)	42,200	12,400
Goodwill	900	900
Total assets	$88,006	$55,820
LIABILITIES AND STOCKHOLDERS' EQUITY		
Accounts payable	$ 9,700	$ 4,700
Accrued payables	4,000	3,300
Income tax payable	1,700	600
Dividend payable	700	500
Bonds payable (net)	28,502	13,242
Capital lease obligations	4,771	5,228
Deferred income taxes	7,200	6,000
Preferred stock	5,000	5,000
Common stock	11,900	6,400
Additional paid-in capital	4,100	4,200
Retained earnings	14,333	9,850
Less: Treasury stock	(3,900)	(3,200)
Total liabilities and stockholders' equity	$88,006	$55,820

Footnotes to the Financial Statements of Wagner Stores

1. Trading Securities. Trading securities are carried at fair market value as of the balance sheet date. During 2001, trading securities with a total book value of $250 were sold.

2. Revenue Recognition and Accounts Receivable. Sales are recorded when goods are shipped, and all sales to customers are on account. Accounts receivable are carried at net realizable value with an allowance for uncollectibles. The dollar amounts in the allowance account were $100 and $120 at the end of 2001 and 2000, respectively.

3. Inventory. Inventory is carried at lower-of-cost-or-market value under the first-in, first-out assumption. All inventory purchases are made on account.

4. Note Receivable. On January 1, 2000, the company received an installment note in exchange for services. The note is accounted for under the effective interest method

Wagner Stores
Statement of Cash Flows
(in thousands of dollars)
For the Year Ended December 31, 2001

	2001	
Operating activities:		
Net income	$ 8,083	
Noncurrent adjustments:		
Depreciation	1,200	
Loss on write-down of equipment lines	3,200	
Increase in deferred income taxes	1,200	
Amortization of discount on long-term debt	260	
Equity income not received in cash	(300)	
Realized and unrealized gains on trading securities	(150)	
Gain on sale of vehicles	(200)	
Current adjustments:		
Decrease in net accounts receivable	2,150	
Increase in inventory	(4,400)	
Decrease in prepaid insurance	700	
Increase in accounts payable	5,000	
Increase in accrued payables	700	
Increase in income tax payable	1,100	
Net cash from operating activities		$18,543
Investing activities:		
Investments in trading securities	$ (400)	
Proceeds from sales of trading securities	300	
Investment in affiliate	(2,300)	
Receipts of principal on notes receivable	734	
Investments in property, plant, and equipment	(34,500)	
Proceeds from sales of vehicles	500	
Net cash used by investing activities		(35,666)
Financing activities:		
Proceeds from bond issuance	$15,000	
Principal payments on capital leases	(457)	
Proceeds from common stock issuance	5,800	
Treasury stock purchases	(2,500)	
Proceeds from treasury stock issuances	800	
Dividend payments	(2,800)	
Net cash from financing activities		15,843
Decrease in cash balance		$ (1,280)
Beginning cash balance (12/31/00)		6,200
Ending cash balance (12/31/01)		$ 4,920

and specifies that the company receive a fixed amount of cash at the end of 2000, 2001, 2002, 2003, and 2004.

5. Investment in Affiliate. For several years, the company has held a 45 percent interest in Truax Incorporated, a financial holding company, which in turn holds interests in a wide variety of financial institutions. At the end of 2001, the company acquired a 25 percent interest in Billingsly Financial. The company uses the equity method to account for these investments.

6. Property, Plant, and Equipment. This category includes all properties used in the operations of the business, including assets acquired through capitalized leases. Straight-line methods are used to depreciate the assets in this category. Accumulated depreciation totaled $2,700 and $3,000 as of the end of 2001 and 2000, respectively. During 2001, one of the company's lines of equipment was discontinued, and the book value of this line was written off the books. In addition, the company sold a small fleet of vehicles with an original cost of $800.

7. Goodwill. The company acquired 100 percent of the outstanding stock of Machen Suppliers at the beginning of 2000, accounting for the acquisition as a purchase and recognizing goodwill.

8. Accounts Payable. Accounts payable includes only outstanding account balances with the company's inventory suppliers.

9. Accrued Payables. Accrued payables refer to the company's general operating expenses.

10. Bonds Payable. On January 1, 1999, the company issued ten-year bonds with a face value of $16,000 and a stated interest rate of 5 percent. Interest payments are made at the end of each year, and the bonds were issued at a discount to yield an 8 percent effective interest rate. The company has the option to call these bonds at a premium of 2 percent above the face value. The market value of these bonds as of December 31, 2001, is $14,350. At the end of 2001, the company issued additional ten-year bonds at face value. These bonds have a stated interest rate of 9 percent.

11. Lease Obligations. The company leases most of its facilities and machinery. Lease payments during 2001 totaled $7,180. Projected future lease payments under capitalized leases are $980 per year until December 31, 2007. Projected future lease payments under operating leases are $6,200 at the end of each year for the next twenty years. Both projections exclude executory costs.

12. Deferred Income Taxes. Deferred income taxes arise due to timing differences between financial reporting and tax reporting. In general, the company attempts to minimize its income tax liability by accelerating expense recognition and deferring revenue recognition within the rules of the Internal Revenue Service. For example, the company uses straight-line depreciation for financial reporting purposes and accelerated methods for income tax reporting purposes. Such practices have accumulated a deferred income tax obligation, which is reported on the balance sheet. The company's effective income tax rate is 35 percent, which is expected to be constant in the foreseeable future.

13. Pension Obligation. The company carries a defined contribution pension plan on all its employees. During 2001, the company contributed $1,500 to the plan, which is reflected in the general operating section of the income statement.

14. Stock Option Plan. The company maintains a stock option plan, which compensates certain executives with ten-year options to purchase the company's stock at a price that equals the stock's market value as of the date of the issuance. Certain options were exercised during 2001.

15. Stockholders' Equity. At December 31, 2000, the company had issued 640 shares of $10 par value stock, 400 of which were held in treasury. During 2001, the company issued 500 shares of $10 par value common stock; 150 shares were issued when executive stock options were exercised; and 224 additional treasury shares were acquired. At the end of 2001, the company issued a 7.5 percent stock dividend on all outstanding shares.

In addition, the company has 500 shares of preferred stock outstanding, which pays annual dividends at a rate of 10 percent of the par value. The nonvoting preferred shares are cumulative and nonparticipating, and the preferred stockholders have an option to require redemption at par value beginning in 2003.

16. Other Income (Losses). The Other Income (Losses) Account consists of the following items:

Interest revenue earned on note receivable	**$ 266**
Realized and unrealized gains on trading securities	**150**
Equity income	**1,500**
Gain on sale of vehicles	**200**
Interest expense	**(1,583)**
Loss on write-down of inventory to market	**(2,600)**
Loss on discontinued equipment	**(3,200)**
Net loss	**$(5,267)**

Glossary

A

accelerated methods of depreciation Accelerated methods of depreciation are used to depreciate fixed assets. Under these methods, more costs are allocated to earlier periods than are allocated to later periods. Examples include double-declining-balance and sum-of-the-years'-digits. These methods are considered conservative since they recognize large amounts of depreciation in the early years of an asset's life.

accounting equation The accounting equation is the basis for the four financial statements. It is a mathematical equation stating that the dollar value of a company's assets equals the dollar value of its liabilities plus the dollar value of its stockholders' equity. The balance sheet is a statement of this equation; transactions are recorded on the financial statements in a way that maintains the equality of this equation.

accounting period An accounting period is the period of time between the preparation of the financial statements. Statements are often prepared monthly, quarterly, semiannually, or annually. Most companies report on a calendar-year basis, but for various reasons, some companies report on other 365-day cycles, called fiscal years.

accounts payable Accounts payable are dollar amounts owed to others for goods, supplies, and services purchased on open account. They arise from frequent transactions between a company and its suppliers that are normally not subject to specific, formal contracts. These extensions of credit are the practical result of a time lag between the receipt of a good, supply, or service and the corresponding payment. Accounts payable are normally included on the balance sheet under current liabilities.

accounts payable turnover *Cost of purchases/Average accounts payable.* Accounts payable turnover measures how quickly, on average, accounts payable are paid to a company's suppliers. It reflects the number of times, during a given period, that these supplier accounts are turned over. Dividing this activity ratio by 365 changes it into an expression indicating how many days, on average, are required to pay off an account.

accounts receivable Accounts receivable is a balance sheet account indicating the dollar amount due from customers from sales made on open account. It arises when revenues are recognized before receipt of the associated cash payment. Accounts receivable is normally included as a current asset and for some companies can be quite large.

accounts receivable turnover *Net credit sales/Average accounts receivable.* Accounts receivable turnover reflects the number of times a company's accounts receivables are recorded and collected during a given period. This ratio is often divided into 365 days, which indicates how many days, on average, receivables are outstanding—often referred to as the collection period.

accrual accounting The accrual basis is a system of accounting that recognizes revenues and expenses when assets and liabilities are created or discharged because of operating activities. Accrual accounting differs from cash flow accounting, which reflects only cash inflows and outflows, and is the basis upon which the statement of cash flows is prepared. Statements prepared under accrual accounting, like the income statement, are designed to measure earning power.

accruals Accruals are accounting entries designed to ensure that the assets and liabilities created or discharged due to the operating activities of the current period are recognized as revenues or expenses on the income statement of that period. The recognition on the income statement occurs at a time different from the related cash flow, so a receivable or payable must be recorded on the balance sheet. Common examples include accrued payables, bad debts, warranties, and deferred revenues.

accrued payables Accrued payables are obligations on the balance sheet that must be recognized at the end of each period because they build up over time. Accrued payables are normally included as current liabilities because they are expected to be paid with the use of assets presently listed as current on the balance sheet. Accrued payables normally include obligations associated with salaries, wages, interest, warranties, and taxes.

accumulated depreciation Accumulated depreciation is a contra asset account on the balance sheet that reflects the dollar value of the total depreciation that has been previously recognized on the fixed assets up to the date of the balance sheet.

activity method The activity method is a method of depreciating fixed assets or depleting natural resource costs that allocates the cost of the long-lived asset to future periods on the basis of its activity. This method is used primarily in the mining, oil, and gas industries to deplete the costs associated with acquiring the rights to and extracting natural resources. The estimated life under the activity method is expressed in terms of units of activity (e.g., miles driven, units produced, barrels extracted) instead of years, as is done under the other common methods of depeciation (e.g., straight-line, double-declining-balance, sum-of-the-years'-digits).

activity ratios Activity ratios measure the speed with which assets or accounts payable move through operations. They involve the calculation of a number called turnover, which indicates the number of times during a given period that assets (or payables) are acquired, disposed of, and replaced. Dividing 365 by the turnover number produces the average number of days during the year that the assets (or payables) were carried on the balance sheet. Turnover is commonly calculated for accounts receivable, inventory, fixed assets, total assets, and accounts payable.

actuary An actuary is a statistician who estimates risks for a wide variety of purposes, including the determination of insurance premiums, the funding of pension and health plans, and other purposes that involve assessing future demographic trends.

additional paid-in capital Additional paid-in capital is included in the stockholders' equity section of the balance sheet and reflects capital contributions to the firm over and above the par value of issued common stock or preferred stock. It can also appear as the result of issuing stock dividends, stock options, and treasury stock.

aging schedule Aging is a method of estimating and analyzing uncollectible accounts receivable that categorizes individual accounts on the basis of the amount of time each has been outstanding. Each category is then multiplied by a different uncollectible percentage, under the assumption that older accounts are more likely than new accounts to be uncollectible. This method is used primarily by management to identify and maintain control over uncollectible accounts receivables.

allowance method The allowance method, under generally accepted accounting principles (GAAP), is the preferred method to account for uncollectibles and sales returns, both of which have a direct effect on the reported value of accounts receivable. The allowance method involves estimating the dollar amount of the uncollectibles or sales returns at the end of each accounting period and, based on that estimate, records an entry that reduces both net income and the balance in accounts receivable with a contra account called "allowance for uncollectibles."

amortization Amortization is the systematic allocation of a deferred charge (e.g., prepaid expense, fixed asset, bond discount or premium, deferred revenue, intangible asset) over its life. Amortization is often used to describe the allocation of the cost of intangible assets to earnings, but prepaid expenses and discounts and premiums on long-term receivables and payables are also amortized to earnings. Depreciation is the amortization of fixed assets, and depletion is the amortization of natural resource costs.

analytic review Analytic review is an important part of financial statement analysis that focuses on whether balances in financial statement accounts deviate from expected levels and seeks to explain why such deviations occur. It includes analyzing common-size financial statements to identify relative changes in the sizes of financial accounts across periods as well as comparing these changes in an effort to infer management actions.

annual report An annual report is a document that a company publishes each year, containing the financial statements, a description of the company and its operations, an audit report, a management letter, footnotes to the financial statements containing supporting schedules, and other financial and nonfinancial information.

annuity An annuity is a periodic cash flow of an equal amount over time. Bond interest payments, lease and rental payments, and insurance payments are examples of annuities.

appropriation of retained earnings An appropriation refers to the act of making a portion of the retained earnings account unavailable for the payment of dividends. Such restrictions can be imposed contractually or voluntarily and are designed to ensure that cash is available in the future for some specific purpose.

asset An asset is an item listed on the left side of the balance sheet that has been acquired by the company in an objectively measurable transaction and has future economic benefit—additional purchasing power, cash, or the ability to generate revenues.

asset depreciation range (ADR) The Asset Depreciation Range (ADR) System contains guidelines published by the Internal Revenue Service that define the minimum allowable useful lives and maximum depreciation rates for various kinds of long-lived assets. These lives are used when depreciating long-lived assets in the computation of taxable income.

asset impairment An asset impairment occurs when the value of an asset is judged to be permanently reduced. See **asset retirement** and **restructuring charges.**

asset mix Asset mix is the combination of assets listed on the balance sheet as of a given date. For example, the percent of current assets, long-term investments, fixed assets, and intangibles to total assets can represent a company's asset mix. Common-size analysis across time can identify changes in a company's asset mix.

asset retirement An asset retirement refers to the discontinuation of the use of a fixed asset.

asset turnover *Sales/Average total assets.* Asset turnover measures how efficiently a company is using its assets to produce sales. A high ratio indicates that a company is producing a large amount of sales with relatively few assets.

audit An audit is an examination conducted by an individual or entity, having no financial interest in the company (i.e., independent), to determine whether the financial statements of the company fairly reflect its financial condition as well as whether the statements have been prepared in conformance with generally accepted accounting principles. The outcome of the audit is an audit report, or opinion letter, signed by the auditor, which states the extent of the auditor's activities and the conclusions.

audit committee The audit committee is a subcommittee of the board of directors, made up entirely of nonmanagement directors, that works with management to choose the external auditor and monitor the audit so that it is conducted in a thorough, objective, and independent manner.

audit opinion See **audit report.**

audit report The audit report, which is written and signed by the external auditor, states whether, and to what extent, the information in the financial statements fairly reflects the financial performance and condition of the company.

authorized shares Authorized shares refers to the number of shares of stock a corporation is entitled to issue by its corporate charter, which is normally granted by the state in which the company is incorporated. Additional authorizations must be approved by the board of directors and are often subject to shareholder vote. Both preferred and common shares must be authorized before they can be issued.

available-for-sale securities Available-for-sale securities refer to relatively small investments (less than 20 percent of the outstanding voting stock) in marketable equity or debt securities that are not considered trading securities. Available-for-sale securities are readily marketable but are not intended to be sold in the near future—they can be listed as either current or noncurrent depending upon management's intention, and they are carried on the balance sheet at fair market value.

averaging assumption In addition to first-in, first-out (FIFO) and last-in, first-out (LIFO), averaging is one of the three most common inventory cost flow assumptions. Under the average method, cost of goods sold and ending inventory are determined by computing a weighted average cost of the items sold and the items remaining, respectively.

B

bad debts See **uncollectibles.**

balance sheet The balance sheet is a financial statement that indicates the financial condition of a business as of a given point in time. It includes assets, liabilities, and stockholders' equity, and it represents a statement of the basic accounting equation. The assets and liabilities are divided into current and noncurrent classifications on the basis of liquidity, and comparisons of assets and liabilities often provide an indication about the company's ability to meet obligations as they come due (i.e., solvency).

bank reconciliation A bank reconciliation is a document that lists items explaining the difference between the cash balance indicated in the company's ledger and the cash balance indicated in the company's bank statement. Differences between the two balances arise from outstanding checks, unrecorded deposits, and bank charges. Maintaining up-to-date bank reconciliations is one component of a good internal control system.

basic earnings per share See **earnings per share.**

betterment A betterment is a material expenditure made after the acquisition of a long-lived asset that improves the asset by increasing its life, increasing the quality or quantity of its output, or decreasing the cost of operating it.

"Big 5" The five public accounting firms that audit most of the large companies in the United States are known as the Big 5. They are Arthur Anderson & Co., Deloitte & Touche, Ernst & Young, KPMG Peat Marwick, and PricewaterhouseCoopers.

board of directors The board of directors is a group of individuals, elected annually by the stockholders of a corporation to represent the interests of those stockholders. In addition to setting overall corporate policies, the board has the power to declare dividends, set executive compensation, and hire and fire management. The board also appoints and monitors the compensation committee and audit committees.

bond Bonds are debt securities issued by an entity to a large number of investors to raise cash. The issuing company, in return, normally agrees to make cash interest payments to the bondholders until a specific future date (called maturity), usually five to thirty years in the future, at which time a large principal payment is made and the obligation is terminated. Companies issue bonds to raise large amounts of cash, and they are normally issued (sold) to the public through a third party (called an underwriter), such as an investment banker or financial institution. After bonds are initially issued, they are generally freely negotiable; that is, they can be purchased and sold in the open market.

bonds payable Bonds payable represents a balance sheet liability reflecting the book value of bonds that have been previously issued and are presently outstanding. This liability is normally considered to be long-term, except for the portion that is due within the time period of current liabilities. Bonds payable are carried on the balance sheet at the present value of the future cash (interest and principal) payments specified by the terms of the bonds, discounted at the effective interest rate.

book gain/loss A book gain (or loss) is the difference between the value received (or given up) and the book value of the asset (or liability) disposed of. If, for example, an asset with a book value of $10,000 is sold for $12,000, a $2,000 book gain is recognized. Selling the same asset for $7,000 would create a book loss of $3,000.

book value Book value is the value of an account, a company, or a share of stock as indicated by the balance sheet. It is often referred to as balance sheet value.

borrowing capacity Borrowing capacity is the ability of a company to raise capital by issuing debt securities or other borrowings. Borrowing capacity is critical for successful businesses because debt financing is a method of raising much needed capital to support operations, invest in assets, or pay off outstanding debts.

business acquisition In a business acquisition, a company (investor) acquires a controlling interest (51 percent or more of the voting stock) in another (investee) company. The investor company is called the parent, and the investee company is called the subsidiary; both companies normally continue to operate. The financial statements of the parent are prepared on a consolidated basis, where the assets, liabilities, income, and cash flows of the combined entity are included together. The financial statements of the subsidiary are unaffected.

business combination See **merger.**

business environment A business environment is the economic setting in which a company's operating, investing, and financing activities are conducted. The business environment consists of many items, most of which are not within management's control—including interest rates, market values of certain assets, competitive forces, the general state of the economy, changes in customer tastes and preferences, characteristics of the workforce, and government regulation.

business segment A business segment is a separate line of business, production line, or class of customer representing an operation that is independent of a company's other operations. Many large companies have multiple lines of business, and if material, the assets, liabilities, revenues, and profits associated with these separate lines are disclosed in the footnotes to the financial statements.

C

call provision A provision in a debt contract that allows the issuing company to repurchase outstanding debt (e.g., bonds) after a specified date for a specified price is a call provision. Call provisions protect issuing companies from situations where market interest rates drop significantly. In such cases, issuing companies can exercise their call provisions (repurchase the debt) and reissue debt at lower interest rates.

capital Capital refers to funds (usually cash) generated by a company to support its operations. In a general sense, capital can refer to funds produced through issuing either debt or equity securities, but the capital section of the balance sheet normally refers to owners' or stockholders' equity—sources of equity capital.

capital lease A capital lease is a lease treated as a purchase for purposes of financial accounting. If, at the date of the lease agreement, a lease meets criteria, it is classified and accounted for as a capital lease by the lessee. Under a capital lease, the lessee is considered to have the economic ownership of the leased asset, which is financed through the periodic lease payments. The resulting accounting treatment recognizes both a balance sheet asset and a liability, which are initially placed on the books at the present value of the future cash payments, discounted at the effective rate of interest. The asset is then depreciated, and the effective-interest method is used to amortize the liability.

capital structure Capital structure refers to a company's financing sources: (1) borrowings or liabilities, (2) contributed capital, and (3) retained earnings. It is represented by the right side of the balance sheet—liabilities and stockholders' equity.

capital structure leverage *Average total assets/Average stockholders' equity.* Capital structure leverage or financial leverage indicates the extent to which a company relies on debt financing. As the ratio increases (decreases), the amount of debt financing is greater (less). A ratio of "1" indicates that there is no debt in the company's capital structure.

capitalization ratios Capitalization ratios help analysts evaluate the capital structure of a company or, in general, the composition of the liability and stockholders' equity side of the balance sheet. They include: (1) debt/equity, (2) debt ratio, (3) contribution of financial leverage to return on equity, (4) capital structure leverage, and (5) common earnings leverage.

capitalize To capitalize an expenditure means to place the cost of an expenditure on the balance sheet as an asset. Expenditures can either be expensed or capitalized.

cash discount When a good or service is sold on credit, the selling company wishes to collect the cash as soon as possible. To encourage prompt payment, many companies offer cash discounts on the gross sales price. Cash discounts specify that an amount of cash less than the gross sales price is sufficient to satisfy the obligation.

cash equivalent Cash equivalents are securities that can be converted into cash in a very short time. Examples include commercial paper and other debt instruments with maturity dates less than three months in the future. Such items are often included in the definition of cash for purposes of the balance sheet and the statement of cash flows.

cash flow Cash flow is the movement of cash associated with a company's operating, investing, and financing activities. Cash flow involves inflows and outflows of cash, and a company's cash flow is considered to be strong if it can generate large amounts of cash relatively quickly. Cash flow is an important part of solvency, and an historical description of cash flow is provided by the statement of cash flows.

cash flow accounting Cash flow accounting is a system that keeps a balance of cash and a record of cash inflows and outflows. The statement of cash flows is based on cash flow accounting.

cash flow from financing Cash flow from financing activities represents cash generated during a particular period through a company's financing activities. These cash flows are disclosed in the financing section of the statement of cash flows and reflect cash flows associated with additional long-term borrowings and repayments, equity issuances and treasury stock purchases, and dividend payments.

cash flow from investing Cash flow from investing activities includes cash inflows and outflows during a particular period from a company's investing activities. These flows are disclosed in the investing section of the statement of cash flows and reflect cash inflows and outflows associated with the acquisition and sale of a company's investments and long-lived assets.

cash flow from operations Cash flows from operating activities include cash receipts and payments during a particular period associated with a company's operating activities. Also called net cash flow from operations, these flows are disclosed in the operating section of the statement of cash flows and can be computed and presented in either of two ways: (1) a direct method, which lists the cash flow effects of each income statement item, or (2) the more common indirect method, which adjusts net income for differences between accruals and operating cash flows.

cash flow projection Cash flow projection is the process of predicting the amount and timing of future cash inflows and outflows and plays an important role in financial statement analysis.

cash management Cash management is the manner in which a company plans and executes the inflows and outflows of cash.

certificate of deposit A certificate of deposit is a short-term bank obligation that pays a given rate of interest for a specified period of time, ending on the maturity date. Often interest penalties are assessed when cash is withdrawn prior to the maturity date.

certified public accountant A certified public accountant (CPA) is an individual who has met a set of educational requirements to sit for the national CPA exam, passed the exam, and met the experience requirements of the states in which he or she practices. Certified public accountants must also pass an ethics exam, periodically participate in continuing education courses, and maintain their membership with the American Institute of Certified Public Accountants (AICPA). CPAs are empowered to sign audit reports.

classified balance sheet A classified balance sheet is a balance sheet that is divided into classifications—including current assets, long-term investments, fixed assets, intangible assets, current liabilities, long-term liabilities, and stockholders' equity.

clean audit opinion See **standard audit report.**

collateral Collateral represents assets designated to be paid to a creditor in case of default on a loan by a debtor—often referred to as security on the loan. The balance sheet, which contains a listing of a company's assets, and the footnotes to the financial statements may help to identify various sources of collateral. Lenders often require that loans be backed by collateral, as a way of reducing the cost associated with default.

collection period See **accounts receivable turnover.**

commercial paper Commercial paper is a fast-growing means of providing short-term financing; it represents short-term notes (30 to 270 days) issued for cash by companies with good credit ratings to other companies.

common earnings leverage (*Net income − Preferred stock dividends*)/(*Net income + Interest expense [1 − Tax rate]*). Common earnings leverage measures the portion of the return to the stockholders relative to the return to all capital providers (stockholders and creditors). Higher levels of this ratio indicate that greater amounts of the return generated by the company are available to the stockholders.

common stock Common stock is a certificate that represents an ownership (equity) interest in a corporation, carrying with it the right to receive dividends if they are declared and the right to vote for the corporation's board of directors at the annual shareholders' meeting. It also carries with it the right to the assets of the corporation, but this right is subordinate to that of the corporate creditor. Issuing common stock is a popular way used by corporations to raise capital.

common-size financial statements Common-size financial statements express dollar values as percentages of other dollar values on the same statement. On a common-size income statement, for example, expense items and the various measures of income (e.g., operating income, net income) are expressed as percentages of sales. On a common-size balance sheet, assets and liabilities are expressed as percentages of total assets (or liabilities plus stockholders' equity).

compensating balance Compensating balances are minimum cash balances that must be maintained in savings or checking accounts until certain loan obligations are satisfied. Compensating balances help financial institutions reduce the risks of default on outstanding loans by ensuring that at least some cash is available for scheduled loan payments.

compensation committee The compensation committee is a subcommittee of the board of directors charged with establishing the compensation packages of the company's officers. It is made up entirely of outside directors (not part of company management).

compensation contracts Compensation contracts specify the form and amount of compensation paid to the executives, managers, or employees of a company.

conservatism Conservatism is an exception to the principles of accounting measurement stating that when in doubt, financial statements should understate assets, overstate liabilities, accelerate the recognition of losses, and delay the recognition of gains.

consignment A consignment is an agreement by which a consignor (owner) transfers inventory to a consignee (receiver) who takes physical possession and places the items up for sale. When the inventory is sold, the consignee collects the sales proceeds, keeps a percentage, and returns the remainder to the consignor.

consistency Consistency is a principle of accounting measurement that states although there is considerable choice among accounting methods, companies should choose a set of methods and use them from one period to the next.

consolidated financial statements Consolidated financial statements include a company's assets and liabilities as well as the assets and liabilities of its majority-owned subsidiaries. See **business acquisition and merger.**

contingency A contingency represents an existing condition, situation, or set of circumstances involving uncertainty concerning a possible gain or loss to a company. The uncertainty will ultimately be resolved when one or more future events occurs or fails to occur.

contingent liability See **contingency** and **loss contingency.**

contra account A contra account is a balance sheet account that offsets another balance sheet account.

contributed capital Contributed capital represents that portion of the stockholders' equity section of the balance sheet of a corporation, reflecting contributions from stockholders. It represents the amount of a company's assets that have been generated through issuances of stock (common and preferred), including the dollar amounts of both the stock and additional paid-in capital accounts.

controlling interest Technically, a controlling interest is ownership of 51 percent or more of the outstanding voting stock of a company. In such cases, consolidated financial statements must be prepared. Control may be possible, however, with less than 51 percent of the stock. A significant influence on either the board of directors or operations of the company, especially in cases where the remaining ownership is spread across many entities, may also represent control.

convertible bonds Convertible bonds are bonds that can be converted to other corporate securities (usually common stock) during some specified period of time. Convertible bonds combine the benefits of a bond (guaranteed interest) with the privilege of exchanging it for stock (potential appreciation and dividends) at the holder's option. They are considered hybrid securities because they possess features of both debt and equity.

copyright Copyrights are exclusive rights granted by law to control literary, musical, or artistic works. They are granted for fifty years beyond the life of the creator. The cost of acquiring a copyright is capitalized on the balance sheet as an intangible asset and normally amortized over its legal life, not to exceed forty years.

corporation A corporation is a legal entity, separate and distinct from its owners (stockholders), who annually elect a board of directors, which in turn represents the stockholders' interests in the management of the business. A corporation has an indefinite life, which continues regardless of changes in ownership. Stockholders of a corporation are usually free to transfer their ownership interests. In a corporation, the liability of the stockholders is limited to the dollar amount of their investments, and in this way, the corporate structure provides a shield that protects the personal assets of the shareholders from corporate creditors. Companies in need of large amounts of capital therefore normally take the corporate form.

cost See **historical cost.**

cost expiration Cost expiration is the process of converting a capitalized cost to an expense. Accounting entries recorded at the end of the period are often used to expire previously capitalized costs, which appear as assets on the balance sheet.

cost method Under the cost method of accounting, assets are carried on the balance sheet at their original (historical) costs, and when an asset is sold, a gain or loss is recognized on the difference between the balance sheet value of the asset and the proceeds from the sale.

cost of capital If a company has available cash, cost of capital is the expected return foregone by investing the cash in a project rather than in comparable financial securities. If a company does not have available cash, it is the cost of acquiring the cash—i.e., the cost of raising debt (effective interest) capital or the cost of raising equity capital (dilution).

cost of goods sold Cost of goods sold appears on the income statement, indicating the cost of inventory sold during the period. In retail companies, cost of goods sold consists primarily of the cost of acquiring the inventory; in manufacturing companies, cost of goods sold consists of material, labor, and overhead costs.

covenant See **debt covenant.**

CPA See **certified public accountant.**

credit quality Credit quality refers to the likelihood that an individual or entity will pay an outstanding account in a timely manner. Customers or clients with high credit quality have a history of paying their obligations on time.

credit rating A credit rating is an assessment by an independent agency of the risk associated with a company and especially its outstanding debts. Credit ratings are usually expressed in alphabetic and/or numerical grades (e.g., AA1), and credit-rating agencies include Standard & Poor's, Dun and Bradstreet, and Moody's Investors Service.

credit terms Credit terms are the contractual terms associated with outstanding credit (accounts receivable and accounts payable) accounts.

creditor A creditor is an individual or entity to which a company owes money or services or to which the company has an outstanding debt.

cumulative preferred stock Cumulative preferred stock is a type of preferred stock with a cumulative feature, which means that when a company misses a dividend on cumulative preferred stock, the missed dividend becomes a dividend in arrears. Most preferred stock is cumulative.

current assets Current assets are assets on the balance sheet expected to be converted to cash or expired in one year or the operating cycle, whichever is longer.

current cost See **replacement cost.**

current liabilities Current liabilities are obligations listed on the balance sheet that are expected to be paid with the use of current assets listed on the balance sheet.

current maturity of long-term debts Current maturity of long-term debt is a balance sheet current liability representing that portion of a long-term liability due in the current period. This liability is expected to require the use of current assets.

current ratio *Current assets/Current liabilities.* The current ratio is often used to assess the solvency position of a company and is normally an important part of financial statement analysis.

D

debenture A debenture is an unsecured bond.

debt Debt is a form of financing a borrowing that involves an obligation, stated in a formal contract, which indicates the time period of the obligation in addition to the amount and timing of the required cash payments. Often, the contract also identifies security (collateral) in the case of default and other provisions (debt covenants) normally designed to protect the interests of the lender.

debt covenant A debt covenant is an agreement between a company's debtholders and its managers that often restricts the managers' behavior. These restrictions are usually designed to protect the debtholder's investment (i.e., increase the likelihood of receiving the contractual debt payments on a timely basis), and they are often written in terms of numbers and ratios taken from the financial statements. Violating a debt covenant puts the issuing company (debtor) into technical default.

debt investment A debt investment involves the purchase of a debt security or a loan of goods or services to another entity, with the expectation that some payment (principal and interest) will be received in return. Debt investments are usually backed by contracts that specify the terms of the arrangement—maturity date interest and principal payments, security, and collateral as well as other features that transfer risk from one party to the other (e.g., debt covenants, call provisions).

debt ratio *Total liabilities/Total assets.* Assets are generated from three sources: borrowings, contributions from owners, and profitable operations not paid out in the form of dividends. The debt ratio reflects that portion provided by borrowings.

debt redemptions See **redemption.**

debt/equity ratio *Total liabilities (both current and noncurrent)/Stockholders' equity. (Note: Sometimes contractual debt only is used in the numerator.)* The debt/equity ratio indicates the extent to which a company can sustain losses without jeopardizing the interests of its creditors. Creditors have priority claims over stockholders, and in case of liquidation, the creditors have first right to a company's assets. From an individual creditor's standpoint, therefore, the amount of equity in the company's capital structure can be viewed as a buffer, helping to ensure that there are sufficient assets to cover individual claims.

default A default occurs when an individual or entity fails to make a contractual payment on a debt. See **technical default.**

deferred cost A deferred cost is a miscellaneous category of assets listed on the balance sheet that often includes prepaid expenses extending beyond the current accounting period and intangible assets such as organizational costs, capitalized legal fees, and other startup costs.

deferred income See **deferred revenue.**

deferred income taxes Deferred income taxes can appear in either the liability or asset section of the balance sheet—arising when companies recognize revenues and expenses for financial reporting and income tax purposes in different time periods. Deferred income tax liabilities (assets) arise in periods when temporary timing differences between tax and financial reporting cause taxable income to be different from net income on the income statement. Deferred tax liabilities (assets) represent expected increases (decreases) in taxes payable in future periods when these temporary timing differences reverse—at which time the deferred income tax liabilities (assets) are written off the books.

deferred revenue Deferred revenue is a balance sheet liability reflecting services yet to be performed by a company for which cash payments have already been collected. Deferred revenues are also referred to as payments in advance, deferred income, and unearned revenues.

defined benefit pension plan In a defined benefit pension plan, an employer promises to provide each employee with a specified benefit at retirement. This promise is difficult to plan for because the benefits are received by the employees in the future. The benefits must be predicted, and the employer must contribute enough cash to a pension fund so that the contributions plus the earnings on the fund assets will be sufficient to provide the promised benefits. See **defined contribution pension plan.**

defined contribution pension plan In a defined contribution pension plan, an employer agrees only to make a series of contributions of a specified amount to a pension fund. These periodic cash payments are often based on employee wages or salaries, and each employee's percentage interest in the total fund is determined by the proportionate share contributed by the employer on the employee's behalf. Under this type of plan, the employer makes no promises regarding how much the employees will receive upon retirement.

depletion Depletion is the amortization of the costs incurred to acquire rights to mine natural resources. For mining and oil and gas companies, such costs can be substantial, and these costs are normally depleted as the natural resource is extracted, using the activity method.

depreciation Depreciation is the periodic allocation of the cost of a fixed asset to the income statement over the asset's useful life. Such allocation is necessary if the costs are to be matched against the benefits produced by the asset. For financial reporting purposes, management has much discretion over how depreciation is computed. For income tax purposes, there is much less leeway.

depreciation base The depreciation (amortization) base is the portion of the cost of a long-lived asset subject to depreciation or amortization—capitalized cost less estimated salvage value.

depreciation expense A depreciation expense is an item on the income statement, reducing net income, that reflects the depreciation recognized on a company's fixed assets during the period of time covered by the income statement. Depreciation is a cost expiration; it does not represent a cash outflow.

diluted earnings per share Diluted earnings per share is a disclosure required by generally accepted accounting principles (GAAP) for companies that have the potential for significant dilution. This ratio, which must be disclosed on the face of the income statement, is computed by adjusting the earnings per share ratio for an estimate of the equity securities likely to be issued in the near future. Diluted earnings per share is less than earnings per share because the potential for additional equity issuances increases the denominator of the earnings per share ratio.

dilution Dilution is the reduction in a stockholder's relative ownership interest due to the issuance of additional equity securities to others.

dilutive securities Dilutive securities are outstanding securities that can lead to future equity issuances. Shareholders and potential shareholders should be aware of dilutive securities because when the options on dilutive securities are exercised, the equity positions of the existing shareholders are diluted. Fully

diluted earnings per share, which is a required disclosure under generally accepted accounting principles (GAAP), reflects the dilutive effects of these kinds of securities.

direct method Under the direct method of presentation in the operating section of the statement of cash flows, the cash effects of the operating expenses are subtracted from the cash effects of the operating revenues in the computation of net cash from operating activities. This form of presentation is called the direct method because the cash inflows and outflows are taken directly from the cash account in the ledger—that is, they represent real cash flows.

direct write-off method The direct write-off method of accounting for bad debts records bad debt expense and removes the outstanding receivable from the balance sheet at the point in time when a specific account is deemed uncollectible. This method of accounting for bad debts is normally considered unacceptable under generally accepted accounting principles (GAAP) because it does not attempt to record all expected bad debts in the same period in which the sales revenue is recorded, thereby violating the matching principle.

discount on bond payable Discount on bond payable is a contra liability account representing the amount by which the face (maturity) value of a bond exceeds the present value of the bond's future cash payments, discounted at the effective rate of interest as of the date when the bonds were issued. Such discounts are amortized over the remaining life of the bond issuance under the effective interest method, increasing periodic interest expense to reflect the fact that the bonds were issued at a discount (i.e., the proceeds at the initial bond issuance were less than the face value of the bond).

discount rate Discount rate is used to describe the rate used in present value computations. To compute the present value of a future cash flow, for example, the cash flows are discounted at the discount rate. In this sense, the discount rate reflects the company's cost of capital—the cost of its debt and/or its equity.

dissimilar asset Dissimilar asset is a classification of long-lived assets used in determining the proper method of accounting for long-lived asset exchanges. The methods used to account for exchanges of dissimilar assets are different from those used to account for exchanges of similar assets. When dissimilar assets are exchanged, book gains or losses are recognized on the transactions—in the amount of the difference between the market value of that received and the market value of that given up. When similar assets are exchanged, book gains or losses are not recognized. Instead, the difference between the market value of that received and the market value of that given up serves to adjust (increase or decrease) the cost of the asset received in the exchange. See **trade-in.**

divestiture A divestiture is the sale of an asset or investment and normally refers to the sale of a major equity interest in another company.

dividend yield *Dividends per share/Market price per share.* Dividend yield indicates the cash return on the stockholders' investment. Recall that a return on an investment in common stock can come in two forms: dividends and market price appreciation. This financial ratio measures the size of the first. Dividend yields tend to be relatively small, especially for fast-growing companies that choose to pay little or no dividends.

dividends Dividends are payments made to the stockholders of a corporation that provide a return on their equity investments. Dividends are declared by the board of directors and are normally paid in the form of cash, although dividends in the form of other assets and shares of stock in the company are not unusual.

dividends in arrears Dividends in arrears are missed dividends on preferred stock with a cumulative feature. Dividends in arrears are not listed on the balance sheet as liabilities, but they must be disclosed in the footnotes to the financial statements, and they must be paid if and when the company declares a dividend.

double taxation Double taxation is a phenomenon that occurs when corporate profits and dividends received by the shareholders are both subject to federal income taxes. Double taxation occurs because the Internal Revenue Service treats corporations and their shareholders as separate taxable entities. It is a major disadvantage of the corporate form of business.

double-declining-balance method Double-declining-balance is the most extreme form of accelerated depreciation. Each period, depreciation expense is computed by multiplying the book value of the depreciable asset (cost − accumulated depreciation) by two times the straight-line rate (1/estimated useful life). This conservative method recognizes large amounts of depreciation expense in the early periods of the asset's life and small amounts in the later periods. It is very popular for tax purposes.

DuPont Model Using the DuPont Model to analyze financial ratios provides an important starting point for financial statement analysis. While there are a number of different forms of this model, all are designed to explain the changes in return on equity by breaking it down into the following components: Profit Margin, Asset Turnover, and Financial Leverage.

E

earned capital Earned capital is a measure of the amount of a company's assets that has been generated through profitable operations and not paid out in the form of dividends. On the balance sheet, earned capital is part of the stockholders' equity section and is comprised primarily of retained earnings.

earning power Earning power is the ability of a company to generate profits and increase net assets in the future. Net income, especially the persistent components of net income, is considered an indication of earning power.

earnings See **net income.**

earnings per share *Net income/Average number of common shares outstanding.* Earnings per share or basic earnings per share is perhaps the best known of all financial ratios, largely because it is often treated by the financial press as the primary measure of a company's performance. According to generally accepted accounting principles (GAAP), earnings per share must appear on the face of the income statement and be calculated in accordance with an elaborate set of complex rules. See **diluted earnings per share.**

earnings persistence Earnings persistence is the extent to which a particular earnings dollar amount can be expected to continue in the future and thus generate future cash flows. Earnings amounts with high levels of persistence are expected to continue in the future, while those with low levels of persistence are not.

earnings quality Earnings quality refers to the extent to which net income reported on the income statement differs from true earnings. This difference is the result of two factors: (1) financial reports based on an objective application of generally accepted accounting principles (GAAP) are inherently limited and (2) management uses its subjective discretion to apply GAAP when preparing the statements. Low earnings quality means that GAAP financial statements do not accurately reflect the company's true financial situation and/or management has used much of its discretion in preparing the financial statements.

economic entity assumption The economic entity assumption states that the financial statements refer to entities that are distinct from both their owners and all other economic entities. This assumption is important in determining the methods to account for consolidated financial statements, investments in equity securities, and business segments.

economic value added Economic value added (EVA) represents the extent to which a return generated by management exceeds the cost of the capital (debt and equity) invested to generate that return.

effective interest method The effective interest method is used to value long-term liabilities (e.g., bonds) and long-term notes receivable and the related interest charges, so that the book value of the note represents an estimate of the present value of the note's future cash flows. The future cash flows are discounted using the effective rate of interest as of the date the note was issued. The effective interest method is required under generally accepted accounting principles (GAAP).

effective interest rate The effective rate of interest is the actual rate of interest on an obligation or receivable, and it often differs from the stated interest rate. It is that rate which, when used to discount the future cash payments associated with the obligation or receivable, results in a present value equal to the fair market value of that which was initially exchanged for the obligation or receivable. Generally accepted accounting principles (GAAP) require that the effective interest rate be used to compute the periodic interest expense and revenue that appears on the income statement.

equity Equity is an ownership interest. Equity holders in a company own common stocks that have been issued by that company. Two rights are associated with owning a common stock—(1) the right to vote for the board of directors at the annual shareholders' meeting and (2) the right to receive dividends if they are declared by the board. The stockholders' equity section of the balance sheet represents the investment made by the equity holders in the company and is a measure of the assets that would remain for the equity holders after all liabilities have been paid.

equity investment An equity investment is the purchase of an ownership interest (e.g., common stock) in a company.

equity issuance An equity issuance is the sale of common shares (stock). Equity issuances raise funds—often large amounts—for a variety of reasons, including business acquisitions, investments in long-lived assets, payments on outstanding debt, or simply to support operations.

equity method The equity method is used to account for equity investments in the amount of 20 to 50 percent of the investee company's outstanding common (voting) stock. Such a significant influence on the investee company indicates a substantive economic relationship between the two companies and may also be evidenced, for example, by representation on the board of directors, the interchange of management personnel between companies, frequent or significant transactions between companies, or the technical dependency of one company on the other.

equity security See **equity investment.**

ERISA The Employment Retirement Income Securities Act passed by Congress in 1974 requires employers to fund their pension plans at specified minimum levels and provide other safeguards designed to protect employees. See **defined benefit pension plan.**

escrow Escrow is the state of an item (e.g., cash) that has been put into the custody of a third party until certain conditions are fulfilled. Damage deposits on rental agreements, for example, are often held in escrow until the end of the rental period.

exchange rate The exchange rate is the value of one currency expressed in terms of another currency. Like the prices of all goods and services, the exchange rates among currencies vary from one day to the next.

Companies that transact in more than one currency face the risks associated with fluctuating exchange rates, which can give rise to gains and losses—some of which are reflected on the financial statements. Hedging is a strategy that can be used to reduce such risks.

expense An expense is the outflow of assets or the creation of liabilities in an effort to generate revenues for a company. Examples include cost of goods sold, salaries, interest, advertising, taxes, utilities, depreciation, and others. Revenues less expenses is equal to net income—the income statement. While some expenses involve cash outflows, many do not; expenses can be accrued (e.g., salaries, wages, interest) or the result of cost expirations (e.g., depreciation, amortization).

expensed Expensed means to treat an expenditure as an expense by running the account through the income statement and closing it to retained earnings. Expense items appearing on the income statement have been expensed.

external financing External financing refers to the generation of funds to support operations and growth through the issuance of debt and/or equity, instead of retained earnings. Externally financed companies normally have capital structures with relatively large balances in debt and/or equity.

extraordinary item Extraordinary items appear on the income statement and represent the financial effects of events that are significantly different from the typical, customary business activities of an entity. Such events are not expected to recur frequently in the ordinary activities of the business. Extraordinary items are neither usual nor frequent.

F

face value See **maturity value.**

fair market value Fair market value is the dollar amount at which an item can be sold—exchanged for cash.

fees earned See **service revenue.**

financial accounting Financial accounting is a process through which managers report financial information about an economic entity to a variety of individuals who use this information for various decision-making purposes. The financial accounting process produces the financial statements and the associated footnotes.

financial accounting standards Financial accounting standards represent the official statements of the Financial Accounting Standards Board (FASB) and its predecessor bodies as well as the official statements from the Securities and Exchange Commission (SEC). The complete set of financial accounting standards currently in force comprise generally accepted accounting principles (GAAP).

Financial Accounting Standards Board The Financial Accounting Standards Board (FASB) is the profes-

sional body currently responsible for establishing financial accounting standards. The FASB consists of seven well-compensated, full-time individuals who have severed all ties from previous employers and represent many business backgrounds. Since 1973, this private-sector body has issued well over 100 statements of financial accounting standards, covering a wide variety of topics.

financial condition Financial condition refers to the economic strength of a company as of a specific point in time. The balance is designed to measure financial condition.

financial flexibility Financial flexibility refers to a company's capacity to raise cash through methods other than operations. Examples include short- and long-term borrowings, issuing equity, or selling assets. Financially flexible companies can readily borrow, issue equity, and/or sell liquid assets that are not essential to their operations.

financial performance Financial performance refers to the economic success of a company over a specified time period. The income statement is designed to measure financial performance.

financial ratio analysis Financial ratio analysis is one of several techniques used to analyze financial statements in an effort to assess earning power, solvency, and earnings persistence. Financial ratio analysis involves computing and analyzing ratios that use two or more financial statement numbers. These ratios are often divided into five categories: (1) profitability, (2) solvency, (3) activity, (4) capitalization, and (5) market ratios. The DuPont Model is used by many analysts as a starting point when analyzing ratios, especially the differences in return on equity and return on assets across time and across companies.

financial statement analysis Financial statement analysis is the process of reading, studying, and analyzing the information contained in the annual report and other relevant documents to predict the future financial performance and condition of a company. Financial statement analysis involves assessing (1) earning power, (2) solvency, (3) earnings persistence, and (4) earnings quality.

financial statements Financial statements are a summary of the financial condition and performance of a company, prepared by its management and in some cases reviewed by independent auditors. The financial statements consist of the income statement, balance sheet, statement of cash flows, statement of stockholders' equity, and related footnotes. The ability to read, understand, and interpret the financial statements is a key element of financial statement analysis.

financing activities Financing activities are the activities of a company that affect its capital structure. They involve the collection of capital through equity or debt issuances and any related payments such as dividends, debt payments, and treasury stock purchases.

first-in, first-out First-in, first-out (FIFO) is a cost flow assumption used to value inventory and cost of goods sold. It assumes that the first items purchased are the first items sold. FIFO is one of three commonly used cost flow assumptions; last-in, first-out (LIFO) and averaging are the other two.

fiscal period assumption The fiscal period assumption states that the life of an economic entity can be divided into fiscal periods and that performance can be measured over those periods. This assumption allows the measurement of income for a given period of time (quarterly or annually) and raises questions about how the benefits and costs of a company should be allocated across periods for financial accounting purposes.

fiscal year Fiscal years end on dates other than December 31. Most companies report on a calendar-year (December 31) basis (e.g. seasonality), but for various reasons, some companies report on other 365-day cycles, called fiscal years.

fixed asset turnover *Net sales/Average fixed assets.* Fixed asset turnover is a measure of how efficiently a company is using its fixed assets. For many companies, this activity ratio is an important component of asset turnover and, in general, financial ratio analysis.

fixed assets Fixed assets, sometimes called property, plant, and equipment, is a category of long-lived assets including buildings, machinery, and equipment.

FOB destination FOB (free on board) destination represents freight terms indicating that the seller is responsible for the sold merchandise until it is received by the buyer. Goods shipped FOB destination are considered owned by the seller until they reach their destination. See **FOB shipping point.**

FOB shipping point FOB (free on board) shipping point describes freight terms indicating that the seller is responsible for the sold merchandise only to the point from where it is shipped. Goods shipped FOB shipping point are considered owned by the seller until they reach the designated shipper, at which time they become the responsibility of the buyer. See **FOB destination.**

footnotes Footnotes are descriptions and schedules included in the annual report that further explain the numbers on the financial statements. The footnotes are audited by the independent auditor, and they are considered part of the financial statements.

forward contract A forward contract enables the holder to buy or sell an asset or liability at a future date at a prespecified price. Forward contracts are also written to enable the holder to buy or sell currencies at a prespecified exchange rate. Companies enter into forward contracts often to hedge the risks of holding assets and/or liabilities denominated in foreign currencies.

freight-in Freight-in, also called transportation-in, is the freight cost associated with purchased inventory.

frequent transactions A frequent transaction is an operating transaction that affects the income statement and is expected to recur repeatedly in the foreseeable future. See **extraordinary item.**

G

gain contingency A gain contingency refers to an event that leads to a possible future outcome involving an increase in assets or a decrease in liabilities. See **loss contingency.**

generally accepted accounting principles Generally accepted accounting principles (GAAP) are the standards that guide the preparation of financial accounting statements in the United States. See **financial accounting standards.**

going concern A going concern is an entity that is expected to exist into the foreseeable future. No financial problems indicating financial failure over the planning horizon are apparent. Going concern is an assumption that underlies the financial statements, and auditors are expected to qualify their audit reports if there is doubt about the ability of the audited company to continue as a going concern.

goods in transit Goods in transit are between the buyer and the seller as of the end of an accounting period. See **freight-in, FOB destination,** and **FOB shipping point.**

goodwill Goodwill refers to items of value to a company that are not listed on the balance sheet. Sometimes, however, goodwill is recognized on the balance sheet—when a company purchases another company in a business acquisition for a dollar amount greater than the fair market value of the purchased company's net assets. This purchased goodwill is the difference between the purchase price and the purchased company's net assets; it represents the purchaser's assessment that the purchased company is worth more as a working unit than is indicated by the value of its individual assets and liabilities.

government accounting See **nonprofit entity** and **not-for-profit accounting.**

gross margin *Gross profit/Sales.* Gross margin measures the extent to which the selling price of sold inventory exceeds its cost.

gross profit Gross profit is equal to sales revenues minus cost of good sold. See **gross margin.**

H

hedging Hedging is a strategy used by management to reduce the risk associated with fluctuations in the values of assets and liabilities.

hidden reserves Hidden reserves refer to subjectively understated assets or overstated liabilities. Building hidden reserves is a reporting strategy used by management that allows it to "smooth" reported earnings from one period to the next. It is accomplished by subjectively recognizing accounting losses, normally in periods of high income, which reduces earnings in the current period and ensures that these losses are not recognized in future periods when reported earnings may be lower.

historical cost Historical cost is the dollar amount incurred to acquire an asset (investment) or bring it to sellable (inventory) or serviceable (long-lived asset) condition. Historical cost is also referred to as original cost or cost.

human capital Human capital refers to a company's human resources, including its workforce and management.

human resources See **human capital.**

hurdle rate See **cost of capital.**

hybrid security Hybrid securities have characteristics of both debt and equity. Issuing these securities is becoming an increasingly popular means of corporate financing.

I

income See **net income.**

income smoothing Income smoothing is an expression used to describe a management practice where accounting discretion is used to maintain a smooth earnings stream across time. See **hidden reserves.**

income statement The income statement is a financial statement, prepared on an accrual basis, indicating the performance of a company during a particular period (usually a quarter or a year). It consists of revenues minus expenses, leading to net income, an important indication of a company's earnings power.

independent auditor Independent auditors have no personal or financial interest in their clients. To ensure objective audits, the audit profession requires that auditors maintain complete independence from their clients when conducting audits.

indirect method Under the indirect method, the operating section of the statement of cash flows contains a series of adjustments that reconcile net income with net cash from operations. This form of presentation is called the indirect method because net cash from operating activities is computed indirectly—starting with net income and then adjusting it for the differences between accrual and cash flow accounting.

industry An industry is a classification of a group of companies based on the similarity of their operations, product lines, and/or customers. Three basic categories are manufacturing, retailing, and services (general and financial).

inflation Inflation refers to the eroding of the purchasing power of a monetary unit over time. In an inflationary environment, a dollar at the beginning of a period of time will buy fewer goods and services than at the end of the period.

input market The input market is where an entity purchases the inputs for its operations. Historical cost, which is used extensively on the balance sheet, represents the cost of a company's inputs (e.g., inventory and long-lived assets) when they were acquired previously. Replacement cost, which is used selectively on the balance sheet (e.g., lower of cost or market applied to inventory), represents the current cost of a company's inputs.

installment obligation An installment obligation requires periodic payments covering both interest and principal. Installment obligations are normally represented in the long-term liability section of the balance sheet, but the current installment is often carried as a current liability.

intangible asset Intangible assets are characterized by the rights, privileges, and benefits of possession rather than by physical existence. Also, they are normally considered to have a higher degree of uncertainty than tangible assets.

intention to convert Intention to convert is a phrase that describes one of the criteria by which an investment in a security is classified in the current assets section of the balance sheet. For an asset to be listed as current, management must intend and be able to convert the investment into cash within the time period that defines current assets.

interest Interest is the price, usually expressed as an annual percentage rate, associated with transferring (borrowing or lending) money for a period of time. See **stated interest rate** and **effective interest rate.**

interest coverage ratio See **times interest earned.**

interest-bearing obligation Interest-bearing obligations are notes requiring periodic interest payments determined as a percentage of face value; notes with stated annual rates of interest greater than zero. Interest-bearing obligations differ from non–interest-bearing obligations, where no interest payments are made until the maturity date. Both interest- and non–interest-bearing notes (receivables and payables) are accounted for under the effective interest method.

internal control system The internal control system consists of procedures and records designed and followed by company personnel to ensure that (1) the company's assets are adequately protected from loss or misappropriation and (2) all relevant and measurable economic events are accurately reflected in the company's financial statements.

internal financing Internal financing refers to the generation of funds to support operations and growth through profits instead of debt or equity capital. Internally financed companies normally have capital structures with relatively large balances in retained earnings, usually a sign of financial strength.

Internal Revenue Code The Internal Revenue Code contains the official federal income tax laws. The Internal

Revenue Service monitors and enforces adherence to these laws.

Internal Revenue Service The Internal Revenue Service is the government agency charged with monitoring and enforcing the payment of federal income taxes. See **Internal Revenue Code.**

interperiod tax allocation Interperiod tax allocation refers to the methods used to account for the timing differences that arise between tax and financial reporting across periods. It involves accounting for deferred income taxes.

intraperiod tax allocation Intraperiod tax allocation is the practice of disclosing the income tax effect of certain nonoperating items on the income statement or statement of retained earnings with the item itself. The income taxes associated with operating income are disclosed on the income statement in a single line item immediately below operating income. The effects on income of nonoperating items—such as disposals of segments, extraordinary items, changes in accounting principles, and prior-period adjustments—are disclosed on the financial statements net of their income tax effects.

inventory Inventory refers to items or products that are either available for sale in the normal course of business or support the operations of the business. See **merchandise inventory** and **supplies inventory.**

inventory turnover *Cost of goods sold/Average inventory.* Inventory turnover measures the speed with which inventories move through operations. This activity ratio compares the amount of inventory carried by a company to the volume of goods sold during the period, reflecting how quickly, in general, inventories are sold. By dividing this ratio into 365 days, it can be converted to an expression indicating how many days it takes, on average, to turn over the inventory.

investing activities Investing activities involve the management of a company's long-term assets. The investment activities of a given period are summarized in the investing section of the statement of cash flows, involving primarily purchases and sales of fixed assets and investments in equity securities.

L

land Land refers to real estate held for investment purposes, usually appearing in the long-term investments section of the balance sheet. Land used in the operations of a business is considered a long-lived asset and is normally referred to as property. Land is carried at historical cost on the balance sheet, not fair market value, and is normally not subject to depreciation.

last-in, first-out Last-in, first-out (LIFO) is a cost flow assumption used to value inventory and cost of goods sold. It assumes that the last items purchased are the first items sold. LIFO is one of three commonly used

cost flow assumptions; FIFO (first-in, first-out) and averaging are the other two. See **LIFO conformity rule, LIFO liquidation,** and **LIFO reserve.**

lease A lease is a contract granting use or occupation of property during a specified period of time in exchange for some form of payment, usually cash. Leases are a popular way to finance business activities. Companies often lease, rather than purchase, land, buildings, machinery, equipment, and other holdings, primarily to avoid the risks and associated costs of ownership. For purposes of financial accounting, leases are divided into two categories: operating leases and capital leases.

leasehold obligation Leasehold obligations are the balance sheet liabilities associated with capital leases reported by the lessee. This liability is equal to the present value of the future payments associated with a capital lease, discounted at the effective interest rate existing at the original date of the lease. Leasehold obligations are listed on the balance sheet as long-term and are accounted for under the effective interest method.

leverage Leverage involves borrowing funds and investing them in assets that produce returns exceeding the after-tax cost of the borrowing. In such cases, a company is managing its debt effectively and creating benefits for the stockholders, which should manifest themselves as increases in the return-on-equity ratio.

liability A liability is a probable future sacrifice of economic benefits arising from present obligations of a particular entity to transfer assets or provide services to other entities in the future as a result of past transactions or events.

life of a bond The life of a bond is the period of time from the issuance of the bond to the maturity date, at which time the face value is paid to the bondholders. See **bond.**

LIFO conformity rule The LIFO conformity rule is a federal income tax requirement stating that if a company uses the LIFO cost flow assumption to value inventory for tax purposes, it must also use the LIFO assumption when preparing its financial statements. Consequently, those companies that use LIFO to save taxes must report the LIFO cost of goods sold amount on the income statement—normally leading to lower reported net income values.

LIFO liquidation A LIFO liquidation occurs when companies that use the LIFO cost flow assumption have sales that exceed production. LIFO users must pay close attention to inventory levels because when inventory liquidations occur, abnormally high profits can be reported. This is due to matching inventory having old (often lower) costs against current revenues.

LIFO reserve The LIFO reserve is the difference between inventory reported under LIFO and inventory reported under FIFO. Under GAAP, companies that use LIFO are required to report what inventory would have been had they used FIFO. The difference between these two amounts (the LIFO reserve) represents the accumulated amount by which net income reported by the LIFO user has been understated, relative to FIFO, since the adoption of LIFO. The increase (decrease) in the LIFO reserve over the current period, when added to (subtracted from) LIFO net income for that period, is equal to FIFO net income (before taxes) for that period.

line of credit A line of credit is a borrowing arrangement granted to a company by a bank or group of banks, allowing it to borrow up to a certain maximum dollar amount, with interest being charged only on the outstanding balance.

liquidation Liquidation is the process of selling assets for cash. When companies go through liquidation, they normally sell their existing assets for cash, which is used to pay off creditors in order of priority. Any remaining cash is distributed to the stockholders. Liquidation is also used to describe an inventory reduction, where sales in a given period exceed inventory production or acquisition. See, for example, **LIFO liquidation.**

liquidity Liquidity is the speed with which an asset can be converted into cash. Assets on the balance sheet are listed roughly in order of liquidity. For example, current assets are considered to be more liquid than intangible assets. Of the current assets, cash is considered to be more liquid than accounts receivable, which is more liquid than inventory, which is more liquid than prepaid expenses.

listed company A listed company has its equity shares listed on a public stock exchange. See **stock market** and **stock price.**

loan contract A loan contract is a written agreement describing the terms of a borrowing arrangement, including the timing of cash payments (interest and principal), the maturity date, collateral (security) in case of default, and restrictions on the actions of management (called covenants).

loan covenant See **debt covenant.**

long-lived assets Long-lived assets are used in the operations of a business, providing benefits that extend beyond the current operating period. Examples include property, plant, and equipment, and intangible assets.

long-term debt Long-term debt refers to obligations listed on the balance sheet, backed by formal contract, expected to be paid with the use of assets listed as noncurrent on the balance sheet. See **debt and liability.**

long-term debt ratio *Total long-term liabilities/Total assets.* The long-term debt ratio reflects that portion of assets provided by long-term borrowings.

long-term investments Long-term investments refer to assets on the balance sheet that are not intended to be sold in the near term, expecting to generate benefits over a time period extending beyond that which defines current assets.

loss A loss occurs when the expenses of a given period exceed the revenues. Loss also refers to a situation where an item on the balance sheet is exchanged for something with a value lower than the item's book value.

loss contingency A loss contingency (or contingent loss) is an existing condition, situation, or set of circumstances involving uncertainty concerning a possible loss to a company that will ultimately be resolved when one or more future events occurs or fails to occur. See **contingency** and **gain contingency.**

lower-of-cost-or-market rule Lower-of-cost-or-market is a rule applied to accounting for inventories, which states that the balance sheet value of inventory will be its historical cost or its market value, whichever is lower.

M

MACRS The Modified Accelerated Cost Recovery System is the set of rules defining the maximum amount of depreciation that can be recognized on a fixed asset for the purpose of determining taxable income in a given year. To determine this amount, a fixed asset is placed into one of eight categories, based on its estimated useful life as specified in the Asset Depreciation Range (ADR) system. Each of the eight categories is then linked with an allowable depreciation method.

maintenance expenditure A maintenance expenditure is a postacquisition expenditure that serves to repair or maintain a fixed asset in its present operating condition.

management accounting Management accounting systems produce information used for decisions within a company. Such systems produce reports that cover such areas as performance evaluation, production output, product costs, and capital budgeting. This information is not available to individuals outside the company.

management discretion Management discretion refers to the latitude exercised by management when applying accounting methods. Management can choose from a variety of accounting methods, estimates, and assumptions when preparing the financial statements and still be within the guidelines defined by GAAP. The financial statements are also influenced by the timing and execution of transactions planned in advance by management. By using its discretion in these ways, management can make choices that serve its own interest—choices that may or may not be in the best interest of the company's owners. This discretion also makes it difficult for analysts to ascertain a company's true financial condition and performance from the financial reports.

management letter The management letter appears in the annual report and normally states that management is responsible for the preparation and integrity of the financial statements. While management letters differ from one company to the next, most contain references to GAAP, ethical and social responsibilities, the quality and reliability of the company's internal control system, the independent audit, and the audit committee of the board of directors.

manufacturing company Manufacturing companies acquire raw materials and, through a process, combine labor and overhead to manufacture inventory. Manufacturing companies are normally characterized by large investments in property, plant and equipment, and inventory.

margin See **profit margin** and **gross margin.**

mark-to-market accounting Under mark-to-market accounting, investments are carried on the balance sheet at their market values. Realized gains and losses are recognized on the income statement; and unrealized gains and losses are either reflected on the income statement or in the stockholders' equity section of the balance sheet, depending on the nature of the investment. See **marketable securities.**

markdown A markdown is a reduction in sales price normally due to decreased demand for an item. Markdowns are very common in the retail industry, especially at the close of the seasons. These discounts are designed to accelerate sales of old items (boosting inventory turnover), making room for new inventories.

market price The market price is the price at which an asset can be exchanged in the open (output) market as of a particular point in time. See **fair market value** and **stock price.**

market ratios The market ratios are the financial ratios that measure returns to common stockholders due to changes in the market price of the common stock and the receipt of dividends.

market share Market share is the proportion of the total market for a particular good or service held by a company. For example, if the total market for boys' tennis shoes is $50 million per year and Company A sells boys' tennis shoes valued at $5 million in a given year, Company A has a 10 percent market share. Market share and changes in market share measure how well a company is competing with other firms in a given market.

market value See **market price** or **fair market value.**

market-to-book ratio (*Number of outstanding common shares × Market price per share*)/*Net assets*. The market-to-book ratio indicates the extent to which the market believes that stockholders' equity on the balance sheet reflects the company's true market value.

marketable securities Marketable securities are investments that are readily marketable and intended to be sold within the time period of current assets. They are carried on the balance sheet at current market prices, and for many purposes (on the statement of cash flows, for example), marketable securities are considered the same as cash, primarily because they can be liquidated immediately and converted into cash. See **short-term investments.**

matching principle The matching principle is a measurement principle of financial accounting stating that performance is measured by matching efforts against benefits in the time period in which the benefits are realized. Net income on the income statement is the result of matching expenses against revenues in the time period when the revenues are realized. The matching principle is applied by first recognizing revenues and then matching against those revenues the expenses required to generate them.

materiality Materiality is an exception to the principles of financial accounting stating that only those transactions dealing with dollar amounts large enough to make a difference to financial statement users need be accounted for in a manner consistent with GAAP. The dollar amounts of some transactions are so small that the method of accounting has virtually no impact on the decisions based upon information in the financial statements. Such transactions are referred to as immaterial, and management is allowed to account for them as expediently as possible.

maturity date The maturity date is the date when a loan agreement ends. As of the maturity date, if all payments (interest and principal) have been made on the loan, the associated debt is satisfied. For most bonds, the face value of the bond is paid to the holder on the maturity date.

maturity value The maturity value is the dollar amount written on the face of the note or bond certificate that is paid to the holder at the maturity date. Face value and par value are terms often used interchangeably with maturity value.

measurement theory Underlying assets, liabilities, revenues, and expenses—the key components of the financial statements—is a theoretical framework consisting of assumptions, principles, and exceptions. The assumptions include economic entity, stable dollar, fiscal period, and going concern; the principles include objectivity, matching, revenue recognition, and consistency; and the exceptions include materiality and conservatism.

merchandise inventory Merchandise inventory represents items held for sale in the ordinary course of business. It is especially important to retail and manufacturing enterprises, whose performance depends significantly on their ability to market their inventory. Indeed, the demand for such companies' products is often the most important determinant of their success.

merger A merger is a business combination whereby two or more companies combine to form a single legal entity. In most cases, the assets and liabilities of the smaller company are merged into those of the larger company, and the stock of the smaller, merged company is retired.

misclassification Misclassification involves including a financial statement account in an inappropriate section of the financial statements.

mortgage A mortgage is a cash loan exchanged for an installment note that is secured by real estate. The mortgage gives the holder the right to take possession of the real estate in case of default.

mortgage payable A mortgage payable is a balance sheet account that indicates the outstanding obligation associated with a mortgage. Mortgage payables are included in the long-term liability section of the balance sheet, except for that portion expected to use assets presently listed as current. This portion is included as a current liability.

multinational corporation Multinational corporations have their home in one country but operate and have subsidiaries operating within and under the laws of other countries.

multistep format Under a multistep format, the income statement is designed in a way that separates cost of goods sold from operating expenses, highlighting gross profit. This format also separates usual and frequent operating items from those that are unusual and/or infrequent, often referred to as other revenues and expenses or extraordinary items.

N

natural resource cost Natural resource costs are the costs of acquiring the rights to extract natural resources. Natural resource costs, which appear in the long-lived asset section of the balance sheet, are quite large in the extractive (e.g., oil, gas, mining) industries, and they are normally depleted under the activity (units-of-production) method.

net assets Net assets equals total assets minus total liabilities, or stockholders' equity. A company's net assets are also referred to as the company's book value, balance sheet value, and net worth.

net book value Net book value is the dollar value assigned to an item on the balance sheet. When used in reference to an entire company, net book value is equal to net assets or stockholders' equity. The net book value of a company is also referred to as simply the company's book value, balance sheet value, stockholders' equity, and net worth.

net credit sales Net credit sales is equal to gross sales on account less an estimate of sales returns and allowances.

net earnings See **net income.**

net income Net income is the difference between the revenues generated by a company in a particular time period and the expenses required to generate those revenues. Net income is the "bottom line" of the income statement.

net of tax To disclose an item net of tax on the income statement means to reduce its dollar value by the income tax effect associated with the item.

net operating income Net operating income is equal to the operating revenues minus operating expenses. It is also referred to as operating income.

net profit See **net income.**

net realizable value Net realizable value is the net cash amount expected from the sale of an item, usually equal to the selling price of the item less the cost to complete and sell it.

net sales Net sales is equal to gross sales less an estimate of sales returns and allowances.

net worth See **net assets** or **net book value.**

non–interest-bearing notes Non–interest-bearing notes are debt instruments that do not require periodic interest payments determined as a percentage of the face value; the entire interest amount is paid at maturity. Non–interest-bearing notes have stated annual rates of interest equal to zero, but the effective (actual) rate of interest is greater than zero.

nonoperating items Nonoperating items appear on the income statement below net operating income and are considered unusual and/or infrequent. Nonoperating items are considered less persistent than operating items.

nonparticipating preferred stock Nonparticipating preferred stock, a common form, carries the right—if dividends are declared—only to an amount designated by the dividend percentage expressed in the terms of the preferred stock. Unlike participating preferred stock, there is no right to an additional dividend.

nonprofit entity A nonprofit entity is an organization where the operations are not designed to make a profit. Rather, most nonprofit entities generate funds through contributions, user fees, or taxes and use these funds to achieve some organizational or social purpose. Nonprofit entities are also referred to as not-for-profit and/or government entities.

nonsufficent funds penalty A nonsufficient funds penalty is an assessment charged by banks against their customers for writing checks that are not backed by adequate funds.

not-for-profit accounting See **nonprofit entity.**

notes payable Notes payables are obligations evidenced by formal notes. They involve direct borrowings from financial institutions, or other companies, and often are established to finance the purchase of long-lived assets. Notes payable appear on the balance sheet in either the current or long-term debt section.

notes receivable Notes receivable are assets backed by formal loan contracts. They normally arise from issuing loans, the sale of inventory, or the provision of a service and are often listed in the long-term assets section of the balance sheet.

O

objectivity Objectivity is a principle of financial accounting measurement stating that the values of transactions and the assets and liabilities created by them must be verifiable, i.e., backed by documents and prepared in a systematic and reasonable manner.

obsolescence Obsolescence, often referred to as physical obsolescence, is the state of an asset when repairs are no longer economically feasible.

off-balance-sheet financing Off-balance-sheet financing is a reporting strategy designed to depict a company as less reliant on debt than it actually is. For example, managers have been known to structure financing transactions and choose certain accounting methods so that liabilities need not be reported on the balance sheet.

open account An open account is an informal credit trade agreement used in cases where frequent credit transactions are conducted and a running balance of the obligation or receivable is maintained. If payments are made regularly within reasonable time periods, interest charges are not usually assessed. Open account is normally used to describe the trade terms underlying accounts receivable and accounts payable.

operating activities Operating activities are the activities of a company associated with the acquisition and sale of a company's products and services.

operating cycle Operating cycle is the time it takes, in general, for a company to begin with cash, convert the cash to inventory (or a service), sell the inventory (or service), and receive cash payment.

operating days *Accounts receivable turnover (days) + Inventory turnover (days) − Accounts payable turnover (days)*. Operating days combines three turnover measures in a way that indicates the time period over which a company's major working capital requirements must be financed. As this measure increases, it indicates a longer time period, a greater working capital investment, and higher financing requirements. See **operating cycle.**

operating expenses Operating expenses are the costs incurred to generate operating revenues associated with the normal activities of a company. They are disclosed in the operating section of the income statement, leading to net operating income.

operating income See **net operating income.**

operating lease An operating lease is treated as a simple rental for financial reporting purposes, where the periodic lease payments are treated as an expense, and no asset or liability is recognized on the balance sheet. See **capital lease** and **off-balance-sheet financing.**

operating margin Operating margin equals net operating income divided by sales. It indicates the number of cents of operating income earned from every dollar of sales.

operating performance An operating performance represents a company's ability to increase its net assets through operating activities.

operating revenues Operating revenues are revenues generated through the usual and frequent transactions of a company. They are disclosed in the operating section of the income statement, leading to net operating income.

operating transactions Operating transactions are usual and frequent transactions involving the acquisition and sale of a company's inventories or services.

opinion letter See **audit report.**

ordinary stock dividend An ordinary stock dividend is a relatively small dividend paid in the form of a company's own equity shares. It is normally expressed as a percent of a company's outstanding shares. For example, a 5 percent stock dividend declared by a company with 100,000 shares outstanding would involve the issuance of 5,000 (100,000 × 0.05) new shares to the stockholders. Under an ordinary stock dividend, the number of shares issued represents less than 25 percent of the number of shares outstanding before the issuance. Ordinary stock dividends are also just called stock dividends.

organizational forms The most common forms of business organization are sole proprietorship, partnership, subchapter S corporation, and corporation.

original cost See **historical cost.**

other gains and losses Other gains and losses appear in the nonoperating section of the income statement and refer to transactions that are either unusual or infrequent, but not both. This section of the income statement is also called other revenues and expenses.

other revenues and expenses See **other gains and losses.**

output market The output market is the market where an entity sells the outputs from its operations. Fair market value, market price, and net realizable value are all output market values.

outstanding shares Outstanding shares are shares of stock that have been issued and are presently held by stockholders. They have not been repurchased (as treasury stock) by the company.

overhead Overhead refers to manufacturing costs that cannot be directly linked to particular products.

overstating financial performance and condition Overstating financial performance and condition, sometimes called providing a favorable financial picture, is a reporting strategy in which management attempts to depict a more favorable picture of the financial statements by overstating the company's financial performance and condition.

owners' equity Owners' equity refers to the section of the balance sheet that measures the results of the activities (contributions and withdrawals) of the owners of a partnership or sole proprietorship. See **stockholders' equity,** the term used to describe these activities for the owners (stockholders) of a corporation.

P

paper profits Paper profits is an expression used to describe profits that appear on the income statement but do not reflect increases in a company's economic wealth. Paper profits can be created by cosmetic changes in accounting estimates, judgments, and methods. Quality of earnings assessment is designed to identify and remove paper profits from the financial statements.

par value In the context of preferred stock, par value is often used in the determination of the amount of the annual preferred dividend payment. It also determines the dollar amount disclosed in the preferred stock account on the balance sheet. In the context of common stock, par value has little economic significance, but it is used to determine the dollar amount disclosed in the common stock account on the balance sheet.

parent company Parent companies own controlling interests in other companies, called subsidiaries. The consolidated financial statements of the parent company include the financial statements of all subsidiaries under its control. See **business acquisition** and **merger.**

participating preferred stock Participating preferred stock carries the right, if dividends are declared, not only to an annual dividend amount (determined by the dividend percentage expressed in the terms of the preferred stock) but also to a portion of the remaining dividend paid to the common stockholders. Most preferred stock is nonparticipating.

partnership A partnership is an organizational form where two or more people agree, by means of a contract, on how the business is to be conducted and how the profits and losses will be shared. A partnership is not a legal entity; the partners are legally liable for each other's business activities and the partnership itself is not subject to federal income taxes. The partners, themselves, are taxed on their share of the partnership profit.

patent Patents are granted by the U.S. Patent Office and give the holders exclusive rights to use, manufacture, or sell a product or process for a period of ten years. See **intangible asset.**

payments in advance See **deferred revenue.**

pension A pension is a sum of money paid to a retired or disabled employee, the amount of which is usually determined by the employee's years of service. For most large companies, pensions are an important part of the employees' compensation packages, and they are part of almost all negotiated wage settlements. There are two primary types of pension plans: a defined-contribution plan and a defined-benefit plan.

percentage-of-credit-sales approach The percentage-of-credit-sales approach is a method of estimating bad debts that multiplies a given percentage by the credit sales of a given accounting period. Percentage-of-credit-sales is a common method of estimating uncollectibles, used in conjunction with the allowance method, when accounting for accounts receivable.

periodic method The periodic method is a method of keeping track of and controlling inventories. It records each purchase as it occurs but does not record inventory outflows at each sale, taking an inventory count to determine the inventory balance only at the end of the accounting period. The periodic method is relatively inexpensive to maintain, but it fails to provide a continuous and up-to-date record of inventories. It also does not provide a mechanism to keep close inventory control.

perpetual method The perpetual method is a method designed to keep track of, and close control over, inventories. It maintains an up-to-date record, recording each purchase as it occurs and recording an inventory outflow at each sale. The perpetual method is becoming increasingly popular, especially with retailers, because it helps to maintain close control over inventories. Also, computer systems have dramatically reduced the cost of using this method. Bar code sensor systems, for example, are used to implement the perpetual method.

physical obsolescence See **obsolescence.**

portfolio A portfolio is a group of securities, investments, or assets held by an individual or company.

postacquisition expenditures Postacquisition expenditures refer to costs incurred subsequent to the acquisition or manufacture of a long-lived asset. They serve either to improve the existing asset (betterment) or merely to maintain it (maintenance expenditure).

postretirement costs Postretirement costs refer to health care and insurance costs incurred by employees after retirement. Most large companies cover a portion of such costs, and similar to pensions, such coverage is part of employee compensation and is earned over an employee's years of service.

preemptive right A preemptive right, which is attached to some equity shares, allows the holder to purchase a proportionate interest in any new equity issuance. It enables shareholders to maintain their relative equity interests, reducing the dilutive effect associated with a new issuance.

preferred stock Preferred stock is issued by companies to raise capital. It has special rights that make it a hybrid between debt and equity. These rights relate either to the receipt of dividends or to claims on assets in case of liquidation.

premium on bonds payable Bond premium is a financial statement account, included in the liability section of the balance sheet and added to the bond liability, representing the fact that the proceeds of a bond issuance exceeded the face value (i.e., the bonds were issued at an effective rate of interest greater than the stated rate of interest). Bond premiums are amortized over the life of the bonds, reducing interest expense. See **effective interest method.**

prepaid expenses Prepaid expense is an asset account that reflects payments for certain items (e.g., insurance and rent) before the corresponding service or right is actually used. Prepaid expenses are considered assets because they represent benefits to be enjoyed by the company in the future. For most companies, prepaid expenses are a relatively small, often insignificant, part of total assets.

present value Present value is a technique used to place a value, as of the present day, on a set of future cash flows. It is computed by discounting future cash flows at an interest rate that reflects a company's cost of capital.

price/earnings ratio *Market price per share/Earnings per share.* The price/earnings (P/E) is a measure of the extent to which the stock market believes that a company's current reported earnings signals future cash inflows.

prime interest rate The prime interest rate is the rate charged by a bank to its best (lowest-risk) customers.

principal Principal is the sum of money owed as a debt, upon which interest is calculated. In the case of a bond, the principal can be referred to as the face value, par value, or maturity value.

prior period adjustment Prior period adjustment refers to the financial effects of certain events that result in direct adjustments to the retained earnings account. They are relatively unusual and are disclosed on the statement of stockholders' equity, normally representing corrections of errors made in prior periods.

private company Private companies have equity shares that are not listed and traded on the public stock exchanges.

proceeds Proceeds refers to the amount of cash collected on a sale, a borrowing, a bond issuance, or a stock issuance.

production capacity Production capacity refers to the number of goods or services a company can produce over a specified period of time given its resources. Production capacity tends to increase when (1) companies expand through business acquisitions and investments in long-lived assets and/or (2) companies increase the efficiency of their available resources.

Companies act to increase production capacity when present capacity is insufficient to meet the existing and/or future demand for the company's products and services.

production efficiency Production efficiency refers to the number of items produced (of a given quality) divided by the cost of producing those items. Companies are continually attempting to improve production efficiency by producing more high-quality output at lower costs.

pro forma financial statements Pro forma financial statements are financial statements projected into the future.

profit See **net income.**

profit and loss statement See **income statement.**

profit margin See **return on sales.**

profitability See **earning power.**

profitability ratios Profitability ratios assess performance, normally measured in terms of some measure of earnings as a percent of some level of activity or investment. Profitability ratios are designed to measure earning power and include return on equity, return on assets, earnings per share, return on sales (profit margin), and times interest earned.

property Property is a long-lived asset account representing the real estate upon which a company's operations are conducted. It is not subject to depreciation and normally not held for sale in the normal course of business. It is carried on the balance sheet at historical cost.

property, plant, and equipment See **fixed assets.**

prospectus A prospectus is a document containing a set of pro forma financial statements and other relevant information (e.g., contractual terms of debt agreements) that is filed with the SEC when a company issues equity or debt to the public.

proxy statement A proxy statement is mailed to the stockholders of the company, inviting them to attend and vote for the board of directors at the annual shareholders' meeting. It also contains extensive information about the company and the compensation packages of the board of directors and management.

public accounting firms Public accounting firms are concerned primarily with providing independent audits of financial statements prepared by companies. The result of the audit is an opinion letter, signed by a certified public accountant, that provides a brief description of the auditor's procedures and responsibilities and states whether the statements present fairly the financial condition and performance of the company and are in conformance with GAAP. In addition to auditing, public accounting firms also perform tax and business advisory services for their clients.

purchase method Under the purchase method of accounting for business acquisitions, the assets and liabilities of the acquired company (subsidiary) are added to those of the parent at their fair market values as of the time of the acquisition. The difference between the purchase price and the fair market value of the subsidiary's assets is recorded as goodwill.

purchasing power Purchasing power is the amount of goods and services a monetary amount can buy at a given point in time. See **inflation.**

Q

qualified audit report A qualified audit report departs from the language in the standard audit report. The departure can be due to any of a wide variety of reasons—some of which are serious, others are not. See **audit report.**

quick ratio (*Cash + Marketable securities accounts receivable*)/*Current liabilities*. The quick ratio compares a company's highly liquid assets to its current liabilities, providing a measure of the portion of the current liabilities that could be paid off in the near future.

R

rate of return See **return on investment.**

readily marketable Readily marketable refers to how quickly an asset can be converted to cash. It is normally used in the context of short-term investments (marketable securities) and describes securities that can be sold, and converted into cash, on demand. Securities traded on the public stock exchanges are considered readily marketable.

realized gain or loss A realized gain or loss occurs when an asset (liability) is exchanged for another asset (liability) with a market value that differs from the book value of the asset (liability) given up.

recognized gain or loss A recognized gain or loss occurs when a gain or loss is recorded on the financial statements. All gains and losses disclosed on the income statement are recognized.

redemption Redemption normally refers to the repurchase of outstanding debt (e.g., bonds) either before or at the maturity date. Depending on the terms of the debt, such repurchases can be at the option of either the issuing company or the debtholders, and the price of the repurchase can be prespecified or at the market price existing at the time of the transaction.

refinancing A refinancing occurs when a company satisfies an outstanding debt by issuing another outstanding debt. A company may also refinance by first redeeming debt and then issuing new debt.

related party transaction A related party transaction occurs when a company executes a transaction with an owner, an officer, or someone with a special interest in the welfare of the company. These transactions should be viewed cautiously by analysts because they may be designed to benefit the related party, often at the expense of the other stakeholders in the company.

replacement cost Replacement cost is the current price a company would have to pay in the input market to replace an existing asset while maintaining operations at the present level.

reporting strategies Reporting strategies are policies used by management when choosing accounting methods, normally designed to achieve specific reporting objectives. There are four common strategies: (1) overstating financial performance and condition, (2) building hidden reserves, (3) taking a bath, and (4) off-balance-sheet financing.

residual interest Residual interest represents the right of the common stockholders to receive corporate assets in case of liquidation, after the creditors and preferred stockholders, in that order, have received their shares. The stockholders' equity section of the balance sheet represents one rough measure of the value of the stockholders' residual interest.

restrictive covenant See **debt covenant.**

restructuring charges A restructuring charge is an expense or loss that appears on the income statement in a given year, reflecting anticipated future costs. Many companies restructure their operations, planning to close plants, lay off employees, and incur other related expenses, choosing to record a charge to income in a period prior to the time they actually close the plants, lay off the employees, etc.

retail company A retail company purchases inventory and attempts to sell it for a price greater than its cost. Retailers purchase inventory from manufacturers or wholesalers and sell it to customers—providing primarily a distribution service, doing little to change or improve the inventory product.

retained earnings Retained earnings is an account listed in the stockholders' equity section of the balance sheet, representing the dollar amount of the company's assets generated through prior profits and not paid out in the form of dividends.

retirement In the context of business activities, retirement normally refers to either discontinuing the use of a fixed asset or purchasing outstanding debt.

return on assets (*Net income + Interest expense* [*1 − Tax rate*])/*Average total assets*. Return on assets measures the returns to both the stockholders (net income) and the creditors (interest expense) on their total investment in the firm (average total assets). The cost of interest is reduced by (1 − Tax rate) because interest is tax deductible. Changes in this ratio can be explained by changes in return on sales and asset turnover. See **DuPont Model, financial statement analysis, and profitability ratios.**

return on equity (*Net income − Preferred stock dividends*)/*Average stockholders' equity*. Return on equity compares the profits generated by a company to the investment made by the company's stockholders. Net income, which appears in the numerator, is viewed as the return to the company's owners, while the balance sheet value of stockholders' equity, which appears in the denominator, represents the amount of resources invested by the stockholders. Changes in this ratio can be explained by changes in return on assets, common earnings leverage, and capital structure leverage.

return on equity from financial leverage *Return on equity − Return on assets*. The difference between the two ratios measures the extent to which the return to the stockholders exceeds the return to all capital providers, including creditors. When return on equity is greater (less) than return on assets, it is a measure of the economic benefit (loss) to stockholders from financial leverage. When a company has no liabilities, then the return on equity will equal return on assets.

return on investment *(Market price[n+1] − Market price[n] + Dividends[n+1])/Market price[n]*. Return on investment provides a measure of the pretax performance of an investment in a share of common stock. The numerator reflects the pretax return to the stockholder (market price appreciation and dividends), and the denominator reflects the amount of the stockholders' investment.

return on sales *(Net Income + Interest expense [1 − Tax rate])/Net sales*. Return on sales provides an indicator of operating efficiency—increasing if operating expenses increase (decrease) at a slower (faster) rate than net sales. An efficient company, for example, will generate increased net sales with a constant level of operating expenses. Changes in this ratio can be analyzed by examining how the items on the income statement changed as a percentage of sales (i.e., common-size income statement).

revaluation adjustment Revaluation adjustments are designed to bring the dollar amount of certain accounts on the financial statements in line with the existing facts.

revenue Revenue refers to inflows or other enhancements of assets of an entity or settlement of its liabilities (or a combination of both) during a period from delivering or producing goods, rendering services, or other activities that constitute the entity's ongoing major or central operations.

revenue recognition Revenue recognition is a principle of accounting measurement that determines when revenue from the sale of a good or the provision of a service is entered into the financial statements. Revenue recognition is a critical question in the matching process because the expenses incurred to generate revenues should not be reflected on the income statement until the revenues are recognized. The sale of a good or provision of a service normally involves a series of steps—including ordering the good or service, producing it, transferring it to the customer, and receiving payment. The principle of revenue recognition helps to determine at which of these steps the revenue should be recorded in the books.

reverse account analysis Reverse account analysis (also called T-account analysis) is a mechanical process that involves examining the activity in a given balance sheet account to acquire information not directly disclosed in the financial statements or footnotes.

risk Risk refers to variation in the returns of a given investment. Risky investments are characterized by large fluctuations in their returns across time—providing large returns in some periods while providing small, zero, or even negative returns in other periods. Risk, when applied to a potential borrower, refers to the probability of receiving timely interest and principal loan payments, sometimes called the risk of default. Equity and debt investors normally require larger expected returns to compensate for bearing additional risk.

risk premium Risk premium refers to the percentage return on investment over and above the risk-free rate that reflects the level of risk associated with an uncertain investment. The risk-free rate plus the risk premium equals the expected rate of return that must be met before an investment will be accepted. In short, larger expected returns are necessary for higher-risk investments.

risk-free return The risk-free return is the return provided by riskless securities (e.g., treasury notes, certificates of deposit). It varies across time due to macroeconomic factors such as economic activity, inflation, exchange rates, and monetary policy but recently has been relatively stable at 5 percent–7 percent.

S

sales Sales is a revenue associated with the sale of a good or product. Sales for a given period is computed by multiplying the number of items sold by the sales price, and it is typically the major revenue for manufacturers and retail companies.

sales growth Sales growth is an important indicator of a company's performance over a period of time. It can be determined by comparing sales dollar amounts on the income statement across reporting periods. It normally reflects changes in customer demand for a company's goods or services—due to changing prices and/or quantities sold.

sales returns Sales returns refer to recorded sales that are subsequently returned to the seller. The returns may be due to faulty merchandise and customer dissatisfaction; in a large number of cases, relatively open returns are part of normal business practices.

salvage value Salvage value refers to the dollar value of a long-lived asset at the completion of its useful life. Salvage values must be estimated before long-lived assets are placed into service so that the depreciable base can be depreciated, or amortized, over the estimated useful life. Estimating salvage values is extremely subjective, so many companies assume them to be zero.

secured note Secured notes are formal promissory notes backed by assets (collateral) that are distributed to creditors in the event of default.

Securities and Exchange Commission In 1934, the U.S. Congress created the Securities and Exchange Commission, a federal agency with powers to implement and enforce the Securities Act of 1933 and the Securities Exchange Act of 1934. The Securities Act of 1933 requires that companies issuing securities on the public security markets file a registration statement (Form S-1) with the SEC prior to the issuance. The SEC Act of 1934 states that companies with securities listed on the public security markets must (1) annually file audited financial reports with the SEC (Form 10-K), (2) file quarterly financial statements with the SEC (Form 10-Q), and (3) provide audited financial reports annually to the stockholders. The SEC is also currently active in establishing financial accounting standards.

security See **collateral.**

service company A service company provides a service, as opposed to a good, for its clients or customers. Service companies carry no inventories and do not recognize cost of goods sold on the income statement. Service revenue or fees earned represent its main revenues. The service industry is normally divided into two groups: general services and financial services.

service revenue Service revenue (also called fees earned) represents revenues from the provision of services. This account is normally found in the operating section of the income statement.

SG&A SG&A refers to selling, general, and administrative expenses—often one of the most important expense categories on the income statement.

shareholder See **stockholders.**

short-term debt Short-term debt refers to obligations on the balance sheet, backed by formal contract, expected to be paid with the use of assets presently listed as current on the balance sheet. Short-term debt is normally listed in current liabilities.

short-term investments Short-term investments consist of investments in equity securities, bonds, and similar financial instruments that are both readily marketable and intended by management to be sold within the time period that defines current assets. Companies often purchase these kinds of securities to earn income with cash that would otherwise be idle for a short time. These investments are carried on the balance sheet at fair market value and, according to GAAP, must be classified as either trading securities or available-for-sale securities.

similar asset Similar assets are those that perform essentially the same function. See **trade-in.**

sole proprietorship A sole proprietorship is considered to be a partnership with a single partner. It is not a legal entity and therefore not subject to federal income taxes. The sole proprietor is taxed and is personally liable for the activities of the business.

solvency Solvency refers to a company's ability to meet debts as they come due. Assessing solvency is a very important part of financial statement analysis.

solvency ratios Solvency ratios refer to financial ratios designed to measure a company's ability to meet its debts as they come due. The current and quick ratios are the two solvency ratios.

specific identification Specific identification is a procedure used to value cost of goods sold and inventory. It is used when companies can specifically identify the inventory items acquired and sold during the period, as well as those that remain at the end of the period. In such cases, the actual costs of the items sold and retained can be allocated to cost of goods sold and inventory, respectively.

stable dollar assumption The stable dollar assumption states that the value of the monetary unit used to measure a company's performance and financial condition is stable across time. That is, the inflation rate is assumed to be zero. This assumption allows mathematical operations (addition, subtraction, multiplication, and division) to be performed on account values that are established at different points in time.

standard audit report A standard audit report, often referred to as an unqualified report, states that the auditor was able to conduct an appropriate audit and render an opinion that the financial statements were prepared in accordance with GAAP and fairly reflect the financial performance and condition of the company. See **qualified audit report.**

stated interest rate The stated interest rate is the annual rate of interest stated on the face of a formal promissory note or bond certificate. The stated interest rate times the face value determines the periodic interest payments.

statement of cash flows The statement of cash flows is a financial statement that provides a summary of the activity in a company's cash account over a period of time. This statement divides cash activity into three categories: (1) operating, (2) investing, and (3) financing activities.

statement of retained earnings The statement of retained earnings represents the portion of the statement of stockholders' equity that reconciles the balance in the retained earnings account at the beginning of an accounting period with the balance at the end of the period. It normally takes the following form: beginning retained earnings plus (minus) net income (loss) less dividends equals ending retained earnings. See **internal financing.**

statement of stockholders' equity The statement of stockholders' equity is a financial statement included in the annual reports of major U.S. companies. It explains the changes in the accounts of the stockholders' equity section of the balance sheet during an accounting period. GAAP requires that these changes be described somewhere in the annual report, and many companies include them in the footnotes.

stock In the United States, the term stock normally refers to common or preferred stock. On occasion, especially outside the United States (e.g. Britain), the term stock refers to inventory.

stock dividend See **ordinary stock dividend.**

stock market The stock market consists of a number of stock exchanges where equity securities are traded in a public forum. The New York Stock Exchange, the American Stock Exchange, and the Over-the-Counter (OTC) market are located in the United States and are the most active in the world. However, there are a number of other exchanges located in virtually all major cities outside the United States.

stock options A stock option is an option to purchase common stock at a prespecified price during a specific time period.

stock price Stock price is the market price of an equity security that has been previously issued and is presently listed on one of the public stock markets. Stock prices increase and decrease as investor expectations about a company change.

stock split Stock splits are used by corporations to increase the number of shares outstanding and simultaneously reduce the market price. Stock splits are expressed in terms of a ratio that describes how the existing shares are to be divided. In a 2:1 split, for example, the existing shareholders each receive an additional share for every share owned. Consequently, the number of outstanding shares are doubled, and the market price per share is approximately cut in half. A 3:1 stock split effectively triples the number of outstanding shares, which the company executes by distributing two additional shares for each one outstanding. In a 3:2 stock split, one additional share is issued for every two outstanding.

stock split in the form of a dividend Stock splits in the form of dividends are relatively large stock dividends where 25 percent or more of the outstanding stock is issued, as a dividend, to the existing shareholders. They are treated as stock splits.

stockholders Stockholders (also called shareholders) are individuals or entities that hold ownership interests in a corporation. These interests include (1) the right to vote in the elections of the board of directors, (2) the right to receive dividends if they are declared by the board of directors, (3) a residual interest to the corporation's assets in the event of liquidation, and in some cases, (4) a preemptive right. *Stockholder* and *shareholder* are used interchangeably.

stockholders' equity Stockholders' equity is the section of a corporate balance sheet that represents the stockholders' interests in the corporation. It consists primarily of contributed capital and retained earnings. The total dollar value of stockholders' equity also represents the company's net book value and its net worth.

straight-line method The straight-line method is a procedure for depreciating or amortizing long-lived assets that recognizes equal amounts of depreciation or amortization in each year of the asset's useful life. To compute straight-line depreciation for a given period, divide the depreciation base by the estimated useful life. Straight-line is the most common method for depreciating fixed assets and amortizing intangible assets.

subchapter S corporation A subchapter S corporation is primarily the same as a corporation with one important difference: it is taxed like a partnership. It is popular with many small businesses because it has the advantages of a corporation (e.g., stockholders are liable only up to the amount of their investment) without one of the major disadvantages (double taxation).

subsidiary A subsidiary is a company with the majority of its common stock owned by another company, called the parent. Normally, the subsidiary prepares its own financial statements separately from the parent, but these statements are usually not available to the public because the shares of the subsidiary owned by the parent are no longer publicly listed. Under GAAP, the parent must prepare consolidated financial statements.

sum-of-the-years'-digits method Sum-of-the-years'-digits is a method of accelerated depreciation that is less extreme than the double-declining-balance method. To compute depreciation for a given period, the depreciation base is multiplied by a ratio—the remaining estimated life serves as the numerator and the sum of the estimated life's digits serves as the denominator. This method recognizes relatively large amounts of depreciation in the early periods of an asset's life and smaller amounts in later periods.

supplies inventory Supplies inventory refers to items available to support the operations of a business, such as office supplies and spare parts. Supplies inventory can be listed on the balance sheet under either current assets (e.g., office supplies) or long-lived assets (e.g., spare parts used to maintain long-lived assets). Supplies inventory is normally a relatively small asset on the balance sheet.

T

T-account analysis See **reverse account analysis.**

takeover In a takeover, an investor, group of investors, or another company purchases enough of the outstanding voting stock to gain a controlling interest (51 percent or more) in the acquired company. Takeovers are often classified as "unfriendly" (the existing board of directors and management are removed) or "friendly" (the existing board of directors and management are maintained). The threat of a takeover creates an important incentive for the board of directors and management to act responsibly and in the interest of the shareholders. Takeovers are accounted for under either the purchase or pooling-of-interests method.

taking a bath Taking a bath is a reporting strategy that recognizes excessive losses or expenses in a single period. This strategy helps to ensure that future periods will show improved performance because losses and expenses recognized in the current period will not have to be recognized in the future.

tax accounting Tax accounting systems produce information that is reported to the Internal Revenue Service and is used in the computation of the company's tax liability.

tax deductible An expense is tax deductible if—according to tax law—it is an allowable reduction of taxable income, the dollar amount upon which the tax liability is based. Many transactions are structured so that the related costs and expenses can be deducted for tax purposes.

taxable income Taxable income is the number used to determine income tax liability. It is computed by subtracting tax-deductible expenses from revenues that must be included for tax purposes. Deductible expenses and includible revenues are determined primarily by the Internal Revenue Code. Taxable income normally differs from net income reported on the income statement, which is based on GAAP.

technical default In a technical default, a company violates the terms of a debt covenant. For example, a debt covenant may require that the company maintain a current ratio of at least 1.0. If the company allows the ratio to fall below 1.0, it is in technical default. Technical default normally leads to renegotiation of the debt terms and is normally a negative signal for the company.

technical obsolescence Technical obsolescence is the state of an asset when technical advances have rendered its services as no longer useful.

term loan Term loans are paid in installments over a period longer than one year from the operating cash flow of a business.

times interest earned *Net income before interest and taxes/Interest expense.* Times interest earned, also referred to as interest coverage, is a financial ratio that measures the extent to which a company's annual profits cover its annual interest expense. The profit number in the numerator should reflect the primary, recurring business operations of the company and should be calculated before income taxes because interest is deductible for tax purposes. The denominator, interest expense, can usually be found on the income statement.

trade-in In a trade-in, an old asset (and usually cash) is exchanged for a new asset. The methods used to account for trade-ins depend upon whether the assets in the exchange are similar or dissimilar.

trademark or trade name Granted by the U.S. Patent Office, a trademark or trade name is a word, phrase, or symbol that distinguishes or identifies a particular enterprise or product. Trademarks last for a fixed period of time but can be renewed indefinitely. See **intangible asset.**

trading securities Trading securities are relatively small investments (less than 20 percent of the outstanding voting stock) in marketable equity (or debt) securities that are purchased and held principally for the purpose of selling them in the very near future with the objective of generating a profit on short-term price changes. Trading securities are always listed as current assets on the balance sheet and are carried at market value. Changes in the market prices of trading securities are reflected as income or loss on the income statement, normally in the nonoperating section.

transportation-in See **freight-in.**

treasury notes Treasury notes are obligations of the federal government that pay interest at a specified rate for a specific period of time, usually less than six months. These notes are very low risk, and companies often purchase treasury notes to temporarily earn interest with excess cash. Such investments are classified as short-term on the balance sheet. The rate paid by treasury notes can also be used as a measure of the riskless rate of return. See **short-term investments.**

treasury stock Treasury stock is previously issued stock that has been repurchased by the issuing company and held in the corporate treasury. It is often reissued at a later date.

U

uncollectibles Uncollectibles, sometimes called bad debts, refer to outstanding accounts or notes receivable that will never be received. Under GAAP, management is required to estimate the value of uncollectibles periodically and recognize an expense on the income statement as well as reduce receivables on the balance sheet.

unearned revenue See **deferred revenue.**

uniformity Uniformity would be achieved if all businesses used the same accounting methods.

unqualified audit report See **standard audit report.**

unrealized gain or loss An unrealized gain or loss occurs when the market value of an asset (liability) on the balance sheet changes and no exchange has taken place. When the market value of an asset increases, for example, an unrealized gain occurs.

unsecured notes Unsecured notes are formal, promissory notes (contracts) that are not backed by any form of security—collateral. For this reason, they tend to be high risk but normally can only be successfully issued by strong companies. The presence of unsecured debt on the balance sheet of a company, therefore, is often a signal of financial strength; that company's creditors apparently have not required that the debt be secured by the company's assets. Unsecured bonds are called debentures.

useful life The useful life of an asset is the estimated time period, or activity, over which a long-lived asset is expected to provide revenue-producing services. The estimated lives of intangible assets can be as long as forty years, while fixed asset lives normally range from three to thirty years. The estimated useful life of an automobile may be more appropriately expressed in terms of miles driven (e.g., 150,000 miles), instead of years.

usual transactions Usual transactions are part of the normal operating activities of a company. They involve the sale of a company's merchandise inventory or the provision of services expected in the normal course of business. If these transactions occur frequently, they are considered operating transactions and are disclosed as part of net operating income. If they occur infrequently, they are considered nonoperating items and classified as such on the income statement.

V

valuation base Valuation base refers to the values (e.g., historical cost, replacement cost, fair market value, net realizable value, present value) used to determine the dollar amount of an entity's assets and liabilities on the balance sheet.

W

warranty A warranty is an agreement by which a seller promises to remove deficiencies in the quantity, quality, or performance of a product sold to a buyer.

window dressing Window dressing is a phrase used to describe the activity of managers who use accounting methods, judgments, and estimates or make operating decisions purely to make the financial statements appear more attractive to financial statement users.

working capital *Current assets − Current liabilities.* Working capital measures the extent to which a company's current assets cover its current liabilities. It is viewed as a measure of solvency and is often used in debt covenants to ensure that the borrower maintains a sufficient buffer of current assets to current liabilities. Like the current and quick ratio, however, working capital is a relatively weak measure of a company's solvency position.

Subject Index

Company Index